D0536919

In MyManagementLab you are treated as an individual with specific learning needs.

GET A BETTER GRADE!

eText
Access the eText while you study—without leaving the online environment!

Annotated Figures and Tables from the Text
Detailed explanations—in addition to what's in the text—help you understand the concepts.

Robbins Self-Assessment Library
The Self-Assessment Library is an interactive library of 51 behavioural questionnaires that will help you discover yourself and give you insight into how you might behave as a manager.

Diversity, Passport, and PRISM
"Diversity" contains interactive exercises that put you in the role of a manager making decisions related to age, gender, or ethnic diversity; "Passport" is a module of global case scenarios in which you will make decisions; "PRISM" (practical interactive skills modules) consists of 12 interactive decision-tree style comprehensive exercises that let you try out different management skills.

Content and tools to enrich your
learning experience and foster
interest and mastery of the subject.

PERSONALIZED
LEARNING!

Glossary Flashcards
Use these quick and fun flashcards to
study the text's key terms.

Auto-graded Tests and Assignments
MyManagementLab comes with two
preloaded Sample Tests per chapter (the
Pre-Test and the Post-Test). Work through
these diagnostic tests to identify areas you
haven't fully understood. The Sample
Tests generate a personalized Study Plan,
designed specifically to suit your studying
needs. Instructors can assign these Sample
Tests or create assignments, quizzes, and
tests using a mix of publisher-supplied
content and their own custom exercises.

Personalized Study Plan
When you use MyManagementLab,
you're treated as an individual with
specific learning needs. Because you
have limited study time, it's important
for you to be as effective as possible
during that time. A personalized
Study Plan is generated from your
results on Sample Tests and instructor
assignments. You can clearly see
which topics you have mastered and,
more importantly, which ones
you still need to work on.

PEARSON
mymanagementlab™

management

ninth canadian edition

management

ninth canadian edition

Stephen P. Robbins
SAN DIEGO STATE UNIVERSITY

Mary Coulter
SOUTHWEST MISSOURI STATE UNIVERSITY

Nancy Langton
SAUDER SCHOOL OF BUSINESS, UNIVERSITY OF BRITISH COLUMBIA

PEARSON

Prentice
Hall

Toronto

Library and Archives Canada Cataloguing in Publication

Robbins, Stephen P., 1943–
            Management / Stephen P. Robbins, Mary Coulter, Nancy
Langton.—9th Canadian ed.

Includes index.
ISBN 978-0-13-206873-4

            1. Management—Textbooks.   2. Management—Canada—Textbooks.
I. Coulter, Mary   II. Langton, Nancy   III. Title.

HD31.R5647 2009   658.4   C2007-904645-2

ISBN-13: 978-0-13-206873-4
ISBN-10: 0-13-206873-7

Vice President, Editorial Director: Gary Bennett
Acquisitions Editor: Karen Elliott
Executive Marketing Manager: Cas Shields
Developmental Editor: Su Mei Ku
Senior Production Editor: Jennifer Handel
Copy Editor: Claudia Forgas
Proofreader: Sheila Wawanash
Senior Production Coordinator: Patricia Ciardullo
Composition: Joan M. Wilson
Permissions and Photo Research: Lisa Brant
Art Director: Julia Hall
Cover Design: Opus House Incorporated/Sonya Thursby
Interior Design: Opus House Incorporated/Sonya Thursby
Cover Image: Stock Illustration Source

1 2 3 4 5   12 11 10 09 08

Printed and bound in the United States of America.

BRIEF CONTENTS

CONTENTS

PART ONE
Defining the Manager's Terrain   2

PART TWO
Planning　134

PART FOUR
Leading   364

PREFACE

Welcome to the ninth Canadian edition of *Management*, by Stephen Robbins, Mary Coulter, and Nancy Langton. This edition takes a fresh approach to management coverage through:

- relevant examples
- updated theory coverage
- a pedagogically sound design

General Content and Approach

The underlying philosophy of our textbook is that "Management Is for Everyone." Students who are not managers, or do not envision themselves as managers, do not always understand why studying management is important or relevant. We use examples from a variety of settings and provide several different end-of-chapter applications, such as *Management for You Today*, to help students understand the relevance of studying management for their day-to-day lives.

In this edition, we have continued to make enhancements that add to both learning and instruction:

- Greater emphasis on presenting a variety of managers, some in unusual (i.e., not large corporate) settings, and some with nontraditional decisions. In the chapter openers, you will meet a school superintendent coping with dress code issues, a pet-food company facing challenges in a global economy, a company trying to work well with its local Aboriginal community, and the CEO in charge of putting on the Olympics in Vancouver. It is hoped that these examples will highlight for students that management takes place in a variety of contexts.

- Significantly increased Canadian content, with an attempt for broader coverage throughout Canada, and examples that cover many different types of organizations: large, small, public and private sector, unionized and non-unionized, privately held and publicly held. Each of these settings provides different challenges for managers, and yet often there are commonalities. The examples help students understand what is the same and what is different.

- Up-to-date statistics wherever possible, and more discussion of the Canadian, rather than the American, scene

- More international examples

- Up-to-date theory and empirical findings in all chapters

- Greater emphasis on strategic management

- Greater coverage of ethics, with more examples

Material Provided in Supplements

Our reviewers tell us that management courses need more than a "one size fits all" textbook. To address the need for flexibility, we continue to offer two supplements, *History of Management Trends* and *Operations Management*. Both of these features have been carefully designed to indicate that the material is important and up to date, and can be used to suit the different needs of management courses.

Chapter Pedagogical Features

We have continued to enhance the ninth Canadian edition through a rich variety of pedagogical features, including the following:

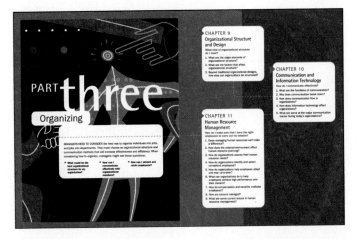

- A part-opening map shows the interconnectedness of the chapters within each part.

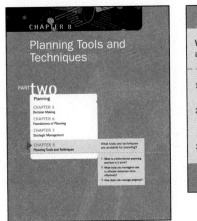
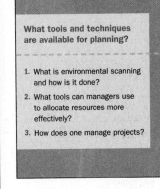

- Outcomes-based questions at the opening of each chapter guide student learning. These questions are repeated in the margin at the start of each major chapter section to reinforce the learning outcome.

- A vignette opens each chapter and is threaded throughout the chapter to help students apply a story to the concepts they are learning.
- The vignette is followed by *Think About It* questions that give students a chance to put themselves into the shoes of managers in various situations.

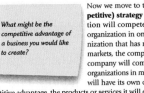

- Integrated questions (in the form of green notes) throughout the chapters help students relate management to their everyday lives.

Q&A 3.4

Prism 5

Diversity in Action 1

Vancouver 2010
www.vancouver2010.com

- References in the margin to *Q&A*, *PRISM*, and *Diversity in Action* throughout the chapters enhance students' learning. These references refer students to the MyManagementLab website (www.pearsoned.ca/mymanagementlab) where students can complete exercises to better their understanding or learn more about a management concept or issue. For example, the *Q&A* feature anticipates questions that students might have about specific areas of management. The answers to these questions are found on the MyManagementLab website.

- Weblinks, provided in the margins, give students access to Internet resources for companies and organizations discussed in the text, broadening their grasp of real-world issues.

- *Management Reflections* appear at appropriate places in chapters. These are longer examples designed to enhance student learning. While some of the *Reflections* are at a general managerial level, others focus on International Issues, Ethics, and Innovation.

- *Tips for Managers* provides "take-aways" from each chapter—things that managers and would-be managers can start to put into action right now, based on what they have learned in the chapter.

- *Summary and Implications* provides responses to the outcomes-based questions at the beginning of each chapter.

End-of-Chapter Applications

Taking the best of our end-of-chapter features from the eighth Canadian edition and adding new ones, we have created a rich section of applications, *Management @ Work*. This section provides students with a variety of opportunities to apply the material right now, even if they are not managers. It includes the following:

- NEW! *Reading for Comprehension*. Students can review their understanding of the chapter content.

- NEW! *Linking Concepts to Practice*. Students can see the application of theory to management situations.

- *Self-Assessment*. This feature includes one self-assessment exercise for the student to fill out, and refers students to the MyManagementLab website where they can access additional interactive self-assessment exercises that will help them discover things about themselves, their attitudes, and their personal strengths and weaknesses. (For more details, see the Supplements section on pages xxi–xxiii.)

- NEW structure! *Management for You Today*. Students can apply chapter material to their daily lives, helping them see that planning, leading, organizing, and controlling are useful in one's day-to-day life too. This feature is divided into two parts:

  - *Dilemma*, which presents an everyday scenario for students to resolve using management tools

  - *Becoming a Manager*, which provides suggestions for students on activities and actions they can do right now to help them in preparing to become a manager.

- *Working Together: Team-Based Exercise*. Students get a chance to work together in groups to solve a management challenge.

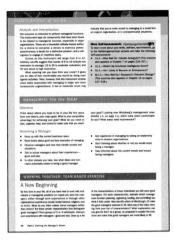

- NEW structure! *Ethics in Action*. This feature gives students an opportunity to consider ethical issues that relate to chapter material. It has two parts:

  - *Ethical Dilemma Exercise*, which focuses on ethical dilemmas that employees of organizations may face

  - *Thinking Critically About Ethics*, which encourages students to think critically about ethical issues they may encounter

- *Case Application*. This is a decision-focused case that asks students to determine what they would do if they were in the situation described.

- NEW! *Developing Your Diagnostic and Analytical Skills*. In this feature, students have the opportunity to apply chapter material to analyze a case. This feature effectively adds a second case to each chapter.

- NEW structure! *Developing Your Interpersonal Skills*. To reflect the importance being placed on skills, each chapter has this skills-based feature that encompasses the four management functions. The feature includes lessons about a particular skill, steps in developing the skill, a practice assignment to use the skill (often a mini-case), and a set of reinforcement assignments to further work on accomplishing the skill.

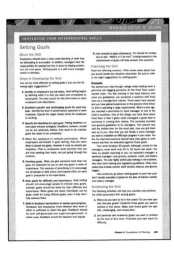

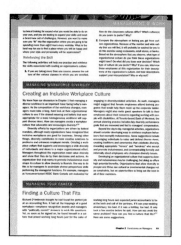

- *Managing Workforce Diversity*. This feature appears in some of the chapters and informs students about what can be done to make workplaces more inclusive.
- *Managing Your Career*. Appearing in some of the chapters, this feature uses short scenarios about the careers of fictional individuals to encourage students to start thinking about their own careers.

New to the Ninth Canadian Edition

In addition to the new pedagogical features highlighted above, we have introduced other new learning aids and made significant changes to content.

MyManagementLab

An access code to MyManagementLab at www.pearsoned.ca/mymanagementlab is included with this textbook. MyManagementLab is an online study tool for students and an online homework and assessment tool for faculty. Also on the site is the *Robbins OnLine Learning System* (*R.O.L.L.S.*), with the *Q&A* feature and additional exercises on managing diversity, ethics, and global management. A MyManagementLab box at the end of each part in the textbook directs students to these additional exercises. The site also includes the Self-Assessment Library, study maps, and other study and learning tools.

For more details on MyManagementLab, see the Supplements section on pages xxi–xxiii.

New Cases

Our reviews tell us that management courses need more cases. Besides offering cases at the end of each chapter (*Case Application* and *Developing Your Diagnostic and Analytical Skills*), we have responded to this request in other ways.

End-of-Part Case

NEW! A case featuring Starbucks appears at the end of each part of the text. The five parts of the case illustrate how the concepts and functions of management can be applied to a real-life corporation. The case can be used in parts, or it can serve as an integrating case at the end of the term.

End-of-Part Video Cases

Two video cases appear at the end of each part, for a total of ten videos. A number of these come from CBC Venture programs. The videos generally focus on several management issues within a part. The cases were carefully selected by David Delcorde of the University of Ottawa to provide instructors with audiovisual material to engage their students' attention. The videos are available in VHS (0-13-515225-9) and DVD format (0-13-515228-3).

End-of-Book Cases

NEW! Two longer cases, "The YMCA of London, Ontario," written by Pat MacDonald, and "Sarnia Food Fresh Grocery Store: The Icing on the Cake," written by J. David Whitehead and Jennifer Baker of Brock University, have been included at the end of the book. These two cases are lengthier and integrate a number of management issues.

Chapter-by-Chapter Highlights

Below, we highlight all the new material that has been added to each chapter.

Chapter 1: Introduction to Management and Organizations

- Enhanced the discussion of characteristics of organizations
- Provided a new emphasis on ethics

Chapter 2: Constraints on Managers: Organizational Culture and the Environment

- Expanded the discussion on how managers can use organizational culture to shape their work units
- Elaborated the discussion on Canada's legal environment and how it affects managers

Chapter 3: Managing in a Global Environment

- Revised and updated section on how organizations operate in a global environment
- New! Discussion of "born globals"
- Revised the discussion of how organizations can choose to structure themselves internationally
- Added a section on Hofstede's Framework for Assessing Cultures
- Expanded the discussion on globalization
- New! Pro- and anti-globalization arguments, including a summary table

Chapter 4: Corporate Social Responsibility and Managerial Ethics

- New! Four-stage model of the progression of an organization's social responsibility, including exhibit
- New! Lengthy discussion of what constitutes social responsibility
- New! Discussion of impact of social responsibility on bottom line
- New! The "greening" of management and how organizations go green
- Provided a discussion on Canada's legal position on ethics and bribery issues

Chapter 5: Decision Making

- Improved the discussion of satisficing and bounded rationality
- New! Group decision making
- Revised the discussion of decision-making biases and errors
- Provided a discussion on highly reliable organizations

Chapter 6: Foundations of Planning

- Included a longer discussion of challenges in planning

Chapter 7: Strategic Management

- Improved the discussion of strategic management
- New! Discussion of how business models relate to strategy
- Significantly revised the section on the steps in the strategic management process
- New! Discussion of how to sustain competitive advantage
- Improved the discussion of corporate strategy
- New! How to develop strategic flexibility
- New! Tips for Managers—Creating Strategic Flexibility

Chapter 8: Planning Tools and Techniques

- Linked the material in the chapter to planning for the 2010 Olympics to provide a realistic overview of planning tools and techniques
- Improved the discussion of forecasting
- Enhanced the discussion on benchmarking

Chapter 9: Organizational Structure and Design

- Provided a greater emphasis on "today's view" of the six key elements of organizational structure
- New! Tips for Managers—How to Delegate Effectively
- New! Today's organizational design challenges, including:
  - Keeping employees connected
  - Building a learning organization
  - Managing global structural issues

Chapter 10: Communication and Information Technology

- Updated information on the cost of information overload
- New! Tips for Managers—Suggestions for Giving Feedback
- New! Managing communication in an Internet world

Chapter 11: Human Resource Management

- Revised the discussion of high performance work practices
- New! Impact of economic conditions on human resource practices
- New! Problems with using written tests during the recruitment process
- New! Developed a section on what happens when performance falls short, including:
  - Discipline
  - Employee counselling
- New! Workplace romances
- New! Helping survivors respond to layoffs
- New! Layoff-survivor sickness
- New! What do college and university grads want from their jobs?

Chapter 12: Leadership

- New! Big Five personality traits and their relationship to leadership
- New! Discussion on applicability of transformational leadership in non-North American cultures
- New! Discussion on how women are perceived in the workplace
- New! Tips for Managers—Getting Back to Basics

Chapter 13: Motivating Employees

- New! Stock option programs and tips for designing them
- New! Suggestions for motivating employees

Chapter 14: Understanding Groups and Teams

- Significantly reorganized (and shortened) the chapter so that the focus is on teams, and how to build more effective teams
- New! Exhibit highlighting difference between groups and teams
- New! Stronger focus on effective group processes: building cohesiveness, managing conflict, and preventing social loafing
- New! Tips for Managers—Increasing Group Cohesiveness
- Expanded the discussion on resolving conflict

Chapter 15: Foundations of Control

- Completely reorganized this chapter, significantly increasing the depth of discussion on control
- New! Effects of feedback on goal setting
- New! How is information used in control?
- New! Controlling information

Chapter 16: Managing Change and Innovation

- More focused discussion on what is organizational change
- New! Global organizational development
- New! Karoshi in Japan (death from overwork)

Supplements

With this edition of *Management*, we have introduced MyManagementLab, which provides students with an assortment of tools to help enrich and expedite learning. MyManagementLab is an online study tool for students and an online homework and assessment tool for faculty. MyManagementLab lets students assess their understanding through auto-graded tests and assignments, develop a personalized study plan to address areas of weakness, and practice a variety of learning tools to master management principles. Some of these tools are described below:

- *Auto-Graded Tests and Assignments* MyManagementLab comes with two sample tests per chapter. These were prepared by David Parker, George Brown College. Students can work through these diagnostic tests to identify areas they have not fully understood. The sample tests generate a personalized study plan. Instructors can also assign these sample tests or create assignments, quizzes, or tests using a mix of publisher-supplied content and their own custom exercises.

mymanagementlab

- *Personalized Study Plan* In MyManagementLab, students are treated as individuals with specific learning needs. Students have limited study time so it is important for them to be as effective as possible. A personalized study plan is generated from each student's results on sample tests and instructor assignments. Students can clearly see the topics they have mastered—and, more importantly, the concepts they need to work on.

- *eText* Students can study without leaving the online environment. They can access the eText online, including animated text figures prepared by Cathy Heyland, Selkirk College.

- *Robbins OnLine Learning System (R.O.L.L.S.)* R.O.L.L.S. features the following tools:
  - *Robbins Self-Assessment Library*. The Self-Assessment Library helps students create a skills portfolio. It is an interactive library of 51 behavioural questionnaires that help students discover things about themselves, their attitudes, and their personal strengths and weaknesses. Learning more about themselves gives students interesting insights into how they might behave as a manager and motivates them to learn more about management theories and practices that can help them better understand what it takes to be a successful manager.
  - *Q&A*. The questions from each chapter that students ask most frequently are answered by the authors—in both written and audio format. It's like having an instructor standing over their shoulder at the times students need it the most.
  - *Diversity in Action*. These interactive exercises put students in the challenging role of a manager making decisions related to age, gender, or ethnic diversity.
  - *Passport: Managing in a Global Environment*. This multimedia module illustrates the globalization challenges that managers face. There are three to four global case scenarios that students can do at the end of each part. These cases span thirteen different countries. Students will find a map and click a desired country to get information about that country (video and written information is provided). Using this information, students make decisions about the most appropriate ways to handle the managerial problems described in the case scenarios.
  - *Ethics*. In these interactive exercises, students are put in the role of a manager making decisions about current ethical issues.
  - *PRactical Interactive Skills Modules (PRISM)*. This module consists of 12 interactive decision-tree–style comprehensive exercises that provide students with an opportunity to try out different management skills and learn why certain approaches are better than others.

- *Study Maps* These extensive maps show students how *all* of the management concepts and functions discussed in *all* of the chapters in a part are related.

- *Glossary Flashcards* This study aid is useful for students' review of key concepts.

- *Management in the News* These mini cases were developed from current news articles and include questions for students to answer. These cases will be updated twice a year.

- *Research Navigator* Research Navigator helps students quickly and efficiently make the most of their research time by providing four exclusive databases of reliable source content including the EBSCO Academic Journal and Abstract Database, New York Times Search by Subject Archive, "Best of the Web" Link Library, and Financial Times Article Archive and Company Financials.

For instructors, we have created an outstanding supplements package, all conveniently available online through MyManagementLab in the special instructor area, downloadable from our product catalogue at www.pearsoned.ca, or available on a single CD-ROM. The Instructor's Resource CD-ROM (978-0-13-515227-0) contains the following:

- Instructor's Resource Manual (includes video teaching notes and detailed lecture outlines) prepared by Terri Champion, Niagara College

- PowerPoint Slides, prepared by Jody Merritt, St. Clair College
- TestGen, prepared by Ron Shay, Kwantlen University College

The video cases are available in VHS (978-0-13-515225-6) and DVD format (978-0-13-515228-7). These cases were prepared by David Delcorde, University of Ottawa.

Acknowledgments

A number of people worked hard to give this ninth Canadian edition of *Management* a new look. Su Mei Ku, who has been my developmental editor on almost all of my projects, again outdid her always excellent performance. Her wit, good humour, helpfulness, support, and organizational skills made working on this textbook immensely easier.

I received incredible support for this project from a variety of people at Pearson Education Canada. Karen Elliott, Acquisitions Editor, was simply terrific in encouraging a fresh look for this book. Julia Hall and her design team translated my thoughts about what this book should look like, creating an exciting new design. I particularly appreciate her responsiveness to suggestions for changes. I appreciated working with Jen Handel again in her role as the Production Editor for this project. Her professionalism, good will, and cheerfulness make the production process a surprisingly enjoyable task. Steve O'Hearn, President of Higher Education, and Gary Bennett, Vice-President, Editorial Director, are extremely supportive on the management side of Pearson Education Canada, and this kind of support makes it much easier for an author to get work done and meet dreams and goals. Lisa Brant once again was very helpful in doing the photo research, and made some incredible finds in her search for photos to highlight management concepts. There are a variety of others at Pearson who also had their hand in making sure that the manuscript would be transformed into this book, and then delivered to your hands. To all of them I extend my thanks for jobs well done. The Pearson sales team is an exceptional group, and I know they will do everything possible to make this book successful. I continue to appreciate and value their support and interaction, particularly that of Cas Shields, Executive Marketing Manager, and Ewan French, my local sales representative.

Claudia Forgas was copyeditor for the project and did an amazing job of making sure everything was in place and written clearly. Sheila Wawanash was the proofreader, and was extremely diligent about checking for consistency throughout the text. I enjoyed the opportunity to work with both of them again. Their keen eyes helped to make the pages as clean as they are. They also help me remember the necessary qualities of virtual teams.

Finally, I want to acknowledge the many reviewers of this textbook for their detailed and helpful comments:

Terri Champion, Niagara College

Aaron Dresner, Concordia University

Richard Field, University of Alberta

Cyndi Hornby, Fanshawe College

Michelle Inness, University of Alberta

Martha Reavley, University of Windsor

Lori Saar, Lethbridge College

Ron Shay, Kwantlen University College

Patti Stoll, Seneca College

Susan Thompson, Trent University

W.J. Whistance-Smith, Ryerson University

Heather White, Georgian College

I dedicate this book to my father, Peter X. Langton. He was a man of many talents, and his understanding of organizations may have been greater than my own. To my family I give silent acknowledgment for everything else.

Nancy Langton
January 2008

ABOUT THE AUTHORS

Stephen P. Robbins received his PhD from the University of Arizona and has taught at the University of Nebraska at Omaha, Concordia University in Montreal, the University of Baltimore, Southern Illinois University at Edwardsville, and San Diego State University. Dr. Robbins' research interests have focused on conflict, power, and politics in organizations, behavioural decision making, and the development of effective interpersonal skills. His articles on these and other topics have appeared in journals such as *Business Horizons*, the *California Management Review*, *Business and Economic Perspectives*, *International Management*, *Management Review*, *Canadian Personnel and Industrial Relations*, and *The Journal of Management Education*.

Dr. Robbins is the world's bestselling textbook author in the areas of management and organizational behaviour. His most recent textbooks include *Organizational Behavior*, 12th ed. (Prentice Hall, 2007), *Essentials of Organizational Behavior*, 9th ed. (Prentice Hall, 2008), *Fundamentals of Management*, 6th ed., with David DeCenzo (Prentice Hall, 2008), and *Supervision Today!*, 5th ed., with David DeCenzo (Prentice Hall, 2007). In addition, Dr. Robbins is the author of the global best-sellers *The Truth About Managing People*, 2nd ed. (Financial Times Press, 2008) and *Decide & Conquer* (Financial Times Press, 2004).

An avid participant in masters' track-and-field competition, Dr. Robbins has set numerous indoor and outdoor age-group world sprint records since turning 50 in 1993. He has won more than a dozen indoor and outdoor US national titles at 60, 100, 200, and 400 meters, and has won seven gold medals at the World Masters Championships.

Mary Coulter received her PhD in Management from the University of Arkansas in Fayetteville. Before completing her graduate work, she held different jobs, including high school teacher, legal assistant, and government program planner. She has taught at Drury University, the University of Arkansas, Trinity University, and since 1983, at Southwest Missouri State University. Dr. Coulter's research interests have focused on competitive strategies for not-for-profit arts organizations and the use of new media in the educational process. Her research on these and other topics has appeared in such journals as *International Journal of Business Disciplines*, *Journal of Business Strategies*, *Journal of Business Research*, *Journal of Nonprofit and Public Sector Marketing*, and *Case Research Journal*. In addition to *Management*, Dr. Coulter has published other books with Prentice Hall including *Strategic Management in Action*, now in its fourth edition, and *Entrepreneurship in Action*. When she is not busy teaching or writing, she enjoys puttering around in her flower gardens, playing the piano, reading different types of books, and enjoying many different activities with her husband Ron and her daughters Sarah and Katie.

Nancy Langton received her PhD from Stanford University. Since completing her graduate studies, Dr. Langton has taught at the University of Oklahoma and the University of British Columbia. Currently a member of the Organizational Behaviour and Human Resources division in the Sauder School of Business, University of British Columbia, and academic director of the Business Families Centre at UBC, she teaches at the undergraduate, MBA, and PhD level, and conducts executive programs on family business issues, time management, attracting and retaining employees, as well as women and management issues. Dr. Langton has received several major research grants from the Social Sciences and Humanities Research Council of Canada, and her research interests have focused on human resource issues in the workplace, including pay equity, gender equity, and leadership and communication styles. She is currently conducting longitudinal research with entrepreneurs in the Greater Vancouver Region, trying to understand the relationship between their human resource practices and the success of their businesses. Her articles on these and other topics have appeared in such journals as *Administrative Science Quarterly*, *American Sociological Review*, *Sociological Quarterly*, *Journal of Management Education*, *Gender, Work and Organizations* and *Organization Studies*. She has won Best Paper commendations from both the Academy of Management and the Administrative Sciences Association of Canada, and in 2003 won the Best Women's Entrepreneurship Paper Award given by the Center for Women's Business Research for her work with Jennifer Cliff (University of Alberta) and Howard Aldrich (University of North Carolina). She has also published two textbooks on organizational behaviour with Pearson Education Canada, and this is her third textbook on management.

Dr. Langton routinely wins high marks from her students for teaching. She has been nominated many times for the Commerce Undergraduate Society Awards, and has won several honourable mention plaques. In 1998, she won the Sauder School of Business' most prestigious award for teaching innovation, The Talking Stick. The award was given for Dr. Langton's redesign of the undergraduate organizational behaviour course as well as for the many activities that were a spin-off of these efforts. In 2001, she was part of the Sauder School's MBA Core design team that won the national Alan Blizzard award, which recognizes innovation in teaching.

In Dr. Langton's "other life," she teaches the artistry of quiltmaking, and one day hopes to win first prize at *Visions*, the juried show for quilts as works of art. When she is not designing quilts, she is either reading novels (often suggested by a favourite correspondent), or studying cookbooks for new ideas. All of her friends would say that she makes from scratch the best pizza in all of Vancouver.

PART one

Defining the Manager's Terrain

MANAGERS COORDINATE WORK activities to achieve organizational goals. Their ability to act is affected by both the internal culture of the organization and the constraints of the external environment—including the global environment. Managers must also deal with complicated ethical and social responsibility issues as they plan, organize, lead, and control. When considering the terrain, managers might ask these questions:

- What is my role as a manager?
- What constraints do I face as a manager both within the organization

- and from the external environment?
- How does the global environment affect my ability to manage?

- What can I do to be an ethical and socially responsible manager?

CHAPTER 1
Introduction to Management and Organizations

What can I learn from the study of management?

1. What makes someone a manager?
2. What is management and what do managers do?
3. What characteristics define an organization?
4. What are the challenges to managing?
5. Does studying management make a difference?

CHAPTER 2
Constraints on Managers: Organizational Culture and the Environment

What constraints do managers face?

1. How much control do managers have?
2. What effect does culture have on managerial actions?
3. What kinds of cultures can managers create?
4. What influence does the environment have on managers?

CHAPTER 3
Managing in a Global Environment

How does the world outside Canada affect how Canadians run their businesses?

1. What are the different ways of viewing global differences?
2. What kinds of alliances affect trade relations among countries in the world?
3. How do organizations do business globally?
4. What are the challenges of doing business globally?

CHAPTER 4
Corporate Social Responsibility and Managerial Ethics

What does it take to be an ethical and socially responsible manager?

1. What is corporate social responsibility?
2. Can being socially responsible help performance?
3. How do organizations go green?
4. How do values influence management?
5. What is ethics and how can ethical behaviour be encouraged?

CHAPTER 1

Introduction to Management and Organizations

What can I learn from the study of management?

1. What makes someone a manager?
2. What is management and what do managers do?
3. What characteristics define an organization?
4. What are the challenges to managing?
5. Does studying management make a difference?

▶ ▶ ▶ Brian Scudamore was an 18-year-old university student in need of money when he founded Vancouver-based 1-800-GOT-JUNK?, North America's largest junk-removal service.[1] "An inspiration came to me when I was in a McDonald's drive-through in Vancouver. I saw a beaten-up pickup truck with plywood panels advertising junk pickup and hauling."

At first, hauling junk was meant to get him through university. However, by the third year of his studies, the business had grown enough that he dropped out of school to manage it full time.

Scudamore started his business in 1989 with a $700 pickup truck, but now has over 300 franchises throughout Canada, the United States, Australia, and the United Kingdom. He says he based his business model on Federal Express, which offers on-time service and up-front rates. Scudamore's drivers wear clean uniforms and drive shiny, clean trucks.

Scudamore learned about business by doing business. He also learned that it is important for managers to involve employees in decision making: "As soon as I stopped trying to be the CEO who's got everything under control, there was an instant shift," he says. "My managers started seeing me as someone they could disagree with—and that makes all of us stronger."

Think About It

What kinds of skills do managers need? Put yourself in Brian Scudamore's shoes. What kinds of leadership skills would you need to manage franchises in four countries? Is managing in a franchise organization different from managing in a large corporation, a small business, or a government organization?

1-800-GOT-JUNK?
www.1800gotjunk.com

Brian Scudamore is a good example of what today's successful managers are like and the skills they must have to deal with the problems and challenges of managing in the twenty-first century. These managers may not be who or what you might expect. They range in age from under 18 to over 80. They run large corporations, as well as entrepreneurial start-ups. They are found in government departments, hospitals, small businesses, nonprofit agencies, museums, schools, and even such nontraditional organizations as political campaigns and consumer cooperatives—in every country on the globe.

No matter where managers are found, the fact is that they have exciting and challenging jobs! Organizations need managers more than ever in these uncertain, complex, and chaotic times. *Managers do matter!* How do we know that managers matter to organizations? A Gallup Organization study based on interviews with 2 million employees at 700 companies found that the single most important variable in employee productivity and loyalty was not pay or benefits or workplace environment; it was the quality of the relationship between employees and their direct supervisors.[2] In addition, a KPMG/Ipsos Reid study of Canadian companies found that those that made the top 10 list for great human resource practices also scored high on financial performance and investment value. Six of the "Most Respected Corporations for Human Resources Management" placed in the top 10 on both financial measures, and nine scored in the top 10 of at least one of the financial measures.[3]

This textbook is about the important managerial work that Brian Scudamore and the millions of other managers like him do. It recognizes the reality facing today's managers—new technologies and new ways of organizing work are altering old approaches. Today's successful managers must be able to blend tried-and-true management approaches with new ones. In this chapter, we introduce you to managers and management by looking at who managers are, what management is, what managers do, and what an organization is. We also consider the key challenges managers face today. Finally, we wrap up the chapter by discussing why it's important to study management.

Who Are Managers?

▶ ▶ ▶ As founder of 1-800-GOT-JUNK?, Brian Scudamore manages the largest junk-removal service in North America.[4] He attended Dawson College in Montreal, and then spent one year each at Concordia and the University of British Columbia studying business before dropping out to run his business full time. Part of his job is making sure that those who run the 1-800-GOT-JUNK? franchises around the world are successful in carrying out his business model. "By relying on franchise owners to come in and share some of the risk, I realized I could expand the firm without having to turn to outside investors or other funding sources," Scudamore said. "To me, this was a solid plan for growth."

Think About It

What makes Brian Scudamore a manager?

1. What makes someone a manager?

It used to be fairly simple to define who managers were: They were the organizational members who told others what to do and how to do it. It was easy to differentiate managers from nonmanagerial employees; nonmanagerial employees were those organizational members who worked directly on a job or task and had no one reporting to them. But it isn't quite that simple anymore. The changing nature of organizations and work has, in many organizations, blurred the clear lines of distinction between managers and nonmanagerial employees. Many traditional nonmanagerial jobs now include managerial activities, particularly for employees working in teams.[5]

Q&A 1.1

Today, how do we define who managers are? A **manager** is someone who works with and through other people by coordinating their work activities in order to accomplish organizational goals. A manager's job is not about *personal* achievement—it's about helping *others* do their work and achieve. That may mean coordinating the work of a departmental group, or it might mean supervising a single person. It could involve coordinating the work activities of a team composed of people from several different departments or even people outside the organization, such as temporary employees or employees who work for the organization's suppliers. Keep in mind, also, that managers may have other work duties not related to coordinating and integrating the work of others. For example, an insurance claims supervisor may also process claims in addition to coordinating the work activities of other claims clerks.

manager
Someone who works with and through other people by coordinating their work activities in order to accomplish organizational goals.

Types of Managers

Is there some way to classify managers in organizations? In traditionally structured organizations (often pictured as being shaped like a pyramid where the number of employees is greater at the bottom than at the top), managers are often described as first-line, middle, or top (see Exhibit 1-1). Identifying exactly who the managers are in these organizations isn't difficult, although they may have a variety of titles. **First-line managers** are at the lowest level of management and manage the work of nonmanagerial employees who are directly or indirectly involved with the production or creation of the organization's products. They are often called *supervisors* but may also be called shift managers, district managers, department managers, office managers, or even foremen. **Middle managers** include all levels of management between the first-line level and the top level of the organization. These

first-line managers
Managers at the lowest level of the organization who manage the work of nonmanagerial employees who are directly or indirectly involved with the production or creation of the organization's products.

middle managers
Managers between the first-line level and the top level of the organization who manage the work of first-line managers.

Donna Rodrigues, principal of the University Park Campus School in Worcester, Massachusetts, has used her management skills to help raise standards among her teachers and students. She improved the curriculum, outlawed swearing and fighting, sent teachers to the homes of students who were absent too often, and promised parents that all their children would attend classes. Rodrigues, a middle manager within the school district hierarchy, believes that treating the students like adults helps motivate them to perform at their best.

managers manage the work of first-line managers and may have titles such as regional manager, project leader, plant manager, or division manager. At or near the top of the organization are the **top managers**, who are responsible for making organization-wide decisions and establishing the plans and goals that affect the entire organization. These individuals typically have titles such as executive vice-president, president, managing director, chief operating officer, chief executive officer, or chairman of the board. In the chapter-opening case, Brian Scudamore is a top-level manager for 1-800-GOT-JUNK? He is involved in creating and implementing broad and comprehensive changes that affect the entire organization.

top managers
Managers at or near the top level of the organization who are responsible for making organization-wide decisions and establishing the plans and goals that affect the entire organization.

Not all organizations get work done using this traditional pyramidal form, however. Some organizations, for example, are more flexible and loosely structured with work being done by ever-changing teams of employees who move from one project to another as work demands arise. Although it's not as easy to tell who the managers are in these organizations, we do know that someone must fulfill that role—that is, there must be someone who works with and through other people by coordinating their work to accomplish organizational goals.

Q&A 1.2

Exhibit 1-1

Managerial Levels

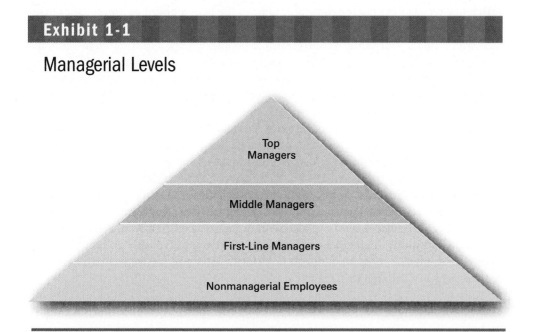

What Is Management and What Do Managers Do?

▶ ▶ ▶ Managers plan, lead, organize, and control, and Brian Scudamore certainly carries out all of these tasks.[6] He has to coordinate the work activities of his entire company efficiently and effectively. With franchises located in four countries, he has to make sure that work is carried out consistently to protect his brand. He also has to support his managers. He does this by providing a call centre operation in Vancouver that provides all the job booking arrangements, no matter where the caller is from. By providing this service, franchise managers at other locations can focus on the business of picking up junk. He continually works on plans to expand the business: "One of our goals at 1-800-GOT-JUNK? has been to become a globally admired company with a presence in 10 different countries by 2012." Scudamore adds, "It's important to stay focused when entering new markets. No matter how well you do your research, there will always be unexpected details that have to be managed differently."

Think About It

As a manager, Brian Scudamore needs to plan, lead, organize, and control, and he needs to be efficient and effective. How might Scudamore balance the needs of efficiency and effectiveness in his role as founder and CEO of 1-800-GOT-JUNK? What skills are needed for him to plan, lead, organize, and control effectively? What challenges does he face performing these functions while running an international business?

---

2. What is management and what do managers do?

management
Coordinating work activities so that they are completed efficiently and effectively with and through other people.

Simply speaking, management is what managers do. But that simple statement does not tell us much, does it? A more thorough explanation is that **management** is coordinating work activities so that they are completed *efficiently* and *effectively* with and through other people. Management researchers have developed three specific categorization schemes to describe what managers do: functions, roles, and skills. In this section, we consider the challenges of balancing efficiency and effectiveness, and then examine the approaches that look at what managers do. In reviewing these categorizations, it might be helpful to understand that management is something that is a learned talent, rather than something that comes "naturally." Many people do not know how to be a manager when they first are appointed to that role.

Efficiency and Effectiveness

efficiency
Getting the most output from the least amount of inputs; referred to as "doing things right."

Efficiency refers to getting the most output from the least amount of inputs, or as management expert Peter Drucker explained, "doing things right."[7] Because managers deal with scarce inputs—including resources such as people, money, and equipment—they are concerned with the efficient use of those resources by getting things done at the least cost.

It's not enough just to be efficient, however. Management is also concerned with being effective, completing activities so that organizational goals are achieved. **Effectiveness** is often described as "doing the right things"—that is, those work activities that will help the organization reach its goals. For instance, hospitals may try to be efficient by reducing the number of days that patients stay in hospital. This may not be effective, however, if patients get sick at home shortly after being released from hospital.

effectiveness
Completing activities so that organizational goals are achieved; referred to as "doing the right things."

Whereas efficiency is concerned with the means of getting things done, effectiveness is concerned with the ends, or attainment of organizational goals (see Exhibit 1-2). Management is concerned, then, not only with getting activities completed and meeting organizational goals (effectiveness) but also with doing so as efficiently as possible. In successful organizations, high efficiency and high effectiveness typically go hand in hand. Poor management is most often due to both inefficiency and ineffectiveness or to effectiveness achieved through inefficiency.

Q&A 1.3

Exhibit 1-2

Efficiency and Effectiveness in Management

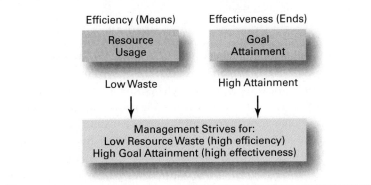

Management Functions

Think about a manager you have had. To what extent did he or she engage in planning, organizing, leading, and controlling?

According to the functions approach, managers perform certain activities or duties as they efficiently and effectively coordinate the work of others. What are these activities or functions? In the early part of the twentieth century, a French industrialist named Henri Fayol first proposed that all managers perform five functions: planning, organizing, commanding, coordinating, and controlling.[8] Today, most management textbooks (including this one) are organized around the **management functions**: planning, organizing, leading, and controlling (see Exhibit 1-3). But you do not have to be a manager in order to have a need to plan, organize, lead and control, so understanding these processes is important for everyone. Let's briefly define what each of these functions encompasses.

management functions
Planning, organizing, leading, and controlling.

Planning

If you have no particular destination in mind, then you can take any road. However, if you have someplace in particular you want to go, you have got to plan the best way to get there. Because organizations exist to achieve some particular purpose, someone must clearly define that purpose and the means for its achievement. Managers performing the **planning** function define goals, establish an overall strategy for achieving those goals, and develop plans to integrate and coordinate activities. This can be done by the CEO

planning
A management function that involves defining goals, establishing a strategy for achieving those goals, and developing plans to integrate and coordinate activities.

Exhibit 1-3

Management Functions

Planning	Organizing	Leading	Controlling	
Defining goals, establishing strategy, and developing subplans to coordinate activities	Determining what needs to be done, how it will be done, and who is to do it	Directing and motivating all involved parties and resolving conflicts	Monitoring activities to ensure that they are accomplished as planned	*Lead to* → Achieving the organization's stated purpose

and senior management team for the overall organization. Middle-level managers often have a planning role within their units. First-line managers have a more limited role in the planning process, but may need to use planning to adequately schedule work and employees. Planning, by the way, is not just for managers. For instance, as a student, you need to plan for exams and your financial needs.

Organizing

organizing
A management function that involves determining what tasks are to be done, who is to do them, how the tasks are to be grouped, who reports to whom, and where decisions are to be made.

Managers are also responsible for arranging work to accomplish the organization's goals. We call this function **organizing**. When managers organize, they determine what tasks are to be done, who is to do them, how the tasks are to be grouped, who reports to whom (that is, they define authority relationships), and where decisions are to be made. When you work in a student group, you engage in some of these same organizing activities—deciding on a division of labour, and what tasks will be carried out to get an assignment completed.

Leading

leading
A management function that involves motivating subordinates, directing the work of individuals or teams, selecting the most effective communication channels, and resolving employee behaviour issues.

Every organization includes people, and a manager's job is to work with and through people to accomplish organizational goals. This is the **leading** function. When managers motivate subordinates, direct the work of individuals or teams, select the most effective communication channel, or resolve employee behaviour issues, they are leading. Knowing how to manage and lead effectively is an important, and sometimes difficult, skill as it requires the ability to successfully communicate. Leading is not just for managers, however. As a student, you might want to practise leadership skills when working in groups or club activities. You might also want to evaluate whether you need to improve your leadership skills in anticipation of the needs of future jobs.

Controlling

controlling
A management function that involves monitoring actual performance, comparing actual performance to a standard, and taking correct action when necessary.

The final management function is **controlling**. After the goals are set (planning), the plans formulated (planning), the structural arrangements determined (organizing), and the people hired, trained, and motivated (leading), there has to be some evaluation of whether things are going as planned (controlling). To ensure that work is going as it should, managers must monitor and evaluate the performance of employees, technology, and systems. Actual performance must be compared with the previously set goals. If performance of individuals or units does not match the goals set, it's management's job to get performance back on track. This process of monitoring, comparing, and correcting is what we mean by the controlling function. Individuals, whether working in groups or alone, also face the responsibility of controlling; that is, they make sure the goals and actions are achieved and take corrective action when necessary.

Just how well does the functions approach describe what managers do? Do managers always plan, organize, lead, and then control? In reality, what a manager does may not always happen in this logical and sequential order. But that does not negate the importance of the basic functions that managers perform. Regardless of the order in which the functions are performed, the fact is that managers do plan, organize, lead, and control as they manage.

The continued popularity of the functions approach to describe what managers do is a tribute to its clarity and simplicity. But some have argued that this approach isn't appropriate or relevant.[9] So let's look at another perspective.

Management Roles

 Henry Mintzberg
www.henrymintzberg.com

management roles
Specific categories of managerial behaviour.

Henry Mintzberg, a prominent management researcher at McGill University, studied actual managers at work. He says that what managers do can best be described by looking at the roles they play at work. His studies allowed him to conclude that managers perform 10 different but highly interrelated management roles.[10] The term **management roles** refers to specific categories of managerial behaviour. (Think of the different roles you play and the different behaviours you are expected to perform in these roles as a student, a sibling, an employee, a volunteer, and so forth.) As shown in Exhibit 1-4, Mintzberg's 10 management roles are grouped around interpersonal relationships, the transfer of information, and decision making.

The **interpersonal roles** involve working with people (subordinates and persons out-side the organization) or performing duties that are ceremonial and symbolic in nature. The three interpersonal roles include being a figurehead, leader, and liaison. The **informational roles** involve receiving, collecting, and disseminating information. The three informa-tional roles include monitor, disseminator, and spokesperson. Finally, the **decisional roles** involve making significant choices that affect the organization. The four decisional roles include entrepreneur, disturbance handler, resource allocator, and negotiator.

A number of follow-up studies have tested the validity of Mintzberg's role categories among different types of organizations and at different levels within given organizations.[11] The evidence generally supports the idea that managers—regardless of the type of organization or level in the organization—perform similar roles. However, the emphasis that managers give to the various roles seems to change with their organizational level.[12] Specifically, the roles of disseminator, figurehead, negotiator, liaison, and spokesperson are more impor-tant at the higher levels of the organization; while the leader role (as Mintzberg defined it) is more important for lower-level managers than it is for either middle- or top-level managers.

interpersonal roles
Management roles that involve working with people or performing duties that are ceremonial and symbolic in nature.

informational roles
Management roles that involve receiving, collecting, and disseminating information.

decisional roles
Management roles that involve making significant choices that affect the organization.

Exhibit 1-4

Mintzberg's Management Roles

Role	Description	Examples of Identifiable Activities
Interpersonal		
Figurehead	Symbolic head; obliged to perform a number of routine duties of a legal or social nature	Greeting visitors; signing legal documents
Leader	Responsible for the motivation of subordinates; responsible for staffing, training, and associated duties	Performing virtually all activities that involve subordinates
Liaison	Maintains self-developed network of outside contacts and informers who provide favours and information	Acknowledging mail; doing external board work; performing other activities that involve outsiders
Informational		
Monitor	Seeks and receives a wide variety of internal and external information to develop a thorough understanding of organization and environment	Reading periodicals and reports; maintaining personal contacts
Disseminator	Transmits information received from outsiders or from subordinates to members of the organization	Holding informational meetings; making phone calls to relay information
Spokesperson	Transmits information to outsiders on organization's plans, policies, actions, results, etc.	Holding board meetings; giving information to the media
Decisional		
Entrepreneur	Searches organization and its environment for opportunities and initiates "improvement projects" to bring about changes	Organizing strategy and review sessions to develop new programs
Disturbance handler	Responsible for corrective action when organization faces important, unexpected disturbances	Organizing strategy and review sessions that involve disturbances and crises
Resource allocator	Responsible for the allocation of organizational resources of all kinds—making or approving all significant organizational decisions	Scheduling; requesting authorization; performing any activity that involves budgeting and the programming of subordinates' work
Negotiator	Responsible for representing the organization at major negotiations	Participating in union contract negotiations

Source: H. Mintzberg, *The Nature of Managerial Work* (New York: Harper & Row, 1973), pp. 93–94. Copyright © 1973 by Henry Mintzberg. Reprinted by permission of Harper & Row, Publishers, Inc.

Functions vs. Roles

So which approach to describing what managers do is correct—functions or roles? Each has merit. However, the functions approach still represents the most useful way of conceptualizing the manager's job. "The classical functions provide clear and discrete methods of classifying the thousands of activities that managers carry out and the techniques they use in terms of the functions they perform for the achievement of goals."[13] Many of Mintzberg's roles align well with one or more of the functions. For instance, resource allocation is part of planning, as is the entrepreneurial role, and all three of the interpersonal roles are part of the leading function. Although most of the other roles fit into one or more of the four functions, not all of them do. The difference can be explained by the fact that all managers do some work that isn't purely managerial.[14] Our decision to use the management functions to describe what managers do does not mean that Mintzberg's role categories are invalid, as he clearly offers important insights into managers' work.

Management Skills

As you can see from the preceding discussion, a manager's job is varied and complex. Managers need certain skills to perform the duties and activities associated with being a manager. What types of skills does a manager need? Research by Robert L. Katz found that managers needed three essential skills: technical skills, human skills, and conceptual skills.[15]

technical skills
Knowledge of and expertise in a specialized field.

Technical skills include knowledge of and expertise in a certain specialized field, such as engineering, computers, accounting, or manufacturing. These skills are more important at lower levels of management since these managers are dealing directly with employees doing the organization's work.

human skills
The ability to work well with other people both individually and in a group.

Human skills involve the ability to work well with other people both individually and in a group. Because managers deal directly with people, this skill is crucial for managers at all levels! Managers with good human skills are able to get the best out of their people. They know how to communicate, motivate, lead, and inspire enthusiasm and trust. These skills are equally important at all levels of management. Management professor Jin Nam Choi, of McGill University, reports that research shows that 40 percent of managers either leave or stop performing within 18 months of starting at an organization "because they have failed to develop relationships with bosses, colleagues or subordinates."[16] Choi's comment underscores the importance of developing human skills.

conceptual skills
The mental ability to analyze and generate ideas about abstract and complex situations.

Finally, **conceptual skills** involve the mental ability to analyze and generate ideas about abstract and complex situations. These skills help managers see the organization as a whole, understand the relationships among various subunits, and visualize how the organization fits into its broader environment. These skills are most important at the top management levels.

Exhibit 1-5 shows the relationship of the three skills to each level of management. Note that the three skills are important to more than one function. Additionally, in very flat organizations with little hierarchy, human, technical, and conceptual skills would be needed throughout the organization.

Exhibit 1-5

Skills Needed at Different Management Levels

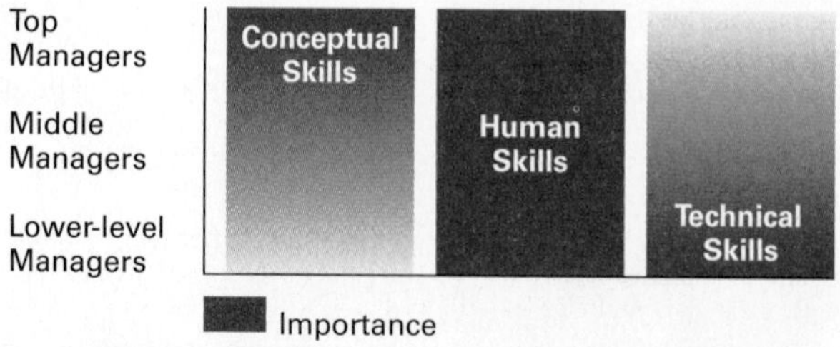

Top Managers
Middle Managers
Lower-level Managers

Conceptual Skills
Human Skills
Technical Skills

■ Importance

As you study the management functions in more depth, *Developing Your Diagnostic and Analytical Skills* and *Developing Your Interpersonal Skills*, found at the end of most chapters, will give you the opportunity to practise some of the key skills that are part of doing what a manager does. Skill-building exercises cannot make you an instant managerial expert, but they can provide you with a basic understanding of and appreciation for some of the skills you will need to master in order to become an effective manager. (To learn more about becoming a better mentor, see *Developing Your Interpersonal Skills—Mentoring* on pages 27–28, at the end of the chapter.)

What Is an Organization?

▶ ▶ ▶ Brian Scudamore is the founder of 1-800-GOT-JUNK?[17] Though he has a board of advisers, he is the only shareholder of the company. He explains why he has no other shareholders: "I believe in one captain of a ship." Therefore, he gets to set his own plans and goals. The company has over 250 franchises in 4 countries, which means that Scudamore's management skills have to include awareness of the challenges of managing in other countries.

Think About It

Do managers act differently if they work for large organizations rather than smaller ones? How does owning a franchise business affect the role of the manager?

Managers work in organizations. But what is an organization? An **organization** is a deliberate arrangement of people who act together to accomplish some specific purpose. Your college or university is an organization; so are fraternities and sororities, government departments, churches, Amazon.ca, your neighbourhood video store, the United Way, the Toronto Raptors basketball team, and Canadian Tire. These are all organizations because they have three common characteristics, as shown in Exhibit 1-6:

1. *Distinct purpose.* This purpose is typically expressed in terms of a goal or a set of goals that the organization hopes to accomplish.

2. *Composed of people.* One person working alone is not an organization, and it takes people to perform the work that is necessary for the organization to achieve its goals.

3. *Deliberate structure.* Whether that structure is open and flexible or traditional and clearly defined, the structure defines members' work relationships.

3. What characteristics define an organization?

organization
A deliberate arrangement of people who act together to accomplish some specific purpose.

Exhibit 1-6

Characteristics of Organizations

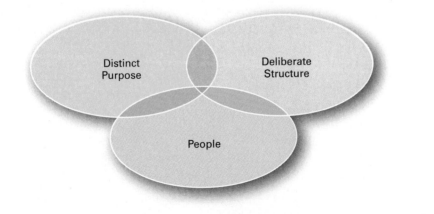

In summary, the term *organization* refers to an entity that has a distinct purpose, includes people or members, and has some type of deliberate structure.

Although these three characteristics are important to our definition of *what* an organization is, the concept of an organization is changing. It's no longer appropriate to assume that all organizations are going to be structured like Air Canada, Petro-Canada, or General Motors, with clearly identifiable divisions, departments, and work units. Just how is the concept of an organization changing? Exhibit 1-7 lists some differences between traditional organizations and new organizations. As these lists show, today's organizations are becoming more open, flexible, and responsive to changes.[18]

Does your college or university or an organization in which you have worked represent a "new organization"? Why or why not?

Why are organizations changing? Because the world around them has changed and continues to change. Societal, economic, political, global, and technological changes have created an environment in which successful organizations (those that consistently attain their goals) must embrace new ways of getting work done. As we stated earlier, even though the concept of organizations may be changing, managers and management continue to be important to organizations.

The Size of Organizations

Managers don't just manage in large organizations, which represent only about 2 percent of organizations in Canada. Small businesses (those that employ fewer than 100 individuals) represent 98 percent of all Canadian companies. These businesses employ almost half of all Canadian workers. Small businesses also contribute significantly to the economy. Businesses employing 50 or fewer individuals generated about 22 percent of total GDP in 2005.[19] Organizations of every size need managers. Moreover, in 2007, about 16 percent of the labour force was self-employed, meaning that these people were managing themselves.[20]

Managers are also not confined to manufacturing work, as only 12 percent of Canadians work in manufacturing organizations. Nineteen percent work in public sector jobs (those in the local, provincial, or federal government), while most Canadians (around 76 percent) work in the service sector of the economy.[21] The government is actually a large

Exhibit 1-7

The Changing Organization

Traditional Organization	New Organization
• Stable	• Dynamic
• Inflexible	• Flexible
• Job-focused	• Skills-focused
• Work is defined by job positions	• Work is defined in terms of tasks to be done
• Individual-oriented	• Team-oriented
• Permanent jobs	• Temporary jobs
• Command-oriented	• Involvement-oriented
• Managers always make decisions	• Employees participate in decision making
• Rule-oriented	• Customer-oriented
• Relatively homogeneous workforce	• Diverse workforce
• Workdays defined as 9 to 5	• Workdays have no time boundaries
• Hierarchical relationships	• Lateral and networked relationships
• Work at organizational facility during specific hours	• Work anywhere, anytime

employer in Canada. For instance, Canada Post, a Crown corporation, is the fifth-largest employer in Canada, employing over 70 000, behind only Onex, George Weston, Loblaw Companies, and Magna International.[22]

The Types of Organizations

Managers work in a variety of situations, and thus the people to whom they are held accountable vary considerably. Large organizations in the **private sector** are often **publicly held**, which means that their shares are available on the stock exchange for public trading. Managers of these companies report to a board of directors that is responsible to shareholders (also known as stockholders). There are also numerous **privately held organizations** (whose shares are not available on the stock market), both large and small. Privately held organizations can be individually owned, family owned, or owned by some other group of individuals. A number of managers work in the **nonprofit sector**, where the emphasis is on providing charity or services rather than on making a profit. Examples of such organizations include the SPCA (Society for the Prevention of Cruelty to Animals), the Royal Ontario Museum, and Vancouver's Bard on the Beach Festival. Other organizational forms such as **NGOs** (nongovernmental organizations), partnerships, and cooperatives also require managers.

Many managers work in the **public sector** as **civil servants** for the provincial, federal, and local governments. The challenges of managing within government departments can be quite different from the challenges of managing in publicly held organizations. Critics argue that it is less demanding to work for governments because there are few measurable performance objectives, allowing employees to feel less accountable for their actions.

Some managers and employees work for **Crown corporations** such as Canada Post, the CBC, and the Business Development Bank of Canada. Crown corporations are structured like private sector corporations, and have boards of directors, CEOs, and so on, but are owned by governments rather than shareholders. Employees in Crown corporations are not civil servants, and managers in Crown corporations are more independent than the senior bureaucrats who manage government departments.

Many of Canada's larger organizations are actually subsidiaries of American parent organizations (for example, Sears, Safeway, General Motors, and Ford Motor Company). These managers often report to American top managers, and are not always free to set their own goals and targets. Conflicts can arise between how Canadian managers and the American managers to whom they report think things should be done.

 Canada Post
www.canadapost.ca

private sector
The part of the economy that is run by organizations which are free from direct government control; organizations in this sector operate to make a profit.

publicly held organization
A company whose shares are available on the stock exchange for public trading by brokers/dealers.

privately held organization
A company whose shares are not available on the stock exchange but are privately held.

nonprofit sector
The part of the economy that is run by organizations which operate for purposes other than making a profit (that is, providing charity or services).

NGO
An organization that is independent from government control and whose primary focus is on humanitarian, development, and environmental sustainability activities.

public sector
The part of the economy that is controlled by government.

civil servant
A person who works in a local, provincial, or federal government department.

Crown corporation
A commercial company owned by the government but independently managed.

What Challenges Do Managers Face?

▶ ▶ ▶ As CEO of 1-800-GOT-JUNK?, Brian Scudamore both manages a head office in Vancouver and oversees the operations of his more than 250 franchise partners.[23] "There's about 105 people in our head office and my role is really just to be the cheerleader and make sure that we've got a very clear vision as to where we're going," Scudamore says.

When he chooses franchise partners, he looks for individuals who can follow systems willingly. "While running a successful franchise does require an entrepreneurial spirit, highly independent types who like things done their way will probably find the franchise model too restrictive," he says. Franchisees must wash their trucks once a day and follow a strict uniform code. They and their waste haulers must also have technological know-how. Service representatives use a computer program called JunkNet that the company developed to administer jobs. Also, franchisees use GPS devices to map out the quickest route to a pickup.

Maintaining the consistency of the 1-800-GOT-JUNK? brand from country to country has been a challenge. For example, in the United Kingdom, 1-800-GOT-JUNK? became Gotjunk.com, because the phone keys on European phones don't include letters. In Australia, although the population may be similar to Canada's, Scudamore says, "It's so far away (an 18-hour flight) that we couldn't possibly babysit it."

4. What are the challenges to managing?

Managers have always had to deal with changes taking place inside and outside their organizations. In today's world, where managers everywhere are dealing with corporate ethics scandals, demands to be more socially responsible, challenges of managing a diverse workforce, and globalization, change is constant. We briefly describe these challenges below, and then throughout this textbook we discuss their impact on the way managers plan, organize, lead, and control.

Ethics

While Canadian corporations were not directly implicated in many of the biggest corporate scandals of recent years, Canada has had its own share of financial mismanagement. For example, Conrad Black, the former CEO of Hollinger International who used the company as his personal piggy bank, was recently found guilty of obstruction of justice and three counts of mail fraud. Even the RCMP is not immune to being accused of financial mismanagement. David Brown, the former head of the Ontario Securities Commission, who was assigned to investigate the RCMP case, found that there was mismanagement by senior RCMP officers in the administration of the force's pension and insurance fund. Moreover, he discovered that those who reported fund problems to former RCMP commissioner Giuliano Zaccardelli "faced career damage."[24]

What do we mean by ethics? The term **ethics** refers to rules and principles that define right and wrong behaviour.[25] Unfortunately, the ethics of a situation are not always black and white. Consider the following: For some decisions, you can make choices exercising complete freedom of choice, with no regard to others. For other decisions, there is a set of laws that guides your behaviour. In between, there is a set of situations where you might want to consider the impact of your decision on others, even though there are no laws regarding your behaviour. This is the grey area of behaviour. Laws often develop because people did not act responsibly when they had a choice—for instance, not that long ago, drinking and driving did not have the penalties that it does now. Many people have talked about laws banning cellphones in various situations for much the same reason: Individuals do not think about the impact of their use on others.

Ontario Securities Commission

www.osc.gov.on.ca

ethics

Rules and principles that define right and wrong behaviour.

An internal investigation at Hollinger International concluded that Conrad Black used most of the company's profits between 1997 and 2004 for his own personal gain. The report suggested that Black colluded with others to take more than $400 million (US) from the publishing company. He was found guilty of four of the multiple charges of fraud brought against him in July 2007.

What has happened to managerial ethics? This important aspect of managerial behaviour seems to have been forgotten or ignored when we see managers put their self-interest ahead of the interests of others who might be affected by their decisions. While most managers continue to behave in a highly ethical manner, recent ethical abuses that were so widely publicized indicated a need to "upgrade" ethical standards. Efforts to improve the ethical behaviour of managers are being made at two levels. First, ethics education is being widely emphasized in university and college classrooms. Second, organizations themselves are taking a more active role in creating *and using* codes of ethics, providing ethics training programs, and hiring ethics officers. We want to prepare you to deal with the ethics dilemmas you are likely to face. We cover ethics and decision making extensively in Chapter 4. We have also included an *Ethical Dilemma Exercise* and a *Thinking Critically About Ethics* feature at the end of almost every chapter. Business ethics is critical to all stakeholders and the performance of a company.

Workforce Diversity

Another challenge facing managers is coordinating the work efforts of diverse organizational members in accomplishing organizational goals. Today's organizations are characterized by **workforce diversity**—the mix of people in organizations in terms of gender, race, ethnicity, disability, sexual orientation, and age, and demographic characteristics such as education and socio-economic status. Perhaps the most significant demographic force affecting workforce diversity during the next decade will be the aging of the population.[26]

Canada is a very diverse country, although this might not be apparent to everyone. Based on the 2006 census, on average 19.8 percent of Canada's population are foreign-born.[27] This varies widely across the country, however. Ontario has the highest proportion of foreign-born individuals, 28.3 percent of its population. British Columbia is second, with 27.5 percent of its population being foreign-born. Toronto and Vancouver have much higher rates than their respective provinces. In these cities, foreign-born individuals make up about 45.7 and 39.6 percent of the population, respectively. By contrast, in Newfoundland and Labrador only 1.7 percent of the population are foreign-born; in Nunavut this figure is 1.5 percent; in Manitoba it is 13.3 percent, and in Alberta it is 16.2 percent. There are many more women and minorities—including people with disabilities and gays and lesbians—in the workforce than ever before, and most experts agree that diversity is steadily increasing.

The challenge for managers is to make their organizations more accommodating to diverse groups of people by addressing different lifestyles, family needs, and work styles. Smart managers recognize that diversity can be an asset because it brings a broad range of viewpoints and problem-solving skills to a company, and also helps organizations better understand a diverse customer base. We highlight many diversity-related issues and discuss how companies are responding to them in our *Managing Workforce Diversity* feature at the end of a number of chapters throughout this textbook.

workforce diversity
The mix of people in organizations in terms of gender, race, ethnicity, disability, sexual orientation, and age, and demographic characteristics such as education and socio-economic status.

Globalization

Management is no longer constrained by national borders and has to confront the challenges of operating in a global market.[28] Globalization has become such an important topic that we devote one chapter to it (Chapter 3) and integrate discussion of its impact on the various management functions throughout this textbook.

Canada has been slow historically to face the global challenge, although the relatively small size of many Canadian firms may be partly a factor in this.[29] The *Fortune* list of the world's top 500 global companies of 2006 includes only 14 Canadian firms, and none of these appears in the top 200. The majority of the firms listed are American, but there are several entries from Britain, France, Germany, Japan, and China.[30] Managers who make no attempt to learn and adapt to changes in the global environment end up reacting rather than innovating; their organizations often become uncompetitive and fail.[31]

Textile workers in Italy are facing some of the challenges of globalization as inexpensive imports from Asia force the Italian clothing industry to cut jobs. But Italy's 120 000-member textile union, Filtea, is taking a controversial stand. The union leadership believes that the best way to protect Italian workers and their jobs is not to impose protective duties or quotas or to strike, but rather to press for better working conditions, tax breaks for corporate research, and ultimately better Italian products that will be more competitive through streamlined manufacturing processes.

Managing in an E-Business World

Can you imagine not using email? Do you expect advertisements to have web addresses included in their messages? Fifteen years ago email and web addresses were not the norm. Today's managers function in an e-business world. In fact, as a student, your learning may increasingly be taking place in an electronic environment. While critics have questioned the viability of Internet-based companies (dot-coms), especially after the high-tech collapse in 2000 and 2001, e-business is here for the long term. E-business offers many advantages to organizations—small or large, profit or nonprofit, global or domestic—in all industries.[32]

e-business (electronic business)
A way of doing business that relies on electronic (Internet-based) linkages with employees, managers, customers, clients, suppliers, and partners to efficiently and effectively achieve goals.

e-commerce (electronic commerce)
The sales and marketing component of e-business.

E-business (electronic business) is a way of doing business that relies on electronic (Internet-based) linkages with employees, managers, customers, clients, suppliers, and partners to efficiently and effectively achieve goals. E-business includes **e-commerce (electronic commerce)**, which is essentially the sales and marketing component of e-business.[33] Firms such as Dell (computers), Indigo Books & Music, and Future Shop (electronics) are engaged in e-commerce, because they sell items over the Internet.

Not every organization is, or needs to be, a total e-business. Exhibit 1-8 illustrates three categories of e-business involvement.[34] The first category is an e-business *enhanced* organization, a traditional organization that sets up e-business capabilities, usually e-commerce, while maintaining its traditional structure. Another category is an e-business *enabled*

Exhibit 1-8

Categories of E-Business Involvement

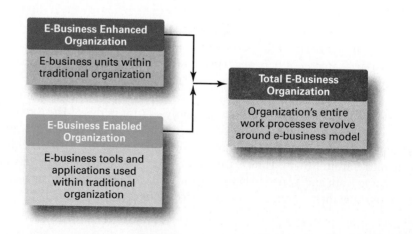

organization, which uses the Internet to perform its traditional business functions better, but not to sell anything. In other words, the Internet enables members of the organization to do their work more efficiently and effectively. Numerous organizations use electronic linkages to communicate with employees, customers, or suppliers, and to support them with information. The last category is a *total* e-business organization. Organizations such as Amazon.ca, Yahoo! Canada, Napster, and eBay are total e-business organizations; their whole existence revolves around the Internet.

Each of these different categories of e-business involvement presents unique management challenges, both in terms of managing employees, and also in interacting with customers and clients. The high failure rate of the dot-coms underscores just how important good management is for e-business organizations.

Customers

Because of globalization and e-business, customers have access to more sources than ever before to find the supplies and services they want. Every organization needs customers. Without customers, most organizations would cease to exist. Yet focusing on customers has long been thought to be the responsibility of marketing types. "Let the marketers worry about customers" is how many managers felt. We are discovering, however, that employee attitudes and behaviours play a big role in customer satisfaction. For instance, an analysis of a Qantas Airways passenger survey confirms this. Passengers were asked to rate their "essential needs" in air travel. Almost every factor listed by passengers was directly influenced by the actions of Qantas employees—from prompt baggage delivery, to courteous and efficient cabin crews, to assistance with connections, to quick and friendly check-ins.[35] Managers everywhere are beginning to understand that delivering consistent high-quality service is essential for success and survival in today's competitive environment and that employees are an important part of that equation.[36] The implication is clear—managers must create a customer-responsive organization where employees are friendly and courteous, accessible, knowledgeable, prompt in responding to customer needs, and willing to do what is necessary to please customers.[37] We examine customer-service management and its importance to planning, organizing, leading, and controlling in several chapters.

Working part-time at an auto-body shop while pursuing his master's degree, engineering student Joe Born wondered whether an industrial paint buffer could smooth out the scratches that had ruined one of his favourite music CDs. This idea worked like a charm, and after receiving a patent on it, Born spent four years perfecting SkipDR, an inexpensive disc-repair kit that he marketed successfully to Best Buy, Radio Shack, and Wal-Mart. Born's new company, Digital Innovations, now sells 50 different products to clean and repair CDs, DVDs, video games, and office equipment and is worth about $25 million (US).

 Qantas
www.qantas.com.au

Innovation

"Nothing is more risky than not innovating."[38] Innovation means doing things differently, exploring new territory, and taking risks. Innovation isn't just for high-tech and technologically advanced organizations. In today's world, organizational managers—at all levels and in all areas—need to encourage their employees to be on the lookout for new ideas and new approaches, not just in the products or services the organization provides, but in everything that is done. We examine innovation and its importance to planning, organizing, leading, and controlling in several chapters.

Knowledge Management and Learning Organizations

Today's managers confront an environment in which change takes place at an unprecedented rate. As a result, many past management approaches and principles—created for a world that was more stable and predictable—no longer apply.

Organizations of the twenty-first century must be able to learn and respond quickly. They should be **learning organizations**—that is, ones that have developed the capacity to continuously learn, adapt, and change.[39] Such organizations need managers who can effectively challenge conventional wisdom, manage the organizations' knowledge bases, and make necessary changes. Exhibit 1-9 on page 20 clarifies how a learning organization is different from a traditional organization.

learning organization
An organization that has developed the capacity to continuously learn, adapt, and change.

Exhibit 1-9

Learning Organization vs. Traditional Organization

	Traditional Organization	Learning Organization
Attitude toward change	If it's working, don't change it.	If you aren't changing, it won't be working for long.
Attitude toward new ideas	If it wasn't invented here, reject it.	If it was invented or reinvented here, reject it.
Who is responsible for innovation?	Traditional areas such as R & D	Everyone in organization
Main fear	Making mistakes	Not learning; not adapting
Competitive advantage	Products and service	Ability to learn; knowledge and expertise
Manager's job	Control others	Enable others

knowledge management
Cultivating a learning culture in which an organization's members systematically gather knowledge and share it with others in the organization to achieve better performance.

Ernst & Young
www.ey.com

Part of a manager's responsibility is to understand the value of knowledge as an important resource, just like cash, raw materials, or office equipment. **Knowledge management** involves cultivating a learning culture in which an organization's members systematically gather knowledge and share it with others in the organization to achieve better performance.[40] For instance, accountants and consultants at Ernst & Young, a professional-services firm, document best practices they have developed, unusual problems they have dealt with, and other work information. This knowledge is then shared with all employees through computer-based applications and through COIN (community of interest) teams that meet regularly throughout the company.

Why Study Management?

5. Does studying management make a difference?

Q&A 1.4

You may be wondering why you need to study management. If you are an accounting major, a marketing major, or any major other than management, you may not understand how studying management is going to help you in your career. We can explain the value of studying management by looking at the universality of management, the reality of work, and how management applies to anyone wanting to be self-employed.

The Universality of Management

universality of management
The reality that management is needed in all types and sizes of organizations, at all organizational levels, in all organizational work areas, and in organizations in all countries around the globe.

Just how universal is the need for management in organizations? We can say with absolute certainty that management is needed in all types and sizes of organizations, at all organizational levels, in all organizational work areas, and in all organizations, no matter what countries they are located in. This is known as the **universality of management** (see Exhibit 1-10). Managers in all these settings will plan, organize, lead, and control. However, this is not to say that management is done the same way in all settings. The differences in what a supervisor in a software applications testing facility at Microsoft does vs. what the CEO of Microsoft does are a matter of degree and emphasis, not of function. Because both are managers, both will plan, organize, lead, and control, but how they do so will differ.

Since management is universally needed in all organizations, we have a vested interest in improving the way organizations are managed. Why? We interact with organizations every single day of our lives. Are you irritated when none of the salespeople in a department store seems interested in helping you? Do you get annoyed when you call your computer's technical help desk because your CD-ROM drive is no longer working, go through 7 voice menus, and then get put on hold for 15 minutes? These are all examples of problems created by poor management. Organizations that are well managed—and we share many examples of these throughout the text—develop a loyal customer base, grow, and prosper. Those that are poorly managed find themselves with a declining customer base and reduced revenues. By studying management, you will be able to recognize poor

Exhibit 1-10

Universal Need for Management

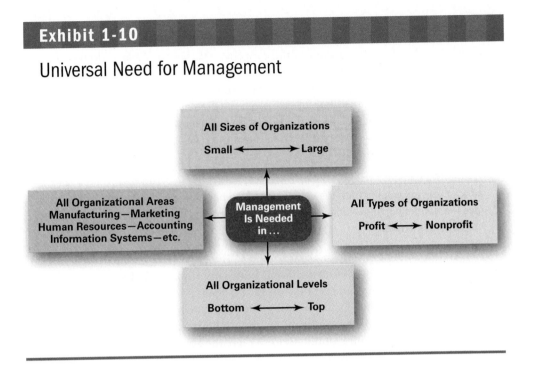

management and work to get it corrected. In addition, you will be able to recognize good management and encourage it, whether it's in an organization with which you are simply interacting or whether it's in an organization in which you are employed.

The Reality of Work

Another reason for studying management is the reality that most of you, once you graduate and begin your career, will either manage or be managed. For those who plan on management careers, an understanding of the management process forms the foundation upon which to build your management skills. For those of you who don't see yourselves in management positions, you are still likely to have to work with managers. Also, assuming that you will have to work for a living and recognizing that you are very likely to work in an organization, you will probably have some managerial responsibilities even if you are not managers. Our experience tells us that you can gain a great deal of insight into the way your manager behaves and the internal workings of organizations by studying management. Our point is that you don't have to aspire to be a manager to gain something valuable from a course in management.

Self-Employment

You may decide that you want to run your own business rather than work for someone else. This will require that you manage yourself, and may involve managing other people as well. Thus, an understanding of management is equally important, whether you are a manager in someone else's business or running your own business.

SUMMARY AND IMPLICATIONS

1. **What makes someone a manager?** Managers work with and through other people by coordinating employee work activities in order to accomplish organizational goals. Managers may have personal goals, but management is not about *personal* achievement—it's about helping *others* to achieve for the benefit of the organization as a whole.

▶ ▶ ▶ As we saw with Brian Scudamore, he is not only a visionary who guides the company but also a cheerleader who helps everyone in the organization do a better job.

2. What is management and what do managers do?   Management is coordinating work activities so that they are done efficiently and effectively. *Efficiency* means "doing things right" and getting things done at the least cost. *Effectiveness* means "doing the right things" and refers to completing activities that will help achieve the organization's goals. To do their jobs, managers plan, organize, lead, and control. This means they set goals and plan how to achieve those goals; they figure out what tasks need to be done, and who should do them; they motivate individuals to achieve goals, and communicate effectively with others; and they put accountability measures into place to make sure that goals are achieved efficiently and effectively.

▶ ▶ ▶ In Brian Scudamore's role as CEO of 1-800-GOT-JUNK?, he sets the goals for the overall organization, working with the various franchise partners. One of the challenges he faces is determining how rapidly his company can expand without weakening the reputation of his brand.

3. What characteristics define an organization?   There is no single type of organization. Managers work in a variety of organizations, both large and small. They also work in a variety of industries, including manufacturing and the service sector. The organizations they work for can be publicly held (meaning shares are traded on the stock exchange and managers are responsible to shareholders), privately held (meaning shares of the company are not available to the public), public sector (where the government is the employer), or nonprofit (where the emphasis is on providing charity or services rather than on making a profit).

▶ ▶ ▶ 1-800-GOT-JUNK? is a privately held organization. As its owner, Brian Scudamore is ultimately responsible to himself. Most managers, however, report to someone else.

4. What are the challenges to managing?   Perhaps one of the greatest managerial challenges is the crisis in ethical responsibility that is damaging confidence in today's organizations. Managers need to ensure that organizational members behave ethically. They also need to consider whether their own actions are socially responsible. Managers face the challenge of coordinating the work of a diverse workforce with differing needs. In addition, operating in today's global marketplace presents its own challenges and puts increasing pressure on managers. Customers and clients have access to more sources than ever before to meet their needs, particularly because of the growing number of e-businesses. Managers must be increasingly concerned with customer service and managing innovation to remain competitive. Finally, we live in a world of information overflow, and managers need to figure out how to manage all of that information and help their organizations become learning organizations. Even though all managers might not face all of these challenges, they should be aware of them, able to recognize them, and ready to handle them should they arise.

▶ ▶ ▶ Brian Scudamore introduced GPS tracking to his trucks so that drivers receive the quickest directions to job locations and dispatchers know where trucks are at any given time, making it easier to schedule additional pickups throughout the day. Scudamore is focused on providing excellent customer service.

5. Does studying management make a difference?   There are many reasons why students end up in management courses. Some of you are already managers, and are hoping to learn more about the subject. Some of you hope to be managers someday. And some of you might not have ever thought about being managers. Career aspirations are only one reason to study management, however. Any organization you encounter will have managers, and it is often useful to understand their responsibilities, challenges, and experience. Understanding management also helps us improve organizations.

CHAPTER 1

Management @ Work

READING FOR COMPREHENSION

1. How does a manager's job change with his or her level in the organization?

2. Why are efficiency and effectiveness important to management?

3. What are the four functions of management? Briefly describe each of them.

4. What are the three categories of management roles proposed by Mintzberg? Provide an example of each.

5. What are the three skills that affect managerial effectiveness?

6. What is an organization? Why are managers important to an organization's success?

7. Why is an understanding of management important even if you don't plan to be a manager?

LINKING CONCEPTS TO PRACTICE

1. Is your instructor a manager? Discuss in terms of management functions, roles, and skills.

2. Is there one best "style" of management? Why or why not?

3. What characteristics of new organizations appeal to you? Why? Which do not? Why?

4. In today's economic environment, which is more important to organizations—efficiency or effectiveness? Explain your choice.

5. Can you think of situations where management does not matter to organizations? Explain.

6. How do societal trends (for example, text messaging instead of using the phone, or Baby Boomers reaching retirement age) influence the practice of management? What are the implications for someone studying management?

SELF-ASSESSMENT

How Motivated Am I to Manage?

For each of the following statements, circle the level of agreement or disagreement that you personally feel:[41]

> 1 = Strongly Disagree
> 2 = Moderately Disagree
> 3 = Slightly Disagree
> 4 = Neither
> 5 = Slightly Agree
> 6 = Moderately Agree
> 7 = Strongly Agree

1. I have a generally positive attitude toward those holding positions of authority over me. 1 2 3 4 5 6 7
2. I enjoy competition and striving to win for myself and my work group. 1 2 3 4 5 6 7
3. I like to tell others what to do and have no problem with imposing sanctions to enforce my directives. 1 2 3 4 5 6 7
4. I like being active, assertive, and protecting the members of my work group. 1 2 3 4 5 6 7
5. I enjoy the idea of standing out from the group, behaving in a unique manner, and being highly visible. 1 2 3 4 5 6 7
6. I am willing to perform routine, day-to-day administrative tasks and duties. 1 2 3 4 5 6 7

Scoring Key

Add up your responses to the six items.

Analysis and Interpretation

Not everyone is motivated to perform managerial functions. This instrument taps six components that have been found to be related to managerial success, especially in larger organizations. These are a favourable attitude toward authority; a desire to compete; a desire to exercise power; assertiveness; a desire for a distinctive position; and a willingness to engage in repetitive tasks.

Scores on this instrument will range from 6 to 42. Arbitrary cut-offs suggest that scores of 6 to 18 indicate low motivation to manage; 19 to 29 is moderate motivation; and 30 and above is high motivation.

What meaning can you draw from your score? It gives you an idea of how comfortable you would be doing managerial activities. Note, however, that this instrument emphasizes tasks associated with managing in larger and more bureaucratic organizations. A low or moderate score may indicate that you're more suited to managing in a small firm, an organic organization, or in entrepreneurial situations.

More Self-Assessments mymanagementlab

To learn more about your skills, abilities, and interests, go to the MyManagementLab website and take the following self-assessments:

- I.A.4.—How Well Do I Handle Ambiguity? (This exercise also appears in Chapter 7 on pages 216–217.)
- I.E.1.—What's My Emotional Intelligence Score?
- I.E.4.—Am I Likely to Become an Entrepreneur?
- III.C.1.—How Well Do I Respond to Turbulent Change? (This exercise also appears in Chapter 16 on pages 537–538.)

MANAGEMENT FOR YOU TODAY

Dilemma

Think about where you hope to be in your life five years from now (that is, your major goal). What is your competitive advantage for achieving your goal? What do you need to plan, organize, lead, and control to make sure that you reach your goal?

Looking over Mintzberg's management roles (Exhibit 1-4, on page 11), which roles seem comfortable for you? What areas need improvement?

Becoming a Manager

- Keep up with the current business news.
- Read books about good and bad examples of managing.
- Observe managers and how they handle people and situations.
- Talk to actual managers about their experiences—good and bad.
- In other classes you take, see what ideas and concepts potentially relate to being a good manager.

- Get experience in managing by taking on leadership roles in student organizations.
- Start thinking about whether or not you would enjoy being a manager.
- Stay informed about the current trends and issues facing managers.

WORKING TOGETHER: TEAM-BASED EXERCISE

A New Beginning

By this time in your life, all of you have had to work with individuals in managerial positions (or maybe you were the manager), either through work experiences or through other organizational experiences (social, hobby/interest, religious, and so forth). What do you think makes some managers better than others? Are there certain characteristics that distinguish good managers? Form groups of 3 or 4 individuals. Discuss your experiences with managers—good and bad. Draw up a list of the characteristics of those individuals you felt were good managers. For each characteristic, indicate which management function (planning, organizing, leading, and controlling) you think it falls under. Also identify which of Mintzberg's 10 roles the good managers seemed to fill. Were any of the roles missing from your list of characteristics? What explanation can you give for this? As a group, be prepared to explain the functions and roles that good managers are most likely to fill.

ETHICS IN ACTION

Ethical Dilemma Exercise: Are Canadian Executives Paid Too Much?

Are we paying executives too much? Is an average salary in 2006 in excess of $9 million justifiable?[42] In any debate, there are two sides to the issue. One fact that supports paying this amount is that these executives have tremendous organizational responsibilities. They not only have to manage the organization in today's environment, but also must keep it moving into the future. Their jobs are not 9-to-5 jobs, but rather 6 to 7 days a week, often 10 to 14 hours a day. If jobs are evaluated on the basis of skills, knowledge, abilities, and responsibilities, executives should be highly paid.[43] Furthermore, there is the issue of motivation and retention. If you want these individuals to succeed and stay with the company, you must provide a compensation package that motivates them to stay. Incentives based on various measures also provide the impetus for them to excel.

Most of the research done on executive salaries questions the linkage to performance. Even when profits are down, many executives are paid handsomely. In fact, Canadian corporate executives are some of the most highly paid people in the world (although American CEOs are paid more). Additionally, pay does not always seem directly related to performance.[44] If one takes into account company performance when evaluating a CEO's pay, Jeffrey Orr and Robert Gratton of Montreal-based Power Financial together were overpaid $66 888 000 in 2006; Ian Telfer and Robert McEwen of Vancouver-based Goldcorp together were overpaid $32 725 000; and David Stein of Markham, Ontario-based CoolBrands International was overpaid $8 072 000 for the same year.[45]

Do you believe that Canadian executives are overpaid? Explain your opinion.

Thinking Critically About Ethics

How far should a manager go to achieve efficiency or effectiveness? Suppose that you are the catering manager at a local country club and you are asked by the club manager to lie about information you have on your work group's efficiency. Suppose that by lying you will save an employee's job. Is that okay? Is lying always wrong, or might it be acceptable under certain circumstances? What, if any, would those circumstances be? What about simply misrepresenting information that you have? Is that always wrong, or might it be acceptable under certain circumstances? When does "misrepresenting" become "lying"?

CASE APPLICATION

Lipschultz Levin & Gray

You might be surprised to find a passionate emphasis placed on people at an accounting firm.[46] Yet at Lipschultz Levin & Gray (**www.thethinkers.com**), self-described "head bean counter" Steven P. Siegel recognizes that his people make the organization. He describes his primary responsibility as assuring that LLG's clients have the best professionals working for them. And the best way to do this, Siegel feels, is by developing the creativity, talent, and diversity of its staff so that new knowledge can be acquired and shared without getting hung up on formal organizational relationships or having employees shut away in corner offices.

Siegel's commitment to his people starts with the company's mission:

> LLG's goal is to be the pre-eminent provider of the highest quality accounting, tax and consulting services. We seek to accomplish this goal by leaving no stone unturned in exploring new and superior alternatives of supplying our services, and developing such methods on a global basis. Our environment promotes creativity, individual development, group interchange, diversity, good humor, family and community, all for the purpose of assisting in our clients' growth.

To further demonstrate that commitment, Siegel has implemented several significant changes at LLG. Because he is convinced that people do their best intellectual work in nontraditional settings, every telltale sign of what most people consider boring, dull accounting work has been eliminated. None of the firm's employees or partners has an office or desk to call his or her own. Instead, everyone is part of a nomadic arrangement where stuff (files, phones, laptops) is wheeled to a new spot every day. Everywhere you look in the company's office, you see versatility, comfort, and individuality. For instance, a miniature golf course is located in the middle of everything. The motivation behind this open office design is to create opportunities for professionals to gather—on purpose or by accident—without walls, cubicles, or offices to get in the way.

Visitors to LLG realize that the firm is different as soon as they walk in the door. A giant, wall-mounted abacus (remember the image of bean counters) decorates the interior. And visitors are greeted by a "Welcome Wall" with a big-screen television that flashes a continuous slide show of one-liners about business, life, and innovation. The setting may be fun and lighthearted, but the LLG team is seriously committed to serving its clients. So serious, in fact, that they state:

> We have one goal. To "Delight" you. Good, even great, is not enough any more. We will "Dazzle" you and we will guarantee it; We will deliver our service with integrity, hon-

esty and openness in everything we do for you and with you; We will absolutely respect the confidentiality of our working relationship; We will return your phone calls, facsimiles and e-mails within 24 hours; We will always provide exceptional service, designed to help you add significant value to your business; We will meet the deadlines we set together with you; We will communicate with you frequently, building a win-win relationship with you; and You will always know in advance our fee arrangement for any service.

Yesterday, one of Siegel's new employees complained in an email to him that the work environment is too informal, and that employees need their own desks. This employee has done well in her first few months on the job. Siegel is meeting with her in an hour. What should he say to her?

DEVELOPING YOUR DIAGNOSTIC AND ANALYTICAL SKILLS

Managing the Virus Hunters

Imagine what life would be like if your product were never finished, if your work were never done, if your market shifted 30 times a day.[47] The computer-virus hunters at Symantec don't have to imagine. That is the reality of their daily work life. At the company's Response Lab in Santa Monica, California, described as the "dirtiest of all our networks at Symantec," software analysts collect viruses and other suspicious code and try to figure out how they work so security updates can be provided to the company's customers. By the door to the lab, there is even a hazardous materials box marked "Danger," where they put all the discs, tapes, and hard drives with the nasty viruses that need to be carefully and completely disposed of. Symantec's situation may seem unique, but the company, which makes content and network security software for both consumers and businesses, reflects the realities facing many organizations today: quickly shifting customer expectations and continuously emerging global competitors that have drastically shortened product life cycles. Managing talented people in such an environment can be quite challenging as well.

Vincent Weafer, a native of Ireland, has been the leader of Symantec's virus-hunting team since 1999. Back then, he said, "There were less than two dozen people, and ... nothing really happened. We'd see maybe five new viruses a day, and they would spread in a matter of months, not minutes." Now, Symantec's virus hunters around the world deal with some 20 000 virus samples each month, not all of which are unique, stand-alone viruses. The response-centre team is a diverse group whose members were not easy to find. Says Weafer, "It's not as if colleges are creating thousands of anti-malware or security experts every year that we can hire. If you find them in any part of the world, you just go after them." The response-

centre team's makeup reflects that. For instance, one senior researcher is from Hungary; another is from Iceland; and another works out of her home in Melbourne, Florida. But they all share something in common: They are all motivated by solving problems.

The launch of the Blaster.B worm in August 2003 changed the company's approach to dealing with viruses. The domino effect of Blaster.B and other viruses spawned by it meant the front-line software analysts were working around the clock for almost two weeks. The "employee burnout" potential made the company realize that its virus-hunting team would now have to be much deeper talent-wise. Now, the response centre's team numbers in the hundreds, and managers can rotate people from the front lines, where they are responsible for responding to new security threats that crop up, into groups where they can help with new-product development. Others write internal research papers. Still others are assigned to develop new tools that will help their colleagues battle the next wave of threats. There is even an individual who tries to figure out what makes the virus writers tick—and the day never ends for these virus hunters. When Santa Monica's team finishes its day, colleagues in Tokyo take over. When the Japanese team finishes its day, it hands off to Dublin, who then hands back to Santa Monica for the new day. It's a frenetic, chaotic, challenging work environment that spans the entire globe. But Weafer says his goals are to "try to take the chaos out, to make the exciting boring," to have a predictable and well-defined process for dealing with the virus threats, and to spread work evenly to the company's facilities around the world. It's a managerial challenge that Weafer has embraced.

Questions

1. Keeping professionals excited about work that is routine and standardized *and* chaotic is a major challenge for Vincent Weafer. How could he use technical, human, and conceptual skills to maintain an environment that encourages innovation and professionalism among the virus hunters?

2. What management roles is Weafer playing as he (a) has weekly security briefing conference calls with co-workers around the globe, (b) assesses the feasibility of adding a new network security consulting service, and (c) keeps employees focused on the company's commitments to customers?

3. Go to Symantec's website (**www.symantec.com**) and look up information about the company. What can you tell about its emphasis on customer service and innovation? In what ways does the organization support its employees in servicing customers and in being innovative?

4. What could other managers learn from Vincent Weafer's and Symantec's approach?

DEVELOPING YOUR INTERPERSONAL SKILLS

Mentoring

About the Skill

A mentor is someone in the organization, usually older, more experienced, and in a higher-level position, who sponsors or supports another employee (a protégé) who is in a lower-level position in the organization. A mentor can teach, guide, and encourage. Some organizations have formal mentoring programs, but even if your organization does not, mentoring should be an important skill for you to develop.

Steps in Developing the Skill

You can be more effective at mentoring if you use the following six suggestions as you mentor another person:[48]

1. **Communicate honestly and openly with your protégé.** If your protégé is going to learn from you and benefit from your experience and knowledge, you are going to have to be open and honest as you talk about what you have done. Bring up the failures as well as the successes. Remember that mentoring is a learning process, and in order for learning to take place you are going to have to be open and honest in "telling it like it is."

2. **Encourage honest and open communication from your protégé.** You need to know as the mentor what your protégé hopes to gain from this relationship. You should encourage the protégé to ask for information and be specific about what he or she wants to gain.

3. **Treat the relationship with the protégé as a learning opportunity.** Don't pretend to have all the answers and all the knowledge, but do share what you have learned through your experiences. In your conversations and interactions with your protégé, you may be able to learn as much from that person as he or she does from you. So be open to listening to what your protégé is saying.

4. **Take the time to get to know your protégé.** As a mentor, you should be willing to take the time to get to know your protégé and his or her interests. If you are not willing to spend that extra time, you should probably not embark on a mentoring relationship.

5. **Remind your protégé that there is no substitute for effective work performance.** In any job, effective work performance is absolutely essential for success. It does not matter how much information you provide as a mentor if the protégé is not willing to strive for effective work performance.

6. **Know when it's time to let go.** Successful mentors know when it's time to let the protégé begin standing on his or her own. If the mentoring relationship has been effective, the protégé will be comfortable and confident in handling new and increasing work responsibilities. Just because the mentoring relationship is over does not mean that you never have contact with your protégé. It just means that the relationship becomes one of equals, not one of teacher and student.

Practising the Skill

Read the following scenario. Write some notes about how you would handle the situation described. Be sure to refer to the six suggestions for mentoring.

Scenario

Lora Slovinsky has worked for your department in a software design firm longer than any other of your employees. You value her skills and commitment, and you frequently ask for her judgment on difficult issues. Very often, her ideas have been better than yours and you have let her know through both praise and pay increases how much you appreciate her contributions. Recently, though, you have begun to question Lora's judgment. The fundamental problem is in the distinct difference in the ways you both approach your work. Your strengths lie in getting things done on time and under budget.

Although Lora is aware of these constraints, her creativity and perfectionism sometimes make her prolong projects, continually looking for the best approaches. On her most recent assignment, Lora seemed more intent than ever on doing things her way. Despite what you felt were clear guidelines, she was two weeks late in meeting an important customer deadline. While her product quality was high, as always, the software design was far more elaborate than what was needed at this stage of development. Looking over her work in your office, you feel more than a little frustrated and certain that you need to address matters with Lora. What will you say?

Reinforcing the Skill

The following activities will help you practise and reinforce the skills associated with mentoring:

1. If there are individuals on your campus who act as mentors (or advisers) to first-time students, make an appointment to talk to one of these mentors. They may be upper-division students, professors, or staff employees. Ask them about their roles as mentors and the skills they think it takes to be an effective mentor. How do the skills they mention relate to the behaviours described here?
2. Athletic coaches often act as mentors to their younger assistant coaches. Interview a coach about her or his role as a mentor. What types of things do coaches do to instruct, teach, advise, and encourage their assistant coaches? Could any of these activities be transferred to an organizational setting? Explain.

MANAGING YOUR CAREER

Career Opportunities in Management

Production at Ford Motor Company of Canada's Windsor, Ontario, cylinder block casting plant ends, laying off 500 people. DaimlerChrysler Canada lays off 2000 employees, mostly in Windsor and Brampton, Ontario. Commonwealth Plywood slashes 1200 jobs by closing its 18 factories in Quebec.[49]

Do these numbers suggest that management jobs are disappearing? You might think so based on news reports showing widespread layoffs. The truth is this: There are abundant management jobs, and the future looks bright as Baby Boomers retire and need to be replaced. Statistics Canada reports that managerial jobs will be hit very hard by the retirement of Baby Boomers in the next 10 to 15 years. Fifty-five percent of managers were 40 years or older in 1999, the last time that such data were collected.[50] Not all of these openings will be in the organizations or fields that you would expect, however. The demand for managers in traditional, large organizations, and particularly in the area of traditional manufacturing, is not going to be as strong as the demand for managers in small and medium-sized organizations in the services field, particularly in information and health care services. Do keep in mind that a good place to land a management position can be a smaller organization.

History of Management Trends

Walk down almost any street in Vancouver, and you will spot a number of people carrying paper cups of coffee, picked up from one of the many local coffee shops found on many corners.[1] The per capita coffee consumption in Canada is high, an average of 402 cups of coffee per year, almost 25 percent more than Americans, and 161 percent more than Europeans. Vancouverites do their share to keep the numbers up.

Christine Corkan noticed the number of coffee drinkers and the coffee shops in Vancouver and realized that there were lots of places where one could not easily get a cup of coffee in the city. Trendy coffee shops tend not to be located next door to community parks, for instance, where people play soccer, baseball, and field hockey. From that observation, her business, Java Jazz Mobile Café, was born.

Java Jazz offers coffee, tea, and cold drinks, as well as baked goods, smoothies, and fresh fruit from the side of a cube van outfitted with a small kitchen run on a generator. Corkan aims to fill the niche where other concessions are not available, and can be hired for any private event in the area that wants to have coffee and beverages available on-site.

Corkan started developing her business with $35 000, almost all of it loaned to her by a friend at 5 percent interest. With the money, she had to purchase and furnish the van and buy beverages and serving cups.

In August, two months after starting the business, Corkan felt she was doing well. Her previous job was with Air Canada. "I made more in two days with Java Jazz than I make in a month at the airport," she said. "I have the first payment already saved for my loan and it's not due until November."

It is important for managers such as Corkan to understand how to run a business, a new experience for her, compared with working for Air Canada. Corkan would do well to learn more about different management theories, as they provide a framework for managing one's business, dealing with employees when she brings them on, and understanding the environment of the business. One of the keys to her success will be understanding as much as she can about how management works. Below we review the history of management thought. As you read through it, you may want to identify some of the tips that would help you be a better manager.

Looking at management history can help us understand today's management theory and practice. It can help us see what did work and what did not. In this supplement, we introduce you to the origins of many contemporary management concepts and show how they have evolved to reflect the changing needs of organizations and society as a whole. Q&A S1.1

Historical Background of Management

Organized endeavours directed by people responsible for planning, organizing, leading, and controlling activities have existed for thousands of years. The Egyptian pyramids and the Great Wall of China, for instance, are tangible evidence that projects of tremendous scope, employing tens of thousands of people, were undertaken well before modern times. The pyramids are a particularly interesting example. The construction of a single pyramid occupied more than 100 000 workers for 20 years.[2] Who told each worker what to do? Who ensured that there would be enough stones at the site to keep workers busy? The answer to such questions is managers. Regardless of what managers were called at the time, someone had to plan what was to be done, organize people and materials to do it, lead and direct the workers, and impose some controls to ensure that everything was done as planned.

While organizations and managers have been around for thousands of years, two pre-twentieth-century events are particularly significant to the study of management.

First, in 1776, Adam Smith published *The Wealth of Nations*, in which he argued for the economic advantages that organizations and society would gain from the **division of labour**, the breakdown of jobs into narrow and repetitive tasks. Using the pin indus-

try as an example, Smith claimed that 10 individuals, each doing a specialized task, could together produce about 48 000 pins a day. However, if each person worked alone performing each task separately, it would be quite an accomplishment to produce even 10 pins a day! Smith concluded that division of labour increased productivity by increasing each person's skill and dexterity, by saving time lost in changing tasks, and by creating labour-saving inventions and machinery. The continued popularity of job specialization—for example, specific tasks performed by members of a hospital surgery team, specific meal preparation tasks done by employees in restaurant kitchens, or specific positions played by players on a hockey team—is undoubtedly due to the economic advantages cited by Adam Smith.

The second important pre-twentieth-century influence on management is the **Industrial Revolution**. Starting in the eighteenth century in Great Britain, the revolution eventually crossed the Atlantic to North America. What the Industrial Revolution did was substitute machine power for human power. This made it more economical to manufacture goods in factories rather than at home. Managers were needed to forecast demand, ensure that enough material was on hand to make products, assign tasks to people, direct daily activities, and so forth. However, it was not until the early 1900s that the first major step was taken toward developing a formal theory to guide managers in running these large organizations.

In the next sections, we present the six major approaches to management: scientific management, general admin-

istrative theory, quantitative, organizational behaviour, systems, and contingency (see Exhibit S1-1 on page 32). Each of the six perspectives contributes to our overall understanding of management. However, each is also a limited view of a particular aspect of management. We begin our journey into management's past by looking at the first major theory of management—scientific management.

Scientific Management

If you had to pinpoint the year modern management theory was born, 1911 might be a logical choice. That was the year Frederick Winslow Taylor's *The Principles of Scientific Management* was published. Its contents were widely accepted by managers around the world. The book described the theory of **scientific management**: the use of scientific methods to define the "one best way" for a job to be done.

Important Contributions

Important contributions to scientific management theory were made by Frederick W. Taylor and Frank and Lillian Gilbreth. Let's look at what they did.

Frederick W. Taylor

Taylor did most of his work at the Midvale and Bethlehem Steel Companies in Pennsylvania. As a mechanical engineer with a Quaker and Puritan background, he was continually shocked at how employees performed. He observed that they used vastly different techniques to do the

division of labour
The breakdown of jobs into narrow and repetitive tasks.

Industrial Revolution
The substitution of machine power for human power, which led to mass production.

scientific management
The use of the scientific method to determine the "one best way" for a job to be done.

Exhibit S1-1

Development of Major Management Theories

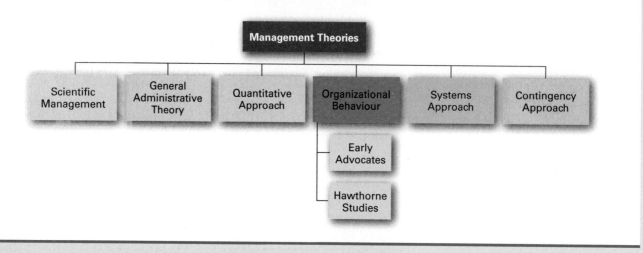

same job and were inclined to "take it easy" on the job. Taylor believed that employee output was only about one-third of what was possible. Virtually no work standards existed. Employees were placed in jobs with little or no concern for matching their abilities and aptitudes with the tasks they were required to do. Taylor set out to correct the situation by applying the scientific method to shop-floor jobs and spent more than two decades passionately pursuing the "one best way" for each job to be done.

Taylor's experiences at Midvale led him to define clear guidelines for improving production efficiency. He argued that four principles of management (see *Tips for Managers—Taylor's Four Principles of Management*) would result in prosperity for both employees and managers.[3] Through his studies of manual work using scientific principles, Taylor became known as the "father" of scientific management. His ideas spread in the United States, France, Germany, Russia, and Japan, and inspired others to study and develop methods of scientific management. His most prominent followers were Frank and Lillian Gilbreth.

Frank and Lillian Gilbreth

A construction contractor by trade, Frank Gilbreth gave up that career to study scientific management after hearing Taylor speak at a professional meeting. Frank and his wife, Lillian, a psychologist, studied work to eliminate wasteful hand and body motions. The Gilbreths also experimented with the design and use of the proper tools and equipment for optimizing work performance.[4]

Frank is probably best known for his experiments in bricklaying. By carefully analyzing the bricklayer's job, he reduced the number of motions in laying exterior brick from 18 to about 5, and on laying interior brick the motions were reduced from 18 to 2. Using Gilbreth's techniques, the bricklayer could be more productive and less fatigued at the end of the day.

The Gilbreths were among the first researchers to use motion pictures to study hand and body motions. They invented a device called a micro-chronometer, which recorded an employee's motions and the amount of time spent doing each motion. Wasted motions missed by the naked eye could be identified and eliminated. The Gilbreths also devised a classification scheme to label 17 basic hand motions (such as search, grasp, hold), which they

TIPS FOR MANAGERS

Taylor's Four Principles of Management

- Develop a **science for each element of an individual's work**, which will replace the old rule-of-thumb method.

- **Scientifically select** and then train, teach, and develop employees.

- **Heartily cooperate with employees** so as to ensure that all work is done in accordance with the principles of the science that has been developed.

- **Divide work and responsibility almost equally** between management and employees. Management takes over all work for which it is better fitted than the employees.

called **therbligs** ("Gilbreth" spelled backward with the *th* transposed). This scheme allowed the Gilbreths a more precise way of analyzing an employee's exact hand movements.

How Do Today's Managers Use Scientific Management?

The guidelines that Taylor and others devised for improving production efficiency are still used in organizations today.[5] When managers analyze the basic work tasks that must be performed, use time-and-motion study to eliminate wasted motions, hire the best qualified employees for a job, and design incentive systems based on output, they are using the principles of scientific management. But current management practice isn't restricted to scientific management. In fact, we can see ideas from the next major approach—general administrative theory—being used as well. Q&A S1.2

General Administrative Theory

Another group of writers looked at the subject of management but focused on the entire organization. These **general administrative theorists** developed more general theories of what managers do and what constitutes good management practice. Let's look at some important contributions that grew out of this perspective.

Important Contributions

The two most prominent theorists behind general administrative theory were Henri Fayol and Max Weber.

Henri Fayol

We mention Fayol in Chapter 1 because he described management as a universal set of functions that included planning, organizing, com-

---

TIPS FOR MANAGERS

Fayol's 14 Principles of Management

- **Division of work.** Specialization increases output by making employees more efficient.

- **Authority.** Managers must be able to give orders, and authority gives them this right.

- **Discipline.** Employees must obey and respect the rules that govern the organization.

- **Unity of command.** Every employee should receive orders from only one superior.

- **Unity of direction.** The organization should have a single plan of action to guide managers and employees.

- **Subordination of individual interests to the general interest.** The interests of any one employee or group of employees should not take precedence over the interests of the organization as a whole.

- **Remuneration.** Employees must be paid a fair wage for their services.

- **Centralization.** This term refers to the degree to which subordinates are involved in decision making.

- **Scalar chain.** The line of authority from top management to the lowest ranks is the scalar chain.

- **Order.** People and materials should be in the right place at the right time.

- **Equity.** Managers should be kind and fair to their subordinates.

- **Stability of tenure of personnel.** Management should provide orderly personnel planning and ensure that replacements are available to fill vacancies.

- **Initiative.** Employees who are allowed to originate and carry out plans will exert high levels of effort.

- **Esprit de corps.** Promoting team spirit will build harmony and unity within the organization.

---

manding, coordinating, and controlling. Because his ideas were important, let's look more closely at what he had to say.[6]

Fayol wrote during the same time period as Taylor. While Taylor was concerned with first-line managers and the scientific method, Fayol's attention was directed at the activities of *all* managers.

He wrote from personal experience because he was the managing director of a large French coal-mining firm.

Fayol described the practice of management as something distinct from accounting, finance, production, distribution, and other typical business functions. His belief that management was an activity common to all human

therbligs
A classification scheme for labelling 17 basic hand motions.

general administrative theorists
Writers who developed general theories of what managers do and what constitutes good management practice.

Exhibit S1-2

Weber's Ideal Bureaucracy

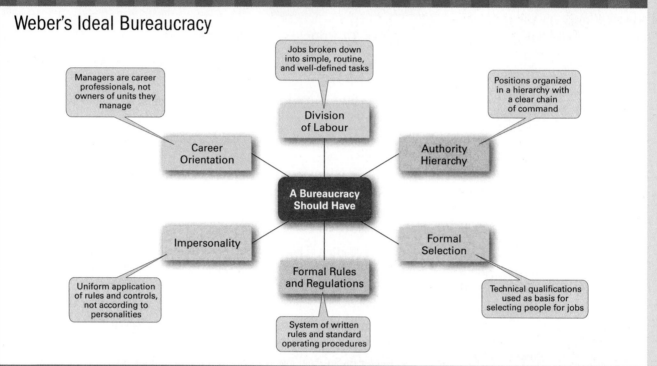

Managers are career professionals, not owners of units they manage

Jobs broken down into simple, routine, and well-defined tasks

Positions organized in a hierarchy with a clear chain of command

Career Orientation

Division of Labour

Authority Hierarchy

A Bureaucracy Should Have

Impersonality

Formal Rules and Regulations

Formal Selection

Uniform application of rules and controls, not according to personalities

System of written rules and standard operating procedures

Technical qualifications used as basis for selecting people for jobs

---

endeavours in business, government, and even in the home led him to develop 14 **principles of management**—fundamental rules of management that could be taught in schools and applied in all organizational situations. These principles are shown in *Tips for Managers—Fayol's 14 Principles of Management* on page 33. Q&A S1.3

Max Weber

Weber (pronounced VAY-ber) was a German sociologist who studied organizational activity. Writing in the early 1900s, he developed a theory of authority structures and relations.[7] Weber described an ideal type of organization that he called a **bureaucracy**—a form of organization characterized by division of labour, a clearly defined hierarchy, detailed rules and regulations, and impersonal relationships. Weber recognized that this "ideal bureaucracy" did not exist in reality. Instead, he intended it as a basis for theorizing about how work could be done in large groups. His theory became the model structural design for many of today's large orga-

nizations. The features of Weber's ideal bureaucratic structure are outlined in Exhibit S1-2.

Bureaucracy, as described by Weber, is a lot like scientific management in its ideology. Both emphasize rationality, predictability, impersonality, technical competence, and authoritarianism. Although Weber's writings were less operational than Taylor's, the fact that his "ideal type" still describes many contemporary organizations attests to the importance of his work.

How Do Today's Managers Use General Administrative Theory?

Some of our current management ideas and practices can be directly

traced to the contributions of the general administrative theorists. For instance, the functional view of the manager's job can be attributed to Fayol. In addition, his 14 principles serve as a frame of reference from which many current management concepts have evolved.

Weber's bureaucracy was an attempt to formulate an ideal prototype for organizations. Although many characteristics of Weber's bureaucracy are still evident in large organizations, his model isn't as popular today as it was in the twentieth century. Many contemporary managers feel that bureaucracy's emphasis on strict division of labour, adherence to formal rules and regulations, and impersonal application of rules and controls takes away the individual employee's creativity

principles of management
Fundamental rules of management that could be taught in schools and applied in all organizational situations.

bureaucracy
A form of organization characterized by division of labour, a clearly defined hierarchy, detailed rules and regulations, and impersonal relationships.

and the organization's ability to respond quickly to an increasingly dynamic environment. However, even in highly flexible organizations of talented professionals—such as Calgary-based WestJet Airlines, Toronto-based ING Bank of Canada, or Ottawa-based Corel—some bureaucratic mechanisms are necessary to ensure that resources are used efficiently and effectively.

The Quantitative Approach

The **quantitative approach** involves the use of quantitative techniques to improve decision making. This approach also has been called *operations research* or *management science.*

Important Contributions

The quantitative approach evolved out of the development of mathematical and statistical solutions to military problems during World War II. After the war was over, many of the techniques that had been used to solve military problems were applied to businesses. One group of military officers, nicknamed the Whiz Kids, joined Ford Motor Company in the mid-1940s and immediately began using statistical methods and quantitative models to improve decision making. Two of these individuals whose names you might recognize are Robert McNamara (who went on to become president of Ford, US Secretary of Defense, and head of the World Bank and was recently featured in the documentary *The Fog of War*) and Charles "Tex" Thornton (who founded Litton Industries).

What exactly does the quantitative approach do? It involves applications of statistics, optimization models, information models, and computer simulations to management activities. Linear programming, for instance, is a technique that managers use to improve resource allocation decisions. Work scheduling can be more efficient as a result of critical-path scheduling analysis. The economic order quantity model helps managers determine optimum inventory levels. Each of these is an example of quantitative techniques being applied to improve managerial decision making.

How Do Today's Managers Use the Quantitative Approach?

The quantitative approach contributes directly to management decision making in the areas of planning and control. For instance, when managers make budgeting, scheduling, quality control, and similar decisions, they typically rely on quantitative techniques. The availability of software programs has made the use of quantitative techniques somewhat less intimidating for managers, although they must still be able to interpret the results. We cover some of the more important quantitative techniques in Chapters 8 and 15.

The quantitative approach has not influenced management practice as much as the next approach we are going to discuss—organizational behaviour—for a number of reasons. These include the fact that many managers are unfamiliar with and intimidated by the quantitative tools, behavioural problems are more widespread and visible, and it is easier for most students and managers to relate to real, day-to-day people problems than to the more abstract activity of constructing quantitative models.

quantitative approach
The use of quantitative techniques to improve decision making.

organizational behaviour (OB)
The field of study concerned with the actions (behaviour) of people at work.

Organizational Behaviour

As we know, managers get things done by working with people. This explains why some writers have chosen to look at management by focusing on the organization's human resources. The field of study concerned with the actions (behaviour) of people at work is called **organizational behaviour (OB)**. Much of what currently makes up the field of human resource management, as well as contemporary views on motivation, leadership, trust, teamwork, and conflict management, has come out of OB research.

Early Advocates

Although a number of people in the late 1800s and early 1900s recognized the importance of the human factor to an organization's success, four stand out as early advocates of the OB approach: Robert Owen, Hugo Münsterberg, Mary Parker Follett, and Chester Barnard. The contributions of these individuals were varied and distinct, yet they all believed that people were the most important asset of the organization and should be managed accordingly. Their approach was very different from the emphasis on bureaucracy and structured arrangements to improve workflow. In particular, their ideas provided the foundation for such management practices as employee selection procedures, employee motivation programs, employee work teams, and organization–environment management techniques. Exhibit S1-3 on page 36 summarizes the most important ideas of the early advocates of OB.

Exhibit S1-3

Early Advocates of OB

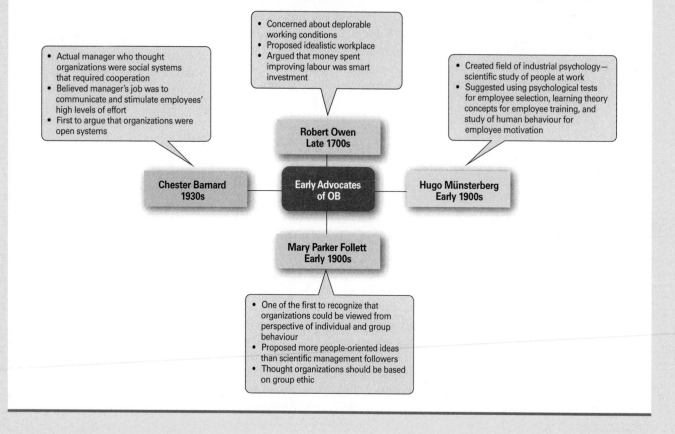

- Concerned about deplorable working conditions
- Proposed idealistic workplace
- Argued that money spent improving labour was smart investment

- Actual manager who thought organizations were social systems that required cooperation
- Believed manager's job was to communicate and stimulate employees' high levels of effort
- First to argue that organizations were open systems

- Created field of industrial psychology—scientific study of people at work
- Suggested using psychological tests for employee selection, learning theory concepts for employee training, and study of human behaviour for employee motivation

Robert Owen
Late 1700s

Chester Barnard
1930s

Early Advocates of OB

Hugo Münsterberg
Early 1900s

Mary Parker Follett
Early 1900s

- One of the first to recognize that organizations could be viewed from perspective of individual and group behaviour
- Proposed more people-oriented ideas than scientific management followers
- Thought organizations should be based on group ethic

The Hawthorne Studies

Without question, the most important contribution to the developing OB field came out of the **Hawthorne Studies**, a series of studies conducted at the Western Electric Company Works in Cicero, Illinois. These studies, which started in 1924, were initially designed by Western Electric industrial engineers as a scientific management experiment. They wanted to examine the effect of various illumination levels on employee productivity. As in any good scientific experiment, control and experimental groups were set up, with the experimental group being exposed to various lighting intensities, and the control group working under a constant intensity. If you were the industrial engineers in charge of this experiment, what would you have expected to happen? It's logical to think that individual output in the experimental group would

be directly related to the intensity of the light. However, they found that as the level of light was increased in the experimental group, output for both groups increased. Then, much to the surprise of the engineers, as the light level was decreased in the experimental group, productivity continued to increase in both groups. In fact, a productivity decrease was observed in the experimental group *only* when the level of light was reduced to that of a moonlit night. What would explain these unexpected results? The engineers were not sure, but concluded that illumination intensity was not directly related to group productivity, and that something else must have contributed to the results. They were not able to pinpoint what that "something else" was, though.

Hawthorne Studies
A series of studies during the 1920s and 1930s that provided new insights into individual and group behaviour.

In 1927, the Western Electric engineers asked Harvard professor Elton Mayo and his associates to join the study as consultants. Thus began a relationship that would last through 1932 and encompass numerous experiments in the redesign of jobs, changes in workday and workweek length, introduction of rest periods, and individual vs. group wage plans.[8] For example, one experiment was designed to evaluate the effect of a group piecework incentive pay system on group productivity. The results indicated that the incentive plan had less effect on an employee's output than did group pressure, acceptance, and security. The researchers concluded that social norms, or group standards, were the key determinants of individual work behaviour.

Scholars generally agree that the Hawthorne Studies had a dramatic impact on management beliefs about the role of human behaviour in organizations. Mayo concluded that behaviour and attitudes are closely related, that group influences significantly affect individual behaviour, that group standards establish individual employee output, and that money is less a factor in determining output than are group standards, group attitudes, and security. These conclusions led to a new emphasis on the human behaviour factor in the management of organizations and the attainment of goals.

However, these conclusions were criticized. Critics attacked the research procedures, analyses of findings, and conclusions.[9] From a historical standpoint, it's of little importance whether the studies were academically sound or their conclusions justified. What *is* important is that they stimulated an interest in human behaviour in organizations. Q&A S1.4

How Do Today's Managers Use the Behavioural Approach?

The behavioural approach has largely shaped today's organizations. From the way managers design motivating jobs to the way they work with employee teams to the way they use open communication, we can see elements of the behavioural approach. Much of what the early OB advocates proposed and the conclusions from the Hawthorne Studies provided the foundation for our current theories of motivation, leadership, group behaviour and development, and numerous other behavioural topics that we address fully in later chapters.

The Systems Approach

During the 1960s, researchers began to analyze organizations from a systems perspective, a concept taken from the physical sciences. A **system** is a set of interrelated and interdependent parts arranged in a manner that produces a unified whole. The two basic types of systems are closed and open. **Closed** systems are not influenced by and do not interact with their environment. This is very much how Air Canada operated when it was a Crown corporation. Because it was in a regulated industry, it did not need to worry about competition. When the Canadian airline industry was deregulated, Air Canada was slow to adapt to the new competitive environment and went into bankruptcy protection in order to restructure its operations and attempt to become a more open system.[10]

Open systems dynamically interact with their environment. Today, when we describe organizations as systems, we mean open systems. Exhibit S1-4 shows a diagram of an organization from an open systems perspective. As you can see, an organization takes in inputs (resources) from the environment and transforms or processes these resources into outputs that are distributed into the environment. The organization is "open" to its environment and interacts with that environment.

system
A set of interrelated and interdependent parts arranged in a manner that produces a unified whole.

closed systems
Systems that are not influenced by and do not interact with their environment.

open systems
Systems that dynamically interact with their environment.

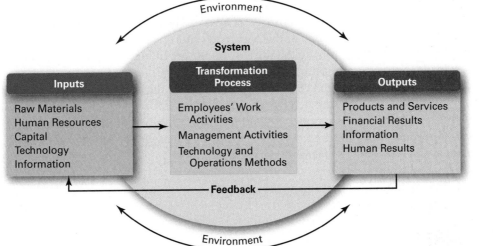

Exhibit S1-4

The Organization as an Open System

Exhibit S1-5

Popular Contingency Variables

Organization Size. As size increases, so do the problems of coordination. For instance, the type of organization structure appropriate for an organization of 50 000 employees is likely to be inefficient for an organization of 50 employees.

Routineness of Task Technology. To achieve its purpose, an organization uses technology. Routine technologies, such as assembly lines, require organizational structures, leadership styles, and control systems that differ from those required by customized or nonroutine technologies where individuals continually have to make decisions about how their jobs are to be done, such as in the emergency room of a hospital.

Environmental Uncertainty. The degree of uncertainty caused by environmental changes influences the management process. What works best in a stable and predictable environment may be totally inappropriate in a rapidly changing and unpredictable environment.

Individual Differences. Individuals differ in terms of their desire for growth, autonomy, tolerance of ambiguity, and expectations. These and other individual differences are particularly important when managers select motivation techniques, leadership styles, and job designs.

The Systems Approach and Managers

How does the systems approach contribute to our understanding of management thinking? Systems researchers envisioned an organization as being made up of "interdependent factors, including individuals, groups, attitudes, motives, formal structure, interactions, goals, status, and authority."[11] What this means is that managers coordinate the work activities of the various parts of the organization and ensure that all the interdependent parts of the organization are working together so that the organization's goals can be achieved. For example, the systems approach would recognize that, no matter how efficient the production department might be, if the marketing department does not anticipate changes in customer tastes and work with the product development department to create products customers want, the organization's overall performance will suffer. This approach is very different from the "silo" approach in some organizations, where each individual unit operates almost in isolation from other units.

In addition, the systems approach implies that decisions and actions taken in one organizational area will affect others and vice versa. For example, if the purchasing department does not acquire the right quantity and quality of inputs, the production department will not be able to do its job effectively.

Finally, the systems approach recognizes that organizations are not self-contained. They rely on their environments for essential inputs and as sources to absorb their outputs. No organization can survive for long if it ignores government regulations, supplier relations, or the varied external constituencies upon which it depends. (We cover these external forces in Chapter 2.)

How relevant is the systems approach to management? Quite relevant. Think, for example, of a day-shift manager at a local Harvey's restaurant who every day must coordinate the work of employees filling customer orders at the front counter and the drive-through windows, direct the delivery and unloading of food supplies, and address any customer concerns that come up. This manager "manages" all parts of the "system" so that the restaurant meets its daily sales goals. Q&A S1.5

The Contingency Approach

Early management thinkers such as Taylor, Fayol, and Weber gave us principles of management that they generally assumed to be universally applicable. Later research found exceptions to many of their principles. For example, division of labour is valuable and widely used, but jobs can become *too* specialized. Bureaucracy is desirable in many situations, but in other circumstances, other structural designs are *more* effective. Management is not (and cannot be) based on simplistic principles to be applied in all situations. Different and changing situations require managers to use different approaches and techniques. The **contingency approach** (sometimes called the *situational approach*) says that organizations are different, face different situations (contingencies), and require different ways of managing.

contingency approach An approach that says that organizations are different, face different situations (contingencies), and require different ways of managing.

The Contingency Approach and Managers

A contingency approach to management is intuitively logical because organizations and even units within the same organization are diverse—in size, goals, work, and the like. It would be surprising to find universally applicable management rules that would work in *all* situations. But, of course, it's one thing to say that the method of managing "depends on the situation" and another to say what the situation is. Management researchers have been working to identify these "what" variables. Exhibit S1-5 describes four popular contingency variables. The list is by no means comprehensive—more than 100 different "what" variables have been identified—but it represents those most widely used and gives you an idea of what we mean by the term *contingency variable*. As you can see, the contingency variables can have a significant impact on managers. The primary value of the contingency approach is that it stresses there are no simplistic or universal rules for managers to follow. Q&A S1.6

Summarizing Management Theory

It would not be unusual for you to read through this supplement on the history of management theory and wonder whether any of it is relevant to you. Theoretical perspectives and the research that is generated to help examine theories lead us to a more solid understanding of how managers should manage. The theories we present above appear in a historical sequence, but that does not mean that as a new theory was developed, the previous one became irrelevant. Instead, if you carefully consider the theories, you will note that they are somewhat self-contained, each addressing a separate aspect of the various considerations that managers face. Exhibit S1-6 highlights for you the different emphases of these theories, so that you can see how each contributes to a better understanding of management as a whole.

Exhibit S1-6

Emphases of Major Management Theories

Constraints on Managers:
Organizational Culture and the Environment

**What constraints do
managers face?**

1. How much control do managers have?

2. What effect does culture have on managerial actions?

3. What kinds of cultures can managers create?

4. What influence does the environment have on managers?

▶ ▶ ▶ Bruce Beairsto wonders how to deal with the fashion sense (or sometimes lack of sense) he sees in secondary students.[1] The Richmond, BC, school board superintendent, in charge of all 51 public schools in the district, is working to change the culture of the schools he oversees.

Some students have been pushing the fashion envelope, showing up for class with revealing tops and low-cut jeans with thongs sticking out. As Beairsto notes, "School is not the mall, not the beach. It's a place of learning."

Beairsto put together a committee of 16 high school students, who together with some parents, teachers, school administrators, and support staff developed clothing guidelines. The guidelines demonstrate "an appropriate respect for the perspectives and sensibilities of others in the school community, recognizing that in a diverse community there will be a wide range of values and beliefs that may relate to clothing."

To signal the importance of dressing appropriately on school grounds, the dress code will be applied to anyone who enters school buildings. The aim is to encourage a culture of respect within schools. "What we are against is clothing that distracts from learning," says Beairsto.

Think About It

What is it like to be the manager of 51 schools in a district, where some people are complaining about what students are wearing? Put yourself in Bruce Beairsto's shoes. What would be the best way to convince teenagers that perhaps they should dress more appropriately at school? How will the school's culture affect Beairsto's ability to introduce a new dress code? How will factors outside the school, such as parental views, or the type of clothing available, affect his decisions?

Bruce Beairsto's managerial responsibilities include making sure the climate for learning is a positive one for students in all 51 schools in the Richmond, BC, school district. He recognizes how important organizational culture is to his organization in getting teachers, students, parents, and the rest of the staff working together. He has seen how the lack of clear clothing guidelines created a situation where at least some students pushed the boundaries on what is appropriate to wear to school. He also recognizes the challenges he would face as a manager if he simply imposed his views on students, teachers, and parents, so he has brought these groups together to create a new set of guidelines. The aim is to create a more supportive learning environment for everyone.

But how much actual impact does a manager like Beairsto have on an organization's success or failure? Can Beairsto simply impose a dress code? Will students go along readily if he does? Will the parents accept Beairsto simply imposing a dress code? What if they feel they cannot afford to buy the recommended clothing? These questions raise more general questions about managing: Do managers control their environment, or are they controlled by it? Are they affected more by outside circumstances or those within the organization? In this chapter, we consider the influence of an organization's internal culture and its external environment on managers' actions. We begin our exploration by considering whether managers have complete control or no control over these factors.

The Manager: How Much Control?

1. How much control do managers have?

omnipotent view of management
The view that managers are directly responsible for an organization's success or failure.

symbolic view of management
The view that managers have only a limited effect on substantive organizational outcomes because of the large number of factors outside their control.

The dominant view in management theory and society in general is that managers are directly responsible for an organization's success or failure. We will call this perspective the **omnipotent view of management**. In contrast, some observers have argued that much of an organization's success or failure is due to external forces outside managers' control. This perspective has been labelled the **symbolic view of management**. Let's look more closely at each of these perspectives so that we can try to clarify just how much credit or blame managers should receive for their organizations' performance.

The Omnipotent View

In Chapter 1 we discussed the importance of managers to organizations. This view reflects a dominant assumption in management theory: The quality of an organization's managers determines the quality of the organization itself. It's assumed that differences in an organization's effectiveness or efficiency are due to the decisions and actions of its managers. Good managers anticipate change, exploit opportunities, correct poor performance, and lead their organizations toward their goals, which may be changed if necessary. When profits are up, managers take the credit and reward themselves with bonuses, stock options, and the like. When profits are down, top managers are often fired in the belief that "new blood" will bring improved results. For instance, it took less than two weeks after the close of the 2004 Olympic Games in Athens for Swimming Canada to fire national coach Dave Johnson, after the swim team failed to win one medal. As Swimming Canada president Rob Colburn noted: "We made the decision on the facts and figures and the clear feeling that we needed to go in another direction. It was time—11 years. And 11 years for any coach is a long run."[2]

Q&A 2.1

The view of managers as omnipotent is consistent with the stereotypical picture of the take-charge business executive who can overcome any obstacle in carrying out the organization's goals. This omnipotent view, of course, is not limited to business organizations. We can also use it to help explain the high turnover among college and professional sports coaches, who can be considered the "managers" of their teams. Coaches who lose more games than they win are seen as ineffective. They are fired and replaced by new coaches who, it is hoped, will correct the inadequate performance.

In the omnipotent view, when organizations perform poorly, someone has to be held accountable regardless of the reasons, and in our society, that "someone" is the manager. Of course, when things go well, we need someone to praise. So managers also get the credit—even if they had little to do with achieving positive outcomes.

The Symbolic View

When tunnelling for the Canada Line transit system started tearing up Vancouver's Cambie Street, a busy shopping area, customers stopped coming to the stores and restaurants. The street was noisy, there was no parking, and the area was a traffic nightmare. Facing a significant drop in customers, Christian Gaudreault, owner of Tomato Fresh Food Café, moved his restaurant elsewhere. Giriaj Gautam, who runs the Cambie General Store, has found his sales down 25 percent and hopes he can hang on until construction finishes up in the area, more than a year after it started. Was the declining revenue the result of decisions and actions by Gaudreault and Gautam, or was it the result of factors beyond their control? Similarly, when a massive power outage hit Ontario, mad cow disease struck in Alberta, and the avian flu killed chickens in British Columbia, were these the result of managerial actions or circumstances outside managers' control? The symbolic view would suggest the latter.

When both Home Hardware and Army and Navy closed their stores in downtown Regina, Blue Mantle, a thrift store in the same area, faced a loss of customer traffic and sales. As a result, Dave Barrett, the store's manager at the time, closed Blue Mantle soon after. He explained his decision: "When Home Hardware closed, and department store Army and Navy closed, that cut away a lot of our traffic to the store. We used to have lots of seniors that would swing over to our place." He also noted that the state of the economy was a factor in the store closing.[3] The Roman Catholic Archdiocese of Regina eventually re-opened Blue Mantle after receiving numerous requests from customers, and now runs the store with volunteers.

The symbolic view says that a manager's ability to affect outcomes is influenced and constrained by external factors.[4] In this view, it's unreasonable to expect managers to significantly affect an organization's performance. Instead, an organization's results are influenced by factors managers do not control, such as the economy, customers, government policies, competitors' actions, industry conditions, control over proprietary technology, and decisions made by previous managers.

According to the symbolic view, managers merely symbolize control and influence.[5] How? They create meaning out of randomness, confusion, and ambiguity or try to innovate and adapt. Because managers have a limited effect on organizational outcomes, their actions involve developing plans, making decisions, and engaging in other managerial activities for the benefit of stockholders, customers, employees, and the public. However, the part that managers actually play in organizational success or failure is minimal.

Reality Suggests a Synthesis

In reality, managers are neither helpless nor all powerful. Internal and external constraints that restrict a manager's decision options exist within every organization. Internal constraints arise from the organization's culture, and external constraints come from the organization's environment.

As Exhibit 2-1 shows, managers operate within the constraints imposed by the organization's culture and environment. Yet, despite these constraints, managers are not powerless. They can still influence an organization's performance. In the remainder of this chapter, we discuss how an organization's culture and environment impose constraints

Q&A 2.2

Parameters of Managerial Discretion

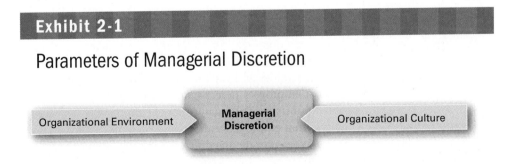

Organizational Environment → **Managerial Discretion** ← Organizational Culture

on managers. However, as we will see in other chapters, these constraints don't mean that a manager's hands are tied. As Bruce Beairsto, in our chapter-opening vignette, recognized, managers can and do influence their culture and environment.

The Organization's Culture

▶ ▶ ▶   Every organization has a culture, a way that those in the organization interact with each other and with their clients or customers.[6] In the Richmond, BC, public school district, school board superintendent Bruce Beairsto worried that the lack of dress code standards was interfering with the culture of learning expected within schools. Beairsto noted that some of the boys said they were distracted by the clothes some of the girls were wearing to class. In drafting the policy on what was appropriate to wear to school, an emphasis was placed on clothes that "demonstrate respect for the rights and perspective of others...and demonstrate a respect for the school context and the wearer's responsibilities as a member of the school community." Not all school districts have dress codes, and, of course, some schools require students to wear uniforms. Beairsto decided that as the manager in charge of the schools, he would like to keep a somewhat relaxed culture in the schools, but one that also demonstrates respect.

Think About It

What is organizational culture and how does it affect Bruce Beairsto's ability to manage? Is the impact of culture different if the organization is a school rather than a business organization?

---

2. What effect does culture have on managerial actions?

We know that every person has a unique personality—a set of relatively permanent and stable traits that influence the way we act and interact with others. When we describe someone as warm, open, relaxed, shy, or aggressive, we are describing personality traits. An organization, too, has a personality, which we call its *culture*.

What Is Organizational Culture?

EnCana
www.encana.com

Calgary-based EnCana was formed by a merger between Alberta Energy Company (AEC) and PanCanadian Energy Corporation.[7] It was not easy bringing the two companies together, as they were marked by two very different corporate cultures. PanCanadian was known as warm and fuzzy, with a risk-averse operating style. AEC was a much more aggressive company. "If you had to distill the two companies, PanCanadian managed for profitability while AEC managed for growth," says Brian Prokop, a research analyst with Calgary-based investment firm Peters & Co. Under the merger, EnCana retains AEC's culture of growth. Each EnCana employee must follow the written goals of a "principled meritocracy," which are spelled out in the company's corporate constitution. EnCana employees are not to become "egotistical or arrogant, cynical, unwilling to adapt or change or play internal politics or games but rather strive to be the best they can be." Thus, the organizational culture supports what EnCana, and its CEO, Randall Eresman, is trying to achieve.

organizational culture
A system of shared meaning and beliefs held by organizational members that determines, in large degree, how employees act.

How does the culture of your college or university differ from that of your high school?

What is **organizational culture**? It's a system of shared meaning and beliefs held by organizational members that determines, in large degree, how they act toward each other and outsiders. It represents a common perception held by an organization's members that influences how they behave. In every organization, there are values, symbols, rituals, myths, and practices that have evolved over time.[8] These shared values and experiences determine, in large degree, what employees perceive and how they respond to their world.[9] When faced with problems or issues, the organizational culture—the "way we do things around here"—influences what employees can do and how they conceptualize, define, analyze, and resolve issues. When considering different job offers, it makes sense to

Q&A 2.3, Q&A 2.4   evaluate whether you can fit into the organization's culture.

Our definition of organizational culture implies three things:

- Culture is a *perception.* Individuals perceive the organizational culture on the basis of what they see, hear, or experience within the organization.
- Culture is *shared.* Even though individuals may have different backgrounds or work at different organizational levels, they tend to describe the organization's culture in similar terms.
- Culture is a *descriptive* term. It's concerned with how members perceive the organization, not with whether they like it. It describes rather than evaluates.

Research suggests that seven dimensions capture the essence of an organization's culture.[10] These dimensions are described in Exhibit 2-2. Each dimension ranges from low (it's not very typical of the culture) to high (it's very typical of the culture). Appraising an organization on these seven dimensions gives a composite picture of the organization's culture. In many organizations, one of these cultural dimensions often is emphasized more than the others and essentially shapes the organization's personality and the way organizational members work. For instance, at Sony Corporation the focus is on product innovation. The company "lives and breathes" new-product development (outcome orientation), and employees' work decisions, behaviours, and actions support that goal. In contrast, WestJet Airlines has made its employees a central part of its culture (people orientation). Exhibit 2-3 on page 46 describes how the dimensions can be combined to create significantly different organizations.

Q&A 2.5

Strong vs. Weak Cultures

Although all organizations have cultures, not all cultures have an equal impact on employees' behaviours and actions. **Strong cultures**—cultures in which the key values are deeply held and widely shared—have a greater influence on employees than do weak cultures.

strong cultures
Organizations in which the key values are deeply held and widely shared.

Exhibit 2-2

Dimensions of Organizational Culture

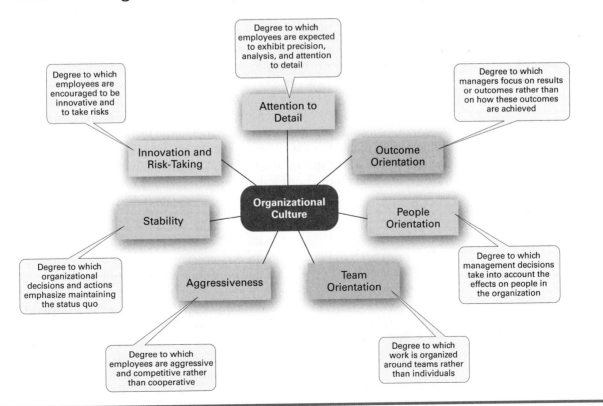

Exhibit 2-3

Contrasting Organizational Cultures

Organization A	Organization B
• Managers must fully document all decisions. • Creative decisions, change, and risks are not encouraged. • Extensive rules and regulations exist for all employees. • Productivity is valued over employee morale. • Employees are encouraged to stay within their own department. • Individual effort is encouraged.	• Management encourages and rewards risk-taking and change. • Employees are encouraged to "run with" ideas, and failures are treated as "learning experiences." • Employees have few rules and regulations to follow. • Productivity is balanced with treating its people right. • Team members are encouraged to interact with people at all levels and functions. • Many rewards are team-based.

The more employees accept the organization's key values and the greater their commitment to those values, the stronger the culture is. This explains why Bruce Beairsto brought together a team of students, parents, teachers, school administrators, and support staff to establish a new dress code for students. He wanted to ensure that he could get greater commitment to the code once it was put in place.

Q&A 2.6

Whether an organization's culture is strong, weak, or somewhere in between depends on factors such as the size of the organization, how long it has been around, how much turnover there has been among employees, and the intensity with which the culture started.

Some organizations do not make clear what is important and what is not, and this lack of clarity is a characteristic of weak cultures. In such organizations, culture is unlikely to greatly influence managers. Most organizations, however, have moderate to strong cultures. There is relatively high agreement on what is important, what defines "good" employee behaviour, what it takes to get ahead, and so forth.

An increasing body of evidence suggests that strong cultures are associated with high organizational performance.[11] It's easy to understand why a strong culture enhances performance. After all, when values are clear and widely accepted, employees know what they are supposed to do and what is expected of them, so they can act quickly to take care of problems, thus preventing any potential performance decline. However, the drawback is that the same strong culture also might prevent employees from trying new approaches, especially

Q&A 2.7

during periods of rapid change.[12] Strong cultures do not always yield *positive* results, however. Enron had a very strong, and unethical, culture. This enabled employees and top management to engage in unethical behaviour that was concealed from public scrutiny.

Subcultures

dominant culture

A system of shared meanings that expresses the core values of a majority of the organization's members; it gives the organization its distinct personality.

subcultures

Minicultures within an organization, typically defined by department designations and geographical separation.

Do the different instructors you have emphasize different things, such as innovative projects, a disciplined classroom, use of humour?

Organizations do not necessarily have one uniform culture. In fact, most large organizations have a dominant culture and numerous sets of subcultures.[13]

When we talk about an organization's culture, we are referring to its *dominant* culture. A **dominant culture** expresses the core values that are shared by the majority of an organization's members. It's this macro view of culture that gives an organization its distinct personality.[14] **Subcultures** tend to develop in large organizations to reflect the common problems, situations, or experiences that members face. The existence of subcultures in an organization suggests that individual managers play a role in moulding a common culture in their own units. By conveying and then reinforcing core values, managers can influence the common culture of the employees in their unit.

Subcultures are likely to be defined by department designations and geographical separation. An organization's marketing department, for example, can have a subculture that is uniquely shared by members of that department. It will include the **core values** of the dominant culture, plus additional values unique to members of the marketing department. Similarly, offices or units of the organization that are physically separated from the organization's main operations may take on a different personality. Again, the core values are essentially retained but modified to reflect the separated unit's distinct situation.

The Source of Culture

An organization's current customs, traditions, and general way of doing things are largely due to what it has done before and the degree of success it has had with those endeavours. The original source of an organization's culture usually reflects the vision or mission of the organization's founders. Their focus might be aggressiveness or it might be treating employees as family. The founders establish the early culture by projecting an image of what the organization should be. They are not constrained by previous customs or approaches. And the small size of most new organizations helps the founders instill their vision in all organizational members. Frank Stronach had a strong impact on the culture of the organization he founded, Magna International, as the following *Management Reflection* shows.

MANAGEMENT REFLECTION

Magna Culture Creates Ownership

How much impact does a founder have on an organization's culture? Frank Stronach, founder of Aurora, Ontario-based Magna International, and currently chair of the board, still has a profound effect on Magna's culture, even though he is no longer CEO.[15] Magna's Corporate Constitution and the Employee's Charter provide the roadmap for the company's Fair Enterprise culture, first introduced by Stronach. Stronach believes that employees should show a "strong sense of ownership and entrepreneurial energy." To encourage a sense of ownership, 10 percent of pre-tax profits go toward profit-sharing programs for his employees. Managers' salaries are set "below industry standards" to encourage managers to earn more through profit-sharing bonuses. To further encourage managerial responsibility, Magna's managers are given considerable autonomy over buying, selling, and hiring. Stronach's policies of profit-sharing and empowerment have created a workforce that has made Magna one of the largest and most profitable companies in the country. ■

Magna International
www.magna.com

The impact of a founder on an organization's culture isn't unique to North America. At Hyundai Corporation, the giant Korean conglomerate, the culture reflects the fierce, competitive style of its founder, Chung Ju Yung. Other well-known contemporary examples of founders from Canada and other countries who have had an enormous impact on their organization's culture include Ted Rogers of Toronto-based Rogers Communications, Bill Gates of Microsoft, the late Anita Roddick of The Body Shop, and Richard Branson of the Virgin Group.

Though founders play an important role in establishing the culture of an organization, if an organization does not have a strong culture, any manager has some ability to create the culture he or she wants within their individual unit. By understanding how employees learn culture, which we discuss below, managers can shape the culture of their own units.

How an Organization's Culture Continues

Once a culture is in place, certain organizational practices help maintain it. For instance, during the employee selection process, managers typically judge job candidates not only on the requirements of the job but also on how well they might fit into the organization.

PRISM 3

At Stacy's Pita Chip Company, the environment is spotless but utilitarian, the equipment is used, and everything goes back into the business. Mark Andrus and Stacy Madison have bootstrapped their low-fat snack chip business to reach sales of over $1.3 million (US). The low-cost, hard-driving culture they have developed retains a sense of humour too, as is evident in the company's "dress code," shown here.

Intuit Canada
www.intuit.ca

socialization
The process that adapts employees to the organization's culture.

At the same time, job candidates find out information about the organization and determine whether or not they are comfortable with what they see. (See *Developing Your Interpersonal Skills— Reading an Organization's Culture* on pages 68–69 and *Managing Your Career* on pages 69–70, at the end of the chapter.)

The actions of top executives also have a major impact on the organization's culture. Through what they say and how they behave, top-level managers establish norms that filter down through the organization. This can have a positive effect on employees' willingness to take risks or to provide exceptional customer service, for instance. IBM's CEO, Sam Palmisano, wanted employees to value teamwork, so he chose to take several million dollars from his 2003 bonus and give it to his top executives to emphasize teamwork. He said, "If you say you're about a team, you have to be a team. You've got to walk the talk, right?"[16] Or it also can have the opposite effect if top managers' behaviour is self-serving, as we saw in the corporate ethics scandals of 2002.

Finally, an organization must help employees adapt to its culture through a process called **socialization**. Through the socialization process, new employees learn the organization's way of doing things. Socialization is more effective if companies hire individuals who fit into the culture. For instance, when potential job candidates look at the career section of Intuit Canada's website, they can determine whether or not they will fit into Intuit's culture.[17] The company informs job seekers that Intuit provides employees with "substantial work assignments." It also lets them know that it is looking for candidates who "are high performers, have the ability to work in teams and are willing and eager to learn and grow."

Socialization provides another benefit to organizations. It minimizes the possibility that new employees, who are unfamiliar with their new organization's culture, might disrupt the beliefs and customs that are in place.

Exhibit 2-4 summarizes how an organization's culture is established and maintained. The original culture is derived from the founders' philosophy. This, in turn, strongly influences the criteria used in hiring. The actions of the current top managers set the general expectations as to what is acceptable behaviour and what is not. Socialization processes, if successful, will match new employees' values to those of the organization during the selection process and provide support during that critical time when employees have joined the organization and are learning the ropes. (To determine what culture suits you, see *Self-Assessment— What's the Right Organizational Culture for Me?* on pages 64–65, at the end of the chapter.)

Exhibit 2-4

How an Organization's Culture Is Established and Maintained

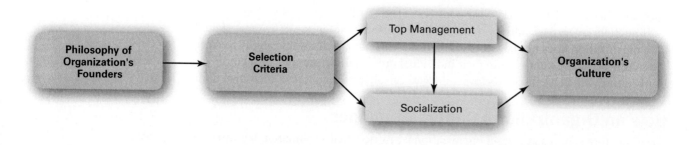

Taking its cue from the show *Survivor*, Osaka, Japan-based noodle maker Nissin Foods sent new managers on a wilderness survival trip recently. On a remote island, "Managers had to dig toilets, make fire from dry leaves, catch fish and…make their own chopsticks out of bamboo." Company spokesman Masanaga Oguchi noted that the managers "would appreciate our product in a situation where they have to go through a lot of trouble just to make hot water." The socialization into management through the survival trip taught the new managers to work together as a team and introduced them to customers' needs.[18]

How Employees Learn Culture

Culture is transmitted to employees in a number of ways. The most significant are stories, rituals, material symbols, and language.

Stories

An organization's "stories" typically are related to significant people or events, such as the organization's founders, rule breaking, reactions to past mistakes, and so forth.[19] For instance, at 3M, the product innovation stories are legendary. There is the story about the 3M scientist who spilled chemicals on her tennis shoe and came up with Scotchgard. Then there is the story about Art Fry, a researcher who wanted a better way to mark the pages of his church hymnal and invented the Post-it Note. These stories reflect what made 3M great and what it will take to continue that success.[20] An organization's stories help employees learn the culture by anchoring the present in the past, providing explanations and legitimacy for current practices, and showing what is important to the organization.[21]

3M
www.3m.com

Rituals

The annual employee golf tournament is an important ritual for Vancouver-based TrashBusters.com, an environmentally conscious company that removes people's clutter. Players have to find all of their equipment from the garbage they have collected, and are also expected to wear outrageous second-hand golf clothes. This ritual is in keeping with founder Mike McKee's philosophy of reducing environmental waste.

Corporate rituals are repetitive sequences of activities that express and reinforce the values of the organization, what goals are most important, and which people are important.[22] One of the best-known corporate rituals is Mary Kay Cosmetics' annual awards ceremony for its sales representatives.[23] Looking like a cross between a circus and a Miss America pageant, the ceremony takes place in a large auditorium, on a stage in front of a large, cheering audience, with all the participants dressed in glamorous evening clothes. Salespeople are rewarded for their success in achieving sales goals with a variety of flashy gifts including gold and diamond pins, furs, and pink Cadillacs. This "show" acts as a motivator by publicly acknowledging outstanding sales performance. In addition, the ritual aspect reinforces late founder Mary Kay's determination and optimism, which enabled her to overcome personal hardships, start her own company, and achieve material success. It conveys to salespeople that reaching their sales goals is important, and through hard work and encouragement they too can achieve success. With Mary Kay's passing in late

Mary Kay Canada
www.marykay.ca

2001, the need to preserve her memory has become even stronger. Regional directors have been known to visit the Texas head office of the firm, where they can sit in her bathtub for good luck![24]

Material Symbols

When you walk into different businesses, do you get a "feel" for the place—formal, casual, fun, serious, and so forth? These feelings demonstrate the power of material symbols in creating an organization's personality. The layout of an organization's facilities, how employees dress, the types of automobiles provided to top executives, and the availability of corporate aircraft are examples of material symbols. Others include the size of offices, the elegance of furnishings, executive "perks" (extra "goodies" provided to managers such as health club memberships, use of company-owned resort facilities, and so forth), the existence of employee lounges or on-site dining facilities, and reserved parking spaces for certain employees. At Toronto-based Willow Manufacturing, everyone from the CEO down wears a uniform, to convey the message that everyone is a member of the team. Managers at Bolton, Ontario-based Husky Injection Molding Systems convey the sense of an egalitarian workplace by having employees and management share the parking lot, dining room, and even washrooms.

Material symbols convey to employees who is important, the degree of equality desired by top management, and the kinds of behaviour (for example, risk-taking, conservative, authoritarian, participative, individualistic) that are expected and appropriate.

Language

Many organizations and units within organizations use language as a way to identify members of a culture. By learning this language, members attest to their acceptance of the culture and their willingness to help preserve it. For instance, Microsoft employees have their own unique vocabulary: *work judo* (the art of deflecting a work assignment to someone else without making it appear that you are avoiding it); *eating your own dog food* (a strategy of using your own software programs or products in the early stages as a way of testing them even if the process is disagreeable); *flat food* (goodies from the vending machine that can be slipped under the door to a colleague who is working feverishly on deadline); *facemail* (actually talking to someone face-to-face, which is considered a technologically backward means of communicating); *death march* (the countdown to shipping a new product), and so on.[25]

Over time, organizations often develop unique terms to describe equipment, key personnel, suppliers, customers, processes, or products related to their business. New employees are frequently overwhelmed with acronyms and jargon that, after a short period of time, become a natural part of their language. Once learned, this language acts as a common denominator that unites members of a given culture.

How Culture Affects Managers

Because an organization's culture constrains what its employees can and cannot do, it is particularly relevant to managers. These constraints are rarely explicit. They are not written down. It's unlikely that they will even be spoken. But they are there, and all managers quickly learn what to do and what not to do in their organization. For instance, you will not find the following values written down anywhere, but each comes from a real organization.

Q&A 2.8

- Look busy even if you are not.
- If you take risks and fail around here, you will pay dearly for it.
- Before you make a decision, run it by your manager so that he or she is never surprised.
- We make our product only as good as the competition forces us to.
- What made us successful in the past will make us successful in the future.
- If you want to get to the top here, you have to be a team player.

The link between values such as these and managerial behaviour is fairly straightforward. If an organization's culture supports the belief that profits can be increased by cost cutting and that the company's best interests are served by achieving slow but steady increases in quarterly earnings, managers are unlikely to pursue programs that are innovative, risky, long term, or expansionary. For organizations that value and encourage workforce diversity, the organizational culture, and thus managers' decisions and actions, will be supportive of diversity efforts. (See *Managing Workforce Diversity—Creating an Inclusive Workplace Culture* on page 69, at the end of the chapter, for more information on creating a workplace that encourages diversity.) In an organization whose culture conveys a basic distrust of employees, managers are more likely to use an authoritarian leadership style than a democratic one. Why? The culture establishes for managers what is appropriate behaviour.

An organization's culture, especially a strong one, constrains a manager's decision-making options in all four management functions. Exhibit 2-5 shows the major areas of a manager's job that are influenced by the culture in which he or she operates.

Current Organizational Culture Issues Facing Managers

Calgary-based WestJet Airlines is renowned for its attention to customers. Nike's innovations in running-shoe technology are legendary. Royal Bank (RBC Financial Group) consistently takes top honours for corporate social responsibility. How have these organizations achieved such reputations? Their organizational cultures have played a crucial role. Let's look at three current cultural issues managers should consider: creating an ethical culture, creating an innovative culture, and creating a customer-responsive culture.

3. What kinds of cultures can managers create?

Creating an Ethical Culture

The content and strength of an organization's culture influences its ethical climate and the ethical behaviour of its members.[26] A strong organizational culture will exert more influence on employees than a weak one. If the culture is strong and supports high ethical standards, it should have a very powerful and positive influence on employee behaviour. Likewise, a strong culture that encourages unethical behaviour will have a powerful influence on employees, as the following *Management Reflection* shows.

Exhibit 2-5

Managerial Decisions Affected by Organizational Culture

Planning
- The degree of risk that plans should contain
- Whether plans should be developed by individuals or teams
- The degree of environmental scanning in which management will engage

Organizing
- How much autonomy should be designed into employees' jobs
- Whether tasks should be done by individuals or in teams
- The degree to which department managers interact with each other

Leading
- The degree to which managers are concerned with increasing employee job satisfaction
- What leadership styles are appropriate
- Whether all disagreements—even constructive ones—should be eliminated

Controlling
- Whether to impose external controls or to allow employees to control their own actions
- What criteria should be emphasized in employee performance evaluations
- What repercussions will result from exceeding one's budget

Manager Rules with Iron Fist

Can a manager encourage individuals to act unethically? At scandal-ridden WorldCom, Canadian-born CEO Bernie Ebbers ruled with an iron fist.[27] Hiding information from directors and auditors was an expected practice, with executives told to "follow orders." Employees were routinely criticized publicly if they did not follow orders. "Show those numbers to the [expletive deleted] auditors and I'll throw you out the [expletive deleted] window," a senior executive told an employee in an email. When company executives suggested that WorldCom needed a corporate code of conducts, Ebbers suggested that drafting one would be "a colossal waste of time." ∎

An organizational culture most likely to shape high ethical standards is one that is high in risk tolerance, low to moderate in aggressiveness, and focused on means as well as outcomes. Managers in such a culture are supported for taking risks and innovating, are discouraged from engaging in uncontrolled competition, and will pay attention to *how* goals are achieved as well as to *what* goals are achieved.

What can managers do to create a more ethical culture? *Tips for Managers—Creating a More Ethical Culture* on page 53 provides some suggestions.

Creating an Innovative Culture

Cirque du Soleil
www.cirquedusoleil.com

Cirque du Soleil, the Montreal-based creator of circus theatre, is known for its innovation. Its managers state that the organization's culture is based on involvement, communication, creativity, and diversity (which they see as a key to innovation).[28] Although Cirque du Soleil is in an industry (entertainment) where continual innovations are crucial to success, the fact is that successful organizations in all types of industries need cultures that support innovation.

Organizational culture is what makes Cirque du Soleil so special. Employees focus on solutions rather than blame. Consensus is not a virtue because CEO Daniel Lamarre feels that the best ideas get lost if everyone has to compromise. Lamarre encourages dissent, and tempers fly during discussions, but the results are the creative, dynamic shows that the Cirque produces.

What does an innovative culture look like? According to Swedish researcher Goran Ekvall, it is characterized by the following:

- *Challenge and involvement.* How much employees are involved in, motivated by, and committed to the long-term goals and success of the organization.
- *Freedom.* The degree to which employees can independently define their work, exercise discretion, and take initiative in their day-to-day activities.
- *Trust and openness.* The degree to which employees are supportive of and respectful to each other.
- *Idea time.* The amount of time individuals have to elaborate on new ideas before taking action.
- *Playfulness/humour.* How much spontaneity, fun, and ease there is in the workplace.
- *Conflict resolution.* The degree to which individuals make decisions and resolve issues based on the good of the organization vs. personal interest.
- *Debates.* How much employees are allowed to express their opinions and put forth their ideas for consideration and review.
- *Risk-taking.* How much managers tolerate uncertainty and ambiguity, and whether employees are rewarded for taking risks.[29]

Being able to create a culture that embraces innovative approaches is not easy, and might be even more difficult for law firms, but one such firm has been quite successful in this regard, as the following *Management Reflection* shows.

MANAGEMENT REFLECTION

Borden Ladner Gervais' Culture Encourages Collaboration

How do you get lawyers from different law firms to work together after separate firms merge? When Borden Ladner Gervais (BLG), a national law firm, was created out of the merger of five regional firms (Ladner Downs in Vancouver; Howard Mackie in Calgary; Borden & Elliot in Toronto; Scott & Aylen in Ottawa; and McMaster Gervais in Montreal), the challenge was to downplay regional rivalries and create a truly national law firm.[30] Each of the smaller firms was considered a "boutique" firm, specializing in particular aspects of law. Following the merger, profits were pooled centrally and then divided across the five regional firms, rather than letting each region keep its own profits. This approach to profit-sharing encourages BLG lawyers to work with each other across regions, getting the best results for clients.

BLG has a strong culture that emphasizes a collaborative management style, with a national council composed of the managing partners of the five regional firms. The CEO (or national managing partner), Sean Weir, needs the consent of the national council for major decisions. Consensus is achieved at the national level through conference calls of the firm's five regional managing partners. The partners work regionally to sell national decisions and build consensus at the regional level.

Clients benefit considerably from the consensus and the pooled resources it brings. For instance, before the merger, when the Vancouver region signed a biotech client, it would have outsourced the technology expertise it needed. Now, the region is able to ask a lawyer from the Ottawa office to work on this type of project. More than a third of BLG's 200 largest clients use lawyers in more than one office, indicating the depth of sharing that occurs across the firm. ■

Borden Ladner Gervais
www.blgcanada.com

Creating a Customer-Responsive Culture

Four Seasons Hotels and Resorts
www.fourseasons.com

Isadore Sharp, chair and CEO of Toronto-based Four Seasons Hotels and Resorts, believes keenly in customer service. Creating a customer-responsive culture starts with employee selection, where every candidate faces four or five interviews, to ensure they have the right attitude. As part of employee training, all new employees spend one night in the hotel as a guest to help them understand the perspective of the customer. Sharp notes that the hotel chain has "30 000 employees who are always thinking of new ways to make our guest experience more rewarding."[31]

Harrah's Entertainment, the Las Vegas-based national gaming company, is also devoted to customer service, and for good reason. Company research showed that customers who were satisfied with the service they received at a Harrah's casino increased their gaming expenditures by 10 percent, and those who were extremely satisfied increased their gaming expenditures by 24 percent. When customer service translates into these types of results, of course managers would want to create a customer-responsive culture![32]

But what does a customer-responsive culture look like? Research shows that six characteristics are routinely present in successful, service-oriented organizations:

- *Outgoing and friendly employees.* Successful service-oriented organizations hire employees who are outgoing and friendly.
- *Few rigid rules, procedures, and regulations.* Service employees need to have the freedom to meet changing customer service requirements.
- *Widespread use of empowerment.* Employees are empowered to decide what is necessary to please the customer.
- *Good listening skills.* Employees in customer-responsive cultures have the ability to listen to and understand messages sent by the customer.
- *Role clarity.* Service employees act as links between the organization and its customers, which can create considerable ambiguity and conflict. Successful customer-responsive cultures reduce employees' uncertainty about their roles and the best way to perform their jobs.
- *Employees attentive to customer needs.* They are willing to take the initiative, even when it's outside their normal job requirements, to satisfy a customer's needs.[33]

Based on these characteristics, what can managers do to make their cultures more customer-responsive? *Tips for Managers—Creating a More Customer-Responsive Culture* provides some suggestions.

TIPS FOR MANAGERS

Creating a More Customer-Responsive Culture

- ✏ Hire service-contact people with the **personality and attitudes consistent with customer service**—friendliness, enthusiasm, attentiveness, patience, concern about others, and listening skills.

- ✏ **Train customer-service people continually** by focusing on improving product knowledge, listening actively, showing patience, and displaying emotions.

- ✏ Socialize new service-contact people to the **organization's goals and values**.

- ✏ Design customer-service jobs so that **employees have as much control as necessary** to satisfy customers.

- ✏ Empower service-contact employees with the **discretion to make day-to-day decisions** on job-related activities.

- ✏ As the leader, **convey a customer-focused vision** and demonstrate through decisions and actions the commitment to customers.

In general, to create any type of culture (and to reinforce the culture), managers need to communicate the elements of the culture, model the appropriate behaviours, train employees to carry out the new actions, and reward desired behaviours, while creating negative incentives for straying from the desired behaviour.[34]

The Environment

▶ ▶ ▶ Schools, just like other organizations, respond to the environment around them. That is why we have seen discussions of some schools banning particular textbooks, or others where students are encouraged to be very active in community affairs. Richmond, BC, where Bruce Beairsto is school board superintendent, is a multicultural community "where two-thirds of the population is made up of immigrant families that have varying ideas about appropriate clothing."[35] It is not only the local environment that affects the schools, however. Teens are influenced by stars such as Lindsay Lohan and Christina Aguilera. Stephanie Ip, 16, says that the media have too much influence in choice of fashion: "There's no more distinction between a pop star or someone who's famous and someone who's a normal 14-year-old girl. She's wearing what Britney Spears could be wearing. There's no distinction anymore—and there should be." Beairsto's challenge as a manager is to understand the environment around him, and then adopt a dress code that will convey an appropriate message, without being overbearing or unreasonable. He even acknowledges: "We're not against skin," he says. "Everything they buy seems to have a little bit of skin showing."

Think About It

Bruce Beairsto has to consider how students, teachers, parents, and the local community will respond to his decisions. To what extent does being a school board superintendent reflect the same management challenges as being the CEO of a manufacturing company?

In the supplement to Chapter 1, our discussion of an organization as an open system explained that an organization interacts with its environment as it takes in inputs and distributes outputs. Anyone who questions the impact of the external environment on managing should consider the following:

4. What influence does the environment have on managers?

- Canadians spent $652.7 million on bottled water in 2005, and sales of bottled water increased 20 percent in 2006. But complaints by environmentalist David Suzuki and others that bottled water is not good for the environment are starting to be heard by consumers.[36]

- In May 2006, Skype, which provides people with the technology to make free calls over the Internet, announced that customers could also call land-line phones and cellphones in Canada and the United States for free.

As these two examples show, there are forces in the environment that play a major role in shaping managers' actions. In this section, we identify some of the critical environmental forces that affect managers and show how they constrain managerial discretion.

Defining the External Environment

The term **external environment** refers to forces and institutions outside the organization that potentially can affect the organization's performance. The external environment is made up of three components, as shown in Exhibit 2-6 on page 56: the specific environment, the general environment, and the global environment. We discuss the first two types of external environment in this chapter. Today, globalization is one of the major factors affecting managers of both large and small organizations. We address the global environment in Chapter 3.

external environment
Outside forces and institutions that potentially can affect the organization's performance.

The Specific Environment

The **specific environment** includes those external forces that have a direct and immediate impact on managers' decisions and actions and are directly relevant to the achievement of the organization's goals. Each organization's specific environment is unique and changes with conditions. For instance, Timex and Rolex both make watches, but their specific environments differ because they operate in distinctly different market niches. What forces make up the specific environment? The main ones are customers, suppliers, competitors, and pressure groups.

specific environment
The part of the external environment that is directly relevant to the achievement of an organization's goals.

Customers Organizations exist to meet the needs of customers. It's the customer or client who consumes or uses the organization's output. This is true even for government organizations and other nonprofits.

Customers obviously represent potential uncertainty to an organization. Their tastes can change or they can become dissatisfied with the organization's products or service. Of course, some organizations face considerably more uncertainty as a result of their

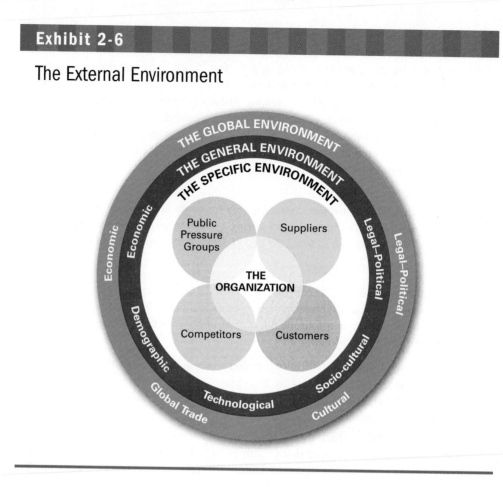

Exhibit 2-6

The External Environment

 Club Med
www.clubmed.com

customers than do others. For example, what comes to mind when you think of Club Med? Club Med's image was traditionally one of carefree singles having fun in the sun at exotic locales. Club Med found, however, that as its target customers married and had children, these same individuals were looking for family-oriented vacation resorts where they could bring the kids. Although Club Med responded to the changing demands of its customers by offering different types of vacation experiences, including family-oriented ones, the company found it hard to change its image.

Suppliers   When you think of an organization's suppliers, you typically think in terms of organizations that provide materials and equipment. For Canada's Wonderland in Toronto, that includes organizations that sell soft drinks, computers, food, flowers and other nursery stock, concrete, and paper products. But the term *suppliers* also includes providers of financial and labour inputs. Stockholders, banks, insurance companies, pension funds, and other similar organizations are needed to ensure a continuous supply of money. Labour unions, colleges and universities, occupational associations, trade schools, and local labour markets are sources of employees. When the sources of employees dry up, it can constrain managers' decisions and actions. For example, a lack of qualified nurses, a serious problem plaguing the health care industry, is making it difficult for health care providers to meet demand and keep service levels high.

Managers seek to ensure a steady flow of needed inputs at the lowest price available. Because these inputs represent uncertainties—that is, their unavailability or delay can significantly reduce the organization's effectiveness—managers typically go to great lengths to ensure a steady, reliable flow. The application of e-business techniques is changing the way that organizations deal with suppliers. For example, Toyota Motor Corporation established electronic linkages with suppliers to ensure that it has the right materials at the right time and in the right place. Although these linkages might help managers manage uncertainty, they certainly don't eliminate it.

When the Internet search engine Google decided to accept heavy censorship of its Chinese site in compliance with Communist Party requirements, its founders said the widely criticized compromise was made to allow Internet access to a fifth of the world's population. Among those who disagreed with Google's compromise were these members of Students for a Free Tibet.

Competitors   All organizations have one or more competitors. Even though it's a monopoly, Canada Post competes with FedEx, UPS, and other forms of communication such as the telephone, email, and fax. Nike competes with Reebok, Adidas, and Fila, among others. Coca-Cola competes with Pepsi and other soft drink companies. Nonprofit organizations such as the Royal Ontario Museum and Girl Guides also compete for dollars, volunteers, and customers.

Managers cannot afford to ignore the competition. When they do, they suffer. For instance, until the 1980s, three major US broadcast networks—ABC, CBS, and NBC—virtually controlled what you watched on television. Now, with digital cable, satellite, TiVo, DVD players, and the web, customers have a much broader choice of what to watch. CNN encouraged viewers to participate in the US presidential debates in the summer of 2007 by submitting their questions to candidates through YouTube. As technological capabilities continue to expand, broadcast networks will face even more competition from individuals who place content on the web. The Internet has virtually eliminated geographic boundaries, making it possible, through the power of Internet marketing, for a small maple syrup maker in Montreal to compete with the likes of Pillsbury, Quaker Oats, and Smucker's.

These examples illustrate that competitors—in terms of pricing, new products developed, services offered, and so forth—represent an environmental force that managers must monitor and to which they must be prepared to respond.

Public Pressure Groups   Managers must recognize the special-interest groups that attempt to influence the actions of organizations. For instance, both Wal-Mart and Home Depot have had difficulty getting approval to build stores in Vancouver. Neighbourhood activists worry about traffic density brought about by big-box stores, and in the case of both stores there is concern that local businesses will fail if the stores move in. Home Depot's director of real estate called Vancouver City Hall's review process "confusing and unfair" and "unlike anything in [his] experience."[37] Local hardware store owners and resident groups have lobbied against the store to city planners, hoping to keep big-box stores out of the Kitsilano neighbourhood.

As social and political attitudes change, so too does the power of public pressure groups. For example, through their persistent efforts, groups such as MADD (Mothers Against Drunk Driving) and SADD (Students Against Destructive Decisions) have managed to make changes in the alcoholic beverage and restaurant and bar industries, and raised public awareness about the problem of drunk drivers.

The General Environment

The **general environment** includes the broad economic, legal–political, socio-cultural, demographic, and technological conditions that *may* affect the organization. Changes in any of these areas usually do not have as large an impact as changes in the specific environment do, but managers must consider them as they plan, organize, lead, and control.

general environment
Broad external conditions that may affect the organization.

Peter B. Moore, founder, chief executive, and chair of Barrie, Ontario-based Moore Packaging, which makes corrugated boxes, knows how changes in the general environment can seriously affect one's business. From 2000 to 2005, the company experienced double-digit sales growth each year, but he does not expect the rest of the decade to be quite as successful. "The corrugated packaging market is kind of stagnating right now as far as growth is concerned," Moore says. "Manufacturing companies have shut down and we come and go as they come and go. I used to say everything made goes in a box, but I didn't realize it would be going into a box in China."

Economic Conditions   Interest rates, inflation, changes in disposable income, stock market fluctuations, and the stage of the general business cycle are some of the economic factors that can affect management practices in an organization. For example, many specialty retailers such as IKEA, Roots, Birks, and Williams-Sonoma are acutely aware of the impact consumer disposable income has on their sales. When consumers' incomes fall or when their confidence about job security declines, as happened during much of the late 1980s and through much of the 1990s, they will postpone purchasing anything that isn't a necessity. Even charitable organizations such as the United Way or the Heart and Stroke Foundation feel the impact of economic factors. During economic downturns, not only does the demand for their services increase, but also their contributions typically decrease.

Legal–Political Conditions   Federal, provincial, and local governments influence what organizations can and cannot do. Some federal legislation has significant implications. For example, the Canadian Human Rights Act makes it illegal for any employer or provider of service that falls within federal jurisdiction to discriminate on the following grounds: race, national or ethnic origin, colour, religion, age, sex (including pregnancy and childbirth), marital status, family status, mental or physical disability (including previous or present drug or alcohol dependence), pardoned conviction, or sexual orientation. The act covers federal departments and agencies; Crown corporations; chartered banks; national airlines; interprovincial communications and telephone companies; interprovincial transportation companies; and other federally regulated industries, including certain mining operations.

Canada's Employment Equity Act of 1995 protects several categories of employees from employment barriers: Aboriginal peoples (whether First Nation, Inuit, or Métis); persons with disabilities; members of visible minorities (non-Caucasian in race or nonwhite in colour); and women. This legislation aims to ensure that members of these four groups are treated equitably. Employers covered by the Canadian Human Rights Act are also covered by the Employment Equity Act.

Many provinces have their own legislation, including employment equity acts, to cover employers in their provinces. Companies sometimes have difficulty complying with equity acts, as recent audits conducted by the Canadian Human Rights Commission show. In an

Canadian Human Rights Commission
www.chrc-ccdp.ca

audit of 180 companies, only Status of Women Canada; Elliot Lake, Ontario-based AJ Bus Lines; the National Parole Board; Canadian Transportation Agency; Les Méchins, Quebec-based Verreault Navigation; and Nortel Networks were compliant on their first try.[38]

The Competition Act of 1986 created the Bureau of Competition Policy (now called the Competition Bureau) to maintain and encourage competition in Canada. For example, if two major competing companies consider merging, they come under scrutiny from the bureau. Heather Reisman and Gerry Schwartz's purchase of Chapters in 2001 needed approval before they could merge Chapters with their Indigo bookstores. Before approving the merger, the bureau imposed a number of conditions, including the sale or closing of 20 stores and a code of conduct for dealing with publishers. The code of conduct was the result of publishers' complaints about the way Chapters had treated them in the past. These rules affected the way Indigo/Chapters could do business until 2006.[39] Beyond that time, the bookseller was allowed to operate without restraint by the Competition Bureau.[40]

To protect farmers, the Canadian government has created marketing boards that regulate the pricing and production of such things as milk and eggs. Those who decide that they want to manufacture small amounts of cheese in Canada would have great difficulty doing so because the Canadian government does not open production quotas to new producers very often. Marketing boards restrict imports of some products, but the unintended result is that foreign governments oppose exports from Canada.

Organizations spend a great deal of time and money meeting government regulations, but the effects of these regulations go beyond time and money.[41] They also reduce managerial discretion by limiting the choices available to managers. In a 2004 COMPAS survey of business leaders, most respondents cited interprovincial trade barriers as a significant hurdle to doing business in this country, calling the barriers "bad economics."[42] A more recent article backed up the views of these Canadian business leaders, arguing that nearly half of the productivity advantage that the United States has over Canada could be accounted for by interprovincial trade barriers.[43]

Other aspects of the legal–political conditions are the political climate, the general stability of a country where an organization operates, and the attitudes that elected government officials hold toward business. In Canada, for example, organizations have generally operated in a stable political environment. However, management can be a global activity. Managers who work for companies with locations outside of Canada should be aware of the political climate in the countries in which they operate because these conditions will likely influence managerial decisions and actions.

Socio-cultural Conditions   Vancouver-based A&W Food Services of Canada announced in January 2007 that it would become "the first national hamburger chain to provide customers across Canada with 'zero or significantly lower' trans fat in menu items." A&W marketing director Mike Atkinson explained the reason for the change: "Our customers wanted us to cut trans fats from our menu items so that's what we've done, without compromising taste and quality."[44] Burlington, Ontario-based Voortman Cookies was the first Canadian cookie maker to drop trans fats from its products. President and co-founder Harry Voortman said he dropped the trans fats after his daughter, Lynn, a naturopathic doctor, became concerned enough that she stopped eating her father's cookies altogether.[45] The *CBC Video Case Incident—The Fast-Food Industry and Trans Fats: Fad or Legitimate Concern for Society?* on page 132 also explores the issue as it applies to managers in the food industry.

Why are A&W and Voortman changing their products? Because health officials and consumers are increasingly anxious about the link between TFAs (trans fatty acids) and heart disease.[46] Managers must adapt their practices to the changing expectations of the society in which they operate. As societal values, customs, and tastes change, managers also must change. For instance, as employees have begun seeking more balance in their lives, organizations have had to adjust by offering family leave policies, more flexible work hours, and on-site child care facilities. These trends may pose a potential constraint to managers' decisions and actions. If an organization does business in other countries, managers need to be familiar with those countries' values and cultures, and manage in ways that recognize and embrace those specific socio-cultural aspects.

Competition Bureau
www.competition.
ic.gc.ca

A&W Food Services of Canada
www.aw.ca

Voortman Cookies
www.voortmancookies.
com

Demographic Conditions Demographic conditions encompass trends in the physical characteristics of a population such as gender, age, level of education, geographic location, income, and family composition. Changes in these characteristics may constrain how managers plan, organize, lead, and control. In Canada, population researchers have labelled specific age cohorts. These include the Depression group (born 1912–1921), the World War II group (born 1922–1927), the Post-war group (born 1928–1945), Baby Boomers (born 1946–1964), Generation X (born 1965–1977), and Generation Y (born 1978–2000). Although each of these groups has its own unique characteristics, members of Generation Y are of particular interest because they are thinking, learning, creating, shopping, and playing in fundamentally different ways that will greatly impact managers and organizations.

Technological Conditions In terms of the general environment, the most rapid changes have occurred in technology. We live in a time of continuous technological change. For instance, the human genetic code has been cracked. Just think of the implications of such an incredible breakthrough! Information gadgets are getting smaller and more powerful. We have automated offices, electronic meetings, robotic manufacturing, lasers, integrated circuits, faster and more powerful microprocessors, synthetic fuels, and entirely new models of doing business in an electronic age. Companies that capitalize on technology, such as Research In Motion (RIM), eBay, and Google, prosper. In addition, many successful retailers such as Wal-Mart use sophisticated information systems to keep on top of current sales trends. Similarly, hospitals, universities, airports, police departments, and even military organizations that adapt to major technological advances have a competitive edge over those that do not. The whole area of technology is radically changing the fundamental ways that organizations are structured and the way that managers manage.

How the Environment Affects Managers

Knowing *what* the various components of the environment are is important to managers. However, understanding *how* the environment affects managers is equally important. The environment affects managers through the degree of environmental uncertainty that is present and through the various stakeholder relationships that exist between the organization and its external constituencies.

PRISM 4

Assessing Environmental Uncertainty

environmental uncertainty
The degree of change and the degree of complexity in an organization's environment.

Not all environments are the same. They differ by what we call their degree of **environmental uncertainty**, which is the degree of change and the degree of complexity in an organization's environment (see Exhibit 2-7).

The first of these dimensions is the degree of change. If the components in an organization's environment change frequently, we call it a *dynamic* environment. If change is minimal, we call it a *stable* one. A stable environment might be one in which there are no new competitors, few technological breakthroughs by current competitors, little activity by pressure groups to influence the organization, and so forth. For instance, Zippo Canada, best known for its Zippo lighters, faces a relatively stable environment. There are few competitors and there is little technological change. Probably the main environmental concern for the company is the declining trend in tobacco smokers, although the company's lighters have other uses and global markets remain attractive.

Zippo Canada
www.zippo.ca

In contrast, the recorded music industry faces a highly uncertain and unpredictable environment. Digital formats like MP3, music-swapping Internet services like Kazaa, and the ability to buy and download individual songs from companies like iTunes and Puretracks have turned the industry upside down. Although music companies traditionally earned revenues by selling physical products such as LP records, cassettes, and CDs, the digital future represents chaos and uncertainty. This environment can definitely be described as dynamic.

What about rapid change that is predictable? Is that considered a dynamic environment? Bricks-and-mortar retail department stores provide a good example. They typically make one-quarter to one-third of their sales in December. The drop-off from December to January is significant. However, because the change is predictable, we don't consider the environment to

Exhibit 2-7

Environmental Uncertainty Matrix

		Degree of Change	
		Stable	**Dynamic**
Degree of Complexity	**Simple**	**Cell 1** Stable and predictable environment Few components in environment Components are somewhat similar and remain basically the same Minimal need for sophisticated knowledge of components	**Cell 2** Dynamic and unpredictable environment Few components in environment Components are somewhat similar but are in continual process of change Minimal need for sophisticated knowledge of components
	Complex	**Cell 3** Stable and predictable environment Many components in environment Components are not similar to one another and remain basically the same High need for sophisticated knowledge of components	**Cell 4** Dynamic and unpredictable environment Many components in environment Components are not similar to one another and are in continual process of change High need for sophisticated knowledge of components

be dynamic. When we talk about the degree of change, we mean change that is unpredictable. If change can be accurately anticipated, it's not an uncertainty that managers must confront.

The other dimension of uncertainty describes the degree of **environmental complexity**. The degree of complexity refers to the number of components in an organization's environment and the extent of the knowledge that the organization has about those components. For example, Hasbro, the second-largest toy manufacturer (behind Mattel), has simplified its environment by acquiring many of its competitors such as Tiger Electronics, Wizards of the Coast, Kenner Toys, Parker Brothers, and Tonka Toys. The fewer competitors, customers, suppliers, government agencies, and so forth that an organization must deal with, the less complexity and, therefore, the less uncertainty there is in its environment.

Complexity is also measured in terms of the knowledge an organization needs to have about its environment. For instance, managers at the online brokerage E*TRADE must know a great deal about their Internet service provider's operations if they want to ensure that their website is available, reliable, and secure for their stock-trading customers. On the other hand, managers of grocery stores have a minimal need for sophisticated knowledge about their suppliers.

How does the concept of environmental uncertainty influence managers? Looking again at Exhibit 2-7, each of the four cells represents different combinations of the degree of complexity and the degree of change. Cell 1 (an environment that is stable and simple) represents the lowest level of environmental uncertainty. Cell 4 (an environment that is dynamic and complex) represents the highest. Not surprisingly, managers' influence on organizational outcomes is greatest in cell 1 and least in cell 4.

Because uncertainty is a threat to an organization's effectiveness, managers try to minimize it. Given a choice, managers would prefer to operate in environments such as those in cell 1. However, they rarely have full control over that choice. In addition, most industries today are facing more dynamic changes, making their environments more uncertain.

Managing Stakeholder Relationships

Managers are also affected by the nature of the relationships they have with external stakeholders. The more obvious and secure these relationships become, the more influence managers will have over organizational outcomes.

Who are **stakeholders**? We define them as groups in the organization's external environment that are affected by and/or have an effect on the organization's decisions and actions. These groups have a stake in or are significantly influenced by what the organization does. In turn, these groups can influence the organization. For example, think of the groups

environmental complexity
The number of components in an organization's environment and the extent of the organization's knowledge about those components.

Hasbro
www.hasbro.com

stakeholders
Any constituencies in the organization's external environment that are affected by the organization's decisions and actions.

Starbucks
www.starbucks.com

that might be affected by the decisions and actions of Starbucks—coffee bean farmers, employees, specialty coffee competitors, local communities, and so forth. Some of these stakeholders also may impact decisions and actions of Starbucks' managers. The idea that organizations have stakeholders is now widely accepted by both management academics and practising managers.[47]

Q&A 2.9

With what types of stakeholders might an organization have to deal? Exhibit 2-8 identifies some of the most common. Note that these stakeholders include internal and external groups. Why? Because both can affect what an organization does and how it operates. However, we are primarily interested in the external groups and their impact on managers' discretion in planning, organizing, leading, and controlling. This does not mean that the internal stakeholders are not important, but we explain these relationships, primarily with employees, throughout the rest of the book.

Why is stakeholder-relationship management important? Why should managers even care about managing stakeholder relationships?[48] One reason is that it can lead to other organizational outcomes, such as improved predictability of environmental changes, more successful innovations, a greater degree of trust among stakeholders, and greater organizational flexibility to reduce the impact of change. But does it affect organizational performance? The answer is yes! Management researchers who have looked at this issue are finding that managers of high-performing companies tend to consider the interests of all major stakeholder groups as they make decisions.[49]

Another reason given for managing external stakeholder relationships is that it's the "right" thing to do. What does this mean? It means that an organization depends on these external groups as sources of inputs (resources) and as outlets for outputs (goods and services), and managers should consider the interests of these external groups as they make decisions and take actions. We address this issue in more detail in Chapter 4 as we look at the concepts of managerial ethics and corporate social responsibility.

How can external stakeholder relationships be managed? There are four steps:

1. *Identify the organization's stakeholders.* Which of the various groups might be impacted by decisions that managers make and which groups might influence those decisions? Those groups that are likely to be influenced by and have influence on organizational decisions are the organization's stakeholders.

Exhibit 2-8

Organizational Stakeholders

2. *Determine what particular interests or concerns the stakeholders might have.* These interests or concerns could be product quality, financial issues, safe working conditions, environmental protection, and so forth.

3. *Decide how critical each stakeholder is to the organization's decisions and actions.* Some stakeholders are more critical to the organization's decisions and actions than others. For instance, a critical stakeholder of the University of British Columbia would be the province's legislature since it controls how much budget money the university gets each year. On the other hand, the university's computer hardware and software suppliers are important but not critical.

4. *Determine how to manage the different stakeholder relationships.* This decision depends on how critical the stakeholder is to the organization and how uncertain the environment is.[50]

The more critical the stakeholder and the more uncertain the environment, the more managers need to rely on establishing explicit stakeholder partnerships rather than just acknowledging their existence.

SUMMARY AND IMPLICATIONS

1. How much control do managers have? The omnipotent view of management suggests that managers are directly responsible for an organization's success or failure. While this is the dominant view of managers, there is another perspective. The symbolic view of management argues that much of an organization's success or failure is due to external forces outside managers' control. The reality is probably somewhere in between these two views, with managers often able to exert control, but also facing situations over which they have no control.

▶ ▶ ▶ Bruce Beairsto, the Richmond, BC, school board superintendent, shows the importance of being aware of how little control one often has. While he could have imposed a dress code on his own, it likely would have met a lot of resistance. By involving many others, he has a better chance of the code being accepted.

2. What effect does culture have on managerial actions? Culture influences how people within an organization act. A strong culture where everyone supports the goals of the organization makes it easier for managers to achieve goals. A weak culture, where people do not feel connected to the organization, can make things more difficult for managers. Managers can also influence culture, through how it is conveyed to employees, which employees are hired, and how rewards occur in organizations.

▶ ▶ ▶ In Bruce Beairsto's case, the culture of a learning environment suggests open discussion before action, and that is why he put together a committee to determine the new dress code policy.

3. What kinds of cultures can managers create? Managers can create a variety of cultures. In this chapter we discussed ethical, innovative, and customer-responsive cultures. By having a culture that is consistent with goals and values, managers can more easily encourage employees to achieve organizational goals.

4. What influence does the environment have on managers? The environment plays a major role in shaping managers' decisions and actions. Managers have to be responsive to customers and suppliers while being aware of competitors and public pressure groups. As well, economic, legal–political, socio-cultural, demographic, and technological conditions affect the issues managers face in doing their job.

▶ ▶ ▶ Bruce Beairsto, in trying to determine an appropriate dress code for students, had to acknowledge the concerns of students, parents, and teachers. He was also aware that teens are very much influenced by external factors, including the media and what retailers are selling. Thus, his dress code policy had to work within those constraints.

CHAPTER 2

Management @ Work

READING FOR COMPREHENSION

1. Contrast the actions of managers according to the omnipotent and symbolic views.

2. What are the seven dimensions of organizational culture?

3. What is the impact of a strong culture on organizations and managers?

4. What is the source of an organization's culture? How does organizational culture continue?

5. How do employees learn an organization's culture?

6. What are the characteristics of an ethical culture, an innovative culture, and a customer-responsive culture?

7. What forces influence the specific and the general environments?

8. Discuss the two dimensions of environmental uncertainty.

9. What are the four steps in managing external stakeholder relationships?

LINKING CONCEPTS TO PRACTICE

1. Classrooms have cultures. Describe your classroom culture using the seven dimensions of organizational culture. Does the culture constrain your instructor? How?

2. Refer to Exhibit 2-3 on page 46. How would a first-line manager's job differ in these two organizations? How about a top manager's job?

3. Can culture be a liability to an organization? Explain.

4. Why is it important for managers to understand the external forces that are acting on them and their organizations?

5. Describe an effective culture for (a) a relatively stable environment and (b) a dynamic environment. Explain your choices.

6. "Businesses are built on relationships." What do you think this statement means? What are the implications for managing the external environment?

7. What would be the drawbacks in not managing stakeholder relationships?

SELF-ASSESSMENT

What's the Right Organizational Culture for Me?

For each of the following statements, circle the level of agreement or disagreement that you personally feel:[51]

1 = Strongly Agree   2 = Agree   3 = Uncertain   4 = Disagree   5 = Strongly Disagree

1. I like the thrill and excitement of taking risks.   1 2 3 4 5

2. I prefer managers who provide detailed and rational explanations for their decisions.   1 2 3 4 5

3. If a person's job performance is inadequate, it's irrelevant how much effort he or she made.   1 2 3 4 5

4. No person's needs should be compromised in order for a department to achieve its goals.   1 2 3 4 5

5. I like being part of a team and having my performance assessed in terms of my contribution
   to the team.   1 2 3 4 5

6. I like to work where there isn't a great deal of pressure and where people are essentially easygoing.   1 2 3 4 5

7. I like things to be stable and predictable.   1 2 3 4 5

Scoring Key

For items 1, 3, 4, 5, 6, use marked scores. For items 2 and 7, reverse the score (that is, Strongly Agree = 5, Agree = 4, Uncertain = 3, Disagree = 2, Strongly Disagree = 1). Add up all the scores.

Analysis and Interpretation

Your total score will range from 7 to 35. Scores of 21 or lower indicate that you are more comfortable in a formal, mechanistic, rule-oriented, and structured culture. This is often associated with large corporations and government agencies. The lower your number, the stronger your preference for this type of culture. Scores above 22 indicate a preference for informal, humanistic, flexible, and innovative cultures, which are more likely to be found in high-tech companies, small businesses, research units, or advertising agencies. The higher your score above 22, the stronger your preference for these humanistic cultures.

Organizational cultures differ. So do individuals. The better you are able to match your personal preferences to an organization's culture, the more likely you are to find satisfaction in your work, the less likely you are to leave, and the greater the probability that you will receive positive performance evaluations.

More Self-Assessments mymanagementlab

To learn more about your skills, abilities, and interests, go to the MyManagementLab website and take the following self-assessment:

- III.B.3.—Am I Experiencing Work/Family Conflict?

MANAGEMENT FOR YOU TODAY

Dilemma

You are considering organizing an event to raise funds for a special cause (children living in poverty, breast cancer research, illiteracy, or another cause of your choice). Think about who you might invite to this event (that is, your "customers"—those who will buy tickets to the event). What type of event might appeal to them? What suppliers might you approach for help in organizing the event? What legal issues might you face in setting up this event? After considering all these specific environmental forces, describe the challenges you could face in holding this event.

Becoming a Manager

- When you read current business or general news stories, see if omnipotent or symbolic views of management are being described.

- Notice aspects of organizational culture as you interact with different organizations.

- Read books about different organizations and entrepreneurs to better understand how an organization's culture forms and how it's maintained.

- Start thinking about the type of organizational culture in which you are going to be most comfortable.

- If you belong to a student organization, evaluate its culture. What does the culture look like? How do new members learn the culture? How is the culture maintained?

- When you evaluate companies for class assignments (for this class and others you may be enrolled in), get in the habit of looking at the stakeholders that might be impacted by these companies' decisions and actions.

- Practise defining the general and specific environments of different organizations and notice how they are similar and different.

WORKING TOGETHER: TEAM-BASED EXERCISE

Assessing the Organization's Environment

Although all organizations face environmental constraints, the forces in their specific and general environments differ. Form a small group with 3 or 4 other class members and choose 2 organizations in different industries. Describe the specific and general environmental forces that affect each organization. How are your descriptions different for the 2 organizations? How are they similar? Now, using the same 2 organizations, see if you can identify their important stakeholders. Also, indicate whether these stakeholders are critical for the organization and why they are or are not. As a group, be prepared to share your information with the class and to explain your choices.

ETHICS IN ACTION

Ethical Dilemma Exercise: How Far Should a Company Go to Please Investors?

Managing relations with a variety of stakeholder groups is a challenge in any situation—but it's even more difficult when the culture tolerates or encourages ethically questionable behaviour.[52] This is what happened at Computer Associates. When Computer Associates reported year after year of impressive sales growth, the stock price soared and investors cheered. During one quarter, however, the company failed to meet earnings expectations, and the stock price plummeted more than 40 percent in a single day as investors fled.

Because CEO Sanjay Kumar and a few top executives had wanted to please investors by keeping up the appear-ance of continued growth, they began booking software sales *before* the contracts were signed. They also told salespeo-ple to change or remove dates on some contracts to clear the way for backdating those deals. Eventually the accounting irregularities made the press—touching off a lengthy inves-tigation that eventually led to Kumar and four former execu-tives pleading guilty to securities fraud.

Imagine this is your second day at work as a manager supervising a team of financial analysts in a major technology corporation. Your boss, the chief financial officer, calls you in and asks you to have your team find "creative" ways of improving sales figures. What should you do?

Thinking Critically About Ethics

Do you think it's possible for a manager with high ethical standards to live by the values in an organizational culture that tolerates, or even encourages, unethical practices? How could a manager deal with such situations?

CASE APPLICATION

RCMP

The Royal Canadian Mounted Police, which has long enjoyed respect both nationally and internationally, has faced a pro-longed period of public criticism and investigation in recent years.[53] A spring 2007 inquiry into the 1985 Air India bombing revealed that the RCMP was aware of a terrorist threat, and even devised a security plan, but did not follow through with it. A two-year federal inquiry into Syrian-born Canadian Maher Arar's arrest and deportation concluded in fall 2006 that the RCMP gave American authorities inaccurate and misleading information that "very likely" led to the actions taken against Arar. In 2005, Auditor General Sheila Fraser found that the RCMP had received more than $3 million from the Liberal Party's sponsorship scandal, with some of that money being put into a nongovernment bank account, which violated the law.

Questions about RCMP management reached new levels of concern in April 2007, after a group of senior RCMP officers alleged that RCMP senior management were engaged in a cover-up of the mismanagement of the force's pension plan. A day later, Minister of Public Safety Stockwell Day appointed David Brown, a lawyer and former head of the Ontario Securities Commission, to investigate and report on his find-ings by mid-June 2007.

Brown's report concluded that the forces were "horribly broken." He noted that he had heard employees use such terms as "poisoned work environment," "abusive work envi-ronment," and a "culture of entitlement at the top." He felt that some of what he found in his investigation provided some credibility for these comments.

Brown placed much of the blame for the problems at the RCMP on the personality and autocratic leadership style of Giuliano Zaccardelli, the former police commissioner. Zaccardelli had resigned in December 2006, after giving con-flicting testimony on the Arar affair. Brown noted "only the brave or the foolhardy were willing to tell [Zaccardelli] career-limiting things he wished not to hear."

Brown found that the organizational structure of the RCMP "is completely at odds with the reality of running a $3-billion enterprise." He noted that the RCMP is run in a paramilitary style. Members of the force are required to obey every lawful order of a superior officer, however question-able. In other words, members are not supposed to ques-tion orders or suggest that they might be flawed.

Brown pointed to a "breach of trust" and failure of lead-ership as reasons why the RCMP's pension crisis was allowed to get out of hand. "In an already fractured culture, senior management was projecting an attitude of disinterest and callousness in respect of an issue of legitimate concern to every single member of the force: their pensions. In the process, the commissioner lost his troops," he wrote.

Brown's conclusions did not surprise Linda Duxbury, a professor at Carleton University's Sprott School of Business. She had conducted a study of 300 RCMP members, tracking changes in their attitudes between 2000 and 2003. She found that "front-line officers and middle managers had lost all trust and faith in their leaders." These rank-and-file members complained about "disconnected" senior leadership, poor communication flow, and weak "people management" by top managers. Meanwhile, Duxbury found, senior management thought the RCMP was a great place to work.

About a month after Brown's report was issued, William Elliott, formerly a national security adviser, was the first civilian appointed to head the RCMP. Many civilians applauded the appointment of an outsider who had never worn a police uniform, hoping this would be the beginning of fundamental change at the RCMP. Many of the RCMP, however, felt differently. "It's like making you the captain of the hockey team and you can't skate," said retired RCMP staff sergeant Ron Lewis.

Elliott acknowledged that it would be a "very, very daunting and challenging task" to rebuild the Mounties' culture. He now wonders how he will go about doing so.

What can Commissioner Elliott do to change the culture of the RCMP?

A Perfect Response to an Imperfect Storm

Twelve days.[54] That is how long it took for Mississippi Power to restore electric power to the heavily damaged areas of southern Mississippi after Hurricane Katrina slammed into the Mississippi Gulf Coast on August 29, 2005, with 233 kilometres-per-hour winds and pounding rain. That is remarkable, given the devastation that news photos and television newscasts so graphically displayed. It's something that even the federal and state governments could not accomplish. How bad was the damage company employees dealt with? One hundred percent of the company's customers were without power. Sixty-five percent of its transmission and distribution facilities were destroyed. And yet, this organization of 1250 employees did what it had to do, despite the horrible circumstances and despite the fact that more than half of its employees suffered substantial damage to their own homes. It speaks volumes about the cultural climate that the managers of Mississippi Power had created.

As a corporate subsidiary of utility holding company Southern Company, Mississippi Power provides electric services to more than 190 000 customers in the Magnolia State. When Hurricane Katrina turned toward Mississippi, managers at Mississippi Power swung into action with a swift and ambitious disaster plan. After Katrina's landfall, Mississippi Power's management team responded "with a style designed for speed and flexibility, for getting things done amid confusion and chaos." David Ratcliffe, senior executive of Southern Company said, "I could not be prouder of our response." What factors led to the company's ability to respond as efficiently and effectively as it did?

One key element is the company's can-do organizational culture, which is evidenced by the important values inscribed on employees' identification tags: "Unquestionable Trust, Superior Performance, Total Commitment." Because the values were visible daily, employees knew their importance. They knew what was expected of them, in a disaster response or in just doing their everyday work. In addition, through employee training and managerial example, the organization had "steeped its culture" in Stephen Covey's book *The 7 Habits of Highly Effective People*. (The company's training building—the Covey Center—flooded during the storm.) These ingrained habits—be proactive; begin with the end in mind; put first things first; think win–win; seek first to understand, then to be understood; synergize; and sharpen the saw—also guided employee decisions and actions.

Another important element in the company's successful post-storm response was the clear lines of responsibility of the 20 "storm directors," who had clear responsibility and authority for whatever task they had been assigned. These directors had the power to do what needed to be done, backed by unquestionable trust from their bosses. Said one, "I don't have to ask permission."

Finally, the company's decentralized decision-making approach contributed to the way in which employees were able to accomplish what they did. The old approach of responding to a disaster with top-down decision making had been replaced by decision making being pushed further down to the electrical substation level, a distribution point that serves some 5000 people. Crews working to restore power reported to these substations and had a simple mission—get the power back on. "Even out-of-state line crews, hired on contract and working unsupervised, were empowered to engineer their own solutions." What the crews often did to "get the power back on" was quite innovative and entrepreneurial. For instance, one crew "stripped a generator off an ice machine to get a substation working." Mississippi Power's president Anthony Topazi said, "... This structure made things happen faster than we expected. People were getting more done."

All in all, employees at Mississippi Power, working in difficult, treacherous, and often dangerous situations, did what they had to do. They got the job done. In recognition of the company's outstanding efforts to restore power in the wake of Hurricane Katrina, Mississippi Power was honoured with an "Emergency Response Award" by the Edison Electric

Institute in January 2006. It's an award that all the company's employees can be proud of.

Questions

1. Using Exhibit 2-2 on page 45, describe the culture at Mississippi Power. Why do you think this type of culture might be important to an electric power company? On the other hand, what might be the drawbacks of such a culture?

2. Describe how you think new employees at Mississippi Power "learn" the company's culture.

3. What stakeholders might be important to Mississippi Power? What concerns might each of these stakeholders have? Would these stakeholders change if there was a disaster to which the company had to respond?

4. What could other organizations learn from Mississippi Power about the importance of organizational culture?

DEVELOPING YOUR INTERPERSONAL SKILLS

Reading an Organization's Culture

About the Skill

The ability to read an organization's culture can be a valuable skill. For instance, if you are looking for a job, you will want to choose an organization whose culture is compatible with your values and in which you will feel comfortable. If you can accurately assess a potential employer's culture before you make your job decision, you may be able to save yourself a lot of anxiety and reduce the likelihood of making a poor choice. Similarly, you will undoubtedly have business transactions with numerous organizations during your professional career, such as selling a product or service, negotiating a contract, arranging a joint work project, or merely seeking out who controls certain decisions in an organization. The ability to assess another organization's culture can be a definite plus in successfully performing those pursuits.

Steps in Developing the Skill

For the sake of simplicity, we are going to look at this skill from the perspective of a job applicant. We will assume that you are interviewing for a job, although this skill can be generalized to many situations. You can be more effective at reading an organization's culture if you use the following five suggestions:[55]

1. **Observe the physical surroundings.** Pay attention to signs, posters, pictures, photos, style of dress, length of hair, degree of openness between offices, and office furnishings and arrangements.

2. **Take note of those with whom you meet.** Did you meet the person who would be your immediate supervisor? Or did you meet with potential colleagues, managers from other departments, or senior executives? Based on what they revealed, to what degree do people interact with others who may not be in their particular work area or at their particular organizational level?

3. **Characterize the style of the people you meet.** Are they formal? Casual? Serious? Laid-back? Open? Not willing to provide information?

4. **Look at the organization's human resource manual.** Are formal rules and regulations printed there? If so, how detailed are these policies?

5. **Ask questions of the people with whom you meet.** The most valid and reliable information tends to come from asking the same questions of many people (to see how closely their responses align) and by talking with individuals whose jobs link them to the outside environment. Questions that will give you insights into organizational processes and practices might include: What is the background of the founders? What is the background of current senior managers? What are their functional specialties? Were they promoted from within or hired from outside? How does the organization integrate new employees? Is there a formal orientation program? Are there formal employee training programs? How does your manager define his or her job success? How would you define fairness in terms of reward allocations? Can you identify some people here who are on the "fast track"? What do you think has put them on the fast track? Can you identify someone in the organization who seems to be considered an oddball or deviant? How has the organization responded to this person? Can you describe a decision that someone made that was well received? Can you describe a decision that did not work out well? What were the consequences for the decision maker? Could you describe a crisis or critical event that has occurred recently in the organization? How did top management respond? What was learned from this experience?

Practising the Skill

Read the following scenario. Write some notes about how you would handle the situation described. Be sure to refer to the five suggestions for reading an organization's culture.

Scenario

You have spent the first three years after college graduation as a freelance graphic designer, and now you are looking at pursuing a job as an account executive at a graphic design firm. You feel that the scope of assignments and potential for technical training far exceed what you would be able to do on your own, and you are looking to expand your skills and meet a brand-new set of challenges. However, you want to make sure you "fit" into the organization where you are going to be spending more than eight hours every workday. What is the best way for you to find a place where you will be happy and where your style and personality will be appreciated?

Reinforcing the Skill

The following activities will help you practise and reinforce the skills associated with reading an organization's culture:

1. If you are taking more than one course, assess the culture of the various classes in which you are enrolled.

How do the classroom cultures differ? Which culture(s) do you seem to prefer? Why?

2. Compare the atmosphere or feeling you get from various organizations. Because of the number and wide variety that you will find, it will probably be easiest for you to do this exercise using restaurants, retail stores, or banks. Based on the atmosphere that you observe, what type of organizational culture do you think these organizations might have? On what did you base your decision? Which type of culture do you prefer? Why? If you can, interview three employees at this organization for their descriptions of the organization's culture. Did their descriptions support your interpretation? Why or why not?

MANAGING WORKFORCE DIVERSITY

Creating an Inclusive Workplace Culture

We know from our discussion in Chapter 1 that managing a diverse workforce is an important issue facing today's managers. As the composition of the workforce changes, managers must take a long, hard look at their organizational culture to see if the shared meaning and beliefs that were appropriate for a more homogeneous workforce will support diverse views. How can managers create a workplace culture that advocates and encourages diversity?[56]

Diversity efforts by organizations are driven by federal mandate, although many organizations have recognized that inclusive workplaces are good for business. Among other things, diversity contributes to more creative solutions to problems and enhances employee morale. Creating a workplace culture that supports and encourages a wide diversity of individuals and views is a major organizational effort. Managers throughout the organization must value diversity and show that they do by their decisions and actions. An organization that truly wants to promote inclusiveness must shape its culture to allow diversity to flourish. One way to do this is for managers to assimilate diverse perspectives while performing the managerial functions. For example, managers at Vancouver-based HSBC Bank Canada are evaluated for

engaging in diversity-related activities. As such, managers might suggest that female employees attend training programs that would help them move up the corporate ladder. Managers might also invite guest speakers to talk to their employees about their concerns regarding working with people with disabilities. At Toronto-based Bank of Montreal, the annual planning process includes key diversity performance goals that are measured and tied to managers' compensation.

Beyond the day-to-day managerial activities, organizations should consider developing ways to reinforce employee behaviours that exemplify inclusiveness. Some suggestions include encouraging individuals to value and defend diverse views, creating traditions and ceremonies that celebrate diversity, rewarding appropriate "heroes" and "heroines" who accept and promote inclusiveness, and communicating formally and informally about employees who champion diversity issues.

Developing an organizational culture that supports diversity and inclusiveness may be challenging, but doing so offers high potential benefits. Organizations that allow diversity to prosper and thrive see cultural or environmental changes not as constraints, but as opportunities to bring out the best in all of their members.

MANAGING YOUR CAREER

Finding a Culture That Fits

Richard D'Ambrosio thought he had found the perfect job at an accounting firm. It had all the trappings of a good workplace—employee recognition awards and managers with "politically correct" answers to work–life questions. Yet, as soon as he signed on, he found himself in a culture that prized working long hours just for the sake of working long

hours and expected junior accountants to be at the beck and call of the partners. If it was your wedding anniversary, too bad. If it was a holiday, too bad. It only took a few months before he quit. How can you avoid the same problem? How can you find a culture that fits?[57] Here are some suggestions.

First, figure out what suits you. For instance, do you like working in teams or on your own? Do you like to go out after work with colleagues or go straight home? Are you comfortable in a more formal or a more casual environment? Then, narrow your job search to those kinds of employers.

Once you have gotten through the initial job screening process and you start interviewing, the real detective work begins. And it involves more than investigating the "official" information provided by the employer. Try to uncover the values that drive the organization. Ask questions such as what are its proudest accomplishments? Or how did it respond to past emergencies and crises? Ask, "If I have an idea, how do I make it happen?" Ask if you can talk to someone who is on the "fast track" to promotions and find out what they are doing and why they are being rewarded. Ask how you will be evaluated— after all, if you are going to be in the game, shouldn't you know how the score is kept? Also, look for nonverbal clues. What do people have at their desks—family pictures or only work stuff? Are office doors closed or open? Are there doors? How does the physical climate feel? Is it relaxed and casual or more formal? Do people seem to be helping each other as they work? Are the washrooms dirty? This might indicate a low value placed on anything to do with employees. Look at the material symbols and who seems to have access to them. And finally, during your investigation, do pay particular attention to the specific department or unit where you would work. After all, this would be where you would spend the majority of your working hours. Can you see yourself being happy there?

Managing in a Global Environment

How does the world outside Canada affect how Canadians run their businesses?

1. What are the different ways of viewing global differences?

2. What kinds of alliances affect trade relations among countries in the world?

3. How do organizations do business globally?

4. What are the challenges of doing business globally?

▶ ▶ ▶ Worry about pet food contamination swept across North America in February and March of 2007, upon news that at least 15 cats and 1 dog had died after eating possibly poisoned food.[1] There were also unconfirmed reports that hundreds of pets in Canada had suffered kidney failure. Though pet owners were reporting pet illnesses in February, the first recall of pet food did not occur until March 16, 2007, when Mississauga, Ontario-based Menu Foods asked retailers to remove 60 million packages of its wet pet foods off grocery and pet food store shelves. At the time, the company was not entirely sure why pets were getting sick, but something seemed to be wrong with its pet food.

For consumers, the pet food recall caused immediate confusion. There is no brand called "Menu Foods" on pet food shelves. Instead, 889 separate items under 100 different brand names had to be taken off grocery shelves. Menu Foods processes most of North America's most popular brands of wet pet food packaged in cans and foil pouches. It produces about 75 percent of private-label pet food brands in Canada (for companies such as Wal-Mart Canada, Sobeys, and Pet Valu) and between 40 and 50 percent of private-label pet food brands in the United States (for companies such as PetSmart, Safeway, and Wal-Mart).

At the time of the recall, Menu Foods was a virtually unknown company, particularly to consumers. Suddenly, this Canadian company had Americans worried about the wisdom of importing food from foreign sources, including Canada. Ironically, the contaminated ingredient in the recalled pet food came from an American company, Nevada-based ChemNutra, that had purchased the ingredient from a company in China.

Think About It

Should large corporations have to report the source of all ingredients in the food products they manufacture? Put yourself in the shoes of Menu Foods' CEO. What responsibilities does an organization have when sourcing food ingredients globally?

The Menu Foods example illustrates that the global marketplace presents opportunities and challenges for managers. With the entire world as a market and national borders becoming increasingly irrelevant, the potential for organizations to grow expands dramatically. (To determine your fit for a position as an international manager, see *Self-Assessment—Am I Well-Suited for a Career as a Global Manager?* on pages 91–92, at the end of the chapter.)

However, as our opening dilemma also implies, even large, successful organizations with talented managers face challenges in managing in the global environment. Managers must deal with cultural, economic, and political differences. Meanwhile, new competitors can suddenly appear at any time from any place on the globe. Managers who don't closely monitor changes in their global environment or who don't take the specific characteristics of their location into consideration as they plan, organize, lead, and control are likely to find limited global success. In this chapter, we discuss the issues managers face in managing in a global environment.

Menu Foods Income Fund
www.menufoods.com

Q&A 3.1

What's Your Global Perspective?

1. What are the different ways of viewing global differences?

It's not unusual for Germans, Italians, or Indonesians to speak three or four languages. Most Japanese schoolchildren begin studying English in the early elementary grades. On the other hand, even though we are officially a bilingual country, many Canadians tend to think of English as the only international business language and don't see a need to study other languages.

> *How comfortable are you being around people from different cultures?*

Monolingualism is just one of the ways that people can be unfamiliar with the cultures of others. Successful global management requires enhanced sensitivity to differences in national customs and practices. Management practices that work in Vancouver might not be appropriate in Bangkok or Berlin. However, not everyone recognizes that others have different ways of living and working, particularly those who suffer from **parochialism**, which is viewing the world narrowly through one's own perspective.[2] Parochialism is a significant obstacle for managers working in a global business world. If managers fall into the trap of ignoring others' values and customs and rigidly applying an attitude of "ours is better than theirs" to foreign cultures, they will find it difficult to compete with other managers and organizations around the world that *are* seeking to understand foreign customs and market differences.

parochialism
A narrow view of the world; an inability to recognize the differences of other people.

ethnocentric attitude
The belief that the best work approaches and practices are those of the home country.

polycentric attitude
The view that the managers in the host country know the best work approaches and practices for running their businesses.

geocentric attitude
A world-oriented view that focuses on using the best approaches and people from around the globe.

Individuals can take a variety of approaches in their attitudes toward other cultures.[3] Exhibit 3-1 summarizes the key points about three possible global attitudes. Let's look at each more closely.

An **ethnocentric attitude** is the belief that the best work approaches and practices are those of the *home* country (the country in which the company's headquarters are located). Managers with an ethnocentric attitude believe that people in foreign countries do not have the skills, expertise, knowledge, or experience that people in the home country do. They would not trust foreign employees with key decisions or technology.

A **polycentric attitude** is the view that the managers in the *host* country (the foreign country in which the organization is doing business) know the best work approaches and practices for running their businesses. Managers with a polycentric attitude view every foreign operation as different and hard to understand. Thus, these managers are likely to leave their foreign facilities alone and let foreign employees figure out how best to do things.

Q&A 3.2

The last type of global attitude that managers might have is a **geocentric attitude**, which is a *world-oriented* view that focuses on using the best approaches and people from around the globe. Managers with this type of attitude believe that it's important to have a global view both at the organization's headquarters in the home country *and* in the various foreign work facilities. For instance, the CEO of Home Décor (a disguised name), a fast-growing manufacturer of household accessories, is a Chinese immigrant who describes the company's strategy as "combining Chinese costs with Japanese quality, European design, and American marketing."[4] With a geocentric attitude, major issues and decisions are viewed globally by looking for the best approaches and people regardless of origin.

Later in this chapter and throughout the rest of the book, you will see how a geocentric attitude toward managing requires eliminating parochial attitudes and carefully developing an understanding of cultural differences between countries. It is important to realize that while in some organizations all managers may express the same perspective toward the world (perhaps because the company has a strong culture), different views can also be held by individual managers, so the company does not necessarily present a unified front when dealing with people from another culture. However, the way that a company chooses to go global may indicate an overall perspective on the best way to do business in other countries.

The British Broadcasting Company's balanced and unbiased reporting on the war in Iraq, led by news people such as Rageh Omaar, demonstrates the geocentric attitude this British-based international firm brings to its product, the news. "BBC doesn't just have a British view," says the firm's director of World Service and Global News. "It has a worldview for the world."

Exhibit 3-1

Key Information About Three Global Attitudes

	Ethnocentric	Polycentric	Geocentric
Orientation	Home Country	Host Country	World
Advantages	• Simpler structure • More tightly controlled	• Extensive knowledge of foreign market and workplace • More support from host government • Committed local managers with high morale	• Extensive understanding of global issues • Balance between local and global objectives • Best people and work approaches used regardless of origin
Drawbacks	• More ineffective management • Inflexibility • Social and political backlash	• Duplication of work • Reduced efficiency • Difficult to maintain global objectives because of intense focus on local traditions	• Difficult to achieve • Managers must have both local and global knowledge

---

Understanding the Global Environment

▶ ▶ ▶ After Menu Foods recalled its pet food, one legislator reminded Americans that it might not be safe to rely on foreign sources of food.[5] "We really don't know what else is out there and yet we've increased food imports and reduced inspections," says Bob Etheridge, a Democratic representative from North Carolina.

Some US legislators and farm groups have called for fewer imports, a reconsideration of the free-trade agreement, fees from Canada and other countries so that the United States can conduct more inspections of food, and labels indicating country of origin on all food products. Should such legislation be passed, Menu Foods may find its dominant role in the pet food market shrinking.

The immediate impact of the pet food recall affects Menu Foods, but some are worried that the scandal could affect Canada's economy, which saw about $14 billion (US) in sales of food to the United States in 2006. "This is an ongoing issue that we have anxiety over," says Canadian Minister of Trade David Emerson.

Think About It

How might the tainted pet food scandal affect the Canadian pet food industry's trade relations with the United States and Mexico?

As we discussed in Chapter 1, management is no longer constrained by national borders. Managers in all sizes and types of organizations are faced with the opportunities and challenges of managing in a global environment. For instance, managers at Menu Foods capitalized on the opportunity of the global environment by buying ingredients from companies around the world. This allowed them to make their company into a leading pet food manufacturer in North America. However, relying on ingredients that originated from China, which did not follow the same food product inspection standards as those in North American countries, has proven to be extremely costly to the company.

What is the global environment like? An important feature is global trade. Global trade is not new. Countries and organizations have been trading with each other for centuries. "Trade is central to human health, prosperity, and social welfare."[6] When trade is allowed to flow freely, countries benefit from economic growth and productivity gains because

2. What kinds of alliances affect trade relations among countries in the world?

they specialize in producing the goods they are best at and importing goods that are more efficiently produced elsewhere. Global trade is being shaped by two forces: regional trading alliances and the agreements negotiated through the World Trade Organization.

Regional Trading Alliances

Just a few years ago, global competition was best described in terms of country against country—the United States vs. Japan, France vs. Germany, Mexico vs. Canada. Now, global competition has been reshaped by the creation of regional trading alliances, such as the European Union, the North American Free Trade Agreement, and the Association of Southeast Asian Nations.

The European Union

European Union (EU)

A union of 27 European countries that forms an economic and political entity.

Europa—The European Union Online
http://europa.
eu/index_en.htm

euro

A single common European currency.

The signing of the Maastricht Treaty (named for the Dutch town where the treaty was signed) in February 1992 created the **European Union (EU)**, a unified economic and trade entity with 12 member countries—Belgium, Denmark, France, Greece, Ireland, Italy, Luxembourg, the Netherlands, Portugal, Spain, the United Kingdom, and Germany. By 2007, the EU comprised 27 countries. Three other countries (Croatia, Former Yugoslav Republic of Macedonia, and Turkey) have submitted applications to join the EU.[7] The economic power represented by the EU is considerable. The original EU member countries cover a population base of 375 million people, and the current 27 member countries encompass a population of over 490 million.[8] (See Exhibit 3-2.)

Before the creation of the EU, each member country had border controls, taxes, and subsidies; nationalistic policies; and protected industries. Now, as a single market, the EU has no barriers to travel, employment, investment, and trade. The EU took an enormous step toward full unification in 1999 when 12 of its countries became part of the Economic and Monetary Union, the formal system responsible for the development of the **euro**, a single European currency. Today, 13 European countries use the euro, and eight more will adopt the euro before 2010.[9] The primary reason these countries joined together was to assert their economic position against the strength of the United States and Japan. Working in sep-

Exhibit 3-2

European Union Countries

arate countries with barriers against one another, European industries could not develop the efficiency of American and Japanese businesses.

The EU was dealt a blow during May 2005 when voters in France and the Netherlands rejected the planned new European Union constitution.[10] Despite this setback, the EU will continue to evolve and grow as an economic power in one of the world's richest markets. European businesses will continue to play an important role in the global economy. For instance, Unilever PLC of the United Kingdom is a powerful force in consumer products, Daimler AG of Germany is a solid competitor in automobiles, and Nokia of Finland is a dominant player in cellphones.

North American Free Trade Agreement

When agreements in key issues covered by the **North American Free Trade Agreement (NAFTA)** were reached by the Canadian, US, and Mexican governments in August 1992, a vast economic bloc was created where barriers to free trade were reduced. Since NAFTA went into effect, Canada has become the United States' number one trading partner.[11] In 2006, Canadian exports to the United States were $362 billion, which accounted for almost 79 percent of our total exports.[12] Canada's exports to Mexico have quadrupled since the NAFTA agreement was signed, and its foreign investments in Mexico increased by a factor of five.[13] Westcoast Energy, Scotiabank, and BCE are just a few Canadian companies that have expanded their operations to Mexico. Many economists argue that reducing the barriers to trade (tariffs, import licensing requirements, customs user fees) has resulted in a strengthening of the economic power of all three countries. Free trade did not eliminate all trade problems between Canada and the United States, however, as the recent softwood lumber negotiations show.

North American Free Trade Agreement (NAFTA)
An agreement among the Canadian, American, and Mexican governments in which barriers to free trade were reduced.

 **NAFTA**
www.dfait-maeci.gc.ca/
nafta-alena/
menu-en.asp

Association of Southeast Asian Nations

The **Association of Southeast Asian Nations (ASEAN)** is a trading alliance of 10 Southeast Asian nations (see Exhibit 3-3). The ASEAN region has a population of about 500 million with a combined gross domestic product of $1071 billion (US).[14] During the years

Association of Southeast Asian Nations (ASEAN)
A trading alliance of 10 Southeast Asian countries.

Exhibit 3-3

ASEAN Members

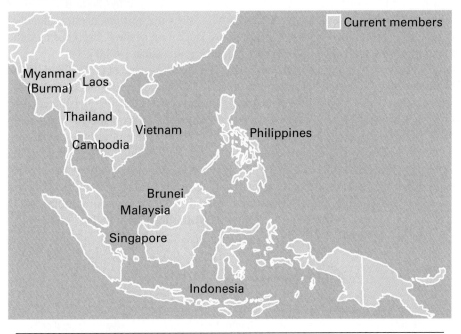

Source: Based on J. McClenahen and T. Clark, "ASEAN at Work," *IndustryWeek*, May 19, 1997, p. 42.

ahead, the Southeast Asian region promises to be one of the fastest-growing economic regions of the world. It will be an increasingly important regional economic and political alliance whose impact eventually could rival that of both NAFTA and the EU.

Other Trade Alliances

Other regions around the world continue to look at creating regional trading alliances. For instance, Latin American nations have moved to become part of free-trade blocs. Colombia, Mexico, and Venezuela led the way when all three signed an economic pact in 1994 eliminating import duties and tariffs (in 2006, Venezuela left the bloc and Panama asked to be included). Negotiators from 34 countries in the Caribbean region, South America, and Central America continue to work on a Free Trade Area of the Americas (FTAA) agreement, which was to have been operational no later than 2005.[15] However, at a November 2005 summit, the leaders of these 34 nations failed to reach any agreement, leaving the future of the FTAA up in the air.[16] The benefits to Canada of an FTAA are not clear. Most of these markets are quite small compared with Mexico and the United States. Already in existence is another free-trade bloc known as the Southern Cone Common Market, or Mercosur, which was formed in 1991 among Brazil, Argentina, Uruguay, and Paraguay. Ecuador and Peru are associate members and Venezuela is in the process of gaining full membership.

The 53-nation African Union came into existence in July 2002.[17] Members of this alliance plan to create an economic development plan and work to achieve greater unity among Africa's nations. Like members of other trade alliances, these countries hope to gain economic, social, cultural, and trade benefits from their association.

Also, the South Asian Association for Regional Cooperation (SAARC), composed of seven nations (India, Pakistan, Sri Lanka, Bangladesh, Bhutan, Nepal, and the Maldives), started eliminating tariffs on January 1, 2006.[18] Its aim, like all the other regional trading alliances, is to allow for the free flow of goods and services.

The World Trade Organization

Global growth and trade among nations does not just happen on its own. Systems and mechanisms are needed so that efficient and effective trading relationships can develop. Indeed, one of the realities of globalization is that countries are interdependent—that is, what happens in one can impact others, whether positively or negatively. For example, the severe Asian financial crisis in the late 1990s had the potential to totally disrupt economic growth around the globe and bring on a worldwide recession. But it did not. Why? Because there were mechanisms in place to prevent that from happening—mechanisms that encouraged global trade and averted the potential crisis. One of the most important of these mechanisms is the multilateral trading system called the **World Trade Organization (WTO)**.[19]

The WTO was formed in 1995 and evolved from the General Agreement on Tariffs and Trade (GATT), an agreement in effect since the end of World War II. Today, the WTO is the only *global* organization dealing with the rules of trade among nations. Its membership consists of 150 member countries and 31 observer governments (which have a specific time frame within which they must apply to become members). At its core are the various trade agreements, negotiated and ratified by the vast majority of the world's trading nations. The goal of the WTO is to help businesses conduct trade between countries (importing and exporting) without undesired side effects. Although a number of vocal critics have staged visible protests and criticized the WTO, claiming that it destroys jobs and the natural environment, the WTO appears to play an important role in monitoring and promoting global trade.

World Trade Organization (WTO)
A global organization of 150 countries that deals with the rules of trade among nations.

 World Trade Organization
www.wto.org

Doing Business Globally

▶ ▶ ▶ Menu Foods was founded in 1971 and bought its first US factory in New Jersey in 1977, hoping to use that factory to launch an expansion into the US market.[20] Today, the global company has four pet food processing plants, one in Mississauga and three in the United States (Emporia, Kansas; Pennsauken, New Jersey; and North Sioux City, South Dakota). The company has processing plants in Canada and the United States so that it can process pet food products close to the areas it serves to reduce product costs, including freight costs. According to the company's website, "Menu's ability to serve [retailers] from four locations provides it with service and freight cost advantages compared to other single or two plant private-label competitors."

Menu Foods buys the ingredients for its pet food from a variety of companies, which in turn may buy ingredients for its products from companies around the world. As the tainted pet food investigation found, an ingredient that originated from China was responsible for the deaths caused by Menu Foods' various pet foods. Because Menu Foods relies on suppliers for some of its ingredients, it may not always be aware of the original source of every ingredient it uses.

Think About It

How is Menu Foods structured to do business globally? Would it make sense for Menu Foods to form a strategic alliance or a joint venture, or create a foreign subsidiary in countries that produce its ingredients? How might it choose partners to do so, if that strategy were chosen?

Organizations in different industries *and* from different countries are pursuing global opportunities. In this section, we look at different types of international organizations and how they do business in the global marketplace.

3. How do organizations do business globally?

Different Types of International Organizations

Multinational Corporations

Organizations doing business globally are not anything new. DuPont started doing business in China in 1863. H.J. Heinz Company was manufacturing food products in the United Kingdom in 1905. Ford Motor Company set up its first overseas sales branch in France in 1908. By the 1920s, other companies, including Fiat, Unilever, and Royal Dutch Petroleum Company/Shell had gone international. But it was not until the mid-1960s that international companies became commonplace. Today, there are very few companies that do not have some type of international dealings. However, in spite of the fact that doing business internationally is so widespread, there is no one generally accepted approach to describing the different types of international companies—they are called different things by different authors. However, we are going to use the terms *multinational, multidomestic, global,* and *transnational* to describe the various types of international organizations.[21] A **multinational corporation (MNC)** is a broad term usually used to refer to any and all types of international companies that maintain operations in multiple countries.

multinational corporations (MNCs)
A broad term that refers to any and all types of international companies that maintain operations in multiple countries.

Multidomestic Corporations

A **multidomestic corporation** is an MNC that maintains significant operations in more than one country but decentralizes management to the local country. This type of organization does not attempt to manage foreign operations from its home country. Instead, local employees typically are hired to manage the business, and marketing strategies are tailored to that country's unique characteristics. This type of global organization reflects the polycentric attitude (see page 74). For example, Switzerland-based Nestlé can be described as a multidomestic corporation. With operations in almost every country on the globe, its managers match the company's products to its consumers. In parts of Europe, Nestlé sells products that are not available in North America or Latin America. Another example of a multidomestic corporation is Frito-Lay, a division of PepsiCo, which markets a Doritos chip in the British market that differs in both taste and texture from the Canadian and US versions. Many consumer companies manage their global businesses using this approach because they must adapt their products and services to meet the needs of the local markets.

multidomestic corporation
An international company that decentralizes management and other decisions to the local country.

Global Companies

A **global company** is an international company that centralizes its management and other decisions in the home country. These companies treat the world market as an integrated whole and focus on the need for global efficiency. Although these companies may have

global company
An international company that centralizes management and other decisions in the home country.

considerable global holdings, management decisions with company-wide implications are made from headquarters in the home country. This approach to globalization reflects the ethnocentric attitude (see page 74). Some examples of companies that can be considered global companies include Montreal-based transport manufacturer Bombardier, Montreal-based aluminum producer Rio Tinto Alcan, Tokyo-based consumer electronics firm Sony, Frankfurt-based Deutsche Bank AG, and New York City-based financial services provider Merrill Lynch.

Transnational or Borderless Organizations

transnational or borderless organization
A type of international company in which artificial geographical barriers are eliminated.

Many companies are going global by eliminating structural divisions that impose artificial geographical barriers. This type of global organization is called a **transnational** or **borderless organization**. The transnational or borderless organization approaches global business with a geocentric attitude. For example, IBM dropped its organizational structure based on country and reorganized into industry groups such as business solutions, software, IT services, and financing. Bristol-Myers Squibb changed its consumer business to become more aggressive in international sales and created a management position responsible for worldwide consumer medicines such as Bufferin and Excedrin. And Spain's Telefónica eliminated the geographic divisions between Madrid headquarters and its widespread phone companies. The company is organized, instead, along business lines such as Internet services, cellphones, and media operations. Borderless management is an attempt by organizations to increase efficiency and effectiveness in a competitive global marketplace.[22]

Born Globals

born global
An international company that chooses to go global from inception.

Our classification of different types of international organizations tends to describe large international businesses. However, there is an increasing number of businesses called **born globals** that choose to go global from inception.[23] These companies (also known as *international new ventures*, or *INVs*) commit resources (material, people, financing) upfront to doing business in more than one country and are likely to continue to play an increasingly important role in international business.

How Organizations Go International

global sourcing
Purchasing materials or labour from around the world wherever it is cheapest.

When organizations do go international, they often use different approaches depending on whether they are just starting or whether they have been doing business internationally for awhile (see Exhibit 3-4). During the initial stages of going international, managers look at ways to get into a global market without having to invest a lot of capital. At this stage, companies may start with **global sourcing** (also called *global outsourcing*), which is purchasing materials or labour from around the world wherever it is cheapest. The goal: Take advantage of lower costs in order to be more competitive. For instance, in fall 2006, Montreal-based Bell Canada contracted with Sitel India and two other Indian companies to provide technical support and customer care to Canadian customers.[24] Although global

Exhibit 3-4

How Organizations Go International

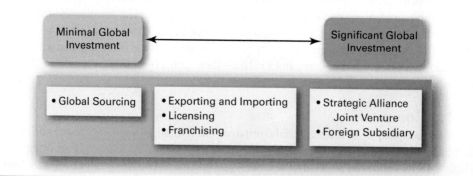

sourcing is often the first step to going international, many organizations continue to use this approach even as they become more international because of the competitive advantages it offers. Beyond global sourcing, however, each successive stage of becoming more international requires more investment and thus entails more risk for the organization.

Importing and Exporting

An organization can go international by **exporting** its products to other countries—that is, by making products at home and selling them overseas. In addition, an organization can go international by **importing** products—that is, by selling products at home that are made abroad. Both exporting and importing are small steps toward being a global business and usually involve minimal investment and minimal risk. Many organizations start doing business globally this way. Many, especially small businesses, continue with exporting and importing as the way they do business globally. For instance, Haribhai's Spice Emporium, a small business in Durban, South Africa, exports spices and rice to customers all over Africa, Europe, and the United States. However, other organizations have built multimillion-dollar businesses by importing or exporting. For instance, that is what Montreal-based Mega Brands (formerly Mega Bloks) has done. Mega Brands is Canada's largest toy company, with sales in over 100 countries. The company also holds the number one position in Spain, and has 43 percent of the UK market share.[25] The company operates in eight countries, with more than 1000 employees. Mega Brands is only one example of Canada's increasing reliance on export business. The value of merchandise exported from Canada totalled $359 billion in 2002, up 38 percent from 1993.[26] Transportation equipment manufacturing, primary metal manufacturing, and paper manufacturing account for the largest volume of Canadian exports.

> *If a company wants to do business in other countries, what choices does it have?*

exporting
An approach to going global that involves making products at home and selling them abroad.

importing
An approach to going global that involves acquiring products made abroad and selling them at home.

 **Mega Brands**
www.megabloks.com

Licensing and Franchising

Some managers use licensing or franchising in the early stages of doing business internationally. Licensing and franchising are similar in that they both involve one organization giving another the right to use its brand name, technology, or product specifications in return for a lump-sum payment or a fee usually based on sales. The only difference is that **licensing** is primarily used by manufacturing organizations that make or sell another company's products and **franchising** is primarily used by service organizations that want to use another company's name and operating methods. For example, Russian consumers can enjoy McDonald's hamburgers because McDonald's Canada opened the first Russian franchise in Moscow. Franchises have also made it possible for Mexicans to dine on Richmond, BC-based Boston Pizza and Koreans to consume frozen yogourt from Markham, Ontario-based Coolbrands' Yogen Früz. Anheuser-Busch licenses the right to brew and market Budweiser beer to other brewers, such as Labatt in Canada, Modelo in Mexico, and Kirin in Japan. Licensing and franchising involve more investment and risk than exporting and importing because the company's brand is more at stake.

licensing
An approach to going global in which a manufacturer gives another organization the right to use its brand name, technology, or product specifications.

franchising
An approach to going global in which a service organization gives a person or group the right to sell a product, using specific business methods and practices that are standardized.

Strategic Alliances

Typically, once an organization has been doing business internationally for awhile and has gained experience in international markets, managers may decide to make a more direct investment. One way they can do this is through **strategic alliances**, which are partnerships between a domestic and a foreign company in which both share resources and knowledge in developing new products or building production facilities. The partners also share the risks and rewards of this alliance. It is not always easy to find a partner, however. When Starbucks decided to open coffee shops in France, it was turned down by four major French food companies it approached as joint venture partners. Jean-Paul Brayer, former head of one of the food companies Starbucks approached, commented, "Their contract was way too expensive. It was a win–win situation—but only for Starbucks."[27] Starbucks ended up partnering with a Spanish firm, Grupo VIPS, and together they opened the first Parisian Starbucks in January 2004. By 2007, there were more than 50 Starbucks in Paris.[28]

strategic alliances
An approach to going global that involves a partnership between a domestic and a foreign company in which both share resources and knowledge in developing new products or building production facilities.

Fast-food giant KFC, like many big franchise firms, is opening more new outlets overseas. Along the way, the company is making appropriate changes in its menu offerings, such as substituting juice and fruit for Coke and fries. This Shanghai promotion features new egg tarts.

A specific type of strategic alliance in which the partners agree to form a separate, independent organization for some business purpose is called a **joint venture**. For example, Hewlett-Packard has had numerous joint ventures with various suppliers around the globe to develop different components for its computer equipment, such as Tokyo-based Hitachi, which supplies hard drives for HP. These partnerships provide a faster and more inexpensive way for companies to compete globally than doing it on their own.

joint venture
An approach to going global in which the partners agree to form a separate, independent organization for some business purpose; it is a type of strategic alliance.

Foreign Subsidiaries

Managers can make a direct investment in a foreign country by setting up a **foreign subsidiary**, a separate and independent production facility or office. This subsidiary can be managed as a multidomestic corporation (foreign control), a global company (domestic control), or as a transnational/borderless organization (global control). As you can probably guess, this arrangement involves the greatest commitment of resources and poses the greatest amount of risk. Many of the larger companies operating in Canada are actually subsidiaries of US corporations, including GM Canada, Procter & Gamble Canada, and McDonald's Canada. Canadian subsidiaries manage their operations and set their own targets and goals, but they also report to head office in the United States. Canada has been a good investment opportunity for American firms. The low Canadian dollar from the early 1990s until 2003 resulted in lower costs and higher productivity. However, the rise in the Canadian dollar may change the number of US companies doing business in Canada. Employers in Canada have long paid far less for health premiums for their employees than they would in the United States because of Canada's health care system. The fall 2007 settlement that General Motors made with the United Auto Workers (UAW) brings into question whether Canada's health care advantage will continue. The American car manufacturer and the UAW agreed that the union would be responsible for paying its retired workers' health care costs going forward. This is expected to lower GM's labour and benefits costs to $55 an hour (from $75 an hour). This lower cost of benefits puts GM's costs close to Japan's $48-an-hour costs, and much lower than Canada's $70-an-hour costs for autoworkers.[29]

foreign subsidiary
An approach to going global that involves a direct investment in a foreign country by setting up a separate and independent production facility or office.

Managing in a Global Environment

▶ ▶ ▶   Menu Foods was forced to remove 60 million packages of its wet pet foods off grocery and pet food store shelves in March 2007.[30] The pet food had been contaminated with melamine, a non-food product. Investigators found that the melamine had been mixed with wheat gluten (an ingredient in pet food) at XuZhou Anying factory in China. Employees apparently deliberately mixed the melamine into the wheat gluten because melamine mimics protein when mixed with gluten. The resulting product would then appear to have a higher nutrient value than it actually did.

China's animal feed producer had been supplementing the feed with melamine for a number of years. "Many companies buy melamine scrap to make animal feed, such as fish feed," says Ji Denghui, general manager of the Fujian Sanming Dinghui Chemical Company, which sells melamine. The additive is inexpensive, thus it reduces product costs. Ji also explains, "I don't know if there's a regulation on it. Probably not. No law or regulation says 'don't do it,' so everyone's doing it. The laws in China are like that, aren't they? If there's no accident, there won't be any regulation."

> ### Think About It
> How have the global legal–political and economic environments affected Menu Foods' ability to produce its pet food? What could Menu Foods do to protect itself from importing tainted ingredients from countries that have fewer regulations about food processing than Canada or the United States?

Assume for a moment that you are a manager going to work for a branch of a global organization in a foreign country. You know that your environment will differ from the one at home, but how? What should you be looking for?

Any manager who finds himself or herself in a foreign country faces new challenges. In this section, we look at some of those challenges and offer guidelines for responding. Although our discussion is presented through the eyes of a Canadian manager, our analytical framework could be used by any manager who has to manage in a foreign environment, regardless of national origin.

4. What are the challenges of doing business globally?

Q&A 3.3

The Legal–Political Environment

Canadian managers are accustomed to stable legal and political systems. Changes are slow, and legal and political procedures are well established. The stability of laws governing the actions of individuals and institutions allows for accurate predictions. The same cannot be said for all countries. Managers in a global organization must stay informed of the specific laws in countries where they do business.

Also, some countries have a history of unstable governments. Managers of businesses in these countries face dramatically greater uncertainty as a result of political instability. For instance, political interference is a fact of life in some Asian countries. Many large businesses have postponed doing business in China because the government controls what organizations do and how they do it. As Chinese consumers gain more power, however, that attitude is likely to change.

The legal–political environment does not have to be unstable or revolutionary to be a concern to managers. Just the fact that a country's laws and political system differ from those of Canada is important. Managers must recognize these differences to understand the constraints under which they operate and the opportunities that exist.

The Economic Environment

The global manager must be aware of economic issues when doing business in other countries. First, it's important to have an understanding of the type of economic system under which the country operates. The two major types are a market economy and a command economy. A **market economy** is one in which resources are primarily owned and controlled by the private sector. A **command economy** is one in which all economic decisions are planned by a central government. In actuality, no economy is purely market or command. For instance, Canada and the United States are two countries at the market end of the spectrum, but their governments do have some control over economic activities. The economies of Vietnam and North Korea, however, would be more command-based. Then there is China, a country that is more command-based, but is moving to be more market-based. Why would managers need to know about a country's economic system? Because it has the

market economy
An economic system in which resources are primarily owned and controlled by the private sector.

command economy
An economic system in which all economic decisions are planned by a central government.

potential to constrain decisions and actions. Other economic issues a manager might need to understand include currency exchange rates, inflation rates, and diverse tax policies.

The Cultural Environment

In what ways do you think culture affects doing business in other countries?

A large global oil company found that employee productivity in one of its Mexican plants was off 20 percent and sent a US manager to find out why. After talking to several employees, the manager discovered that the company used to have a monthly fiesta in the parking lot for all the employees and their families. Another US manager had cancelled the fiestas, saying they were a waste of time and money. The message employees were getting was that the company did not care about their families anymore. When the fiestas were reinstated, productivity and employee morale soared.

At Hewlett-Packard, a cross-global team of American and French engineers were assigned to work together on a software project. The American engineers sent long, detailed emails to their counterparts in France. The French engineers viewed the lengthy emails as patronizing and replied with quick, concise emails. This made the American engineers think that their French colleagues were hiding something from them. The situation spiralled out of control and negatively affected output until team members went through cultural training.[31]

As we know from Chapter 2, organizations have different cultures. Countries have cultures too. **National culture** is the values and attitudes shared by individuals from a specific country that shape their behaviour and beliefs about what is important.[32]

national culture
The values and attitudes shared by individuals from a specific country that shape their behaviour and beliefs about what is important.

Which is more important to a manager—national culture or organizational culture? For example, is an IBM facility in Germany more likely to reflect German culture or IBM's corporate culture? Research indicates that national culture has a greater effect on employees than does their organization's culture.[33] German employees at an IBM facility in Munich will be influenced more by German culture than by IBM's culture. This means that as influential as organizational culture may be on managerial practice, national culture is even more influential.

Q&A 3.4

Legal, political, and economic differences among countries are fairly obvious. The Japanese manager who works in Canada or his or her Canadian counterpart in Japan can get information about a country's laws or tax policies without too much difficulty. Getting information about a country's cultural differences isn't quite that easy! The primary reason is that it's hard for natives to explain their country's unique cultural characteristics to someone else. For instance, if you are a Canadian raised in Canada, how would you characterize Canadian culture? In other words, what are Canadians like? When Wal-Mart moved to Japan, it had to rethink some of its approach to customer service, as the following *Management Reflection* shows.

National culture influences many aspects of competing abroad. India now has about 350 000 engineering graduates each year; the United States has 70 000. Organizations that need employees with engineering skills in order to be competitive are going to have to understand national cultures, such as that of India.

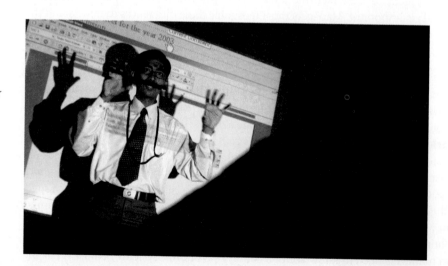

The Big Box Goes to Japan

What does Wal-Mart need to do to be successful in Japan?   When Wal-Mart bought 38 percent of Seiyu, Japan's fourth-largest retailer, in 2003 to get a foothold in Japan, it tried to maintain the classic Wal-Mart culture, while trying to meet the needs of Japanese customers.[34] Rather than loudly announcing its presence, Wal-Mart operated behind the Seiyu name. Employees at Seiyu had to adopt the Wal-Mart culture, however, starting the day much like their North American Wal-Mart counterparts, chanting "Give me an S" and eventually spelling out S-E-I-Y-U. The Japanese manager follows the chant by asking, "Who's number 1?" Employees respond with "Customers!" and punch their fists in the air.

The chant might have translated easily, but big-box stores in Japan are not an easy sell. Customers do not necessarily understand the concept of "everyday low prices." When Wal-Mart first came to town, the company mailed circulars advertising low prices to local neighbourhoods, but tried to stop the practice, as the company did not see the point of constantly advertising their everyday low prices. Unfortunately, Japanese customers are used to circulars announcing sales, and Seiyu had to continue the practice.

Wal-Mart faces several challenges in meeting customer needs in Japan. Homes are smaller, so bulk buying is less common, and many people rely on public transportation, making it difficult to bring big items home. Japanese customers demand high quality in clothing, and have high standards for freshness in food. Richard Galanti, chief financial officer of Costco, which has also opened stores in Japan, notes that "the definition of fresh seafood in Japan is different than that in [North America]. Fresh means live in some cases."

By 2007, Wal-Mart had not successfully penetrated the Japanese market, and had posted five years of losses. At Wal-Mart headquarters, executives remain hopeful that the company will fare better in Japan than it did in Germany and South Korea, two countries Wal-Mart exited in 2006 after it did not achieve expected sales. n

Wal-Mart
www.walmart.com

Hofstede's Framework for Assessing Cultures

One of the most widely referenced approaches to helping managers better understand differences between national cultures was developed by Geert Hofstede. His research found that managers and employees vary on five dimensions of national culture, which are as follows:

1   *Individualism vs. collectivism.* Individualism is the degree to which people in a country prefer to act as individuals rather than as members of groups. In an individualistic society, people are supposed to look after their own interests and those of their immediate family and do so because of the large amount of freedom that an individualistic society allows its citizens. The opposite is collectivism, which is characterized by a social framework in which people prefer to act as members of groups and expect others in groups of which they are a part (such as a family or an organization) to look after them and to protect them.

1   *Power distance.* Hofstede used the term *power distance* as a measure of the extent to which a society accepts the fact that power in institutions and organizations is distributed unequally. A high power distance society accepts wide differences in power in organizations. Employees show a great deal of respect for those in authority. Titles, rank, and status carry a lot of weight. In contrast, a low power distance society plays down inequalities as much as possible. Superiors still have authority, but employees are not afraid of or in awe of the boss.

1   *Uncertainty avoidance.* Uncertainty avoidance describes the degree to which people tolerate risk and prefer structured over unstructured situations. People in low uncertainty avoidance societies are relatively comfortable with risks. They are also relatively tolerant of behaviour and opinions that differ from their own because they don't feel threatened by them. On the other hand, people in a society that is

Geert Hofstede Cultural Dimensions
http://feweb.uvt.nl/
center/hofstede/
index.htm

high in uncertainty avoidance feel threatened by uncertainty and ambiguity and experience high levels of anxiety in such situations, which manifests itself in nervousness, high stress, and aggressiveness.

- *Achievement vs. nurturing.* The fourth cultural dimension, like individualism/collectivism, is a dichotomy. Achievement reflects the degree to which values such as assertiveness, the acquisition of money and material goods, and competition prevail. Nurturing is a national cultural attribute that emphasizes relationships and concern for others.[35]

- *Long-term and short-term orientation.* This cultural attribute looks at a country's orientation toward life and work. People in cultures with long-term orientation look to the future and value thrift and persistence. Also, in these cultures, leisure time is not so important and it is believed that the most important events in life will occur in the future. A short-term orientation values the past and present and emphasizes respect for tradition and fulfilling social obligations. Leisure time is important, and it is believed that the most important events in life happen in the past and in the present.

Although we don't have the space to review Hofstede's entire results for all the countries he studied, we provide 12 examples of the first four variables in Exhibit 3-5. The long-term orientation variable isn't included in this table because scores for some of the countries were not reported. However, the top five countries with higher long-term orientation (LTO) scores are China, Hong Kong, Taiwan, Japan, and South Korea. Countries such as Sweden, Germany, Australia, United States, United Kingdom, and Canada had lower LTO scores, which reflect a more short-term orientation.[36]

Developing Your Interpersonal Skills—Becoming More Culturally Aware, on pages 95–96, encourages you to think about how to become more comfortable when interacting with people from different cultures.

Exhibit 3-5

Examples of Hofstede's Cultural Dimensions

Country	Individualism/ Collectivism	Power Distance	Uncertainty Avoidance	Achievement/ Nurturing[a]
Australia	Individual	Small	Moderate	Strong
Canada	Individual	Moderate	Low	Moderate
England	Individual	Small	Moderate	Strong
France	Individual	Large	High	Weak
Greece	Collective	Large	High	Moderate
Italy	Individual	Moderate	High	Strong
Japan	Collective	Moderate	High	Strong
Mexico	Collective	Large	High	Strong
Singapore	Collective	Large	Low	Moderate
Sweden	Individual	Small	Low	Weak
United States	Individual	Small	Low	Strong
Venezuela	Collective	Large	High	Strong

[a]A weak achievement score is equivalent to high nurturing.

Source: Based on G. Hofstede, "Motivation, Leadership, and Organization: Do American Theories Apply Abroad?" *Organizational Dynamics,* Summer 1980, pp. 42–63.

The GLOBE Framework for Assessing Cultures

Although Hofstede's cultural dimensions have been the main framework for differentiating among national cultures, much of the data on which they are based are somewhat outdated. Since the time of Hofstede's original studies, there have been a number of changes in the global environment, suggesting the need for an updated assessment of cultural dimensions, which the GLOBE project provides.[37] The GLOBE (Global Leadership and Organizational Behavior Effectiveness) research program, which began in 1993, continues to investigate cross-cultural leadership behaviours. Using data from over 18 000 middle managers in 62 countries, the GLOBE research team identified nine dimensions on which national cultures differ:

GLOBE Research Project
www.thunderbird.edu/
wwwfiles/ms/globe/

1 *Assertiveness.* The degree to which a society encourages people to be tough, confrontational, assertive, and competitive vs. modest and tender.

1 *Future orientation.* The degree to which a society encourages and rewards future-oriented behaviours such as planning, investing in the future, and delaying gratification.

1 *Gender differentiation.* The degree to which a society maximizes gender-role differences as measured by how much status and decision-making responsibilities women have.

1 *Uncertainty avoidance.* The degree to which a society relies on social norms and procedures to alleviate the unpredictability of future events.

1 *Power distance.* The degree to which members of a society expect power to be unequally shared.

1 *In-group collectivism.* In contrast to focusing on societal institutions, this dimension encompasses the degree to which members of a society take pride in membership in small groups, such as their family and circle of close friends, and the organizations in which they are employed.

1 *Performance orientation.* The degree to which a society encourages and rewards group members for performance improvement and excellence.

1 *Humane orientation.* The degree to which a society encourages and rewards individuals for being fair, altruistic, generous, caring, and kind to others.

1 *Individualism/collectivism.* The degree to which individuals are encouraged by societal institutions to be integrated into groups within organizations and society.

How do different countries rank on these nine dimensions? Exhibit 3-6 on page 88 provides examples.

The Pros and Cons of Globalization

What is your attitude toward globalization? Is your attitude favourable or unfavourable?

Doing business globally today isn't easy! Advocates praise the economic and social benefits that come from globalization. Yet that very globalization has created challenges and controversy because of the impact it can have on the world's poor (for instance, child labour has been used to produce North American goods). However, if one country's economy falters, it potentially could have a domino effect on other countries with which it does business.

Some have said that globalization is dead, including Canadian philosopher John Ralston Saul. However, Joel Bakan, a University of British Columbia law professor who wrote *The Corporation* and co-produced the documentary of the same name, claims, "It's overly optimistic to say globalization is dead."[38]

Although supporters of globalization praise it for its economic benefits, there are those who think that it is simply a euphemism for "Americanization"—that is, the way US cultural values and US business philosophy are said to be slowly taking over the world.[39] Critics claim that this attitude of the "almighty American dollar wanting to spread the

Exhibit 3-6

GLOBE Rankings

Dimension	Countries Rating		
	Low	Medium	High
Assertiveness	Sweden New Zealand Switzerland	Egypt Ireland Philippines	Spain United States Greece
Future orientation	Russia Argentina Poland	Slovenia Egypt Ireland	Denmark Canada Netherlands
Gender differentiation	Sweden Denmark Slovenia	Italy Brazil Argentina	South Korea Egypt Morocco
Uncertainty avoidance	Russia Hungary Bolivia	Israel United States Mexico	Austria Denmark Germany
Power distance	Denmark Netherlands South Africa	England France Brazil	Russia Spain Thailand
Individualism/collectivism (with the first column indicating the most collectivist and the last column indicating the most individualistic)	Denmark Singapore Japan	Hong Kong United States Egypt	Greece Hungary Germany
In-group collectivism	Denmark Sweden New Zealand	Japan Israel Qatar	Egypt China Morocco
Performance orientation	Russia Argentina Greece	Sweden Israel Spain	United States Taiwan New Zealand
Humane orientation	Germany Spain France	Hong Kong Sweden Taiwan	Indonesia Egypt Malaysia

Source: M. Javidan and R. J. House, "Cultural Acumen for the Global Manager: Lessons from Project GLOBE," *Organizational Dynamics*, Spring 2001, pp. 289–305. Copyright © 2001. Reprinted with permission from Elsevier.

American way to every single country" has created many problems.[40] Exhibit 3-7 outlines the major pro- and anti-globalization arguments. Some of the dominant opponents of globalization include the International Institute for Sustainable Development; the International Forum on Globalization; Greenpeace; the Canadian-based Centre for Research on Globalization; and Canadian author, journalist, and activist Naomi Klein, who is well-known for her book *No Logo: Taking Aim at the Brand Bullies*. Some of the main supporters of globalization include London-based International Policy Network, Washington-based Competitive Enterprise Institute, and the Cato Institute.

Because Canada is not seen as a country that wants to spread Canadian values and culture, Canadian managers may have some advantages over their American counterparts in doing business internationally. Managers will need to be aware of how their decisions and actions will be viewed, not only by those who may agree, but, more importantly, by those who may disagree. They will need to adjust their leadership styles and management approaches to accommodate these diverse views. Yet, as always, they will need to do this while still being as efficient and effective as possible in reaching the organization's goals.

Exhibit 3-7

Sample Positions of Anti- and Pro-Globalization Groups

Anti-Globalization Positions	**Pro-Globalization Positions**
⅃ Globalization is a synonym for Western imperialism.	⅃ Globalization promotes economic prosperity; it offers access to foreign capital, export markets, and advanced technology.
⅃ Trade liberalization may hinder economic development for poorer countries.	⅃ Globalization encourages the efficient use of natural resources and raises environmental awareness and, thus, helps protect the environment.
⅃ There are environmental, social, and economic costs to globalization.	⅃ Globalization minimizes government intervention, which can hinder development, in business and in people's lives.
⅃ Globalization erodes the power of local organizations and local decision-making methods.	⅃ Globalization is a positive force that has encouraged the development of markets, which can bring about prosperity.
⅃ Globalization can lead to the exploitation of workers' rights and human rights.	
⅃ Globalization usually benefits wealthy countries at the expense of poor countries.	
⅃ Lessening or removing trade regulations hurts the poor by pushing up the price of necessities, such as seeds for planting crops and medicine.	

Source: Based on "Who Are the Players?" *Globalisation Guide,* http://www.globalisationguide.org/02.html (accessed July 6, 2007).

SUMMARY AND IMPLICATIONS

1. What are the different ways of viewing global differences? We can view global differences from ethnocentric, polycentric, and geocentric perspectives. An ethnocentric attitude is the belief that the best work approaches and practices are those of the *home* country (the country in which the company's headquarters are located). The polycentric attitude is the view that the managers in the *host* country (the foreign country in which the organization is doing business) know the best work approaches and practices for running their businesses. The geocentric attitude, which is a *world-oriented* view, focuses on using the best approaches and people from around the globe.

▶ ▶ ▶ Menu Foods likely understood the best practices for doing business in Canada and the United States, but may not have taken enough precautions to understand that food regulations in China were almost nonexistent.

2. What kinds of alliances affect trade relations among countries in the world? Global trade is affected by two forces: regional trading alliances and the agreements negotiated through the World Trade Organization (WTO). Regional trading alliances include the European Union (EU), the North American Free Trade Agreement (NAFTA), the Association of Southeast Asian Nations (ASEAN), and others. These regional alliances specify how trade is conducted among countries. The goal of the WTO, which consists of 150 member countries and 31 observer governments, is to help businesses (importers and exporters) conduct their business through the various trade agreements, negotiated and ratified by the vast majority of the world's trading nations.

▶ ▶ ▶ Menu Foods used a variety of suppliers to get the ingredients to make its pet food, and some of these ingredients came from foreign countries with different quality standards. When things like this happen, there are often calls for more restrictive trade arrangements for countries with lower standards than North America has.

3. **How do organizations do business globally?** Organizations can take on a variety of structures when they go global, including multinational corporations, multidomestic corporations, global companies, and transnational or borderless organizations. An organization can take lower-risk and lower-investment strategies for going global through importing or exporting, hiring foreign representation, or contracting with foreign manufacturers. It can also increase its presence in another country by joining with another business to form a strategic alliance or joint venture. Or it can set up a foreign subsidiary in order to have a full presence in the foreign country.

▶ ▶ ▶ Menu Foods is a global company that produces private-label and brand-name pet foods for retailers in Canada, the United States, and Mexico. Its headquarters are in Canada, and it has four manufacturing facilities in Canada and the United States. It processes pet food products close to the areas it serves to reduce product costs, including freight costs, so that it can remain competitive.

4. **What are the challenges of doing business globally?** When managers do business in other countries, they will be affected by the global legal–political and economic environments of those countries. Differing laws and political systems can create constraints as well as opportunities for managers. The type of economic system in some countries can place restrictions on how foreign companies are able to conduct business. In addition, managers must be aware of the culture of the countries in which they do business to understand *how* business is done and what customers expect.

▶ ▶ ▶ Menu Foods learned the challenge of relying on pet food ingredients that originate from countries with different food safety standards and regulations. Though Menu Foods' ingredient supplier was American, that company was merely a distributor for Chinese-produced goods. As Menu Foods discovered, in a very unfortunate way, the wheat gluten its company had used in numerous brands was not produced according to the same food safety standards and regulations that exist in Canada and the United States.

Management @ Work

READING FOR COMPREHENSION

1. Contrast ethnocentric, polycentric, and geocentric attitudes toward global business.

2. What is the Association of Southeast Asian Nations?

3. What is the role of the World Trade Organization?

4. Contrast multinational corporations, multidomestic corporations, global companies, and transnational or borderless organizations.

5. Define importing, exporting, licensing, and franchising.

6. Define strategic alliances, joint ventures, and foreign subsidiaries.

7. What are the nine GLOBE dimensions for assessing cultures?

8. What are some of the pros and cons of globalization?

LINKING CONCEPTS TO PRACTICE

1. What are the managerial implications of a transnational or borderless organization?

2. Compare the advantages and drawbacks of the various approaches to going global.

3. What challenges might confront a Mexican manager transferred to Canada to manage a manufacturing plant in Winnipeg? Will these be the same for a

Canadian manager transferred to Guadalajara, Mexico? Explain.

4. Can the GLOBE framework presented in this chapter be used to guide managers in a Thai hospital or a government agency in Venezuela? Explain.

5. In what ways do you think global companies select and train managers differently than domestic companies do? What impact might the Internet have on this? Explain.

SELF-ASSESSMENT

Am I Well-Suited for a Career as a Global Manager?

For each of the following statements, circle the level of agreement or disagreement with how well the statement describes you:[41]

1 = Very Strongly Disagree
2 = Strongly Disagree
3 = Disagree
4 = Neither Agree nor Disagree
5 = Agree
6 = Strongly Agree
7 = Very Strongly Agree

1. When working with people from other cultures, I work hard to understand their perspectives.   1 2 3 4 5 6 7

2. I have a solid understanding of my organization's products and services.   1 2 3 4 5 6 7

3. I am willing to take a stand on issues.   1 2 3 4 5 6 7

4. I have a special talent for dealing with people.   1 2 3 4 5 6 7

5. I can be depended on to tell the truth regardless of circumstances.   1 2 3 4 5 6 7

6. I am good at identifying the most important part of a complex problem or issue.   1 2 3 4 5 6 7

7. I clearly demonstrate commitment to seeing the organization succeed.   1 2 3 4 5 6 7

8. I take personal as well as business risks.   1 2 3 4 5 6 7

9. I have changed as a result of feedback from others. 1 2 3 4 5 6 7

10. I enjoy the challenge of working in countries other than my own. 1 2 3 4 5 6 7

11. I take advantage of opportunities to do new things. 1 2 3 4 5 6 7

12. I find criticism hard to take. 1 2 3 4 5 6 7

13. I seek feedback even when others are reluctant to give it. 1 2 3 4 5 6 7

14. I don't get so invested in things that I cannot change when something does not work. 1 2 3 4 5 6 7

Scoring Key

Reverse your scoring for item 12 (that is, 1 = 7, 2 = 6, 3 = 5, etc.), and then add up your total score. Your total score will range from 14 to 98. The higher your score, the greater your potential for success as an international manager.

Analysis and Interpretation

In today's global economy, being a manager often means being a global manager. But unfortunately, not all managers are able to transfer their skills smoothly from domestic environments to global ones. Your results here can help you assess whether your skills align with those needed to succeed as an international manager.

MANAGEMENT FOR YOU TODAY

Dilemma

You are part of a multicultural team of eight students, two from each of Canada, China, Africa, and Germany. You are trying to put together a business plan for a small business that could be operated in your community. This is a course assignment, but winning proposals have the opportunity to be funded, up to $10 000. Your team is struggling to come up with a workable idea, and cannot even agree on a potential course of action to get the project completed. What might be some of the multicultural differences that could be getting in your way? What could you do to smooth over some of these differences? How might each student's global perspective be affecting team performance?

Becoming a Manager

- Learn as much as you can about other countries.
- Familiarize yourself with current global political, economic, and cultural issues.
- If given the opportunity, try to have your class projects or reports (in this class and other classes) cover global issues or global companies.
- Talk to instructors or students who may be from other countries and ask them what the business world is like in their countries.
- If you have the opportunity, travel to other countries.
- Go see a foreign film.

WORKING TOGETHER: TEAM-BASED EXERCISE

Assessing People's Global Aptitudes

Moving to a foreign country isn't easy, no matter how many times you have done it or how receptive you are to new experiences. Successful global organizations are able to identify the best candidates for global assignments, and one of the ways they do this is through individual assessments prior to assigning people to global facilities. Form groups of 3 to 5 individuals. Your newly formed team, the Global Assignment Task Force, has been given the responsibility for developing a global aptitude assessment form for Zara, the successful European clothing retailer.[42] The company is starting to become well known in North America, and Zara's managers have positioned the company for continued global success. That success is based on a simple principle—in fashion, nothing is as important as time to market.

Zara's store managers (more than 600 worldwide) offer suggestions every day on cuts, fabrics, and even new lines. After reviewing the ideas, a team at headquarters in A Coruña, Spain, decides what to make. Designers draw up the ideas and send them over the company's intranet to nearby factories. Within days, the cutting, dyeing, sewing, and assembling starts. In three weeks, the clothes will be in stores from

Barcelona to Berlin to Bangkok. That is 12 times faster than its rivals. Zara has a twice-a-week delivery schedule that restocks old styles and brings in new designs. Rivals tend to get new designs once or twice a season.

Because Zara is expanding its global operations significantly, it wants to make sure that it's sending the best possible people to the various global locations. Your team's assignment is to come up with a rough draft of a form to assess people's global aptitudes. Think about the characteristics, skills, attitudes, and so on that you think a successful global employee would need. Your team's draft should be at least one half page but not longer than one page. Be prepared to present your ideas to your classmates and instructor.

ETHICS IN ACTION

Ethical Dilemma Exercise: What Should a Company Do When It Faces Opposition to Expansion in Another Country?

Montreal-based Rio Tinto Alcan is the world's largest primary aluminum producer.[43] The company has some 68 000 employees and 430 facilities in 61 countries; it posted a profit of $129 million in 2005. The company plans to develop a $1.8-billion strip mine and refinery in Orissa state, 1200 kilometres southeast of New Delhi, India.

The company has only recently been given permission to begin developing the mine. For a number of years, local people have expressed concern that the mining activities will uproot the Adivasis, some of India's indigenous tribes. Several years ago, the protests against developing the mine grew violent when state police fired guns at the Adivasis, killing three protesters. Rio Tinto Alcan's plans were put on hold while government officials conducted an inquiry into the deaths. The government concluded that tribal areas "cannot afford to remain backward for the sake of so-called environmental protection."

Bhagawan Majhi serves as sarpanch (chief) of Kucheipadar village, where the violence took place. He has led the opposition to the mines since he was a teen, and says, "Our fight will continue until the government revokes its agreement with the company."

Rio Tinto Alcan insists on carrying through with the mine, even though one of its partners in the project, Norway-based

Hydro (formerly Norsk Hydro), decided to quit the project after three of its employees were kidnapped by tribal members.

Rio Tinto Alcan spokespeople claim that the mine can actually improve the life of the Adivasis. The company promises to create more than 1000 jobs, and each tribal family will be given at least one. Employees will get a health clinic that others in the area can use. Majhi does not believe that the Adivasis will be better off with the mine. For one thing, the Baphlimali Hill, which is sacred to their tribe, will be ruined. He also says that land is more important than jobs. "What will we do with the money? We don't know how to do business," he notes. He also talks about how the lives of villagers who accepted money from Rio Tinto Alcan in exchange for drilling rights have been ruined: "They spent it on alcohol, they married two or three women, they bought wristwatches and motorcycles," Majhi says.

Rio Tinto Alcan's CEO, Travis Engen, was given notice two weeks before the annual general meeting that several shareholders would protest the company's plans to develop the mine on Adivasis lands. He knows that he must respond to their complaints at the meeting. Does it make sense to simply abandon the mining plans in the face of protests? What should he tell shareholders at the meeting about Alcan's future plans for the region?

Thinking Critically About Ethics

Foreign countries often have lax product-labelling laws. As the international product manager for a Canadian pharmaceutical company, you are responsible for the profitability of a new drug to be sold outside Canada. The drug's side effects can be seri-

ous, although not fatal. Adding this information to the label or even putting an informational insert into the package will add to the product's cost, threatening profitability margins. What will you do? Why? What factors will influence your decision?

National Basketball Association

Using an exceptionally well-executed game plan, the National Basketball Association (NBA) is trying to emerge as the first truly global sports league.[44] The game was invented in 1891 by Canadian James Naismith, from Almonte, Ontario, and the Toronto Raptors and Vancouver Grizzlies were the first non-US cities to join the league, during the 1995–1996 season.

The desire to transform the once-faltering domestic sport into a global commercial success reflects a keen understanding of managing in a global environment. And much of the credit should go to NBA commissioner David Stern, who has been consciously building the NBA into a global brand.

Professional basketball sparked the interest of fans and players around the globe in the mid-1990s, and the NBA cashed in on the game's universal appeal. At one time, if you had asked someone in China what the most popular basketball team was, the answer would have been the "Red Oxen" from Chicago (the Bulls). Today, the NBA's centre of attention comes from China. Yao Ming, the 2.2-metre-tall centrepiece of the Houston Rockets, has a personality that appeals to fans around the world. But he is not the only global player in the league. Others include the Dallas Mavericks' Dirk Nowitzki from Germany; Pau Gasol of the Memphis Grizzlies, a native of Spain; San Antonio Spurs' guard Tony Parker from France; Denver Nuggets' forward Nenê Hilario from Brazil; and Utah Jazz guard Gordan Giricek from Croatia. The Raptors' first-round draft pick in 2004, Rafael Araujo, is from Brazil. What started as a trickle in the 1980s with occasional foreign stars like Hakeem Olajuwon (Nigeria) and the late Dražen Petrović (Croatia), has turned into a flood. A total of 60 players from 28 countries and territories outside the United States were playing in the NBA as of July 2007. These include Canadian players Jamaal Magloire of the Portland Trailblazers and Steve Nash of the Pheonix Suns. Seventeen Canadian basketball players have played in the NBA over the years. The NBA wants to prove that the game can be played globally also.

What strategies can Stern take to increase consumer familiarity with basketball both domestically and globally? How can he develop a greater basketball presence in Canada?

When Yes Does Not Always Mean Yes, and No Does Not Always Mean No

When a major chip-manufacturing project ran more than a month late, David Sommers, vice-president for engineering at Adaptec, felt that perhaps the company's Indian engineers "didn't understand the sense of urgency" in getting the project completed.[45] In the Scottish highlands, Bill Matthews, the general manager of McTavish's Kitchens, is quite satisfied with his non-Scottish employees—cooks who are German, Swedish, or Slovak and waitresses who are mostly Polish. Other highland hotels and restaurants also have a large number of Eastern European staff. Despite the obvious language barriers, these Scottish employers are finding ways to help their foreign employees adapt and be successful. When Lee Epting of Forum Nokia gave a presentation to a Finnish audience and asked for feedback, he was told, "That was good." Based on his interpretation of that phrase, he assumed that it must have been just an okay presentation…nothing spectacular. However, because Finns tend to be generally much quieter and more reserved than North Americans, that response actually meant, "That was great, off the scale."

It's not easy being a successful global manager, especially when it comes to dealing with cultural differences. Research by Wilson Learning Worldwide says there is an "iceberg of culture, of which we can only see the top 15 percent—food, appearance, and language." Although these elements themselves can be complicated, it's the other 85 percent of the "iceberg" that is not apparent initially that managers need to be especially concerned about. What does that include? Workplace issues such as communication styles, priorities, role expectations, work tempo, negotiation styles, nonverbal communication, attitudes toward planning, and so forth. Understanding these issues requires developing a global mindset and skill set. Many organizations are relying on cultural awareness training to help them do just that.

Having outsourced some engineering jobs to India, Axcelis Technologies had its North American-based employees go through a training program where they role-played scenarios with one person pretending to be Indian and the other his North American co-worker. One of the company's human resource directors said, "At first I was skeptical and wondered what I'd get out of the class, but it was enlightening for me. Not everyone operates like we do in North America." In our global world, successful managers must learn to recognize and appreciate cultural differences and to understand how to work effectively and efficiently with employees, no matter their nationality.

Questions

1. What global attitude do you think would most support, promote, and encourage cultural awareness? Explain.

2. Would legal–political and economic differences play a role as companies design appropriate cultural awareness training for employees? Explain.

3. Pick one of the countries mentioned in the case and do some cultural research on it. What did you find out

about the culture of that country? How might this information affect the way a manager in that country plans, organizes, leads, and controls?

4. UK-based company Kwintessential has several cultural awareness "quizzes" on its website (**www.kwintessential. co.uk/resources/culture-tests.html**). Go to the company's website and try two or three of these. Were you surprised at your score? What does your score tell you about your cultural awareness?

5. What advice might you give to a manager who has little experience working with people in other countries?

DEVELOPING YOUR INTERPERSONAL SKILLS

Becoming More Culturally Aware

About the Skill

"Understanding and managing people who are similar to us are challenges—but understanding and managing those who are *dissimilar from us and from each other* can be even tougher." Workplaces around the world are becoming increasingly diverse. Thus, managers need to recognize that not all employees want the same thing, act in the same manner, and can be managed in the same way. What is a diverse workforce? It's one that is heterogeneous in terms of gender, race, ethnicity, age, and other characteristics that reflect differences. Valuing diversity and helping a diverse workforce achieve its maximum potential are becoming indispensable skills for more and more managers.

Steps in Developing the Skill

The diversity issues an individual manager might face are many. They might include communicating with employees whose familiarity with the language might be limited; creating career development programs that fit the skills, needs, and values of a variety of employees; helping a diverse team cope with a conflict over goals or work assignments; or learning which rewards are valued by different groups of employees. You can improve your handling of diversity issues if you use the following eight suggestions:[46]

1. **Fully accept diversity.** Successfully valuing diversity starts with each individual accepting the principle of multiculturalism. Accept the value of diversity for its own sake—not simply because you have to. Accepting and valuing diversity is important because it's the right thing to do. And it's important that you reflect your acceptance in all you say and do.

2. **Recruit broadly.** When you have job openings, work to get a diverse applicant pool. Although referrals from current employees can be a good source of applicants, they tend to produce candidates similar to the current workforce.

3. **Select fairly.** Make sure that the selection process does not discriminate. One suggestion is to use job-specific tests rather than general aptitude or knowledge tests. Such tests measure specific skills, not subjective characteristics.

4. **Provide orientation and training for minorities.** Making the transition from outsider to insider can be particularly difficult for an employee who belongs to a minority group. Provide support either through a group or through a mentoring arrangement.

5. **Sensitize nonminorities.** Not only do you personally need to accept and value diversity, but as a manager you need to encourage all your employees to do so. Many organizations do this through diversity training programs, where employees examine the cultural norms of different groups. The most important thing a manager can do is show by his or her actions that diversity is valued.

6. **Strive to be flexible.** Part of valuing diversity is recognizing that different groups have different needs and values. Be flexible in accommodating employees' requests.

7. **Seek to motivate individually.** Motivating employees is an important skill for any manager; motivating a diverse workforce has its own special challenges. Managers must be more in tune with the background, cultures, and values of employees. What motivates a single mother of two

young children who is working full time to support her family is likely to be different from the needs of a young, single, part-time employee or an older employee who is working to supplement his or her retirement income.

8. **Reinforce employee differences.** Encourage individuals to embrace and value diverse views. Create traditions and ceremonies that promote diversity. Celebrate diversity by accentuating its positive aspects. However, also be prepared to deal with the challenges of diversity, such as mistrust, miscommunication, lack of cohesiveness, attitudinal differences, and stress.

Practising the Skill

Read the descriptions of the following employees who work for the same organization. After reading each description, write a short paragraph describing what you think the goals and priorities of each employee might be. With what types of employee issues might the manager of each employee have to deal? How could these managers exhibit the value of diversity?

Lester is 57 years old, a college graduate, and a vice-president of the firm. His two children are married, and he is a grandparent of three beautiful grandchildren. He lives in a condo with his wife, who does volunteer work and is active in their church. Lester is healthy and likes to stay active, both physically and mentally.

Sanjyot is a 30-year-old clerical worker who came to Canada from Indonesia 10 years ago. She completed high school after moving to Canada and has begun to attend evening classes at a local college. Sanjyot is a single parent with two children under the age of eight. Although her health

is excellent, one of her children suffers from a severe learning disability.

Yuri is a recent immigrant from one of the former Soviet republics. He is 42 years old and his English communication skills are quite limited. He has an engineering degree from his country, but since he is not licensed to practise in Canada, he works as a parts clerk. He is unmarried and has no children but feels an obligation to his relatives back in his home country. He sends much of his paycheque to them.

Reinforcing the Skill

The following activities will help you practise and reinforce the skills associated with becoming more culturally aware:

1. Indicate which employees (age, gender, ethnicity, family status, and so forth) you think might be motivated by the following additional employee benefits: on-site daycare, fitness centre, tuition reimbursement, job sharing, English classes, having a mentor, being a mentor, performance bonus plan, more time off, flextime, enhanced retirement benefits, supervisory training, subsidized dependant care, discounts on company products, religious holidays, free candy and snacks in the employee break room, on-site physician, country club membership, and on-site dry cleaning services. Looking at your responses, what are the implications for a manager?

2. Ask friends from other cultures what kinds of biases they encounter in school or at work. Think about how you, as a manager, might deal with instances of these types of biases.

3. Come up with a list of suggestions that you personally can use to improve your sensitivity to diversity issues.

Corporate Social Responsibility and Managerial Ethics

PART one

Defining the Manager's Terrain

CHAPTER 1
Introduction to Management and Organizations

CHAPTER 2
Constraints on Managers: Organizational Culture and the Environment

CHAPTER 3
Managing in a Global Environment

▶ **CHAPTER 4**
Corporate Social Responsibility and Managerial Ethics

What does it take to be an ethical and socially responsible manager?

1. What is corporate social responsibility?

2. Can being socially responsible help performance?

3. How do organizations go green?

4. How do values influence management?

5. What is ethics and how can ethical behaviour be encouraged?

▶ ▶ ▶ Lana Hill is the Aboriginal community investment coordinator for Fort McMurray, Alberta-based Syncrude Canada.[1] In her position, she helps Syncrude encourage and sustain the growth and well-being of local Aboriginal communities. She works with Syncrude's Aboriginal Relations Team to ensure that Syncrude's commitments to Aboriginal development are achieved.

Syncrude, the largest producer of light sweet crude oil from oil sands, is the largest industrial employer of Aboriginal people in Canada. More than 400 of the company's 4500 employees are from Aboriginal communities, with over 200 of them filling administrative, professional, and technical positions. Another 350 Aboriginals work for Syncrude's contractors. The company says its "commitment to the Aboriginal people of our region is not only motivated by our responsibility as a good corporate citizen, but by our desire to be a good neighbour."

Syncrude helps develop the skills of Aboriginal people so that they can compete for jobs in the oil-sands industry on

an equal footing. The Aboriginal Relations Team knows that it's not as simple as just hiring Aboriginal people, "because you don't just take someone from a small community, put them in a big corporation environment, and expect that people will survive there, because that's quite a bit of a culture shock."

Syncrude has done well in encouraging Aboriginal development. In 2006, for its corporate social responsibility in the area of Aboriginal relations, Syncrude received Gold Level accreditation in the Progressive Aboriginal Relations (PAR) program. It is the first company that has won this top standing three times.

Think About It

Can a company be socially responsible and achieve good financial performance? Put yourself in the Aboriginal Relations Team's shoes. What advantages does Syncrude gain through working with its Aboriginal community? Would there be any reason not to form such relationships with the community?

Deciding how much social responsibility is enough—for instance, looking at when it's better to simply focus on profits—is just one example of the complicated types of ethical and social responsibility issues that managers may have to address as they plan, organize, lead, and control. As managers go about their business, social factors can and do influence their actions. In this chapter, we introduce you to the issues surrounding social responsibility and managerial ethics. Our discussion of these topics appears here in the textbook because both corporate social responsibility and ethics are responses to a changing environment and are influenced by organizational culture (Chapter 2); they have an influence upon how we do business globally (Chapter 3); and they are important considerations when making decisions (Chapter 5).

Syncrude Canada
www.syncrude.ca

What Is Corporate Social Responsibility?

1. What is corporate social responsibility?

Internet file-sharing sites allow music and video lovers all over the world to obtain and share their favourite recordings for free. Large global corporations want to lower their costs and be more competitive by locating in countries where human rights are not a high priority, and justify doing so by saying that they are bringing in jobs and helping to strengthen local economies. Automobile manufacturers build gas-guzzling sport utility vehicles that have the potential to seriously injure people in smaller, more fuel-efficient vehicles because customers want them and are willing to pay the prices. Are these companies being socially responsible? What factors influenced managers' decisions in these situations?

Managers regularly face decisions that have a dimension of social responsibility: Employee relations, philanthropy, pricing, resource conservation, product quality and safety, and doing business in countries that violate human rights are some of the more obvious. How do managers make such decisions? Let's begin by looking at two different perspectives.

Q&A 4.1

Two Views of Corporate Social Responsibility

A great deal of attention has been focused on the extent to which organizations and management should act in socially responsible ways. On one side, there is the classical—or purely economic—view, and on the other side is the socio-economic view.

The Classical View

classical view
The view that management's only social responsibility is to maximize profits.

The **classical view** says that management's only social responsibility is to maximize profits. The most outspoken advocate of this approach is economist and Nobel laureate Milton Friedman.[2] He argues that managers' primary responsibility is to operate the business in the best interests of the stockholders (the owners of a corporation). What are those interests? Friedman contends that stockholders have a single concern: financial return. He also argues that any time managers decide to spend the organization's resources for "social good," they are adding to the costs of doing business. These costs have to be passed on to consumers either through higher prices or absorbed by stockholders through a smaller profit returned as dividends. Do understand that Friedman isn't saying that organizations should *not* be socially responsible; he thinks they should. But the extent of that responsibility is to maximize organizational profits for stockholders.

Is it wrong for Canadian companies to employ children to work in factories in countries where child labour is legal?

Joel Bakan, professor of law at the University of British Columbia, author of *The Corporation*, and co-director of the documentary of the same name, is more critical of organizations than Friedman, though he finds that current laws support corporate behaviour that some might find troubling. Bakan suggests that today's corporations have many of the same characteristics as a psychopathic personality (for example, self-interested, lacking empathy, manipulative, and reckless in their disregard of others). Bakan notes that even though companies have a tendency to act psychopathically, this is not why they are fixated on profits. Rather, though they may have social responsibilities, the only *legal* responsibility corporations have is to maximize organizational profits for stockholders.[3] He suggests that more laws and more restraints need to be put in place if corporations are to behave more socially responsibly, as current laws direct corporations to be responsible to their shareholders, and make little mention of responsibility toward other stakeholders.

The Socio-economic View

socio-economic view
The view that management's social responsibility goes beyond making profits to include protecting and improving society's welfare.

The **socio-economic view** says that management's social responsibility goes beyond making profits to include protecting and improving society's welfare. This position is based on the belief that corporations are *not* independent entities responsible only to stockholders. They also have a responsibility to the larger society that endorses their creation through various laws and regulations and supports them by purchasing their products and services. In addition, proponents of this view believe that business organizations are not just mere

At Charlottetown, PEI-based APM Group, a construction and property development company, Terry Palmer, APM Group vice-president of finance (left), Tim Banks, president, Duane Lamont, vice-president of construction, and Pam Mullally, director of accounting, think about the bottom line when they review plans for new subdivisions APM might build. However, they also know that social responsibility is a guiding principle for the company. So they also evaluate each project's impact on the environment, focus on design that promotes energy conservation, and strive to create a healthy economic community through the building plan.

economic institutions. Society expects and even encourages businesses to become involved in social, political, and legal issues. For example, proponents of the socio-economic view would say that Avon Products was being socially responsible when it initiated its Breast Cancer Crusade to provide women with breast cancer education and early detection screening services, and which, after 14 years, has raised more than $450 million worldwide.[4]

Educational programs implemented by Brazilian cosmetics manufacturer Natura Cosmeticos SA in public primary schools in São Paulo to improve children's literacy and decision-making skills are also viewed as socially responsible.[5] Why? Through these programs, the company's managers are protecting and improving society's welfare. More and more organizations around the world are embracing the socio-economic view, as shown by a recent survey of more than 4200 managers in 116 countries in which respondents overwhelmingly agreed that the role of corporations in society goes far beyond just meeting stockholder obligations.[6] Some even try to measure their "Triple Bottom Line," which takes into account not only financial responsibilities, but social and environmental ones as well.[7]

Natura Cosmeticos SA
www.natura.net

Comparing the Two Views

The key differences between the two views of corporate social responsibility are easier to understand if we think in terms of the people to whom organizations are responsible. Classicists would say that shareholders, or owners, are the only legitimate concern. Those supporting the socio-economic view would respond that managers should be responsible to any group affected by the organization's decisions and actions—that is, the stakeholders (such as employees and community members).[8] Exhibit 4-1 shows a four-stage model of the progression of an organization's social responsibility.[9]

Exhibit 4-1

To Whom Is Management Responsible?

	Corporate Social Responsibility		
Lesser →			Greater
Stage 1 Owners and Management	**Stage 2** Employees	**Stage 3** Constituents in the Specific Environment	**Stage 4** Broader Society

Would you be willing to stop eating your favourite snack if you found out the company did not use environmentally friendly packaging for its products?

At stage 1, managers are following the classical view of social responsibility and obey all laws and regulations while caring for stockholders' interests. At stage 2, managers expand their responsibilities to another important stakeholder group—employees. Because they want to attract, keep, and motivate good employees, stage 2 managers improve working conditions, expand employee rights, increase job security, and focus on human resource concerns.

At stage 3, managers expand their responsibilities to other stakeholders in the specific environment, primarily customers and suppliers. Socially responsible actions for these stakeholders might include fair prices, high-quality products and services, safe products, good supplier relations, and similar actions. Their philosophy is that they can meet their responsibilities to stakeholders only by meeting the needs of these other stakeholders.

Finally, at stage 4, which characterizes the highest socio-economic commitment, managers feel they have a responsibility to society as a whole. They view their business as a public entity and therefore feel that it's important to advance the public good. The acceptance of such responsibility means that managers actively promote social justice, preserve the environment, and support social and cultural activities. They do these things even if such actions may negatively affect profits.

Arguments For and Against Corporate Social Responsibility

Another way to decide whether organizations should be socially responsible is to look at the arguments for and against corporate social responsibility. Exhibit 4-2 outlines the major points that have been presented.[10]

Q&A 4.2

How much and what type of social responsibility businesses should pursue continues to be a topic of interest and heated debate. But if we decide that organizations *should* be socially responsible, what does that mean? Now is a good time to define what we mean by the term *social responsibility*.

From Obligations to Responsiveness to Responsibility

Few concepts have been described in as many different ways as *corporate social responsibility*. For instance, it's been called "profit making only," "going beyond profit making," "voluntary activities," and "concern for the broader social system."[11] We can understand corporate social responsibility better if we first compare it to two similar concepts: social obligation and social responsiveness.[12] A firm that follows a **social obligation** approach engages in social actions because of its obligation to meet certain economic and legal responsibilities. The firm does *only* what it's obligated to do, which indicates that it follows the classical view of social responsibility. In contrast to social obligation, however, both social responsiveness and social responsibility go beyond merely meeting basic economic and legal standards.

A firm that follows a **social responsiveness** approach engages in social actions in response to some popular **social need**. Managers in a socially responsive firm are guided by social norms and make practical decisions about the societal actions in which they take part.[13] For instance, managers at Toronto-based CIBC identified three themes—supporting youth, contributing to community development, and involving CIBC employees—to guide them in deciding which projects and organizations to support.[14] By making these choices, managers were "responding" to what they felt were important social needs; that is, things important to the community.

A socially *responsible* organization views things a little differently. It goes beyond what it's obligated to do or may choose to do because of some popular social need. Rather, it does what it can to help improve society because it's the right thing to do. We define **corporate social responsibility** as a firm's efforts, beyond those required by law and economics, to

social obligation
When a firm engages in social actions because of its obligation to meet certain economic and legal responsibilities.

social responsiveness
When a firm engages in social actions in response to some popular social need.

social need
A need of a segment of society caused by factors such as physical and mental disabilities; language barriers; and cultural, social, or geographical isolation.

corporate social responsibility
A firm's obligation, beyond that required by law and economics, to do the right things and act in ways that are good for society.

Exhibit 4-2

Arguments For and Against Corporate Social Responsibility

For	Against
Public expectations Public opinion now supports businesses pursuing economic and social goals.	**Violation of profit maximization** Business is being socially responsible only when it pursues its economic interests.
Long-run profits Socially responsible companies tend to have more secure long-run profits.	**Dilution of purpose** Pursuing social goals dilutes business's primary purpose—economic productivity.
Ethical obligation Businesses should be socially responsible because responsible actions are the right thing to do.	**Costs** Many socially responsible actions do not cover their costs and someone must pay those costs.
Public image Businesses can create a favourable public image by pursuing social goals.	**Too much power** Businesses have a lot of power already, and if they pursue social goals they will have even more.
Better environment Business involvement can help solve difficult social problems.	**Lack of skills** Business leaders lack the necessary skills to address social issues.
Discouragement of further governmental regulation By becoming socially responsible, businesses can expect less government regulation.	**Lack of accountability** There are no direct lines of accountability for social actions.
Balance of responsibility and power Businesses have a lot of power, and an equally large amount of responsibility is needed to balance against that power.	
Stockholder interests Social responsibility will improve a business's stock price in the long run.	
Possession of resources Businesses have the resources to support public and charitable projects that need assistance.	
Superiority of prevention over cures Businesses should address social problems before they become serious and costly to correct.	

do the right things and act in ways that are good for society. Note that this definition assumes that a firm obeys laws and pursues economic interests, but it also emphasizes that it has to differentiate between right and wrong.

Social responsibility adds an ethical imperative to do those things that make society better and not to do those that could make it worse. As Exhibit 4-3 on page 104 shows, social responsibility requires business to determine what is right or wrong and to engage in ethical business activities. A socially responsible organization does what is right because it feels it has a responsibility to act that way. For example, Vancouver-based Mountain Equipment Co-op, which makes outdoor sports clothing and gear, has a green building policy. Its Ottawa and Winnipeg stores were the first and second Canadian retail buildings to comply with standards requiring a 50 percent reduction in energy consumption over regular buildings. CEO Peter Robinson says, "The bottom line is that sustainability is good business: for the ledger books and for the planet."[15] That's the attitude of a socially responsible manager and organization.

Mountain Equipment Co-op
www.mec.ca

How should we view an organization's social actions? In Canada, a company that meets pollution control standards established by the federal government or that does not discriminate against employees over the age of 40 in promotion decisions is meeting its social obligation and nothing more because there are laws mandating these actions. However, when

Exhibit 4-3

Corporate Social Responsibility vs. Social Responsiveness

	Corporate Social Responsibility	Social Responsiveness
Major consideration	Ethical	Pragmatic
Focus	Ends	Means
Emphasis	Obligation	Responses
Decision framework	Long term	Medium and short term

Source: Adapted from S. L. Wartick and P. L. Cochran, "The Evolution of the Corporate Social Performance Model," *Academy of Management Review* 10, no. 4 (1985), p. 766.

it provides on-site child care facilities for employees, packages products in 100 percent recycled paper, or announces that it will not purchase, process, or sell any tuna caught along with dolphins, it is being socially responsive. Why? Working parents and environmentalists have voiced these social concerns and demanded such actions.

Many companies in Canada and around the world practise social responsiveness. For example Mississauga, Ontario-based Purolator Courier developed its Tackle Hunger campaign because no major Canadian corporations were tackling this important issue. The program visits Canadian Football League (CFL) cities annually, and fans can have their picture taken with the Grey Cup if they bring a nonperishable food item or make a cash donation. In addition, Purolator donates the quarterback's weight in food to the local food bank whenever he gets sacked in a regular season game. Between 2003 and 2007, the program contributed almost 460 000 kilograms of food to food banks.[16]

Advocates believe that social responsiveness replaces philosophical talk with practical, market-oriented action. They see it as a more tangible and achievable goal than social responsibility.[17] Rather than assessing what is good for society in the long term and making moral judgments, managers in a socially responsive organization identify the prevailing social norms and then change their social involvement to respond to changing societal conditions. For instance, environmental stewardship seems to be an important social norm at present, and many companies are looking at ways to be environmentally responsible. Alcoa of Australia developed a novel way to recycle the used linings of aluminum smelting pots, and Japanese auto parts manufacturer DENSO generates its own electricity and steam at many of its facilities. Other organizations are addressing other popular social issues. For instance, Winnipeg-based CanWest Global Communications (publisher of *National Post*, *Gazette* (Montreal), *Ottawa Citizen*, *Leader-Post* (Regina), *StarPhoenix* (Saskatoon), and *Vancouver Sun*, among other newspapers), hosts an annual Raise-A-Reader day to raise funds ($2.7 million in 2007) to support literacy programs in Canada.[18] These are examples of socially responsive actions for today.

Corporate Social Responsibility and Economic Performance

▶ ▶ ▶ Syncrude Canada is one of the largest nongovernmental employers of Aboriginal people in Canada.[19] As part of Syncrude's commitment to being a good neighbour, the company gives preference to local suppliers so that the local population can benefit economically from Syncrude's presence. Syncrude also supports literacy programs for schools and has employment counsellors to help Aboriginal families learn about the company and the expectations for employees of the company.

Are these programs worth the effort? From a business perspective, Syncrude is the largest single source of oil in Canada and the world's largest producer of light sweet crude oil from oil sands. The company has won a number of awards for its corporate social responsibility activities, including the Gold Level accreditation in the Progressive Aboriginal Relations (PAR) program, which is sponsored by the Canadian Council for Aboriginal Business. It is one of only seven companies in Canada to receive this award. Syncrude is also the safest employer in the industry, and has been rated in the top 100 places to work several times in recent years.

Think About It

Does it always pay off for a company to be socially responsible? What else might Syncrude do to advance its socially responsible record?

In this section, we look at the question: How do socially responsible activities affect a company's economic performance? Findings from a number of research studies can help us answer this question.[20]

The majority of these studies show a positive relationship between social involvement and economic performance. For instance, one study found that firms' corporate social performance was positively associated with both *prior* and *future* financial performance.[21] But we should be cautious about making any sweeping generalizations from these findings because of the methodological limitations associated with trying to measure "corporate social responsibility" and "economic performance."[22] Most of these studies determined a company's social performance by analyzing the content of annual reports, citations of the company's social actions in news articles, and "reputation" indexes based on public perception. Such criteria certainly have drawbacks as reliable measures of corporate social responsibility. Still, a more recent and methodologically rigorous reanalysis of several of these studies concluded that managers can afford to be (and should be) socially responsible.[23]

Another way to look at the issue of corporate social responsibility and economic performance is by evaluating socially responsible mutual stock funds. These mutual funds provide a way for individual investors to support socially responsible companies. Typically, these funds do not invest in companies that are involved in liquor, gambling, tobacco, nuclear power, weapons, price fixing, or fraud, or in companies that have poor product safety, employee relations, and environmental track records. A recent survey indicates that the amount of money invested in Canadian socially responsible investment assets grew to $500 billion in 2006, from $65.5 billion in 2004.[24] How have these funds performed overall? A 2007 survey by Toronto-based *Corporate Knights* magazine found that the funds performed similarly to mainstream funds.[25]

We can also look at what consumers say about corporate social responsibility. A recent survey conducted by GlobeScan, which specializes in corporate issues, found that "83 percent of Canadians believe that corporations should go beyond their traditional economic role; 51 percent say they have punished a socially irresponsible company in the past year."[26] As for naming a socially responsible company, 43 percent of Canadians said they could not do so.

What conclusion can we draw from all of this? The most meaningful one is that there is little evidence to say that a company's social actions hurt its long-term economic performance. Given political and societal pressures on business to be socially involved, managers would be wise to take social goals into consideration as they plan, organize, lead, and control. Jason Mogus, president of Vancouver-based Communicopia, agrees: "The times that we are in right now are tough times for a lot of high-tech firms, and the ones that are thriving are the ones that really did build community connections and have strong customer and employee loyalty." Says Mogus, "If everyone's just there for the stock price and it goes underwater, then what you have is a staff of not very motivated workers."[27]

2. Can being socially responsible help performance?

The Greening of Management

▶ ▶ ▶ As part of Syncrude Canada's work with the Aboriginal communities that surround its oilsands fields, the company seeks to develop environmental practices that show respect for the lands it mines.[28] By partnering with the Fort McKay First Nation, Syncrude re-established a herd of 300 wood bison on land that was once used as an open-pit mine. The company also seeks to reduce its use of fresh water from the Athabasca River through its water recycling and conservation programs. In recognition of the links between increasing global temperatures and greenhouse gas emissions, Syncrude engages in energy conservation and focuses some of its efforts on trying to control greenhouse gas emissions. The company has restored about 22 percent of the land it has mined to its natural state, making it the industry leader in land reclamation.

Think About It

Why has Syncrude chosen to follow an approach to business that incorporates environmental sustainability? What benefits does being green provide to a company?

3. How do organizations go green?

Rachel Carson's *Silent Spring*, a book about the negative effects of pesticides on the environment that was published in 1962, is often cited as having launched the environmental movement. Until that time, few people (and organizations) paid attention to the environmental consequences of their decisions and actions.[29] Although there were some groups concerned with conserving natural resources, about the only popular reference to saving the environment you would have seen was the ubiquitous printed request "Please Do Not Litter."

Since then, a number of highly publicized environmental disasters (mercury poisoning in Japan [from 1932 to 1968], Three Mile Island [1979] and Chernobyl [1986] nuclear power plant accidents, and Exxon Valdez oil spill [1989]) have increased environmental awareness among individuals, groups, and organizations. Increasingly, managers began to confront questions about an organization's impact on the natural environment. The recognition by business of the close link between its decisions and activities and their impact on the natural environment is referred to as the **greening of management**. Let's look at some green issues managers may have to address.

greening of management
The recognition by business of the close link between its decisions and activities and their impact on the natural environment.

Global Environmental Problems

Some of the more serious global environmental problems include natural resource depletion, global climate change, pollution (air, water, and soil), industrial accidents, and toxic wastes. How did these problems occur? Much of the blame can be placed on industrial activities in developed (economically wealthy) countries over the last half-century.[30] Various reports have shown that wealthy societies account for more than 75 percent of the world's energy and resource consumption, and create most of the industrial, toxic, and consumer waste.[31] An equally unsettling picture is that as the world population continues to grow and as emerging countries become more market-oriented and well off, global environmental problems can be expected to worsen.[32] However, many managers and organizations around the world have embraced their responsibility to respect and protect the natural environment. What role *can* organizations play in addressing global environmental problems? In other words, how can they go green?

How Organizations Go Green

Managers and organizations can do many things to protect and preserve the natural environment.[33] Some do no more than what is required by law—that is, they fulfill their social obligation. However, others have made radical changes to make their products and production processes cleaner. For instance, Paris, France-based Total SA, one of the world's largest integrated oil companies, is cleaning up and greening up by implementing tough new rules on oil tanker safety and working with groups such as Global Witness and Greenpeace. UPS, the world's largest package delivery company, has taken numerous environmental actions, such as retrofitting its aircraft with advanced technology and fuel-efficient engines; developing a powerful computer network that efficiently dispatches its fleet of brown trucks; and using alternative fuel to run its trucks. There are many more examples of organizations committed to being green. Although these examples are interesting, they don't tell us much about *how* organizations go green. One model of environmental responsibility uses the phrase *shades of green* to describe the different approaches that organizations take.[34] (See Exhibit 4-4.)

The first approach is the *legal* (or *light green*) *approach*—that is, simply doing what is required legally. Organizations that follow this approach exhibit little environmental sensitivity. They

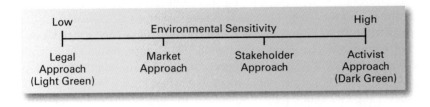

Exhibit 4-4

Approaches to Being Green

Low	Environmental Sensitivity		High
Legal Approach (Light Green)	Market Approach	Stakeholder Approach	Activist Approach (Dark Green)

Source: Based on R. E. Freeman, J. Pierce, and R. Dodd, *Shades of Green: Business Ethics and the Environment* (New York: Oxford University Press, 1995).

obey laws, rules, and regulations willingly and without legal challenge and may even try to use the law to their own advantage, but that is the extent of their being green. For example, many durable product manufacturers have taken the legal approach and comply with the relevant environmental laws and regulations, but go no further. This approach is a good illustration of social obligation—these organizations simply follow the legal requirements to prevent pollution and protect the environment.

As an organization becomes more sensitive to environmental issues, it may adopt the *market approach,* where organizations respond to the environmental preferences of their customers. Whatever customers demand in terms of environmentally friendly products will be what the organization provides. For example, DuPont developed a new type of herbicide that helped farmers around the world reduce their annual use of chemicals by more than 20 million kilograms. By developing this product, the company was responding to the demands of its customers (farmers) who wanted to minimize the use of chemicals on their crops.

Organizations that follow the *stakeholder approach* work to meet the environmental demands of multiple stakeholders such as employees, suppliers, and the community. For instance, Hewlett-Packard has several corporate environmental programs in place for its supply chain (suppliers), product design and product recycling (customers and society), and work operations (employees and community). Both the market approach and the stakeholder approach are good illustrations of social responsiveness.

Richard Kouwenhoven, manager of digital services of Burnaby, BC-based Hemlock Printers, founded by his father, has been one of the leaders in his generation's push to have the company, already known for its green practices, become a leader in sustainable paper use.

Finally, if an organization pursues an *activist* (also called a *dark green*) *approach,* it looks for ways to respect and preserve the earth and its natural resources. Organizations that follow the activist approach exhibit the highest degree of environmental sensitivity. For example, Ecover, a Belgian company that produces cleaning products from natural soaps and renewable raw materials, operates a near-zero-emissions factory. This ecological factory is an environmentally sound engineering marvel with a huge grass roof that keeps the factory cool in summer and warm in winter, and a water treatment system that runs on wind and solar energy. The company chose to build this type of facility because of its deep commitment to protecting and preserving the environment. The activist approach is a good illustration of corporate social responsibility.

Evaluating the Greening of Management

As organizations become "greener," we find more and more of them issuing detailed reports on their environmental performance, many of them through the guidelines developed by the

Global Reporting Initiative
www.globalreporting.org

Global Reporting Initiative (GRI). Founded in 1997, the GRI is an independent entity that develops and disseminates globally applicable Sustainability Reporting Guidelines. Using G3 guidelines (reporting principles, reporting guidance, and standard disclosures), over 1000 organizations around the globe voluntarily report their efforts in promoting environmental sustainability.[35] These reports, which can be found in the database on the GRI website, describe the numerous "green" actions these organizations are pursuing.

Another way that organizations can show their commitment to being green is by adopting ISO 14001 standards. The nongovernmental ISO (International Organization for Standardization) is the world's largest developer of standards. Although ISO has developed more than 15 000 international standards, it's probably best known for its ISO 9000 (quality management) and ISO 14000 (environmental management) standards. Organizations that want to become ISO 14000 compliant must develop a total environmental management system for meeting environmental challenges. This means that the organization must minimize the effects of its activities on the environment and continually improve its environmental performance. If the organization can meet these standards, it can state that it is ISO 14001 compliant. Although these standards are voluntary, over 760 000 organizations in 154 countries have implemented ISO 9000 and ISO 14000 standards. In addition to its environmental management standards, the ISO is developing an international standard to be released in 2008 that will provide guidelines for social responsibility. This voluntary standard, which will be known as ISO 26000, will not include requirements, so organizations will not be able to become "certified" if they meet the standards. However, ISO believes that organizations that meet these guidelines will demonstrate that they are behaving in a socially responsible way that meets the "generalized requirements of society."[36]

Global 100 Most Sustainable Corporations in the World
www.global100.org

The final way to evaluate whether a company is "green" is by its inclusion in the list of the Global 100 Most Sustainable Corporations in the World, a project that was launched in 2005 as a collaboration between the Toronto-based media company Corporate Knights and the research firm Innovest Strategic Value Advisers. To be named to this list, a company must have displayed an ability to effectively manage environmental and social factors. The companies that comprise the Global 100 are announced each year at the renowned World Economic Forum in Davos, Switzerland. The Canadian companies on the 2007 list were Montreal-based Alcan, Calgary-based Enbridge, Toronto-based Royal Bank of Canada, Toronto-based Sun Life Financial, and Calgary-based TransCanada Pipelines.[37]

Values-Based Management

▶ ▶ ▶ Syncrude Canada practises values-based management.[38] As part of its values, the company "is committed to a strong local economy and the development of local businesses and local aboriginal businesses." Because of these values, Syncrude solicits business with local Aboriginal businesses, and "all things being equal, preference [is] given first to local aboriginal businesses." In 2006, Syncrude spent $132 million on 27 active contracts with Aboriginal firms in the Wood Buffalo region of Alberta. Syncrude representatives also held more than 130 direct meetings with Aboriginal stakeholders that year to discuss "employment opportunities, land reclamation and environmental stewardship, and ways in which Syncrude [could] support community objectives for such things as education, training and community enhancement."

Think About It

Does Syncrude's policy of giving preference to local Aboriginal businesses, all things being equal, create disadvantages for other local companies? What might be the pros and cons of such a policy?

4. How do values influence management?

values-based management
An approach to managing in which managers establish and uphold an organization's shared values.

Values-based management is an approach to managing in which managers establish and uphold an organization's shared values. An organization's values reflect what it stands for and what it believes in. As we discussed in Chapter 2, the shared organizational values form the organization's culture and serve many purposes.[39]

Vancouver-based Mountain Equipment Co-op (MEC) practises values-based management. MEC passionately pursues environmental preservation. Its strong environmental commitment influences employees' actions and decisions in areas such as product design, manufacturing, marketing, shipping, and store design. For instance, in designing its store in Montreal, the company favoured using recycled building materials.[40] Although contractors quoted cheaper prices for using new material, MEC held out, to be consistent with the company's values.

Purposes of Shared Values

Exhibit 4-5 shows the four purposes of shared organizational values. One purpose is to guide managers' decisions and actions.[41] For instance, at Tom's of Maine, a manufacturer of all-natural personal care products, the corporate Statement of Beliefs guides managers as they plan, organize, lead, and control. One of the company's eight beliefs states, "We believe that different people bring different gifts and perspectives to the team and that a strong team is founded on a variety of gifts."[42] This statement expresses to managers the value of diversity—diversity of opinions, diversity of abilities—and serves as a guide for managing teams of people. Another belief states, "We believe in products that are safe, effective, and made of natural ingredients." Again, think how this statement might influence and guide company managers.

A second purpose of shared values is to shape employee behaviour by communicating what the organization expects of its members. Shared values also influence marketing efforts. Finally, shared values are a way to build team spirit in an organization.[43] When employees embrace the stated organizational values, they develop a deeper personal commitment to their work and feel obligated to take responsibility for their actions. Because the shared values influence the way work is done, employees become more enthusiastic about working together as a team to support the values they believe in. At companies such as Bolton, Ontario-based Husky Injection Molding, Vancouver-based Weyerhaeuser, Vancouver-based Vancity, Toronto-based Home Depot Canada, and numerous others, employees know what is expected of them on the job. The shared organizational values not only guide the way they work, but serve to unite them in a common quest. Just how do shared organizational values affect employee actions? They can promote employee loyalty in a hot job market, as the following *Management Reflection* shows.

When Mountain Equipment Co-op opened its first Montreal store in 2003, the building was the first in Quebec to meet Natural Resource Canada's C-2000 standard. The store is much more energy efficient than conventional retail buildings. The building was made with reused building materials; and water for toilet flushing and landscape irrigation comes from roof water runoff. MEC has a high commitment to social and environmental responsibility, and its products come from factories that meet high labour, health, and safety standards.

Q&A 4.3

Exhibit 4-5

Purposes of Shared Values

SHARED ORGANIZATIONAL VALUES

Guide Managers' Decisions and Actions

Shape Employee Behaviour

Influence Marketing Efforts

Build Team Spirit

Pacific Insight Electronics Values Its Employees

Can strong corporate values make a difference?   With a strong economy and a short-age of workers throughout British Columbia, it's not easy for companies to attract or retain employees.[44] But Nelson, BC-based Pacific Insight Electronics (PI) has no trouble find-ing people who want to work for the company. PI finished at number 11 in *BCBusiness*'s Top 25 Best Companies to Work For in BC in 2006.

Employees praise the company for its strong corporate values related to "team-work, respect, integrity, productivity and communication." The company is also praised for living by the Golden Rule: "Treat people how you want to be treated," says human resource manager Amanda Laurie.

Employees receive birthdays off with pay, turkeys at Thanksgiving, and Christmas par-ties, which all help support the idea that they are treated well. The company also tries to provide flexibility for employees' personal needs by offering full- and part-time work. They also have a parent shift for those who need more options to manage their family lives. Even student schedules are considered. "We hire students for the summer, hire them back at Christmas…we work around their courses," says Laurie.

The company has a policy of promoting from within. Employees may start as pro-duction assistants, but they can advance to any number of other positions over time. "We have a lot of career paths," says Laurie.

Ultimately, PI's strong corporate values have contributed to the company's success. In 2006, the company doubled the previous year's earnings, achieving a record profit of $2.9 million. ∎

Managerial Ethics

▶ ▶ ▶ Like many companies today, Syncrude Canada has an ethics policy. The policy affirms the company's intention to act ethically in all its dealings, and is guided by the following six prin-ciples:[45]

- We have the courage and conviction to do what is right.
- We lead with courage and wisdom, being ethical in all our endeavours and accountable for our actions.
- We interact with care, honesty, and respect.
- We uphold the dignity and worth of everyone involved in our relationships with each other, our community, and the environment.
- We continuously improve.
- We seize opportunities to learn, and actively apply those learnings in order to continuously improve in every aspect of our business.

Think About It

How would you expect a code of ethics to be related to a company's social responsibility deci-sions? How would you design a code of ethics for a company that decides it wants to develop socially responsible policies toward the Aboriginal community?

5. What is ethics and how can ethical behaviour be encouraged?

Managers—at all levels, in all areas, and in all kinds of organizations—will face ethical issues and dilemmas. As managers plan, organize, lead, and control, they must consider eth-ical dimensions.

What do we mean by ethics? As you may recall from Chapter 1, **ethics** refers to rules and principles that define right and wrong behaviour.[46] In this section, we examine the ethical dimensions of managerial decisions. Many decisions that managers make require them to consider who may be affected—in terms of the result as well as the process.[47] To better understand the complicated issues involved in managerial ethics, we look at four different views of ethics and the factors that influence a person's ethics, and offer some suggestions for what organizations can do to improve the ethical behaviour of employees.

ethics
Rules and principles that define right and wrong behaviour.

Q&A 4.4

Four Views of Ethics

There are four views of ethics: the utilitarian view, the rights view, the theory of justice view, and the integrative social contracts theory.[48]

The Utilitarian View of Ethics

The **utilitarian view of ethics** says that ethical decisions are made solely on the basis of their outcomes or consequences. Utilitarian theory uses a quantitative method for making ethical decisions by looking at how to provide the greatest good for the greatest number. Following the utilitarian view, a manager might conclude that laying off 20 percent of the workforce in her plant is justified because it will increase the plant's profitability, improve job security for the remaining 80 percent, and be in the best interest of stockholders. Utilitarianism encourages efficiency and productivity and is consistent with the goal of profit maximization. However, it can result in biased allocations of resources, especially when some of those affected by the decision lack representation or a voice in the decision. Utilitarianism can also result in the rights of some stakeholders being ignored.

utilitarian view of ethics
A view of ethics that says that ethical decisions are made solely on the basis of their outcomes or consequences.

The Rights View of Ethics

The **rights view of ethics** is concerned with respecting and protecting individual liberties and privileges such as the rights to privacy, freedom of conscience, free speech, life and safety, and due process. This would include, for example, protecting the free speech rights of employees who report legal violations by their employers. The positive side of the rights perspective is that it protects individuals' basic rights, but the drawback is that it can hinder productivity and efficiency by creating a work climate that is more concerned with protecting individuals' rights than with getting the job done. For instance, an individual's right to privacy might make it difficult to make special arrangements for employees who have an illness that prevents them from carrying out all of their job responsibilities.

rights view of ethics
A view of ethics that is concerned with respecting and protecting individual liberties and privileges.

The Theory of Justice View of Ethics

According to the **theory of justice view of ethics**, managers impose and enforce rules fairly and impartially and do so by following all legal rules and regulations. A manager following this view would decide to provide the same rate of pay to individuals who are similar in their levels of skills, performance, or responsibility and not base that decision on arbitrary differences such as gender, personality, race, or personal favourites. Using standards of justice also has pluses and minuses. It protects the interests of those stakeholders who may be underrepresented or lack power, but it can encourage a sense of entitlement that might make employees reduce risk-taking, innovation, and productivity.

theory of justice view of ethics
A view of ethics in which managers impose and enforce rules fairly and impartially and do so by following all legal rules and regulations.

The Integrative Social Contracts Theory

The **integrative social contracts theory** proposes that ethical decisions be based on existing ethical norms in industries and communities in order to determine what constitutes right and wrong. This view of ethics is based on the integration of two "contracts": the general social contract that allows businesses to operate and defines the acceptable ground rules, and a more specific contract among members of a community that addresses acceptable ways of behaving. For instance, in deciding what wage to pay employees in a new factory in Ciudad Juarez, Mexico, Canadian managers following the integrative social contracts theory would base the decision on existing wage levels in the community, rather than paying what Canadians might consider a "fair wage" in that situation. Although this theory focuses on looking at existing practices, the problem is that some of these practices may be unethical.[49]

integrative social contracts theory
A view of ethics that proposes that ethical decisions be based on existing ethical norms in industries and communities in order to determine what constitutes right and wrong.

Which approach to ethics do most businesspeople follow? Not surprisingly, most follow the utilitarian approach.[50] Why? It's consistent with such business goals as efficiency, productivity, and profits. However, that perspective needs to change because the world facing managers is changing. Trends toward individual rights, social justice, and community standards mean that managers need ethical standards based on nonutilitarian criteria. This is an obvious challenge for managers because making decisions on such criteria involves far more ambiguities than using utilitarian criteria such as efficiency and profits. The result, of course, is that managers increasingly find themselves struggling with the question of the right thing to do. The *CBC Video Case Incident—Stem Cell Research* on page 133 looks at some of the ethical questions surrounding stem cell research.

Factors That Affect Employee Ethics

Whether a person acts ethically or unethically when faced with an ethical dilemma is the result of complex interactions between their stage of moral development and several moderating variables including individual characteristics, the organization's structural design, organizational culture, and the intensity of the ethical issue (see Exhibit 4-6). People who lack a strong moral sense are much less likely to do the wrong things if they are constrained by rules, policies, job descriptions, or strong cultural norms that disapprove of such behaviours. Conversely, intensely moral individuals can be corrupted by an organizational structure and culture that permits or encourages unethical practices. Let's look more closely at the factors that influence whether individuals will behave ethically or unethically.

Stage of Moral Development

Research confirms the existence of three levels of moral development, each composed of two stages.[51] At each successive stage, an individual's moral judgment becomes less and less dependent on outside influences. The three levels and six stages are described in Exhibit 4-7.

The first level is labelled *preconventional*. At this level, a person's choice between right and wrong is based on the personal consequences involved, such as physical punishment, reward, or exchange of favours. Ethical reasoning at the *conventional* level indicates that moral values reside in maintaining expected standards and living up to the expectations of others. At the *principled* level, individuals make a clear effort to define ethical principles apart from the authority of the groups to which they belong or society in general.

We can draw some conclusions from research on the levels and stages of moral development.[52] First, people proceed through the six stages sequentially. They move up the moral ladder, stage by stage. Second, there is no guarantee of continued moral development. An individual's moral development can stop at any stage. Third, the majority of adults are at stage 4. They are limited to obeying the rules and will be inclined to behave ethically,

Exhibit 4-6

Factors That Affect Ethical and Unethical Behaviour

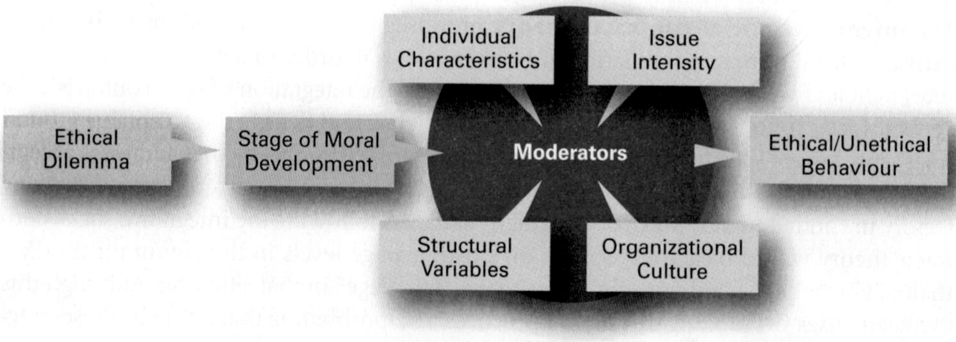

Exhibit 4-7

Stages of Moral Development

Level		Description of Stage
	Principled	6. Following self-chosen ethical principles even if they violate the law
		5. Valuing rights of others and upholding absolute values and rights regardless of the majority's opinion
	Conventional	4. Maintaining conventional order by fulfilling obligations to which you have agreed
		3. Living up to what is expected by people close to you
Preconventional		2. Following rules only when doing so is in your immediate interest
		1. Sticking to rules to avoid physical punishment

Source: Based on L. Kohlberg, "Moral Stages and Moralization: The Cognitive-Development Approach," in *Moral Development and Behavior: Theory, Research, and Social Issues*, ed. T. Lickona (New York: Holt, Rinehart & Winston, 1976), pp. 34–35.

although for different reasons. For instance, a manager at stage 3 is likely to make decisions that will receive peer approval; a manager at stage 4 will try to be a "good corporate citizen" by making decisions that respect the organization's rules and procedures; and a stage 5 manager is likely to challenge organizational practices that he or she believes to be wrong.

Individual Characteristics

Every person joining an organization has a relatively entrenched set of **values**. Our values—developed at a young age from parents, teachers, friends, and others—represent basic convictions about what is right and wrong. Thus, managers in the same organization often possess very different personal values.[53] Although *values* and *stage of moral development* may seem similar, they are not. Values are broad and cover a wide range of issues; the stage of moral development is a measure of independence from outside influences.

values
Basic convictions about what is right and wrong.

Two personality variables also have been found to influence an individual's actions according to his or her beliefs about what is right or wrong: ego strength and locus of control. **Ego strength** is a personality measure of the strength of a person's convictions. People who score high on ego strength are likely to resist impulses to act unethically and instead follow their convictions. That is, individuals high in ego strength are more likely to do what they think is right. We would expect employees with high ego strength to be more consistent in their moral judgments and actions than those with low ego strength.

ego strength
A personality measure of the strength of a person's convictions.

Locus of control is a personality attribute that reflects the degree to which people believe they control their own fate. People with an *internal* locus of control believe that they control their own destinies; those with an *external* locus believe that what happens to them is due to luck or chance. How does this influence a person's decision to act ethically or unethically? Externals are less likely to take personal responsibility for the consequences of their behaviour and are more likely to rely on external forces to guide their actions. Internals, on the other hand, are more likely to take responsibility for consequences and rely on their own internal standards of right and wrong to guide their actions.[54] Also, employees with an internal locus of control are likely to be more consistent in their moral judgments and actions than those with an external locus of control.

locus of control
A personality attribute that reflects the degree to which people believe they control their own fate.

Structural Variables

An organization's structural design influences whether employees behave ethically. Some structures provide strong guidance, whereas others create ambiguity and uncertainty. Structural designs that minimize ambiguity and uncertainty through formal rules and regulations and those that continuously remind employees of what is ethical are more likely to encourage ethical behaviour.

Other organizational mechanisms that influence ethics include performance appraisal systems and reward allocation procedures. Some organizational performance appraisal systems focus exclusively on outcomes, such as number of sales. Others evaluate means as well as ends, such as how customer-oriented employees are when customers speak with them. When employees are evaluated only on outcomes, they may be pressured to do "whatever is necessary" to look good on the outcome variables, and not be concerned with how they got those results. Recent research suggests that "success may serve to excuse unethical behaviors."[55] Just think of the impact of this type of thinking. The danger is that if managers take a more lenient view of unethical behaviours for successful employees, other employees will model their behaviour on what they see.

Closely associated with the performance appraisal system is the way rewards are allocated. The more that rewards or punishments depend on specific goal outcomes, the more pressure there is on employees to do whatever they must to reach those goals and perhaps compromise their ethical standards. Although these structural factors are important influences on employees, they are not the most important. What *is* the most important?

Research continues to show that the behaviour of managers is the single most important influence on an individual's decision to act ethically or unethically.[56] People look to see what those in authority are doing and use that as a benchmark for acceptable practices and expectations.

Organizational Culture

The content and strength of an organization's culture also influence ethical behaviour.[57] An organizational culture most likely to encourage high ethical standards is one that is high in risk tolerance, control, and conflict tolerance. Employees in such a culture are encouraged to be aggressive and innovative, are aware that unethical practices will be discovered, and feel free to openly challenge expectations they consider to be unrealistic or personally undesirable.

Q&A 4.5

As we discussed in Chapter 2, a strong culture will exert more influence on employees than a weak one. If the culture is strong and supports high ethical standards, it has a very powerful and positive influence on an employee's decision to act ethically or unethically. The Boeing Company, for example, has a strong culture that has long stressed ethical dealings with customers, employees, the community, and stockholders. To reinforce the importance of ethical behaviours, the company developed a series of serious and thought-provoking posters designed to get employees to recognize that their individual decisions and actions are important to the way the organization is viewed. (See the following examples.)

Boeing
www.boeing.com

The Boeing Company's imaginative poster series reinforces the core values of integrity and ethical behaviour for its employees.

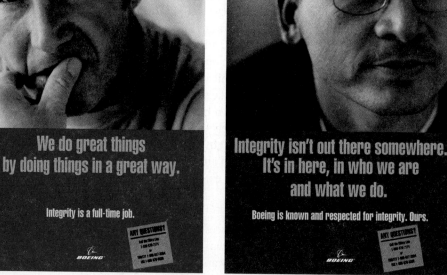

Issue Intensity

A student who would never consider breaking into an instructor's office to steal an accounting exam does not think twice about asking a friend who took the same course from the same instructor last semester what questions were on the exam. Similarly, a manager might think nothing about taking home a few office supplies yet be highly concerned about the possible embezzlement of company funds.

These examples illustrate the final factor that affects a manager's ethical behaviour: the intensity of the ethical issue itself.[58] As Exhibit 4-8 shows, six characteristics determine issue intensity: greatness of harm, consensus of wrong, probability of harm, immediacy of consequences, proximity to victim(s), and concentration of effect.[59] These six factors determine how important an ethical issue is to an individual. According to these guidelines, the larger the number of people harmed, the more agreement that the action is wrong, the greater the likelihood that the action will cause harm, the more immediately that the consequences of the action will be felt, the closer the person feels to the victim(s), and the more concentrated the effect of the action on the victim(s), the greater the issue intensity. When an ethical issue is important—that is, the more intense it is—the more we should expect employees to behave ethically.

Ethics in an International Context

Are ethical standards universal? Hardly! Social and cultural differences between countries are important factors that determine ethical and unethical behaviour. For example, the manager of a Mexican firm bribes several high-ranking government officials in Mexico City to secure a profitable government contract. Such a practice would be seen as unethical, if not illegal, in Canada, but is standard business practice in Mexico.

Q&A 4.6

Should Canadian companies operating in Saudi Arabia adhere to Canadian ethical standards, or should they follow local standards of acceptable behaviour? If Airbus (a European company) pays a "broker's fee" to a middleman to get a major contract with a Middle Eastern airline, should Montreal-based Bombardier be restricted from doing the same because such practices are considered improper in Canada?

In Canada and many other Western countries, engaging in bribery to conduct business in one's home country is considered unethical and often illegal. Bribing foreign public

Exhibit 4-8

Determinants of Issue Intensity

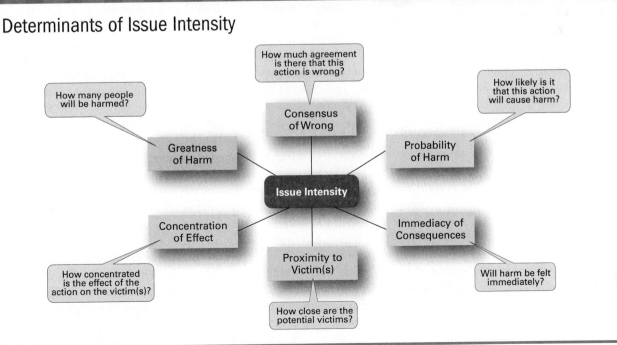

TIPS FOR MANAGERS

The Global Compact

Human Rights

Principle 1: Businesses should support and respect the protection of international human rights within their sphere of influence; and

Principle 2: make sure that they are not complicit in human rights abuses.

Labour Standards

Principle 3: Businesses should uphold the freedom of association and the effective recognition of the right to collective bargaining;

Principle 4: the elimination of all forms of forced and compulsory labour;

Principle 5: the effective abolition of child labour; and

Principle 6: the elimination of discrimination in respect of employment and occupation.

Environment

Principle 7: Businesses should support a precautionary approach to environmental challenges;

Principle 8: undertake initiatives to promote greater environmental responsibility; and

Principle 9: encourage the development and diffusion of environmentally friendly technologies.

Anti-Corruption

Principle 10: Businesses should work against corruption in all its forms, including extortion and bribery.

Source: United Nations Global Compact website, http://www.unglobalcompact.org (accessed July 11, 2007).

officials is widespread, however. The US government found bribery in more than 400 competitions for international contracts between 1994 and 2001.[60] Another study found that some Asian governments were far more tolerant of corruption than others. Singapore, Japan, and Hong Kong scored relatively low on corruption (0.83, 2.5, and 3.77 out of 10, respectively), while Vietnam, Indonesia, India, the Philippines, and Thailand scored as the most corrupt of the 12 Asian countries surveyed.[61]

Canada has no national laws regarding codes of ethics, although a coalition of Canadian companies developed an international code of ethics in 1997.[62] The code is voluntary and deals with issues such as the environment, human rights, business conduct, treatment of employees, and health and safety standards. Supporters of the Canadian code include the Alliance of Manufacturers & Exporters Canada, the Conference Board of Canada, and the Canadian Council of Chief Executives (formerly the Business Council on National Issues). Montreal-based Rio Tinto Alcan, Calgary-based Komex International, Shell Canada, and Talisman Energy are among the companies that have signed the code. Former foreign affairs minister and current president of the University of Winnipeg, Lloyd Axworthy viewed the code as a way of putting Canadian values into the international arena.[63] It's important for individual managers working in foreign cultures to recognize the various social, cultural, and political and legal influences on what is appropriate and acceptable behaviour.[64] And global organizations must clarify their ethical guidelines so that employees know what is expected of them while working in a foreign location, which adds another dimension to making ethical judgments.

At the World Economic Forum in 1999, the United Nations secretary-general challenged world business leaders to "embrace and enact" the Global Compact, a document outlining 10 principles for doing business globally in the areas of human rights, labour, and the environment.[65] These principles are listed in *Tips for Managers—The Global Compact*. Global organizations have been asked to incorporate these guidelines into their business activities. The goal: a more sustainable and inclusive global economy. Today, over 3000 companies and international labour organizations from all regions of the world participate in the Global Compact. Organizations that make a commitment to the Global Compact and its 10 principles do so because they believe that the world business community plays a significant role in improving economic and social conditions.

Improving Ethical Behaviour

Managers can do a number of things if they are serious about reducing unethical behaviour in their organizations. They can seek to hire individuals with high ethical standards, establish codes of ethics and rules for decisions, lead by example, delineate job goals and undertake performance appraisals, provide ethics training, conduct independent social audits, and support individuals facing ethical dilemmas. Taken individually, these actions will probably not have much impact. But when all or most of them are implemented as part of a comprehensive ethics program, they have the potential to significantly improve an organization's ethical climate. The key term here, however, is *potential*. There are no guarantees that a well-designed ethics program will lead to the desired outcome. Sometimes corporate ethics programs can be little more than public relations gestures, having minimal influence on managers and employees. For instance, retailer Sears has a long history of encouraging ethical business practices and, in fact, has a corporate Office of Compliance and Ethics.

However, the company's ethics programs did not stop managers from illegally trying to collect payments from bankrupt charge-account holders or from routinely deceiving automotive–service centre customers in California into thinking they needed unnecessary repairs. (To help you think more about your own ethics, see *Self-Assessment—How Do My Ethics Rate?* on pages 122–123, at the end of the chapter.)

Employee Selection

Given that individuals are at different stages of moral development and possess different personal value systems and personalities, the selection process—interviews, tests, background checks, and so forth—could be used to eliminate ethically questionable applicants. The selection process should be viewed as an opportunity to learn about an individual's level of moral development, personal values, ego strength, and locus of control.[66] But it isn't easy! Even under the best circumstances, individuals with questionable standards of right and wrong will be hired. However, this should not be a problem if other ethics controls are in place.

Codes of Ethics and Rules for Decisions

Toronto-based Royal Bank of Canada has had a corporate code of conduct for more than 25 years. Christina Donely, the bank's senior adviser on employee relations and policy governance, says that the code "focuses on outlining behaviours that support honesty and integrity … and covers environmental [and] social issues."[67] However, that is not the way it is in all organizations. The US government passed the Sarbanes-Oxley Act in 2002 to crack down on business wrongdoing in publicly traded companies. Following the American example, the Canadian Securities Administrators put into effect best corporate governance practices in March 2004, although these are not as tough as the American rules.[68] As well, the securities regulators of the 10 provinces and 3 territories have proposed that all public companies adopt written codes of ethics and conduct, or explain why they do not have one.[69] But these proposals carry no enforcement requirements or mechanisms.

Ambiguity about what is and is not ethical can be a problem for employees. A **code of ethics**, a formal statement of an organization's primary values and the ethical rules it expects its employees to follow, is a popular choice for reducing that ambiguity. About 60 percent of Canada's 650 largest corporations have some sort of ethics code. Codes of ethics are also becoming more popular globally. A survey of business organizations in 22 countries found that 78 percent have formally stated ethics standards and codes of ethics.[70]

What should a code of ethics look like? It's been suggested that codes should be specific enough to show employees the spirit in which they are supposed to do things yet loose enough to allow for freedom of judgment.[71] A survey of companies' codes of ethics found their content tended to fall into three categories: (1) Be a dependable organizational citizen; (2) don't do anything unlawful or improper that will harm the organization; and (3) be good to customers.[72]

How well do codes of ethics work? In reality, they are not always effective in encouraging ethical behaviour in organizations. While no comparable Canadian data are available, a survey of employees in US businesses with ethics codes found that 75 percent of those surveyed had observed ethical or legal violations in the previous 12 months, including such things as deceptive sales practices, unsafe working conditions, sexual harassment, conflicts of interest, and environmental violations.[73] These findings suggest that companies with codes of ethics may not do enough monitoring. For instance, David Nitkin, president of Toronto-based EthicScan Canada, an ethics consultancy, notes that "only about 15% of [larger Canadian corporations with codes of ethics] have designated an ethics officer or ombudsman" or provide an ethics hotline, and that less than 10 percent offer whistleblower protection.[74] Vancouver public employees were concerned enough about whistleblower protection that it was one of the major stumbling blocks in reaching an agreement for a new collective agreement in summer 2007, leading to a 12-week strike.

Does this mean that codes of ethics should not be developed? No. But there are some suggestions managers can follow. First, an organization's code of ethics should be developed and then communicated clearly to employees. Second, all levels of management should

Royal Bank of Canada
www.rbc.com

code of ethics
A formal statement of an organization's primary values and the ethical rules it expects its employees to follow.

EthicScan Canada
www.ethicscan.ca

continually affirm the importance of the code of ethics and the organization's commitment to it, and consistently discipline those who break it. When managers consider the code of ethics important, regularly affirm its content, and publicly reprimand rule breakers, a code of ethics can supply a strong foundation for an effective corporate ethics program.[75] Finally, an organization's code of ethics might be designed around the 12 questions listed in Exhibit 4-9, which can be used to guide managers as they handle ethical dilemmas in decision making.[76]

Ethical Leadership

PRISM 4

Doing business ethically requires a commitment from top managers. Why? Because it's the top managers who uphold the shared values and set the cultural tone. They are role models in terms of both words and actions, although what they *do* is far more important than what they *say*. If top managers, for example, take company resources for their personal use, inflate their expense accounts, or give favoured treatment to friends, they imply that such behaviour is acceptable for all employees. (To learn more about how trust works, see *Developing Your Interpersonal Skills—Building Trust* on pages 126–127, at the end of the chapter.)

Top managers also set the cultural tone by their reward and punishment practices. The choices of who and what are rewarded with pay increases and promotions send a strong signal to employees. As we said earlier, when an employee is rewarded for achieving impressive results in an ethically questionable manner, it indicates to others that those ways are acceptable. When wrongdoing is uncovered, managers who want to emphasize their commitment to doing business ethically must punish the offender and publicize the fact by making the outcome visible to everyone in the organization. This practice sends a message that doing wrong has a price and it's not in employees' best interests to act unethically!

A 2002 ethics survey by KPMG found that 82 percent of Canadian organizations had initiatives that promoted ethical practices, and about 56 percent had a senior manager responsible for handling ethical issues.[77]

Exhibit 4-9

12 Questions Examining the Ethics of a Business Decision

1. Have you defined the problem accurately?

2. How would you define the problem if you stood on the other side of the fence?

3. How did this situation occur in the first place?

4. To whom and to what do you give your loyalty as a person and as a member of the corporation?

5. What is your intention in making this decision?

6. How does this intention compare with the probable results?

7. Whom could your decision or action injure?

8. Can you discuss the problem with the affected parties before you make the decision?

9. Are you confident that your position will be as valid over a long period of time as it seems now?

10. Could you disclose without qualm your decision or action to your boss, your chief executive officer, the board of directors, your family, society as a whole?

11. What is the symbolic potential of your action if understood? If misunderstood?

12. Under what conditions would you allow exceptions to your stand?

Source: Reprinted by permission of *Harvard Business Review*. An exhibit from "Ethics Without the Sermon" by L. L. Nash. November–December 1981, p. 81. Copyright © 1981 by the President and Fellows of Harvard College. All rights reserved.

Job Goals and Performance Appraisal

Employees in three Internal Revenue Service offices (the American equivalent of Canada Revenue Agency) were found in the washrooms flushing tax returns and other related documents down the toilets. When questioned, they openly admitted doing it, but offered an interesting explanation for their behaviour. The employees' supervisors had been putting increasing pressure on them to complete more work in less time. If the piles of tax returns were not processed and moved off their desks more quickly, they were told, their performance reviews and salary raises would be adversely affected. Frustrated by few resources and an overworked computer system, the employees decided to "flush away" the paperwork on their desks. Although these employees knew what they did was wrong, it illustrates the impact of unrealistic goals and performance appraisals on behaviour.[78] Under the stress of unrealistic job goals, otherwise ethical employees may feel they have no choice but to do whatever is necessary to meet those goals.

Ethical leadership starts with being a good role model. When Reuben Mark, CEO of Colgate-Palmolive, found himself unexpectedly in possession of proprietary information about competitor Dial Corporation, he returned it, unread and unopened, to Dial's CEO.

Whether an individual achieves his or her job goals is usually a key issue in performance appraisal. Keep in mind, though, that if performance appraisals focus only on economic goals, ends will begin to justify means. If an organization wants its employees to uphold high ethical standards, the performance appraisal process should include this dimension. For example, a manager's annual review of employees might include a point-by-point evaluation of how their decisions measured up against the company's code of ethics, as well as how well job goals were met.

Ethics Training

More and more organizations are setting up seminars, workshops, and similar ethics training programs to encourage ethical behaviour. A 2002 ethics survey by KPMG found that 71 percent of Canadian provided ethics training (up from 21 percent in 1997), although most provided fewer than eight hours per year.[79] But these training programs are not without controversy. The primary debate is whether you can actually teach ethics. Critics, for instance, stress that the effort is pointless because people establish their individual value systems when they are young. Proponents, however, note that several studies have found that values can be learned after early childhood. In addition, they cite evidence that shows that teaching ethical problem solving can make an actual difference in ethical behaviours;[80] that training has increased individuals' level of moral development;[81] and that, if it does nothing else, ethics training increases awareness of ethical issues in business.[82]

Q&A 4.7

Ethics training sessions can provide a number of benefits.[83] They reinforce the organization's standards of conduct. They are a reminder that top managers want employees to consider ethical issues in making decisions. They clarify what practices are and are not acceptable. Finally, when employees discuss common concerns among themselves, they get reassurance that they are not alone in facing ethical dilemmas, which can strengthen their confidence when they have to take unpopular but ethically correct stances.

Independent Social Audits

An important element of deterring unethical behaviour is the fear of being caught. Independent social audits, which evaluate decisions and management practices in terms of the organization's code of ethics, increase the likelihood of detection. These social audits can be routine evaluations, performed on a regular basis just as financial audits are, or they can occur randomly with no prior announcement. An effective ethical program should probably have both. To maintain integrity, auditors should be responsible to the company's board of directors and present their findings directly to the board. This arrangement gives the auditors clout and lessens the opportunity for retaliation from those being audited.

Chief Superintendent Fraser Macaulay was one of several RCMP officers who complained to Giuliano Zaccardelli, then RCMP commissioner, about how problems with the RCMP's pension and insurance plans were investigated. Consistent with the way many whistle-blowers are treated, Zaccardelli did not follow up with an investigation, and Macaulay was told that he "was on an island by [him]self."

Formal Protective Mechanisms

Q&A 4.8 Our last recommendation is for organizations to provide formal mechanisms to protect employees who face ethical dilemmas so that they can do what is right without fear of reprimand. An organization might designate ethics counsellors. When employees face an ethics dilemma, they could go to these advisers for guidance. As a sounding board, the ethics counsellor would let employees openly state their ethics problem, the problem's cause, and their own options. After the options are clear, the adviser might take on the role of advocate who champions the ethically "right" alternatives. Other organizations have appointed ethics officers who design, direct, and modify the organization's ethics programs as needed.

It is important that managers assure employees who raise ethical concerns or issues to others inside or outside the organization that they will face no personal or career risks. These individuals, often called **whistle-blowers**, can be a key part of any company's ethics program because they are willing to step forward and expose unethical behaviour, no matter what the cost, professional or personal. Former prime minister Paul Martin tabled the Public Servants Disclosure Protection Act in March 2004 to protect those who expose government wrongdoings and financial mismanagement. Many critics complained that the act does not go far enough to protect whistle-blowers, and hoped Parliament would have tabled a tougher bill.

whistle-blowers
Individuals who raise ethical concerns or issues to others inside or outside the organization.

SUMMARY AND IMPLICATIONS

1. What is corporate social responsibility?   We define corporate social responsibility as a business's obligation, beyond that required by law and economics, to pursue long-term goals that are good for society. Not everyone would agree that businesses have any responsibility to society. The classical view says that management's only responsibility is to maximize profits; stockholders, or owners, are the only legitimate concern. The socio-economic view says that management's responsibility goes beyond maximizing profits; any group affected by the organization's decisions and actions—that is, its stakeholders—are also its concern.

▶ ▶ ▶ Syncrude Canada takes a socio-economic view toward corporate social responsibility. The company emphasizes being a good neighbour to the Aboriginal community and helping to develop community members to become employees.

2. Can being socially responsible help performance? Some evidence suggests that socially responsible firms perform better, and they are certainly appreciated by many members of society. There is little evidence to say that a company's social actions hurt its long-term economic performance. Given political and societal pressures on business to be socially involved, managers would be wise to take social goals into consideration as they plan, organize, lead, and control.

▶ ▶ ▶ Syncrude has been able to be a successful company, even as it supports a socially responsible approach to doing business.

3. How do organizations go green? One model of environmental responsibility uses the phrase *shades of green* to describe the different approaches that organizations take to going green.[84] Organizations that follow a *legal* (or *light green*) *approach* simply do what is required legally. Organizations that follow a *market approach* respond to the environmental preferences of their customers. Organizations that follow a *stakeholder approach* work to meet the environmental demands of multiple stakeholders such as employees, suppliers, and the community. Organizations that follow an *activist* (also called a *dark green*) *approach* look for ways to respect and preserve the earth and its natural resources.

▶ ▶ ▶ Syncrude takes an activist approach to going green. The company has developed a variety of water recycling and conservation programs. It engages in energy conservation and tries to control greenhouse gas emissions. The company has re-established bison on land it once used as an open-pit mine. Syncrude is the industry leader in land reclamation.

4. How do values influence management? An organization's values reflect what it stands for and what it believes in. Thus, an organization's values are reflected in the decisions and actions of employees. Shared values form an organization's culture and serve to (a) guide managers' decisions and actions, (b) shape employee behaviour, (c) influence marketing efforts, and (d) build team spirit.

▶ ▶ ▶ Syncrude values its relationships with the Aboriginal community, and its policies reflect that.

5. What is ethics and how can ethical behaviour be encouraged? Ethics refers to rules and principles that define right and wrong behaviour. Ethical behaviour is encouraged (or discouraged) through organizational culture. A strong culture that supports ethical standards will have a powerful and positive influence on managers and employees. To improve ethical behaviour, managers can hire individuals with high ethical standards, design and implement a code of ethics, lead by example, delineate job goals and undertake performance appraisals, provide ethics training, perform independent social audits, and provide formal protective mechanisms for employees who face ethical dilemmas.

▶ ▶ ▶ Syncrude, like many companies, has an ethics policy to help guide the decisions and actions of its employees.

Management @ Work

READING FOR COMPREHENSION

1. Contrast the classical and socio-economic views of corporate social responsibility.

2. What role do stakeholders play in the four stages of corporate social responsibility?

3. Can being socially responsible help organizational performance?

4. What are the four approaches to going green?

5. What is values-based management?

6. How do the four views of ethics differ?

7. What factors affect the ethical and unethical behaviour of employees?

8. How can managers encourage ethical behaviour in their organizations?

LINKING CONCEPTS TO PRACTICE

1. What does social responsibility mean to you personally? Do you think business organizations should be socially responsible? Explain.

2. Do you think values-based management is just a "do-gooder" ploy? Explain your answer.

3. Internet file-sharing programs are popular among college and university students. These programs work by allowing anyone to access any local network where desired files are located. These programs can severely limit the use of local networks by those working at colleges and universities if many students are exchanging music and video files at any given time. There is also some question about whether sharing copyrighted files is legal. What ethical and social responsibilities does a college or university have in this situation? To whom does it have a responsibility? What guidelines might you suggest for campus decision makers?

4. What are some problems that could be associated with employee whistle-blowing for (a) the whistle-blower and (b) the organization?

5. Describe the characteristics and behaviours of someone you consider an ethical person. How could the types of decisions and actions this person engages in be encouraged in a workplace?

SELF-ASSESSMENT

How Do My Ethics Rate?

For each of the following statements, circle the level of agreement or disagreement that you personally feel:[85]

1 = Strongly Disagree
2 = Disagree
3 = Neither Agree nor Disagree
4 = Agree
5 = Strongly Agree

1. The only moral of business is making money.	1 2 3 4 5
2. A person who is doing well in business does not have to worry about moral problems.	1 2 3 4 5
3. Act according to the law, and you cannot go wrong morally.	1 2 3 4 5
4. Ethics in business is basically an adjustment between expectations and the ways people behave.	1 2 3 4 5
5. Business decisions involve a realistic economic attitude and not a moral philosophy.	1 2 3 4 5
6. "Business ethics" is a concept for public relations only.	1 2 3 4 5

7. Competitiveness and profitability are important values.   1 2 3 4 5

8. Conditions of a free economy will best serve the needs of society. Limiting competition can only hurt society and actually violates basic natural laws.   1 2 3 4 5

9. As a consumer, when making an auto insurance claim, I try to get as much as possible regardless of the extent of the damage.   1 2 3 4 5

10. While shopping at the supermarket, it is appropriate to switch price tags on packages.   1 2 3 4 5

11. As an employee, I can take home office supplies; it doesn't hurt anyone.   1 2 3 4 5

12. I view sick days as vacation days that I deserve.   1 2 3 4 5

13. Employees' wages should be determined according to the laws of supply and demand.   1 2 3 4 5

14. The business world has its own rules.   1 2 3 4 5

15. A good businessperson is a successful businessperson.   1 2 3 4 5

Scoring Key

Compare your scores on each statement against the mean (average) scores of management students (N = 243).

Analysis and Interpretation

In comparing your scores to those of the average of a set of management students, determine whether you score higher or lower than the average student. What does this say about your ethics compared to others?

Statement	Management Students Mean	Statement	Management Students Mean
1	3.09	9	3.44
2	1.88	10	1.33
3	2.54	11	1.58
4	3.41	12	2.31
5	3.88	13	3.36
6	2.88	14	3.79
7	3.62	15	3.38
8	3.79		

More Self-Assessments mymanagementlab

To learn more about your skills, abilities, and interests, go to the MyManagementLab website and take the following self-assessments:

- I.B.1.—What Do I Value?
- I.C.3.—What Rewards Do I Value Most? (This exercise also appears in Chapter 13 on pages 427–428.)
- III.B.1.—What's the Right Organizational Culture for Me? (This exercise also appears in Chapter 2 on pages 64–65.)

MANAGEMENT FOR YOU TODAY

Dilemma

What things are you willing to do in order to be a more socially responsible citizen? Are there things that would be easy for you to give up in order to help promote the use of less energy and less packaging? Are there things that you would not give up, even though doing so might mean a more green environment for others?

Becoming a Manager

- Clarify your own personal views on how much social responsibility you think an organization should have.
- Research different companies' codes of ethics.
- Think about the organizational values that are important to you.

- When faced with an ethical dilemma, use the 12 questions in Exhibit 4-9 on page 118 to help you make a decision.
- Work through the *Ethics in Action* dilemmas found in each chapter in this textbook.

WORKING TOGETHER: TEAM-BASED EXERCISE

Assessing Ethical and Unethical Behaviour

You have obviously already faced many ethical dilemmas in your life—at school, in social settings, and even at work. Form groups of 3 to 5 individuals. Appoint a spokesperson to present your group's findings to the class. Each member of the group is to think of some unethical behaviours he or she has observed in organizations. The incidents could be something experienced as an employee, customer, or client, or an action observed informally.

Once everyone has identified some examples of ethically questionable behaviours, the group should identify three impor-

tant criteria that could be used to determine whether a particular action is ethical. Think carefully about these criteria. They should differentiate between ethical and unethical behaviour. Write your choices down. Use these criteria to assess the examples of unethical behaviour described by group members.

When asked by your professor, the spokesperson should be ready to describe several of the incidents of unethical behaviour witnessed by group members, your criteria for differentiating between ethical and unethical behaviour, and how you used these criteria for assessing these incidents.

ETHICS IN ACTION

Ethical Dilemma Exercise: Can an Environmental Organization Balance Its Values with Making Money?

The Sierra Club lobbies for stricter antipollution regulations, pushes companies to use more eco-friendly products and techniques, and leads wilderness trips to promote appreciation for nature.[86] In short, the Sierra Club goes well beyond bare-minimum legal requirements by pursuing an activist approach to preserving the earth for future generations.

To raise money for its mission, the nonprofit recently began licensing its name for a broad array of products, including jackets, coffee, and toys. The organization receives royalties of 5 percent to 20 percent of each product's retail price, and the manufacturers must include environmental advocacy information with every item. "We can raise money even as we promote environmentally conscious consumption," explained the executive director.

Imagine you are a manager reporting to Johanna O'Kelley, Sierra Club's director of licensing. O'Kelley wants to increase the number of environmentally friendly products on which the club's name appears. You get a bonus for each positive recommendation you make, based on the retail price of the product. A manufacturer has just proposed a Sierra Club bed cover containing organically grown cotton and coloured with vegetable dyes. However, the cover will have to contain some synthetic fibres to keep threads of the filler from working their way through the top. Bed covers sell for a lot more money than the coffee mugs you recently recommended for the club's logo. Should you recommend that the bed cover be licensed? Review Exhibit 4-8 on page 115 as you think about this dilemma.

Thinking Critically About Ethics

In an effort to be (or at least appear to be) socially responsible, many organizations donate money to philanthropic and charitable causes. In addition, many organizations ask their employees to make individual donations to these causes. Suppose you are the manager of a work team, and you know that several of your employees cannot afford to pledge money right now because of various personal and financial prob-

lems. You have also been told by your supervisor that the CEO has been known to check the list of individual contributors to see who is and is not "supporting these very important causes." What would you do? What ethical guidelines might you suggest for individual and organizational contributions to philanthropic and charitable causes?

CASE APPLICATION

City of Ottawa

Many Ottawa residents and some city councillors were up in arms after Richard Hewitt, deputy city manager of Public Works and Services, and some councillors and city employees

were spotted at an Ottawa Senators game during the 2007 playoff season.[87] Hewitt and the others were seated in a corporate box owned by Waste Management of Canada.

Waste Management owns a dump at Carp Road, and wants to either expand the dump or build a new incinerator there. Changes to the Carp Road site need city hall approval. However, the plans are opposed by nearby residents, the mayor, and the councillors who live in wards near the dump.

Hewitt's department is in charge of garbage collection and disposal. While ultimate approval for what happens at Carp Road will come from Ontario's Ministry of the Environment, Hewitt is supposed to represent the city's interests in the landfill expansion application process. Concerned citizens wondered whether Waste Management offered the tickets to get favourable treatment from the city.

The City of Ottawa has a code of employee ethics that states, "Employees shall neither offer nor accept any gifts, favours, hospitality or entertainment that could reasonably be construed as being given in anticipation of future, or recognition of past, 'special consideration' by the city."

Is accepting hockey playoff tickets a violation of this policy? Some citizens and councillors spoke out:

- "Sounds like a conflict of interest to me. It looks as if they're accepting a bribe. It doesn't look good," said Vivian Katz, a local citizen.
- "I think they should be able to take a break from their stressful jobs, I don't see a conflict of interest," said Steve Birk, a local citizen.
- "The city's code of conduct says staff aren't supposed to receive benefits from the people we do business with. It's clear, and I think accepting valuable, hard-to-get playoff tickets is a clear violation of the code," said Alex Cullen, a city councillor.

Hewitt defended his behaviour, however. "I feel I am in line with the city policy. I try to be cognizant of the policy on all occasions. There's a certain business element to these situations."

The city's ethics policy outlines possible exceptions to the general guidelines to not accept gifts: "Hospitality may be acceptable within strict limits as a part of some reciprocal business relationships or to develop a network which is of benefit to the city. An employee may pay for or accept customary business hospitality, such as meals." The policy cautions that entertainment activities must "clearly be seen as legitimately serving a definite business purpose," and be "appropriately related to the responsibilities of the individual."

Hewitt and the city staff who were at the game are governed by the city's ethics policy. Councillors, however, are not. There was widespread disagreement about whether councillors should be covered by the policy. Councillors Clive Doucet, Diane Holmes, and Rainer Bloess argued that the rules should apply to staff and councillors alike. "What's good for the goose is good for the gander," Bloess said.

Mayor Larry O'Brien suggested that elected officials needed more leeway, however. He feared that a strict policy might discourage corporations from sponsoring city events. He noted that earlier in the year he had been in a company's luxury box for a Senators game. Later in the year, he phoned that company, which then paid for the big-screen televisions that were installed in Sens Plaza outside city hall for the Stanley Cup games. Citizens benefited by being able to watch the games in an enjoyable setting.

"Businesses do wonderful things for this community, and I think all councillors want to clarify the issues surrounding ethics," O'Brien said. "But we don't want to cut off our noses to spite our faces." Councillor Holmes disagrees. "Accepting things creates an obligation to return the favour. It's just human nature."

Are playoff tickets part of "the normal course of business?" Do such gifts influence a manager's decisions? Should elected officials be allowed to accept gifts of substantial value, and under what circumstances?

DEVELOPING YOUR DIAGNOSTIC AND ANALYTICAL SKILLS

You've Got Questions...

At Texas-based RadioShack Corporation, whose brand-positioning slogan reads, "You've Got Questions, We've Got Answers," the events of early February 2006 surely had the company's board of directors and top executives wondering whether the questions they had about former CEO David Edmondson would ever be answered to their satisfaction.[88] The problems began when the company's hometown newspaper, the Fort Worth Star-Telegram, ran a story by reporter Heather Landy that the "unaccredited bible college from which Mr. Edmondson claimed two degrees said he had not graduated." The paper also reported that its investigation showed that on two occasions, Edmondson had been charged with (but not convicted of) driving while intoxicated. In addition,

the paper reported that shortly after being named CEO, he was arrested on a third DWI (drinking while intoxicated) charge. "It was this last incident, scheduled to go to trial in April 2006, that had made the Star-Telegram sufficiently skeptical to begin checking out the local CEO."

Edmondson joined RadioShack in 1994, worked his way up the corporate ladder, and had been a senior executive since 1998. He served two years as senior vice-president before being named as the company's president and chief operating officer in 2000. When RadioShack's board of directors announced in January 2005 that CEO Len Roberts was transitioning out of the CEO position but would remain as the executive chairman of the board, it also announced that it had selected David

Edmondson as the new CEO. This CEO transition had been a planned succession, given that the two men had worked side-by-side for 10 years in revitalizing the company. Roberts had "always believed that one of the most important jobs of a CEO was to select, groom and mentor a successor," and he felt he had done that with the hiring of Edmondson. As the company's website stated, "From the first time he met Edmondson, Roberts instinctively knew that Edmondson had the potential to one day become the company's CEO." He mentored Edmondson, grooming him to take over the top spot someday.

When Roberts stepped down, Edmondson was named RadioShack's new CEO. During his 13 months' tenure in this position, the company struggled with flat sales and a lagging stock price. Three days after the newspaper story ran, Edmondson offered two apologies in a conference call with investors: one for the performance of the company and one for having lied about his educational background. He then announced a turnaround plan for the company that included the closing of 400 to 700 of the company's 7000 stores and dropping slow-moving products from its stores' inventory. He also reiterated that he was going to stay on as CEO. The stock market reacted with RadioShack's share price falling to a three-year low. In a later phone news conference that same day, Edmondson replied to a question about whether the company had fired other employees for submitting false résumés by stating, "I would not want to comment on that." He also refused to comment on whether his conduct violated the company's ethics code. At this point, RadioShack's board was still supporting its CEO.

However, by February 21, just days after he told investors that he intended to stay on as CEO, Edmondson had resigned. Board chairman Roberts announced the resignation, stating that it was a "tough decision," but a mutual decision between the board and Edmondson. He said, "When our company's credibility becomes based on a single individual, it is time for a change. One of the most important things we have as a corporation is integrity and trust. We have to restore that back to the company."

Although the situation at RadioShack certainly seems to have nowhere to go but up, new questions have been raised about the severance package Edmondson received. According to a regulatory filing, he received a cash payout worth at least $1.03 million (US) in addition to payments for accrued and unpaid vacation and salary. RadioShack did not state the total value of the severance package, which also included four months of insurance coverage and the right to exercise outstanding stock options and stock awards. An examination of the company's website at the time showed the following stated in bold print on the front cover of the company's code of ethics: "Revision 02.21.06."

Questions

1. Evaluate this situation from the viewpoint of David Edmondson's ethical leadership. What could RadioShack have done differently?

2. What stakeholders were likely affected by this situation? What concerns might each stakeholder have had? Were any of the stakeholders' concerns in conflict with each other? Explain. What effect might this situation have had on employees?

3. Do you think the board's decision to fire Edmondson was "tough," as Len Roberts suggested? Why or why not? Why do you think Roberts would have described this decision as such?

4. What impact do you think the company's severance package to Edmondson might have?

5. Could an organization ever prevent a situation like this from happening? Why or why not? What could they do? How could the company's code of ethics play a role? Go to the company's website (**www.radioshack.com**) and take a look at its code.

DEVELOPING YOUR INTERPERSONAL SKILLS

Building Trust

About the Skill

When individuals evaluate companies for their social responsibility policies, trust plays an important role in how the company is viewed. Trust is also important in the manager's relationships with his or her employees. Given the importance of trust, managers should actively seek to foster it within their work group.

Steps in Developing the Skill

You can be more effective at building trust among your employees if you use the following eight suggestions:[89]

1. **Practise openness.** Mistrust comes as much from what people don't know as from what they do. Being open with employees leads to trust. Keep people informed. Make clear the criteria you use in making decisions. Explain the rationale for your decisions. Be forthright and candid about problems. Fully disclose all relevant information.

2. **Be fair.** Before making decisions or taking actions, consider how others will perceive them in terms of objectivity and fairness. Give credit where credit is due. Be objective and impartial in performance appraisals. Pay attention to equity perceptions in distributing rewards.

3. **Speak your feelings.** Managers who convey only hard facts come across as cold, distant, and unfeeling. When you share your feelings, others will see that you are real and human. They will know you for who you are and their respect for you is likely to increase.

4. **Tell the truth.** Being trustworthy means being credible. If honesty is critical to credibility, then you must be perceived as someone who tells the truth. Employees are more tolerant of hearing something "they don't want to hear" than of finding out that their manager lied to them.

5. **Be consistent.** People want predictability. Mistrust comes from not knowing what to expect. Take the time to think about your values and beliefs and let those values and beliefs consistently guide your decisions. When you know what is important to you, your actions will follow, and you will project a consistency that earns trust.

6. **Fulfill your promises.** Trust requires that people believe that you are dependable. You need to ensure that you keep your word. Promises made must be promises kept.

7. **Maintain confidences.** You trust those whom you believe to be discreet and those on whom you can rely. If people open up to you and make themselves vulnerable by telling you something in confidence, they need to feel assured you will not discuss it with others or betray that confidence. If people perceive you as someone who leaks personal confidences or someone who cannot be depended on, you have lost their trust.

8. **Demonstrate competence.** Develop the admiration and respect of others by demonstrating technical and professional ability. Pay particular attention to developing and displaying your communication, negotiation, and other interpersonal skills.

Practising the Skill

Read the following scenario. Write some notes about how you would handle the situation described. Bear in mind that the employees feel that they have been betrayed because the vacation that they had come to expect has been taken away from them. In determining what to do, be sure to refer to the eight suggestions for building trust.

Scenario

Donna Romines is the shipping department manager at Tastefully Tempting, a gourmet candy company based in New Brunswick. Orders for the company's candy come from around the world. Your six-member team processes these orders. Needless to say, the two months before Christmas are quite hectic. Everybody counts the days until December 24, when the phones finally stop ringing off the wall, at least for a few days.

When the company was first founded five years ago, after the holiday rush the owners would shut down Tastefully Tempting for two weeks after Christmas. However, as the business has grown and moved into Internet sales, that practice has become too costly. There is too much business to be able to afford that luxury. The rush for Valentine's Day starts as orders pour in the week after Christmas. Although the two-week post-holiday company-wide shutdown was phased out formally last year, some departments found it difficult to get employees to gear up once again after the Christmas break. The employees who came to work after Christmas accomplished little. This year, though, things have got to change. You know that the cultural "tradition" will not be easy to overcome, but your shipping team needs to be ready to tackle the orders that have piled up. How will you handle the situation?

Reinforcing the Skill

The following activities will help you practise and reinforce the skills associated with building trust:

1. Keep a one-week log describing ways that your daily decisions and actions encouraged people to trust you or to not trust you. What things did you do that led to trust? What things did you do that may have led to distrust? How could you have changed your behaviour so that the situations of distrust could have been situations of trust?

2. Review recent issues of a business periodical (for example, *BusinessWeek, Fortune, Forbes, Fast Company, IndustryWeek,* or the *Wall Street Journal*) for articles where trust (or lack of trust) may have played a role. Find two articles and describe the situation. Explain how the person(s) involved might have used skills in developing trust to handle the situation.

Continuing Case: Starbucks

Community. Connection. Caring. Committed. Coffee.[1] Five Cs that describe the essence of Starbucks Corporation—what it stands for and what it wants to be as a business. With over 14 000 outlets in 42 countries, Starbucks is the world's number one specialty coffee retailer. It's also a company that truly epitomizes the challenges facing managers in today's globally competitive environment. To help you better understand these challenges, we are going to take an in-depth look at Starbucks through these continuing cases, which you will find at the end of every part in the textbook. Each of these five part-ending continuing cases will look at Starbucks from the perspective of the material presented in that part. Although each case "stands alone," you will be able to see the progression of the management process as you work through each one.

So how does Starbucks epitomize the five Cs—community, connection, caring, committed, and coffee? That is what you will discover as you complete the remaining continuing cases. Keep in mind that as you do the other cases, there may be information included in this introduction you might want to review.

The Beginning

"We aren't in the coffee business, serving people. We're in the people business, serving coffee." That is the philosophy of Howard Schultz, chairman and chief global strategist of Starbucks. It's a philosophy that has shaped—and continues to shape—the company.

The first Starbucks, which opened in Seattle's famous Pike Place Market in 1971, was founded by Gordon Bowker, Jerry Baldwin, and Zev Siegl. The company was named for the coffee-loving first mate in the book *Moby Dick,* which also influenced the design of Starbucks' distinctive two-tailed siren logo. Schultz, a successful New York City businessperson, first walked into Starbucks in 1981 as a sales representative for a Swedish kitchenware manufacturer. He was hooked immediately. He knew that he wanted to work for this company, but it took almost a year before he could persuade the owners to hire him. After all, he *was* from New York and he had not grown up with the values of the company. The owners thought Schultz's style and high energy would clash with the existing culture. But Schultz was quite persuasive and was able to allay the owners' fears. They asked him to join the company as director of retail operations and marketing, which he enthusiastically did. Schultz's passion for the coffee business was obvious. Although some of the company's employees resented the fact that he was an "outsider," Schultz had found his niche and he had lots of ideas for the company. As he says, "I wanted to make a positive impact."

About a year after joining the company, while on a business trip to Milan, Schultz walked into an espresso bar and right away knew that this concept could be successful in the United States. He said, "There was nothing like this in America. It was an extension of people's front porch. It was an emotional experience. I believed intuitively we could do it. I felt it in my bones." Schultz recognized that although Starbucks treated coffee as produce, something to be bagged and sent home with the groceries, the Italian coffee bars were more like an experience ... a warm, community experience. That is what Schultz wanted to recreate in the United States. However, Starbucks' owners were not really interested in making Starbucks big and did not really want to give the idea a try. So Schultz left the company in 1985 to start his own small chain of espresso bars in Seattle and Vancouver called Il Giornale. Two years later, when Starbucks' owners finally wanted to sell, Schultz raised $3.8 million from local investors to buy them out. That small investment has made him a very wealthy person indeed, and allowed him to open his first Canadian store in Vancouver. In 1996, Starbucks went east, opening five stores in the greater Toronto area. In 2007, Starbucks had over 500 stores across Canada.

Company Facts

Starbucks' main product is coffee ... more than 30 blends and single-origin coffees. In addition to fresh-brewed coffee, here is a sampling of other products the company also offers:

- *Handcrafted beverages:* Hot and iced espresso beverages, coffee and noncoffee blended beverages, and Tazo® teas
- *Merchandise:* Home espresso machines, coffee brewers and grinders, premium chocolates, coffee mugs and coffee accessories, compact discs, and other assorted items
- *Fresh food:* Baked pastries, sandwiches, and salads
- *Global consumer products:* Starbucks Frappuccino® coffee drinks, Starbucks Iced Coffee drinks, Starbucks Coffee Liqueurs, Starbucks Discoveries® coffee drinks (in Japan and Taiwan), Starbucks DoubleShot® espresso drinks, and a line of super-premium ice creams
- *Starbucks Card:* A reloadable stored-value card

Pike Place Market was the site of the first Starbucks coffee shop, opened in 1971, in Seattle, Washington.

- *Starbucks Entertainment:* A selection of music, books, and film from new and established talent
- *Brand portfolio:* Starbucks Entertainment, Ethos™ Water, Seattle's Best Coffee, Tazo® teas, Starbucks Hear Music, Ethos Water, and Torrefazione Italia Coffee.

At the end of 2006, the company had over 145 000 full and part-time partners (employees) around the world. Howard Schultz is the chairman of Starbucks. Jim Donald is the president and CEO. Some of the other "interesting" top-level executive positions include senior vice-president of total pay, senior vice-president of coffee and global procurement, senior vice-president of global business systems solutions, senior vice-president of culture and leadership development, and senior vice-president of corporate social responsibility.

Starbucks Culture and Environment

As managers manage, they must be aware of the terrain or broad environment within which they plan, organize, lead, and control. The characteristics and nature of this "terrain" will influence what managers and other employees do and how they do it. And more importantly, it will affect how efficiently and effectively managers do their job of coordinating and overseeing the work of other people so that goals—organizational and work-level or work unit—can be accomplished. What does Starbucks' terrain look like and how is the company adapting to that terrain?

An organization's culture is a mix of written and unwritten values, beliefs, and codes of behaviour that influence the way work gets done and the way that people behave in organizations. And the distinct flavour of Starbucks' culture can be traced to the original founders' philosophies and Schultz's unique beliefs about how a company should be run. The three friends (Bowker, Baldwin, and Siegl) who founded Starbucks in 1971 as a store in Seattle's historic Pike Place Market district did so for one reason: They loved coffee and tea and wanted Seattle to have access to the best. They had no intention of building a business empire. Their business philosophy, although never written down, was simple: "Every company must stand for something; don't just give customers what they ask for or what they think they want; and assume that your customers are intelligent and seekers of knowledge." The original Starbucks was a company passionately committed to world-class coffee and dedicated to educating its customers, one on one, about what great coffee can be. It was these qualities that ignited Schultz's passion for the coffee business and inspired him to envision what Starbucks could become. Schultz continues to have that passion for his business—he is the visionary and soul behind Starbucks. He visits at least 30 to 40 stores a week, talking to partners (employees) and to customers. His ideas for running a business have been called "unconventional," but Schultz does not care. He says, "We can be extremely profitable and competitive, with a highly regarded brand, and also be respected for treating our people well." One member of the company's board of directors says about him, "Howard is consumed with his vision of Starbucks. That means showing the good that a corporation can do for its workers, shareholders, and customers."

The company's mission is as follows: "To establish Starbucks as the premier purveyor of the finest coffee in the world while maintaining our uncompromising principles as we grow." What are those principles that guide the decisions and actions of company partners from top to bottom?

- "Provide a great work environment and treat each other with respect and dignity."
- "Embrace diversity as an essential component in the way we do business."
- "Apply the highest standards of excellence to the purchasing, roasting, and fresh delivery of our coffee."
- "Develop enthusiastically satisfied customers all of the time."
- "Contribute positively to our communities and our environment."
- "Recognize that profitability is essential to our future success."

Starbucks' culture emphasizes keeping employees motivated and content. One thing that has been important to Schultz from day one is the relationship that he has with his employees. He treasures those relationships and feels that they are critically important to the way the company develops its relationships with its customers and the way it is viewed by the public. He says, "We know that our people are the heart and soul of our success." Starbucks' employees worldwide serve millions of customers each week. That is a lot of opportunities to either satisfy or disappoint the customer. The experiences customers have in the stores ultimately affect the company's relationships with its customers. That is why Starbucks has created a unique relationship with its employees. Starbucks provides all employees who work more than 20 hours a week health care benefits and stock options. Schultz says, "The most important thing I ever did was give our partners [employees] bean stock [options to buy the company's stock]. That's what sets us apart and gives us a higher-quality employee, an employee that cares more." And Starbucks does care about its employees. For instance, when a manager of a downtown Vancouver outlet was murdered while saving the life of a fellow employee who was being attacked by a man with a butcher's knife, Schultz attended the memorial service. In addition, about a dozen Starbucks stores were closed for that evening, allowing about 400 Starbucks employees to attend the service. Schultz spoke at the ceremony and later read a statement to the media: "I have been incredibly moved by the words and gestures from the many people who were touched by Tony's life … We will never forget Tony. His heroism and joyful spirit will touch us forever." It probably should not come as a surprise that Starbucks has the lowest level of employee attrition (leaving) of any comparable retailer.

As a global company with revenues well over $7 billion, Starbucks' executives recognize they must be aware of the impact the environment has on their decisions and actions. It recently began lobbying legislators in Washington, DC, on issues including lowering trade barriers, health care costs, and tax breaks. It's something that Schultz did not really want to do, but he recognizes that such efforts could be important to the company's future.

Global Challenges

Although Starbucks does business in 42 countries, about 85 percent of Starbucks' revenues come from the US market. Much of the company's future growth, however, is likely to be global. In fact, the company has targeted four markets for major global expansion: China, Brazil, India, and Russia. As Starbucks continues its global push, it not only has to be concerned with the product, but it also must address staffing issues as well. The president of Starbucks Coffee International says, "These emerging markets have a great deal to offer. They are rich in culture, heritage, and untapped resources, possessing, in many cases, an eager workforce keen to better their lives, which in turn improves the social and economic situation in their respective country."

Starbucks entered the Chinese market in 1999 and currently has 140 stores there, which it feels is an accomplish-

Starbucks chairman Howard Schultz (on left).

ment, given the fact that this is a country of tea drinkers. However, Starbucks feels there are untapped opportunities as China becomes a stronger economic force and as young, newly affluent urban Chinese workers embrace drinking quality coffee products. One of the major problems that Starbucks encountered in China—an imitator by the name of Shanghai Xing Ba Ke coffee shops (loosely translated as "Shanghai Starbucks") that was creating customer confusion—has been resolved. A Chinese court ordered the imitator to pay Starbucks rmb500 000 (approximately $62 000) for copying the Starbucks name and logo. This trademark protection victory was an important one for Starbucks.

Corporate Social Responsibility and Ethics

Good coffee is important to Starbucks, but equally important is doing good. Starbucks takes that commitment seriously. Its website states, "Corporate Social Responsibility. It's the way we do business. Contributing positively to our communities and environment is so important to Starbucks that it's a guiding principle of our mission statement. We jointly fulfill this commitment with partners [employees], at all levels of the company, by getting involved together to help build stronger communities and conserve natural resources." Here is a list of some of the things that Starbucks has done in relation to its corporate social responsibilities:

- Requires its stores to donate to local causes and charities
- Made part-time employees eligible for health and pension benefits
- Works to protect the rainforest
- Introduced recycled-content paper cups in early 2006
- Introduced a bottled-water product called Ethos and will donate 5 cents per bottle sold to boost clean-water supplies in poorer countries
- Provided assistance to coffee farmers and their families in southwest Mexico and northwest Guatemala after Hurricane Stan in October 2005

- Launched an international program to offer better pay to coffee farmers who treat their workers and the environment decently

In 2001, the company began issuing an annual corporate social responsibility report, which addresses the company's decisions and actions in relation to its products, society, the environment, and the workplace. These reports are not simply a way for Starbucks to brag about its socially responsible actions, but are intended to stress the importance of doing business in a responsible way and to hold employees and managers accountable for their actions.

Starbucks also takes its ethical commitments seriously. Each top-level manager who has financial responsibilities signs a "Code of Ethics" that affirms his or her commitment to balancing, protecting, and preserving stakeholders' interests. All store employees (partners) have resources ("Standards of Business Conduct," the *Partner Guide*, the *Safety, Security and Health Standards Manual*) to help them in doing their jobs ethically. And the company created a process for employees to raise complaints and concerns they may have over questionable accounting and internal accounting controls.

Questions

1. What management skills do you think would be most important for Howard Schultz to have? Why? What skills do you think would be most important for a Starbucks store manager to have? Why?
2. How might the following management theories/approaches be useful to Starbucks: scientific management, organizational behaviour, quantitative approach, systems approach?
3. Choose three of the current trends and issues facing managers and explain how Starbucks might be impacted. What might be the implications for first-line managers? Middle managers? Top managers?
4. Give examples of how Howard Schultz might perform the interpersonal roles, the informational roles, and the decisional roles.
5. Look at Howard Schultz's philosophy of Starbucks. How will this affect the way the company is managed?
6. Go to the company's website (**www.starbucks.com**) and find the list of senior officers. Pick one of those positions and describe what you think that job might involve. Try

to envision what types of planning, organizing, leading, and controlling this person would have to do.

7. What do you think of the company's guiding principles? Describe how the company's guiding principles would influence how a barista at a local Starbucks store does his or her job. Describe how these principles would influence how one of the company's top executives does his or her job.
8. Do you think Howard Schultz views his role more from the omnipotent or from the symbolic perspective? Explain.
9. What has made Starbucks' culture what it is? How is that culture maintained?
10. Does Starbucks encourage a customer-responsive culture? An ethical culture? Explain.
11. Describe some of the specific and general environmental components that are likely to impact Starbucks.
12. How would you classify the uncertainty of the environment in which Starbucks operates? Explain.
13. What stakeholders do you think Starbucks might be most concerned with? Why? What issue(s) might each of these stakeholders want Starbucks to address?
14. Why do you think Howard Schultz is uncomfortable with the idea of legislative lobbying? Do you think his discomfort is appropriate? Why or why not?
15. What types of global economic and legal–political issues might Starbucks face?
16. You are responsible for developing a global cultural awareness program for Starbucks' executives who are leading the company's international expansion efforts. Describe what you think will be important for these executives to know.
17. Go to the company's website (**www.starbucks.com**) and find the latest corporate social responsibility annual report. Choose one of the key areas in the report (or your instructor may assign one of these areas). Describe and evaluate what the company has done in this key area.
18. What do you think the company's use of the term *partners* instead of *employees* implies? What is your reaction to this? Do you think it matters what companies call their employees? (For instance, Wal-Mart calls its employees *associates*.) Why or why not?
19. What does Starbucks' terrain look like and how is the company adapting to that terrain?
20. How effective is Starbucks at recognizing and managing its terrain? Explain.

VIDEO CASE INCIDENTS

The Fast-Food Industry and Trans Fats: Fad or Legitimate Concern for Society?

Trans fats (such as partially hydrogenated oils) are fats that are artificially created through a chemical process that solidifies the oil and limits the body's ability to regulate cholesterol. These fats are considered to be the most harmful to one's health.

BanTransFats.com is an organization established to provoke a ban on the use of trans fats in food. The organization's 2003 lawsuit against Kraft resulted in the company eliminating the use of trans fats in Oreo cookies and reducing or eliminating the use of trans fats in 650 other Kraft products. After the lawsuit, the US Food and Drug Administration (FDA) changed its labelling rule to include trans fats. This has had a significant effect on the elimination of trans fats in a range of fast foods in the United States and Canada.

On June 28, 2006, a task force formed by Health Canada recommended that total trans fats in vegetable oils and spreadable margarines should be limited to 2 percent of total fat content. It also recommended that trans fats be limited to 5 percent of total fat content for all other foods. These recommendations have been publicly supported by the Canadian Restaurant and Foodservices Association (CRFA).

While banning trans fats is good for societal health, it is not as good for business; restaurants use trans fats because they are far cheaper than other fats. To preserve profits, restaurants may be forced to pass on the increased costs to consumers through higher prices. If regulations do not ultimately require a "ban" but only a "significant reduction," are fast-food companies moving toward eliminating trans fats due to a legitimate concern for society or to ensure that competitive ground is not lost? Are the increased costs to the food sector offset by health care savings? Given so much varying nutritional information and the realities of competition, how can the fast-food industry react to these changes, remain profitable, and be perceived as being socially responsible?

QUESTIONS

1. *For discussion:* How might the issue of trans fats be perceived by holders of the classical vs. the socio-economic views of corporate social responsibility?

2. *For debate:* "Since every person has the right to decide what to eat, ingesting trans fats seems to be more a matter of making informed decisions and, as such, the fast-food industry should not bear the entire responsibility for the illnesses that are believed to arise from eating its products." Do you agree or disagree with this statement?

3. *For analysis:* How does this case demonstrate the importance of stakeholder management?

4. *For application:* Pick a fast-food restaurant of your choice and, using the Internet and other sources, determine whether the elimination of trans fats from its products is mentioned in its corporate social responsibility activities. Based on your research, do you feel this company is eliminating trans fats out of genuine concern for society, for competitive advantage, to avoid or reduce government regulation, or some combination of these factors?

Sources: "Fast Food Fads," *CBC Venture*, January 30, 2005, 935, VA–2081 C; C. Ness, "Tiburon Lawyer Getting the Trans Fat Out," *San Francisco Chronicle*, February 4, 2007, http://sfgate.com/cgi-bin/article.cgi?f=/c/a/2007/02/04/LVGI5NRT291. DTL; http://www.bantransfats.com; "Diet Wars," *Frontline*, http://www.pbs.org/wgbh/pages/frontline/teach/diet/worksheet_pre2.html; and J. M. Hirsch, "Obesity Often Blamed on Food Companies," *CTV.ca*, March 20, 2006, http://www.ctv.ca/servlet/ArticleNews/story/CTVNews/20060320/food_obesity_blame_060320?s_name=&no_ads=.

Stem Cell Research

Stem cells are undifferentiated cells that have the unique potential to produce any kind of cell in the body; they are "generic" cells with indefinite self-renewal capabilities. Stem cell research holds much promise in potentially curing diseases such as Alzheimer's and Parkinson's, diabetes, heart disease, arthritis, cancer, and spinal cord injuries.

In 2000, the government of Canada established the Canadian Institutes of Health Research (CIHR) as the premier funding agency for health research in Canada. To be eligible for funding, stem cells for research can only be derived from three major sources: very early embryos, fetal reproductive organs, and adult tissue. The conditions under which stem cell research would be eligible for CIHR funding include: the use of pre-existing human embryonic stem cell lines; using surplus embryos originally created for reproductive purposes; when the persons for whom the embryos were created give free and informed consent for their use in research; and when there are no commercial transactions involved in embryo creation and use.

The ethical issues surrounding stem cell research are complex. As Peter Calamai states, "The ethical crux is usually framed as a dilemma: to potentially save the lives of people afflicted with degenerative diseases...through the use of embryonic stem cells, it appears necessary to sacrifice the potential life of an embryo."

Professor Ron Worton, a researcher in the genetics of human disease, noted that the embryos used would most likely die anyway since they are derived from "surplus" fertilized eggs remaining after treatment at fertility clinics. Professor Bernard Dickens, emeritus professor of health law and policy, noted that embryos have no legal rights in Canadian law; no one could be prosecuted for homicide for killing a fetus. Professor Abby Lipman, a professor of epidemiology, biostatistics, and occupational health, contended that the major threats to the health of Canadian women are from problems "much less exotic than the diseases being tackled by embryonic research," and the push by "vested interests" for such research means that poor women run the risk of being considered simply as producers of raw material for third parties.

In a *Science AAAS* article, Gretchen Vogel reports on the experience of the Bedford Stem Cell Research Foundation and its successful efforts to recruit donors of oocytes (eggs produced by the ovary before fertilization) for embryonic stem cell experiments. The group advertised in the *Boston Globe* in September 2000 and by word of mouth from 2003. By the end of 2005, 23 donors had yielded 274 oocytes at an average cost of $3673 per egg. Adding the costs of psychological and physical evaluations and medical expenses, the cost per woman of each completed donation cycle amounted to $27 200. The costs of obtaining materials for this research are obviously significant. Might ethical issues eventually emerge in biotechnology research in developing countries if poor women are transformed into producers of "raw materials" for third parties?

QUESTIONS

1. *For discussion:* Describe how each of the four perspectives of ethics applies to the ethics of stem cell research.

2. *For debate:* Do you feel that stem cell research is ethical? Would your position change if a loved one was afflicted by a disease that could potentially be cured through stem cell research?

3. *For analysis:* Professor Lipman contended that the major threats to the health of Canadian women are from poverty, abuse, and other woes, and that stem cell research means that poor women run the risk of being considered simply as producers of "raw material" for third parties. Do you agree or disagree with Professor Lipman?

4. *For application:* Using the Internet and other sources, define stem cell research. Given this definition, develop a "Code of Ethical Conduct" for a biotechnology lab engaged in stem cell research.

Sources: "Stem Cell," *National* (CBC), February 12, 2007; http://en.wikipedia.org/wiki/Stem_cell_research; http://www.sciencecoalition.org; "Stem Cell Research and Ethics"; *The Royal Society of Canada*, http://www.rsc.ca/print.php?lang_id=1&page_id=195; "CIHR Releases Human Pluripotent Stem Cell Research Guidelines," Canadian Institutes of Health Research, March 4, 2002, http://www.cihr-irsc.gc.ca/e/8000.html; http://www.repro-med.net/glossary.php; http://www.sciencemag.org/cgi/content/full/313/5784/155b; and M. Bhardwaj and D. Macer, "Policy and Ethical Issues in Applying Biotechnology in Developing Countries," *Medical Science Monitor* 9, no. 2 (2003), http://www.MedSciMonit.com/pub/vol_9/no_2/3030.pdf.

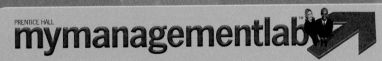

PRENTICE HALL

mymanagementlab™

After you have completed your study of Part 1, do the following exercises at the MyManagementLab website (www.pearsoned.ca/mymanagementlab):

- *You're the Manager: Putting Ethics into Action* (Lindblad Expeditions)

- *Passport, Scenario 1* (Paula Seeger, Java World), *Scenario 2* (Charles Mathidi, QSI) , *and Scenario 3* (André Fasset, PhenomGaming)

PART two

Planning

PLANNING INVOLVES DEFINING the organization's goals, establishing an overall strategy for achieving those goals, and developing a comprehensive set of plans to integrate and coordinate organizational work. When planning, managers might ask these questions:

- **Where is my company now, and where should it go in the future?**

- **How do I make plans for the future and carry them out?**

- **What analysis can I use to understand where the company is and where it can go?**

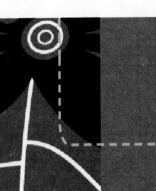

CHAPTER 5
Decision Making

How do I make good decisions?

1. What are the steps in the decision-making process?
2. What factors affect how decisions are made?
3. How can managers make more effective decisions?

CHAPTER 6
Foundations of Planning

How do I make plans to carry out decisions?

1. What does planning involve?
2. How do managers set goals and develop plans?
3. What are the challenges in planning?

CHAPTER 7
Strategic Management

What analysis can I use to make decisions?

1. What is strategic management?
2. What are the steps in strategic management?
3. What kinds of strategies can managers use?
4. How does today's dynamic environment affect strategic management?

CHAPTER 8
Planning Tools and Techniques

What tools and techniques are available for planning?

1. What is environmental scanning and how is it done?
2. What tools can managers use to allocate resources more effectively?
3. How does one manage projects?

Decision Making

How do I make good decisions?

1. What are the steps in the decision-making process?

2. What factors affect how decisions are made?

3. How can managers make more effective decisions?

▶ ▶ ▶ Sandra Wilson, chair and CEO of Burnaby, BC-based Robeez Footwear, faced a very big decision in spring 2006.[1] At the time, Robeez was the leading worldwide manufacturer of soft-soled leather footwear for young children. Wilson wondered what the company should do next. Robeez was poised for growth, but needed outside capital in order to expand. Was it time to take on a new partner or sell the company? Would bringing in an outside investor take the company, which she considered her baby, out of her hands? Was there a company to which Wilson might sell Robeez that had the desire, drive, and expertise to achieve her vision for growth?

Wilson started her home-based business after she "stumbled across the idea to design baby shoes by watching [her] son and [her] friend's young children." She received immediate encouragement from friends who saw her shoes. To test her idea in the marketplace, she made 20 pairs of shoes by hand, and took them to a retailer gift show. From that show she received orders from 15 retailers. This was enough to launch her business, Robeez Footwear, named for her young son, Robert.

Initially, Wilson handled all aspects of her business herself, from design to production to marketing and distribution. By 2006, however, 20 years after she had started the company, she employed 400 people and sold shoes in North America, Europe, and Australia. It was time for Wilson to decide the next steps for her business. "We experienced significant growth at Robeez, particularly over the last three or four years," said Wilson. "We have a real vision about where we want to take the Robeez brand and we feel there is a lot of potential for growth with the brand."

Think About It

How do CEOs make important decisions? Put yourself in Sandra Wilson's shoes. What steps would you take to determine whether Robeez should take on a partner or be sold to another company? How could Wilson evaluate the effectiveness of the decision she is about to make? What decision criteria might she use?

Like managers everywhere, Sandra Wilson needs to make good decisions. Making good decisions is something that every manager strives to do, since the overall quality of managerial decisions has a major influence on organizational success or failure. In this chapter, we examine the concept of decision making and how managers make decisions.

Robeez Footwear
www.robeez.com

The Decision-Making Process

While watching a sports competition, have you ever felt that you could make better decisions than the coaches on the field or court? Soccer fans outside Helsinki, Finland, get to do just that, as the following *Management Reflection* shows.

1. What are the steps in the decision-making process?

Fans Help Soccer Coach Make Decisions

Can you really coach a team by getting input from 300 fans? In the Helsinki suburb of Pukinmaki, the fans of PK-35, an amateur soccer team, get that chance![2] The coach does not make decisions about what to do on the field by himself, but instead relies on 300 fans who text message their instructions via their cellphones. Each week, the coach posts between 3 and 10 questions about training, team selection, and game tactics to the fans. They have three minutes to respond via cellphone text messaging, and they receive immediate feedback on what others think.

Does shared decision making work? During the first season of the experiment, the team won first place in its division and was promoted to the next higher division. Although we are unlikely to see this type of wireless interactive decision making any time soon in organizations, it does illustrate that decisions, and maybe even how they are made, play a role in performance. ■

decision
A choice from two or more alternatives.

Individuals must continually make **decisions**. That is, they make choices from two or more alternatives. For instance, you have made decisions about what post-secondary institution to attend, and what your likely major will be. Top managers make decisions about their organization's goals, where to locate manufacturing facilities, what new markets to move into, and what products or services to offer. Middle and first-line managers make decisions about weekly or monthly production schedules, problems that arise, pay raises, and disciplining employees. Individual employees make decisions about how well they will do their job, whether or not they will go to work, even whether they will look for another job. How do people make their decisions?

Although decision making is typically described as the act of choosing among alternatives, that view is simplistic. Why? Because decision making is a comprehensive process.[3] Even for something as straightforward as deciding where to go for lunch, you do more than just choose burgers or pizza. You may consider various restaurants, how you will get there, who might go with you. Granted, you may not spend a lot of time contemplating a lunch decision, but you still go through a process when making that decision. What *does* the decision-making process involve?

decision-making process
A set of eight steps that includes identifying a problem, selecting an alternative, and evaluating the decision's effectiveness.

Exhibit 5-1 illustrates the **decision-making process**, a set of eight steps that begins with identifying a problem and decision criteria, and allocating weights to those criteria; moves to developing, analyzing, and selecting an alternative that can resolve the problem; then moves to implementing the alternative; and concludes with evaluating the decision's effectiveness. Many individuals use most or all of the steps implicitly, if not explicitly. Often, when a poor decision is made, it is because one of the steps was not carefully considered.

This process is as relevant to your personal decision about what movie to see on a Friday night as it is to a corporate action such as a decision to use technology in managing client relationships. The process also can be used to describe both individual and group decisions. Let's take a closer look at the process in order to understand what each step involves. We will use an example—a manager deciding which laptop computers are best to purchase—to illustrate.

Step 1: Identify a Problem

problem
A discrepancy between an existing and a desired state of affairs.

Do you follow these steps when making a decision?

The decision-making process begins with the existence of a **problem**, or, more specifically, a discrepancy between an existing and a desired state of affairs.[4] Take Amanda, a sales manager whose sales representatives need new laptops because their old ones are inadequate to do their jobs efficiently and effectively. For simplicity's sake, assume that Amanda has determined that it's not economical to simply

Exhibit 5-1

The Decision-Making Process

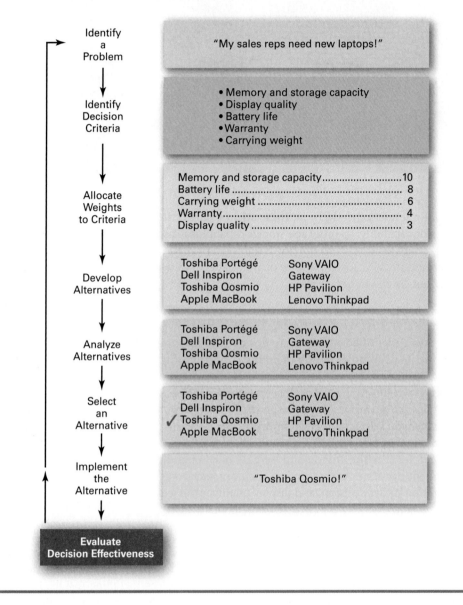

Identify a Problem — "My sales reps need new laptops!"

Identify Decision Criteria —
- Memory and storage capacity
- Display quality
- Battery life
- Warranty
- Carrying weight

Allocate Weights to Criteria —
Memory and storage capacity 10
Battery life 8
Carrying weight 6
Warranty 4
Display quality 3

Develop Alternatives —
Toshiba Portégé, Dell Inspiron, Toshiba Qosmio, Apple MacBook, Sony VAIO, Gateway, HP Pavilion, Lenovo Thinkpad

Analyze Alternatives —
Toshiba Portégé, Dell Inspiron, Toshiba Qosmio, Apple MacBook, Sony VAIO, Gateway, HP Pavilion, Lenovo Thinkpad

Select an Alternative —
Toshiba Portégé, Dell Inspiron, ✓ Toshiba Qosmio, Apple MacBook, Sony VAIO, Gateway, HP Pavilion, Lenovo Thinkpad

Implement the Alternative — "Toshiba Qosmio!"

Evaluate Decision Effectiveness

---

add memory to the old laptops and that it's the organization's policy that managers purchase new computers rather than lease them. Now we have a problem. The sales reps' current laptops are not efficient or effective enough for sales reps to do their jobs properly. Amanda has a decision to make.

Step 2: Identify Decision Criteria

Once a manager has identified a problem, the **decision criteria** important to resolving the problem must be identified. That is, managers must determine what is relevant in making a decision. Every decision maker has criteria, whether explicitly stated or not, that guide his or her decisions. These criteria are generally determined by one's objectives. For instance, when you buy a car, your objective might be to have a car that shouts "status symbol." Or you might want a car that is low maintenance. With your objective in mind, you might consider speed, fuel efficiency, colour, manufacturer, size, and so on as criteria on which to evaluate which car to buy. In our laptop purchase example, Amanda has to assess what

decision criteria
Criteria that define what is relevant in making a decision.

The choice of a new laptop relies on specific decision criteria like price, convenience, memory and storage capacity, display quality, battery life, warranty, and even carrying weight.

factors are relevant to her decision. These might include criteria such as price, convenience, multimedia capability, memory and storage capabilities, display quality, battery life, expansion capability, warranty, and carrying weight. After careful consideration, she decides that memory and storage capacity, display quality, battery life, warranty, and carrying weight are the relevant criteria in her decision.

Step 3: Allocate Weights to Criteria

If the criteria identified in step 2 are not equally important, the decision maker must weight the items in order to give them the correct priority in the decision. How do you weight criteria? A simple approach is to give the most important criterion a weight of 10 and then assign weights to the rest against that standard. Thus, a criterion with a weight of 10 would be twice as important as one given a 5. Of course, you could use 100 or 1000 or any number you select as the highest weight. The idea is to prioritize the criteria you identified in step 2 by assigning a weight to each.

Q&A 5.1

Exhibit 5-2 lists the criteria and weights that Amanda developed for her computer replacement decision. As you can see, memory and storage capacity is the most important criterion in her decision, and display quality is the least important.

Step 4: Develop Alternatives

The fourth step requires the decision maker to list viable alternatives that could resolve the problem. No attempt is made to evaluate the alternatives, only to list them. Our sales manager, Amanda, identified eight laptops as possible choices, including Toshiba Portégé, Dell Inspiron, Toshiba Qosmio, Apple MacBook, Sony VAIO, Gateway, HP Pavilion, and Lenovo Thinkpad.

PRISM 12

Exhibit 5-2

Criteria and Weights for Laptop Replacement Decision

Criterion	Weight
Memory and storage capacity	10
Battery life	8
Carrying weight	6
Warranty	4
Display quality	3

Step 5: Analyze Alternatives

Once the alternatives have been identified, a decision maker must critically analyze each one. How? By appraising it against the criteria established in steps 2 and 3. From this comparison, the strengths and weaknesses of each alternative become evident. Exhibit 5-3 shows the assessed values Amanda gave each of her eight alternatives after she had talked to some computer experts and read the latest information from computer magazines and from the web.

Keep in mind that the ratings given the eight laptop models listed in Exhibit 5-3 are based on the personal assessment made by Amanda. Some assessments can be done objectively. For instance, carrying weight is easy to determine by looking at descriptions online or in computer magazines. However, the assessment of display quality is more of a personal judgment. The point is that most decisions by managers involve judgments—the criteria chosen in step 2, the weights given to the criteria in step 3, and the analysis of alternatives in step 5. This explains why two computer buyers with the same amount of money may look at two totally different sets of alternatives or even rate the same alternatives differently.

Exhibit 5-3 represents only an assessment of the eight alternatives against the decision criteria. It does not reflect the weighting done in step 3. If you multiply each alternative (Exhibit 5-3) by its weight (Exhibit 5-2), you get Exhibit 5-4 (see page 142). The sum of these scores represents an evaluation of each alternative against both the established criteria and weights. There are times when a decision maker might not have to do this step. If one choice had scored 10 on every criterion, you would not need to consider the weights. Similarly, if the weights were all equal, you could evaluate each alternative merely by summing up the appropriate lines in Exhibit 5-3. In this instance, for example, the score for the Toshiba Portégé would be 36 and the score for Gateway would be 35.

Step 6: Select an Alternative

What does it mean if the "best" alternative does not feel right to you after going through the decision-making steps?

Step 6 is choosing the best alternative from among those considered. Once all the pertinent criteria in the decision have been weighted and viable alternatives analyzed, we simply choose the alternative that generated the highest total in step 5. In our example (see Exhibit 5-4), Amanda would choose the Toshiba Qosmio because it scored highest (249 total) on the basis of the criteria identified, the weights given to the criteria, and her assessment of each laptop's ranking on the criteria. It's the "best" alternative and the one she should choose.

That said, occasionally, when one gets to this step, the alternative that looks best according to the numbers may not feel like the best solution (for example, your intuition might sug-

Exhibit 5-3

Assessed Values of Laptops Using Decision Criteria

	Memory and Storage Capacity	Battery Life	Carrying Weight	Warranty	Display Quality
Toshiba Portégé	10	3	10	8	5
Dell Inspiron	8	7	7	8	7
HP Pavilion	8	5	7	10	10
Apple MacBook	8	7	7	8	7
Sony VAIO	7	8	7	8	7
Gateway	8	3	6	10	8
Toshiba Qosmio	10	7	8	6	7
Lenovo Thinkpad	4	10	4	8	10

Exhibit 5-4

Evaluation of Laptop Alternatives Against Weighted Criteria

	Memory and Storage Capacity	Battery Life	Carrying Weight	Warranty	Display Quality	Total
Toshiba Portégé	100	24	60	32	15	231
Dell Inspiron	80	56	42	32	21	231
HP Pavilion	80	40	42	40	30	232
Apple MacBook	80	56	42	32	21	231
Sony VAIO	70	64	42	32	21	229
Gateway	80	24	36	40	24	204
Toshiba Qosmio	100	56	48	24	21	249
Lenovo Thinkpad	40	80	24	32	30	206

gest some other alternative). Often the reason is that the individual did not give the correct weight to one or more criterion (perhaps because one criterion was actually much more important than the individual realized initially, when assigning weights). Thus, if the individual finds that the "best alternative" does not seem like the right alternative, the decision maker needs to decide if a review of the criteria is necessary before implementing the alternative.

Step 7: Implement the Alternative

Step 7 is concerned with putting the decision into action. This involves conveying the decision to those affected by it and getting their commitment to it. Managers often fail to get buy-in from those around them before making a decision, even though successful implementation requires participation. One study found that managers used participation in only 20 percent of decisions, even though broad participation in decisions led to successful implementation 80 percent of the time. The same study found that managers most commonly tried to implement decisions through power or persuasion (used in 60 percent of decisions). These tactics were successful in only one of three decisions, however.[5] If the people who must carry out a decision participate in the process, they're more likely to enthusiastically support the outcome than if you just tell them what to do. Parts 3, 4, and 5 of this book discuss how decisions are implemented by effective planning, organizing, and leading.

Q&A 5.2

Step 8: Evaluate Decision Effectiveness

Q&A 5.3

The last step in the decision-making process involves evaluating the outcome of the decision to see if the problem has been resolved. Did the alternative chosen in step 6 and implemented in step 7 accomplish the desired result? In Part 5 of this book, where we look at the controlling function, we will see how to evaluate the results of decisions.

What if the evaluation shows the problem still exists? The manager would need to assess what went wrong. Was the problem incorrectly defined? Were errors made in the evaluation of the various alternatives? Was the right alternative selected but poorly implemented? Answers to questions like these might send the manager back to one of the earlier steps. It might even require redoing the whole decision process.

The Manager as Decision Maker

▶ ▶ ▶ As chair and CEO, Sandra Wilson needed to make a decision about the future of Robeez Footwear.[6] "We recognized that if we wanted to execute the plans and achieve the vision for where we could take this company, we needed to look for ... someone with the financial backing and expertise to help us continue to build Robeez," says Wilson.

Should Wilson seek a new partner for Robeez or sell the company? She weighed the pros and cons of each choice. For example, taking on a new partner would provide the company with the money to expand to more markets. The downside would be the possibility of losing control over the quality of the product. Selling Robeez to another company could provide Robeez with the resources and experience necessary to continue its momentum of growth. However, if Robeez were manufactured by another company, the corporate culture that underlies Robeez' success might change and negatively affect the brand.

Think About It

What biases might enter into Sandra Wilson's decision making, and how might she overcome these? How can Wilson improve her decision making, given that she is dealing with uncertainty and risk? How might escalation of commitment affect her decision?

Everyone in an organization makes decisions, but decision making is particularly important in a manager's job.[7] As Exhibit 5-5 shows, decision making is part of all four managerial functions. That is why managers—when they plan, organize, lead, and control—are frequently called *decision makers*.

The decision-making process described in Exhibit 5-1 on page 139 suggests that individuals make rational, carefully scripted decisions. But is this the best way to describe the decision-making situation and the person who makes the decisions? We look at those issues in this section. We start by looking at three perspectives on how decisions are made.

2. What factors affect how decisions are made?

Making Decisions: Rationality, Bounded Rationality, and Intuition

Our model of the decision-making process implies that individuals engage in **rational decision making**. By that we mean that people make consistent, value-maximizing choices within specified constraints.[8] What are the underlying assumptions of rationality, and how valid are those assumptions?

rational decision making
Making decisions that are consistent and value-maximizing within specified constraints.

Assumptions of Rationality

A decision maker who was perfectly rational would be fully objective and logical. He or she would carefully define a problem and would have a clear and specific goal. Moreover, making decisions using rationality would consistently lead to selecting the alternative that maximizes the likelihood of achieving that goal. Exhibit 5-6 on page 144 summarizes the assumptions of rationality.

Exhibit 5-5

Decisions in the Management Functions

Planning
- What are the organization's long-term objectives?
- What strategies will best achieve those objectives?
- What should the organization's short-term objectives be?
- How difficult should individual goals be?

Leading
- How do I handle employees who appear to be low in motivation?
- What is the most effective leadership style in a given situation?
- How will a specific change affect worker productivity?
- When is the right time to stimulate conflict?

Organizing
- How many employees should I have report directly to me?
- How much centralization should there be in the organization?
- How should jobs be designed?
- When should the organization implement a different structure?

Controlling
- What activities in the organization need to be controlled?
- How should those activities be controlled?
- When is a performance deviation significant?
- What type of management information system should the organization have?

Exhibit 5-6

Assumptions of Rationality

Lead to

- The problem is clear and unambiguous.
- A single, well-defined goal is to be achieved.
- All alternatives and consequences are known.
- Preferences are clear.
- Preferences are constant and stable.
- No time or cost constraints exist.
- Final choice will maximize payoff.

Rational Decision Making

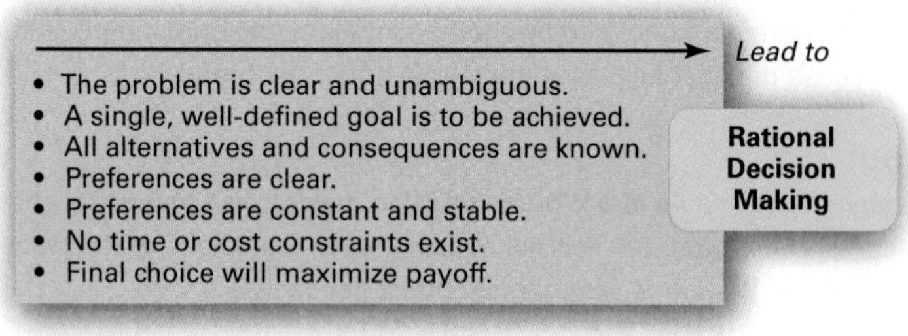

Would you say you make decisions rationally or do you rely on gut instinct?

The assumptions of rationality apply to any decision—personal or managerial. However, because we are concerned with managerial decision making, we need to add one further assumption. Rational managerial decision making assumes that decisions are made in the best interests of the organization. That is, the decision maker is assumed to be maximizing the organization's interests, not his or her own interests.

How realistic are these assumptions? Not all problems are simple, with clear goals and limited alternatives. Often there are time pressures involved in decision making. There can be high costs in seeking out and evaluating alternatives. For these reasons, most decisions that managers face in the real world don't meet the assumptions of rationality.[9] So how are most decisions in organizations usually made? The concept of bounded rationality can help answer that question.

Bounded Rationality

bounded rationality
Limitations on a person's ability to interpret, process, and act on information.

satisfice
To accept solutions that are "good enough."

Q&A 5.4

Most decisions that managers make don't fit the assumptions of perfect rationality (where all the steps above are followed, and all alternatives are known and fully understood). Instead, managers make those decisions under assumptions of **bounded rationality**. That is, they make decisions rationally, but are limited (bounded) by their ability to process information.[10] Because they cannot possibly analyze all information on all alternatives, managers **satisfice** rather than maximize. That is, they accept a solution that is both satisfactory and sufficient. When managers satisfice, they limit their review of alternatives to some of the more conspicuous ones. Rather than carefully evaluate each alternative in great detail, managers settle on an alternative that is "good enough"—one that meets an acceptable level of performance. The first alternative that meets the "good enough" criterion ends the search.

Let's look at an example. Suppose that you are a finance major and upon graduation you want a job, preferably as a personal financial planner, with a minimum salary of $50 000 and within 100 kilometres of your hometown. You accept a job offer as a business credit analyst—not exactly a personal financial planner but still in the finance field—at a bank 50 kilometres from home at a starting salary of $55 000. A more comprehensive job search would have revealed a job in personal financial planning at a trust company only 25 kilometres from your hometown and starting at a salary of $57 000. Because the first job offer was satisfactory (or "good enough"), you behaved in a boundedly rational manner by accepting it, although according to the assumptions of perfect rationality, you did not

Q&A 5.5

maximize your decision by searching all possible alternatives and then choosing the best.

Intuition

Q&A 5.6

When managers at stapler maker Swingline saw the company's market share declining, they decided to use a logical scientific approach to help them address the issue. For three years, they exhaustively researched stapler users before deciding what new products to develop.

Do you prefer to make decisions intuitively? Are these good decisions?

However, at newcomer Accentra, founder Todd Moses used a more intuitive decision approach to come up with his line of unique PaperPro staplers. His stapler sold 1 million units in 6 months in a market that only sells 25 million units in total annually—a pretty good result for a new product.[11]

Like Todd Moses, managers regularly use their intuition, which may actually help improve their decision making.[12] What is **intuitive decision making**? It's making decisions on the basis of experience, feelings, and accumulated judgment. Researchers studying managers' use of intuitive decision making identified five different aspects of intuition, which are described in Exhibit 5-7.[13]

Making a decision on intuition or "gut feeling" does not necessarily happen independently of rational analysis; rather, the two complement each other. A manager who has had experience with a particular, or even similar, type of problem or situation often can act quickly with what appears to be limited information. Such a manager does not rely on a systematic and thorough analysis of the problem or identification and evaluation of alternatives but instead uses his or her experience and judgment to make a decision.

How accurate is intuitive decision making? A recent study suggests that complex decisions may be better if made "in the absence of attentive deliberation."[14] (To discover your own intuitive abilities, see *Self-Assessment—How Intuitive Am I?* on pages 159–160, at the end of the chapter.)

Intuition played a strong part in Barbara Choi's decision to locate her firm, a cosmetics and personal care products manufacturer, in Valley Springs Industrial Center in Los Angeles. In Chinese, the numbers of the building's address signify continued growth.

intuitive decision making
Making decisions on the basis of experience, feelings, and accumulated judgment.

Types of Problems and Decisions

Managers at eating establishments in Whitehorse, Yukon, make decisions weekly about purchasing food supplies and scheduling employee work shifts. It's something they have done numerous times. But in 2007, they faced a different kind of decision—one they had never encountered—how to adapt to a newly enacted no-smoking ban in public places, which includes restaurants and bars. And this situation is not all that unusual. Managers in all kinds of organizations will face different types of problems and decisions as they do their jobs. Depending on the nature of the problem, a manager can use different types of decisions.

Exhibit 5-7

What Is Intuition?

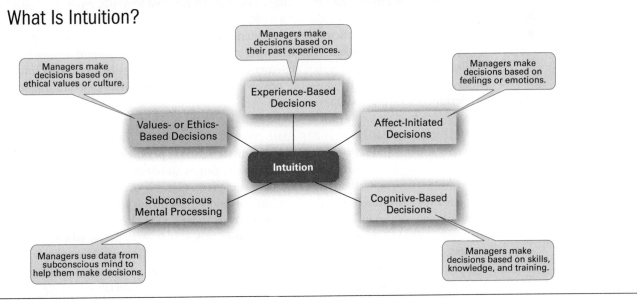

Managers make decisions based on ethical values or culture.

Managers make decisions based on their past experiences.

Managers make decisions based on feelings or emotions.

Values- or Ethics-Based Decisions

Experience-Based Decisions

Affect-Initiated Decisions

Intuition

Subconscious Mental Processing

Cognitive-Based Decisions

Managers use data from subconscious mind to help them make decisions.

Managers make decisions based on skills, knowledge, and training.

Source: Based on L. A. Burke and M. K. Miller, "Taking the Mystery Out of Intuitive Decision Making," *Academy of Management Executive*, October 1999, pp. 91–99.

Structured Problems and Programmed Decisions

Some problems are straightforward. The goal of the decision maker is clear, the problem is familiar, and information about the problem is easily defined and complete. Examples of these types of problems could include what to do when a customer returns a purchase to a store, a supplier delivers an important product late, a news team wants to respond to a fast-breaking event, or a student wants to drop a class. Such situations are called **structured problems** because they are straightforward, familiar, and easily defined. When situations are structured, there is probably some standardized routine for handling problems that may arise. For example, when a restaurant server spills a drink on a customer's coat, the manager offers to have the coat cleaned at the restaurant's expense. This is what we call a **programmed decision**, a repetitive decision that can be handled by a routine approach. Because the problem is structured, the manager does not have to go to the trouble and expense of following an involved decision process. Programmed decisions can have negative consequences, however, particularly when decision makers deal with diverse populations/clients/customers. For instance, it may be difficult to have one's coat cleaned immediately if one is away from home on a business trip in the middle of winter. Employees of Ottawa-based JDS Uniphase were not happy with the programmed decision they received from the Canada Revenue Agency about hefty taxes they were asked to pay on their company stock options. When JDS stock was trading for $300, employees were saddled with tax bills of several hundred thousand dollars for their stock options, even though they had not cashed in their options. When employees asked the Canada Revenue Agency how they could be expected to pay such big tax bills when they earned only $50 000 per year, the agency responded unsympathetically that they had to pay up.[15]

Managers make programmed decisions by falling back on procedures, rules, and policies.

A **procedure** is a series of interrelated sequential steps that a decision maker can use to respond to a structured problem. The only real difficulty is in identifying the problem. Once it's clear, so is the procedure. For instance, when bad weather grounds airplanes, airlines have procedures for helping customers who miss their flights. Customers may request being put up in hotels for the night. The customer service agent knows how to make this decision—follow the established airline procedure for dealing with customers when flights are grounded.

A **rule** is an explicit statement that tells a decision maker what he or she can or cannot do. Rules are frequently used because they are simple to follow and ensure consistency. For example, rules about lateness and absenteeism permit supervisors to make disciplinary decisions rapidly and fairly.

A **policy** is a guideline for making a decision. In contrast to a rule, a policy establishes general parameters for the decision maker rather than specifically stating what should or should not be done. Policies typically contain an ambiguous term that leaves interpretation up to the decision maker. "The customer always comes first and should always be *satisfied*" is an example of a policy statement. While ambiguity of policies is often intended to allow more flexibility in action, not all employees and customers are comfortable with flexibly determined policies.

Unstructured Problems and Nonprogrammed Decisions

Many organizational situations involve **unstructured problems**, which are problems that are new or unusual and for which information is ambiguous or incomplete. Whether to build a new manufacturing facility in Beijing is an example of an unstructured problem.

Nonprogrammed decisions are unique and nonrecurring and require custom-made solutions. For instance, if an office building were to be flooded because sprinklers went off accidentally, CEOs with businesses in the building would have to decide when and how to start operating again, and what to do for employees whose offices were completely ruined. When a manager confronts an unstructured problem, there is no cut-and-dried solution. It requires a custom-made response through nonprogrammed decision making.

Few managerial decisions in the real world are either fully programmed or nonprogrammed. These are extremes, and most decisions fall somewhere in between. Few programmed decisions are designed to eliminate individual judgment completely. At the

structured problems
Problems that are straightforward, familiar, and easily defined.

programmed decisions
Repetitive decisions that can be handled by a routine approach.

procedure
A series of interrelated sequential steps that a decision maker can use to respond to a structured problem.

rule
An explicit statement that tells a decision maker what he or she can or cannot do.

policy
A guideline for making a decision.

Q&A 5.7

unstructured problems
Problems that are new or unusual and for which information is ambiguous or incomplete.

nonprogrammed decisions
Decisions that are unique and nonrecurring and require custom-made solutions.

Many people believe that China will become the next big market for powerful brand-name products, and Zong Qinghou, founder of China's Wahaha beverage group, plans to be ready. But brand names are a new concept in Chinese markets, and Zong prefers his own first-hand information to market research. He will face many nonprogrammed decisions as he tries to make his brand a success at home and eventually abroad.

other extreme, even a unique situation requiring a nonprogrammed decision can be helped by programmed routines. It's best to think of decisions as *mainly* programmed or *mainly* non-programmed, rather than as completely one or the other.

The problems confronting managers usually become more unstructured as they move up the organizational hierarchy. Why? Because lower-level managers handle the routine decisions themselves and let upper-level managers deal with the decisions they find unusual or difficult. Similarly, higher-level managers delegate routine decisions to their subordinates so that they can deal with more difficult issues.[16]

One of the more challenging tasks facing managers as they make decisions is analyzing decision alternatives (step 5 in the decision-making process). In the next section, we look at analyzing alternatives under different conditions.

Decision-Making Conditions

When managers make decisions, they face three conditions: certainty, risk, and uncertainty. What are the characteristics of each?

Certainty

The ideal condition for making decisions is one of **certainty**, that is, a condition in which a decision maker can make accurate decisions because the outcome of every alternative is known. For example, when Saskatchewan's finance minister is deciding in which bank to deposit excess provincial funds, he knows the exact interest rate being offered by each bank and the amount that will be earned on the funds. He is certain about the outcomes of each alternative. As you might expect, most managerial decisions are not like this.

> How much do risk and uncertainty affect your decisions?

certainty
A condition in which a decision maker can make accurate decisions because the outcome of every alternative is known.

Risk

A far more common condition is one of **risk**, a condition in which a decision maker is able to estimate the likelihood of certain outcomes. The ability to assign probabilities to outcomes may be the result of personal experiences or secondary information. With risk, managers have historical data that let them assign probabilities to different alternatives. Let's work through an example.

Suppose that you manage a ski resort in Whistler, BC. You are thinking about adding another lift to your current facility. Obviously, your decision will be influenced by the additional revenue that the new lift would generate, and additional revenue will depend on snowfall. The decision is made somewhat clearer because you have fairly reliable weather data

risk
A condition in which a decision maker is able to estimate the likelihood of certain outcomes.

Exhibit 5-8

Expected Value for Revenues from the Addition of One Ski Lift

Event	Expected Revenues	¥ Probability	=	Expected Value of Each Alternative
Heavy snowfall	$850 000	0.3		$255 000
Normal snowfall	725 000	0.5		362 500
Light snowfall	350 000	0.2		70 000
				$687 500

from the past 10 years on snowfall levels in your area—three years of heavy snowfall, five years of normal snowfall, and two years of light snowfall. Can you use this information to help you make your decision about adding the new lift? If you have good information on the amount of revenues generated during each level of snow, the answer is yes.

You can calculate expected value—the expected return from each possible outcome—by multiplying expected revenues by snowfall probabilities. The result is the average revenue you can expect over time if the given probabilities hold. As Exhibit 5-8 shows, the expected revenue from adding a new ski lift is $687 500. Of course, whether that justifies a decision to build or not depends on the costs involved in generating that revenue—such as the cost to build the lift, the additional annual operating expenses for the lift, the interest rate for borrowing money, and so forth.

Uncertainty

What happens if you have a decision where you are not certain about the outcomes and cannot even make reasonable probability estimates? We call such a condition **uncertainty**. Managers do face decision-making situations of uncertainty. Under these conditions, the choice of alternative is influenced by the limited amount of information available to the decision maker and by the psychological orientation of the decision maker. The optimistic manager will follow a *maximax* choice (maximizing the maximum possible payoff) in order to get the largest possible gain. The pessimist will follow a *maximin* choice (maximizing the minimum possible payoff) to make the best of a situation should the worst possible outcome occur. The manager who desires to minimize his maximum "regret" will opt for a *minimax* choice, to avoid having big regrets after decisions play out. Let's look at these different choice approaches using an example.

A marketing manager at Visa has determined four possible strategies (S_1, S_2, S_3, and S_4) for promoting the Visa card throughout western Canada. The marketing manager also knows that major competitor MasterCard has three competitive actions (CA_1, CA_2, CA_3) it's using to promote its card in the same region. For this example, we will assume that the Visa executive had no previous knowledge that would allow her to place probabilities on the success of any of the four strategies. She formulates the matrix shown in Exhibit 5-9 to show the various Visa strategies and the resulting profit to Visa depending on the competitive action used by MasterCard.

In this example, if our Visa manager is an optimist, she will choose S_4 because that could produce the largest possible gain: $28 million. Note that this choice maximizes the maximum possible gain (the *maximax* choice).

If our manager is a pessimist, she will assume that only the worst can occur. The worst outcome for each strategy is as follows: S_1 = $11 million; S_2 = $9 million; S_3 = $15 million; S_4 = $14 million. These are the most pessimistic outcomes from each

Visa
www.visa.com

MasterCard
www.mastercard.com

Exhibit 5-9

Payoff Matrix

(in millions of dollars) Visa Marketing Strategy	MasterCard's Response		
	CA$_1$	CA$_2$	CA$_3$
S$_1$	13	14	11
S$_2$	9	15	18
S$_3$	24	21	15
S$_4$	18	14	28

strategy. Following the *maximin* choice, she would maximize the minimum payoff; in other words, she would select S$_3$ ($15 million is the largest of the minimum payoffs).

In the third approach, managers recognize that once a decision is made, it will not necessarily result in the most profitable payoff. There may be a "regret" of profits given up—*regret* referring to the amount of money that could have been made had a different strategy been used. Managers calculate regret by subtracting all possible payoffs in each category from the maximum possible payoff for each given event, in this case for each competitive action. For our Visa manager, the highest payoff, given that MasterCard engages in CA$_1$, CA$_2$, or CA$_3$, is $24 million, $21 million, or $28 million, respectively (the highest number in each column). Subtracting the payoffs in Exhibit 5-9 from those figures produces the results shown in Exhibit 5-10.

The maximum regrets are S$_1$ = $17 million; S$_2$ = $15 million; S$_3$ = $13 million; and S$_4$ = $7 million. The *minimax* choice minimizes the maximum regret, so our Visa manager would choose S$_4$. By making this choice, she will never have a regret of giving up profits of more than $7 million. This result contrasts, for example, with a regret of $15 million had she chosen S$_2$ and MasterCard had taken CA$_1$.

Although managers will try to quantify a decision when possible by using payoff and regret matrices, uncertainty often forces them to rely more on intuition, creativity, hunches, and "gut feel." Canadian Tire built a better tent by giving people an environment that encouraged them to think creatively, as the following *Management Reflection* shows.

Exhibit 5-10

Regret Matrix

(in millions of dollars) Visa Marketing Strategy	MasterCard's Response		
	CA$_1$	CA$_2$	CA$_3$
S$_1$	11	7	17
S$_2$	15	6	10
S$_3$	0	0	13
S$_4$	6	7	0

An "Innovation Room" Unleashes Creativity

Can bringing people together to play help produce a better tent?   Managers at Toronto-based Canadian Tire know that sitting around a boardroom table trying to make a decision is more likely to yield an obvious solution, rather than one that no one has thought about before.[17] So they created an "innovation room" that is "a cross between a kindergarten classroom and a fantasy land."

When they decided to come up with new ideas for camping gear, they invited friends and family who had an interest in camping to meet in the innovation room. The room has crayons, LEGO sets, a canoe, and a sundeck. There is even a "tree" made of ski poles, skateboards, and other items Canadian Tire sells.

Managers knew that there was a growing demand for tents with lighting, but were not sure how to develop a product that would sell. By getting people together in the innovation room, where they could play and toss around ideas, the idea emerged for a solar-lit tent. The tent is now a big seller.

"It's really about unlocking and unleashing creativity and getting people to just let loose and dream a little and have fun," says Glenn Butt, a senior vice-president at Canadian Tire. "It's a process that usually ends up with some very unique and different products and concepts."■

(To learn more about creativity and decision making, see *Developing Your Interpersonal Skills—Solving Problems Creatively* on pages 164–165, at the end of the chapter.)

Regardless of the decision that needs to be made and the conditions that affect it, each manager has his or her own style of making decisions.

directive style
A decision-making style characterized by a low tolerance for ambiguity and a rational way of thinking.

analytic style
A decision-making style characterized by a high tolerance for ambiguity and a rational way of thinking.

Decision-Making Styles

Suppose that you were a new manager at The Bay or at the local YMCA. How would you make decisions? Decision-making styles differ along two dimensions.[18] The first dimension is an individual's *way of thinking*. Some of us are more rational and logical in the way we process information. A rational type processes information in order and makes sure that it's logical and consistent before making a decision. Others tend to be creative and intuitive. An intuitive type does not have to process information in a certain order and is comfortable looking at it as a whole.

The other dimension is an individual's *tolerance for ambiguity*. Some of us have a low tolerance for ambiguity. These types need consistency and order in the way they structure information so that ambiguity is minimized. On the other hand, some of us can tolerate high levels of ambiguity and are able to process many thoughts at the same time. (To assess your tolerance for ambiguity, see *Self-Assessment—How Well Do I Handle Ambiguity?* on pages 216–217, in Chapter 7.) When we diagram these two dimensions, four decision-making styles are evident: directive, analytic, conceptual, and behavioural (see Exhibit 5-11). Let's look more closely at each style.

- *Directive style.* Individuals with a **directive style** have a low tolerance for ambiguity and are rational in their way of thinking. They are efficient, logical, practical, and impersonal. Directive types make fast decisions and focus on the short run. Their efficiency and speed in making decisions often result in their making decisions with minimal information and assessing few alternatives.

- *Analytic style.* Individuals with an **analytic style** have much greater tolerance for ambiguity than do directive types. They want more information before making a decision and consider more alternatives than directive-style decision makers do. Analytic-style decision

The choice of an advertising agency is often made by those with a conceptual approach to decision making. Marketing executives from Virgin Atlantic Airways saw presentations from five ad agencies before choosing Crispin Porter & Bogusky, a small firm whose inventive proposal showed how efficiently the airline's $19 million ad budget could be spent. The marketing team from Virgin allowed 10 weeks to make a decision; it took four days. The winning team is pictured here with the paper airplanes that played a part in their pitch.

Exhibit 5-11

Decision-Making Styles

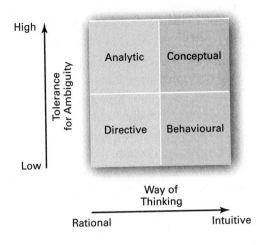

Source: S. P. Robbins and D. A. DeCenzo, *Supervision Today*, 2nd ed. (Upper Saddle River, NJ: Prentice Hall, 1998), p. 166.

makers are characterized as careful decision makers with the ability to adapt to or cope with unique situations.

- *Conceptual style.* Individuals with a **conceptual style** tend to be very broad in their outlook and consider many alternatives. They are intuitive, focus on the long run, and are very good at finding creative solutions to problems. They are also adaptive and flexible.

- *Behavioural style.* Individuals with a **behavioural style** have a low tolerance for ambiguity and an intuitive way of thinking. They are sociable, friendly, and supportive. They work well with others, are concerned about the achievements of those around them, and are receptive to suggestions from others. They often use meetings to communicate, although they try to avoid conflict. Acceptance by others is important to this decision-making style.

conceptual style
A decision-making style characterized by a high tolerance for ambiguity and an intuitive way of thinking.

behavioural style
A decision-making style characterized by a low tolerance for ambiguity and an intuitive way of thinking.

Q&A 5.8, Q&A 5.9

Although these four decision-making styles are distinct, most managers have characteristics of more than one style. It's probably more realistic to think of a manager's dominant style and his or her alternative styles. Although some managers will rely almost exclusively on their dominant style, others are more flexible and can shift their style depending on the situation.

Managers should also recognize that their employees may use different decision-making styles. Some employees may take their time, carefully weighing alternatives and considering riskier options (analytic style), while other employees may be more concerned about getting suggestions from others before making decisions (behavioural style). This does not make one approach better than the other. It just means that their decision-making styles are different. (See *Managing Workforce Diversity—The Value of Diversity in Decision Making* on page 165, at the end of the chapter, for the issues associated with valuing diversity in decision making.)

Group Decision Making

Many organizational decisions are made by groups. It's a rare organization that does not at some time use committees, task forces, review panels, study teams, or similar groups to make decisions. In addition, studies show that managers may spend up to 30 hours a week in group meetings.[19] Undoubtedly, a large portion of that time is spent identifying problems, developing solutions, and determining how to implement the solutions. It's possible,

Do you think individuals or groups make better decisions?

in fact, for groups to be assigned any of the eight steps in the decision-making process. In this section, we look at the advantages and disadvantages of group decision making, discuss when groups would be preferred, and review some techniques for improving group decision making.

What advantages do group decisions have over individual decisions?

- *More complete information and knowledge.* A group brings a diversity of experience and perspectives to the decision process that an individual cannot.
- *More diverse alternatives.* Because groups have a greater amount and diversity of information, they can identify more diverse alternatives than an individual.
- *Increased acceptance of a solution.* Group members are reluctant to fight or undermine a decision they have helped develop.
- *Increased legitimacy.* Decisions made by groups may be perceived as more legitimate than decisions made unilaterally by one person.

If groups are so good at making decisions, how did the phrase "A camel is a horse put together by a committee" become so popular? The answer, of course, is that group decisions also have disadvantages:

- *Increased time to reach a solution.* Groups almost always take more time to reach a solution than it would take an individual.
- *Opportunity for minority domination.* The inequality of group members creates the opportunity for one or more members to dominate others. A dominant and vocal minority frequently can have an excessive influence on the final decision.
- *Ambiguous responsibility.* Group members share responsibility, but the responsibility of any single member is diluted.
- *Pressures to conform.* There can be pressures to conform in groups. This pressure undermines critical thinking in the group and eventually harms the quality of the final decision.[20]

Groupthink

Have you ever been in a situation in which several people were sitting around discussing a particular item and you had something to say that ran contrary to the consensus views of the group, but you remained silent? Were you surprised to learn later that others shared your views and also had remained silent? What you experienced is what Irving Janis termed **groupthink**.[21] This is a form of conformity in which group members withhold deviant, minority, or unpopular views in order to give the appearance of agreement. As a result, groupthink undermines critical thinking in the group and eventually harms the quality of the final decision.

groupthink
The withholding by group members of different views in order to appear to be in agreement.

Groupthink applies to a situation in which a group's ability to appraise alternatives objectively and arrive at a quality decision is jeopardized. Because of pressures for conformity, groups often deter individuals from critically appraising unusual, minority, or unpopular views. Consequently, an individual's mental efficiency, reality testing, and moral judgment deteriorate. How does groupthink occur? The following are examples of situations in which groupthink is evident:

- Group members rationalize any resistance to the assumptions they have made.
- Members apply direct pressures on those who momentarily express doubts about any of the group's shared views or who question the validity of arguments favoured by the majority.
- Those members who have doubts or hold differing points of view seek to avoid deviating from what appears to be group consensus.
- There is an illusion of unanimity. If someone does not speak, it is assumed that he or she is in full accord.

Does groupthink really hinder decision making? Yes. Several research studies have found that groupthink symptoms were associated with poorer-quality decision outcomes.[22] But groupthink can be minimized if the group is cohesive, fosters open discussion, and has an impartial leader who seeks input from all members.[23]

Individual and Group Decision Making: When Is One More Effective Than the Other?

Determining whether a group or an individual will be more effective in making a particular decision depends on the criteria you use to assess effectiveness.[24] Exhibit 5-12 indicates when group decisions are preferable to those made by an individual.

Keep in mind, however, that the effectiveness of group decision making is also influenced by the size of the group. Although a larger group provides greater opportunity for diverse representation, it also requires more coordination and more time for members to contribute their ideas. So groups probably should not be too large. Evidence indicates, in fact, that groups of five, and to a lesser extent, seven, are the most effective.[25] Having an odd number in the group helps avoid decision deadlocks. Also, these groups are large enough for members to shift roles and withdraw from unfavourable positions but still small enough for quieter members to participate actively in discussions.

Decision-Making Biases and Errors

When managers make decisions, not only do they use their own particular style, but many use "rules of thumb," or **heuristics**, to simplify their decision making. Rules of thumb can be useful to decision makers because they help make sense of complex, uncertain, and ambiguous information.[26] Even though managers may use rules of thumb, that does not mean those rules are reliable. Why? Because they may lead to errors and biases in processing and evaluating information. Exhibit 5-13 on page 154 identifies seven common decision-making biases and errors. Let's take a quick look at each.[27]

> **heuristics**
> Rules of thumb that managers use to simplify decision making.

- *Overconfidence bias.* Decision makers tend to think they know more than they do or hold unrealistically positive views of themselves and their performance. For instance, a sales manager brags that his presentation was so good that there is no doubt the sale will be his. Later he learns that he lost the sale because the client found him obnoxious.

- *Selective perception bias.* Decision makers selectively organize and interpret events based on their biased perceptions. This influences the information they pay attention to, the problems they identify, and the alternatives they develop. For instance, before Joanne meets with two job candidates, she learns that one went to her alma mater. She does not seriously consider the other job candidate because she believes that graduating from the same university as she did makes the candidate superior.

Exhibit 5-12

Group vs. Individual Decision Making

Criteria of Effectiveness	Groups	Individuals
Accuracy	✔	
Speed		✔
Creativity	✔	
Degree of acceptance	✔	
Efficiency		✔

Exhibit 5-13

Common Decision-Making Biases and Errors

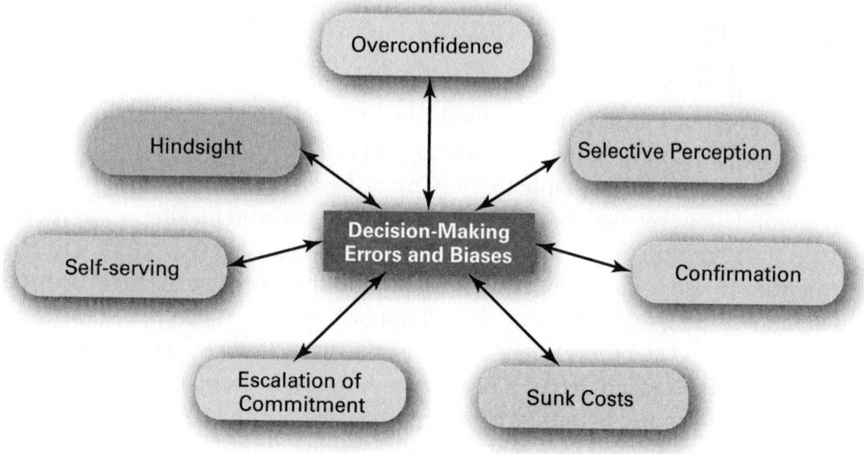

- *Confirmation bias.* Decision makers seek out information that reaffirms their past choices and discount information that contradicts past judgments. These people tend to accept at face value information that confirms their preconceived views and are critical and skeptical of information that challenges these views. For instance, Pierre continues to give business to the same supplier, even though the supplier has been late on several deliveries. Pierre thinks the supplier is a nice person, and the supplier keeps promising to deliver on time.

- *Sunk-costs error.* Decision makers forget that current choices cannot correct the past. They incorrectly fixate on past expenditures of time, money, or effort in assessing choices rather than on future consequences. For instance, Amita has spent thousands of dollars and several months introducing new procedures for handling customer complaints. Both customers and employees are complaining about the new procedures. Amita does not want to consider the possibility that the procedures are needlessly complicated because of the investment in time and money she has already made.

- *Escalation-of-commitment error.* Decisions can also be influenced by a phenomenon called **escalation of commitment**, which is an increased commitment to a previous decision despite evidence that it might have been wrong.[28] For example, studies of the events leading up to the space shuttle *Columbia* disaster in 2003 point to an escalation of commitment by decision makers to ignore the possible damage that foam striking the shuttle at takeoff might have had, even though the decision was questioned by certain individuals. Why would decision makers want to escalate commitment to a bad decision? Because they don't want to admit that their initial decision might have been flawed. Rather than search for new alternatives, they simply increase their commitment to the original solution.

- *Self-serving bias.* Decision makers take credit for their successes and blame failure on outside factors. For instance, Jessie dismisses his team's efforts when he wins a contract, although he blames them for the small error that was in the final report.

- *Hindsight bias.* Decision makers falsely believe that they would have accurately predicted the outcome of an event once that outcome is actually known. For instance, after a client cancelled a contract that had been drawn up, Cindy tells her manager she knew ahead of time that was going to happen, even though she had had no such thoughts before the contract was cancelled. After the fact, some outcomes seem more obvious than they did beforehand.

escalation of commitment
An increased commitment to a previous decision despite evidence that it might have been wrong.

How can managers avoid the negative effects of these decision-making errors and biases? The main thing is being aware of them and then trying not to exhibit them. Beyond that, managers also should pay attention to "how" they make decisions and try to identify the heuristics they typically use and critically evaluate how appropriate those are. Finally, managers might want to ask those around them to help identify weaknesses in their decision-making style and try to improve on them.

Summing Up Managerial Decision Making

How can we best sum up managerial decision making? Exhibit 5-14 provides an overview. Because it's in their best interests, managers *want* to make good decisions—that is, choose the "best" alternative, implement it, and determine whether or not it takes care of the problem—the reason a decision was needed in the first place. Their decision-making process is affected by four factors, including the decision-making approach being followed, the decision-making conditions, the type of problem being dealt with, and the decision maker's own style of decision making. In addition, certain decision-making errors and biases may impact the process. Each of these factors plays a role in determining how a manager makes a decision. So whether that decision involves addressing an employee's habitual tardiness, resolving a problem with product quality, or determining whether to enter a new market, remember that it has been shaped by a number of factors.

Exhibit 5-14

Overview of Managerial Decision Making

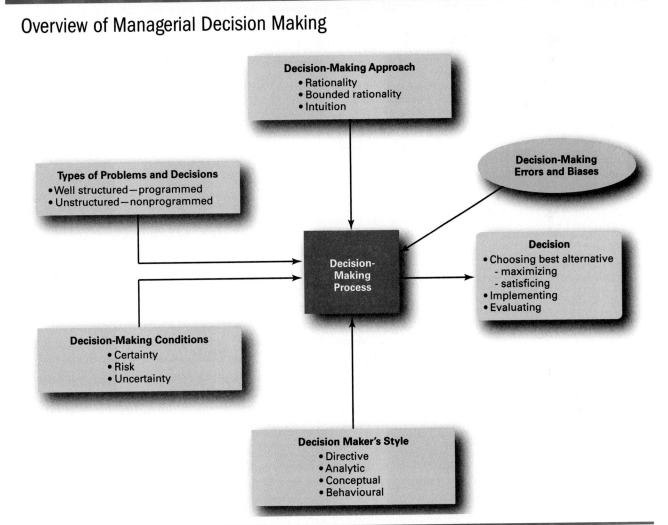

Decision Making for Today's World

▶ ▶ ▶ On September 6, 2006, Sandra Wilson sold Robeez Footwear to Stride Rite, her largest client, for $30.5 million.[29] Wilson will stay on as a consultant to Stride Rite for the Robeez brand and help add children's accessories and clothing to the shoe line. As a consultant, she will be able to ensure that her vision for Robeez' design and brand continues.

The deal is also a coup for Stride Rite because it will help the company gain entry into the upscale department stores that carry Robeez. According to a financial analyst, "By having Robeez sold in stores like Saks and Bloomingdale's, that gives [Stride Rite] a better opportunity to also sell the Stride Rite product in those same retail channels."

Wilson found the decision to sell her company an emotional one. She signed the deal the same day her son Robert started high school. "I've had to say goodbye to two babies," she said. "This was probably the toughest decision I'm ever going to have to make, but I'm really looking forward to working with the Robeez team and Stride Rite in the next year."

Think About It
How can Sandra Wilson be sure she made the right decision?

3. How can managers make more effective decisions?

Stride Rite
www.striderite.com

Today's business world revolves around making decisions, often risky ones, usually with incomplete or inadequate information, and under intense time pressure. In a recent survey of managers, 77 percent said that the number of decisions made during a typical workday had increased, and more than 43 percent said that the amount of time given to each decision had decreased.[30] Most managers are making one decision after another, and, as if that were not challenging enough, more is at stake than ever before. Bad decisions can cost millions. What do managers need to do to make effective decisions in today's fast-moving world? Here are a few guidelines:

- *Know when it's time to call it quits.* When it's evident that a decision is not working, don't be afraid to pull the plug. As we said earlier, many decision makers block or distort negative information because they don't want to believe that their decision was bad. They become so attached to the decision that they refuse to recognize when it's time to move on. In today's dynamic environment, this type of thinking simply will not work.

- *Practise the five whys.* When the environment is highly uncertain, one way to encourage good decision making is to get people to think more broadly and deeply about the issues. Because of the intense time pressure that managers face, it may be tempting to do just a superficial analysis. The "five whys" approach suggests that employees learn to ask "why" not just once, but five times.[31] Asking "why" this is happening usually results in a superficial explanation of the problem the first time; subsequent "whys" force decision makers to probe more deeply into the causes of the problem and possible solutions.

- *Use an effective decision-making process.* An effective decision-making process has these six characteristics: "(1) It focuses on what's important; (2) It's logical and consistent; (3) It acknowledges both subjective and objective thinking and blends analytical with intuitive thinking; (4) It requires only as much information and analysis as is necessary to resolve a particular dilemma; (5) It encourages and guides the gathering of relevant information and informed opinion; and (6) It's straightforward, reliable, easy to use, and flexible."[32]

The remaining suggestions for making decisions in today's world come from Karl Weick, an organizational psychologist who has made a career of studying organizations and how people work. He says that the best way for managers to respond to unpredictability and uncertainty is "by building an organization that expertly spots the unexpected when it crops up and then quickly adapts to the changed environment."[33] He calls these organizations *highly reliable organizations (HROs)* and says they share five habits:

- *They are not tricked by their success.* HROs are preoccupied with their failures. They are alert to the smallest deviations and react early and quickly to anything that does not fit with their expectations. Weick talks about Navy aviators who describe "leemers—a gut feeling that something isn't right." Typically, these leemers turn out to be accurate. Something, in fact, is wrong. Organizations need to create climates where people feel safe trusting their leemers.

- *They defer to the experts on the front line.* Front-line employees—those who interact day in and day out with customers, products, suppliers, and so forth—have first-hand knowledge of what can and cannot be done, what will and will not work. Get their input. Let them make decisions.

- *They let unexpected circumstances provide the solution.* One of Weick's better-known works is his study of the Mann Gulch fire in Montana that killed 13 smoke jumpers in 1949. The event was a massive, tragic organizational failure. However, the reaction of the foreman illustrates how effective decision makers respond to unexpected circumstances. When the fire was nearly on top of his men, he invented the escape fire—a small fire that consumed all the brush around the team, leaving an area where the larger fire could not burn. His action was contrary to everything firefighters are taught (that is, you don't start fires—you extinguish them), but at the time it was the best decision.

- *They embrace complexity.* This characteristic is similar to the five whys we discussed earlier. Because business is complex, these organizations recognize that it "takes complexity to sense complexity." Rather than simplifying data, which we instinctively try to do when faced with complexity, these organizations aim for deeper understanding of the situation. They tap into their complexity to help them adapt more effectively.

- *They anticipate, but also anticipate their limits.* These organizations do try to anticipate as much as possible, but they recognize that they cannot anticipate everything. As Weick says, they don't "think, then act. They think by acting. By actually doing things, you'll find out what works and what doesn't."

Making decisions in today's fast-moving world is not easy. Successful managers have good decision-making skills to effectively and efficiently plan, organize, lead, and control. (The *CBC Video Case Incident—Ben & Jerry's in Canada* on page 254 provides an example of a manager who understands the importance of making good decisions.)

SUMMARY AND IMPLICATIONS

1. What are the steps in the decision-making process? The steps include identifying a problem and the decision criteria; allocating weights to those criteria; developing, analyzing, and selecting an alternative that can resolve the problem; implementing the alternative; and evaluating the decision's effectiveness.

▶ ▶ ▶ Sandra Wilson, Robeez Footwear chair and CEO, identified that her company was poised for growth. She had to determine the relevant criteria and their weights to make a decision about whether or not to seek a new partner or sell the company. Which would be the best alternative?

2. What factors affect how decisions are made? It is often assumed that managers make decisions that follow the steps of the rational decision-making model. However, not all decisions follow that model, for a variety of reasons. Often managers work with bounded rationality, because they are not able to collect and process all the information on all possible alternatives. Or they might make a satisficing decision—one that is "good enough" rather than the "best." Managers sometimes use intuition to enhance their decision-making process. Managers also need to decide whether they should make decisions themselves, or encourage a team to help make the decision. Teams can make better decisions in many cases, but the time to make the decision generally increases. Managers are affected by a variety of biases and errors: overconfidence bias, selective perception bias, confirmation bias, sunk-costs error, escalation-of-commitment error, self-serving bias, and hindsight bias.

▶ ▶ ▶ Sandra Wilson was aware of a variety of positives and negatives in the decision to either bring in a new partner or sell Robeez. It was important for her to recognize that her preference for growth and the desire to see her creative vision for the brand continue might affect how she made her decision.

3. How can managers make more effective decisions? When making a decision, managers need to think broadly and deeply about issues, and then know when it's time to call it quits. To be effective decision makers, they should focus on what is important; be logical and consistent; acknowledge both subjective and objective thinking; consider only as much information and analysis as is necessary; gather relevant information and informed opinion; and be flexible.

▶ ▶ ▶ Sandra Wilson decided that selling Robeez to Stride Rite was the right thing to do. There are advantages and disadvantages to most decisions, and it is important to weigh these thoroughly before reaching a conclusion.

CHAPTER 5

Management @ Work

READING FOR COMPREHENSION

1. Why is decision making often described as the essence of a manager's job?

2. How is implementation important to the decision-making process?

3. What is a satisficing decision? How does it differ from a maximizing decision?

4. How do certainty, risk, and uncertainty affect decision making?

5. What is groupthink? How does it affect decision making?

6. Describe the decision-making biases and errors managers may exhibit.

7. How does escalation of commitment affect decision making? Why would managers make this type of error?

LINKING CONCEPTS TO PRACTICE

1. How might an organization's culture influence the way managers make decisions?

2. Would you call yourself a systematic or an intuitive thinker? What are the decision-making implications of these labels? What are the implications for choosing an employer?

3. All of us bring biases to the decisions we make. What would be the drawbacks of having biases? Could there be any advantages to having biases? Explain. What are the implications for decision making?

4. How can managers blend the guidelines for making effective decisions in today's world with the rationality and bounded rationality models of decision making, or can they? Explain.

5. Why do good managers sometimes make bad decisions? How can managers improve their decision-making skills?

SELF-ASSESSMENT

How Intuitive Am I?

For each of the following questions, select the response that first appeals to you:[34]

1. When working on a project, I prefer to
   a. be told what the problem is, but be left free to decide how to solve it.
   b. get very clear instructions about how to go about solving the problem before I start.

2. When working on a project, I prefer to work with colleagues who are
   a. realistic.
   b. imaginative.

3. I most admire people who are
   a. creative.
   b. careful.

4. The friends I choose tend to be
   a. serious and hard-working.
   b. exciting and often emotional.

5. When I ask a colleague for advice on a problem I have, I
   a. seldom or never get upset if he/she questions my basic assumptions.
   b. often get upset if he/she questions my basic assumptions.

6. When I start my day, I
   a. seldom make or follow a specific plan.
   b. usually make a plan first to follow.

7. When working with numbers, I find that I
   a. seldom or never make factual errors.
   b. often make factual errors.

8. I find that I

   a. seldom daydream during the day and really don't enjoy doing so when I do it.

   b. frequently daydream during the day and enjoy doing so.

9. When working on a problem, I

   a. prefer to follow the instructions or rules when they are given to me.

   b. often enjoy circumventing the instructions or rules when they are given to me.

10. When I try to put something together, I prefer to have

   a. step-by-step written instructions on how to assemble the item.

   b. a picture of how the item is supposed to look once assembled.

11. I find that the person who irritates me the most is the one who appears to be

   a. disorganized.

   b. organized.

12. When an unexpected crisis comes up that I have to deal with, I

   a. feel anxious about the situation.

   b. feel excited by the challenge of the situation.

Scoring Key

For items 1, 3, 5, 6, and 11, score as follows:	a = 1, b = 0
For items 2, 4, 7, 8, 9, 10, and 12, score as follows:	a = 0, b = 1
Your total score will range between 0 and 12.	

Analysis and Interpretation

Decision making isn't all systematic logic. Good decision makers also have developed, through experience, an intuitive ability that complements rational analysis. This ability is particularly valuable when decision makers face high levels of uncertainty, when facts are limited, when there is little previous precedent, when time is pressing, or when there are multiple plausible alternatives to choose among and there are good arguments for each.

If you have an intuitive score greater than 8, you prefer situations where there is a lack of structure and rules. You can handle uncertainty, spontaneity, and openness. Whether this ability is a plus in your job depends to a great extent on the culture of your organization. Where rationality is highly valued, reliance on intuition is likely to be seen as a negative quality. In open and creative-type cultures, intuitive ability is more likely to be valued.

More Self-Assessments mymanagementlab

To learn more about your skills, abilities, and interests, go to the MyManagementLab website and take the following self-assessments:

- I.A.4.—How Well Do I Handle Ambiguity? (This exercise also appears in Chapter 7 on pages 216–217.)
- I.D.1.—What's My Decision-Making Style?
- III.C.1.—How Well Do I Respond to Turbulent Change? (This exercise also appears in Chapter 16 on pages 537–538.)

MANAGEMENT FOR YOU TODAY

Dilemma

Suppose your uncle said that he would help you open your own business. You are not sure whether you really want to run your own business, or work for a large consulting firm. However, you have always been interested in running a restaurant. How would you go about making a decision on what kind of restaurant you might open? How would you decide whether you should take your uncle up on his offer?

Becoming a Manager

- Pay close attention to decisions you make and how you make them.
- When you feel you have not made a good decision, assess how you could have made a better one. Which step of the decision-making process could you have improved?
- Work at developing good decision-making skills.
- Read books about decision making.
- Ask people you admire for advice on how they make good decisions.

WORKING TOGETHER: TEAM-BASED EXERCISE

A Life or Death Situation

The situation described in this problem is based on actual cases in which men and women lived or died depending upon the survival decision they made. Your "life" or "death" will depend on how well your group can share its present knowledge of a relatively unfamiliar problem, so that the group can make decisions that will lead to your survival.[35]

It is approximately 2:30 p.m. on October 5, and you have just crash-landed in a float plane on the east shore of Laura Lake in the subarctic region of the Northern Quebec–Newfoundland and Labrador border. The pilot was killed in the crash, but the rest of you are uninjured. Each of you is wet up to the waist and has perspired heavily. Shortly after the crash, the plane drifted into deep water and sank with the pilot's body pinned inside. The pilot was unable to contact anyone before the crash. However, ground sightings indicate that you are 48 kilometres south of your intended course and approximately 22 air miles east of Schefferville, your original destination and the nearest known habitation. Schefferville (pop. 240) is an iron ore–mining town approximately 300 air miles north of the St. Lawrence, 720 kilometres east of the James Bay/Hudson Bay area, 1290 kilometres south of the Arctic Circle, and 480 kilometres west of the Atlantic Coast. It is reachable only by air or rail, all roads ending a few kilometres from town. Your party was expected to return from northwestern Labrador to Schefferville no later than October 19 and filed a flight plan with Transport Canada via Schefferville radio to that effect.

The immediate area is covered with small evergreen trees (4 to 10 centimetres in diameter). Scattered in the area are a number of hills having rocky and barren tops. Tundra (treeless plains) makes up the valleys between the hills and consist only of small scrubs. Approximately 25 percent of the area in the region is covered by long, narrow lakes that run northwest to southeast. Innumerable streams and rivers flow into and connect the lakes. Temperatures during October vary between −4°C and 2°C, although it sometimes can go as high as 10°C and as low as −18°C. Heavy clouds cover the sky three-quarters of the time, with only one day in ten being fairly clear. Thirteen to eighteen centimetres of snow are on the ground. However, the actual depth varies enormously because the wind sweeps the exposed areas clear and builds drifts 0.9 to 1.5 metres deep in other areas. The wind speed averages 20 to 25 kilometres/hour and is mostly out of the west-northwest.

You are all dressed in insulated underwear, socks, heavy wool shirts, pants, knit gloves, sheepskin jackets, knitted wool toques, and heavy leather hunting boots. Collectively, your personal possessions include $150 in bills, 4 loonies, 4 quarters, 2 dimes, 1 nickel, and 3 pennies; 1 pocket knife (2 blades and an awl, which resembles an ice pick); 1 stub lead pencil; and an air map.

Before the plane drifted away and sank, you were able to salvage the 15 items listed on the attached chart. Your task is to rank these items according to their importance to your survival, from "1" for the most important up to "15" for the least important.

You may assume the following:

- The number of survivors is the same as the number on your team.

- You are the actual people in the situation.

- The team has agreed to stick together.

- All items are dry and in good condition.

Items	Step 1: Your ranking	Step 2: Team ranking	Step 3: Survival experts' ranking	Step 4: Difference between steps 1 and 3	Step 5: Difference between steps 2 and 3
A magnetic compass					
A 4-litre can of maple syrup					
A sleeping bag per person (arctic type; down-filled with liner)					
A bottle of water purification tablets					
A 6 m x 6 m piece of heavy duty canvas					

continued

Items	Step 1: Your ranking	Step 2: Team ranking	Step 3: Survival experts' ranking	Step 4: Difference between steps 1 and 3	Step 5: Difference between steps 2 and 3
13 wood matches in a metal screwtop, water-proof container					
75 m of 0.5-cm braided nylon rope, 20 kg test					
An operating 4-battery flashlight					
3 pairs of snowshoes					
A fifth of Bacardi rum (151 proof)					
Safety-razor shaving kit with mirror					
A wind-up alarm clock					
A hand axe					
1 aircraft inner tube for a 35-cm wheel (punctured)					
A book entitled *Northern Star Navigation*					
Total				Individual	Team

ETHICS IN ACTION

Ethical Dilemma Exercise: Can Investment Advice Be "Perfectly Objective"?

Competitive problems are rarely well structured, as the managers at Greenfield Brokerage know.[36] Over the years, the firm has successfully competed with well-established rivals by making nonprogrammed decisions. For example, management decided to charge customers less for trading stocks, bonds, and mutual funds and to implement technology giving customers more trading choices. Because the competitive environment is constantly changing, Greenfield's advertising managers can never be certain about the outcome of decisions concerning how to promote the firm's competitive advantages.

Not long ago, some competing brokerage firms paid hefty fines to settle charges stemming from conflicts of interest involving their research and recommendations to customers. In the aftermath of these scandals, Greenfield's managers decided on an advertising campaign to stress that Greenfield does things differently. One tongue-in-cheek commercial took viewers behind the scenes at a fictitious competitor's office,

where brokers chanted "Buy, buy, buy." A broker looked at a restaurant takeout menu as he told a customer on the phone, "I have your portfolio right here, and I think you should buy." Some networks rejected these aggressive commercials. The ads also raised questions about potential conflicts of interest created by Greenfield brokers steering business to in-house traders and mutual funds.

Imagine you are an advertising manager at Greenfield. Your advertising agency has suggested a newspaper ad in which a fictitious competing broker is quoted as saying, "My investment advice is perfectly objective, even though I work on commission." A Greenfield broker is then quoted as saying, "I don't work on commission like other brokers do, so my investment advice is perfectly objective." How certain are you that your advice is perfectly objective when Greenfield benefits from every client it gets? (Review Exhibits 5-13 on page 154 and 5-14 on page 155 as you think about this dilemma.)

Thinking Critically About Ethics

You are in charge of hiring a new employee to work in your area of responsibility, and one of your friends from college needs a job. You think he's minimally qualified for the position, and you feel that you could find a better-qualified and more experienced candidate if you kept looking. What will you do? What factors will influence your decision? What will you tell your friend?

C. F. Martin Guitar Company

The C. F. Martin Guitar Company (**www.mguitar.com**) has been producing acoustic instruments since 1833.[37] A Martin guitar is among the best that money can buy. Current CEO Christian Frederick Martin IV—better known as Chris—continues to be committed to the guitar maker's craft. During 2002, the company sold about 77 000 instruments and hit a record $77 million in revenue. Despite this success, Chris is facing some serious issues.

Martin Guitar is an interesting blend of old and new. Although the equipment and tools may have changed over the years, employees remain true to the principle of high standards of musical excellence. Building a guitar to meet these standards requires considerable attention and patience. In a 1904 catalogue, a family member explained, "How to build a guitar to give this tone is not a secret. It takes care and patience." Now, well over a century later, this statement is still an accurate reflection of the company's philosophy.

From the very beginning, quality has played an important role in everything that Martin Guitar does. Part of that quality approach includes a long-standing ecological policy. The company depends on natural wood products to make its guitars, but a lot of the wood supply is vanishing. Chris has long embraced the responsible use of traditional wood materials, going so far as to encourage suppliers to find alternative species. Based on thorough customer research, Martin Guitar introduced guitars that used structurally sound woods with natural cosmetic defects that were once considered unacceptable. In addition, Martin Guitar follows the directives of CITES, the Convention on International Trade in Endangered Species of Wild Fauna and Flora (**www.cites. org**), even though it has the potential to affect Martin Guitar's ability to produce the type of quality products it has in the past. This treaty barred the export of the much-desired Brazilian rosewood, which is considered endangered. A guitar built from the remaining supply of this popular wood has a hefty price tag—$39 999 and up. Similar prices may be in line for the leading alternative, Honduras mahogany. Chris says, "All of us who use wood for the tone [it makes] are scrambling. Options are limited."

Although the company is rooted in its past, Chris is wondering whether he should go in new directions. For instance, he could try selling guitars in the under-$800 segment, a segment that accounts for 65 percent of the acoustic guitar industry's sales. A less expensive guitar would not look, smell, or feel like the company's pricier models. But Chris thinks that it would sound better than guitars in that price range made by other companies. Chris explains, "My fear is that if we don't look at alternatives, we'll be the company making guitars for doctors and lawyers. If Martin just worships its past without trying anything new, there won't be a Martin left to worship."

What should Chris do? Why?

Some Solutions Create More Problems

With sentences handed down to executives involved in the Enron scandal, the conviction of Martha Stewart in March 2004 of lying to federal investigators during a stock-scandal investigation, and the conviction of Conrad Black for using millions of Hollinger International's profits between 1997 and 2004 for his own personal gain, being a CEO appears to be losing some of its lustre.[38] Why these individuals did what they did and why they made such decisions that proved to be so wrong is difficult to say. You just have to wonder what underlies the CEO decision-making process. Take the case of Robert Milton, CEO of Montreal-based Air Canada.

Air Canada has been struggling financially for a number of years. As the company went into bankruptcy in the early 2000s, Milton pleaded with the union leaders representing the company's 25 000 employees to consider accepting significant pay and benefits cuts. Milton built the case that this was a last resort and that without the employees' acceptance of the cuts, the company was doomed.

The company emerged from bankruptcy in late 2004, but employees have not seen pay raises in awhile. Milton informed employees in spring 2006 that Air Canada would find it "hard" to increase wages in labour contract talks later in the year because other carriers have reduced pay. He added that expecting pay raises was not realistic, "given that in most places around North America wages are going down very, very significantly."

Meanwhile, the company distributed $266 million to its shareholders, leading union members to conclude that the company was doing better than the CEO was acknowledging. That money, had it been distributed to employees, would have resulted in a $10 000 bonus for each one. Employees were furious, and demanded that Milton step down. However, Milton explained his logic for not giving that money to employees: "By

providing a return of capital to our shareholders, ACE is rewarding investors for their confidence while maintaining a firm foundation for future prosperity."

Questions

1. How do you think poor decision making contributed to the failures of Conrad Black and Robert Milton? Discuss.

2. How could the eight-step decision-making process have helped Milton make a better decision? Explain.

3. What role, if any, did escalation of commitment play in Milton's decision? Defend your opinion.

DEVELOPING YOUR INTERPERSONAL SKILLS

Solving Problems Creatively

About the Skill

Creativity is a frame of mind. You need to expand your mind's capabilities—that is, open up your mind to new ideas. Every individual has the ability to improve his or her creativity, but many people simply don't try to develop that ability. In a global business environment, where changes are fast and furious, organizations desperately need creative people. The uniqueness and variety of problems that managers face demand that they be able to solve problems creatively.

Steps in Developing the Skill

You can be more effective at solving problems creatively if you use the following 10 suggestions:[39]

1. **Think of yourself as creative.** Although this may be a simple suggestion, research shows that if you think you cannot be creative, you will not be. Believing in your ability to be creative is the first step in becoming more creative.

2. **Pay attention to your intuition.** Every individual has a subconscious mind that works well. Sometimes answers will come to you when you least expect them. Listen to that "inner voice." In fact, most creative people keep a notepad near their beds and write down ideas when the thoughts come to them. That way, they don't forget them.

3. **Move away from your comfort zone.** Every individual has a comfort zone in which certainty exists. But creativity and the known often do not mix. To be creative, you need to move away from the status quo and focus your mind on something new.

4. **Determine what you want to do.** This includes such things as taking time to understand a problem before

beginning to try to resolve it, getting all the facts in mind, and trying to identify the most important facts.

5. **Look for ways to tackle the problem.** This can be accomplished by setting aside a block of time to focus on it; working out a plan for attacking it; establishing subgoals; imagining or actually using analogies wherever possible (for example, could you approach your problem like a fish out of water and look at what the fish does to cope? Or can you use the things you have to do to find your way when it's foggy to help you solve your problem?); using different problem-solving strategies such as verbal, visual, mathematical, theatrical (for example, you might draw a diagram of the decision or problem to help you visualize it better or you might talk to yourself out loud about the problem, telling it as you would tell a story to someone); trusting your intuition; and playing with possible ideas and approaches (for example, look at your problem from a different perspective or ask yourself what someone else, such as your grandmother, might do if faced with the same situation).

6. **Look for ways to do things better.** This may involve trying consciously to be original, not worrying about looking foolish, eliminating cultural taboos (like gender stereotypes) that might influence your possible solutions, keeping an open mind, being alert to odd or puzzling facts, thinking of unconventional ways to use objects and the environment (for instance, thinking about how you could use newspaper or magazine headlines to help you be a better problem solver), discarding usual or habitual ways of doing things, and striving for objectivity by being as critical of your own ideas as you would those of someone else.

7. **Find several right answers.** Being creative means continuing to look for other solutions even when you think you

have solved the problem. A better, more creative solution just might be found.

8. **Believe in finding a workable solution.** Like believing in yourself, you also need to believe in your ideas. If you don't think you can find a solution, you probably won't.

9. **Brainstorm with others.** Creativity isn't an isolated activity. Bouncing ideas off others creates synergy.

10. **Turn creative ideas into action.** Coming up with creative ideas is only part of the process. Once the ideas are generated, they must be implemented. Keeping great ideas in your mind, or on papers that no one will read, does little to expand your creative abilities.

Practising the Skill

Read the following scenario. Write some notes about how you would handle the situation. Be sure to refer to the 10 suggestions for solving problems creatively.

Scenario

Every time the phone rings, your stomach clenches and your palms start to sweat. And it's no wonder! As sales manager for Brinkers, a machine tool parts manufacturer, you are besieged by calls from customers who are upset about late deliveries. Your manager, Carter Hererra, acts as both production manager and scheduler. Every time your sales representatives negotiate a sale, it's up to Carter to determine whether or not production can actually meet the delivery date

the customer specifies. And Carter invariably says, "No problem." The good thing about this is that you make a lot of initial sales. The bad news is that production hardly ever meets the shipment dates that Carter authorizes. And he does not seem to be all that concerned about the aftermath of late deliveries. He says, "Our customers know they're getting outstanding quality at a great price. Just let them try to match that anywhere. It can't be done. So even if they have to wait a couple of extra days or weeks, they're still getting the best deal they can." Somehow the customers don't see it that way, however. And they let you know about their unhappiness. Then it's up to you to try to soothe the relationship. You know this problem has to be taken care of, but what possible solutions are there? After all, how are you going to keep from making your manager or the customers angry?

Reinforcing the Skill

The following activities will help you practise and reinforce the skills associated with solving problems creatively:

1. Take out a couple of sheets of paper. How many words can you make using the letters in the word *brainstorm*? (There are at least 95.) If you run out of words before time is up, it's OK to quit early. But try to be as creative as you can.

2. List on a piece of paper some common terms that apply to both water and finance. How many were you able to come up with?

MANAGING WORKFORCE DIVERSITY

The Value of Diversity in Decision Making

Have you decided what your major is going to be? How did you decide? Do you feel your decision is a good one? Is there anything you could have done differently to make sure that your decision was the best one?[40]

Making good decisions is tough! Managers are continually making decisions—for instance, developing new products, establishing weekly or monthly goals, implementing advertising campaigns, reassigning employees to different work groups, resolving customers' complaints, or purchasing new laptops for sales representatives. One important suggestion for making better decisions is to tap into the diversity of the work group. Drawing upon the ideas of diverse employees can prove valuable to a manager's decision making. Why? Diverse employees can provide fresh perspectives on issues. They can offer differing interpretations on how a problem is defined and may be more open to trying new ways of doing things. Diverse employees usually are more creative in generating alternatives and more flexible in resolving issues. And getting input from diverse sources increases the likelihood of finding creative and unique solutions.

Even though diversity in decision making can be valuable, there are drawbacks. The lack of a common perspective usually means that more time is spent discussing the issues. Communication may be a problem, particularly if language barriers are present. In addition, seeking out diverse opinions can make the decision-making process more complex, confusing, and ambiguous. In addition, with multiple perspectives on the decision, it may be difficult to reach a single agreement or to agree on specific actions. Although these drawbacks are valid concerns, the value of diversity in decision making outweighs the potential disadvantages.

Now, about that decision on a major. Did you ask others for their opinions? Did you seek out advice from professors, family members, friends, or co-workers? Getting diverse perspectives on an important decision like this could help you make the best one! Managers also should consider the value to be gained from diversity in decision making.

Taking Risks

"IYAD-WYAD-YAG-WYAG: If you always do what you've always done, you'll always get what you've always got! So if your life is ever going to improve, you'll have to take chances" (Anonymous).[41]

How will you approach your various career moves in the time you spend working over the course of your lifetime? Will you want to do what you have always done? Or will you want to take chances, and how comfortable will you be taking chances? Taking career risks does not have to be a gamble. Responsible risk-taking can make outcomes more predictable. Here are some suggestions for being a responsible, effective risk-taker in career decisions.

It's important to thoroughly evaluate the risk. Before committing to a career risk, consider what you could lose or who might be hurt. How important are those things or those people to you? Explore whether you can reach your goal in another way, thus making the risk unnecessary. Find out everything you can about what is involved with taking this career risk—the timing; the people involved; the changes it will entail; and the potential gains and losses, both in the short run and the long run. Examine closely your feelings about taking this risk: Are you afraid? Are you ready to act now? Will you know if you have risked more than you can afford to lose? Finally, ensure your employability. The most important thing you can do is ensure you have choices by keeping your skills current and continually learning new skills.

As with any decision involving risk, the more information you have available, the better able you are to assess the risk. Then, armed with this information, you can make a more informed decision. And even though you will not be able to eliminate all the negatives associated with taking the risk, you can, at least, know about them.

Foundations of Planning

PART **two**

How do I make plans to carry out decisions?

1. What does planning involve?

2. How do managers set goals and develop plans?

3. What are the challenges in planning?

▶ ▶ ▶ Blue Man Group is one of the hottest performance groups today.[1] Its theatrical productions have run in New York, Boston, Chicago, and Las Vegas for years. Currently, the group has shows in Berlin, Oberhausen, Amsterdam, New York City, Boston, Chicago, Las Vegas, and Orlando. It also opened a show in Toronto in 2005, which ran until 2007. Blue Man performances are a mix of mime, percussion music, and splashing paint.

The group was founded in 1988 by three guys who decided it was time to stage a funeral for the 1980s. They put on bald wigs, painted themselves blue, and carried a coffin filled with items representing the worst of the decade (such as yuppies and Rambo) into New York City's Central Park. MTV recorded the ceremony.

Encouraged by their friends, the trio (Chris Wink, Matt Goldman, and Phil Stanton) started giving small performances around the city. None of the three had formal training in music or acting. They really had not planned to become performers. Three years later, they had performed on national TV, spitting paint on *The Tonight Show* and *Live with Regis and Kathie Lee*. They also had an off-Broadway show called *Tubes*.

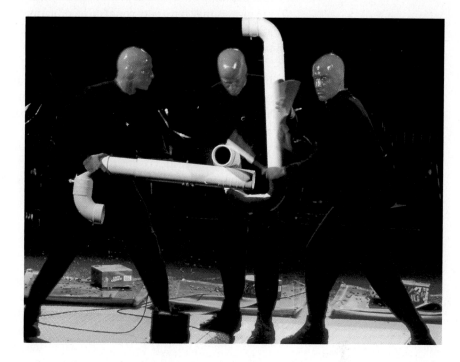

Wink, Goldman, and Stanton were also starting to burn out. They were working six days a week, had gone three years without a break, and performed 1200 consecutive shows. Once success started, the three just kept going, not giving thought to how to manage the show or their time. They did not have time to create new material, so they were just performing the same show over and over.

They had a small crew who had "never worked in theater and [did not] have a clue, just like us," says Wink. They spent 90 minutes each night making themselves up before a performance. Then they were part of the cleanup crew. They were so tired that they did not have time for a personal life. How did they get into this situation? "We've never planned ahead," explained Wink.

Think About It

How much planning should organizations do? Put yourself in Blue Man Group's shoes. How can it make sure that the show goes on, should one of its members get injured?

Managers everywhere need to plan. In this chapter, we present the basics of planning: what it is, why managers plan, and how they plan. Then we conclude by looking at some contemporary issues in planning.

What Is Planning?

As we stated in Chapter 1, **planning** involves defining goals, establishing an overall strategy for achieving those goals, and developing a comprehensive set of plans to integrate and coordinate the work needed to achieve the goals. It's concerned with both ends (what's to be done) and means (how it's to be done). For instance, you and your classmates may want to organize a large graduation dinner dance. To do so, you would consider the goals, the strategy, and the plans and assign committees to get the work done.

1. What does planning involve?

planning
A management function that involves defining goals, establishing a strategy for achieving those goals, and developing plans to integrate and coordinate activities.

Planning can be either formal or informal. In informal planning, nothing is written down, and there is little or no sharing of goals with others. Informal planning is general and lacks continuity. Although it's more common in smaller organizations, where the owner-manager has a vision of where he or she wants the business to go and how to get there, informal planning does exist in some large organizations as well. At the same time, some small businesses may have very sophisticated planning processes and formal plans. (For a look at your response to planning, see *Self-Assessment—How Good Am I at Personal Planning?* on pages 243–244, in Chapter 8.)

Q&A 6.1

When we use the term *planning* in this book, we mean *formal* planning. In formal planning, specific goals covering a period of years are defined. These goals are written and shared with organization members. Then a specific action program for the achievement of these goals is developed; that is, managers clearly define the path they want to take to get the organization and the various work units from where they are to where the managers want them to be.

Setting goals, establishing strategies to achieve those goals, and developing a set of plans to integrate and coordinate activities seem pretty complicated. Given that fact, why should managers want to plan? Does planning impact performance? We address these issues in the following sections.

Purposes of Planning

Are you a planner or a doer? Do you prefer to make plans or just act?

We can identify at least four reasons for planning:

- *Planning provides direction to managers and nonmanagers alike.* When employees know where the organization or work unit is going and what they must contribute to reach goals, they can coordinate their activities, cooperate with each other, and do what it takes to accomplish those goals. Without planning, departments and individuals might work at cross purposes, preventing the organization from moving efficiently toward its goals. This would also be true if you and your friends were planning your grad party—if you did not coordinate and cooperate, you might not actually get the party organized in time.

- *Planning reduces uncertainty by forcing managers to look ahead, anticipate change, consider the impact of change, and develop appropriate responses.* Even though planning cannot eliminate change or uncertainty, managers plan in order to anticipate change and develop the most effective response to it. Similarly, by planning a grad party ahead of time, you can make sure that it's held at a desired location, rather than at the only one that was left because you waited until the last minute.

- *Planning reduces overlapping and wasteful activities.* When work activities are coordinated around established plans, redundancy can be minimized. Furthermore, when means and ends are made clear through planning, inefficiencies become obvious and can be corrected or eliminated.

- *Planning establishes the goals or standards that are used in controlling.* If we are unsure of what we are trying to accomplish, how can we determine whether we have actually achieved it? In planning, we develop the goals and the plans. Then, through controlling, we compare actual performance against the goals, identify any significant deviations, and take any necessary corrective action. Without planning, there would be no way to control outcomes.

Victoria Hale founded the nonprofit Institute for OneWorld Health with an informal plan. Inspired by a conversation with a cab driver about pharmaceutical science, Hale went back to an essay she had written years earlier about diseases that would benefit from drug development efforts. Using that as her preliminary business plan, she incorporated the Institute the next day. The institute's goal is to persuade companies with important but not profitable drugs to donate those to the institute for tax and public relations benefits. The institute then uses grants and donations to distribute the drugs to needy patients around the world.

Ron Zambonini, former CEO of Ottawa-based Cognos (acquired by IBM in 2008), notes that planning went out of fashion during the dot-com years. He found that in both California and in Ottawa, entrepreneurs worked "90 hours a week, but the whole goal [was] not to build a business or a company. [All they really wanted was] someone to buy them out."[2] Unfortunately, many of those companies were not bought out, but folded. Planning might have helped them be more successful.

Planning and Performance

Are you skeptical of planning? Do you wonder whether planning really pays off?

Is planning worthwhile? Do managers and organizations that plan outperform those that don't? Intuitively, you would expect the answer to be a resounding yes. While studies of performance in organizations that plan are generally positive, we cannot say that organizations that formally plan *always* outperform those that don't plan.

Numerous studies have looked at the relationship between planning and performance.[3] We can draw the following four conclusions from these studies. First, generally speaking, formal planning is associated with higher profits, higher return on assets, and other positive financial results. Second, the quality of the planning process and the appropriate implementation of the plans probably contribute more to high performance than does the extent of planning. Third, in those studies in which formal planning did not lead to higher performance, the external environment often was the culprit. Government regulations, powerful labour unions, and other critical environmental forces constrain managers' options and reduce the impact of planning on an organization's performance. Fourth, the planning/performance relationship is influenced by the planning time frame. Organizations need at least four years of systematic formal planning before performance is affected.

Q&A 6.2

How Do Managers Plan?

▶ ▶ ▶ One evening, after three years of nonstop performing with Blue Man Group, Phil Stanton cut his hand with a router.[4] The group had never planned for what to do if one of them was injured. They had one understudy, one of the show's drummers, but only because their investors had insisted on it as a backup plan. While he had studied the show, he had never even rehearsed in it. When Stanton cut his hand, the drummer had to go onstage as a Blue Man. Because the group members wear bald wigs and paint themselves blue, no one in the audience knew that Stanton was missing. The show was a success even without him.

That success made the co-founders of Blue Man (Chris Wink, Matt Goldman, and Phil Stanton) realize that it would be quite easy to clone Blue Man, which would increase the number of shows they could do, and also give the co-founders time off. Finally, three years after they had started performing, they could think more about how to expand their show.

The group's next hurdle came when it opened a second venue, in Boston. The co-founders split their time between their New York venue and Boston, but it meant that they were less "hands on" at their shows. Quality started to slip. They finally realized they needed a specific plan to guide the 38 new performers they were bringing on board, so they locked themselves in an apartment and talked through their creative vision in great detail. The result? A 132-page operating manual that tells the story of the Blue Man show and allows the show to be reproduced by others. Ironically, by writing the plan, though it is a somewhat unorthodox one, the co-founders were able to express artistic ideals that had been understood among them but never stated before. Today, the former drummer who was their first understudy trains new Blue Man performers. Wink, Goldman, and Stanton make only occasional appearances onstage.

Think About It

How did planning make Blue Man Group performers more successful?

Planning is often called the primary management function because it establishes the basis for all the other functions that managers perform. Without planning, managers would not know what to organize, lead, or control. In fact, without plans, there would not be anything to organize, lead, or control! So how do managers plan?

2. How do managers set goals and develop plans?

goals
Desired outcomes for individuals, groups, or entire organizations.

plans
Documents that outline how goals are going to be met and describe resource allocations, schedules, and other necessary actions to accomplish the goals.

Planning involves two important elements: goals and plans. **Goals** are desired outcomes for individuals, groups, or entire organizations.[5] Goals are objectives, and we use the two terms interchangeably. They provide the direction for all management decisions and form the criteria against which actual work accomplishments can be measured. That is why they are often called the foundation of planning. You have to know the desired target or outcome before you can establish plans for reaching it. **Plans** are documents that outline how goals are going to be met and that typically describe resource allocations, schedules, and other necessary actions to accomplish the goals. As managers plan, they are developing both goals and plans.

In the next section, we consider how to establish goals.

Approaches to Establishing Goals

Every organization has some purpose for being in business. This purpose is generally derived from an organization's mission statement, which answers the question: What is our reason for being in business? We describe mission statements more thoroughly in Chapter 7 when we discuss strategic management. For now, it is important to note that the organization's mission helps managers determine the organization's goals. Goals provide the direction for all management decisions and actions and form the criteria against which actual accomplishments are measured. Everything organizational members do should be oriented toward helping their work units and the organization achieve its goals. These goals can be established through a process of traditional goal setting or management by objectives.

Traditional Goal Setting

traditional goal setting
An approach to setting goals in which goals are set at the top of the organization and then broken into subgoals for each organizational level.

In **traditional goal setting**, goals are set at the top of the organization and then broken into subgoals for each organizational level. This traditional perspective works reasonably well when an organization is hierarchically structured. For example, the president of a manufacturing business tells the vice-president of production what he expects manufacturing costs to be for the coming year and tells the marketing vice-president what level he expects sales to reach for the year. These goals then are passed down to the next organizational level and written to reflect the work responsibilities of that level, passed down to the next level, and so forth. Then, at some later point, performance is evaluated to determine whether the assigned goals have been achieved. This traditional perspective assumes that top managers know what is best because they see the "big picture." Thus, the goals that are established and passed down to each succeeding level serve to direct and guide, and in some ways constrain, individual employees' work behaviours. Employees work to meet the goals that have been assigned in their areas of responsibility.

Goals are the outcomes we desire. At the Bronx Zoo, where Patrick Thomas, curator of mammals, recently gazed into the eyes of Siberian tiger "Taurus" through a sheet of 2.5-centimetre-thick glass, "Our goal is to have animals engaged in normal behaviors." Thomas goes on to say of the new tiger habitat, "You want the exhibit to inspire visitors to care about saving tigers." The 1.2-hectare Tiger Mountain is particularly important: its 6 residents represent the mere 5000 tigers left in the wild.

One of the problems with this traditional approach is that if top managers define the organization's goals in broad terms—achieving "sufficient" profits or increasing "market leadership"—these ambiguous goals have to be made more specific as they flow down through the organization. At each level, managers define the goals, applying their own interpretations and biases as they make them more specific. However, what often happens is that goals lose clarity and unity as they make their way down from the top of the organization to lower levels. Exhibit 6-1 illustrates what can happen in this situation.

When the hierarchy of organizational goals *is* clearly defined, however, it forms an integrated network of goals, or a **means–ends chain**. This means that higher-level goals (or ends) are linked to lower-level goals, which serve as the means for their accomplishment. In other words, the achievement of goals at lower levels becomes the means to reach the goals at the next level (ends), and the accomplishment of goals at that level becomes the means to achieve the goals at the next level (ends), and so forth and so on, up through the different levels of the organization. That is how the traditional goal-setting approach is supposed to work. For instance, if top management wants to increase sales by 10 percent for the year, the marketing and sales departments need to develop action plans that will yield these results. The manufacturing division needs to develop plans for how to produce more product. An individual salesperson may need to make more calls to new clients, or convince current clients that they need more product. Thus, each of the lower levels (individual employee, sales, marketing, production) becomes means to achieving the corporate end of increasing sales.

Management by Objectives

Instead of traditional goal setting, many organizations use **management by objectives (MBO)**, an approach in which specific performance goals are jointly determined by employees and their managers, progress toward accomplishing these goals is periodically reviewed, and rewards are allocated on the basis of this progress. Rather than using goals only as controls, MBO uses them to motivate employees as well. Employees will be more committed to goals that they help set.

Management by objectives consists of four elements: goal specificity, participative decision making, an explicit time period, and performance feedback.[6] Its appeal lies in its focus on the accomplishment of participatively set objectives as the reason for and motivation behind individuals' work efforts. Exhibit 6-2 on page 174 lists the steps in a typical MBO program.

Do MBO programs work? Studies of actual MBO programs confirm that MBO increases employee performance and organizational productivity. A review of 70 programs, for example, found organizational productivity gains in 68 of them.[7] This same review also identified top management's commitment and involvement as important conditions for MBO to succeed.

Q&A 6.3

means–ends chain
An integrated network of goals in which the accomplishment of goals at one level serves as the means for achieving the goals, or ends, at the next level.

management by objectives (MBO)
An approach to setting goals in which specific performance goals are jointly determined by employees and their managers, progress toward accomplishing those goals is periodically reviewed, and rewards are allocated on the basis of this progress.

Exhibit 6-1

The Downside of Traditional Goal Setting

Exhibit 6-2

Steps in a Typical MBO Program

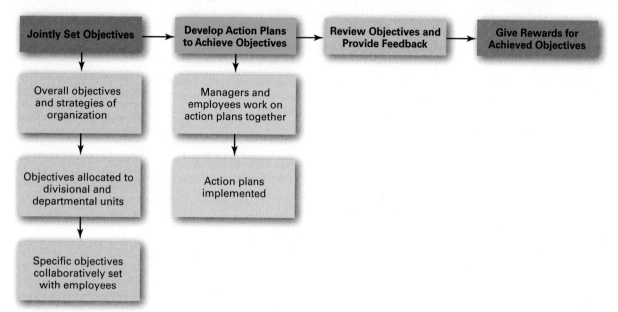

One problem of MBO programs is that they may not be as effective in times of dynamic environmental change. An MBO program needs some stability for employees to work toward accomplishing the set goals. If new goals must be set every few weeks, there is no time for employees to work on accomplishing the goals and measuring that accomplishment. Another problem of MBO programs is that an employee's overemphasis on accomplishing his or her goals without regard to others in the work unit can be counterproductive. A manager must work closely with all members of the work unit to ensure that employees are not working at cross purposes. Finally, if MBO is viewed simply as an annual exercise in filling out paperwork, employees will not be motivated to accomplish the goals. (For a look at your response to achieving goals, see *Self-Assessment—What's My Attitude Toward Achievement?* on pages 184–185, at the end of the chapter.)

Q&A 6.4

Characteristics of Well-Designed Goals

Goals are not all created equal! Some goals are better than others. How do you tell the difference? What makes a "well-designed" goal?[8] Exhibit 6-3 outlines the characteristics of well-designed goals.

A well-designed goal should be *written in terms of outcomes* rather than actions. The desired end result is the most important element of any goal and, therefore, the goal should be written to reflect this. Next, a goal should be *measurable and quantifiable*. It's much easier to determine if a goal has been met if it's measurable. For instance, suppose one of your goals is to "produce a high-quality product." What exactly do you mean by high quality? Because there are numerous ways to define quality, the goal should state specifically how you will measure whether or not the product is high quality. This means that even in areas where it may be difficult to quantify your intent, you should try to find some specific way or ways to measure whether that goal is accomplished. Why have the goal if you cannot measure whether it's been met?

Have you occasionally failed at your goals? How can you develop more achievable goals?

In addition to specifying a quantifiable measure of accomplishment, a well-designed goal should also be *clear as to a time frame*. Open-ended goals may seem preferable because of their flexibility. However, goals without a time frame make an organization less flexible

Exhibit 6-3

Characteristics of Well-Designed Goals

- Written in terms of outcomes rather than actions
- Measurable and quantifiable
- Clear time frame

- Challenging yet attainable
- Written down
- Communicated to all necessary organizational members

because you are never sure when the goal has been met or when you should call it quits because the goal will never be met regardless of how long you work at it. A well-designed goal will specify a time frame for accomplishment.

A well-designed goal should also be *challenging but attainable*. Goals that are too easy to accomplish are not motivating, and neither are goals that are not attainable even with exceptional effort. A well-designed goal should also be *written down*. Although actually writing down goals may seem too time-consuming, the process of writing the goals forces people to think them through. In addition, the written goals become visible and tangible evidence of the importance of working toward something. Finally, a well-designed goal is *communicated to all organizational members* who need to know the goal. Why? Making people aware of goals ensures that they are all "on the same page" and working in ways to secure the accomplishment of the organization's goals. The following *Management Reflection* shows what can happen when an organization does not set goals for growth and must cope with booming sales.

MANAGEMENT REFLECTION

Kicking Horse Coffee Learns the Benefits of Planning

Should a company plan for success?   For Canada's top seller of organic coffee, Invermere, BC-based Kicking Horse Coffee, rapid growth and expansion meant that the company could not keep up with the soaring demand for its product.[9] As they started expanding into markets east of Manitoba, Kicking Horse founders Elana Rosenfeld (CEO) and Leo Johnson (president) did not really consider whether they had the capacity to meet an increase in demand. Rather, they focused on getting into new markets. Rosenfeld got a "wake-up call" about the need for planning. As a result, the founders developed detailed sales forecasts and considered capital needs. They also started to examine space, people, and equipment needs. The owners realized that they needed to be more disciplined about the opportunities they pursued, including deciding that they would not supply ground coffee to grocery stores.

The new strategic plan makes sure that demand for coffee can be met and that Kicking Horse can grow fast, while still keeping its promise to employees: "never any overtime." Rosenfeld explains why she has become so committed to planning: "Part of planning is articulating who you are and what you believe in so you can stay on the path." ∎

Steps in Goal Setting

What steps should managers follow in setting goals? The goal-setting process consists of five steps.

1. *Review the organization's mission.* The **mission** is the purpose of an organization. The broad statement of what the organization's purpose is and what it hopes to accomplish provides an overall guide to what organizational members think is important. (We look more closely at organizational mission in Chapter 7.) It's important to review these statements before writing goals because the goals should reflect the intent of the company's mission.

mission
The purpose of an organization.

Planning is definitely not just for managers. When families in the *Vancouver Sun*'s distribution area were asked to take the newspaper's "car free challenge" for a month, they learned that planning became a much greater part of their lives. The three families pictured above took the challenge and found that figuring out how long a journey took and the best way to get there required being more aware of their schedules than when they could just grab their car keys and drive off.

2. *Evaluate available resources.* You don't want to set goals that are impossible to achieve given your available resources. Even though goals should be challenging, they should be realistic. After all, if the resources you have to work with will not allow you to achieve a goal no matter how hard you try or how much effort is exerted, that goal should not be set. That would be like the person with a $50 000 annual income and no other financial resources setting a goal of building an investment portfolio worth $1 million in three years. No matter how hard he or she works at it, it's not going to happen.

3. *Determine the goals individually or with input from others.* These goals reflect desired outcomes and should be consistent with the organization's mission and goals in other organizational areas. These goals should be measurable, specific, and include a time frame for accomplishment.

4. *Write down the goals and communicate them to all who need to know.* We have already explained the benefit of writing down and communicating goals.

5. *Review results and whether goals are being met.* If goals are not being met, make changes to the goals, as needed. For any plan to be effective, reviews need to be done, and this would be expected for any industry.

(For suggestions on setting work goals for employees, see *Developing Your Interpersonal Skills—Setting Goals* on page 189, at the end of the chapter.)

Developing Plans

Once goals have been established, written down, and communicated, a manager is ready to develop plans for pursuing the goals.

Types of Plans

The most popular ways to describe an organization's plans are by their breadth (strategic vs. operational), time frame (short term vs. long term), specificity (directional vs. specific), and frequency of use (single use vs. standing). These planning classifications are not independent. As Exhibit 6-4 illustrates, strategic plans are long term, directional, and single use. Operational plans are short term, specific, and standing. Let's describe each of these types of plans.

Strategic plans are plans that apply to the entire organization, establish the organization's overall goals, and seek to position the organization in terms of its environment. Plans that specify the details of how the overall goals are to be achieved are called **operational plans**. How do the two types of plans differ? Strategic plans tend to cover a longer time frame and a broader view of the organization. Strategic plans also include the formulation of goals, whereas operational plans define ways to achieve the goals. Also, operational plans tend to cover short time periods—monthly, weekly, and day-to-day.

The difference in years between short term and long term has shortened considerably. It used to be that long term meant anything over seven years. Try to imagine what you would like to be doing in seven years, and you can begin to appreciate how difficult it was for managers to establish plans that far in the future. As organizational environments have become more uncertain, the definition of *long term* has changed. We define **long-term plans** as those with a time frame beyond three years.[10] For instance, an organization may develop a five-year plan for increasing its sales in Asia. We define **short-term plans** as those with a time frame of one year or less. For instance, a company may decide that it will increase sales by 10 percent over the next year. The intermediate term is any time

strategic plans
Plans that apply to the entire organization, establish the organization's overall goals, and seek to position the organization in terms of its environment.

operational plans
Plans that specify the details of how the overall goals are to be achieved.

long-term plans
Plans with a time frame beyond three years.

short-term plans
Plans with a time frame of one year or less.

Exhibit 6-4

Types of Plans

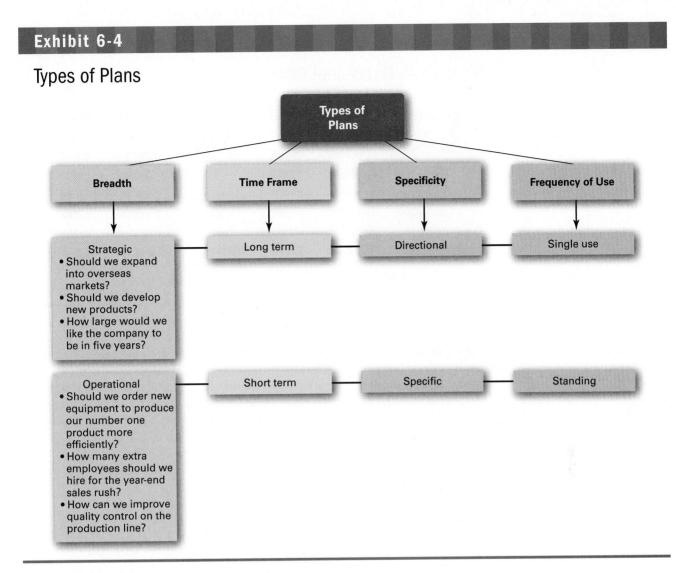

period in between. Although these time classifications are fairly common, an organization can designate any time frame it wants for planning purposes.

Intuitively, it would seem that specific plans would be preferable to directional, or loosely guided, plans. **Specific plans** are plans that are clearly defined and that leave no room for interpretation. They have clearly defined objectives. There is no ambiguity and no problem with misunderstanding. For example, a manager who seeks to increase his or her unit's work output by 8 percent over a given 12-month period might establish specific procedures, budget allocations, and schedules of activities to reach that goal. The drawbacks of specific plans are that they require clarity and a sense of predictability that often do not exist. This clarity and predictability worked well for Blue Man Group, however, because they wanted to create a very uniform product.

When uncertainty is high and managers must be flexible in order to respond to unexpected changes, directional plans are preferable. **Directional plans** are flexible plans that set out general guidelines. They provide focus but don't lock managers into specific goals or courses of action. (Exhibit 6-5 on page 178 illustrates how specific and directional plans differ, with the directional plan indicating only the intent to get from "A" to "B" and the specific plan identifying the exact route that one would take to go from "A" to "B.") Instead of detailing a specific plan to cut costs by 4 percent and increase revenues by 6 percent in the next six months, managers might formulate a directional plan for improving profits by 5 to 10 percent over the next six months. The flexibility inherent in directional plans must be weighed against the loss of clarity provided by specific plans.

specific plans
Plans that are clearly defined and that leave no room for interpretation.

directional plans
Plans that are flexible and that set out general guidelines.

Exhibit 6-5

Specific vs. Directional Plans

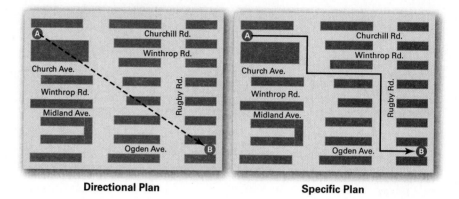

Directional Plan   Specific Plan

single-use plan

A one-time plan specifically designed to meet the needs of a unique situation.

standing plans

Ongoing plans that provide guidance for activities performed repeatedly.

Some plans that managers develop are ongoing, while others are used only once. A **single-use plan** is a one-time plan specifically designed to meet the needs of a unique situation. For instance, when Charles Schwab introduced its online discount stock-brokerage service, top-level executives used a single-use plan to guide the creation and implementation of the new service. In contrast, **standing plans** are ongoing plans that provide guidance for activities performed repeatedly. Standing plans include policies, rules, and procedures, which we defined in Chapter 5. An example of a standing plan would be the discrimination and harassment policy developed by the University of Saskatchewan. It provides guidance to university administrators, faculty, and staff as they perform their job duties.

Contingency Factors in Planning

Q&A 6.5

What kinds of plans are needed in a given situation? Will strategic or operational plans be needed? How about specific or directional plans? In some situations, long-term plans make sense; in others, they do not. What are these situations? The process of developing plans is influenced by three contingency factors and by the planning approach followed. Three contingency factors affect planning: the level in the organization, the degree of environmental uncertainty, and the length of future commitments.[11]

Exhibit 6-6 shows the relationship between a manager's level in the organization and the type of planning done. For the most part, operational planning dominates managers' plan-

Exhibit 6-6

Planning in the Hierarchy of Organizations

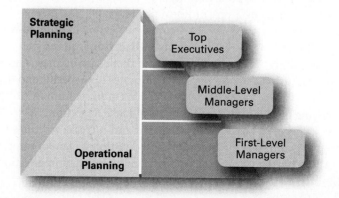

ning efforts at lower levels. At upper organizational levels, planning becomes more strategy oriented.

The second contingency factor that affects planning is environmental uncertainty. When environmental uncertainty is high, plans should be specific, but flexible. Managers must be prepared to amend plans as they are implemented. At times, managers may even have to abandon their plans.[12] For example, at Continental Airlines, former CEO Gordon M. Bethune and his management team established a specific goal of focusing on a key concern of customers—on-time flights—to help the company become more competitive in the highly uncertain airline industry. Because of the high level of uncertainty, the management team identified a "destination, but not a flight plan," and changed plans as necessary to achieve that goal of on-time service. Also, it's important for managers to continue formal planning efforts through periods of environmental uncertainty because studies have shown that it takes at least four years of such efforts before any positive impact on organizational performance is seen.[13]

Continental Airlines
www.continental.com

The last contingency factor affecting planning is related to the time frame of plans. The more that current plans affect future commitments, the longer the time frame for which managers should plan. This **commitment concept** means that plans should extend far enough to meet those commitments made when the plans were developed. Planning for too long or too short a time period is inefficient and ineffective. To see how important the commitment concept is to planning, just look at the heated conversations that have occurred throughout British Columbia's Lower Mainland ever since Vancouver was awarded the 2010 Olympic Winter Games. Planning for the event has led to conflicts over public transportation. Some have been fully committed to the construction of a rail-based rapid transit line (called the Canada Line), stating that the line would be needed when the Olympics comes to town. Others have raised concerns that the cost estimates for the line will prove to be too low and the public will be expected to pay for the additional costs. Many Lower Mainland residents thus worry that plans for the Canada Line have not adequately factored in all the costs and the promise to stay within budget will not be met.

commitment concept
Plans should extend far enough to meet those commitments made today.

Approaches to Planning

How an organization plans can best be understood by looking at *who* does the planning. In the traditional approach, planning is done entirely by top managers who are often assisted by a **formal planning department**, a group of planning specialists whose sole responsibility is to help write the various organizational plans. In this approach, plans developed by top managers flow down through other organizational levels, much like the traditional approach to goal setting. As they flow down through the organization, plans are tailored to the particular needs of each level. Although this approach helps make managerial planning thorough, systematic, and coordinated, all too often the focus is on developing "the plan," a thick binder (or binders) full of meaningless information, that gets stuck away on a shelf and is never used by anyone for guiding or coordinating work efforts.

formal planning department
A group of planning specialists whose sole responsibility is to help write the various organizational plans.

In a survey of managers about formal top-down organizational planning processes, over 75 percent said that their company's planning approach was unsatisfactory.[14] A common complaint was that "plans are documents that you prepare for the corporate planning staff and later forget." Although this traditional top-down approach to planning is still used by many organizations, it can be effective only if managers understand the importance of creating a workable, usable document that organization members actually draw on for direction and guidance, not a document that looks impressive but is never used.

Another approach to planning is to involve more organizational members in the process. In this approach, plans are not handed down from one level to the next, but instead are developed by organization members at the various levels and in the various work units to meet their specific needs. For instance, at Dell's server manufacturing facility in Austin, Texas, employees from production, supply management, and channel management meet weekly to make plans based on current product demand and supply. In addition, work teams set their own daily schedules and track their progress against those schedules. If a team falls behind, team members develop "recovery" plans to try to get back on schedule.[15] When organizational members are more actively involved in planning, they see that the plans are more than just something written down on paper. They can actually see that the plans are used in directing and coordinating work.

Current Issues in Planning

▶ ▶ ▶ When Blue Man Group started out, it was just three guys having fun, mocking the 1980s, and then working their ideas through mime and percussion.[16] They did not feel they had time to plan. Many people feel the same way. Recall, though, that the three co-founders (Chris Wink, Matt Goldman, and Phil Stanton) were able to do only as many shows as they could physically attend when they started out. By figuring out a way to clone themselves, they could do many more shows, and also have the opportunity to tour Canada and the United States, which they recently did in 2007. Touring has meant even more planning. The move to planning has certainly made the group successful: Blue Man Group Productions has about 450 employees, their productions attract 1 million people a year, and they bring in millions of dollars in revenues annually. Their first CD, *Audio,* was nominated for a Grammy in 1999 and one of their songs made the soundtrack for *Terminator 3: Rise of the Machines.*

However, Blue Man's time in Toronto was short-lived. The production closed only 18 months after it opened, although the group had planned to be there forever. The group's debut at Toronto's Panasonic Theatre got off to a rocky start. Four unions called on the public to boycott the production after Blue Man refused to negotiate a collective agreement with any of them and decided to use non-union performers instead. "We maybe made assumptions that were naive or, I hope not, arrogant," said Wink during a visit to Toronto. "But we assumed that things would be more like they were in the States."

Think About It

Blue Man Group clearly learned to develop plans in order to grow the company and create more opportunities. What could the group have done to better plan for their Toronto production? How did context contribute to the group's short run in Toronto?

3. What are the challenges in planning?

We conclude this chapter by addressing two contemporary issues in planning. Specifically, we look at criticisms of planning, and then at how managers can plan effectively in dynamic environments.

Criticisms of Planning

What if you really don't like to make plans?

Formalized organizational planning became popular in the 1960s and, for the most part, it is still popular today. It makes sense for an organization to establish some direction. But critics have challenged some of the basic assumptions underlying planning. What are the primary criticisms directed at formal planning?

- *Planning may create rigidity.*[17] Formal planning efforts can lock an organization into specific goals to be achieved within specific timetables. When these goals are set, the assumption may be that the environment will not change during the time period the goals cover. If that assumption is faulty, managers who follow a plan may face trouble. Rather than remaining flexible—and possibly throwing out the plan—managers who continue to do the things required to achieve the original goals may not be able to cope with the changed environment. Forcing a course of action when the environment is fluid can be a recipe for disaster.

- *Plans cannot be developed for a dynamic environment.*[18] Most organizations today face dynamic environments. If a basic assumption of making plans—that the environment will not change—is faulty, then how can you make plans at all? Today's business environment is often chaotic at best. By definition, that means random and unpredictable. Managing under those conditions requires flexibility, and that may mean not being tied to formal plans.

Q&A 6.6

- *Formal plans cannot replace intuition and creativity.*[19] Successful organizations are typically the result of someone's innovative vision. But visions have a tendency to become formalized as they evolve. Formal planning efforts typically involve a thorough investigation of the organization's capabilities and opportunities and a mechanical analysis that reduces the vision to some type of programmed routine. That approach can spell disaster for an organization. Apple Inc. learned this the hard way. In the late 1970s and throughout the 1980s, Apple's success was attributed, in part, to the innovative and creative approaches of co-founder Steve Jobs. Eventually, Jobs was forced to leave, and with his departure came increased organizational formality, including detailed planning—the same things that Jobs despised so much because he felt that they hampered creativity. During the 1990s, the situation at Apple became so bad that Jobs was brought back as CEO to get Apple back on track. The company's renewed focus on innovation led to the debut of the iMac in 1998, the iPod in 2001, a radically new look for the iMac in 2002, an online music store in 2003, and the iPhone in 2007.

- *Planning focuses managers' attention on today's competition, not on tomorrow's survival.*[20] Formal planning has a tendency to focus on how to capitalize on existing business opportunities within an industry. It often does not allow managers to consider creating or reinventing an industry. Consequently, formal plans may result in costly blunders and high catch-up costs when other competitors take the lead. On the other hand, companies such as Intel, General Electric, Nokia, and Sony have found success forging into uncharted waters, spawning new industries as they go.

- *Formal planning reinforces success, which may lead to failure.*[21] It's hard to change or discard previously successful plans—to leave the comfort of what works for the anxiety of the unknown. Successful plans, however, may provide a false sense of security, generating more confidence in the formal plans than is warranted. Many managers will not face the unknown until they are forced to do so by environmental changes. By then, it may be too late!

- *Just planning is not enough.* It's not enough for managers just to plan. They have to start doing![22] When executives at the *Wall Street Journal* decided that they had to do something to respond to a prolonged slump in financial and technology advertising, they developed a plan for how best to accomplish that goal. Then they set about doing it. One of the first things they did was to make some design changes by adding more colour to the paper's pages, redesigning the typeface, and making other format changes. Another thing they did to bring in more readers was launch a Saturday edition in September 2005. Next on the agenda: cutting down the size of the newspaper with the smaller format, starting in January 2007.[23] As this example shows, just planning to do something does not get it done. Planning to have enough money so you can retire at age 35 is not enough. You have to put that plan into motion and do it. Managers need to plan, but they also need to see that the plan is carried out.

How valid are these criticisms? Should managers forget about planning? No! Although the criticisms have merit when directed at rigid, inflexible planning, today's managers can be effective planners if they understand planning in dynamic, uncertain environments.

Effective Planning in Dynamic Environments

The external environment is continuously changing. For instance, Wi-Fi is revolutionizing all kinds of industries, from airlines to automobile manufacturing to consumer electronics. The power of the Internet also is being used by companies in new and unique ways, including product design and logistics. Consumers continue to increase the amounts they spend on eating out instead of cooking at home.

How can managers effectively plan when the external environment is continually changing? We have already discussed uncertain environments as one

Q&A 6.7

Terri Williamson put her background in chemistry and professional branding to good use when she decided to create a line of cosmetics under the brand name "Glow." She planned carefully, checking the Internet to be sure the product name was available, creating a distinctive look and feel for the packaging of her product line, hand-picking the Hollywood location of her store, and mixing and remixing essential oils and other ingredients in her home to come up with a distinctive sandalwood scent. Williamson's plans were coming to fruition in 2001 and 2002, with steadily rising sales among her celebrity clients, when everything changed. Jennifer Lopez unveiled her own new fragrance called "Glow by J.Lo," and Williamson's Glow Industries began a trademark infringement suit. The suit has since been settled out of court between the two parties.

of the main contingency factors that affects the types of plans managers develop. Because dynamic environments are more the norm than the exception for today's managers, let's revisit how to plan in an uncertain environment. (To determine your own reactions to continual change, see *Self-Assessment—How Well Do I Respond to Turbulent Change?* on pages 537–538, in Chapter 16.)

In an uncertain environment, managers need to develop plans that are specific, but flexible. Although this may seem contradictory, it's not. To be useful, plans need some specificity, but the plans should not be cast in stone. Managers must recognize that planning is an ongoing process; the plans serve as a road map, although the destination may be changing constantly due to dynamic market conditions. They should be willing to change directions if environmental conditions warrant. This flexibility is particularly important as plans are implemented. Managers must stay alert to environmental changes that could impact the effective implementation of plans and make changes as needed. Keep in mind, also, that it's important to continue formal planning efforts, even when the environment is highly uncertain, in order to see any effect on organizational performance. It's the persistence in planning efforts that contributes to significant performance improvement. Why? It seems that, as with most activities, managers "learn to plan" and the quality of their planning improves when they continue to do it.[24]

Finally, effective planning in dynamic environments means flattening the organizational hierarchy as the responsibility for establishing goals and developing plans is pushed to lower organizational levels, since there is little time for goals and plans to flow down from the top. Managers must train their employees in setting goals and establishing plans and then trust that they will do so. Doing so can lead to innovation, as the following *Management Reflection* shows.

MANAGEMENT REFLECTION
▶ Focus on International Issues

Employees Do Some of the Planning at Wipro

How do you move from an anonymous conglomerate to a global company?   Just a short decade ago, Wipro in Bangalore, India, was "an anonymous conglomerate selling cooking oil and personal computers, mostly in India. Today, it is a US$2.3 billion-a-year global company, and most of its business comes from information-technology services."[25] Accenture, EDS, IBM, and the big US accounting firms know all too well the competitive threat Wipro represents. Not only are Wipro's employees low cost, but they are knowledgeable and skilled. They also play an important role in the company's planning. Since the information services industry is continually changing, employees are taught to analyze situations and to define the scale and scope of a client's problems in order to offer the best solutions. They are the ones on the front line with the clients, and it's their responsibility to establish what to do and how to do it. It's an approach that has positioned Wipro for success no matter how the industry changes. ■

SUMMARY AND IMPLICATIONS

1. What does planning involve?
Planning is the process of defining specific goals that cover a period of years. These goals are written and shared with organizational members. Once the goals are agreed upon, specific action plans are created to achieve the goals. Planning's purpose is to provide direction, reduce uncertainty, reduce overlapping and wasteful activities, and establish the goals or standards used in controlling. Without planning, managers would not know what to organize, lead, or control.

▶ ▶ ▶ In Blue Man Group's case, lack of planning in the early years led to exhaustion and near burnout of its co-founders. The co-founders claimed they did not have time to plan.

that use strategic management do have higher levels of performance. And that makes strategic management pretty important!

Another reason strategic management is important has to do with the fact that organizations of all types and sizes face continually changing situations. These changes may be minor or significant, but they are still changes with which managers must cope. That is where strategic management comes in. By following the steps in the strategic management process, managers examine relevant variables in deciding what to do and how to do it. When managers use the strategic management process, they can better cope with uncertain environments. (To understand your ability to deal with the ambiguity that managers often face, see *Self-Assessment—How Well Do I Handle Ambiguity?* on pages 216–217, at the end of the chapter.)

Strategic management is also important because of the nature of organizations. They are composed of diverse divisions, units, functions, and work activities—manufacturing, marketing, accounting, and so forth—that need to be coordinated and focused on achieving the organization's goals. Strategic management clarifies what is important to everyone in an organization and gives employees reasons for doing what they do.

Finally, strategic management is important because it's involved in many of the decisions that managers make. Most of the significant current business events reported in the various business publications involve strategic management. For instance, recently, there were reports that Toronto-based Sears Canada, one of the largest retailers of apparel in Canada, asked for rebates from suppliers, whom it felt were profiting from the rise in the value of the loonie; Oakville, Ontario-based Tim Hortons introduced caramel-flavoured iced cappuccino; and Calgary-based WestJet Airlines hired bilingual flight attendants in anticipation of offering flights into Quebec City. All of these events are examples of managers making strategic decisions.

How widespread is the use of strategic management? One survey of business owners found that 69 percent had strategic plans, and among those owners 89 percent responded that they found their plans effective.[7] They stated, for example, that strategic planning gave them specific goals and provided their staff with a unified vision. Although a few management writers claim that strategic planning is "dead," most continue to emphasize its importance.[8]

Today, strategic management has moved beyond for-profit business organizations to include government agencies, hospitals, and other nonprofit organizations. For instance, when Canada Post found itself in intense competitive battles with overnight package–delivery companies, courier services, and email, its CEO used strategic management to help pinpoint important issues and design appropriate strategic responses. Although strategic management in nonprofits has not been as well researched as that in for-profit organizations, we know it's important for these organizations as well. The City of Vancouver, in collaboration with several other partners, has created a program to help nonprofit organizations develop strategic plans, as the following *Management Reflection* shows.

MANAGEMENT REFLECTION

Helping Nonprofits Help Themselves

Can nonprofit organizations benefit from strategic planning?   Partners in Organizational Development (POD) believes so.[9] The organization provides grants to nonprofit social services, arts, and environmental organizations in British Columbia to help them improve and change. Because nonprofits may not have the internal resources needed to develop a strategic plan, funding is available that allows nonprofits to work with consultants to develop their plans.

The program was established in 1989 as a partnership of the Vancouver Foundation, United Way of the Lower Mainland, the Department of the Secretary of State, and the City of Vancouver. The program's aim is to help nonprofit organizations adapt to an increasingly complex environment. Because of the "financial uncertainty, demographic shifts, heightened competition and growing service demands" that these groups face, strong management practices are essential, and the development of a strategic plan helps accomplish that. Not all of the funding goes to strategic planning initiatives, but the latest awards went to help a number of organizations create strategic plans, including the Kamloops Child Development Society, Nanaimo Community Gardens Society, Community Arts Council of Vancouver, Nanaimo Conservatory of Music, Chinook Institute for Community Stewardship, and Stanley Park Ecology Society. ■

The Strategic Management Process

▶ ▶ ▶ As Heather Reisman considers the future of Indigo Books & Music, she recognizes that consumers have changed the way in which they get information and entertainment.[10] Book reading is down, as is television watching, while Internet use is up. Thus, Reisman has to respond to this new reality by figuring out ways to attract more consumers to the company's bookstores and websites. Reisman is considering starting the equivalent of Facebook for book lovers, which would be housed on the Indigo website. By creating a community of book lovers, she hopes to entice people to buy more books.

Think About It

What other strategies could Heather Reisman use to create more crossovers between books and the Internet? Would some strategies be more effective than others?

2. What are the steps in strategic management?

strategic management process
A six-step process that encompasses strategic planning, implementation, and evaluation.

The **strategic management process**, as illustrated in Exhibit 7-1, is a six-step process that encompasses strategic planning, implementation, and evaluation. Although the first four steps describe the planning that must take place, implementation and evaluation are just as important! Even the best strategies can fail if management does not implement or evaluate them properly. Let's examine the six steps in detail.

Step 1: Identify the Organization's Current Mission, Goals, and Strategies

Q&A 7.2

How would you develop a strategic plan for the next five or ten years of your life? What would be your mission, goals, and strategies?

Every organization needs a mission—a statement of the purpose of an organization. The mission answers the question, What is our reason for being in business? Defining the organization's mission forces managers to carefully identify the scope of its products or services. For example, Indigo Books & Music's mission statement is "to provide a service-driven, stress-free approach to satisfying the booklover."[11] The mission of WorkSafeBC (the Workers' Compensation Board of

Exhibit 7-1

The Strategic Management Process

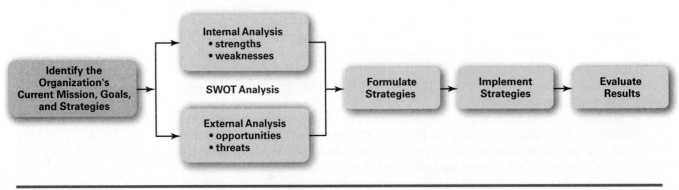

British Columbia) is to "promot[e] workplace health and safety for the workers and employers of [the] province."[12] The mission of eBay is "to build an online marketplace that enables practically anyone to trade practically anything almost anywhere in the world."[13] These statements provide clues to what these organizations see as their reason for being in business. Exhibit 7-2 provides a description of the typical components of a mission statement.

It's also important for managers to identify goals and strategies consistent with the mission being pursued. For instance, based on its mission statement, the WCB established the following goals:[14]

- Promote the prevention of workplace injury, illness, and disease
- Rehabilitate those who are injured and provide timely return to work
- Provide fair compensation to replace workers' loss of wages while recovering from injuries
- Ensure sound financial management for a viable workers' compensation system

Exhibit 7-2

Components of a Mission Statement

Customers	**Who are the organization's customers?**
	We believe our first responsibility is to the doctors, nurses, and patients, to mothers and all others who use our products and services. (Johnson & Johnson)
Markets	**Where does the organization compete geographically?**
	To invoke the senses, evoke the imagination and provoke the emotions of people around the world! (Cirque du Soleil)
Concern for survival, growth, and profitability	**Is the organization committed to growth and financial stability?**
	We expand our thinking and grow faster than the industry average, and we enjoy being seen as a young aggressive company. We believe that we do not have to compromise our integrity to be profit driven. (G.A.P Adventures)
Philosophy	**What are the organization's basic beliefs, values, and ethical priorities?**
	Ducks Unlimited Canada (DUC) envisions Canada as a nation that can sustain use by people and wildlife without endangering the amount or functions of natural lands. DUC leads wetland conservation for waterfowl, other wildlife and people in North America. (Ducks Unlimited Canada)
Concern for public image	**How responsive is the organization to societal and environmental concerns?**
	As a vital measure of integrity, we will ensure the health and safety of our communities, and protect the environment in all we do. (Dow Chemical)
Products or services	**What are the organization's major products or services?**
	To enrich the lives of everyone in WestJet's world by providing safe, friendly, affordable air travel. (WestJet Airlines)
Technology	**Is the organization technologically current?** **Pushing the limits of what technology can accomplish**
	Pushing the limits means focusing more of our resources and attention on what we do not know rather than on controlling what we already know. The fact that something has not worked in the past does not mean that it cannot be made to work in the future; and the fact that something did work in the past doesn't mean that it can't be improved upon. (Syncrude Canada)
Self-concept	**What are the organization's major competitive advantage and core competencies?**
	CBC Television, as Canada's national public television broadcaster, has a cultural mandate to tell compelling, original, audacious and entertaining Canadian stories in a way that Canadians want to watch, and in large numbers. (CBC Television)
Concern for employees	**Are employees a valuable asset of the organization?**
	We recognize contributions and celebrate accomplishments. (Tourism BC)

Source: Based on company websites; and F. David, *Strategic Management*, 11th ed. (Upper Saddle River, NJ: Prentice Hall, 2007), p. 70.

As we explained in Chapter 6, goals are the foundation of planning. A company's goals provide the measurable performance targets that employees strive to reach. Knowing the company's current goals gives managers a basis for assessing whether those goals need to be changed. For the same reasons, it's important for managers to identify the organization's current strategies.

Step 2: Internal Analysis

resources
An organization's assets—financial, physical, human, intangible—that are used to develop, manufacture, and deliver products or services to customers.

capabilities
An organization's skills and abilities that enable it to do the work activities needed in its business.

core competencies
An organization's major value-creating skills, capabilities, and resources that determine its competitive advantage.

Q&A 7.3, Q&A 7.4

strengths
Any activities the organization does well or any unique resources that it has.

weaknesses
Activities the organization does not do well or resources it needs but does not possess.

Q&A 7.5

> *What are your strengths and weaknesses for developing a successful career?*

The internal analysis provides important information about an organization's specific resources and capabilities. An organization's **resources** are its assets—financial, physical, human, intangible—that are used by the organization to develop, manufacture, and deliver products or services to its customers. Its **capabilities** are its skills and abilities in doing the work activities needed in its business. The major value-creating capabilities and skills of the organization are known as its **core competencies**.[15] Both resources and core competencies can determine the organization's competitive weapons. For instance, Fujio Cho, Toyota Motor Corporation's chair, called the company's Prius, "a giant leap into the future," but the highly popular car is simply one more example of the company's resources and core competencies in product research and design, manufacturing, marketing, and managing its human resources. Toyota is renowned worldwide for its effectiveness and efficiency. Experts who have studied the company point to its ability to nourish and preserve employee creativity and flexibility in a work environment that is fairly rigid and controlled.[16]

After doing the internal analysis, managers should be able to identify organizational strengths and weaknesses. Any activities the organization does well or any unique resources that it has are called **strengths**. **Weaknesses** are activities the organization does not do well or resources it needs but does not possess. This step forces managers to recognize that their organizations, no matter how large or successful, are constrained by the resources and capabilities they have.

Doing an internal analysis of an organization's financial and physical assets is fairly easy because information on those areas is readily available. However, evaluating an organization's intangible assets—things such as employees' skills, talents, and knowledge; databases and other IT assets; organizational culture; and so forth—is a bit more challenging. Organizational culture, specifically, is one crucial part of the internal analysis that is often overlooked.[17] It's crucial because strong and weak cultures do have different effects on strategy, and the content of a culture has a major effect on strategies pursued. In a strong culture, almost all employees have a clear understanding of what the organization is about. This clarity makes it easy for managers to convey to new employees the organization's core competencies and strengths. The negative side of a strong culture, of course, is that it may be more difficult to change organizational strategies. Successful organizations with strong cultures may become prisoners of their own successes. Research has also shown that the kind of culture an organization has can promote or hinder its strategic actions. Firms with "strategically appropriate cultures" outperformed corporations with less appropriate cultures.[18] What is a strategically appropriate culture? It's one that supports the firm's chosen strategy. For instance, Avis, the number two US car rental company, has for a number of years stood on top of its category in an annual survey of brand loyalty. By creating a culture where employees obsess over every step of the rental car experience, Avis has built an unmatched record for customer loyalty.[19]

Another intangible asset that is important, but tricky to assess during an internal analysis, is corporate reputation. Does the fact that Montreal-based aluminum producer Rio Tinto Alcan is ranked as one of Canada's "most admired corporations" make a difference? Does the fact that Calgary-based WestJet Airlines made the list of Canada's 10 Most Admired Corporate Cultures™ for 2006 mean anything? Does the fact that Coca-Cola has the world's most powerful global brand give it any edge? Studies of reputation and corporate performance show that it can have a positive impact.[20] As one researcher said, "A strong, well-managed reputation can and should be an asset for any organization."[21]

Step 3: External Analysis

What changes in the world are happening that might affect how your career may unfold over time? How might this affect your strategic plan?

PRISM 3

In Chapter 2, we described the external environment as an important constraint on a manager's actions. Analyzing that environment is a critical step in the strategy process. Managers in every organization need to do an external analysis. They need to know, for instance, what the competition is doing, what pending legislation might affect the organization, or what the labour supply is like in locations where it operates. In analyzing the external environment, managers should examine both the specific and general environments to see what trends and changes are occurring. At Indigo Books & Music, managers noted that individuals were reading fewer books, and using the Internet more. This observation required Indigo to rethink how to encourage more people to rely on Indigo stores for gift items and connections with other book lovers. (To learn more about analyzing the environment, see *Developing Your Interpersonal Skills—Scanning the Environment* on page 220, at the end of the chapter.)

After analyzing the environment, managers need to assess what they have learned in terms of opportunities that the organization can exploit, and threats that it must counteract. **Opportunities** are positive trends in external environmental factors; **threats** are negative trends. For Indigo Books & Music managers, one opportunity is the increased use of the Internet, and managers have looked for ways to get more revenue from this medium. Threats to Indigo include a decreasing number of people who read books and greater competition from alternative sources of entertainment, including movies, radio, and television programs.

opportunities
Positive trends in external environmental factors.

threats
Negative trends in external environmental factors.

One last thing to understand about external analysis is that the same environment can present opportunities to one organization and pose threats to another in the same industry because of their different resources and capabilities. For example, WestJet Airlines has prospered in a turbulent industry, while Air Canada has struggled through a painful restructuring.

The combined external and internal analyses are called the **SWOT analysis** because it's an analysis of the organization's *s*trengths, *w*eaknesses, *o*pportunities, and *t*hreats. Based on the SWOT analysis, managers can identify a strategic niche that the organization might exploit (see Exhibit 7-3 on page 198). For Instance, owner Leonard Lee started Ottawa-based Lee Valley Tools in 1982 to help individual woodworkers, and later gardeners, find just the right tools for their tasks. This niche strategy enabled Lee Valley to grow into one of North America's leading garden and woodworking catalogue companies for over 25 years. (The *CBC Video Case Incident—Joe Six-Pack and Four Canadian Entrepreneurs* on pages 254–255 shows how two new beer companies are entering the Canadian market through different strategies.)

SWOT analysis
An analysis of the organization's strengths, weaknesses, opportunities, and threats.

Managers of the New Horizons seniors' residence at Bloor and Dufferin streets in Toronto know how to recognize a good opportunity. In 2003, the nonprofit home was losing a lot of money, and half of its rooms were empty. The double-cohort was about to hit Toronto post-secondary schools, and New Horizons had rooms and rents that would appeal to student budgets. So New Horizons decided to open the residence to college and university students. Both seniors and students feel they benefit from the situation, and New Horizons is on a better financial footing these days.

Exhibit 7-3

Identifying the Organization's Opportunities

SWOT analysis was very effective in keeping jobs at Proctor & Gamble Canada's Brockville, Ontario, plant, as the following *Management Reflection* shows.

MANAGEMENT REFLECTION

Loss of Detergent Production Turns into Victory

How does a Canadian CEO convince his American bosses that there is advantage to staying in Canada? SWOT analysis saved the jobs of employees at Proctor & Gamble Canada's Brockville, Ontario, plant.[22] Tim Penner, president of the Toronto-based company, knew that the parent company (based in Cincinnati, Ohio) planned to consolidate the production of laundry detergent in the United States, which would eliminate the jobs of the Brockville employees. Penner, in search of a new opportunity, suggested to head office that P&G move manufacture of fabric softener sheets and electrostatic cleaning sheets for the Swiffer sweeper to Brockville. Penner outlined the strengths of the Ontario plant, including a highly educated workforce known for its commitment and productivity. With Penner's strategic thinking, Brockville's loss of laundry detergent production turned into a victory for Canadian jobs. More recently, Penner convinced the US head office to allow the Brockville plant to produce Tide to Go. Penner says his job includes "aggressively selling Canada [to US head office] as a possible site for new products and reorganized operations." Penner's strategy has paid off. When he became president in 1999, P&G Canada was the seventh-largest revenue generator in the world for the US multinational. By 2007, Penner had taken the Canadian subsidiary to third place, and increased annual sales from $1.5 billion to over $2.9 billion. ∎

Step 4: Formulate Strategies

Q&A 7.6

Once the SWOT analysis is complete, managers need to develop and evaluate strategic alternatives and then select strategies that capitalize on the organization's strengths and exploit environmental opportunities or that correct the organization's weaknesses and buffer it against threats. Strategies need to be established for the corporate, business, and functional levels of the organization, which we will describe shortly. This step is complete when managers have developed a set of strategies that gives the organization a relative advantage over its rivals.

Step 5: Implement Strategies

Q&A 7.7

After strategies are formulated, they must be implemented. No matter how effectively an organization has planned its strategies, it cannot succeed if the strategies are not implemented properly. Involving all members of the organization in strategic planning can be effective, as the following *Management Reflection* shows.

Concentra Financial Involves All Employees in Decision Making

Would involving all employees in a strategic plan make a company more successful or less successful? Myrna Bentley, president and CEO of Saskatoon, Saskatchewan-based Concentra Financial Services Association (formerly, Co-operative Trust Company of Canada) understands the importance of employee involvement in implementing the results of SWOT analysis.[23] Her company provides financial intermediary and trusteeship services to credit unions, corporate clients, mortgage brokers, and deposit agents across Canada. "When we did our SWOT analysis, we involved all the staff and sent that information through to the management team, which spent time working through it. As a result we have business plan deliverables ...that are directly fed through the organization from the front-line level," Bentley says. The SWOT analysis paid off, as the company's revenues increased 58 percent between 2004 and 2006.

Bentley's inclusion of employees pays off in other ways as well. In 2006, the company was recognized for being one of Canada's Top 50 Best Managed Companies for the fourth year in a row and was named one of Canada's Top 100 Employers from 2001 to 2004. ∎

Exhibit 7-4 indicates different things organizations can do to implement a new strategy. The rest of the chapters in this book address a number of issues related to strategy

Exhibit 7-4

Ways to Implement Strategy

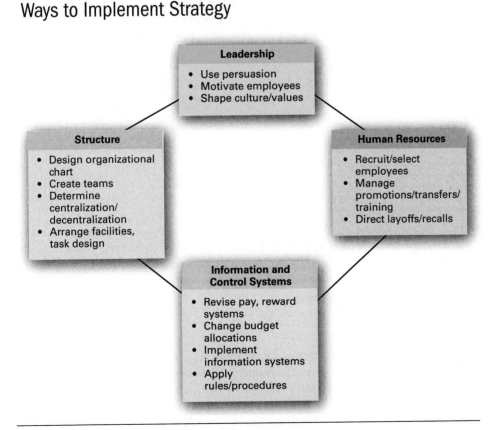

Source: Adapted from Jay R. Galbraith and Robert K. Kazanjian, *Strategy Implementation: Structure, Systems, and Process,* 2nd ed. (St. Paul, MN: West, 1986), p. 115.

implementation. For instance, in Chapter 9, we discuss the strategy–structure relationship. In Chapter 11, we show that if new strategies are to succeed, they often require hiring new people with different skills, transferring some current employees to new positions, or laying off some employees. Also, since more organizations are using teams, the ability to build and manage effective teams is an important part of implementing strategy (we cover teams in Chapter 14). Finally, top management leadership is a necessary ingredient in a successful strategy. So, too, is a motivated group of middle- and lower-level managers to carry out the organization's specific strategies. Chapters 12 and 13 discuss ways to improve leadership effectiveness and offer suggestions on motivating people.

Step 6: Evaluate Results

Q&A 7.8

The final step in the strategic management process is evaluating results. How effective have the strategies been? What adjustments, if any, are necessary? We discuss this step in our coverage of the control process in Chapter 15.

Types of Organizational Strategies

▶ ▶ ▶ Indigo Books & Music first started to implement its expansion plans in 2001, by buying its major competitor, Chapters (and chapters.ca).[24] This move gave Indigo a broader market base with a number of new stores, as well as the platform to launch a successful online business.

The plans Reisman contemplated in 2007 seek to further grow the company. Reisman planned to open at least 12 new stores by the end of 2008, with 6 of them in the large superstore format. She also hoped to expand some stores in Toronto and Montreal. To build stronger ties with consumers, she planned to create a social-networking site for book lovers. She also planned to launch "Indigo TV," a channel that would broadcast author interviews and book-related programming throughout certain stores, and host an online photo album site where people can upload and display their pictures.

Think About It

Indigo Books & Music has chosen a growth strategy. What other ways might the company grow? What other strategies might you recommend to Heather Reisman?

3. What kinds of strategies can managers use?

There are three types of organizational strategy: corporate, business, and functional (see Exhibit 7-5). They relate to the particular level of the organization that introduces the strategy. Managers at the top level of the organization typically are responsible for corporate strategies; for example, Heather Reisman plans Indigo Books & Music's growth strategy. Managers at the middle level typically are responsible for business strategies; for example, Indigo's executive vice-president, online, is responsible for the company's Internet business. Departmental managers typically are responsible for functional strategies; for example, Indigo's senior vice-president, human resource/organization development, is responsible for human resource policies, employee training, and staffing. Let's look at each level of organizational strategy.

Corporate Strategy

corporate strategy
An organizational strategy that evaluates what businesses a company is in, should be in, or wants to be in, and what it wants to do with those businesses.

If you were to develop your own company, what business would it be in? Why?

Corporate strategy is a strategy that evaluates what businesses a company is in, should be in, or wants to be in, and what it wants to do with those businesses. It's based on the mission and goals of the organization and the roles that each business unit of the organization will play. Take PepsiCo, for instance. Its mission is to be a successful producer and marketer of beverage and packaged food products, and its strategy for pursuing that mission and various

Exhibit 7-5

Levels of Organizational Strategy

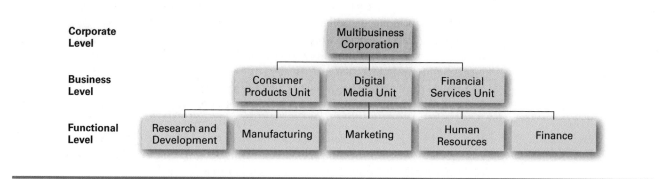

Corporate Level			Multibusiness Corporation		
Business Level		Consumer Products Unit	Digital Media Unit	Financial Services Unit	
Functional Level	Research and Development	Manufacturing	Marketing	Human Resources	Finance

goals is through its different businesses, including North American Soft Drinks, Frito-Lay, Gatorade, Tropicana Products, and PepsiCo International. At one time, PepsiCo had a restaurant division that included Taco Bell, Pizza Hut, and KFC, but because of intense competitive pressures in the restaurant industry and the division's inability to contribute to corporate growth, PepsiCo made a strategic decision to spin off that division as a separate and independent business entity, now known as YUM! Brands. What types of corporate strategies do organizations, such as PepsiCo, use?

In choosing what businesses to be in, senior management can choose among three main types of corporate strategies: growth, stability, and renewal. To illustrate, Wal-Mart, Ganong Bros., and General Motors are companies that seem to be going in different directions. Wal-Mart is rapidly expanding its operations and developing new business and retailing concepts. Managers at St. Stephen, New Brunswick-based Ganong Bros. ("Canada's Chocolate Family"), on the other hand, are content to maintain the status quo and focus on the candy industry. Meanwhile, sluggish sales and an uncertain outlook in the automobile industry have prompted GM to take drastic measures in dealing with its problems. Each of these organizations is using a different type of corporate strategy. Let's look closer at each type.

PepsiCo
www.pepsico.com

growth strategy
A corporate strategy that seeks to increase the organization's operations by expanding the number of products offered or markets served, either through its current business(es) or through new business(es).

Growth

Even though it's the world's number one retailer, Wal-Mart continues to grow internationally and in the United States. Because it plans to open over 625 new stores in 2008,[25] its corporate strategy is definitely growth! A **growth strategy** is used when an organization wants to grow and does so by expanding the number of products offered or markets served, either through its current business(es) or through new business(es). As a result of its growth strategy, the organization may increase sales revenues, number of employees, market share, or other quantitative measures. How can organizations grow? Through concentration, vertical integration, horizontal integration, or diversification.

Concentration Growth through *concentration* is achieved when an organization concentrates on its primary line of business and increases the number of products offered or markets served in this primary business. No other firms are acquired or merged with; instead the company chooses to grow by increasing its own business operations. For instance, Oakville, Ontario-based Tim Hortons opens about 200 new stores a year, and is currently focusing most of its new openings on small-town western Canada, and Quebec. It also plans an aggressive expansion in the United States, where it had 288 stores in 2006 and hopes to have 500 by 2008.[26]

When Stewart Gilliland took over as CEO of Labatt Breweries in January 2004, he discovered that with its strategy of concentration, the company had been more a follower than a leader. He vowed to change that immediately by putting a "fresh emphasis on quality, brewing process and taste among his company's many products, including its flagship Blue brand."

Vertical Integration A company also might choose to grow by *vertical integration*, which is an attempt to gain control of inputs (backward vertical integration), outputs (forward vertical integration), or both. In backward vertical integration, the organization attempts to gain control of its inputs by becoming its own supplier. For instance, French hospitality giant Accor concentrates in two areas: hotels and travel services. The company owns a variety of hotels, including the Sofitel, Motel 6, and Red Roof Inns chains. The company also owns the Frantour travel agencies, which comprise more than 300 travel agencies in France.[27] In forward vertical integration, the organization gains control of its outputs (products or services) by becoming its own distributor. For example, several manufacturers with strong brands—including Coach, Apple, LACOSTE, and LEGO—have opened select stores where customers can buy products. In other words, they have become their own distributor.

Horizontal Integration In *horizontal integration*, a company grows by combining with other organizations in the same industry—that is, combining operations with competitors. Inbev of Belgium, which owns Alexander Keith's and Labatt, is the leading brewer in the world; it is a dominant player in North America, South America, Europe, Australia, and parts of Asia and Africa because of its acquisition of local breweries. Horizontal integration has been considered frequently in the Canadian banking industry in recent years as well.

Because combining with competitors might decrease the amount of competition in an industry, Competition Bureau Canada assesses the impact of proposed horizontal integration strategies and must approve such plans before they are allowed to go forward in this country. Other countries have similar bodies that protect fair competition. For instance, the Federal Trade Commission examines proposals for horizontal integration in the United States. In early 2007, Sirius Satellite Radio and XM Satellite Radio announced that they would merge to create a single satellite radio network in the United States and Canada. The companies face significant hurdles in the United States to finalizing their agreement because the merger would create a monopoly in satellite radio. The merger is not guaranteed for the companies' satellite services in Canada either. In this case, both the Competition Bureau Canada and the Canadian Radio-television and Telecommunications Commission (CRTC) would need to approve any merger between Sirius Canada and XM Canada before it could happen.

related diversification
When a company grows by combining with firms in different, but related, industries.

unrelated diversification
When a company grows by combining with firms in different and unrelated industries.

Diversification Finally, an organization can grow through *diversification*, either related or unrelated. In **related diversification** a company grows by merging with or acquiring firms in different, but related, industries. So, for instance, Toronto-based George Weston Foods is involved in the baking and dairy industries, while its ownership of Loblaw Companies provides for the distribution of Weston's food products. In **unrelated diversification**, a company grows by merging with or acquiring firms in different and unrelated industries. Toronto-based Brookfield Asset Management (formerly Brascan) is one of the few Canadian conglomerates that pursues a diversified strategy. Under CEO Bruce Flatt, Brascan has focused its development in three areas: real estate (Brookfield Properties), financial services (Brookfield Asset Management), and power generation (Brookfield Power). The company also owns 56 percent of Fraser Papers, a leading manufacturer of specialized printing, publishing, and converting papers, and 40 percent of Norbord, a paperboard company.[28] However, unrelated diversification has fallen out of favour in recent years because too much diversification can cause managers to lose control of their organizations' core business. This can reduce value rather than create it.[29] For instance, Toronto-based Sears Canada announced in March 2004 that it was getting out of the automotive business by closing 13 of its 49 auto centres, and selling the rest to Vernon, BC-based Kal Tire, Toronto-based Active Green & Ross, and Laval, Quebec-based President Tire. In doing this, Sears was returning to its roots. According to Vincent Power, Sears Canada's communication director, "We're a traditional department store and we want to focus our capital investment on traditional merchandise such as apparel, home fashions, furnishings and appliances."[30]

Many companies use a combination of these approaches to grow. For instance, McDonald's has grown using the concentration strategy by opening more than 32 000 outlets in more than 100 countries, of which about 30 percent are company-owned. In addition, it's used horizontal integration by purchasing Boston Market, Chipotle Mexican Grill (which it spun off as a separate entity in 2006), and Donato's Pizza chains (which it sold in late 2003). It also has a minority stake in the UK-based sandwich shops Pret A Manger. McDonald's newest twist on its growth strategy is a move into the premium coffee market with its McCafé coffee shops.

Stability

A **stability strategy** is a corporate strategy characterized by an absence of significant change in what the organization is currently doing. Examples of this strategy include continuing to serve the same clients by offering the same product or service, maintaining market share, and sustaining the organization's business operations. The organization does not grow, but it does not fall behind, either.

Although it may seem strange that an organization might not want to grow, there are times when its resources, capabilities, and core competencies are stretched to their limits, and expanding operations further might jeopardize its future success. When might managers decide that the stability strategy is the most appropriate choice? One situation might be that the industry is in a period of rapid upheaval with external forces drastically changing and making the future uncertain. At times like these, managers might decide that the prudent course of action is to sit tight and wait to see what happens.

Another situation where the stability strategy might be appropriate is if the industry is facing slow- or no-growth opportunities. In this instance, managers might decide to keep the organization operating at its current levels before making any strategic moves. This period of stability would allow them time to analyze their strategic options. The grocery industry is one that is growing very slowly. This fact, plus the all-out assault of Wal-Mart into grocery retailing, for instance, led managers at Toronto-based grocery chain A&P Canada to use a stability strategy.

Finally, owners and managers of small businesses, such as small neighbourhood grocers, often purposefully choose to follow a stability strategy. Why? They may feel that their business is successful enough just as it is, that it adequately meets their personal goals, and that they don't want the hassles of a growing business.

Renewal

The popular business periodicals frequently report stories of organizations that are not meeting their goals or whose performance is declining. When an organization is in trouble, something needs to be done. Managers need to develop strategies that address organizational weaknesses that are leading to performance declines. These strategies are called **renewal strategies**. There are two main types of renewal strategies, retrenchment and turnaround.

A **retrenchment strategy** reduces the company's activities or operations. Retrenchment strategies include cost reductions, layoffs, closing underperforming units, or closing entire product lines or services.[31] There is no shortage of companies that have pursued a retrenchment strategy. A partial list includes some big corporate names: Procter & Gamble, Sears Canada, Corel, and Nortel Networks. When an organization is facing minor performance setbacks, a retrenchment strategy helps it stabilize operations, revitalize organizational resources and capabilities, and prepare to compete once again. Brampton, Ontario-based Loblaw Companies is hoping that reducing office staff by 20 percent and centralizing procurement and merchandising operations will help offset problems the supermarket chain has had in expanding its stores to better compete with Wal-Mart's supercentres.[32]

What happens if an organization's problems are more serious? What if the organization's profits are not just declining, but instead there are no profits, just losses? General Motors reported a net loss in 2005 of $3.4 billion.[33] Kodak had a $1.3 billion loss in 2005.[34] These types of situations call for a more drastic strategy. The **turnaround strategy** is a renewal strategy for times when the organization's performance problems are more critical.

For both renewal strategies, managers cut costs and restructure organizational operations. However, a turnaround strategy typically involves a more extensive use of these measures than does a retrenchment strategy. For instance, one of GM's more drastic measures in its turnaround strategy was making buyout offers to about 113 000 workers. GM hoped that

stability strategy
A corporate strategy characterized by an absence of significant change in what the organization is currently doing.

renewal strategy
A corporate strategy designed to address organizational weaknesses that are leading to performance declines.

retrenchment strategy
A short-run renewal strategy.

turnaround strategy
A renewal strategy for situations in which the organization's performance problems are more serious.

at least 30 000 employees would accept the offer so it could get to 100 percent plant capacity by 2008 and avoid having to potentially file for bankruptcy.[35]

Corporate Portfolio Analysis

When an organization's corporate strategy involves a number of businesses, managers can manage this collection, or portfolio, of businesses using a corporate portfolio matrix.[36] The first portfolio matrix—the **BCG matrix**—developed by the Boston Consulting Group, introduced the idea that an organization's businesses could be evaluated and plotted using a 2 × 2 matrix (see Exhibit 7-6) to identify which ones offered high potential and which were a drain on organizational resources.[37] The horizontal axis represents *market share*, which was evaluated as either low or high; and the vertical axis indicates anticipated *market growth*, which also was evaluated as either low or high. Based on its evaluation, businesses can be placed in one of four categories:

- *Cash cows* (low growth, high market share). Businesses in this category generate large amounts of cash, but their prospects for future growth are limited.
- *Stars* (high growth, high market share). These businesses are in a fast-growing market, and hold a dominant share of that market. Their contribution to cash flow depends on their need for resources.
- *Question marks* (high growth, low market share). These businesses are in an attractive market, but hold a small share of that market. Therefore, they have the promise of performance, but need to be developed more for that to happen.
- *Dogs* (low growth, low market share). Businesses in this category do not produce, or consume, much cash. However, they hold no promise for improved performance.

What are the strategic implications of the BCG matrix? Managers should "milk" cash cows for as much as they can, limit any new investment in them, and use the large amounts of cash generated to invest in stars and question marks with strong potential to improve market share. Heavy investment in stars will help take advantage of the market's growth and help maintain high market share. The stars, of course, will eventually develop into cash cows as their markets mature and sales growth slows. The hardest decision for managers is related to the question marks. After careful analysis, some will be sold off and others turned into stars. The dogs should be sold off or liquidated as they have low market share in markets with low growth potential.

Exhibit 7-6

The BCG Matrix and Strategic Implications

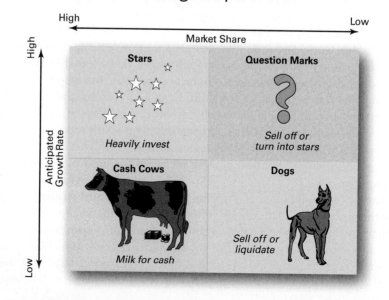

A corporate portfolio matrix, such as the BCG matrix, can be a useful strategic management tool. It provides a framework for understanding diverse businesses and helps managers establish priorities for making resource allocation decisions.

Business Strategy

> What might be the competitive advantage of a business you would like to create?

Now we move to the business level. A **business (or competitive) strategy** is a strategy focused on how an organization will compete in each of its businesses. For a small organization in only one line of business or the large organization that has not diversified into different products or markets, the competitive strategy simply describes how the company will compete in its primary or main market. For organizations in multiple businesses, however, each division will have its own competitive strategy that defines its competitive advantage, the products or services it will offer, the customers it wants to reach, and the like. For example, the French company LVMH Moët Hennessy-Louis Vuitton SA has different business-level strategies for its divisions, such as Donna Karan fashions, Louis Vuitton leather goods, Guerlain perfume, TAG Heuer watches, Dom Pérignon champagne, and other luxury products. Each division has developed its own unique approach for competing. When an organization is in several different businesses, these single businesses that are independent and formulate their own strategies are often called **strategic business units (SBUs)**.

business (or competitive) strategy An organizational strategy that focuses on how the organization will compete in each of its businesses.

strategic business units (SBUs) Single businesses of an organization in several different businesses that are independent and formulate their own strategies.

The Role of Competitive Advantage

Developing an effective business or competitive strategy requires an understanding of competitive advantage, a key concept in strategic management.[38] **Competitive advantage** is what sets an organization apart: that is, its distinct edge. That distinct edge comes from the organization's core competencies, which, as we know from earlier in this chapter, might be in the form of organizational capabilities—the organization does something that others cannot do or does it better than others can do it. For example, Dell has developed a competitive advantage in its ability to create a direct-selling e-commerce channel that is highly responsive to customers. WestJet Airlines has a competitive advantage because of its lower operating costs compared with rival Air Canada and its skills at giving passengers what they want—quick, convenient, and fun service. Those core competencies that lead to competitive advantage also can come from organizational assets or resources—the organization has something that its competitors do not have. For instance, Wal-Mart's state-of-the-art information system allows it to monitor and control inventories and supplier relations more efficiently than its competitors, which Wal-Mart has turned into a cost advantage. Harley-Davidson, Nike, and Coca-Cola all have well-known global trademarks that they use to get premium prices for their products.

competitive advantage What sets an organization apart: its distinct edge.

Quality as a Competitive Advantage

If implemented properly, quality can be a way for an organization to create a sustainable competitive advantage.[39] That is why many organizations apply quality management concepts to their operations in an attempt to set themselves apart from competitors.

To the degree that an organization can satisfy a customer's need for quality, it can differentiate itself from competitors and attract a loyal customer base. Moreover, constant improvement in the quality and reliability of an organization's products or services may result in a competitive advantage that cannot be taken away.[40]

Sustaining Competitive Advantage

Given the fact that every organization has resources and capabilities, what makes some organizations more successful than others? Why do some professional hockey teams consistently win championships or draw large crowds? Why do some organizations have consistent and continuous growth in revenues and profits? Why do some colleges, universities, or departments experience continually increasing enrolments? Why do some companies consistently appear at the top of lists ranking the "best," or the "most admired," or the "most profitable"? Although every organization has resources (assets) and capabilities (how work gets done) to do whatever it's in business to do, not every one is able to effectively exploit its resources and to develop the core competencies that can provide it with a competitive advantage. It's not enough for an organization simply to create a competitive advantage; it must be able to sustain it—that is, to keep its edge despite competitors' actions or evolutionary changes in the industry. But that is not easy to do. Market instabilities, new technology, and other types of significant, but unpredictable, changes can challenge managers' attempts at creating a long-term, sustainable competitive advantage. However, by using strategic management, managers can better position their organizations to get a sustainable competitive advantage.

Competitive Strategies

Many important ideas in strategic management have come from the work of Michael Porter.[41] Porter's major contribution has been to explain how managers can create and sustain a competitive advantage that will give a company above-average profitability. An important element in doing this is an industry analysis.

Porter proposes that some industries are inherently more profitable (and, therefore, more attractive to enter and remain in) than others. For example, the pharmaceutical industry is one with historically high profit margins, and the airline industry has notoriously low ones. But a company can still make a lot of money in a "dull" industry and lose money in a "glamorous" industry. The key is to exploit a competitive advantage.

In any industry, five competitive forces dictate the rules of competition. Together, these five forces (see Exhibit 7-7) determine industry attractiveness and profitability. Managers assess an industry's attractiveness using these forces:

- *Threat of new entrants.* Factors such as economies of scale, brand loyalty, and capital requirements determine how easy or hard it is for new competitors to enter an industry.

- *Threat of substitutes.* Factors such as switching costs and buyer loyalty determine the degree to which customers are likely to buy a substitute product.

Exhibit 7-7

Forces in an Industry Analysis

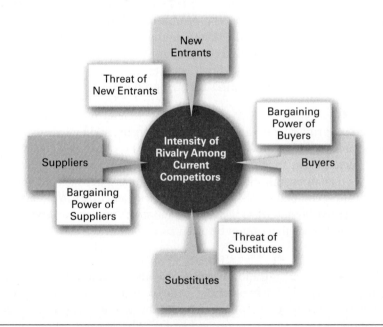

Source: Based on M. E. Porter, *Competitive Strategy: Techniques for Analyzing Industries and Competitors* (New York: Free Press, 1980).

In trying to find a niche for his bread-making company, Dokse Perklin, founder of Mississauga, Ontario-based Le Bon Croissant, realized that he could do something that grocery stores and restaurants could not: ensure high-quality bakery products while controlling costs. "Hotels, grocery chains, restaurant chains [and] institutions just can't afford to bake on premises anymore," Perklin says. "They can't find the staff, they can't effectively control overheads, they can't ensure consistent quality." So Perklin filled that need, and has created a bread-baking business that ships frozen unbaked and baked goods throughout Canada, the United States, the Caribbean, and Asia.

- *Bargaining power of buyers.* Factors such as number of customers in the market, customer information, and the availability of substitutes determine the amount of influence that buyers have in an industry.

- *Bargaining power of suppliers.* Factors such as the degree of supplier concentration and availability of substitute inputs determine the amount of power that suppliers have over firms in the industry.

- *Current rivalry.* Factors such as industry growth rate, increasing or falling demand, and product differences determine how intense the competitive rivalry will be among firms currently in the industry.

Once managers have assessed the five forces and determined what threats and opportunities exist, they are ready to select an appropriate competitive strategy. According to Porter, no firm can be successful by trying to be all things to all people. He proposes that managers select a strategy that will give the organization a competitive advantage, which he says arises out of either having lower costs than all other industry competitors or by being significantly different from competitors. On that basis, managers can choose one of three strategies: cost leadership, differentiation, or focus. Which one managers select depends on the organization's strengths and core competencies and its competitors' weaknesses (see Exhibit 7-8 on page 208).

Cost Leadership Strategy When an organization sets out to be the lowest-cost producer in its industry, it's following a **cost leadership strategy**. A low-cost leader aggressively searches out efficiencies in production, marketing, and other areas of operation. Overhead is kept to a minimum, and the firm does everything it can to cut costs. You will not find expensive art or interior décor at offices of low-cost leaders. For example, at Wal-Mart's headquarters in Bentonville, Arkansas, office furnishings are sparse and drab but functional.

cost leadership strategy
A business strategy in which the organization sets out to be the lowest-cost producer in its industry.

Exhibit 7-8

Requirements for Successfully Pursuing Porter's Competitive Strategies

Generic Strategy	Commonly Required Skills and Resources	Common Organizational Requirements
Cost Leadership	Sustained capital investment and access to capital Process engineering skills Intense supervision of labour Products designed for ease in manufacture Low-cost distribution system	Tight cost control Frequent, detailed control reports Structured organization and responsibilities Incentives based on meeting strict quantitative targets
Differentiation	Strong marketing abilities Product engineering Creative flair Strong capability in basic research Corporate reputation for quality or technological leadership Long tradition in the industry or unique combination of skills drawn from other businesses Strong cooperation from channels	Strong coordination among functions in R & D, product development, and marketing Subjective measurement and incentives instead of quantitative measures Amenities to attract highly skilled labour, scientists, or creative people
Focus	Combination of the foregoing skills and resources directed at the particular strategic target	Combination of the foregoing organizational requirements directed at the particular strategic target

Source: Reprinted from M. E. Porter, *Competitive Strategy: Techniques for Analyzing Industries and Competitors* (New York: Free Press, 1980), pp. 40–41.

Although low-cost leaders don't place a lot of emphasis on "frills," the product or service being sold must be perceived as comparable in quality to that offered by rivals or at least be acceptable to buyers. Examples of companies that have used the low-cost leader strategy include Wal-Mart, Hyundai, and WestJet Airlines.

Differentiation Strategy   The company that seeks to offer unique products that are widely valued by customers is following a **differentiation strategy**. Sources of differentiation might be exceptionally high quality, extraordinary service, innovative design, technological capability, or an unusually positive brand image. The key to this competitive strategy is that whatever product or service attribute is chosen for differentiating must set the firm apart from its competitors and be significant enough to justify a price premium that exceeds the cost of differentiating. For instance, St. Stephen, New Brunswick-based Ganong Bros., a small chocolate maker, differentiates itself from bigger boxed-chocolate makers by focusing on the assorted chocolates and fruit jellies market. This allows it to rank second in Canada in that market. Its Fruitfull brand, made with real fruit purée and packaged like chocolates, has a 43 percent share of fruit jelly sales.[42] Vancouver-based Vancouver City Savings Credit Union differentiates itself from competitors through a focus on the community and the customer, as the following *Management Reflection* shows.

differentiation strategy
A business strategy in which a company seeks to offer unique products that are widely valued by customers.

Ganong Brothers
www.ganong.com

Vancouver City Savings Credit Union
www.vancity.com

Vancity Champions the Underdog

How does a small bank compete against the larger ones? Vancouver City Savings Credit Union (Vancity) does not hope to be like the country's Big Five banks.[43] It is much smaller, for one thing. Profit is not the bank's only goal, and only 20 percent of executive compensation is based on profit. Even so, the bank makes enough profit each year to return 30 percent of the profits to its members and the community. When Tamara Vrooman assumed the role of CEO in September 2007, she emphasized how Vancity is not simply about profit. "I am thrilled to be joining an organization that is well-known, successful, not afraid to take risks, and is thoughtful in terms of what it means to be a co-operative, a banker, an employer, and a member of the community."[44]

Vancity is sometimes mocked for its "left coast ways," but it is not afraid to be clear about its mission: The bank is committed to the community, social responsibility, and the environment. This is also what makes the bank unique. According to former CEO Dave Mowat: "Every day of our lives we're trading on our differentiation…We have to do it a little bit different, a little bit better to give value-added to draw people to our organization. There isn't an end point where we can win on scale." What the bank can win on is customer service, as Mowat explains, by providing "that extra bit of customization."

While Vancity has many wealthy clients, it likes to work with the less fortunate. It has set up a branch in Canada's poorest neighbourhood, East Vancouver, something other banks were reluctant to do. Mowat believes these clients can be just as trustworthy when you take the time to get to know them. Vancity is so dedicated to customer service that its customer satisfaction rating is at 85 percent, compared with 60 percent for the big banks. ∎

Practically any successful consumer product or service can be identified as an example of the differentiation strategy: Calgary-based WestJet Airlines (customer service); Waterloo,

How can a Canadian company compete against imports from low-labour-cost countries like China? Mississauga, Ontario-based Dahl Brothers Canada, which makes valves and fittings for plumbing and hot-water heating systems, found a way. "Where we compete is on design, quality, response time and choice," president Jannike Godfrey says. "By doing that, we can hold our own against imports."

The Ortiz brothers, Nicolas, George, and Oliver, have earned almost $400 million in revenues in a country of only 3.5 million people by creating IKI, now the second-largest supermarket chain in Lithuania. IKI's 67 stores and 15 convenience outlets cater to the once-Communist country's long-unmet niche market for luxury goods like French cheese, American personal-care products, free-range chickens, and gourmet mushrooms. The brothers recently opened IKI stores in Latvia and are planning to expand to Estonia.

Ontario-based Research In Motion, the maker of the BlackBerry (quality and innovative design); Vancouver-based Martha Sturdy (furniture design and brand image); and Ottawa-based Lee Valley Tools (product design).

focus strategy
A business strategy in which a company pursues a cost or differentiation advantage in a narrow industry segment.

Focus Strategy The first two of Porter's competitive strategies seek a competitive advantage in the broad marketplace. However, the **focus strategy** involves a cost advantage (cost focus) or a differentiation advantage (differentiation focus) in a narrow industry segment. That is, managers select a market segment in an industry and attempt to exploit it rather than serve the broad market. Segments can be based on product variety, type of end buyer, distribution channel, or geographical location of buyers. For example, at Compania Chilena de Fosforos SA, a large Chilean wood products manufacturer, Vice-Chair Gustavo Romero Zapata devised a focus strategy to sell chopsticks in Japan. Competitors, and even other company managers, thought he was crazy. However, by focusing on this segment, Romero's strategy managed to create more demand for his company's chopsticks than it had mature trees with which to make the products. Whether a focus strategy is feasible depends on the size of the segment and whether the organization can support the additional cost of focusing. Although research suggests that the focus strategy may be the most effective choice for small businesses because they typically do not have the economies of scale or internal resources to successfully pursue one of the other two strategies, there are large organizations that successfully use the focus strategy.[45] For example, Denmark's Bang & Olufsen, whose profit was over $56 million in 2005–2006, focuses on high-end audio equipment sales.[46] Whether a focus strategy is feasible depends on the size of the segment and whether the organization can make money serving that segment.

stuck in the middle
A situation in which an organization is unable to develop a competitive advantage through cost or differentiation.

Stuck in the Middle What happens if an organization is unable to develop a competitive advantage through either cost or differentiation? Porter uses the term **stuck in the middle** to describe those organizations that find it very difficult to achieve long-term success. Porter goes on to note that successful organizations frequently get into trouble by reaching beyond their competitive advantage and ending up stuck in the middle. The Hudson's Bay Company department store in recent years seems to have had this strategy, avoiding the low-cost strategy of its sister store, Zellers, and avoiding the strategies of higher-end fashion boutiques such as Holt Renfrew.

However, research has shown that organizations *can* pursue a cost leadership and a differentiation strategy at the same time and achieve high performance.[47] However, it's not easy to pull off! To do so successfully means an organization must be strongly committed to keeping costs low *and* establishing solid sources of differentiation. For example, companies such as Molson, Toyota, Intel, and Coca-Cola differentiate their products while at the same time maintaining low-cost operations.

Exhibit 7-9

Examples of Functional Strategies

Function	Ways to Provide Cost Leadership Advantage	Ways to Provide Differentiation Advantage
Sales and marketing	• Find new customers • Find low-cost advertising methods	• Promote brand-name awareness and loyalty • Tailor products to suit customers' needs
Materials management	• Use just-in-time inventory system/computerized warehousing • Develop long-term relationships with suppliers and customers	• Develop long-term relationships with suppliers to provide high-quality inputs • Reduce shipping time to customers
Research and development	• Design products that can be made more cheaply • Improve efficiency of machinery and equipment	• Create new products • Improve existing products
Manufacturing	• Develop skills in low-cost manufacturing	• Increase product quality and reliability
Human resource management	• Reduce turnover and absenteeism • Raise employee skills	• Hire highly skilled employees • Develop innovative training programs

Source: G. R. Jones and J. M. George, *Contemporary Management*, 4th ed. (New York: McGraw-Hill/Irwin, 2006), p. 290. Reprinted by permission of McGraw-Hill Education.

Functional Strategy

Functional strategies are the strategies used by an organization's various functional departments to support the business strategy. Traditional functional departments include manufacturing, marketing, human resources, research and development, and finance. Exhibit 7-9 illustrates functional strategies that can be used to support either cost leadership or differentiation strategies at the business level.

functional strategy
A strategy used by a functional department to support the business strategy of the organization.

Problems occur when employees and customers don't understand a company's strategy. For instance, Air Canada did not articulate a clear strategy in creating Tango and Zip to operate alongside the parent airline. By spring 2004, Tango had become a fare category rather than a brand, and it was announced that Zip would no longer operate as a separate carrier. By contrast, WestJet Airlines communicates a very clear strategy to its employees: enjoyable flights and an affordable experience for travellers. Employees are to ensure these while keeping costs down and improving turnaround time. Aware of the strategy, all WestJet employees know what is expected of them in a crisis, and all employees help in whatever ways are necessary to meet this strategy.

Strategic Management in Today's Environment

▶ ▶ ▶ Indigo Books & Music is using its e-business to achieve growth.[48] While amazon.ca has more visitors to its site, chapters.indigo.ca turns more of its visitors into buyers. By creating a social-networking site, the company hopes consumers will share thoughts on their favourite books and, ultimately, encourage others to buy those books. While having a social-networking site like Facebook would be a first for a book retailer, not everyone is sure this strategy will pay off. David Gray, president of Vancouver-based retail consultancy Sixth Line Solutions, notes that "everyone is rushing to do the next Facebook, and people only have so much time."

4. How does today's dynamic environment affect strategic management?

There is no better example of the strategic challenges faced by managers in today's dynamic environment than the recorded music industry. Global music sales tumbled 5 percent in 2006—the seventh drop in a row—and industry executives are braced for more declines.[49] However, digital sales were up 85 percent in the same year. As well, cellphone ring-tone sales doubled from 2004 to 2005, but challenges still remain.[50] Rampant global piracy (according to the IFPI—an organization that represents the worldwide recording industry—one in three music discs sold worldwide is an illegal copy), economic uncertainty, and intense competition from other forms of entertainment have devastated the music industry. Its very nature continues to change, and managers are struggling to find strategies that will help their organizations succeed in such an environment.[51] But the music industry is not the only industry dealing with such enormous strategic challenges. Managers in all kinds of organizations face increasingly intense global competition and the increased demands of higher performance expectations by investors and customers. How have managers responded to these new realities? In this section, we will look at some current issues in strategy, including the need for strategic flexibility, and how managers are designing strategies to emphasize e-business, customer service, and innovation.

Strategic Flexibility

Jürgen Schrempp, former CEO of DaimlerChrysler, stated, "My principle always was…move as fast as you can and [if] you indeed make mistakes, you have to correct them. It's much better to move fast, and make mistakes occasionally, than move too slowly."[52] You would not think that smart individuals who are paid lots of money to manage organizations would make mistakes when it comes to strategic decisions. But even when managers "manage strategically" by following the strategic management process, there is no guarantee that the chosen strategies will lead to positive outcomes. Reading any of the current business periodicals would certainly support this assertion. But the key for managers is responding quickly when it's obvious that the strategy is not working. In other words, they need **strategic flexibility**—the ability to recognize major external environmental changes, to quickly commit resources, and to recognize when a strategic decision is not working. Given the environment that managers face today—oftentimes, highly uncertain and changing—strategic flexibility seems absolutely necessary. What can managers do to enhance their ability to quickly shift strategies as needed? *Tips for Managers—Creating Strategic Flexibility* provides some suggestions.

strategic flexibility
The ability to recognize major external environmental changes, to quickly commit resources, and to recognize when a strategic decision was a mistake.

New Directions in Organizational Strategies

What strategies are important for today's environment? We think there are three: e-business, customer service, and innovation.

E-business Strategies

As we discussed in Chapter 1, e-business techniques offer many advantages to organizations, whether simply through e-commerce (the sales and marketing component) or through being a total e-business.

There is no doubt that the Internet has changed and is changing the way organizations do business. Using the Internet, companies have, for instance, (1) created knowledge bases that employees can tap into any time, anywhere; (2) turned customers into collaborative partners who help design, test, and launch new products; (3) become virtually paperless in specific tasks such as purchasing and filing expense reports; (4) managed logistics in real time; and (5) changed the nature of numerous work tasks throughout the organization.

Using e-business techniques, managers can formulate strategies that contribute to the development of a sustainable competitive advantage.[53] A cost leader can use e-business techniques to reduce costs in a variety of ways. It might use online bidding and order processing to eliminate the need for sales calls and to decrease sales-force expenses; it could use web-based inventory control systems that reduce storage costs; or it might use online testing and evaluation of job applicants. For example, General Electric applied e-business techniques as it initiated several Internet-based purchasing activities in order to reduce costs.

A differentiator needs to offer products or services that customers perceive and value as unique. How could e-business techniques contribute? The differentiator might use Internet-based knowledge systems to shorten customer response times; provide rapid online responses to service requests; or automate purchasing and payment systems so that customers have detailed status reports and purchasing histories. Dell is an excellent example of a company that has exploited the differentiation advantage made possible by e-business techniques.

Finally, since the focuser targets a narrow market segment with customized products, it might provide chat rooms or discussion boards for customers to interact with others who have common interests; design niche websites that target specific groups with specific interests; or use websites to perform standardized office functions such as payroll or budgeting.

Research has shown that an important e-business strategy might be a clicks-and-bricks strategy. A clicks-and-bricks firm is one that uses both online (clicks) and traditional stand-alone locations (bricks).[54] A number of companies, such as Indigo Books & Music, London Drugs, and Canadian Tire, have stores, as well as websites, that allow consumers to shop online. Findings suggest that Canadians like to do their research on the web and then go to nearby stores to pick up items rather than have them shipped to their home. Nevertheless, in 2005, Canadians spent $7.9 billion on goods and services online, and it is projected that this spending will double by 2009.[55] While online purchases by Canadians represent a small fraction of personal spending on goods and services, this area is growing. So stores' "clicks-and-bricks" strategy works...and works well!

Today's Internet-enriched environment provides managers with many opportunities to design strategies that can help their organizations achieve a sustainable competitive advantage. At their disposal is a variety of e-business tools and techniques. The key challenge for managers is to know which ones to use, where, and when. Well-chosen e-business strategies can help an organization succeed.

Customer Service Strategies

Companies that emphasize customer service need strategies that cultivate that atmosphere from top to bottom. What kinds of strategies does that take? It takes giving customers what they want, communicating effectively with them, and providing employees with customer service training. Let's look first at the strategy of giving customers what they want.

New Balance Athletic Shoe was the first of the athletic shoe manufacturers to give customers a truly unique product: shoes in varying widths. Previously, no other athletic shoe manufacturer had shoes for narrow or wide feet in almost any size.[56] It should come as no surprise that an important customer service strategy is giving customers what they want, a major aspect of an organization's overall marketing strategy.

Another important customer service strategy involves communication. Managers should know what is going on with customers. They need to find out what customers liked and did not like about their purchase encounter—from their interactions with employees to their experience with the actual product or service. But communication is not a one-way street. It's also important to let customers know what is going on with the organization that

---

TIPS FOR MANAGERS

Creating Strategic Flexibility

- Know what is happening with strategies currently being used by **monitoring and measuring results**.

- Encourage employees to **be open about disclosing and sharing negative information**.

- **Get new ideas and perspectives from outside** the organization.

- Have **multiple alternatives** when making strategic decisions.

- **Learn from mistakes**.

Source: Based on K. Shimizu and M. A. Hitt, "Strategic Flexibility: Organizational Preparedness to Reverse Ineffective Strategic Decisions," *Academy of Management Executive*, November 2004, pp. 44–59.

might affect future purchase decisions. Having an effective customer communication system is an important customer service strategy.

Finally, we have discussed previously the importance of an organization's culture in emphasizing customer service. And this requires that employees be trained to provide exceptional customer service. For example, Singapore Airlines is well-known for its customer treatment. "On everything facing the customer, they do not scrimp," says an analyst based in Singapore.[57] Employees are expected to "get service right," leaving employees with no doubt about the expectations as far as how to treat customers. Singapore Airlines' service strategy is a good example of what managers must do if customer service is an important organizational goal and an important part of the company's culture.

Innovation Strategies

When Procter & Gamble purchased the Iams pet food business, it did what it always does—it used its renowned research division to look for ways to transfer technology from its other divisions to make new products.[58] One of the outcomes of this cross-divisional combination was a new tartar-fighting ingredient from toothpaste that is included in all of its dry adult pet foods.

As this example shows, innovation strategies are not necessarily focused on just the radical, breakthrough products. They can include the application of existing technology to new uses. Organizations of all kinds and sizes have successfully used both approaches. What types of innovation strategies do organizations need in today's environment? Those strategies should reflect their philosophy about innovation, which is shaped by two strategic decisions: innovation emphasis and innovation timing.

Managers must first decide where the emphasis of their innovation effort will be. Is the organization's focus going to be basic scientific research, product development, or process improvement? Basic scientific research requires the heaviest commitment in terms of resources because it involves the nuts-and-bolts activities and work of scientific research. In numerous industries (for instance, genetics engineering, information technology, or pharmaceuticals), an organization's expertise in basic research is the key to a sustainable competitive advantage. However, not every organization requires this extensive commitment to scientific research to achieve high performance levels. Instead, many depend on product development strategies. Although this strategy also requires a significant resource investment, it's not in the areas associated with scientific research. Instead, the organization takes existing technology and improves on it or applies it in new ways, just as Procter & Gamble did when it applied tartar-fighting knowledge to pet food products. Both of these first two strategic approaches to innovation (basic scientific research and product development) can help an organization achieve high levels of differentiation, which is a significant source of competitive advantage.

Finally, the last strategic approach to innovation emphasis is a focus on process development. Using this strategy, an organization looks for ways to improve and enhance its work processes. The organization introduces new and improved ways for employees to do their work in all organizational areas. This innovation strategy can lead to an organization's lowering costs, which, as we know, can be a significant source of competitive advantage.

Once managers have determined the focus of their innovation efforts, they must decide on their innovation timing strategy. Some organizations want to be the first with innovations whereas others are content to follow or mimic the innovations. An organization that is first to bring a product innovation to the market or to use a new process innovation is called a **first mover**. Being a first mover has certain strategic advantages and disadvantages, as shown in Exhibit 7-10. Some organizations pursue this route, hoping to develop a sustainable competitive advantage. Others have successfully developed a sustainable competitive advantage by being the followers in the industry. They let the first movers pioneer the innovations and then mimic their products or processes. Which approach managers choose depends on their organizations' innovation philosophies and specific resources and capabilities.

first mover
An organization that is first to bring a product innovation to the market or to use a new process innovation.

Exhibit 7-10

First-Mover Advantages and Disadvantages

Advantages	Disadvantages
• Reputation for being innovative and industry leader	• Uncertainty over exact direction technology and market will go
• Cost and learning benefits	• Risk of competitors' imitating innovations
• Control over scarce resources and keeping competitors from having access to them	• Financial and strategic risks
• Opportunity to begin building customer relationships and customer loyalty	• High development costs

SUMMARY AND IMPLICATIONS

1. What is strategic management? Strategic management is that set of managerial decisions and actions that determines the long-run performance of an organization. It is an important task of managers and involves all of the basic management functions—planning, organizing, leading, and controlling.

▶ ▶ ▶ Heather Reisman, CEO of Indigo Books & Music, announced a new growth strategy in June 2007 that recognizes the influence of the digital age on book sales. She hopes that the strategy she has chosen will pay off.

2. What are the steps in strategic management? The strategic management process is a six-step process that encompasses planning, implementation, and evaluation. The first four steps involve planning: identifying the organization's current mission, goals, and strategies; analyzing the internal environment; analyzing the external environment; and formulating strategies. The fifth step is implementing the strategy, and the sixth step is evaluating the results of the strategy. Even the best strategies can fail if management does not implement or evaluate them properly.

▶ ▶ ▶ Indigo is currently building on its use of the Internet to help increase sales. The company will want to evaluate the success of its strategy over time and may want to reconsider it if online purchases do not increase significantly or fall.

3. What kinds of strategies can managers use? There are three types of organizational strategy: corporate, business, and functional. They relate to the particular level of the organization that introduces the strategy. At the corporate level, organizations can engage in growth, stability, and renewal strategies. At the business level, strategies look at how an organization should compete in each of its businesses: through cost leadership, differentiation, or focus. At the functional level, strategies support the business strategy.

▶ ▶ ▶ Indigo is trying a differentiation strategy primarily by offering consumers a unique social-networking site for book lovers.

4. How does today's dynamic environment affect strategic management? Managers face more uncertainty and risk and greater change in today's continually changing environment, making it necessary to scan the environment more frequently and adjust strategy accordingly. Important new strategies in today's environment are e-business, the need to be more customer focused, and an emphasis on innovative approaches.

▶ ▶ ▶ For example, Indigo's plan to place greater emphasis on online sales through its social-networking site for book lovers focuses on all three new strategies mentioned. Changes in the environment can also lead to changes in an industry's regulations. In Indigo's case, its strategy is affected by government regulations that protect the Canadian book industry from foreign competition. If those regulations were revised to allow more foreign book retailers in Canada (amazon.ca, a subsidiary of amazon.com, was allowed to enter the Canadian market in 2002), Indigo may see more competition and might need to revise its strategy.

CHAPTER 7

Management @ Work

READING FOR COMPREHENSION

1. Describe the six-step strategic management process.

2. What is a SWOT analysis?

3. Explain the three growth strategies.

4. Describe the role of competitive advantage in business strategies.

5. What are Porter's five competitive forces?

6. What are the three competitive strategies organizations can implement?

7. How can quality provide a competitive advantage? Give an example.

8. Describe the three new directions in organizational strategies.

LINKING CONCEPTS TO PRACTICE

1. Perform a SWOT analysis on a local business you think you know well. What, if any, competitive advantage does this organization have?

2. Should ethical considerations be included in analyses of an organization's internal and external environments? Why or why not?

3. How might the process of strategy formulation, implementation, and evaluation differ for (a) large businesses, (b) small businesses, (c) nonprofit organizations, and (d) global businesses?

4. How could the Internet be helpful to managers as they follow the steps in the strategic management process?

5. "The concept of competitive advantage is as important for nonprofit organizations as it is for for-profit organizations." Do you agree or disagree with this statement? Explain your position, using examples to make your case.

6. Find examples of five different organizational mission statements. Using the mission statements, describe what types of corporate and business strategies each organization might use to fulfill that mission statement. Explain your rationale for choosing each strategy.

SELF-ASSESSMENT

How Well Do I Handle Ambiguity?

For each of the following statements, circle the level of agreement or disagreement that you personally feel:[59]

1 = Completely Disagree
4 = Neither Agree nor Disagree
7 = Completely Agree

1. An expert who does not come up with a definite answer probably does not know too much.   1 2 3 4 5 6 7

2. I would like to live in a foreign country for a while.   1 2 3 4 5 6 7

3. The sooner we all acquire similar values and ideals, the better.   1 2 3 4 5 6 7

4. A good teacher is one who makes you wonder about your way of looking at things.   1 2 3 4 5 6 7

5. I like parties where I know most of the people more than ones where all or most of the people are complete strangers.   1 2 3 4 5 6 7

6. Teachers or supervisors who hand out vague assignments give a chance for one to show initiative and originality.   1 2 3 4 5 6 7

7. A person who leads an even, regular life in which few surprises or unexpected happenings arise really has a lot to be grateful for.   1 2 3 4 5 6 7

8. Many of our most important decisions are based on insufficient information.   1 2 3 4 5 6 7

9. There is really no such thing as a problem that cannot be solved.   1 2 3 4 5 6 7

10. People who fit their lives to a schedule probably miss most of the joy of living.   1 2 3 4 5 6 7

11. A good job is one in which what is to be done and how it is to be done are always clear.   1 2 3 4 5 6 7

12. It is more fun to tackle a complicated problem than to solve a simple one.   1 2 3 4 5 6 7

13. In the long run, it is possible to get more done by tackling small, simple problems than large and complicated ones.   1 2 3 4 5 6 7

14. Often the most interesting and stimulating people are those who don't mind being different and original.   1 2 3 4 5 6 7

15. What we are used to is always preferable to what is unfamiliar.   1 2 3 4 5 6 7

16. People who insist upon a yes or no answer just don't know how complicated things really are.   1 2 3 4 5 6 7

Scoring Key

For odd-numbered questions, add the total points. For even-numbered questions, use reverse scoring (1 = 7, 2 = 6, 3 = 5, etc.) to determine your points. Your total score is the sum of the even- and odd-numbered questions.

Analysis and Interpretation

A completely tolerant person would score 15 and a completely intolerant person 105. Research shows that people typically score from 20 to 80, with a mean of 45.

In today's dynamic work environment, where changes occur at an ever faster pace, the ability to tolerate ambiguity becomes a valuable asset. A high tolerance for ambiguity (scores lower than 40) makes you more likely to be able to function in a work world where there is less certainty about expectations, performance standards, and career progress. A low tolerance for ambiguity (scores higher than 60) makes you more likely to be comfortable in more stable, well-defined situations. People can work toward becoming more (or less) comfortable with ambiguity.

More Self-Assessments mymanagementlab

To learn more about your skills, abilities, and interests, go to the MyManagementLab website and take the following self-assessments:

- I.A.5.—How Creative Am I?
- III.C.1.—How Well Do I Respond to Turbulent Change? (This exercise also appears in Chapter 16 on pages 537–538.)

MANAGEMENT FOR YOU TODAY

Dilemma

In Chapter 6, you were asked to develop your personal vision and a mission statement. To supplement that exercise, develop a SWOT analysis for considering what you want to be doing in five years. What are your strengths and weaknesses? What are the opportunities and threats in carrying out this plan?

Becoming a Manager

- As you keep up with the current business news, pay attention to organizational strategies that managers are using. What types of strategies are the successful organizations using?
- Use SWOT analysis when you apply for jobs—after all, why would you want to work for some organization that has a lot of weaknesses or is facing significant threats?
- Talk to managers about strategy. Ask them how they know when it's time to try a different strategy.

Identifying Organizational Strategies

Examples of organizational strategies are found everywhere in business and general news periodicals. You should be able to recognize the different types of strategies from these news stories.

Form groups of 3 or 4 individuals. Using news stories in the business and popular press, find examples of five dif-

ferent organizational strategies. Determine whether the examples are corporate, business, or functional strategies, and explain why your group made that choice. Be prepared to share your examples with the class.

Ethical Dilemma Exercise: What Are the Real Costs of Selling Used Books?

What happens when a new entrant shakes up an entire industry and changes the competitive situation?[60] Consider the book retailing industry. In Japan, the Bookoff chain stirred up controversy by manoeuvring around the country's law forbidding discounts on new books. Instead, Bookoff buys used books from customers, cleans them up, and sells them for half the original price. Even as Bookoff has expanded to 700 stores, competitors are upset because they cannot legally cut their prices to compete. Moreover, the Japan Booksellers Federation complains that teenagers could be shoplifting books from other stores to sell to Bookoff.

In the United States, amazon.com has used the Internet to successfully compete against long-established store chains such as Barnes & Noble. Amazon.com also allows dealers and individuals to sell used books alongside the new books posted on its online system.

Even though people buy and sell used books (and other items) through auctions on eBay—sales from which authors

receive no royalties—amazon.com is primarily a retailer competing with other retailers on and off the web. amazon.com's practice has drawn some protests. The Authors Guild in the United States wants its members to boycott amazon.com because authors receive no royalties from sales of used books, only sales of new books.

Imagine that you are a manager for Indigo Books & Music with responsibility for expanding revenues by broadening the range of products offered in Indigo's stores. Although expanding further into the used book market might increase Indigo's sales, you are somewhat concerned about the impact this might have on author royalties. You are also worried that the Canadian Authors Association might decide to start a boycott if you sell significant numbers of used books. This could harm your in-store sales. What should you do? (Review Exhibit 7-7 on page 206 as you think about this challenge.)

Thinking Critically About Ethics

Many company websites have an "About Us" page that provides information about the company and its products or services—past, present, and, often, future. This information is available for anyone to read, even competitors. In an intensely competitive industry where it's difficult for a company to sur-

vive, much less be successful, would it be wrong for managers to include misleading, or even false information? Why or why not? Suppose that the industry was not intensely competitive? Would you feel differently? Explain.

Haier Group

You may not be familiar with the Haier Group (sounds like "higher"), but if you have ever shopped for a refrigerator, microwave, wine cellar, or air conditioner at Wal-Mart, Sears, or Home Depot, you have undoubtedly seen, if not purchased,

the company's products.[61] Haier's name surfaced in North American headlines in late 2005, when it made a bid to purchase domestic appliance maker Maytag, which operates in both Canada and the US. Haier exports its products to more than 100 countries and regions, and its revenue in 2005 was over $14 billion.

Haier Group is China's largest home-appliance maker, and CEO Zhang Ruimin has ambitious goals for his company. Whereas the United States has General Electric, Germany has Mercedes-Benz, and Japan has Sony, China has yet to produce a comparable global competitor. Zhang is hoping to change that. Haier enjoys enviable prestige in China (a survey of "young, fashionable" Chinese ranked Haier as the country's third-most-popular brand behind Shanghai Volkswagen and Motorola, with Coca-Cola fourth), but Zhang is not satisfied. He wants to gain worldwide recognition, build the company

into China's first truly global brand, and be listed on the *Fortune* Global 500. But accomplishing those goals may mean losing the "Chinese-ness." In an online survey conducted in 2005 by Interbrand, 79 percent of the respondents believed that a "made in China" label hurts Chinese brands, with the biggest challenge to Chinese companies being to change the impression of Chinese products as cheap, poor value, poor quality, and unreliable. Product recalls during 2007 have increased concern about products manufactured in China.

What can Zhang do to build his brand globally while addressing the concerns of those who worry about the quality and safety of Chinese products?

DEVELOPING YOUR DIAGNOSTIC AND ANALYTICAL SKILLS

XXL No More!

For more than a decade, McDonald's was the leader in pioneering what it thought customers wanted—larger and larger portions.[62] Although its menu had remained relatively stable, McDonald's management was always looking for ways to improve sales and fend off strong competition from the likes of Wendy's and Burger King. It would also periodically add items to its menu to address small changes in people's fast-food desires, but these items often met with additional competition from other fast-food restaurants such as Taco Bell or even SUBWAY. The one thing that McDonald's did to boost sales and create a marketing coup was the addition of the Supersized Meal. Starting in the early 1990s, customers at McDonald's could add to their meal an extra-large soda and an extra-large order of french fries by simply saying, "Supersize it." Nearly 1 in 10 customers took advantage of the company's offer to "supersize" their meal for just 39 cents (US).

But since this expanded offering hit stores, McDonald's has come under fire. Public concern with the fattening of North America was often focused on McDonald's. The company's primary products were high in fat content, high in calories, and high in carbohydrates. Public pressure was mounting to the point that individuals sued McDonald's for causing their physical ailments brought about from obesity. Likened to the nicotine controversy surrounding cigarette smoking, lawyers were trying to make the connection that eating McDonald's food was addictive and a primary cause of obesity—especially among young people. Criticism reached its height early in 2004, when the effects of eating McDonald's food was the subject of an award-winning documentary. In it, producer Morgan Spurlock chronicled the 30-day effects of eating only McDonald's food for all of his meals. At the end of the month-long experiment, Spurlock spoke of his deteriorating health due solely to eating this fast food—and the 24 pounds he gained during this time frame.

Changes in public health consciousness and competitive pressures, along with this documentary film, led McDonald's to announce in March 2004 that it would eliminate all supersized offerings. McDonald's management claims that such action was warranted to simplify its menu offerings and to promote efficiency in the organization. Additionally, McDonald's has also begun altering its menu offerings. It now offers salads as an entrée meal, has reduced the fat content of its milk from 2 to 1 percent, and is attempting to promote itself as being more health conscious.

McDonald's action was largely driven by the reality that its sales had plummeted, as had its stock price. Competition from "health-friendly" alternatives was having a major effect on the company's revenues. McDonald's was losing market share and something had to be done. The company's announcement of the elimination of the supersized option and the addition of healthier substitutes is being viewed as a move that is entirely responsive to the changing market environment—something that executives at Burger King and Wendy's are watching very closely.

Questions

1. Explain how the environment affected McDonald's plans to discontinue offering supersized meals.

2. Describe how McDonald's can use the decision to stop selling supersized meals as a competitive advantage.

3. Would you classify this action by McDonald's as a growth strategy, a stability strategy, or a renewal strategy? Defend your choice.

4. Do you believe McDonald's was socially responsive in its actions to discontinue supersizing? Why or why not?

Scanning the Environment

About the Skill

Anticipating and interpreting changes that are taking place in the environment is an important skill that managers need. Information that comes from scanning the environment can be used in making decisions and taking actions. Managers at all levels of an organization need to know how to scan the environment for important information and trends.

Steps in Developing the Skill

You can be more effective at scanning the environment if you use the following five suggestions:[63]

1. **Decide which type of environmental information is important to your work.** Perhaps you need to know changes in customers' needs and desires, or perhaps you need to know what your competitors are doing. Once you know the type of information that you would like to have, you can look at the best ways to get that information.

2. **Regularly read and monitor pertinent information.** There is no scarcity of information to scan, but what you need to do is read those information sources that are pertinent. How do you know information sources are pertinent? They are pertinent if they provide you with the information that you identified as important.

3. **Incorporate the information that you get from your environmental scanning into your decisions and actions.** Unless you use the information you are getting, you are wasting your time getting it. Also, the more that you find you are using information from your environmental scanning, the more likely it is that you will want to continue to invest time and other resources into gathering it. You will see that this information is important to your being able to manage effectively and efficiently.

4. **Regularly review your environmental scanning activities.** If you find that you are spending too much time getting nonuseful information, or if you are not using the pertinent information that you have gathered, you need to make some adjustments.

5. **Encourage your subordinates to be alert to information that is important.** Your employees can be your "eyes and ears" as well. Emphasize to them the importance of gathering and sharing information that may affect your work unit's performance.

Practising the Skill

Read the following scenario. Write some notes about how you would handle the situation described. Be sure to refer to the five suggestions for scanning the environment.

Scenario

You are the assistant to the president at your college or university. You have been asked to prepare a report outlining the external information that you think is important for her to monitor. Think of the types of information that the president would need in order to do an effective job of managing the college or university right now and over the next three years. Be as specific as you can in describing this information. Also, identify where this information could be found.

Reinforcing the Skill

The following activities will help you practise and reinforce the skills associated with scanning the environment:

1. Select an organization with which you are familiar either as an employee or perhaps as a frequent customer. Assume that you are the top manager in this organization. What types of information from environmental scanning do you think would be important to you? Where would you find this information? Now assume that you are a first-line manager in this organization. Would the types of information you would get from environmental scanning change? Explain.

2. Assume that you are a regional manager for a large bookstore chain. What types of environmental and competitive information are you able to identify using the Internet? For each source, what information did you find that might help you do your job better?

Doing a Personal SWOT Analysis

A SWOT analysis can be a useful tool for examining your own skills, abilities, career preferences, and career opportunities. Doing a personal SWOT analysis involves taking a hard look at what your individual strengths and weaknesses are, and then assessing the opportunities and threats of various career paths that might interest you.[64]

Step 1: Assess your personal strengths and weaknesses. All of us have special skills, talents, and abilities. Each of us enjoys certain activities and not others. For example, some people hate sitting at a desk all day; others panic at the thought of having to interact with strangers. List the activities you enjoy and the things you are good at. Also, identify some things you don't enjoy and are not so good at. It's important to recognize our weaknesses so that we can either try to correct them or stay away from careers in which those things would be important. List your important individual strengths and weaknesses and highlight those you think are particularly significant.

Step 2: Identify career opportunities and threats. We know from this chapter and Chapter 2 that different industries face different external opportunities and threats. It's important to identify these external factors for the simple reason that your initial job offers and future career advancement can be significantly influenced by the opportunities and threats. A company that is in an industry where there are significant negative trends will offer few job openings or career advancement opportunities. On the other hand, job prospects will be bright in industries that have significant positive external trends. List two or three industries you have an interest in and critically evaluate the opportunities and threats facing those industries.

Step 3: Outline your five-year career goals. Taking your SWOT assessments, list four or five career goals that you would like to accomplish within five years of graduation. These goals might include things such as the type of job you would like to have, how many people you might be managing, or the type of salary you would like to be making. Keep in mind that ideally you should try to match your individual strengths with industry opportunities.

Step 4: Outline a five-year career action plan. Now it's time to get specific! Write a specific career action plan for accomplishing each of the career goals you identified in the previous step. State exactly what you will do, and by when, in order to meet each goal. If you think you will need special assistance, state what it is and how you will get it. For example, your SWOT analysis may indicate that in order to achieve your desired career goal, you need to take more courses in management. Your career action plan should indicate when you will take those courses. Your specific career action plan will provide you with guidance for making decisions, just as an organization's plans provide direction to managers.

Planning Tools and Techniques

PART two

Planning

**What tools and techniques
are available for planning?**

1. What is environmental scanning
   and how is it done?

2. What tools can managers use
   to allocate resources more
   effectively?

3. How does one manage projects?

▶ ▶ ▶ John Furlong (third from right in photo) has one of the most interesting and enviable jobs in the country—but also one of the most difficult and demanding.[1] He is the CEO of Vancouver 2010, the board of directors charged with getting everything ready for the 2010 Olympic Winter Games. The task is massive. He was appointed in early 2004, giving him six years to get everything ready for the two-week event.

One of Furlong's early tasks was to put together his leadership team, shown here. The overall operating budget for the Olympics when Vancouver won the bid was about $1.5 billion. Projects include developing new transportation lines and building nearly $470 million worth of Olympic venues. Furlong has been hiring staff, arranging for television rights, and mobilizing thousands of volunteers. He cannot miss his deadlines, as the dates of the games are already scheduled. And he was warned by the federal and provincial governments that he cannot exceed budget.

The budget shortfalls from the 2004 Athens Summer Olympics may give Furlong reason to plan expenditures carefully. To the average Olympics visitor, the Athens games seemed well organized: Everything happened on schedule, and there were no major problems. However, last-minute

construction, trying to finish six stadiums on time, and security and terrorism-prevention costs resulted in "a bill that could cripple the country's economy for a generation," one more than twice the original amount budgeted for the games. Montreal serves as another example for what happens when budgeting and planning is not kept under control. In February 2006, Montreal announced that it had finally paid back its $2 billion debt for holding the 1976 Olympic games.

Being CEO of the Olympics is "an almost impossible job with a steep learning curve and little margin for error," says Furlong. Not one CEO has made it from start to finish in the past four Olympics. Will Furlong be any different?

Think About It

With six years to plan, what does the CEO of the 2010 Olympics need to do to keep the project on task and on budget? Put yourself in John Furlong's shoes. What tools can he use to keep the construction projects for the Olympic venues on track? How can he make sure that everything gets done on time? What planning tools might he use to accomplish his goals?

In this chapter, we discuss some basic planning tools and techniques that managers in any business—large or small—can use. We begin by looking at some techniques for assessing the environment. Then we review techniques for allocating resources. Finally, we discuss some contemporary planning techniques, including project management and scenario planning. (To learn more about how well you deal with planning, see *Self-Assessment— How Good Am I at Personal Planning?* on pages 243–244, at the end of the chapter.)

Vancouver 2010
www.vancouver2010.com

Techniques for Assessing the Environment

1. What is environmental
scanning and how is it done?

In our description of the strategic management process in Chapter 7, we discussed the importance of assessing the organization's environment. In this section, we review three techniques to help managers do that: environmental scanning, forecasting, and benchmarking. There are a variety of software tools that can do the actual analysis of data, once collected. For instance, Ottawa-based Cognos (acquired by IBM in 2008), a world leader in business intelligence, has developed software that allows companies throughout the world to access their corporate data, analyze this data and prepare reports, plan budgets, and share information throughout the companies.

Environmental Scanning

> *What kinds of information might you look for to learn about competitors?*

How can managers become aware of significant environmental changes, such as a new law in Nova Scotia that permits shopping on Sunday? Or Wal-Mart Canada opening more Supercentres that include a discount grocery store? Or the precipitous decline in the working-age populations in Japan, Germany, Italy, and Russia? Managers in both small and large organizations use **environmental scanning,** which is the screening of large amounts of information to anticipate and interpret changes in the environment. Extensive environmental scanning is likely to reveal issues and concerns that could affect an organization's current or planned activities. (See *Developing Your Interpersonal Skills— Scanning the Environment* on page 220, in Chapter 7.)

environmental scanning
The screening of large amounts of information to anticipate and interpret changes in the environment.

PRISM 3

Tupperware Canada
www.tupperware.ca

Rubbermaid
www.rubbermaid.com

Borders Group is the United States' second-largest book retailer. In its efforts to boost sales at its US stores, the firm emphasizes market research, a specialized form of environmental scanning. Relying less on "gut" reactions to new titles, the traditional strategy of the past, Borders aggressively seeks input from focus groups, exit interviews, and customer polls, and it calls on publishers to help it manage some 250 categories ranging from thrillers to cookbooks, determining what titles to carry, how many of each, and how the books will be displayed.

Research has shown that companies with advanced environmental scanning systems have increased their profits and revenue growth.[2] Organizations that don't keep on top of environmental changes are likely to experience the opposite! For instance, Tupperware, the food-storage container company, enjoyed unprecedented success during the 1960s and 1970s, selling its products at home-hostessed parties where housewives played games, socialized, and saw product demonstrations. However, as North American society changed— more women working full time outside the home, an increasing divorce rate, and young adults waiting longer to marry—the popularity of Tupperware parties began to decline because no one had time to go to them. The company's North American market share fell from 60 percent to 40 percent while Rubbermaid, a competitor that marketed its plastic food-storage containers in retail outlets, increased its market share from 5 percent to 40 per-

cent. By the early 1990s, most women had no desire to go to a Tupperware party, or knew how to find Tupperware products elsewhere. Yet Tupperware's president, obviously clueless about the changed environment, predicted that before the end of the 1990s, the party concept would be popular once again. In 2006, Tupperware was still struggling to find its niche.[3] This example shows how a once successful company can suffer by failing to recognize how the environment has changed.

Competitor Intelligence

One of the fastest-growing areas of environmental scanning is **competitor intelligence**.[4] It's a process by which organizations gather information about their competitors and get answers to questions such as, Who are they? What are they doing? How will what they are doing affect us? Let's look at an example of how one organization used competitor intelligence in its planning.

Dun & Bradstreet (D&B), a leading provider of business credit, marketing, and purchasing information, has an active business intelligence division. The division manager received a call from an assistant vice-president for sales in one of the company's geographic territories. This person had been on a sales call with a major customer and the customer happened to mention in passing that another company had visited and made a major presentation about its services. What was interesting was that, although D&B had plenty of competitors, this particular company wasn't one of them. The manager gathered together a team that sifted through dozens of sources (research services, Internet, personal contacts, and other external sources) and quickly became convinced that there was something to this; that this company was "aiming its guns right at us." Managers at D&B jumped into action to develop plans to counteract this competitive attack.[5]

Competitor intelligence experts suggest that 80 percent of what managers need to know about competitors can be found out from their own employees, suppliers, and customers.[6] Competitor intelligence does not have to involve spying. Customers, advertisements, promotional materials, marketing research, press releases, reports filed with government agencies, annual reports, want ads, newspaper reports, distributors, and industry studies are examples of readily accessible sources of information. Attending trade shows and debriefing the sales force can be other good sources of competitor information. Monitoring job ads by competitors gives some indication of the kinds of positions the competitor is trying to fill; the frequency of the ads may indicate that there is a lot of turnover, or that the company is expanding rapidly.[7] Many firms regularly buy competitors' products and have their own engineers study them (through a process called *reverse engineering*) to learn about new technical innovations. In addition, the Internet has opened up vast sources of competitor intelligence, as many corporate websites include new-product information and press releases. As Professor Marc-David Seidel of UBC's Sauder School of Business notes, "There are actually a lot of private firms that get hired to do this kind of work—the really dark stuff... These are ethical decisions. It's a fairly grey line."[8]

The concerns about competitor intelligence pertain to the ways in which competitor information is gathered. For instance, at Procter & Gamble, executives hired competitive intelligence firms to spy on its competitors in the hair care business. At least one of these firms misrepresented themselves to competitor Unilever's employees, trespassed at Unilever's hair care headquarters in Chicago, and went through trash dumpsters to gain information. When P&G's CEO found out, he immediately fired the individuals responsible and apologized to Unilever.[9] Competitor intelligence becomes illegal corporate spying when it involves the theft of proprietary materials or trade secrets by any means. The difficult decisions about competitive intelligence arise because often there is a fine line between what is considered *legal and ethical* and what is considered *legal but unethical*. Although the top manager at one competitive intelligence firm contends that 99.9 percent of intelligence gathering is legal, there is no question that some people or companies will go to any lengths—many unethical— to get information about competitors.[10] Often participants will claim that what is legal or ethical is a grey area. For instance, when Air Canada accused WestJet Airlines of gathering information about its routes in an illegal manner, WestJet said that there was no indication the data were confidential, as the *Management Reflection* on the next page shows.

competitor intelligence
Environmental scanning activity that seeks to identify who competitors are, what they are doing, and how their actions will affect the organization.

 D&B Canada
www.dnb.com

Q&A 8.1

Proctor & Gamble
www.pg.com
Unilever
www.unilever.com

Air Canada Accuses WestJet Airlines of Espionage

Should managers access a competitor's website just because they can? When Jeffrey Lafond received a severance package from Air Canada in 2000, he was given a password for an Air Canada employee travel website that listed all of the company's flights and passenger loads.[11] The intended use for the password to the site was for Lafond to book two free flights of his choice every year through 2005.

Lafond subsequently became a financial analyst at WestJet Airlines. In March 2003, Mark Hill, WestJet co-founder and vice-president of strategic planning, saw Lafond accessing the Air Canada employee travel website. Intrigued, Hill asked for Lafond's password so that he could view the website himself.

Hill admits to spending about 90 minutes every night going into the website and counting Air Canada's load factors. He complained about this use of his time to Don Bell, WestJet's vice-president of customer service and another airline co-founder. As a result, Bell assigned Sven Hanson, a WestJet IT staff member, the task of developing a system to automatically download and analyze Air Canada's load factors. Air Canada claims that WestJet entered Air Canada's employee travel website 240 000 times between May 2003 and March 2004, using Lafond's password.

Lafond admits that he did ask WestJet to protect him financially, should Air Canada ever find out that he had given out his password. He was concerned: "I could have been liable for somebody else accessing the [Air Canada] database, I guess."

WestJet's lawyers rejected Air Canada's claims of corporate espionage. They said that while the website was password protected, "At all material times, there was nothing on the website stating it was confidential." They further argued that "Air Canada does not provide persons given access to the website any terms or conditions stating the information on the website is confidential or limiting the use of the information to a particular purpose."

In a countersuit, WestJet accused Air Canada of collecting garbage from Hill's house, in an effort to determine exactly how he was using Air Canada's data. Hill countersued Air Canada for trespassing. Neither airline denied the charges made against them, though both suggested that the harm to the other was minimal.

WestJet president and CEO Clive Beddoe apologized to shareholders in July 2004, and Hill resigned at the same time, stating that it was in the best interests of him and the company. In May 2006, to put an end to the lawsuits, WestJet admitted that senior executives stole confidential information, and apologized to Air Canada. It agreed to pay Air Canada $5.5 million for its legal fees and donate $10 million to children's charities in the name of both airlines. ■

Global Scanning

One type of environmental scanning that is particularly important is global scanning. Because world markets are complex and dynamic, managers have expanded the scope of their scanning efforts to gain vital information on global forces that might affect their organizations.[12] The value of global scanning to managers, of course, is largely dependent on the extent of the organization's global activities. For a company that has significant global interests, global scanning can be quite valuable. For instance, Mitsubishi has elaborate information networks and computerized systems to monitor global changes. This has led to the creation of one of the "most technologically advanced automotive-manufacturing facilities in the world."[13]

The sources that managers use for scanning the domestic environment are too limited for global scanning. Managers need to globalize their perspectives and information sources. For instance, they can subscribe to information clipping services that review world newspapers and business periodicals and provide summaries of desired information. Also, there are numerous electronic services that provide topic searches and automatic updates in global areas of special interest to managers.

Forecasting

The second technique managers can use to assess the environment is forecasting. Forecasting is an important part of planning, and managers need forecasts that will allow them to predict future events effectively and in a timely manner. Environmental scanning establishes the basis for **forecasts**, which are predictions of outcomes. Virtually any component in the organization's environment can be forecasted. Let's look at how managers forecast and how effective forecasts are.

Q&A 8.2

forecasts
Predictions of outcomes.

Forecasting Techniques

Forecasting techniques fall into two categories: quantitative and qualitative. **Quantitative forecasting** applies a set of mathematical rules to a series of past data to predict outcomes. These techniques are preferred when managers have sufficient hard data that can be used. **Qualitative forecasting**, in contrast, uses the judgment and opinions of knowledgeable individuals to predict outcomes. Qualitative techniques typically are used when precise data are limited or hard to obtain. Exhibit 8-1 describes some popular forecasting techniques.

Today, many organizations collaborate on forecasts by using Internet-based software known as CPFR®, which stands for collaborative planning, forecasting, and replenishment.[14] CPFR offers a standardized way for retailers and manufacturers to use the Internet to exchange data. Each organization relies on its own data about past sales trends, promotion plans, and other factors to calculate a demand forecast for a particular product. If their respective forecasts differ by a certain amount (say 10 percent), the retailer and manufacturer use the Internet to exchange more data and written comments until they arrive

quantitative forecasting
Forecasting that applies a set of mathematical rules to a series of past data to predict outcomes.

qualitative forecasting
Forecasting that uses the judgment and opinions of knowledgeable individuals to predict outcomes.

Exhibit 8-1

Forecasting Techniques

Technique	Description	Application
Quantitative		
Time series analysis	Fits a trend line to a mathematical equation and projects into the future by means of this equation	Predicting next quarter's sales on the basis of four years of previous sales data
Regression models	Predicts one variable on the basis of known or assumed other variables	Seeking factors that will predict a certain level of sales (for example, price, advertising expenditures)
Econometric models	Uses a set of regression equations to simulate segments of the economy	Predicting change in car sales as a result of changes in tax laws
Economic indicators	Uses one or more economic indicators to predict a future state of the economy	Using change in GNP to predict discretionary income
Substitution effect	Uses a mathematical formula to predict how, when, and under what circumstances a new product or technology will replace an existing one	Predicting the effect of HDTVs on the sale of traditional-style tube TVs
Qualitative		
Jury of opinion	Combines and averages the opinions of experts	Polling the company's human resource managers to predict next year's college and university recruitment needs
Sales force composition	Combines estimates from field sales personnel of customers' expected purchases	Predicting next year's sales of industrial lasers
Customer evaluation	Combines estimates from established customers' purchases	Surveying major car dealers by a car manufacturer to determine types and quantities of products desired

at a single and more accurate forecast. This collaborative forecasting helps both organizations do a better job of planning.

Forecasting Effectiveness

The goal of forecasting is to provide managers with information that will facilitate decision making. Despite forecasting's importance to planning, managers have had mixed success with it. In a survey of financial managers in organizations in the United States, United Kingdom, France, and Germany, 84 percent of the respondents said their financial forecasts were inaccurate by 5 percent or more; 54 percent of the respondents reported inaccuracy of 10 percent or more.[15] Forecasting techniques are most accurate when the environment is not rapidly changing. The more dynamic the environment, the more likely managers are to forecast ineffectively. Also, forecasting is relatively ineffective in predicting nonseasonal events such as recessions, unusual occurrences, discontinued operations, and the actions or reactions of competitors.

Q&A 8.3

Although forecasting has a mixed record, there are ways to improve its effectiveness:[16]

- *Use simple forecasting methods.* They tend to do as well as, and often better than, complex methods that may mistakenly confuse random data for meaningful information. For instance, Brampton, Ontario-based Loblaw Companies did not need to use complex mathematical techniques to predict that Wal-Mart would be their next big competitor. Loblaw prepared for Wal-Mart's growing grocery inventory by increasing its proportion of nonfood items, and adding clothes, pharmaceuticals, and small appliances to a number of stores. Loblaw has also focused on customer convenience by forming "strategic alliances with coffee shops, fitness studios, photo marts, wine shops, dry cleaners and other companies to provide its customers with the convenience of one-stop-shopping in a Loblaws atmosphere."[17]

Loblaw Companies
www.loblaws.ca

- *Look at involving more people in the process.* At *Fortune* 100 companies, it's not unusual to have 1000 to 5000 managers providing forecasting input. These businesses are finding that the more people are involved in the process, the more they can improve the reliability of the outcomes.[18]
- *Compare every forecast with "no change."* A no-change forecast is accurate approximately half the time.
- *Use rolling forecasts that look 12 to 18 months ahead, instead of using a single, static forecast.* These types of forecasts can help managers spot trends better and help their organizations be more adaptive in changing environments.[19]
- *Don't rely on a single forecasting method.* Make forecasts with several models and average them, especially when making long-range forecasts.
- *Don't assume that you can accurately identify turning points in a trend.* What is typically perceived as a significant turning point often turns out to be simply a random event.
- Shorten the length of forecasts to improve their accuracy because accuracy decreases as the period you are trying to predict increases.

Forecasting is a managerial skill and as such can be practised and improved. Forecasting software has made the task somewhat less mathematically challenging, although the "number crunching" is only a small part of the activity. Interpreting the forecast and incorporating that information into planning decisions is the challenge facing managers.

Benchmarking

benchmarking
The search for the best practices among competitors or noncompetitors that lead to their superior performance.

Suppose that you are a talented pianist or gymnast. To make yourself better, you want to learn from the best, so you watch outstanding musicians or athletes for motions and techniques they use as they perform. That is what is involved in the final technique we are going to discuss for assessing the environment—**benchmarking**. This is the search for the best practices among competitors or noncompetitors that lead to their superior performance.[20] Does benchmarking work? Studies show that users have achieved 69 percent faster growth and 45 percent greater productivity.[21]

Wipro, a business-process outsourcing company in Bangalore, India, actively benchmarks Toyota's smoothly run manufacturing processes, looking for ways to operate its own labour-intensive business more efficiently. P. V. Priya (centre in photo), medical claims supervisor for Wipro, starts each day in a stand-up meeting with her team in the "War Zone," where she congratulates them on work done and asks for suggestions about how to improve team performance.

The basic idea behind benchmarking is that managers can improve performance by analyzing and then copying the methods of the leaders in various fields. Companies such as Sudbury, Ontario-based ABS Manufacturing and Distributing, a manufacturer of valves and gaskets for mining, and pulp and paper companies; Toronto-based Mr. Convenience, which leases furniture and appliances to Toronto consumers and businesses; and Mississauga, Ontario-based computer security firm BorderWare use benchmarking as a standard tool in their quest for performance improvement. Canadian business schools use benchmarking to set goals for where they want to rank. Rotman, Schulich, Ivey, and Sauder are just a few of the business schools that follow national and international rankings in their quest to be the "number one business school in Canada."

Some companies have chosen some pretty unusual benchmarking partners. Southwest Airlines, for example, studied Indy 500 pit crews, who can change a race tire in under 15 seconds, to see how they could make gate turnarounds even faster. IBM studied Las Vegas casinos for ways to discourage employee theft. Even governments use benchmarking. The federal government passed a bill in March 2004, requiring all departments to benchmark their fees and performance standards against those of Canada's trading partners. The penalty if departments fail to meet their benchmarks? They will have to refund some of the fees they have been collecting for services. Toronto-area Liberal MP Roy Cullen introduced the bill after complaints from Bayer and BASF, companies in his riding, that claimed they paid fees equivalent to what they paid in other countries, but waited far longer to get new chemicals approved.[22]

What does benchmarking involve? Exhibit 8-2 illustrates the four steps typically used in benchmarking.

Q&A 8.4

Exhibit 8-2

Steps in Benchmarking

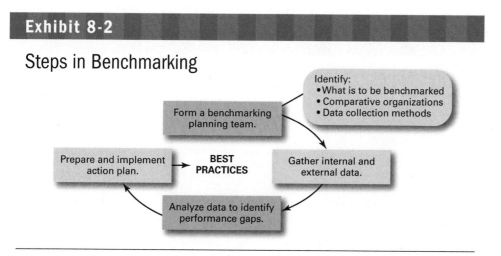

Source: Based on Y. K. Shetty, "Aiming High: Competitive Benchmarking for Superior Performance," *Long Range Planning*, February 1993, p. 42.

Techniques for Allocating Resources

▶ ▶ ▶ As CEO of Vancouver 2010, John Furlong has to allocate a variety of resources properly.[23] Capital advances of $35 million went to the University of British Columbia for a curling centre and a hockey arena, and to the City of Richmond for a speed skating oval. One athletes' village is under way in the False Creek area of Vancouver and another has been built in the Callahan Valley, near Whistler, along with a Nordic centre. At Whistler, construction includes a centre for bobsled, skeleton, and luge. The convention centres in Vancouver and Whistler will also be expanded. The $600 million upgrade to the Sea-to-Sky Highway, the route to Whistler, is under way. The Canada Line (a rail-based rapid transit line) that will link Vancouver International Airport to the downtown area is under construction, causing frustration to shop owners along its path. These are just the major construction projects. Furlong also needs to hire hundreds of people, negotiate lucrative television deals, mobilize volunteers, and focus the world's attention on Vancouver and British Columbia for 16 days in February 2010. On June 29, 2007, exactly four years after Vancouver won the bid for the 2010 Winter Olympics, organizers were pleased with the planning to date. The budget was on track (with finances better than expected), and construction of many of the sporting venues was well ahead of schedule.

Despite the good news, with just a few years to go, Furlong, and the Olympics themselves, have to avoid the scandals that often afflict Olympic games and their planning. He knows that he will continue to face considerable political pressure from those who think Olympic dollars would be better spent on improving the lives of Vancouver's homeless. Will Furlong be able to get the job done on time and on budget?

Think About It

What are the tools John Furlong can use to keep this massive Olympic project on task and on budget? How can he make sure resources are allocated appropriately?

2. What tools can managers use to allocate resources more effectively?

resources
The assets of the organization, including financial, physical, human, intangible, and structural/cultural factors.

As we know from Chapter 6, once an organization's goals have been established, an important aspect of planning is determining how those goals are going to be accomplished. Before managers can organize and lead in order to implement the goals, they must have resources. **Resources** are the assets of the organization, including financial (debt, equity, retained earnings, and other financial holdings); physical (equipment, buildings, raw materials, or other tangible assets); human (experience, skills, knowledge, and competencies of people); intangible (brand names, patents, reputation, trademarks, copyrights, registered designs, and databases); and structural/cultural (history, culture, work systems, working relationships, level of trust, policies, and structure) factors. How are these resources allocated effectively and efficiently so that organizational goals are met? That is what we want

Exhibit 8-3

Techniques for Allocating Resources

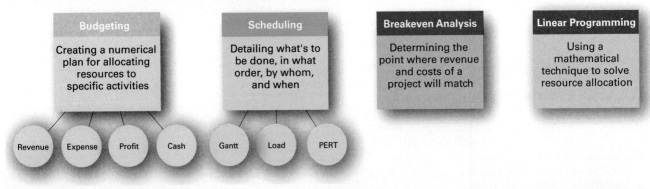

to look at in this section. Although managers can choose from a number of techniques for allocating resources (many of which are covered in courses on accounting, finance, human resources, and operations management), we discuss four techniques here: budgeting, scheduling, breakeven analysis, and linear programming. Exhibit 8-3 summarizes the differences among these techniques.

Budgeting

Most of us have had some experience, as limited as it might be, with budgets. We probably learned at a very early age that unless we allocated our "revenues" carefully, our weekly allowance was spent on "expenses" before the week was half over.

A **budget** is a numerical plan for allocating resources to specific activities. Managers typically prepare budgets for revenues, expenses, and large capital expenditures such as equipment. It's not unusual, though, for budgets to be used for improving time, space, and use of material resources. These types of budgets substitute nondollar numbers for dollar amounts. For example, the costs of such items as person-hours, capacity use, or units of production can be budgeted for daily, weekly, or monthly activities. Exhibit 8-4 on page 232 describes the different types of budgets that managers might use.

budget
A numerical plan for allocating resources to specific activities.

Q&A 8.5

Have you ever made a budget? How difficult was it to create and follow it?

Why are budgets so popular? Probably because they are applicable to a wide variety of organizations and work activities within organizations. We live in a world in which almost everything is expressed in monetary units. Dollars, pesos, euros, yen, and the like are used as a common measuring unit within a country. It seems only logical, then, that monetary budgets would be a useful tool for allocating resources and guiding work in such diverse departments as manufacturing and marketing research or at various levels in an organization. Budgets are one planning technique that most managers, regardless of organizational level, use. It's an important managerial activity because it forces financial discipline and structure throughout the organization.

Many managers don't like preparing budgets because they feel the process is time-consuming, inflexible, inefficient, and ineffective.[24] How can the budgeting process be improved? *Tips for Managers—Improving Budgeting* provides some suggestions. Organizations such as Texas Instruments, IKEA, Volvo, and Svenska Handelsbanken have incorporated several of these suggestions as

TIPS FOR MANAGERS

Improving Budgeting

↗ **Collaborate** and **communicate**.

↗ Be **flexible**.

↗ Understand that **goals should drive budgets**—budgets should not determine goals.

↗ **Coordinate budgeting** throughout the organization.

↗ **Use budgeting/planning software** when appropriate.

↗ Remember that **budgets are tools**.

↗ Remember that **profits result from smart management**, not because you budgeted for them.

Richard Hayne, founder and CEO of Urban Outfitters, sees his chain's budgeting process as "two sides of the brain working together." Budget controls at headquarters are tight, but the two brand presidents, who make quarterly plans determined by the budget and by fashion forecasts, have enough flexibility to change direction within a week based on what items are selling well. Despite daily monitoring, Urban Outfitters' individual merchandise buyers also have wide latitude; they can take markdowns when they need to instead of waiting for decisions from headquarters. "If you take the markdown when you need it," says the company's chief financial officer, "you have a better chance of selling it."

Exhibit 8-4

Types of Budgets

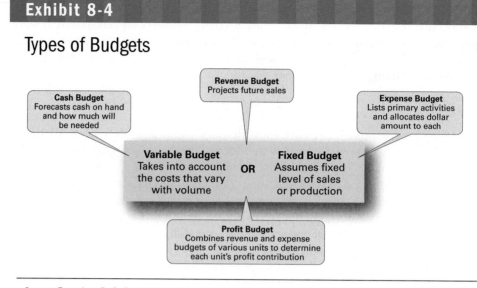

Source: Based on R. S. Russell and B. W. Taylor III, *Production and Operations Management* (Upper Saddle River, NJ: Prentice Hall, 1995), p. 287.

they revamped their budgeting processes. (For an explanation of the mechanics of the budgeting process, see *Developing Your Interpersonal Skills—Budgeting* on pages 247–248, at the end of the chapter.)

Scheduling

scheduling
Detailing what activities have to be done, the order in which they are to be completed, who is to do each, and when they are to be completed.

Ann is a manager at a Roots store in Toronto. Every week, she determines employees' work hours and the store area where each employee will be working. If you observed any group of supervisors or department managers for a few days, you would see them doing much the same—allocating resources by detailing what activities have to be done, the order in which they are to be completed, who is to do each, and when they are to be completed. These managers are **scheduling**. In this section, we review some useful scheduling devices including Gantt charts, load charts, and PERT network analysis.

Gantt Charts

Gantt chart
A scheduling chart developed by Henry Gantt that shows output, both planned and actual, over a period of time.

The **Gantt chart** was developed during the early 1900s by Henry Gantt, an associate of the scientific management expert Frederick Taylor. The idea behind a Gantt chart is simple. It's essentially a bar graph with time on the horizontal axis and the activities to be sched-

The trendy Zara clothing retailer continues to expand across Europe, the Americas, Asia, and Africa at a steady pace, its success relying heavily on its innovative product delivery schedule. New goods are shipped from the warehouse to Zara's more than 1000 stores every few days, instead of only once a season, as many competitors do. Maintaining the marketing advantage of this carefully managed schedule will be Zara's big challenge as it continues its global expansion.

uled on the vertical axis. The bars show output, both planned and actual, over a period of time. The Gantt chart visually shows when tasks are supposed to be done and compares that with the actual progress on each. It's a simple but important device that lets managers detail easily what has yet to be done to complete a job or project and to assess whether an activity is ahead of, behind, or on schedule.

Exhibit 8-5 depicts a simplified Gantt chart for book production developed by a manager in a publishing company. Time is expressed in months across the top of the chart. The major work activities are listed down the left side. Planning involves deciding what activities need to be done to get the book finished, the order in which those activities need to be completed, and the time that should be allocated to each activity. Where a box sits within a time frame reflects its planned sequence. The shading represents actual progress. The chart also serves as a control tool because the manager can see deviations from the plan. In this example, both the design of the cover and the printing of first pages are running behind schedule. Cover design is about three weeks behind, and printing first pages is about two weeks behind schedule. Given this information, the manager might need to take some action to either make up for the two lost weeks or ensure that no further delays will occur. At this point, the manager can expect that the book will be published at least two weeks later than planned if no action is taken.

As John Furlong plans for the 2010 Olympics in Vancouver, he likely has developed a similar chart that incorporates planning between 2005 and 2010. The chart should indicate what needs to be done (goals), the actual progress (so he can keep track of whether projects such as building Olympic sites and housing are on track), and reporting dates for projects (so that those managing the projects keep him informed of progress and delays).

Load Charts

A **load chart** is a modified Gantt chart. Instead of listing activities on the vertical axis, load charts list either entire departments or specific resources. This arrangement allows managers to plan and control capacity use. In other words, load charts schedule capacity by work areas.

For example, Exhibit 8-6 on page 234 shows a load chart for six production editors at the same publishing company. Each editor supervises the production and design of several books. By reviewing a load chart, the executive editor, who supervises the six production editors, can see who is free to take on a new book. If everyone is fully scheduled, the executive editor might decide not to accept any new projects, to accept new projects and delay others, to have the editors work overtime, or to employ more production editors. In Exhibit 8-6, only Antonio and Maurice are completely scheduled for the next six months. The other editors have some unassigned time and might be able to accept new projects or be available to help other editors who get behind.

load chart
A modified Gantt chart that schedules capacity by entire departments or specific resources.

Exhibit 8-5

A Gantt Chart

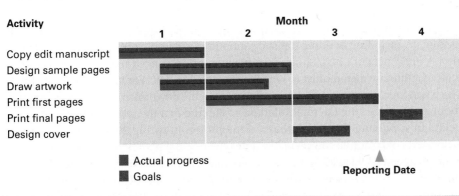

Activity — Month — 1 2 3 4

Copy edit manuscript
Design sample pages
Draw artwork
Print first pages
Print final pages
Design cover

■ Actual progress
■ Goals

▲ Reporting Date

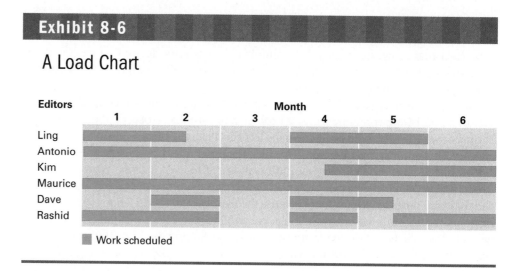

Exhibit 8-6

A Load Chart

As John Furlong and his managers plan for the 2010 Olympics in Vancouver, they likely use load charts for the various groups working on Olympic projects. For instance, members of the organizing committee responsible for building Olympic housing in Vancouver and Whistler need to coordinate with city governments of both locations, and meet with architects, contractors, and building inspectors. To make sure that one person is not burdened with the responsibility of meeting with representatives of every area, a load chart can identify the committee members who will handle meetings, and then people can be assigned accordingly. The load chart can also be used to ensure that someone is available for meetings and follow-up when particular decisions come due.

PERT Network Analysis

Gantt and load charts are useful as long as the activities being scheduled are few in number and independent of each other. But what if a manager had to plan a large project such as a departmental reorganization; the implementation of a cost-reduction program; the development of a new product that required coordinating inputs from marketing, manufacturing, and product design; or the Olympics? Such projects require coordinating hundreds and even thousands of activities, some of which must be done simultaneously and some of which cannot begin until preceding activities have been completed. If you are constructing a building, you obviously cannot start putting up the walls until the foundation is laid. How can managers schedule such a complex project? The Program Evaluation and Review Technique (PERT) is highly appropriate for such projects.

A **PERT network** is a flow chart diagram that depicts the sequence of activities needed to complete a project and the time or costs associated with each activity. With a PERT network, a manager must think through what has to be done, determine which events depend on one another, and identify potential trouble spots. PERT also makes it easy to compare the effects alternative actions might have on scheduling and costs. Thus, PERT allows managers to monitor a project's progress, identify possible bottlenecks, and shift resources as necessary to keep the project on schedule.

As John Furlong plans for the 2010 Olympics in Vancouver, he has many projects to coordinate, including building transportation lines, Olympic housing, and Olympic facilities. A PERT network helps him identify when projects need to be completed, and the goals that must be met in order to make the completion date. For instance, the Canada Line, which will link Vancouver International Airport to the downtown area, must be completed about a year before the Olympics start, to make sure that the system is working properly. Delays in approving the initial phase of the project in spring 2004 created worries that the project could not be completed in time. The original plan had assumed that approval would happen by March 2004, but approval came four months later, and only after two negative votes resulted in intense lobbying for the third round of voting to yield a positive outcome. The delays caused the provincial government to allocate more resources to the

PERT network
A flow chart diagram that depicts the sequence of activities needed to complete a project and the time or costs associated with each activity.

project in order to resolve the bottleneck created by concerns over whether the Canada Line planners had been realistic about their budget. Budget concerns will most likely continue to be an issue until completion of the line.

To understand how to construct a PERT network, you need to know four terms. **Events** are end points that represent the completion of major activities. **Activities** represent the time or resources needed to progress from one event to another. **Slack time** is the amount of time an individual activity can be delayed without delaying the whole project. The **critical path** is the longest or most time-consuming sequence of events and activities in a PERT network. Any delay in completing events on this path would delay completion of the entire project. In other words, activities on the critical path have zero slack time.

Developing a PERT network requires that a manager identify all key activities needed to complete a project, rank them in order of occurrence, and estimate each activity's completion time. Exhibit 8-7 explains the steps in this process.

Most PERT projects are complicated and include numerous activities. Such complicated computations can be done with specialized PERT software. However, let's work through a simple example. Assume that you are the superintendent at a construction company and have been assigned to oversee the construction of an office building. Because time really is money in your business, you must determine how long it will take to get the building completed. You have determined the specific activities and events. Exhibit 8-8 on page 236 outlines the major events in the construction project and your estimate of the expected time to complete each. Exhibit 8-9 on page 236 shows the actual PERT network based on the data in Exhibit 8-8. You have also calculated the length of time that each path of activities will take:

A-B-C-D-I-J-K (44 weeks)   A-B-C-E-G-H-J-K (47 weeks)
A-B-C-D-G-H-J-K (50 weeks)   A-B-C-F-G-H-J-K (47 weeks)

Your PERT network shows that if everything goes as planned, the total project completion time will be 50 weeks. This is calculated by tracing the project's critical path (the longest sequence of activities), A-B-C-D-G-H-J-K, and adding up the times. You know that any delay in completing the events on this path would delay the completion of the entire project. Taking six weeks instead of four to put in the floor covering and panelling (Event I) would have no effect on the final completion date. Why? Because that event is not on the critical path. However, taking seven weeks instead of six to dig the subterranean garage

events
End points that represent the completion of major activities in a PERT network.

activities
The time or resources needed to progress from one event to another in a PERT network.

slack time
The amount of time an individual activity can be delayed without delaying the whole project.

critical path
The longest or most time-consuming sequence of events and activities in a PERT network.

Exhibit 8-7

Steps in Developing a PERT Network

1. *Identify every significant activity that must be achieved for a project to be completed.* The accomplishment of each activity results in a set of events or outcomes.

2. *Determine the order in which these events must be completed.*

3. *Diagram the flow of activities from start to finish, identifying each activity and its relationship to all other activities.* Use circles to indicate events and arrows to represent activities. This results in a flow chart diagram called a PERT network. (See Exhibit 8-9.)

4. *Compute a time estimate for completing each activity.* This is done with a weighted average that uses an *optimistic* time estimate (t_o) of how long the activity would take under ideal conditions, a *most likely* estimate (t_m) of the time the activity normally should take, and a *pessimistic* estimate (t_p) that represents the time that an activity should take under the worst possible conditions. The formula for calculating the expected time (t_e) is then

$$t_e = \frac{t_o + 4t_m + t_p}{6}$$

5. *Using the network diagram that contains time estimates for each activity, determine a schedule for the start and finish dates of each activity and for the entire project.* Any delays that occur along the critical path require the most attention because they can delay the whole project.

Outline of Major Events for Constructing an Office Building

Event	Description	Expected Time (in weeks)	Preceding Event
A	Approve design and get permits	10	None
B	Dig subterranean garage	6	A
C	Erect frame and siding	14	B
D	Construct floor	6	C
E	Install windows	3	C
F	Put on roof	3	C
G	Install internal wiring	5	D, E, F
H	Install elevator	5	G
I	Put in floor covering and panelling	4	D
J	Put in doors and interior decorative trim	3	I, H
K	Turn over to building management group	1	J

(Event B) would likely delay the total project. A manager who needed to get back on schedule or to cut the 50-week completion time would want to concentrate on those activities along the critical path that could be completed faster. How might the manager do this? He or she could look to see if any of the other activities *not* on the critical path had slack time in which resources could be transferred to activities that *were* on the critical path.

Breakeven Analysis

breakeven analysis
A technique for identifying the point at which total revenue is just sufficient to cover total costs.

Managers at McCain Foods want to know how many units of its new Solo Gourmet pizzas must be sold in order to break even—that is, the point at which total revenue is just sufficient to cover total costs. **Breakeven analysis** is a widely used resource allocation technique to help managers determine breakeven point.[25]

Breakeven analysis is a simple calculation, yet it's valuable to managers because it points out the relationship between revenues, costs, and profits. To compute breakeven point (BE), a manager needs to know the unit price of the product being sold (P), the variable cost per unit (VC), and total fixed costs (TFC). An organization breaks even when its total revenue is just enough to equal its total costs. But total cost has two parts: fixed and variable. *Fixed costs* are expenses that do not change regardless of volume. Examples include insurance premiums, rent, and property taxes. *Variable costs* change in proportion to output and include raw materials, labour costs, and energy costs.

Breakeven point can be computed graphically or by using the following formula:

$$BE = \frac{TFC}{P - VC}$$

A PERT Network for Constructing an Office Building

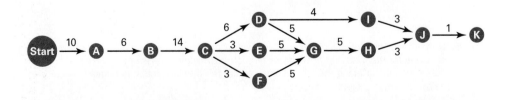

This formula tells us that (1) total revenue will equal total cost when we sell enough units at a price that covers all variable unit costs and (2) the difference between price and variable costs, when multiplied by the number of units sold, equals the fixed costs. Let's work through an example.

Assume that Pierre's Photocopying Service charges $0.10 per photocopy. If fixed costs are $27 000 a year and variable costs are $0.04 per copy, Pierre can compute his breakeven point as follows: $27 000 ÷ ($0.10 – $0.04) = 450 000 copies, or when annual revenues are $45 000 (450 000 copies x $0.10). This same relationship is shown graphically in Exhibit 8-10.

As a planning tool, breakeven analysis could help Pierre set his sales goal. For example, he could determine his profit goal and then calculate what sales level is needed to reach that goal. Breakeven analysis could also tell Pierre how much volume has to increase to break even if he is currently operating at a loss or how much volume he can afford to lose and still break even.

Linear Programming

Kamie Bousman manages a manufacturing plant that produces two kinds of cinnamon-scented home fragrance products: wax candles and a wood-chip potpourri sold in bags. Business is good, and she can sell all of the products she can produce. This is her problem: Given that the bags of potpourri and the scented candles are manufactured in the same facility, how many of each product should she produce to maximize profits? Kamie can use **linear programming** to solve her resource allocation problem.

Although linear programming can be used here, it cannot be applied to all resource allocation problems because it requires that there be limited resources, that the goal be outcome optimization, that there be alternative ways of combining resources to produce a number of output mixes, and that there be a linear relationship between variables (a change in one variable must be accompanied by an exactly proportional change in the other).[26] For Kamie's business, that last condition would be met if it took exactly twice the amount of raw materials and hours of labour to produce two of a given home fragrance product as it took to produce one.

What kinds of problems can be solved with linear programming? Some applications include selecting transportation routes that minimize shipping costs, allocating a limited advertising budget among various product brands, making the optimal assignment of people among projects, and determining how much of each product to make with a limited

linear programming
A mathematical technique that solves resource allocation problems.

Exhibit 8-10

Breakeven Analysis

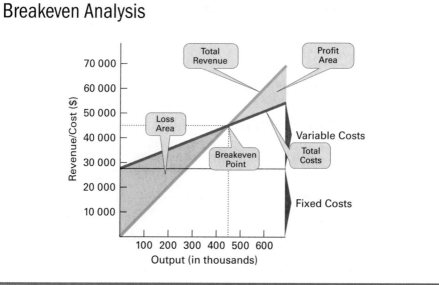

number of resources. Let's return to Kamie's problem and see how linear programming could help her solve it. Fortunately, her problem is relatively simple, so we can solve it rather quickly. For complex linear programming problems, managers can use computer software programs designed specifically to help develop optimizing solutions.

Q&A 8.6   First, we need to establish some facts about Kamie's business. She has computed the profit margins on her home fragrance products at $10 for a bag of potpourri and $18 for a scented candle. These numbers establish the basis for Kamie to be able to express her *objective function* as maximum profit = $10P + $18S, where *P* is the number of bags of potpourri produced and *S* is the number of scented candles produced. The objective function is simply a mathematical equation that can predict the outcome of all proposed alternatives. In addition, Kamie knows how much time each fragrance product must spend in production and the monthly production capacity (1200 hours in manufacturing and 900 hours in assembly) for manufacturing and assembly (see Exhibit 8-11). The production capacity numbers act as *constraints* on her overall capacity. Now Kamie can establish her constraint equations:

$$2P + 4S \leq 1200$$
$$2P + 2S \leq 900$$

Of course, Kamie can also state that $P \geq 0$ and $S \geq 0$, because neither fragrance product can be produced in a volume less than zero.

Kamie has graphed her solution in Exhibit 8-12. The shaded area represents the options that don't exceed the capacity of either department. What does this mean? Well, let's look first at the manufacturing constraint line BE. We know that total manufacturing capacity is 1200 hours, so if Kamie decides to produce all potpourri bags, the maximum she can produce is 600 (1200 hours ÷ 2 hours required to produce a bag of potpourri). If she decides to produce all scented candles, the maximum she can produce is 300 (1200 hours ÷ 4 hours required to produce a scented candle). The other constraint Kamie faces is that of assembly, shown by line DF. If Kamie decides to produce all potpourri bags, the maximum she can assemble is 450 (900 hours' production capacity ÷ 2 hours required to assemble). Likewise, if Kamie decides to produce all scented candles, the maximum she can assemble is also 450 because the scented candles also take 2 hours to assemble. The constraints imposed by these capacity limits establish Kamie's *feasibility region*. Her optimal resource allocation will be defined at one of the corners within this feasibility region. Point C provides the maximum profits within the constraints stated. How do we know? At point A, profits would be 0 (no production of either potpourri bags or scented candles). At point B, profits would be $5400 (300 scented candles × $18 profit and 0 potpourri bags produced = $5400). At point D, profits would be $4500 (450 potpourri bags produced × $10 profit and 0 scented candles produced = $4500). At point C, however, profits would be $5700 (150 scented candles produced × $18 profit and 300 potpourri bags produced × $10 profit = $5700).

Exhibit 8-11

Production Data for Cinnamon-Scented Products

| | Number of Hours Required (per unit) | | |
Department	Potpourri Bags	Scented Candles	Monthly Production Capacity (in hours)
Manufacturing	2	4	1200
Assembly	2	2	900
Profit per unit	$10	$18	

Exhibit 8-12

Graphical Solution to Linear Programming Problem

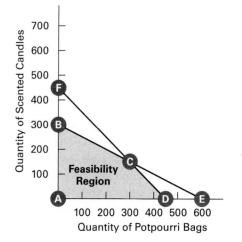

Contemporary Planning Techniques

▶ ▶ ▶ John Furlong is aware of the many projects he needs to complete before Vancouver can host the 2010 Olympics, but he cannot know all the possible distractions and problems that might crop up along the way.[27]

Furlong faces a few challenges. The residents of Vancouver are not unanimous in their support of the Olympics; some fear the possibility of soaring costs and others feel that the money slotted for the Olympics would be better spent on assisting the homeless. The 20-member board of directors that Furlong oversees represents seven different constituency groups: the Canadian Olympic Committee, federal and provincial governments, the City of Vancouver, the municipality of Whistler, the Canadian Paralympic Committee, and First Nations representatives. Furlong must ensure that these groups work with each other in the best interests of the Olympics and set aside individual differences. He must also meet the ongoing demand for information from the media and the public, who are following the Olympic preparations closely. In addition, a number of the shopkeepers whose stores have had limited access because of the Canada Line construction have been lobbying the province to do something so that their businesses can survive road construction that keeps customers away.

Furlong also has to plan for the unexpected. What if a project falls behind? What if the budget gets out of hand because of rising construction costs? What if there is another terrorist attack in the United States in the year before the Olympics? What if a virus like SARS (sudden acute respiratory syndrome) arises in Vancouver as the Olympics begin? What if city employees threaten to strike during the Olympics?

Think About It

What can John Furlong do to improve his chances that the 2010 Olympics will run smoothly, without controversy and scandal? What tools should he use to prepare for the unexpected?

Wi-Fi applications. Life-threatening epidemics. Dolby TrueHD audio. Deflation/inflation worries. Changing competition. Today's managers face the challenges of planning in an environment that is both dynamic and complex. Two planning techniques that are appropriate for this type of environment are project management and scenario planning. Both techniques emphasize *flexibility*, something that is important to make planning more effective and efficient in this type of organizational environment.

3. How does one manage projects?

Project Management

project
A one-time-only set of activities that has a definite beginning and ending point in time.

project management
The task of getting a project's activities done on time, within budget, and according to specifications.

You have a big project to complete. Can you list all the steps you need to take to complete it?

Different types of organizations, from manufacturers such as Bombardier and Boeing to software design firms such as Corel and Microsoft, use projects. A **project** is a one-time-only set of activities that has a definite beginning and ending point in time.[28] Projects vary in size and scope—from Vancouver's plans for the Canada Line to go from the airport to downtown (which includes a lengthy tunnel through the downtown area) to a sorority's holiday formal. **Project management** is the task of getting a project's activities done on time, within budget, and according to specifications.[29]

More and more organizations are using project management because the approach fits well with the need for flexibility and rapid response to perceived market opportunities. When organizations undertake projects that are unique, have specific deadlines, contain complex inter-related tasks requiring specialized skills, and are temporary in nature, these projects often do not fit into the standardized planning procedures that guide an organization's other routine work activities. Instead, managers use project management techniques to effectively and efficiently accomplish the project's goals. What does the project management process involve?

Q&A 8.7

The Project Management Process

In the typical project, work is done by a project team whose members are assigned from their respective work areas to the project and who report to a project manager. The project manager coordinates the project's activities with other departments. When the project team accomplishes its goals, it disbands and members move on to other projects or back to their permanent work areas.

The essential features of the project planning process are shown in Exhibit 8-13. The process begins by clearly defining the project's objectives. This step is necessary because the manager and the team members need to know what is expected. All activities in the project and the resources needed to do them must then be identified. What materials and labour are needed to complete the project? This step may be time-consuming and complex, particularly if the project is unique and there is no history or experience with similar projects. Once the activities and resources have been identified, the sequence of completion needs to be established. What activities must be completed before others can begin? Which can be done simultaneously? This step often uses flow chart diagrams such as a Gantt chart, a load chart, or a PERT network. Next, the project activities need to be scheduled. Time estimates for each activity are done and these estimates are used to develop an overall project schedule and completion date. Then the project schedule is compared to the objectives, and any necessary adjustments are made. If the project completion time is too long, the manager might assign more resources to critical activities so they can be completed faster.

Q&A 8.8

Today, the project management process can take place online, as a number of Internet-based project collaboration software packages are available. For instance, onProject provides web-based software that allows users to share and manage information associated with projects. Suppliers and customers can even be part of the process.[30]

Exhibit 8-13

Project Planning Process

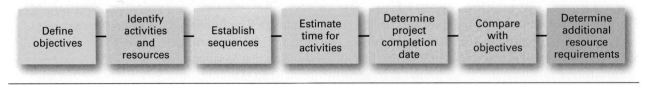

| Define objectives | Identify activities and resources | Establish sequences | Estimate time for activities | Determine project completion date | Compare with objectives | Determine additional resource requirements |

Source: Based on R. S. Russell and B. W. Taylor III, *Production and Operations Management* (Upper Saddle River, NJ: Prentice Hall, 1995), p. 287.

The Role of the Project Manager

The temporary nature of projects makes managing them different from, say, overseeing a production line or preparing a weekly tally of costs on an ongoing basis. There is a specific job to be done. It has to be defined—in detail. And the project manager is responsible for how it's done. For instance, a variety of project managers will be responsible for overseeing construction for the 2010 Olympics, some responsible for athletic venues, others responsible for road construction and housing. They will be responsible for everything from developing plans to paying invoices.

Even with the availability of sophisticated computerized and online scheduling programs and other project management tools, the role of project manager remains difficult because he or she is managing people who typically are still linked to their permanent work areas. The only real influence project managers have is their communication skills and their powers of persuasion. To make matters worse, team members seldom work on just one project. They are usually assigned to two or three at any given time. So project managers end up competing with each other to focus an employee's attention on his or her particular project.

Scenario Planning

We already know how important it is that today's managers monitor and assess the external environment for trends and changes. As they assess the environment, issues and concerns that could affect their organization's current or planned operations are likely to be revealed. All of these will not be equally important, so it's usually necessary to focus on a limited set that are most important and to develop scenarios based on each.

A **scenario** is a consistent view of what the future is likely to be. Developing scenarios also can be described as *contingency planning;* that is, if this is what happens, then these are the actions we need to take. If, for instance, environmental scanning reveals increasing interest by the Alberta government in raising the provincial minimum wage, managers at SUBWAY could create multiple scenarios to assess the possible consequences of such an action. What would be the implications for its labour costs if the minimum wage was raised from its current $7.00 an hour to $7.25? How about $7.50 an hour? What effect would these changes have on the chain's bottom line? How might competitors respond? Different assumptions lead to different outcomes. The intent of scenario planning is not to try to predict the future but to reduce uncertainty by playing out potential situations under different specified conditions.[31] SUBWAY could, for example, develop a set of scenarios ranging from optimistic to pessimistic in terms of the minimum wage issue. It would then be prepared to implement new strategies to get and keep a competitive advantage. According to an expert in scenario planning, "Just the process of doing scenarios causes executives to rethink and clarify the essence of the business environment in ways they almost certainly have never done before."[32]

Although scenario planning is useful in anticipating events that *can be* anticipated, it's difficult to forecast random events—the major surprises that cannot be foreseen. The planning challenge comes from the totally random and unexpected events. For instance, the 9/11 terrorist attacks in New York; Washington, DC; and Pennsylvania were random, unexpected, and a total shock to numerous organizations throughout the world. Scenario planning was of little use because no one could have envisioned this scenario. Similarly, the sudden spread of the SARS virus in Toronto caught everyone by surprise, and many businesses in Ontario learned the hard way about the importance of having contingency plans in place.[33] Over 75 percent of companies said that they did not have a contingency plan in place for public health crises.[34] When SARS hit Toronto, businesses were faced with employees ordered into quarantine. Some companies ordered employees to work from home, others required that

scenario
A consistent view of what the future is likely to be.

The outbreak of SARS shows how unpredictable the environment can be for managers. Organizations had to develop contingency plans to ensure work could continue during a public health crisis.

TIPS FOR MANAGERS

Preparing for Unexpected Events

↗ Identify potential **unexpected events**.

↗ Determine if any of these events would have **early indicators**.

↗ Set up an **information-gathering system** to identify early indicators.

↗ Have appropriate **responses (plans) in place** if these unexpected events occur.

Source: S. Caudron, "Frontview Mirror," *Business Finance,* December 1999, pp. 24–30.

key personnel remain on-site at all times, providing them with makeshift beds and other personal items. More companies have since thought about what to do if key employees are ordered to stay home from work, but can function. Toronto health officials also did not have a complete plan in place, but they had been working on a pandemic influenza plan for the city. Dr. Sheela Basrur, former chief medical officer of health for Ontario, notes how valuable it was to have a draft of the plan available, and then test it with the SARS outbreak: "Although the official planning process had to take a backseat to the response to the actual outbreak, the outbreak has really well informed the plan, so it's now probably better than it ever would have been had we completed it and put it on a shelf before SARS hit."[35]

As difficult as it may be for managers to anticipate and deal with random events, they do not need to be completely vulnerable to the consequences. See *Tips for Managers—Preparing for Unexpected Events.*

Q&A 8.9

Planning tools and techniques can help managers prepare confidently for the future. However, managers should remember that all the tools we have described in this chapter are just that—tools. They will never replace a manager's skills and capabilities in using the information gained to develop effective and efficient plans.

SUMMARY AND IMPLICATIONS

1. What is environmental scanning and how is it done? Environmental scanning screens large amounts of information to anticipate and interpret changes in the environment. One form of scanning is competitor intelligence, an activity that seeks to identify competitors, what they are doing, and how what they are doing will affect the organization. Forecasting and benchmarking are other ways of scanning the environment to provide information that facilitates decision making.

▶ ▶ ▶ As John Furlong prepares for the 2010 Olympic Winter Games, he develops benchmarks for the various projects that must be completed before the games begin, and he uses forecasts to predict outcomes for his projects.

2. What tools can managers use to allocate resources more effectively? Managers can allocate resources more effectively through budgeting, scheduling, breakeven analysis, and linear programming.

▶ ▶ ▶ John Furlong will have to use all of these techniques in order to keep the 2010 Olympics planning on track.

3. How does one manage projects? Project management is the task of getting a project's activities done on time, within budget, and according to specifications. Managers and team members need to share information, which can be done through software, or online through Internet-based collaboration. They also need to prepare for unexpected outcomes, by using scenario planning.

▶ ▶ ▶ John Furlong must be aware of the many factors that could change in the environment during the time leading up to the 2010 Olympics and develop alternative scenarios for problems that might arise and ways to respond to them.

Management @ Work

READING FOR COMPREHENSION

1. How can managers improve the effectiveness of forecasting?

2. What are the four steps in the benchmarking process?

3. Describe the different types of budgets.

4. Why is flexibility so important to today's planning techniques?

5. What are the steps in the project planning process?

6. Why has scenario planning become an important planning tool for managers?

LINKING CONCEPTS TO PRACTICE

1. Do intuition and creativity have any relevance in quantitative planning tools and techniques? Explain.

2. The *Globe and Mail*'s *Report on Business* and other business periodicals often carry reports of companies that have not met their sales or profit forecasts. What are some reasons a company might not meet its forecast? What suggestions could you make for improving the effectiveness of forecasting?

3. "It's a waste of time and other resources to develop a set of sophisticated scenarios for situations that may

never occur." Do you agree or disagree? Explain your position.

4. In what ways is managing a project different from managing a department or other structured work area? In what ways are they the same?

5. "People can use statistics to prove whatever it is they want to prove." What do you think? What are the implications for managers and how they plan?

SELF-ASSESSMENT

How Good Am I at Personal Planning?

For each of the following statements, circle your level of agreement or disagreement as it relates to your school and personal life:[36]

1 = Strongly Disagree
2 = Disagree
3 = Neither Agree nor Disagree
4 = Agree
5 = Strongly Agree

	1	2	3	4	5
1. I am proactive rather than reactive.	1	2	3	4	5
2. I set aside enough time and resources to study and complete projects.	1	2	3	4	5
3. I am able to budget money to buy the things I really want without going broke.	1	2	3	4	5
4. I have thought through what I want to do in school.	1	2	3	4	5
5. I have a plan for completing my major.	1	2	3	4	5
6. My goals for the future are realistic.	1	2	3	4	5

Scoring Key

No overall scoring is necessary.

Analysis and Interpretation

A score of 5 on any item means that you are doing well in planning and goal setting in that area. The authors of this instrument suggest that any item you did not agree with (scores of 1 or 2) indicates you need to gain a better understanding of the importance of goal setting and what is involved in the process.

MANAGEMENT FOR YOU TODAY

Dilemma

In Chapters 6 and 7, you were asked to develop your personal vision and mission statements, and to conduct a SWOT analysis to consider what you want to be doing in five years. What tools could you use to discover potential opportunities or threats that might occur during the next five years? How might you use forecasting techniques to evaluate whether your plan for five years from now makes sense? How could benchmarking help you improve the plan you have for your life?

Becoming a Manager

- Get into the habit of reading general news and business periodicals. Pay attention to events, trends, and changes that are written about.
- Practise competitor intelligence by visiting several different coffee shops in your neighbourhood and observing all the differences in service, product, and clientele across stores. Talk to employees about what they like about working for their employers.
- Take classes to learn about linear programming and forecasting techniques.
- Practise budgeting by applying it to your personal life.
- Try different scheduling tools when faced with class projects that need to be planned and managed.

WORKING TOGETHER: TEAM-BASED EXERCISE

Identifying Organizational Strategies

Benchmarking can be an important tool and source of information for managers. It also can be useful to students. Form groups of 3 or 4 individuals. In your small group, discuss study habits that each of you has found effective from your years of being in school. As a group, come up with a bulleted list of at least eight suggestions in the time period allotted by your instructor. When the instructor calls time, each group should combine with one other group and share your ideas, again in the time allotted by your instructor. In this larger group, be sure to ask questions about suggestions that each respective small group had. Each small group should make sure that it understands the suggestions of the other small group it's working with. When the instructor calls time, each small group will then present and explain the study habit suggestions of the other small group it was working with. After all groups have presented, the class will come up with what it feels are the "best" study habits of all the ideas presented.

ETHICS IN ACTION

Ethical Dilemma Exercise: What Factors Should Managers Consider When Making a Revenue Forecast?

Managers rely on forecasts for predicting many future events, especially when planning revenues and profits.[37] Forecasts are also important to financial analysts and investors assessing a company's investment potential and to bankers determining a company's ability to repay borrowed funds. For example, HealthSouth met many ambitious growth forecasts as it developed into a large chain of clinics and surgical centres across the United States with billions of dollars in annual revenues. Once its acquisitions slowed, however, HealthSouth had difficulty living up to lofty forecasts.

Then, according to a former chief financial officer, CEO Richard Scrushy pressured his managers: "If we weren't making the numbers, he'd say, 'Go figure it out.'" Even after repeatedly reassuring financial analysts that their estimates would be met, HealthSouth was forced to announce lower than expected results because of changes in government regulations. The stock price plummeted. Scrushy continued pushing his managers to find ways of avoiding disappointing results. During one high-level staff meeting, he reportedly told his executives, "I want each of the [divisional] presidents to email all of their people who miss their budget. I don't care whether it's by a dollar." Two weeks later, with

government investigators gathering evidence of fraud, HealthSouth fired Scrushy. Ultimately, 11 former managers pleaded guilty to fraud charges, and Scrushy was named in a $1.4 billion fraud lawsuit.

Imagine you are the financial manager of a HealthSouth clinic preparing revenue forecasts for the coming quarter. Too high a number will set unrealistic expectations for senior managers, analysts, investors, and bankers to use in decision making; too low a number will make you and your facility look bad to upper management. What techniques should you consider in setting your revenue estimate? (Review Exhibit 8-1 on page 227 as you think about this ethical challenge.)

Thinking Critically About Ethics

Here are some techniques that have been suggested for gathering competitor information: (1) Get copies of lawsuits and civil suits that may have been filed against competitors. These court proceedings are public records and can expose surprising details. (2) Call the Better Business Bureau and ask if competitors have had complaints filed against them because of fraudulent product claims or questionable business practices. (3) Pretend to be a journalist and call competitors to ask questions. (4) Get copies of your competitors' in-house

newsletters and read them. (5) Buy a single share of competitors' stock so you get the annual report and other information the company sends out. (6) Send someone from your organization to apply for a job at a competitor and have that person ask specific questions. (7) Dig through a competitor's trash.

Which, if any, of these are unethical? Defend your choices. What ethical guidelines would you suggest for competitor intelligence activities?

CASE APPLICATION

Peerless Clothing

At Montreal-based Peerless Clothing, chair and CEO Alvin Segal wonders about the future of manufacturing in Montreal.[38] The family-owned business is the largest domestic producer of fine tailored clothing in North America, manufacturing clothes under such labels as Calvin Klein, Ralph Lauren, and Izod, as well as private-label store brands. The garment industry has suffered setbacks in recent years, and while Peerless is known for the quality of its men's suits, continuing to manufacture suits in Montreal may not be the company's best strategy.

The company was founded in 1919 by Segal's late father Moe. Segal started working in the family business in Montreal as a teenager in 1951. Although he started off on the factory floor, five years later he was the plant manager and then became president in 1970.

Segal took the opportunity to expand into the US market after the 1989 free-trade agreement, a decision that has paid off well. Eighty percent of the company's production is sold in the United States. With the rising strength of the Canadian dollar and much-lower-priced suits available from China, Segal and the others worry that they may not be able to compete effectively for much longer.

Corporate controller Tony Nardi thinks that if Peerless were a public company, responsible to outside shareholders,

the company would be run quite a bit differently. It would also be a lot smaller, with less manufacturing done in Canada. "Dollar to dollar, it makes no sense to keep this factory open," he explains. "You make the same suit overseas and you make twice the amount of money."

Vice-chairman Elliot Lifson believes that relying completely on overseas manufacturers to produce the company's suits could come with substantial risks. While production costs in China are lower, other problems arise when clothing is produced so far away. Because it takes longer for suits to be delivered, the company would need larger inventories, which in turn means building new and larger warehouses. A "Canadian operation can provide fast turnarounds for North American retailers," Lifson argues. In addition, the Montreal head office and the company's factory on Pie IX Boulevard represent knowledge and expertise that would be lost if the company downsized and outsourced the manufacturing of its suits.

In the past three years, Peerless has started outsourcing suits to overseas manufacturers, with about 65 percent of its product coming from Asia and being shipped directly to a warehouse in St. Albans, Vermont. This has turned out to be a successful strategy, and it is estimated that annual sales have grown about 20 percent in each of the past three years, to more than $500 million. However, while five years ago the Montreal factory used to produce 38 000 suits a week, production is down to about 23 000 suits a week because of increased production in Asia.

Remaining in Montreal is important to Segal, because his father started the business there and the company is well-known for its corporate citizenship in the community. Peerless hires many new Canadians and Segal feels loyalty to his 1800 factory workers, who represent 60 cultural and linguistic groups. It is not uncommon for immigrants to "fly into Montreal one day, and show up at Peerless the next, often carrying a referral from a friend or family member who works there," Lifson reports. Twenty-two Peerless employees became Canadian citizens in the company's cafeteria in 2004.

Segal is known for innovation in the garment industry. He spent 15 years, starting in the late 1970s, buying about $1 million of computerized equipment that allowed assembly-line efficiencies for creating suits without the need of tailors. Instead, computer-assisted cutting, sewing, and gluing machines crank out high-quality suits at a lower cost. Segal was the first to bring this technology to North America, although it has been in use in Europe since after World War II. Segal, who thinks of himself as a manufacturing specialist, explains the benefit of the technology: "You produce a hand-tailored look without the hand tailoring." The focus on innovation meant that Segal was able to enter the US market quickly after the passage of the North American Free Trade Act and take a substantial share of the men's clothing market.

Now, however, he faces a new challenge. When Asian companies first started producing clothes for the North American market several years ago, production quality was low. Almost 90 percent of the clothing Peerless imported from Asia needed repairs before they could be shipped to customers. By 2007, however, only 10 percent of the clothing needed repairs.

Segal wonders how he can use planning tools and techniques to help him evaluate whether to keep his garment factory in Montreal operating, something he very much wants to do. He has come to you for advice.

DEVELOPING YOUR DIAGNOSTIC AND ANALYTICAL SKILLS

A New Pitch for an Old Classic

Andrew E. Friedman is a new breed of manager in America's favourite pastime—the classic game of baseball.[39] As the general manager of the Tampa Bay Devil Rays (his formal title is executive vice-president of baseball operations), Friedman is responsible for overseeing and directing the team's overall baseball operations. And he is doing it his way—by relying on financial models and data mining to help improve the team's performance and valuation. For the 2006 season, *Sports Illustrated* ranked the team 24th overall out of the 30 MLB (Major League Baseball) teams. Its payroll of $35 million puts it at the bottom of the league in terms of players' salaries. However, Friedman uses his own numbers approach to assess the value of his team and to help it realize its maximum potential.

With a degree in management and finance from Tulane University in New Orleans, Friedman understands the language of business. He spent five years on Wall Street before joining the Devil Rays organization as director of baseball development. Having played on Tulane's baseball team until an injury sidelined him, Friedman is no stranger to the game. However, in baseball, quantitative, statistics-based methods of player talent assessment, team valuation, and contract negotiations are not the usual approach to doing business. That is why Friedman is not concerned about having the lowest payroll of any major league team because his assessment—based upon a valuation technique used on Wall Street—places the real value of the Devil Rays' payroll at closer to $50 million.

Friedman also uses a quantitative approach to trading players. He says, "I am purely market driven. I love players I think that I can get for less than they are worth. It's positive arbitrage, the valuation asymmetry in the game." He and team owner Stuart Sternberg and team president Matt Silverman recently put their philosophy of quantitative, statistics-based talent assessment into action as they made their first big trade, "exchanging their all-star closer, Danys Baez, for two untested starting pitchers from the Los Angeles Dodgers, Edwin Jackson and Chuck Tiffany." The trio is betting that the two prospects will blossom into top-rated starting pitchers—"perhaps the most elusive and highly valued commodity in baseball today." Despite the emphasis on stats and quantitative analysis, the Devil Rays management team understands that it "cannot be a substitute for old-fashioned scouting and talent assessment, an area it also wants to strengthen."

Although there may be a new pitch to an old classic, computers, BlackBerrys, and economic models cannot, and will probably never, provide all the answers. However, it is hoped that the tools and techniques can help the organization achieve, as its owner says, its maximum potential.

Questions

1. What other planning tools and techniques might be useful to Andrew Friedman as he oversees and directs the team's operations? Be specific.

2. In baseball, where the traditional approach to assessing player potential and performance has involved watching the individual play in different settings (scouting the player) and where most of the team management would not have a business background, how might you overcome the doubts of "traditionalists"

about the benefits of using quantitative forecasting techniques?

3. What are some ways that Friedman might evaluate whether his quantitative forecasting techniques are working? Be specific.

Budgeting

About the Skill

Managers do not have unlimited resources to do their jobs. Most managers will have to deal with a budget, a numerical plan for allocating resources to specific activities. As planning tools, budgets indicate what activities are important and how many resources should be allocated to each activity. However, budgets are not used just in planning. They are also used in controlling. As control tools, budgets provide managers with quantitative standards against which to measure and compare resource consumption. By pointing out deviations between standard and actual consumption, managers can use the budget for control purposes.

Steps in Developing the Skill

You can develop your skills at budgeting if you use the following seven suggestions:[40]

1. **Determine which work activities are going to be pursued during the coming time period.** An organization's work activities are a result of the goals that have been established. Your control over which work activities your unit will be pursuing during a specific time period will depend on how much control you normally exercise over the work that must be done in order to meet those goals. In addition, the amount of control you have often depends on your managerial level in the organization.

2. **Decide which resources will be necessary to accomplish the desired work activities: that is, those that will ensure goals are met.** Although there are different types of budgets used for allocating resources, the most common ones involve monetary resources. However, you also may have to budget time, space, material resources, human resources, capacity utilization, or units of production.

3. **Gather cost information.** You will need accurate cost estimates of those resources you need. Old budgets may be of some help, but you will also want to talk with your manager, colleagues, and key employees, and use other contacts you have developed inside and outside your organization.

4. **Once you know which resources will be available to you, assign the resources as needed to accomplish the desired work activities.** In many organizations, managers are given a monthly, quarterly, or annual budget to work with. The budget will detail which resources are available during the time period. As the manager, you have to assign the resources in an efficient and effective manner to ensure that your unit goals are met.

5. **Review the budget periodically.** It's wise to do so. Don't wait until the end of the time period to monitor whether you are over or under budget.

6. **Take action if you find that you are not within your budget.** Remember that a budget also serves as a control tool. If resources are being consumed more quickly than budgeted, you may need to determine why and take corrective action.

7. **Use past experience as a guide when developing your budget for the next time period.** Although every budgeted time period will be different, it is possible to use past experience to pinpoint trends and potential problems. This knowledge can help you prepare for any circumstances that may arise.

Practising the Skill

Read the following scenario. Write some notes about how you would handle the situation described. Be sure to refer to the seven suggestions for budgeting.

Scenario

You have recently been appointed advertising manager for a new monthly health and lifestyle magazine, *Global Living for Life*, being developed by the magazine division of LifeTime Publications. You were previously an advertising manager on one of the company's established magazines. In this new position, you will report to the new magazine's publisher, Molly Tymon.

Estimates of first-year subscription sales for *Global Living for Life* are 125 000 copies. Newsstand sales should add another 5000 copies a month to that number, but your concern is with developing advertising revenue for the magazine.

You and Molly have set a goal of selling advertising space totalling $6 million during the magazine's first year. You think you can do this with a staff of 10 people. Because this is a completely new publication, there is no previous budget for your advertising group. You have been asked by Molly to submit a preliminary budget for your group.

Write up a report (no longer than two pages in length) that describes in detail how you would go about fulfilling this request by Molly. For example, where would you get budget categories? Whom would you contact? Present your best ideas for creating this budget for your department.

Reinforcing the Skill

The following activities will help you practise and reinforce the skills associated with budgeting:

1. Create a personal budget for the next month. Be sure to identify sources of income and planned expenditures. At the end of the month, answer the following questions:
   (a) Did your budget help you plan what you could and could not do this month?
   (b) Did unexpected situations arise that were not included in the budget? How did you handle those?
   (c) How is a personal budget similar to and different from a budget that a manager might be responsible for?

2. Interview three managers from different organizations. Ask them about their budgeting responsibilities and the "lessons" they have learned about budgeting.

Continuing Case: Starbucks

One thing that all managers do is plan.[1] The planning they do may be extensive or it may be limited. It might be for the next week or month or it might be for the next couple of years. It might cover a work group or it might cover an entire division. No matter what type or extent of planning a manager does, the important thing is that planning takes place. Without planning, there would be nothing for managers to organize, lead, or control. Based on the numerous accomplishments that Starbucks has achieved through the efforts of its employees, managers, no doubt, have done their planning.

Company Goals

As of August 2007, Starbucks had over 14 000 outlets in 42 countries. However, that is a far cry from where the company wants and intends to be someday. President and CEO Jim Donald says Starbucks' long-term goal is 15 000 US stores and 30 000 stores globally. In 2006, the company opened 2199 new stores around the world and reached well over $7 billion in revenues. Goals for the next three to five years include attaining total net revenue growth of 20 percent and earnings per share growth between 20 and 25 percent.

In addition to its financial and other growth goals, Starbucks has an even "glitzier" goal. It wants to have a hand in helping define society's pop culture menu. Although this goal takes Starbucks beyond its coffee roots, it seems to fit well with the unconventional approach to business that Howard Schultz, the company's chairman and chief global strategist, has followed from the beginning.

Company Strategies

Starbucks has been called the most dynamic retail brand conceived over the last two decades. It has been able to rise above the commodity nature of its product and become a global brand leader by reinventing the coffee experience. Millions of times each week, a customer receives a drink from a Starbucks barista. It's a reflection of the success that Schultz has had in creating something that never really existed in North America—café life. Even though Toronto-based Second Cup started operating in 1975 and Starbucks did not come to Canada until 1987, Starbucks dominates the Canadian marketplace. Second Cup has 360 cafés across Canada (and over 15 cafés internationally), while Starbucks has over 500 stores across the country.

Schultz has created a cultural phenomenon. Starbucks is changing what we eat and drink. It's altering where we work and play. It's shaping how we spend time and money. No one is more surprised by this cultural impact than Schultz. He says, "It amazes all of us how we've become part of popular culture. Our customers have given us permission to extend the experience."

Starbucks has found a way to appeal to practically every customer demographic, as its customers cover a broad base. It's not just the affluent or the urban professionals, and it's not just the intellectuals or the creative types who frequent Starbucks. You will find soccer moms, construction workers, bank tellers, and clerical assistants at Starbucks. And despite the high price of its products, customers pay it because they think it's worth it. What they get for that price is some of the finest coffee available commercially, custom preparation, and, of course, that Starbucks ambiance—the music, the comfy chairs, the aromas, the hissing steam from the espresso machine—all invoking that warm feeling of community and connection that Schultz experienced on his first business trip to Italy and knew instinctively could work elsewhere.

There is no hiding the fact that Starbucks' broad strategy is to grow into a global empire. Schultz says, "We are in the second inning of a nine-inning game. We are just beginning to tap into all sorts of new markets, new customers, and new products." But any growth that Starbucks pursues is done with great care and planning. President and CEO Jim Donald says that all company growth is governed by whether quality can be maintained. If there is any uncertainty about quality, a new strategy won't fly, no matter how good it might seem. Starbucks has designed its growth strategies to exploit the customer connections it has so carefully nurtured and the brand equity it has so masterfully built. And company executives have taken the company in new directions even while continuing to grow store numbers and locations and increasing same-store sales.

As the world's number one specialty coffee retailer, Starbucks sells coffee drinks, food items, coffee beans, and coffee-related accessories and equipment. In addition, Starbucks sells whole-bean coffees through a specialty sales group and grocery stores. Starbucks has grown beyond coffee into related businesses such as coffee-flavoured ice cream and ready-to-drink coffee beverages. These Starbucks-branded products have been developed with other companies. For instance, its Frappuccino® and DoubleShot™ coffee drinks were developed with Pepsi-Cola. Its Starbucks Ice Cream was developed with Dreyer's. In 2006, Starbucks launched its ready-to-drink coffee drink, Starbucks Iced Coffee, through a joint venture with Pepsi-Cola. The company extended its success at brand extensions to selected global markets when it launched a fresh Starbucks-branded premium ready-to-drink chilled coffee called Starbucks Discoveries™ in convenience stores in Taiwan and Japan. This product was enthusiastically embraced by customers immediately. In addition, Starbucks markets a selection of premium tea products since its acquisition of Tazo, LLC.

Starbucks has also pursued other strategic initiatives to enhance its core business. For instance, in November 2001, the company launched the Starbucks Card, a prepaid card. Since that time, more than 77 million Starbucks Cards have been activated and loaded with more than $1 billion. The director of Starbucks global card services says, "We've been pleasantly surprised by the card business, by how fast it's grown in percentage of tender, and how people use the card. It offers so many opportunities to grow from there. It's one of our fastest-growing channels." Industry experts say that part of the reason for its success is its dual use—as gift cards and for customer loyalty. Also important to its success, however, is the fact that the company has made it easy to purchase, reload, and use. The company is on the leading edge in finding innovative ways to get the prepaid cards into potential customers' hands, such as parent–student cards, gift-card malls, and business gifts and incentives.

Having conquered the coffee business, one of the company's most interesting brand extensions has been music. Selling music at Starbucks began when a store manager made tapes for his store. These tapes proved to be so popular that the company began licensing music compilation CDs for sale. Initially, Schultz had to be persuaded about this product and recalls, "I began to understand that our customers looked to Starbucks as a kind of editor. It was like ... we trust you. Help us choose." And if you think about it, music has always been part of the café or coffeehouse experience. In addition to selling its private-label CDs, the company launched the HearMusic Café in Santa Monica, California, in March 2004. At these stores, customers burn their own compilation CDs. After sampling selections, if they choose to buy, customers can walk up to a music "bar" and order a custom CD with any variation of songs and have it delivered to their table when it's completed. Based on the success Starbucks has had with music, it decided to selectively link the Starbucks brand with certain kinds of movies, the first being *Akeelah and the Bee.* The president of Starbucks entertainment division says, "Movies are a very important part of our entertainment strategy. The thought was to start with music, build

A customer selects songs for burning to a CD as another orders coffee at a Starbucks' HearMusic Café.

some success, establish credibility, and then move into films." Eventually, the company wants to be a destination not just for java but also for music, movies, books, and more.

Not everything that Starbucks touches turns to gold. One of its big flops was a magazine called *Joe,* launched by the company and *Time.* It lasted three issues before being called off. A carbonated coffee beverage product called Mazagran, developed with Pepsi-Cola, never made it to market. As well, Starbucks decided to close its Torrefazione Italia cafés when they did not meet the goals set for them.

There is no doubt that Howard Schultz has built and continues to build Starbucks to be big. Growth has been funded through cash flow, not by selling stock or by using debt financing. Some of the new ideas to be implemented include an aggressive rollout of drive-through windows, which now number 35 Canadian locations and more than 1000 US locations; a co-branded website between Yahoo! and Starbucks where online daters can arrange to meet and drink free coffee; a partnership between Starbucks and Kellogg that created a hot breakfast product; and two new banana-based blended drinks.

Questions

1. Starbucks has some pretty specific goals it wants to achieve. Given this, do you think managers would be more likely to make rational decisions, bounded rationality decisions, or intuitive decisions? Explain.
2. Give examples of decisions that Starbucks managers might make under conditions of certainty. Under conditions of risk. Under conditions of uncertainty.

3. Make a list of Starbucks' goals. Describe what type of goal each is. Then, describe how that stated goal might affect how the following employees do their jobs: (a) a part-time store employee—a barista—in Winnipeg; (b) a quality assurance technician at one of the company's roasting plants; (c) a regional sales manager; (d) the senior vice president of new markets; and (e) the president and CEO.

4. Discuss the types of growth strategies that Starbucks has used. Be specific.

5. Evaluate the growth strategies Starbucks is using. What do you think it will take for these strategies to be successful?

6. What competitive advantage(s) do you think Starbucks has? What will it have to do to maintain that (those) competitive advantage(s)?

7. Do you think the Starbucks brand can become too saturated—that is, extended to too many different products? Why or why not?

8. What companies might be good benchmarks for Starbucks? Why? What companies might want to benchmark Starbucks? Why?

9. Describe how the following Starbucks managers might use forecasting, budgeting, and scheduling (be specific): (a) a retail store manager; (b) a regional marketing manager; (c) the manager of global trends; and (d) the president and CEO.

10. Describe Howard Schultz as a strategic leader.

11. Is Starbucks "living" its mission? Explain. (You can find the company mission on its website (**www.starbucks.com**) or in the continuing case found at the end of Part 1.

VIDEO CASE INCIDENTS

Ben & Jerry's in Canada

In May 1978, Ben Cohen and Jerry Greenfield completed a $5 correspondence course on ice-cream making and started Ben & Jerry's in a converted abandoned gas station in Burlington, Vermont. They gambled their life savings of $8000 on a dream of making Vermont's best ice cream. By 1985, Ben & Jerry's had sales of more than $9 million, reaching almost $20 million the following year. Sales hit $237 million by the end of 1999, before the company was acquired by the Anglo-Dutch corporation Unilever in August 2000.

Ben & Jerry's operates on a corporate concept of *linked prosperity* anchored in three key parts to its mission statement. Its *product mission* calls for making, distributing, and selling "the finest quality all natural ice cream ... with a continued commitment to incorporating wholesome, natural ingredients and promoting business practices that respect the earth ..." Its *economic mission* is "to operate the company on a sustainable financial basis of profitable growth ..." and its *social mission* is "to operate the company in a way that actively recognizes the central role that business plays in society by initiating innovative ways to improve the quality of life locally, nationally, and internationally."

Perhaps this is why Morrie Baker and his real estate partner were willing to risk over $1 million of their own money to develop Ben & Jerry's in Canada. But investors were worried that their $1 million could be eaten up very quickly. According to TheFranchiseMall.com, the total investment to open a single Ben & Jerry's franchise could run from $147 000 to $396 000. Planning and decision making is critical. Where should the franchises be set up? How much should be spent on a location? How much customer traffic is necessary to be profitable? Do the locations offer exclusivity or would the location manager offer a site to competitors?

Morrie Baker now owns 20 Canadian shops and takes the view that success comes from execution and proper location choice. While Baker appears to be succeeding in Canada, it seems that elsewhere 10 percent of Ben & Jerry's shops close each year. Baker knows that a winning strategy requires the right decisions at the right times ... within the confines of rationality!

QUESTIONS

1. *For discussion:* Which step of the decision making process presents the greatest risk?

2. *For debate:* "Given the advances of information and communications technology, managerial decision making today is much easier since so much information is so quickly and easily available to aid in the decision-making process." Do you agree or disagree with this statement?

3. *For analysis:* In your view, which of the common decision-making biases and errors would most likely present the greatest risk to a manager deciding on a location for a Ben & Jerry's franchise?

4. *For application:* Using the Internet and other sources, identify some of the corporate social responsibility activities Ben & Jerry's has undertaken as a member of the Unilever company. What do you feel are the most important issues that affect the decision of the company to invest in these activities?

Sources: "Ben & Jerry's Ice Cream Moves into Canada," *CBC Venture*, January 30, 2005, 935, VA–2100 F; Ben and Jerry's website, http://www.benjerry.com/our_company/our_history, http://www.benjerry.com/our_company/research_library/fin/qtr/1999/Q4-99.html, http://www.benjerry.com/our_company/about_us/our_history/timeline/index.cfm; "Unilever Acquisition of Ben & Jerry's," http://benjerry.custhelp.com/cgi-bin/benjerry.cfg/php/enduser/std_adp.php?p_sid=utNxObMi&p_lva=1&p_faqid=136&p_created=955568704&p_sp=cF9zcmNoPTEmcF9ncmlkc29ydD0mcF9yb3dfY25OPTExJnBfc2VhcmNoX3RleHQ9dW5pbGV2ZXImcF9zZWFyY2hfdHlwZT0zJnBfbfY2F0X2x2bDE9fmFueX4mcF9jb3J3zb3J0X2J5PWRmbHQmcF9wYWdlPTE*&p_li=; "Ben and Jerry's," Unilever, http://www.unileverusa.com/ourbrands/foods/benandjerrys.asp; "Ben and Jerry's Franchise," TheFranchiseMall.com, http://www.thefranchisemall.com/franchises/details/10816-0-Ben_and_Jerrys.htm; "Ben and Jerry's Franchise," FranchiseMarketplace.com, http://www.franchisemarketplace.com/franchisedetail.asp?aid=147&franchise=Ben_and_Jerry; and http://www.ethicalcorp.com/content.asp?ContentID=4538.

Joe Six-Pack and Four Canadian Entrepreneurs

Today, Canada's brewing industry comprises two dominant companies: Labatt Breweries of Canada, established in 1847, brewing 60 quality beers, employing 3200 Canadians, and operating six breweries from coast to coast; and Molson Breweries, Canada's oldest brewing company, established in 1786, employing 3000 employees across the country, and operating six breweries. Molson Canada is now an integral part of the Molson Coors Brewing Company, which was formed by the 2005 merger of Molson and Coors.

In recent times, the Canadian market has seen the development of over 40 microbreweries and an endless influx of international beers. Risks for new market entrants are high. How could another start-up beer company and a micro-distillery promoting coolers ever hope to make it?

Black Fly Beverage Company

Black Fly Beverage Company is Ontario's first micro-distillery, founded by husband and wife team Rob Kelly and Cathy Siskind-Kelly in May 2005. Black Fly Coolers are made and bottled in London, Ontario. Setting up the enterprise required considerable funds, and major lenders were reluctant due to the very real risk of failure; most of the start-up funds were raised by the Kellys themselves. The production capacity of their 3300 square foot "pilot" plant is limited to 2.5 million 400-millilitre bottles per year.

In January 2006, Black Fly's original cranberry–blueberry cooler was selling in 140 Liquor Control Board of Ontario (LCBO) outlets and bars in the London area. Today the LCBO distributes the "all Canadian produced" cooler to 450 of its 600 stores. The Kellys are looking for a new plant with at least 10 times the capacity of the existing plant, and are considering expanding their market into all parts of Canada.

Mountain Crest Brewing Company

Meet Manjit and Ravinder Minhas, petroleum-engineering graduates from the University of Calgary. The 20-something siblings started Calgary-based Mountain Crest Brewing Company in 2002. Their strategy is to underprice Molson and Labatt. To do so, they outsourced their brewing to Huber Brewing in Monroe, Wisconsin. Huber offered lower prices than any of the Canadian brewers they approached. In 2006, the siblings bought Huber Brewing to have long-term production stability, renaming it Minhas Craft Brewery in October 2007.

Mountain Crest beer is mainly sold in Alberta and other western provinces. In an effort to have a presence in eastern Canada, the Minhases incorporated Lakeshore Creek Brewing in Ontario in the summer of 2004, wanting to crack the large, highly competitive Ontario market with their Lakeshore Creek brand of premium but inexpensive beer.

Statistics Canada reports that Canadians bought around $7.9 billion worth of beer in 2003; it is estimated that 20 percent of that was spent on value beer. Ontario craft brewers such as Brick Brewery are posting record sales numbers. This is good news for the Minhases!

QUESTIONS

1. *For discussion:* Compare and contrast the Mountain Crest Brewing Company with the Black Fly Beverage Company using the strategic management process.

2. *For debate:* "The weakest part of the strategic management process undertaken by both the Mountain Crest Brewing Company and the Black Fly Beverage Company in their entry into the Ontario market was in their assessment of threats, or in the external analysis process." Do you agree or disagree with this statement?

3. *For analysis:* Which growth strategies would be best suited to each company in the long and short term?

4. *For application:* Using the Internet and other sources, identify two key competitors for both the Mountain Crest Brewing Company (in Ontario) and the Black Fly Beverage Company, and identify each company's sustainable competitive advantage over its key competitors.

Sources: "Joe Six Pack," *CBC Venture*, January 22, 2006, 6, NEP-14756; http://www.blackflycoolers.com; "Entrepreneur: Black Fly Beverage Co.," January 15, 2007, http://www.yoce.ca/entrepreneur_archives.php?sub=featureprofiles&issue=2&m=01&y=2007; http://www.macleans.ca/business/companies/article.jsp?content=200060529_127754_127754; T. Daykin, "Crafting Success," *Milwaukee Journal Sentinel*, October 29, 2007; H. Daniszewski, "Black Fly Grips Sales," *London Free Press*, January 18, 2006, http://www.lfpress.ca/cgi-bin/publish.cgi?p=120093&x=articles&s=shopping; M. Magnan, "Beer War," *Canadian Business*, July 2005, http://www.canadianbusiness.com/shared/print.jsp?content=20050718_69548_69548; "Siblings Brew Up Attack Plan on Big Beer," *Business Edge*, March 31, 2005, http://www.businessedge.ca/article.cfm/newsID/8963.cfm; and Mountain Crest Brewing Company website, http://www.damngoodbeer.ca/beer5.htm.

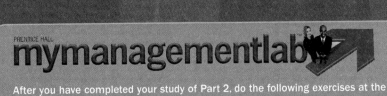

PART three

Organizing

MANAGERS NEED TO CONSIDER the best way to organize individuals into jobs, and jobs into departments. They must choose an organizational structure and communication methods that will increase effectiveness and efficiency. When considering how to organize, managers might ask these questions:

- **What would be the best organizational structure for my organization?**

- **How can I communicate effectively with organizational members?**

- **How can I attract and retain employees?**

CHAPTER 9
Organizational Structure and Design

What kind of organizational structure do I need?

1. What are the major elements of organizational structure?
2. What are the factors that affect organizational structure?
3. Beyond traditional organizational designs, how else can organizations be structured?

CHAPTER 10
Communication and Information Technology

How do I communicate effectively?

1. What are the functions of communication?
2. Why does communication break down?
3. How does communication flow in organizations?
4. How does information technology affect organizations?
5. What are some of the major communication issues facing today's organizations?

CHAPTER 11
Human Resource Management

How do I make sure that I have the right employees to carry out my mission?

1. Does managing human resources well make a difference?
2. How does the external environment affect human resource planning?
3. How do organizations assess their human resource needs?
4. How do organizations identify and select competent employees?
5. How do organizations help employees adapt and stay up-to-date?
6. What can organizations do to help employees achieve high performance over their careers?
7. How do compensation and benefits motivate employees?
8. How are careers managed?
9. What are some current issues in human resource management?

Organizational Structure and Design

PART three

Organizing

What kind of organizational structure do I need?

1. What are the major elements of organizational structure?

2. What are the factors that affect organizational structure?

3. Beyond traditional organizational designs, how else can organizations be structured?

▶ ▶ ▶ Richard A. Peddie is the president and CEO of Maple Leaf Sports & Entertainment (MLSE), which owns the NHL's Toronto Maple Leafs, the NBA's Toronto Raptors, Major League Soccer's Toronto FC, the AHL's Toronto Marlies, Leafs TV, and Raptors NBA TV.[1] MLSE also owns Air Canada Centre (where the Maple Leafs and Raptors play their home games) and is a major investor in BMO Field (where the Toronto FC play their home games). Peddie's job is complex—it includes responsibility for the business affairs of each team ("team operations, sales, marketing, finance, administration, event operations, broadcast, communications, and community development"). Peddie is also responsible for the operation of Air Canada Centre, BMO Field, Ricoh Coliseum in Toronto, and General Motors Centre in Oshawa, Ontario.

To perform his job, Peddie needs a variety of people and departments to help him. One of his jobs, then, is to create an organizational structure for MLSE that supports the operations of the sports teams and the sports facilities. He has a great deal of flexibility in determining some parts of the structure, and less flexibility in determining others. For instance, the number of athletes that can fill positions on a hockey team is deter-

mined by the NHL. Through the draft and trades, Peddie and his coaches have some ability to choose the particular players who fill these positions, however.

Peddie also oversees ticket sales for the four teams. In determining how to manage ticket sales, Peddie can con-

sider whether there should be separate ticket sales departments for each team, whether marketing should be included with or separate from ticket sales, and whether ticket salespeople should be subdivided into specialties: corporate sales, season tickets, playoff tickets, etc.

Think About It

How do you run four sports teams and four sports facilities? Put yourself in Richard Peddie's shoes. He wants to continue to make Maple Leaf Sports & Entertainment successful. What can he do so that MLSE continues to adapt and change? What organizational structure can best ensure his goals?

Richard Peddie's desire to make Maple Leaf Sports & Entertainment successful illustrates how important it is for managers to design an organizational structure that helps accomplish organizational goals and objectives. In this chapter, we present information about designing appropriate organizational structures. We look at the various elements of organizational structure and the factors that influence their design. We also look at some traditional and contemporary organizational designs, as well as organizational design challenges that today's managers face.

Air Canada Centre
www.theaircanadacentre.com

Q&A 9.1

Defining Organizational Structure

No other topic in management has undergone as much change in the past few years as that of organizing and organizational structure. Traditional approaches to organizing work

1. What are the major elements of organizational structure?

organizing
A management function that involves determining what tasks are to be done, who is to do them, how the tasks are to be grouped, who reports to whom, and where decisions are to be made.

organizational structure
How job tasks are formally divided, grouped, and coordinated within an organization.

organizational design
The process of developing or changing an organization's structure.

are being questioned and re-evaluated as managers search out structural designs that will best support and facilitate employees doing the organization's work—ones that can achieve efficiency but also have the flexibility that is necessary for success in today's dynamic environment. Recall from Chapter 1 that **organizing** is defined as the process of creating an organization's structure. That process is important and serves many purposes (see Exhibit 9-1). The challenge for managers is to design an organizational structure that allows employees to do their work effectively and efficiently.

Just what is **organizational structure**? It's the formal arrangement of jobs within an organization. When managers develop or change the structure, they are engaged in **organizational design**, a process that involves decisions about six key elements: work specialization, departmentalization, chain of command, span of control, centralization and decentralization, and formalization.[2]

Work Specialization

When you are working in a team on a course project, does it make sense to specialize tasks? What are the advantages and disadvantages?

work specialization
The degree to which activities in an organization are subdivided into separate job tasks; also known as *division of labour.*

Q&A 9.2

Adam Smith first identified division of labour and concluded that it contributed to increased employee productivity (see the supplement *History of Management Trends* on page 30 for further information). Early in the twentieth century, Henry Ford applied this concept in an assembly line where every Ford employee was assigned a specific, repetitive task.

Today we use the term **work specialization** to describe the degree to which activities in an organization are subdivided into separate job tasks. The essence of work specialization is that an entire job is not done by one individual but instead is broken down into steps, and each step is completed by a different person. Individual employees specialize in doing part of an activity rather than the entire activity.

During the first half of the twentieth century, managers viewed work specialization as an unending source of increased productivity. And for a time it was! Because it was not widely used, when work specialization *was* implemented, employee productivity rose. By the 1960s, however, it had become evident that a good thing could be carried too far. The point had been reached in some jobs where human diseconomies from work specialization—boredom, fatigue, stress, poor quality, increased absenteeism, and higher turnover—more than offset the economic advantages.

Today's View

Most managers today see work specialization as an important organizing mechanism but not as a source of ever-increasing productivity. They recognize the economies it provides in certain types of jobs, but they also recognize the problems it creates—including job dissatisfaction, poor mental health, and a low sense of accomplishment—when it's carried to extremes.[3] McDonald's uses high work specialization to efficiently make and sell its products, and most employees in health care organizations are specialized. However, other

---

Exhibit 9-1

Purposes of Organizing

- Divides work to be done into specific jobs and departments.
- Assigns tasks and responsibilities associated with individual jobs.
- Coordinates diverse organizational tasks.
- Clusters jobs into units.
- Establishes relationships among individuals, groups, and departments.
- Establishes formal lines of authority.
- Allocates and deploys organizational resources.

organizations, such as Bolton, Ontario-based Husky Injection Molding Systems and Ford Australia, have successfully increased job breadth and reduced work specialization. Still, specialization has its place in some organizations. No hockey team has anyone play both goalie and centre positions. Rather, players tend to specialize in their positions.

Departmentalization

Does your college or university have an office of student affairs? A financial aid or student housing department? Once job tasks have been divided up through work specialization, common job tasks have to be grouped back together so that they can be done in a coordinated way. The basis on which jobs are grouped together is called **departmentalization**. Every organization will have its own specific way of classifying and grouping work activities. Exhibit 9-2 on page 262 shows the five common forms of departmentalization.

Functional departmentalization groups jobs by functions performed. This approach can be used in all types of organizations, although the functions change to reflect the organization's purpose and work. **Product departmentalization** groups jobs by product line. In this approach, each major product area is placed under the authority of a manager who is responsible for everything having to do with that product line. For instance, Estée Lauder sells lipsticks, eyeshadow, blush, and a variety of other cosmetics, represented by different product lines. The company's lines include Clinique, Prescriptives, and Origins, in addition to Canadian-created MAC Cosmetics and its own original line of Estée Lauder products, each of which operates as a distinct company. Similarly, while Richard Peddie is the president and CEO of both the Raptors and the Maple Leafs, each team is treated as a separate product line in terms of the rest of its management and operations, with each team being led by its general manager.

Geographical departmentalization groups jobs on the basis of territory or geography, such as the East Coast, western Canada, or central Ontario, or maybe by US, European, Latin American, and Asia–Pacific regions. **Process departmentalization** groups jobs on the basis of product or customer flow. In this approach, work activities follow a natural processing flow of products or even of customers. For instance, many beauty salons have separate employees for shampooing, colouring, and cutting hair, all different processes for having one's hair styled. Finally, **customer departmentalization** groups jobs on the basis of customers who have common needs or problems that can best be met by having specialists for each.

Large organizations often combine forms of departmentalization. For example, a major Japanese electronics firm organizes each of its divisions along functional lines; its manufacturing units around processes; its sales units around seven geographic regions; and sales regions into four customer groupings.

Today's View

Two popular trends in departmentalization are the increasing use of customer departmentalization and the use of cross-functional teams. Customer departmentalization is being used to monitor customers' needs and to respond to changes in those needs. For example, Toronto-based Dell Canada is organized around four customer-oriented business units: home and home office; small business; medium and large business; and government, education, and health care. Burnaby, BC-based TELUS is structured around four customer-oriented business units: consumer solutions (focused on services to homes and individuals); business solutions (focused on services to small and medium-sized businesses and entrepreneurs); TELUS Québec (a TELUS company focused on services for the Quebec marketplace); and partner solutions (focused on services to wholesale customers, such as telecommunications carriers and wireless communications companies). Customer-oriented structures allow companies to better understand their customers and to respond faster to their needs.

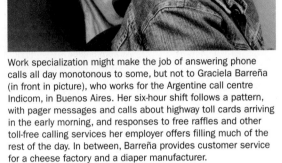

Work specialization might make the job of answering phone calls all day monotonous to some, but not to Graciela Barreña (in front in picture), who works for the Argentine call centre Indicom, in Buenos Aires. Her six-hour shift follows a pattern, with pager messages and calls about highway toll cards arriving in the early morning, and responses to free raffles and other toll-free calling services her employer offers filling much of the rest of the day. In between, Barreña provides customer service for a cheese factory and a diaper manufacturer.

departmentalization
The basis on which jobs are grouped together.

functional departmentalization
Groups jobs by functions performed.

product departmentalization
Groups jobs by product line.

geographical departmentalization
Groups jobs on the basis of territory or geography.

process departmentalization
Groups jobs on the basis of product or customer flow.

customer departmentalization
Groups jobs on the basis of customers who have common needs or problems.

 Dell Canada
www.dell.ca

TELUS
www.telus.com

Exhibit 9-2

The Five Common Forms of Departmentalization

Functional Departmentalization

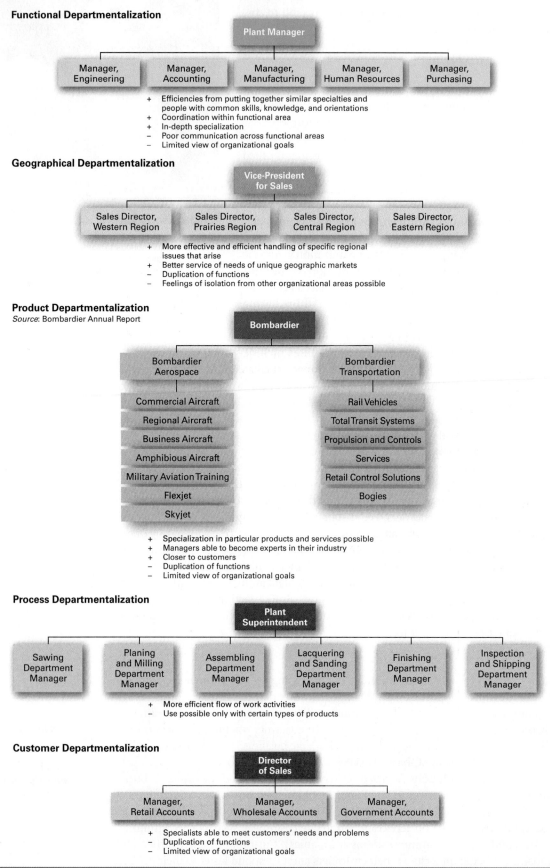

Plant Manager

| Manager, Engineering | Manager, Accounting | Manager, Manufacturing | Manager, Human Resources | Manager, Purchasing |

+ Efficiencies from putting together similar specialties and people with common skills, knowledge, and orientations
+ Coordination within functional area
+ In-depth specialization
− Poor communication across functional areas
− Limited view of organizational goals

Geographical Departmentalization

Vice-President for Sales

| Sales Director, Western Region | Sales Director, Prairies Region | Sales Director, Central Region | Sales Director, Eastern Region |

+ More effective and efficient handling of specific regional issues that arise
+ Better service of needs of unique geographic markets
− Duplication of functions
− Feelings of isolation from other organizational areas possible

Product Departmentalization
Source: Bombardier Annual Report

Bombardier

Bombardier Aerospace
- Commercial Aircraft
- Regional Aircraft
- Business Aircraft
- Amphibious Aircraft
- Military Aviation Training
- Flexjet
- Skyjet

Bombardier Transportation
- Rail Vehicles
- Total Transit Systems
- Propulsion and Controls
- Services
- Retail Control Solutions
- Bogies

+ Specialization in particular products and services possible
+ Managers able to become experts in their industry
+ Closer to customers
− Duplication of functions
− Limited view of organizational goals

Process Departmentalization

Plant Superintendent

| Sawing Department Manager | Planing and Milling Department Manager | Assembling Department Manager | Lacquering and Sanding Department Manager | Finishing Department Manager | Inspection and Shipping Department Manager |

+ More efficient flow of work activities
− Use possible only with certain types of products

Customer Departmentalization

Director of Sales

| Manager, Retail Accounts | Manager, Wholesale Accounts | Manager, Government Accounts |

+ Specialists able to meet customers' needs and problems
− Duplication of functions
− Limited view of organizational goals

Managers use **cross-functional teams**—work teams made up of individuals who are experts in various functional specialties—to increase knowledge and understanding of some organizational tasks. For instance, Scarborough, Ontario-based Aviva Canada, a leading property and casualty insurance group, puts together catastrophe teams to more quickly help policyholders when a crisis occurs. The cross-functional teams, with trained representatives from all relevant departments, are called upon to provide services in the event of a crisis. During the BC wildfires of summer 2003, the catastrophe team worked on both local and corporate issues, including managing information technology, internal and external communication, tracking, resourcing, and vendors. This made it easier to meet the needs of policyholders as quickly as possible.[4] We discuss the use of cross-functional teams more fully in Chapter 14.

cross-functional teams
Work teams made up of individuals who are experts in various functional specialties.

Aviva Canada
www.avivacanada.com

Chain of Command

> *Have you ever worked in an organization where it was not clear what the chain of command was? What effect did this have on employees?*

For many years, the chain-of-command concept was a cornerstone of organizational design. As you'll see, it has far less importance today. But contemporary managers still need to consider its implications when deciding how best to structure their organizations.

The **chain of command** is the continuous line of authority that extends from upper organizational levels to the lowest levels and clarifies who reports to whom. It helps employees answer questions such as, "Who do I go to if I have a problem?" or "To whom am I responsible?"

You cannot discuss the chain of command without discussing these other concepts: authority, responsibility, accountability, unity of command, and delegation. **Authority** refers to the rights inherent in a managerial position to tell people what to do and to expect them to do it.[5] To facilitate decision making and coordination, an organization's managers are part of the chain of command and are granted a certain degree of authority to meet their responsibilities. Some senior managers and CEOs are better at granting authority than others. For instance, when Richard Peddie hired Rob Babcock to be the general manager of the Raptors in 2004, some sportswriters raised concerns over whether Babcock would have enough autonomy to do his job. It was noted that Peddie "has a reputation for meddling with basketball operations."[6] When Babcock was fired in 2006, sportswriters observed that many of his decisions were actually made by senior management.[7]

As managers coordinate and integrate the work of employees, those employees assume an obligation to perform any assigned duties. This obligation or expectation to perform is known as **responsibility**. Responsibility brings with it **accountability**, which is the need to report and justify work to a manager's superiors. When John Muckler was dismissed as general manager of the Ottawa Senators in 2007, the team owner was signalling that he held Muckler accountable for failing to land top players that could have helped the team in their run at the Stanley Cup.[8]

The **unity of command** principle (one of Fayol's 14 principles of management discussed in the supplement *History of Management Trends* on page 30) helps preserve the concept of a continuous line of authority. It states that every employee should receive orders from only one superior. Without unity of command, conflicting demands and priorities from multiple managers can create problems.

Because managers have limited time and knowledge, they may choose to delegate some of their responsibilities to other employees. **Delegation** is the assignment of authority to another person to carry out specific duties, allowing the employee to make some of the decisions. Delegation is an important part of a manager's job, as it can ensure that the right people are part of the decision-making process. What can managers do to be better delegators? *Tips for Managers—Delegating Effectively* on page 264 provides some suggestions.

chain of command
The continuous line of authority that extends from the top of the organization to the lowest level and clarifies who reports to whom.

authority
The rights inherent in a managerial position to tell people what to do and to expect them to do it.

Q&A 9.3

responsibility
The obligation or expectation to perform any assigned duties.

accountability
The need to report and justify work to a manager's superiors.

unity of command
The management principle that states every employee should receive orders from only one superior.

delegation
The assignment of authority to another person to carry out specific duties, allowing the employee to make some of the decisions.

Line and Staff Authority

In many organizations, there is a distinction between line and staff authority. Line managers are responsible for the activities that form the core of the organization's mission, including production and sales. Line managers have the authority to issue orders to those in the chain of command. The president, the production manager, and the sales manager are examples of line managers. Staff managers work in the supporting activities of the organizations (such as human resources or accounting). Staff managers have advisory authority, and cannot issue orders to those in the chain of command (except those in their own department). The vice-president of accounting, the human resource manager, and the marketing research manager are examples of staff managers. For instance, Mardi Walker, senior vice-president, People, for Maple Leafs Sports & Entertainment, may have recommendations about how the Raptors might win more games, but cannot expect that such recommendations to General Manager Bryan Colangelo will be followed. However, as senior vice-president, People, Walker can give advice about managing employee benefits.

Today's View

Early management theorists (Fayol, Weber, Taylor, and others) were enamoured with the concepts of chain of command, authority, responsibility, and unity of command. However, times change, and so have the basic tenets of organizational design. However, it's been hard for some organizations to give up the control that a formal chain of command represents.

In addition, concepts such as chain of command, authority, and so forth are considerably less relevant today because of things like information technology. In a matter of a few seconds, employees throughout the organization can access information that used to be available only to top managers. Also, with computers, employees communicate with anyone else anywhere in the organization without going through formal channels—that is, the chain of command. Moreover, as more organizations use self-managed and cross-functional teams and as new organizational designs with multiple bosses are implemented, these traditional concepts are less relevant.

Span of Control

span of control
The number of employees a manager can efficiently and effectively manage.

How many employees can a manager efficiently and effectively manage? This question of **span of control** is important because, to a large degree, it determines the number of levels and managers an organization has. All things being equal, the wider or larger the span, the more efficient the organization. An example can show why.

Assume that we have two organizations, both of which have almost 4100 employees. As Exhibit 9-3 shows, if one organization has a uniform span of four and the other a span of eight, the wider span will have two fewer levels and approximately 800 fewer managers. If the average manager made $50 000 a year, the organization with the wider span would save $40 million a year in management salaries alone! Obviously, wider spans are more efficient in terms of cost. However, at some point, wider spans reduce effectiveness. When the span becomes too large, employee performance can suffer because managers may no longer have the time to provide the necessary leadership and support.

Q&A 9.4

Today's View

The contemporary view of span of control recognizes that many factors influence the appropriate number of employees that a manager can efficiently *and* effectively manage. These factors include the skills and abilities of the manager and the employees, and characteristics of the work being done. For instance, the more training and experience employees have, the less direct supervision they need. Therefore, managers with well-trained and experienced employees can function quite well with a wider span. Other contingency variables that determine the appropriate span include similarity of employee tasks, the com-

Exhibit 9-3

Contrasting Spans of Control

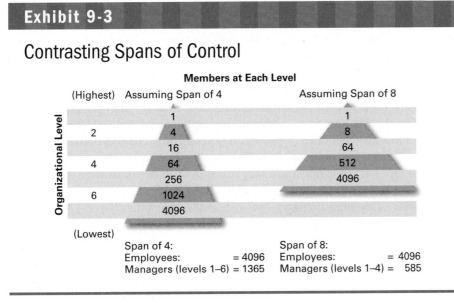

Members at Each Level

(Highest)	Assuming Span of 4	Assuming Span of 8
	1	1
2	4	8
	16	64
4	64	512
	256	4096
6	1024	
	4096	
(Lowest)		

Span of 4:
Employees: = 4096
Managers (levels 1–6) = 1365

Span of 8:
Employees: = 4096
Managers (levels 1–4) =   585

plexity of those tasks, the physical proximity of subordinates, the degree to which standardized procedures are in place, the sophistication of the organization's information system, the strength of the organization's culture, and the preferred style of the manager.[9] Wider spans of control are also possible due to technology—it is easier for managers and their subordinates to communicate with each other, and there is often more information readily available to help employees perform their jobs.

The trend in recent years has been toward larger spans of control, which is consistent with managers' efforts to reduce costs, speed up decision making, increase flexibility, get closer to customers, and empower employees. However, to ensure that performance does not suffer because of these wider spans, organizations are investing heavily in employee training. Managers recognize that they can handle a wider span when employees know their jobs well or can turn to co-workers if they have questions.

Q&A 9.5

Centralization and Decentralization

In some organizations, top managers make all the decisions and lower-level managers and employees simply carry out their orders. At the other extreme are organizations in

Many employees are asked to work in teams to get things done. These Xerox employees are a self-managed team. They make decisions about managing and scheduling production, and they monitor the quality of their output.

which decision making is pushed down to the managers who are closest to the action. The former organizations are centralized, and the latter are decentralized.

centralization
The degree to which decision making is concentrated at a single point in the organization.

Centralization describes the degree to which decision making is concentrated at a single point in the organization. If top managers make the organization's key decisions with little or no input from below, then the organization is centralized. We noted above that Richard Peddie tends to be closely involved in decisions regarding the Raptors. In contrast, the more that lower-level employees provide input or actually make decisions, the more **decentralization** there is. Keep in mind that the concept of centralization/decentralization is relative, not absolute—that is, an organization is never completely centralized or decentralized. Few organizations could function effectively if all decisions were made by only a select group of top managers; nor could they function if all decisions were delegated to employees at the lowest levels. (To learn more about delegating, see *Developing Your Interpersonal Skills—Delegating* on pages 284–285, at the end of the chapter.)

decentralization
The degree to which lower-level employees provide input or actually make decisions.

PRISM 10

What determines whether an organization will move toward more centralization or decentralization? Exhibit 9-4 lists some of the factors that influence the amount of centralization or decentralization an organization uses.[10]

Today's View

As organizations become more flexible and responsive, there is a distinct trend toward decentralizing decision making. In large companies especially, lower-level managers are "closer to the action" and typically have more detailed knowledge about problems and how best to solve them than do top managers. For instance, the Bank of Montreal's some 1000 branches are organized into "communities"—a group of branches within a limited geographical area. Each community is led by a community area manager, who typically works within a 20-minute drive of the area's other branches. This area manager can respond faster and more intelligently to problems in his or her community than could some senior executive at the company's head office. As the company continues its southward expansion into the United States, it continues to use decentralization to successfully manage its various businesses.[11] The following *Management Reflection* considers the case of Cascades, a pulp and paper company, which illustrates a few of the reasons for having a decentralized structure.

Exhibit 9-4

Factors That Influence the Amount of Centralization and Decentralization

More Centralization	More Decentralization
• Environment is stable.	• Environment is complex, uncertain.
• Lower-level managers are not as capable or experienced at making decisions as upper-level managers.	• Lower-level managers are capable and experienced at making decisions.
• Lower-level managers do not want to have a say in decisions.	• Lower-level managers want a voice in decisions.
• Decisions are significant.	• Decisions are relatively minor.
• Organization is facing a crisis or the risk of company failure.	• Corporate culture is open to allowing managers to have a say in what happens.
• Company is large.	• Company is geographically dispersed.
• Effective implementation of company strategies depends on managers' retaining say over what happens.	• Effective implementation of company strategies depends on managers' having involvement and flexibility to make decisions.

Brothers Decentralize to Increase Entrepreneurial Management

Does decentralization lead to better management?   Kingsey Falls, Quebec-based Cascades, a leading manufacturer of packaging products and tissue paper, has more than 100 operating units located in Canada, the United States, and Europe.[12] Alain Lemaire is president and CEO, and his two brothers, Bernard and Laurent, are also senior executives in the business.

Cascades is composed of autonomous units: the Boxboard Group, the Containerboard Group–Norampac, the Specialty Products Group, and the Tissue Group. The companies produce coated boxboard and folding cartons, container-board packaging, specialty paper products, and tissues. Boralex, a company affiliated with Cascades, produces energy and is headed by Bernard Lemaire. The companies are treated as separate entities, based on product, and operate like a federation of small and medium-sized businesses. Each mill within a subsidiary operates as a separate business unit and is accountable for its own bottom line.

The company motivates its employees through profit sharing, although employees share only in the profits generated by their own mill. Because each mill is evaluated separately, managers have to be both more responsible and more accountable for their operations, and encourage employees to take more ownership of their job performance. The Lemaires' emphasis on decentralized, entrepreneurial management has been copied by other Canadian forest products companies, such as Domtar. ■

Cascades
www.cascades.com

Another term for increased decentralization is **employee empowerment**, which is giving more authority to employees to make decisions. We address empowerment more thoroughly in our discussion of leadership in Chapter 12.

employee empowerment
Giving more authority to employees to make decisions.

Formalization

Formalization refers to the degree to which jobs within the organization are standardized and the extent to which employee behaviour is guided by rules and procedures. If a job is highly formalized, then the person doing that job has little freedom to choose what is to be done, when it's to be done, and how he or she does it. Employees can be expected to handle the same input in exactly the same way, resulting in consistent and uniform output. In organizations with high formalization, there are explicit job descriptions, numerous organizational rules, and clearly defined procedures covering work processes. On the other hand, where formalization is low, job behaviours are relatively unstructured and employees have a great deal of freedom to choose how they do their work.

The degree of formalization varies widely between organizations and even within organizations. For instance, at a newspaper, news reporters often have a great deal of discretion in their jobs. They may pick their news topics, find their own stories, research them the way they want, and write them up, usually within minimal guidelines. On the other hand, employees who lay out the newspaper pages don't have that type of freedom. They have constraints—both time and space—that standardize how they do their work.

formalization
The degree to which jobs within the organization are standardized and the extent to which employee behaviour is guided by rules and procedures.

Q&A 9.6

Today's View

Although some formalization is important and necessary for consistency and control, many of today's organizations seem to be less reliant on strict rules and standardization to guide and regulate employee behaviour. For instance, consider the following situation:

It is 2:37 p.m., and a customer at a branch of a large national drugstore chain is trying to drop off a roll of film for same-day developing. Store policy states that film must be dropped off by 2:00 p.m. for this service. The clerk knows that rules like this are supposed to be followed. At the same time, he wants to be accommodating to the customer, and he knows that the film could, in fact, be processed that day. He decides to accept the film and, in so doing, to violate the policy. He just hopes that his manager does not find out.[13]

Has this employee done something wrong? He did "break" the rule. But by breaking the rule, he actually brought in revenue and provided the customer good service: so good, in fact, that the customer may be satisfied enough to come back in the future.

Considering that there are numerous situations like these where rules may be too restrictive, many organizations have allowed employees some freedom to make those decisions that they feel are best under the circumstances. It does not mean that all organizational rules are thrown out the window, because there *will* be rules that are important for employees to follow—and these rules should be explained so employees understand why it's important to adhere to them. But for other rules, employees may be given some leeway in application.[14]

Organizational Design Decisions

2. What are the factors that affect organizational structure?

Organizations don't have the same structures. A company with 30 employees is not going to look like one with 30 000 employees. But even organizations of comparable size don't necessarily have similar structures. What works for one organization may not work for another. How do managers decide what organizational design to use? That decision depends upon certain contingency factors. In this section, we look at two generic models of organizational design and then at the contingency factors that favour each.

Mechanistic and Organic Organizations

Dining in Vancouver can get you two very different experiences. At McDonald's, you will find a limited selection of menu items, most available daily. Employees are not expected to be decision makers. Rather, they are closely supervised and follow well-defined rules and standard operating procedures. Only one employee helps each customer. At Blue Water Café in downtown Vancouver, by contrast, there is no division of labour, and management does not dictate what the kitchen serves. Instead, the chef on duty creates a meal of his choice while you sit at the sushi bar and watch. The chef chooses the meal from the fresh fish of the day that he bought at the market earlier, so each day's menu can be quite original. Waiters work collaboratively, helping each other serve all customers, rather than being assigned to specific tables.

mechanistic organization
An organizational design that is rigid and tightly controlled.

Exhibit 9-5 describes two organizational forms.[15] A **mechanistic organization** is a rigid and tightly controlled structure, much like McDonald's. It's characterized by high specialization, rigid departmentalization, a limited information network (mostly downward communication), narrow spans of control, little participation in decision making by lower-level employees, and high formalization.

Exhibit 9-5

Mechanistic vs. Organic Organization

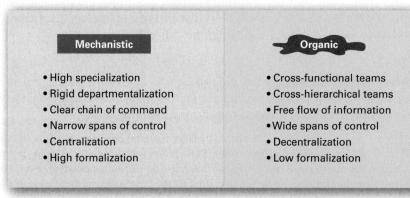

Mechanistic	Organic
• High specialization	• Cross-functional teams
• Rigid departmentalization	• Cross-hierarchical teams
• Clear chain of command	• Free flow of information
• Narrow spans of control	• Wide spans of control
• Centralization	• Decentralization
• High formalization	• Low formalization

Mechanistic organizational structures tend to be efficiency machines and rely heavily on rules, regulations, standardized tasks, and similar controls. This organizational design tries to minimize the impact of differing personalities, judgments, and ambiguity because these human traits are seen as inefficient and inconsistent. Although there is no totally mechanistic organization, almost all large corporations and government agencies have some of these mechanistic characteristics.

In direct contrast to the mechanistic form of organization is the **organic organization**, which is as highly adaptive and flexible a structure as the mechanistic organization is rigid and stable. This structure characterizes the Blue Water Café. Rather than having standardized jobs and regulations, the organic organization is flexible, which allows it to change rapidly as needs require. Organic organizations have a division of labour, but the jobs people do are not standardized. Employees are highly trained and empowered to handle diverse job activities and problems, and these organizations frequently use cross-functional and cross-hierarchical teams. Employees in organic-type organizations require minimal formal rules and little direct supervision, instead relying on a free flow of information and wide span of control. Their high levels of skills and training and the support provided by other team members make formalization and tight managerial controls unnecessary.

Organizations can display a mix of mechanistic and organic features. Wikipedia, the online encyclopedia, is known for its creation and editing of entries by anyone who has Internet access. In this way, it displays a very organic structure. However, behind the scenes there is a more mechanistic structure, where individuals have some authority to monitor abuse and perform other functions to safeguard the credibility of entries and the website overall, as the following *Management Reflection* shows.

organic organization
An organizational design that is highly adaptive and flexible.

MANAGEMENT REFLECTION

Wikipedia's Structure Maintains Order in the Face of Anarchy

Why would a decentralized, free-wheeling website need an organizational structure? Even a seemingly democratic organization such as Wikipedia has an organizational structure.[16] The structure serves to help the online encyclopedia be as accurate as possible. At the bottom of that structure are the 4.6 million registered English-language users. These users are overseen by a group of about 1200 administrators, who have the power to "block other users from the site, either temporarily or permanently." One of their roles is to make sure that users are not vandalizing the site by adding incorrect information deliberately. To become an administrator, one must first be nominated, and then answer a series of five questions. Users then have seven days to register their approval or disapproval of the nominee. The administrators are overseen by a group called "bureaucrats." The bureaucrats can appoint administrators once they determine that users approve of a particular administrator nominee (this requires about a 70 percent approval rating by users). They can also change user names, and they make sure that bot policies (policies regarding automated or semi-automated processes that edit webpages) are followed. Above the bureaucrats are about 30 stewards, who are elected to this position. The stewards can provide (and take away) special access status to Wikipedia. Above the stewards is the seven-person Wikimedia Foundation board of trustees, who are "the ultimate corporate authority." At the top of the Wikipedia organizational chart is the "de facto leader," Jimmy Wales, one of the co-founders of Wikipedia. ■

When is a mechanistic structure preferable, and when is an organic one more appropriate? Let's look at the main contingency factors that influence the decision.

Q&A 9.7

Contingency Factors

Top managers of most organizations typically put a great deal of thought into designing an appropriate structure. What that appropriate structure is depends on four contingency variables: the organization's strategy, size, technology, and degree of environmental uncertainty. It is important to remember that because these variables can change over the life cycle of the organization, managers should consider from time to time whether the current organizational structure is best suited for what the organization is facing.

Q&A 9.8

Strategy and Structure

An organization's structure should facilitate the achievement of goals. Because goals are influenced by the organization's strategies, it's only logical that strategy and structure should be closely linked. More specifically, structure should follow strategy. If managers significantly change the organization's strategy, they should modify the structure to support the new strategy.

Most current strategy frameworks tend to focus on three dimensions:

- *Innovation.* This dimension reflects the organization's pursuit of meaningful and unique innovations.
- *Cost minimization.* This dimension reflects the organization's pursuit of tightly controlled costs.
- *Imitation.* This dimension reflects an organization's attempt to minimize risk and maximize profit opportunities by copying the market leaders.

What organizational structure works best with each?[17] Innovators need the flexibility and free-flowing information of the organic structure, whereas cost minimizers seek the efficiency, stability, and tight controls of the mechanistic structure. Imitators use structural characteristics of both—the mechanistic structure to maintain tight controls and low costs and the organic structure to mimic the industry's innovative directions.

Size and Structure

There is considerable evidence that an organization's size significantly affects its structure.[18] For instance, large organizations—those with 2000 or more employees—tend to have more specialization, departmentalization, centralization, and rules and regulations than do small organizations. However, the relationship is not linear. Rather, beyond a certain point, size becomes a less important influence on structure as an organization grows. Why? Essentially, once an organization has around 2000 employees, it's already fairly mechanistic. Adding 500 employees to an organization with 2000 employees will not have much of an impact. On the other hand, adding 500 employees to an organization that has only 300 members is likely to result in a shift toward a more mechanistic structure.

Technology and Structure

Q&A 9.9

Every organization has at least one form of technology to convert its inputs into outputs. For instance, employees at FedEx Kinko's produce custom print jobs for individual customers. Employees at GM Canada's Oshawa, Ontario, plant build Chevrolet Impala, Chevrolet Monte Carlo, Buick Lacrosse/Allure, and Pontiac Grand Prix cars on a standardized assembly line. And employees at Bayer AG make aspirin and other pharmaceutical products using a continuous-flow production line. Each of these organizations uses a different type of technology.

The initial interest in technology as a determinant of structure can be traced to the work of British scholar Joan Woodward.[19] She studied several small manufacturing firms in southern England to determine the extent to which structural design elements were related to organizational success. Woodward was unable to find any consistent pattern until she segmented the firms into three categories based on the size of their production runs. The three categories, representing three distinct technologies, have increasing levels of complexity and sophistication. The first category, **unit production**, describes the production of items in units or small batches. The second category, **mass production**, describes large-batch manufacturing. Finally, the third and most technically complex group, **process production**,

unit production
The production of items in units or small batches.

mass production
The production of items in large batches.

process production
The production of items in continuous processes.

describes the production of items in continuous processes. A summary of her findings is shown in Exhibit 9-6.

Since Woodward's initial work, numerous studies have been done on the technology–structure relationship. These studies generally demonstrate that organizations adapt their structures to their technology.[20] The processes or methods that transform an organization's inputs into outputs differ by their degree of routineness or standardization. In general, the more routine the technology, the more mechanistic the structure can be. Organizations with more nonroutine technology, such as custom furniture building or online education, are more likely to have organic structures because the product delivery cannot be standardized.[21]

Environmental Uncertainty and Structure

In Chapter 2, we introduced the organization's environment and the amount of uncertainty in that environment as constraints on managerial discretion. Why should an organization's structure be affected by its environment? Because of environmental uncertainty! Some organizations face relatively stable and simple environments; others face dynamic and complex environments. Because uncertainty threatens an organization's effectiveness, managers will try to minimize it. One way to reduce environmental uncertainty is through adjustments in the organization's structure.[22] The greater the uncertainty, the more an organization needs the flexibility offered by an organic structure. On the other hand, in stable, simple environments, mechanistic structures tend to be most effective.

3M has surged ahead of its competitors in sales of products based on applications of nanotechnology. At the same time, R & D spending as a percentage of sales is at a record low, which means the company's research efforts are paying off as never before. The reason? Larry Wendling, vice president of the central R & D lab, reorganized the company's researchers around emerging technologies like nanotechnology, setting lower priorities on old technologies like adhesives. A $1 billion research budget is also a factor, but Wendling credits the reorganization. "The best way to transfer ideas," he says, "is to transfer people."

Today's View

The evidence on the environment–structure relationship helps explain why so many managers today are restructuring their organizations to be lean, fast, and flexible. Global competition, accelerated product innovation by competitors, and increased demands from customers for high quality and faster deliveries are examples of dynamic environmental forces. Mechanistic organizations are not equipped to respond to rapid environmental change and environmental uncertainty. As a result, we are seeing organizations designed to be more organic. However, a purely organic organization may not be ideal. One study

---

Exhibit 9-6

Woodward's Findings on Technology, Structure, and Effectiveness

	Unit Production	**Mass Production**	**Process Production**
Structural Characteristics	• Low vertical differentiation • Low horizontal differentiation • Low formalization	• Moderate vertical differentiation • High horizontal differentiation • High formalization	• High vertical differentiation • Low horizontal differentiation • Low formalization
Most Effective Structure	• Organic	• Mechanistic	• Organic

Source: Based on J. Woodward, *Industrial Organization: Theory and Practice* (London: Oxford University Press, 1965).

found that organic structures may work more effectively if managers establish semistructures that govern "the pace, timing, and rhythm of organizational activities and processes." Thus, introducing a bit of structure while keeping most of the flexibility of the organic structure may reduce operating costs.[23]

Common Organizational Designs

▶ ▶ ▶ Maple Leaf Sports & Entertainment (MLSE) is divided into four operating units: MLSE, Toronto Raptors, Toronto Maple Leafs (Toronto Marlies is an affiliate), and Toronto FC. Richard Peddie is the president and CEO of all four units.[24] The Raptors, the Maple Leafs, the Marlies, and Toronto FC have their own general manager who manages the day-to-day operations of the team, develops recruiting plans, and oversees training. The general managers report to the CEO, and have a number of managers who report to them. MLSE has a divisional structure, whereby its businesses operate separately, on a daily basis.

Think About It

Why do organizations vary in the types of structures they have? How do organizations choose their structures? Why does Maple Leaf Sports & Entertainment have the structure that it does?

3. Beyond traditional organizational designs, how else can organizations be structured?

What organizational designs do Ford Canada, Corel, McCain Foods, Procter & Gamble, and eBay have? In making organizational design decisions, managers can choose from traditional organizational designs and contemporary organizational designs.

Traditional Organizational Designs

In designing a structure to support the efficient and effective accomplishment of organizational goals, managers may choose to follow more traditional organizational designs. These designs—the simple structure, functional structure, and divisional structure—tend to be more mechanistic. Exhibit 9-7 summarizes the strengths and weaknesses of each of these designs.

Simple Structure

simple structure
An organizational structure with low departmentalization, wide spans of control, authority centralized in a single person, and little formalization.

Most organizations start as entrepreneurial ventures with a simple structure consisting of owners and employees. A **simple structure** is an organizational structure with low departmentalization, wide spans of control, authority centralized in a single person, and little formalization.[25] This structure is most commonly used by small businesses in which the owner and manager are one and the same.

Most organizations do not remain simple structures. As an organization grows, it generally reaches a point where it has to add employees. As the number of employees rises, the structure tends to become more specialized and formalized. Rules and regulations are introduced, work becomes specialized, departments are created, levels of management are added, and the organization becomes increasingly bureaucratic. (You can review Weber's concept of bureaucracy in the supplement *History of Management Trends* on page 30.) At this point, a manager might choose to organize around a functional structure or a divisional structure.

Q&A 9.10

Functional Structure

functional structure
An organizational structure that groups similar or related occupational specialties together.

A **functional structure** is an organizational structure that groups similar or related occupational specialties together. It's the functional approach to departmentalization applied to the entire organization. For instance, Revlon is organized around the functions of operations, finance, human resources, and product research and development.

Divisional Structure

divisional structure
An organizational structure that consists of separate business units or divisions.

The **divisional structure** is an organizational structure that consists of separate business units or divisions.[26] In this structure, each unit or division has relatively limited autonomy, with a division manager responsible for performance and with strategic and opera-

Exhibit 9-7

Strengths and Weaknesses of Common Traditional Organizational Designs

Structure	Strengths	Weaknesses
Simple Structure	Fast; flexible; inexpensive to maintain; clear accountability.	Not appropriate as organization grows; reliance on one person is risky.
Functional Structure	Cost-saving advantages from specialization (economies of scale, minimal duplication of people and equipment) and employees are grouped with others who have similar tasks.	Pursuit of functional goals can cause managers to lose sight of what's best for overall organization; functional specialists become insulated and have little understanding of what other units are doing.
Divisional Structure	Focuses on results—division managers are responsible for what happens to their products and services.	Duplication of activities and resources increases costs and reduces efficiency.

tional authority over his or her unit. In divisional structures, however, the parent corporation typically acts as an external overseer to coordinate and control the various divisions, and it often provides support services such as financial and legal. As we noted earlier, Maple Leaf Sports & Entertainment has four divisions, including the three sports teams, the Raptors, the Maple Leafs, and Toronto FC.

Contemporary Organizational Designs

Managers in some contemporary organizations are finding that these traditional hierarchical designs often are not appropriate for the increasingly dynamic and complex environments they face. In response to marketplace demands for being lean, flexible, and innovative, managers are finding creative ways to structure and organize work and to make their organizations more responsive to the needs of customers, employees, and other organizational constituents.[27] For instance, at the Canada Revenue Agency the workforce is spread out, and they rely on shared workspaces, mobile computing, and virtual private networks to get work done. Nevertheless, work gets done effectively and efficiently.[28] Now, we want to introduce you to some of the newest concepts in organizational design. Exhibit 9-8 on page 274 summarizes these contemporary organizational designs.

Team Structure

Larry Page and Sergey Brin, co-founders of Google, have created a corporate structure that "tackles most big projects in small, tightly focused teams."[29] In a **team structure**, the entire organization is made up of work groups or teams that perform the organization's work.[30] Needless to say, employee empowerment is crucial in a team structure because there is no line of managerial authority from top to bottom. Rather, employee teams are free to design work in the way they think is best. However, the teams are also held responsible for all work and performance results in their respective areas. Let's look at some other examples of organizations that are organized around teams.

Whole Foods Market, the largest natural-foods grocer in the United States, opened its first Canadian outlet in Toronto in 2002, its second in Vancouver in 2004, and its third in Oakville, Ontario, in 2005. The stores are structured around teams.[31] Each Whole Foods store is an autonomous profit centre composed of an average of 10 self-managed teams, each with a designated team leader. The team leaders in each store are a team; store leaders in each region are a team; and the company's six regional presidents are a team. At the Sun Life Assurance Company of Canada (US) office in Wellesley Hills, Massachusetts, customer

team structure
An organizational structure in which the entire organization is made up of work groups or teams.

Q&A 9.11

Whole Foods Market
www.wholefoodsmarket.com

Exhibit 9-8

Contemporary Organizational Designs

Structure	Description	Advantages	Disadvantages
Team	A structure in which the entire organization is made up of work groups or teams.	Employees are more involved and empowered. Reduced barriers among functional areas.	No clear chain of command. Pressure on teams to perform.
Matrix–Project	Matrix is a structure that assigns specialists from different functional areas to work on projects but who return to their areas when the project is completed. Project is a structure in which employees continuously work on projects. As one project is completed, employees move on to the next project.	Fluid and flexible design that can respond to environmental changes. Faster decision making.	Complexity of assigning people to projects. Task and personality conflicts.
Boundaryless	A structure that is not defined by or limited to artificial horizontal, vertical, or external boundaries; includes *virtual* and *networked* types of organizations.	Highly flexible and responsive. Draws on talent wherever it's found.	Lack of control. Communication difficulties.

representatives work in eight-person teams trained to expedite all customer requests. When customers call in, they are not switched from one specialist to another, but to one of the teams, which takes care of every aspect of the customer's request.

In large organizations, the team structure complements what is typically a functional or divisional structure. This allows the organization to have the efficiency of a bureaucracy while providing the flexibility that teams provide. To improve productivity at the operating level, for instance, companies such as Toyota's CAPTIN plant (based in Delta, BC), Motorola, and Xerox extensively use self-managed teams. At Saturn and Hewlett-Packard, cross-functional teams are used to design new products or coordinate major projects. Scarborough, Ontario-based Aviva Canada, a property and casualty insurance group, uses a cross-functional team for handling BC wildfire catastrophes. The Cat (which stands for "Catastrophe") team

Acxiom, of Little Rock, Arkansas, needed a new organizational design in order to stay at the cutting edge of its field (data mining). So the company abandoned its old hierarchical structure and adopted a streamlined culture that focuses on teams, like the Global Data Development team shown here, which meets twice each month. Lee Parrish, leader of another Acxiom team, compared the firm's team structure to the hierarchy at his previous employer: "You had a job title.... Here, you have a role. Instead of a lot of wasted motion, you can reach out to people and spend your time working on proactive solutions to problems."

includes specialists in information technology, internal and external communication, tracking, resourcing, and vendor management. Together, team members work to make resolving insurance difficulties after a disaster go much more smoothly.[32]

Matrix and Project Structures

> *Have you ever had to work for two managers at the same time? Was this a positive or negative experience?*

Other popular contemporary designs are the matrix and project structures. The **matrix structure** is an organizational structure that assigns specialists from different functional departments to work on one or more projects being led by project managers. Exhibit 9-9 shows an example of the matrix structure used in an aerospace firm. Along the top are the familiar organizational functions. The specific projects the firm is currently working on are listed along the left-hand side. Each project is managed by an individual who staffs his or her project with people from each of the functional departments. The addition of this vertical dimension to the traditional horizontal functional departments, in effect, "weaves together" elements of functional and product departmentalization, creating a matrix arrangement. One other unique aspect of this design is that it creates a *dual chain of command*. It explicitly violates the classical organizing principle of unity of command. How does a matrix structure work in reality?

Employees in a matrix organization have two managers, their functional department manager and their product or project manager, who share authority. The project managers have authority over the functional members who are part of their project team in areas related to the project's goals. However, decisions such as promotions, salary recommendations, and annual reviews remain the functional manager's responsibility. To work effectively, project and functional managers have to communicate regularly, coordinate work demands on employees, and resolve conflicts together.

Although the matrix structure continues to be an effective organizational structure choice for some organizations, many are using a more "advanced" type of **project structure**, in which employees continuously work on projects. Unlike the matrix structure, a project structure has no formal departments that employees return to at the completion of a project. Instead, employees take their specific skills, abilities, and experiences to other projects. In addition, all work in project structures is performed by teams of employees who become part of a project team because they have the appropriate work skills and abilities. For instance, at Oticon Holding A/S, a Danish hearing-aid manufacturer, there are no departments or employee job titles. All work is project based, and these project teams form, disband, and form again as the work requires. Employees "join" project teams

matrix structure
An organizational structure that assigns specialists from different functional departments to work on one or more projects.

Q&A 9.12

project structure
An organizational structure in which employees continuously work on projects.

Exhibit 9-9

A Matrix Organization in an Aerospace Firm

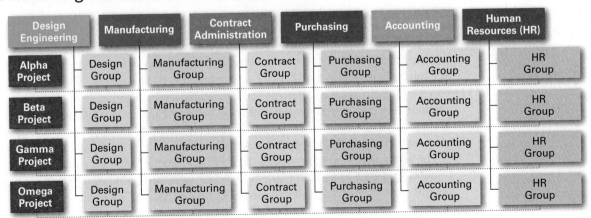

because they bring needed skills and abilities to that project. Once the project is completed, they move on to the next one.[33]

Project structures tend to be fluid and flexible organizational designs. There is no departmentalization or rigid organizational hierarchy to slow down decision making or taking actions. In this type of structure, managers serve as facilitators, mentors, and coaches. They "serve" the project teams by eliminating or minimizing organizational obstacles and by ensuring that the teams have the resources they need to effectively and efficiently complete their work.

Boundaryless Organizations

boundaryless organization
An organization that is not defined by a chain of command, places no limits on spans of control, and replaces departments with empowered teams.

Another approach to contemporary organizational design is the concept of a **boundaryless organization**, an organization whose design is not defined by a predefined structure. Instead, the organization seeks to eliminate the chain of command, places no limits on spans of control, and replaces departments with empowered teams.[34] The term was coined by Jack Welch, former chair of General Electric, who wanted to eliminate vertical and horizontal boundaries within GE and break down external barriers between the company and its customers and suppliers. This idea may sound odd, yet many successful organizations are finding that they can operate more effectively in today's environment by remaining flexible and *un*structured: that the ideal structure for them is *not* having a rigid, predefined structure. Instead, the boundaryless organization seeks to eliminate the chain of command, to have limitless spans of control, and to replace departments with empowered teams.[35]

Q&A 9.13

What do we mean by "boundaries"? In a typical organization, there are internal boundaries—horizontal boundaries imposed by work specialization and departmentalization and vertical boundaries that separate employees into organizational levels and hierarchies. Then, there are external boundaries that separate the organization from its customers, suppliers, and other stakeholders. To minimize or eliminate these boundaries, managers might use virtual or network organizational structures.

So how does a boundaryless organization operate in practice? General Electric is made up of a number of companies including GE Money, which provides financial services to consumers and retailers; GE Water & Process Technologies, which provides water treatment, wastewater treatment, and process systems products; GE Energy, which supplies technology to the energy industry; and NBC Universal Studios, a leading media and entertainment company. One way that the boundaryless organization functions for employees is that anyone working in any division of GE can learn about opportunities available in the other business units, and how to move into those units, if so desired. Outside the company, the boundaryless structure means that some GE customers can send information to the factories to increase inventory when the customer needs more product. Thus, the customer makes a decision about inventory that was once made inside the organization. GE also encourages customers and suppliers to evaluate its service levels, giving direct and immediate feedback to employees.

virtual organization
An organization that has elements of a traditional organization, but also relies on recent developments in information technology to get work done.

Virtual Organizations   A **virtual organization** has elements of a traditional organization, but also relies on recent developments in information technology to get work done.[36] Thus, the organization could consist of a small core of full-time employees that temporarily hires outside specialists to work on opportunities that arise.[37] A virtual organization could also be formed of employees who work from their own home offices, connected by technology, but perhaps getting together face-to-face only rarely. An example of a virtual organization is Strawberry Frog, an international advertising agency based in Amsterdam. The small administrative staff accesses a network of about 50 people around the globe to complete advertising projects. By relying on this web of freelancers around the globe, the company enjoys a network of talent without all the unnecessary overhead and structural complexity.

The inspiration for virtual organizations comes from the film industry. If you look at the film industry, people are essentially "free agents" who move from project to project applying their skills—directing, talent search, costuming, makeup, set design—as needed.

New Westminster, BC-based iGEN Knowledge Solutions uses its virtual form to bring technical solutions to its business clients. iGEN associates work from home offices, connected

iGEN Knowledge Solutions
www.igeninc.com

by wireless technologies, to solve client problems collaboratively. This structure allows faster idea implementation, product development, and service delivery. The company finds it easy to set up operations in different regions of the country without large overhead costs because of its virtual structure.

Some organizations might also consider a new form of virtuality, using the virtual online world of Second Life to create a different type of organization, as the following *Management Reflection* shows.

Trend Micro, a maker of antivirus software, is a virtual organization with financial headquarters in Tokyo, product development people in Taiwan, and sales offices in Silicon Valley. Its computer-virus response centre is in Manila, and its smaller labs are scattered around the world from Munich to Tokyo. Says CEO Steve Chang, "With the Internet, viruses became global. To fight them, we had to become a global company." Trend Micro has responded to virus threats in as little as 30 minutes.

MANAGEMENT REFLECTION
► Focus on Innovation

Avatars and the Business World

Can a Second Life presence bring a company more clients? Vancouver-based Davis LLP is the first Canadian law firm to have a presence in the virtual online world of Second Life.[38] Lawyer Dani Lemon, whose online avatar (a digital version of a real person) is Lemon Darcy, says, "The online world gives [Davis] an opportunity to interact with clients and meet new ones who are comfortable in that setting."

Lemon believes that being part of Second Life will bring new clients to Davis, giving them an opportunity to communicate in new ways. Several of her colleagues have joined her in this virtual office, including Sarah Dale-Harris (BarristerSolicitor Underwood), Pablo Guzman (PabloGuzman Little), Chris Bennett (IPand Teichmann), David Spratley (DaveS Blackadder), and Chris Metcalfe (IP Maximus).

The Second Life office has a boardroom off the lobby that will be used for online conferences, accessing recruiting information for lawyers and students from Davis, and a library with online legal information.

"I think it will be an evolving process," Lemon said of the online office. "We will use it as a networking tool and as a way to meet clients."

The law firm also plans to hold online events in Second Life, conduct seminars, and give talks that might be of value to potential clients. ■

Network Organizations Another structural option for managers who want to minimize or eliminate organizational boundaries is the **network organization**, which is a small core organization that outsources major business functions.[39] This approach allows organizations to concentrate on what they do best and contract out other activities to companies that can do those activities best. Many large organizations use the network structure to outsource manufacturing. Companies like Cisco Systems, Nike, Ericsson, L.L. Bean, and Reebok have found that they can do hundreds of millions of dollars of business without owning manufacturing facilities. For instance, San Jose, California-based Cisco Systems is essentially a research and development company that uses outside suppliers and independent manufacturers to assemble the Internet routers its engineers design. Beaverton, Oregon-based Nike is essentially a product development and marketing company that contracts with outside organizations to manufacture its athletic footwear. And Stockholm, Sweden-based Ericsson contracts its manufacturing and even some of its research and development to more cost-effective contractors in New Delhi, Singapore, California, and other global locations.[40]

While many companies use outsourcing, not all are successful at it. Managers should be aware of some of the problems involved in outsourcing, such as the following:

network organization
A small core organization that outsources major business functions.

- Choosing the wrong activities to outsource
- Choosing the wrong vendor
- Writing a poor contract
- Failing to consider personnel issues
- Losing control over the activity

- Ignoring the hidden costs
- Failing to develop an exit strategy (for either moving to another vendor, or deciding to bring the activity back in-house)

A review of 91 outsourcing activities found that the most likely reasons for an outsourcing venture to fail were writing a poor contract and losing control of the activity.[41]

Canadian managers say they are reluctant to outsource.[42] In a 2004 survey of 603 Canadian companies by Ipsos Reid, 60 percent were not eager to ship software development overseas. While a number of managers said they were concerned with controlling costs (36 percent), almost the same number said they preferred to keep jobs in Canada (32 percent), and one-third were also concerned about losing control of projects that went overseas.

Today's Organizational Design Challenges

As managers look for organizational designs that will best support and facilitate employees doing their work efficiently and effectively in today's dynamic environment, there are certain challenges with which they must contend. These include keeping employees connected, building a learning organization, and managing global structural issues.

Keeping Employees Connected

Many organizational design concepts were developed during the twentieth century, when work tasks were fairly predictable and constant, most jobs were full time and continued indefinitely, and work was done at an employer's place of business under a manager's supervision.[43] That is not what it's like in many organizations today, as you saw in our preceding discussion of virtual and network organizations. A major structural design challenge for managers is finding a way to keep widely dispersed and mobile employees connected to the organization. We cover information on motivating these employees in Chapter 13.

Building a Learning Organization

We first introduced the concept of a learning organization in Chapter 1 as we looked at some of the current issues facing managers. The concept of a learning organization does not involve a specific organizational design per se but instead describes an organizational mindset or philosophy that has design implications.

Q&A 9.14

What is a learning organization? It's an organization that has developed the capacity to continuously learn, adapt, and change.[44] In a learning organization, employees continually acquire and share new knowledge and are willing to apply that knowledge in making decisions or performing their work. Some organizational theorists even go so far as to say that an organization's ability to do this—that is, to learn and to apply that learning—may be the only sustainable source of competitive advantage.[45] What structural aspects does a learning organization need?

Q&A 9.15

First, it's critical for members in a learning organization to share information and collaborate on work activities throughout the entire organization—across different functional specialties and even at different organizational levels. To do this requires minimal structural and physical barriers. In such a boundaryless environment, employees can work together and collaborate in doing the organization's work the best way they can, and learn from each other. Finally, because of this need to collaborate, teams also tend to be an important feature of a learning organization's structural design. Employees work in teams that are empowered to make decisions about doing whatever work needs to be done or resolving issues. With empowered employees and teams, there is little need for "bosses" to direct and control. Instead, managers serve as facilitators, supporters, and advocates.

Managing Global Structural Issues

Are there global differences in organizational structures? Are Australian organizations structured like those in Canada? Are German organizations structured like those in France or Mexico? Given the global nature of today's business environment, this is an issue with which managers need to be familiar. Researchers have concluded that the structures and strategies of organizations worldwide are similar, "while the behavior within them is maintaining its cultural uniqueness."[46] What does this mean for designing effective and efficient structures? When designing or changing structure, managers may need to think about the cultural implications of certain design elements. For instance, one study showed that formalization—rules and bureaucratic mechanisms—may be more important in less economically developed countries, and less important in more economically developed countries, where employees may have higher levels of professional education and skills.[47] Other structural design elements may be affected by cultural differences as well.

A Final Thought

No matter what structural design managers choose for their organizations, the design should help employees do their work in the best—most efficient and effective—way they can. The structure should aid and facilitate organizational members as they carry out the organization's work. After all, the structure is simply a means to an end. (To understand your reaction to organizational structure, see *Self-Assessment—What Type of Organizational Structure Do I Prefer?* on pages 280–281, at the end of the chapter.)

SUMMARY AND IMPLICATIONS

1. What are the major elements of organizational structure? Organizational structure is the formal arrangement of jobs within an organization. Organizational structures can vary due to six key elements: work specialization, departmentalization, chain of command, span of control, centralization and decentralization, and formalization. Decisions about these elements determine how work is organized; how many employees managers supervise; where in the organization decisions are made; and whether employees follow standardized operating procedures or have greater flexibility in how they do their work.

▶ ▶ ▶ For Maple Leafs Sports & Entertainment, it makes sense to separate the operation of the four sports teams because of the work specialization involved. For example, the general manager of the Raptors would not necessarily make good decisions about what Maple Leafs players should do to improve their game.

2. What are the factors that affect organizational structure? There is no one best organizational structure. The appropriate structure depends upon the organization's strategy (innovation, cost minimization, imitation), its size, the technology it uses (unit production, mass production, or process production) and the degree of environmental uncertainty the organization faces.

▶ ▶ ▶ For Maple Leaf Sports & Entertainment, because hockey, basketball, and soccer are in different "industries" with different types of players, it makes sense to organize the teams by industry. Because sports teams are governed by formal rules, the teams have more of a mechanistic structure than an organic one. Each team has a similar organizational structure because size, technology, and environmental uncertainty would not differ in any meaningful way for the teams.

3. Beyond traditional organizational designs, how else can organizations be structured? The traditional structures of organizations are simple, functional, and divisional. Contemporary organizational designs include team structure, matrix and project structures, and boundaryless organizations.

▶ ▶ ▶ Maple Leaf Sports & Entertainment follows a traditional divisional structure for its sport teams. Other structures might be used to operate its sports facilities, such as a project structure or a boundaryless organization, because events and ticket sales can be managed in a variety of ways.

CHAPTER 9

Management @ Work

READING FOR COMPREHENSION

1. Describe what is meant by the term *organizational design*.

2. In what ways can management departmentalize? When should one approach be considered over the others?

3. What is the difference between a mechanistic and an organic organization?

4. Why is the simple structure inadequate in large organizations?

5. Describe the characteristics of a boundaryless organization.

6. Describe the characteristics of a learning organization. What are its advantages?

LINKING CONCEPTS TO PRACTICE

1. Can an organization's structure be changed quickly? Why or why not?

2. Would you rather work in a mechanistic or an organic organization? Why?

3. What types of skills would a manager need to effectively work in a team structure? In a matrix and project structure? In a boundaryless organization?

4. "The boundaryless organization has the potential to create a major shift in the way we work." Do you agree or disagree with this statement? Explain.

5. With the availability of information technology that allows an organization's work to be done anywhere at any time, is organizing still an important managerial function? Why or why not?

SELF-ASSESSMENT

What Type of Organizational Structure Do I Prefer?

For each of the following statements, circle your level of agreement or disagreement:[48]

> 1 = Strongly Disagree
> 2 = Disagree Somewhat
> 3 = Undecided
> 4 = Agree Somewhat
> 5 = Strongly Agree

I prefer to work in an organization where:

1. Goals are defined by those at higher levels.   1   2   3   4   5

2. Clear job descriptions exist for every job.   1   2   3   4   5

3. Top management makes important decisions.   1   2   3   4   5

4. Promotions and pay increases are based as much on length of service as on level of performance.   1   2   3   4   5

5. Clear lines of authority and responsibility are established.   1   2   3   4   5

6. My career is pretty well planned out for me.   1   2   3   4   5

7. I have a great deal of job security.   1   2   3   4   5

8. I can specialize.   1   2   3   4   5

9. My boss is readily available.   1   2   3   4   5

10. Organization rules and regulations are clearly specified. 1 2 3 4 5

11. Information rigidly follows the chain of command. 1 2 3 4 5

12. There is a minimal number of new tasks for me to learn. 1 2 3 4 5

13. Work groups incur little turnover in members. 1 2 3 4 5

14. People accept authority of a leader's position. 1 2 3 4 5

15. I am part of a group whose training and skills are similar to mine. 1 2 3 4 5

Scoring Key

Add up the numbers for each of your responses to get your total score.

Analysis and Interpretation

This instrument measures your preference for working in a mechanistic or organic organizational structure.

Scores above 60 suggest that you prefer a mechanistic structure. Scores below 45 indicate a preference for an organic structure. Scores between 45 and 60 suggest no clear preference.

Because the trend in recent years has been toward more organic structures, you are more likely to find a good organizational match if you score low on this instrument. However, there are few, if any, pure organic structures. Therefore, very low scores may also mean that you are likely to be frustrated by what you perceive as overly rigid structures of rules, regulations, and boss-centred leadership. In general, however, low scores indicate that you prefer small, innovative, flexible, team-oriented organizations. High scores indicate a preference for stable, rule-oriented, more bureaucratic organizations.

More Self-Assessments mymanagementlab

To learn more about your skills, abilities, and interests, go to the MyManagementLab website and take the following self-assessments:

- I.A.4.—How Well Do I Handle Ambiguity? (This exercise also appears in Chapter 7 on pages 216–217.)
- III.A.2.—How Willing Am I to Delegate?
- II.C.3.—How Good Am I at Playing Politics?

MANAGEMENT FOR YOU TODAY

Dilemma

Choose an organization for which you have worked. How did the structure of your job and the organization affect your job satisfaction? Did the tasks within your job make sense? In what ways could they be better organized? What structural changes would you make to this organization? Would you consider making this a taller or flatter organization? How would the changes you have proposed improve responsiveness to customers and your job satisfaction?

Becoming a Manager

- If you belong to a student organization or are employed, notice how various activities and events are organized through the use of work specialization, chain of command, authority, responsibility, and so forth.

- As you read current business periodicals, note what types of organizational structures businesses use and whether or not they are effective.

- Talk to managers about how they organize work and what they have found to be effective.

- Since delegating is part of decentralizing and is an important management skill, complete the *Developing Your Interpersonal Skills—Delegating* module on pages 284–285. Then practise delegating in various situations.

- Look for examples of organizational charts (a visual drawing of an organization's structure), and use them to try to determine what structural design the organization is using.

Delegating Effectively and Ineffectively

In relatively decentralized organizations, managers must delegate authority to another person to carry out specific duties. Read through *Developing Your Interpersonal Skills—Delegating* on pages 284–285. Form groups of 3 or 4 individuals. Your instructor will assign groups to either "effective delegating"

or "ineffective delegating." Come up with a role-playing situation that illustrates what your group was assigned (effective or ineffective delegating), which you will present in class. Be prepared to explain how your situation was an example of effective or ineffective delegating.

Ethical Dilemma Exercise: Is "Just Following Orders" a Valid Defence?

Is a manager acting unethically by simply following orders within the chain of command?[49] One recent survey of human resource managers found that 52 percent of the respondents felt some pressure to bend ethical rules, often because of orders from above or to achieve ambitious goals. This might happen in any organization. At WorldCom, for example, Betty Vinson was a senior manager when she and others received orders, through the chain of command, to slash expenses through improper accounting. She argued against the move. Her manager said he had also objected and was told this was a one-time "fix" to make WorldCom's finances look better. Vinson reluctantly agreed, but she felt guilty and told her manager she wanted to resign. A senior executive persuaded her to stay, and she continued following orders to fudge the accounting.

Soon Vinson realized that the figures would need fudging for some time. After investigators started to probe WorldCom's finances, she and others cooperated with regulators and prosecutors. Ultimately, the company was forced into bankruptcy. Some managers were indicted; some (including Vinson) pleaded guilty to conspiracy and fraud.

Imagine that you are a salesperson at a major corporation. Your manager invites you to an expensive restaurant where she is entertaining several colleagues and their spouses. The manager orders you to put the meal on your expense account as a customer dinner. She says she will approve the expense so you are reimbursed, and higher-level managers will not know that managers and their spouses were in attendance. What would you do? (Review this chapter's *Chain of Command* section, on pages 263–264, as you consider your decision.)

Thinking Critically About Ethics

Changes in technology have cut the shelf life of most employees' skills. A factory or clerical worker used to be able to learn one job and be reasonably sure that the skills acquired to do that job would be enough for most of his or her work years. That is no longer the case. What ethical obligation do

organizations have to assist employees whose skills have become obsolete? What about employees? Do they have an obligation to keep their skills from becoming obsolete? What ethical guidelines might you suggest for dealing with employee skill obsolescence?

Hewlett-Packard

Best known for its printers, cameras, calculators, and computers, Hewlett-Packard has had its share of organizing challenges over the years.[50] Carly Fiorina, who was named CEO of H-P in 1999—a move that made news headlines because H-P was one of the first major US corporations to be headed by a woman—continued the company's strategy of growing by acquiring businesses. Her most controversial acquisition was the $25 billion purchase of rival Compaq Computers—

a decision that was the beginning of the end for Fiorina. The combined companies experienced many problems—financial, cultural, and structural—resulting in poor performance. Her differences with the company's board of directors over the direction H-P was going finally led to her firing in early February 2005. By the end of March 2005, Mark Hurd, CEO of NCR Corporation, had been selected by the board as the new CEO of H-P.

A few weeks after arriving at H-P, Hurd began hearing complaints about the company's salesforce. At a retreat "with 25 top corporate customers, several of them told Mr. Hurd they didn't know whom to call at H-P because of the company's confusing management layers." He also heard the same complaints inside the organization. The company's head of corporate technology told Hurd that "it once took her three months to get approval to hire 100 sales specialists." Another executive said that "his team of 700 salespeople typically spent 33 percent to 36 percent of their time with customers. The rest of the time was spent negotiating internal H-P bureaucracy." Even the sales reps said that they did not get to spend time with customers because they were "often burdened with administrative tasks." Getting a price quote or a sample product to a customer became a time-consuming ordeal. It did not take Hurd long to realize that there was a "fundamental problem" that he had to address.

Delving into H-P's sales structure, Hurd found 11 layers of management between him and customers—way too many, he decided. And the company's sales structure was highly inefficient. For instance, in Europe, H-P had four people from different departments working to close a sales deal, while competitors typically only had three people. "That meant H-P was slower to cut a deal and lost many bids." And the final issue Hurd uncovered: Of the 17 000 people working in corporate sales, less than 60 percent of them directly sold to customers. The rest were support staff or in management.

How should Hurd restructure H-P to restore it to its former position as an industry leader?

DEVELOPING YOUR DIAGNOSTIC AND ANALYTICAL SKILLS

A Learning Organization at Svenska

Svenska Handelsbanken, Sweden's premier bank, is one of the largest banks in the Nordic region.[51] Pär Boman, Svenska's president and group chief executive, oversees a business that is organized around a decentralized structure. This structure has a network consisting of hundreds of branches in Sweden, Denmark, Finland, Norway, and Great Britain, as well as those located in 14 non-European countries such as China, Poland, and Russia. Boman believes that the bank's 30-plus years of developing its branch network have allowed it to consistently grow market share and achieve a return on equity that has been above the average of its competitors. Now these competitors are starting to copy Svenska's structure in an attempt to model the bank's success. But Boman believes the bank's competitive advantage is not simply from having more branches. Rather, he believes it comes from the degree of autonomy that branch managers have.

Svenska's branch managers can choose their customers and product offerings. They can also set staffing numbers and decide salary levels at their branch. All customers, private and corporate, no matter what their size, are the sole responsibility of the branch. That means, for example, that even a large global corporation such as Volvo is managed by a branch bank operation. Yet, to better facilitate customer service, each branch office can buy specialized services it may need in servicing such a large customer. Each branch manager is also responsible for branch performance, which is measured by a ratio of costs divided by revenues. At Svenska, this measure is used to benchmark every branch against each other.

If a branch starts underperforming, the regional office will offer consultative services about what other branches are doing successfully. To stop predatory competition among its own branches, the company has set up strict geographical boundaries. Svenska's number of centralized staff is a relatively small percentage of what its competitors have, and guidelines from headquarters are few and seldom issued. The bank's flat management structure and emphasis on personal responsibility and consensus approach are well suited to the Swedish culture.

Boman wants to continue to build the learning organization the bank has started. He wants to improve its capacity to continuously learn, adapt, and change. That is an interesting goal for a 130-year-old bank that has proven to be successful in the industry.

Questions

1. What do you see as the advantages and disadvantages of Svenska Handelsbanken's structure?

2. Do you believe such a structure could work effectively in other cultures, such as that of the United States, in which there is less emphasis placed on consensus building?

3. What do you believe Pär Boman could do to enhance the learning organization concept at Svenska?

Delegating

About the Skill

Managers get things done through other people. Because there are limits to any manager's time and knowledge, effective managers need to understand how to delegate. *Delegation* is the assignment of authority to another person to carry out specific duties. It allows an employee to make some of the decisions. Delegation should not be confused with participation. In participative decision making, there is a sharing of authority. In delegation, employees make decisions on their own.

Steps in Developing the Skill

A number of actions differentiate the effective delegator from the ineffective delegator. You can be more effective at delegating if you use the following five suggestions:[52]

1. **Clarify the assignment.** Determine what is to be delegated and to whom. You need to identify the person who is most capable of doing the task, and then determine whether or not he or she has the time and motivation to do the task. If you have a willing and able employee, it's your responsibility to provide clear information on what is being delegated, the results you expect, and any time or performance expectations you may have. Unless there is an overriding need to adhere to specific methods, you should delegate only the results expected. Get agreement on what is to be done and the results expected, but let the employee decide the best way to complete the task.

2. **Specify the employee's range of discretion.** Every situation of delegation comes with constraints. Although you are delegating to an employee the authority to perform some task or tasks, you are not delegating unlimited authority. You are delegating authority to act on certain issues within certain parameters. You need to specify what those parameters are so that employees know, without any doubt, the range of their discretion.

3. **Allow the employee to participate.** One of the best ways to decide how much authority will be necessary to accomplish a task is to allow the employee who will be held accountable for that task to participate in that decision. Be aware, however, that allowing employees to participate can present its own set of potential problems as a result of employees' self-interests and biases in evaluating their own abilities.

4. **Inform others that delegation has occurred.** Delegation should not take place behind the scenes. Not only do the manager and employee need to know specifically what has been delegated and how much authority has been given, but so does anyone else who is likely to be affected by the employee's decisions and actions. This includes people inside and outside the organization. Essentially, you need to communicate what has been delegated (the task and amount of authority) and to whom.

5. **Establish feedback channels.** To delegate without establishing feedback controls is to invite problems. The establishment of controls to monitor the employee's performance increases the likelihood that important problems will be identified and that the task will be completed on time and to the desired specifications. Ideally, these controls should be determined at the time of the initial assignment. Agree on a specific time for the completion of the task, and then set progress dates when the employee will report back on how well he or she is doing and any major problems that may have arisen. These controls can be supplemented with periodic checks to ensure that authority guidelines are not being abused, organizational policies are being followed, proper procedures are being met, and the like.

Practising the Skill

Read the following scenario. Write some notes about how you would handle the situation described. Be sure to refer to the five suggestions for delegating.

Scenario

Ricky Lee is the manager of the contracts group of a large regional office supply distributor. His manager, Anne Zumwalt, has asked him to prepare by the end of the month the department's new procedures manual, which will outline the steps followed in negotiating contracts with office products manufacturers who supply the organization's products. Because Ricky has another major project he is working on, he went to Anne and asked her if it would be possible to assign the rewriting of the procedures manual to Bill Harmon, one of his employees, who has worked in the contracts group for about three years. Anne said she had no problems with Ricky reassigning the project as long as Bill knew the parameters and the expectations for the completion of the project. Ricky is preparing for his meeting in the morning with Bill regarding this assignment. Prepare an outline of what Ricky should discuss with Bill to ensure the new procedures manual meets expectations.

Reinforcing the Skill

The following activities will help you practise and reinforce the skills associated with delegating:

1. Interview a manager regarding his or her delegation skills. What activities does he or she *not* delegate? Why?

2. Teach someone else how to delegate effectively. Be sure to identify to this person the behaviours needed to delegate effectively and explain why these behaviours are important.

Communication and Information Technology

PART three

How do I communicate effectively?

1. What are the functions of communication?

2. Why does communication break down?

3. How does communication flow in organizations?

4. How does information technology affect organizations?

5. What are some of the major communication issues facing today's organizations?

▶ ▶ ▶ Facebook, the social networking website, was started in 1995 as a way for university students to connect with each other online.[1] Users could post photos and information about themselves, and keep in contact with friends.

Currently, less than half of Facebook's 24 million members worldwide are in university. Nearly 3 million Canadians use Facebook, with more than half logging in daily. Canada is second only to the United States in the numbers of people on Facebook, and Toronto has the largest regional network in the world (637 956 members in 2007).

Facebook is starting to be recognized as a multifaceted tool by the business community. Some employers prescreen job applicants by searching their Facebook profile. "At its core, Facebook is a place to share information and communicate and people are really starting to see it as an effective utility in their lives," says Brandee Barker, director of communications for Facebook.

It's also an easy way for employers to get information about job candidates and employees. Brian Drum, president of the New York-based executive search firm Drum Associates, says that sites like Facebook make it easy to do "subtle" background checks. "Employers can go to these sites and see what people are saying about themselves," he says.

Employers are also starting to create their own company networks on Facebook, where only those with the company's email address can join. This allows employees from the same company to use Facebook features to communicate with each other.

Think About It

Can social networking websites enhance communication in the workplace? How might social networking websites affect communication in organizations? What risks might using Facebook pose to graduating students looking for their first major job?

Communication between managers and employees provides the information necessary to get work done effectively and efficiently in organizations. As such, there is no doubt that communication is fundamentally linked to managerial performance.[2] In this chapter, we present basic concepts in managerial communication. We describe the interpersonal communication process, channels for communicating, barriers to effective communication, and ways to overcome those barriers. We also look at organizational communication issues including communication flow and communication networks. And, because managerial communication is so greatly influenced by information technology, we look at it as well. Finally, we discuss several contemporary communication issues facing managers.

Facebook
www.facebook.com

Understanding Communication

If you have not studied communication before, you might think that it's a pretty normal process, and that almost anyone can communicate effectively without much thought. So many things can go wrong with communication, though, that it's clear not everyone thinks

1. What are the functions of communication?

about how to communicate effectively. For instance, unlike the character Bill Murray plays in *Groundhog Day,* Neal L. Patterson, CEO of Cerner, a health care software development company based in Kansas City, probably wishes he *could* do over one particular day. Upset with the fact that employees did not seem to be putting in enough hours, he sent an angry and emotional email to about 400 company managers that said, in part:

> We are getting less than 40 hours of work from a large number of our K.C.-based EMPLOYEES. The parking lot is sparsely used at 8 a.m.; likewise at 5 p.m. As managers, you either do not know what your EMPLOYEES are doing, or you do not CARE. You have created expectations on the work effort which allowed this to happen inside Cerner, creating a very unhealthy environment. In either case, you have a problem and you will fix it or I will replace you.... I will hold you accountable. You have allowed things to get to this state. You have two weeks. Tick, tock.[3]

Patterson had a message, and he wanted to get it out to his managers. Although the email was meant only for the company's managers, it was leaked and posted on a Yahoo! discussion site. The tone of the email surprised industry analysts, investors, and, of course, Cerner's managers and employees. The company's stock price dropped 22 percent over the next three days. Patterson apologized to his employees and acknowledged, "I lit a match and started a firestorm." This is a good example of why it's important for individuals to understand the impact of communication.

The importance of effective communication for managers cannot be overemphasized for one specific reason: Everything a manager does involves communicating. Not *some* things, but everything! A manager can't make a decision without information. That information has to be communicated. Once a decision is made, communication must again take place. Otherwise, no one would know that a decision was made. The best idea, the most creative suggestion, the best plan, or the most effective job redesign cannot take shape without communication. Managers need effective communication skills. We are not suggesting that good communication skills alone make a successful manager. We can say, however, that ineffective communication skills can lead to a continuous stream of problems for the manager.

What Is Communication?

communication
The transfer and understanding of meaning.

Communication is the transfer and understanding of meaning. The first thing to note about this definition is the emphasis on the *transfer* of meaning. This means that if no information or ideas have been conveyed, communication has not taken place. The speaker who is not heard or the writer who is not read has not communicated.

More importantly, however, communication involves the *understanding* of meaning. For communication to be successful, the meaning must be conveyed and understood. A letter written in Portuguese addressed to a person who does not read Portuguese cannot be considered communication until it's translated into a language the person does read and understand. Perfect communication, if such a thing existed, would be the receiver's understanding of a transmitted thought or idea exactly as it was intended by the sender.

Another point to keep in mind is that *good* communication is often erroneously defined by the communicator as *agreement* with the message instead of clearly *understanding* the message.[4] If someone disagrees with us, many of us assume that the person just did not fully understand our position. In other words, many of us define good communication as having someone accept our views. But I can clearly understand what you mean and just *not* agree with what you say. In fact, many times, when a conflict has gone on for a long time, people will say it's because the parties are not communicating effectively. That assumption reflects the tendency to think that effective communication equals agreement.

Q&A 10.1

interpersonal communication
Communication between two or more people.

organizational communication
All the patterns, networks, and systems of communication within an organization.

The final point we want to make about communication is that it encompasses both **interpersonal communication**—communication between two or more people—and **organizational communication**—all the patterns, networks, and systems of communication within an organization. Both these types of communication are important to managers in organizations.

Functions of Communication

Why is communication important to managers and organizations? It serves four major functions: control, motivation, emotional expression, and information.[5]

Communication acts to *control* member behaviour in several ways. As we know from Chapter 9, organizations have authority hierarchies and formal guidelines that employees are required to follow. For instance, when employees are required to communicate any job-related grievance first to their immediate manager, or to follow their job description, or to comply with company policies, communication is being used to control. But informal communication also controls behaviour. When work groups tease or harass a member who is working too hard or producing too much (making the rest of the group look bad), they are informally controlling the member's behaviour.

Communication encourages *motivation* by clarifying to employees what is to be done, how well they are doing, and what can be done to improve performance if it's not up to par. As employees set specific goals, work toward those goals, and receive feedback on their progress, communication is required. Managers motivate more effectively if they show support for the employee by communicating constructive feedback, rather than mere criticism.

For many employees, their work group is a primary source of social interaction. The communication that takes place within the group is a fundamental mechanism by which members share frustrations and feelings of satisfaction. Communication, therefore, provides a release for *emotional expression* of feelings and for fulfillment of social needs.

If you have ever had a bad haircut, you have probably never forgotten the experience. And you might never have returned to the stylist again. Dorys Belanger, owner of Montreal-based Au Premier Spa Urbain, says that a bad haircut should not be blamed on the stylist alone. Good communication is "50 percent up to the hairdresser, 50 percent up to the client," she says.

Finally, individuals and groups need *information* to get things done in organizations. Communication provides that information.

No one of these four functions is more important than the others. For groups to work effectively, they need to maintain some form of control over members, motivate members to perform, provide a means for emotional expression, and make decisions. You can assume that almost every communication interaction that takes place in a group or organization is fulfilling one or more of these four functions.

Interpersonal Communication

▶ ▶ ▶ Facebook encourages online interaction rather than face-to-face communication.[6] Because Facebook users write rather than speak directly to each other, they may feel safer saying something on their Facebook page than they would in person. There is concern, however, that the less personal interactions in Facebook may lead to poorer-quality relationships with fewer emotional rewards.

Individuals might also inadvertently incriminate themselves on Facebook. The Ontario Provincial Police have used the site to find out about parties that might have illegal drug use and underage drinking. Facebook makes it easy—it makes such party plans instantly available on the site and provides directions to the location.

Following the lead of Queen's Park and Parliament Hill, the City of Toronto banned its employees from using Facebook while at work in May 2007, because it had become so popular. Managers wanted to remove the temptation to waste "an inordinate amount of time."

Think About It

What effect will the growing use of online social networking sites have on people's ability to communicate face-to-face? Can online social networking lead people to forget to consider the consequences of their communication?

**2. Why does communication
break down?**

message
A purpose to be conveyed.

encoding
Converting a message into
symbols.

channel
The medium a message travels
along.

decoding
A receiver's translation of a
sender's message.

communication process
The seven elements involved in
transferring meaning from one
person to another.

noise
Disturbances that interfere with
the transmission, receipt, or
feedback of a message.

Before communication can take place, a purpose, expressed as a **message** to be conveyed, must exist. It passes between a source (the sender) and a receiver. The message is converted into symbols (called **encoding**) and passed by way of some medium (**channel**) to the receiver, who translates the sender's message (called **decoding**). The result is the transfer of meaning from one person to another.[7] Exhibit 10-1 illustrates the seven elements of the interpersonal **communication process**: the sender, the message, encoding, the channel, the receiver, decoding, and feedback. In addition, note that **noise**—disturbances that interfere with the transmission, receipt, or feedback of a message—can affect the entire process. Typical examples of noise include external factors such as illegible print, phone static, or background sounds of machinery or co-workers. However, noise can be the result of internal factors such as inattention of the receiver, as well as perceptions and personality traits of the receiver. Remember that anything that interferes with understanding can be noise, and noise can create distortion at any point in the communication process.

How Distortions Can Happen in Interpersonal Communication

Distortions can happen with the sender, the message, the channel, the receiver, or the feedback loop. Let's look at each.

Sender

A *sender* initiates a message by *encoding* a thought. Four conditions influence the effectiveness of that encoded message: the skills, attitudes, and knowledge of the sender, and the social–cultural system. How? We will use ourselves, as your textbook authors, as an example. If we don't have the required skills, our message won't reach you, the reader, in the form desired. Our success in communicating to you depends on our writing skills. In addition, any pre-existing ideas (attitudes) that we may have about numerous topics will affect how we communicate. For instance, our attitudes about managerial ethics or the importance of managers to organizations influence our writing. Next, the amount of knowledge we have about a subject affects the message(s) we are transferring. We cannot communicate what we don't know; and if our knowledge is too extensive, it's possible that our writing won't be understood by the readers. Finally, the socio-cultural system in which we live influences us as communication senders. Our beliefs and values (all part of culture) act to influence what and how we communicate.

Message

The *message* itself can distort the communication process, regardless of the kinds of supporting tools or technologies used to convey it. A message is the actual physical product

---

Exhibit 10-1

The Interpersonal Communication Process

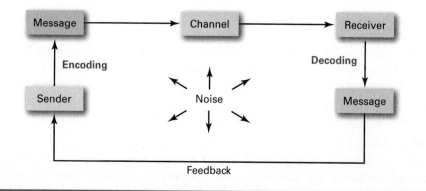

Your instructor chooses to interact with all students via email, rather than hold office hours. How effective do you think email is as the channel of communication in this context?

encoded by the source. It can be a written document, a speech, or even the gestures and facial expressions we make. The message is affected by the symbols used to transfer meaning (words, pictures, numbers, etc.), the content of the message itself, and the decisions that the sender makes in selecting and arranging both the symbols and the content. Noise can distort the communication process in any of these areas.

Channel

The *channel* chosen to communicate the message also has the potential to be affected by noise. Whether it's a face-to-face conversation, an email message, or a company-wide memorandum, distortions can, and do, occur. Managers need to recognize that certain channels are more appropriate for certain messages. (Think back to how Cerner's CEO chose to communicate his frustration with his managers by email and whether that was an appropriate choice.) Obviously, if the office is on fire, a memo to convey the fact is inappropriate! And if something is important, such as an employee's performance appraisal, a manager might want to use multiple channels—perhaps an oral review followed by a written letter summarizing the points. This decreases the potential for distortion. In general, the type of channel chosen will affect the extent to which accurate emotional expression can be communicated. For instance, individuals often make stronger negative statements when using email than they would in holding a face-to-face conversation.[8] Additionally, individuals often give little thought to how their emails might be interpreted, and assume that their intent will be readily apparent to the recipient, even though this is not always the case.[9]

Receiver

The *receiver* is the individual to whom the message is directed. Before the message can be received, however, the symbols in it must be translated into a form that the receiver can understand. This is the *decoding* of the message. Just as the sender was limited by his or her skills, attitudes, knowledge, and socio-cultural system, so is the receiver. And just as the sender must be skillful in writing or speaking, so the receiver must be skillful in reading or listening. A person's knowledge influences his or her ability to receive. Moreover, the receiver's attitudes and socio-cultural background can distort the message. (See *Managing Workforce Diversity—The Communication Styles of Men and Women* on page 316, at the end of the chapter, for more information on how men and women might hear messages differently.)

Communication channels have multiplied with the spread of new technologies such as Wi-Fi, which provides wireless high-speed Internet access. At the more than 170 warehouse-type stores operated by BJ's Wholesale Club, for instance, managers have saved time and money by switching to Wi-Fi for their internal communications. The devices mean that managers like John Barrows can talk to customers, suppliers, or even his manager without having to hike across the aisles to the store's front-office telephone.

Feedback Loop

The final link in the communication process is a *feedback loop*. Feedback returns the message to the sender and provides a check on whether understanding has been achieved. Because feedback can be transmitted along the same types of channels as the original message, it faces the same potential for distortion. Many receivers forget that there is a responsibility involved in communication: to give feedback. For instance, if you sit in a boring lecture, but never discuss with the instructor ways that the delivery could be improved, you have not engaged in communication with your instructor.

When either the sender or the receiver fails to engage in the feedback process, the communication is effectively one-way communication. Two-way communication involves both talking and listening. Many managers communicate badly because they fail to use two-way communication.[10]

Channels for Communicating Interpersonally

Q&A 10.2

Managers have a wide variety of communication channels from which to choose. These include face-to-face, telephone, group meetings, formal presentations, memos, postal (snail) mail, fax machines, employee publications, bulletin boards, other company publications, audio files/DVD video, hot lines, email, computer conferences, voice mail, teleconferences, and videoconferences. All of these communication channels include oral or written symbols, or both. How do you know which to use? Managers can use 12 questions to help them evaluate appropriate communication channels for different circumstances.[11]

1. *Feedback.* How quickly can the receiver respond to the message?
2. *Complexity capacity.* Can the method effectively process complex messages?
3. *Breadth potential.* How many different messages can be transmitted using this method?
4. *Confidentiality.* Can communicators be reasonably sure their messages are received only by those for whom they are intended?
5. *Encoding ease.* Can the sender easily and quickly use this channel?
6. *Decoding ease.* Can the receiver easily and quickly decode messages?
7. *Time–space constraint.* Do senders and receivers need to communicate at the same time and in the same space?
8. *Cost.* How much does it cost to use this method?
9. *Interpersonal warmth.* How well does this method convey interpersonal warmth?
10. *Formality.* Does this method have the needed amount of formality?
11. *Scanability.* Does this method allow the message to be easily browsed or scanned for relevant information?
12. *Time of consumption.* Does the sender or receiver exercise the most control over when the message is dealt with?

Exhibit 10-2 provides a comparison of the various communication methods on these 12 criteria. Which method a manager ultimately chooses should reflect the needs of the sender, the attributes of the message, the attributes of the channel, and the needs of the receiver. For instance, if you need to communicate to an employee the changes being made in her job, face-to-face communication would be a better choice than a memo since you want to be able to address immediately any questions and concerns that she might have. (To find out more about face-to-face communication, see *Self-Assessment—What's My Face-to-Face Communication Style?* on pages 310–312, at the end of the chapter.)

We cannot leave the topic of interpersonal communication without looking at the role of **nonverbal communication**—that is, communication transmitted without words. Some of the most meaningful communications are neither spoken nor written. A loud siren or a red light at an intersection tells you something without words. When an instructor is teaching a class, she does not need words to tell her that her students are bored when their eyes are glazed over or they begin to read the school newspaper in the middle of class. Similarly, when students start putting their papers, notebooks, and books away, the message

nonverbal communication
Communication transmitted without words.

Exhibit 10-2

Comparison of Communication Channels

Channel	Feedback Potential	Complexity Capacity	Breadth Potential	Confiden-tiality	Encoding Ease	Decoding Ease	Time–Space Constraint	Cost	Interpersonal Warmth	Formality	Scan-ability	Consumption Time
							Criteria					
Face-to-face	1	1	1	1	1	1	1	2	1	4	4	S/R
Telephone	1	4	2	2	1	1	3	3	2	4	4	S/R
Group meetings	2	2	2	4	2	2	1	1	2	3	4	S/R
Formal presentations	4	2	2	4	3	2	1	1	3	3	5	Sender
Memos	4	4	2	3	4	3	5	3	5	2	1	Receiver
Postal mail	5	3	3	2	4	3	5	3	4	1	1	Receiver
Fax	3	4	2	4	3	3	5	3	3	3	1	Receiver
Publications	5	4	2	5	5	3	5	2	4	1	1	Receiver
Bulletin boards	4	5	1	5	3	2	2	4	5	3	1	Receiver
Audio files/ DVD videos	4	4	3	5	4	2	3	2	3	3	5	Receiver
Hot lines	2	5	2	2	3	1	4	2	3	3	4	Receiver
Email	3	4	1	2	3	2	4	2	4	3	4	Receiver
Computer conference	1	2	2	4	3	2	3	2	3	3	4	S/R
Voice mail	2	4	2	1	2	1	5	3	2	4	4	Receiver
Teleconference	2	3	2	5	2	2	2	2	3	3	5	S/R
Videoconference	3	3	2	4	2	2	2	1	2	3	5	S/R

Note: Ratings are on a 1–5 scale where 1 = high and 5 = low. Consumption time refers to who controls the reception of communication. S/R means the sender and receiver share control.

Source: P. G. Clampitt, *Communicating for Managerial Effectiveness* (Newbury Park, CA: Sage Publications, 1991), p. 136.

is clear: Class time is about over. The size of a person's office or the clothes he or she wears also convey messages to others. These are all forms of nonverbal communication. The best-known types of nonverbal communication are body language and verbal intonation.

Body language refers to gestures, facial expressions, and other body movements that convey meaning. A person frowning "says" something different from one who is smiling. Hand motions, facial expressions, and other gestures can communicate emotions or temperaments such as aggression, fear, shyness, arrogance, joy, and anger. Knowing the meaning behind someone's body movements and learning how to put forth your best body language can help you personally and professionally.[12] For instance, studies indicate that those who maintain eye contact while speaking are viewed with more credibility than those whose eye contact wanders. People who make eye contact are also deemed more competent than those who do not.

Be aware that what is communicated nonverbally may be quite different from what is communicated verbally. A manager may say it's a good time to discuss a raise, but then keep looking at the clock. This nonverbal signal may indicate that the manager has other things to do right now. Thus, actions can speak louder (and more accurately) than words.

A variety of popular books have been written to help one interpret body language. However, do use some care when interpreting their messages. For instance, while it is often thought that crossing one's arms in front of one's chest shows resistance to a message, it might also mean the person is feeling cold.

Verbal intonation (more appropriately called *paralinguistics*) refers to the emphasis someone gives to words or phrases that convey meaning. To illustrate how intonations can change the meaning of a message, consider the student who asks the instructor a question. The instructor replies, "What do you mean by that?" The student's reaction will vary, depending on the tone of the instructor's response. A soft, smooth vocal tone conveys interest and creates a different meaning from one that is abrasive and puts a strong emphasis on saying the last word. Most of us would view the first intonation as coming from someone sincerely interested in clarifying the student's concern, whereas the second suggests that the person is defensive or aggressive.

The fact that every oral communication also has a nonverbal message cannot be overemphasized. Why? Because the nonverbal component usually carries the greatest impact. "It's not *what* you said, but *how* you said it." People respond to *how* something is said, as well as *what* is said. Managers should remember this as they communicate.

body language
Gestures, facial expressions, and other body movements that convey meaning.

verbal intonation
An emphasis given to words or phrases that conveys meaning.

Q&A 10.3

Barriers to Effective Interpersonal Communication

In addition to the general distortions identified in the communication process, managers face other barriers to effective communication.

Filtering

Filtering is the deliberate manipulation of information to make it appear more favourable to the receiver. For example, when a person tells his or her manager what the manager wants to hear, that individual is filtering information. Does this happen much in organizations? Yes, it does! As information is communicated up through organizational levels, it's condensed and synthesized by senders so those on top don't become overloaded with information. Those doing the condensing filter communications through their personal interests and their perceptions of what is important.

The extent of filtering tends to be a function of the number of vertical levels in the organization and the organizational culture. The more vertical levels there are in an organization, the more opportunities there are for filtering. As organizations become less dependent on strict hierarchical arrangements and instead use more collaborative, cooperative work arrangements, information filtering may become less of a problem. In addition, the ever-increasing use of email to communicate in organizations reduces filtering because communication is more direct as intermediaries are bypassed. Finally, the organizational culture encourages or discourages filtering by the type of behaviour it rewards. The more that organizational rewards emphasize style and appearance, the more managers will be motivated to filter communications in their favour.

filtering
The deliberate manipulation of information to make it appear more favourable to the receiver.

Q&A 10.4

Emotions

How a receiver feels when a message is received influences how he or she interprets it. You will often interpret the same message differently, depending on whether you are happy or upset. Extreme emotions are most likely to hinder effective communication. In such instances, we often disregard our rational and objective thinking processes and substitute emotional judgments. It's best to avoid reacting to a message when you are upset because you are not likely to be thinking clearly.

Information Overload

A marketing manager goes on a week-long sales trip to Spain and does not have access to his email. On his return, he is faced with 1000 messages. It's not possible to fully read and respond to each and every one of those messages without facing **information overload**—when the information we have to work with exceeds our processing capacity. Today's typical employee frequently complains of information overload. Email has added considerably to the number of hours worked per week, according to a recent study by Christina Cavanagh, professor of management communications at the University of Western Ontario's Richard Ivey School of Business.[13] Researchers calculate that 141 billion email messages circulate the globe each day. In 2001, that number was 5.1 billion email messages.[14] One researcher suggests that knowledge workers devote about 28 percent of their days to email.[15] The demands of keeping up with email, phone calls, faxes, meetings, and professional reading create an onslaught of data that is nearly impossible to process and assimilate. What happens when individuals have more information than they can sort and use? They tend to select out, ignore, pass over, or forget information. Or they may put off further processing until the overload situation is over. Regardless, the result is lost information and less effective communication.

information overload
When the information we have to work with exceeds our processing capacity.

Christina Cavanagh
www.christinacavanagh
.com

Q&A 10.5, Q&A 10.6

jargon
Specialized terminology or technical language that members of a group use to communicate among themselves.

Selective Perception

Individuals don't see reality; rather, they interpret what they see and call it "reality." These interpretations are based on an individual's needs, motivations, experience, background, and other personal characteristics. Individuals also project their interests and expectations when they are listening to others. For example, the employment interviewer who believes that young people spend too much time on leisure and social activities will have a hard time believing that young job applicants will work long hours.

Defensiveness

When people feel that they are being threatened, they tend to react in ways that reduce their ability to achieve mutual understanding. That is, they become defensive—engaging in behaviours such as verbally attacking others, making sarcastic remarks, being overly judgmental, and questioning others' motives.[16] When individuals interpret another's message as threatening, they often respond in ways that hinder effective communication.

Language

Words mean different things to different people. Age, education, and cultural background are three of the more obvious variables that influence the language a person uses and the definitions he or she gives to words. News anchor Peter Mansbridge and rap artist Nelly both speak English, but the language each uses is vastly different.

In an organization, employees typically come from diverse backgrounds and have different patterns of speech. Even employees who work for the same organization but in different departments often have different **jargon**—specialized terminology or technical language that members of a group use to communicate among themselves. Keep in mind that while we may speak the same language, our use of that language is far from uniform. Senders tend to assume that the words and phrases they use mean the same to the receiver as they do to them. This, of course, is incorrect and creates communication barriers. Knowing how each of us modifies the language would help minimize those barriers.

Filtering, or shaping information to make it look good to the receiver, might not always be intentional. For John Seral, vice-president and chief information officer of GE Aviation and GE Energy, the problem was that "when the CEO asked how the quarter was looking, he got a different answer depending on whom he asked." Seral solved the problem by building a continuously updated database of the company's most important financial information that gives not just the CEO but also 300 company managers instant access to sales and operating figures on their PCs and BlackBerrys. Instead of dozens of analysts compiling the information, the new system requires only six.

Montreal-based Yellow Pages learned that it could produce better printed telephone directories by studying how online users searched for things—demonstrating that customers and advertisers don't always use the same terms for the same categories, as the following *Management Reflection* shows.

MANAGEMENT REFLECTION

Finding Sushi

Should we look under "sushi" or "restaurants—Japanese" in the phone book when we decide we want raw fish for dinner? Paying attention to how people search for information online can give clearer insights into what organizations need to do to communicate more effectively.[17] Executives at Montreal-based Yellow Pages Group learned this by recording how people searched for telephone listings.

Until recently, sushi restaurants were listed under "restaurants—Japanese" or "restaurants—seafood" in the hard-copy version of the Yellow Pages telephone directory. Online, however, people do not type in those search words to find sushi restaurants. They simply type in "sushi."

In 2007, Yellow Pages executives started reviewing how to more effectively present material in the next edition of their hard-copy phone book so that it makes sense to the end user. They did this by constructing categories that "reflect how people think, speak and search online." "Armouries" and "buttonhole makers" will be dropped from the directory categories, while new categories such as "tapas" and "wine cellars" will be added.

The company has been in the phone book business for 100 years and, with the help of advertisers, has always determined the categories used by people searching the directory. The Internet has allowed Yellow Pages to better address user needs, however. "Now that we're seeing the trends through our online directories—the key words people use—it gives us a good idea of what they are looking for in the print book," says company spokeswoman Annie Marsolais. ∎

Q&A 10.7

National Culture

Communication differences can also arise from the different languages that individuals use to communicate and the national culture they are part of. Interpersonal communication is not conducted the same way around the world. For example, let's compare countries that place a higher value on individualism (such as Canada) with countries where the emphasis is on collectivism (such as Japan).[18]

In Canada, communication patterns tend to be oriented to the individual and clearly spelled out. Canadian managers rely heavily on memos, announcements, position papers, and other formal forms of communication to state their positions on issues. Supervisors may hoard information in an attempt to make themselves look good and as a way of persuading their employees to accept decisions and plans. For their own protection, lower-level employees often engage in this practice as well.

In collectivist countries, such as Japan, there is more interaction for its own sake. The Japanese manager, in contrast to the Canadian manager, engages in extensive verbal consultation with subordinates over an issue first, and draws up a formal document later to outline the agreement that was made. The Japanese value decisions by consensus, and open communication is an inherent part of the work setting. Also, face-to-face communication is encouraged.

Cultural differences can affect the way a manager chooses to communicate. These differences undoubtedly can be a barrier to effective communication if not recognized and taken into consideration.

Cultural differences also affect body language and such things as how closely people stand to each other. In China, for instance, it is not unusual for people to push in queues to get ahead, and even step in front of someone who has left too much space in a lineup. In North America, there is an expectation that people will keep a greater distance between one another and stay in their position in a lineup.

Overcoming the Barriers

On average, an individual must hear new information seven times before he or she truly understands.[19] This might explain why reading your textbook just once may not be enough. In light of this fact and the barriers to communication, what can we do to overcome these barriers? The following suggestions should help make your interpersonal communication more effective.

Use Feedback

Many communication problems can be directly attributed to misunderstanding and inaccuracies. These problems are less likely to occur if individuals use the feedback loop in the communication process, either verbally or nonverbally.

If a speaker asks a receiver, "Did you understand what I said?" the response represents feedback. Good feedback should include more than yes-and-no answers. The speaker can ask a set of questions about a message to determine whether or not the message was received and understood as intended. Better yet, the speaker can ask the receiver to restate the message in his or her own words. If the speaker hears what was intended, understanding and accuracy should improve. Feedback includes subtler methods than directly asking questions or having the receiver summarize the message. General comments can give the speaker a sense of the receiver's reaction to a message. (To learn more about giving feedback, see *Self-Assessment—How Good Am I at Giving Performance Feedback?* on pages 352–353, in Chapter 11).

Of course, feedback does not have to be conveyed in words. Actions *can* speak louder than words. A sales manager sends an email to his or her staff describing a new monthly sales report that all sales representatives will need to complete. If some of them don't turn in the new report, the sales manager has received feedback. This feedback suggests that the sales manager needs to clarify further the initial communication. Similarly, when you are talking to people, you watch their eyes and look for other nonverbal clues to tell whether they are getting your message or not.

Simplify Language

Because language can be a barrier, managers should choose words and structure their messages in ways that will make those messages clear and understandable to the receiver. Remember, effective communication is achieved when a message is both received and *understood*. Understanding is improved by simplifying the language used in relation to the audience intended. This means, for example, that a hospital administrator should always try to communicate in clear, easily understood terms. The language used in messages to the emergency room staff should be purposefully different from that used with office employees. Jargon can facilitate understanding when it's used within a group of those who know what it means, but it can cause many problems when used outside that group.

Listen Actively

Do you know the difference between hearing and listening? When someone talks, we hear. But too often we don't listen. Listening is an active search for meaning, whereas hearing is passive. In listening, two people are engaged in thinking: the sender *and* the receiver.

Many of us are poor listeners. Why? Because it's difficult, and it's usually more satisfying to be on the offensive. Listening, in fact, is often more tiring than talking. It demands intellectual effort. Unlike hearing, **active listening**, which is listening for full meaning without making premature judgments or interpretations, demands total concentration. The average person normally speaks at a rate of about 125 to 200 words per minute. However, the average listener can comprehend up to 400 words per minute.[20] The difference obviously leaves lots of idle time for the brain and opportunities for the mind to wander.

active listening
Listening for full meaning without making premature judgments or interpretations.

Active listening is enhanced by developing empathy with the sender—that is, by placing yourself in the sender's position. Because senders differ in attitudes, interests, needs, and expectations, empathy makes it easier to understand the actual content of a message. An empathetic listener reserves judgment on the message's content and carefully listens to what is being said. The goal is to improve your ability to receive the full meaning of a

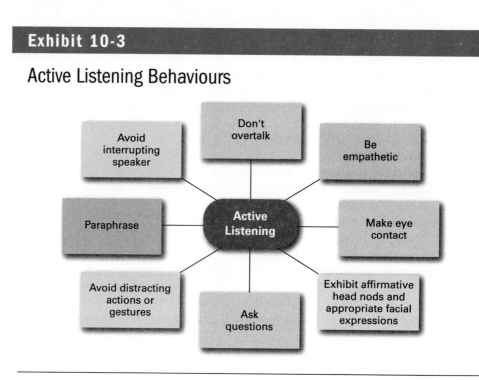

Exhibit 10-3

Active Listening Behaviours

Source: Based on P. L. Hunsaker, *Training in Management Skills* (Upper Saddle River, NJ: Prentice Hall, 2001).

PRISM 11

communication without having it distorted by premature judgments or interpretations. Other specific behaviours that active listeners demonstrate are listed in Exhibit 10-3. (To learn more about active listening, see *Developing Your Interpersonal Skills—Active Listening* on page 315, at the end of the chapter.)

Constrain Emotions

It would be naive to assume that managers always communicate in a rational manner. We know that emotions can severely cloud and distort the transference of meaning. A manager who is emotionally upset over an issue is more likely to misconstrue incoming messages and fail to communicate clearly and accurately. What can the manager do? The simplest answer is to refrain from communicating until he or she has regained composure.

Watch Nonverbal Cues

If actions speak louder than words, then it's important to watch your actions to make sure they align with and reinforce the words that go along with them. The effective communicator watches his or her nonverbal cues to ensure that they convey the desired message.

Organizational Communication

3. How does communication flow in organizations?

An understanding of managerial communication is not possible without looking at the fundamentals of organizational communication. In this section, we look at several important aspects of organizational communication, including formal vs. informal communication, the direction of communication flow, and organizational communication networks.

Formal vs. Informal Communication

formal communication
Communication that follows the official chain of command or is part of the communication required to do one's job.

Communication within an organization is often described as formal or informal. **Formal communication** refers to communication that follows the official chain of command or is part of the communication required to do one's job. For example, when a manager asks an employee to complete a task, he or she is communicating formally. So is the employee who brings a problem to the attention of his or her manager. Any communication that takes place within prescribed organizational work arrangements would be classified as formal.

Informal communication is communication that is not defined by the organization's structural hierarchy. When employees talk with each other in the lunch room, as they pass in hallways, or as they are working out at the company exercise facility, that is informal communication. Employees form friendships and communicate with each other. The informal communication system fulfills two purposes in organizations: (1) It permits employees to satisfy their need for social interaction, and (2) it can improve an organization's performance by creating alternative, and frequently faster and more efficient, channels of communication.

informal communication
Communication that is not defined by the organization's structural hierarchy.

Diversity in Action 1

Direction of Communication Flow

Organizational communication can flow downward, upward, laterally, or diagonally. Let's look at each.

Downward Communication

Every morning, and often several times a day, managers at UPS package delivery facilities gather employees for mandatory meetings that last precisely three minutes. During those 180 seconds, managers relay company announcements and go over local information like traffic conditions or customer complaints. Then, each meeting ends with a safety tip. The three-minute meetings have proved so successful that many of the company's office employees are using the idea.[21]

Any communication that flows downward from managers to employees is **downward communication**. Downward communication is used to inform, direct, coordinate, and evaluate employees. When managers assign goals to their employees, they are using downward communication. Managers are also using downward communication by providing employees with job descriptions, informing them of organizational policies and procedures, pointing out problems that need attention, or evaluating and giving feedback on their performance. Downward communication can take place through any of the communication methods we described earlier. Managers can improve the quality of the feedback they give to employees if they follow the advice given in *Tips for Managers—Suggestions for Giving Feedback*

downward communication
Communication that flows downward from managers to employees.

upward communication
Communication that flows upward from employees to managers.

lateral communication
Communication that takes place among employees on the same organizational level.

Upward Communication

Any communication that flows upward from employees to managers is **upward communication**. Managers rely on their employees for information. Reports are given to managers to inform them of progress toward goals and any current problems. It keeps managers aware of how employees feel about their jobs, their co-workers, and the organization in general. Managers also rely on upward communication for ideas on how things can be improved. Some examples of upward communication include performance reports prepared by employees, suggestion boxes, employee attitude surveys, grievance procedures, manager–employee discussions, and informal group sessions in which employees have the opportunity to identify and discuss problems with their manager or even representatives of top management.

The extent of upward communication depends on the organizational culture. If managers have created a climate of trust and respect and use participative decision making or empowerment, there will be considerable upward communication as employees provide input to decisions. For instance, Ernst & Young encourages employees to evaluate the principals, partners, and directors on how well they create a positive work climate. A partner in the Montreal office was surprised to learn that people in her office found her a poor role model, and she took care to explain her actions more as a result.[22] In a highly structured and authoritarian environment, upward communication still takes place, but is limited in both style and content.

Lateral Communication

Communication that takes place among employees on the same organizational level is called **lateral communication**. In today's

TIPS FOR MANAGERS

Suggestions for Giving Feedback

Managers can use the following tips to give more effective feedback:

- "Relate feedback to existing **performance goals and clear expectations**."

- "Give **specific feedback** tied to observable behaviour or measurable results."

- "Channel feedback toward **key result areas**."

- "Give feedback **as soon as possible**."

- "Give positive **feedback for improvement**, not just final results."

- "**Focus feedback on performance**, not personalities."

- "Base feedback on **accurate and credible information**."

Source: R. Kreitner and A. Kinicki, *Organizational Behavior*, 6th ed. (New York: McGraw-Hill/Irwin, 2004), p. 335. Reprinted by permission of McGraw-Hill Education.

often chaotic and rapidly changing environment, horizontal communication is frequently needed to save time and facilitate coordination. Cross-functional teams, for instance, rely heavily on this form of communication. However, it can create conflicts if employees don't keep their managers informed about decisions they have made or actions they have taken.

Diagonal Communication

diagonal communication
Communication that cuts across both work areas and organizational levels.

Communication that cuts across both work areas *and* organizational levels is **diagonal communication**. When an analyst in the credit department communicates directly with a regional marketing manager—note the different department and different organizational level—about a customer problem, that is diagonal communication. In the interest of efficiency and speed, diagonal communication can be beneficial. Email facilitates diagonal communication. In many organizations, any employee can communicate by email with any other employee, regardless of organizational work area or level. However, just as with lateral communication, diagonal communication has the potential to create problems if employees don't keep their managers informed.

Organizational Communication Networks

communication networks
The variety of patterns of vertical and horizontal flows of organizational communication.

The vertical and horizontal flows of organizational communication can be combined into a variety of patterns called **communication networks**. Exhibit 10-4 illustrates three common communication networks.

Types of Communication Networks

In the *chain* network, communication flows according to the formal chain of command, both downward and upward. The *wheel* network represents communication flowing between a clearly identifiable and strong leader and others in a work group or team. The leader serves as the hub through whom all communication passes. Finally, in the *all-channel* network, communication flows freely among all members of a work team.

As a manager, which network should you use? The answer depends on your goal. Exhibit 10-4 also summarizes the effectiveness of the various networks according to four criteria: speed, accuracy, the probability that a leader will emerge, and the importance of member satisfaction. One observation is immediately apparent: No single network is best

Exhibit 10-4

Three Common Organizational Communication Networks and How They Rate on Effectiveness Criteria

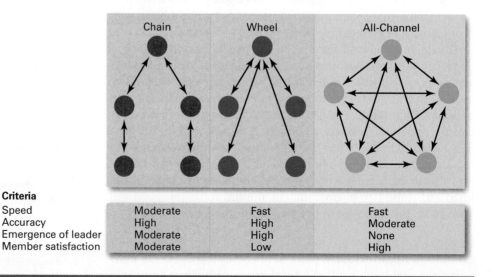

Criteria	Chain	Wheel	All-Channel
Speed	Moderate	Fast	Fast
Accuracy	High	High	Moderate
Emergence of leader	Moderate	High	None
Member satisfaction	Moderate	Low	High

It looks like graffiti, but it's really informal communication at work. Dozens of whiteboards dot the hallways and common areas of Google's Mountain View headquarters in California. Some of the boards are used by product teams swapping ideas, while the two largest are filled with cartoons and jokes. "It's collaborative art," says the company's director of communications and a frequent contributor. "When new hires see the boards, they get a quick, comprehensive snapshot of our personality."

for all situations. If you are concerned with high member satisfaction, the all-channel network is best; if having a strong and identifiable leader is important, the wheel facilitates this; and if accuracy is most important, the chain and wheel networks work best.

The Grapevine   We cannot leave our discussion of communication networks without discussing the **grapevine**—the informal organizational communication network. The grapevine is active in almost every organization. Is it an important source of information? You bet! One survey reported that 75 percent of employees hear about matters first through rumours on the grapevine.[23]

What are the implications for managers? Certainly, the grapevine is an important part of any group or organization communication network and well worth understanding.[24] It identifies for managers those bewildering issues that employees consider important and anxiety producing. It acts as both a filter and a feedback mechanism, picking up on the issues employees consider relevant. More importantly, from a managerial point of view, it *is* possible to analyze what is happening on the grapevine—what information is being passed, how information seems to flow along the grapevine, and what individuals seem to be key conduits of information on the grapevine. By being aware of the grapevine's flow and patterns, managers can stay on top of issues that concern employees, and, in turn, can use the grapevine to disseminate important information. Since the grapevine cannot be eliminated, managers should "manage" it as an important information network.

Rumours that flow along the grapevine also can never be eliminated entirely. Managers can minimize the negative consequences of rumours by limiting their range and impact. How? By communicating openly, fully, and honestly with employees, particularly in situations where employees may not like proposed or actual managerial decisions or actions. Open and honest communication with employees can impact the organization in various ways. A study by Watson Wyatt Worldwide concluded that effective communication "connects employees to the business, reinforces the organization's vision, fosters process improvement, facilitates change, and drives business results by changing employee behavior." For those companies that communicated effectively, total returns to shareholders were 57 percent higher over a five-year period than for companies with less effective communication. And the study also showed that companies that were highly effective communicators were 20 percent more likely to report lower turnover rates.[25]

grapevine
The informal organizational communication network.

Q&A 10.8

Understanding Information Technology

▶ ▶ ▶ Social networking websites such as Facebook and LinkedIn have become resources for employers seeking job candidates.[26] Companies large and small are using these resources to do research, form relationships, and fill positions. More than 350 companies broadcast their job listings to more than 10 million registered users of LinkedIn. A manager looking to fill a key position can use LinkedIn to view posted résumés, read an individual's postings, and can even "check out a competitor's site for potential candidates."

Brian Drum, president of executive search firm Drum Associates, uses social networking sites such as MySpace to see if there is any information about a job candidate's character that might suggest an inability to perform reliably. "Sometimes all we find is meaningless chitchat," says Drum, "but once in a while we'll turn up something useful, like an unflattering picture or a piece of information that really shows what the person is made of."

Some businesses are not just using social networking sites for recruiting, however. They have also added their own company profiles at such sites, where employees can interact with each other. They realize that a number of younger employees are using social networking sites, so they might as well encourage productive use of the medium.

Think About It

What are the benefits to employers of using a source like Facebook to screen job candidates? Should employers consider these postings just private musings and ignore them? Are there advantages to organizations in allowing employees to use social networking sites? If yes, do they outweigh the disadvantages?

4. How does information technology affect organizations?

Technology is changing the way we live and work. Take the following three examples: In a number of countries, employees, managers, housewives, and teens use wireless interactive web phones to send email, surf the web, swap photos, and play computer games. Service technicians at Ajax, Ontario-based Pitney Bowes Canada started using instant messaging rather than pagers, because "it's cheaper and it's two-way."[27] The company knows when messages are received. IBM's 320 000 employees regularly use instant messaging **Q&A 10.9** software for communicating and for workplace collaboration.[28]

The world of communication is not what it used to be. Managers are challenged to keep their organizations functioning smoothly while continually improving work operations *and* staying competitive even though both the organization and the environment are changing rapidly. Although changing technology has been a significant source of the environmental uncertainty facing organizations, these same technological advances have enabled managers to coordinate the work efforts of employees in ways that can lead to increased efficiency and effectiveness. Information technology now touches every aspect of almost every company's business. The implications for the ways individuals communicate are profound. (The *Video Case Incident—Information Technology: Massachusetts General Hospital* on page 361 shows how technology has affected the way health care is provided at a hospital.)

How Information Technology Affects Communication

Information technology has radically changed the way organizational members communicate. For example, it has

- significantly improved a manager's ability to monitor individual or team performance
- allowed employees to have more complete information to make faster decisions
- provided employees with more opportunities to collaborate and share information
- made it possible for employees to be fully accessible, any time, regardless of where they are

Information technology also creates opportunities for organizations. For instance, colleges and universities now have the capability of offering online courses and degrees. This could, over time, decrease the number of students taught in face-to-face contexts and increase the overall number of students because of the accessibility of online courses.

Three developments in information technology seem to be having the most significant impact on managerial communication today: email, instant messaging, and social networking websites.

Email

Email is a quick and convenient way for organizational members to share information and communicate. Many people complain about email overload, however, and it is not always used effectively. A recent study found that opening nasty messages from your boss can harm your health over time.[29] While negative email messages from anyone had health consequences, those from superiors showed the most significant increase in a person's blood pressure.

Q&A 10.10

Have you ever emailed or instant-messaged someone who was just in the next office? Does the reliance on technology make it harder or easier to communicate effectively with people?

Individuals should remember that email can be permanent, which means that a message sent in anger could come back to hurt the sender later on. Email is also not necessarily private communication, and organizations often take the position that they have the right to read your email.

To construct more effective emails, you might want to consider the following tips for writing and sending email offered by Professor Christina Cavanagh of the University of Western Ontario's Richard Ivey School of Business:[30]

- Don't send emails without a subject line.
- Be careful in your use of emoticons and acronyms for business communication.
- Write your message clearly and briefly.
- Copy emails to others only if they really need the information.
- Sleep on angry emails before sending to be sure you are sending the right message.

Instant Messaging

Instant messaging (IM) first became popular among teens and preteens who wanted to communicate online immediately with their friends. Now, it has moved to the workplace. According to the latest research, 11.4 billion IMs were sent worldwide each day in 2004, and this number is expected to increase to more than 45.8 billion by 2008.[31] However, there are a couple of drawbacks to IM. Unlike email, it requires users to be logged on to the organization's computer network in order to be able to communicate with one another. This leaves the network open to security breaches, and some organizations have limited which employees can use IM in the workplace as a result.

Social Networking Websites

Social networking websites such as Facebook, MySpace, and LinkedIn have drawn millions of subscribers who voluntarily post information about themselves that can be viewed by any other subscriber, unless the user deliberately sets privacy restrictions.

Employers and search firms are starting to check the postings of clients, and some even monitor employees to see if there is anything questionable in their character. Despite the public's concern that the government is not doing enough to protect individual privacy, many people feel free to post information (flattering and unflattering) about themselves online that is readily accessible to anyone.

Some employers post job offerings on sites such as Facebook; others post recruitment videos on sites such as YouTube. In a recent twist, some employers have done virtual interviews through Second Life, the online virtual community.[32] Job seekers create an "avatar," a computer-generated image that represents themselves, and then communicate with prospective employers through instant messaging. A recent virtual job fair on Second Life included employers Hewlett-Packard, Microsoft, Verizon, and Sodexho Alliance SA, a food and facilities-management services company.

Individuals who use websites such as Facebook may want to consider the lack of privacy such sites afford when it comes to employers and evaluations. Individuals may forget that once it's written on the web, it's difficult to erase. So while it might seem like a good idea to post photos of drunken partying, this might not leave a good impression on potential employers. As Deanna MacDougal, a partner at Toronto-based IQ Partners, notes, "If your potential employer Googles a name and sees your social life, that can be good but it can also hinder you. Even with password-protected sites, I think the youth need to be a little bit

Technology need not always reduce face-to-face communication. To make contact easier between employees at its call centre and in its information systems department, ASB, a New Zealand bank, adopted an open layout encompassing five areas on three different floors. There is a landscaped park area in the centre, a café, a minigolf green, a TV room, and a barbecue area, all of which help bring people together. Since moving into the new design, bank managers have noted that the volume of interdepartmental emails has dropped, indicating that people are communicating in person more.

more careful." Geoff Bagg, president of Toronto-based The Bagg Group, adds: "I don't think you can segment your life and say, 'This is my private life and this is my work life.' They're all intertwined."[33]

How Information Technology Affects Organizations

Employees—working in teams or as individuals—need information to make decisions and do their work. After describing the communications capabilities managers have at their disposal, it's clear that technology *can* significantly affect the way that organizational members communicate, share information, and do their work. The following *Management Reflection* explores how one Canadian firm reduced cost and improved service for customers using Voice over Internet Protocol (VoIP) technology.

MANAGEMENT REFLECTION
► Focus on Innovation

VoIP Improves Communication and Customer Service

Can saving money increase service?   Johnson, a St John's, Newfoundland-based national insurance company, founded in 1880, recently introduced the latest in long-distance telephone technology: Voice over Internet Protocol (VoIP).[34] The technology, purchased from Cisco Systems, treats long-distance calls as if they were local ones. With appropriate hardware, subscribers can use the same cable that connects their computer to the Internet to connect their telephone to make calls.

It is not just a cost-saving measure, though. C. C. Huang, Johnson's president and CEO, says, "We really believe in Voice over IP [Internet Protocol]. It's helping us provide better customer service, improve our productivity—and outperform the industry." The IP infrastructure allows voice, video, and data to be transferred on a single network.

When customers call in, the network can direct calls to staff members who have the appropriate skills and are available to handle the call. The network is also able to link a caller's phone number to his or her electronic file, making it immediately available to the employee handling the phone call. Employees are able to see their voice mail, email, and faxes on their telephone screens. Huang is enthusiastic about the system because, "We're actually spending less money—and doing more than we have before." ■

Communication and the exchange of information among organizational members are no longer constrained by geography or time. Collaborative work efforts among widely dispersed individuals and teams, information sharing, and the integration of decisions and work throughout an entire organization have the potential to increase organizational efficiency and effectiveness. While the economic benefits of information technology are obvious, managers must not forget to address the psychological drawbacks.[35] For instance, what is the psychological cost of an employee always being accessible? Will there be increased pressure for employees to "check in" even during their off hours? How important is it for employees to separate their work lives and their personal lives? While there are no easy answers to these questions, these are issues that managers will have to face.

The widepsread use of voice mail and email at work has led to some ethical concerns as well. These forms of communication are not necessarily private, because employers have access to them. The federal Privacy Act (which protects the privacy of individuals and provides individuals with a right to access personal information about themselves) and the Access to Information Act (which allows individuals to access government information) apply to all federal government departments, most federal agencies, and some federal Crown corporations. However, many private sector employees are not covered by privacy legislation. Only Quebec's privacy act applies to the entire private sector. Managers need to clearly convey to employees the extent to which their communications will be monitored, and policies on such things as personal Internet and email use.

Current Issues in Communication in Organizations

Managing Communication in an Internet World

At eBay's headquarters, CEO Meg Whitman banned wireless devices such as BlackBerrys from Monday staff meetings. She said, "There was a little grumbling from the top execs who regularly attend the meetings. [However], personal interaction is much more important than instantly answering e-mails."[36]

Managers are learning, the hard way sometimes, that all this new technology has created special communication challenges. The two main ones are (1) legal and security issues and (2) lack of personal interaction.

Chevron paid $2.2 million (US) to settle a sexual-harassment lawsuit stemming from inappropriate jokes being sent by employees over company email.[37] UK firm Norwich Union had to pay £450 000 in an out-of-court settlement after an employee sent an email stating that their competitor Western Provident Association was in financial difficulties.[38]

Although email is a quick and easy way to communicate, managers need to be aware of potential legal problems from inappropriate email usage. Electronic information is potentially admissible in court. For instance, during the Enron trial, prosecutors entered into evidence emails and other documents they say showed that the defendants defrauded investors. Says one expert, "Today, e-mail and instant messaging are the electronic equivalent of DNA evidence."[39] But email's legal problems are not the only issue facing managers. Security concerns are another. Managers need to ensure that confidential information is kept confidential. Employee emails and blogs should not communicate—inadvertently or purposely—proprietary information. Corporate computer and email systems should be protected against hackers and spam. These are serious issues that managers and organizations must address if the benefits that communication technology offers are to be realized.

Another communication challenge posed by the Internet age we live and work in is the lack of personal interaction. Even when two people are communicating face-to-face, understanding is not always achieved. However, when communication takes place in a virtual environment, it can be *really* hard to achieve understanding and collaborate on getting work done. Some companies have gone so far as to ban email on certain days of the week. Others have simply encouraged employees to collaborate more in person. Yet, there are situa-

5. What are some of the major communication issues facing today's organizations?

tions and times when personal interaction is not physically possible—for example, when your colleagues work across the continent or even across the globe. In those instances, real-time collaboration software (such as private workplace wikis, blogs, instant messengers, and other types of groupware) may be a better communication choice than sending an email and waiting for a response.[40]

Managing the Organization's Knowledge Resources

Kara Johnson is a materials expert at product design firm IDEO. To make finding the right materials easier, she built a master library of samples linked to a database that explains their properties and manufacturing processes.[41] What Johnson did was manage knowledge and make it easier for others at IDEO to "learn" and benefit from her knowledge. That is what today's managers need to do with the organization's knowledge resources— make it easy for employees to communicate and share their knowledge so they can learn from each other ways to do their jobs more effectively and efficiently. One way organizations can do this is to create online information databases that employees can access. This is one example of how managers can use communication tools to manage this valuable organizational resource called knowledge.

In addition to online information databases for sharing knowledge, some knowledge management experts suggest that organizations create **communities of practice**, which are "groups of people who share a concern, a set of problems, or a passion about a topic, and who deepen their knowledge and expertise in that area by interacting on an ongoing basis."[42] The keys to this concept are that the group must actually meet in some fashion on a regular basis and use its information exchanges to improve in some way. For example, repair technicians at Xerox tell "war stories" to communicate their experiences and to help others solve difficult problems with repairing machines.[43] This is not to say that communities of practice don't face challenges. They do. For instance, in large global organizations, keeping communities of practice going takes additional effort. To make these communities of practice work, it's important to maintain strong human interactions through communication. Interactive websites, email, and videoconferencing are essential communication tools. In addition, these groups face the same communication problems that individuals face—filtering, emotions, defensiveness, information overload, and so forth. However, groups can resolve these issues by focusing on the same suggestions we discussed earlier: using feedback, simplifying language, listening actively, constraining emotions, and watching nonverbal cues.

Communicating Appropriately and Effectively with Customers

You have been a customer many times; in fact, you probably find yourself in a customer service encounter several times a day. So what does this have to do with communication? As it turns out, a lot! *What* communication takes place and *how* it takes place can have a significant impact on a customer's satisfaction with the service and the likelihood of being a repeat customer. Managers in service organizations need to make sure that employees who interact with customers are communicating appropriately and effectively with those customers. How? By first recognizing the three components in any service delivery process: the customer, the service organization, and the individual service provider.[44] Each plays a role in whether or not communication is working. Obviously, managers don't have a lot of control over what or how the customer communicates, but they can influence the other two.

An organization with a strong service culture already values taking care of customers— finding out what their needs are, meeting those needs, and following up to make sure that their needs were met satisfactorily. Each of these activities involves communication, whether face-to-face, by phone or email, or through other channels. In addition, communication is part of the specific customer service strategies the organization pursues. One strategy that

IDEO
www.ideo.com

communities of practice
Groups of people who share a concern, a set of problems, or a passion about a topic, and who deepen their knowledge and expertise in that area by interacting on an ongoing basis.

many service organizations use is personalization. For instance, at Ritz-Carlton Hotels, customers are provided with more than a clean bed and room. Customers who have stayed at a location previously and indicated that certain items are important to them—such as extra pillows, hot chocolate, or a certain brand of shampoo—will find those items waiting in their room at arrival. The hotel's database allows service to be personalized to customers' expectations. In addition, all employees are asked to communicate information related to service provision. For instance, if a room attendant overhears guests talking about celebrating an anniversary, he or she is supposed to relay the information so something special can be done.[45] Communication plays an important role in the hotel's customer personalization strategy.

Communication also is important to the individual service provider or contact employee. The quality of the interpersonal interaction between the customer and that contact employee does influence customer satisfaction.[46] That is especially true when the service encounter is not up to expectations. People on the front line involved with those "critical service encounters" are often the first to hear about or notice service failures or breakdowns. They must decide *how* and *what* to communicate during these instances. Their ability to listen actively and communicate appropriately with the customer goes a long way in whether or not the situation is resolved to the customer's satisfaction or spirals out of control. Another important communication concern for the individual service provider is making sure that he or she has the information needed to deal with customers efficiently and effectively. If the service provider does not personally have the information, there should be some way to get the information easily and promptly.[47] Hudson's Bay Company uses online customer surveys to learn about customers' store experiences, as the following *Management Reflection* shows.

MANAGEMENT REFLECTION

Mystery Shoppers Dropped for Online Surveys

What is the best way to get feedback about customer service?   Customers of The Bay, Zellers, and Home Outfitters can give feedback about their store experience by filling out an online survey at the Toronto-based Hudson's Bay Company's website.[48] Managers have learned, for instance, that training was lacking in a specific department at a specific store, after a customer described an experience where the clerk could not use the cash register properly or remove anti-theft tags from clothing.

The website for customer feedback is listed on sales receipts, encouraging customers who have had either negative or positive experiences to let the company know. Customers have submitted gripes about a number of issues at Hudson's Bay's stores, including "not enough sale items in stock…[and] no salesperson in sight when you really need one."

In the past, many retail outlets, including The Bay, have hired mystery shoppers to gather information about customer service. Companies are now questioning whether that is the best way to get adequate feedback, however. David Zinman, vice-president of corporate operations at Burnaby, BC-based Best Buy Canada, which owns Richmond, BC-based Future Shop, notes that "You get better-quality information from customers that are actually in there shopping and that aren't on your payroll."

The Texas-based Mystery Shopping Providers Association worries that stores are not getting the best feedback by relying on online surveys. Only about 10 percent of customers fill out the surveys, even though doing so can make them eligible to win 1 million HBC Rewards points. It is not obvious whether stores should continue to use online surveys, or use a mix of mystery shoppers and surveys. However, as we have suggested in this chapter, knowing how to communicate effectively also means knowing how to collect the best data for reliable feedback. ■

Understanding the Importance of "Politically Correct" Communication

Sears tells its employees to use phrases such as "person with a disability" instead of "disabled person" when writing or speaking about people with disabilities. It also suggests that when talking with a customer in a wheelchair for more than a few minutes, employees place themselves at the customer's eye level by sitting down to make a more comfortable atmosphere for everyone.[49] These suggestions, provided in an employee brochure that discusses assisting customers with disabilities, reflect the importance of politically correct communication. How you communicate with someone who is not like you, what terms you use in addressing a customer, or what words you use to describe a colleague who is wheelchair-bound can mean the difference between losing a client, an employee, a lawsuit, a harassment claim, or a job.[50]

Most of us are acutely aware of how our vocabulary has been modified to reflect political correctness. For instance, most of us refrain from using words like *handicapped, blind,* and *elderly,* and use instead terms like *physically challenged, visually impaired,* or *senior.* We must be sensitive to others' feelings. Certain words can and do stereotype, intimidate, and insult individuals. With an increasingly diverse workforce, we must be sensitive to how words might offend others. Although it's complicating our vocabulary and making it more difficult for people to communicate, it is something managers cannot ignore.

Words are the primary means by which people communicate. When we eliminate words from use because they are politically incorrect, we reduce our options for conveying messages in the clearest and most accurate form. For the most part, the larger the vocabulary used by a sender and a receiver, the greater the opportunity to accurately transmit messages. By removing certain words from our vocabulary, we make it harder to communicate accurately. When we further replace these words with new ones whose meanings are less well understood, we have reduced the likelihood that our messages will be received as we had intended them.

We must be sensitive to how our choice of words might offend or alienate others. But we need to acknowledge that politically correct language can restrict communication clarity. Nothing suggests that this increased communication ambiguity is likely to be reduced any time soon. This is just another communication challenge for managers.

SUMMARY AND IMPLICATIONS

1. What are the functions of communication? Communication serves four major functions: control, motivation, emotional expression, and information. In the control function, communication sets out the guidelines for behaviour. Communication motivates by clarifying to employees what is to be done, how well they are doing, and what can be done to improve performance if it's not up to par. Communication provides an opportunity to express feelings and also fulfills social needs. Finally, communication also provides the information to get things done in organizations.

▶ ▶ ▶ Facebook has allowed employers to learn more about potential employees, and some organizations have set up Facebook sites for employees to communicate with each other.

2. Why does communication break down? When a message passes between a sender and a receiver, it needs to be converted into symbols (called *encoding*) and passed to the receiver by some channel. The receiver translates (decodes) the sender's message. At any point in this process, communication can become distorted through noise. A variety of other factors can also affect whether the message is interpreted correctly, including the degree of filtering, the sender's or receiver's emotional state, and whether too much information is being sent (information overload).

▶ ▶ ▶ The value of face-to-face communication is that one receives more information through body language. The rise of online communication, through such tools as email as well as social networking sites such as Facebook, means that communication is often more ambiguous. It also becomes harder to know whether too much information has been revealed because feedback mechanisms may not be as direct.

3. How does communication flow in organizations? Communication can be of the formal or informal variety. Formal communication follows the official chain of command or is part of the communication required to do one's job. Communication can flow downward, upward, laterally to those at the same organizational level, or diagonally, which means that the communication cuts across both work areas and organizational levels. Communication can also flow through networks and through the grapevine.

4. How does information technology affect organizations? Information technology allows managers and employees more access to each other and to customers and clients. It provides more opportunities for monitoring, as well as a greater ability to share information. Information technology also increases flexibility and responsiveness.

▶ ▶ ▶ Even though some workplaces have banned Facebook in the workplace, some employers have found ways to use Facebook as a source of information on job candidates and employees, as well as a business communication tool. Other organizations are exploring how to implement Facebook, knowing that their younger employees are widely using the social networking site already.

5. What are some of the major communication issues facing today's organizations? The major issues covered in this chapter are managing in an Internet world, managing the organization's knowledge resources, communicating effectively and appropriately with customers, and understanding the importance of "politically correct" communication. Organizations today must figure out ways to help employees communicate with one another and share their knowledge to increase the effectiveness of the organization. Organizations have to consider the best ways to communicate with customers so that they can find out what their needs are, meet those needs, and follow up to make sure that their needs were met satisfactorily. Finally, dealing with the challenge of politically correct language means being sensitive to how words might offend others while realizing that sometimes clarity is lost.

Management @ Work

1. What are the four functions of communication?

2. What steps can you take to make interpersonal communication more effective?

3. What can managers do to help them determine which communication channel to use in a given circumstance?

4. Identify four types of channels and when they might be best used.

5. Describe the barriers to effective interpersonal communication. How can they be overcome?

6. Which do you think is more important for a manager: speaking accurately or listening actively? Why?

7. How has information technology enhanced a manager's communication effectiveness?

8. What are the two main challenges of communicating in an Internet world?

LINKING CONCEPTS TO PRACTICE

1. Describe why effective communication is not synonymous with agreement between the communicating parties.

2. Which do you think is more important for a manager: speaking accurately or listening actively? Why?

3. "Ineffective communication is the fault of the sender." Do you agree or disagree with this statement? Explain your position.

4. How might a manager use the grapevine to his or her advantage? Support your response.

5. Is information technology helping managers to be more effective and efficient? Explain your position.

SELF-ASSESSMENT

What's My Face-to-Face Communication Style?

For each of the following statements, circle the level of agreement or disagreement that you personally feel:[51]

1 = Strongly Disagree
3 = Neither Agree nor Disagree
5 = Strongly Agree

1. I am comfortable with all varieties of people.	1 2 3 4 5
2. I laugh easily.	1 2 3 4 5
3. I readily express admiration for others.	1 2 3 4 5
4. What I say usually leaves an impression on people.	1 2 3 4 5
5. I leave people with an impression of me which they definitely tend to remember.	1 2 3 4 5
6. To be friendly, I habitually acknowledge verbally others' contributions.	1 2 3 4 5
7. I have some nervous mannerisms in my speech.	1 2 3 4 5
8. I am a very relaxed communicator.	1 2 3 4 5
9. When I disagree with somebody, I am very quick to challenge them.	1 2 3 4 5
10. I can always repeat back to a person exactly what was meant.	1 2 3 4 5

11. The sound of my voice is very easy to recognize.   1 2 3 4 5

12. I leave a definite impression on people.   1 2 3 4 5

13. The rhythm or flow of my speech is sometimes affected by nervousness.   1 2 3 4 5

14. Under pressure I come across as a relaxed speaker.   1 2 3 4 5

15. My eyes reflect exactly what I am feeling when I communicate.   1 2 3 4 5

16. I dramatize a lot.   1 2 3 4 5

17. Usually, I deliberately react in such a way that people know that I am listening to them.   1 2 3 4 5

18. Usually, I do not tell people much about myself until I get to know them well.   1 2 3 4 5

19. Regularly, I tell jokes, anecdotes, and stories when I communicate.   1 2 3 4 5

20. I tend to constantly gesture when I communicate.   1 2 3 4 5

21. I am an extremely open communicator.   1 2 3 4 5

22. I am vocally a loud communicator.   1 2 3 4 5

23. In arguments I insist upon very precise definitions.   1 2 3 4 5

24. In most social situations I generally speak very frequently.   1 2 3 4 5

25. I like to be strictly accurate when I communicate.   1 2 3 4 5

26. Because I have a loud voice, I can easily break into a conversation.   1 2 3 4 5

27. Often I physically and vocally act out when I want to communicate.   1 2 3 4 5

28. I have an assertive voice.   1 2 3 4 5

29. I readily reveal personal things about myself.   1 2 3 4 5

30. I am dominant in social situations.   1 2 3 4 5

31. I am very argumentative.   1 2 3 4 5

32. Once I get wound up in a heated discussion I have a hard time stopping myself.   1 2 3 4 5

33. I am always an extremely friendly communicator.   1 2 3 4 5

34. I really like to listen very carefully to people.   1 2 3 4 5

35. Very often I insist that other people document or present some kind of proof for what they are arguing.   1 2 3 4 5

36. I try to take charge of things when I am with people.   1 2 3 4 5

37. It bothers me to drop an argument that is not resolved.   1 2 3 4 5

38. In most social situations I tend to come on strong.   1 2 3 4 5

39. I am very expressive nonverbally in social situations.   1 2 3 4 5

40. The way I say something usually leaves an impression on people.   1 2 3 4 5

41. Whenever I communicate, I tend to be very encouraging to people.   1 2 3 4 5

42. I actively use a lot of facial expressions when I communicate.   1 2 3 4 5

43. I very frequently verbally exaggerate to emphasize a point.   1 2 3 4 5

44. I am an extremely attentive communicator.   1 2 3 4 5

45. As a rule, I openly express my feelings and emotions.   1 2 3 4 5

Scoring Key

Step 1: Reverse the score on items 4, 17, and 26 (1 = 5, 2 = 4, 3 = 3, etc.).

Step 2: Add together the scores on the following items to get a final total for each dimension.

1. 5, 7, 9, 20, 44   = _____ (Dominant)
2. 22, 28, 30, 32, 39 = _____ (Dramatic)
3. 2, 10, 13, 37, 41   = _____ (Contentious)
4. 6, 21, 24, 34, 42   = _____ (Animated)
5. 11, 14, 18, 31, 40 = _____ (Impression leaving)
6. 4, 12, 16, 17, 36   = _____ (Relaxed)
7. 15, 23, 27, 29, 45 = _____ (Attentive)
8. 1, 25, 26, 33, 38   = _____ (Open)
9. 3, 8, 19, 35, 43   = _____ (Friendly)

Analysis and Interpretation

This scale measures the following dimensions of communication style:

Dominant—Tends to take charge of social interactions.

Dramatic—Manipulates and exaggerates stories and uses other stylistic devices to highlight content.

Contentious—Is argumentative.

Animated—Uses frequent and sustained eye contact, and many facial expressions, and gestures often.

Impression leaving—Is remembered because of the communicative stimuli that are projected.

Relaxed—Is relaxed and void of nervousness.

Attentive—Makes sure that the other person knows that he or she is being listened to.

Open—Is conversational, expansive, affable, convivial, gregarious, unreserved, somewhat frank, definitely extroverted, and obviously approachable.

Friendly—Ranges from being unhostile to showing deep intimacy.

For each dimension, your score will range from 5 to 25. The higher your score for any dimension, the more that dimension characterizes your communication style. When you review your results, consider to what degree your scores aid or hinder your communication effectiveness. High scores for being attentive and open would almost always be positive qualities. A high score for contentious, on the other hand, could be a negative in many situations.

More Self-Assessments mymanagementlab

To learn more about your skills, abilities, and interests, go to the MyManagementLab website and take the following self-assessments:

- II.A.2.—How Good Are My Listening Skills?
- III.A.3.—How Good Am I at Giving Performance Feedback? (This exercise also appears in Chapter 11 on pages 352–353.)

MANAGEMENT FOR YOU TODAY

Dilemma

Think of a person with whom you have had difficulty communicating. Using the barriers to effective interpersonal communication as a start, analyze what has gone wrong with the communication process with that person. What can be done to improve communication? To what extent did sender and receiver problems contribute to the communication breakdown?

Becoming a Manager

- Practise being a good communicator—as a sender and a listener.
- When preparing to communicate, think about the most appropriate channel for your communication and why it may or may not be the most appropriate.
- Pay attention to your and others' nonverbal communication. Learn to notice the cues.
- Complete the *Developing Your Interpersonal Skills—Active Listening* module on page 312.

Choosing the Right Communication Channel

Purpose

To reinforce the idea that some channels are more appropriate for certain communications than others.

Time Required

Approximately 20 minutes.

Procedure

Form groups of 5 or 6 individuals. Evaluate the most appropriate channel to use to deliver the following information to employees. Justify your choices.

1. The company has just been acquired by a large competitor, and 15 percent of the employees will be laid off within the next three months.

2. A customer has complained about an employee via email. You have investigated and found the complaint justified. How do you convey this to the employee?

3. The founder of the company, who is well-liked, died of a heart attack last night.

4. Bonus decisions have been made. Not all individuals will receive a bonus.

5. An employee has gone above and beyond in meeting a customer's request. You want to acknowledge the employee's efforts.

Ethical Dilemma Exercise: Should CEOs Join the Blogger's World?

More and more organizational members are initiating messages through corporate blogs.[52] Officially known as *weblogs*, these are websites where an individual posts ideas, comments on contemporary issues, and offers other musings. Because anyone can visit the site and read the messages, companies have become concerned about messages that include sensitive data, criticize managers or competitors, use inflammatory language, or contain misrepresentations. Companies are also worried about the reaction of stakeholders who disagree with or are offended by blog postings. Corporate blogs are becoming so popular that companies such as Groove Networks have developed blog policies. In fact, CNN insisted that a reporter suspend a blog where he posted his conflicting thoughts about a career as a war correspondent, even though the reporter had a disclaimer saying the blog was "not affiliated with, endorsed by, or funded by CNN."

But what happens when a CEO sets up a blog? Jonathan Schwartz, CEO of Sun Microsystems, blogs about new technologies, management issues, and more (see **http://blogs. sun.com/jonathan/**). Alan Meckler, the CEO of Jupitermedia, started a blog as "a diary of the ups and downs of trying to

do something monumental"—create a new industry-wide technology conference. This event put Jupitermedia squarely in competition with a well-established event known as Comdex. In early blog entries, Meckler talked bluntly about the competing conference's management. Based on legal advice (and negative feedback from a few conference exhibitors), he softened his tone in later entries. Although he still blogs, Meckler notes, "I'm not stirring the pot anymore, which isn't my nature." What is the most ethical way to deal with a corporate blog, especially one by a senior manager?

Imagine that you are Jupitermedia's public relations director. The CEO has just posted a blog message saying your conference was more financially successful than the competing conference. Because neither company releases profitability details, you know this statement cannot be verified. You don't want Jupitermedia to look bad; you also know that your CEO likes to express himself. What should you do about the CEO's blog? (Review Exhibit 10-1 on page 290 as you think about the ethical challenge posed by this blog communication.)

Thinking Critically About Ethics

According to a survey by Websense, 58 percent of employees spend time at nonwork-related websites.[53] Another survey by salary.com and AOL found that personal Internet surfing was the top method of goofing off at work. Funny stories, jokes, and pictures make their way from one employee's email inbox to another's, to another's, and so forth. An elf bowling game sent by email was a favourite diversion during the holiday season. Although these may seem like fun and harmless activities,

it's estimated that such Internet distractions cost businesses over $54 billion annually. While there is a high dollar cost associated with using the Internet at work for other than business reasons, is there a psychological benefit to be gained by letting employees do something to relieve the stress of pressure-packed jobs? What are the ethical issues for both employees and organizations associated with widely available Internet access at work?

Voyant Technologies

Voyant Technologies makes teleconferencing technology that allows users to call various people at once and invite them to join a conference call.[54] A chance meeting in a headquarters hallway between company CEO Bill Ernstrom and his chief engineer led to the decision to have Voyant's engineers add streaming media to the company's flagship product. Four months and $200 000 later, Ernstrom wished he had never had that conversation, especially after a product manager who had learned of the project produced a marketing report that showed most customers had little interest in streaming anything. That incident underscored a communication challenge that had been ignored for too long: Top engineers were not listening to the product managers—and vice versa.

According to Ernstrom, "We got a long way down the road, built the code, got the engineers excited. Then we found out that we'd sell about 10 units."

The communication barriers experienced by Voyant are not all that unusual in high-tech organizations. The cultural and language gap between computer "geeks" and the more market/business-oriented colleagues happens time and time again. In these types of organizations, the early stages of a new project belong to the engineers. It's crucial to get the technology right, but what they produce is "often elegant technology that has no market, is too complicated, or doesn't match customers' expectations." Ernstrom's challenge is to get the two competing groups to collaborate. How might he do this?

English-Only Rules

Canada is a multicultural country.[55] "One in six Canadians in their 20s are immigrants, and one in five are the children of at least one immigrant parent." In 2006, 45.7 percent of Metropolitan Toronto's population, 39.6 percent of Vancouver's, and 30.7 percent of Montreal's were made up of immigrants.

The 2006 census found that 26 percent of Vancouver's population over age five spoke neither of the country's two official languages as their preferred language. The largest number of people who speak neither English or French as their preferred language speak Chinese (mainly Mandarin or Cantonese). The other dominant language in Vancouver is Punjabi, but many other languages are represented as well. Very few Vancouverites speak French, however (less than 8 percent).

Can an organization in BC require its employees to speak only English on the job? There are many sides to this issue. On the one hand, employers have identified the need to have a common language spoken in the workplace. Employers must be able to communicate effectively with all employees, especially when safety or productive efficiency matters are at stake. This, they claim, is a business necessity. Consequently, if it is a valid requirement of the job, the practice could be permitted. Furthermore, an employer's desire to have one language also stems from the fact that some employees may use bilingual capabilities to harass and insult other employees in a language they cannot understand. With today's increasing concern with protecting employees, especially women, from hostile environments, English-only rules serve as one means of reasonable care.

A counterpoint to this English-only rule firmly rests with the workforce diversity issue. Employees in today's organizations come from all nationalities and speak different languages. What about these individuals' desire to speak their language, to communicate effectively with their peers, and to maintain their cultural heritage? To them, English-only rules are discriminatory in terms of national origin in that they create an adverse impact for non-English-speaking individuals. Moreover, promoting languages of employees might be one way for organizations to avert marketing disasters. For example, marketing campaigns by Kentucky Fried Chicken and Coors have caused some embarrassment when these campaigns are translated literally in the global arena. Specifically, while Kentucky Fried Chicken's "Finger Licking Good" implies great-tasting fried chicken in North America, those same words in Chinese translate into "Eat Your Fingers Off." Likewise, Coors's marketing adage to "Turn It Loose," in Spanish means "Drink Coors and Get Diarrhea." Probably not the images the companies had in mind.

Questions

1. Should employers be permitted to require that only English be spoken in the workplace? Defend your position.

2. What suggestions for communication effectiveness, if any, would you give to organizations that market goods globally? Explain.

Human Resource Management

PART **three**

How do I make sure that I have the right employees to carry out my mission?

1. Does managing human resources well make a difference?

2. How does the external environment affect human resource planning?

3. How do organizations assess their human resource needs?

4. How do organizations identify and select competent employees?

5. How do organizations help employees adapt and stay up-to-date?

6. What can organizations do to help employees achieve high performance over their careers?

7. How do compensation and benefits motivate employees?

8. How are careers managed?

9. What are some current issues in human resource management?

▶ ▶ ▶ Toronto-based Bank of Nova Scotia (also called Scotiabank), Canada's second-largest bank, provides retail, corporate, and investment banking services worldwide.[1]

Scotiabank has more than 970 domestic branches and offices in 50 countries, including Mexico, Ireland, and China. In fiscal year 2006, the bank had total assets of over $379 billion, making it the number two bank by market capitalization. From 1996 to 2006, Scotiabank grew earnings per share at a compound annual rate of 14 percent, and annual dividends more than doubled between 2002 and 2006. Scotiabank has close to 57 000 employees, but President and CEO Rick Waugh worries that too many will be leaving within the next 5 to 10 years. He expects about half of the bank's senior management—vice-presidents and those at higher levels—will retire during that time.

Managing human resources so that an organization has the right people in place at the right time is often thought of as a key role of human resource managers. Waugh thinks that is not enough, however. "Responsibility for leadership development must begin at the very top. HR can and does play an important role facilitating the process, but it must be owned and executed by current leaders," Waugh told attendees at a recent

Conference Board of Canada's National Leadership Summit.

Waugh also wants to make sure that Scotiabank taps the full potential of its workforce. For instance, while women represent about 50 percent of Scotiabank's management-level employees, they have much less representation at the executive level. Waugh will be working with senior managers to make sure that more qualified women get opportunities in senior management.

Think About It

How do companies manage their human resources to achieve better performance? Put yourself in Rick Waugh's shoes. What policies and practices can he adopt to ensure that the bank has a high-quality workforce? What might he do to make sure that Scotiabank will have enough people to fill important roles as Baby Boomers retire?

The challenge facing Rick Waugh in making sure that Scotiabank recruits and retains high-quality employees reflects only a small aspect of the types of human resource management challenges facing today's managers. If an organization does not take its human resource management responsibilities seriously, work performance and goal accomplishment may suffer. The quality of an organization is, to a large degree, merely the sum of the quality of people it hires and keeps. Getting and keeping competent employees are critical to the success of every organization, whether the organization is just starting or has been in business for years. Therefore, part of every manager's job in the organizing function is human resource management.

Scotiabank
www.scotiabank.com

Q&A 11.1

Why Human Resource Management Is Important

1. Does managing human resources well make a difference?

"Our people are our most important asset." Many organizations use this phrase, or something close to it, to acknowledge the important role that employees play in organizational success. These organizations also recognize that *all* managers must engage in some human resource management (HRM) activities—even in large ones that have a separate HRM department. These managers interview job candidates, orient new employees, and evaluate their employees' work performance.

Can HRM be an important strategic tool? *Can* it help establish an organization's sustainable competitive advantage? The answer to these questions seems to be yes. Various studies have concluded that an organization's human resources can be a significant source of competitive advantage.[2] And that is true for organizations around the world, not just Canadian firms. The Human Capital Index, a comprehensive global study of more than 2000 firms conducted by consulting firm Watson Wyatt Worldwide, concluded that people-oriented HR gives an organization an edge by creating superior shareholder value.[3]

Achieving competitive success through people requires a fundamental change in how managers think about their employees and how they view the work relationship. It involves working with and through people and seeing them as partners, not just as costs to be minimized or avoided. That is what organizations such as WestJet Airlines, The Container Store, and Timberland are doing. In addition to their potential importance as part of organizational strategy and their contribution to competitive advantage, an organization's HRM practices have been found to have a significant impact on organizational performance.[4] For instance, one study reported that significantly improving an organization's HRM practices could increase its market value by as much as 30 percent.[5] The term used to describe these practices that lead to such results is **high-performance work practices**. High-performance work practices lead to both high individual and high organizational performance. Exhibit 11-1 lists examples of high-performance work practices. The common thread in these practices is a commitment to improving the knowledge, skills, and abilities of an organization's employees; increasing their motivation; reducing loafing on the job; and enhancing the retention of quality employees while encouraging low performers to leave.

high-performance work practices Work practices that lead to both high individual and high organizational performance.

Human Resources for Non-Human Resource Managers

All managers need to do a good job of handling people and have a reasonable knowledge of people skills. In a smaller organization, managers often have to handle many human resource functions, as well as their other jobs. In larger organizations, the human resource tasks are delegated to the human resource person or department. Consequently, if you are

---

Exhibit 11-1

Examples of High-Performance Work Practices

- Self-managed teams
- Decentralized decision making
- Training programs to develop knowledge, skills, and abilities
- Flexible job assignments
- Open communication
- Performance-based compensation
- Staffing based on person–job and person–organization fit

Source: Based on W. R. Evans and W. D. Davis, "High-Performance Work Systems and Organizational Performance: The Mediating Role of Internal Social Structure," *Journal of Management*, October 2005, p. 760.

an operating manager in a larger organization, you may not need to know all of the intricate details of what a human resource manager faces. The human resource manager will mainly advise you on major issues, including formulating policies and procedures consistent with organizational goals (such as pay and reward policies), handling difficult employee situations, handling recruiting and selection of employees, and developing training programs. Human resource managers also make sure that the organization is in compliance with federal and provincial legislation.

As a manager, it is important for you to be aware that federal and provincial legislation as well as company policies govern many aspects of the employment relationship. Because HR also involves appropriate ways for treating co-workers, even non-managers must be aware of basic HR principles and practices. You may also be interested in human resource issues as they help you understand and manage your own career.

The Human Resource Management Process

Human resource management should not operate in a vacuum. Rather, it should support the organization's corporate strategy.[6] Thus, human resource practices must sustain the organization's distinctive competencies, its competitive advantage (for example, superior customer service, innovation, efficient production), and the long-term objectives of the organization (such as growth or market share).

Certain human resource management activities are necessary to ensure that an organization has qualified people to perform the work required by the organization's strategy. Exhibit 11-2 on page 322 introduces the key components of an organization's **human resource management process**, which consists of eight activities for staffing the organization and sustaining high employee performance. The first three activities ensure that competent employees are identified and selected; the next two activities involve providing employees with up-to-date knowledge and skills; and the final three activities entail making sure that the organization retains competent and high-performing employees. Notice in Exhibit 11-2 that the entire HRM process is influenced by the external environment, as well as the organization's corporate strategy.

2. How does the external environment affect human resource planning?

human resource management process
Activities necessary for staffing the organization and sustaining high employee performance.

Q&A 11.2

Environmental Factors That Influence the Human Resource Management Process

We elaborated on the constraints that the environment puts on managers in Chapter 2, but let's briefly review those environmental factors that most directly influence the HRM process—economic conditions, labour unions, and government legislation.

Economic Conditions

The ability of employers to recruit is dependent upon local (and national) unemployment rates, competition in regional and local labour markets, and industry-specific labour market conditions. For instance, BC is facing a shortage in skilled labour in the leadup to the 2010 Olympics because of the increasing number of jobs available, the decreasing number of people available because of demographic issues, such as the oldest Baby Boomers nearing the age of retirement and Alberta's higher wage rates. Similarly, hospitals across the country face a shortage of nurses, so provinces compete with each other to recruit and retain nurses. When the unemployment rate is high, employers have more potential employees to choose from.

Labour Unions

The Canada Labour Code covers employment by the federal government and Crown corporations and establishes the right of employees to join labour unions if they desire. The provinces and territories have similar legislation to cover workplaces within their areas. This legislation provides a general framework for fair negotiations between management and labour unions and also provides guidelines to make sure that labour disputes do not unduly inconvenience the public.

Q&A 11.3

Exhibit 11-2

The Human Resource Management Process

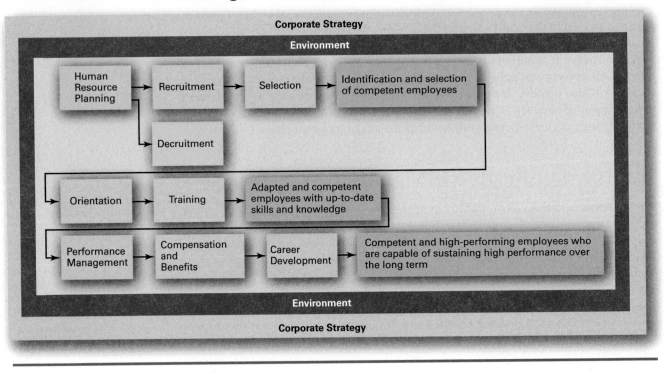

labour union
An organization that represents employees and seeks to protect their interests through collective bargaining.

A **labour union** is an organization that represents employees and seeks to protect their interests through collective bargaining. Labour unions try to improve pay and benefits and working conditions for members. They also try to have greater control over the rules and procedures covering issues such as promotions, layoffs, transfers, and outsourcing.

In unionized organizations, many HRM decisions are regulated by the terms of collective agreements. These agreements usually define such things as recruitment sources; criteria for hiring, promotions, and layoffs; training eligibility; and disciplinary practices. About 31 percent of Canadian employees belong to labour unions, a figure that has been consistent for the past 20 years.[7] By comparison, only about 12.5 percent of the workforce in the United States is unionized, although that percentage is higher in other countries. For instance, in Japan and Germany, respectively, 19.6 percent and 27 percent of the labour force belong to a union. In Mexico, 19 percent of employees belong to a union.[8] Individuals join a labour union for any number of reasons.[9] Wages, working conditions, lack of respect by managers, unfair working hours, job security, and the desire for safer workplaces all contribute to unionization. For example, students working at Montreal's downtown Indigo Books, Music & Café were unhappy with their working conditions and voted to join the Confédération des syndicats nationaux in February 2003.[10]

Government Legislation

The federal government has greatly expanded its influence over HRM by enacting a number of laws and regulations including the Canada Labour Code, employment standards legislation, the Charter of Rights and Freedoms, and the Canadian Human Rights Act. The provincial and territorial governments also have their own labour legislation that governs the workplace.

Legislation Affecting Workplace Conditions   The Canada Labour Code covers employment by the federal government and Crown corporations and establishes the right of employees to join labour unions if they desire. Part II of this legislation outlines the health and safety obligations of federal employers to prevent accidents and injury to their employees.

Each province and territory has health and safety regulations that cover most nonfederal workplaces in its region. This legislation is typically called the Occupational Health and Safety Act or something similar. The act generally does not cover work done in private homes or work done in farming operations (unless separate regulations have been added). There is separate legislation covering workplace hazards: the Workplace Hazardous Materials Information System (WHMIS). This is a comprehensive plan for providing information on the safe use of potentially hazardous materials in the workplace.

Employment standards legislation sets minimum employment standards in the private sector in Canada. It covers such things as the minimum age of employees, hours of work and overtime pay, minimum wages, equal pay, general holidays and annual vacations with pay, parental leave, and termination of employment.

The intent of the Canada Labour Code, Occupational Health and Safety Act, and employment standards legislation is to ensure that all employees have a safe work environment, that they are not asked to work too many hours, and that pay for jobs is not discriminatory.

Anti-Discrimination Legislation The Charter of Rights and Freedoms and the Canadian Human Rights Act require employers to ensure that equal employment opportunities exist for job applicants and current employees. Decisions regarding who will be hired, for instance, or which employees will be chosen for a management training program must be made without regard to race, sex, religion, age, colour, national origin, or disability. (See Exhibit 11-3 on page 324 for examples of prohibited grounds of discrimination in the provinces and territories.)

Trying to balance the "shoulds and should-nots" of these laws often falls within the realm of employment equity. The Employment Equity Act creates four "protected categories"—women, Aboriginal people, people with disabilities, and visible minorities. These groups must not be discriminated against by federally regulated employers and all employers who receive federal contracts worth more than $200 000. Employment equity is intended to ensure that all citizens have an equal opportunity to obtain employment regardless of gender, race or ethnicity, or disabilities. Provincial and territorial governments also have equity legislation. Many organizations have their own employment equity programs to ensure that decisions and practices enhance the employment, upgrading, and retention of members from protected groups. That is, the organization not only refrains from discrimination but also actively seeks to enhance the status of members from protected groups.

Although considerable legislation exists to prevent discrimination, exceptions can occur only when special circumstances exist. For instance, a fire department can deny employment to a firefighter applicant who is confined to a wheelchair, but if that same individual is applying for a desk job, such as fire department dispatcher, the disability cannot be used as a reason to deny employment. The issues involved, however, are rarely that clear-cut. For example, employment laws protect most employees whose religious beliefs require a specific style of dress—robes, long shirts, long hair, and the like. However, if the specific style of dress may be hazardous or unsafe in the work setting (for example, when operating machinery), a company could refuse to hire a person who won't adopt a safer dress code.

Managers are not completely free to choose whom they hire, promote, or fire. Although these laws and regulations have significantly helped to reduce employment discrimination and unfair employment practices, they have, at the same time, reduced managers' discretion over human resource decisions. Because an increasing number of workplace lawsuits are targeting supervisors, as well as their organizations, managers need to be aware of what they can and cannot do by law.[11]

Q&A 11.4

The Canadian Human Rights Act also covers discrimination in pay, under its pay equity guidelines. The act specifies that "It is a discriminatory practice for an employer to establish or maintain differences in wages between male and female employees employed in the same establishment who are performing work of equal value."[12] While it is not always easy to determine what "work of equal value" means, the Equal Wages Guidelines, 1986, helps employers sort this out.[13]

Exhibit 11-3

Prohibited Grounds of Discrimination in Employment*

Prohibited Grounds	FED	BC	ALTA	SASK	MAN	ONT	QUE	NB	PEI	NS	NFLD	NWT	YT
Race or colour	•	•	•	•	•	•	•	•	•	•	•	•	•
Religion	•	•	•	•	•	•	•	•	•	•	•	•	•
Age	•	(19–65)	(18+)	(18–64)	•	(18–65)	•	•	•	•	(19–65)	•	•
Sex (includes pregnancy or childbirth)	•	•	•	•	•	•	•	•	•	•	•	•	•
Marital status	•	•	•	•	•[2]	•[2]	•[3]	•	•	•	•	•	•
Physical/mental disability	•	•	•	•	•	•	•	•	•	•	•	•	•
Sexual orientation	•[4]	•	•	•	•	•	•	•	•	•	•	•	•
National or ethnic origin (includes linguistic background)	•	•	•	•[5]	•	•[6]	•	•	•	•	•	•	•
Family status	•	•	•	•	•	•	•[3]	•	•	•	•	•	•
Dependence on alcohol or drug	•	•[1]	•[1]	•[1]	•[1]	•[1]	•	•[1,7]	•[1]	•[7]			
Ancestry or place of origin												•[5]	
Political belief	•	•		•	•		•	•	•	•	•		•
Based on association	•				•	•	•			•		•	•
Pardoned conviction	•	•			•	•	•			•		•	•
Record of criminal conviction	•	•					•						
Source of income		•	•	•[8]	•	•	•		•			•	•
Place of residence		•							•				
Assignment, attachment, or seizure of pay													
Social condition/origin							•				•		
Language						•	•						•

*Any limitation, exclusion, denial, or preference may be permitted if a bona fide occupational requirement can be demonstrated. Harassment on any of the prohibited grounds is considered a form of discrimination.

1 Complaints accepted based on policy.
2 In Manitoba, includes gender-determined characteristics; in Ontario, includes transgendered persons.
3 Quebec uses the term "civil status."
4 Pursuant to a 1992 Ontario Court of Appeal decision, the Canadian Human Rights Commission now accepts complaints on the grounds of sexual orientation.
5 Defined as nationality.
6 Ontario's code includes both "ethnicity" and "citizenship."
7 Previous dependence only.
8 Defined as "receipt of public assistance."

Source: Compiled from "Prohibited Grounds of Discrimination in Canada," *Canadian Human Rights Commission,* September 2006, http://www.chrc-ccdp.ca/publications/prohibitedgrounds-en.asp.

Human Resource Planning

▶ ▶ ▶ As president and CEO of Scotiabank, Rick Waugh recognizes that providing good service means having good employees.[14] Scotiabank needs to recruit more employees to replace those who move into senior management positions in the next few years.

Think About It

How will changes in the age of the population affect how organizations hire people? How can Scotiabank and other organizations respond successfully? Canada is expected to experience a shortage of 1 million skilled workers by 2020, according to the Conference Board of Canada. Aware of these predictions, managers at many companies are developing plans to ensure that they will have enough qualified people to fulfill their human resource needs.

Human resource planning is the process by which managers ensure that they have the right number and kinds of people in the right places, and at the right times, who are capable of effectively and efficiently performing the tasks necessary to carry out the organization's strategy. Through planning, organizations can avoid sudden talent shortages and surpluses.[15] Human resource planning can be condensed into two steps: (1) assessing current human resources and (2) assessing future human resource needs and developing a program to meet those future needs.

Human resource planning works together with general management planning to make sure that the goals of the organization can be met. If management is planning an expansion, for instance, human resources needs to determine how to recruit more people. If management is planning downsizing, human resources determines how to lay off people in an efficient manner. If management is planning to introduce new technology, human resources should be examining the training needs required to make sure that the introduction of new technology will go smoothly. A human resource manager who thinks strategically will be sure that the skills and training of employees is consistent with where the organization is planning to go in the future.

Assessing Current Human Resources

Managers begin human resource planning by reviewing the organization's current human resource status, usually through a *human resource inventory*. This information is taken from forms filled out by employees, and includes things such as name, education, training, prior employment, languages spoken, special capabilities, and specialized skills. Many firms have introduced HR management information systems (HRMIS) to track employee information for policy and strategic needs. For instance, these systems can be used for salary and benefits administration. They can also be used to track absenteeism, turnover, and health and safety data. More strategically, HRMIS can be used to keep track of employee skills and education, and match these to ongoing needs of the organization. The availability of sophisticated databases makes keeping and getting this information quite easy.

Another part of the assessment of current resources is the **job analysis**, which is an assessment that defines jobs and the behaviours necessary to perform them. For instance, what are the duties of a senior accountant who works for Petro-Canada? What knowledge, skills, and abilities are necessary to be able to adequately perform this job? How do these requirements compare with those for a junior accountant or for an accounting manager? Information for a job analysis can be gathered by directly observing or videotaping individuals on the job, interviewing employees individually or in a group, having employees complete a structured questionnaire, having job "experts" (usually managers) identify a job's specific characteristics, or having employees record their daily activities in a diary or notebook.

With information from the job analysis, managers develop or revise job descriptions and job specifications. A **job description** is a written statement of what a jobholder does, how it is done, and why it is done. It typically describes job content, environment, and conditions of employment. A **job specification** states the minimum qualifications that a

3. How do organizations assess their human resource needs?

human resource planning
The process by which managers ensure that they have the right number and kinds of people in the right places, and at the right times, who are capable of effectively and efficiently performing assigned tasks.

job analysis
An assessment that defines jobs and the behaviours necessary to perform them.

job description
A written statement of what a jobholder does, how it is done, and why it is done.

job specification
A statement of the minimum qualifications that a person must possess to perform a given job successfully.

person must possess to perform a given job successfully. It identifies the human traits, knowledge, skills, and attitudes needed to do the job effectively. The job description and the job specification are both important documents that aid managers in recruiting and selecting employees.

Meeting Future Human Resource Needs

Future human resource needs are determined by the organization's mission, goals, and strategies. Demand for employees is a result of demand for the organization's products or services. On the basis of its estimate of total revenue, managers can attempt to establish the number and mix of employees needed to reach that revenue. In some cases, however, that situation may be reversed. When particular skills are necessary but in short supply, the availability of appropriate human resources determines revenues.

After they have assessed both current capabilities and future needs, managers are able to estimate human resource shortages—both in number and in type—and to highlight areas in which the organization will be overstaffed. Managers can then develop replacement charts for managerial positions, which outline what employees are available to fill future managerial needs, and can indicate who might be ready for promotion, and who might need more training to move into upper-level positions. With all of this information, managers are ready to proceed to the next step in the HRM process.

Staffing the Organization

▶ ▶ ▶ To deal with recruiting issues, Scotiabank has developed a Careers webpage to target young graduates and encourage them to think about working for the bank.[16] "We looked at our audience and their primary medium is the Internet. We're matching the channels with the audience we're trying to attract," says Arlene Russell, vice-president of HR. The site gives corporate information, and users can do job searches and read about what makes Scotiabank a good employer.

Russell notes that e-recruiting is not the only way that the bank seeks job applicants. Scotiabank also uses print advertising and recruitment fairs, for instance. "There are still strengths in all mediums, and I think to really attract job seekers, you have to deliver on all the channels people want," says Russell. "The bottom line is you need to understand who you're speaking to and speak to them in the medium they're comfortable with."

Think About It
What kinds of selection techniques can Scotiabank use to choose suitable employees?

---

4. How do organizations identify and select competent employees?

recruitment
The process of locating, identifying, and attracting capable applicants.

decruitment
Techniques for reducing the organization's workforce.

Once managers know their current human resource status and their future needs, they can begin to do something about any shortages or excesses. If one or more vacancies exist, they can use the information gathered through job analysis to guide them in **recruitment**—that is, the process of locating, identifying, and attracting capable applicants.[17] On the other hand, if human resource planning shows a surplus of employees, management may want to reduce the organization's workforce through **decruitment**.[18]

Recruitment

At a career fair and expo at Edmonton City Centre mall, the Edmonton Police Service tried to convince high school students that they should consider a career with the police force. To show that there are many different opportunities in police service, they brought their vehicles, including police motorcycles and dirt bikes. Explains spokesperson Dean Parthenis, "People may have thought that once you become a police officer, you stay in that position on patrol for the rest of your life. You can if you like. But there's lots of opportunity to move around once you become a police officer."[19] Potential job candidates can be found through several sources, as Exhibit 11-4 shows.[20]

Exhibit 11-4

Major Sources of Potential Job Candidates

Source	Advantages	Disadvantages
Internet	Reaches large numbers of people; can get immediate feedback	Generates many unqualified candidates
Employee Referrals	Knowledge about the organization provided by current employee; can generate strong candidates because a good referral reflects on the recommender	May not increase the diversity and mix of employees
Company Website	Wide distribution; can be targeted to specific groups	Generates many unqualified candidates
College/University Recruiting	Large centralized body of candidates	Limited to entry-level positions
Professional Recruiting Organizations	Good knowledge of industry challenges and requirements	Little commitment to specific organization

> *How would you go about recruiting team members to work on a course project?*

Web-based recruiting, or e-recruiting, has become a popular choice for organizations and applicants. For instance, after the Vancouver Police Department examined the kinds of recruits that would be needed over the next several years, the department decided to launch a recruitment seminar inside Second Life, the online alternative universe. The police recruiters created their own avatars (Second Life personas) dressed "in a specially designed VPD uniform, badge, belt and radio." Inspector Kevin McQuiggen, head of the department's tech crimes division, explains why recruiting on Second Life makes sense: "If people are on Second Life, they're likely to be web-savvy, a quality the police department is looking for in new recruits." The department has seen an increasing number of Internet and technology-related crimes in recent years, and hiring people who can help detect those crimes would be an advantage to the Vancouver police.[21]

Although e-recruiting has been gaining in popularity (Scotiabank, for instance, allows applicants to fill out an information form online and upload their résumé with the form), employers use other recruitment sources as well. Burnaby, BC-based Electronic Arts Canada, following the lead of some other Canadian companies, decided to recruit at universities in recent years to win "the best and the brightest" from computer science programs.[22] Pat York, director of human resources, is pleased with the results, as the interviews have led to hires more than a third of the time.

What recruiting sources have been found to produce superior candidates? The majority of studies have found that employee referrals generally produce the best candidates.[23] The

The Vancouver Police Department has started recruiting through an online presence on Second Life. They created special avatars (shown here) to interview prospective candidates.

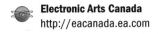

Electronic Arts Canada
http://eacanada.ea.com

explanation is intuitively logical. First, applicants referred by current employees are pre-screened by these employees. Because the recommenders know both the job and the person being recommended, they tend to refer applicants who are well qualified. Also, because current employees often feel that their reputation is at stake with a referral, they tend to refer others only when they are reasonably confident that the referral will not make them look bad.

Decruitment

The other approach to controlling labour supply is through decruitment, which is not a pleasant task for any manager. The decruitment options are shown in Exhibit 11-5. Obviously, people can be fired, but other choices may be more beneficial to the organization. Keep in mind that, regardless of the method used to reduce the number of employees in the organization, there is no easy way to do it, even though it may be absolutely necessary.

Selection

Once the recruiting effort has developed a pool of candidates, the next step in the HRM process is to determine who is best qualified for the job. This step is called the **selection process**, the process of screening job applicants to ensure that the most appropriate candidates are hired. Errors in hiring can have far-reaching implications. However, hiring the right people pays off.

selection process
The process of screening job applicants to ensure that the most appropriate candidates are hired.

What Is Selection?

Selection is an exercise in prediction. It seeks to predict which applicants will be successful if hired. Successful in this case means performing well on the criteria the organization uses to evaluate employees. In filling a sales position, for example, the selection process should be able to predict which applicants will generate a high volume of sales; for a position as a network administrator, it should predict which applicants will be able to effectively oversee and manage the organization's computer network.

Consider, for a moment, that any selection decision can result in four possible outcomes. As shown in Exhibit 11-6, two of these outcomes would be correct, and two would indicate errors.

A decision is correct when the applicant was predicted to be successful and proved to be successful on the job, or when the applicant was predicted to be unsuccessful and would

Exhibit 11-5

Decruitment Options

Option	Description
Firing	Permanent involuntary termination
Layoffs	Temporary involuntary termination; may last only a few days or extend to years
Attrition	Not filling openings created by voluntary resignations or normal retirements
Transfers	Moving employees either laterally or downward; usually does not reduce costs but can reduce intraorganizational supply–demand imbalances
Reduced Workweeks	Having employees work fewer hours per week, share jobs, or perform their jobs on a part-time basis
Early Retirements	Providing incentives to older and more senior employees for retiring before their normal retirement dates
Job Sharing	Having employees share one full-time position

Karen Flavelle, president of Vancouver-based Purdy's Chocolates, agonizes over new hires because she really wants them to fit in with the company's culture. A search for a new personnel director took three years, until she could find someone who would support "the company's practice of rotating store clerks and plant workers into challenging projects to test their suitability for supervisory and management posts." Most managers at Purdy's are promoted from within.

be so if hired. In the first case, we have successfully accepted; in the second case, we have successfully rejected.

Problems arise when errors are made in rejecting candidates who would have performed successfully on the job (reject errors) or accepting those who ultimately perform poorly (accept errors). These problems can be significant. Given today's human resource laws and regulations, reject errors can cost more than the additional screening needed to find acceptable candidates. They can expose the organization to charges of discrimination, especially if applicants from protected groups are disproportionately rejected. The costs

Exhibit 11-6

Selection Decision Outcomes

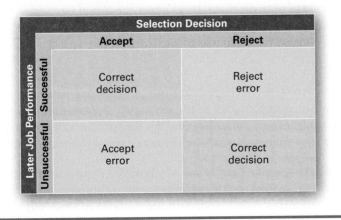

		Selection Decision	
		Accept	**Reject**
Later Job Performance	**Successful**	Correct decision	Reject error
	Unsuccessful	Accept error	Correct decision

of accept errors include the cost of training the employee, the profits lost because of the employee's incompetence, the cost of severance, and the subsequent costs of further recruiting and screening. The major thrust of any selection activity should be to reduce the probability of making reject errors or accept errors while increasing the probability of making correct decisions. How do managers do this? By using selection procedures that are both valid and reliable.

Validity and Reliability

Any selection device that a manager uses should demonstrate **validity**, a proven relationship between the selection device and some relevant job criterion. For example, the law prohibits managers from using a test score as a selection device unless there is clear evidence that, once on the job, individuals with high scores on this test outperform individuals with low test scores. The burden is on managers to show that any selection device they use to differentiate between applicants is related to job performance.

In addition to being valid, a selection device must also demonstrate **reliability**, which indicates whether the device measures the same thing consistently. For example, if a test is reliable, any single individual's score should remain fairly consistent over time, assuming that the characteristics being measured are also stable. No selection device can be effective if it's low in reliability. Using such a device would be like weighing yourself every day on an erratic scale. If the scale is unreliable—randomly fluctuating, say 4 to 7 kilos every time you step on it—the results will not mean much. To be effective predictors, selection devices must possess an acceptable level of consistency.

Types of Selection Devices

Managers can use a number of selection devices to reduce accept and reject errors. The best-known include application forms, written tests, performance-simulation tests, interviews, background investigations, and, in some cases, physical examinations. Let's briefly review each of these devices. Exhibit 11-7 lists the strengths and weaknesses of each of these devices.[24]

Application Forms Almost all organizations require job candidates to fill out an application. The application might be a form on which the person gives his or her name, address, and telephone number. Or it might be a comprehensive personal history profile that details the person's activities, skills, and accomplishments.

Written Tests Typical written tests include tests of intelligence, aptitude, ability, and interest. Such tests have been used for years, although their popularity tends to run in cycles. Today, personality, behavioural, and aptitude assessment tests are popular among businesses. Managers need to be careful regarding their use, however, since legal challenges against such tests have been successful when the tests are not job related or when they elicit information concerning sex, race, age, or other areas protected by the Employment Equity Act.

Managers know that poor hiring decisions are costly and that properly designed tests can reduce the likelihood of poor decisions. In addition, the cost of developing and validating a set of written tests for a specific job has decreased significantly.

A review of the evidence finds that tests of intellectual ability, spatial and mechanical ability, perceptual accuracy, and motor ability are moderately valid predictors for many semi-skilled and unskilled operative jobs in industrial organization.[25] However, an enduring criticism of written tests is that intelligence and other tested characteristics can be somewhat removed from the actual performance of the job itself.[26] For example, a high score on an intelligence test is not necessarily a good indicator that the applicant will perform well as a computer programmer. This criticism has led to an increased use of performance-simulation tests.

Performance-Simulation Tests What better way is there to find out whether an applicant for a technical writing position at Matsushita can write technical manuals than by having him or her do it? Performance-simulation tests are made up of actual job behaviours. The best-known performance-simulation tests are work sampling and assessment centres.

Exhibit 11-7

Selection Devices

Selection Device	Strengths	Weaknesses
Application Forms	Relevant biographical data and facts that can be verified have been shown to be valid performance measures for some jobs. When items on the form have been weighted to reflect job relatedness, this device has proved to be a valid predictor for diverse groups.	Usually only a couple of items on the form prove to be valid predictors of job performance, and then only for a specific job. Weighted-item applications are difficult and expensive to create and maintain.
Written Tests	Tests of intellectual ability, spatial and mechanical ability, perceptual accuracy, and motor ability are moderately valid predictors for many semi-skilled and unskilled lower-level jobs in manufacturing. Intelligence tests are reasonably good predictors for supervisory positions.	Intelligence and other tested characteristics can be somewhat removed from actual job performance, thus reducing their validity.
Performance-Simulation Tests	Tests are based on job analysis data and easily meet the requirement of job relatedness. Tests have proven to be valid predictors of job performance.	They are expensive to create and administer.
Interviews	Interviews must be structured and well organized to be effective predictors. Interviewers must use common questions to be effective predictors.	Interviewers must be aware of the legality of certain questions. Interviews are subject to potential biases, especially if they are not well structured and standardized.
Background Investigations	Verifications of background data are valuable sources of information.	Reference checks are essentially worthless as a selection tool.
Physical Examinations	Physical exams have some validity for jobs with certain physical requirements.	Managers must be sure that physical requirements are job related and do not discriminate.

Work sampling involves presenting applicants with a miniature model of a job and having them perform a task or set of tasks that are central to it. Applicants demonstrate that they have the necessary skills and abilities by actually doing the tasks. This type of test is appropriate for jobs where work is routine or standardized.

Assessment centres are places in which job candidates undergo performance-simulation tests to evaluate managerial potential.[27] In assessment centres, executives, supervisors, or trained psychologists evaluate candidates for managerial positions as they go through extensive exercises that simulate real problems they would confront on the job.[28] Activities might include interviews, in-basket problem-solving exercises, group discussions, and business decision games.

Interviews   The interview, like the application form, is an almost universal selection device.[29] Not many of us have ever got a job without one or more interviews. Because there are so many variables that can impact interviewer judgment, the value of the interview as a selection device has been of considerable debate.[30] Managers can make interviews

work sampling
A selection device in which job applicants are presented with a miniature model of a job and are asked to perform a task or set of tasks that are central to it.

assessment centres
Places in which job candidates undergo performance-simulation tests to evaluate managerial potential.

Q&A 11.5

TIPS FOR MANAGERS

Some Suggestions for Interviewing

↗ Structure a **fixed set of questions** for all applicants.

↗ Have **detailed information about the job** for which applicants are interviewing.

↗ **Minimize any prior knowledge** of applicants' backgrounds, experience, interests, test scores, or other characteristics.

↗ **Ask behavioural questions** that require applicants to give detailed accounts of actual job behaviours.

↗ Use a **standardized evaluation form**.

↗ **Take notes** during the interview.

↗ **Avoid short interviews** that encourage premature decision making.

Source: Based on D. A. DeCenzo and S. P. Robbins, *Human Resource Management,* 7th ed. (New York: Wiley, 2002), p. 200.

more valid and reliable by following the approach presented in *Tips for Managers—Some Suggestions for Interviewing.* (See also *Developing Your Interpersonal Skills—Interviewing* on pages 355–356, at the end of the chapter.)

Another important factor in interviewing job candidates is the legality of certain interview questions. Employment law attorneys warn managers to be extremely cautious in the types of questions they ask candidates. Questions about age, marital status, and child-bearing plans, for instance, are not appropriate. Exhibit 11-8 lists examples of typical interview questions that the Canadian Human Rights Commission suggests managers *should not* ask because they could expose the organization to lawsuits by job applicants.

An approach that some companies are now using is *situational interviews,* in which candidates role play in mock scenarios. For instance, at a Bay Street bank in Toronto, a prospective account representative might be asked to role play dealing with a customer who has an account discrepancy. The interviewers watch the candidate's reaction: how he or she processes the information, how he or she interacts with the "client," his or her body language, and which words he or she chooses.[31]

Some companies also use group interviews, where job candidates are interviewed by multiple people at once. In some settings, the interviews are conducted by different people across the organization, to assess whether the candidate fits in with the organizational culture. In other settings, the work team in which the

Q&A 11.6   candidate will work conducts the interview, to determine whether the candidate will fit into the work team. Candidates may even be asked to perform tasks with the team, to better assess how the candidate works with the team members.

Exhibit 11-8

Examples of "Don't Ask" and "Can Ask" Interview Questions for Managers*

Subject	Don't Ask	Can Ask
Name	About name changes; maiden name	After selection, about previous name if needed to check on previous jobs or education credentials
Address	For addresses outside Canada	About place and duration of current or recent address
Age	For birth certificate, baptismal records, or about age in general	If the applicant is eligible to work under Canadian laws regarding age restrictions
Sex	About pregnancy, childbearing plans, or child care arrangements	If the applicant can meet the job's attendance requirements
Marital status	Whether applicant is single, married, divorced, engaged, separated, widowed, or living common-law Whether an applicant's spouse may be transferred About the spouse's employment	If transfer or travel is part of the job, whether the applicant can meet these requirements Whether there are any circumstances that might prevent completion of a minimum service commitment

(continued)

Exhibit 11-8 (continued)

Subject	Don't Ask	Can Ask
Family status	About the number of children or dependants About child care arrangements	If the applicant can work the required hours and, where applicable, overtime
National or ethnic origin	About birthplace, nationality of ancestors, spouse, or other relatives Whether born in Canada For proof of citizenship	Since those who are entitled to work in Canada must be citizens, permanent residents, or holders of valid work permits, whether the applicant is legally entitled to work in Canada
Military service	About military service in other countries	About Canadian military service where employment preference is given to veterans by law
Language	About mother tongue Where language skills were obtained	If the applicant understands, reads, writes, or speaks languages required for the job
Race or colour	Any questions about race or colour, including colour of eyes, skin, or hair	
Photographs	For photo to be attached to application or sent to interviewer before interview	After selection, for photo to be taken for security passes or company files
Religion	Whether the applicant will work a specific religious holiday About religious affiliation, church membership, frequency of church attendance For references from clergy or religious leader	After stating the required work shift, whether such a schedule poses problems for the applicant
Height and weight	About height and weight unless there is evidence they are genuine occupational requirements	
Disability	For a list of all disabilities, limitations, or health problems Whether the applicant drinks or uses drugs Whether the applicant has ever received psychiatric care or been hospitalized for emotional problems	Whether the applicant has received workers' compensation Whether the applicant has any condition that could affect ability to do the job Whether the applicant has any condition which should be considered in selection
Medical information	Whether the applicant is currently under a physician's care For the name of the family doctor Whether the applicant is receiving counselling or therapy	
Pardoned conviction	Whether the applicant has ever been convicted Whether the applicant has ever been arrested Whether the applicant has a criminal record	If bonding is a job requirement, whether the applicant is eligible
Sexual orientation	About the applicant's sexual orientation	
References	The same restrictions that apply to questions asked of applicants apply to questions asked of employment references.	

*Managers should always check with the human resource department for specific guidance.

Source: Based on information from "Guide to Screening and Selection in Employment (A)," Canadian Human Rights Commission, http://www.chrc-ccdp.ca/publications/screening_employment-en.asp.

Background Investigations   If managers at Lucent Technologies (now Alcatel-Lucent) had done a thorough background check, they might have discovered that the individual who eventually became director of recruitment (who is no longer with the company) was imprisoned for stealing money from student funds while a principal at a California high school and had lied about earning a doctorate at Stanford.[32]

Background investigations are of two types: verifications of application data and reference checks. The first type has proved to be a valuable source of selection information. For instance, Angus Stewart notes that "education fraud is the most common" thing he finds on background checks. He is vice-president of forensics and leader of corporate intelligence at KPMG LLP in Toronto. Quite a lot of people lie "about the degree they received or the institutions they attended," he adds.[33]

KPMG LLP
www.kpmg.ca

Physical Examinations   This device would be useful only for a small number of jobs that have certain physical requirements.

What Works Best and When?

Many selection devices are of limited value to managers in making selection decisions. Exhibit 11-9 summarizes the validity of these devices for particular types of jobs. Managers should use those devices that effectively predict success for a given job.

In addition, managers who treat the recruiting and hiring of employees as if the applicants must be sold on the job and exposed only to an organization's positive characteristics are likely to have a workforce that is dissatisfied and prone to high turnover.[34]

During the hiring process, every job applicant develops a set of expectations about the company and about the job for which he or she is interviewing. When the information an applicant receives is excessively inflated, a number of things happen that have potentially negative effects on the company. First, mismatched applicants are less likely to withdraw from the selection process. Second, because inflated information builds unrealistic expectations, new employees are likely to become quickly dissatisfied and leave the organization. Third, new hires are prone to become disillusioned and less committed to the organization when they face the unexpected harsh realities of the job. In many cases, these individuals may feel that they were misled during the hiring process and may become problem employees.

realistic job preview (RJP)
A preview of a job that includes both positive and negative information about the job and the company.

To increase job satisfaction among employees and reduce turnover, you should consider providing a **realistic job preview (RJP)**. An RJP includes both positive and negative

Exhibit 11-9

Quality of Selection Devices as Predictors

Selection Device	Position			
	Senior Management	Middle and Lower Management	Complex Nonmanagerial	Routine Work
Application Forms	2	2	2	2
Written Tests	1	1	2	3
Work Sampling	—	—	4	4
Assessment Centres	5	5	—	—
Interviews	4	3	2	2
Verification of Application Data	3	3	3	3
Reference Checks	1	1	1	1
Physical Exams	1	1	1	2

Note: Validity is measured on a scale from 5 (highest) to 1 (lowest). A dash means "not applicable."

information about the job and the company. For instance, in addition to the positive comments typically expressed during an interview, the job applicant might be told that there are limited opportunities to talk to co-workers during work hours, that promotional advancement is slim, or that work hours fluctuate so erratically that employees may be required to work during what are usually off hours (nights and weekends). Research indicates that applicants who have been given a realistic job preview hold lower and more realistic job expectations for the jobs they will be performing and are better able to cope with the frustrating elements of the job than are applicants who have been given only inflated information.

Orientation and Skill Development

▶ ▶ ▶ Thirty-year-old Roxann Linton is enthusiastic about her career at Scotiabank.[35] "Working with an international and diverse organization like Scotiabank, there are so many opportunities," says Linton. The young woman was chosen for Leading Edge, Scotiabank's fast-track leadership program. In the application process, she had to prepare a challenging business case analysis, go through psychometric testing, and be interviewed twice by a total of eight executives. The Leading Edge program prepares employees for senior management positions by rotating them through a series of assignments.

Linton worked for the bank for about five years in the bank's internal audit department in Kingston, Jamaica. She then transferred to Halifax and worked in commercial banking. During the first 15 months of the Leading Edge program, Linton managed more than 100 people in the electronic banking contact centre. Her next assignment was as director of special projects at Scotia Cassels Investment Counsel, part of the bank's wealth management division. She launched a new corporate bond fund during her first three months on that assignment. She will have one more 12- to 18-month assignment in another part of the bank, and then she can start applying for vice-president positions.

Think About It

What kinds of orientation and training methods do organizations use to help employees develop their skills and learn about their organization?

Organizations have to introduce new members to the work they will do and the organization. They do this through their orientation programs. As time goes by, employees may need to increase their skills. This is handled through training. We review the strategies that organizations use for orientation and training below.

5. How do organizations help employees adapt and stay up-to-date?

Orientation

Did you participate in some type of organized "introduction to campus life" when you started school? If so, you may have been told about your school's rules and regulations, the procedures for activities such as applying for financial aid, cashing a cheque, or registering for classes, and you were probably introduced to some of the campus administrators. A person starting a new job needs the same type of introduction to his or her job and the organization. This introduction is called **orientation**.

There are two types of orientation. *Work unit orientation* familiarizes the employee with the goals of the work unit, clarifies how his or her job contributes to the unit's goals, and includes an introduction to his or her new co-workers. *Organization orientation* informs the new employee about the organization's objectives, history, philosophy, procedures, and rules. This should include relevant human resource policies and benefits such as work hours, pay procedures, overtime requirements, and fringe benefits. In addition, a tour of the organization's work facilities is often part of the organization orientation.

Managers have an obligation to make the integration of the new employee into the organization as smooth and as free of anxiety as possible. They need to openly discuss employee

orientation
Introduction of a new employee to his or her job and the organization.

beliefs regarding mutual obligations of the organization and the employee.[36] It's in the best interests of the organization and the new employee to get the person up and running in the job as soon as possible. Successful orientation, whether formal or informal, results in an outsider–insider transition that makes the new member feel comfortable and fairly well adjusted, lowers the likelihood of poor work performance, and reduces the probability of a surprise resignation by the new employee only a week or two into the job.

Training

Employee training is an important HRM activity. As job demands change, employee skills have to be altered and updated. In 2006, US business firms budgeted over $55 billion on workforce formal training.[37] Canadian companies spend far less than American firms on training and development, about $852 per employee compared with $1273 by the Americans in 2006.[38] Managers, of course, are responsible for deciding what type of training employees need, when they need it, and what form that training should take.

Types of Training

When organizations invest in employee training, what are they offering? Exhibit 11-10 describes the major types of training that organizations provide.[39] Some of the most popular types of training that organizations provide include sexual harassment, safety, management skills and development, and supervisory skills.[40] For many organizations, employee interpersonal skills training—communication, conflict resolution, team building, customer service, and so forth—is a high priority. For example, Shannon Washbrook, director of training and development for Vancouver-based Boston Pizza International, says, "Our people know the Boston Pizza concept; they have all the hard skills. It's the soft skills they lack." To address that, Washbrook launched Boston Pizza College, a training initiative that uses hands-on, scenario-based learning about many interpersonal skills topics.[41] SaskPower, like Scotiabank, uses training to develop leadership potential, as the following *Management Reflection* shows.

MANAGEMENT REFLECTION

SaskPower Sends Its Leaders to Leadership School

Are leaders made or born? Managers at Regina-based SaskPower believe that leaders are developed, not born.[42] The company has developed a leadership program that is similar to a mini-MBA. It introduces participants to leadership skills and other areas of business. The company selects employees for the program based on leadership potential. Individuals can nominate themselves for the leadership-training program by persuading management with examples of why they would make great managers.

The program works better than the way managers were chosen previously at SaskPower. "It was unorganized, and the 'old boys' network' was still at work," said Bill Hyde, vice-president of human resources. The program also ensures that SaskPower continues to have a skilled workforce and trained managers for the future, when Baby Boomers start retiring in large numbers. ■

Training Methods

Employee training can be delivered in traditional ways including on-the-job training, job rotation, mentoring and coaching, experiential exercises, workbooks and manuals, classroom lectures or videos. Toronto-based Labatt Breweries has created its own beer school at an on-site pub at company headquarters that teaches participants about the qualities of beer.[43] It might seem obvious that those in sales should know the product, but even accountants and human resource specialists from head office learn how to change a keg and clean the lines. They learn that "Keith's is a fast-pouring beer, that Stella Artois is best served in a glass with a stem and that foam bubbles should

Labatt Breweries
www.labatt.com

Toronto-based Labatt Breweries is putting its employees through beer school over the next few years. Beer "professors" at Labatt's beer school teach employees how to pour the perfect glass of beer and how to match food with certain beers.

be sliced from the heads of some beers because 'large CO_2 bubbles will bloat us.'" Labatt's senior management feels that all employees need to be beer experts so that they can help sell the product, even if they are not officially salespeople.

Many organizations are relying more on technology-based training methods because of their accessibility, lower cost, and ability to deliver information. For instance, a computer-based simulation called vLeader (virtual leader) by SimuLearn provides trainees with realistic leadership scenarios, including the following:

"Be in the boardroom in 10 minutes," reads the email from Senior Vice President Alan Young. The CEO is out on his boat, and a storm has knocked out all communication. Worse, there has been a massive fire in the call centre in South America. "We could lose billions," Young says. The board has given senior staff emergency powers. You're a top manager who has been called in to help. What do you do?[44]

Exhibit 11-10

Types of Training

Type	Includes
General	Communication skills, computer systems application and programming, customer service, executive development, management skills and development, personal growth, sales, supervisory skills, and technological skills and knowledge
Specific	Basic life/work skills, creativity, customer education, diversity/cultural awareness, remedial writing, managing change, leadership, product knowledge, public speaking/presentation skills, safety, ethics, sexual harassment, team building, wellness, and others

Source: Based on "2005 Industry Report—Types of Training," *Training*, December 2005, p. 22.

Is college or university training enough for the workplace, or do you need more?

Exhibit 11-11 provides a description of the various traditional and technology-based employee training methods that managers might use. Although web-based or online training had been predicted just a few years ago to become the most popular method of training, it simply has not lived up to expectations, Julie Kaufman, an industry analyst with Toronto-based IDC Canada, recently told attendees at a training and development conference. Most organizations have not yet figured out how to make use of this type of training.[45]

Not all employees have access to training from their companies. Exhibit 11-12a shows that managerial and professional employees are far more likely than blue-collar employees to receive training. Training is not confined to formal activities arranged by employers. In 2002, about one-third of employees engaged in self-learning activities, such as observing others or trying new methods themselves. Exhibit 11-12b shows the dominant methods of self-learning. Finally, employees receive different amounts of training based on the industry in which they are employed. Those in goods-producing industries received substantially less training than those in service-producing industries (18 percent vs. 28 percent). Within the service sector, employees in education, finance, insurance, real estate, health care, and social assistance are most likely to receive training.[46] Because the needs of organizations change frequently, and changes in technology occur rapidly, it is very important for employees to participate in training activities, either through their companies or on their own.

Exhibit 11-11

Employee Training Methods

Traditional Training Methods

- *On-the-job*—Employees learn how to do tasks simply by performing them, usually after an initial introduction to the task.

- *Job rotation*—Employees work at different jobs in a particular area, getting exposure to a variety of tasks.

- *Mentoring and coaching*—Employees work with an experienced worker who provides information, support, and encouragement; also called apprenticing in certain industries.

- *Experiential exercises*—Employees participate in role playing, simulations, or other face-to-face types of training.

- *Workbooks/manuals*—Employees refer to training workbooks and manuals for information.

- *Classroom lectures*—Employees attend lectures designed to convey specific information.

Technology-Based Training Methods

- *CD-ROM/DVD/videotapes/audiotapes*—Employees listen to or watch selected media that convey information or demonstrate certain techniques.

- *Videoconferencing/teleconferencing/satellite TV*—Employees listen or participate as information is conveyed or techniques demonstrated.

- *E-learning*—Internet-based learning where employees participate in multimedia simulations or other interactive modules.

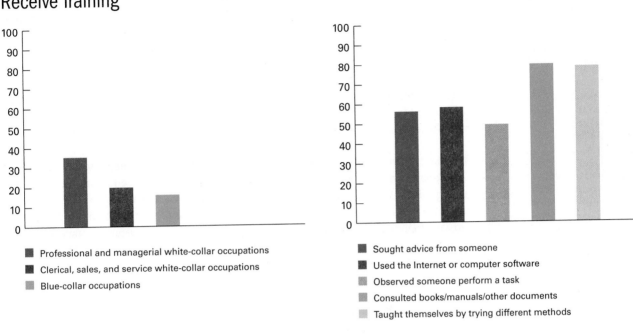

Exhibit 11-12a

Occupations of Employees Who Receive Training

- ■ Professional and managerial white-collar occupations
- ■ Clerical, sales, and service white-collar occupations
- ■ Blue-collar occupations

Exhibit 11-12b

How Employees Train Themselves

- ■ Sought advice from someone
- ■ Used the Internet or computer software
- ■ Observed someone perform a task
- ■ Consulted books/manuals/other documents
- ■ Taught themselves by trying different methods

Source: V. Peters, "Working and Training: First Results of the 2003 Adult Education and Training Survey," Statistics Canada, Culture, Tourism and the Centre for Education Statistics Division, 2004, Catalogue no. 81-595-MIE—No. 015.

Managing and Rewarding Performance

Managers need to know whether their employees are performing their jobs efficiently and effectively or whether there is need for improvement. Employees are often compensated based on those evaluations. (For more on giving evaluations, see *Self-Assessment—How Good Am I at Giving Performance Feedback?* on pages 352–353, at the end of the chapter.)

6. What can organizations do to help employees achieve high performance over their careers?

Performance Management

What techniques might you want to use if you had to evaluate the members of your student project group?

Evaluating employee performance is part of a **performance management system**, which is a process of establishing performance standards and appraising employee performance in order to arrive at objective human resource decisions, as well as to provide documentation to support those decisions. Performance appraisal is a critical part of a performance management system. Some companies invest far more effort in it than others.

performance management system
A process of establishing performance standards and evaluating performance in order to arrive at objective human resource decisions, as well as to provide documentation to support those decisions.

Performance appraisal is not easy to do, and many managers do it poorly. Both managers and employees often dread the appraisal process. A recent survey found that 41 percent of employees report having had a least one incident of being demotivated after feedback from their managers.[47] Let's look at some different methods of doing performance appraisal. Performance appraisal can also be subject to politics, not unlike the 2002 Olympic Winter Games ice skating controversy where the French judge was accused of manipulating her scores to allow the Russian skaters to win the gold over Jamie Salé and David Pelletier. (To learn more about performance appraisal, see *Developing Your Interpersonal Skills—Providing Feedback* on pages 497–498, in Chapter 15.)

Performance Appraisal Methods

Managers can choose from seven major performance appraisal methods. The advantages and disadvantages of each of these methods are shown in Exhibit 11-13.

written essay
A performance appraisal method in which the evaluator writes out a description of an employee's strengths and weaknesses, past performance, and potential.

Written Essays The **written essay** is a performance appraisal method in which the evaluator writes out a description of an employee's strengths and weaknesses, past performance, and potential. The evaluator also makes suggestions for improvement.

critical incidents
A performance appraisal method in which the evaluator focuses on the critical behaviours that separate effective from ineffective job performance.

Critical Incidents The use of **critical incidents** focuses the evaluator's attention on critical, or key, behaviours that separate effective from ineffective job performance. The evaluator writes down anecdotes that describe what an employee did that was especially effective or ineffective. The key here is that only specific behaviours, not vaguely defined personality traits, are cited.

graphic rating scales
A performance appraisal method in which the evaluator rates an employee on a set of performance factors.

Graphic Rating Scales One of the most popular performance appraisal methods is **graphic rating scales**. This method lists a set of performance factors such as quantity and quality of work, job knowledge, cooperation, loyalty, attendance, honesty, and initiative. The evaluator then goes down the list and rates the employee on each factor using an incremental scale, which usually specifies five points. For instance, a factor such as job knowledge might be rated from 1 ("poorly informed about work duties") to 5 ("has complete mastery of all phases of the job").

behaviourally anchored rating scales (BARS)
A performance appraisal method in which the evaluator rates an employee on examples of actual job behaviours.

Behaviourally Anchored Rating Scales Another popular performance appraisal method is **behaviourally anchored rating scales (BARS)**. These scales combine major elements from the critical incident and graphic rating scale approaches. The evaluator rates an employee according to items along a numeric scale, but the items are examples of actual job behaviours rather than general descriptions or traits.

multiperson comparisons
A performance appraisal method by which one individual's performance is compared with that of others.

Multiperson Comparisons **Multiperson comparisons** compare one individual's performance with that of others.[48] Made popular by former General Electric CEO Jack Welch, employees were rated as top performers (20 percent), middle performers (70 percent), or bottom performers (10 percent). It was believed that by using this type of "rank and yank," or forced ranking, appraisal, the company would rid itself of slackers and thus be more productive. However, critics of such systems say that they unfairly penalize groups made up of

Exhibit 11-13

Advantages and Disadvantages of Performance Appraisal Methods

Method	Advantage	Disadvantage
Written Essays	Simple to use	More a measure of evaluator's writing ability than of employee's actual performance
Critical Incidents	Rich examples; behaviourally based	Time-consuming; lack quantification
Graphic Rating Scales	Provide quantitative data; less time-consuming than others	Do not provide depth of job behaviour assessed
BARS	Focus on specific and measurable behaviours	Time-consuming; difficult to develop job behaviours
Multiperson Comparisons	Compare employees with one another	Unwieldy with large number of employees; legal concerns
MBO	Focuses on end goals; results oriented	Time-consuming
360-Degree Feedback	Thorough	Time-consuming

star performers and hinder risk-taking and collaboration.[49] For instance, Sprint used forced rankings for a year and discontinued the program because it found more effective ways to differentiate performance.[50] Are forced rankings a good idea or a bad idea? Research has shown that in companies that used forced rankings and fired the bottom 5 percent to 10 percent of employees, productivity increased an impressive 16 percent over the first couple of years. But then in subsequent years, productivity gains dropped off considerably.[51] So companies are questioning the wisdom of strict forced rankings. Even GE has been looking at ways to make its system more flexible and has encouraged its managers to use more common sense in assigning rankings.[52]

Management by Objectives   We previously introduced management by objectives (MBO) when we discussed planning in Chapter 6. MBO is also a mechanism for appraising performance. In fact, it's often used for assessing managers and professional employees.[53] With MBO, employees are evaluated according to how well they accomplish specific goals that have been established by them and their managers.

360-Degree Feedback   **360-degree feedback** is a performance appraisal method that uses feedback from supervisors, employees, and co-workers. In other words, this appraisal uses information from the full circle of people with whom the manager interacts. Of the 101 large Canadian organizations surveyed by professors Mehrdad Debrayen and Stephane Brutus of the John Molson School of Business at Concordia University, 43 percent used 360-degree feedback.[54] Toronto-based Hill & Knowlton Canada, a public relations firm, uses 360-degree feedback to help employees learn what they need to get to the next level of the organization. The feedback has had the added benefit of reducing turnover to 18 percent.[55]

Users caution that, although it's effective for career coaching and helping a manager recognize his or her strengths and weaknesses, this method is not appropriate for determining pay, promotions, or terminations. Managers using 360-degree feedback also have to carefully consider the pros and cons of using anonymous evaluations.[56]

Not all organizations conduct performance evaluations; in particular, smaller organizations often do not. Consequently, it can be useful as an employee to ask your manager for an annual appraisal, if you do not routinely receive one. The feedback will allow you to determine your goals for the following year, and identify anything for which you need improvement or training.

What Happens When Performance Falls Short?

So far, this discussion has focused on the performance management system. But what if an employee is not performing in a satisfactory manner? What can you do?

If, for some reason, an employee is not meeting his or her performance goals, a manager needs to find out why. If it is because the employee is mismatched for the job (a hiring error) or because he or she does not have adequate training, something relatively simple can be done; the manager can either reassign the individual to a job that better matches his or her skills or train the employee to do the job more effectively. If the problem is associated not with the employee's abilities but with his or her desire to do the job, it becomes a **discipline** problem. In that case, a manager can try counselling and, if necessary, can take disciplinary action such as verbal and written warnings, suspensions, and even termination.

Employee counselling is a process designed to help employees overcome performance-related problems. Rather than viewing the performance problem as something that needs to be punished (discipline), employee counselling attempts to uncover why employees have lost their desire or ability to work productively. More important, it is designed to find ways to fix the problem. In many cases, employees don't go from being productive one day to being unproductive the next. Rather, the change happens gradually and may be a function of what is occurring in their personal lives. Employee counselling attempts to assist employees in getting help to resolve whatever is bothering them.

360-degree feedback
A performance appraisal method that uses feedback from supervisors, employees, and co-workers.

discipline
Actions taken by a manager to enforce an organization's standards and regulations.

employee counselling
A process designed to help employees overcome performance-related problems.

Compensation and Benefits

7. How do compensation and
benefits motivate employees?

Most of us expect to receive appropriate compensation from our employer. Developing an effective and appropriate compensation system is an important part of the HRM process.[57] Why? Because it helps attract and retain competent and talented individuals who help the organization accomplish its mission and goals. In addition, an organization's compensation system has been shown to have an impact on its strategic performance.[58]

Q&A 11.7

*How would you know
whether your employer
was paying you fairly?*

Managers must develop a compensation system that reflects the changing nature of work and the workplace in order to keep people motivated. Organizational compensation can include many different types of rewards and benefits such as base wages and salaries, wage and salary add-ons, and incentive payments, as well as other benefits and services such as vacation time, extended health care, training allowances, and pensions. Benefits can often amount to one-third or more of an individual's base salary and should be viewed by the employee as part of the total compensation package.

How do managers determine who gets paid $9 an hour and who gets $350 000 a year? Several factors influence the differences in compensation and benefit packages for different employees. Exhibit 11-14 summarizes these factors, which are both job-based and business- or industry-based.

skill-based pay

A pay system that rewards
employees for the job skills and
competencies they can
demonstrate.

Many organizations use an alternative approach to determining compensation called **skill-based pay**. Under this type of pay system, an employee's job title does not define his or her pay category; skills do.[59] Research shows that this type of pay system seems to be more successful in manufacturing organizations than in service organizations and organizations pursuing technical innovations.[60] Skill-based pay systems seem to mesh nicely with the changing nature of jobs and today's work environment. As one expert noted, "Slowly, but surely, we're becoming a skill-based society where your market value is tied to what you can do and what your skill set is. In this new world where skills and knowledge are what really count, it does not make sense to treat people as jobholders. It makes sense to treat them as people with specific skills and to pay them for these skills."[61] On the other hand, many organizations are using variable pay systems, in which an individual's compensation is contingent on performance—81 percent of Canadian and Taiwanese organizations use variable pay plans, and 78 percent of US organizations do.[62] In Chapter 13, we discuss how pay systems, such as pay-for-performance programs, can be used to motivate employees.

Although many factors influence the design of an organization's compensation system, flexibility is a key consideration. The traditional approach to paying people reflected a time of job stability when an employee's pay was largely determined by seniority and job level. Given the dynamic environments that many organizations face in which the skills that are absolutely critical to organizational success can change in a matter of months, the trend is to make pay systems more flexible and to reduce the number of pay levels. However, whatever approach managers take, they must establish a fair, equitable, and motivating compensation system that allows the organization to recruit and keep a productive workforce.

Public vs. Private Sector Pay

There are differences between public and private sector pay structures. On average, all three levels of government (federal, provincial, and local) pay about 9 percent more to their employees, compared with what equivalent jobs in the private sector would be paid. Public sector employees generally have better benefit plans and are more likely to be covered by pension plans as well. Not everyone gets paid better in the public sector, however. While women and less-skilled employees generally get higher wages for working in the public sector, managers, especially male managers, do not see this same advantage. Moreover, at the federal level, senior managers are paid less than they might earn in the private sector. There is greater wage compression in the public sector. In the private sector, individuals in managerial, administrative, or professional occupations are paid 41 percent more, on average, than

Exhibit 11-14

Factors That Influence Compensation and Benefits

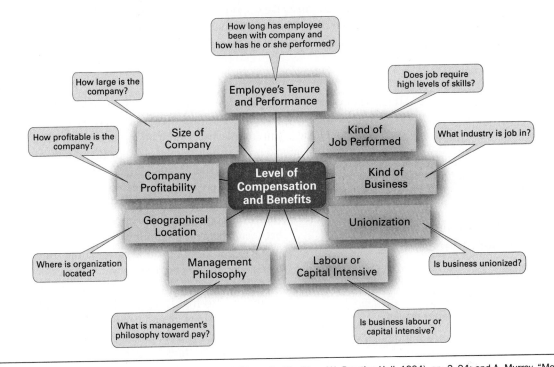

Sources: Based on R. I. Henderson, *Compensation Management*, 6th ed. (Upper Saddle River, NJ: Prentice Hall, 1994), pp. 3–24; and A. Murray, "Mom, Apple Pie, and Small Business," *Wall Street Journal*, August 15, 1994, p. A1.

those in service occupations. In the public sector, it is not uncommon for managers to be paid only 10 percent more than other employees.[63] What accounts for the public–private sector differences? Public sector pay rates are affected by labour union equity initiatives that seek to ensure women are paid equivalent wages to men for substantially similar work. The private sector is much more responsive to "market wages," which do not always result in equal pay rates for jobs that are similar, but done predominantly by one gender.[64]

Career Development

The term *career* has several meanings. In popular usage, it can mean advancement ("she is on a management career track"), a profession ("he has chosen a career in accounting"), or a lifelong sequence of jobs ("his career has included 12 jobs in 6 organizations"). For our purposes, we define a **career** as the sequence of positions held by a person during his or her lifetime.[65] Using this definition, it's apparent that we all have, or will have, a career. Moreover, the concept is as relevant to unskilled labourers as it is to software designers or physicians. But career development is not what it used to be![66]

The Way It Was

Although career development has been an important topic in management courses for years, we have witnessed some dramatic changes in the concept. Career development programs were typically designed by organizations to help employees advance their work lives within a specific organization. The focus of such programs was to provide the information, assessment, and training needed to help employees realize their career goals. Career development was also a way for organizations to attract and retain highly talented people. Those purposes have all but disappeared in today's workplace. Widespread organizational changes

8. How are careers managed?

career
A sequence of positions held by a person during his or her lifetime.

have led to uncertainty about the concept of a traditional organizational career. Downsizing, restructuring, and other organizational adjustments have brought us to one significant conclusion about career development: The individual—not the organization—is responsible for his or her own career! You, therefore, must be prepared to do what is necessary to advance your career. You must take responsibility for designing, guiding, and developing your own career.[67] Both organizations and individuals are adjusting to the notion that organizational members have to look out for themselves and become more self-reliant.

Q&A 11.8

You and Your Career Today

The idea of increased personal responsibility for one's career has been described as a *boundaryless career* in which individuals rather than organizations define career progression, organizational loyalty, important skills, and marketplace value.[68] The challenge for individuals is that there are no norms and few rules to guide them in these new circumstances. Instead, individuals assume primary responsibility for career planning, career goal setting, and education and training.[69]

Q&A 11.9

One of the first career decisions you have to make is a career choice. The optimum career choice is one that offers the best match between what you want out of life and your interests, abilities, and market opportunities. Good career choice outcomes should result in a series of positions that give you an opportunity to be a good performer, make you want to maintain your commitment to your career, lead to highly satisfying work, and give you the proper balance between work and personal life. A good career match, then, is one in which you are able to develop a positive self-concept, to do work that you think is important, and to lead the kind of life you desire.[70] Exhibit 11-15 describes the factors Canadian, US, and UK college and university students are looking for in their jobs. As you look at these results, think about what is important to you.

Once you have identified a career choice, it's time to initiate the job search. We are not going to get into the specifics of job hunting, writing a résumé, or interviewing successfully, although those career actions are important. Let's fast forward through all that and assume that your job search was successful. It's time to go to work! How do you survive and excel in your career? See *Tips for Managers—Some Suggestions for a Successful Management Career.*[71] By taking an active role in managing your career, your work life can be more exciting, enjoyable, and satisfying.

TIPS FOR MANAGERS

Some Suggestions for a Successful Management Career

- Develop a **network**.
- Continue **upgrading** your skills.
- Consider **lateral career moves**.
- Stay **mobile**.
- Support your **boss**.
- Find a **mentor**.
- **Don't stay too long** in your first job.
- Stay **visible**.
- Gain control of **organizational resources**.
- Learn the **power structure**.
- Present **the right image**.
- Do **good work**.
- Select your **first job carefully**.

Exhibit 11-15

What Do College and University Grads Want from Their Jobs?

Top Factors for Canadian Students	Top Factors for US Students	Top Factors for UK Students
• Opportunities for advancement in position	• Work–life balance	• International career opportunities
• Good people to work with	• Annual base salary	• Flexible working hours
• Good people to report to	• Job stability and security	• Variety of assignments
• Work–life balance	• Recognition for a job done well	• Paid overtime
• Initial salary	• Increasingly challenging tasks	
	• Rotational programs	

Sources: Based on E. Pooley, "Hire Education: How to Recruit Top University Graduates," *Canadian Business*, September 11–24, 2006; S. Shellenbarger, "Avoiding the Next Enron: Today's Crop of Soon-to-Be Grads Seeks Job Security," *Wall Street Journal*, February 16, 2006; "MBAs Eye Financial Services and Management Consulting," *HRMarketer.com*, June 7, 2005; and J. Boone, "Students Set Tighter Terms for Work," *FinancialTimes.com*, May 21, 2005.

Current Issues in Human Resource Management

▶ ▶ ▶ Scotiabank prides itself on its work with the Aboriginal community.[72] The bank sponsors scholarships, events, and programs for community members, and also supports Aboriginal business initiatives.

The bank actively recruits from the Aboriginal community. Scotiabank's recruiting strategy is based "on the medicine wheel and the teachings of the medicine wheel, in terms of all the components [of the medicine wheel] need to exist in balance together," says Michele Baptiste, national manager of Aboriginal relations with Scotiabank. The bank has also approached the Aboriginal Human Resource Development Council of Canada to assist "in recruitment and retention of Aboriginal people across the country," according to Baptiste.

Think About It

How are companies managing diversity in their workplaces? To what extent are they addressing issues such as work–life balance? Should they be doing so?

We conclude this chapter by looking at some contemporary human resource issues facing today's managers: managing workforce diversity, dealing with sexual harassment, helping employees manage work–life balance, and managing downsizing.

9. What are some current issues in human resource management?

Workforce Diversity

We have discussed the changing makeup of the workforce in several places throughout this textbook and provided insights in our *Managing Workforce Diversity* feature in several chapters. In this section, we consider how workforce diversity is directly affected by basic HRM activities including recruitment, selection, and orientation and training.

Recruitment

To improve workforce diversity, managers need to widen their recruiting net. For example, the popular practice of relying on employee referrals as a source of job applicants tends to produce candidates who are similar to present employees. However, some organizations, such as Toronto-based Tele-Mobile (TELUS Mobility), have recruited and hired diverse individuals by relying on referrals from their current employees. But not every organization has the employee resources needed to achieve workforce diversity through employee referrals. So managers may have to look for job applicants in places where they might not have looked before. To increase diversity, managers from such companies as Calgary-based Suncor Energy, Saskatoon, Saskatchewan-based Cameco, and Toronto-based Scotiabank and TELUS Mobility are increasingly turning to nontraditional recruitment sources such as women's job networks, over-50 clubs, urban job banks, disabled people's training centres, ethnic newspapers, and gay rights organizations. This type of outreach should enable the organization to broaden its pool of diverse applicants. When IKEA went to Seville, Spain, it followed an alternative recruiting strategy, as the following *Management Reflection* shows.

MANAGEMENT REFLECTION
▶ Focus on International Issues

IKEA Taps into New Labour Force

Should you hire people with no previous experience? When Swedish-based IKEA opened up a store in Seville, its fifth location in Spain, the company decided to search for a different type of employee.[73] The company advertised for "single mothers, students, people with disabilities and long-term unemployed." They did not even require working experience. Andalusia, the region where the store was opening, has an 18.5 percent unemployment rate, and 30 000 applicants responded to IKEA's ads.

Employers in Spain had never recruited from these categories of workers before. IKEA's model for employment is unique: It targets people who really need jobs. The company provides training to its employees to help them overcome any initial hurdles from lack of experience. People with disabilities were hired for customer service, administration, and logistics. Juvencio Maeztu, the store manager, explained the store's hiring policy: "We were more interested in finding people with the right motivation than with the right college degrees."

IKEA's strategy of hiring the previously "unhirable" may well pay off in Spain. With the country's high unemployment rates and IKEA's plan to have 35 stores in Spain by 2015, those in Spain looking for jobs have renewed hope they will be able to find work. ■

Selection

Once a diverse set of applicants exists, efforts must be made to ensure that the selection process does not discriminate. Moreover, applicants need to be made comfortable with the organization's culture and be made aware of management's desire to accommodate their needs. For instance, at TD Canada Trust, managers are trained to respond positively to requests by employees who need a prayer room or whose religions require them to stop working by sundown.[74]

Orientation and Training

The outsider–insider transition is often more challenging for women and minorities than for white males. Many organizations provide special workshops to raise diversity awareness issues. Some organizations aggressively pursue diversity efforts only after being hit with legal claims. For instance, Advantica, the parent company of Denny's restaurants, was hit with a series of legal claims in the early 1990s. It responded with aggressive minority hiring and a supplier-diversity effort. The company has been ranked in the top 10 of *Fortune* magazine's "America's 50 Best Companies for Minorities" for seven years straight. Coca-Cola, which settled a class-action suit by black employees for more than $250 million (US) in November 2000, has made strides in its diversity efforts, including launching a formal mentoring program and required diversity training for employees.[75]

Sexual Harassment

Sexual harassment is a serious issue in both public and private sector organizations. A recent survey by York University found that 48 percent of working women in Canada reported they had experienced some form of "gender harassment" in the year before they were surveyed.[76] A 1996 RCMP survey found that 6 out of every 10 female Mounties said they had experienced sexual harassment.[77] In 2006, Nancy Sulz, who worked as an RCMP officer in British Columbia, was awarded $950 000 for her complaint against the detachment, which included claims of sexual harassment.[78] Barbara Orser, a research affiliate with the Conference Board of Canada, notes that "sexual harassment is more likely to occur in workplace environments that tolerate bullying, intimidation, yelling, innuendo and other forms of discourteous behaviour."[79] And sexual harassment is not a problem just in Canada. During 2005, more than 12 600 complaints were filed with the US Equal Employment Opportunity Commission (EEOC). Although most complaints are filed by women, the percentage of charges filed by males has risen every year but two since 1992.[80] Sexual harassment is a global issue: Charges have been filed against employers in such countries as Japan, Australia, the Netherlands, Belgium, New Zealand, Sweden, Ireland, and Mexico.[81]

Even though discussions of sexual harassment cases often focus on the large awards granted by a court, there are other concerns for employers. Sexual harassment creates an unpleasant work environment and undermines employees' ability to perform their jobs.

Sexual harassment is defined by the Supreme Court of Canada as unwelcome behaviour of a sexual nature in the workplace that negatively affects the work environment or leads to adverse job-related consequences for the employee.[82] Sexual harassment can occur between members of the opposite sex or of the same sex. Although such activity is generally covered under employment discrimination laws, in recent years this problem has gained

sexual harassment
Any unwelcome behaviour of a sexual nature in the workplace that negatively affects the work environment or leads to adverse job-related consequences for the employee.

more recognition. By most accounts, prior to the mid-1980s this problem was generally viewed as an isolated incident, with the individual at fault being solely responsible (if at all) for his or her actions.

Many problems associated with sexual harassment involve interpreting the Supreme Court's definition to determine exactly what constitutes illegal behaviour. For many organizations, conveying what an offensive or hostile environment looks like is not completely black and white. For instance, while it is relatively easy to focus on problems where an individual employee is harassed, this may not address more systemic problems in the workplace. Other employees can also be negatively affected when they witness offensive conduct.[83] Thus managers at all levels need to be attuned to what makes fellow employees uncomfortable—and if they don't know, they should ask.[84]

What can an organization do to protect itself against sexual harassment claims?[85] The courts want to know two things: Did the organization know about, or should it have known about, the alleged behaviour? and What did management do to stop it? With the number and dollar amounts of the awards against organizations increasing, there is a greater need for management to educate all employees on sexual harassment matters and have mechanisms available to monitor employees. Managers at all levels have a duty to create and maintain a harassment-free work environment. One final area of interest we want to discuss in terms of sexual harassment is workplace romances.

Q&A 11.10

Workplace Romances

If you are employed, have you ever dated someone at work? If not, have you ever been attracted to someone in your workplace and thought about pursuing a relationship? Such situations are more common than you might think—40 percent of employees surveyed by the *Wall Street Journal* said that they have had an office romance. And another survey found that 54 percent of single men and 40 percent of single women said they would be open to dating a co-worker.[86] The environment in today's organizations with mixed-gender work teams and working long hours is undoubtedly contributing to this situation. "People realize they're going to be at work such long hours, it's almost inevitable that this takes place," said one survey director. But a workplace romance is something that can potentially become a really big problem for organizations.[87] In addition to the potential conflicts and retaliation between co-workers who decide to stop dating or to end a romantic relationship, the more serious problems stem from the potential for sexual harassment accusations, especially when it's between supervisor and subordinate. The standard used by judicial courts has been that workplace sexual conduct is prohibited sexual harassment *if* it is unwelcome. If it's welcome, it still may be inappropriate, but usually is not unlawful. However, a recent ruling by the California Supreme Court concerning specifically a supervisor–subordinate relationship that got out of hand is worth noting. That ruling said the "completely consensual workplace romances can create a hostile work environment for others in the workplace."[88]

What should organizations do about workplace romances? The best bet is to have some type of policy regarding workplace dating among co-workers, particularly in terms of educating employees about the potential for sexual harassment. However, because possible liability is more serious when it comes to supervisor–subordinate relationships, organizations need to be more proactive in these situations in terms of discouraging such relationships and perhaps even requiring supervisors to report any such relationships to the HR department. At some point, the organization may even want to consider banning such relationships, although an outright ban may be difficult to put into practice.

Work–Life Balance

Professors Linda Duxbury of the Sprott School of Business at Carleton University and Chris Higgins of the University of Western Ontario are the leading Canadian researchers on the issue of work–life balance. Their research shows that employees are working long hours, and are also increasingly being asked to work a number of unpaid hours a week.[89] This affects employees' abilities to manage their family lives.

What kinds of work–life balance issues can arise that might affect an employee's job performance? Here are some examples:

- Is it okay for someone to bring his baby to work because of an emergency crisis with normal child care arrangements?

- Is it okay to expect an employee to work 60 or more hours a week?

- Should an employee be given the day off to watch her child perform in a school event?

What kinds of work–life balance issues are affecting your life right now?

In the 1980s, organizations began to recognize that employees don't leave their families and personal lives behind when they walk into work. An organization hires a person who has a personal life outside the office, personal problems, and family commitments. Although managers cannot be sympathetic to every detail of an employee's family life, we *are* seeing organizations more attuned to the fact that employees have sick children, elderly parents who need special care, and other family issues that may require special arrangements. In response, most major organizations have taken actions to make their workplaces more family-friendly by offering **family-friendly benefits**, which include a wide range of work and family programs to help employees.[90] They have introduced programs such as on-site child care, summer day camps, flextime, job sharing, leaves for school functions, telecommuting, and part-time employment.

family-friendly benefits
Benefits that accommodate employees' needs for work–life balance.

Work–life conflicts are as relevant to male employees with children and women without children as they are for female employees with children. Heavy workloads and increased travel demands, for instance, are making it increasingly hard for many employees, male and female, to meet both work and personal responsibilities. A *Fortune* survey found that 84 percent of male executives surveyed said that "they'd like job options that let them realize their professional aspirations while having more time for things outside work." Also, 87 percent of these executives believed that any company that restructured top-level management jobs in ways that would both increase productivity and make more time available for life outside the office would have a competitive advantage in attracting talented employees.[91] Younger employees, particularly, put a higher priority on family and a lower priority on jobs, and are looking for organizations that give them more work flexibility.[92]

Today's progressive workplace is becoming more accommodating to the varied needs of a diverse workforce. It provides a wide range of scheduling options and benefits that allow employees more flexibility at work and allow employees to better balance or integrate their work and personal lives. Despite these organizational efforts, work–life programs have room for improvement. Workplace surveys still show high levels of employee stress stemming from work–life conflicts. And large groups of women and minority employees remain unemployed or underemployed because of family responsibilities and bias in the workplace.[93] So what can managers do?

Research on work–family life balance has provided some new insights. For instance, we are beginning to see evidence that there are positive outcomes when individuals are able to combine work and family roles.[94] As a participant in a recent study noted, "I think being a mother and having patience and watching someone else

Does being rigid about not offering flextime harm employers? Surrey, BC, mom Sheila Whitehead thinks so. She quit her job as a marketing manager for a pharmaceuticals company when she could not get the flextime she needed to spend more time with her four-year-old-daughter, Abigail, and her other two young children. She says that employers are "missing out on incredibly talented people who simply don't want the rigid nine-to-five hours." She's created a website, beyond9to5.com, to help match employers with employees who want to have more flexible work hours.

grow has made me a better manager. I am better able to be patient with other people and let them grow and develop in a way that is good for them."[95] In addition, individuals who have family-friendly workplace support appear to be more satisfied on the job.[96] This finding seems to strengthen the notion that organizations benefit by creating a workplace in which employee work–family life balance is possible. And the benefits show up in financial results as well. Research has shown a significant, positive relationship between work–family initiatives and an organization's stock price.[97]

However, managers need to understand that people do differ in their preferences for work–family life scheduling options and benefits.[98] Some people prefer organizational initiatives that better *segment* work from their personal lives. Others prefer programs that facilitate *integration*. For instance, flextime schedules segment because they allow employees to schedule work hours that are less likely to conflict with personal responsibilities. On the other hand, on-site child care integrates by blurring the boundaries between work and family responsibilities. People who prefer segmentation are more likely to be satisfied and committed to their jobs when offered options such as flextime, job sharing, and part-time hours. People who prefer integration are more likely to respond positively to options such as on-site child care, gym facilities, and company-sponsored family picnics.

Helping Survivors Respond to Layoffs

Downsizing is the planned elimination of jobs in an organization. When an organization has too many employees—which can happen when it needs to cut costs, is faced with declining market share, or has grown too aggressively—one option for shoring up profits is by eliminating some of those surplus employees through downsizing. Well-known companies such as Air Canada, Nortel, Shaw Communications, Domtar, BCE, and GM Canada and others have had to downsize in recent years.[99] How can managers best manage a downsized workplace? Expect disruptions in the workplace and in employees' personal lives. Stress, frustration, anxiety, and anger are typical reactions of both individuals being laid off and the job survivors. But are there things managers can do to lessen the pain? Yes.[100]

Open and honest communication is critical. Individuals who are being let go need to be informed as soon as possible. In providing assistance to employees being downsized, the law requires some form of severance pay in lieu of proper notice. Benefit extensions to help employees while they find new plans must also be covered for a specified period of time. Managers want to be sure they're following any laws that might affect the length of time pay and benefits must be offered and the types of pay and benefits that must be provided. In addition, many organizations provide job search assistance.

It may surprise you to learn that both victims and survivors experience feelings of frustration, anxiety, and loss.[101] But layoff victims get to start over with a clean slate and a clear conscience. Survivors don't. A new syndrome seems to be popping up in more and more organizations: **layoff-survivor sickness**, a set of attitudes, perceptions, and behaviours of employees who survive involuntary staff reductions.[102] Symptoms include job insecurity, perceptions of unfairness, guilt, depression, stress from increased workload, fear of change, loss of loyalty and commitment, reduced effort, and an unwillingness to do anything beyond the required minimum.

downsizing
The planned elimination of jobs in an organization.

layoff-survivor sickness A set of attitudes, perceptions, and behaviours of employees who remain after involuntary employee reductions; it includes insecurity, guilt, depression, stress, fear, loss of loyalty, and reduced effort.

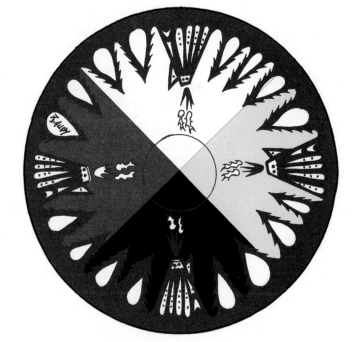

Michele Baptiste, national manager of Aboriginal relations with Scotiabank, created the bank's Aboriginal employment strategy. It is based on the teachings of the medicine wheel (an example of which is shown here). The idea behind the medicine wheel is that the four major components of an individual (mental, spiritual, emotional, physical) have to be in balance. Baptiste emphasizes that Scotiabank takes a holistic approach to Aboriginal relations, bringing together employment, business, and community involvement.

To address this survivor syndrome, managers may want to provide opportunities for employees to talk to counsellors about their guilt, anger, and anxiety.[103] Group discussions can also provide an opportunity for the survivors to vent their feelings. Some organizations have used downsizing as the spark to implement increased employee participation programs such as empowerment and self-managed work teams. In short, to keep morale and productivity high, every attempt should be made to ensure that those individuals who are still working in the organization know that they are needed and valuable.

SUMMARY AND IMPLICATIONS

1. Does managing human resources well make a difference? Studies show that an organization's human resources can be a significant competitive advantage. Often, employees are thought of as costs to be minimized or avoided. However, when employees are considered partners, they are more likely to be motivated, leading to greater organizational performance.

▶ ▶ ▶ Scotiabank is often rated as one of Canada's top employers, and also as a good place for women to work.

2. How does the external environment affect human resource planning? When managers hire employees, they must follow laws that have been written to protect employees and the workplace, including the Canada Labour Code, employment standards legislation, the Charter of Rights and Freedoms, and the Canadian Human Rights Act. Therefore, managers are not completely free to choose whom they hire, promote, or fire.

▶ ▶ ▶ Practically speaking, managers such as Rick Waugh of Scotiabank cannot simply hire their friends, or decide to exclude from hire a particular minority group. While Scotiabank's employees are not unionized, managers within a unionized environment are obligated to uphold the collective agreement negotiated with the labour union.

3. How do organizations assess their human resource needs? Human resource managers do a human resource inventory to discover what skills and capabilities current employees have. They map that inventory against what might be needed in the future, based on the organization's mission, goals, and strategies.

▶ ▶ ▶ Because President and CEO Rick Waugh would like to see more women in senior management positions, Scotiabank needs to assess which of its female employees have the skills and leadership qualities to move into senior management.

4. How do organizations identify and select competent employees? Organizations first need to assess their current and future needs for employees, to make sure they have enough of the right people to accomplish the organization's goals. When selecting new employees, organizations need to determine whether potential employees will be successful once they are on the job. To do this, managers use application forms, written tests, performance-simulation tests, interviews, background investigations, and, in some cases, physical examinations to screen employees. Managers need to make sure that they do not engage in discrimination in the hiring process.

▶ ▶ ▶ One way that Scotiabank identifies potential employees is through applications from its Careers webpage, which targets young graduates and encourages them to think about working for the bank.

5. How do organizations help employees adapt and stay up-to-date? Organizations, particularly larger ones, have orientation programs for new employees. The orientation introduces the new employee to his or her job, and also to the organization. As job demands change, employees may need to have their skills updated through training programs. Companies use a variety of training methods, from on-the-job training to classroom work to technology-based training.

▶ ▶ ▶ Among other programs, Scotiabank has Leading Edge, the bank's fast-track leadership program.

6. What can organizations do to help employees achieve high performance over their careers? Organizations should develop performance standards for employees, and then evaluate employees on a regular basis. Through performance appraisal, employees learn whether they are performing effectively, or whether they need to improve, including getting additional training.

7. How do compensation and benefits motivate employees? Organizations develop compensation and benefit programs that will motivate employees to achieve high performance. Many organizations have implemented skill-based pay systems, which reward employees for the job skills and competencies they can demonstrate. On average, all three levels of government (federal, provincial, and local) pay about 9 percent more to their employees, compared with what equivalent jobs in the private sector would be paid. Public sector employees generally have better benefit and pension plans.

8. How are careers managed? A career is the sequence of positions held by a person during his or her lifetime. Career development programs used to be created by organizations to help employees advance within the organization. Today, employees are encouraged to create their own development programs, in addition to whatever their companies provide, because often employees work for multiple organizations during their careers. Thus, more responsibility rests on employees to manage their own careers.

9. What are some current issues in human resource management? The major current issues in human resource management include managing downsizing, managing workforce diversity, dealing with sexual harassment, workplace romances, helping employees manage work–life balance, and managing downsizing.

▶ ▶ ▶ Scotiabank prides itself on its work with the Aboriginal community, sponsoring scholarships, events, and programs for community members and also supporting Aboriginal business initiatives. The bank also permits flex hours, flex days, job sharing, and telecommuting so that employees can find the right "work life" to match their personal needs.

CHAPTER 11

Management @ Work

READING FOR COMPREHENSION

1. Describe the environmental factors that most directly influence the human resource management process.

2. Contrast reject errors and accept errors. Which are more likely to open an employer to charges of discrimination? Why?

3. What is the relationship between job analysis, recruitment, and selection?

4. What are the major problems of the interview as a selection device?

5. What are the benefits and drawbacks of realistic job previews? (Consider this question from the perspective of both the organization and the employee.)

6. How are orientation and employee training alike? How are they different?

7. Describe three performance appraisal methods, as well as the advantages and disadvantages of each.

8. What is skill-based pay?

9. How do recruitment, selection, orientation, and training directly affect workforce diversity?

LINKING CONCEPTS TO PRACTICE

1. How does human resource management affect all managers?

2. Are there limits on how far a prospective employer should delve into an applicant's personal life by means of interviews or tests? Explain.

3. Should an employer have the right to choose employees without government interference in the hiring process? Explain your position.

4. Studies show that women's salaries still lag behind men's, and even with equal opportunity laws and regulations women are paid about 73 percent of what men

are paid. How would you design a compensation system that would address this issue?

5. What drawbacks, if any, do you see in implementing flexible benefits? (Consider this question from the perspective of both the organization and the employee.)

6. What, in your view, constitutes sexual harassment? Describe how companies can minimize sexual harassment in the workplace.

SELF-ASSESSMENT

How Good Am I at Giving Performance Feedback?

For each of the following pairs, identify the statement that most closely matches what you normally do when you give feedback to someone else.[104]

1. a. Describe the behaviour. **b.** Evaluate the behaviour.

2. a. Focus on the feelings that the behaviour evokes. **b.** Tell the person what he or she should be doing differently.

3. a. Give specific instances of the behaviour. **b.** Generalize.

4. a. Deal only with behaviour that the person can control. **b.** Sometimes focus on something the person can do nothing about.

5. a. Tell the person as soon as possible after the behaviour. **b.** Sometimes wait too long.

6. a. Focus on the effect the behaviour has on me. **b.** Try to figure out why the individual did what he or she did.

7. a. Balance negative feedback with positive feedback. **b.** Sometimes focus only on the negative.

8. a. Do some soul searching to make sure that the reason I am giving the feedback is to help the other person or to strengthen our relationship. **b.** Sometimes give feedback to punish, win, or dominate the other person.

Scoring Key

Total the number of "a" responses, and then total the number of "b" responses, and then form an a/b ratio. For instance, if you have 6 "a" responses and 2 "b" responses, your a/b ration would be 6/2.

Analysis and Interpretation

Along with listening skills, feedback skills comprise the other primary component of effective communication. This instrument is designed to assess how good you are at providing feedback.

In this assessment instrument, the "a" responses are your self-perceived strengths and the "b" responses are your self-perceived weaknesses. By looking at the proportion of your "a" and "b" responses, you will be able to see how effective you feel you are when giving feedback and determine where your strengths and weaknesses lie.

More Self-Assessments mymanagementlab

To learn more about your skills, abilities, and interests, go to the MyManagementLab website and take the following self-assessments:

- I.B.3.—How Satisfied Am I with My Job?
- III.B.3.—Am I Experiencing Work–Family Conflict?

MANAGEMENT FOR YOU TODAY

Dilemma

Your instructor has asked class members to form teams to work on a major class project. You have worked on teams before, and have not always been pleased with the results. This time you are determined to have a good team experience. You have reason to believe that how people are recruited to and selected for teams might make a difference. You also

know that evaluating performance and giving feedback are important. You have also heard that training can make a difference. With all of this in mind, write up a plan that indicates how you might recruit an excellent set of team members and make sure that they perform well throughout.

Becoming a Manager

- Using the Internet, research different companies that interest you and check out what they say about careers or their people.
- If you are working, note what types of human resource management activities your managers do. What do they do that seems to be effective? Ineffective? What can you learn from this?

- Do career research in your chosen career by finding out what it's going to take to be successful in that career.
- Complete *Developing Your Interpersonal Skills—Interviewing* on pages 355–356, at the end of this chapter, and *Developing Your Interpersonal Skills—Becoming More Culturally Aware* on pages 95–96, in Chapter 3.

WORKING TOGETHER: TEAM-BASED EXERCISE

Recruiting for Diversity

You work as director of human resources for a gift registry website based in Toronto. Your company currently has 30 employees, but due to the popularity of your site, the company is growing rapidly. To handle customer demand, at least 30 additional employees are going to be needed in the next three months. In filling those positions, the company's CEO is committed to increasing employee diversity because she feels that this will add unique

perspectives on the types of gift services provided by the company. She has asked you to head up a team to propose some specific practices for recruiting diverse individuals.

Form teams of 3 or 4 individuals. Identify specific steps that your company can take to recruit diverse individuals. Be creative and be specific. Write down your proposed steps and be prepared to share your ideas with the class.

ETHICS IN ACTION

Ethical Dilemma Exercise: But I Deserve an "A"!

Everybody wants an A ranking; nobody wants a C ranking.[105] Yet the multiperson ranking system used by Goodyear Tire & Rubber Company forced managers to rank 10 percent of the workforce as A performers, 80 percent as B performers, and 10 percent as C performers. Those ranked as A performers were rewarded with promotions; those ranked as C performers were told they could be demoted or fired for a second C rating. Goodyear abandoned its 10-80-10 system just before some C employees who had been fired filed a lawsuit claiming age discrimination. "It is very unfair to start with the assumption that a certain percentage of your employees are unsatisfactory," said one of the plaintiffs. "It was very subjective and designed to weed out the older people."

Like Goodyear, a growing number of companies have followed the lead of General Electric in regularly ranking employees. Many companies give poor performers an opportunity to improve before taking action. However, critics say the ranking system forces managers to penalize employees on poorly performing teams. They also say the ranking system can lead to age, gender, or race discrimination. In response, companies are training managers to use more objective measures for appraisals, such as monitoring progress toward preset goals.

Imagine that you are a General Electric executive who must rank 20 percent of your subordinate managers as top performers, 70 percent as average, and 10 percent as needing improvement. Retaining incompetent or unmotivated managers is unfair to the rest of the staff and sends mixed signals. On the other hand, even if all your managers are competent, you must put 10 percent into the bottom category. Now it's appraisal time and you do not feel that any of your employees deserve to be in the bottom category. What should you do? (Review Exhibit 11-13 on page 340 as you consider this ethical challenge.)

Thinking Critically About Ethics

What you say online *can* come back to haunt you. Organizations are using Google, MySpace, and Facebook to check out applicants and current employees. In fact, some organizations see Google as a way to get "around discrimination laws, inasmuch as employers can find out all manner of information—some of it for a nominal fee—that is legally off-limits in interviews: your age, your marital status, fraternity pranks, stuff you wrote in college, political affiliations and so forth." And for those individuals who like to rant and rave about employers, there might be later consequences. That is why some individuals pull their Facebook profiles. What do you think of what these companies are doing? What positives and negatives are there to such behaviour? What are the ethical implications? What guidelines might you suggest for an organization's selection process?

CASE APPLICATION

Mitsubishi Motors North America

When Rich Gilligan took over as plant manager at Mitsubishi Motors North America's (MMNA) manufacturing facility in Normal, Illinois, in 1998, the plant had two notorious distinctions: It was one of the most automated yet least productive plants in the industry, and it was known as the place sued by the US government for the sexual harassment of its female employees.[106] That lawsuit was what most people knew about Mitsubishi Motors.

The high-profile case told the story of a dismal workplace: "sexual graffiti written on fenders about to pass female line employees; pornographic pictures taped on walls; male employees taunting women with wrenches and air compressors; women asked by male employees to bare their breasts; other women fondled; and women who complained of being fired or passed over for promotion." Almost from the beginning, the plant had a bad reputation regarding the employment of women. People in the local community looked with suspicion at plant employees. One of the shift managers said, "We had guys who had no bad marks asked to stop coaching girls' softball teams just because they worked at that plant." After numerous employee complaints, the Equal Employment Opportunity Commission (EEOC) entered the picture and filed suit on behalf of 500 female employees, charging the company with sexual harassment. The case dragged on for three years, further draining employee morale and damaging an already distant relationship between American employees and Japanese managers. That is the environment that Gilligan inherited.

Right before Gilligan was hired, MMNA settled the EEOC lawsuit for more than $44 million (US)—still the largest sexual harassment settlement in US history. The money was distributed to more than 400 women, many of whom still work at the plant. The EEOC settlement also dictated a makeover of the work environment.

Gilligan needs to change the culture of the plant, and improve productivity and quality. He knows that Mitsubishi's mission statement is "We are a spirited, diverse workforce.

We are a culture that looks for, and rewards, hard work and dedication. We are winners." Although each member of the Mitsubishi Group is independent, they are supposed to share the guiding principles of the Sankoryo, first announced in the 1930s by founder Koyata Iwasaki and revised to reflect today's realities:

- *Shoki Hoko:* Strive to enrich society, both materially and spiritually, while contributing toward the preservation of the environment.

- *Shoji Komei:* Maintain principles of transparency and openness, conducting business with integrity and fairness.
- *Ritsugyo Boeki:* Expand business, based on an all-encompassing global perspective.

Conduct like this is not what was happening at MMNA as Gilligan took over. What could Gilligan do to improve the culture and increase productivity?

The Benefits of Benefits

Can the benefits offered to employees be a factor in encouraging individuals to apply for and accept jobs in an organization? Would your response to a job viewed as less than desirable, in which the work hours are long and the pay is low, be the same if it had benefits? For some people, benefits are critical to whether they take and keep a job. Take the case of Patsy Sechrest.

Patsy Sechrest is among a growing number of contemporary employees who cannot afford to retire. She is in her twenty-eighth year as an employee at a family restaurant in BC. She works over 50 hours a week, earning $9.00 per hour and arriving to work at 4:05 a.m. each day. Sechrest, like many others over 50 years old, continues to work simply because she needs the money and the extended health benefits (eye care, dental care, prescription drugs, massage, and physiotherapy) that working provides. Compounding this issue is the fact that Sechrest and her husband live in a depressed area that was hit hard by the closing of a local pulp and paper mill.

Sechrest is also dealing with health ailments that have created a financial burden for her family. Making just over $20 000 annually, she is one of the more fortunate ones. Her employer provides generous extended health benefits. Without it, she would be financially devastated and in physical pain. Due to arthritis, she needs to see a massage ther-

apist and a physiotherapist regularly. Her health insurance pays most of the costs. Without the health insurance coverage, she simply could not have afforded the alternative medical treatments she receives.

For Patsy Sechrest, work and therapist visits have become a way of life. She is not bitter at the hand she has been dealt, but rather she is thankful for what her employer has provided—a paying job and extended health benefits. She expects to hang on to both for as long as she can!

Questions

1. How do benefits, such as those that the family restaurant provides, assist organizations in competing for and retaining employees?

2. Do you believe employee benefits should be membership-based (you get them simply because you work for the company) or performance-based (you earn them)? Defend your position.

3. Do you believe providing extended health care benefits for employees is a competitive necessity or a socially responsible action by the organization? Defend your position.

Interviewing

About the Skill

The interview is used almost universally as part of the employee selection process. Not many of us have ever got a job without having gone through one or more interviews. Interviews can be valid and reliable selection tools, but they need to be structured and well organized.

Steps in Developing the Skill

You can be an effective interviewer if you use the following seven suggestions for interviewing job candidates:[107]

1. **Review the job description and job specification.** Be sure that prior to the interview, you have reviewed pertinent information about the job. Why? Because this will

provide you with valuable information on which to assess the job candidate. Furthermore, knowing the relevant job requirements will help eliminate interview bias.

2. **Prepare a structured set of questions you want to ask all job applicants.** By having a set of prepared questions, you ensure that you will get the information you want. Furthermore, by asking similar questions, you are able to better compare all candidates' answers against a common base.

3. **Before meeting a candidate, review his or her application form and résumé.** By doing this, you will be able to create a complete picture of the candidate in terms of what is represented on the résumé or application and what the job requires. You can also begin to identify areas to explore during the interview; that is, areas that are not clearly defined on the résumé or application but that are essential to the job can become a focal point in your discussion with the candidate.

4. **Open the interview by putting the applicant at ease and by providing a brief preview of the topics to be discussed.** Interviews are stressful for job candidates. Opening the discussion with small talk, such as the weather, can give the candidate time to adjust to the interview setting. By providing a preview of topics to come, you are giving the candidate an agenda. This helps the candidate begin framing what he or she will say in response to your questions.

5. **Ask your questions and listen carefully to the candidate's answers.** Select follow-up questions that flow naturally from the answers given. Focus on the candidate's responses as they relate to information you need to ensure that the person meets your job requirements. If you are still uncertain, use a follow-up question to probe further for information.

6. **Close the interview by telling the applicant what is going to happen next.** Applicants are anxious about the status of your hiring decision. Be upfront with candidates regarding others who will be interviewed and the remaining steps in the hiring process. Let the person know your time frame for making a decision. In addition, tell the applicant how you will notify him or her about your decision.

7. **Write your evaluation of the applicant while the interview is still fresh in your mind.** Don't wait until the end of the day, after interviewing several people, to write your analysis of each person. Memory can (and often will) fail you! The sooner you write your impressions after an interview, the better chance you have of accurately noting what occurred in the interview and your perceptions of the candidate.

Practising the Skill

Read the following list and do the actions. Be sure to refer to the seven suggestions for conducting effective interviews.

1. Break into groups of 3.

2. Take up to 10 minutes to compose five challenging job interview questions that you think should be relevant in the hiring of new graduates for a sales-management training program at Kraft Canada. Each hiree will spend 18 to 24 months as a sales representative calling on retail grocery and restaurant accounts. After this training period, successful performers can be expected to be promoted to the position of district sales supervisor.

3. Exchange your five questions with another group.

4. Each group should allocate one of the following roles to their 3 members: interviewer, applicant, and observer. The person playing the applicant should rough out a brief résumé of his or her background and experience and then give it to the interviewer.

5. Role play a job interview. The interviewer should include, but not be limited to, the five questions provided by the other group.

6. After the interview, the observer should evaluate the interviewer's behaviour in terms of the effective interview suggestions.

Reinforcing the Skill

The following activities will help you practise and reinforce the skills associated with interviewing:

1. On your campus, there is probably a job and career placement service provided for graduates. If possible, talk with two or three graduating students who have been interviewed by organizations through this campus service. Ask them to share what happened during their interviews. Then write a brief report describing what you found out and comparing the students' experiences with the suggestions for effective interviewing.

2. Interview a manager about the interview process he or she uses in hiring new employees. What types of information does the manager try to get during an interview? (Be sure that as you interview this manager you are using the suggestions for good interviewing! Although you are not "hiring" this person, you are looking for information, which is exactly what managers are looking for during a job interview.)

Continuing Case: Starbucks

Organizing is an important task of managers.[1] Once the organization's goals and plans are in place, the organizing function sets in motion the process of seeing that those goals and plans are pursued. When managers organize, they are defining what work needs to get done and creating a structure that enables work activities to be completed efficiently and effectively by organizational members hired to do that work. As Starbucks continues its global expansion and pursues innovative strategic initiatives, managers must deal with the realities of continually organizing and reorganizing its work efforts.

Structuring Starbucks

Like many start-up businesses, Starbucks' original founders organized their company around a simple structure based on each person's unique strengths: Zev Siegl became the retail expert; Jerry Baldwin took over the administrative functions; and Gordon Bowker was the dreamer who called himself "the magic, mystery, and romance man" and recognized from the start that a visit to Starbucks could "evoke a brief escape to a distant world." As Starbucks grew to the point where Jerry recognized that he needed to hire professional and experienced managers, Howard Schultz joined the company, bringing his skills in sales, marketing, and merchandising. When the original owners eventually sold the company to Schultz, he was able to take the company on the path to becoming what it is today and what it hopes to be in the future.

As Starbucks has expanded, its organizational structure has changed to accommodate that growth. However, the company prides itself on its "lean" corporate structure. Howard Schultz is chairman and chief global strategist and Jim Donald is president and CEO. Schultz has focused on hiring a team of executives from companies like Wal-Mart, Dell, and PepsiCo. He says, "I wanted to bring in people who had experience working at $10 billion companies." These senior corporate officers include the following: president of Starbucks Coffee US, president of Starbucks Coffee International, 4 executive vice-presidents, and 29 senior vice-presidents. In addition to the president of Starbucks Coffee Canada, Colin Moore, the senior vice-president positions include senior vice-president of finance, senior vice-president of coffee and global procurement, and senior vice-president of corporate social responsibility. (A complete list of upper-level managers can be found in the company's annual report on its website: **www.starbucks.com**.)

Although the executive team provides the all-important strategic direction, the "real" work of Starbucks gets done at the company's support centre, zone offices, retail stores, and roasting plants. The support centre provides support to and assists all other aspects of corporate operations in the areas of accounting, finance, information technology, and sales and supply chain management.

The zone offices oversee the regional operations of the retail stores and provide support in human resource management, facilities management, account management, financial management, and sales management. The essential link between the zone offices and each retail store is the district manager, each of whom oversees 8 to 10 stores apiece, which is down from the dozen or so stores they used to oversee. Since district managers need to be out working with the stores, most use mobile technology that allows them to spend more time in the stores and still remain connected to their own office. A company executive says, "These are the most important people in the company. And while their primary job is outside the office and in those stores, they still need to be connected."

In the retail stores, hourly employees (baristas) service customers under the direction of assistant store managers and store managers. These managers are responsible for the day-to-day operations of each Starbucks location. One of the organizational challenges for many store managers has been the company's decision to add more drive-through windows to retail stores, which appears to be a smart strategic move since the average annual volume at a store with a drive-through window is about 30 percent higher than a store without one. However, a drive-through window often takes up to four people to operate: one to take orders, one to operate the cash register, one to work the espresso machine, and a "floater" who can fill in where needed. And these people have to work rapidly and carefully to get the cars in and out in a timely manner, since the drive-through lane can get congested quickly.

Finally, without coffee to sell, there would be no Starbucks. The coffee beans are processed at the company's domestic roasting plants in Washington, Pennsylvania, Nevada, and internationally in Amsterdam. At each roasting plant, the production team produces the coffee and the distribution team manages the inventory and distribution of products and equipment to company stores. Because product quality is so essential to Starbucks' success, each person in the roasting plants must be focused on maintaining quality control at every step in the process.

Communication at Starbucks

Keeping organizational communication flowing in all directions is important to Starbucks. And that commitment starts at the top. Howard Schultz visits at least 30 to 40 stores a week. Not only does this give him an upfront view of what is happening out in the field, it gives partners a chance to talk with the top guy in the company. Jim Donald also likes to "get out in the field" by visiting the stores and roasting facilities. Despite these efforts by the top executives, results from the most current employee survey indicated communication needed improvement. Managers listened and made some changes.

An initial endeavour was the creation of Starbucks Broadcast News, an internal video newsletter that conveys information to partners about company news and announcements. Another change was the implementation of an internal communication audit that asks randomly selected partners for feedback on how to make company communication more effective. In addition, partners can voice concerns about actions or decisions where they "believe the company is not operating in a manner consistent with Starbucks' Guiding Principles" to the mission review team, a group formed in 1991 and consisting of company managers and partners. In 2005, more than 4200 contacts were made with this team in North America. The concept has worked so well that many of Starbucks' international units have provided similar communication forums to their partners.

People Management at Starbucks

"Our ability to accomplish what we set out to do is based primarily on the people we hire.... We recognize that the right people, offering their ideas and expertise, will enable us to continue our success," says Starbucks' website.

Since the beginning, Starbucks has strived to be an employer that nurtured employees and gave them opportunities to grow and be challenged. The company says it is "pro-partner" and has always been committed to providing a flexible and progressive work environment and treating one another with respect and dignity.

As Starbucks continues its expansion, it needs to make sure it has the right number of the right people in the right place at the right time. What kinds of people are "right" for Starbucks? The company states that it wants "people who are adaptable, self-motivated, passionate, creative team players." Starbucks uses a variety of methods to attract potential partners. The company has an interactive and easy-to-use

online career centre. Job seekers—who must be at least 16 years old—can search and apply online for jobs in any geographic location. Starbucks also has recruiting events in various locations in Canada throughout the year, which allow job seekers to talk to recruiters and partners face-to-face about working at Starbucks. In addition, job seekers for part-time and full-time hourly positions can submit an application at any Starbucks store location. The company also has a limited number of internship opportunities for students during the summer.

Starbucks' workplace policies provide for employment equity and strictly prohibit discrimination. Diversity and inclusion are very important to Starbucks. That commitment to diversity starts at the top. During 2005, CEO Jim Donald and 12 senior executives participated in a 360-degree diversity assessment to identify their strengths and areas that needed improvement. Also during 2005, an executive diversity learning series was developed for individuals at the vice-president level and above to build their diversity competencies. In 2006, a full-day diversity immersion exercise was launched.

Although diversity training is important to Starbucks, it is not the only training provided. The company continually invests in training programs and career development initiatives: baristas, who get a "green apron book" that exhorts them to be genuine and considerate, receive 23 hours of initial training; an additional 29 hours of training as shift supervisor; 112 hours as assistant store manager; and 320 hours as store manager. District manager trainees receive 200 hours of training. And every partner takes a class on coffee education, which focuses on Starbucks' passion for coffee and understanding the core product. In addition, Starbucks offers a variety of classes ranging from basic computer skills to conflict resolution to management training. Starbucks' partners are not "stuck" in their jobs. The company's rapid growth creates tremendous opportunities for promotion and advancement for all store partners. If they desire, they can utilize career counselling, executive coaching, job rotation, mentoring, and leadership development to help them create a career path that meets their needs. In 2006, Starbucks was named one of *Training* magazine's Top 100. One example of the company's training efforts: When oxygen levels in coffee bags were too high in one of the company's roasting plants (which affected product freshness), partners were retrained on procedures and given additional coaching. After the training, the number of bags of coffee placed on "quality hold" declined by 99 percent.

One human resource issue that has haunted Starbucks is its position on labour unions. The company states on its website, "We firmly believe that the direct employment relationship which we currently have with our partners is the best way to help ensure a great work environment. We believe we do not need a third party to act on behalf of our partners. We prefer to deal directly with them in a fair and respectful manner, just as we have throughout our history." Starbucks prides itself on how it treats its employees. However, the Canadian Auto Workers represents about 140 Starbucks workers at 10 stores in Vancouver.

Change and Innovation at Starbucks

Starbucks has always thought "outside the box." It took the concept of the corner coffee shop and totally revamped the coffee experience. The company has always had the ability to roll out new products relatively quickly. If a new product seems like it would appeal to customers—the popular pumpkin spice latte is one example—Starbucks often skips product testing and does not use focus groups to assess the product. Innovation is so important, in fact, that the category management group is responsible for changing the items on the shelves every six weeks. And Starbucks relies heavily on its partners to be the driving force behind innovations. As we said earlier, Starbucks is firmly committed to its belief that "We recognize that the right people, offering their ideas and expertise, will enable us to continue our success."

Questions

1. What types of departmentalization are being used? Explain your choices. (Hint: In addition to information in the case, you might want to look at the list of corporate executives on the company's website.)

2. Do you think it's a good idea to have a president for the US division and for the international divisions? What are the advantages of such an arrangement? Disadvantages?

3. What examples of the six organizational structural elements do you see discussed in the case? Describe.

4. Considering the expense associated with having more managers, what are some reasons why you think Starbucks decided to decrease the number of stores each district manager was responsible for, thus increasing the number of managers needed? Other than the expense, can you think of any disadvantages to this decision?

5. Give some examples of the types of communication taking place at Starbucks.

6. Suppose that you are a Starbucks store manager in St. John's, Newfoundland and Labrador. How do you find out what is going on in the company? How might you communicate concerns or issues that you have?

7. Jim Donald has said that Starbucks' long-term goal is to have 15 000 US stores and 30 000 stores globally. In addition, the company has set a financial goal of attaining total net revenue growth of 20 percent and earnings per share growth between of 20 to 25 percent. How will the organizing function contribute to the accomplishment of these goals?

8. Starbucks has said that it wants people who are "adaptable, self-motivated, passionate, and creative team players." How does the company ensure that its hiring and selection process identifies those kinds of people?

9. Select one of the job openings posted on the company's website. Do you think the job description and job specification for this job are adequate? Why or why not? What changes might you suggest?

10. Evaluate Starbucks' training efforts. What types of training are available?

11. Pretend that you are a local Starbucks' store manager. You have three new hourly partners (baristas) joining your team. Describe the orientation you would provide these new hires.

12. Which of the company's Guiding Principles affect the organizing function of management? Explain how the one(s) you chose would affect how Starbucks' managers deal with (a) structural issues; (b) communication issues; and (c) HRM issues. (Hint: The Guiding Principles can be found on the company's website or, in the continuing case in Part 1, under "Starbucks Culture and Environment" on page 129.)

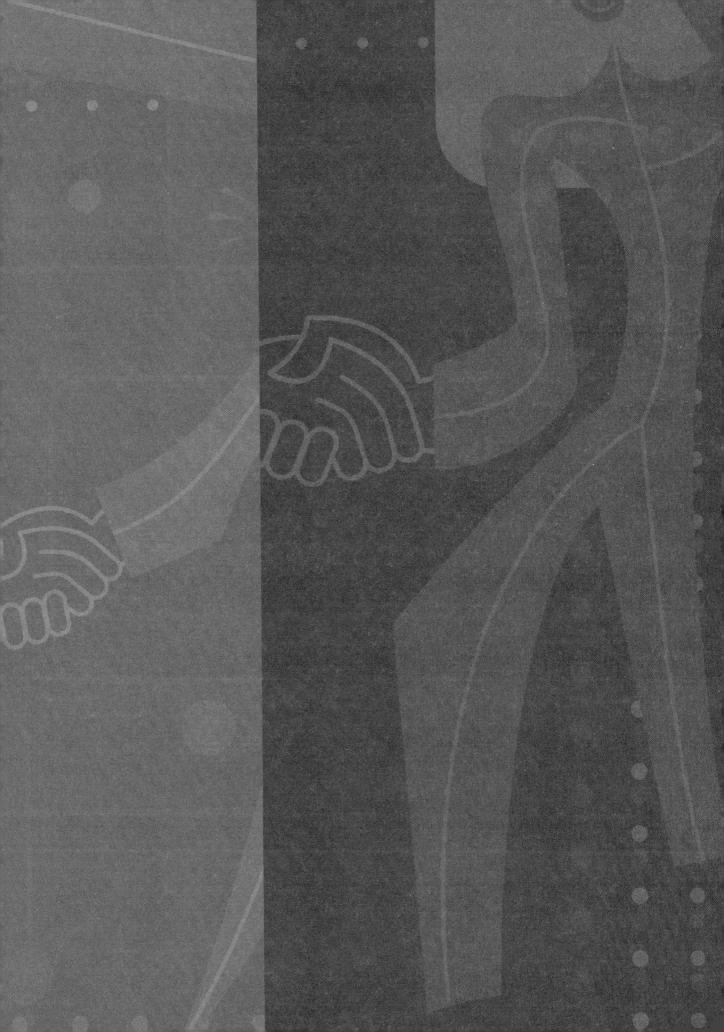

PART four

Leading

MANAGERS MUST LEARN HOW TO LEAD. They need to motivate employees and influence individuals and teams. When considering how to lead, managers might ask these questions:

- **What do I need to do to become an effective leader?**

- **How can I motivate my employees?**

- **How can I build productive teams in my workplace?**

Leadership

PART **four**

Leading

What does it take to be a good leader?

1. How do leaders and managers differ?

2. What do trait and behavioural theories tell us about leadership?

3. How do contingency theories of leadership improve our understanding of leadership?

4. What do charismatic and transformational leaders do?

5. How can managers use power and trust to enhance leadership?

6. What are some current issues in leadership?

▶ ▶ ▶ When Rossana Di Zio Magnotta first started Vaughan, Ontario-based Festa Juice with her husband, Gabe, the company sold imported grape juice to people who were making wine at home.[1] A scientist by training, she helped with the technical side of the business by applying biochemistry and microbiology to winemaking. Her intention was to offer free advice about winemaking to her customers, even testing some of their samples to see how they could improve their wine.

Her scientific background did not impress her customers, however, who were mainly first-generation Italian and Portuguese men. They had trouble believing a Canadian woman (even if she had Italian ancestry) could possibly know how to make wine. "They would say they were 'born in the grapes,' and start talking to me about the old country," she said.

Rather than feel undermined by the questioning of her winemaking ability, Magnotta became inspired to win over her customers by writing a step-by-step guide to winemaking, "Making Wine the Festa Way." The booklet was translated into Italian and Spanish, and was given away to every Festa Juice purchaser.

Because of the helpful advice Magnotta provided, it was not too long before customers started asking the company to sell wine, rather than juice and advice. After much consideration, the husband and wife team decided to buy Charal Winery, which had a license and a few pieces of equipment, although no land. They renamed the company Magnotta Winery and launched their new business in late 1990. The business has been very successful, and is now the third-largest winery in Ontario. Its 2006 net earnings were $2.8 million on net sales of $23 million. It has also been voted one of Canada's 50 Best Managed Companies seven years in a row, starting in 1999.

Think About It

What does it mean to be a leader for today's organizations? Put yourself in Rossana Di Zio Magnotta's shoes. What kinds of challenges does she face as a leader in the male-dominated winery business? What can she do to encourage support for her leadership style from both men and women?

Why is leadership so important? Because it's the leaders in organizations who make things happen. If leadership is so important, it's only natural to ask: What differentiates leaders from nonleaders? What is the most appropriate style of leadership? And what can you do if you want to be seen as a leader? In this chapter, we try to answer these and other questions about leaders.

 **Magnotta Winery**
www.magnotta.com

Managers vs. Leaders

leader
Someone who can influence others and provide vision and strategy to the organization.

leadership
The process of influencing individuals or groups toward the achievement of goals.

Let's begin by clarifying the distinction between managers and leaders. *Leadership* and *management* are two terms that are often confused. What is the difference between them?

Professor Rabindra Kanungo at McGill University finds that management scholars are beginning to reach a consensus that leadership and supervision/management are different.[2] Exhibit 12-1 illustrates the distinctions Kanungo sees between managership and leadership. **Leaders** provide vision and strategy to the organization; managers implement that vision and strategy, coordinate and staff the organization, and handle the day-to-day problems that occur. **Leadership** is the process of influencing individuals or groups toward the achievement of goals.

Can managers be leaders? Should leaders be managers? Because no one yet has shown that leadership ability is a handicap to a manager, ideally, we believe that all managers *should* be leaders. One of the major functions of management is to lead. However, not all leaders have the capabilities or skills of effective managers, and thus not all leaders should be managers. The fact that an individual can set vision and strategy does not mean that he or she can also plan, organize, and control.

Can Anyone Be a Leader?

Organizations around the globe spend billions of dollars, yen, and euros on leadership training and development.[3] These efforts take many forms—from $50 000 leadership programs offered by universities such as Harvard to sea kayaking experiences at Outward Bound Canada. Nevertheless, some people don't have what it takes to be a leader. For instance, evidence indicates that leadership training is more likely to be successful with individuals who are high self-monitors than with low self-monitors. Such individuals have the flexibility to change their behaviour as different situations may require. In addition, organizations may find that individuals who are more motivated to lead are more receptive to leadership development opportunities.[4]

PRISM 2

What kinds of things can individuals learn that might be related to being a more effective leader? It may be a bit optimistic to think that "vision creation" can be taught, but implementation skills can be taught. People can be trained to develop "an understand-

---

Exhibit 12-1

Distinguishing Managership from Leadership

Managership	Leadership
1. Engages in day-to-day caretaker activities: maintains and allocates resources	Formulates long-term objectives for reforming the system: Plans strategy and tactics
2. Exhibits supervisory behaviour: acts to make others maintain standard job behaviour	Exhibits leading behaviour: acts to bring about change in others congruent with long-term objectives
3. Administers subsystems within organizations	Innovates for the entire organization
4. Asks how and when to engage in standard practice	Asks what and why to change standard practice
5. Acts within established culture of the organization	Creates vision and meaning for the organization
6. Uses transactional influence: Induces compliance in manifest behaviour using rewards, sanctions, and formal authority	Uses transformational influence: Induces change in values, attitudes, and behaviour using personal examples and expertise
7. Relies on control strategies to get things done by subordinates	Uses empowering strategies to make followers internalize values
8. Status quo supporter and stabilizer	Status quo challenger and change creator

Source: R. N. Kanungo, "Leadership in Organizations: Looking Ahead to the 21st Century," *Canadian Psychology* 39, nos. 1–2 (1998), p. 77. Copyright 1998 The Canadian Psychological Association.

Conservative MP Steven Fletcher is motivated to be a leader. A car accident left him quadriplegic when he was 23, and this inspired him to take charge of his life. He won his first political campaign, to be president of the University of Manitoba Students Union. He later became president of the Progressive Conservative Party of Manitoba. When he was elected MP, he defeated his riding's incumbent Liberal candidate. He says many of his constituents are not aware that he is quadriplegic until they meet him.

ing about content themes critical to effective visions."[5] We can also teach skills such as trust building and mentoring. And leaders can be taught situational analysis skills. They can learn how to evaluate situations, how to modify situations to make them fit better with their style, and how to assess which leader behaviours might be most effective in given situations.

Is Leadership Always Necessary?

In order to lead, leaders need followers. Part of their job, then, is establishing relationships with individuals, so that followers can help leaders achieve their visions. Some situations may make it more difficult for leaders to develop followers. For instance, followers who have experience, training, professional orientation, or need for independence are less likely to need a leader's support. Thus leaders need to be aware of the characteristics of their followers when trying to achieve their goals.

Leadership, like motivation, is an organizational behaviour topic that has been heavily researched, and most of that research has been aimed at answering the question, What is an effective leader? We begin our study of leadership by looking at some early leadership theories.

Early Leadership Theories

▶ ▶ ▶ When Rossana Di Zio Magnotta and her husband, Gabe, decided to start Magnotta Winery, their intention was to sell their wine through the Liquor Control Board of Ontario (LCBO).[6] Their timing for the opening of the business could not have been worse. The economy was in the midst of a downturn. As Magnotta explains, "On December 7th, 1990, we opened up shop and immediately got hit with the recession that was rolling across the country." At the same time, the LCBO informed Magnotta and her husband that there was no room in the stores to shelve Magnotta wine. These obstacles had not been part of their business planning.

Magnotta and her husband ended up waging a 10-year battle with the LCBO in order to get their wines into LCBO stores. She explains, "We had no choice, it was either fight or die."

Think About It

A president and CEO of any company has to manage people effectively. Are there specific traits or behaviours that leaders such as Rossana Di Zio Magnotta should have?

Q&A 12.1

2. What do trait and behavioural theories tell us about leadership?

People have been interested in leadership since they started gathering together in groups to accomplish goals. However, it was not until the early part of the twentieth century that researchers began to study leadership. These early leadership theories focused on the *leader* (trait theories) and how the *leader interacted* with his or her group members (behavioural theories).

Trait Theories

Think about some of the managers you have encountered. How did their traits affect whether they were good or bad managers?

Leadership research in the 1920s and 1930s focused on leader traits—characteristics that might be used to differentiate leaders from nonleaders. The intent was to isolate traits that leaders possessed and nonleaders did not. Some of the traits studied included physical stature, appearance, social class, emotional stability, fluency of speech, and sociability. Despite the best efforts of researchers, it proved to be impossible to identify a set of traits that would *always* differentiate leaders (the person) from nonleaders. Maybe it was a bit optimistic to think that there could be consistent and unique traits that would apply universally to all effective leaders, whether they were in charge of Toyota Motor Corporation, the Moscow Ballet, Ted's Outfitters Shop, or Queen's University. However, more recent attempts to identify traits consistently associated with leadership (the process, not the person) have been more successful. Seven traits associated with effective leadership include drive, the desire to lead, honesty and integrity, self-confidence, intelligence, job-relevant knowledge, and extraversion.[7] These traits are briefly described in Exhibit 12-2.

Q&A 12.2

Researchers have begun organizing traits around the Big Five personality framework.[8] They have found that most of the dozens of traits that emerged in various leadership reviews fall under one of the Big Five personality traits (extraversion, agreeableness, conscientiousness, emotional stability, and openness to experience). This approach has resulted in consistent and strong support for traits as predictors of leadership.

Researchers agreed that traits alone were not sufficient for explaining effective leadership since explanations based solely on traits ignored the interactions of leaders and their group members, as well as situational factors. Possessing the appropriate traits only made it more likely that an individual would be an effective leader. Therefore, leadership research from

---

Exhibit 12-2

Seven Traits Associated with Leadership

1. **Drive.** Leaders exhibit a high effort level. They have a relatively high desire for achievement; they are ambitious; they have a lot of energy; they are tirelessly persistent in their activities; and they show initiative.

2. **Desire to lead.** Leaders have a strong desire to influence and lead others. They demonstrate the willingness to take responsibility.

3. **Honesty and integrity.** Leaders build trusting relationships between themselves and followers by being truthful or nondeceitful and by showing high consistency between word and deed.

4. **Self-confidence.** Followers look to leaders for an absence of self-doubt. Leaders, therefore, need to show self-confidence in order to convince followers of the rightness of their goals and decisions.

5. **Intelligence.** Leaders need to be intelligent enough to gather, synthesize, and interpret large amounts of information, and they need to be able to create visions, solve problems, and make correct decisions.

6. **Job-relevant knowledge.** Effective leaders have a high degree of knowledge about the company, industry, and technical matters. In-depth knowledge allows leaders to make well-informed decisions and to understand the implications of those decisions.

7. **Extraversion.** Leaders are energetic, lively people. They are sociable, assertive, and rarely silent or withdrawn.

Sources: S. A. Kirkpatrick and E. A. Locke, "Leadership: Do Traits Really Matter?" *Academy of Management Executive*, May 1991, pp. 48–60; and T. A. Judge, J. E. Bono, R. Ilies, and M. Werner, "Personality and Leadership: A Qualitative and Quantitative Review," *Journal of Applied Psychology*, August 2002, pp. 765–780.

the late 1940s to the mid-1960s concentrated on the preferred behavioural styles that leaders demonstrated. Researchers wondered whether there was something unique in what effective leaders *did*—in other words, in their *behaviour*.

Behavioural Theories

Rick Waugh, president and CEO of Scotiabank, has very little in common with his predecessors who led the bank before him. Both Cedric Ritchie, CEO in the 1970s and 1980s, and Peter Godsoe, who succeeded Ritchie, are described as "autocratic, undemocratic and one-man army" when others reflect on their leadership styles.[9] Waugh, who was appointed president and CEO in 2003, is seen as kinder and gentler. "He is always open to discussion," says Laurent Lemaire, executive vice-chairman of pulp-and-paper manufacturer Cascades and a member of Scotiabank's executive and risk committee and human resources committee. "He will listen to you bring ideas."[10] Scotiabank has been quite successful under different leaders, and moved from the number five to the number two bank in Canada under Godsoe. But this example shows that leaders can behave in very different ways, even when working for the same organization. What do we know about leader behaviour, and how can it help us in our understanding of what an effective leader is?

Behavioural theories of leadership identify behaviours that differentiate effective leaders from ineffective leaders. Researchers hoped that the behavioural theories approach would provide more definitive answers about the nature of leadership than did the trait theories. There are four main leader behaviour studies we need to examine. (Exhibit 12-3 provides a summary of the major leader behavioural dimensions and the conclusions of each of the studies.)

University of Iowa Studies

The University of Iowa studies (conducted by Kurt Lewin and his associates) explored three leadership styles.[11] The **autocratic style** describes a leader who tends to centralize

behavioural theories
Leadership theories that identify behaviours that differentiate effective leaders from ineffective leaders.

autocratic style
A leadership style where the leader tends to centralize authority, dictate work methods, make unilateral decisions, and limit employee participation.

Exhibit 12-3

Behavioural Theories of Leadership

	Behavioural Dimension	Conclusion
University of Iowa	*Democratic style:* involving subordinates, delegating authority, and encouraging participation *Autocratic style:* dictating work methods, centralizing decision making, and limiting participation *Laissez-faire style:* giving group freedom to make decisions and complete work	Democratic style of leadership was most effective, although later studies showed mixed results.
Ohio State	*Consideration:* being considerate of followers' ideas and feelings *Initiating structure:* structuring work and work relationships to meet job goals	High-high leader (high in consideration and high in initiating structure) achieved high subordinate performance and satisfaction, but not in all situations.
University of Michigan	*Employee oriented:* emphasizes interpersonal relationships and taking care of employees' needs *Production oriented:* emphasizes technical or task aspects of job	Employee-oriented leaders were associated with high group productivity and higher job satisfaction.
Managerial Grid	*Concern for people:* measures leader's concern for subordinates on a scale of 1 to 9 (low to high) *Concern for production:* measures leader's concern for getting job done on a scale of 1 to 9 (low to high)	Leaders performed best with a 9,9 style (high concern for production and high concern for people).

authority, dictate work methods, make unilateral decisions, and limit employee participation. The **democratic style** describes a leader who tends to involve employees in decision making, delegate authority, encourage participation in deciding work methods and goals, and use feedback as an opportunity for coaching employees. Finally, the **laissez-faire style** describes a leader who generally gives the group complete freedom to make decisions and complete the work in whatever way it sees fit.

Lewin and his associates researched which one of the three leadership styles was most effective. Their results seemed to indicate that the democratic style contributed to both good quantity and quality of work. Had the answer to the question of the most effective leadership style been found? Unfortunately, it was not that simple. Later studies of the autocratic and democratic styles showed mixed results. For instance, the democratic style sometimes produced higher performance levels than the autocratic style, but at other times it produced lower or equal performance levels. More consistent results were found, however, when a measure of subordinate satisfaction was used. Group members' satisfaction levels were generally higher under a democratic leader than under an autocratic one.[12] (To learn more about your leadership style, see *Self-Assessment—What's My Leadership Style?* on pages 395–397, at the end of the chapter.)

Now leaders faced a dilemma! Should they focus on achieving higher performance or on achieving higher member satisfaction? This recognition of the dual nature of a leader's behaviour—that is, focusing on the task and on the people—was also a key characteristic of the other behavioural studies.

Ohio State Studies

The Ohio State studies identified two important dimensions of leader behaviour.[13] Beginning with more than 1000 behavioural dimensions, the researchers eventually narrowed the list down to just two categories that accounted for most of the leadership behaviour described by group members: initiating structure and consideration.

Initiating structure refers to the extent to which a leader is likely to define and structure his or her role and the roles of group members in the search for goal attainment. It includes behaviour that attempts to organize work, work relationships, and goals. **Consideration** refers to the extent to which a leader has job relationships characterized by mutual trust and respect for group members' ideas and feelings. A leader who is high in consideration helps group members with personal problems, is friendly and approachable, and treats all group members as equals. He or she shows concern for (is considerate of) his or her followers' comfort, well-being, status, and satisfaction.

Were these behavioural dimensions adequate descriptions of leader behaviour? Research found that a leader who is high in both initiating structure and consideration behaviours (a **high-high leader**) achieved high group task performance and satisfaction more frequently than one who is low on either dimension or both. However, the high-high style did not always yield positive results. Enough exceptions were found to indicate that perhaps situational factors needed to be integrated into leadership theory.

University of Michigan Studies

Leadership studies conducted at the University of Michigan's Survey Research Center at about the same time as those being done at Ohio State had a similar research objective: Identify behavioural characteristics of leaders that are related to performance effectiveness. The Michigan group also came up with two dimensions of leadership behaviour, which they labelled employee oriented and production oriented.[14] *Employee-oriented* leaders tend to emphasize interpersonal relationships; they take a personal interest in the needs of their followers and accept individual differences among group members. In contrast, *production-oriented* leaders tend to emphasize the technical or task aspects of the job; they are concerned mainly with accomplishing their group's tasks and regard group members as a means to that end. The conclusions of the Michigan researchers strongly favoured leaders who are employee oriented, as they were associated with high group productivity and high job satisfaction.

democratic style
A leadership style where the leader tends to involve employees in decision making, delegate authority, encourage participation in deciding work methods and goals, and use feedback as an opportunity for coaching employees.

laissez-faire style
A leadership style where the leader tends to give the group complete freedom to make decisions and complete the work in whatever way it sees fit.

Q&A 12.3

initiating structure
The extent to which a leader is likely to define and structure his or her role and the roles of group members in the search for goal attainment.

consideration
The extent to which a leader has job relationships characterized by mutual trust and respect for group members' ideas and feelings.

high-high leader
A leader high in both initiating structure and consideration behaviours.

The Managerial Grid

The behavioural dimensions from these early leadership studies provided the basis for the development of a two-dimensional grid for appraising leadership styles. This **managerial grid**, developed by R. R. Blake and Jane S. Mouton, uses the behavioural dimensions "concern for people" and "concern for production" and evaluates a leader's use of these behaviours, ranking them on a scale from 1 (low) to 9 (high).[15] Although the grid (shown in Exhibit 12-4) has 81 potential categories into which a leader's behavioural style might fall, emphasis has been placed on five: impoverished management (1,1), task management (9,1), middle-of-the-road management (5,5), country club management (1,9), and team management (9,9). Of these five styles, Blake and Mouton concluded that managers performed best when using a 9,9 style. Unfortunately, the grid offers no answers to the question of what makes a manager an effective leader; it only provides a framework for conceptualizing leadership style. In fact, there has been little substantive evidence to support the conclusion that a 9,9 style is most effective in all situations.[16]

managerial grid
A two-dimensional grid of leadership behaviours—concern for people and concern for production—that results in five different leadership styles.

Exhibit 12-4

The Managerial Grid

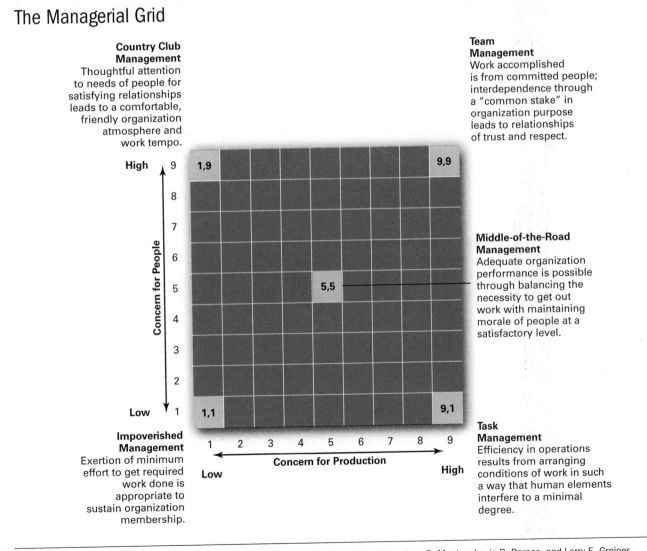

Country Club Management
Thoughtful attention to needs of people for satisfying relationships leads to a comfortable, friendly organization atmosphere and work tempo.

Team Management
Work accomplished is from committed people; interdependence through a "common stake" in organization purpose leads to relationships of trust and respect.

Middle-of-the-Road Management
Adequate organization performance is possible through balancing the necessity to get out work with maintaining morale of people at a satisfactory level.

Impoverished Management
Exertion of minimum effort to get required work done is appropriate to sustain organization membership.

Task Management
Efficiency in operations results from arranging conditions of work in such a way that human elements interfere to a minimal degree.

Source: Reprinted by permission of Harvard Business Review. An exhibit from R. R. Blake, Jane S. Mouton, Louis B. Barnes, and Larry E. Greiner, "Breakthrough in Organization Development," *Harvard Business Review*, November–December 1964, p. 136. Copyright © 1964 by the President and Fellows of Harvard College. All rights reserved.

A lengthy review of the results of behavioural studies support the idea that people-oriented behaviours are related to follower satisfaction, motivation, and leader effectiveness while production-oriented behaviours are slightly more strongly related to performance by the leader, the group, and the organization.[17]

Contingency Theories of Leadership

3. How do contingency theories of leadership improve our understanding of leadership?

Contingency theories of leadership developed after it became clear that identifying traits or key behaviours was not enough to understand what made good leaders. Contingency researchers considered whether different situations required different styles of leadership. To illustrate how situations might affect the ability to lead, consider the fate of some of the Americans who have been recruited to run Canadian companies. Hudson's Bay Company hired American Bill Fields and Zellers hired American Millard Barron to replicate their US retail successes in Canada. Neither was able to do so. Successful Texas oilman J. P. Bryan was given two chances to restore profitability at Canadian companies—Gulf Canada Resources (now ConocoPhillips) and Canadian 88 Energy (now Pengrowth Energy Trust)—and failed in both attempts.[18] These examples suggest that one's leadership style may need to be adjusted for different companies and employees, and perhaps even for different countries.

Do you know what your leadership style is? What impact might that have on how you lead?

In this section, we examine four contingency theories of leadership—Fiedler contingency model, Hersey and Blanchard's Situational Leadership®, leader participation model, and path-goal theory. Each theory looks at defining leadership style and the situation, and attempts to answer *if–then* contingencies (that is, *if* this is the situation, *then* this is the best leadership style to use). All of these theories focus on the relationship of the leader to followers, and there is broad support for the idea that this relationship is important.[19]

Fiedler Contingency Model

Fiedler contingency model
A leadership theory that proposes effective group performance depends on the proper match between the leader's style of interacting with his or her followers and the degree to which the situation gives the leader control and influence.

least-preferred co-worker (LPC) questionnaire
A questionnaire that measures whether a leader is task oriented or relationship oriented.

The first comprehensive contingency model for leadership was developed by Fred Fiedler.[20] The **Fiedler contingency model** proposes that effective group performance depends on the proper match between the leader's style of interacting with his or her followers and the degree to which the situation allows the leader to control and influence. The model was based on the premise that a certain leadership style would be most effective in different types of situations. The key was to define those leadership styles and the different types of situations and then to identify the appropriate combinations of style and situation.

Fiedler proposed that a key factor in leadership success was an individual's basic leadership style, either task oriented or relationship oriented. To measure a leader's style, Fiedler developed the **least-preferred co-worker (LPC) questionnaire**. This questionnaire contains 16 pairs of contrasting adjectives—for example, pleasant-unpleasant, cold-warm, boring-interesting, and friendly-unfriendly. Respondents are asked to think of all the co-workers they have ever had and to describe that one person they *least enjoyed* working with by rating him or her on a scale of 1 to 8 (the 8 always describes the positive adjective out of the pair and the 1 always describes the negative adjective out of the pair) for each of the 16 sets of adjectives. Fiedler believed that you could determine a person's basic leadership style on the basis of the responses to the LPC questionnaire. The questionnaire is reproduced in Exhibit 12-5.

Leaders who describe the least-preferred co-worker in relatively positive terms (in other words, a "high" LPC score—a score of 64 or more) are primarily interested in good personal relations with co-workers. That is, if leaders describe the person they least liked to work with in favourable terms, their style would be described as *relationship oriented*. In contrast, leaders who describe the least-preferred co-worker in relatively unfavourable terms (a low LPC score—a score of 35 or less) are primarily interested in productivity and getting the job done; that is, they are *task oriented*. Fiedler did acknowledge that there was a small group of people who fell in between these two extremes and who did not have a cut-and-dried leadership

Exhibit 12-5

Fiedler's Least-Preferred Co-worker Questionnaire: A Measure of Leader Style

Instructions: Think of the person with whom you can work least well. He/she may be someone you work with now, or he/she may be someone you knew in the past.

He/she does not have to be the person you like least well, but should be the person with whom you had the most difficulty in getting a job done. Describe this person as he/she appears to you.

Pleasant	8	7	6	5	4	3	2	1	Unpleasant
Friendly	8	7	6	5	4	3	2	1	Unfriendly
Rejecting	1	2	3	4	5	6	7	8	Accepting
Helpful	8	7	6	5	4	3	2	1	Frustrating
Unenthusiastic	1	2	3	4	5	6	7	8	Enthusiastic
Tense	1	2	3	4	5	6	7	8	Relaxed
Distant	1	2	3	4	5	6	7	8	Close
Cold	1	2	3	4	5	6	7	8	Warm
Cooperative	8	7	6	5	4	3	2	1	Uncooperative
Supportive	8	7	6	5	4	3	2	1	Hostile
Boring	1	2	3	4	5	6	7	8	Interesting
Quarrelsome	1	2	3	4	5	6	7	8	Harmonious
Self-assured	8	7	6	5	4	3	2	1	Hesitant
Efficient	8	7	6	5	4	3	2	1	Inefficient
Gloomy	1	2	3	4	5	6	7	8	Cheerful
Open	8	7	6	5	4	3	2	1	Guarded

Scoring: Add up all the circled responses for an overall score. High LPC leaders have scores of 64 or more. Low LPC leaders have scores of 35 or less.

Source: F. E. Fiedler and M. M. Chemers, *Improving Leadership Effectiveness: The Leader Match Concept*, 2nd ed. (New York: John Wiley and Sons, 1984).

personality style. It's important to point out that Fiedler assumed that a person's leadership style was always the same (fixed), regardless of the situation. In other words, a relationship-oriented leader would always be one, and the same was true for a task-oriented leader.

After an individual's leadership style had been assessed through the LPC, it was necessary to evaluate the situation in order to match the leader with the situation. Fiedler's research uncovered three contingency dimensions that defined the key situational factors for determining leader effectiveness:

- **Leader–member relations.** The degree of confidence, trust, and respect employees have for their leader; rated as either good or poor.
- **Task structure.** The degree to which job assignments are formalized and procedurized; rated as either high or low.
- **Position power.** The degree of influence a leader has over power-based activities such as hiring, firing, discipline, promotions, and salary increases; rated as either strong or weak.

Fiedler evaluated leadership situations in terms of these three contingency variables, and concluded that there are eight possible situations in which a leader could find himself or herself (see the bottom of the chart in Exhibit 12-6 on page 376). Each of these situations was described in terms of its favourableness (or situational control) for the leader. Situations I, II, and III were classified as very favourable for the leader. Situations IV, V, and VI were moderately favourable for the leader. Situations VII and VIII were very unfavourable for the leader.

Q&A 12.4

leader–member relations
One of Fiedler's situational contingencies that describes the degree of confidence, trust, and respect employees have for their leader.

task structure
One of Fiedler's situational contingencies that describes the degree to which job assignments are formalized and procedurized.

position power
One of Fiedler's situational contingencies that describes the degree of influence a leader has over power-based activities such as hiring, firing, discipline, promotions, and salary increases.

Exhibit 12-6

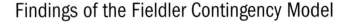

Findings of the Fieldler Contingency Model

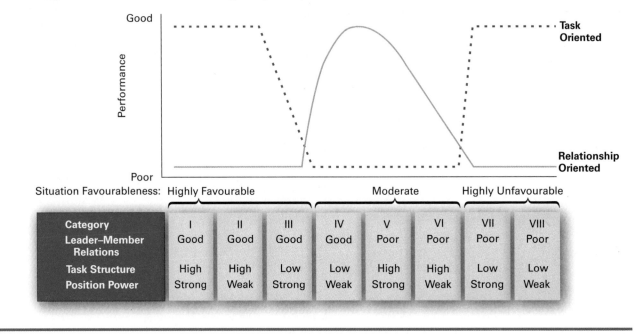

Situation Favourableness:	Highly Favourable			Moderate			Highly Unfavourable	
Category	I	II	III	IV	V	VI	VII	VIII
Leader–Member Relations	Good	Good	Good	Good	Poor	Poor	Poor	Poor
Task Structure	High	High	Low	Low	High	High	Low	Low
Position Power	Strong	Weak	Strong	Weak	Strong	Weak	Strong	Weak

Once Fiedler had described the leader variables and the situational variables, he was ready to define the specific contingencies for leadership effectiveness. To do so, he studied 1200 groups where he compared relationship-oriented vs. task-oriented leadership styles in each of the eight situational categories. He concluded that task-oriented leaders performed better in either very favourable situations or very unfavourable situations. (See the top of Exhibit 12-6 where performance is shown on the vertical axis and situation favourableness is shown on the horizontal axis.) In a high control situation, a leader can "get away" with task orientation, because the relationships are good and followers are easily influenced.[21] In a low control situation (which is characterized by poor relations, ill-defined task, and low influence), task orientation may be the only thing that makes it possible to get something done. On the other hand, relationship-oriented leaders performed better in moderately favourable situations. In a moderate control situation, being relationship oriented may smooth the way to getting things done.

Since Fiedler treated an individual's leadership style as fixed, there were only two ways to improve leader effectiveness. First, you could bring in a new leader whose style better fit the situation. For instance, if the group situation was rated as highly unfavourable but was led by a relationship-oriented leader, the group's performance could be improved by replacing that person with a task-oriented leader. The second alternative was to change the situation to fit the leader. This could be done by restructuring tasks or increasing or decreasing the power that the leader had over factors such as salary increases, promotions, and disciplinary actions.

Reviews of the major studies undertaken to test the overall validity of Fiedler's model have shown considerable evidence to support the model.[22] However, his theory was not without criticism. For instance, additional variables were probably needed to fill in some gaps in the model. Moreover, there were problems with the LPC, and the practicality of it needed to be addressed. In addition, it's probably unrealistic to assume that a person cannot change his or her leadership style to fit the situation. Effective leaders can, and do, change their styles to meet the needs of a particular situation. Finally, the contingency variables were difficult for practitioners to assess.[23] Despite its shortcomings, the Fiedler contingency model showed that effective leadership style needed to reflect situational factors.

Hersey and Blanchard's Situational Leadership®

Paul Hersey and Ken Blanchard developed a leadership theory that has gained a strong following among management development specialists.[24] This contingency theory of leadership, called **Situational Leadership® (SL)**, focuses on followers' readiness. Hersey and Blanchard argue that successful leadership is achieved by selecting the right leadership style, which is contingent upon the level of the followers' readiness. Before we proceed, there are two points we need to clarify: why a leadership theory focuses on the followers, and what is meant by the term *readiness*.

The emphasis on the followers in leadership effectiveness reflects the reality that it is the followers who accept or reject the leader. Regardless of what the leader does, effectiveness depends on the actions of his or her followers. This is an important dimension that has been overlooked or underemphasized in most leadership theories. **Readiness**, as defined by Hersey and Blanchard, refers to the extent to which people have the ability and willingness to accomplish a specific task.

SL uses the same two leadership dimensions that Fiedler identified: task and relationship behaviours. However, Hersey and Blanchard go a step further by considering each as either high or low and then combining them into four specific leadership styles (see Exhibit 12-7), described as follows:

- *Telling* (high task–low relationship): The leader defines roles and tells people what, how, when, and where to do various tasks.
- *Selling* (high task–high relationship): The leader provides both directive and supportive behaviour.
- *Participating* (low task–high relationship): The leader and follower share in decision making; the main role of the leader is facilitating and communicating.
- *Delegating* (low task–low relationship): The leader provides little direction or support.

Situational Leadership®
A leadership theory that focuses on the readiness of followers.

Q&A 12.5

readiness
The extent to which people have the ability and willingness to accomplish a specific task.

Exhibit 12-7

Hersey and Blanchard's Situational Leadership®

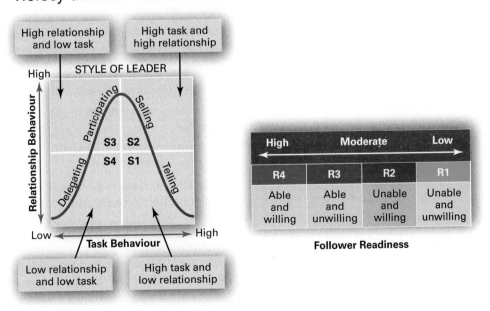

The final component in the theory is the four stages of follower readiness:

- *R1:* People are both *unable* and *unwilling* to take responsibility for doing something. They are neither competent nor confident.
- *R2:* People are *unable* but *willing* to do the necessary job tasks. They are motivated but currently lack the appropriate skills.
- *R3:* People are *able* but *unwilling* to do what the leader wants.
- *R4:* People are both *able* and *willing* to do what is asked of them.

SL essentially views the leader–follower relationship as similar to that of a parent and a child. Just as a parent needs to give up control as a child becomes more mature and responsible, so, too, should a leader. As followers reach high levels of readiness, the leader responds not only by continuing to decrease control over their activities, but also by continuing to decrease relationship behaviour. SL says if followers are *unable* and *unwilling* to do a task, the leader needs to give clear and specific directions; if followers are *unable* and *willing*, the leader needs to display high task orientation to compensate for the followers' lack of ability and high relationship orientation to get followers to "buy into" the leader's desires; if followers are *able* and *unwilling*, the leader needs to use a supportive and participative style; and if employees are both *able* and *willing*, the leader does not need to do much.

SL has intuitive appeal. It acknowledges the importance of followers and builds on the logic that leaders can compensate for ability and motivational limitations in their followers. Yet research efforts to test and support the theory generally have been disappointing.[25] Why? Possible explanations include internal inconsistencies in the model itself as well as problems with research methodology. So despite its appeal and wide popularity, any endorsement should be made with caution.

Leader Participation Model

Another early contingency theory of leadership, developed by Victor Vroom and Phillip Yetton, is the **leader participation model**, which relates leadership behaviour and participation to decision making.[26] Developed in the early 1970s, the model argued that leader behaviour must adjust to reflect the task structure—whether it is routine, nonroutine, or in between. Vroom and Yetton's model is what we call *normative*. That is, it provides a sequential set of rules (norms) to follow in determining the form and amount of participation a leader should exercise in decision making in different types of situations.

The leader participation model has changed as research continues to provide additional insights into effective leadership style.[27] The current model reflects *how* and *with whom* decisions are made and uses variations of the same five leadership styles identified in the original model:[28]

- *Decide.* Leader makes the decision alone and either announces or sells it to the group.
- *Consult individually.* Leader presents the problem to group members individually, gets their suggestions, and then makes the decision.
- *Consult group.* Leader presents the problem to group members in a meeting, gets their suggestions, and then makes the decision.
- *Facilitate.* Leader presents the problem to the group in a meeting and, acting as facilitator, defines the problem and the boundaries within which a decision must be made.
- *Delegate.* Leader permits the group to make the decision within prescribed limits.

The current model also expands upon the decision-making contingencies leaders look at in determining what leadership style would be most effective.[29] These contingencies—decision significance, importance of commitment, leader expertise, likelihood of commitment, group support, group expertise, and team competence—are either present (H for high) or absent (L for Low). Exhibit 12-8 shows a current leader participation model—the Time-Driven Model, which is short term in its orientation and concerned with making effective decisions with minimum cost. To use the model, a leader goes from left to right determining whether each contingency factor is high or low. After assessing all these contingencies, the most effective

leader participation model
A leadership theory that relates leadership behaviour and participation to decision making.

Exhibit 12-8

Time-Driven Model

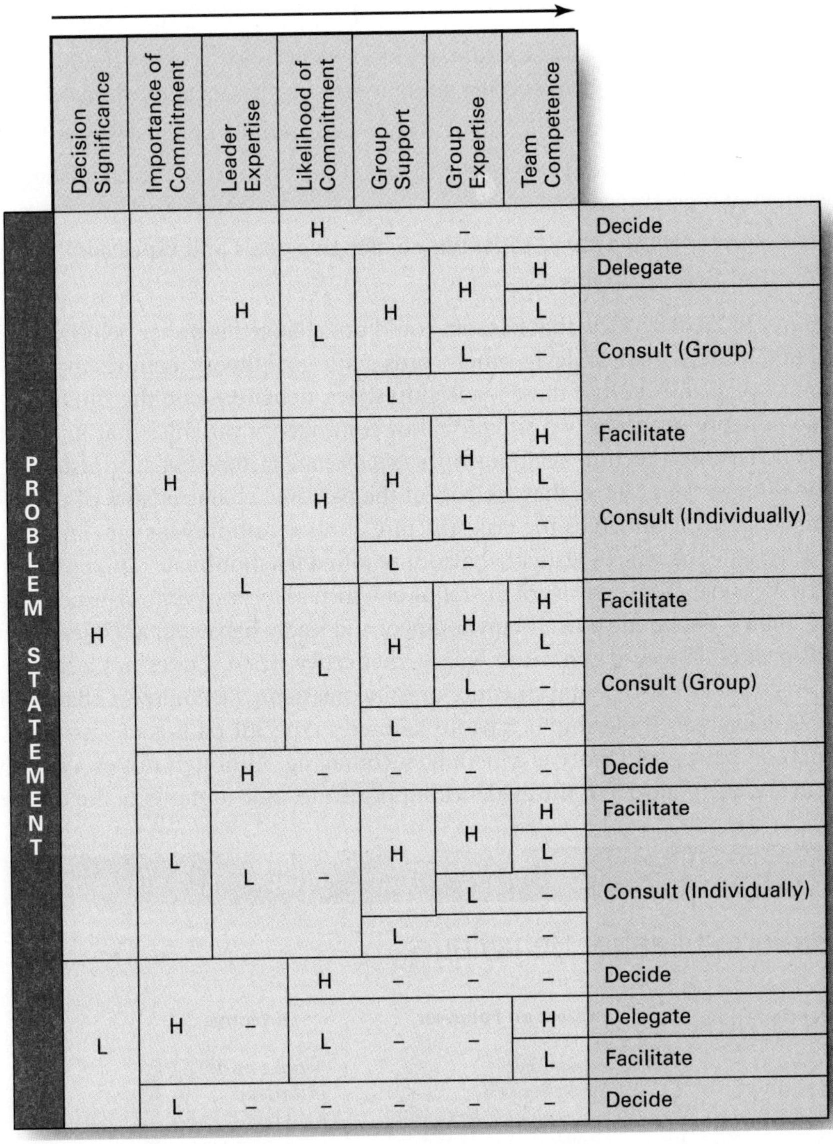

Decision Significance	Importance of Commitment	Leader Expertise	Likelihood of Commitment	Group Support	Group Expertise	Team Competence	
H	H	H	H	–	–	–	Decide
H	H	H	L	H	H	H	Delegate
H	H	H	L	H	H	L	Consult (Group)
H	H	H	L	H	L	–	Consult (Group)
H	H	H	L	L	–	–	Consult (Group)
H	H	L	H	H	H	H	Facilitate
H	H	L	H	H	H	L	Consult (Individually)
H	H	L	H	H	L	–	Consult (Individually)
H	H	L	H	L	–	–	Consult (Individually)
H	H	L	L	H	H	H	Facilitate
H	H	L	L	H	H	L	Consult (Group)
H	H	L	L	H	L	–	Consult (Group)
H	H	L	L	L	–	–	Consult (Group)
H	L	H	–	–	–	–	Decide
H	L	L	–	H	H	H	Facilitate
H	L	L	–	H	H	L	Consult (Individually)
H	L	L	–	H	L	–	Consult (Individually)
H	L	L	–	L	–	–	Consult (Individually)
L	H	–	H	–	–	–	Decide
L	H	–	L	–	–	H	Delegate
L	H	–	L	–	–	L	Facilitate
L	L	–	–	–	–	–	Decide

Source: Adapted from V. Vroom, "Leadership and the Decision-Making Process," *Organizational Dynamics* 28, no. 4 (2000), p. 87.

leadership style is identified on the far right-hand side of the model. Another model—the Development-Driven Model—is structured the same way but emphasizes making effective decisions with maximum employee development outcomes and places no value on time.

Path-Goal Theory

Currently, one of the most respected approaches to understanding leadership is **path-goal theory**, which states that it's the leader's job to assist his or her followers in attaining their goals and to provide the direction and/or support needed to ensure that their goals are compatible with the overall objectives of the group or organization. Developed by University of Toronto professor Martin Evans in the late 1960s, it was subsequently expanded upon by Robert House (formerly at the University of Toronto, but now at the Wharton School of Business). Path-goal theory is a contingency model of leadership that takes key elements

path-goal theory
A leadership theory that says it's the leader's job to assist his or her followers in attaining their goals and to provide the necessary direction and/or support to ensure that their goals are compatible with the overall objectives of the group or organization.

from the expectancy theory of motivation (see Chapter 13, pages 414–415).[30] The term *path-goal* is derived from the belief that effective leaders clarify the path to help their followers get from where they are to the achievement of their work goals and make the journey along the path easier by reducing roadblocks and pitfalls.

Path-goal theory identifies four leadership behaviours:

- *Directive leader.* Leader lets subordinates know what is expected of them, schedules work to be done, and gives specific guidance on how to accomplish tasks.
- *Supportive leader.* Leader is friendly and shows concern for the needs of followers.
- *Participative leader.* Leader consults with group members and uses their suggestions before making a decision.
- *Achievement-oriented leader.* Leader sets challenging goals and expects followers to perform at their highest level.

In contrast to Fiedler's view that a leader could not change his or her behaviour, House assumed that leaders are flexible. In other words, path-goal theory assumes that the same leader can display any or all of these leadership styles, depending on the situation.

Path-goal theory proposes two situational or contingency variables that moderate the leadership behaviour–outcome relationship: *environmental* factors that are outside the control of the follower and factors that are part of the personal characteristics of the *follower*. Environmental factors—such as the task structure, formal authority system, and the work group—determine the type of leader behaviour required if subordinate outcomes are to be maximized. Personal characteristics of the follower—such as locus of control, experience, and perceived ability—determine how the environment and leader behaviour are interpreted. The theory proposes that leader behaviour will be ineffective when it does not address situations arising from environmental structure or is inconsistent with follower characteristics. Exhibit 12-9 illustrates leadership behaviour tailored to specific path-goal situations.

Research on path-goal theory is generally encouraging. Although not every study has found support, the majority of the evidence supports the logic underlying the theory.[31] In

Exhibit 12-9

Path-Goal Situations and Preferred Leader Behaviours

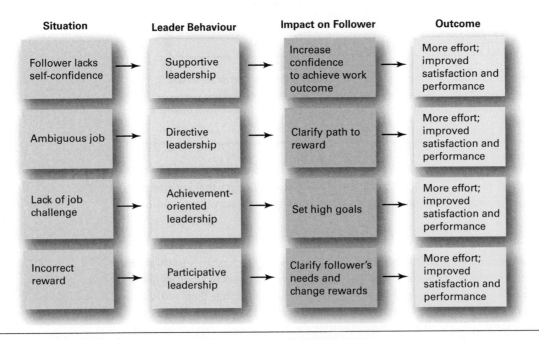

Source: R. L. Daft, *Management*, 7th ed. (Mason, OH: Thomson, 2005), p. 566. By permission.

summary, employee performance and satisfaction are likely to be positively influenced when the leader compensates for shortcomings in either the employee or the work setting. However, if the leader spends time explaining tasks that are already clear or when the employee has the ability and experience to handle them without interference, the employee is likely to see such directive behaviour as redundant or even insulting.

Q&A 12.6

Q&A 12.7

Leading Change

▶ ▶ ▶ When the Liquor Control Board of Ontario (LCBO) decided not to give Magnotta Winery any shelf space, Rossana Di Zio Magnotta and her husband, Gabe, settled on two strategies.[32] They decided to sell the wine themselves and also wage a battle against the LCBO, protesting the decision not to stock their wines.

To gain customers, the Magnottas used an innovative marketing strategy, selling their wine at $3.95 a bottle. This was significantly less than the price of wine of similar quality selling at the LCBO. Their strategy got publicity in the newspapers, and soon people were travelling to their winery in Vaughan, Ontario, to purchase wine.

At the same time, they conducted a campaign to get their wine into LCBO stores. Customers who were fans of the winery were urged to go into LCBO stores and ask to purchase the wine, creating the impression of demand for the wine. The battle against the LCBO lasted 10 years, but by 2000, the LCBO started carrying some Magnotta icewines.

Think About It
Mobilizing people to work toward a leader's vision is a difficult task. How do leaders like Rossana Di Zio Magnotta get individuals to support their vision and help carry it out?

Most of the leadership theories presented so far in this chapter have described **transactional leaders**; that is, leaders who guide or motivate their followers in the direction of established goals by clarifying role and task requirements.[33] But other leadership is needed for leading change in organizations. Two types of leadership that have been identified in situations where leaders have inspired change are charismatic–visionary leadership and transformational leadership.

4. What do charismatic and transformational leaders do?

transactional leaders
Leaders who guide or motivate their followers in the direction of established goals by clarifying role and task requirements.

Charismatic–Visionary Leadership

Have you ever encountered a charismatic leader? What was this person like?

Jeff Bezos, founder and CEO of Amazon.com, is a person who exudes energy, enthusiasm, and drive.[34] He is fun-loving (his legendary laugh has been described as a flock of Canadian geese on nitrous oxide), but has pursued his vision for Amazon with serious intensity and has demonstrated an ability to inspire his employees through the ups and downs of a rapidly growing company. Bezos is what we call a **charismatic leader**—that is, an enthusiastic, self-confident leader whose personality and actions influence people to behave in certain ways.

charismatic leader
An enthusiastic, self-confident leader whose personality and actions influence people to behave in certain ways.

Characteristics of Charismatic Leaders
Several authors have attempted to identify the personal characteristics of charismatic leaders.[35] The most comprehensive analysis identified five such characteristics that differentiate charismatic leaders from noncharismatic ones: They have a vision, are able to articulate that vision, are willing to take risks to achieve that vision, are sensitive to both environmental constraints and follower needs, and exhibit behaviours that are out of the ordinary.[36]

Q&A 12.8

Effects of Charismatic Leadership
What can we say about the charismatic leader's effect on his or her followers? There is an increasing body of evidence that shows impressive correlations between charismatic leadership and high performance and satisfaction among followers.[37] Research shows that

people who work for charismatic leaders are motivated to exert extra work effort and express greater satisfaction, because they like their leaders.[38] One of the most cited studies of the effects of charismatic leadership was done at the University of British Columbia in the early 1980s by Jane Howell (now at the University of Western Ontario) and Peter Frost.[39] They found that those who worked under a charismatic leader generated more ideas, produced better results, reported higher job satisfaction, and showed stronger bonds of loyalty. Howell concludes, "Charismatic leaders know how to inspire people to think in new directions."[40]

Charismatic leadership also affects overall company performance. Robert House and colleagues studied 63 American and 49 Canadian companies (including Nortel Networks, Molson, Gulf Canada, and Manulife Financial) and found that "between 15 and 25 percent of the variation in profitability among the companies was accounted for by the leadership qualities of their CEO."[41] Charismatic leaders led more profitable companies. However, a recent study of the impact of a charismatic CEO on subsequent organizational performance found no relationship.[42] Despite this, charisma is still believed to be a desirable leadership quality.

Charismatic leadership may have a downside, however, as we see from the recent accounting scandals and high-profile bankruptcies of North American companies. WorldCom's Bernard Ebbers and Enron's Kenneth Lay "seemed almost a breed apart, blessed with unique visionary powers" when their companies were increasing stock prices at phenomenal rates in the 1990s.[43] After the scandals, however, there was some agreement that CEOs with less vision and more ethical and corporate responsibility might be more desirable.

Becoming Charismatic

Can people learn to be charismatic leaders? Or are charismatic leaders born with their qualities? Although a small number of experts still think that charisma cannot be learned, most believe that individuals can be trained to exhibit charismatic behaviours.[44] For example, researchers have succeeded in teaching undergraduate students to "be" charismatic. How? They were taught to articulate a sweeping goal, communicate high performance expectations, exhibit confidence in the ability of subordinates to meet those expectations, and empathize with the needs of their subordinates; they learned to project a powerful, confident, and dynamic presence; and they practised using a captivating and engaging voice tone. The researchers also trained the student leaders to use charismatic nonverbal behaviours including leaning toward the follower when communicating, maintaining direct eye contact, and having a relaxed posture and animated facial expressions. In groups with these "trained" charismatic leaders, members had higher task performance, higher task adjustment, and better adjustment to the leader and to the group than did group members who worked in groups led by noncharismatic leaders.

One last thing we need to say about charismatic leadership is that it may not always be needed to achieve high levels of employee performance. It may be most appropriate when the follower's task has an ideological purpose or when the environment involves a high degree of stress and uncertainty.[45] This may explain why, when charismatic leaders surface, it's more likely to be in the arenas of politics, religion, or war; or when a business firm is starting up or facing a survival crisis. For example, Martin Luther King Jr. used his charisma to bring about social equality through nonviolent means; and Steve Jobs achieved unwavering loyalty and commitment from Apple Inc.'s technical staff in the early 1980s by articulating a vision of personal computers that would dramatically change the way people lived.

Visionary Leadership

visionary leadership
The ability to create and articulate a realistic, credible, and attractive vision of the future that improves upon the present situation.

Although the term *vision* is often linked with charismatic leadership, **visionary leadership** goes beyond charisma since it's the ability to create and articulate a realistic, credible, and attractive vision of the future that improves upon the present situation.[46] This vision, if properly selected and implemented, is so energizing that it "in effect jump-starts the future by calling forth the skills, talents, and resources to make it happen."[47]

A vision should offer clear and compelling imagery that taps into people's emotions and inspires enthusiasm to pursue the organization's goals. It should be able to generate possibilities that are inspirational and unique and offer new ways of doing things that are clearly better for the organization and its members. Visions that are clearly articulated and have powerful imagery are easily grasped and accepted. For instance, Michael Dell (founder of Dell) created a vision of a business that sells and delivers a finished PC computer directly to a customer in less than a week. The late Mary Kay Ash's vision of women as entrepreneurs selling products that improved their self-image guided her cosmetics company, Mary Kay Cosmetics. (The *CBC Video Case Incident—Millionaire on a Mission* on page 461 shows a leader, Bill Young, who created a vision of a company that provides support to businesses that hire people who often have difficulties finding employment.)

What skills do visionary leaders have? Once the vision is identified, these leaders appear to have three skills that are related to effectiveness in their visionary roles.[48] First is the *ability to explain the vision to others* by making the vision clear in terms of required goals and actions through clear oral and written communication. The second skill is the *ability to express the vision not just verbally but* through behaviour, which requires behaving in ways that continuously convey and reinforce the vision. The third skill is the *ability to extend or apply the vision to different leadership contexts.* For instance, the vision has to be as meaningful to the people in accounting as it is to those in production, and to employees in Halifax as it is to those in Toronto.

Transformational Leadership

Some leaders are able to inspire followers to transcend their own self-interests for the good of the organization, and are capable of having a profound and extraordinary effect on their followers. These are **transformational leaders**, and examples include Frank Stronach, chair of Aurora, Ontario-based Magna International; and Mogens Smed, CEO of Calgary-based DIRTT (Doing It Right This Time) and former CEO of SMED International. Prime Minister Stephen Harper was named *Time* magazine's 2006 Canadian Newsmaker of the Year, in part because of his transformational style. *Time* contributing editor Stephen Handelman explained the choice as follows: "[Harper] has set himself the messianic tasks of remaking Canadian federalism by curbing Ottawa's spending powers and overhauling Canada's health care and social welfare system." Handelman predicted that should Harper win a Conservative majority in the next election, "He may yet turn out to be the most transformational leader since Trudeau."[49]

> **transformational leaders**
> Leaders who inspire followers to transcend their own self-interests for the good of the organization, and who have a profound and extraordinary effect on their followers.

Transformational leaders pay attention to the concerns and developmental needs of individual followers; they change followers' awareness of issues by helping those followers look at old problems in new ways; and they are able to excite, arouse, and inspire followers to put out extra effort to achieve group goals.[50]

Transformational leaders turn followers into believers on a mission, working toward what they believe is really important. "The transforming leader provides followers with a cause around which they can rally."[51] Transformational leadership is more than charisma since the transformational leader attempts to empower followers to question not only established views but even those views held by the leader.[52] The four factors that characterize transformational leadership (the "four I's") are presented in *Tips for Managers—How to Be a Transformational Leader.*

The evidence supporting the superiority of transformational leadership over transactional leadership is overwhelmingly impressive. For instance, studies that looked at managers in different settings, including the military and business, found that transformational leaders were evaluated as more effective, higher performers, and more promotable than their transactional counterparts.[53] In addition, evidence indicates that transformational leadership is strongly correlated with lower turnover rates, higher productivity, and higher employee satisfaction.[54] Finally, subordinates of transformational leaders may trust their leaders and their organizations more and feel that they are being fairly treated, which in turn may positively influence their work motivation (see Chapter 13).[55] However, transformational leadership should be used with some caution in non–North American contexts because its effectiveness may be affected by cultural values concerning leadership.[56]

TIPS FOR MANAGERS

How to Be a Transformational Leader

- **Individualized consideration:** Pay attention to the needs of individual followers to help them reach their full potential.

- **Intellectual stimulation:** Provide "ways and reasons for followers to change the way they think about" things.

- **Inspirational motivation:** "Set an example of hard work, give 'pep' talks, [and] remain optimistic in times of crisis."

- **Idealized influence:** Show respect for others, building confidence and trust about the mission in followers.

Source: B. J. Avolio, D. A. Waldman, and F. J. Yammarino, "Leading in the 1990s: The Four I's of Transformational Leadership," *Journal of European Industrial Training* 15, no. 4 (1991), pp. 9–16.

Managing Power and Developing Trust

5. How can managers use power and trust to enhance leadership?

Earlier in the chapter, we defined *leadership* as "the process of influencing individuals or groups toward the achievement of goals." In order to lead, then, leaders must be skillful at using power effectively and developing trust.

Managing Power

Q&A 12.9

Where do leaders get their power—that is, their capacity to influence work actions or decisions? Five sources of leader power have been identified: legitimate, coercive, reward, expert, and referent.[57]

legitimate power
The power a leader has as a result of his or her position in the organization.

Legitimate power and authority are the same. Legitimate power represents the power a leader has as a result of his or her position in the organization. People in positions of authority are also likely to have reward and coercive power, but legitimate power is broader than the power to coerce and reward.

coercive power
The power a leader has through his or her ability to punish or control.

Coercive power is the power that rests on the leader's ability to punish or control. Followers react to this power out of fear of the negative results that might occur if they did not comply. As a manager, you typically have some coercive power, such as being able to suspend or demote employees or to assign them work they find unpleasant or undesirable.

reward power
The power a leader has to give positive benefits or rewards.

Reward power is the power to give positive benefits or rewards. These rewards can be anything that another person values. In an organizational context, that might include money, favourable performance appraisals, promotions, interesting work assignments, friendly colleagues, and preferred work shifts or sales territories.

expert power
The influence a leader has based on his or her expertise, special skills, or knowledge.

Expert power is influence that's based on expertise, special skills, or knowledge. As jobs have become more specialized, managers have become increasingly dependent on staff "experts" to achieve the organization's goals. If an employee has skills, knowledge, or expertise that is critical to the operation of a work group, that person's expert power is enhanced.

referent power
The power a leader has because of his or her desirable resources or personal traits.

Finally, **referent power** is the power that arises because of a person's desirable resources or personal traits. If I admire and identify with you, you can exercise power over me because I want to please you. Referent power develops out of admiration of another and a desire to be like that person. If you admire someone to the point of modelling your behaviour and attitudes after him or her, that person has referent power over you.

Most effective leaders rely on several different sources of power to affect the behaviour and performance of their followers. For example, a lieutenant leading a crew on a state-of-the-art submarine might employ several different types of power in managing the crew and equipment. He gives orders to the crew (legitimate), praises them (reward), and disciplines those who commit infractions (coercive). As an effective leader, he also strives to have expert power (based on his expertise and knowledge) and referent power (based on his being admired) to influence his crew.[58] (See also *Developing Your Interpersonal Skills—Acquiring Power* on pages 400–401, at the end of the chapter.)

PRISM 5

Developing Trust

In 2003, after union members reluctantly agreed to $850 million a year in concessions that they believed were necessary to keep their company from bankruptcy, Air Canada's employees were stunned at president and CEO Robert Milton's after-the-fact disclosure of lucrative compensation policies and pension protections designed to retain key executives. Milton and his chief restructuring officer, Calin Rovinescu, were to receive 1 percent of the airline's shares, potentially worth an estimated $21 million, if the proposed takeover by Victor Li was successful. Any trust that employees had in Milton's ability to lead the airline into the future was eroded. In 2004, the deal with Li collapsed when union members could not agree to further concessions relating to their pension plans.[59]

Milton's behaviour illustrates how fragile leader trust can be. In today's uncertain environment, an important consideration for leaders is building trust and credibility. Before we can discuss ways leaders can build trust and credibility, we have to know what trust and credibility are and why they are so important.

The main component of credibility is honesty. Surveys show that honesty is consistently singled out as the number one characteristic of admired leaders. "Honesty is absolutely essential to leadership. If people are going to follow someone willingly, whether it be into battle or into the boardroom, they first want to assure themselves that the person is worthy of their trust." In addition to being honest, credible leaders are competent and inspiring.[60] They are personally able to communicate effectively their confidence and enthusiasm. Thus, followers judge a leader's **credibility** in terms of his or her honesty, competence, and ability to inspire.

Trust is closely entwined with the concept of credibility, and, in fact, the terms are often used interchangeably. **Trust** is defined as the belief in the integrity, character, and ability of a person. Followers who trust a leader are willing to be vulnerable to the leader's actions because they are confident that their rights and interests will not be abused.[61] Research has identified five dimensions that make up the concept of trust:[62]

- *Integrity:* Honesty and truthfulness
- *Competence:* Technical and interpersonal knowledge and skills
- *Consistency:* Reliability, predictability, and good judgment in handling situations
- *Loyalty:* Willingness to protect a person, physically and emotionally
- *Openness:* Willingness to share ideas and information freely

credibility
The degree to which someone is perceived as honest, competent, and able to inspire.

trust
The belief in the integrity, character, and ability of a person.

Of these five dimensions, integrity seems to be the most critical when someone assesses another's trustworthiness.[63] However, both integrity and competence were seen in our earlier discussion of leadership traits as consistently associated with leadership.

Workplace changes have reinforced why such leadership qualities are so important. For instance, the trend toward empowerment (which we discuss later in this chapter, on page 388) and self-managed work teams has reduced or eliminated many of the traditional control mechanisms used to monitor employees. If a work team is free to schedule its own work, evaluate its own performance, and even make its own hiring decisions, trust becomes critical. Employees have to trust that managers will treat them fairly, and managers have to trust that employees will conscientiously fulfill their responsibilities.

Also, leaders have to increasingly lead others who may not be in their immediate work group—members of cross-functional teams, individuals who work for suppliers or customers, and perhaps even people who represent other organizations through strategic alliances. These situations don't allow leaders the luxury of falling back on their formal positions for influence. Many of these relationships, in fact, are fluid and fleeting. So the ability to quickly develop trust is crucial to the success of the relationship.

Why is it important that followers trust their leaders? Research has shown that trust in leadership is significantly related to positive job outcomes, including job performance, organizational citizenship behaviour, job satisfaction, and organizational commitment.[64] Given the importance of trust in effective leadership, how should leaders build trust? See *Tips for Managers—Suggestions for Building Trust.*[65] (To learn more about trust, see *Developing Your Interpersonal Skills—Building Trust* on pages 126–127, in Chapter 4.)

TIPS FOR MANAGERS

Suggestions for Building Trust

- Practise **openness**.
- Be **fair**.
- Speak your **feelings**.
- Tell the **truth**.
- Show **consistency**.
- Fulfill your **promises**.
- Maintain **confidences**.
- Demonstrate **competence**.

PRISM 4

Current Leadership Issues

▶ ▶ ▶ When Rossana Di Zio Magnotta first started trying to help her customers learn how to make wine, she ran into a significant hurdle.[66] Her customers, many of whom were first-generation Italian and Portuguese male immigrants, did not believe that a woman could know how to make wine. They constantly told her stories that implied that they knew more about wine-making than she did.

Magnotta knew that if she simply asserted her knowledge, her customers might become resentful. Instead, she wrote a step-by-step guide on winemaking, and then started distributing it with each purchase of winemaking materials. This way, her customers would not feel threatened by her expertise, and were able to make better wine. The booklet significantly increased her business. "One Italian would bring three of his brothers and when I got one Portuguese guy I got five of his cousins, so all of a sudden my business became an instant success," she explains. All by leading behind the scenes.

Think About It

Do men and women lead differently? Do men and women face different challenges in moving to the top of an organization? What factors might have affected Rossana Di Zio Magnotta's ability to be seen as an effective leader?

6. What are some current issues in leadership?

Leaders today face some important leadership issues. In this section, we look at some of these issues, including providing ethical leadership, providing online leadership, empowering employees, providing team leadership, cross-cultural leadership, and gender differences and leadership.

Providing Ethical Leadership

The topic of leadership and ethics has received surprisingly little attention. Only recently have ethics and leadership researchers begun to consider the ethical implications in leadership.[67] Why now? One reason is a growing general interest in ethics throughout the field of management. Another, without a doubt, is the recent corporate financial scandals that have increased the public's and politicians' concerns about ethical standards.

Ethics is part of leadership in a number of ways. For instance, transformational leaders have been described as fostering moral virtue when they try to change the attitudes and behaviours of followers.[68] We can also see an ethical component to charisma. Unethical leaders may use their charisma to enhance their power over followers and use that power for self-serving purposes. On the other hand, ethical leaders may use their charisma in more socially constructive ways to serve others.[69] We also see a lack of ethics when leaders abuse their power and give themselves large salaries and bonuses while, at the same time, they seek to cut costs by laying off employees. And, of course, trust, which is important to ethical behaviour, explicitly deals with the leadership traits of honesty and integrity.

As we have seen recently, leadership is not values-free. Providing moral leadership involves addressing the *means* that a leader uses in trying to achieve goals, as well as the content of those goals. As a recent study concluded, ethical leadership is more than being ethical; it's reinforcing ethics through organizational mechanisms such as communication and the reward system.[70] Thus, before we judge any leader to be effective, we should consider both the moral content of his or her goals *and* the means used to achieve those goals.

Providing Online Leadership

Would you expect your job as leader to be more difficult if employees are working from home, connected by computer?

How do you lead people who are physically separated from you and where interactions are basically reduced to written online communications? Pat O'Day, manager of a five-person virtual team at KPMG International, understands the challenges of providing online leadership. To help his team be more effective, O'Day says, "We communicate through email and conference calls and meet in person four times a year."[71]

What little research has been done in online leadership has focused on managing virtual teams.[72] This research suggests that there are three fundamental challenges in providing online leadership: communication, performance management, and trust.

Communication

In a virtual setting, leaders may need to learn new communication skills in order to be seen as effective. To effectively convey online leadership, managers must realize that they have choices in words, structure, tone, and style of their online communications and be alert to expressions of emotions. For instance, in face-to-face communications, harsh *words* can be softened by nonverbal action. A smile and comforting gestures, for instance, can lessen the blow behind words like *disappointed, unsatisfactory, inadequate,* or *below expectations.* In online interactions, that nonverbal aspect does not exist.

The *structure* of words in online communication has the power to motivate or demotivate the receiver. Is the message made up of full sentences or just phrases? The latter, for instance, is likely to be seen as curt and more threatening. Similarly, a message in ALL CAPS is the equivalent of shouting.

Leaders also need to be sure the *tone* of their message correctly conveys the emotions they want to send. Is the message formal or informal? Does it convey the appropriate level of importance or urgency? Also, is the leader's writing style consistent with his or her oral style? For instance, if a leader's written communication is more formal than his or her oral style, it will likely create confusion for employees and hinder the effectiveness of the message.

Online leaders must also choose a *style.* Do they use emoticons, abbreviations, jargon, and the like? Do they adapt their style to their audience? Observation suggests that some managers are having difficulty adjusting to computer-based communications. For instance, they use the same style with their bosses that they use with their staff. Or they selectively use online communication to "hide" when delivering bad news. Finally, online leaders need to develop the skills of "reading between the lines" in the messages they receive so they can decipher the emotional components.

Performance Management

Another challenge of online leadership is managing performance. How? By defining, facilitating, and encouraging it.[73] As leaders *define* performance, it's important to ensure that all members of a virtual team understand the team's goals, their responsibilities in achieving those goals, and how goal achievement is going to be assessed. There should be no surprises or uncertainties about performance expectations. Although these are important managerial responsibilities in all situations, they are particularly critical in virtual work environments as there are no face-to-face interactions to convey expectations or address performance problems.

Online leaders also have a responsibility to *facilitate* performance. This means reducing or eliminating obstacles to successful performance and providing adequate resources to get the job done. This can be particularly challenging, especially if the virtual team is global, since the physical distance separating the leader and the team means it's not easy to get team members the resources they may need.

Finally, online leaders are responsible for *encouraging* performance by providing sufficient rewards that virtual employees really value. As we will see in Chapter 13, motivating employees can be difficult, even in work settings where there is face-to-face interaction. In a virtual setting, the motivational challenge can be even greater because the leader is not there in person to encourage, support, and guide. So what can online leaders do? They can ask virtual employees what rewards are most important to them—pay, benefits, technology upgrades, opportunities for professional development, or whatever. Then, they can make sure the rewards are provided in a timely manner after major work goals have been achieved. Finally, any rewards program must be perceived as fair. This expectation is not any different from that of leaders in nonvirtual settings—employees want and expect rewards to be distributed fairly.

Online leadership encompasses many new tasks, even for managers in firms that have already established themselves in the brick-and-mortar world as Costco has. Costco's Internet company, Costco.com, offers shoppers only a fraction of the products they can find in one of its warehouse stores. Susan Castillo, vice-president of e-commerce, has made the site a success with unexpected items like hot tubs and diamond jewellery instead of "safe" items like books and CDs. Castillo likes relying on the Internet to control performance. "We know immediately whether something is successful simply by how many people order it," she says. "That's the joy of the Internet. You can see minute by minute what members are ordering."

Trust

The final challenge of providing online leadership is the issue of trust. In a virtual setting, there are numerous opportunities to violate trust. One possible trust issue is whether the system is being used to monitor and evaluate employees. The technology is there to do so, but leaders must consider whether that is really the best way to influence employee behaviour. For instance, T. J. Rodgers, founder and CEO of Cypress Semiconductor, found out the hard way that it might not be.[74] He built an in-house system that tracked goals and deadlines. If a department missed its target, the software shut down its computers and cancelled the manager's next paycheque. After realizing the system encouraged dishonesty, Rodgers ditched it. The experience made him understand that it was more important to create a culture where trust among all participants is expected and required. In fact, the five dimensions of trust we described earlier—integrity, competence, consistency, loyalty, and openness—would be vital to the development of such a culture.

Cypress Semiconductor
www.cypress.com

Empowering Employees

As we have described elsewhere in the text, managers are increasingly leading by empowering their employees. **Employee empowerment** involves giving more authority to employees to make decisions. Millions of individual employees and employee teams are making the key operating decisions that directly affect their work. They are developing budgets, scheduling workloads, controlling inventories, solving quality problems, and engaging in similar activities that until very recently were viewed exclusively as part of the manager's job.[75]

employee empowerment
Giving more authority to employees to make decisions.

Why are more and more companies empowering employees? One reason is the need for quick decisions by those people who are most knowledgeable about the issues—often those at lower organizational levels. If organizations are to successfully compete in a dynamic global economy, they have to be able to make decisions and implement changes quickly. Another reason is the reality that organizational downsizing has left many managers with larger spans of control. In order to cope with the increased work demands, managers had to empower their people. Although empowerment is not appropriate for all circumstances, when employees have the knowledge, skills, and experience to do their jobs competently and when they seek autonomy and possess an internal locus of control, it can be beneficial. (To learn more about another way that managers cope with increased work demands, see *Developing Your Interpersonal Skills—Delegating*, pages 284–285, in Chapter 9.)

Empowerment should be used cautiously, however. Professor Jia Lin Xie of the University of Toronto's Rotman School of Management found that people who lack confidence can become ill from being put in charge of their own work. Xie and her colleagues found that "workers who had high levels of control at work, but lacked confidence in their abilities or blamed themselves for workplace problems, were more likely to have lower antibody levels and experienced more colds and flus."[76]

One of the difficulties with empowerment is that companies do not always introduce it properly. Professor Dan Ondrack of the University of Toronto's Rotman School of Management points out that for employees to be empowered, four conditions need to be met:[77]

- There must be a clear definition of the values and mission of the company.
- The company must help employees acquire the relevant skills.
- Employees need to be supported in their decision making, and not criticized when they try to do something extraordinary.
- Employees need to be recognized for their efforts.

Providing Team Leadership

Q&A 12.10

Since leadership is increasingly taking place within a team context and more organizations are using work teams, the role of the leader in guiding team members has become increasingly important. The role of team leader *is* different from the traditional leadership role. Many leaders are not equipped to handle the change to employee teams. As one consultant noted, "Even the most capable managers have trouble making the transition because all the command-and-control type things they were encouraged to do before are no longer appropriate. There's no reason to have any skill or sense of this."[78] This same consultant estimated that "probably 15 percent of managers are natural team leaders; another 15 percent could never lead a team because it runs counter to their personality—that is, they're unable to sublimate their dominating style for the good of the team. Then there's that huge group in the middle: Team leadership doesn't come naturally to them, but they can learn it."[79]

Paul Okalik (left) was the first sitting premier of Nunavut and has been chosen to serve a second term. Okalik heads a nonpartisan government run by consensus, built from the principles of parliamentary democracy and Aboriginal values. Okalik's leadership skills include team building. He was the key negotiator in the settlement that led to the creation of Nunavut, and in his role as premier he must balance the needs of the Inuit and Qallunaaq (non-Inuit) residents in Nunavut.

The challenge for many managers is learning how to become an effective team leader. They have to learn skills such as having the patience to share information, being able to trust others and to give up authority, and understanding when to intervene. Effective team leaders have mastered the difficult balancing act of knowing when to leave their teams alone and when to get involved. New team leaders may try to retain too much control at a time when team members need more autonomy, or they may abandon their teams at times when team members need support and help.[80] (To learn more about team leadership, see *Self-Assessment—How Good Am I at Building and Leading a Team?* on pages 452–453, in Chapter 14.)

One study of organizations that had reorganized themselves around employee teams found certain common responsibilities of all leaders. These included coaching, facilitating, handling disciplinary problems, reviewing team and individual performance, training, and communication.[81] However, a more meaningful way to describe the team leader's job is to focus on two priorities: (1) managing the team's external boundary and (2) facilitating the team process.[82] These priorities entail four specific leadership roles (see Exhibit 12-10).

> *What has been your biggest challenge when trying to lead team members?*

Team leaders are *liaisons with external constituencies.* These may include upper management, other organizational work teams, customers, or suppliers. The leader represents the team to other constituencies, secures needed resources, clarifies others' expectations of the team, gathers information from the outside, and shares that information with team members.

Team leaders are *troubleshooters.* When the team has problems and asks for assistance, team leaders sit in on meetings and try to help resolve the problems. Troubleshooting rarely involves technical or operational issues because the team members typically know more about the tasks being done than does the leader. The leader is most likely to contribute by asking penetrating questions, helping the team talk through problems, and getting needed resources to tackle problems.

Exhibit 12-10

Specific Team Leadership Roles

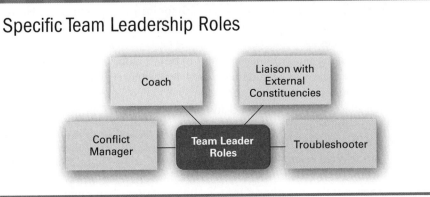

Team leaders are *conflict managers*. They help identify issues such as the source of the conflict, who is involved, the issues, the resolution options available, and the advantages and disadvantages of each. By getting team members to address questions such as these, the leader minimizes the disruptive aspects of intrateam conflicts.

Finally, team leaders are *coaches*. They clarify expectations and roles, teach, offer support, and do whatever else is necessary to help team members keep their work performance high. Team leaders are required in a variety of situations, as the following *Management Reflection* shows.

MANAGEMENT REFLECTION

Derek Jeter Inspires the New York Yankees

Can a shortstop really lead the team?   Leaders come in a variety of forms and contexts. New York Yankees shortstop Derek Jeter is team captain and definitely his team's leader.[83] Jeter is known as a player who adjusts to any situation—his only goal is to win.

Yankees owner George Steinbrenner refers to Jeter as "an inspiration for all of our nation's youth." Jeter's very bruised face appeared in sports sections across North America in July 2004 after a crucial catch in the twelfth inning to help the Yankees win a big game against the Boston Red Sox. As Jeter ran to catch the ball, he had to make a split-second decision: catch the ball, but crash into the stands and injure himself, or let the ball fall, and hope no one scored.

Jeter caught the ball, cut his chin, and bruised his right cheek and right shoulder. He was immediately taken to hospital to get seven stitches. Meanwhile, his teammates, two runs down but inspired by his heroics, came back to win the game. "The team would have been devastated to lose the game after Jeter's selflessness," says Yankees General Manager Brian Cashman.

Jeter's a leader on and off the field. In the clubhouse and the dugout he checks up on the other players and lets them know he is available to talk with them. Paul Quantrill, the former Toronto Blue Jays pitcher who was Jeter's teammate in 2004–2005, says Jeter "will do what it takes for the team to win, to beat you, so you'd better be careful." Jeter's entire team looks up to him. "It's the real deal," Quantrill says. "He carries himself the right way.…He's very approachable, he's one of the guys, but he's a rock star." ■

Cross-Cultural Leadership

One general conclusion that surfaces from leadership research is that effective leaders do not use any single style. They adjust their style to the situation. Although not mentioned explicitly, national culture is certainly an important situational variable in determining which leadership style will be most effective. What works in one country may not be effective in another. For instance, a study comparing German and English managers found a significant difference in their preference for an emphasis on production in the workplace. In Germany, procedures and high standards are part of the culture, and therefore, "the ideal leader in Germany is not expected to have to push for increased production." However, English managers indicated a preference for leaders to push for increased production. Because German employees are promoted more on the basis of technical competence than on relationships with managers, employees expect to be left alone to do their work, without a lot of guidance once the basic plan is understood. By contrast, English employees expect more direction from their managers.[84]

National culture affects leadership style because it influences how followers will respond. Leaders cannot (and should not) just choose their styles randomly. They are constrained by the cultural conditions their followers have come to expect. Exhibit 12-11 provides some findings from selected examples of cross-cultural leadership studies. Since most leadership theories were developed in the United States, using US subjects, they have an American bias. They emphasize follower responsibilities rather than rights; assume self-gratification rather than commitment to duty or altruistic motivation; assume centrality of work and democratic value orientation; and stress rationality rather than spirituality, religion, or superstition.[85]

The GLOBE (Global Leadership and Organizational Behavior Effectiveness) research program, which we introduced in Chapter 3, is the most extensive and comprehensive cross-cultural study of leadership ever undertaken. One of the findings of the GLOBE program is that there are some universal aspects to leadership. Specifically, a number of elements of transformational leadership appear to be associated with effective leadership regardless of what country the leader is in.[86] Which elements appear to be universal? Vision, foresight, providing encouragement, trustworthiness, dynamism, positiveness, and proactiveness. These findings led two members of the GLOBE team to conclude that "effective business leaders in any country are expected by their subordinates to provide a powerful and proactive vision to guide the company into the future, strong motivational skills to stimulate all employees to fulfill the vision, and excellent planning skills to assist in implementing the vision."[87] Some people suggest that these transformational leadership characteristics hold universal appeal as a result of the use of common technologies and management practices among businesses around the world, as well as global competitiveness and multinational influences.

Gender Differences and Leadership

There was a time when the question "Do males and females lead differently?" could be accurately characterized as a purely academic issue—interesting, but not very relevant. That time has certainly passed! Many women now hold management positions, and many more around the world will continue to join the management ranks. For instance, women fill 37 percent of managerial roles in Canada, although only 22 percent of the senior management roles (down from 27 percent in 1996), and 6.7 percent of the highest corporate titles—CEO, chief financial officer, or chief operating officer.[88] They are highly involved in smaller companies, however. Industry Canada reports that in 2000, 45 percent of all small to medium-sized enterprises had at least one female owner.[89] Moreover, women start almost half of all small businesses in Canada today and, among young people, women start almost 80 percent of small businesses.[90]

In other economically developed countries, the percentage of female managerial and administrative employees is as follows: Australia—37 percent; France—37 percent;

Exhibit 12-11

Selected Cross-Cultural Leadership Findings

- Korean leaders are expected to be paternalistic toward employees.
- Arab leaders who show kindness or generosity without being asked to do so are seen by other Arabs as weak.
- Japanese leaders are expected to be humble and speak frequently.
- Scandinavian and Dutch leaders who single out individuals with public praise are likely to embarrass, not energize, those individuals.
- Malaysian leaders are expected to show compassion while using more of an autocratic than a participative style.
- Effective German leaders are characterized by high performance orientation, low compassion, low self-protection, low team orientation, high autonomy, and high participation.

Sources: Based on J. C. Kennedy, "Leadership in Malaysia: Traditional Values, International Outlook," *Academy of Management Executive*, August 2002, pp. 15–17; F. C. Brodbeck, M. Frese, and M. Javidan, "Leadership Made in Germany: Low on Compassion, High on Performance," *Academy of Management Executive*, February 2002, pp. 16–29; M. F. Peterson and J. G. Hunt, "International Perspectives on International Leadership," *Leadership Quarterly*, Fall 1997, pp. 203–231; R. J. House and R. N. Aditya, "The Social Scientific Study of Leadership: Quo Vadis?" *Journal of Management* 23, no. 3 (1997), p. 463; and R. J. House, "Leadership in the Twenty-First Century," in *The Changing Nature of Work*, ed. A. Howard (San Francisco: Jossey-Bass, 1995), p. 442.

Germany—37 percent; Poland—33 percent; Sweden—30 percent; and Japan—10 percent.[91] Misconceptions about the relationship between leadership and gender can adversely affect hiring, performance evaluation, promotion, and other human resource decisions for both men and women. For instance, evidence indicates that a "good" manager is still perceived as predominantly masculine.[92]

A warning before we proceed: This topic is controversial. If male and female styles differ, is one inferior? If there is a difference, is one gender more effective in leading than the other? These are important questions and we will address them shortly.

A number of studies focusing on gender and leadership style have been conducted in recent years.[93] Their general conclusion is that males and females *do* use different styles. Specifically, women tend to adopt a more democratic or participative style. Women are more likely to encourage participation, share power and information, and attempt to enhance followers' self-worth. They lead through inclusion and rely on their charisma, expertise, contacts, and interpersonal skills to influence others. Women tend to use transformational leadership, motivating others by transforming their self-interest into organizational goals. Men are more likely to use a directive, command-and-control style. They rely on formal position authority for their influence. Men use transactional leadership, handing out rewards for good work and punishment for bad.[94] There is an interesting qualifier to the above findings. The tendency for female leaders to be more democratic than males declines when women are in male-dominated jobs. Apparently, group norms and male stereotypes influence women and they tend to act more autocratically.[95]

Another issue to consider is how male and female leaders are perceived in the workplace. A recent study sheds some light on this topic.[96] One major finding of this research was that men consider women to be less skilled at problem solving, which is one of the qualities often associated with effective leadership. Another finding was that both men and women believe women to be superior to men at "take care" behaviours and men superior to women at "take charge" behaviours. Such gender-based stereotyping creates challenges both for organizations and for leaders within those organizations. Organizations need effective leaders at all levels, but they need to ensure that stereotypical perceptions don't limit who those leaders might be.[97]

Although it's interesting to see how male and female leadership styles differ, a more important question is whether they differ in effectiveness. Although some researchers have shown that males and females tend to be equally effective as leaders,[98] an increasing number of studies have shown that women executives, when rated by their peers, employees, and bosses, score higher than their male counterparts on a wide variety of measures, including getting extra effort from subordinates and overall effectiveness in leading. Subordinates also reported more satisfaction with the leadership given by women.[99] See Exhibit 12-12 for a scorecard on where female managers do better, based on a summary of five studies. Why these differences? One possible explanation is that in today's organizations, flexibility, teamwork and partnering, trust, and information sharing are rapidly replacing rigid structures, competitive individualism, control, and secrecy. In these types of workplaces, effective managers must use more social and interpersonal behaviours. They listen, motivate, and provide support to their people. They inspire and influence rather than control. And women seem to do those things better than men.[100]

Although women seem to rate highly on those leadership skills needed to succeed in today's dynamic global environment, we don't want to fall into the same trap as the early leadership researchers who tried to find the "one best leadership style" for all situations. We know that there is no one *best* style for all situations. Instead, which leadership style is effective will depend on the situation. So even if men and women differ in their leadership styles, we should not assume that one is always preferable to the other.

How can managers stay in touch with their employees and be better leaders? *Tips for Managers—Getting Back to Basics* provides some suggestions.

TIPS FOR MANAGERS

Getting Back to Basics

↗ Give people **a reason to come to work**.

↗ **Be loyal** to the organization's people.

↗ **Spend time with people** who do the real work of the organization—people down at the loading dock, or in the checkout line, or out on sales calls.

↗ **Be more open** and **more candid** about what business practices are acceptable and proper and how the unacceptable ones should be fixed.

Source: A. Webber, "Above-It-All CEOs Forget Workers," *USA Today*, November 11, 2002, p. 13A.

Exhibit 12-12

Where Female Managers Do Better: A Scorecard

None of the five studies set out to find gender differences. They stumbled on them while compiling and analyzing performance evaluations.

Skill (Each check mark denotes which group scored higher on the respective studies.)	MEN	WOMEN
Motivating Others		✓ ✓ ✓ ✓
Fostering Communication		✓ ✓ ✓ ✓ *
Producing High-Quality Work		✓ ✓ ✓ ✓ ✓
Strategic Planning	✓ ✓	✓ ✓ *
Listening to Others		✓ ✓ ✓ ✓ ✓
Analyzing Issues	✓ ✓	✓ ✓ *

* In one study, women's and men's scores in these categories were statistically even.

Data: Hagberg Consulting Group, Management Research Group, Lawrence A. Pfaff, Personnel Decisions International Inc., Advanced Teamware Inc.

Source: R. Sharpe, "As Leaders, Women Rule," *BusinessWeek*, November 20, 2000, p. 75.

SUMMARY AND IMPLICATIONS

1. How do leaders and managers differ? Managers are appointed to their positions. They have formal authority, and it is this authority that gives them their ability to influence employees. In contrast, leaders can be appointed or can emerge from within a work group. They provide vision and strategy and are able to influence others for reasons beyond formal authority. Though ideally all managers should be leaders, not all leaders can be managers, because they do not all have the ability to plan, organize, and control.

▶ ▶ ▶ Rossana Di Zio Magnotta has demonstrated the ability to both lead and manage at Magnotta Winery.

2. What do trait and behavioural theories tell us about leadership? Researchers agree that traits alone are not sufficient for explaining effective leadership. Possessing the appropriate traits only makes it more likely that an individual would be an effective leader. In general, behavioural theories have identified useful behaviours that managers should have, but the research could not identify when these behaviours were most useful.

▶ ▶ ▶ Rossana Di Zio Magnotta notes that one of her most useful leadership traits is being tough and willing to stand up to adversity.

3. How do contingency theories of leadership improve our understanding of leadership? Contingency theories acknowledge that different situations require different leadership styles. The theories suggest that leaders may need to adjust their style to the needs of different organizations and employees, and perhaps different countries.

4. What do charismatic and transformational leaders do? While most leaders are transactional, guiding followers to achieve goals by clarifying role and task requirements, charismatic and transformational leaders inspire and influence their followers. Charismatic leaders are enthusiastic and self-confident leaders whose personality and actions motivate followers. They are known for having and articulating a vision, and for being willing to take risks to achieve that vision. Transformational leaders turn followers into believers on a mission, and encourage followers to go beyond their own self-interests for the greater good. Transformational leadership is more than charisma, since the transformational leader attempts to empower followers to question established views and even those views held by the leader.

▶ ▶ ▶ Rossana Di Zio Magnotta found that motivating customers to help with the winery's dispute with the Liquor Control Board of Ontario reinforced the idea that the wines should be carried in the stores. By mobilizing customers, she got free attention to the LCBO.

5. How can managers use power and trust to enhance leadership?   Most effective leaders rely on several different sources of power—legitimate, coercive, reward, expert, and referent power—to affect the behaviour and performance of their followers. An important consideration for leaders today is building trust and credibility with employees. Trust in leadership has been found to have a significant effect on positive job outcomes, including job performance, organizational citizenship behaviour, job satisfaction, and organizational commitment.

6. What are some current issues in leadership?   The major leadership issues today are providing ethical leadership, providing online leadership, empowering employees, providing team leadership, cross-cultural leadership, and gender differences and leadership.

▶ ▶ ▶ Rossana Di Zio Magnotta's experience with Italian and Portuguese male customers illustrates the differences men and women can face in the workplace. She had to find a way to make her male customers comfortable with her expertise, something a man in her position would probably not have had to do.

Management @ Work

READING FOR COMPREHENSION

1. Discuss the strengths and weaknesses of trait theories of leadership.

2. What is the managerial grid? Contrast this approach to leadership with that developed by the Ohio State and University of Michigan studies.

3. How is a least-preferred co-worker (LPC) determined? What is the importance of one's LPC for the Fiedler contingency model for leadership?

4. What are the two contingency variables of the path-goal theory of leadership?

5. What similarities, if any, can you find among Fiedler's contingency model, Hersey and Blanchard's Situational Leadership®, and path-goal theory?

6. Describe the difference between a transactional leader and a transformational leader.

7. What sources of power are available to leaders? Which ones are most effective?

8. What are the five dimensions of trust?

LINKING CONCEPTS TO PRACTICE

1. What types of power are available to you? Which ones do you use most? Why?

2. Do you think that most managers in real life use a contingency approach to increase their leadership effectiveness? Discuss.

3. If you ask people why a given individual is a leader, they tend to describe the person in terms such as *competent, consistent*, *self-assured*, *inspiring a shared vision*, and *enthusiastic*. How do these descriptions fit with leadership concepts presented in the chapter?

4. What kinds of campus activities could a full-time student do that might lead to the perception that he or she is a charismatic leader? In pursuing those activities, what might the student do to enhance this perception of being charismatic?

5. Do you think trust evolves out of an individual's personal characteristics or out of specific situations? Explain.

SELF-ASSESSMENT

What's My Leadership Style?

The following items describe aspects of leadership behaviour.[101] Respond to each item according to the way you would be most likely to act if you were the leader of a work group. Use this scale for your responses:

A = Always
F = Frequently
O = Occasionally
S = Seldom
N = Never

1. I would most likely act as the spokesperson of the group.	A	F	O	S	N
2. I would encourage overtime work.	A	F	O	S	N
3. I would allow group members complete freedom in their work.	A	F	O	S	N
4. I would encourage the use of uniform procedures.	A	F	O	S	N
5. I would permit group members to use their own judgment in solving problems.	A	F	O	S	N

6. I would stress being ahead of competing groups. A F O S N

7. I would speak as a representative of the group. A F O S N

8. I would needle group members for greater effort. A F O S N

9. I would try out my ideas in the group. A F O S N

10. I would let group members do their work the way they think best. A F O S N

11. I would be working hard for a promotion. A F O S N

12. I would be able to tolerate postponement and uncertainty. A F O S N

13. I would speak for the group when visitors were present. A F O S N

14. I would keep the work moving at a rapid pace. A F O S N

15. I would turn group members loose on a job and let them go to it. A F O S N

16. I would settle conflicts when they occur in the group. A F O S N

17. I would get swamped by details. A F O S N

18. I would represent the group at outside meetings. A F O S N

19. I would be reluctant to allow group members any freedom of action. A F O S N

20. I would decide what shall be done and how it shall be done. A F O S N

21. I would push for increased production. A F O S N

22. I would let some group members have authority that I should keep. A F O S N

23. Things would usually turn out as I predicted. A F O S N

24. I would allow the group a high degree of initiative. A F O S N

25. I would assign group members to particular tasks. A F O S N

26. I would be willing to make changes. A F O S N

27. I would ask group members to work harder. A F O S N

28. I would trust group members to exercise good judgment. A F O S N

29. I would schedule the work to be done. A F O S N

30. I would refuse to explain my actions. A F O S N

31. I would persuade group members that my ideas are to their advantage. A F O S N

32. I would permit the group to set its own pace. A F O S N

33. I would urge the group to beat its previous record. A F O S N

34. I would act without consulting the group. A F O S N

35. I would ask that group members follow standard rules and regulations. A F O S N

Scoring Key

1. Circle the numbers 8, 12, 17, 18, 19, 30, 34, and 35.

2. Write a 1 in front of the circled number if you responded Seldom or Never.

3. Also write a 1 in front of any remaining (uncircled) items if you responded Always or Frequently to these.

4. Circle the 1s that you have written in front of the following questions: 3, 5, 8, 10, 15, 18, 19, 22, 24, 26, 28, 30, 32, 34, and 35.

5. Count the circled 1s. This is your score for "Concern for People."

6. Count the uncircled 1s. This is your score for "Task."

Analysis and Interpretation

This leadership instrument taps the degree to which you are task or people oriented. Task orientation is concerned with getting the job done, whereas people orientation focuses on group interactions and the needs of individual members.

The cutoff scores separating high and low scores are approximately as follows. For task orientation, high is a score above 10; low is below 10. For people orientation, high is a score above 7; low is below 7.

The best leaders are ones who can balance their task/people orientation to various situations. A high score on both would indicate this balance. If you are too task oriented, you tend to be autocratic. You get the job done but at a high emotional cost. If you are too people oriented, your leadership style may be overly laissez-faire. People are likely to be happy in their work but sometimes at the expense of productivity.

Your score should also help you to put yourself in situations that increase your likelihood of success. So, for instance, evidence indicates that when employees are experienced and know their jobs well, they tend to perform best with a people-oriented leader. If you are people oriented, then this is a favourable situation for you. But if you are task oriented, you might want to pass on this situation.

More Self-Assessments mymanagementlab

To learn more about your skills, abilities, and interests, go to the MyManagementLab website and take the following self-assessments:

- II.B.2.—How Charismatic Am I?
- II.B.4.—Do Others See Me as Trustworthy?
- II.B.6.—How Good Am I at Building and Leading a Team? (This exercise also appears in Chapter 14 on pages 452–453.)

MANAGEMENT FOR YOU TODAY

Dilemma

Your school is developing a one-day orientation program for new students majoring in business. You have been asked to consider leading the group of students who will design and implement the orientation program. Develop a 2- to 3-page "handout" that shows whether the position is a natural fit for you. To do this

(1) identify your strengths and weaknesses in the sources of power you can bring to the project; and (2) discuss whether you would be a transactional or transformational leader and why. Provide a strong concluding statement about whether or not you would be the best leader for this task.

Becoming a Manager

- As you interact with various organizations, note different leadership styles.
- Think of people that you would consider effective leaders and try to determine why they are effective.
- If you have the opportunity, take leadership development courses.

- Practise building trust in relationships that you have with others.
- Read books on great leaders (not just business leaders) and on leadership development topics.

WORKING TOGETHER: TEAM-BASED EXERCISE

Conveying Bad News

You are the new manager of customer-service operations at Preferred Bank Card, a credit card issuer with offices throughout Ontario. Your predecessor, who was very popular with the customer-service representatives and who is still with the company, concealed from your team members how far behind they are on their goals this quarter. As a result, your team members are looking forward to a promised day off that they are not entitled to and will not be getting. It's your job to tell them the bad news. How will you do it?

Form groups of no more than 4 individuals. Discuss this situation and how you would handle it. Then create a role-playing situation that illustrates your group's proposed approach. Be ready to perform your role play in front of the class. Also, be prepared to provide the rest of the class with the specific steps that your group suggested be used in this situation.

Ethical Dilemma Exercise: Is an Eye for an Eye Fair Play?

What happens when a charismatic leader's relentless pursuit of a vision encourages extreme or even ethically questionable behaviour?[102] Consider the CEO of a company that hired an investigator to dive into other firms' dumpsters for information about their dealings with a major competitor. The same CEO's company has used precisely timed news releases as strategic weapons against particular rivals. And the same CEO's company once announced a hostile takeover bid for a direct competitor with the stated intention of not actively selling its products but acquiring its best customers and employees. This CEO, described by the *Wall Street Journal* as "a swashbuckling figure in Silicon Valley," is Larry Ellison of Oracle.

Ellison's charismatic leadership has built Oracle into a software powerhouse. Although it is locked in fierce competition with Microsoft and other giants, it does not ignore smaller rivals such as i2 Technologies. Oracle once issued a news release belittling i2's attempt at developing a certain type of software only minutes before i2's CEO was to meet with

influential analysts. Such hardball tactics are hardly random or spontaneous. When Oracle pursued an unwelcome acquisition bid for rival PeopleSoft, the two CEOs traded barbed quotes for weeks as the companies battled in courtrooms and in the media. PeopleSoft's CEO, a former Oracle executive, described the situation as "enormously bad behavior from a company that's had a history of it." Nevertheless, Oracle finally bought PeopleSoft in 2005.

Imagine that you are the CEO of i2 Technologies, which makes inventory and supply tracking systems that compete with Oracle's large-scale business software suites. In five minutes, you will be meeting with a roomful of financial analysts who make buy or sell recommendations to investors. Your goal is to showcase your company's accomplishments, outline your vision for its future, and encourage a positive recommendation so your stock price will go even higher. You just heard about Oracle's news release belittling your product in development—and you suspect the analysts also know about it. How will you handle the news release?

Thinking Critically About Ethics

Your boss is not satisfied with the way one of your colleagues is handling a project, and she reassigns the project to you. She tells you to work with this person to find out what he has done already and to discuss any other necessary information that he might have. She wants your project report by the end of the month. This person is pretty upset and angry over the reassignment and will not give you the information you

need to even start, much less complete, the project. You will not be able to meet your deadline unless you get this information.

What type of power does your colleague appear to be using? What type of influence could you possibly use to gain his cooperation? What could you do to resolve this situation successfully, yet ethically?

Grafik Marketing Communications

When more seasoned employees take less experienced employees under their wings, we call this mentoring.[103] The wisdom and guidance of these seasoned individuals serve to assist less experienced employees in obtaining the necessary skills and socialization to succeed in the organization. It is also helpful in facilitating an individual's career progress. Technology, however, is starting to change some of this traditional mentoring process in terms of who does the mentoring. For Judy Kirpich, for example, technological advancements have resulted in significant increases in mentoring in her organization, Grafik Marketing Communications. However, the company's senior managers are the ones who need to be mentored. They do not have the technological

savvy of the younger employees who have grown up on computers, resulting in what is called reverse mentoring.

Kirpich is considering introducing reverse mentoring, a practice started years ago at General Electric. Then-CEO Jack Welch recognized that his senior managers needed to become more proficient with using technology—especially the Internet. Accordingly, Welch had several hundred senior managers partner with younger employees in the organization. Not only were these managers able to learn about the Internet, but reverse mentoring also enhanced intergenerational understanding and gave senior decision makers a new perspective on younger consumer products and service needs. It also helped the organization in brainstorming for new and creative ideas.

Reverse mentoring, however, is not without drawbacks. For these younger employees to mentor properly, they must be trained. They must understand how to be patient with those individuals who may have a technology phobia. These reverse mentors need to recognize that their mentoring is limited to offering advice solely on relevant technology topics. They must also understand and acknowledge the need for confidentiality because many senior managers may be reluctant to have this mentoring relationship widely known.

Reverse mentoring can also lead to the problem of subordinates forgetting that the leader is still in charge. Furthermore, when reverse mentors exist, organizational members must be made aware that problems arising out of favouritism are a reality.

Kirpich wants to move reverse mentoring forward at Grafik Marketing Communications. However, she is aware of the many problems that could arise. What advice would you give her about successfully implementing reverse mentoring?

DEVELOPING YOUR DIAGNOSTIC AND ANALYTICAL SKILLS

Radical Leadership

Ricardo Semler, CEO of Semco Group of São Paulo, Brazil, is considered by many to be a radical. He has never been the type of leader that most people might expect to be in charge of a multimillion-dollar business.[104] Why? Semler breaks all the traditional "rules" of leading and managing. He is the ultimate hands-off leader who does not even have an office at the company's headquarters. As the "leading proponent and most tireless evangelist" of participative management, Semler says his philosophy is simple: Treat people like adults and they will respond like adults.

Underlying the participative management approach is the belief that "organizations thrive best by entrusting employees to apply their creativity and ingenuity in service of the whole enterprise, and to make important decisions close to the flow of work, conceivably including the selection and election of their bosses." And according to Semler, his approach works ... and works well. But how does it work in reality?

At Semler, you will not find most of the trappings of organizations and management. There are no organization charts, no long-term plans, no corporate values statements, no dress codes, and no written rules or policy manuals. The company's 3000 employees decide their work hours and their pay levels. Subordinates decide who their bosses will be, and they also review their boss's performance. The employees also elect the corporate leadership and decide most of the company's new strategic initiatives. Each person has one vote—including Ricardo Semler.

At one of the company's plants outside São Paulo, there are no supervisors telling employees what to do. On any given day, an employee may decide to "run a grinder or drive a forklift, depending on what needs to be done." João Vendramin Neto, who is in charge of Semco's manufacturing, says that "the workers know the organization's objectives and they use common sense to decide for themselves what they should do to hit those goals."

Why did Semler decide that his form of radical leadership was necessary, and does it work? Semler did not pursue such radical self-governance out of some altruistic ulterior motive. Instead, he felt it was the only way to build an organization that was flexible and resilient enough to flourish in chaotic and turbulent times. He maintains that this approach has enabled Semco to survive the roller-coaster nature of Brazilian politics and economy. Although the country's political leadership and economy have gone from one extreme to another and countless Brazilian banks and companies have failed, Semco has survived. And not just survived—prospered. Semler says, "If you look at Semco's numbers, we've grown 27.5 percent a year for 14 years." Semler attributes this fact to flexibility ... of his company and, most importantly, of his employees.

Questions

1. Describe Ricardo Semler's leadership style. What do you think the advantages and drawbacks of his style might be?

2. What challenges might a radically "hands-off" leader face? How could those challenges be addressed?

3. How could future leaders be identified in this organization? Would leadership training be important to this organization? Discuss.

4. What could other businesses learn from Semler's approach to leadership?

Acquiring Power

About the Skill

The exercise of power is a natural process in any group or organization, and to perform their jobs effectively, managers need to know how to acquire and use power—the capacity of a leader to influence work actions or decisions. We discussed the concept of power earlier in the chapter and identified five different sources: legitimate, coercive, reward, expert, and referent power. Why is having power important? Because power makes you less dependent on others. When a manager has power, he or she is not as dependent on others for critical resources. And if the resources a manager controls are important, scarce, and nonsubstitutable, her power will increase because others will be more dependent on her for those resources.

Steps in Developing the Skill

You can be more effective at acquiring power if you use the following eight suggestions:[105]

1. **Frame arguments in terms of organizational goals.** To be effective at acquiring power means camouflaging your self-interests. Discussions over who controls what resources should be framed in terms of the benefits that will accrue to the organization; do not point out how you personally will benefit.

2. **Develop the right image.** If you know your organization's culture, you already understand what the organization wants and values from its employees in terms of dress, associates to cultivate and those to avoid, whether to appear risk taking or risk aversive, the preferred leadership style, the importance placed on getting along well with others, and so forth. With this knowledge, you are equipped to project the appropriate image. Because the assessment of your performance is not always a fully objective process, you need to pay attention to style as well as substance.

3. **Gain control of organizational resources.** Controlling organizational resources that are scarce and important is a source of power. Knowledge and expertise are particularly effective resources to control. They make you more valuable to the organization and, therefore, more likely to have job security, chances for advancement, and a receptive audience for your ideas.

4. **Make yourself appear indispensable.** Because we are dealing with appearances rather than objective facts, you can enhance your power by appearing to be indispensable. You don't really have to be indispensable as long as key people in the organization believe that you are.

5. **Be visible.** If you have a job that brings your accomplishments to the attention of others, that is great. However, if you don't have such a job, you will want to find ways to let others in the organization know what you are doing by highlighting successes in routine reports, having satisfied customers relay their appreciation to senior executives, being seen at social functions, being active in your professional associations, and developing powerful allies who speak positively about your accomplishments. Of course, you will want to be on the lookout for those projects that will increase your visibility.

6. **Develop powerful allies.** To get power, it helps to have powerful people on your side. Cultivate contacts with potentially influential people above you, at your own level, and at lower organizational levels. These allies often can provide you with information that is otherwise not readily available. In addition, having allies can provide you with a coalition of support if and when you need it.

7. **Avoid "tainted" members.** In almost every organization, there are fringe members whose status is questionable. Their performance and/or loyalty may be suspect. Keep your distance from such individuals.

8. **Support your manager.** Your immediate future is in the hands of your current manager. Because he or she evaluates your performance, you will typically want to do whatever is necessary to have your manager on your side. You should make every effort to help your manager succeed, make her look good, support her if she is under siege, and spend the time to find out the criteria she will use to assess your effectiveness. Don't undermine your manager. And don't speak negatively of her to others.

Practising the Skill

Read the following scenario. Write some notes about how you would handle the situation described. Be sure to refer to the eight suggestions for acquiring power.

Scenario

You used to be the star marketing manager for Hilton Electronics. But for the past year, you have been outpaced again and again by Conor, a new manager in the design department, who has been accomplishing everything expected of her and more. Meanwhile, your best efforts to do your job well have been sabotaged and undercut by Leonila—your and Conor's manager. For example, before last year's international consumer electronics show, Leonila moved $30 000 from your budget to Conor's. Despite your best efforts, your marketing team could not complete all the marketing materials normally developed to showcase all of your organization's new products at this important industry show. Leonila has chipped away at your staff and budget ever since. Although you have been able to meet most of your goals with fewer staff and less budget, Leonila has continued to slice away resources of your group. Just last week, she eliminated two positions in your team of eight marketing specialists to make room for a new designer and some extra equipment for Conor. Leonila is clearly taking away your resources while giving Conor whatever she wants and more. You think it's time to do something, or soon you will not have any team or resources left. How should you approach the problem?

Reinforcing the Skill

The following activities will help you practise and reinforce the skills associated with acquiring power:

1. Keep a one-week journal of your behaviour describing incidences when you tried to influence others around you. Assess each incident by asking: Were you successful at these attempts to influence them? Why or why not? What could you have done differently?

2. Review recent issues of a business periodical (such as *BusinessWeek, Fortune, Forbes, Fast Company, IndustryWeek, Canadian Business, PROFIT,* or the *Wall Street Journal*). Look for articles on reorganizations, promotions, or departures from management positions. Find at least two articles where you believe power issues are involved. Relate the content of the articles to the concepts introduced in this *Developing Your Interpersonal Skills* feature.

MANAGING YOUR CAREER

The Ins and Outs of Office Politics

You have probably heard the term *office politics* before and probably have experienced it if you have ever worked in an organization. Office politics is a fact of life in organizations.[106] Since organizations are made up of individuals and groups with different values, goals, and interests, this sets up the potential for conflict over resources such as budgets, space allocations, project responsibilities, and salary adjustments. To gain control over these resources, people exert power. People want to carve out a niche from which to exert influ-

ence, to earn awards, and to advance their careers. When employees convert their power into action, we describe them as being engaged in office politics. Those with good political skills effectively use their various sources of power to get what they need and want. Although you may not like the idea of engaging in office politics, it is important that you know how to be politically adept. You can use the suggestions found in this chapter's *Developing Your Interpersonal Skills* to improve your political effectiveness.

Motivating Employees

How do I motivate people to accomplish organizational goals?

1. What is motivation?
2. How can needs help one be motivated?
3. What are the contemporary theories of motivation?
4. What are some current issues in motivation?
5. How can managers motivate employees?

▶ ▶ ▶ How do you motivate employees in an industry where absenteeism rates average 5 percent of all working hours, but can be as high as 10 percent in urban areas?[1] What do you do when the turnover rate of managers averages 20 percent, and the turnover rate of nonmanagerial employees averages 30 percent?

Sir Terry Leahy, CEO of UK-based Tesco, faces these problems daily. The company has over 3200 supermarkets, hypermarkets, and convenience stores in the United Kingdom, Ireland, Central Europe, and Asia. Once a discount supermarket, Tesco has built itself as a dressier, mid-market retailer while becoming the number one food retailer in the United Kingdom.

The company is trying to keep its Generation Y employees (Generation Y includes those born between 1979 and 1994) motivated, while also trying to accommodate the needs of other groups of employees, including ethnic minorities and mothers returning to the workplace. Not all of the jobs are interesting, and many can be quite repetitive, like stocking shelves or running groceries past scanners for hours on end.

Leahy believes in starting with the basics in dealing with employees. "We've built Tesco around sound values and principles," he says. Therefore, he makes sure that employees are treated with respect. But he is also concerned about performance: "If that's bad and there's no good reason, I get cross."

Think About It

What are the different motivation tools that managers use? Put yourself in Sir Terry Leahy's shoes. How should he motivate his managers so that he will have less turnover? What can he do to keep his shelf-stockers and cashiers motivated?

Motivating and rewarding employees is one of the most important, and one of the most challenging, activities that managers perform. Successful managers, like Sir Terry Leahy, understand that what motivates them personally may have little or no effect on others. Just because *you* are motivated by being part of a cohesive work team, don't assume everyone is. Or the fact that you are motivated by challenging work does not mean everyone is. Effective managers who want their employees to put forth maximum effort recognize that they need to know how and why employees are motivated and to tailor their motivational practices to satisfy the needs and wants of those employees.

In this chapter, we take a look at what motivation is, early motivation theories, and contemporary theories. Then, we discuss some current motivation issues and provide practical suggestions managers can use to motivate employees.

Tesco
www.tesco.com

What Is Motivation?

All managers need to be able to motivate their employees, and that requires understanding what motivation is. Many people incorrectly view motivation as a personal trait—that is, a trait that some people have and others don't. Our knowledge of motivation tells us that we cannot label people that way. What we *do* know is that motivation is the result of the interaction between a person and a situation. Certainly, individuals differ in motivational drive, but, overall, motivation varies from situation to situation. For instance, your level of motivation probably differs among the various courses you take each term. As we analyze the concept of motivation, keep in mind that the level of motivation varies both between individuals and within individuals at different times.

1. What is motivation?

motivation
An individual's willingness to exert high levels of effort to reach organizational goals, conditioned by the degree to which that effort satisfies some individual need.

need
An internal state that makes certain outcomes appear attractive.

Motivation refers to an individual's willingness to exert high levels of effort to reach organizational goals, conditioned by the effort's ability to satisfy some individual need. Although, in general, motivation refers to effort exerted toward any goal, here it refers to organizational goals because our focus is on work-related behaviour.

Three key elements can be seen in this definition: effort, organizational goals, and need. The *effort* element is a measure of intensity or drive.[2] A motivated person tries hard. But high levels of effort are unlikely to lead to favourable job performance unless the effort is channelled in a direction that benefits the organization.[3] Therefore, we must consider the quality of the effort as well as its intensity. Effort that is directed toward, and consistent with, *organizational goals* is the kind of effort that we should be seeking. Finally, we will treat motivation as a *need-satisfying* process, as shown in Exhibit 13-1.

A **need** is an internal state that makes certain outcomes appear attractive. An unsatisfied need creates tension, which an individual reduces by exerting effort. Because we are interested in work behaviour, this tension-reduction effort must be directed toward organizational goals. Therefore, inherent in our definition of motivation is the requirement that the individual's needs be compatible with the organization's goals. When the two don't match, individuals may exert high levels of effort that run counter to the interests of the organization. Incidentally, this is not all that unusual. Some employees regularly spend a lot of time talking with friends at work to satisfy their social need. There is a high level of effort, but little, if any, is being directed toward work.

What motivates you?

Finding ways to motivate employees to achieve high levels of performance is an important organizational problem, and managers keep looking for a solution. A recent Canadian Policy Research Network survey found that only 40 percent of Canadians are very satisfied with their jobs. By comparison, 47 percent of American workers are happy with their work, and 54 percent of Danish workers report high satisfaction.[4] In light of these results, it's no wonder that both academic researchers and practising managers want to understand and explain employee motivation.

Early Theories of Motivation

▶ ▶ ▶ Management at Tesco was interested in discovering what concerns their employees had and how these might be addressed.[5] They conducted research on their employees and found that many of their staff were single and worked mainly to have the money to travel overseas and participate in leisure activities. Their research also found that these employees "were unlikely to take much pride in their work, would lack commitment and would have little hesitation about going to work elsewhere if the pay were better."

Think About It

What kinds of needs do employees have? How can they be addressed?

Exhibit 13-1

The Motivation Process

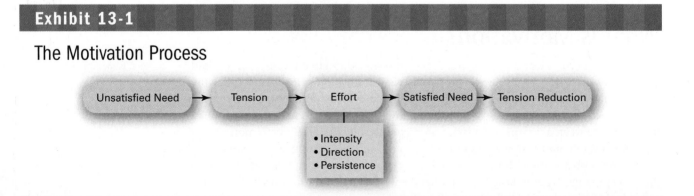

We begin by looking at three early theories of motivation that, although questionable in terms of validity, are probably the most widely known approaches to employee motivation. These three theories are *Maslow's hierarchy of needs, McGregor's Theory X and Theory Y,* and *Herzberg's motivation-hygiene theory.* Although more valid explanations of motivation have been developed, you should know these early theories because (1) they represent the foundation from which contemporary motivation theories were developed, and (2) practising managers continue to regularly use these theories and their terminology to explain employee motivation.

2. How can needs help one be motivated?

Maslow's Hierarchy of Needs Theory

The best-known theory of motivation is probably Abraham Maslow's **hierarchy of needs theory**.[6] Maslow was a psychologist who proposed that within every person is a hierarchy of five needs:

1. **Physiological needs**. Food, drink, shelter, sexual satisfaction, and other physical requirements.

2. **Safety needs**. Security and protection from physical and emotional harm, as well as assurance that physical needs will continue to be met.

3. **Social needs**. Affection, belongingness, acceptance, and friendship.

4. **Esteem needs**. Internal esteem factors such as self-respect, autonomy, and achievement, and external esteem factors such as status, recognition, and attention.

5. **Self-actualization needs**. Growth, achieving one's potential, and self-fulfillment; the drive to become what one is capable of becoming.

Maslow argued that each level in the needs hierarchy must be substantially satisfied before the next is activated and that once a need is substantially satisfied, it no longer motivates behaviour. In other words, as each need is substantially satisfied, the next need becomes dominant. In terms of Exhibit 13-2 on page 406, an individual moves up the needs hierarchy. From the standpoint of motivation, Maslow's theory proposed that, although no need is ever fully satisfied, a substantially satisfied need will no longer motivate an individual. Therefore, according to Maslow, if you want to motivate someone, you need to understand what level that person is on in the hierarchy and focus on satisfying needs at or above that level. Managers who accepted Maslow's hierarchy attempted to change their organizations and management practices so that employees' needs could be satisfied.

In addition, Maslow separated the five needs into higher and lower levels. Physiological and safety needs were considered *lower-order needs;* social, esteem, and self-actualization needs were considered *higher-order needs.* The difference was that higher-order needs are satisfied internally while lower-order needs are predominantly satisfied externally.

Maslow's needs theory received wide recognition during the 1960s and 1970s, especially among practising managers, probably because of its intuitive logic and ease of understanding. However, Maslow provided no empirical support for his theory, and several studies that sought to validate it could not.[7]

McGregor's Theory X and Theory Y

Do you need to be rewarded by others or are you a self-motivator?

Are individuals intrinsically or extrinsically motivated? Douglas McGregor tried to uncover the answer to this question through his discussion of Theory X and Theory Y.[8] **Extrinsic motivation** comes from outside the person and includes such things as pay, bonuses, and other tangible rewards. **Intrinsic motivation** reflects an individual's internal desire to do something, with motivation coming from interest, challenge, and personal satisfaction. Individuals show intrinsic motivation when they deeply care about their work, look for ways to improve the work, and are fulfilled by doing it well.[9]

Q&A 13.1

hierarchy of needs theory
Maslow's theory that there is a hierarchy of five human needs: physiological, safety, social, esteem, and self-actualization; as each need becomes satisfied, the next need becomes dominant.

physiological needs
A person's need for food, drink, shelter, sexual satisfaction, and other physical requirements.

safety needs
A person's need for security and protection from physical and emotional harm, as well as assurance that physical needs will continue to be met.

social needs
A person's need for affection, belongingness, acceptance, and friendship.

esteem needs
A person's need for internal esteem factors such as self-respect, autonomy, and achievement, and external esteem factors such as status, recognition, and attention.

self-actualization needs
A person's need to grow and become what he or she is capable of becoming.

extrinsic motivation
Motivation that comes from outside the person and includes such things as pay, bonuses, and other tangible rewards.

intrinsic motivation
Motivation that comes from the person's internal desire to do something, due to such things as interest, challenge, and personal satisfaction.

Exhibit 13-2

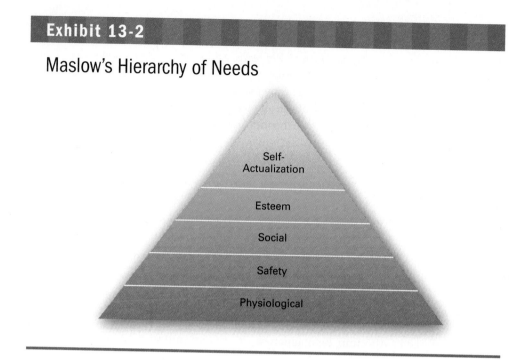

Maslow's Hierarchy of Needs

McGregor's **Theory X** offers an essentially negative view of people. It assumes that employees have little ambition, dislike work, want to avoid responsibility, and need to be closely controlled to work effectively. It suggests that people are almost exclusively driven by extrinsic motivators. **Theory Y** offers a positive view. It assumes that employees can exercise self-direction, accept and actually seek out responsibility, and consider work a natural activity. It suggests that people are more intrinsically motivated. McGregor believed that Theory Y assumptions best captured the true nature of employees and should guide management practice.

What did McGregor's analysis imply about motivation? The answer is best expressed in the framework presented by Maslow. Theory X assumed that lower-order needs dominated individuals, and Theory Y assumed that higher-order needs dominated individuals. McGregor himself held to the belief that the assumptions of Theory Y were more valid than those of Theory X. Therefore, he proposed that participation in decision making, responsible and challenging jobs, and good group relations would maximize employee motivation.

Q&A 13.2

Our knowledge of motivation tells us that neither theory alone fully accounts for employee behaviour. What we know is that motivation is the result of the interaction of the individual and the situation. Individuals differ in their basic motivational drive. As well, while you may find completing a homework assignment boring, you might enthusiastically plan a surprise party for a friend. These points underscore that the level of motivation varies both *between* individuals and *within* individuals at different times. They also suggest that managers should try to make sure that situations are motivating for employees.

Herzberg's Motivation-Hygiene Theory

Frederick Herzberg's **motivation-hygiene theory** proposes that intrinsic factors are related to job satisfaction and motivation, whereas extrinsic factors are associated with job dissatisfaction.[10] Believing that individuals' attitudes toward work determined success or failure, Herzberg investigated the question "What do people want from their jobs?" He asked people for detailed descriptions of situations in which they felt exceptionally good or bad about their jobs. These findings are shown in Exhibit 13-3.

Herzberg concluded from his analysis that the replies people gave when they felt good about their jobs were significantly different from the replies they gave when they felt bad. Certain characteristics were consistently related to job satisfaction (factors on the left side

Exhibit 13-3

Herzberg's Motivation-Hygiene Theory

Motivators	Hygiene Factors
• Achievement • Recognition • Work Itself • Responsibility • Advancement • Growth	• Supervision • Company Policy • Relationship with Supervisor • Working Conditions • Salary • Relationship with Peers • Personal Life • Relationship with Subordinates • Status • Security

Extremely Satisfied	Neutral	Extremely Dissatisfied

of the exhibit), and others to job dissatisfaction (factors on the right side). Those factors associated with job satisfaction were intrinsic and included things such as achievement, recognition, and responsibility. When people felt good about their work, they tended to attribute these characteristics to themselves. On the other hand, when they were dissatisfied, they tended to cite extrinsic factors such as supervision, company policy, interpersonal relationships, and working conditions.

In addition, Herzberg believed that the data suggested that the opposite of satisfaction was not dissatisfaction, as traditionally had been believed. Removing dissatisfying characteristics from a job would not necessarily make that job more satisfying (or motivating). As shown in Exhibit 13-4, Herzberg proposed that his findings indicated the existence of a dual continuum: The opposite of "satisfaction" is "no satisfaction," and the opposite of "dissatisfaction" is "no dissatisfaction."

According to Herzberg, the factors that led to job satisfaction were separate and distinct from those that led to job dissatisfaction. Therefore, managers who sought to eliminate factors that created job dissatisfaction could bring about workplace harmony but not necessarily motivation. The extrinsic factors that create job dissatisfaction were called **hygiene factors**. When these factors are adequate, people won't be dissatisfied, but they won't be satisfied (or motivated) either. To motivate people in their jobs, Herzberg suggested emphasizing **motivators**, the intrinsic factors such as achievement, recognition, and challenge that increase job satisfaction.

hygiene factors
Factors that eliminate job dissatisfaction, but don't motivate.

motivators
Factors that increase job satisfaction and motivation.

Exhibit 13-4

Contrasting Views of Satisfaction-Dissatisfaction

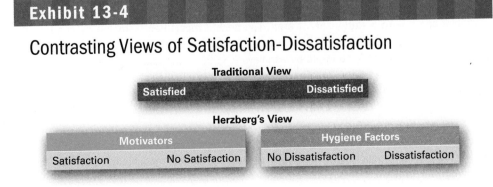

Traditional View

Satisfied	Dissatisfied

Herzberg's View

Motivators		Hygiene Factors	
Satisfaction	No Satisfaction	No Dissatisfaction	Dissatisfaction

Herzberg's theory enjoyed wide popularity from the mid-1960s to the early 1980s, but criticisms arose concerning his procedures and methodology. Although today we say the theory was simplistic, it has had a strong influence on how we currently design jobs, as the following *Management Reflection* shows.

MANAGEMENT REFLECTION

Machine Shop Cleans Up Its Act

Can the design of a machine shop affect employee morale?   Langley, BC-based Pazmac Enterprises uses insights from Herzberg's theory to organize its workplace.[11] The employees at the machine shop enjoy perks often associated with employees in the high-tech industry. Owner Steve Scarlett provides opportunities for his employees to be involved in decision making. "I believe business needs to be planned diplomatically—we talk things out," says Scarlett. He ensures good relationships among employees, and he also shows concern about employees' hygiene needs, reflecting Herzberg. Usually machine shops are noisy and messy, the floors are covered with oil, and employees wear dirty overalls. Pazmac, however, is spotlessly clean. The lunch room is tastefully designed, and the men's washroom is plush, with potpourri bowls and paintings on the walls.

Scarlett believes that employees should be treated the way he himself would like to be treated, which explains why he provides an on-site swimming pool, personal trainers, weekly yoga classes, and professional counselling services for employees. Scarlett clearly considers both hygiene factors and motivator factors in dealing with his employees. His strategy has paid off. The company has had very little employee turnover in recent years, and a number of employees have worked there for more than 15 years. ■

While needs theories give us some insights into motivating employees by stressing the importance of addressing individuals' needs, they don't provide a complete picture of motivation. For that we turn to some contemporary theories of motivation that explain the processes managers can use to motivate employees.

Contemporary Theories of Motivation

▶ ▶ ▶ One of the challenges of motivating employees is linking productivity to rewards. Compounding this challenge for Tesco is that some jobs are very boring.[12] Clare Chapman, Tesco's director of human resources, says, "We're trying to take the routine out of the workplace, and build in more interest." The company eliminated the boring task of unloading soft drinks by ordering merchandising units that come fully stocked, ready to be wheeled into the store.

Tesco also encourages employees to buy shares of the company, so that staff can "share in the success they helped to create," says reward manager Helen O'Keefe. To help employees understand the potential benefits of shares, the annual benefit report includes share price graphs and a reward statement for staff. The benefit report helps employees see how the share price performs over the longer term and in comparison with the shares of other companies.

Sir Terry Leahy says he wants his employees to take four things from the job: "They find it interesting, they're treated with respect, they have the chance to get on, and they find their boss is helpful and not their biggest problem." All of these rewards make it easier for employees to perform well.

Think About It

How can you link productivity to rewards so that employees feel motivated? What other things can be done at Tesco to ensure that employees feel motivated?

The theories and approaches we discuss in this section represent contemporary explanations of employee motivation. Although these may not be as well known as some of the theories we just discussed, they do have reasonable degrees of valid research support.[13] What are these contemporary motivation theories and approaches? We look at three: designing motivating jobs, equity theory, and expectancy theory.

3. What are the contemporary theories of motivation?

Designing Motivating Jobs

Have you ever had a job that was really motivating? What were its characteristics?

Because managers are primarily interested in how to motivate individuals on the job, we need to look at ways to design motivating jobs. If you look closely at what an organization is and how it works, you will find that it's composed of thousands of tasks. These tasks, in turn, are combined into jobs. We use the term **job design** to refer to the way tasks are combined to form complete jobs. The jobs that people perform in an organization should not evolve by chance. Managers should design jobs deliberately and thoughtfully to reflect the demands of the changing environment, the organization's technology, and its employees' skills, abilities, and preferences.[14] When jobs are designed with those things in mind, employees are motivated to work hard. What are some ways that managers can design motivating jobs?[15]

job design
The way tasks are combined to form complete jobs.

Q&A 13.3

Job Enlargement

As we saw earlier, in Chapter 9, job design historically has concentrated on making jobs smaller and more specialized. Yet when jobs are narrow in focus and highly specialized, motivating employees is a real challenge. One of the earliest efforts at overcoming the drawbacks of job specialization involved the horizontal expansion of a job through increasing **job scope**—the number of different tasks required in a job and the frequency with which these tasks are repeated. For instance, a dental hygienist's job could be enlarged so that in addition to dental cleaning, he or she is pulling patients' files, refiling them when finished, and cleaning and storing instruments. This type of job design option is called **job enlargement**.

Efforts at job enlargement that focused solely on increasing the number of tasks have had less than exciting results. As one employee who experienced such a job redesign said, "Before, I had one lousy job. Now, thanks to job enlargement, I have three lousy jobs!" However, one study that looked at how *knowledge* enlargement activities (expanding the scope of knowledge used in a job) affected employees found benefits such as more satisfaction, enhanced customer service, and fewer errors.[16] Even so, most job enlargement efforts provided few challenges and little meaning to employees' activities, although they addressed the lack of variety in overspecialized jobs.

job scope
The number of different tasks required in a job and the frequency with which these tasks are repeated.

job enlargement
The horizontal expansion of a job through increasing job scope.

Job Enrichment

Another approach to designing motivating jobs is the vertical expansion of a job by adding planning and evaluating responsibilities—**job enrichment**. Job enrichment increases **job depth**, which is the degree of control employees have over their work. In other words, employees are empowered to assume some of the tasks typically done by their managers. Thus, the tasks in an enriched job should allow employees to do a complete activity with increased freedom, independence, and responsibility. These tasks should also provide feedback so that individuals can assess and correct their own performance. For instance, in an enriched job, our dental hygienist, in addition to dental cleaning, could schedule appointments (planning) and follow up with clients (evaluating). Although job enrichment can improve the quality of work, employee motivation, and satisfaction, the research evidence on the use of job enrichment programs has been inconclusive.[17]

job enrichment
The vertical expansion of a job by adding planning and evaluating responsibilities.

job depth
The degree of control employees have over their work.

Job Characteristics Model

Even though many organizations have implemented job enlargement and job enrichment programs and experienced mixed results, neither of these job design approaches provided a conceptual framework for analyzing jobs or for guiding managers in designing motivating jobs. The **job characteristics model (JCM)** offers such a framework.[18] It identifies

job characteristics model (JCM)
A framework for analyzing jobs and designing motivating jobs that identifies five core job dimensions, their interrelationships, and their impact on employees.

five core job dimensions, their interrelationships, and their impact on employee productivity, motivation, and satisfaction.

According to the JCM, any job can be described in terms of five core dimensions, defined as follows:

1. **Skill variety**. The degree to which a job requires a variety of activities so that an employee can use a number of different skills and talents.

2. **Task identity**. The degree to which a job requires completion of a whole and identifiable piece of work.

3. **Task significance**. The degree to which a job affects the lives or work of other people.

4. **Autonomy**. The degree to which a job provides substantial freedom, independence, and discretion to the individual in scheduling the work and determining the procedures to be used in carrying it out.

5. **Feedback**. The degree to which carrying out work activities required by a job results in the individual's obtaining direct and clear information about the effectiveness of his or her performance.

Exhibit 13-5 presents the model. Notice how the first three dimensions—skill variety, task identity, and task significance—combine to create meaningful work. What we mean is that if these three characteristics exist in a job, we can predict that the person will view his or her job as important, valuable, and worthwhile. Notice, too, that jobs that possess autonomy give the job incumbent a feeling of personal responsibility for the results, and that if a job provides feedback, the employee will know how effectively he or she is performing.

From a motivational standpoint, the JCM suggests that internal rewards are obtained when an employee *learns* (knowledge of results through feedback) that he or she *personally* (experienced responsibility through autonomy of work) has performed well on a task that he or she *cares about* (experienced meaningfulness through skill variety, task identity, and/or task significance).[19] The more these three conditions characterize a job, the greater the employee's motivation, performance, and satisfaction and the lower his or her absenteeism and likelihood of resigning. As the model shows, the links between the job dimensions and the outcomes are moderated by the strength of the individual's growth need (the person's desire for self-esteem and self-actualization). This means that individuals with a high growth need are more likely to experience the critical psychological states and respond positively when their jobs include the core dimensions than are individuals with a low growth need. This may explain the mixed results with job enrichment: Individuals with low growth needs don't tend to achieve high performance or satisfaction by having their jobs enriched. (For further insights into motivating employees, see *Developing Your Interpersonal Skills—Designing Motivating Jobs* on page 431, at the end of the chapter.)

The JCM provides specific guidance to managers for job redesign (see Exhibit 13-6). The following suggestions, which are based on the JCM, specify the types of changes in jobs that are most likely to lead to improvement in each of the five core job dimensions. You will notice that two of these suggestions incorporate the earlier job design concepts we discussed (job enlargement and job enrichment), although the other suggestions also involve more than vertically and horizontally expanding jobs.

- *Combine tasks.* Managers should put fragmented tasks back together to form a new, larger module of work (job enlargement) to increase skill variety and task identity.

- *Create natural work units.* Managers should design tasks that form an identifiable and meaningful whole to increase employee "ownership" of the work and encourage employees to view their work as meaningful and important rather than as irrelevant and boring.

- *Establish client relationships.* The client is the external or internal user of the product or service that the employee works on.

skill variety
The degree to which a job requires a variety of activities so that an employee can use a number of different skills and talents.

task identity
The degree to which a job requires completion of a whole and identifiable piece of work.

task significance
The degree to which a job affects the lives or work of other people.

autonomy
The degree to which a job provides substantial freedom, independence, and discretion to the individual in scheduling work and determining the procedures to be used in carrying it out.

feedback
The degree to which carrying out work activities required by a job results in the individual's obtaining direct and clear information about the effectiveness of his or her performance.

PRISM 1

It is easy to identify the task that Manuela Frank and Erika Seres perform at Audi's headquarters in Ingolstadt, Germany. Their job is to ensure that new cars have no unappealing odours. "You can't smell more than six specimens at a time," says Seres (right), "because after that, you are not discerning. Like wine tasters, we have rules."

Exhibit 13-5

Job Characteristics Model

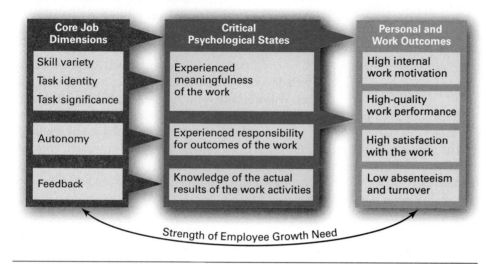

Source: J. R. Hackman and J. L. Suttle, eds., *Improving Life at Work* (Glenview, IL: Scott, Foresman, 1977). With permission of the authors.

Whenever possible, managers should establish direct relationships between employees and their clients to increase skill variety, autonomy, and feedback. For instance, at many restaurants you can find feedback cards on the tables to indicate the quality of service received during a meal.

- *Expand jobs vertically.* Vertical expansion (job enrichment) gives employees responsibilities and controls that were formerly reserved for managers. It partially closes the gap between the "doing" and the "controlling" aspects of the job and increases employee autonomy.

- *Open feedback channels.* Feedback lets employees know how well they are performing in their jobs and whether their performance is improving, deteriorating, or remaining constant. Ideally, employees should receive performance feedback directly as they do their jobs rather than from managers on an occasional basis.

Exhibit 13-6

Guidelines for Job Redesign

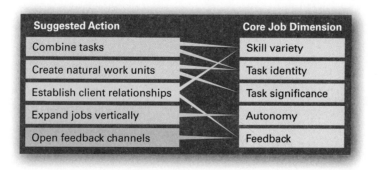

Source: J. R. Hackman and J. L. Suttle, eds., *Improving Life at Work* (Glenview, IL: Scott, Foresman, 1977). With permission of the authors.

Equity Theory

Q&A 13.4

Have you ever thought someone else's pay was unfair compared with yours?

After graduating from the University of New Brunswick, Mike Wilson worked in Northern Alberta as a civil engineer. He liked his job, but he became frustrated with his employer. "If you did a great job, you were treated just the same as if you did a poor job," he says.[20] Wilson decided to return home to work in the business his father had started in 1965—Dorchester, New Brunswick-based Atlantic Industries, which designs, fabricates, and builds corrugated steel structures. Wilson's hard work at Atlantic Industries has paid off: He received the 2005 Ernst & Young Entrepreneur of the Year Award for the Atlantic Region.

Wilson's decision to leave his job in Northern Alberta can be explained by equity theory. The term *equity* is related to the concept of fairness and equal treatment compared with others who behave in similar ways. There is considerable evidence that employees compare their job inputs and outcomes relative to others' and that inequities influence the degree of effort that employees exert.[21]

equity theory
The theory that an employee compares his or her job's inputs–outcomes ratio with that of relevant others and then responds to correct any inequity.

Equity theory, developed by J. Stacey Adams, proposes that employees perceive what they get from a job situation (outcomes) in relation to what they put into it (inputs) and then compare their inputs–outcomes ratio with the inputs–outcomes ratio of relevant others (see Exhibit 13-7). If an employee perceives her ratio to be equal to those of relevant others, a state of equity exists. In other words, she perceives that her situation is fair—that justice prevails. However, if the ratio is perceived as unequal, inequity exists and she views herself as underrewarded or overrewarded. Not all inequity (or equity) is real. It is important to underscore that it is the individual's *perception* that determines the equity of the situation.

What will employees do when they perceive an inequity? Equity theory proposes that employees might (1) distort either their own or others' inputs or outcomes, (2) behave in some way to induce others to change their inputs or outcomes, (3) behave in some way to change their own inputs or outcomes, (4) choose a different comparison person, or (5) quit their jobs. These types of employee reactions have generally proved to be accurate.[22] A review of the research consistently confirms the equity thesis: Employee motivation is influenced significantly by relative rewards, as well as by absolute rewards. Whenever employ-

Exhibit 13-7

Equity Theory

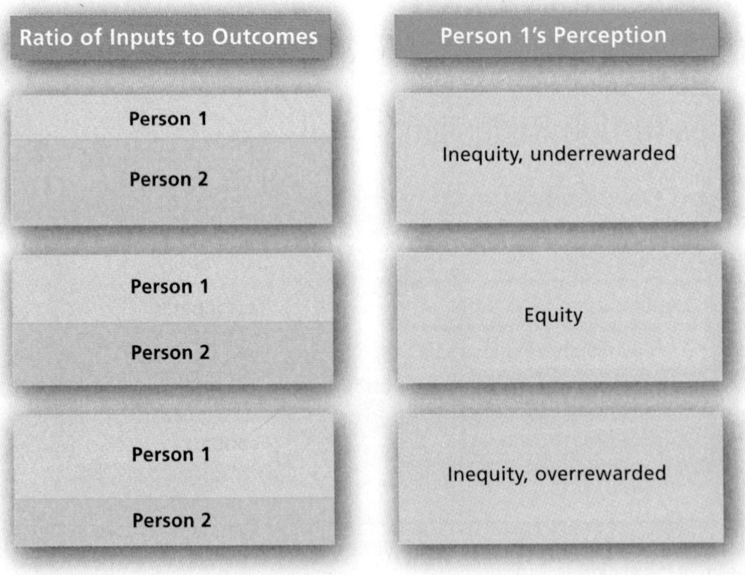

Ratio of Inputs to Outcomes	Person 1's Perception
Person 1 Person 2	Inequity, underrewarded
Person 1 Person 2	Equity
Person 1 Person 2	Inequity, overrewarded

ees perceive inequity, they will act to correct the situation.[23] The result might be lower or higher productivity, improved or reduced quality of output, increased absenteeism, or voluntary resignation.

When Toronto city councillors faced inequity in their pay, they responded by voting themselves a raise, as the following *Management Reflection* shows.

MANAGEMENT REFLECTION

City Councillors End "Inequitable" Pay

What is fair pay for city councillors?   Toronto city councillors voted themselves an 8.9 percent pay raise effective January 2007, shortly before it became obvious that extensive budget cuts were going to be needed to manage the city.[24] On a percentage basis, the pay raise seems high compared with what the average Ontarian received as a pay raise in 2006. Other government employees might have wondered if they should raise their salaries as well.

But what should a municipal councillor be paid? In 2007, members of the Quebec Parliament earned annual salaries of $82 073, heads of federal Crown corporations started at $109 000, Ontario's premier, Dalton McGuinty, earned $198 620, and members of the BC legislature earned $98 000, plus expenses. With the raise, Toronto's councillors earn $95 000 a year. Despite working at different levels of government—federal, provincial, and local—all of these officials make complex decisions, and need many of the same skills. Many of them could make more money working in the private sector.

When the Toronto councillors voted themselves a pay raise, they were not thinking about possible budget shortfalls. Instead, they were responding to the idea that they were underpaid compared with other government decision makers who performed duties similar to their own. As councillors for the largest city in the country, with the largest budget, they were advised by a consulting firm that they should rank in the "top 25 per cent of salaries of councillors across the country." Their salary before the raise was one of the lowest in the country. ■

The **referent** against which individuals compare themselves is an important variable in equity theory.[25] Three referent categories have been defined: other, system, and self. The *other* category includes other individuals with similar jobs in the same organization but also includes friends, neighbours, or professional associates. On the basis of what they hear at work or read about in newspapers or trade journals, employees compare their pay with that of others. The *system* category includes organizational pay policies and procedures and the administration of the system. Whatever precedents have been established by the organization regarding pay allocation are major elements of this category. The *self* category refers to inputs–outcomes ratios that are unique to the individual. It reflects past personal experiences and contacts and is influenced by criteria such as past jobs or family commitments. The choice of a particular set of referents is related to the information available about the referents as well as to their perceived relevance. At Surrey, BC-based Back in Motion Rehab (named the #1 Best Workplace in Canada for 2007 by *Canadian Business*), management decided that the highest-paid director's base salary should be less than two times the salary of the average staff member.[26] Because this policy uses the average staff member's pay as a referent, it sends the message that the output of the average staff member is truly valued.

Historically, equity theory focused on **distributive justice**, which is the perceived fairness of the amount and allocation of rewards among individuals. Recent equity research has focused on looking at issues of **procedural justice**, which is the perceived fairness of the process used to determine the distribution of rewards. This research shows that distributive justice has a greater influence on employee satisfaction than procedural justice, while procedural justice tends to affect an employee's organizational commitment, trust in his or her manager, and intention to quit.[27] What are the implications of these findings for managers?

referents
Those things individuals compare themselves against in order to assess equity.

distributive justice
Perceived fairness of the amount and allocation of rewards among individuals.

procedural justice
Perceived fairness of the process used to determine the distribution of rewards.

They should consider openly sharing information on how allocation decisions are made, follow consistent and unbiased procedures, and engage in similar practices to increase the perception of procedural justice. When managers increase the perception of procedural justice, employees are likely to view their managers and the organization as positive even if they are dissatisfied with pay, promotions, and other personal outcomes.

In conclusion, equity theory shows that, for most employees, motivation is influenced significantly by relative rewards, as well as by absolute rewards, but some key issues are still unclear.[28] For instance, how do employees define inputs and outcomes? How do they combine and weigh their inputs and outcomes to arrive at totals? When and how do the factors change over time? And how do people choose referents? Despite these problems, equity theory does have an impressive amount of research support and offers us some important insights into employee motivation. Managers need to pay attention to equity issues when making plans to motivate their employees.

Expectancy Theory

The most comprehensive and widely accepted explanation of employee motivation to date is Victor Vroom's **expectancy theory**.[29] Although the theory has its critics,[30] most research evidence supports it.[31]

Expectancy theory states that an individual tends to act in a certain way based on the expectation that the act will be followed by a given outcome and on the attractiveness of that outcome to the individual. It includes three variables or relationships (see Exhibit 13-8):

- *Expectancy, or effort–performance linkage.* The probability perceived by the individual that exerting a given amount of effort will lead to a certain level of performance.

- *Instrumentality, or performance–reward linkage.* The degree to which the individual believes that performing at a particular level is instrumental in attaining the desired outcome.

- *Valence, or attractiveness of reward.* The importance that the individual places on the potential outcome or reward that can be achieved on the job. Valence considers both the goals and needs of the individual. (See also *Self-Assessment—What Rewards Do I Value Most?* on pages 427–428, at the end of the chapter.)

This explanation of motivation might sound complex, but it really is not. It can be summed up in these questions: How hard do I have to work to achieve a certain level of performance, and can I actually achieve that level? What reward will I get for working at that level of performance? How attractive is the reward to me, and does it help me achieve my goals? Whether you are motivated to put forth effort (that is, to work) at any given time depends on your particular goals and your perception of whether a certain level of performance is necessary to attain those goals.

expectancy theory
The theory that an individual tends to act in a certain way based on the expectation that the act will be followed by a given outcome and on the attractiveness of that outcome to the individual.

Exhibit 13-8

Simplified Expectancy Model

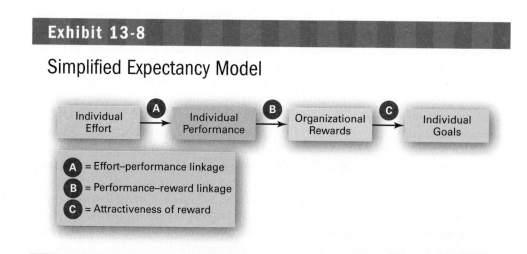

A = Effort–performance linkage
B = Performance–reward linkage
C = Attractiveness of reward

The key to expectancy theory is understanding an individual's goal and the link between effort and performance, between performance and rewards, and, finally, between rewards and individual goal satisfaction. Expectancy theory recognizes that there is no universal principle for explaining what motivates individuals and thus stresses that managers need to understand why employees view certain outcomes as attractive or unattractive. After all, we want to reward individuals with those things they value as positive. Also, expectancy theory emphasizes expected behaviours. Do employees know what is expected of them and how they will be evaluated? Finally, the theory is concerned with perceptions. Reality is irrelevant. An individual's own perceptions of performance, reward, and goal outcomes, not the outcomes themselves, will determine his or her motivation (level of effort). Exhibit 13-9 suggests how managers might increase employee motivation, using expectancy theory.

Q&A 13.5

Integrating Contemporary Theories of Motivation

We have presented three contemporary motivation theories. You might be tempted to view them independently, but doing so would be a mistake. Many of the ideas underlying the theories are complementary, and you will better understand how to motivate people if you see how the theories fit together.[32]

Expectancy theory predicts that an employee will exert a high level of effort if he or she perceives that there is a strong relationship between effort and performance, performance and rewards, and rewards and satisfaction of personal goals. Each of these relationships is, in turn, influenced by certain factors. The level of individual performance is determined not only by the level of individual effort but also by the individual's ability to perform and by whether the organization has a fair and objective performance evaluation system. The performance–reward relationship will be strong if the individual perceives that it is performance (rather than seniority, personal favourites, or some other criterion) that is rewarded. The final link in expectancy theory is the rewards–goal relationship. Needs theories come into play at this point. Motivation would be high to the degree that the rewards an individual received for his or her high performance satisfied the dominant needs consistent with his or her individual goals.

Rewards also play a key part in equity theory. Individuals will compare the rewards (outcomes) they have received from the inputs or efforts they made with the inputs–outcomes ratio of relevant others. If inequities exist, the effort expended may be influenced.

Finally, the JCM suggests that task characteristics (job design) influence job motivation at two places. First, jobs that are designed around the five core dimensions are likely to lead to higher actual job performance because the individual's motivation will be stimulated by the job itself—that is, he or she will increase the linkage between effort and performance. Second, jobs that are designed around the five core dimensions also increase an employee's control over key elements in his or her work. Therefore, jobs that offer autonomy, feedback, and similar task characteristics help to satisfy the individual goals of employees who desire greater control over their work.

Exhibit 13-9

Steps to Increasing Motivation, Using Expectancy Theory

Improving Expectancy	Improving Instrumentality	Improving Valence
Improve the ability of the individual to perform.	**Increase the individual's belief that performance will lead to reward.**	**Make sure that the reward is meaningful to the individual.**
• Make sure employees have skills for the task. • Provide training. • Assign reasonable tasks and goals.	• Observe and recognize performance. • Deliver rewards as promised. • Indicate to employees how previous good performance led to greater rewards.	• Ask employees what rewards they value. • Give rewards that are valued.

Current Issues in Motivation

▶ ▶ ▶ One of the challenges managers at Tesco faced was how to motivate its many different employee groups: students, new graduates, mothers returning to the workplace, and ethnic minorities.[33] In a survey of its employees, the company found that older female employees wanted flexible hours and stimulating work, but they were not looking to be promoted. Young college graduates working in head office wanted a challenging, well-paid career and time to pursue personal interests and family life. Many employees noted they wanted managers who helped them.

Tesco has come up with a variety of practices to meet employee needs, including career breaks of up to eight months, discounts on family holidays, driving lessons, and magazine subscriptions. Tesco has a website that offers career and financial advice and discounts on meals, cinema tickets, and travel for its 16- to 24-year-old employees who are in school or have recently left school. The company created the "A-Level Options" program to give young people who did not want a post-secondary education the opportunity to be fast-tracked into management. Clare Chapman, Tesco's human resource director, says the company has not limited specific rewards for specific groups. "It's more a question of being mindful of the needs of all staff instead of catering for one or two types of attitude."

Think About It

What factors need to be considered when motivating employees who have very different needs? Is there anything else Tesco can do to motivate young people?

4. What are some current issues in motivation?

So far, we have covered a lot of the theoretical bases of employee motivation. Understanding and predicting employee motivation continues to be one of the most popular areas in management research. However, even current studies of employee motivation are influenced by several significant workplace issues—issues such as motivating a diverse workforce, designing effective rewards programs, and improving work–life balance. Let's take a closer look at each of these issues.

Motivating a Diverse Workforce

To maximize motivation among today's workforce, managers need to think in terms of *flexibility*. For instance, studies tell us that men place more importance on having autonomy in their jobs than do women. In contrast, the opportunity to learn, convenient and flexible work hours, and good interpersonal relations are more important to women.[34] Baby Boomers may need more flextime as they manage the needs of their children and their aging parents. Gen-Xers want employers to add to their experience so they develop portable skills. Meanwhile, Gen-Yers want more opportunities and the ability to work in teams.[35] Managers need to recognize that what motivates a single mother with two dependent children who is working full time to support her family may be very different from the needs of a single part-time employee or an older employee who is working only to supplement his or her retirement income. A diverse array of rewards is needed to motivate employees with such diverse needs.

Motivating Employees from Diverse Cultures

In today's global business environment, managers cannot automatically assume that motivational programs that work in one location are going to work in others. Most current motivation theories were developed in the United States by Americans about Americans.[36] Maybe the most blatant pro-American characteristic in these theories is the strong emphasis on individualism and quantity-of-life cultural characteristics. For instance, expectancy theory emphasizes goal accomplishment, as well as rational and individual thought. Let's look at several theories to see if there is any cross-cultural transferability.

Maslow's hierarchy of needs proposes that people start at the physiological level and then move progressively up the hierarchy in order. This hierarchy, if it has any application at all, aligns with American culture. In countries like Japan, Greece, and Mexico, where uncertainty-avoidance characteristics are strong (that is, individuals prefer structured situations), security needs would be on the top of the needs hierarchy. Countries that score high on quality-of-life characteristics (that is, individuals value relationships and are concerned with the welfare of others)—Denmark, Sweden, Norway, the Netherlands, and Finland—would have social needs on top.[37] We would predict, for instance, that group work will motivate employees more when a country's culture scores high on quality-of-life characteristics.

Equity theory has a relatively strong following in the United States. That is not surprising given that US-style reward systems are based on the assumption that employees are highly sensitive to equity in reward allocations. And in the United States, equity is meant to closely tie pay to performance. However, recent evidence suggests that even in collectivist cultures (where individuals expect that others will look after and protect them), especially in the former socialist countries of Central and Eastern Europe, employees expect rewards to reflect their individual needs, as well as their performance.[38] Moreover, consistent with a legacy of communism and centrally planned economies, employees exhibited a greater "entitlement" attitude—that is, they expected outcomes to be greater than their inputs.[39] These findings suggest that US-style pay practices may need modification, especially in Russia and former communist countries, in order to be perceived as fair by employees.

It can be difficult or even misleading to apply Western theories of motivation to employees like Rina Masuda of Sharp Corp. Masuda uses a soldering iron to quickly and delicately repair tiny computer chips, a task so extraordinarily precise that she is among only a few thousand of all Japan's workers honoured with the title of "super technician," or *supaa ginosha*. These workers receive certificates and pins, but seldom money. "The soldering I do by hand is far superior to anything that machines can do," says Masuda, her pride expressing the common view that recognition and honour are enough.

Despite these cross-cultural differences in motivation, don't assume there are no cross-cultural consistencies. For instance, the desire for interesting work seems important to almost all employees, regardless of their national culture. In a study of seven countries, employees in Belgium, Great Britain, Israel, and the United States ranked "interesting work" number one among 11 work goals. And this factor was ranked either second or third in Japan, the Netherlands, and Germany.[40] Similarly, in a study comparing job-preference outcomes among graduate students in the United States, Canada, Australia, and Singapore, growth, achievement, and responsibility were rated the top three and had identical rankings.[41] Both of these studies suggest some universality to the importance of intrinsic factors identified by Herzberg in his motivation-hygiene theory. Another recent study examining workplace motivation trends in Japan also seems to indicate that Herzberg's model is applicable to Japanese employees.[42] For a discussion of diversity initiatives in the workplace, see *Managing Workforce Diversity—Developing Employee Potential: The Bottom Line of Diversity* on page 432, at the end of the chapter.

Motivating Minimum-Wage Employees

Suppose that in your first managerial position after graduating, you are responsible for managing a work group composed of minimum-wage employees. Offering more pay to these employees for high levels of performance is out of the question: Your company just cannot afford it.[43] In addition, these employees have limited education and skills. What are your motivational options at this point? One of the toughest motivational challenges facing many managers today is how to achieve high performance levels from minimum-wage employees.

Q&A 13.6

One trap we often fall into is thinking that people are motivated only by money. Although money is important as a motivator, it's not the only reward that people seek and that managers can use. What are some other types of rewards? Many companies use employee recognition programs such as employee of the month, quarterly employee performance award ceremonies, or other celebrations of employee accomplishment. For

At Vancouver-based Electronic Arts Canada, managers believe the company should pay attention to employee needs in order to motivate them. The cafeteria at Electronic Arts is well stocked with employee favourites, and employees can purchase takeout dinners at good prices for their families if they do not have time to cook dinner.

instance, at many fast-food restaurants such as McDonald's and Wendy's, you will often see plaques hanging in prominent places that feature the "Crew Member of the Month." These types of programs highlight employees whose performance has been of the type and level the organization wants to encourage. Many managers also recognize the power of praise, but you need to be sure that these "pats on the back" are sincere and done for the right reasons; otherwise, employees can interpret such actions as manipulative.

We know from the motivation theories presented earlier that rewards are only part of the motivation equation. We need to look at other elements, such as empowerment and career development assistance. We can look to job design and expectancy theories for these insights. In service industries such as travel and hospitality, retail sales, child care, and maintenance, where pay for front-line employees generally does not get much higher than the minimum-wage level, successful companies are empowering these front-line employees with more authority to address customers' problems. If we use the JCM to examine this change, we can see that this type of job redesign provides enhanced motivating potential because employees now experience increased skill variety, task identity, task significance, autonomy, and feedback. Also, employees facing this situation often want to better themselves professionally. They need guidance, assistance in self-assessment, and training. By providing these to minimum-wage employees, you are preparing them for the future—one that hopefully promises better pay. For many, this is a strong motivator![44]

Motivating Professional and Technical Employees

In contrast to a generation ago, the typical employee today is more likely to be a highly trained professional with a post-secondary degree than a blue-collar factory worker. What special concerns should managers be aware of when trying to motivate a team of engineers at London, Ontario-based EllisDon, software designers at Vancouver-based Electronic Arts, or a group of consultants at Toronto-based Accenture Canada?

Professionals are typically different from nonprofessionals.[45] They have a strong and long-term commitment to their field of expertise. Their loyalty is more often to their profession than to their employer. To keep current in their field, they need to regularly update their knowledge, and because of their commitment to their profession they rarely define their workweek as 8:00 a.m. to 5:00 p.m., five days a week.

What motivates professionals? Money and promotions typically are low on their priority list. Why? They tend to be well paid and enjoy what they do. In contrast, job challenge tends to be ranked high. They like to tackle problems and find solutions. Their chief reward in their job is the work itself. Professionals also value support. They want others to think that what they are working on is important.[46] That may be true for all employees, but professionals tend to be focused on their work as their central life interest, whereas nonprofessionals typically have other interests outside work that can compensate for needs not met on the job. The preceding points imply that managers should provide professional and technical employees with new assignments and challenging projects. Give them autonomy to follow their interests and allow them to structure their work in ways they find productive. Reward them with educational opportunities—training, workshops, conferences—that allow them to keep current in their field and to network with their peers. Also reward them with recognition. Managers should ask questions and engage in other actions that demonstrate to their professional and technical employees that the managers are sincerely interested in what they are doing.

Motivating Contingent Workers

As full-time jobs have been eliminated through downsizing and other organizational restructurings, the number of openings for part-time, contract, and other forms of temporary work have increased. Contingent workers don't have the security or stability that permanent employees have, and they don't identify with the organization or display the commitment that other employees do. Temporary employees also typically get little or no benefits such as health care or pensions.[47]

There is no simple solution for motivating contingent employees. For that small set of individuals who prefer the freedom of their temporary status—for instance, some students, working mothers, retirees—the lack of stability may not be an issue. In addition, temporariness might be preferred by highly compensated physicians, engineers, accountants, or financial planners who don't want the demands of a full-time job. But these are the exceptions. For the most part, temporary employees are not temporary by choice.

What will motivate involuntarily temporary employees? An obvious answer is the opportunity to become a permanent employee. In cases in which permanent employees are selected from a pool of temps, the temps will often work hard in hopes of becoming permanent. A less obvious answer is the opportunity for training. The ability of a temporary employee to find a new job is largely dependent on his or her skills. If the employee sees that the job he or she is doing can help develop marketable skills, then motivation is increased. From an equity standpoint, you should also consider the repercussions of mixing permanent and temporary workers when pay differentials are significant. When temps work alongside permanent employees who earn more, and get benefits, too, for doing the same job, the performance of temps is likely to suffer. Separating such employees or perhaps minimizing interdependence between them might help managers decrease potential problems.[48]

Designing Effective Rewards Programs

Employee rewards programs play a powerful role in motivating for appropriate employee behaviour. In this section, we look at how managers can design effective rewards programs by using employee recognition programs and pay-for-performance programs. First, though, we should examine the issue of the extent to which money motivates.

The Role of Money

The most commonly used reward in organizations is money. As one author notes, "Money is probably the most emotionally meaningful object in contemporary life: only food and sex are its close competitors as common carriers of such strong and diverse feelings, significance, and strivings."[49]

Little research attention has been given to individual differences in people's feelings about money, although some studies indicate that money is not employees' top priority.[50] A survey of 2000 Canadians discovered that trustworthy senior management and a good balance between work and personal or family life mattered more than pay or benefits when it came to employee satisfaction.[51] In another survey that looked at Canadian attitudes about work, one respondent explained, "Of course money is important, but that's not what's going to make you jump out of bed in the morning." Another noted, "Everyone here would take more money and more time off—that's a given. But some of the things that really make the job a good or bad one are your relations with your boss."[52]

A number of studies suggest that an individual's attitude toward money is correlated with personality traits and demographic factors.[53] People who value money score higher on "attributes like sensation seeking, competitiveness, materialism, and control." People who desire money score higher on self-esteem, need for achievement, and Type A personality measures. Men seem to value money more than women. These studies suggest that individuals who value money will be more motivated by it than individuals who value other things.

What these findings suggest is that when organizations develop reward programs, they need to consider very carefully what individuals value.

Employee Recognition Programs

Employee recognition programs provide managers with opportunities to give employees personal attention and express interest, approval, and appreciation for a job well

employee recognition programs Reward programs that provide managers with opportunities to give employees personal attention and express interest, approval, and appreciation for a job well done.

done.[54] These programs can take many forms. For instance, you can personally congratulate an employee in private for a good job. You can send a handwritten note or an email message acknowledging something positive that the employee has done. For employees with a strong need for social acceptance, you can publicly recognize accomplishments. To enhance group cohesiveness and motivation, you can celebrate team successes. For instance, you can throw a pizza party to celebrate a team's accomplishments.

A survey of Canadian firms in 2006 by Hewitt Associates found that 35 percent of companies recognized individual or group achievements with cash or merchandise.[55] Do employees think employee recognition programs are important? You bet! One of the consistent themes that has emerged in the seven years that Hewitt Associates has studied the 50 Best Companies to Work for in Canada is the importance of recognition. A large number of the winning companies show appreciation for their employees frequently and visibly.[56]

Pay-for-Performance Programs

What's in it for me? That is a question every person consciously or unconsciously asks before engaging in any form of behaviour. Our knowledge of motivation tells us that people act in order to satisfy some need. Before they do anything, therefore, they look for a payoff or reward. Although many different rewards may be offered by organizations, most of us are concerned with earning an amount of money that allows us to satisfy our needs and wants. In fact, a large body of research suggests that pay is far more motivational than some motivation theorists such as Maslow and Herzberg suggest.[57] Because pay is an important variable in motivation, we need to look at how we can use pay to motivate high levels of employee performance. This concern explains the logic behind pay-for-performance programs.

Pay-for-performance programs are variable compensation plans that pay employees on the basis of some performance measure.[58] Piece-rate pay plans, wage-incentive plans, profit-sharing plans, lump-sum bonuses, and stock option programs are examples. What differentiates these forms of pay from more traditional compensation plans is that instead of paying a person for time on the job, pay is adjusted to reflect some performance measure. These performance measures might include such things as individual productivity, team or work group productivity, departmental productivity, or the overall organization's profit performance.

pay-for-performance programs Variable compensation plans that pay employees on the basis of some performance measure.

Q&A 13.7

Pay-for-performance is probably most compatible with expectancy theory. Specifically, individuals should perceive a strong relationship between their performance and the rewards they receive if motivation is to be maximized. If rewards are allocated only on nonperformance factors—such as seniority, job title, or across-the-board pay raises—then employees are likely to reduce their efforts.

Pay-for-performance programs are popular. The number of employees affected by variable pay plans has been rising in Canada. A 2007 survey of 314 firms by Hewitt Associates found that 80 percent of respondents have variable pay programs in place, compared with 43 percent in 1994.[59] Pay-for-performance programs are more common for non-unionized employees than unionized ones, although more than 30 percent of unionized companies had such plans in 2002.[60] Prem Benimadhu, an analyst with the Conference Board of Canada, notes, "Canadian unions have been very allergic to variable compensation."[61] In addition to wage uncertainty, employees may object to pay for performance if they feel that factors out of their control might affect the extent to which bonuses are possible.

In 2005, some 78 percent of large US companies had some form of variable pay plan.[62] About 22 percent of Japanese companies have company-wide pay-for-performance plans.[63] However, one Japanese company, Fujitsu, dropped its performance-based program after eight years because it proved to be "flawed and a poor fit with Japanese culture."[64] Management found that some employees set goals as low as possible for fear of falling short. Others set extremely short-term goals. As a result, Fujitsu executives felt that ambitious projects that could produce hit products were being avoided.

Do pay-for-performance programs work? The evidence is mixed, at best.[65] One recent study that followed the careers of 1000 top economists found that they put in more effort early in their careers, at a time when productivity-related incentives had a larger impact.[66] A recent study of Finnish white-collar employees found that higher levels of payment and more frequent payments positively affected productivity, while lower levels of payment did not improve productivity.[67] A Canadian study looked at both unionized and non-unionized workplaces, and found that variable pay plans result in "increased productivity, a safer work environment, a better understanding of the business by employees, and little risk of employees losing base pay," according to Prem Benimadhu.[68] But there are studies that question the effectiveness of pay-for-performance approaches, suggesting they can lead to less group cohesiveness in the workplace.[69]

If the organization uses work teams, managers should consider group-based performance incentives that will reinforce team effort and commitment. But whether these programs are individual based or team based, managers do need to ensure that they are specific about the relationship between an individual's pay and his or her expected level of appropriate performance. Employees must clearly understand exactly how performance—theirs and the organization's—translates into dollars on their paycheques.[70] Ottawa-based Lee Valley Tools uses quarterly newsletters to employees to let them know how much profit is forecast. This helps employees understand how hard work will pay off for them. Robin Lee, the company's president, says that "sharing information and profits promotes an atmosphere in which hard work, innovation and efficiency pay off for everybody."[71]

As mentioned earlier, organizations can use a variety of programs to reward employees for performance. The most common forms are profit-sharing and stock option programs.

Profit-Sharing Plans

In a **profit-sharing plan**, the employer shares profits with employees based on a predetermined formula. Employees may receive direct cash bonuses or stock options. Though senior executives are most likely to be involved in profit-sharing plans, such plans can be applied to employees at any level.

Be aware that profit-sharing plans focus on past financial results. They don't necessarily focus employees on the future, because employees and managers look for ways to cut costs today, without considering future organizational needs.

Three Canadian studies by Professor Richard J. Long of the University of Saskatchewan's College of Commerce show that a profit-sharing plan is most effective in workplaces where there is more involvement by employees, more teamwork, and a managerial philosophy that encourages participation.[72]

profit-sharing plan
An organization-wide plan in which the employer shares profits with employees based on a predetermined formula.

Stock Option Programs

During 2003, Lino Saputo, chair of Montreal-based Saputo, one of the largest cheese producers in North America, received a salary of $600 000, bonuses of $330 000, and no stock options. Eugene Melnyk, chair of Mississauga, Ontario-based Biovail, a pharmaceutical company, received a salary of $830 463, no bonus, and $56.4 million in long-term incentives. Total compensation for the two men over the period 2000–2003 was quite different: Saputo received $2.43 million, just a little more than 10 percent of the $202 million Melnyk received. Yet by March 2004, Biovail's shares had declined 74 percent from their high in December 2001, while Saputo's share price was similar to what it was at its high in early 2002.[73] These results mirror a 2006 study of the largest Canadian public companies by the Ontario Teachers' Pension Plan, which found little evidence that the amount paid to Canada's top executives was related to the performance of their companies.[74]

Executive bonus and stock option programs have come under fire because they seem to fly in the face of the belief that executive pay aligns with the organization's performance. What are stock option programs, and what are they designed to do?

Some companies try to encourage employees to adopt the perspective of top management by making them owners of their firms, either through stock options or employee stock ownership plans. **Stock options** are a financial incentive that gives employees the right to purchase shares of company stock, at some time in the future, at a set price. **Employee stock ownership plans (ESOPs)** are company-established benefit plans in which employees acquire stock as part of their benefits.

The original idea behind stock options was to turn employees into owners and give them strong motivation to work hard to make the company successful.[75] If the company was successful,

Saputo
www.saputo.ca

Biovail
www.biovail.com

stock options
A financial incentive that gives employees the right to purchase shares of company stock, at some time in the future, at a set price.

employee stock ownership plan (ESOP)
A company-established benefit plan in which employees acquire stock as part of their benefits.

the value of the stock went up, making the stock options valuable. In other words, there was a link between performance and reward. The popularity of stock options as a motivational and compensation tool skyrocketed during the dot-com boom in the late 1990s. Because many dot-coms could not afford to pay employees the going market-rate salaries, stock options were offered as performance incentives. However, the shakeout among dot-com stocks in 2000 and 2001 illustrated one of the inherent risks of offering stock options. As long as the market was rising, employees were willing to give up a large salary in exchange for stock options. However, when stock prices tanked, many individuals who joined and stayed with a dot-com for the opportunity to get rich through stock options found those stock options had become worthless. The declining stock market became a powerful demotivator.

Despite the risk of potential lost value and the widespread abuse of stock options, managers might want to consider them as part of their overall motivational program. An appropriately designed stock option program can be a powerful motivational tool for the entire workforce.[76] Exhibit 13-10 lists several recommendations for designing stock option programs.

Improving Work–Life Balance

While many employees continue to work an eight-hour day, five days a week, with fixed start and end times, organizations have started to implement programs to help employees manage their lives outside of work. Many of the work–life balance programs that organiza-

Exhibit 13-10

Recommendations for Designing Stock Option Programs

Design Question	Choices	Recommendations
Who receives them?	• Broad-based or restricted	• Match company growth prospects, management style, and organizational culture.
How many?	• Large or small percentage of employee income • Many or few options in previous grants	• Match company growth prospects. • Know that large previous grants may increase recipient risk aversion.
What terms?	• Vesting* • Maturity	• Should match business cycle. • Terms shorter than 10 years can create stronger pay-for-performance relationships.
How often?	• Fixed or variable schedule	• Predictable grants may reduce incentive alignment prospects. • Internal equity issues may result from schedules that result in a variety of exercise prices.
What price?	• Fair market value • Premium • Discounted • Indexed	• Employees must view stock option exercise prices as feasible and believe that chosen benchmarks are appropriate.
What ownership?	• Holding requirements after exercise • Ownership guidelines	• Requiring recipients to hold some of their shares after exercise encourages better incentive alignment. • Clear general ownership guidelines can also increase incentive alignment.

* Vesting refers to the time that must pass before a person can exercise the option.

Source: P. Brandes, R. Dharwadkar, and G. V. Lemesis, "Effective Employee Stock Option Design: Reconciling Stakeholder, Strategic, and Motivational Factors," *Academy of Management Executive,* February 2003, p. 84.

tions have implemented are a response to the varied needs of a diverse workforce. (The *Video Case Incident—Work–Life Balance and Motivation: Ernst & Young* on page 462 looks at the initiatives introduced by the accounting firm to create work–life balance for its employees.) At Electronic Arts Canada, employees are given help with their family and personal needs, as the following *Management Reflection* shows.

MANAGEMENT REFLECTION

Electronic Arts Canada Meets Family Needs

Can your workplace really make life easier?   It is not always easy to make sure that employees working in the computer game–designing industry do not decide to take a job elsewhere.[77] At Vancouver-based Electronic Arts Canada (EA), the world's leading game developer, the human resource department makes sure that employees do not think about looking for jobs elsewhere.

During the 1990s, it became commonplace for high-tech firms to offer free beverages, including lattes, and other perks that suited 20-something employees. EA has found that different perks are needed now that these same employees have moved into their thirties and beyond.

One emphasis at EA is having more family-friendly policies in the workplace. During spring break, children accompany their parents to work, and there are high chairs in the company cafeteria. New parents get generous leave time. Employees can even take dinner home to their families. Employees can buy a chicken and rice dish and spareribs for "a comparative bargain at $18 to feed [a] family," says the company's HR manager. The cafeteria offers breakfast, lunch, dinner, and snacks, and even provides Atkins, HeartSmart, and vegetarian meals.

The firm tries to make it easier for its employees to balance work life with family life. It takes care of many of the errands people might have to do at night or on weekends by providing drop-off dry cleaning services, a hairdresser and a barber who regularly show up to give haircuts, and a seamstress who does alterations. On Fridays, employees can have their cars washed.

EA also has a gym, with Pilates classes and a personal trainer, and a massage therapist is on site several days a week. ■

In addition to helping with errands and meals, contemporary companies are looking at a variety of scheduling options, including flextime, job sharing, and telecommuting to help employees balance work and personal life.

Flexible Work Schedules

Many organizations have developed flexible working schedules that recognize different needs. For instance, a **compressed workweek** is a workweek in which employees work longer hours per day but fewer days per week. The most common form is four 10-hour days (a 4-40 program). To fit employees' needs, however, organizations could design whatever schedules they want. Another alternative is **flexible work hours** (also popularly known as **flextime**), a scheduling option in which employees are required to work a specific number of hours per week but are free to vary those hours within certain limits. In a flextime schedule, there are certain common core hours when all employees are required to be on the job, but starting, ending, and lunch-hour times are flexible. Flextime is one of the most desired benefits among employees.[78] Employers have responded; a survey of 314 Canadian employers shows that 81 percent of them were offering flexible work options in 2007, including flexible hours, working from home some or all of the time, and compressed workweeks. [79]

compressed workweek
A workweek in which employees work longer hours per day but fewer days per week.

flexible work hours (flextime)
A scheduling option in which employees are required to work a specific number of hours per week but are free to vary those hours within certain limits.

Job Sharing

In Great Britain, McDonald's is experimenting with an unusual program—dubbed the Family Contract—to reduce absenteeism and turnover at some of its restaurants. Under

job sharing
The practice of having two or more people split a full-time job.

this Family Contract, employees from the same immediate family can fill in for one another for any work shift without having to clear it first with their manager.[80] This type of job scheduling, which can be effective in motivating a diverse workforce, is called **job sharing**— the practice of having two or more people split a full-time job. Although something like McDonald's Family Contract may be appropriate for a low-skilled job, other organizations might offer job sharing to professionals who want to work but don't want the demands and hassles of a full-time position. For instance, at global accounting firm Ernst & Young, employees in many of the company's locations— Bermuda, New Zealand, and South Africa, for instance—can choose from a variety of flexible work arrangements, including job sharing.

Telecommuting

telecommuting
A job arrangement in which employees work at home and are linked to the workplace by computer and other technology.

Another alternative made possible by information technology is **telecommuting**, in which employees work at home and are linked to the workplace by computer and other technology. Since many jobs are computer- and Internet-oriented, this job arrangement might be considered to be ideal for some people, as there is no commuting, the hours are flexible, there is freedom to dress as you please, and there are few or no interruptions from colleagues. However, keep in mind that not all employees embrace the idea of telecommuting. A number of employees enjoy the informal interactions at work that satisfy their social needs and provide a source of new ideas.

Q&A 13.8

Do flexible work arrangements motivate employees? Although such arrangements might seem highly motivational, both positive and negative relationships have been found. For instance, a recent study looking at the impact of telecommuting on job satisfaction found that job satisfaction initially increased as the extent of telecommuting increased, but as the number of hours spent telecommuting increased, job satisfaction started to level off, decreased slightly, and then stabilized.[81]

From Theory to Practice: Suggestions for Motivating Employees

5. How can managers motivate employees?

We have covered a lot of information about motivation. If you are a manager concerned with motivating your employees, what specific recommendations can you draw from the theories and issues presented in this chapter? Although there is no simple, all-encompassing set of guidelines, the following suggestions draw on what we know about motivating employees:

- *Recognize individual differences.* Almost every contemporary motivation theory recognizes that employees are not identical.[82] They have different needs, attitudes, personalities, and other important individual variables. Managers may not be giving enough consideration to what employees really want in terms of pay and benefits from the workplace. A recent survey of 446 employers by Western Compensation and Benefits Consultants found that 94 percent listed competitive base salary as an important incentive. Only 52 percent of employers listed flexible scheduling as a good incentive.[83] Meanwhile, a Statistics Canada survey found that employees want "challenging work, continuous learning, flexible work arrangements and better communication with their employers."[84] In the Western Compensation survey, 87 percent of companies reported having difficulties attracting new employees in 2006. Companies may need to pay more attention to what their employees say that they want.

- *Match people to jobs.* There is a great deal of evidence showing the motivational benefits of carefully matching people to jobs. For example, high achievers should have jobs that allow them to participate in setting moderately challenging goals and that involve autonomy and feedback. Also, keep in mind that not everybody is motivated by jobs that are high in autonomy, variety, and responsibility.

- *Individualize rewards.* Because employees have different needs, what acts as a reinforcer for one may not for another. Managers should use their knowledge of employee differences to individualize the rewards they control, such as pay, promotions, recognition, desirable work assignments, autonomy, and participation.

- *Link rewards to performance.* Managers need to make rewards contingent on performance. Rewarding factors other than performance will reinforce only those other factors. Important rewards such as pay increases and promotions should be given for the attainment of specific goals. Managers should also look for ways to increase the visibility of rewards, making them potentially more motivating.

- *Check the system for equity.* Employees should perceive that rewards or outcomes are equal to the inputs. On a simple level, experience, ability, effort, and other obvious inputs should explain differences in pay, responsibility, and other obvious outcomes. And remember that one person's equity is another's inequity, so an ideal reward system should probably weigh inputs differently in arriving at the proper rewards for each job.

- *Use recognition.* Recognize the power of recognition. In a stagnant economy where cost cutting is widespread (as it was from 2001 to 2005), using recognition is a low-cost means to reward employees. And it's a reward that most employees consider valuable.

- *Don't ignore money.* It's easy to get so caught up in setting goals, creating interesting jobs, and providing opportunities for participation that you forget that money is a major reason why most people work. Some studies indicate that money is not the top priority of employees. Professor Graham Lowe at the University of Alberta and a colleague found that relationships in the workplace are more important than pay or benefits in determining job satisfaction.[85] Nevertheless, the allocation of performance-based wage increases, piecework bonuses, and other pay incentives is important in determining employee motivation. We are not saying that managers should focus solely on money as a motivational tool. Rather, we are simply stating the obvious—that is, if money is removed as an incentive, people are not going to show up for work. The same cannot be said for removing performance goals, enriched work, or participation.

Andrew Robinson, who runs an information security company in Portland, ME, has taken the idea of matching people to jobs a step further than most by matching future employees to potential jobs. Robinson runs a free after-school program to teach students like these about "ethical hacking," or the fine art of protecting computer systems by hacking them first. Of the 50 students in the program, Robinson says, "They have all the skills that they need to cause trouble, and some of them may have even started doing some of those things just for fun." His point to the students is, "Here's how you can do this legally, within a moral and ethical framework, and make a good amount of money doing it."

SUMMARY AND IMPLICATIONS

1. What is motivation? Motivation refers to the processes that account for an individual's willingness to exert high levels of effort to reach organizational goals, conditioned by the effort's ability to satisfy some individual need.

▶ ▶ ▶ At Tesco, one challenge was to motivate employees so that there would be less turnover.

2. How can needs help one be motivated? Needs theories point out that individuals have needs that, when fulfilled, will motivate individuals to perform well. While the theories do not account for all aspects of motivation, they do inform managers that individuals have different needs that should be considered when developing reward plans.

▶ ▶ ▶ Managers at Tesco discovered that different employee groups, such as students and mothers returning to the workplace, had different needs, and tried to address these needs to keep employees motivated.

3. What are the contemporary theories of motivation? It is possible to make jobs more motivating by designing them better. The job characteristics model proposes that employees will be more motivated if they have greater autonomy and feedback and the work is meaningful. Equity theory proposes that employees compare their rewards and their productivity with others, and then determine whether they have been treated fairly. Individuals who perceive that they are underrewarded will try to adjust their behaviour to correct this imbalance. Expectancy theory explores the link between people's belief in whether they can do the work assigned, their belief in whether they will get the rewards promised, and the extent to which the reward is something they value. Most research evidence supports expectancy theory.

▶ ▶ ▶ Tesco encourages employees to buy shares of the company, so that they can "share in the success they helped to create" and see the link between performance and reward.

4. What are some current issues in motivation? Current issues in motivation include motivating a diverse workforce, designing effective rewards programs, and improving work–life balance.

▶ ▶ ▶ One of Tesco's challenges was motivating employees who had somewhat repetitive jobs.

5. How can managers motivate employees? Managers can motivate employees by recognizing individual differences, matching people to jobs, individualizing rewards, linking rewards to performance, checking the system for equity, using recognition, and not ignoring that money is a major reason why most people work.

▶ ▶ ▶ Tesco has worked hard to recognize the different needs of students and mothers returning to the workplace. The company also uses recognition to motivate employees and reduce turnover.

CHAPTER 13

Management @ Work

READING FOR COMPREHENSION

1. How do needs affect motivation?

2. Contrast lower-order and higher-order needs in Maslow's needs hierarchy.

3. Describe how Theory X and Theory Y managers approach motivation.

4. Define the five core dimensions of the job characteristics model.

5. What are some of the possible consequences of employees' perceiving an inequity between their inputs and outcomes and those of others?

6. What are some advantages of using pay-for-performance programs to motivate employee performance? Are there drawbacks? Explain.

7. What are the advantages of flextime from an employee's perspective? From management's perspective?

8. What can an organization do to create a more motivating environment for employees?

LINKING CONCEPTS TO PRACTICE

1. Most of us have to work for a living, and a job is a central part of our lives. So why do managers have to worry so much about employee motivation issues?

2. Describe a task you have done recently for which you exerted a high level of effort. Explain your behaviour using the following motivation approaches: (1) the hierarchy of needs theory, (2) motivation-hygiene theory, (3) equity theory, and (4) expectancy theory.

3. If you had to develop an incentive system for a small company that makes tortillas, which elements from which motivation approaches or theories would you

use? Why? Would your choice be the same if it was a software design firm?

4. What motivation theories or approaches could be used to encourage and support workforce diversity efforts? Explain.

5. Many job design experts who have studied the changing nature of work say that people do their best work when they are motivated by a sense of purpose rather than by the pursuit of money. Do you agree? Explain your position.

SELF-ASSESSMENT

What Rewards Do I Value Most?

Below are 10 work-related rewards. For each, identify the number that best describes the value that a particular reward has for you personally. Use the following scale to express your feelings:[86]

1 = No Value at All
2 = Slight Value
3 = Moderate Value
4 = Great Value
5 = Extremely Great Value

1. Good pay	1 2 3 4 5	
2. Prestigious title	1 2 3 4 5	
3. Vacation time	1 2 3 4 5	
4. Job security	1 2 3 4 5	
5. Recognition	1 2 3 4 5	

6. Interesting work	1 2 3 4 5
7. Pleasant conditions	1 2 3 4 5
8. Chances to advance	1 2 3 4 5
9. Flexible schedule	1 2 3 4 5
10. Friendly co-workers	1 2 3 4 5

Scoring Key

To assess your responses, prioritize them into groups. Put all the rewards you gave a 5 together. Do the same for your other responses. The rewards you gave 5s or 4s are the ones that you most desire and which your employer should emphasize with you.

Analysis and Interpretation

What motivates you does not necessarily motivate me. So employers that want to maximize employee motivation should determine what rewards each employee individually values. This instrument can help you understand which work-related rewards have the greatest value to you.

Compare the rewards that your employer offers with your scores. The greater the disparity, the more you might want to consider looking for opportunities at another organization with a reward structure that better matches your preferences.

More Self-Assessments mymanagementlab

To learn more about your skills, abilities, and interests, go to the MyManagementLab website and take the following self-assessments:

- I.C.1.—What Motivates Me?
- I.C.4.—What's My View on the Nature of People?
- I.C.8.—How Sensitive Am I to Equity Differences?

MANAGEMENT FOR YOU TODAY

Dilemma

You are in a team with six other management students, and you have a major case analysis due in four weeks. The case project will count for 25 percent of the course mark. You are the team's leader. Several team members are having diffi- culty getting motivated to get started on the project. Identify ways you could motivate your team members, using needs theories, expectancy theory, and equity theory. How will you motivate yourself?

Becoming a Manager

- Start paying attention to times when you are highly motivated and times when you are not as motivated. What accounts for the difference?

- When working on teams for class projects or on committees in student organizations, try different approaches to motivating others.

- If you are working, assess your job using the job characteristics model. How might you redesign your job to make it more motivating?

- As you visit various businesses, note what, if any, employee recognition programs these businesses use.

- Talk to practising managers about their approaches to employee motivation. What have they found works?

WORKING TOGETHER: TEAM-BASED EXERCISE

What Is Most Important to You in a Job?

List five criteria (for example: pay, recognition, challenging work, friendships, status, the opportunity to do new things, the opportunity to travel, and so forth) that would be most impor- tant to you in a job. Rank them by order of importance. Break into small groups (3 or 4 other class members) and compare your responses. What patterns, if any, did you find?

ETHICS IN ACTION

Ethical Dilemma Exercise: Are Some Employees More Deserving Than Others?

Employees who feel unfairly forced into accepting deep cuts in salary and benefits may not be the most motivated employees.[87] This is the situation facing many major North American airlines as they struggle for survival. To stay in business, management at Air Canada and other carriers have pressured unionized pilots, mechanics, and flight attendants for concessions on pay and work rules again and again.

Still, many North American airline employees are resentful that their compensation will not return to previous levels until the end of 2008—at the earliest. Air Canada employees are not even sure there will be an airline in 2008. Moreover, there is concern that cuts in management's compensation will not last as long as those for unionized employees. Many employees are bitter about what they see as inequitable treatment. "We know we had to help the airline," says one flight attendant. "But we think they took more than they needed from us." This sense of inequity could dampen motivation and make a huge difference in the way employees work together and the way they deal with customers.

Imagine that you were just promoted and now manage one of your airline's mechanical maintenance facilities at a regional airport. Your manager just told you that the airline has lost a large number of managers to jobs outside the industry. To stop defections and retain good managers, your company has decided to return managers to full pay and benefits within 12 months. However, employees must wait much longer. You sympathize with your employees' gripes about compensation cuts, and you know they have little hope of getting maintenance jobs at other airlines. Although you like your new job and would welcome full pay, you could easily move to another industry. What, if anything, would you do about the nonmanagerial employees who will continue working with the pay cuts? (Look back at this chapter's discussion of equity theory as you consider this ethical challenge.)

Thinking Critically About Ethics

You have been hired as a phone sales representative at G.A.P Adventures in Toronto. In this job, you help customers who call in to book vacations by finding what works best for them and their needs. You check airline flights, times, and fares, and also help with rental car and hotel reservations.

Most car rental firms and hotels run contests for the sales representative who books the most cars or most hotel rooms. The contest winners receive very attractive rewards! For instance, if you book just 50 clients for one rental car company, your name is put in a draw for $1000. If you book 100 clients, the draw is for $2500. And if you book 200 clients, you receive an all-expenses-paid, one-week Caribbean vacation. So the incentives are attractive enough to encourage you to "steer" customers toward one of those companies even though it might not be the best or cheapest for them. Your manager does not discourage participation in these programs.

Do you see anything wrong with this situation? Explain. What ethical issues do you see for (a) the employee, (b) the organization, and (c) the customer? How could an organization design performance incentive programs that encourage high levels of performance without compromising ethics?

CASE APPLICATION

Best Buy

Customer-centricity.[88] That is the new strategic focus that Brad Anderson, CEO of Best Buy, is betting on to keep the company from becoming a retailing casualty like Woolworth or Kmart. What is customer-centricity? Simply, it's figuring out which customers are the most profitable and doing whatever it takes to please them so they want to come back often and spend money. As the biggest consumer electronics retailer in North America, Best Buy has a lot at stake. And its 100 000-plus employees will play a crucial role in this new approach, which shifts the focus from "pushing gadgets to catering to customers."

"At Best Buy, People Are the Engines That Drive Our Success." That is the upfront and central phrase on the company's web-based career centre. And to Best Buy, it's not an empty slogan. The company has tried to create an environment in which employees, wherever they are, have numerous opportunities to learn, work, play, and achieve. One way they do that is by providing facts and figures to employees on everything from new technology to industry changes to company actions. At store meetings or on the intranet, employees can get the information they need to do their jobs and do them well.

Like many other companies, Best Buy has "struggled to meet the demands of its business—how to do things better, faster, and cheaper than its competitors—with an increasingly stressed-out workforce." Its culture has always rewarded long hours and sacrifice. For instance, one manager used a plaque to recognize the employee "who turns on the lights in the morning and turns them off at night." However, that approach has been taking its toll on employees. Best Buy is having difficulty retaining its best and brightest managers and executives.

Anderson wants to know why the company does not have an "innovative incentive program to foster our innovative culture." He has come to you for advice. What is the best way for the company to get employees on board so that they will be more customer-centric in their approach?

DEVELOPING YOUR DIAGNOSTIC AND ANALYTICAL SKILLS

Motivation at Classic Hospitality

The reality of service work in a hotel is that a substantial portion of your work involves days of boredom punctuated by hours of tedium.[89] You basically spend your time in isolation, often doing work that will make the quality of a guest's stay better. You are typically low paid and advancement is often lacking. But that is not necessarily the case at Hotel Lombardy, a hotel that is part of the Classic Hospitality Consortium. If you are like Charles Hegeman, what you thought was a quick job to make a few extra bucks to travel across North America has turned into a career with Classic that has lasted over five years.

The hospitality industry in general has a terrible record of employee loyalty. Because the jobs are often viewed as low-paying service jobs, turnover is unbelievably high. In fact, most companies in the hospitality industry experience turnover rates at around 160 percent annually. That means that they have an entirely new set of employees every eight months. Continuity of quality service, as you can imagine, can be extremely difficult under such circumstances.

But Classic Hospitality views jobs at its hotels differently. It has made a corporate commitment to attract good employees and to encourage the best employees to stay. Although company officials recognize there is a lot of competition for these employees, they believe that they can find a way to motivate this group of individuals and keep them longer. For instance, because of the excellent work Hegeman did as a front office clerk, he was promoted to front office manager. After a period of time in that job with outstanding performance, Hegeman notified hotel management that he was ready for a promotion. Working with him to match his skills and abilities to hotel needs, management promoted Hegeman to sales manager in another of Classic's properties.

In addition to internal advancement, Classic Hospitality offers employees bonuses, recognition, and even transportation assistance. For example, the cleaning staff has a checklist that they must complete when cleaning a guest room. Periodically a supervisor will evaluate how well the staff performed their jobs. If over a six-month period a staff member has achieved a 95 percent or greater effectiveness rating, that individual is given an extra week's pay. And on those really busy nights when hotel occupancy exceeds 80 percent, which makes the employees' jobs just that much harder, each hotel staff member is given a $100 bonus. Needless to say, employees are very happy when the hotel is full!

No discussion of employee life at Classic Hospitality would be complete without mentioning the company's focus on family. Each year the organization holds an annual holiday party, inviting employees, their spouses, and children to attend as a way of saying thanks for the hard work they have done. Management knows that the work hours often take employees away from their families. The holiday party is just one additional means of letting employees and their loved ones know that they matter to Classic.

Is this form of motivation effective? By most accounts it is, considering, as we mentioned previously, that the turnover rate in the hospitality industry typically is around 160 percent annually. Turnover at Classic Hospitality is less than 25 percent. That is a tremendous savings for the corporation—something that company officials appear to share with their loyal employees.

Questions

1. If you were interested in working in the hospitality industry, would you consider a job at Classic Hospitality? Why or why not?

2. How many activities in this case study can you tie in to specific motivation theories? List the activities, the motivation theory, and how the activities apply.

3. Do you believe that bonus programs, such as an extra week's pay if at least 95 percent effectiveness of a job is achieved, transportation assistance, and the like, would work in other types of jobs? If yes, which ones, and why? If no, why not?

Designing Motivating Jobs

About the Skill

As a manager, you may need to give input into the design or redesign of jobs at some point. How will you ensure that these jobs are motivating? What can you do regarding job design that will maximize your employees' motivation and performance? The job characteristics model, which defines five core job dimensions (skill variety, task identity, task significance, autonomy, and feedback) and their relationships to employee motivation, provides a basis for designing motivating jobs.

Steps in Developing the Skill

The following five suggestions, based on the job characteristics model, specify the types of changes in jobs you can make as a manager that are most likely to improve motivation in employees:[90]

1. **Combine tasks.** Put existing specialized and divided tasks back together to form a new, larger module of work. This step will increase skill variety and task identity.

2. **Create natural work units.** Design work tasks that form an identifiable and meaningful whole. This step will increase "ownership" of the work and will encourage employees to view their work as significant and important rather than as irrelevant and boring.

3. **Establish client relationships.** The client is the user of the product or service that is the basis for an employee's work. Whenever possible, establish direct relationships between employees and their clients. This step will increase skill variety, autonomy, and feedback for the employees.

4. **Expand jobs vertically.** Vertical expansion of a job means giving employees responsibilities and controls that were formerly the manager's. It partially closes the gap between the "doing" and "controlling" aspects of the job. This step will increase employee autonomy.

5. **Open feedback channels.** By increasing feedback, employees not only learn how well they are performing their jobs but also whether their performance is improving, deteriorating, or remaining at a constant level. Ideally, this feedback should be received directly as the employee does the job, rather than from his or her manager on an occasional basis.

Practising the Skill

Read the following scenario. Write some notes about how you would handle the situation described. Be sure to refer to the five suggestions for designing motivating jobs.

Scenario

You work for Sunrise Deliveries, a freight transportation company that makes local deliveries of products for your customers. In your position, you supervise Sunrise's six delivery drivers. Each morning, your drivers drive their pre-loaded trucks to their destinations and wait for the products to be unloaded. There is a high turnover rate in the job. In fact, most of your drivers don't stay longer than six months. Not only is this turnover getting expensive, but it's been hard to develop a quality customer-service program when you have constantly got new faces. You have also heard complaints from the drivers that "all they do is drive." What will you do to retain and motivate the delivery drivers?

Reinforcing the Skill

The following activities will help you practise and reinforce the skills associated with designing motivating jobs:

1. Think of the worst job you have ever had. Analyze the job according to the five dimensions identified in the job characteristics model. Redesign the job in order to make it more satisfying and motivating.

2. Interview two people in two different job positions on your campus. Ask them questions about their jobs, using the job characteristics model as a guide. Using the information provided, list recommendations for making the jobs more motivating.

Developing Employee Potential: The Bottom Line of Diversity

One of a manager's more important goals is helping employees develop their potential.[91] This is particularly important in managing talented employees from a variety of cultures who can bring new perspectives and ideas to the business but who may find that the workplace environment is not as conducive as it could be to accepting and embracing these different perspectives. For instance, managers at Alcatel-Lucent's distinguished Bell Labs have worked hard to develop an environment in which the ideas of nonwhite employees are encouraged openly.

What can managers do to ensure that employees from different cultures have the opportunity to develop their potential? One thing they can do is to make sure that there are role models of different cultures in leadership positions so that others see that there are opportunities to grow and advance. Having motivated, talented, hard-working, and enthusiastic diverse employees who excel in decision-making roles can be a powerful motivator to other employees of the same or similar backgrounds to work hard to develop their own potential. A mentoring program in which diverse employees are given the opportunity to work closely with organizational leaders can be a powerful tool. At SGI, for instance, new employees become part of a mentoring group called "Horizons." Through this mentoring group, diverse employees have the opportunity to observe and learn from key company decision makers.

Another way for managers to develop the potential of their diverse employees is to offer developmental work assignments that provide a variety of learning experiences in different organizational areas. Daimler, for example, started its Corporate University, which offers a comprehensive series of learning opportunities for all employees. The company's director of diversity and work/family says that employees who are provided the opportunity to learn new processes and how to use new technology are more likely to excel at their work and to stay with the company. These types of developmental opportunities are particularly important for diverse employees because they empower employees with tools that are critical to professional development.

Consider organizations for which you have worked. Did any of them have diversity initiatives? What did they do to either recruit employees from various cultures or make them feel more welcome? Were the company's policies effective in managing diversity?

What Do You Want from Your Job?

Since you are reading this textbook, you are likely enrolled in a class that is helping you earn credit toward a degree.[92] You are probably also taking the courses you need to earn a degree because you hope to get a good job (or a better job, if you are already working) on graduating. With all this effort you are putting forth, have you ever stopped to think about what you really want from your job? A high salary? Work that challenges you? Autonomy and flexibility? Perhaps the results of a recent survey of employees will give you some insights into what you might want from your job. The top reasons that employees stay with their jobs are as follows.

Reason	Percentage of Respondents
Like co-workers	71 percent
Pleasant work environment	68 percent
Easy commute	68 percent
Challenging work	65 percent
Flexible work hours	54 percent

Do any of these characteristics describe what you want from your job? Whether they do or don't, you should spend some time reflecting on what you want your job to provide you. Then, when it's time to embark on that all-important job search, look for situations that will offer what you are looking for.

Understanding Groups and Teams

PART four

What is the best way to create and manage teams?

1. What are the stages of team development?

2. How do individuals become team players?

3. How can groups become effective teams?

4. What are some of the current challenges in managing teams?

▶ ▶ ▶ When you are putting together the Canadian team for the 2006 Winter Olympics in Turin, do you go with the proven winners of the 2004 World Cup of Hockey and the 2002 Winter Olympics or put together a new team?[1]

That was the challenge facing Wayne Gretzky and management as they prepared to announce the 24-man roster for Team Canada on December 21, 2005.

Gretzky's 2004 World Cup hockey team beat Finland 3 to 2 in Toronto, taking first place. His 2002 Olympic hockey team beat the Americans 5 to 2 in Salt Lake City, winning the gold medal. It was the first time Canada had won Olympic gold for hockey since 1952.

When Steve Tambellini, filling in for Gretzky, whose mother's funeral had been earlier that week, announced the new team in December 2005, 20 of the players had played for either the World Cup team, the 2002 Olympic team, or both. Only three new players were added to the team. There were certainly questions about some of the decisions. Was it right to leave off Pittsburgh Penguin Sidney Crosby, who was having a strong debut season in the NHL? Why include contro-

versial Canuck Todd Bertuzzi, after he attacked Colorado Avalanche player Steve Moore, ending his career? Most importantly, what about 2010? Shouldn't there be some younger players getting experience now in preparation for playing for Olympic gold in Vancouver?

Team Canada assistant coach Wayne Fleming defended against those who complained that there were not enough new faces on the team. This would be a team that would have "instant chemistry, with very little preparation time." Better to go with experience, in other words.

Think About It

What is the best way to choose an effective team? Put yourself in Wayne Gretzky's shoes. Are there other players he should have chosen instead? Could he have put together a better team?

Work teams are one of the realities—and challenges—of managing in today's dynamic global environment. Thousands of organizations have made the move to restructure work around teams rather than individuals. Why? What do these teams look like? What stages of development do teams go through? And, like the challenge Wayne Gretzky faced, how can managers create effective teams? These are a few of the types of questions we answer in this chapter. First, however, let's begin by developing our understanding of group behaviour.

Hockey Canada
www.hockeycanada.ca

Understanding Groups and Teams

Because most organizational work is done by individuals who are part of a work group, it's important for managers to understand group behaviour. Why? Because individuals act differently in groups than they do when they are alone. Therefore, if we want to understand organizational behaviour more fully, we need to study groups.

1. What are the stages of team development?

What Is a Group?

A **group** is defined as two or more interacting and interdependent individuals who come together to achieve particular goals. Groups can be either formal or informal. *Formal groups* are work groups defined by the organization's structure that have designated work assignments and specific tasks. In formal groups, appropriate behaviours are established by and directed toward organizational goals. Exhibit 14-1 provides some examples of different types of formal groups in today's organizations.

Diversity in Action 3

In contrast, *informal groups* are social. These groups occur naturally in the workplace in response to the need for social contact. For example, three employees from different departments who regularly eat lunch together are an informal group. Informal groups tend to form around friendships and common interests.

What Is a Team?

Most of you are already familiar with teams, especially if you have watched organized sports events. Although a sports team has many of the same characteristics as a work team, work teams *are* different from work groups and have their own unique traits (see Exhibit 14-2 for a description of the differences). Work groups interact primarily to share information and to make decisions to help each member do his or her job more efficiently and effectively. These groups have no need or opportunity to engage in collective work that requires joint effort. On the other hand, **work teams** are groups whose members work intensely on a specific common goal using their positive synergy, individual and mutual accountability, and complementary skills. In a work team, the combined individual efforts of team members result in a level of performance that is greater than the sum of those individual inputs. How? By generating positive **synergy** through coordinated effort.

Though teams and groups do differ, we sometimes use *groups* and *teams* interchangeably in our theoretical discussions below (conforming to how scholars have written their research). This simply underscores that in some cases the processes for groups and teams are similar, although teams involve more synergy.

Types of Teams

Teams can do a variety of things. They can design products, provide services, negotiate deals, coordinate projects, offer advice, and make decisions.[2] The four most common types of teams you are likely to find in an organization are problem-solving teams, self-managed teams, cross-functional teams, and virtual teams.

Problem-Solving Teams

If we look back at when work teams were just beginning to gain in popularity, most were what we call **problem-solving teams**, which are teams of 5 to 12 employees from the same department or functional area who are involved in efforts to improve work activities or to solve specific problems. In problem-solving teams, members share ideas or offer

Exhibit 14-1

Examples of Formal Groups

Command Groups: Groups that are determined by the organizational chart and composed of individuals who report directly to a given manager.

Task Groups: Groups composed of individuals brought together to complete a specific job task; their existence is often temporary because once the task is completed, the group disbands.

Cross-Functional Teams: Groups that bring together the knowledge and skills of individuals from various work areas, or groups whose members have been trained to do one another's jobs.

Self-Managed Teams: Groups that are essentially independent and, in addition to their own tasks, take on traditional managerial responsibilities such as hiring, planning and scheduling, and performance evaluations.

Google's website explains that the company looks for exceptional people, and one of the skills they need is the ability to work as a team member. "We work in small teams, which we believe promotes spontaneity, creativity, and speed," the company says, "and team achievements are highly valued."

suggestions on how work processes and methods can be improved. However, these teams are rarely given the authority to unilaterally implement any of their suggested actions.

Self-Managed Teams

Self-managed teams are a formal group of employees who operate without a manager and are responsible for a complete work process or segment. Unlike problem-solving teams, the self-managed team is responsible for getting the work done *and* for managing itself. This usually includes planning and scheduling work, assigning tasks to members, collectively controlling the pace of work, making operating decisions, and taking action on problems. For instance, a self-managed team operates Muskoseepi Park in Grande Prairie, Alberta. Team members are accountable to each other and do not have direct supervision on a daily basis.

How effective are self-managed teams? Most organizations that use them find them successful and plan to expand their use in the coming years.[3] For instance, the evidence indicates that self-managed work teams often perform better than teams with formally appointed leaders.[4] Leaders can obstruct high performance when they interfere with self-managed teams.[5] However, managers cannot forget to consider cultural differences when deciding

self-managed team

A work team that operates without a manager and is responsible for a complete work process or segment.

Exhibit 14-2

Groups vs. Teams

Work Group	Team
• Strong, clearly focused leader	• Shared leadership roles
• Individual accountability	• Individual and mutual accountability
• The group's purpose is the same as the broader organizational mission	• Specific team purpose that the team itself delivers
• Individual work products	• Collective work products
• Runs efficient meetings	• Encourages open-ended discussion and active problem-solving meetings
• Measures its effectiveness indirectly by its influence on others (such as financial performance of the business)	• Measures performance directly by assessing collective work products
• Discusses, decides, and delegates together	• Discusses, decides, and does real work

Source: J. R. Katzenbach and D. K. Smith, "The Discipline of Teams," *Harvard Business Review*, July–August 2005, p. 164. Reprinted with permission of Harvard Business Review.

whether to use self-managed teams. For instance, evidence suggests that these types of teams have not fared well in Mexico, largely due to that culture's low tolerance of ambiguity and uncertainty and employees' strong respect for hierarchical authority.[6]

Cross-Functional Teams

cross-functional team
Work teams made up of individuals who are experts in various functional specialties.

Cross-functional teams, which we introduced in Chapter 9, are work teams made up of individuals who are experts in various functional specialties. Many organizations use cross-functional teams. For example, Calgary-based Canadian Pacific Railway (CPR) uses cross-functional teams to figure out ways to cut costs. Individuals from all of the functional areas affected by the spending review (such as supply services, operations, and finance) make up the team.[7] Organic organizations, which we discussed in Chapter 9, are generally structured around cross-functional teams.

Q&A 14.1

Virtual Teams

virtual team
A type of work team that uses computer technology to link physically dispersed members in order to achieve a common goal.

Virtual teams are teams that use computer technology to link physically dispersed members in order to achieve a common goal. For instance, Microsoft's staff in Richmond, BC, is part of a virtual team that works for managers in Redmond, Washington, and other global centres. They collaborate with colleagues throughout the world.[8]

In a virtual team, members collaborate online with tools such as wide-area networks, videoconferencing, email, fax, or even websites where the team can hold online conferences.[9] Virtual teams can do all the things that other teams can—share information, make decisions, and complete tasks; however, they can suffer from the absence of paraverbal and nonverbal cues and limited social contact. Professor Mark Mortensen of McGill University's Faculty of Management notes a major difficulty in working long distance: "You may be in Montreal and are working with someone in Bangalore, India. You send an e-mail to someone there and get no response. You send another and get no response and then you get annoyed. Later, you find out that it was a national holiday and no one was working."[10] An additional concern about virtual teams is whether members are able to build the same kind of trust that face-to-face teams build.[11]

However, two recent studies examining how virtual teams work on projects indicate that virtual teams can develop close interaction and trust; these qualities simply evolve differently than in face-to-face groups.[12] The researchers found that initial electronic messages set the tone and determined the extent to which trust developed on a virtual team. For example, on one team the appointed leader sent an introductory message that had a distrustful tone. This team suffered low morale and poor performance throughout the project. Virtual teams should start with an electronic form of "courtship," with members providing some personal information early on. Teams should assign clear roles to members, so members can identify with each other. By engaging in spontaneous communication with virtual team members, managers can also reduce the likelihood and impact of conflict.[13]

Managing virtual teams effectively has become more important as more employees engage in telecommuting, an alternative work arrangement we discussed in Chapter 13.

Stages of Team Development

Have you ever noticed the stages a team goes through in learning how to work together?

Team development is a dynamic process. Most teams and groups are in a continual state of change, although there is a general pattern that describes how most of them evolve. Professor Bruce Tuckman of Ohio State University developed a five-stage model of group development. His research found that teams pass through a standard sequence of five stages.[14] As shown in Exhibit 14-3, these five stages are *forming, storming, norming, performing,* and *adjourning.*

forming
The first stage of team development, in which people join the group and then define the team's purpose, structure, and leadership.

Stage I, **forming**, has two aspects. First, people join the team either because of a work assignment or for some other benefit desired (such as status, self-esteem, affiliation, power, or security).

Exhibit 14-3

Stages of Team Development

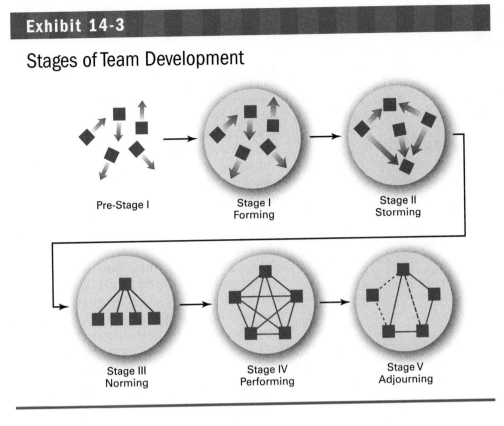

Pre-Stage I	Stage I Forming	Stage II Storming

Stage III Norming	Stage IV Performing	Stage V Adjourning

Once the team's membership is in place, the second part of the forming stage begins: the task of defining the team's purpose, structure, and leadership. This phase is characterized by a great deal of uncertainty. Members are "testing the waters" to determine what types of behaviour are acceptable. This stage is complete when members begin to think of themselves as part of a team.

Stage II, **storming**, is one of intragroup conflict. Members accept the existence of the team but resist the control that the team imposes on individuality. Further, there is conflict over who will control the team. When this stage is complete, there will be a relatively clear hierarchy of leadership within the team and agreement on the team's direction.

Stage III is one in which close relationships develop and the team demonstrates cohesiveness. There is now a strong sense of team identity and camaraderie. This **norming** stage is complete when the team structure solidifies and the team has assimilated a common set of expectations of what defines correct member behaviour.

Stage IV is **performing**. The team structure at this point is fully functional and accepted by team members. Team energy has moved from getting to know and understand each other to performing the task at hand.

Performing is the last stage in the development of permanent work teams. Temporary teams—such as project teams, task forces, and similar groups that have a limited task to perform—have a fifth stage, **adjourning**. In this stage, the team prepares to disband. High levels of task performance are no longer the team's top priority. Instead, attention is directed at wrapping up activities. Responses of team members vary at this stage. Some are upbeat, basking in the team's accomplishments. Others may be saddened by the loss of camaraderie and friendships gained during the work team's life.

Many of you have probably experienced each of these stages in working on a class team project. Team members are selected and then meet for the first time. There is a "feeling out" period to assess what the team is going to do and how it's going to do it. This is usually rapidly followed by a battle for control: Who is going to be in charge? Once this issue

Q&A 14.2

storming
The second stage of team development, which is characterized by intragroup conflict.

norming
The third stage of team development, which is characterized by close relationships and cohesiveness.

performing
The fourth stage of team development, in which the team structure is fully functional and accepted by team members.

adjourning
The final stage of team development for temporary teams, in which members are concerned with wrapping up activities rather than task performance.

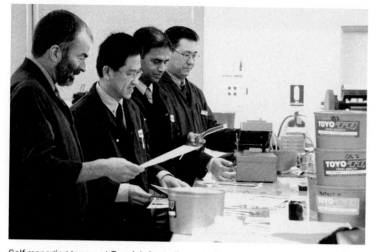

Self-managing teams at Toyo Ink Australia are in the performing stage. There are no more time clocks because team members are responsible for the amount of work they do, and they will soon also be in charge of planning and organizing their own vacation times. Information sharing is more efficient, and communication with management has increased as well.

is resolved and a "hierarchy" agreed on, the team identifies specific aspects of the task, who is going to do them, and dates by which the assigned work needs to be completed. General expectations are established and agreed upon by each member. These decisions form the foundation for what you hope will be a coordinated team effort culminating in a project well done. Once the team project is completed and turned in, the team breaks up. Of course, some teams don't get much beyond the first or second stage; these teams typically have serious interpersonal conflicts, turn in disappointing work, and get lower grades.

Should you assume from the preceding discussion that a team becomes more effective as it progresses through the first four stages? Some researchers argue that effectiveness of work teams increases at advanced stages, but that is not always the case.[15] Also, teams don't always proceed clearly from one stage to the next. Sometimes teams are able to skip the storming stage, if the goals and roles are spelled out clearly. Sometimes, several stages may be going on simultaneously, as when teams are storming and performing at the same time. Individuals within a team may also be at different stages, with some performing, while others are still in the forming or norming stage. When individuals are shy, it may take them longer to reach the performing stage, and it may be helpful for team members to support and encourage each other through the stages. Teams sometimes regress to previous stages. Therefore, don't always assume that all teams precisely follow this development process or that Stage IV (performing) is always the most preferable. It's better to think of this model as a general framework. It underscores the fact that teams are dynamic entities, and it can help you better understand the problems and issues that are most likely to surface during a team's life.

Diversity in Action 1

Turning Individuals into Team Players

▶ ▶ ▶ When Wayne Gretzky put together Team Canada for the 2006 Winter Olympics, he had to balance out many considerations.[16] His 2002 Winter Olympic team and his 2004 World Cup of Hockey team had done a terrific job in representing Canada. Still, having some younger players gain experience for the 2010 Winter Olympics in Vancouver might be a consideration.

Gretzky put together a team with a lot of experience, particularly international experience. He seemed less concerned with the players' recent performance in the league. Since Mario Lemieux and Steve Yzerman, two veterans whom Gretzky had relied on for leadership roles in previous team Canada, were unavailable, Gretzky may have felt experienced players would fill the leadership void. Choosing the players was not the end of the task, however. Gretzky had to get the collection of individuals to play like a team.

Think About It

What does it take to turn an individual into a team player?

---

2. How do individuals become team players?

So far, we have made a strong case for the value and growing popularity of work teams, but not every employee is inherently a team player. Some people prefer to be recognized for their individual achievements. In some organizations, too, work environments are such that only the strong survive. Creating teams in such an environment may meet some resistance. Countries differ in terms of the degree to which individuals are encouraged by societal institutions to be integrated into groups. Teams fit well in countries that score high on collectivism, where working together is encouraged. But what if an organization wants to introduce teams into an individualistic society, like that of Canada? The job becomes more difficult.

Q&A 14.3

The Challenges of Creating Team Players

One substantial barrier to work teams is the individual resistance that may exist. Employees' success, when they are part of teams, is no longer defined in terms of individual performance. Instead, success is a function of how well the team as a whole performs. To perform well as team members, individuals must be able to communicate openly and honestly with one another, to confront differences and resolve conflicts, and to place lower priority on personal goals for the good of the team. For many employees, these are difficult and sometimes impossible assignments. The *Ethical Dilemma Exercise* on page 454 looks at a situation in which an employee does not want to be a team member.

The challenge of creating team players will be greatest when the national culture is highly individualistic and the teams are being introduced into an established organization that has historically valued individual achievement.[17] These organizations prospered by hiring and rewarding corporate stars, and they bred a competitive work climate that encouraged individual achievement and recognition. In this context, employees can experience culture shock caused by a sudden shift in the focus to teamwork.[18]

Team players just don't appear. There is a lot of hard work required to get team members to gel. That is why baseball players, like the Toronto Blue Jays, go to spring training every year—to prepare themselves as a team for the upcoming baseball season.

In contrast, the challenge for management is less demanding when teams are introduced in places in which employees have strong collectivist values—such as Japan or Mexico. The challenge of forming teams will also be less in new organizations that use teams as their initial form of structuring work. For instance, Saturn Corporation (an American organization owned by General Motors) was designed around teams from its start. Everyone at Saturn was hired on the understanding that they would be working in teams, and the ability to be a good team player was a hiring prerequisite. *Managing Workforce Diversity—The Challenge of Managing Diverse Teams* on page 457 asks you to consider how to help team members from different cultures work together more effectively.

What Roles Do Team Members Play?

A **role** refers to a set of expected behaviour patterns attributed to someone who occupies a given position in a social unit. In a group, individuals are expected to perform certain roles because of their position in the group. **Task-oriented roles** tend to be oriented toward task accomplishment, while **maintenance roles** are oriented toward maintaining group member satisfaction and relationship.[19] Think about groups that you have been in and the roles that you played. Were you continually trying to keep the group focused on getting its work done? If so, you were filling a task accomplishment role. Or were you more concerned that group members had the opportunity to offer ideas and that they were satisfied with the experience? If so, you were performing a maintenance role to preserve the harmony of the group. Both roles are important to the ability of a group to function effectively and efficiently, and some group members are flexible and play both roles. One study found that the most effective teams had a leader who performed both the task-oriented and the maintenance roles.[20] In some groups, unfortunately, there are people who take on neither role, and participate very little in the team functions. It is not helpful if there are too many people who do not take on a role.

role
A set of expected behaviour patterns attributed to someone who occupies a given position in a social unit.

task-oriented roles
Roles performed by group members to ensure that the tasks of the group are accomplished.

maintenance roles
Roles performed by group members to maintain good relations within the group.

Q&A 14.4

Shaping Team Behaviour

There are several options available for managers who are trying to turn individuals into team players. The three most popular ways include proper selection, employee training, and rewarding the appropriate team behaviours. Let's look at each of these.

Selection

Some individuals already possess the interpersonal skills to be effective team players. When hiring team members, in addition to checking on the technical skills required to successfully perform the job, the organization should ensure that applicants can fulfill team roles.

As we have mentioned before, some applicants have been socialized around individual contributions and, consequently, lack team skills, as might some current employees whose jobs are being restructured into teams. When faced with such candidates, a manager can do several things. First, and most obvious, if a candidate's team skills are woefully lacking, don't hire that candidate. If successful performance requires interaction, rejecting such a candidate is appropriate. On the other hand, a good candidate who has only some basic team skills can be hired on a probationary basis and required to undergo training to shape him or her into a team player. If the skills are not learned or practised, the individual may have to be let go for failing to achieve the skills necessary for performing successfully on the job.

Training

Performing well in a team involves a set of behaviours. As we discussed in the preceding chapter, new behaviours can be learned. Even a large portion of people who were raised on the importance of individual accomplishment can be trained to become team players. Training specialists can conduct workshops that allow employees to experience the satisfaction that teamwork can provide. The workshops usually cover such topics as team problem solving, communications, negotiations, conflict resolution, and coaching skills. It's also not unusual for these employees to be exposed to the five stages of team development that we discussed earlier.[21] At Verizon, for example, trainers focus on how a team goes through various stages before it gels. Employees are reminded of the importance of patience, because teams take longer to do some things—such as make decisions—than do employees acting alone.[22]

Rewards

The organization's reward system needs to encourage cooperative efforts rather than competitive ones. For instance, Lockheed Martin Aeronautics Company has organized its 20 000-plus employees into teams. Rewards are structured to return a percentage of the increase in the bottom line to the team members on the basis of achievements of the team's performance goals.

Promotions, pay raises, and other forms of recognition should be given to employees who are effective collaborative team members. This does not mean that individual contribution is ignored, but rather that it is balanced with selfless contributions to the team. Examples of behaviours that should be rewarded include training new colleagues, sharing information with teammates, helping resolve team conflicts, and mastering new skills in which the team is deficient.[23] Finally, managers cannot forget the inherent rewards that employees can receive from teamwork. Work teams provide camaraderie. It's exciting and satisfying to be an integral part of a successful team. The opportunity to engage in personal development and to help teammates grow can be a very satisfying and rewarding experience for employees.[24]

Turning Groups into Effective Teams

▶ ▶ ▶ Wayne Gretzky had many excellent players to choose from for the team that would play in the 2006 Winter Olympics.[25] One strategy for choosing players might have been to pick the absolute best players for each position, examining their records during the previous season. Alternatively, it might have made sense to pick very good players who also know how to work well with other team members. Gretzky chose the latter strategy, picking 20 players who had been on either the 2004 World Cup of Hockey team or the 2002 Winter Olympic team.

Hockey Canada president Bob Nicholson explained the thinking behind Gretzky's strategy: "We've always stated that we want to have players with experience at the Olympics, world championships and players who have won a Cup. You want players around [the Olympics] who have won."

Clearly, Gretzky felt that a team, particularly the Olympic team, was more than just the sum of its parts. Gretzky's choice of team members did not pay off, however. Unlike Team Canada's performance in the 2004 World Cup, going undefeated in the six playoff games and never once trailing in a game, Canada was eliminated in the quarter-finals of the 2006 Winter Olympics, and played three scoreless games on the way to Olympic defeat. Hockey Canada president Bob Nicholson summarized what went wrong: "Seventeen power plays [in the three shutout losses] and zero goals, who would have ever expected that? It wasn't one player, it was a group of individuals that couldn't put the puck in the net."

Think About It

How can managers create effective teams?

Teams are not automatic productivity enhancers. They can also be disappointments. So the challenge is to create effective teams. Effective teams have a number of characteristics, which we review below. In addition, teams need to build group cohesiveness, manage group conflict, and prevent social loafing to perform well. (For more insights into creating effective teams, see *Developing Your Interpersonal Skills—Creating Effective Teams* on pages 456–457, at the end of the chapter.)

3. How can groups become effective teams?

PRISM 9

Characteristics of Effective Teams

How do you build an effective team? Have you ever done so?

Research on teams provides insights into the characteristics associated with effective teams.[26] Let's look more closely at these characteristics, which are shown in Exhibit 14-4.

Clear Goals

High-performance teams have a clear understanding of the goals to be achieved. Members are committed to the team's goals; they know what they are expected to accomplish and understand how they will work together to achieve these goals.

Relevant Skills

Effective teams are composed of competent individuals who have the necessary technical and interpersonal skills to achieve the desired goals while working well together. This last point is important since not everyone who is technically competent has the interpersonal skills to work well as a team member.

Exhibit 14-4

Characteristics of Effective Teams

Mutual Trust

Effective teams are characterized by high mutual trust among members. That is, members believe in each other's ability, character, and integrity. But as you probably know from personal relationships, trust is fragile. For team members to have mutual trust, they must believe that the team is capable of getting the task done and that "the team will not harm the individual or his or her interests."[27] Maintaining this trust requires careful attention by managers.

Unified Commitment

Unified commitment is characterized by dedication to the team's goals and a willingness to expend extraordinary amounts of energy to achieve them. Members of an effective team exhibit intense loyalty and dedication to the team and are willing to do whatever it takes to help their team succeed.

Good Communication

Not surprisingly, effective teams are characterized by good communication. Members convey messages, verbally and nonverbally, to each other in ways that are readily and clearly understood. Also, feedback helps to guide team members and to correct misunderstandings. Like a couple who has been together for many years, members on high-performing teams are able to quickly and efficiently share ideas and feelings.

Negotiating Skills

Effective teams are continually making adjustments as to who does what. This flexibility requires team members to possess negotiating skills. Since problems and relationships are regularly changing in teams, members need to be able to confront and reconcile differences.

Appropriate Leadership

Effective leaders can motivate a team to follow them through the most difficult situations. How? By clarifying goals, demonstrating that change is possible by overcoming inertia, increasing the self-confidence of team members, and helping members to more fully realize their potential. Increasingly, effective team leaders act as coaches and facilitators. They help guide and support the team, but don't control it. (See also *Self-Assessment—How Good Am I at Building and Leading a Team?* on pages 452–453, at the end of the chapter.)

Internal and External Support

The final condition necessary for an effective team is a supportive climate. Internally, the team should have a sound infrastructure, which means having proper training, a clear and reasonable measurement system that team members can use to evaluate their overall performance, an incentive program that recognizes and rewards team activities, and a supportive human resource system. The right infrastructure should support members and reinforce behaviours that lead to high levels of performance. Externally, managers should provide the team with the resources needed to get the job done.

Building Group Cohesiveness

Q&A 14.5

Intuitively, it makes sense that groups in which there is a lot of internal disagreement and lack of cooperation are less effective in completing their tasks than are groups in which members generally agree, cooperate, and like each other. Research in this area has focused on **group cohesiveness**, or the degree to which members are attracted to each other and share the group's goals. Cohesiveness is important because it has been found to be related to a group's productivity.[28]

group cohesiveness
The degree to which group members are attracted to each other and share the group's goals.

Research has generally shown that highly cohesive groups are more effective than are less cohesive ones.[29] However, the relationship between cohesiveness and effectiveness is more complex. A key moderating variable is the degree to which the group's attitude lines up with its goals or with the goals of the organization.[30] The more cohesive a group is, the more its members will follow its goals. If the goals are desirable (for instance, high output, quality work, cooperation with individuals outside the group), a cohesive group is more productive than a less cohesive group. But if cohesiveness is high and attitudes are unfavourable, productivity decreases. If cohesiveness is low and goals are supported, productivity increases,

Exhibit 14-5

The Relationship between Cohesiveness and Productivity

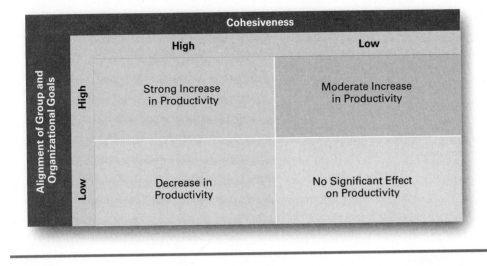

conflict
Perceived differences that result in some form of interference or opposition.

traditional view of conflict
The view that all conflict is bad and must be avoided.

human relations view of conflict
The view that conflict is a natural and inevitable outcome in any group and has potential to be a positive force in contributing to a group's performance.

interactionist view of conflict
The view that some conflict is absolutely necessary for a group to perform effectively.

but not as much as when both cohesiveness and support are high. When cohesiveness is low and goals are not supported, cohesiveness has no significant effect on productivity. These conclusions are illustrated in Exhibit 14-5.

Q&A 14.6

Most studies of cohesiveness focus on *socio-emotional cohesiveness:* the "sense of togetherness that develops when individuals derive emotional satisfaction from group participation."[31] There is also *instrumental cohesiveness:* the "sense of togetherness that develops when group members are mutually dependent on one another because they believe they could not achieve the group's goal by acting separately." Teams need to achieve a balance of these two types of cohesiveness to function well. *Tips for Managers—Increasing Group Cohesiveness* indicates how to increase both socio-emotional and instrumental cohesiveness.

Managing Group Conflict

Another important group process is how a group manages conflict. As a group performs its assigned tasks, disagreements inevitably arise. When we use the term **conflict**, we are referring to *perceived* differences that result in some form of interference or opposition. Whether the differences are real or not is irrelevant. If people in a group perceive that differences exist, then there is conflict. Our definition encompasses the full range of conflict—from subtle or indirect acts to overt acts such as strikes, riots, or wars.

Over the years, three different views have evolved regarding conflict.[32] One view argues that conflict must be avoided—that it indicates a problem within the group. We call this the **traditional view of conflict**. A second view, the **human relations view of conflict**, argues that conflict is a natural and inevitable outcome in any group and need not be negative but, rather, has potential to be a positive force in contributing to a group's performance. The third and most recent perspective proposes that not only can conflict be a positive force in a group but that some conflict is *absolutely necessary* for a group to perform effectively. This third approach is called the **interactionist view of conflict**.

TIPS FOR MANAGERS

Increasing Group Cohesiveness

Increasing socio-emotional cohesiveness

- Keep the group relatively **small**.
- Strive for a **favourable public image** to increase the status and prestige of belonging.
- Encourage **interaction** and **cooperation**.
- Emphasize members' **common characteristics** and interests.
- **Point out environmental threats** (for example, competitors' achievements) to rally the group.

Increasing instrumental cohesiveness

- Regularly update and **clarify the group's goal(s)**.
- Give every group member a **vital "piece of the action."**
- Channel each group member's special talents toward the **common goal(s)**.
- **Recognize** and equitably reinforce **every member's contributions**.
- Frequently remind group members **they need each other** to get the job done.

Source: R. Kreitner and A. Kinicki, *Organizational Behavior*, 6th ed. (New York: Irwin, 2004), p. 460. Reprinted by permission of McGraw-Hill Education.

Exhibit 14-6

Conflict and Group Performance

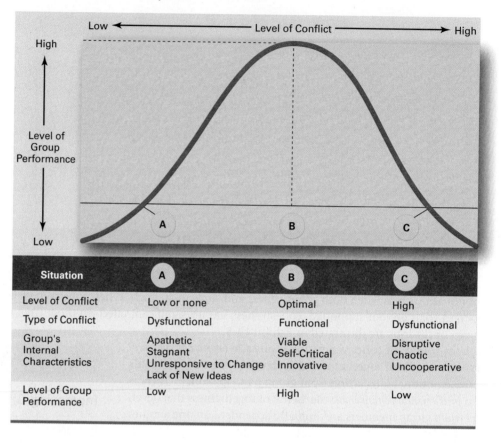

Situation	A	B	C
Level of Conflict	Low or none	Optimal	High
Type of Conflict	Dysfunctional	Functional	Dysfunctional
Group's Internal Characteristics	Apathetic Stagnant Unresponsive to Change Lack of New Ideas	Viable Self-Critical Innovative	Disruptive Chaotic Uncooperative
Level of Group Performance	Low	High	Low

functional conflicts
Conflicts that support the goals of the work group and improve its performance.

dysfunctional conflicts
Conflicts that are destructive and prevent a group from achieving its goals.

task conflict
Conflict over content and goals of the work.

relationship conflict
Conflict based on interpersonal relationships.

process conflict
Conflict over how the work gets done.

The interactionist view does not suggest that all conflicts are good. Some conflicts are seen as supporting the goals of the work group and improving its performance; these are **functional conflicts** of a constructive nature. Other conflicts are destructive and prevent a group from achieving its goals. These are **dysfunctional conflicts**. Exhibit 14-6 illustrates the challenge facing managers. They want to create an environment in which there is healthy conflict that will help the group reach a high level of performance.

What differentiates functional from dysfunctional conflict? The evidence indicates that you need to look at the *type* of conflict.[33] Three types have been identified: task, relationship, and process.

Task conflict relates to the content and goals of the work. **Relationship conflict** is based on interpersonal relationships. **Process conflict** relates to how the work gets done. Studies demonstrate that relationship conflicts are almost always dysfunctional. Why? It appears that the friction and interpersonal hostilities inherent in relationship conflicts increase personality clashes and decrease mutual understanding, thereby hindering the completion of organizational tasks. On the other hand, low levels of process conflict and low to moderate levels of task conflict are functional. For process conflict to be productive, it must be kept to a minimum. Intense arguments about who should do what become dysfunctional when they create uncertainty about task roles, increase the time taken to complete tasks, and lead to members working at cross-purposes. A low to moderate level of task conflict consistently demonstrates a positive effect on group performance because it stimulates discussions of ideas that help groups be more innovative.[34] Because we have yet to devise a sophisticated measuring instrument for assessing whether a given task, relationship, or process conflict level is optimal, too high, or too low, the manager must make intelligent judgments.

Q&A 14.7

When group conflict becomes dysfunctional, what can managers do? They can select from five conflict-resolution options: avoiding, accommodating, forcing, compromising, and collaborating.[35] (See Exhibit 14-7 for a description of each of these techniques.) Keep in mind that no one option is ideal for every situation. Which approach to use depends upon the manager's desire to be more or less cooperative and more or less assertive.

Q&A 14.8

Preventing Social Loafing

One of the more important findings related to group size is **social loafing**, which is the tendency for individuals to expend less effort when working with others than when working individually.[36] Social loafing is much more likely to happen in larger groups. The finding directly challenges the logic that the group's productivity should at least equal the sum of the productivity of each group member. What causes social loafing? It may be caused by a belief that others in the group are not doing their fair share. If you see others as lazy or inept, you can reestablish equity by reducing your effort. Another explanation is the dispersion of responsibility. Because the results of the group cannot be attributed to any one person, the relationship between an individual's input and the group's output is clouded. In such situations, individuals may be tempted to become "free riders" and coast on the group's efforts. In other words, there will be a reduction in efficiency when individuals think that their contribution cannot be measured.

The implications of social loafing are significant for managers. When managers use collective work situations to enhance morale and teamwork, they must also have a way to identify individual efforts. If this is not done, they must weigh the potential losses in

social loafing
The tendency of individuals to expend less effort when working collectively than when working individually.

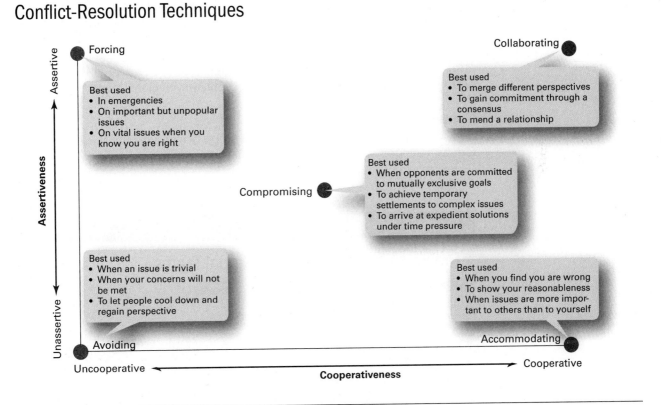

Exhibit 14-7

Conflict-Resolution Techniques

Forcing
Best used
• In emergencies
• On important but unpopular issues
• On vital issues when you know you are right

Collaborating
Best used
• To merge different perspectives
• To gain commitment through a consensus
• To mend a relationship

Compromising
Best used
• When opponents are committed to mutually exclusive goals
• To achieve temporary settlements to complex issues
• To arrive at expedient solutions under time pressure

Avoiding
Best used
• When an issue is trivial
• When your concerns will not be met
• To let people cool down and regain perspective

Accommodating
Best used
• When you find you are wrong
• To show your reasonableness
• When issues are more important to others than to yourself

Assertiveness (Assertive ↑ / Unassertive ↓)
Cooperativeness (Uncooperative ← / Cooperative →)

Sources: Adapted from K. W. Thomas, "Conflict and Negotiation Processes in Organizations," in *Handbook of Industrial and Organizational Psychology*, vol. 3, 2nd ed., ed. M. D. Dunnette and L. M. Hough (Palo Alto, CA: Consulting Psychologists Press, 1992), p. 668; and C. K. W. De Dreu, A. Evers, B. Beersma, E. S. Kluwer, and A. Nauta, "A Theory-Based Measure of Conflict Management Strategies in the Workplace," *Journal of Organizational Behavior* 22, no. 6 (September 2001), pp. 645–668. With permission.

productivity from using groups against any possible gains in employee satisfaction.[37] However, this conclusion does have a Western bias. It's consistent with individualistic cultures, such as Canada and the United States, that are dominated by self-interest. It's not consistent with collectivist societies, in which individuals are motivated by in-group goals. For instance, in studies comparing employees from the United States with employees from the People's Republic of China and Israel (both collectivist societies), the Chinese and Israelis showed no propensity to engage in social loafing. In fact, they actually performed better in a group than when working alone.[38]

Current Challenges in Managing Teams

4. What are some of the current challenges in managing teams?

Managers face some challenges in managing teams, especially global teams. They also have to determine when it is best to use a team.

Managing Global Teams

Two characteristics of today's organizations are obvious: (1) They are global, and (2) work is increasingly done by groups or teams. This means that any manager is likely, at some point in time, to have to manage a global team. What do we know about managing global teams? We know that there are both drawbacks and benefits in using global teams (see Exhibit 14-8). Let's look at some of the issues associated with managing global teams.

Group Member Resources in Global Teams

In global organizations, understanding the relationship between group performance and group member resources is more challenging because of the unique cultural characteristics represented by members of a global team. In addition to recognizing team members' abilities, skills, knowledge, and personality, managers need to be familiar with and clearly understand the cultural characteristics of the groups and the group members they manage.[39] For instance, is the global team from a culture in which uncertainty avoidance is high? If so, members will not be comfortable dealing with unpredictable and ambiguous tasks. Also, as managers work with global teams, they need to be aware of the potential for stereotyping, which has been shown to be a problem with global teams.[40]

Group Structure

Some of the structural areas where we see differences in managing global teams include conformity, status, social loafing, and cohesiveness.

Exhibit 14-8

Drawbacks and Benefits of Global Teams

Drawbacks	Benefits
• Dislike team members	• Greater diversity of ideas
• Mistrust team members	• Limited groupthink
• Stereotyping	• Increased attention on understanding others' ideas, perspectives, etc.
• Communication problems	
• Stress and tension	

Source: Based on N. Adler, *International Dimensions in Organizational Behavior*, 4th ed. (Cincinnati, OH: SouthWestern, 2002), pp. 141–147.

Conformity

Research suggests that Solomon Asch's findings on conformity—that group pressures for conformity can have an effect on an individual member's judgment and attitudes—are culture-bound.[41] For instance, as might be expected, conformity to social norms tends to be higher in collectivist cultures than in individualistic cultures. Despite this, however, groupthink tends to be less of a problem in global teams because members are less likely to feel pressured to conform to the ideas, conclusions, and decisions of the group.[42]

Status

The importance of status varies between cultures. The French, for example, are extremely status conscious. Also, countries differ on the criteria that confer status. For instance, status for Latin Americans and Asians tends to come from family position and formal roles held in organizations. In contrast, although status is important in countries like Canada and Australia, it tends to be less "in your face." And it tends to be given based on accomplishments rather than on titles and family history. Managers should be sure to understand who and what holds status when interacting with people from a culture different from their own. A Canadian manager who does not understand that office size is not a measure of a Japanese executive's position or who fails to grasp the importance the British place on family genealogy and social class is likely to unintentionally offend others and lessen his or her interpersonal effectiveness.

Social Loafing

As we noted earlier, employees from the People's Republic of China and Israel (both collectivist societies) were less likely to engage in social loafing than were employees from the United States.[43]

Cohesiveness

Cohesiveness is another group structural element where managers may face special challenges. In a cohesive group, members are unified and "act as one." There is a great deal of camaraderie and group identity is high. In global teams, however, cohesiveness is often more difficult to achieve because of higher levels of mistrust, miscommunication, and stress.[44]

Group Processes

The processes global teams use to do their work can be particularly challenging for managers. For one thing, communication problems often arise because not all team members may be fluent in the team's working language. This can lead to inaccuracies, misunderstandings, and inefficiencies.[45] However, research has also shown that a multicultural global team is better able to make use of the diversity of ideas represented if a wide range of information is used.[46]

Managing conflict in global teams, especially when those teams are virtual teams, is not easy. Conflict in multicultural teams can interfere with how information is used by the team. However, research shows that in collectivistic cultures, a collaborative conflict-management style can be most effective.[47]

The Manager's Role

Despite the challenges associated with managing global teams, there are things managers can do to provide the group with an environment in which efficiency and effectiveness are enhanced.[48] First, because communication skills are vital, managers should focus on developing those skills. Also, as we have said earlier, managers must consider cultural differences when deciding what type of global team to use. For instance, evidence suggests that self-managed teams have not fared well in Mexico, largely due to that culture's low tolerance of ambiguity and uncertainty and employees' strong respect for hierarchical authority.[49] Finally, it is vital that managers be sensitive to the unique differences of each member of the global team. But it is also important that team members be sensitive to each other as well.

Beware! Teams Are Not Always the Answer

Do you ever find you are tired of working in a team?

Despite considerable success in the use of teams, they are not necessarily appropriate in all situations. Teamwork takes more time and often more resources than individual work; also, it has increased communication demands, and the number of conflicts to be managed and meetings to be run. In the rush to enjoy the benefits of teams, some managers have introduced them into situations where the work is better done by individuals. A 2003 study by Statistics Canada found that the introduction of teamwork lowered turnover in the service industries, for both high- and low-skilled employees. However, manufacturing companies experienced higher job turnover if they had introduced teamwork and formal teamwork training, compared with not doing so (15.8 percent vs. 10.7 percent).[50]

How do you know if the work of your group would be better done in teams? Three questions can help determine whether a team fits the situation:[51]

- *Can the work be done better by more than one person?* Simple tasks that don't require diverse input are probably better left to individuals.

- *Does the work create a common purpose or set of goals for the people in the group that is more than the sum of individual goals?* For instance, many new-car dealer service departments have introduced teams that link customer-service personnel, mechanics, parts specialists, and sales representatives. Such teams can better manage collective responsibility for ensuring that customer needs are properly met.

- *Are the members of the group interdependent?* Teams make sense where there is interdependence between tasks; where the success of the whole depends on the success of each one; *and* where the success of each one depends on the success of the others. Soccer, for instance, is an obvious *team* sport because of the interdependence of the players. Swim teams, by contrast, are not really teams, but groups of individuals whose total performance is merely the sum of the individual performances.

Researchers have outlined the conditions under which organizations would find teams more useful: "when work processes cut across functional lines; when speed is important (and complex relationships are involved); when the organization mirrors a complex, differentiated, and rapidly changing market environment; when innovation and learning have priority; when the tasks that have to be done require online integration of highly interdependent performers."[52]

SUMMARY AND IMPLICATIONS

1. What are the stages of team development?   The five stages are forming, storming, norming, performing, and adjourning. These stages describe how teams evolve over time, although teams do not necessarily go through these stages in a completely linear fashion. Some researchers argue that effectiveness of work teams increases at advanced stages, but it's not that simple. That assumption may be generally true, but what makes a team effective is a complex issue. It's better to think of this model as a general framework of how teams develop.

▶ ▶ ▶ When Team Canada started practising for the 2006 Winter Olympics, individual hockey players knew how to play the game, but team members were supposed to learn how to work together, even though they were usually opponents.

2. How do individuals become team players?   Many individuals resist being team players. To improve the odds that a team will function well, managers can select the right people to be on a team, train individuals in how to work on teams, and make sure that rewards encourage individuals to be cooperative team players.

▶ ▶ ▶ Wayne Gretzky put together a set of players for the 2006 Winter Olympics who had international playing experience, hoping this would be enough to create a winning team.

3. How can groups become effective teams? The characteristics associated with effective teams include clear goals, relevant skills, mutual trust, unified commitment, good communication, negotiating skills, appropriate leadership, and internal and external support. Teams also need to build group cohesiveness, manage group conflict, and prevent social loafing to be effective.

▶ ▶ ▶ For Team Canada players, perhaps the most important factors in working toward winning the 2004 World Cup of Hockey were learning to trust each other, communicating well, and having the right leadership. The same team chemistry was not apparent in the 2006 Winter Olympics.

4. What are some of the current challenges in managing teams? Managers face a variety of challenges in managing teams, especially global teams. The cultural differences of the team members may lead to more conflict, at least initially. As well, there may be an increase in communication difficulties. Another challenge that managers face is to consider whether a team is really necessary to get the work done.

Management @ Work

READING FOR COMPREHENSION

1. Contrast (1) self-managed and cross-functional teams and (2) virtual and face-to-face teams.

2. How do virtual teams enhance productivity?

3. What problems might surface in teams during each of the five stages of team development?

4. Describe three ways managers can try to encourage individuals to become team players.

5. Why do you believe mutual trust is important to developing high-performing work teams?

6. Why might a manager want to stimulate conflict in a group or team? How could conflict be stimulated?

LINKING CONCEPTS TO PRACTICE

1. How do you explain the rapidly increasing popularity of work teams in countries such as Canada and the United States, whose national cultures place a high value on individualism?

2. Think of a team to which you belong (or have belonged). Trace its development through the five stages of team development shown in Exhibit 14-3 on page 439. How closely did its development parallel the team development model? How might the team development model have been used to improve the team's effectiveness?

3. "All work teams are work groups, but not all work groups are work teams." Do you agree or disagree with the statement? Discuss.

4. Would you prefer to work alone or as part of a team? Why? Support your response with data from your self-assessments.

5. Describe a situation in which individuals, acting independently, outperform teams in an organization.

SELF-ASSESSMENT

How Good Am I at Building and Leading a Team?

Use the following rating scale to respond to the 18 statements on building and leading an effective team:[53]

1 = Strongly Disagree	3 = Slightly Disagree	5 = Agree
2 = Disagree	4 = Slightly Agree	6 = Strongly Agree

1. I am knowledgeable about the different stages of development that teams can go through in their life cycles. 1 2 3 4 5 6

2. When a team forms, I make certain that all team members are introduced to one another at the outset. 1 2 3 4 5 6

3. When the team first comes together, I provide directions, answer team members' questions, and clarify goals, expectations, and procedures. 1 2 3 4 5 6

4. I help team members establish a foundation of trust among one another and between themselves and me. 1 2 3 4 5 6

5. I ensure that standards of excellence, not mediocrity or mere acceptability, characterize the team's work. 1 2 3 4 5 6

6. I provide a great deal of feedback to team members regarding their performance. 1 2 3 4 5 6

7. I encourage team members to balance individual autonomy with interdependence among other team members. 1 2 3 4 5 6

8. I help team members become at least as committed to the success of the team as to their own personal success. 1 2 3 4 5 6

9. I help members learn to play roles that assist the team in accomplishing its tasks as well as building strong interpersonal relationships.   1 2 3 4 5 6

10. I articulate a clear, exciting, passionate vision of what the team can achieve.   1 2 3 4 5 6

11. I help team members become committed to the team vision.   1 2 3 4 5 6

12. I encourage a win-win philosophy in the team; that is, when one member wins, every member wins.   1 2 3 4 5 6

13. I help the team avoid groupthink or making the group's survival more important than accomplishing its goal.   1 2 3 4 5 6

14. I use formal process management procedures to help the group become faster, more efficient, and more productive, and to prevent errors.   1 2 3 4 5 6

15. I encourage team members to represent the team's vision, goals, and accomplishments to outsiders.   1 2 3 4 5 6

16. I diagnose and capitalize on the team's core competence.   1 2 3 4 5 6

17. I encourage the team to achieve dramatic breakthrough innovations, as well as small continuous improvements.   1 2 3 4 5 6

18. I help the team work toward preventing mistakes, not just correcting them after the fact.   1 2 3 4 5 6

Scoring Key

To calculate your total score, add up your scores on the 18 individual items.

Analysis and Interpretation

The authors of this instrument propose that it assesses team development behaviours in 5 areas: diagnosing team development (statements 1, 16); managing the forming stage (2–4); managing the norming stage (6–9, 13); managing the storming stage (10–12, 14, 15); and managing the performing stage (5, 17, 18). Your score will range between 18 and 108, with higher scores indicating greater ability at building and leading an effective team.

Based on a norm group of 500 business students, the following can help estimate where you are in relation to others.

Total score of 95 or more = You are in the top quartile
72–94 = You are in the second quartile
60–71 = You are in the third quartile
Less than 60 = You are in the bottom quartile

More Self-Assessments mymanagementlab

To learn more about your skills, abilities, and interests, go to the MyManagementLab website and take the following self-assessments:

- II.A.2.—How Good Are My Listening Skills?
- II.B.4.—Do Others See Me as Trustworthy?

MANAGEMENT FOR YOU TODAY

Dilemma

One of your instructors has just informed your class that you will be working on a new major assignment worth 30 percent of your course mark. The assignment is to be done in teams of 7. Realistically, you will need to function as a virtual team, as it turns out that each of you has a different work and class schedule, so that there is almost no time when more than 3 people could meet face-to-face. As you know, virtual teams have benefits, but they can also have problems. How will you build group cohesiveness in this team? What norms might help the team function, and how should the norms be decided? What will you do to prevent social loafing?

Becoming a Manager

- Use any opportunities that come up to work in a group. Note things such as stages of team development, roles, norms, social loafing, and so forth.

- When confronted with conflicts, pay attention to how you manage or resolve them.

- In group projects, try different techniques for improving the group's creativity.

- When you see a successful team, try to assess what makes it successful.

WORKING TOGETHER: TEAM-BASED EXERCISE

Puzzle Building

What happens when a group is presented with a task that must be completed within a certain time frame? Does the group exhibit characteristics of the stages of team development? Your instructor will divide the class into groups and give you instructions about building a puzzle or watching others do so.

Note: Instructors can find the instructions for this exercise in the Instructor's Resource Manual.

ETHICS IN ACTION

Ethical Dilemma Exercise: Does Everyone Have to Be a Team Player?

You are a production manager at a Saturn plant. One of your newest employees in supply chain management is Barbara Petersen, who has a bachelor's degree in engineering and a master's degree in business.

You have recently been chosen to head up a cross-functional team to look at ways to reduce inventory costs. This team would essentially be a permanent task force. You have decided to have team members come from supplier relations, cost accounting, transportation, and production systems. You have also decided to include Barbara on the team. While she has been at Saturn only for four months, you have been impressed with her energy, smarts, and industriousness. You think this would be an excellent assignment for her to increase her visibility in the company and expand her understanding of the company's inventory system.

When you gave Barbara the good news, you were surprised by her response. "I'm not a team player. I didn't join clubs in high school. I was on the track team and I did well,

but track is an individual sport. We were a team only in the sense that we rode together in the same bus to away meets. In university, I avoided the whole sorority thing. Some people may call me a loner. I don't think that's true. I can work well with others, but I hate meetings and committees. To me, they waste so much time. And when you work with a group, you've got all these different personalities that you have to adjust for. I'm an independent operator. Give me a job and I'll get it done. I work harder than anyone I know—and I give my employer 150 percent. But I don't want my performance to be dependent on the other people in my group. They may not work as hard as I will. Someone is sure to shirk some of their responsibilities. I just don't want to be a team player."

What do you do? Should you give Barbara the option of joining the inventory cost reduction team? Is it unethical for you to require someone like Barbara to do his or her job as part of a team?

Thinking Critically About Ethics

You have been hired as a summer intern in the events planning department of a public relations firm in Calgary. After working there about a month, you conclude that the attitude in the office is "anything goes." Employees know that supervisors will not discipline them for ignoring company rules. For example, employees have to turn in expense reports, but the process is a joke; nobody submits receipts to verify reimbursement, and nothing is ever said. In fact, when you tried to turn in your receipts with your expense report, you were told, "Nobody else turns in receipts and you don't really need to, either."

You know that no expense cheque has ever been denied because of failure to turn in a receipt, even though the employee handbook says that receipts are required. Also, your co-workers use company phones for personal long-distance calls even though that is prohibited by the employee handbook. And one permanent employee told you to "help yourself" to any paper, pens, or pencils you might need here or at home. What are the norms of this group? Suppose that you were the supervisor in this area. How would you go about changing the norms?

Samsung Electronics

Samsung Electronics is now the world's largest and most profitable consumer electronics company.[54] In 2006, it ranked higher than Sony as the world's most valuable consumer electronics brand, according to the most recent valuable global brands survey done by the Interbrand Consulting Group. Its clever product designs have won over consumers and won numerous awards.

Samsung Group was founded as a trucking company in the 1930s and in the 1960s became one of several *chaebol* (large conglomerates) "shaped by the Korean government and protected from foreign competition by import duties and other government-sponsored regulations." The electronics division, Samsung Electronics, is by far the largest and most global of the Samsung businesses.

At the company's design centre just a few blocks away from headquarters, in Seoul, designers work in small teams with three to five members coming from various specialty areas and levels of seniority. Even though Korean culture has loosened up somewhat, respect for elders and a reluctance to speak out of turn are still the norm. But here at Samsung's design centre, there is no dress code and team members work as equals. Everyone—even the younger staffers, who often have their hair dyed green or pink—is encouraged to speak up and challenge their superiors.

Although Samsung Electronics is sitting on top now, Kim Byung Cheol, a senior executive, is worried about his company's future. Why? Because Samsung "still has not mastered one crucial factor: originality." Much of Samsung's success in electronics can be traced to its ability to mimic and enhance others' inventions, but it has never been the design innovator. Kim says, "We are at a pivotal moment for the company. If we don't become an innovator, we could end up like one of those Japanese companies, mired in difficulties." What can Kim and his managers do to encourage innovation and originality with the design centre teams?

Team Ferrari

Imagine working for an organization that employs more than 2000 individuals with each one having the identical focus.[55] Imagine, too, that company management in this organization wants you to work only so hard but still be the best at what you do. If you are employed by Ferrari, these elements are not hard to imagine.

Luca Cordero, president and managing director of Ferrari, believes that his employees truly make a difference in producing one of the world's greatest sports cars. Cordero recognizes that to be the best, he needs employees who understand how to work together and how to achieve common goals. That is because at Ferrari there are no assembly lines. Rather, teams of employees combine their efforts to produce an outstanding automobile noted for its quality in the automobile industry. You simply will not find traditional assembly lines in the Ferrari factory, nor will you find production quotas. Auto assembly time is not measured in seconds—rather, team tasks often last over 90 minutes for each portion of a car. Then the team proudly takes its finished work on to the next team so its work can begin. Management of the company wants no more than 4000 Ferraris produced in each year, even though the company could sell considerably more.

Employees at Ferrari truly enjoy being part of a team. They cite the fact that working in a common direction is one of the most satisfying elements in their job. They also appreciate what management does for them. They are offered a state-of-the-art fitness centre, annual physicals at the company's on-site clinic, an employee cafeteria, and home-based training for employees to learn English. They feel as if Cordero and his team treat them as associates, not just as cogs in the Ferrari wheel. As one Ferrari employee stated "For many of us, working for Ferrari is like working in the Vatican."

Is the team concept at Ferrari working? By all accounts it is. The company recently celebrated its first $1 billion year of sales, which resulted in over $60 million in profits. Profits over the past several years continue to rise, and more importantly for Ferrari's management, there is more than a two-year waiting list for most Ferrari models.

Questions

1. Why do you believe the team concept at Ferrari works so well? Cite specific examples to support your position.

2. Do you believe such a system could be replicated in other automotive manufacturers? If so, in what kind of organizations? If not, why not?

3. Using Exhibit 14-4 on page 443, describe each of the characteristics of effective teams as they relate to this case. Use examples when appropriate. If a characteristic was not specifically cited in the case, describe how it may have been part of this situation.

Creating Effective Teams

About the Skill

A team is different from a group because its members are committed to a common purpose, have a set of specific performance goals, and hold themselves mutually accountable for the team's results. Teams can produce outputs that are greater than the sum of the individual contributions of its members. The primary force that makes a work group an effective team—that is, a real high-performing team—is its emphasis on performance.

Steps in Developing the Skill

Managers and team leaders have a significant impact on a team's effectiveness. You can be more successful at creating an effective team if you use the following nine suggestions:[56]

1. **Establish a common purpose.** An effective team needs a common purpose to which all members aspire. This purpose is a vision. It's broader than any specific goals. This common purpose provides direction, momentum, and commitment for team members.

2. **Assess team strengths and weaknesses.** Team members will have different strengths and weaknesses. Knowing these strengths and weaknesses can help the team leader build upon the strengths and compensate for the weaknesses.

3. **Develop specific individual goals.** Specific individual goals help lead team members to achieve higher performance. In addition, specific goals facilitate clear communication and help maintain the focus on getting results.

4. **Get agreement on a common approach for achieving goals.** Goals are the ends a team strives to attain. Defining and agreeing upon a common approach ensures that the team is unified on the means for achieving those ends.

5. **Encourage acceptance of responsibility for both individual and team performance.** Successful teams make members individually and jointly accountable for the team's purpose, goals, and approach. Members understand what they are individually responsible for and what they are jointly responsible for.

6. **Build mutual trust among members.** When there is trust, team members believe in the integrity, character, and ability of each other. When trust is lacking, members are unable to depend on each other. Teams that lack trust tend to be short-lived.

7. **Maintain an appropriate mix of team member skills and personalities.** Team members come to the team with different skills and personalities. To perform effectively, teams need three types of skills. First, teams need people with technical expertise. Next, they need people with problem-solving and decision-making skills to identify problems, generate alternatives, evaluate those alternatives, and make competent choices. Finally, teams need people with good interpersonal skills.

8. **Provide needed training and resources.** Team leaders need to make sure that their teams have both the training and the resources to accomplish their goals.

9. **Create opportunities for small achievements.** Building an effective team takes time. Team members have to learn to think and work as a team. New teams cannot be expected to hit home runs every time they come to bat, especially at the beginning. Instead, team members should be encouraged to try for small achievements at the beginning.

Practising the Skill

Read the following scenario. Write some notes about how you would handle the situation described. Be sure to refer to the nine suggestions for creating effective teams.

Scenario

You are the leader of a five-member project team that has been assigned the task of moving your engineering firm into the new booming area of high-speed rail construction. You and your team have been researching the field, identifying business opportunities, negotiating alliances with equipment vendors, and evaluating high-speed rail experts and consultants from around the world. Throughout the process, Tonya, a highly qualified and respected engineer, has challenged everything you say during team meetings and in the workplace. For example, at a meeting two weeks ago, you presented the team with a list of 10 possible high-speed rail projects that had been identified by the team and started evaluating your organization's ability to compete for them. Tonya contradicted all your comments, questioned your statistics, and was pessimistic about the possibility of contracts. After this latest display of displeasure, two other group members, Liam and Ahmed, came to you and complained that Tonya's actions were damaging the team's effectiveness. You had put Tonya on the team for her unique expertise and insight. What should you say to Tonya, and how can you help get the team on the right track to reach its full potential?

Reinforcing the Skill

The following activities will help you practise and reinforce the skills associated with creating effective teams:

1. Interview three managers at different organizations. Ask them about their experiences in managing teams. What behaviours have they found successful in creating an effective team? What about those behaviours that have not been successful in creating an effective team?

2. After completing a team project for one of your classes, assess the team's effectiveness by answering the following questions: Did everyone on the team know exactly why the team did what it did? Did team members have a significant amount of input into or influence on decisions that affected them? Did team members have open, honest, timely, and two-way communications? Did everyone on the team know and understand the team's priorities? Did the team members work together to resolve destructive conflicts? Was everyone on the team working toward accomplishing the same thing? Did team members understand the team's unwritten rules of how to behave within the group?

MANAGING WORKFORCE DIVERSITY

The Challenge of Managing Diverse Teams

Understanding and managing teams composed of people who are similar can be difficult![57] Add in diverse members and managing teams can be even more of a challenge. However, the benefits to be gained from the diverse perspectives, skills, and abilities often more than offset the extra effort. How can you meet the challenge of coordinating a diverse work team? It's important to stress four critical interpersonal behaviours: understanding, empathy, tolerance, and communication.

You know that people are not the same, yet they need to be treated fairly and equitably. And differences (cultural, physical, or other) can cause people to behave in different ways. Team leaders need to understand and accept these differences. Each and every team member should be encouraged to do the same.

Empathy is closely related to understanding. As a team leader, you should try to understand others' perspectives.

Tolerance is another important interpersonal behaviour in managing diverse teams. The fact that you understand that people are different and you empathize with them does not mean that it's any easier to accept different perspectives or behaviours. But it's important to be tolerant in dealing with diverse ages, gender, and cultural backgrounds—to allow team members the freedom to be themselves. Part of being tolerant is being open-minded about different values, attitudes, and behaviours.

Finally, open communication is important to managing a diverse team. Diversity problems may intensify if people are afraid or unwilling to openly discuss issues that concern them. Communication within a diverse team needs to be two-way. If a person wants to know whether a certain behaviour is offensive to someone else, it's best to ask. Likewise, a person who is offended by a certain behaviour of someone else should explain his or her concerns and ask that person to stop. As long as these communication exchanges are handled in a nonthreatening, low-key, and friendly manner, they generally will have a positive outcome. Finally, it helps to have an atmosphere within the team that supports and celebrates diversity.

Put yourself in the place of an Asian woman who has joined a team of Caucasian and Hispanic men. How can you be made to feel more welcome and comfortable with the team? As the Asian woman, what could you do to help the team get along well together and also help your transition to the team?

Continuing Case: Starbucks

Once people are hired or brought into organizations, managers must oversee and coordinate their work so that organizational goals can be pursued and achieved.[1] This is the leading function of management. And it's an important one! However, it also can be quite challenging! Managing people successfully means understanding their attitudes, behaviours, personalities, individual and team work efforts, motivation, conflicts, and so forth. That is not an easy thing to do. In fact, understanding how people behave and why they do the things they do is downright difficult at times. Starbucks has worked hard to create a workplace environment in which employees (partners) are *encouraged to* and *want to* put forth their best efforts. Chairman and Chief Global Strategist Howard Schultz says, "We all want the same thing as people—to be respected and valued as employees and appreciated as customers."

Starbucks—Focus on Individuals and Teamwork

Even with some 145 000 full- and part-time partners around the world, one thing that has been important to Howard Schultz from day one is the relationship he has with employees. He says, "We know that our people are the heart and soul of our success." And one way that Starbucks demonstrates the concern it has for the relationship with its partners is through an attitude survey that is administered approximately every 18 months. This survey "gives partners a voice in shaping their partner experience." It also measures "overall satisfaction and, more important, partner engagement—the degree to which partners are connected to the company." It's been an effective way for Starbucks to show that it cares about what its employees think.

The most recent partner view survey was conducted in fiscal 2005 with partners in the United States and Canada and in the international regional support centres in Europe/Middle East/Africa, Asia Pacific and Latin America, at Starbucks Coffee Trading Company in Switzerland, at Starbucks Coffee Agronomy Company in Costa Rica, and at the coffee roasting facility in Amsterdam. Well over half (64 percent) of partners responded to the survey—much higher than the number of respondents to the previous survey in 2003 in which the partner response rate was only 46 percent. Responses to

questions about partner satisfaction and partner engagement were extremely positive: 87 percent of partners said they were satisfied or very satisfied, and 73 percent said they were engaged with the company. (The numbers in 2003 were 82 percent satisfied and 73 percent engaged.) In addition, partners specifically said they "Know what is expected of them at work; believe someone at work cares about them; and work for managers who promote work/life balance." But partners identified some areas where they felt improvements were needed. These included, "Celebrate successes more; provide more effective coaching and feedback; and improve communication with partners." Starbucks' managers took specific actions to address these concerns.

Every organization needs employees who will be able to do their jobs efficiently and effectively. Starbucks states that it wants employees who are "adaptable, self-motivated, passionate, creative team players." As you can see, this "ideal" Starbucks' partner should have individual strengths and should be able to work as part of a team. In the retail store setting, especially, individuals must work together as a team to provide the experience that customers expect when they walk into a Starbucks. If that does not happen, the company's ability to pursue its mission and goals are likely to be affected.

Starbucks—Motivating Employees

A story from Howard Schultz's childhood provides some clues into what has shaped his philosophy about how to treat people. Schultz's father worked hard at various blue-collar jobs. However, when he did not work, he did not get paid. When his father broke his ankle when Howard was 7 years old, the family "had no income, no health insurance, no worker's compensation, nothing to fall back on." The image of his father "slumped on the couch with his leg in a cast unable to work or earn money left a lasting impression." Many years later, when his father died of lung cancer, "he had no savings, no pension, and more important, he had never attained fulfillment and dignity from work he found meaningful." The sad realities of the types of work environments his father endured had a powerful effect on Howard, and he vowed that if he were "ever in a position where I could make a difference, I wouldn't leave people behind." And those personal experiences

Locals and tourists alike enjoy Starbucks beverages in Shanghai, China.

have shaped the way that Starbucks cares for its partners—the relationships and commitments the company has with each and every employee.

One of the best reflections of how Starbucks treats its eligible part- and full-time partners is its Total Pay package, which includes competitive base pay, bonuses, a comprehensive health plan, paid time-off plans, stock options, a savings program, and partner perks (which includes a pound of coffee each week). Although specific benefits differ between regions and countries, all Starbucks international partners share the "Total Pay" philosophy. For instance, in Malaysia and Thailand, partners are provided extensive training opportunities to further their careers, in addition to health insurance, paid vacation, sick leave, and other benefits. In Turkey, the "Total Pay" package for Starbucks' partners includes transportation subsidies and access to a company doctor who provides free treatment.

Partner (employee) recognition is important to Starbucks. The company currently has 18 formal recognition programs in place that partners can use as tools to encourage, reward, and inspire one another. These programs range from formal company awards to informal special acknowledgments given by co-workers. One of the newest "tools"—developed in response to suggestions on the partner survey—is an on-the-spot recognition card that celebrates partner and team successes.

To assist partners who are facing particularly difficult circumstances (such as natural disaster, fire, illness), the company has a CUP (Caring Unites Partners) fund that provides financial support. After Hurricanes Katrina and Rita in 2005, more than 300 partners from the Gulf Coast region received more than $225 000 (US) in assistance from the CUP fund. This is the type of caring and compassion that Schultz vowed to provide after seeing his father not able to work and have an income because of a broken ankle. The company's president and CEO, Jim Donald, supports and reinforces this philosophy. He says, "Spending money to put people first is smart money."

In 2005, Starbucks Canada ranked sixth among the "Most Admired Corporate Cultures" in a study conducted by Waterstone Human Capital and *Canadian Business* and was named one of "Canada's Most Responsible Companies" by *Report on Business* magazine.

Starbucks—Fostering Leadership

Not surprisingly, Howard Schultz has some definite views about leading and leadership. He says, "Being a great leader means finding the balance between celebrating success and not embracing the status quo. Being a great leader also means identifying a path we need to go down and creating enough confidence in our people so they follow it and don't veer off course because it's an easier route to go." He also has this to say about leadership: "The art of leadership is making sure we don't allow the scale and size of the company to change the methodology of how we conduct ourselves. We have to be careful not to let our values be compromised by an ambition to grow."

Since 1982, Howard Schultz has led Starbucks in a way that has allowed the company to successfully grow and meet and exceed its goals *and* to do so ethically and responsibly. From the creation of the company's Guiding Principles to the various innovative strategic initiatives, Schultz has never veered from his belief about what Starbucks, the company, could be and should be.

Unlike many companies, Starbucks and Howard Schultz have taken their leadership succession responsibilities seriously. In 2000, when Schultz was still CEO, he decided to move into the chairman's position. His replacement, Orin Smith (president and chief operating officer of Starbucks Coffee US), had been "groomed" to take over the CEO position. Smith made it a top priority to plan his own succession. First, he established an exit date—in 2005 at age 62. Then he monitored the leadership skills development of his top executives. Two years into the job, Smith recognized that the internal candidates most likely to replace him would still be too "unseasoned" to assume the CEO position by his stated exit date. At that point, the decision was made to look externally for a promising successor. That is when Jim Donald was hired from Pathmark, a regional grocery chain, where he was chairman, president, and CEO. For three years, Donald was immersed in Starbucks' business as president of the largest division, the North American unit, before assuming the CEO position in 2005, as planned.

Starbucks also recognizes the importance of having individuals with excellent leadership skills throughout the company. In addition to the leadership development training for upper-level managers, Starbucks offers a program called Learning to Lead for hourly employees (baristas) to develop leadership skills. This training program also covers store operations and effective management practices. In addition, Starbucks offers to managers at all organizational levels additional training courses on coaching and providing feedback to help managers improve their people skills.

Questions

1. Do the overwhelmingly positive results from the partner view survey surprise you? Why or why not? Do you think giving employees an opportunity to express their opinions in something like an attitude survey is beneficial? Why or why not?

2. How might the results of the partner survey affect the way a local store manager does his or her job? How about a district manager? How about the senior vice-president of store development? Do you think there are differences in the impact of employee surveys on how managers at different organizational levels lead? Why or why not?

3. Discuss the "ideal" Starbucks employee in terms of the various personality trait theories.

4. Describe in your own words the workplace environment that Starbucks has tried to create. What impact might such an environment have on motivating employees?

5. Using the job characteristics model in Exhibit 13-5 on page 411, redesign a part-time hourly employee's job to be more motivating. Do the same with a store manager's job.

6. Does Starbucks "care" too much for its partners? Can a company ever treat its employees too well? Why or why not?

7. Howard Schultz says, "We all want the same thing as people—to be respected and valued as employees and appreciated as customers." Does the company respect and value its partners (employees)? Explain. What do you think this implies for its employee relationships?

8. CEO Jim Donald says, "Spending money to put people first is smart money." Do you agree or disagree? Why?

9. Describe Howard Schultz's leadership style. Would his approach be appropriate in other types of organizations? Why or why not?

10. Do you agree that leadership succession planning is important? Why or why not?

11. What is Starbucks doing "right" with respect to the leading function? Are they doing anything "wrong?" Explain.

12. Which of the company's Guiding Principles influence the leading function of management? Explain how the one(s) you chose would affect how Starbucks' managers deal with (a) work team behaviour issues; (b) motivational techniques; and (c) leadership styles or approaches.

VIDEO CASE INCIDENTS

Millionaire on a Mission

Bill Young is a millionaire with a heart. After making millions leading high-growth entrepreneurial organizations, he decided to invest in helping others. He founded Toronto-based Social Capital Partners (SCP) in 2001. SCP provides support to businesses that hire people who often have difficulties finding employment: youths, single mothers, Aboriginal peoples, new immigrants, people with disabilities, and those with substance abuse issues.

SCP provides start-up capital to business ventures that it thinks will be able to grow and turn a profit within about three years. The business owners must commit to helping improve the lives of their employees by making them financially self-sufficient while providing training and other support as necessary.

The types of businesses supported by SCP are known as "social enterprises." They look like typical businesses, except most of their employees come from groups that rely heavily on government assistance to live and have found it nearly impossible to get full-time jobs for a variety of reasons. These businesses have a "double bottom line": "a financial bottom line like traditional businesses but also a social bottom line—getting people who have traditionally faced significant employment barriers back into the economic mainstream."

SCP funds a number of social enterprises, including Winnipeg-based Inner City Renovation (ICR). ICR, founded in August 2002, is a construction and renovation company that works mainly on nonprofit housing projects. The company's work helps address the lack of affordable housing in Winnipeg, and also provides employment to Aboriginal peoples who live in the inner city. Employees often work on houses in their own neighbourhoods, which means that their work is also improving their local environment. ICR's employees earn a steady income, and also learn a skilled trade that they can use in the future. An Aboriginal social worker on staff helps employees address personal problems, including alcohol and chemical dependency.

By mid-2004, SCP and Winnipeg-based Community Ownership Solutions had invested $100 000 in ICR. The company generated almost $1 million in revenue after its first year, but also suffered a $350 000 loss. By the end of 2005, however, the company generated more than $1 million in revenue, with a loss of only $3000. Young acknowledges that ICR is a "wonderful learning experience. It's not like it's gone smoothly. It's such an exciting model, this notion of combining housing and employment. It's taking a radically different approach to structural social problems in a lot of urban areas. There are exciting implications, if we can make this work."

QUESTIONS

1. *For analysis:* What leadership style(s) might be effective when dealing with employees who have personal challenges, such as those who are employed by Inner City Renovation?

2. *For analysis:* From a leadership perspective, what are the advantages and disadvantages of leading a company identified as a social enterprise?

3. *For application:* Inner City Renovation would like to reduce the absenteeism and turnover rates of its employees. How should it go about doing this?

4. *For application:* What are some of the challenges that Bill Young faces in trying to identify social enterprises to invest in?

5. *For debate:* "Only money motivates employees. Inner City Renovation should pay its employees more in order to solve its turnover problems." Do you agree or disagree with this statement? Explain.

Sources: "Social Capitalist," *CBC Venture*, February 29, 2004, 916, VA–2050 D; http://www. socialcapitalpartners.ca/index.html (accessed January 23, 2005); M. Cook, "Chasing the Double Bottom Line: Series: The Charity Industry," *Ottawa Citizen*, March 1, 2004, p. D7; and http://www.socialcapitalpartners.ca/articles/ ICRReport%20Card%202005.ppt.

Work–Life Balance and Motivation: Ernst & Young

Ernst & Young, the third-largest US accounting firm, increased its employee retention rate by 5 percent as a result of a human resource initiative to put "people first." By creating a feedback-rich culture, building great résumés for its 160 000 employees in New York City and around the world, and giving employees time and freedom to pursue personal goals, Ernst & Young has reaped the benefits of a highly motivated workforce. The company uses mandatory goal setting, provides employees with learning opportunities in areas of interest, and measures human resource processes using an employee survey to evaluate the workplace environment. While conceding that everyone is somewhat motivated by money, Jim Freer, vice-chair of people, believes that the way a person is treated is the determining factor in a person's level of performance. "People don't leave organizations," he says. "They leave managers."

QUESTIONS

1. *For analysis:* How might the job characteristics model be useful to managers at Ernst & Young?

2. *For analysis:* Recently, Ernst & Young was barred from accepting any new audit clients in the United States for six months after an SEC administrative judge called Ernst & Young "reckless," "highly unreasonable," and "negligent" in forming a business relationship with an audit client, PeopleSoft. As a student intern at the firm, how might this affect your career plans? Explain.

3. *For application:* In light of the damage to the firm's public image and the consequential six-month ban on new business, what steps would you take as a manager to maintain employee motivation at Ernst & Young?

4. *For application:* How would you suggest that diversity initiative managers at Ernst & Young create an inclusive environment that will motivate employees from diverse cultural backgrounds to excel?

5. *For debate:* According to Richard Whiteley, author of *Love the Work You're With,* by discovering your purpose in life, you can increase your job satisfaction. Would you agree that Ernst & Young's "people first" initiative supports this viewpoint? Explain why you feel the human resource initiative either supports or contradicts Richard Whiteley's premise.

Sources: "Ernst & Young" (video), Pearson Prentice Hall Management Video Library; and M. Goldstein, "Ernst & Young Hit Hard in PeopleSoft Case," *The Street*, April 16, 2004, http://www.thestreet.com/_tscs/markets/matthewgoldstein/10154603.html.

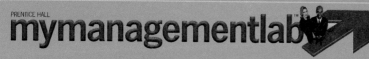

PRENTICE HALL

mymanagementlab

After you have completed your study of Part 4, do the following exercises at the MyManagementLab website (www.pearsoned.ca/mymanagementlab):

- *You're the Manager: Putting Ethics into Action* (Avon Products)
- *Passport, Scenario 1* (Robert Mathis, DaimlerChrysler), *Scenario 2* (Mary Chang), and *Scenario 3* (Jean Claude Moreau, Bon Appétit)

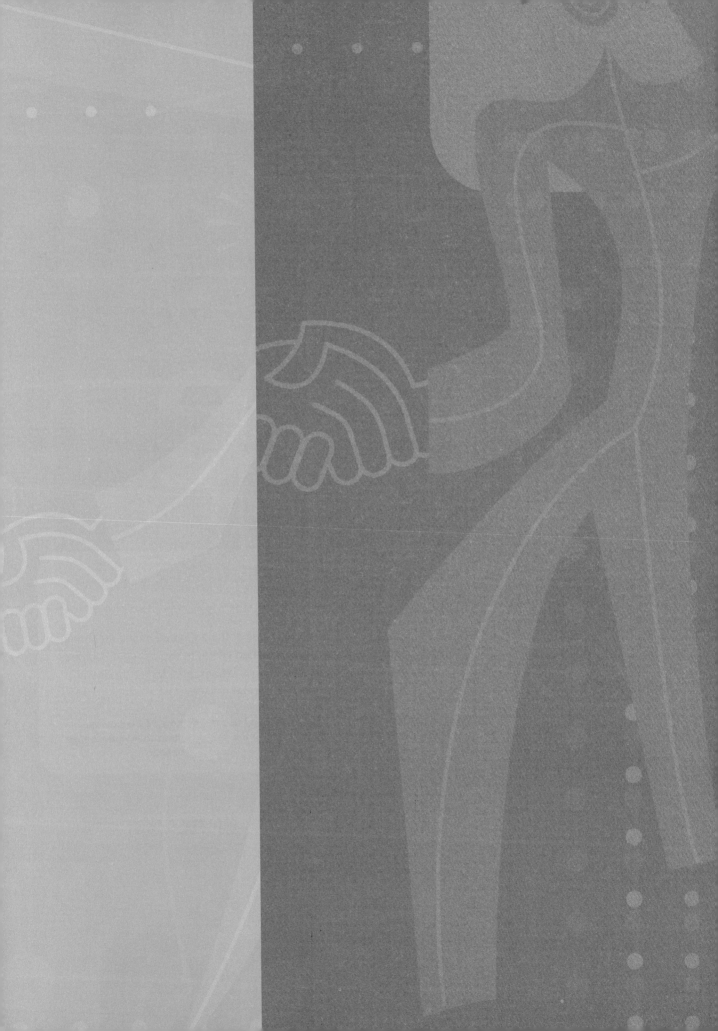

PART five

Controlling

MANAGERS NEED TO MONITOR the activities of the organization and determine whether they are accomplishing their planned goals. In evaluating outcomes, they sometimes have to change directions. When considering the issue of control, managers might ask these questions:

- **How do I evaluate the decisions I implement?**
- **What tools can I use to measure performance?**
- **How do I encourage innovation and manage change?**

Foundations of Control

PART **five**

How do I evaluate the effectiveness of my plans?

1. What is control?

2. What is the control process?

3. When should controls be introduced?

4. What methods of control do managers use?

5. How do financial and information controls help managers monitor performance?

6. What are some current issues in control?

▶ ▶ ▶ When Li Ka-shing first invested in Calgary-based Husky Oil (now Husky Energy) in 1986, buying 52 percent of its shares, the company had just posted its first year-end loss in the company's history.[1] The company had no cash on hand, shares had dropped to half of their 1981 value, and the company's debt was growing. Bob Blair, then the CEO at Husky, turned to Li. "We required a lot of capital, more than Husky could generate from its own cash flow," says Blair, in explaining why he approached his friend Li, a wealthy Hong Kong businessman, to invest in the company. In 1991, Li and his holding company bought 43 percent more of the company.

After the 1991 investment, Li immediately sent John Chin-Sung Lau (at right) to Calgary to turn the company around. Li wanted to halt the company's large losses and "wild expansions" of Husky's previous management. Appointed vice-president at the time, Lau had difficulty working with Husky president Art Price. Lau found Price to be "a hopeless free-

spender," just trying to maintain his position as president.

Lau had a difficult task in front of him to make Husky profitable.

Think About It

What is organizational control? Put yourself in John Lau's shoes. How can he use control to make Husky successful? What did he need to do to turn Husky Energy into one of Canada's largest oil and gas enterprises?

In today's competitive global marketplace, managers want their organizations to achieve high levels of performance, and one way they can do that is by searching out the best practices successful organizations are using. By comparing themselves against the best, managers look for specific performance gaps and areas for improvement—areas where better controls over the work being done are needed.

As we will see in this chapter, John Lau understands the importance of management controls. No matter how thorough the planning, a decision still may be poorly implemented without a satisfactory control system in place. This chapter describes controls for monitoring and measuring performance. It also looks at how to create a well-designed organizational control system.

Husky Energy
www.huskyenergy.ca

What Is Control?

Both the viewing public and NASA officials were devastated by the tragic *Columbia* shuttle disaster in February 2003. Investigations of the tragedy suggest that organizational safety controls may not have been as thorough as they should have been.[2] When problems were

1. What is control?

spotted, managers might have been too quick to dismiss them as non-life-threatening, and in this situation that choice might have led to disastrous consequences. Although most managers will not face such tragic consequences if they ignore signs that something may be wrong, this example does point out the importance of control.

control
The process of monitoring activities to ensure that they are being accomplished as planned, and correcting any significant deviations.

Q&A 15.1, Q&A 15.2

What is **control**? It's the process of monitoring activities to ensure that they are being accomplished as planned, and correcting any significant deviations. All managers should be involved in the control function even if their units are performing as planned. Managers cannot really know whether their units are performing properly until they have evaluated what activities have been done and have compared the actual performance with the desired standard.[3] An effective control system ensures that activities are completed in ways that lead to the attainment of the organization's goals. The criterion that determines the effectiveness of a control system is how well it facilitates goal achievement. The more it helps managers achieve their organization's goals, the better the control system.[4]

Performance Standards

performance
The end result of an activity.

organizational performance
The accumulated end results of all the organization's work activities.

Q&A 15.3

To achieve control, performance standards must exist. These standards are the specific goals created during the planning process. **Performance** is the end result of an activity. Whether that activity is hours of intense practice before a concert or race or whether it's carrying out job responsibilities as efficiently and effectively as possible, performance is what results from that activity.

Managers are concerned with **organizational performance**—the accumulated end results of all the organization's work activities. It's a complex but important concept. Managers need to understand the factors that contribute to high organizational performance. After all, they don't want (or intend) to manage their way to mediocre performance. They *want* their organizations, work units, or work groups to achieve high levels of performance, no matter what mission, strategies, or goals are being pursued.

Measures of Organizational Performance

All managers must know what organizational performance measures will give them the information they need. The most frequently used organizational performance measures include organizational productivity, organizational effectiveness, and industry and company rankings.

Organizational Productivity

productivity
The overall output of goods or services produced divided by the inputs needed to generate that output.

Productivity is the overall output of goods or services produced divided by the inputs needed to generate that output. Organizations strive to be productive. They want the most goods and services produced using the least amount of inputs. Output is measured by the sales revenue an organization receives when those goods and services are sold (selling price × number sold). Input is measured by the costs of acquiring and transforming the organizational resources into the outputs.

Organizational Effectiveness

Q&A 15.4

organizational effectiveness
A measure of how appropriate organizational goals are and how well an organization is achieving those goals.

In Chapter 1, we defined managerial effectiveness as goal attainment. Can the same interpretation apply to organizational effectiveness? Yes, it can. **Organizational effectiveness** is a measure of how appropriate organizational goals are and how well an organization is achieving those goals. It's a common performance measure used by managers in designing strategies, work processes, and work activities, and in coordinating the work of employees.

Industry and Company Rankings

Q&A 15.5, Q&A 15.6

There is no shortage of different types of industry and company rankings. The rankings for each list are determined by specific performance measures. For instance, the companies listed in *Report on Business Magazine*'s Top 1000: Canada's Power Book are measured by assets. They are ranked according to after-tax profits in the most recent fiscal year, excluding extraordinary gains or losses.[5] The companies listed in the 50 Best Employers in Canada are ranked based on answers given by managers to a leadership team survey, an employee opinion survey, and a human resource survey designed by Hewitt Associates, a compensation and benefits consultant.[6] The companies listed in the *PROFIT* 100: Canada's Fastest Growing Companies are ranked based on their percentage sales growth over the past five years. Private and publicly traded companies that are over 50 percent Canadian-owned and are headquartered in Canada nominate themselves, and then *PROFIT* editors collect further information about eligible companies.[7]

Why Is Control Important?

Planning can be done, an organizational structure can be created to efficiently facilitate the achievement of goals, and employees can be motivated through effective leadership. Still, there is no assurance that activities are going as planned and that the goals managers are seeking are, in fact, being attained. Control is important, therefore, because it's the final link in the four management functions. It's the only way managers know whether organizational goals are being met and, if not, the reasons why. The value of the control function lies in its relation to planning, empowering employees, and protecting the organization and workplace.

Q&A 15.7

How can control help a team perform better on a course project?

In Chapter 6, we described goals as the foundation of planning. Goals give specific direction to managers. However, just stating goals or having employees accept your goals is no guarantee that the necessary actions to accomplish those goals have been taken. As the old saying goes, "The best-laid plans often go awry." The effective manager needs to follow up to ensure that what others are supposed to do is, in fact, being done and that their goals are in fact being achieved. In reality, managing is an ongoing process, and controlling activities provide the critical link back to planning (see Exhibit 15-1). If managers did not control, they would have no way of knowing whether their goals and plans were on target and what future actions to take.

Q&A 15.8

Another reason control is important is employee empowerment. Many managers are reluctant to empower their employees because they fear employees will do something wrong for which the manager will be held responsible. Thus, many managers are tempted to do things themselves and avoid empowering. This reluctance, however, can be reduced if managers develop an effective control system that provides information and feedback on employee performance.

Exhibit 15-1

The Planning–Controlling Link

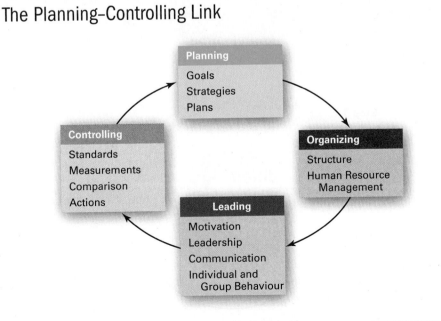

The final reason that managers control is to protect the organization and the physical workplace.[8] Given today's environment, with heightened security alerts and surprise financial scandals, managers must have plans in place to protect the organization's employees, data, and infrastructure.

The Control Process

2. What is the control process?

control process
A three-step process that includes measuring actual performance, comparing actual performance against a standard, and taking managerial action to correct deviations or inadequate standards.

The **control process** is a three-step process: measuring actual performance, comparing actual performance against a standard, and taking managerial action to correct deviations or inadequate standards (see Exhibit 15-2). The control process for managers is similar to what you might do as a student at the beginning of the term: set goals for yourself for studying and marks, and then evaluate your performance after midterms, determining whether you have studied enough or need to study more in order to meet whatever goals you set for your marks. (To learn more about how proactive you are, see *Self-Assessment— How Proactive Am I?* on pages 493–494, at the end of the chapter.)

Measuring Performance

To determine what actual performance is, a manager must acquire information about it. The first step in control, then, is measuring. Let's consider how we measure and what we measure.

How We Measure

Four sources of information frequently used by managers to measure actual performance are personal observations, statistical reports, oral reports, and written reports. Exhibit 15-3 summarizes the advantages and drawbacks of each approach. For most managers, using a combination of approaches increases both the number of input sources and the probability of getting reliable information.

What We Measure

What we measure is probably more critical to the control process than *how* we measure. Why? The selection of the wrong criteria can result in serious dysfunctional consequences. Besides, what we measure determines, to a great extent, what people in the organization will attempt to excel at.[9] For instance, if employees are evaluated by the number of big-ticket items they sell, they may not help customers who are looking for less expensive items.

Exhibit 15-2

The Control Process

Exhibit 15-3

Common Sources of Information for Measuring Performance

	Advantages	Drawbacks
Personal Observations (Management by Walking Around)	• Get first-hand knowledge • Information isn't filtered • Intensive coverage of work activities	• Subject to personal biases • Time-consuming • Can distract employees
Statistical Reports	• Easy to visualize • Effective for showing relationships	• Provide limited information • Ignore subjective factors
Oral Reports	• Fast way to get information • Allow for verbal and nonverbal feedback	• Information is filtered • Information cannot be documented
Written Reports	• Comprehensive • Formal • Easy to file and retrieve	• Take more time to prepare

Some control criteria are applicable to any management situation. For instance, because all managers, by definition, coordinate the work of others, criteria such as employee satisfaction or turnover and absenteeism rates can be measured. Most managers also have budgets set in dollar costs for their areas of responsibility. Keeping costs within budget is, therefore, a fairly common control measure. However, any comprehensive control system needs to recognize the diversity of activities that managers do. For instance, a production manager at a paper tablet manufacturer might use measures such as quantity of paper tablets produced per day and per labour-hour, scrap rate, and/or percentage of rejects returned by customers. On the other hand, the manager of an administrative unit in a government agency might use the number of client requests processed per hour or the average time required to process paperwork. Marketing managers often use measures such as percentage of market held, average dollars per sale, number of customer visits per salesperson, or number of customer impressions per advertising medium.

Most jobs and activities can be expressed in tangible and measurable terms. However, when a performance indicator cannot be stated in quantifiable terms, managers should use subjective measures. Although subjective measures have significant limitations, they are better than having no standards at all and ignoring the control function. If an activity is important, the excuse that it's difficult to measure is unacceptable.

Comparing Performance against Standard

The comparing step determines the degree of variation between actual performance and the standard. Although some variation in performance can be expected in all activities, it's critical to determine the acceptable **range of variation** (see Exhibit 15-4 on page 472). Deviations that exceed this range become significant and need the manager's attention. In the comparison stage, managers are particularly concerned with the size and direction of the variation. An example can help make this concept clearer.

range of variation
The acceptable degree of variation between actual performance and the standard.

Chris Tanner is sales manager for Beer Unlimited, a distributor of specialty beers in the Prairies. Chris prepares a report during the first week of each month that describes sales for the previous month, classified by brand name. Exhibit 15-5 on page 472 displays both the sales goal (standard) and the actual sales figures for the month of July.

Should Chris be concerned about July's sales performance? Sales were a bit higher than originally targeted, but does that mean there were no significant deviations? Even though overall performance was generally quite favourable, several brands might need to be examined more closely by Chris. However, the number of brands that deserve attention depends

Q&A 15.9

Exhibit 15-4

Defining the Acceptable Range of Variation

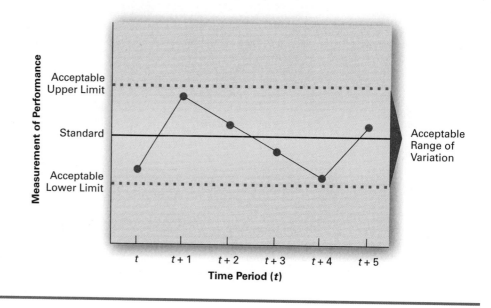

on what Chris believes to be *significant*. How much variation should Chris allow before corrective action is taken?

The deviation on three brands (Maple Brown Ale, Full Moon, Black Cat Lager) is very small and does not need special attention. On the other hand, are the shortages for Premium Lager and Blanche de Chambly brands significant? That is a judgment Chris must make. Premium Lager sales were 15 percent below Chris' goal. This deviation is

Exhibit 15-5

Sales Performance Figures for July, Beer Unlimited

Brand	Standard	(number of cases) Actual	Over (Under)
Premium Lager (Okanagan Spring, Vernon, BC)	1075	913	(162)
India Pale Ale (Alexander Keith's, Halifax)	800	912	112
Maple Brown Ale (Upper Canada Brewery, Toronto)	620	622	2
Blanche de Chambly (Brasseries Unibroue, Quebec)	160	110	(50)
Full Moon (Alley Kat, Edmonton)	225	220	(5)
Black Cat Lager (Paddock Wood Brewing, Saskatoon, Saskatchewan)	80	65	(15)
Bison Blonde Lager (Agassiz, Winnipeg)	170	286	116
Total cases	**3130**	**3128**	**(2)**

significant and needs attention. Chris should look for a cause. In this instance, Chris attributes the decrease to aggressive advertising and promotion programs by the big domestic producers, Anheuser-Busch and Miller. Because Premium Lager is his company's number one selling microbeer, it's most vulnerable to the promotion clout of the big domestic producers. If the decline in sales of Premium Lager is more than a temporary slump (that is, if it happens again next month), then Chris will need to cut back on inventory stock.

An error in understating sales can be as troublesome as an overstatement. For instance, is the surprising popularity of Bison Blonde Lager (up 68 percent) a one-month anomaly, or is this brand becoming more popular with customers? If the brand is increasing in popularity, Chris will want to order more product to meet customer demand, so as not to run short and risk losing customers. Again, Chris will have to interpret the information and make a decision. Our Beer Unlimited example illustrates that both overvariance and undervariance in any comparison of measures may require managerial attention.

Benchmarking of Best Practices

We first introduced the concept of benchmarking in Chapter 8. Remember that **benchmarking** is the search for the best practices among competitors or noncompetitors that lead to their superior performance. The **benchmark** is the standard of excellence against which to measure and compare.[10] At its most fundamental level, benchmarking means learning from others.[11] As a tool for monitoring and measuring organizational performance, benchmarking can be used to help identify specific performance gaps and potential areas of improvement.[12] To ensure the company is on track, Montreal-based BouClair, a home-decorating store, benchmarks everything against past performance and also against what other leading retailers are doing. "If a particular department or category is up 40% in sales over last year but we said we expected it to grow at 60%, then we are going to investigate and find out why," Gerry Goldberg, president and CEO, says.[13] "Then we look at our own same-store sales increases and compare them to the best companies out there. That's how we measure our efficiency and our productivity."

Managers should not look just at external organizations for best practices. It is also important for them to look inside their organization for best practices that can be shared. Research shows that best practices frequently already exist within an organization but usually go unidentified and unused.[14] In today's environment, organizations striving for high performance levels cannot afford to ignore such potentially valuable information. Some companies already have recognized the potential of internally benchmarking best practices as a tool for monitoring and measuring performance. For example, to improve diversity within the company, Saskatoon, Saskatchewan-based Yanke Group, a trucking company, is committed to hiring Aboriginal peoples and people with disabilities. Yanke reviews its employment equity benchmarks quarterly.[15] Toyota Motor Corporation developed a suggestion-screening system to prioritize best practices based on potential impact, benefits, and difficulty of implementation. General Motors sends employees—from upper management to line employees—to different plants where they learn about internal and external best practices.[16] Exhibit 15-6 on page 474 provides a summary of what managers must do to implement an internal benchmarking best-practices program.

benchmarking
The search for the best practices among competitors or noncompetitors that lead to their superior performance.

benchmark
The standard of excellence against which to measure and compare.

Yanke Group
www.yanke.ca

Q&A 15.10

SYSCO is a food-services distribution firm, headquartered in Houston, Texas, that has more than 170 subsidiary companies. A recent innovation developed by its human resource department is the Innovation Key Metrics Benchmark System, which provides executives at all SYSCO's regional offices with scorecards showing how well their company has performed against others in the SYSCO family. A database of its business practices also lets SYSCO executives look up subsidiary companies of similar size and learn about what has made them strong in particular areas. Site visits to these benchmark firms are encouraged.

Taking Managerial Action

The third and final step in the control process is taking managerial action. Managers can choose among three possible courses of action: They can do nothing; they

Exhibit 15-6

Steps to Successfully Implement an Internal Benchmarking Best-Practices Program

1. *Connect best practices to strategies and goals.* The organization's strategies and goals should dictate what types of best practices might be most valuable to others in the organization.

2. *Identify best practices throughout the organization.* Organizations must have a way to find out what practices have been successful in different work areas and units.

3. *Develop best-practices reward and recognition systems.* Individuals must be given an incentive to share their knowledge. The reward system should be built into the organization's culture.

4. *Communicate best practices throughout the organization.* Once best practices have been identified, that information needs to be shared with others in the organization.

5. *Create a best-practices knowledge-sharing system.* There needs to be a formal mechanism for organizational members to continue sharing their ideas and best practices.

6. *Nurture best practices on an ongoing basis.* Create an organizational culture that reinforces a "we can learn from everyone" attitude and emphasizes sharing information.

Source: Based on T. Leahy, "Extracting Diamonds in the Rough," *Business Finance*, August 2000, pp. 33–37.

can correct the actual performance; or they can revise the standard. Because "doing nothing" is fairly self-explanatory, let's look more closely at the other two options.

Correct Actual Performance

If the source of the performance variation is unsatisfactory work, the manager will want to take corrective action. Examples of such corrective action might include changing strategy, structure, compensation practices, or training programs; redesigning jobs; or firing employees. Toronto-based Celestica redesigned its manufacturing process to cut waste, as this *Management Reflection* shows.

MANAGEMENT REFLECTION

Celestica Works to Improve the Bottom Line

Can changing the manufacturing process reduce the bottom line?   Toronto-based Celestica, an electronics manufacturer, has spent most of this decade introducing control mechanisms to improve the company's fortunes.[17] Between 2001 and 2005, the company cut 29 600 jobs and restructured its operations five times. The company saw its revenues decline significantly between 2001 and 2003, and finally started to see a profit at the end of 2006. The introduction of a number of controls is given credit for the turnaround.

One of the areas that Celestica worked on was improving manufacturing operations. It did so by watching how factory workers carried out their duties, and then designing more efficient processes. Workers at its Monterrey, Mexico, plant "reduced equipment setup time by 85 percent, shortened time between receiving an order and shipping it by 71 percent, reduced floor space used by 34 percent, reduced consumables by 25 percent, reduced scrap by 66 percent and reduced the investment in surface-mount technology (SMT) lines by 49 percent." ■

A manager who decides to correct actual performance has to make another decision: Should immediate or basic corrective action be taken? **Immediate corrective action** corrects problems at once to get performance back on track. **Basic corrective action** looks at how and why performance has deviated and then proceeds to correct the source of deviation. It's not unusual for managers to rationalize that they don't have the time to take basic corrective action and therefore must be content to perpetually "put out fires" with immediate corrective action. Effective managers, however, analyze deviations and, when the benefits justify it, take the time to pinpoint and correct the causes of variance.

To return to our Beer Unlimited example, taking immediate corrective action on the negative variance for Premium Lager, Chris might contact the company's retailers and have them immediately drop the price on Premium Lager by 5 percent. However, taking basic corrective action would involve more in-depth analysis by Chris. After assessing how and why sales deviated, Chris might choose to increase in-store promotional efforts, increase the advertising budget for this brand, or reduce future purchases from the brewery. The action Chris takes will depend on the assessment of the brand's potential profitability.

immediate corrective action
Corrective action that corrects problems at once to get performance back on track.

basic corrective action
Corrective action that looks at how and why performance deviated and then proceeds to correct the source of deviation.

Q&A 15.11

Revise the Standard

It's possible that the variance was a result of an unrealistic standard; that is, the goal may have been too high or too low. In such instances, it's the standard that needs corrective attention, not the performance. For instance, if individuals are exceeding the standard, or have no problem meeting the standard, this might suggest that the standard should be raised. In our example, Chris might need to raise the sales goal (standard) for Bison Blonde Lager to reflect its growing popularity.

The more troublesome problem is revising a performance standard downward. If an employee, work team, or work unit falls significantly short of reaching its goal, their natural response is to shift the blame for the variance to the goal. For instance, students who make a low grade on a test often attack the grade cut-off standards as too high. Rather than accept the fact that their performance was inadequate, students argue that the standards are unreasonable. Similarly, salespeople who fail to meet their monthly quotas may attribute the failures to unrealistic quotas. It may be true that when a standard is too high, it can result in a significant variation and may even contribute to demotivating those employees being measured. But keep in mind that if employees or managers don't meet the standard, the first thing they are likely to attack is the standard. If you believe that the standard is realistic, fair, and achievable, hold your ground. Explain your position, reaffirm to the employee, team, or unit that you expect future performance to improve, and then take the necessary corrective action to turn that expectation into reality.

Corrective action can take many forms. On the selling floor of Home Depot stores, where one contractor spent 20 minutes waiting for a Home Depot forklift operator to arrive so he could load some purchased drywall, the need to improve customer service led to changes in the composition of the workforce. Senior management realized that stores had hired too many part-time employees, whose commitment to the job and knowledge about the do-it-yourself business sometimes lagged behind those of full-timers. Home Depot scaled back from a 50-50 mix to a new balance of 40 percent part-time and 60 percent full-time employees, and customer service has since improved.

Summary of Managerial Decisions

Exhibit 15-7 summarizes the manager's decisions in the control process. Standards evolve out of goals that are developed during the planning process. These goals then provide the basis for the control process, which is essentially a continuous flow between measuring, comparing, and taking managerial action. Depending on the results of comparing, a manager's decision about what course of action to take might be to do nothing, revise the standard, or correct the performance.

When to Introduce Control

3. When should controls be introduced?

Managers can implement controls *before* an activity begins, *during* the time the activity is going on, and *after* the activity has been completed. The first type is called *feedforward control*, the second is *concurrent control*, and the last is *feedback control* (see Exhibit 15-8).

Feedforward Control

feedforward control
A type of control that focuses on preventing anticipated problems, since it takes place before the actual activity.

The most desirable type of control—**feedforward control**—prevents anticipated problems since it takes place before the actual activity.[18] Let's look at some examples of feedforward control.

When working on a project, do you anticipate problems ahead of time or wait until they occur?

When McDonald's Canada opened its first restaurant in Moscow, it sent company quality control experts to help Russian farmers learn techniques for growing high-quality potatoes and bakers to learn processes for baking high-quality breads. Why? Because McDonald's strongly emphasizes product quality no matter what the geographical location. It wants a cheeseburger in Moscow to taste like one in Winnipeg. Still another example of feedforward control is the scheduled

Exhibit 15-7

Managerial Decisions in the Control Process

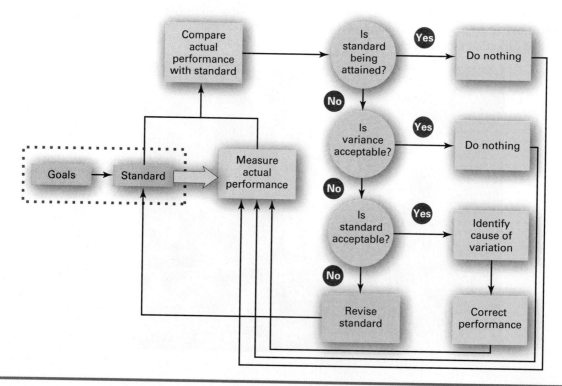

Exhibit 15-8

Types of Control

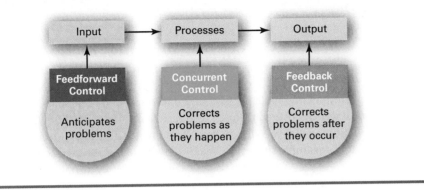

Input	Processes	Output

Feedforward Control — Anticipates problems

Concurrent Control — Corrects problems as they happen

Feedback Control — Corrects problems after they occur

preventive maintenance programs on aircraft done by airlines. These are designed to detect and, it is hoped, to prevent structural damage that might lead to an accident.

The key to feedforward controls is taking managerial action *before* a problem occurs. Feedforward controls are desirable because they allow managers to prevent problems rather than having to correct them later after the damage (such as poor-quality products, lost customers, lost revenue, and so forth) has already been done. Unfortunately, these controls require timely and accurate information that often is difficult to get. As a result, managers frequently end up using the other two types of control. (The *Video Case Incident—Creativity and the Bottom Line: Mullen PR* on page 547 shows the controls that are used in the advertising industry.)

Concurrent Control

Concurrent control, as its name implies, takes place while an activity is in progress. When control is enacted while the work is being performed, management can correct problems before they become too costly.

The best-known form of concurrent control is direct supervision. When managers use **management by walking around**, which is a term used to describe a manager being out in the work area, interacting directly with employees, they are using concurrent control. When a manager directly oversees the actions of employees, he or she can monitor their actions and correct problems as they occur. Although, obviously, there is some delay between the activity and the manager's corrective response, the delay is minimal. Problems usually can be addressed before much resource waste or damage has been done. Also, technical equipment (computers, computerized machine controls, and so forth) can be programmed for

concurrent control
A type of control that takes place while an activity is in progress.

management by walking around
A term used to describe a manager being out in the work area, interacting directly with employees.

Yun Jong-Yong, CEO of Samsung Electronics, describes how he practises an effective kind of concurrent control. "I spend much of my time visiting our domestic and overseas work sites to examine operations from the ground, receiving face-to-face reports and indicating areas for improvement. This gives me the opportunity to freely discuss matters with the person directly involved, from the top management to the junior staff of that work site.... I still believe that no [technological] innovation can replace the valuable information that is gathered through direct discussions."

concurrent controls. For instance, you may have experienced concurrent control when using a computer program such as word-processing software that alerts you to misspelled words or incorrect grammatical usage. In addition, many organizational quality programs rely on concurrent controls to inform employees if their work output is of sufficient quality to meet standards.

Q&A 15.12

Feedback Control

feedback control
A type of control that takes place after a work activity is done.

The most popular type of control relies on feedback. In **feedback control**, the control takes place *after* the activity is done. For instance, when McDonald's executives learned that a suspected criminal ring had allegedly stolen millions of dollars in top prizes in their customer games, it was discovered through feedback control.[19] Even though the company took corrective action once it was discovered, the damage had already occurred.

As the McDonald's example shows, the major drawback of this type of control is that by the time the manager has the information, the problems have already occurred—leading to waste or damage. But for many activities, feedback is the only viable type of control available. For instance, financial statements are an example of feedback controls. If, for example, the income statement shows that sales revenues are declining, the decline has already occurred. So at this point, the manager's only option is to try to determine why sales have decreased and to correct the situation.

Have you used feedback with team members after completing a team project?

Feedback controls do have two advantages.[20] First, feedback provides managers with meaningful information on how effective their planning efforts were. Feedback that indicates little variance between standard and actual performance is evidence that the planning was generally on target. If the deviation is significant, a manager can use that information when formulating new plans to make them more effective. Second, feedback control can enhance employee motivation. People want information on how well they have performed and feedback control provides that information. However, managers should be aware that recent research suggests that while individuals raise their goals when they receive positive feedback, they lower their goals when they receive negative feedback.[21] (To learn how to give feedback effectively, see *Developing Your Interpersonal Skills—Providing Feedback* on pages 497–498 at the end of the chapter.)

Methods of Control

▶ ▶ ▶ Everyone seems to agree that John Lau, president and CEO of Husky Energy, is a difficult and demanding boss.[22] He represents the Li family's interests in the company, and the Li family "favours a top down, autocratic environment, crammed with checks and balances." As one former executive of the company noted, "If you want to learn manufacturing cost control, unit cost measurement, they are great at it." Lau, trained as an accountant, brought to Husky the financial models that Li uses with his own companies to control costs and improve performance. Husky gets top shareholder returns as a result, but the company is viewed as tough on its employees.

Think About It

What methods of control are available to managers? How do managers introduce controls? What impact might controls have on employees?

4. What methods of control do managers use?

Ideally, every organization would like to efficiently and effectively reach its goals. Does this mean that the control systems organizations use are identical? In other words, would Matsushita, Husky Energy, and WestJet Airlines have the same types of control systems? Probably not. There are generally three approaches to designing control systems: market, bureaucratic, and clan controls.[23] (See Exhibit 15-9.)

Exhibit 15-9

Characteristics of Three Approaches to Designing Control Systems

Type of Control	Characteristics
Market	Uses external market mechanisms, such as price competition and relative market share, to establish standards used in system. Typically used by organizations whose products or services are clearly specified and distinct and that face considerable marketplace competition.
Bureaucratic	Emphasizes organizational authority. Relies on administrative and hierarchical mechanisms, such as rules, regulations, procedures, policies, standardization of activities, well-defined job descriptions, and budgets to ensure that employees exhibit appropriate behaviours and meet performance standards.
Clan	Regulates employee behaviour by the shared values, norms, traditions, rituals, beliefs, and other aspects of the organization's culture. Often used by organizations in which teams are common and technology is changing rapidly.

Market Control

Market control is an approach to control that emphasizes the use of external market mechanisms, such as price competition and relative market share, to establish the standards used in the control system. Organizations that use the market control approach often have divisions that are set up as profit centres and evaluated by the percentage of total corporate profits contributed. For instance, at Japan's Matsushita, which supplies a wide range of products throughout the world, the various divisions (audiovisual and communication networks, components and devices, home appliances, and industrial equipment) are evaluated according to the profits each generates.

market control
An approach to control that emphasizes the use of external market mechanisms, such as price competition and relative market share, to establish the standards used in the control system.

Bureaucratic Control

Another approach to control is **bureaucratic control**, which emphasizes organizational authority and relies on administrative rules, regulations, procedures, and policies. Husky Energy provides a good example of bureaucratic control. Although managers at Husky's various divisions are allowed some freedom to run their units as they see fit, they are expected to adhere closely to their budgets and stay within corporate guidelines.

bureaucratic control
An approach to control that emphasizes organizational authority and relies on administrative rules, regulations, procedures, and policies.

Clan Control

Clan control is an approach to control in which employee behaviours are regulated by the shared values, norms, traditions, rituals, beliefs, and other aspects of the organization's culture. While market control relies on external standards and bureaucratic control is based on strict hierarchical mechanisms, clan control is dependent on the individuals and the groups in the organization (the clan) to identify appropriate and expected behaviours and performance measures. For instance, at Calgary-based WestJet Airlines, individuals are well aware of the expectations regarding appropriate work behaviour and performance standards, as the following *Management Reflection* shows.

clan control
An approach to control in which employee behaviour is regulated by the shared values, norms, traditions, rituals, beliefs, and other aspects of the organization's culture.

MANAGEMENT REFLECTION

WestJet Airlines' Employees Control Costs

Can employees be encouraged to think just like owners?   WestJet Airlines' founder and former CEO, Clive Beddoe, encouraged his employees to keep costs low.[24] The airline has a much better profit margin than Air Canada and its other rivals. Beddoe introduced a generous profit-sharing plan to ensure that employees felt personally responsible for the profitability of the airline. The company's accountants insist that profit-sharing turns employees into "cost cops" looking for waste and savings. "We are one of the few companies that has to justify [to employees] its Christmas party every year," Derek Payne, vice-president of finance, boasts ruefully.

WestJet encourages teamwork and gives employees a lot of freedom to determine and carry out their day-to-day duties. There are no rigid job descriptions for positions, and employees are required to help with all tasks. Sometimes pilots are recruited to load baggage. When a plane reaches its destination, all employees onboard, even those not working the flight, are expected to prepare the plane for its next takeoff. The company saves $2.5 million annually in cleaning costs by having everyone work together. Planes get turned around much more quickly as well, usually within about a half-hour. When necessary, though, the employees have been able to do it in as little as six minutes. WestJet's profit-sharing program encourages employees to do their best because they see a clear link between their performance, the profits of the company, and their rewards. Not all companies that have profit-sharing programs provide employees with such clear links between behaviour and performance. ∎

Clan control requires careful selection and socialization of employees who will support the organization's culture. This includes making sure to manage diversity in the workforce (see *Managing Workforce Diversity—Diversity Success Stories* on page 499).

Financial and Information Controls

▶ ▶ ▶ For Husky Energy president and CEO John Lau, the bottom line is the measure of organizational performance.[25] When he started at Husky in 1991, it was not doing well financially. By 1993, it had a loss of $250 million on the books. In 2006, the company had $2.7 billion in net earnings, clearly an outstanding turnaround. Judith Romanchuk, an investment banker, notes that Lau has taken the company from "minor league player with a 'crumbling foundation' to a major producer" with holdings in both Canada and China.

Lau also measures performance by the number of barrels of oil equivalent (BOE) produced daily. When he started, Husky was producing 28 000 barrels daily. In 2006, the company produced 359 700 BOE daily. Lau has grown volume 10 percent a year since 2004 and expects to reach 500 000 BOE daily by 2008. By 2020, he expects the company will extract half a million BOEs daily from the Alberta oil sands alone.

Think About It

How can managers use financial and information controls to make sure that their organizations are performing well?

5. How do financial and information controls help managers monitor performance?

One of the primary purposes of every business firm is to earn a profit. To achieve this goal, managers need financial controls and accurate information. Managers might, for instance, carefully analyze quarterly income statements for excessive expenses. They might also perform several financial ratio tests to ensure that sufficient cash is available to pay ongoing expenses, that debt levels have not risen too high, or that assets are being used productively. Or they might look at some newer financial control tools such as EVA (economic value added) to see if the company is creating economic value. Managers can control information and use it to control other organizational activities.

Traditional Financial Control Measures

Q&A 15.13

Traditional financial control measures include ratio analysis and budget analysis. Exhibit 15-10 on page 481 summarizes some of the most popular financial ratios used in organizations. Liquidity ratios measure an organization's ability to meet its current debt obligations. Leverage ratios examine the organization's use of debt to finance its assets and whether it's able to meet the interest payments on the debt. Activity ratios assess how efficiently the firm is using its assets. Finally, profitability ratios measure how efficiently and effectively the firm is using its assets to generate profits.

These ratios are calculated using information from the organization's two primary financial statements (the balance sheet and the income statement); they compare two figures and express them as a percentage or ratio. Because you have undoubtedly discussed these ratios in introductory accounting and finance courses, or you will in the near future, we are not going to elaborate on how they are calculated. Instead, we mention these ratios only briefly here to remind you that managers use such ratios as internal control devices for monitoring how efficiently and profitably the organization uses its assets, debt, inventories, and the like.

We discussed budgets as a planning tool in Chapter 8. When a budget is formulated, it's a planning tool because it gives direction to work activities. It indicates what activities are important and how much in resources should be allocated to each activity. But budgets are also used for controlling.

Budgets provide managers with quantitative standards against which to measure and compare resource consumption. By pointing out deviations between standard and actual consumption, they become control tools. If the deviations are judged to be significant enough to require action, the manager will want to examine what has happened and try to uncover the reasons behind the deviations. With this information, he or she can take whatever action is necessary. For example, if you use a personal budget for monitoring and controlling your monthly expenses, you might find one month that your miscellaneous expenses were higher than you had budgeted for. At that point, you might cut back spending in another area or work extra hours to try to get more income.

Exhibit 15-10

Popular Financial Ratios

Objective	Ratio	Calculation	Meaning
Liquidity	Current ratio	$\dfrac{\text{Current assets}}{\text{Current liabilities}}$	Tests the organization's ability to meet short-term obligations
	Acid test	$\dfrac{\text{Current assets less inventories}}{\text{Current liabilities}}$	Tests liquidity more accurately when inventories turn over slowly or are difficult to sell
Leverage	Debt to assets	$\dfrac{\text{Total debt}}{\text{Total assets}}$	The higher the ratio, the more leveraged the organization
	Times interest earned	$\dfrac{\text{Profits before interest and taxes}}{\text{Total interest charges}}$	Measures how far profits can decline before the organization is unable to meet its interest expenses
Activity	Inventory turnover	$\dfrac{\text{Sales}}{\text{Inventory}}$	The higher the ratio, the more efficiently inventory assets are being used
	Total asset turnover	$\dfrac{\text{Sales}}{\text{Total assets}}$	The fewer assets used to achieve a given level of sales, the more efficiently management is using the organization's total assets
Profitability	Profit margin on sales	$\dfrac{\text{Net profit after taxes}}{\text{Total sales}}$	Identifies the profits that various products are generating
	Return on investment	$\dfrac{\text{Net profit after taxes}}{\text{Total assets}}$	Measures the efficiency of assets to generate profits

Other Financial Control Measures

In addition to the traditional financial tools, managers are using measures such as EVA (economic value added) and MVA (market value added). The fundamental concept behind these financial tools is that companies are supposed to take in capital from investors and make it worth more. When managers do that, they have created wealth. When they take in capital and make it worth less, they have destroyed wealth.

Economic value added (EVA) is a tool that measures corporate and divisional performance. It's calculated by taking after-tax operating profit minus the total annual cost of capital.[26] EVA is a measure of how much economic value is being created by what a company does with its assets, less any capital investments the company has made in its assets. As a performance control tool, EVA focuses managers' attention on earning a rate of return over and above the cost of capital. About 30 percent of Canadian companies use EVA, including Montreal-based Rio Tinto Alcan, Montreal-based Domtar, Markham, Ontario-based Robin Hood Multifoods, and Montreal-based cable company Cogeco.[27] When EVA is used as a performance measure, employees soon learn that they can improve their organization's or business unit's EVA either by using less capital (that is, figuring out how to spend less) or by investing capital in high-return projects (that is, projects that will bring in more money, with fewer expenses). Former Molson CEO Daniel O'Neill was well rewarded for EVA improvement to the company in 2002. He "closed several breweries, laid off hundreds of staff and slashed overhead costs, using the savings to modernize remaining breweries," all of which sent Molson shares soaring. O'Neill received a $2.4 million bonus for his efforts.[28]

Market value added (MVA) adds a market dimension since it is a tool that measures the stock market's estimate of the value of a firm's past and expected capital investment projects. If the company's market value (value of all outstanding stock plus company's debt) is greater than all the capital invested in it (from shareholders, bondholders, and retained earnings), it has a positive MVA, indicating that managers have created wealth. If the company's market value is less than all the capital invested in it, the MVA will be negative, indicating that managers have destroyed wealth. Studies have shown that EVA is a predictor of MVA and that consecutive years of positive EVA generally lead to a high MVA.[29]

To understand that EVA and MVA measure different things, let's consider three companies that had the highest MVA in the United States in 2006 and the amount of wealth they created for their shareholders (in US dollars): General Electric ($281 billion), Exxon Mobil ($223 billion), and Microsoft ($221 billion). While these three companies had relatively similar MVA, they had very different real profits (measured by EVA). Exxon Mobil had the highest EVA ($28.9 billion), followed by Microsoft ($9.1 billion), and then GE ($8.2 billion). Microsoft, with a lower MVA than General Electric, delivered a higher EVA.[30]

Information Controls

Gordon Bobbitt found hundreds of phone records from Rogers littering the streets of Toronto in April 2007. These records contained contact information, financial details, and, in some cases, social insurance numbers. This case was just one instance of consumer records that were not handled properly. Earlier in 2007, CIBC and retailer TJX Companies (operator of Winners and Home Sense) had breaches of security with consumer data. In 2006, the RCMP processed about 7800 cases of identity theft, which represented $16.3 million in individual losses.[31]

There are two ways to view information controls: (1) as a tool to help managers control other organizational activities and (2) as an organizational area that managers need to control. Let's look first at information as a control tool.

How Is Information Used in Controlling?

Information is critical to monitoring and measuring an organization's activities and performance. Managers need the right information at the right time and in the right amount. Without information, they would find it difficult to measure, compare, and take action as part of the controlling process. Inaccurate, incomplete, excessive, or delayed information will seriously impede performance.

economic value added (EVA)
A financial tool that measures corporate and divisional performance, calculated by taking after-tax operating profit minus the total annual cost of capital.

market value added (MVA)
A financial tool that measures the stock market's estimate of the value of a firm's past and expected capital investment projects.

Q&A 15.14

For instance, in measuring actual performance, managers need information about what is, in fact, happening within their area of responsibility, about what the standards are in order to be able to compare actual performance with the standard, and to help them determine acceptable ranges of variation within these comparisons. And they rely on information to help them develop appropriate courses of action if there are or are not significant deviations between actual and standard. Information can also be used to control costs, as the following *Management Reflection* shows.

MANAGEMENT REFLECTION

Air Canada Improves Maintenance Procedures

How can wireless technology make maintenance more efficient?   Air Canada's former vice-president of IT and CIO, Alice Keung, found that maintenance costs at Air Canada were skyrocketing because line maintenance (unscheduled repairs to a plane's equipment, instruments, or body) was not handled very effectively.[32] In particular, pilots or mechanics would send a note to the Toronto maintenance facility by teletype or fax or put a note in the plane's log, noting a repair issue. Mechanics often would not get these notes, or the plane would arrive but the mechanic would not have the necessary parts to perform a quick maintenance procedure.

Keung realized that maintenance procedures could be significantly streamlined if mechanics had easy and immediate access to information about repairs that needed to be made, as well as maintenance manuals and diagrams. Mechanics were given tablet-sized display screens mounted on their trucks and connected to a wireless local area network. This made the information easily available, and the display was large enough to show maintenance diagrams when needed.

The technology significantly improved maintenance productivity. Mechanics spent less time travelling back and forth to the hangar to get additional parts, since they could determine what they needed more quickly. Mechanics could also make sure that parts were waiting when planes landed, so simple repairs could be performed without delaying flights. "That all has a bottom-line impact," Keung says. ■

As you can see, information is an important tool in monitoring and measuring organizational performance. Most of the information tools that managers use arise out of the organization's management information system.

Although there is no universally agreed-upon definition of a **management information system (MIS)**, we will define it as a system used to provide management with needed information on a regular basis. In theory, this system can be manual or computer-based, although all current discussions focus on computer-supported applications. The term *system* in MIS implies order, arrangement, and purpose. Further, an MIS focuses specifically on providing managers with *information*, not merely *data*. These two points are important and require elaboration.

A library provides a good analogy. Although it can contain millions of volumes, a library does not do users much good if they cannot find what they want quickly. That is why librarians spend a great deal of time cataloguing a library's collections and ensuring that materials are returned to their proper locations. Organizations today are like well-stocked libraries. There is no lack of data. There is, however, an inability to process that data so that the right information is available to the right person when he or she needs it. Likewise, a library is almost useless if it has the book you need immediately, but either you cannot find it or the library takes a week to retrieve it from storage. An MIS, on the other hand, has organized data in some meaningful way and can access the information in a reasonable amount of time. **Data** are raw, unanalyzed facts, such as numbers, names, or quantities. Raw unanalyzed facts are relatively useless to managers. When data are analyzed and processed, they become **information**. An MIS collects data and turns them into relevant information for managers to use.

management information system (MIS)
A system used to provide management with needed information on a regular basis.

data
Raw, unanalyzed facts.

information
Processed and analyzed data.

Controlling Information

As critically important as an organization's information is to everything it does, managers must have comprehensive and secure controls in place to protect that information. Such controls can range from data encryption to system firewalls to data backups, and other techniques as well.[33] Problems can lurk in places that an organization might not even have considered, like search engines. Sensitive, defamatory, confidential, or embarrassing organizational information has found its way into search engine results. For instance, detailed monthly expenses and employee salaries on the National Speleological Society's website turned up in a Google search.[34] Laptop computers are also proving to be a weak link in an organization's data security. For instance, Boston-based mutual fund company Fidelity Investments disclosed that a stolen laptop had the personal information of almost 200 000 current and former Hewlett-Packard employees.[35] Even RFID (radio frequency identification) tags, now being used by more and more organizations to track and control products, may be vulnerable to computer viruses.[36] Needless to say, whatever information controls are used must be monitored regularly to ensure that all possible precautions are in place to protect the organization's important information.

Current Issues in Control

▶ ▶ ▶ Husky Energy, like all public organizations, has a board of directors that looks after the interests of shareholders.[37] In recent years, corporate governance has come under scrutiny because of corporate scandals. Many boards were not overseeing management as well as they might have.

Husky has strengthened its board policies in recent years. The primary duty of Husky's board is to "approve, monitor and provide guidance on the strategic planning process." While the president and CEO and senior management team create the strategic plan, the board has to review and approve it. The board's role also includes identifying the principal risks of Husky's business and managing and monitoring these risks, as well as approving Husky's strategic plans, annual budget, and financial plans.

Think About It

Why has corporate governance become so important in recent years? What are the advantages of having a strong corporate board? Would there be any disadvantages?

6. What are some current issues in control?

The employees of Tempe, Arizona-based Integrated Information Systems thought there was nothing wrong with exchanging copyrighted digital music over a dedicated office server they had set up. Like office betting on college basketball games, it was technically illegal, but harmless, or so they thought. But after the company had to pay a $1.3 million (US) settlement to the Recording Industry Association of America, managers wished they had controlled the situation better.[38]

Control is an important managerial function. What types of control issues do today's managers face? We look at five: balanced scorecard, corporate governance, cross-cultural differences, workplace concerns, and customer interactions.

Balanced Scorecard

The balanced scorecard approach to performance measurement was introduced as a way to evaluate organizational performance from more than just the financial perspective.[39] The **balanced scorecard** is a performance measurement tool that examines four areas—financial, customer, internal business process, and learning/growth assets—that contribute to a company's performance. Exhibit 15-11 illustrates how the balanced scorecard is measured. The financial area looks at activities that improve the short- and long-term performance of the organization. The customer area looks at the customer's view of the organization, whether customers return, and whether they are satisfied. The internal business process looks at how production and operations, such as order fulfilment, are carried out. The learning and growth area looks at how well the company's employees are being managed for the company's future.

According to this approach, managers should develop goals in each of the four areas and then measure to determine if these goals are being met. For instance, a company might

balanced scorecard
A performance measurement tool that looks at four areas—financial, customer, internal business process, and learning and growth assets—that contribute to a company's performance.

Q&A 15.15

Exhibit 15-11

The Balanced Scorecard

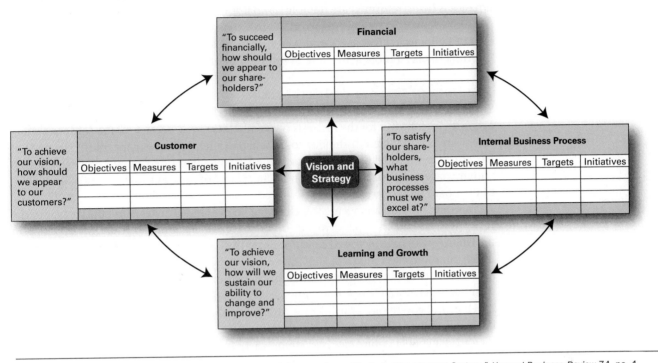

Source: R. S. Kaplan and D. P. Norton, "Using the Balanced Scorecard as a Strategic Management System," *Harvard Business Review* 74, no. 1 (January–February 1996), pp. 75–85.

include cash flow, quarterly sales growth, and return on investment (ROI) as measures for success in the financial area. It might include percentage of sales coming from new products as a measure of customer goals. It might include dollars spent toward training, or number of courses taken by employees as a measure of learning and growth. The intent of the balanced scorecard is to emphasize that all of these areas are important to an organization's success and that there should be a balance among them.

Although a balanced scorecard makes sense, managers still tend to focus on areas that drive their organization's success.[40] Their scorecards reflect their strategies. If those strategies centre on the customer, for example, then the customer area is likely to get more attention than the other three areas. Yet you really cannot focus on measuring only one performance area because, ultimately, other performance areas will be affected.

Many companies are starting to use the balanced scorecard as a control mechanism, including Bell Canada, British Airways, and Hilton Hotels. In 2003, the Ontario Hospital Association developed a scorecard for 89 hospitals, designed to evaluate four main areas: clinical use and outcomes, financial performance and financial condition of the hospital, patient satisfaction, and how the hospital was investing for the future. The scorecard was purposefully designed to recognize the synergies among each of these measures. After hospitals were evaluated on the scorecard measures, the results of the scorecard evaluations were made available to patients, giving them an objective basis for choosing a hospital. The association has provided the reports for every year since then, except 2004, on its website.[41]

Ontario Hospital Association
www.oha.com

Corporate Governance

Although Andrew Fastow, Enron's former chief financial officer, had an engaging and persuasive personality, that still does not explain why Enron's board of directors failed to raise even minimal concerns about management's questionable accounting practices. The board even allowed Fastow to set up off-balance-sheet partnerships for his own profit at the expense of Enron's shareholders.

corporate governance
The system used to govern a corporation so that the interests of corporate owners are protected.

Corporate governance, the system used to govern a corporation so that the interests of corporate owners are protected, failed abysmally at Enron, as it did at many of the other companies caught in recent financial scandals. In the aftermath of these scandals, there have been increased calls for better corporate governance. Two areas in which corporate governance is being reformed are the role of boards of directors and financial reporting. The concern over corporate governance exists in Canada and globally.[42] For example, 75 percent of senior executives at US and Western European corporations expect their boards of directors to take a more active role in improving corporate governance.[43]

The Role of Boards of Directors

The original purpose of a board of directors was to have a group, independent from management, looking out for the interests of shareholders who, because of the corporate structure, were not involved in the day-to-day management of the organization. However, it has not always worked that way in practice. Board members often enjoy a cozy relationship with managers in which board members "take care" of the CEO and the CEO "takes care" of the board members.

This quid pro quo arrangement is changing. In the United States, since the passage of the Sarbanes-Oxley Act in 2002, demands on board members of publicly traded companies in the United States have increased considerably.[44] The Canadian Securities Administrators rules, which came into effect in March 2004, strive to tighten board responsibility somewhat, though these rules are not as stringent as those developed in the United States. To help boards do their job better, researchers at the Corporate Governance Center at Kennesaw State University developed 10 governance principles for American public companies that have been endorsed by the Institute of Internal Auditors in the United States. These principles are equally relevant for Canadian public companies (see Exhibit 15-12 for a list of these principles).

Exhibit 15-12

Twenty-First Century Governance Principles for Public Companies

1. *Interaction:* Sound governance requires effective interaction among the board, management, the external auditor, and the internal auditor.

2. *Board purpose:* The board of directors should understand that its purpose is to protect the interests of the corporation's stockholders, while considering the interests of other stakeholders (for example, creditors and employees).

3. *Board responsibilities:* The board's major areas of responsibility should be monitoring the CEO, overseeing the corporation's strategy, and monitoring risks and the corporation's control system. Directors should employ healthy skepticism in meeting these responsibilities.

4. *Independence:* The major stock exchanges should define an "independent" director as one who has no professional or personal ties (either current or former) to the corporation or its management other than service as a director. The vast majority of the directors should be independent in both fact and appearance so as to promote arm's-length oversight.

5. *Expertise:* The directors should possess relevant industry, company, functional area, and governance expertise. The directors should reflect a mix of backgrounds and perspectives. All directors should receive detailed orientation and continuing education to assure they achieve and maintain the necessary level of expertise.

6. *Meetings and information:* The board should meet frequently for extended periods of time and should have access to the information and personnel it needs to perform its duties.

7. *Leadership:* The roles of board chair and CEO should be separate.

8. *Disclosure:* Proxy statements and other board communications should reflect board activities and transactions (e.g., insider trades) in a transparent and timely manner.

9. *Committees:* The nominating, compensation, and audit committees of the board should be composed only of independent directors.

10. *Internal audit:* All public companies should maintain an effective, full-time internal audit function that reports directly to the audit committee.

Source: P. D. Lapides, D. R. Hermanson, M. S. Beasley, J. V. Carcello, F. T. DeZoort, and T. L. Neal. Corporate Governance Center, Kennesaw State University, March 26, 2002.

Financial Reporting

In addition to expanding the role of boards of directors, the Canadian Securities Administrators rules require more financial disclosure by organizations but, unlike the Sarbanes-Oxley Act of the United States, do not require senior managers to provide a qualitative assessment of a company's internal compliance control. Still, these types of changes should lead to somewhat better information—that is, information that is more accurate and reflective of the firm's financial condition.

Cross-Cultural Differences

The concepts of control that we have discussed so far are appropriate for an organization whose units are not geographically separated or culturally distinct. But what about global organizations? Will control systems be different, and what should managers know about adjusting controls for cross-cultural differences?

Methods of controlling people and work can be quite different in different countries. The differences we see in organizational control systems of global organizations are primarily in the measurement and corrective action steps of the control process. In a global corporation, managers of foreign operations tend to be less directly controlled by the home office, if for no other reason than that distance keeps managers from being able to observe work directly. Because distance creates a tendency to formalize controls, the home office of a global company often relies on extensive formal reports for control. The global company also may use the power of information technology to control work activities. For instance, the Japanese-based retailer Seven & i Holdings, which owns the 7-Eleven convenience store chain, uses automated cash registers not only to record sales and monitor inventory, but also to schedule tasks for store managers and to track managers' use of the built-in analytical graphs and forecasts. If managers don't use them enough, they are told to increase their activities.[45]

Technology's impact on control is most evident in comparisons of technologically advanced nations with those that are less technologically advanced. In countries such as Canada, the United States, Japan, Great Britain, Germany, and Australia, global managers use indirect control devices—especially computer-generated reports and analyses—in addition to standardized rules and direct supervision to ensure that work activities are going as planned. In less technologically advanced countries, managers tend to rely more on direct supervision and highly centralized decision making as means of control.

Also, constraints on what corrective actions managers can take may affect managers in foreign countries because laws in some countries do not allow managers the option of closing facilities, laying off employees, taking money out of the country, or bringing in a new management team from outside the country.

Finally, another challenge for global companies in collecting data for measurement and comparison is comparability. For instance, a company's manufacturing facility in Mexico might produce the same products as a facility in Scotland. However, the Mexican facility might be much more labour intensive than its Scottish counterpart (to take strategic advantage of lower labour costs in Mexico). If the top-level executives were to control costs by, for example, calculating labour costs per unit or output per employee, the figures would not be comparable. Global managers must address these types of control challenges.

Workplace Concerns

Today's workplace presents considerable control challenges for managers. From monitoring employees' computer use at work to protecting the workplace from disgruntled employees, managers must control the workplace to ensure that the organization's work can be carried out efficiently and effectively as planned. In this section, we look at two major workplace concerns: workplace privacy and employee theft.

Workplace Privacy

If you work, do you think you have a right to privacy at your workplace? What can your employer find out about you and your work? You might be surprised by the answers!

Do you think it is right for your employer to monitor your email and web surfing at work?

Employers can (and do), among other things, read your email (even those marked "personal" or "confidential"), tap your telephone, monitor your work by computer, store and review computer files, and monitor you in an employee washroom or dressing room. And these actions are not all that uncommon. Nearly 57 percent of Canadian companies have Internet-use policies restricting employees' personal use of the Internet.[46] Employees of the City of Vancouver are warned that their computer use is monitored, and a desktop agent icon of a spinning head reminds them that they are being watched. Exhibit 15-13 summarizes the percentage of employers engaging in different forms of workplace monitoring.

Why do managers feel they must monitor what employees are doing? A big reason is that employees are hired to work, not to surf the web checking stock prices, placing bets at online casinos, or shopping for presents for family or friends. A 2003 Ipsos Reid poll found Canadians spend 1.6 billion hours a year online at work for personal reasons, an average of 4.5 hours a week per employee. The amount of personal time has doubled from 2000.[47] That is a significant cost to businesses.

Another reason that managers monitor employee email and computer use is that they don't want to risk being sued for creating a hostile workplace environment because of offensive messages or an inappropriate image displayed on a co-worker's computer screen. Concern about racial or sexual harassment is one of the reasons why companies might want to monitor or keep backup copies of all email. This electronic record can help establish what actually happened and can help managers react quickly.[48]

Finally, managers want to ensure that company secrets are not being leaked.[49] Although protecting intellectual property is important for all businesses, it's especially important in high-tech industries. Managers need to be certain that employees are not, even inadvertently, passing information on to others who could use that information to harm the company.

Even with the workplace monitoring that managers can do, Canadian employees do have some protection through the Criminal Code, which prohibits unauthorized interception of electronic communication. The Personal Information Protection and Electronic Documents Act, which went into effect in early 2004, gives employees some privacy protection, but it does not make workplace electronic monitoring illegal. Under existing laws, if an individual is aware of a corporate policy of surveillance and does not formally object, or remains at the job, the monitoring is acceptable.[50] Unionized employees may have a bit more privacy with respect to their computers. The Canada Labour Code requires employers operating under a collective agreement to disclose information about plans for technological change. This might provide unions with an opportunity to bargain over electronic surveillance.

Exhibit 15-13

Types of Workplace Monitoring by Employers

Internet use	54.7%
Telephone use	44.0%
Email messages	38.1%
Computer files	30.8%
Job performance using video cameras	14.6%
Phone conversations	11.5%
Voice mail messages	6.8%

Source: Based on S. McElvoy, "E-Mail and Internet Monitoring and the Workplace: Do Employees Have a Right to Privacy?" *Communications and the Law*, June 2002, p. 69.

Because of the potentially serious costs, and given the fact that many jobs now entail work that involves using a computer, many companies are developing and enforcing workplace monitoring policies. The responsibility for this falls on managers. It's important to develop some type of viable workplace monitoring policy. What can managers do to maintain control but do so in a way that is not demeaning to employees? They should develop a clear and unambiguous computer-use policy and make sure that every employee knows about it. For instance, managers should tell employees upfront that their computer use may be monitored at any time and provide clear and specific guidelines as to what constitutes acceptable use of company email systems and the web. For instance, the Bank of Montreal blocks access to "some of the dubious sites that are high risk," such as Playboy.com and other pornographic sites. The bank has developed policies about appropriate and inappropriate use of the Internet, which are emailed to all employees several times a year.[51]

Employee Theft

Would you be surprised to find out that up to 75 percent of Canadian organizations have reported experiencing employee theft and fraud?[52] It's a costly problem—Air Canada, which has run a campaign against employee theft, noted that the airline "is right in line with industry standards for employee theft, and that means as much as 9 per cent of stock such as office supplies and on-board products is taken each year."[53] Employee theft cost Canadian retail businesses more than $8 million a day in 2002, the most recent data available.[54]

Employee theft is defined as any unauthorized taking of company property by employees for their personal use.[55] It can range from embezzlement to fraudulent filing of expense reports to removing equipment, parts, software, and office supplies from company premises. While retail businesses have long faced serious potential losses from employee theft, loose financial controls at start-ups and small companies and the ready availability of information technology have made employee stealing an escalating problem in all kinds and sizes of organizations. It's a control issue that managers need to educate themselves about and with which they must be prepared to deal.[56]

Why do employees steal? The answer depends on whom you ask.[57] Experts in various fields—industrial security, criminology, clinical psychology—all have different perspectives. Industrial security people propose that people steal because the opportunity presents itself through lax controls and favourable circumstances. Criminologists say that it's because people have financial pressures (such as personal financial problems) or vice-based pressures (such as gambling debts). Clinical psychologists suggest that people steal because they can rationalize whatever they are doing as correct and appropriate behaviour ("everyone does it," "they had it coming," "this company makes enough money and they will never miss anything this small," "I deserve this for all that I put up with," and so forth).[58] Although each of these approaches provides compelling insights into employee theft and has been instrumental in program designs to deter it, unfortunately employees continue to steal.

What can managers do to deter or reduce employee theft or fraud? We can use the concepts of feedforward, concurrent, and feedback controls to identify actions managers can take.[59] Exhibit 15-14 on page 490 summarizes several possible control measures.

Customer Interactions

Every month, every local branch of Enterprise Rent-a-Car conducts telephone surveys with customers.[60] Each branch earns a ranking based on the percentage of its customers who say they were "completely satisfied" with their last Enterprise experience—a level of satisfaction referred to as "top box." Top box performance is important to Enterprise because completely satisfied customers are far more likely to be repeat customers. And by using this service-quality index measure, employees' careers and financial aspirations are linked with the organizational goal of providing consistently superior service to each and every customer. Managers at Enterprise understand the connection between employees and customers and the importance of controlling these interactions.

employee theft
Any unauthorized taking of company property by employees for their personal use.

Enterprise Rent-a-Car Canada
www.enterpriserentacar.ca

Exhibit 15-14

Control Measures for Deterring or Reducing Employee Theft or Fraud

Feedforward	Concurrent	Feedback
Use careful prehiring screening.	Treat employees with respect and dignity.	Make sure employees know when theft or fraud has occurred—not naming names but letting people know this is not acceptable.
Establish specific policies defining theft and fraud and discipline procedures.	Openly communicate the costs of stealing.	Use the services of professional investigators.
Involve employees in writing policies.	Let employees know on a regular basis about their successes in preventing theft and fraud.	Redesign control measures.
Educate and train employees about the policies.	Use video surveillance equipment if conditions warrant.	Evaluate your organization's culture and the relationships of managers and employees.
Have professionals review your internal security controls.	Install "lock-out" options on computers, telephones, and email.	
	Use corporate hot lines for reporting incidences.	
	Set a good example.	

Sources: Based on A. H. Bell and D. M. Smith, "Protecting the Company Against Theft and Fraud," *Workforce Online*, December 3, 2000, http://www.workforce.com; J. D. Hansen, "To Catch a Thief," *Journal of Accountancy*, March 2000, pp. 43–46; and J. Greenberg, "The Cognitive Geometry of Employee Theft," in *Dysfunctional Behavior in Organizations: Nonviolent and Deviant Behavior*, eds. S. B. Bacharach, A. O'Leary-Kelly, J. M. Collins, and R. W. Griffin (Stamford, CT: JAI Press, 1998), pp. 147–193.

There is probably no better area to see the link between planning and controlling than in customer service. If a company proclaims customer service as one of its goals, it quickly and clearly becomes apparent whether or not that goal is being achieved by seeing how satisfied customers are with their service. How can managers control the interactions between the goal and the outcome when it comes to customers? The concept of a service profit chain can help (see Exhibit 15-15).

service profit chain
The service sequence from employees to customers to profit.

The **service profit chain** is the service sequence from employees to customers to profit.[61] According to this concept, the company's strategy and service delivery system influences how employees serve customers—their attitudes, behaviours, and service capability. Service capability, in turn, enhances how productive employees are in providing service and the quality of that service. The level of employee service productivity and service quality influences customer perceptions of service value. When service value is high, it has a positive impact on customer satisfaction, which leads to customer loyalty. And customer loyalty improves organizational revenue growth and profitability.

So what does the concept of a service profit chain mean for managers? Managers who want to control customer interactions should work to create long-term and mutually beneficial relationships among the company, employees, and customers. How? By creating a work environment that not only enables employees to deliver high levels of quality service, but makes them feel they are capable of delivering top-quality service. In such a service climate, employees are motivated to deliver superior service.

There is no better example of the service profit chain in action than WestJet Airlines. WestJet is the most consistently profitable Canadian airline, and its customers are fiercely loyal. This is because the company's operating strategy (hiring, training, rewards and recognition, teamwork, and so forth) is built around customer service. Employees consistently deliver outstanding service value to customers. And WestJet's customers reward the company by coming back. It's through efficiently and effectively controlling these customer interactions that companies like WestJet and Enterprise have succeeded.

Exhibit 15-15

The Service Profit Chain

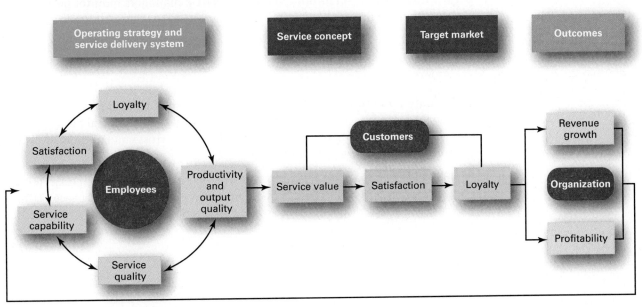

Sources: Adapted and reprinted by permission of Harvard Business Review. An exhibit from J. L. Heskett, T. O. Jones, G. W. Loveman, W. E. Sasser Jr., and L. A. Schlesinger, "Putting the Service Profit Chain to Work," *Harvard Business Review*, March–April 1994, p. 166. Copyright by the President and Fellows of Harvard College. All rights reserved. See also J. L. Heskett, W. E. Sasser, and L. A. Schlesinger, *The Service Profit Chain* (New York: Free Press, 1997).

SUMMARY AND IMPLICATIONS

1. What is control? Control is the process of monitoring activities to ensure that they are being accomplished as planned and correcting any significant deviations. Managers can measure a variety of performances, but the most frequently used ones are organizational productivity, organizational effectiveness, and industry rankings.

▶▶▶ When Li Ka-shing first bought Husky Energy, he immediately introduced financial controls to improve the company's bottom line. He also hired John Lau to stop the losses and halt the expansions that previous managers had introduced. These measures were put in place to make the company profitable.

2. What is the control process? The control process is a three-step process: measuring actual performance, comparing actual performance against a standard, and taking managerial action to correct deviations or inadequate standards.

3. When should controls be introduced? Managers can implement controls before an activity begins (feedforward control), during the time the activity is going on (concurrent control), and after the activity has been completed (feedback control).

4. What methods of control do managers use? There are three different approaches to designing control systems: market, bureaucratic, and clan control. Market control emphasizes the use of external market mechanisms, such as price competition and relative market share, to establish the standards used in the control system. Bureaucratic control emphasizes organizational authority and relies on administrative rules, regulations, procedures, and policies. Under clan control, employee behaviours are regulated by the shared values, norms, traditions, rituals, beliefs, and other aspects of the organization's culture.

▶ ▶ ▶ Control is often needed to improve organizational performance, as John Lau found when he took over Husky Energy and had to halt the company's large losses and the "wild expansions" of the company's previous management.

5. How do financial and information controls help managers monitor performance?
Managers can use financial and information controls to monitor performance.

▶ ▶ ▶ At Husky Energy, John Lau uses traditional financial controls, as well as other measures, including the number of barrels of oil equivalent (BOE) produced by the company daily.

6. What are some current issues in control?
Some important current issues in control include the balanced scorecard (looking at financial, customer, internal business process, and learning and growth assets), corporate governance, cross-cultural differences, workplace concerns, and customer interactions.

▶ ▶ ▶ Husky Energy has a board of directors that looks after the interests of shareholders. The primary duty of Husky's board is to "approve, monitor and provide guidance on the strategic planning process." The board also approves Husky's strategic plans, annual budget, and financial plans.

Chapter 15

Management @ Work

READING FOR COMPREHENSION

1. What is the role of control in management?

2. Name four sources managers can use to acquire information about actual organizational performance.

3. What are three approaches to designing control systems?

4. Contrast immediate and basic corrective action.

5. What can management do to implement a benchmarking best-practices program?

6. What are the advantages and disadvantages of feedforward control?

7. Describe the financial control measures managers can use.

8. What challenges do managers of global organizations face with their control systems?

LINKING CONCEPTS TO PRACTICE

1. What would an organization have to do to change its dominant control approach from bureaucratic to clan? From clan to bureaucratic?

2. How could you use the concept of control in your own personal life? Be specific. (Think in terms of feedforward, concurrent, and feedback controls, as well as controls for the different areas of your life.)

3. When do electronic surveillance devices such as computers, video cameras, and telephone monitoring step

over the line from "effective management controls" to "intrusions on employee rights"?

4. "Every individual employee in the organization plays a role in controlling work activities." Do you agree, or do you think control is something that only managers are responsible for? Explain.

5. Why do you think feedback control is the most popular type of control? Justify your response.

SELF-ASSESSMENT

How Proactive Am I?

For each of the following statements, circle the level of agreement or disagreement that you personally feel:[62]

1 = Strongly Disagree

4 = Neither Agree nor Disagree

7 = Strongly Agree

1. I am constantly on the lookout for new ways to improve my life.	1	2	3	4	5	6	7
2. I feel driven to make a difference in my community, and maybe the world.	1	2	3	4	5	6	7
3. I tend to let others take the initiative to start new projects.	1	2	3	4	5	6	7
4. Wherever I have been, I have been a powerful force for constructive change.	1	2	3	4	5	6	7
5. I enjoy facing and overcoming obstacles to my ideas.	1	2	3	4	5	6	7
6. Nothing is more exciting than seeing my ideas turn into reality.	1	2	3	4	5	6	7
7. If I see something I don't like, I fix it.	1	2	3	4	5	6	7
8. No matter what the odds, if I believe in something I will make it happen.	1	2	3	4	5	6	7
9. I love being a champion for my ideas, even against others' opposition.	1	2	3	4	5	6	7

10. I excel at identifying opportunities.

$\quad$ 1 $\quad$ 2 $\quad$ 3 $\quad$ 4 $\quad$ 5 $\quad$ 6 $\quad$ 7

11. I am always looking for better ways to do things.

$\quad$ 1 $\quad$ 2 $\quad$ 3 $\quad$ 4 $\quad$ 5 $\quad$ 6 $\quad$ 7

12. If I believe in an idea, no obstacle will prevent me from making it happen.

$\quad$ 1 $\quad$ 2 $\quad$ 3 $\quad$ 4 $\quad$ 5 $\quad$ 6 $\quad$ 7

13. I love to challenge the status quo.

$\quad$ 1 $\quad$ 2 $\quad$ 3 $\quad$ 4 $\quad$ 5 $\quad$ 6 $\quad$ 7

14. When I have a problem, I tackle it head-on.

$\quad$ 1 $\quad$ 2 $\quad$ 3 $\quad$ 4 $\quad$ 5 $\quad$ 6 $\quad$ 7

15. I am great at turning problems into opportunities.

$\quad$ 1 $\quad$ 2 $\quad$ 3 $\quad$ 4 $\quad$ 5 $\quad$ 6 $\quad$ 7

16. I can spot a good opportunity long before others can.

$\quad$ 1 $\quad$ 2 $\quad$ 3 $\quad$ 4 $\quad$ 5 $\quad$ 6 $\quad$ 7

17. If I see someone in trouble, I help out in any way I can.

$\quad$ 1 $\quad$ 2 $\quad$ 3 $\quad$ 4 $\quad$ 5 $\quad$ 6 $\quad$ 7

Scoring Key

Add up the numbers for each of your responses to get your total score.

Analysis and Interpretation

This instrument assesses proactive personality. Research finds that the proactive personality is positively associated with entrepreneurial intentions.

Your proactive personality score will range between 17 and 149. The higher your score, the stronger your proactive personality. High scores on this questionnaire suggest you have strong inclinations toward becoming an entrepreneur.

More Self-Assessments mymanagementlab

To learn more about your skills, abilities, and interests, go to the MyManagementLab website and take the following self-assessments:

- I.E.2.—What Time of Day Am I Most Productive?
- II.B.5.—How Good Am I at Disciplining Others?
- III.A.2.—How Willing Am I to Delegate?
- III.A.3.—How Good Am I at Giving Performance Feedback? (This exercise also appears in Chapter 11 on pages 352–353.)

MANAGEMENT FOR YOU TODAY

Dilemma

Your parents have let you know that they are expecting a big party for their 25th wedding anniversary, and that you are in charge of planning it. Develop a timeline for carrying out the project, and then identify ways to monitor progress toward getting the party planned. How will you know that your plans have been successful? At what critical points do you need to examine your plans to make sure that everything is on track?

Becoming a Manager

- Identify the types of controls you use in your own personal life and whether they are feedforward, concurrent, or feedback controls.
- When preparing for major class projects, identify some performance measures that you can use to help you determine whether or not the project is going as planned.
- Try to come up with some ways to improve your personal efficiency and effectiveness.

Controlling Cheating

You are a professor in the School of Business at a local university. Several of your colleagues have expressed an interest in developing some specific controls to minimize opportunities for students to cheat on homework assignments and exams. You and some other faculty members have volunteered to write a report outlining some suggestions that might be used.

Form teams of 3 or 4 and discuss this topic. Write a bulleted list of your suggestions from the perspective of controlling possible cheating (1) before it happens, (2) while in-class exams or assignments are being completed, and (3) after it has happened. Please keep the report brief (no more than two pages). Be prepared to present your suggestions before the rest of the class.

ETHICS IN ACTION

Ethical Dilemma Exercise: Should Surfing Adult Websites on a Personal Laptop at Work Be Considered Private?

Pornography and offensive email are two major reasons why many companies establish strict policies and monitor their employees' use of the Internet.[63] Citing legal and ethical concerns, managers are determined to keep inappropriate images and messages out of the workplace. "As a company, if we don't make some effort to keep offensive material off our network, we could end up on the wrong end of a sexual harassment lawsuit or other legal action that could cost the company hundreds of thousands of dollars," says the technology manager at one small business. "To a company our size, that would be devastating." Another reason is cost. Unauthorized Internet activity not only wastes valuable work time but it ties up network resources. Thus, many companies have installed electronic systems to screen email messages and monitor what employees do online. In some companies, one person is designated to review incoming emails and delete offensive messages.

Having a clear policy and a monitoring system are only first steps. Management must be sure that employees are aware of the rules—and understand that the company is

serious about cleaning up any ethics violations. British Telecom (BT), for example, twice sent emails to remind all its employees that looking at online pornography was grounds for dismissal. Despite the warnings, management had to fire 200 employees in an 18-month period. Going further, the company told police about 10 employees' activities, and one has already been sentenced to prison. "We took this decision for the good of BT," explained a spokesperson, "and since we have taken this action, the problem has reduced dramatically."

Imagine that you are the administrative assistant for a high-ranking executive at BT. One afternoon you receive an urgent phone call for your manager. You knock on his office door but get no answer, so you open the door, thinking you will leave a note on his desk. Then you notice that your manager is absorbed in watching a very graphic adult website on his personal laptop. As you quietly back out of the office, you wonder how to handle this situation. Review this chapter's "Workplace Privacy" section on pages 487–489 as you consider this ethical challenge.

Thinking Critically About Ethics

Duplicating software for co-workers and friends is a widespread practice, but software in Canada is protected by copyright laws. Copying software is punishable by fines of up to $20 000. Businesses can be held accountable if their employees use unlicensed software on company computers.

Is reproducing copyrighted software ever an acceptable practice? Explain. Is it wrong for employees of a business to

pirate software but permissible for struggling students who cannot afford to buy their own software? As a manager, what types of ethical guidelines could you establish for software use? What if you were a manager in another country where software piracy was an accepted practice?

Air Canada and WestJet Airlines

Without information, managers cannot make good decisions.[64] In order to make good decisions, then, companies need to protect their information. Executives at Air Canada thought they had. However, managers were shocked when they discovered that outsiders had penetrated their website to steal data. Their experience raises some troubling questions about the security of company information in the Internet age.

One of Air Canada's former employees, Jeffrey Lafond, had a password for an Air Canada employee travel website that listed all of the company's flights and passenger loads. The password had been given to him as part of a severance package in 2000. It was meant to enable Lafond to book two free flights of his choice a year through 2005.

Lafond subsequently became a financial analyst at WestJet Airlines, and Mark Hill, WestJet co-founder and vice-president of strategic planning, learned of Lafond's ability to access the Air Canada website. Hill asked for Lafond's password, so that he could access the website himself.

Hill used the password to count Air Canada's load factors, spending about 90 minutes an evening doing so. Because it was so time-consuming to do this by hand, Don Bell, WestJet's vice-president of customer service and another airline co-founder, asked a WestJet IT staff member to create a program to automatically download and analyze Air Canada's load factors. Air Canada claims that WestJet entered Air Canada's website 240 000 times between May 2003 and March 2004, using Lafond's password.

Air Canada filed a lawsuit against WestJet. In a countersuit, WestJet accused Air Canada of collecting garbage from Hill's house in an effort to determine exactly how he was using Air Canada's data.

In May 2006, to put an end to the lawsuits, WestJet admitted that senior executives stole confidential information and apologized to Air Canada. They agreed to pay Air Canada $5.5 million for its legal fees and donate $10 million to children's charities.

Should Lafond have given Hill his password? What other ethical issues do you see in this case? What should Air Canada's chief information officer do to ensure that information is available to those who need it, but not available to outsiders who may use the information for competitive advantage?

A Control Concern at BC Ferries

Just after midnight on March 22, 2006, the *Queen of the North* ferry, part of the BC Ferries system, hit rocks off Gil Island, south of Prince Rupert.[65] It was immediately clear that the ferry was in trouble, and within 15 minutes, "all" the passengers and crew were off the ship and in the ferry's lifeboats. As local townspeople and the Coast Guard rescued the passengers from the lifeboats, the ferry sank, a little more than an hour after first striking the rocks. Initial media reports celebrated the fact that all 99 passengers and crew had managed to get off the ferry safely, and with no major injuries. The crew was widely praised for conducting an orderly evacuation, something employees practise and train for at regular intervals.

On day two, passengers were reported missing. How could the ferry crew not know that there had still been people onboard? While international regulations require that ferries record identifying information about all passengers (name, gender, and whether they are adults, children, or infants), Ottawa does not require BC's ferry fleet to meet international standards. Transport Canada guidelines also do not require the collection of passenger names. Ferry staff do not even take a head count after loading, so the number of passengers is only roughly determined by the number of tickets sold. Moreover, there is no system in place to count passengers as they move from the ship to lifeboats, should such a situation arise. Thus, the initial reports from BC Ferries that "all 99" passengers and crew survived were based on the simple belief that everyone had been evacuated.

In the days following the sinking, demands for explanations of what had gone wrong arose. Jackie Miller, president of the BC Ferry and Marine Workers Union, which represented the ferry employees, called for a public inquiry into safety issues of the entire ferry fleet, citing another ferry sinking and an engine room fire in recent years. "We have grave concerns," Miller said. "A lot of us have been continuously worried. BC Ferries has been incredibly lucky, thank God, that we haven't had a major loss of life as a result of the three major marine incidents."

However, Rod Nelson, regional director of communications for Transport Canada, reported that the *Queen of the North* passed an annual safety inspection less than 3 weeks earlier, including a lifeboat drill on March that required that passengers be evacuated in less than 30 minutes. "They did very well at it, and they obviously did very well when it happened for real," Nelson said.

The internal investigation BC Ferries conducted in the months after the sinking concluded that "human factors were the primary cause" of what happened. "The ship never altered course at all. It never changed its speed, it just ran ahead into Gil Island," BC Ferries' president, David Hahn, said. There were two people on the bridge that evening (from where the ship is navigated), the acting fourth officer and the quartermaster, who had not yet written her bridge watchman's exam. The report stated that the fourth officer "failed to make a necessary course alteration or verify such alteration was made in accordance with pre-established fleet routing directives and good seamanship."

During the investigation, crew members responsible for navigating the ship that night claimed that they were unfamiliar with newly installed steering equipment. In addition, they had turned off a monitor displaying their course, because they could not turn on the night settings. The bridge crew used the equipment "in a way different than as instructed," the report noted, although this was not cited as a cause of running aground. The report also concluded that the crew maintained a "casual watch-standing behaviour," had "lost situational awareness," and "failed to appreciate the vessel's impending peril." Transcripts of radio calls that evening noted that music was heard playing on the bridge.

Regarding the evacuation, though the crew was praised for acting quickly, several things made the evacuation more difficult than need be. There was no master key to the sleeping cabins; rather, multiple keys had to be tried. A chalk X is supposed to be drawn on searched cabin doors, but no one had chalk. As well, only 53 of the 55 cabins were confirmed to have been searched.

Questions

1. Describe the type(s) of control that could be used to improve the BC Ferries service to prevent an accident such as this occurring again. Give specific examples.

2. Assume that you are the president of BC Ferries. You have read the report of the investigation and noted some of the problems found. What would you do? Explain your reasoning.

3. Would some types of controls be more important than others in this situation?

DEVELOPING YOUR INTERPERSONAL SKILLS

Providing Feedback

About the Skill

Ask a manager how often he or she gives feedback to employees, and you are likely to get an answer followed by a qualifier! If the feedback is positive, it's likely to be given promptly and enthusiastically. However, negative feedback is often treated very differently and often avoided. Most of us don't enjoy receiving negative feedback and managers don't particularly enjoy communicating bad news. They fear offending the other person or having to deal with the recipient's defensiveness. The result is that negative feedback is often avoided, delayed, or substantially distorted. However, it is important for managers to provide both positive and negative feedback. It is also important during formal reviews that managers bring up the good things employees have done over the evaluation period, even if they have already commented on them informally. Employees expect managers to remember these things and to be congratulated again.[66]

Steps in Developing the Skill

You can be more effective at providing feedback if you use the following six suggestions:[67]

1. **Focus on specific behaviours.** Feedback should be specific rather than general. Avoid such statements as, "You have a bad attitude" or "I'm really impressed with the good job you did." They are vague, and although they provide information, they don't tell the recipient enough to correct the "bad attitude" or on what basis you concluded that a "good job" had been done so the person knows what behaviours to repeat or to avoid.

2. **Keep feedback impersonal.** Feedback, particularly the negative kind, should be descriptive rather than judgmental or evaluative. No matter how upset you are, keep the feedback focused on job-related behaviours and never criticize someone personally because of an inappropriate action.

3. **Keep feedback goal oriented.** Feedback should not be given primarily to "unload" on another person. If you have to say something negative, make sure it's directed toward the recipient's goals. Ask yourself whom the feedback is supposed to help. If the answer is you, bite your tongue and hold the comment. Such feedback undermines your credibility and lessens the meaning and influence of future feedback.

4. **Time feedback well.** Feedback is most meaningful to a recipient when there is a very short interval between his or her behaviour and the receipt of feedback about that behaviour. Moreover, if you are particularly concerned with changing behaviour, delays in providing feedback on the undesirable actions lessen the likelihood that the feedback will be effective in bringing about the desired change. Of course, making feedback prompt merely for the sake of promptness can backfire if you have insufficient information, if you are angry, or if you are otherwise emotionally upset. In such instances, "well timed" could mean "somewhat delayed."

5. **Ensure understanding.** Make sure your feedback is concise and complete so that the recipient clearly and fully understands your communication. It may help to have the recipient rephrase the content of your feedback to find out whether or not it fully captured the meaning you intended.

6. **Direct negative feedback toward behaviour that the recipient can control.** There is little value in reminding a person of some shortcoming over which he or she has no control. Negative feedback should be directed at behaviour that the recipient can do something about. In addition, when negative feedback is given concerning something that the recipient can control, it might be a good idea to indicate specifically what can be done to improve the situation.

Practising the Skill

Read the following scenario. Write some notes about how you would handle the situation described. Be sure to refer to the six suggestions for providing feedback.

Scenario

Craig is an excellent employee whose expertise and productivity have always met or exceeded your expectations. But recently he has been making work difficult for other members of your advertising team. Like his co-workers, Craig researches and computes the costs of media coverage for your advertising agency's clients. The work requires laboriously leafing through several large reference books to find the correct base price and add-on charges for each radio or television station and time slot, calculating each actual cost, and compiling the results in a computerized spreadsheet. To make things more efficient and convenient, you have always allowed your team members to bring the reference books they are using to their desks while they are using them. Lately, however, Craig has been piling books around him for days and sometimes weeks at a time. The books interfere with the flow of traffic past his desk and other people have to go out of their way to retrieve the books from Craig's pile. It's time for you to have a talk with Craig. What will you say?

Reinforcing the Skill

The following activities will help you practise and reinforce the skills associated with providing feedback:

1. Think of three things that a friend or family member did well recently. Did you praise the person at the time? If not, why? The next time someone close to you does something well, give him or her positive feedback.

2. You have a good friend who has a mannerism (for instance, speech, body movement, style of dress, or whatever) that you think is inappropriate and detracts from the overall impression that he or she makes. Come up with a plan for talking with this person. What will you say? When will you talk with your friend? How will you handle his or her reaction?

Diversity Success Stories

Canadian companies are making progress in their diversity programs.[68] Although many still have a long way to go, some companies are doing their best to make employees of all races into full and active participants in their businesses. *Canadian Business* and Rogers OMNI TV recently identified top places for visible minorities and Aboriginal peoples to work. Each of the companies on this list has made a strong commitment to diversity at every organizational level and in every aspect—from new hires to suppliers, and even to the charitable causes supported. Who are some of these diversity champions? The top 10 are Call-Net Enterprises (now part of Rogers), Canadian Imperial Bank of Commerce, TD Bank Financial Group, Bank of Nova Scotia, Bank of Montreal, HSBC Bank Canada, TELUS Mobility, Canadian Western Bank, Citizens Bank of Canada, and Westcoast Energy (now Duke Energy Gas Transmission Canada).

At Vancouver-based HSBC Bank Canada, 43.3 percent of the employees are from visible minorities. "Diversity is core to our business," says Executive Vice-president Sarah Morgan-Silvester.

Canadian Business recently recognized Ottawa-based Nasittuq Corporation, which monitors 47 radar stations that protect Canadian skies from threats, as one of Canada's most inclusive workplaces for Aboriginal peoples. Nasittuq runs a training program that introduces Inuit to the North Warning System. Graduates are then hired by Nasittuq or find jobs with other companies because of the skills they have acquired.

How can companies use control mechanisms to make sure that they have a diverse workforce? Do you think companies should make special efforts to recruit employees with diverse characteristics? Why or why not? What would be the business advantages of doing so?

Operations Management

It's one of the oldest post offices in North America. Sepomex (*Servicio Postal Mexicano*), Mexico's state postal system, was established over four centuries ago in 1580. In August 1986, it became a semi-independent decentralized organization with the mandate to "serve as the public post office in Mexico." Carlos Rodarte is the head of regional operations for Sepomex, a job that entails many operational challenges.[1]

The Mexican postal system handles some 700 million letters a year, which may sound like a lot. But that number translates into just 7 pieces of mail per person. Compare that to Brazil, where the postal system handles 8 billion mailings a year, or 46 letters per person. It's clear that "Mexico's postal system is underused by a skeptical public." Data collected by a Mexican polling organization found that "a shocking 29 percent of Mexicans hadn't even heard of Sepomex. Of those familiar with the mail service, 32 percent considered it to be slow and almost the same percentage preferred to use private messengers to hand-deliver documents, a common practice in Latin American cities."

Rodarte is trying to improve both the efficiency and the effectiveness of the country's postal system. He oversees Pantaco, the dispatch centre where most of the country's mail passes through at some point. He has made improvements there including installing a new roof to make the building look more modern, and investing in cutting-edge technology like security cameras, barcode scanners, and machines that can read and sort 70 letters per minute. In addition, Mexico's Transport and Communications Ministry provided more funds to Sepomex, almost doubling capital outlays in 2005. These additional funds will go toward purchasing new vehicles, renovating dilapidated post offices, and making other infrastructure improvements. In addition, one of the things that Rodarte does to test his "own company's efficiency" is to send postcards to himself from almost every place he travels. However, there are still operational challenges to tackle, especially in the area of quality.

It is important for managers everywhere to have well-thought-out and well-designed operating systems, organizational control systems, and quality programs in order to survive in the increasingly competitive global environment. With these systems in place, organizations will be able to produce high-quality products and services at prices that meet or beat those of their competitors. One of the keys to managerial success is in understanding operations management.

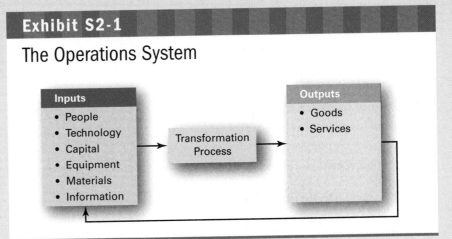

Exhibit S2-1

The Operations System

Inputs
- People
- Technology
- Capital
- Equipment
- Materials
- Information

Transformation Process

Outputs
- Goods
- Services

What Is Operations Management and Why Is It Important?

What is **operations management**? The term refers to the design, operation, and control of the transformation process that converts such resources as labour and raw materials into goods and services that are sold to customers. Exhibit S2-1 portrays, in a very simplified fashion, the fact that every organization has an operations system that creates value by transforming inputs into outputs. The system takes in inputs—people, technology, capital, equipment, materials, and information—and transforms them, through various processes, procedures, work activities, and so forth, into finished goods and services. And just as every organization produces something, so every unit in an organization also produces something. Marketing, finance, research and development, human resources, and accounting convert inputs into outputs such as sales, increased market share, high rates of return on capital, new and innovative products, motivated and committed employees, and accounting reports. As a manager, you will need to be familiar with operations management concepts, regardless of the area you manage, in order to achieve your goals efficiently and effectively. Q&A S2.1

Why is operations management so important to organizations and man-

agers? There are three reasons: It encompasses both services and manufacturing, it's important in effectively and efficiently managing productivity, and it plays a strategic role in an organization's competitive success.

Services and Manufacturing

Every organization produces something. Unfortunately, this fact is often overlooked except in obvious cases such as in the manufacturing of cars, cellphones, or outboard engines. After all, **manufacturing organizations** produce physical goods. It's easy to see the operations management (transformation) process at work in these types of organizations because raw materials are turned into recognizable physical products. But that transformation process is not as readily evident in **service organizations** because they produce nonphysical outputs in the form of services. For instance, hospitals provide medical and health care services that help people manage their personal health, airlines provide transportation services that move people

from one location to another, a cruise line provides a vacation and entertainment service, schools provide education, and the list goes on and on. All of these service organizations transform inputs into outputs.

Service organizations dominate the global economy today. Most of the world's industrialized nations are predominantly service economies. In Canada, for instance, over 69 percent of all economic activity is in the services sector; in the United States, it's 78 percent. The economy of most industrialized countries are over 50 percent services.[2]

Managing Productivity

One jetliner has some 4 million parts. Efficiently assembling such a finely engineered product requires intense focus. Boeing and Airbus, the two major global manufacturers, have copied techniques from Toyota. However, not every technique can be copied because airlines demand more customization than do car buyers, and there are significantly more rigid safety regulations for jetliners than for cars.[3]

operations management
The design, operation, and control of the transformation process that converts resources into goods and services.

manufacturing organizations
Organizations that produce physical goods.

service organizations
Organizations that produce nonphysical outputs in the form of services.

Exhibit S2-2

Deming's 14 Points for Improving Management's Productivity

1. Plan for the long-term future.

2. Never be complacent concerning the quality of your product.

3. Establish statistical control over your production processes and require your suppliers to do so as well.

4. Deal with the best and fewest number of suppliers.

5. Find out whether your problems are confined to particular parts of the production process or stem from the overall process itself.

6. Train workers for the job that you are asking them to perform.

7. Raise the quality of your line supervisors.

8. Drive out fear.

9. Encourage departments to work closely together rather than to concentrate on departmental or divisional distinctions.

10. Do not adopt strictly numerical goals.

11. Require your workers to do quality work.

12. Train your employees to understand statistical methods.

13. Train your employees in new skills as the need arises.

14. Make top managers responsible for implementing these principles.

Source: W. E. Deming, "Improvement of Quality and Productivity Through Action by Management," *National Productivity Review*, Winter 1981–1982, pp. 12–22. With permission. Copyright 1981 by Executive Enterprises, Inc., 22 West 21st St., New York, NY 10010-6904. All rights reserved.

Although most organizations don't make products that have 4 million parts, improving productivity has become a major goal in virtually every organization. By **productivity**, we mean the overall output of goods or services produced divided by the inputs needed to generate that output. For countries, high productivity can lead to economic growth and development. Employees can receive higher wages and company profits can increase without causing inflation. For individual organizations, increased productivity provides a more competitive cost structure and the ability to offer more competitive prices. Q&A S2.2

Organizations that hope to succeed globally are looking for ways to improve productivity. For example, McDonald's drastically reduced the amount of time it takes to cook its french fries—now only 65 seconds as

compared with the 210 seconds it once took, saving time and other resources.[4] Toronto-based Canadian Imperial Bank of Commerce automated its purchasing function, saving several million dollars annually.[5] And Škoda, the Czech Republic car company owned by Germany's Volkswagen AG, improved its productivity through an intensive restructuring of its manufacturing process. The company recently produced its 5-millionth car.[6]

Productivity is a composite of people and operations variables. To improve productivity, managers must focus on both. W. Edwards Deming, a management consultant and quality expert, believed that managers, not workers, were the primary source of increased productivity. He outlined 14 points for improving management's productivity (see Exhibit S2-2). A close look at these suggestions reveals Deming's understanding of the interplay between people and operations. High productivity cannot come solely from good "people management." The

truly effective organization will maximize productivity by successfully integrating people into the overall operations system.

Strategic Role of Operations Management

The era of modern manufacturing originated over 100 years ago in North America, primarily in Detroit's automobile factories. The success that North American manufacturers experienced during World War II led manufacturing executives to believe that troublesome production problems had been conquered. These executives focused, instead, on improving other functional areas such as finance and marketing and gave manufacturing little attention.

However, as Canadian and US executives neglected production, managers in Japan, Germany, and other countries took the opportunity to develop modern, computer-based, and technologically advanced facilities that

productivity
The overall output of goods or services produced divided by the inputs needed to generate that output.

fully integrated manufacturing operations into strategic planning decisions. The competition's success realigned world manufacturing leadership. North American manufacturers soon discovered that foreign goods were being made not only less expensively but also with better quality. Finally, by the late 1970s, Canadian and American executives recognized that they were facing a true crisis, and they responded. They invested heavily in improving manufacturing technology, increased the corporate authority and visibility of manufacturing executives, and began incorporating existing and future production requirements into the organization's overall strategic plan. Today, successful organizations recognize the crucial

role that operations management plays as part of the overall organizational strategy to establish and maintain global leadership.[7] Q&A S2.3

The strategic role that operations management plays in successful organizational performance can be seen clearly through an understanding of how operations are planned and then controlled.

Planning Operations

As we have noted in several places throughout this book, planning must precede control. Therefore, before we can introduce operations management control techniques, we need to review a few of the more important decisions related to planning operations.

Four key decisions—capacity, facilities location, process, and facilities layout—provide the long-term strategic direction for operations planning. They determine the proper size of an operating system, where the physical facilities should be located, the best methods for transforming inputs into outputs, and the most efficient layout of equipment and workstations. Once these decisions have been made, three short-term decisions—the aggregate plan, the master schedule, and a material requirements plan—need to be established. These short-term decisions provide the tactical plans for the operating system. In this section, we review these seven types of planning decisions (see Exhibit S2-3).

Exhibit S2-3

Decisions Made in Planning Operations

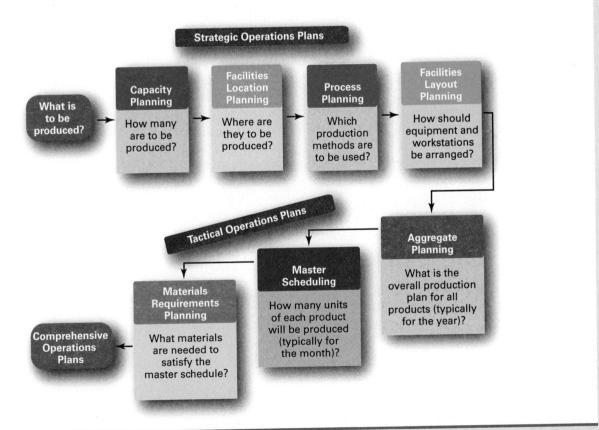

Capacity Planning

Assume that you have decided to go into the boat-building business. On the basis of your analysis of the market and other environmental factors (see Chapter 7), you believe that there is a market for a premium-quality 8.5-metre sailboat. You know *what* you want to produce. What is your next step? You need to determine *how many* boats you expect to build. This decision, in turn, will determine the proper size of your plant and other facility-planning issues. When managers assess their operating system's capabilities for producing a desired number of output units for each type of product anticipated during a given period, they are engaged in **capacity planning**.

Capacity planning begins by converting the sales demand forecasts (see Chapter 8) into capacity requirements. If you produce only one type of boat, plan to sell the boats for an average of $50 000 each, and anticipate generating sales of $2.5 million during the first year, you will need to be able to handle 50 boats ($50 000 × 50 = $2 500 000). Those are your physical capacity requirements. This calculation is obviously much more complex if you are producing dozens of different products.

If your organization is already established, you compare the sales demand forecast against your production capacity. Then you can determine whether you will need to add to or subtract from your existing capacity. Keep in mind that you don't have to be in a manufacturing business to use capacity planning. It is just as relevant for determining the number of beds needed in a hospital or the maximum number of sandwiches that a SUBWAY outlet can serve during the lunch rush hour.

Once you have converted the forecast into physical capacity requirements, you will be able to develop a set of alternative capacity plans that will meet the requirements. You often will have to make some modifications; that is, you will have to expand or reduce capacity. In the long term, you can alter the size of your operation significantly and permanently by buying new equipment or¡ by selling off existing facilities. In the short term, however, you will be forced to make more temporary modifications. You can add an extra work shift, increase overtime, or reduce employee work hours; you can temporarily shut down operations or subcontract work out to other organizations. If you manufacture a product that can be stored (like sailboats), you can build inventories during slack periods to be used when demand exceeds capacity.

Facilities Location Planning

When you determine the need for additional capacity, you must design and choose a facility. This process is called **facilities location planning**. Where you choose to locate will depend on which factors have the greatest impact on total production and distribution costs. These include availability of needed labour skills, labour costs, energy costs, proximity to suppliers or customers, and the like. Rarely are all these factors of equal importance. The kind of business you are in dictates your critical contingencies, which then dictate, to a large degree, the optimal location.

For example, the need for skilled technical specialists has led an increasing number of high-tech firms to locate in the Vancouver area. The area's high concentration of colleges and universities makes it easy for firms that require employees with computer, engineering, and research skills to find and hold on to such people. Similarly, it's not by chance that many manufacturers whose transformation processes are labour intensive have moved their manufacturing facilities overseas to places such as Taiwan and Malaysia. When labour costs are a critical contingency, organizations will locate their facilities where labour wage rates are low. For instance, Toronto-based Bata Shoes manufactures most of its shoes outside Canada because of the low labour costs in less developed countries.[8] When customer convenience is critical, as it is for many retail stores, the location decision is often dictated by concerns such as proximity to a highway or pedestrian traffic.

What contingencies are going to be critical in your sailboat business? Obviously, you will need employees with boat-building skills, and they are most likely to be plentiful in coastal areas such as the Maritimes and British Columbia. Shipping costs of the final product are likely to be a major expenditure. To keep your prices competitive, you might want to locate close to your customers. That again suggests the East Coast, West Coast, or possibly the Great Lakes region. Weather might be an additional factor. It might be less expensive to build boats outside in Vancouver's milder climate than in the harsh winter climate of the Maritimes. If labour availability, shipping costs, and weather are your critical contingencies, you still have some latitude in your location decision. After you choose a region, you still must select a community and a specific site.

Process Planning

In **process planning**, management determines how a product or service will be produced. Process planning encompasses evaluating the available production methods and selecting

capacity planning
Assessing an operating system's capabilities for producing a desired number of output units for each type of product anticipated during a given period.

facilities location planning
The design and location of an operations facility.

process planning
Determining how a product or service will be produced.

those that will best achieve the operating objectives.

For any given production process, whether in manufacturing or the service sector, there are always alternative conversion methods. Designing a restaurant, for instance, allows for a number of process choices: Should we inventory fast food (as McDonald's does)? Should we have limited-option fast food (as Burger King and Wendy's do)? Should we have cafeteria-style delivery, drive-in, take-out, a no-option fixed menu, or complex meals prepared to order? Key questions that ultimately determine how an organization's products or services will be produced include the following: Will the technology be routine or nonroutine? What degree of automation will be used? Should the system be developed to maximize efficiency or flexibility? How should the product or service flow through the operations systems?[9] In our sailboat manufacturing example, the boats could be made by an assembly-line process. If you decide to keep them highly standardized, you might find a routine transformation process to be most cost efficient. But if you want each boat to be made to a customer's order, you will require a different technology and a different set of production methods.

Process planning is complex. Deciding on the best combinations of processes in terms of costs, quality, labour efficiency, and similar considerations is difficult because the decisions are interrelated. A change in one element of the production process often has spillover effects on a number of other elements. As a result, the detailed planning is usually left to production and industrial engineers under the overall guidance of top managers.

Facilities Layout Planning

The final strategic decision in operations planning is to assess and select among alternative layout options for equipment and workstations. This step is called **facilities layout planning**. The objective of facilities layout planning is to find a physical arrangement that will best facilitate production efficiency and that will also be appealing to employees and customers.

Layout planning begins by assessing space needs. Space has to be provided for work areas, tools and equipment, storage, maintenance facilities, restrooms, offices, lunch areas and cafeterias, waiting rooms, and even parking lots. Then, on the basis of the previously decided process plans, various layout configurations can be evaluated to determine how efficient each is for handling the workflow. A number of layout-planning devices are available to help make these decisions; they range from simple, scaled-to-size paper cutouts to sophisticated computer software programs that can manipulate hundreds of variables and print out alternative layout designs.[10]

There are basically three workflow layouts.[11] The **process layout** arranges components (such as work centres, equipment, or departments) together according to similarity of function. Exhibit S2-4 on page 506 illustrates the process layout at a medical clinic. In **product layout**, the components are arranged according to the progressive steps by which the product is made. Exhibit S2-5 on page 506 illustrates a product layout in a plant that manufactures aluminum tubing. The third approach, the **fixed-position layout**, is used when, because of its size or bulk, the product remains at one location. The product stays in place, and tools, equipment, and human skills are brought to it. Movie lot sound stages and the manufacturing of airplanes and cruise ships illustrate the fixed-position layout. The building of your 8.5-metre sailboats is likely to use either a product or a fixed-position layout.

Aggregate Planning

Since the strategic decisions have been made, we move to the tactical operations decisions. The first of these deals with planning the overall production activities and the operating resources needed to do them. This is called **aggregate planning** and often deals with a time frame of up to a year.

The aggregate plan provides a "big picture." On the basis of the sales demand forecast and capacity plan, the aggregate plan establishes inventory levels and production rates and estimates the size of the total operation's labour force on a monthly basis for approximately the next 12 months. The focus is on generalities, not specifics. Categories of products, not individual items, are considered. A paint company's aggregate plan would look at the total number of gallons of house paint to be manufactured but would avoid decisions about colour or size of container. As such, the aggregate plan is particularly valuable to large operations that have a varied product line.

For small, one-product firms, the aggregate plan will look like the master schedule, only it covers a longer time frame. When completed, the aggregate plan often points out two basic decisions: the best overall production rate to adopt and the overall number of workers to be employed during each period in the planning time frame.[12]

facilities layout planning
Assessing and selecting among alternative layout options for equipment and workstations.

process layout
A layout that arranges components together according to similarity of function.

product layout
A layout that arranges components according to the progressive steps by which a product is made.

fixed-position layout
A layout in which the product stays in place, and tools, equipment, and human skills are brought to it.

aggregate planning
Planning the overall production activities and the operating resources needed to do them.

Exhibit S2-4

A Process Layout at a Medical Clinic

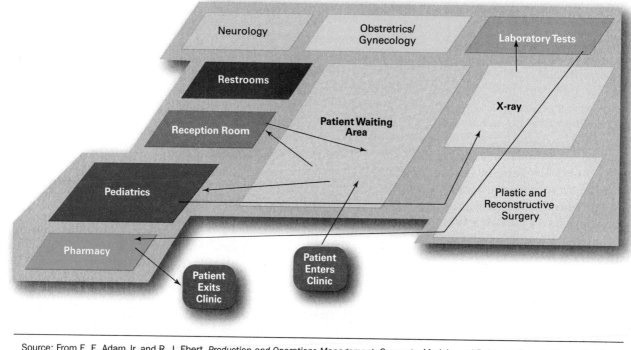

Source: From E. E. Adam Jr. and R. J. Ebert, *Production and Operations Management: Concepts, Models, and Behavior*, 5th ed. (Upper Saddle River, NJ: Prentice Hall, 1992), p. 254. With permission of Ronald J. Ebert.

Exhibit S2-5

A Product Layout at an Aluminum-Tubing Plant

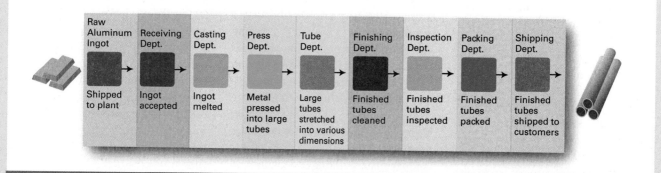

Master Scheduling

The **master schedule** is derived from the aggregate plan. It specifies the following: quality and type of each item to be produced; how, when, and where they should be produced for the next day, week, or month; labour force levels; and inventory.

The first requirement of master scheduling is *disaggregation:* that is, breaking the aggregate plan down into detailed operational plans for each of the products or services the organization produces.[13] After that, these plans

master schedule
A schedule that specifies quality and type of each item to be produced; how, when, and where they should be produced; labour force levels; and inventory.

Exhibit S2-6

Developing a Master Schedule from an Aggregate Plan

From the Aggregate Plan (units per month)

Month	July	August	September	October	November
Heavy-Duty Transmission	100	125	120	130	120
Standard Transmission	75	80	70	100	100
Economy Transmission	75	45	60	70	80
Total	**250**	**250**	**250**	**300**	**300**

Master Schedule for Heavy-Duty Transmission (units)

		July				August			
Week		1	2	3	4	5	6	7	8
Heavy-Duty Model #s	1176	0	10	0	15	0	0	20	0
	1177	0	10	0	10	0	5	10	0
	1178	0	5	10	0	0	15	0	10
	1179	10	0	5	0	10	15	0	0
	1180	15	0	10	0	20	0	0	20
		Total 100				**Total 125**			

need to be scheduled against one another in a master schedule.

Exhibit S2-6 shows a master schedule for a manufacturer of automobile transmissions. The top portion of the figure informs lower-level managers (through the aggregate plan) that top managers have authorized the capacity, inventory, and people to produce 100 heavy-duty transmissions in July, 125 in August, and so forth. The lower part of the figure illustrates a master schedule. For example, it shows how lower-level managers consider the July production for 100 heavy-duty transmissions and determine which models to make. They determine not only what specific models to make each week, but also how many. During the first week of July, for instance, 10 units

of Model 1179 and 15 units of Model 1180 will be assembled.

Material Requirements Planning

After the specific products have been determined, each should be analyzed to determine the precise materials and parts that it requires. **Material requirements planning (MRP)** is a system that uses these data for purchasing, inventory, and priority planning purposes.

Using a computer, managers can analyze product design specifications to pinpoint all the materials and parts necessary to produce the product. By merging this information with computerized inventory records, management will know the quantities of each

part in inventory and when each is likely to be used up. When lead times and safety stock requirements are established and entered into the computer, MRP ensures that the right materials are available when needed.

Newly enhanced MRP software is offering production planners and schedulers even more decision support. This "constraint based" scheduling software takes into account such factors as equipment shutdowns, labour shortages, production bottlenecks, and raw material shortfalls in determining when and where resources should be allocated.[14]

material requirements planning (MRP)
A system that dissects products into the materials and parts necessary for purchasing, inventory, and priority planning purposes.

Controlling Operations

Once an operating system has been designed and implemented, its key elements must be monitored. Below, we discuss ways to control costs, maintenance, and quality.

Cost Control

Unlike Japanese managers, Canadian and US managers treat cost control as a project that happens from time to time. Japanese managers regard cost control as something done continuously.[15] Although cost control is often viewed as a function controlled by the accounting department, with managers asked to look for causes for deviations from cost standards, cost control really should be a continuing concern of managers.

Many organizations have adopted the cost-centre approach to controlling costs. Work areas, departments, or entire manufacturing plants are identified as distinct **cost centres**, and their managers are held responsible for the cost performance of their units. Any unit's total costs are made up of two types of costs: direct and indirect. **Direct costs** are costs incurred in proportion to the output of a particular good or service. Labour and materials typically fall into this category. On the other hand, **indirect costs** are largely unaffected by changes in output. Even if output is zero, these costs are still incurred. Insurance expenses and the salaries of staff employees are examples of typical indirect costs. This direct–indirect distinction is important. Cost-centre managers are held responsible for all direct costs in their unit, but indirect costs are not necessarily within their control. However, because all costs are controllable at some level in the organization, top managers should identify where the control lies and should hold lower-level managers accountable for costs under their control.[16]

Maintenance Control

Delivering goods or services in an efficient and effective manner requires operating systems with high equipment utilization and a minimum amount of downtime. Therefore, managers need to be concerned with maintenance control. The importance of maintenance control, however, depends on the process technology used. A breakdown in a standardized assembly-line process can affect hundreds of employees. On an automobile or refrigerator assembly line, it's not unusual for a serious breakdown on one machine to bring an entire manufacturing plant to a halt. In contrast, most systems using more general-purpose and redundant processes have less interdependency between activities; therefore, a machine breakdown is likely to have less of an impact. Nevertheless, an equipment breakdown—like an inventory stockout—may mean higher costs, delayed deliveries, or lost sales.

There are three approaches to maintenance control.[17] **Preventive maintenance** is performed before a breakdown occurs. **Remedial maintenance** is a complete overhaul, replacement, or repair of the equipment when it breaks down. **Conditional maintenance** refers to overhaul or repair in response to an inspection and measurement of the equipment's state. For instance, when Air Canada tears down its jet engines every 1000 hours, it is engaging in preventive maintenance. When it inspects the plane's tires every 24 hours and changes them when conditions warrant, it is performing conditional maintenance. Finally, if Air Canada's operations policy is to repair window shades or seat pockets on its planes only after the equipment breaks, then it is using remedial maintenance practices.

The Air Canada example points out that the type of maintenance control depends on the costs of a breakdown. The greater the cost in terms of money, time, liability, and customer goodwill, the greater the benefits from preventive maintenance; that is, the benefits can easily justify the costs.

Maintenance control should also be considered in the design of equipment. If downtime is highly inconvenient or costly, reliability can be increased by designing redundancy into the equipment. Nuclear power plants, for example, have elaborate backup systems built in. Similarly, equipment can be designed to facilitate fast or low-cost maintenance. Equipment that has fewer parts has fewer things to go wrong. High-failure items can also be placed in locations that are easily accessible or in independent modular units that can be quickly removed and replaced. Cable television operators follow these guidelines. Breakdowns infuriate customers, so when they occur, managers want to be able to correct them quickly. Speed

cost centre
A unit in which managers are held responsible for all associated costs.

direct costs
Costs incurred in proportion to the output of a particular good or service.

indirect costs
Costs incurred that are largely unaffected by changes in output.

preventive maintenance
Maintenance performed before a breakdown occurs.

remedial maintenance
Maintenance that calls for the overhaul, replacement, or repair of equipment when it breaks down.

conditional maintenance
Maintenance that calls for the overhaul or repair in response to an inspection and measurement of the equipment's state.

is facilitated by centralizing equipment in easy-access locations and making extensive use of modular units. If a piece of equipment fails, the whole module of which it is a part can be pulled or replaced in just a few minutes. Television service is resumed rapidly, and the pulled modular unit can be repaired without time pressures.

Quality Control

What is quality? When you consider a product or service to have quality, what does that mean? Does it mean that the product does not break or quit working—that is, that it's reliable? Does it mean that the service is delivered in a way that you intended? Does it mean that the product does what it's supposed to do? Or does quality mean something else? Exhibit S2-7 provides a description of several quality dimensions. We are going to define **quality** as the ability of a product or service to reliably do what it's supposed to do and to satisfy customer expectations.

How is quality achieved? That is the issue managers must address. A good way to address quality initiatives is to think in terms of the management functions—planning, organizing and leading, and controlling—that need to take place:

- *Planning for quality.* Managers must have quality improvement goals and strategies and plans formulated to achieve those goals. Goals can help focus everyone's attention toward some objective quality standard.

- *Organizing and leading for quality.* Since quality improvement initiatives are carried out by organizational employees, it's important for managers to look at how they can best organize and lead them. Quality-driven organizations rely on well-trained, flexible, and empowered employees.

- *Controlling for quality.* Quality improvement initiatives are

---

Exhibit S2-7

Quality Dimensions of Goods and Services

Product Quality Dimensions

1. Performance—Operating characteristics
2. Features—Important special characteristics
3. Flexibility—Meeting operating specifications over some period of time
4. Durability—Amount of use before performance deteriorates
5. Conformance—Match with pre-established standards
6. Serviceability—Ease and speed of repair or normal service
7. Aesthetics—How a product looks and feels
8. Perceived quality—Subjective assessment of characteristics (product image)

Service Quality Dimensions

1. Timeliness—Performed in promised period of time
2. Courtesy—Performed cheerfully
3. Consistency—Giving all customers similar experiences each time
4. Convenience—Accessibility to customers
5. Completeness—Fully serviced, as required
6. Accuracy—Performed correctly each time

Sources: Adapted from J. W. Dean Jr. and J. R. Evans, *Total Quality: Management, Organization and Society* (St. Paul, MN: West Publishing Company, 1994); H. V. Roberts and B. F. Sergesketter, *Quality Is Personal* (New York: Free Press, 1993); D. Garvin, *Managed Quality: The Strategic and Competitive Edge* (New York: Free Press, 1988); and M. A. Hitt, R. D. Ireland, and R. E. Hoskisson, *Strategic Management*, 4th ed. (Cincinnati, OH: SouthWestern, 2001), p. 211.

---

not possible without having some way to monitor and evaluate their progress. Whether it involves standards for inventory control, defect rate, raw materials procurement, or any other operations management area, controlling for quality is important.

Quality Goals

To publicly demonstrate their quality commitment, many organizations worldwide have pursued challenging quality goals—the two best known being ISO 9000 and Six Sigma. Q&A S2.4, Q&A S2.5

ISO 9000

ISO 9000 is a series of international quality management standards established by the International Organi-

zation for Standardization, which sets uniform guidelines for processes to ensure that products conform to customer requirements. These standards cover everything from contract review to product design to product delivery. The ISO 9000 standards have become the internationally recognized standard for evaluating and comparing companies in the global marketplace. In fact, this type of certification is becoming a prerequisite for doing business globally. Gaining ISO 9000 certification provides proof that a quality operations system is in place.

The latest survey of ISO 9000 certificates showed that the number of registered sites worldwide exceeded 776 608 in 2005, up from 44 388 in 2001. And these certificates had been awarded in 161 countries.[18] The ISO has also developed the ISO 14000 standard for

quality

The ability of a product or service to reliably do what it's supposed to do and to satisfy customer expectations.

environmental management systems, as well as other quality management standards for specific industries.[19]

Six Sigma

Motorola popularized the use of stringent quality standards more than 20 years ago through a trademarked quality improvement program called Six Sigma.[20] Very simply, **Six Sigma** is a quality standard that establishes a goal of no more than 3.4 defects per million units or procedures. What does the name mean? Sigma is the Greek letter that statisticians use to define a standard deviation from a bell curve. The higher the sigma, the fewer the deviations from the norm—that is, the fewer the defects. At One Sigma, two-thirds of whatever is being measured falls within the curve. Two Sigma covers about 95 percent. At Six Sigma, you are about as close to defect-free as you can get.[21] It's an ambitious quality goal! Although it may be an extremely high standard to achieve, many quality-driven businesses are using it and benefiting from it. Some well-known companies pursuing Six Sigma include Air Canada, CIBC, Dow Chemical, Sony, and Nokia. Although manufacturers seem to make up the bulk of Six Sigma users, service companies such as financial institutions, retailers, and health care organizations are beginning to apply it.

Summary

Although it's important for managers to recognize that many positive benefits can accrue from obtaining ISO 9000 or Six Sigma certification, the key benefit comes from the quality improvement journey itself. In other words, the goal of quality certification should be having work processes and an operations system in place that enable organizations to meet customers' needs and employees to perform their jobs in a consistently high-quality way.

Current Issues in Operations Management

It's 11 p.m., and you are reading a text message from your parents saying they want to buy you a computer for your birthday this year and to go ahead and order it. You log on to Dell Canada's website and configure your dream machine that will serve even your most demanding computing needs for the remainder of your school years. You hit the order button, and within three or four days, your dream computer is delivered to your front door, built to your exact specifications, ready to set up and use immediately to type that management assignment due tomorrow. Dell's ability to get the computer to your door so quickly illustrates three of today's most important operations management issues: value chain management, technology, and mass customization.

Value Chain Management

Every organization needs customers if it's going to survive and prosper. Even a nonprofit organization must have "customers" who use its services or purchase its products. Customers want some type of value from the goods and services they purchase or use, and these end-users determine what has value. Organizations must provide that value to attract and keep customers. **Value** is the performance characteristics, features and attributes, and any other aspects of goods and services for which customers are willing to give up resources (usually money). For example, when you purchase Nelly Furtado's new CD at HMV, a new pair of Australian sheepskin Ugg boots online at the company's website, a Harvey's Original Cheeseburger at a drive-through location, or a haircut from your local hair salon, you are exchanging (giving up) money in return for the value you need or desire from these products—providing music during your evening study time, keeping your feet warm *and* fashionable during winter's cold weather, getting rid of your hunger pangs quickly, or looking professionally groomed for the job interview you have next week. Q&A S2.6

How *is* value provided to customers? Through the transformation of raw materials and other resources into some product or service that end-users need or desire where, when, and how they want it. However, that seemingly simple act of turning a variety of resources into something that customers value and are willing to pay for involves a vast array of interrelated work activities performed by different participants (suppliers, manufacturers, and even customers)—that is, it involves the value chain. The **value chain** is the entire series of organizational work activities that add value at each step, beginning with the processing of raw materials and ending with the finished product in the hands of end-users. In its entirety, the value chain can encompass everything from the supplier's suppliers to the customer's customer.[22] Q&A S2.7

ISO 9000
A series of international quality management standards that sets uniform guidelines for processes to ensure that products conform to customer requirements.

Six Sigma
A quality standard that establishes a goal of no more than 3.4 defects per million units or procedures.

value
The performance characteristics, features and attributes, and any other aspects of goods and services for which customers are willing to give up resources.

value chain
The entire series of organizational work activities that add value at each step, beginning with the processing of raw materials and ending with the finished product in the hands of end-users.

Value chain management is the process of managing the entire sequence of integrated activities and information about product flows along the entire value chain. In contrast to supply chain management, which is internally oriented and focuses on efficient flow of incoming materials (resources) to the organization, value chain management is externally oriented and focuses on both incoming materials and outgoing products and services. And while supply chain management is efficiency oriented (its goal is to reduce costs and make the organization more productive), value chain management is effectiveness oriented and aims to create the highest value for customers.[23] Q&A S2.8

Requirements for Value Chain Management

Managing an organization from a value chain perspective is not easy. Approaches to giving customers what they want that may have worked in the past are likely no longer efficient or effective. Today's dynamic competitive environment facing global organizations demands new solutions. Understanding how and why value is determined by the marketplace has led some organizations to experiment with a new **business model**—that is, a strategic design for how a company intends to profit from its broad array of strategies, processes, and activities. For example, IKEA, the home furnishings manufacturer, transformed itself from a small Swedish mail-order furniture operation into the world's largest retailer of home furnishings by reinventing the value chain in the home furnishings industry. The company offers customers well-designed products at substantially lower prices in return for their willingness to take on certain key tasks traditionally done by manufacturers and retailers—assembling furniture and getting it home.[24] The company's definition of a new business model and willingness to abandon old methods and processes has worked well. Q&A S2.9, Q&A S2.10

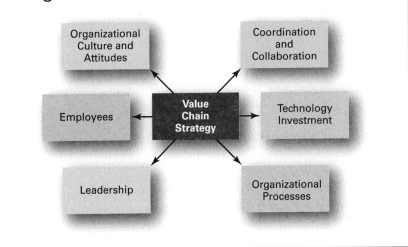

Exhibit S2-8

Six Requirements for Successful Value Chain Management

Exhibit S2-8 summarizes the six main requirements of successful value chain management: coordination and collaboration, technology investment, organizational processes, leadership, employees, and organizational culture and attitudes.

Coordination and Collaboration

For the value chain to achieve its goal of meeting and exceeding customers' needs and desires, comprehensive and seamless integration among all members of the chain is absolutely necessary. Collaborative relationships must be developed. Each partner in the value chain must identify things they may not value but that customers do.

Technology Investment

Successful value chain management is not possible without a significant investment in information technol-

ogy. The payoff from this investment, however, is that information technology can be used to restructure the value chain to better serve end-users.

Organizational Processes

Value chain management radically changes **organizational processes**—that is, the ways that organizational work is done.

When managers decide to manage operations using value chain management, old processes are no longer appropriate. Managers must critically evaluate all organizational processes from beginning to end by looking at core competencies—the organization's major skills, capabilities, and resources—to determine where value is being added. Non-value-adding activities should be eliminated. Questions such as these should be asked for each and every process: Where can internal knowledge be leveraged to improve

value chain management
The process of managing the entire sequence of integrated activities and information about product flows along the entire value chain.

business model
A strategic design for how a company intends to profit from its broad array of strategies, processes, and activities.

organizational processes
The ways that organizational work is done.

the flow of material and information? How can we better configure our product to satisfy both customers and suppliers? How can the flow of material and information be improved? How can we improve customer service?

Leadership

Successful value chain management is not possible without strong and committed leadership. From top organizational levels to lower levels, managers must support, facilitate, and promote the implementation and ongoing practice of value chain management. Managers must make a serious commitment to identifying what value is, how that value can best be provided, and how successful efforts at providing value have been. That type of organizational atmosphere or culture where all efforts are focused on delivering superb customer value is not possible without a serious commitment on the part of the organization's leaders.

Employees

We know from our discussions of management theories throughout this textbook that employees are the organization's most important resource. Without employees, there would be no products produced or services delivered—in fact, there would be no organized efforts in the pursuit of common goals. So, not surprisingly, employees play an important role in value chain management. The three main human resource requirements for value chain management are flexible approaches to job design, an effective hiring process, and ongoing training.

Flexibility is the key to job design in a value chain management organization. Jobs need to be designed around work processes that link all functions involved in creating and providing value to customers. Since the focus needs to be on how each activity performed by an employee can best contribute to the creation and delivery of customer value, employees need

to be flexible in what they do and how they do it.

Flexible jobs require employees who are flexible. In a value chain organization, employees may be assigned to work teams that tackle a given process and are often asked to do different things on different days depending on need. The organization's hiring process must be designed to identify those employees who have the ability to learn and adapt.

Finally, the need for flexibility also requires that there be a significant investment in continual and ongoing employee training. Whether the training involves learning how to use information technology software, how to improve the flow of materials throughout the chain, how to identify activities that add value, how to make better decisions faster, or how to improve any other number of potential work activities, managers must see to it that employees have the knowledge and tools they need to do their jobs efficiently and effectively.

Organizational Culture and Attitudes

The last requirement for value chain management that we need to discuss is the importance of having supportive organizational culture and attitudes. From our extensive description of value chain management, you could probably guess the type of organizational culture and attitudes that are going to support its successful implementation! Those cultural attitudes include sharing, collaborating, openness, flexibility, mutual respect, and trust. And these attitudes encompass not only the internal partners in the value chain, but extend to external partners as well.

Technology

As we know from our previous discussion of value chain management, today's competitive marketplace has put tremendous pressure on organiza-

tions to deliver products and services that customers value in a timely manner. Smart companies are looking at ways to harness technology to improve operations management. For example, Schneider Automation, of North Andover, Massachusetts, implemented its Transparent Factory initiative—a framework for linking plant-floor automation with enterprise-wide business network systems. With millions of device sensors and actuators on its factory floors running on stand-alone software but with no way to connect to the factory's system network, managers saw prime opportunities to capitalize on information technology solutions to manage its operations more effectively and efficiently.[25]

Although manufacturing is being driven by the recognition that the customer is king, managers still need to realize that the organization's production activities must be more responsive. For instance, operations managers need systems that can reveal available capacity, status of orders, and product quality while products are in the process of being manufactured, not just after the fact. To connect more closely with customers, operations across the enterprise, including manufacturing, must be synchronized. To avoid production and delivery bottlenecks, the manufacturing function must be a full partner in the entire business system.

What is making this type of extensive involvement and collaboration possible is technology. Technology is also allowing manufacturing plants to control costs, particularly in the areas of predictive maintenance, remote diagnostics, and utility cost savings. For instance, let's look at how technology is affecting the equipment maintenance function—an important operations management activity. New generations of Internet-compatible equipment contain embedded web servers that can communicate proactively—that is, if a piece of equipment breaks or reaches certain preset parameters that it's about to break, it can ask for help. But technology can do more than sound an alarm or light up an indicator button. For instance, some devices have the ability to initiate email or signal a pager at a supplier, the maintenance department, or a contractor describing the specific problem and requesting parts and service. How much is such e-enabled maintenance control worth? It can be worth quite a lot if it prevents equipment breakdowns and subsequent production downtime, such as for airplanes.

Managers who understand the power of technology to contribute to more effective and efficient performance know that managing operations is more than the traditional view of manufacturing's role in producing the product. Instead, the emphasis is on working together with all the organization's business functions to find solutions to customers' business problems.

Mass Customization

The term *mass customization* may seem peculiar. However, the design-to-order concept is becoming an important operations management issue for today's managers. **Mass customization** provides consumers with a product when, where, and how they want it.[26] For instance, we noted earlier that you can enter the Dell Canada website and build exactly the kind of computer that you want to buy. You can also go to the MINI Cooper Canada site and get exactly the colour and style of MINI that you want to buy. Companies adopting mass customization do so to maintain or attain a competitive advantage.

Mass customization requires flexible manufacturing techniques and continual dialogue with customers.[27] Technology plays an important role in both.

With flexible manufacturing, companies have the ability to quickly re-adjust assembly lines to make products to order. Using technology such as computer-controlled factory equipment, intranets, industrial robots, bar-code scanners, digital printers, and logistics software, companies can manufacture, assemble, and ship customized products with customized packaging to customers in incredibly short time frames. Dell is a good example of a company that uses flexible manufacturing techniques and technology to custom-build computers to customers' specifications.

Technology also is important in the continual dialogue with customers. Using extensive databases, companies can keep track of customers' likes and dislikes. And the Internet has made it possible for companies to have ongoing dialogues with customers to learn about and respond to their exact preferences. For instance, at Lands' End's website (**www.landsend.com**), customers can create their own virtual model to see how the company's clothes will fit them. Amazon.ca uses its website to greet visitors by name and offer personalized recommendations of books and other products. The ability to customize a product to a customer's exact specifications starts an important relationship between the organization and the customer. If the customer likes the product and it provides value, he or she is more likely to be a repeat customer.

mass customization
Providing consumers with a product when, where, and how they want it.

Managing Change and Innovation

PART **five**

How can I manage and encourage change and innovation?

1. What factors create the need for change?

2. Is change ongoing or episodic?

3. How do organizations manage change and resistance to change?

4. What is innovation and how does it occur in organizations?

5. What are some current issues in managing change?

▶ ▶ ▶ By late 2006, Yahoo! was starting to lose its top position in providing web services to Internet users, facing stiff competition for visitors and advertisers from Google, Microsoft's MSN, America Online, and even MySpace.[1] Yahoo!'s shares were slumping, revenue growth was slowed, staff were leaving in alarming numbers, and a crucial project, code-name "Panama," was delayed. In 2005, Yahoo! and Google had the same market share, about 19 percent. A year later, Google's market share was about 25 percent of US online ad revenue, and Yahoo!'s had fallen to 18 percent.

In a memo that has been called "The Peanut Butter Manifesto," a Yahoo! senior vice-president, Brad Garlinghouse, expressed his concern to Yahoo!'s top executives that Yahoo! was losing ground. Garlinghouse argued that Yahoo! was spreading its resources too thin, "Thus we focus on nothing in particular." He recommended that the company undergo a deep reorganization, lay off 15 to 20 percent of the workforce, and make executives accountable for poor performance.

Industry analysts have noted that Yahoo! lost its focus in recent years, missing opportunities taken by YouTube, Facebook, and MySpace. "Yahoo! had

every single asset you would have needed to do those bigger, faster and sooner than anyone else," said Rob Norman, CEO of the WPP Group's GroupM Interaction unit, whose clients buy Yahoo! advertising.

About eight months after "The Peanut Butter Manifesto" was written, Yahoo! finally made a change industry analysts hoped would make the difference. On June 18,

2007, Terry Semel stepped down as Yahoo! CEO. In his place, the company appointed Jerry Yang, one of Yahoo!'s co-founders, as CEO and Susan Decker as president. High hopes were placed on the two to "cut through the bureaucracy and indecision," and lead Yahoo! back to the front of the pack. Six months later, Microsoft made an unsolicited bid to take over Yahoo!.

Think About It

Can large organizations be innovative at the same speed as smaller organizations? Put yourself in Jerry Yang's shoes. You are faced with major competition from several newer, smaller, and innovative organizations. Meanwhile, Yahoo! has grown so bureaucratic in recent years that it has stopped acting rapidly in the face of opportunities. How would you go about making Yahoo! respond more quickly?

Big companies and small businesses, universities and colleges, and governments at all levels are being forced to significantly change the way they do things. Although change has always been a part of the manager's job, it has become even more important in recent years. In this chapter, we describe why change is important and how managers can manage change. Since change is often closely tied to an organization's innovation efforts, we also discuss ways in which managers can stimulate innovation and increase their organization's adaptability. Then, we conclude by looking at some current issues in managing change.

Yahoo! Canada
http://ca.yahoo.com

Forces for Change

1. What factors create the need for change?

If it were not for change, the manager's job would be relatively easy. Planning would be simple because tomorrow would be no different from today. The issue of effective organizational design would also be solved because the environment would be free from uncertainty and there would be no need to adapt. Similarly, decision making would be dramatically streamlined because the outcome of each alternative could be predicted with almost certain accuracy. It would, indeed, simplify the manager's job if, for example, competitors did not introduce new products or services, if customers did not demand new and improved products, if government regulations were never modified, or if employees' needs never changed. But that is not the way it is. Change is an organizational reality.[2] And managing change is an integral part of every manager's job. In Chapter 2, we pointed out the external and internal forces that constrain managers. These same forces also bring about the need for change. Let's briefly look at these forces.

External Forces

Are there external factors that might suggest to you that your college or university might think about doing things differently?

The external forces that create the need for change come from various sources. In recent years, the *marketplace* has affected firms such as Yahoo! as competition from Google, MySpace, and Ask Jeeves intensified. These companies constantly adapt to changing consumer desires as they develop new search capabilities.

Government laws and regulations are a frequent impetus for change. For example, the Canadian Securities Administrators rules, which came into effect in March 2004, require Canadian companies to change the way they disclose financial information and to carry out corporate governance.

Technology also creates the need for change. For example, technological improvements in diagnostic equipment have created significant economies of scale for hospitals. Assembly-line technology in other industries is changing dramatically as organizations replace human labour with robots. In the greeting card industry, email and the Internet have changed the way people exchange greeting cards. Technological change from analog to digital recording has meant the shift from records to CDs, videotapes to DVDs, and film to digital cameras. In just 10 years, DVD players have gone from the test stage to virtually eliminating the videotape rental market. The companies that produce videotapes and the companies that rent them have had to develop new strategies or go out of business.

Profound changes taking place in the Chinese economy are creating labour shortages at hundreds of factories, as seen in the many public job postings at this location in Shenzhen, China. Managers around the world must expect that wages in China may go up as the middle class continues to grow, which will have an impact on the price of manufacturing goods. Some international companies are already considering moving to lower-wage countries such as Vietnam.

The fluctuation in *labour markets* also forces managers to change. Organizations that need certain kinds of employees must change their human resource management activities to attract and retain skilled employees in the areas of greatest need. For instance, health care organizations facing severe nursing shortages have had to change the way they schedule work hours.

Economic changes, of course, affect almost all organizations. For instance, global recessionary pressures force organizations to become more cost efficient. But even in a strong economy, uncertainties about interest rates, federal budget deficits, and currency exchange rates create conditions that may force organizations to change.

Internal Forces

In addition to the external forces just described, internal forces also create the need for change. These internal forces tend to originate primarily from the internal operations of the organization or from the impact of external changes.

A redefinition or modification of an organization's *strategy* often introduces a host of changes. For instance, when Steve Bennett took over as CEO of Intuit (Quicken, QuickBooks, and QuickTax are its best-known products), the company was losing money. By orchestrating a series of well-planned and dramatic strategic changes, he turned Intuit into a profitable company with extremely committed employees, as the following *Management Reflection* shows.

MANAGEMENT REFLECTION
► Focus on Innovation

Steve Bennett Transforms Intuit

Can a company stay entrepreneurial and become more structured? When Steve Bennett was hired as Intuit's CEO in 2000, he had never worked for a high-tech firm.[3] He had spent all of his career with General Electric. Intuit's founder, Scott Cook, was looking for someone who could take Intuit to the next level. The company was struggling to break through the $1 billion (US) revenue wall, and Cook wanted the company to reach $10 billion (US) in revenue.

After he was hired, Bennett spent five weeks interviewing employees at more than 12 of Intuit's locations. He found a company still being run as haphazardly as a start-up venture. "The operation was a mess. It was losing money. Its technology was outdated. Execution was grindingly slow, and nothing was documented."[4] He discovered the organization had a democratic culture that nurtured employees to make sure they felt good. Managers chose whatever brand of PC they wanted to use, the employees were always holding meetings, and different units were responsible for the same product's development and sales support. Bennett felt the employees had to change how they viewed their work: "I wanted them to know that a company can be focused on high performance and still be a good place to work," he says.

Bennett introduced a number of changes, including putting business units in charge of development and customer service, introducing zero-based budgeting, and ordering the same computers for everyone to manage costs. He also flattened the organization, taking on 18 direct reports, rather than 8, so that he could drive change faster. "If you have that many direct reports, you don't have time to meddle in their business. My job is to conduct the orchestra, not to play all the instruments." He also introduced a new motto: "Mind your minutes." Employees were not to be involved in endless meetings, and they were to focus on the things that were really important. ∎

Intuit Canada
www.intuit.ca

In addition, an organization's *workforce* is rarely static. Its composition changes in terms of age, education, ethnic background, sex, and so forth. Take, for instance, an organization in which a large number of seasoned executives, because of financial reasons, decide to continue working instead of retiring. There might be a need to restructure jobs in order to retain and motivate younger managers. Also, the compensation and benefits system might need to be adapted to reflect the needs of this older workforce.

The introduction of new *equipment* represents another internal force for change. Employees may have their jobs redesigned, need to undergo training on how to operate the new equipment, or be required to establish new interaction patterns within their work group.

Finally, *employee attitudes* such as job dissatisfaction may lead to increased absenteeism, more voluntary resignations, and even labour strikes. Such events often lead to changes in management policies and practices.

This chapter's *Managing Workforce Diversity—The Paradox of Diversity* on page 543 notes the challenge managers have when they are balancing competing goals under change: to encourage employees to accept the organization's dominant values and to encourage employees to accept differences.

Two Views of the Change Process

▶ ▶ ▶ For years, Yahoo!, which helped give birth to the commercial Internet in 1994, dominated the Internet services market.[5] Through 2004, things were going well for the company, but then it started to lose its competitive edge.

The company, well known for its banner and video ads, was targeted by both Google (who bought online ad firm DoubleClick) and Microsoft (who bought digital marketing firm aQuantive). Yahoo! tried to make a deal with Facebook but was not successful, while Google bought the leading video-sharing site, YouTube. Yahoo!'s response to competition has been comparatively slow, although it did buy 80 percent of advertising network RightMedia in April 2007.[6]

Because Yahoo! delayed its response to competition from Google, it now faces a bigger challenge. In 2007, Google was worth $160 billion (US) on the stock market while Yahoo!'s shares were worth only $37 billion (US). Moreover, Yahoo! was facing a hostile takeover from Microsoft in early 2008.

Think About It

How does change happen in organizations? Is change a constant process, or can organizations take breaks from worrying about change, as Yahoo! seems to have done in the last few years?

2. Is change ongoing or episodic?

We can use two very different metaphors to describe the change process.[7] One metaphor envisions the organization as a large ship crossing calm waters. The ship's captain and crew know exactly where they are going because they have made the trip many times before. Change comes in the form of an occasional storm, a brief distraction in an otherwise calm and predictable trip. In the other metaphor, the organization is seen as a small raft navigating a raging river with uninterrupted white-water rapids. Aboard the raft are half-a-dozen people who have never worked together before, who are totally unfamiliar with the river, who are unsure of their eventual destination, and who, as if things were not bad enough, are travelling at night. In the white-water rapids metaphor, change is an expected and natural state, and managing change is a continuous process. These two metaphors present very different approaches to understanding and responding to change. Let's take a closer look at each one.

The Calm Waters Metaphor

Up until the late 1980s, the calm waters metaphor pretty much described the situation that managers faced. It's best illustrated by Kurt Lewin's three-step description of the change process.[8] (See Exhibit 16-1.)

According to Lewin, successful change can be planned and requires *unfreezing* the status quo, *changing* to a new state, and *refreezing* to make the change permanent. The status quo can be considered an equilibrium state. To move from this equilibrium, unfreezing is necessary. Unfreezing can be thought of as preparing for the needed change. It can be achieved

Exhibit 16-1

The Change Process

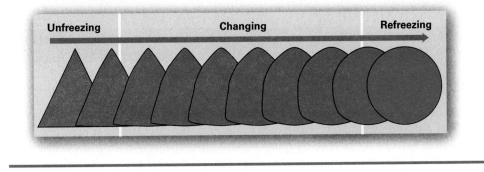

by increasing the *driving forces*, which are forces that drive change and direct behaviour away from the status quo; decreasing the *restraining forces*, which are forces that resist change and push behaviour toward the status quo; or combining the two approaches.

Once unfreezing is done, the change itself can be implemented. However, merely introducing change does not ensure that the change will take hold. The new situation needs to be *refrozen* so that it can be sustained over time. Unless this last step is taken, there is a strong chance that the change will be short-lived as employees revert back to the old equilibrium state—that is, the old ways of doing things. The objective of refreezing, then, is to stabilize the new situation by reinforcing the new behaviours.

Note how Lewin's three-step process treats change simply as a break in the organization's equilibrium state. The status quo has been disturbed and change is necessary to establish a new equilibrium state. However, a calm waters environment is not what most managers face today.[9]

Q&A 16.1

The White-Water Rapids Metaphor

The white-water rapids metaphor is consistent with our discussion of uncertain and dynamic environments in Chapters 2 and 7. It's also consistent with a world that's increasingly dominated by information, ideas, and knowledge.[10] We can see how the metaphor applies to Yahoo!, which currently faces an uncertain and dynamic environment after dominating the Internet services industry for many years.

To get a feeling of what managing change might be like when you have to continuously manoeuvre in uninterrupted and uncertain rapids, consider attending a college or university that has the following rules: Courses vary in length. Unfortunately, when you sign up, you don't know how long a course will run. It might go for 2 weeks or 30 weeks. Furthermore, the instructor can end a course any time he or she wants, with no prior warning. If that is not bad enough, the length of the class changes each time it meets: Sometimes the class lasts 20 minutes; other times it runs for 3 hours. And the time of the next class meeting is set by the instructor during this class. There is one more thing. All exams are unannounced, so you have to be ready for a test at any time. To succeed in this type of environment, you would have to be incredibly flexible and able to respond quickly to changing conditions. Students who are overly structured, "slow" to respond, or uncomfortable with change would not survive.

Growing numbers of managers are coming to accept that their job is much like what a student would face in such a college. The stability and predictability of the calm waters metaphor do not exist. Disruptions in the status quo are not occasional and temporary, and they are not followed by a return to calm waters. Many managers never get out of the rapids. They face constant change, bordering on chaos.

Is the white-water rapids metaphor an exaggeration? No! Although you would expect this type of chaotic and dynamic environment in high-tech industries, even organizations in non-high-tech industries are faced with constant change, as the following *Management Reflection* shows.

MANAGEMENT REFLECTION
► Focus on Innovation

Converse Builds a Better Shoe

How does a shoe company manage in a highly competitive industry?   Converse, an athletic footwear manufacturer based in Massachusetts, filed for Chapter 11 bankruptcy protection in January 2001.[11] The company was having difficulty surviving in the very competitive, and rapidly changing, shoe industry. Teens and preteens (a major target market) demand new and unique styles more often than ever. Competition is hot! Industry leaders Adidas, Reebok, and Nike keep the pressure on everyone else in the industry.

Managers at Converse who wanted to revitalize the brand knew that if they were to get the company out of bankruptcy and become profitable once again, they had to make changes. They decided to revive the once-popular Chuck Taylor line of canvas basketball shoes, make shoes for mountain biking and skateboarding, implement a company-wide quality management program, develop more athletic footwear for the women's and children's markets, and introduce a new collection of Converse brand apparel and accessories. These significant changes were essential if Converse wanted to survive the white-water rapids environment in which it operated. Then, in July 2003, Converse managers announced another significant change. They had agreed to be acquired by Nike for close to $400 million. ■

Putting the Two Views in Perspective

Does *every* manager face a world of constant and chaotic change? No, but the number who don't is dwindling. (See also *Self-Assessment—How Well Do I Respond to Turbulent Change?* on pages 537–538, at the end of the chapter.) Managers in such businesses as telecommunications, computer software, and women's clothing have long confronted a world of white-water rapids. These managers used to envy their counterparts in industries such as banking, utilities, oil exploration, publishing, and air transportation, where the environment was historically more stable and predictable. However, those days of stability and predictability are long gone!

Today, any organization that treats change as the occasional disturbance in an otherwise calm and stable world runs a great risk. Too much is changing too fast for an organization or its managers to be complacent. It's no longer business as usual. And managers must be ready to efficiently and effectively manage the changes facing their organizations or their work areas. Nevertheless, managers have to be certain that change is the right thing to do at any given time. Law firm Brobeck, Phleger & Harrison had a disastrous strategy for change, as the following *Management Reflection* shows.

MANAGEMENT REFLECTION

To Change or Not to Change?

How important is a company's strategy for change?   Brobeck, Phleger & Harrison had been a prominent San Francisco law firm for 70 years when the technology boom happened in the late 1990s.[12] Located in the heart of California's Silicon Valley, the firm saw great opportunity to engage in dot-com and venture capital deals. At first the strategy paid off, with the company handling 74 initial public offerings (IPOs) in 1999.

Many new lawyers were added to the firm, and they were offered huge salaries. Average compensation increased more than 50 percent. The company expanded the number of offices it had throughout the United States, and signed very expensive leases for very large buildings to house the offices. Two years later, the firm handled just three IPOs, but Brobeck continued to increase expenses dramatically. By 2003, Brobeck had lost many of its best-performing partners and was in debt to Citibank for $120 million (US).

Why did everything go so wrong? When Brobeck developed its plan for the technology boom, the firm decided that it would handle only the corporate side of business: "buying and selling shares, taking options in companies." Brobeck refused any business on the commercial side, which might have balanced things when the technology bubble burst. ∎

As Brobeck's experience shows, companies need to carefully consider change strategies, as change can lead to failure. If change is the appropriate course of action, how should it be managed? That's what we'll discuss next.

Q&A 16.2

Managing Organizational Change

▶ ▶ ▶ With Jerry Yang back at the helm of Yahoo!, hopes are that he will be able to inspire the company's employees in a way that CEO Terry Semel did not seem able to do in recent years.[13] Many felt that Semel's background did not help him steer Yahoo! to a more visionary future. Semel was a Warner Bros. movie executive before joining Yahoo! in 2001. Yang is much quieter, but many of the successful Silicon Valley firms, such as Apple and Oracle, are run by their founders. "He's no Steve Jobs," says Ned May, an industry analyst. "But he's a founder. Putting a founder back in the reins will create excitement inside Yahoo!"

Think About It
What advantages might come from bringing back a co-founder to help with the changes needed at Yahoo!?

What Is Organizational Change?

Most managers, at one point or another, will have to make changes in some aspects of their workplace. We classify these changes as **organizational change**—which is any alteration of people, structure, or technology. Organizational changes often need someone to act as a catalyst and assume the responsibility for managing the change process—that is, a **change agent**. Who can be change agents?

We assume that changes are initiated and coordinated by a manager within the organization. However, the change agent could be a nonmanager—for example, a change specialist from the HR department or even an outside consultant whose expertise is in change implementation. For major system-wide changes, an organization often hires outside consultants to provide advice and assistance. Because they are from the outside, they offer an objective perspective that insiders may lack. However, outside consultants are usually at a disadvantage because they have a limited understanding of the organization's history, culture, operating procedures, and people. Outside consultants also are likely to initiate more drastic change than insiders would (which can be either a benefit or a disadvantage) because they don't have to live with the repercussions after the change is implemented. In contrast, internal managers who act as change agents may be more thoughtful, but possibly overcautious, because they must live with the consequences of their decisions.

As change agents, managers are motivated to initiate change because they are committed to improving their organization's performance. Initiating change involves identifying what types of changes might be needed and putting the change process in motion. But that is not all there is to managing organizational change. Managers must manage employee resistance to change. What types of organizational change might managers need to make, and how do managers deal with resistance to change?

3. How do organizations manage change and resistance to change?

organizational change
Any alteration of people, structure, or technology in an organization.

change agent
Someone who acts as a catalyst and assumes the responsibility for managing the change process.

Types of Change

What *can* a manager change? The manager's options fall into three categories: structure, technology, and people (see Exhibit 16-2). Changing *structure* includes any alteration in authority relations, coordination mechanisms, employee empowerment, job redesign, or similar structural variables. Changing *technology* encompasses modifications in the way work is performed or the methods and equipment that are used. Changing *people* refers to changes in employee attitudes, expectations, perceptions, and behaviour.

Changing Structure

We discussed organizational structure issues in Chapter 9. Managers' organizing responsibilities include such activities as choosing the organization's formal design, allocating authority, and determining the degree of formalization. Once those structural decisions have been made, however, they are not final. Changing conditions or changing strategies bring about the need to make structural changes.

What options does the manager have for changing structure? The manager has the same ones we introduced in our discussion of organizational structure and design. A few examples should make this clearer. Recall from Chapter 9 that an organization's structure is defined in terms of work specialization, departmentalization, chain of command, span of control, centralization and decentralization, and formalization. Managers can alter one or more of these *structural elements*. For instance, departmental responsibilities could be combined, organizational levels eliminated, or spans of control widened to make the organization flatter and less bureaucratic. Or more rules and procedures could be implemented to increase standardization. An increase in decentralization can be used to make decision making faster. Even downsizing involves changes in structure.

Another option would be to make major changes in the actual *structural design*. For instance, when Hewlett-Packard acquired Compaq, several structural changes were made as product divisions were dropped, merged, or expanded. Or structural design changes might include a shift from a functional to a product structure or the creation of a project structure design. Hamilton, Ontario-based Dofasco became a more profitable steel producer after revamping its traditional functional structure to a new design that arranges work around cross-functional teams. Some government agencies and private organizations are looking to new organizational ventures, forming public–private partnerships to deal with these changes, as the following *Management Reflection* shows.

Exhibit 16-2

Three Categories of Change

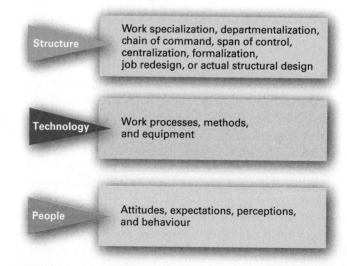

New Ways for Government to Get Jobs Done

Can public–private partnerships work?   Federal and provincial governments are trying to come up with new ways to get much-needed projects completed.[14] Tony Fell, chair of Toronto-based RBC Capital Markets, notes that governments need help financing transportation, water, health care, and education systems, which are "deteriorating at an alarming rate." There is much talk about an innovative way of handling these projects: public–private partnerships (P3s), where the government and the private sector form companies to get things done. Unfortunately, to date most have not been successful. Almost four out of five P3s fail.

Whether they fail because the idea is unworkable, or whether they suffer from an inability of the public sector and the private sector to figure out appropriate ways to work together, is not entirely clear. Gordon Campbell, premier of British Columbia, has been trying to find a successful model to make P3s work. Despite trying to get P3s started that would help with the "$2 billion in public capital projects built annually across the province," only one project has been signed. The private sector seems unwilling to take on risks that the government also does not want to assume.

BC's Canada Line, a rail-based rapid transit line being built between Vancouver International Airport and downtown Vancouver for the 2010 Olympic Winter Games, was the first BC P3 project to launch, but gaining acceptance for the project was not easy. The provincial government was seen as pushing the project through, while labour unions fought it, and Vancouver residents were divided on whether the project should be given a go-ahead.

One successful P3 is Toronto-based Teranet, formed in 1995 to create an electronic database of all of the property title records in Ontario, so that lawyers could research and transfer titles in property deals from their office computers. The company has been profitable from the beginning. "The trouble was, if government tried it alone, it would probably take 30 to 40 years to get done and cost tens of millions of dollars," says Bonnie Foster, vice-president of corporate affairs and an original member of the Teranet management team.

The difficulties governments face in raising money for and managing large projects suggest that innovative ways to build public infrastructure still need to be found. Teranet may be one example of how to create joint ventures that work. ∎

Changing Technology

Managers can also change the technology used to convert inputs into outputs. Most early studies in management—such as the work of Taylor and the Gilbreths described in the supplement to Chapter 1—dealt with efforts aimed at technological change. If you recall, scientific management sought to implement changes that would increase production efficiency based on time-and-motion studies. Today, major technological changes usually involve the introduction of new equipment, tools, or methods; automation; or computerization.

Competitive factors or new innovations within an industry often require managers to introduce *new equipment, tools,* or *operating methods.* For example, coal mining companies in New South Wales, Australia, updated operational methods, installed more efficient coal-handling equipment, and made changes in work practices to be more productive. New innovations do not always inspire organizations to change, however. The Canadian Armed

Computerization has been the engine for all kinds of changes in the business environment, including employee training. Cisco Systems' Internet Learning Solutions Group is charged with developing electronic training programs both for Cisco's own sales force and channel partners and for the company's hundreds of thousands of customers. The team, whose leaders are pictured here, has developed tools ranging from virtual classrooms to video server technology and content development templates. "We really believe that our e-learning programs are a more effective way to grow skills in high volume in a shorter time than in the past," says the group's director.

Forces has been criticized in recent years because it has not taken advantage of new technology to update its equipment.[15]

Automation is a technological change that uses machines for tasks previously done by people. It began in the Industrial Revolution and continues today as one of a manager's options for structural change. Automation has been introduced (and sometimes resisted) in organizations such as Canada Post, where automatic mail sorters are used, and in automobile assembly lines, where robots are programmed to do jobs that blue-collar workers used to perform.

Probably the most visible technological changes in recent years, though, have come through managers' efforts to expand *computerization.* Most organizations have sophisticated information systems. For instance, grocery stores and other retailers use scanners linked to computers that provide instant inventory information. Also, it's very uncommon for an office to not be computerized. At BP, employees had to learn how to deal with the personal visibility and accountability brought about by the implementation of an enterprise-wide information system. The integrative nature of this system meant that what any employee did on his or her computer automatically affected other computer systems on the internal network.[16] The Benetton Group uses computers to link its manufacturing plants outside Treviso, Italy, with the company's various sales outlets and a highly automated warehouse.[17]

Changing People

Changing people—that is, changing their attitudes, expectations, perceptions, and behaviours—is not easy. Yet, for over 30 years now, academic researchers and actual managers have been interested in finding ways for individuals and groups within organizations to work together more effectively. The term **organizational development (OD)**, though occasionally referring to all types of change, essentially focuses on techniques or programs to change people and the nature and quality of interpersonal work relationships.[18] The most popular OD techniques are described in Exhibit 16-3. The common thread in these techniques is that each seeks to bring about changes in the organization's people. For example, executives at Scotiabank, Canada's third-largest bank in terms of market capitalization, knew that the success of a new customer sales and service strategy depended on changing employee attitudes and behaviours. Managers used different OD techniques during the strategic change, including team building, survey feedback, and intergroup development. One indicator of how well these techniques worked in getting people to change was that every branch in Canada implemented the new strategy on or ahead of schedule.[19] (The *Video Case Incident—Modern Manners at the Ritz-Carlton* on page 548 provides another example of how an organization changed its employees' behaviour to better serve its customers.)

Global OD

Much of what we know about OD practices has come from North American research. However, managers need to recognize that although there may be some similarities in the types of OD techniques used, some techniques that work for North American organizations may not be appropriate for organizations or organizational divisions based in other countries.[20] For instance, a study of OD interventions showed that "multirater (survey) feedback as practiced in the United States is not embraced in Taiwan" because the cultural value of "saving face is simply more powerful than the value of receiving feedback from subordinates."[21] What is the lesson for managers? Before using the same techniques to implement behavioural changes, especially across different countries, managers need to be sure that they have taken into account cultural characteristics and whether the techniques "make sense for the local culture."

Managing Resistance to Change

Change can be a threat to people in an organization. Organizations can build up inertia that motivates people to resist changing their status quo, even though change might be beneficial. Why do people resist change and what can be done to minimize their resistance?

Why People Resist Change

Resistance to change is well documented.[22] Why *do* people resist change? An individual is likely to resist change for the following reasons: uncertainty, habit, concern over personal loss, and the belief that the change is not in the organization's best interest.[23]

Q&A 16.3

organizational development (OD) Techniques or programs to change people and the nature and quality of interpersonal work relationships.

Exhibit 16-3

Organizational Development Techniques

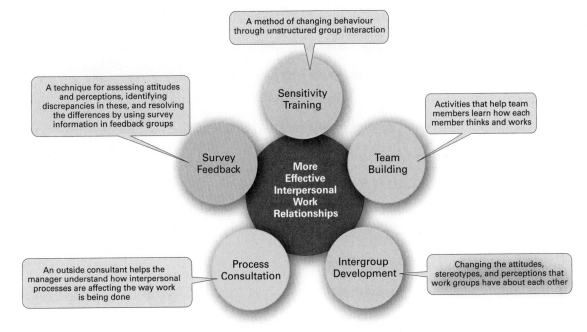

Change replaces the known with ambiguity and uncertainty. When you finish school, you will be leaving an environment where you know what is expected of you to join an organization where things are uncertain. Employees in organizations are faced with similar uncertainty. For example, when quality control methods based on sophisticated statistical models are introduced into manufacturing plants, many quality control inspectors have to learn the new methods. Some inspectors may fear that they will be unable to do so and may, therefore, develop a negative attitude toward the change or behave poorly if required to use the methods.

How would you feel if your company, two years after you started there, changed the software you used to enter your contact and sales information?

Another cause of resistance is that we do things out of habit. Every day, when you go to school or work, you probably go the same way. If you are like most people, you find a single route and use it regularly. As human beings, we are creatures of habit. Life is complex enough—we don't want to have to consider the full range of options for the hundreds of decisions we make every day. To cope with this complexity, we rely on habits or programmed responses. But when confronted with change, this tendency to respond in our accustomed ways becomes a source of resistance.

The third cause of resistance is the fear of losing something already possessed. Change threatens the investment you have already made in the status quo. The more that people have invested in the current system, the more they resist change. Why? They fear the loss of status, money, authority, friendships, personal convenience, or other economic benefits that they value. This helps explain why older employees tend to resist change more than younger employees. Older employees have generally invested more in the current system and thus have more to lose by changing.

A final cause of resistance is a person's belief that the change is incompatible with the goals and interests of the organization. For instance, an employee who believes that a proposed new job procedure will reduce product quality or productivity can be expected to resist the change.

Exhibit 16-4

Helping Employees Accept Change

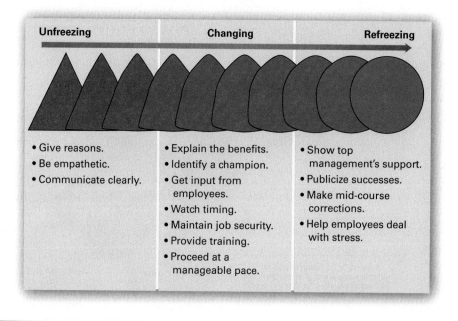

Unfreezing	Changing	Refreezing
• Give reasons. • Be empathetic. • Communicate clearly.	• Explain the benefits. • Identify a champion. • Get input from employees. • Watch timing. • Maintain job security. • Provide training. • Proceed at a manageable pace.	• Show top management's support. • Publicize successes. • Make mid-course corrections. • Help employees deal with stress.

Source: J. Liebowitz and G. J. Iskat, "What to Do When Employees Resist Change," *Supervision* 57, no. 8 (August 1996), pp. 3–5. With permission.

Techniques for Reducing Resistance

When managers see resistance to change as dysfunctional, they can use a variety of actions to deal with it.[24] Exhibit 16-4 shows how to manage resistance at the unfreezing, changing, and refreezing stages. Actions include communicating the reasons for change, getting input from employees, choosing the timing of change carefully, and showing management support for the change process. Providing support to employees to deal with the stress of the change is also important. Depending on the type and source of the resistance, managers might choose to use any of these. In general, resistance is likely to be lower if managers involve people in the change, offer training where needed, and are open to revisions once the change has been implemented. (For more suggestions on reducing resistance, see *Developing Your Interpersonal Skills—Managing Resistance to Change* on pages 541–543, at the end of the chapter.)

PRISM 5

Stimulating Innovation

▶ ▶ ▶ In order to improve its performance, Yahoo! must become more innovative.[25] The company was slow to catch on to the force that online social networking websites, such as Facebook, would become. Unlike Google, Yahoo! has been more interested in displaying content rather than creating content. Under the leadership of Terry Semel, the company became more product centred, turning out so many products that a senior vice-president commented that the company had spread itself too thin.

Yahoo! needs to develop a better technology platform that would integrate the company's entire network of products. It also needs to figure out what to do if MySpace surpasses Yahoo! in audience size (which seemed likely in 2007) and online social networking becomes more popular with advertisers.

Think About It

What can companies do to stimulate and nurture innovation?

"Winning in business today demands innovation."[26] Such is the stark reality facing today's managers. In the dynamic, chaotic world of global competition, organizations must create new products and services and adopt state-of-the-art technology if they are to compete successfully.[27]

For instance, stores such as The Bay and Zellers have faced difficulty competing against Wal-Mart, because they have failed to either adapt or respond to retail industry practices. The Bay, for instance, has had difficulty identifying its target market, and developing clothing lines appropriate to that market. A recent study of bankruptcies among Canadian wholesale and retail firms suggests that bankruptcies for older retailers may be the result of "Internet vendors and 'big-box' outlet stores … eroding the competitive position of established, traditional wholesale and retail businesses."[28] Meanwhile, fast-food restaurants like McDonald's and Krispy Kreme Doughnuts looked out of touch when the "low carb" fad swept the diet industry. How do companies keep up in a quickly changing environment?

When you think of successful innovators, you probably consider companies such as Sony, with its MiniDiscs, PlayStations, Cyber-Shot digital cameras, and OLED display TV. 3M continually introduces new types of Post-it Notes. Intel makes continual advances in chip designs. What is the secret to the success of these innovator champions? What, if anything, can other managers do to make their organizations more innovative? In the following pages, we will try to answer those questions as we discuss the factors behind innovation.

Creativity vs. Innovation

Creativity refers to the ability to combine ideas in a unique way or to make unusual associations between ideas.[29] An organization that stimulates creativity develops unique ways to work or novel solutions to problems. But creativity by itself is not enough. Creative ideas need to be turned into useful products, services, or work methods; this process is defined as **innovation**. Thus, the innovative organization is characterized by its ability to channel creativity into useful outcomes. When managers talk about changing an organization to make it more creative, they usually mean they want to stimulate and nurture innovation.

Sony, 3M, and Intel are aptly described as innovative because they take novel ideas and turn them into profitable products and work methods.

Stimulating and Nurturing Innovation

What has your employer done, if anything, to encourage innovation? Do you think more innovation could be encouraged?

Using the systems approach we introduced in the supplement to Chapter 1, we can better understand how organizations become more innovative.[30] (See Exhibit 16-5 on page 528.) We see from this model that getting the desired outputs (innovative products) involves both the inputs and the transformation of those inputs. Inputs include creative individuals and groups within the organization. But having creative individuals is not enough. It takes the right environment for the innovation process to take hold and prosper as the inputs are transformed. What does this "right" environment—that is, an environment that stimulates innovation—look like? We have identified three sets of variables that have been found to stimulate innovation: the organization's structure, culture, and human resource practices (see Exhibit 16-6 on page 528).

Structural Variables

Research into the effect of structural variables on innovation shows five things.[31] First, organic structures positively influence innovation. Because this type of organization is low in formalization, centralization, and work specialization, organic structures facilitate the flexibility, adaptability, and cross-fertilization necessary in innovation. Second, the easy availability of plentiful resources provides a key building block for innovation. With an abundance of resources, managers can afford to purchase innovations, can afford the cost of instituting innovations, and can absorb failures. Third, frequent interunit communication helps break down barriers to innovation.[32] Cross-functional teams, task forces, and other

4. What is innovation and how does it occur in organizations?

Q&A 16.4

3M Canada
www.3m.com/intl/ca

Intel Canada
www.intel.com/ca

creativity
The ability to combine ideas in a unique way or to make unusual associations between ideas.

innovation
The process of taking creative ideas and turning them into useful products, services, or work methods.

Q&A 16.5

Exhibit 16-5

Systems View of Innovation

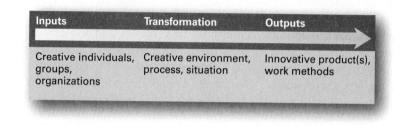

Inputs	Transformation	Outputs
Creative individuals, groups, organizations	Creative environment, process, situation	Innovative product(s), work methods

Source: Adapted from R. W. Woodman, J. E. Sawyer, and R. W. Griffin, "Toward a Theory of Organizational Creativity," *Academy of Management Review*, April 1993, p. 309.

such organizational designs facilitate interaction across departmental lines and are widely used in innovative organizations. Fourth, innovative organizations try to minimize extreme time pressures on creative activities despite the demands of white-water-type environments. Although time pressures may spur people to work harder and may make them feel more creative, studies show that it actually causes them to be less creative.[33] Finally, studies show that when an organization's structure provides explicit support for creativity from work and nonwork sources, an employee's creative performance is enhanced. What kinds of support are beneficial? Things like encouragement, open communication, readiness to listen, and useful feedback.[34] Toronto-based Labatt Breweries, for instance, gathers employees from across the country to an annual "innovation summit" to allow them to present

Exhibit 16-6

Innovation Variables

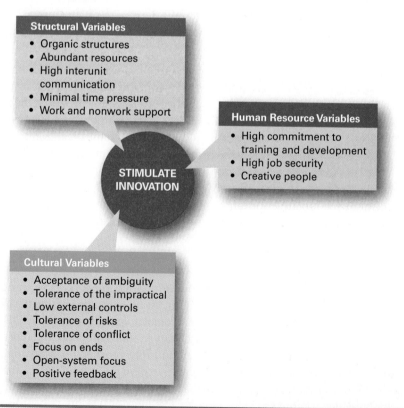

Structural Variables
- Organic structures
- Abundant resources
- High interunit communication
- Minimal time pressure
- Work and nonwork support

Human Resource Variables
- High commitment to training and development
- High job security
- Creative people

STIMULATE INNOVATION

Cultural Variables
- Acceptance of ambiguity
- Tolerance of the impractical
- Low external controls
- Tolerance of risks
- Tolerance of conflict
- Focus on ends
- Open-system focus
- Positive feedback

ideas.[35] At one summit, Don Perron, a power engineer from Labatt's Edmonton brewery, presented an idea to move pumps from the ceiling of the plant to the floor that was accepted. This impressed Perron, who said, "It gives you a sense of satisfaction." His co-workers have become enthusiastic about developing ideas as a result. "It has taken away some of the monotony [of production-line work]," Perron said. Labatt helps employees develop good ideas by investing time and money into the research and development of new ideas.

Cultural Variables

"Throw the bunny" is part of the lingo used by a project team at toy company Mattel. It refers to a juggling lesson in which team members try to learn to juggle two balls and a stuffed bunny. Most people easily learn to juggle two balls but cannot let go of that third object. Creativity, like juggling, is learning to let go—that is, to "throw the bunny." For Mattel, having a culture in which people are encouraged to "throw the bunny" is important to its continued product innovations.[36]

Innovative organizations tend to have similar cultures.[37] They encourage experimentation, reward both successes and failures, and celebrate mistakes. An innovative culture is likely to have the following characteristics:

- *Acceptance of ambiguity.* Too much emphasis on objectivity and specificity constrains creativity. (To learn more about handling ambiguity, see *Self-Assessment— How Well Do I Handle Ambiguity?* on pages 216–217, in Chapter 7.)
- *Tolerance of the impractical.* Individuals who offer impractical, even foolish, answers to what-if questions are not stifled. What at first seems impractical might lead to innovative solutions.
- *Low external controls.* Rules, regulations, policies, and similar organizational controls are kept to a minimum.
- *Tolerance of risk.* Employees are encouraged to experiment without fear of consequences should they fail. Mistakes are treated as learning opportunities.
- *Tolerance of conflict.* Diversity of opinions is encouraged. Harmony and agreement between individuals or units are *not* assumed to be evidence of high performance.
- *Focus on ends.* Goals are made clear, and individuals are encouraged to consider alternative routes to meeting the goals. Focusing on ends suggests that there might be several right answers to any given problem.
- *Open-system focus.* Managers closely monitor the environment and respond to changes as they occur.
- *Positive feedback.* Managers provide positive feedback, encouragement, and support so employees feel that their creative ideas will receive attention.

Human Resource Variables

In this category, we find that innovative organizations actively promote the training and development of their members so their knowledge remains current; offer their employees high job security to reduce the fear of getting fired for making mistakes; and encourage individuals to become "champions" of change. **Idea champions** actively and enthusiastically support new ideas, build support, overcome resistance, and ensure that innovations are implemented. Research finds that these idea champions have common personality characteristics: extremely high self-confidence, persistence, energy, and a tendency to take risks. Champions also display characteristics associated with dynamic leadership. They inspire and energize others with their vision of the potential of an innovation and through their strong personal conviction in their mission. They are also good at gaining the commitment of others to support their mission. In addition, champions have jobs that provide considerable decision-making discretion. This autonomy helps them introduce and implement innovations in organizations.[38] For instance, *Spirit* and *Opportunity*, the two golf-cart-sized exploration rovers that landed on Mars in 2004 to explore its surface, never would have been built had it not been for an idea champion by the name of Donna L. Shirley. As the head of Mars exploration in the 1990s at NASA's Jet Propulsion Laboratory in Pasadena, California, Shirley had been working since the early 1980s on the idea of putting roving vehicles on Mars.

idea champions
Individuals who actively and enthusiastically support new ideas, build support, overcome resistance, and ensure that innovations are implemented.

The toy industry is very competitive and picking the next great toy is not easy. Still, Toronto-based Spin Master is better than most at finding the most innovative new toys. Co-CEOs Anton Rabie and Ronnen Harary and executive vice-president Ben Varadi rely on intuition. They have also created a "culture of ideas" and pick everyone's brains for new ideas, "from inventors and licensing companies to distributors and retailers around the world." They also give a prize to one employee each month for the best idea.

Despite ongoing funding and management support problems, she continued to champion the idea until it was approved in the early 1990s.[39]

Current Issues in Managing Change

▶ ▶ ▶ One of the most difficult challenges Yahoo! CEO Jerry Yang faces in moving the company forward is recapturing the organization's entrepreneurial culture, which it lost under Semel.[40] The culture had become bureaucratic, with lots of separate silos, when what is needed is a sleek, well-run organization. "Jerry won't be able to do much unless he can bring back that entrepreneurial spirit," notes Professor John Sullivan of San Francisco State University's business school.

Shortly after taking over the helm, Yang posted a description of his new job on Yahoo! His vision for the company moving forward includes the following:

- A Yahoo! that executes with speed, clarity, and discipline.
- A Yahoo! that increases its focus on differentiating its products and investing in creativity and innovation.
- A Yahoo! that is better focused on what's important to its users, customers, and employees.

To accomplish his vision, Yang will need "to figure out how he wants the furniture broken," says Kevin Coyne, a strategy consultant and Harvard Business School lecturer. He may not have this chance, however, if Microsoft succeeds in its bid to take over Yahoo!.

Think About It

Is it possible to change a large organization's bureaucratic, slow-moving culture into an entrepreneurial, fast-paced culture?

5. What are some current issues in managing change?

Today's change issues—changing organizational culture, handling employee stress, and making change happen successfully—are critical concerns for managers. What can managers do to change an organization's culture when that culture no longer supports the organization's mission? What can managers do to handle the stress created by today's dynamic and uncertain environment? And how can managers successfully manage the challenges of introducing and implementing change? These are the topics we look at in this section.

Changing Organizational Culture

Q&A 16.6

When W. James McNerney Jr. took over as CEO of 3M, he brought with him managerial approaches from his old employer, General Electric. He soon discovered that what was routine at GE was unheard of at 3M. For instance, he was the only one who showed up at meetings without a tie. His blunt, matter-of-fact, and probing style of asking questions caught many 3M managers off guard. McNerney soon realized that he would need to address the cultural issues before tackling any needed organizational changes.[41] The fact that an organization's culture is made up of relatively stable and permanent characteristics (see Chapter 2) tends to make that culture very resistant to change.[42] A culture takes a long time to form, and once established it tends to become entrenched. Strong cultures are particularly resistant to change because employees have become so committed to them.

The explosion of the space shuttle *Columbia* in 2003 highlights how difficult changing an organization's culture can be. An investigation of the explosion found that the causes were remarkably similar to the reasons given for the *Challenger* disaster 20 years earlier.[43] Although foam striking the shuttle was the technical cause, NASA's organizational culture was the real problem. Joseph Grenny, a NASA engineer, noted that "the NASA culture does not accept being wrong." The culture does not accept that "there's no such thing as a stupid question." Instead, "the humiliation factor always runs high."[44] Consequently, people do not speak up. As this example shows, if, over time, a certain culture becomes inappropriate to an organization and a handicap to management, there might be little a manager can do to change it, especially in the short run. Even under favourable conditions, cultural changes have to be viewed in years, not weeks or even months.

Understanding the Situational Factors

What "favourable conditions" might facilitate cultural change? The evidence suggests that cultural change is most likely to take place when most or all of the following conditions exist:

- *A dramatic crisis occurs.* This can be the shock that weakens the status quo and makes people start thinking about the relevance of the current culture. Examples are a surprising financial setback, the loss of a major customer, or a dramatic technological innovation by a competitor.

- *Leadership changes hands.* New top leadership, who can provide an alternative set of key values, may be perceived as more capable of responding to the crisis than the old leaders were. Top leadership includes the organization's chief executive but might include all senior managers.

- *The organization is young and small.* The younger the organization, the less entrenched its culture. Similarly, it's easier for managers to communicate new values in a small organization than in a large one.

- *The culture is weak.* The more widely held the values and the higher the agreement among members on those values, the more difficult it will be to change. Conversely, weak cultures are more receptive to change than are strong ones.[45]

These situational factors help explain why a company such as Yahoo! faces challenges in reshaping its culture. For the most part, employees like the old ways of doing things and don't always see the company's problems as critical. This may also be why Yahoo! was slow to recognize the importance of Facebook and YouTube to the online scene.

How Can Cultural Change Be Accomplished?

Now we ask the question, If conditions are right, how do managers go about changing culture? The challenge is to unfreeze the current culture, implement the new "ways of doing things," and reinforce those new values. No single action is likely to have the impact necessary to change something that is so ingrained and highly valued. Thus, there needs to be a comprehensive and coordinated strategy for managing cultural change, as shown in the *Tips for Managers—Strategies for Managing Cultural Change.*

TIPS FOR MANAGERS

Strategies for Managing Cultural Change

- Set the tone through management behaviour. Managers, particularly top management, need to be **positive role models**.

- Create **new stories, symbols, and rituals** to replace those currently in vogue.

- Select, promote, and support employees who **adopt the new values** that are sought.

- **Redesign socialization processes** to align with the new values.

- Change the reward system to **encourage acceptance** of a new set of values.

- Replace unwritten norms with **formal rules and regulations** that are tightly enforced.

- **Shake up current subcultures** through transfers, job rotation, and/or terminations.

- Work to get peer-group consensus through **employee participation** and creation of a climate with a high level of trust.

As you can see, these suggestions focus on specific actions that managers can take to change the ineffective culture. Following these suggestions, however, is no guarantee that a manager's change efforts will succeed. Organizational members don't quickly let go of values that they understand and that have worked well for them in the past. Managers must, therefore, be patient. Change, if it comes, will be slow. And managers must stay constantly alert to protect against any return to old, familiar practices and traditions.

Handling Employee Stress

Q&A 16.7

As a student, you have probably experienced stress when finishing class assignments and projects, taking exams, or finding ways to pay rising tuition costs, which may mean juggling a job and school. Then, there is the stress associated with getting a decent job after graduation. Even after you have landed that job, your stress is not likely to stop. For many employees, organizational change creates stress. A dynamic and uncertain environment characterized by mergers, restructurings, forced retirements, and downsizing has created a large number of employees who are overworked and stressed out.[46] In fact, Ipsos Reid recently did a survey of 1500 Canadians with employer-sponsored health care plans. It found that 62 percent reported experiencing "a great deal of stress on the job." Workplace stress was bad enough to cause 34 percent of those surveyed to say that it had made them physically ill.[47] In this section, we review what stress is, what causes it, how to identify its symptoms, and what managers can do to reduce it.

What Is Stress?

stress

The adverse reaction people have to excessive pressure placed on them from extraordinary demands, constraints, or opportunities.

Stress is the adverse reaction people have to excessive pressure placed on them from extraordinary demands, constraints, or opportunities.[48] Let's look more closely at what stress is.

Stress is not necessarily bad. Although it's often discussed in a negative context, stress does have a positive value, particularly when it offers a potential gain. Functional stress allows an athlete, stage performer, or employee to perform at his or her highest level in crucial situations.

However, stress is more often associated with fear of loss. When you take a test at school or have your annual performance review at work, you feel stress because you know that there can be either positive or negative outcomes. A good performance review may lead to a promotion, greater responsibilities, and a higher salary. But a poor review may keep you from getting the promotion. An extremely poor review might lead to your being fired.

What are the things that cause you stress?

Just because the conditions are right for stress to surface does not always mean it will. Stress is highest for individuals who are uncertain whether they will win or lose and lowest for individuals who think that winning or losing is a certainty. In addition, if winning or losing is unimportant, there is no stress. An employee who feels that keeping a job or earning a promotion is unimportant will experience no stress before a performance review.

Causes of Stress

As shown in Exhibit 16-7, the causes of stress can be found in issues related to the organization or in personal factors that evolve out of the employee's private life. Clearly, change of any kind has the potential to cause stress. It can present opportunities, constraints, or demands. Moreover, changes are frequently created in a climate of uncertainty and around issues that are important to employees. It's not surprising, then, that change is a major stressor.

Symptoms of Stress

What signs indicate that an employee's stress level might be too high? Stress shows itself in a number of ways. For instance, an employee who is experiencing high stress may become depressed, accident prone, or argumentative; may have difficulty making routine decisions; may be easily distracted; and so on. As Exhibit 16-8 shows, stress symptoms can be grouped under three general categories: physical, psychological, and behavioural. Of these, the physical symptoms are least relevant to managers. Of greater importance are the psychological and behavioural symptoms, since these directly affect an employee's work.

Exhibit 16-9

Mistakes Managers Make When Leading Change

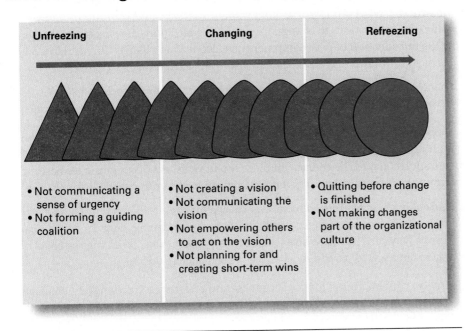

Unfreezing	Changing	Refreezing
• Not communicating a sense of urgency • Not forming a guiding coalition	• Not creating a vision • Not communicating the vision • Not empowering others to act on the vision • Not planning for and creating short-term wins	• Quitting before change is finished • Not making changes part of the organizational culture

Sources: J. P. Kotter, "Leading Change: Why Transformation Efforts Fail," *Harvard Business Review*, March–April 1995, pp. 56–67; and *Management*, First Canadian Edition by Williams/Kondra/Vibert. © 2004. Reprinted with permission of Nelson, a division of Thomson Learning: www.thomsonrights.com. FAX 800-730-2215.

Third, managers need to encourage employees to be change agents—to look for those day-to-day improvements and changes that individuals and teams can make. For instance, a study of organizational change found that 77 percent of changes at the work-group level were reactions to a specific, current problem or to a suggestion from someone outside the work group; and 68 percent of those changes occurred in the course of employees' day-to-day work.[55]

Exhibit 16-10

Characteristics of Change-Capable Organizations

- *Link the present and the future.* Think of work as more than an extension of the past; think about future opportunities and issues and factor them into today's decisions.
- *Make learning a way of life.* Change-friendly organizations excel at knowledge sharing and management.
- *Actively support and encourage day-to-day improvements and changes.* Successful change can come from the small changes as well as the big ones.
- *Ensure diverse teams.* Diversity ensures that things won't be done the way they are always done.
- *Encourage mavericks.* Since their ideas and approaches are outside the mainstream, mavericks can help bring about radical change.
- *Shelter breakthroughs.* Change-friendly organizations have found ways to protect those breakthrough ideas.
- *Integrate technology.* Use technology to implement changes.
- *Build and deepen trust.* People are more likely to support changes when the organization's culture is trusting and managers have credibility and integrity.

Source: Based on P. A. McLagan, "The Change-Capable Organization," *Training & Development*, January 2003, pp. 50–58.

SUMMARY AND IMPLICATIONS

1. What factors create the need for change? Organizations are confronted with the need for change from both external and internal forces. Externally, the marketplace, government laws and regulations, technology, labour markets, and economic changes all put pressure on organizations to change. Internally, organizations may decide to change strategies. The introduction of new equipment can also lead to change. The workforce, both in terms of composition and attitudes, can also lead to demands for change.

▶ ▶ ▶ Yahoo! faces changes because it is a large organization experiencing challenges from ever-changing technology and fast-moving, smaller, and more aggressive organizations.

2. Is change ongoing or episodic? Until the late 1980s, change was viewed as episodic, something that could be planned and managed readily. In between periods of change, organizations "stayed the course." In more recent years, environments have become more uncertain and dynamic, and this has led to more continuous demands for change.

▶ ▶ ▶ Yahoo! has had to respond to various changes in the online world (even as it introduced technological changes itself). To regain its leadership edge as the company moves forward, it has to be able to identify new opportunities on an ongoing basis and figure out a way to provide services that its competitors do not.

3. How do organizations manage change and resistance to change? Managers can change an organization's structure, technology, and people. People tend to resist change, and there are a variety of reasons why they do so. The main reason is that change replaces the known with ambiguity and uncertainty. As well, people do not necessarily like their habits changed; they may fear losing something already possessed (such as status, money, or friendships); and they may believe that the change could actually reduce product quality or productivity.

▶ ▶ ▶ One of the challenges Yahoo! needs to manage is that employees have been used to working in separate silos, not always aware of the big picture of the organization. They may resist working "outside of the box" initially because they have been rewarded for working within subunits, rather than thinking of the overall strategic plan of the organization.

4. What is innovation and how does it occur in organizations? Innovation is the process of taking creative ideas and turning them into useful products, services, or work methods. Organizations that have greater structural flexibility, encourage training and development of employees, and encourage risk-taking and new ideas are more likely to be innovative.

▶ ▶ ▶ At the outset, Yahoo! was a very innovative company, but in recent years its innovations have been more limited, which has allowed Google and Facebook to become serious competitors.

5. What are some of the current issues in managing change? One main consideration in managing change is determining how to introduce change in an existing organizational culture. An organization's culture can make it difficult to introduce change. Another major consideration is how to deal with employee stress while undergoing change.

▶ ▶ ▶ Yahoo!'s culture has been one of separate silos, and now it needs more teamwork from employees. This may create difficulties for CEO Jerry Yang, who has to figure out how to reward team activities rather than individual actions. However, because he was a co-founder of Yahoo!, he may be better suited in introducing such changes successfully than an outsider would be.

Management @ Work

READING FOR COMPREHENSION

1. Define *organizational change.*

2. What are the external and internal forces for change?

3. Why is handling change an integral part of every manager's job?

4. Describe Lewin's three-step change process. How is it different from the change process needed in the white-water rapids metaphor of change?

5. Discuss what it takes to make change happen successfully.

6. Explain why people resist change and how resistance might be managed.

7. How do work overload, role conflict, and role ambiguity contribute to employee stress?

LINKING CONCEPTS TO PRACTICE

1. Can a nonmanagerial employee be a change agent? Explain your answer.

2. "Innovation requires allowing people to make mistakes. However, being wrong too many times can be fatal." Do you agree? Why or why not? What are the implications for nurturing innovation?

3. How are opportunities, constraints, and demands related to stress? Give an example of each.

4. Planned change is often thought to be the best approach to take in organizations. Can unplanned change ever be effective? Explain.

5. Organizations typically have limits to how much change they can absorb. As a manager, what signs would you look for that might suggest that your organization has exceeded its capacity to change?

SELF-ASSESSMENT

How Well Do I Respond to Turbulent Change?

Listed below are a set of statements describing the characteristics of a managerial job. If your job had these features, how would you react to them?[56]

    Use the following rating scale for your answers:

        1 = This feature would be very unpleasant for me.

        2 = This feature would be somewhat unpleasant for me.

        3 = I would have no reaction to this feature one way or another; or it would be about equally enjoyable and unpleasant.

        4 = This feature would be enjoyable and acceptable most of the time.

        5 = I would enjoy this feature very much; it's completely acceptable.

1. I regularly spend 30 to 40 percent of my time in meetings.   1   2   3   4   5

2. A year and a half ago, my job did not exist, and I have been essentially inventing it as I go along.   1   2   3   4   5

3. The responsibilities I either assume or am assigned consistently exceed the authority I have for discharging them.   1   2   3   4   5

4. I am a member of a team and I have no more authority than anyone else on the team.   1   2   3   4   5

5. At any given moment in my job, I have on the average about a dozen phone calls or emails to be returned.   1   2   3   4   5

6. My job performance is evaluated by not only my boss but also by my peers and subordinates.   1   2   3   4   5

7. About three weeks a year of formal management training is needed in my job just to stay current.   1   2   3   4   5

8. My job consistently brings me into close working contact at a professional level with people of many races, ethnic groups, and nationalities, and of both sexes.   1   2   3   4   5

9. For many of my work colleagues, English is their second language.   1   2   3   4   5

10. My boss is from another country and has been in this country for only six months.   1   2   3   4   5

11. There is no objective way to measure my effectiveness.   1   2   3   4   5

12. I report to three different bosses for different aspects of my job, and each has an equal say in my performance appraisal.   1   2   3   4   5

13. On average, about a third of my time is spent dealing with unexpected emergencies that force all scheduled work to be postponed.   1   2   3   4   5

14. On average, I spend about a week every month out of town on business.   1   2   3   4   5

15. I frequently have to work until 8 p.m. to get my day's work completed.   1   2   3   4   5

16. When I have a meeting with the people who report to me, at least one or two will participate by phone or electronic conferencing.   1   2   3   4   5

17. The degree I earned in preparation for this type of work is now obsolete, and I probably should go back for another degree.   1   2   3   4   5

18. My job requires me to read 100 to 200 pages per week of technical materials.   1   2   3   4   5

19. My department is so interdependent with several other departments in the organization that all distinctions about which departments are responsible for which tasks are quite arbitrary.   1   2   3   4   5

20. I am unlikely to get a promotion any time in the near future.   1   2   3   4   5

21. There is no clear career path for me in this job and organization.   1   2   3   4   5

22. During the period of my employment here, either the entire organization or the division I worked in has been reorganized every year or so.   1   2   3   4   5

23. While I have many ideas about how to make things work better, I have no direct influence on either the business policies or the personnel policies that govern my division.   1   2   3   4   5

24. My organization is a defendant in an antitrust suit, and if the case comes to trial, I will probably have to testify about some decisions that were made a few years ago.   1   2   3   4   5

25. Sophisticated new technological equipment and software are continually being introduced into my division, necessitating constant learning on my part.   1   2   3   4   5

26. The computer I have in my office can be monitored by my bosses without my knowledge.   1   2   3   4   5

Scoring Key

To calculate your tolerance-of-change score, add up your responses to all 26 items.

Analysis and Interpretation

This instrument describes a number of characteristics of the changing workplace. The higher your score, the more comfortable you are with change.

The author of this instrument suggests an "average" score is around 78. If you scored over 100, you seem to be accepting the "new" workplace fairly well. If your score was below 70, you are likely to find the manager's job in the twenty-first century unpleasant, if not overwhelming.

More Self-Assessments mymanagementlab

To learn more about your skills, abilities, and interests, go to the MyManagementLab website and take the following self-assessments:

- I.A.4.—How Well Do I Handle Ambiguity? (This exercise also appears in Chapter 7 on pages 216–217.)
- I.A.5.—How Creative Am I?
- III.C.2.—How Stressful Is My Life?
- III.C.3.—Am I Burned Out?

MANAGEMENT FOR YOU TODAY

Dilemma

Think of something that you would like to change in your personal life. It could be your study habits, your fitness and nutrition, the way you interact with others, or anything else that is of interest to you. What values and assumptions have encouraged the behaviour that currently exists (that is, the one you want to change)?

What driving and restraining forces can you address in order to make the desired change?

Becoming a Manager

- Pay attention to how you handle change. Figure out why you resist certain changes and not others.

- Practise using different approaches to managing resistance to change at work or in your personal life.

- Read material that has been written about how to be a more creative person.

- Find ways to be innovative and creative as you complete class projects or work projects.

WORKING TOGETHER: TEAM-BASED EXERCISE

Dealing with Stress

Stress is something that all of us face, and college and university students particularly may have extremely stressful lives. How do you recognize when you are under a lot of stress? What do you do to deal with that stress?

Form teams of 3 or 4 individuals. Each person in the group should describe how he or she knows when he or she is under a lot of stress. What symptoms does each person show? Make a list of these symptoms and categorize them using Exhibit 16-8 on page 533. Then, each person should also describe things that he or she has found to be particularly effective in dealing with stress. Make a list of these stress-handling techniques. Out of that list, identify your top three stress reducers and be prepared to share these with the class.

ETHICS IN ACTION

Ethical Dilemma Exercise: How Can Managers Help Employees Accept Change?

What is the most ethical way to deal with change that will take away some employees' jobs or completely alter the work environment?[57] Managers at the Boots chain, which operates 1400 drugstores and employs 60 000 people in the United Kingdom, faced this issue not long ago. They had just formulated a long-term plan to cut costs and increase efficiency by replacing a group of older distribution facilities with a new automated warehouse. Closing the facilities would take years and save the company millions of dollars—but it would also mean displacing more than 2000 workers. The challenge was to manage the change in a sensitive way and minimize resistance while maintaining high productivity.

To reduce the stress on its workforce, Boots announced the change three years in advance and emphasized that the employees affected by the closures would be offered other jobs in the company. To increase participation and support, the company also held talks with the main union representing employees. Going further, management praised employee performance and kept on communicating about the progress toward constructing the new warehouse and closing individual facilities. Productivity has not suffered so far, although the combination of changing structure and technology will probably add some stress and encounter a degree of internal resistance. This is just the beginning, notes a senior executive: "Boots is changing very fast, probably faster than any other large UK retailer."

Imagine you are the manager of a Boots store. During a staff meeting, one of your employees suggests that the store remain open one hour later on Thursday nights. This would increase sales and help your store compete with a drugstore two blocks away. Although you like the idea, your assistant manager—an outstanding employee—raises a number of objections and keeps complaining even after the meeting ends. What should you do? (Review Exhibit 16-4 on page 526 as you consider this ethical challenge.)

Thinking Critically About Ethics

Although numerous organizations provide stress-reduction programs, many employees choose not to participate. Why? Many employees are reluctant to ask for help, especially if a major source of that stress is job insecurity. After all, there is still a stigma associated with stress. Employees don't want to be perceived as unable to handle the demands of their jobs. Although they may need stress management now more than ever, few employees want to admit that they are stressed. What can be done about this paradox? Do organizations even have an ethical responsibility to help employees deal with stress?

CASE APPLICATION

1-800-GOT-JUNK?

Eighteen thousand expired cans of sardines.[58] Fifty garden gnomes. A mechanical bull. An antique silver set (worth a lot of money). These are just some of the weird items that Vancouver-based 1-800-GOT-JUNK? customers have asked the uniformed people in the freshly scrubbed blue trucks to haul away. Company founder and CEO Brian Scudamore discovered there was a lucrative niche between "trash cans and those big green bins dropped off by" the giant waste haulers. But even in such an uncomplicated business as hauling people's junk, Scudamore must be concerned with managing change and managing innovation.

1-800-GOT-JUNK?, named one of the Best Employers in Canada for 2007 by *Canadian Business*, has a corporate staff of about 300 individuals. "With a vision of creating the 'FedEx' of junk removal," says Scudamore, "I dropped out of university with just one year left to become a full-time JUNKMAN! Yes, my father, a liver transplant surgeon, was not impressed, to say the least." However, in 2006, the company had about 250 franchises and system-wide revenues were over $105 million. Not surprisingly, Scudamore's father is a little more understanding these days about his son's business! Since 1997, the company has grown exponentially. In fact, the company made the list of *Entrepreneur* magazine's 100 fastest-growing franchises in 2005 and 2006.

Hauling junk would be, to most people's minds at least, a pretty simple business. However, the company Scudamore founded is a "curious hybrid." It's been described as a blend of "old economy and new economy." The company's service—hauling away trash—has been done for hundreds, if not thousands, of years. But 1-800-GOT-JUNK? also relies heavily on up-to-date information technology and has the kind of organizational culture that most people associate with high-tech start-ups. The company uses its 1-800-GOT-JUNK? call centre to do the booking and dispatching for all its franchise partners. The franchise partners also use the company's proprietary intranet and customer relationship management site—dubbed JunkNet—to access schedules, customer information, real-time reports, and so forth. Scudamore's philosophy was that this approach allowed franchise partners to "work on the business" instead of "work in the business." On any given day, all a franchisee has to do is open up JunkNet to see the day's schedule. If a new job comes in during a workday, the program automatically sends an alert to the franchisee. Needless to say, the company's franchisees tend to be quite tech-savvy. In fact, some of them have installed GPS devices in their trucks to help find the most efficient routes on a job. Others use online navigation sites. With the price of gas continuing to increase, this type of capability is important.

1-800-GOT-JUNK? also has a culture that would rival any high-tech start-up. The head office is known as the Junktion. Grizzly, Scudamore's dog, comes to the office every day and helps employees relieve stress by playing catch any time, anywhere. Each morning at exactly 10:55, all employees at the Junktion meet for a five-minute huddle, where they share good news, announcements, metrics, and problems they are encountering. Visitors to the Junktion have to join the group huddle also. One of the most conspicuous features of the Junktion—"the first thing one sees upon entering—is the Vision Wall," which contains the "fruits of Scudamore's brainstorms." Other members of the executive team have visions for the company's future as well. Periodically, they will "wander through the offices of Genome Sciences Centre, the tenant occupying the space above them, to visualize a future when Got-Junk has expanded so sufficiently" that it will take over that office space. Company franchisees are also encouraged to take initiative and be creative. For instance, the Toronto franchise, which has 12 trucks, sometimes gets a blue-truck motorcade going down Yonge Street through the heart of the city as a way to be noticed and to publicize its services.

Despite the company's success to date, Scudamore is wondering whether he is prepared to face whatever changes may happen in the environment in the years to come. How would you advise him to create a "change-capable" organization?

DEVELOPING YOUR DIAGNOSTIC AND ANALYTICAL SKILLS

Changes in the Health Care Industry

When you think about the significant changes that have occurred in people's lives over the past five decades, clearly the advances in medical science would be at the top of such a list.[59] Diseases have been eradicated and medical procedures and devices have helped save thousands of lives. But don't be too quick to conclude that the health care industry is a model of innovation and efficiency.

Hospitals, in general, have one of the most archaic and costly operating systems of any group of large organizations. Nearly 95 percent of all hospitals currently use procedures and record-keeping systems that were implemented more than 50 years ago. It's the way it's always been done, and that is how most doctors and technicians prefer it. Individuals in this industry have been highly reluctant to accept and use new technologies.

Doctors and hospital administrators at Prairie General Hospital, however, refuse to be part of the "old guard." Consider the following that happened in the emergency room at Prairie General. A middle-aged patient was brought in by his wife to the emergency room. The patient, who was very overweight, was complaining of shortness of breath and dizziness. Although the patient claimed he was okay, his wife made him go to the hospital. Immediately, the staff at Prairie General went to work. While nurses hooked the patient up to heart-monitoring equipment and checked his vital signs, a resident wheeled over an emergency room cart, which contained a laptop computer. Logging in the patient's identification number, the ER doctor noticed that the patient had an EKG in the past year. Immediately reviewing the past EKG records and comparing it with current heart-monitoring results, the doctor determined the patient was in the midst of having a heart attack. Within 10 minutes of being seen, doctors had determined that the patient was suffering from a blocked artery. Clot-busting drugs were swiftly administered, and the patient was immediately taken to the cardiac lab, where an emergency angioplasty was performed to open up the clogged artery. Within a day, the patient was back on his feet and ready to go home. In most other hospitals, the patient may not have been so lucky!

Prairie General is unusual in the health care industry. This hospital is investing money in technology that enables it to provide better service at a lower cost. Through its system, called CareWeb, more than 1 million patient records are available. Within each of these records are all previous medical orders, such as lab test results and prescriptions, for each patient. When a patient comes to the hospital, that individual's health history is easily retrievable and can be used to assist in the current diagnosis.

What has been the effect of this technology change on Prairie General? The system is saving the hospital more than $1 million each year. It has reduced errors in patient care by more than 90 percent and reduced prescription errors and potential drug interactions by more than 50 percent. Patient charts are now available in moments rather than hours or days. And patients are now discharged more than 30 minutes faster than they had been before CareWeb was implemented.

Cost savings, time savings, increased patient care, and saved lives—all this makes you wonder why every hospital is not making such changes!

Questions

1. Describe the types of changes that have occurred at Prairie General in terms of structure, technology, and people. Cite examples.

2. Why do you believe there is resistance by the medical profession to systems such as CareWeb? Explain.

3. Assume you were going to make a presentation to a group of hospital staff (doctors and administrators) on why they should invest in technology such as CareWeb. How would you attempt to overcome their resistance to change and their attitude about continuing to do what they have always done? Discuss.

DEVELOPING YOUR INTERPERSONAL SKILLS

Managing Resistance to Change

About the Skill

Managers play an important role in organizational change— that is, they often serve as change agents. However, managers may find that change is resisted by employees. After all, change represents ambiguity and uncertainty, or it threatens the status quo. How can this resistance to change be effectively managed?

Steps in Developing the Skill

You can be more effective at managing resistance to change if you use the following three suggestions:[60]

1. **Assess the climate for change.** One major factor why some changes succeed and others fail is the readiness for change. Assessing the climate for change involves asking several questions. The more affirmative answers you get, the more likely it is that change efforts will succeed.

   - Is the sponsor of the change high enough in the hierarchy to have power to effectively deal with resistance?

   - Is senior management supportive of the change and committed to it?

   - Is there a strong sense of urgency from senior managers about the need for change, and is this feeling shared by others in the organization?

   - Do managers have a clear vision of how the future will look after the change?

   - Are there objective measures in place to evaluate the change effort, and have reward systems been explicitly designed to reinforce them?

   - Is the specific change effort consistent with other changes going on in the organization?

   - Are managers willing to sacrifice their personal self-interests for the good of the organization as a whole?

   - Do managers pride themselves on closely monitoring changes and actions by competitors?

   - Are managers and employees rewarded for taking risks, being innovative, and looking for new and better solutions?

   - Is the organizational structure flexible?

   - Does communication flow both down and up in the organization?

   - Has the organization successfully implemented changes in the recent past?

   - Are employee satisfaction with and trust in management high?

   - Is there a high degree of interaction and cooperation between organizational work units?

   - Are decisions made quickly, and do decisions take into account a wide variety of suggestions?

2. **Choose an appropriate approach for managing the resistance to change.** There are five tactics that have been suggested for dealing with resistance to change. Each is designed to be appropriate for different conditions of resistance. They are *education and communication* (used when resistance comes from lack of information or inaccurate information); *participation* (used when resistance stems from people not having all the information they need or when they have the power to resist); *facilitation and support* (used when those with power will lose out in a change); *manipulation and cooptation* (used when any other tactic will not work or is too expensive); and *coercion* (used when speed is essential and change agents possess considerable power). Which one of these approaches will be most effective depends on the source of the resistance to the change.

3. **During the time the change is being implemented and after the change is completed, communicate with employees regarding what support you may be able to provide.** Your employees need to know that you are there to support them during change efforts. Be prepared to offer the assistance that may be necessary to help your employees enact the change.

Practising the Skill

Read the following scenario. Write some notes about how you would handle the situation described. Be sure to refer to the three suggestions for managing resistance to change.

Scenario

You are the nursing supervisor at a local hospital that employs both emergency room and floor nurses. Each of these teams of nurses tends to work almost exclusively with others doing the same job. In your professional reading, you have come across the concept of cross-training nursing teams and giving them more varied responsibilities, which in turn has been shown to improve patient care while lowering costs. You call the two team leaders, Sue and Scott, into your office to explain that you want the nursing teams to move to this approach. To your surprise, they are both opposed to the idea. Sue says she and the other emergency room nurses feel they are needed in the ER, where they fill the most vital role in the hospital. They work special hours when needed, do whatever tasks are required, and often work in difficult and stressful circumstances. They think the floor nurses have relatively easy jobs for the pay they receive. Scott, the leader of the floor nurse team, tells you that his group believes the ER nurses lack the special training and extra experience that the floor nurses bring to the hospital. The floor nurses claim they have the heaviest responsibilities and do the most exacting work. Because they have ongoing contact with patients and families, they believe they should not be called away from vital floor duties to help the ER nurses complete their tasks. What should you do about your idea to introduce more cross-training for the nursing teams?

Reinforcing the Skill

The following activities will help you practise and reinforce the skills associated with effectively managing resistance to change.

1. Think about changes (major and minor) that you have dealt with over the last year. Perhaps these changes involved other people and perhaps they were personal. Did you resist the change? Did others resist the change? How did you overcome your resistance or the resistance of others to the change?

2. Interview managers at three different organizations about changes they have implemented. What was their experience in implementing the change? How did they manage resistance to the change?

MANAGING WORKFORCE DIVERSITY

The Paradox of Diversity

When organizations bring diverse individuals in and socialize them into the culture, a paradox is created.[61] Managers want these new employees to accept the organization's core cultural values. Otherwise, the employees may have a difficult time fitting in or being accepted. At the same time, managers want to openly acknowledge, embrace, and support the diverse perspectives and ideas that these employees bring to the workplace.

Strong organizational cultures put considerable pressure on employees to conform, and the range of acceptable values and behaviours is limited. Therein lies the paradox. Organizations hire diverse individuals because of their unique strengths, yet their diverse behaviours and strengths are likely to diminish in strong cultures as people attempt to fit in.

A manager's challenge in this paradox of diversity is to balance two conflicting goals: to encourage employees to accept the organization's dominant values and to encourage employees to accept differences. When changes are made in the organization's culture, managers need to remember the importance of keeping diversity alive.

How difficult do you think it is for managers to encourage employees to accept differences, while also trying to get them to all be part of the same organizational culture?

MANAGING YOUR CAREER

Reinvent Yourself

Face it. The only constant thing about change is that it is constant.[62] These days, you don't have the luxury of dealing with change only once in a while. No, the workplace seems to change almost continuously. How can you reinvent yourself to deal with the demands of a constantly changing workplace?

Being prepared is not a credo just for the Boy Scouts; it should be your motto for dealing with a workplace that is constantly changing. Being prepared means taking the initiative and being responsible for your own personal career development. Rather than depending on your organization to provide you with career development and training opportunities, do it yourself. Take advantage of continuing education or graduate courses at local colleges and universities. Sign up for workshops and seminars that can help you enhance your skills. Upgrading your skills to keep them current is one of the most important things you can do to reinvent yourself.

It's also important for you to be a positive force when faced with workplace changes. We don't mean that you should routinely accept any change that is being implemented. If you think that a proposed change won't work, speak up. Voice your concerns in a constructive manner. Being constructive may mean suggesting an alternative. However, if you feel that the change is beneficial, support it wholeheartedly and enthusiastically.

The changes that organizations make in response to a dynamic environment can be overwhelming and stressful. However, you can take advantage of these changes by reinventing yourself.

Continuing Case: Starbucks

Once managers have established goals and plans, organized and structured work activities, and developed programs to motivate and lead people to put forth effort to accomplish those goals, the manager's job is not done.[1] Quite the opposite! Managers must now monitor work activities to make sure they are being done as planned and correct any significant deviations. This process is called *controlling*. It's the final link in the management process, and although controlling happens last in the process, that does not make it any less important than any of the other managerial functions. At Starbucks, managers control various functions, activities, processes, and procedures to ensure that desired performance standards are achieved at all organizational levels.

Controlling the Coffee Experience

Why has Starbucks been so successful? Although there are many factors that have contributed to its success, one significant factor has been its ability to provide customers with a unique product of the highest quality delivered with exceptional service. Everything that each Starbucks partner does, from top level to bottom level, contributes to the company's ability to do that efficiently and effectively. And managers need controls in place to help monitor and evaluate what is being done and how it is being done. Starbucks' managers use different types of controls to ensure that Starbucks remains, as its mission states, "the premier purveyor of the finest coffee in the world while maintaining our uncompromising principles as we grow." These controls include transactions controls, security controls, employee controls, and organizational performance controls.

A legal recruiter stops by Starbucks on her way to her office in downtown Calgary and orders her daily Caffè Mocha tall. A construction site supervisor pulls into the drive-through line at the Starbucks store in Montreal, for a cinnamon chip scone and grande Caffè Americano. It's 11 p.m. and, needing a break from studying for her next-day's management exam, a student heads to the local Starbucks for a tasty treat—Tazo® Chai Tea Latte. Now she is ready again to tackle that chapter material on managerial controls.

Every single day, an average of 636 transactions just like these happen at every Starbucks store. Worldwide, about 34 million transactions take place each week. The average sale per transaction is $4.05. These transactions between partners (employees) and customers—the exchange of products for money—are the major source of sales revenue for Starbucks. Measuring and evaluating the efficiency and effectiveness of these transactions for both walk-in customers and customers at drive-through windows is important. As Starbucks has been doing walk-in transactions for a number of years, numerous procedures and processes are in place to make those transactions go smoothly. However, as Starbucks adds more drive-through windows, the focus of the transaction is on being fast as well as on quality, a different metric than for walk-in transactions. When a customer walks into a store and orders, he or she can step aside while the order is being prepared; that is not possible in a drive-through line. Recognizing these limitations, the company is taking steps to improve its drive-through service. For instance, digital timers are placed where employees can easily see them to measure service times; order confirmation screens are used to help keep accuracy rates high; and additional pastry racks have been conveniently located by the drive-through windows.

Security is also an important issue for Starbucks. Keeping company assets (such as people, equipment, products, financial information, and so forth) safe and secure requires security controls. The company's Standards of Business Conduct document states, "Starbucks is committed to providing all partners with a clean, safe and healthy work environment. To achieve this goal, we must recognize our shared responsibilities to follow all safety rules and practices, to cooperate with officials who enforce those rules and practices, to take necessary steps to protect ourselves and other partners, to attend required safety training and to report immediately all accidents, injuries and unsafe practices or conditions." When hired, each partner is provided with a Safety, Security, and Health Standards manual and trained on the requirements outlined in the manual. In addition, managers receive ongoing training about these issues and are expected to keep employees trained and up-to-date on any changes. And at any time, any partner can contact the partner and asset protection department for information and advice.

One security area that has been particularly important to Starbucks has been with its gift cards, in which it does an enormous volume of business. (Review the information on Starbucks Cards in the continuing case at the end of Part 2.) With these gift cards, there are lots of opportunities for an unethical employee to "steal" from the company. The company's director of compliance says that "detecting such fraud can be difficult because there is no visibility from an operations standpoint." However, Starbucks uses transactional data analysis technology to detect multiple card redemptions in a single day and has identified other "telltale" activities that pinpoint possible fraud. When the company's technology detects transaction activity outside the norm, Starbucks' corporate staff is alerted and a panel of company experts reviews the data. Investigators have found individuals at stores who confess to stealing as much as $42 000. When smaller exceptions are noted, the individuals are sent letters asking them to explain what is going on. The director of compliance says, "I view this as a gentle touch on the shoulder saying we can see what is happening." Employees who have been so "notified" often quit.

Starbucks' part-time and full-time hourly partners are the primary—and most important—source of contact between the company and the customer, and outstanding customer service is a top priority at Starbucks. The Standards of Business Conduct document states, "We strive to make every customer's experience pleasant and fulfilling, and we treat our customers as we treat one another, with respect and dignity." What kinds of employee controls does Starbucks use to ensure that this happens? Partners are trained in and are required to follow all proper procedures relating to the storage, handling, preparation, and service of Starbucks' products. In addition, partners are told to notify their managers immediately if they see anything that suggests a product may pose a danger to the health or safety of themselves or of customers. Partners also are taught the warning signs associated with possible workplace violence and how to reduce their vulnerability if faced with a potentially violent situation. In either circumstance, where product or partner safety and security are threatened, store managers have been trained in the appropriate steps to take if such a situation occurs.

The final types of control that are important to Starbucks' managers are the organizational performance and financial controls. Starbucks uses the typical financial control measures, but also looks at growth in sales at stores open at least one year as a performance standard. One issue with which company executives are dealing is that store operating costs have increased. One contributing factor is the health care packages offered to every employee who puts in 20 hours a week. Another factor is that, as the company continues to expand, there are more employees. However, president and CEO Jim Donald is not too worried at this point. He says, "No problem. We could tighten this thing up at a moment's notice, but we're a growing business. Instead, the trick is basic retailing—sell more stuff at more stores." There is a fine balance the company has to achieve between keeping costs low and keeping quality high. However, there are

steps the company has taken to control costs. For instance, new, thinner garbage bags will save the company half a million dollars a year.

In addition to the typical financial measures, corporate governance procedures and guidelines are an important part of Starbucks' financial controls, as they are at any public corporation that is covered by Sarbanes-Oxley legislation. The company has identified guidelines for its board of directors with respect to responsibilities, processes, procedures, and expectations.

Starbucks' Value Chain: From Bean to Cup

The steaming cup of coffee placed in a customer's hand at any Starbucks store location starts as coffee beans (berries) plucked from fields of coffee plants. From harvest to storage to roasting to retail to cup, Starbucks understands the important role each participant in its value chain plays.

Starbucks offers a selection of coffees from around the world, and its coffee buyers personally travel to the coffee-growing regions of Latin America, Africa/Arabia, and Asia/Pacific in order to select and purchase the highest-quality *arabica* beans. Once the beans arrive at any one of the four roasting facilities (in Washington, Pennsylvania, Nevada, or Amsterdam), Starbucks' master professional roasters do their "magic" in creating the company's rich signature roast coffee, a process that is the "cumulative result of expert

roasters knowing coffee and bringing balance to all of its flavor attributes." There are many potential challenges to "transforming" the raw material into the quality product and experience that customers have come to expect at Starbucks. Weather, shipping and logistics, technology, political instability, and so forth all could potentially impact what Starbucks is in business to do.

One issue of great importance to Starbucks is environmental protection. Starbucks has taken actions throughout its entire supply chain to minimize its "environmental footprint." For instance, suppliers are asked to sign a Supplier Code of Conduct that deals with business standards and practices that "produce social, environmental, and economic benefits for the communities where Starbucks does business." Even company stores are focused on the environmental impact of their store operations. Partners at stores around the world have found innovative ways to reuse coffee grounds. For example, in Japan, a team of Starbucks partners realized that coffee grounds could be used as an ingredient to make paper. A local printing company uses this paper to print the official Starbucks Japan newsletter. In Bahrain, partners dry coffee grounds in the sun, package them, and give them to customers as fertilizer for house plants.

Questions

1. What control criteria might be useful to a retail store manager? What control criteria might be appropriate for a barista at one of Starbucks' retail stores (walk-in only)? How about for a store that has a drive-through window?

2. What types of feedforward, concurrent, and feedback controls does Starbucks use? Are there others that might be important to use? If so, describe.

3. What "red flags" might indicate significant deviations from standard for (a) an hourly employee; (b) a store manager; (c) a district manager; (d) the executive vice-president of finance; and (e) the CEO? Are there any similarities? Why or why not?

4. Would it be easy to keep costs low and quality high? Discuss.

5. Evaluate the control measures Starbucks is using with its gift cards from the standpoint of the three steps in the control process.

6. Using the company's most current financial statements, calculate the following financial ratios: current ratio, debt to assets, inventory turnover, total asset turnover, profit margin on sales, and return on investment (see Exhibit 15-10 on page 481). What do these ratios tell managers?

7. Describe and evaluate Starbucks' operations in terms of the service profit chain illustrated in Exhibit 15-15 on page 491.

8. Would you describe Starbucks' production/operations technology in its retail stores as unit, mass, or process? How about in its roasting plants? Explain. (Hint: You might need to review material in Chapter 9, as well, in order to answer this question.)

9. Describe the things Starbucks is doing to manage its value chain. Are these activities appropriate? Why or why not?

10. Can Starbucks manage the uncertainties in its value chain? If so, how? If not, why not?

11. Go to the company's website (**www.starbucks.com**) and find the information on the company's environmental activities from bean to cup. Select one of the steps in the chain (or your instructor may assign one). Describe and evaluate what environmental actions Starbucks is taking. How might these affect the planning, organizing, and leading that take place in these areas?

12. Look at the company's mission and Guiding Principles. How might these affect the way Starbucks uses controls? How do the ways Starbucks controls contribute to pursuing or achieving its mission and Guiding Principles?

13. Would you classify Starbucks' environment as more calm waters or white-water rapids? Explain. How does the company manage change in this type of environment?

14. Using Exhibit 16-6 on page 528, describe Starbucks' innovation environment.

VIDEO CASE INCIDENTS

Creativity and the Bottom Line: Mullen PR

Mullen is a full-service advertising and public relations firm located north of Boston and housed in a 1920s mansion. Its staff of 300 employees bills $640 million a year and has created some of the United States' most compelling commercials and print ads. Mullen's clients include Nextel, Arby's, Lending Tree, Orbitz, and General Motors. Since the dot-com bust, concurrent control has been replaced by preventive control, or "account planning," in the advertising industry. Although he acknowledges the importance of measuring the bottom line, Chief Creative Director Edward Boches, who began his career in the 1970s, still maintains allegiance to the following corporate mission: "to generate enduring creative ideas, to do beautifully crafted work, and to expect the best." After this video was filmed, it was reported in *AdWeek* that the $150 million Nextel Communications account, which Mullen had held since 1996, was under review. Mullen competed against three rival advertising agencies in an effort to keep the account. Ultimately, Nextel awarded its advertising business jointly to TBWA\Chiat\Day New York and MindShare.

QUESTIONS

1. *For analysis:* Why was concurrent control popular in the advertising industry during the dot-com boom of the 1990s?

2. *For analysis:* How does using feedforward control give Mullen a competitive advantage in today's dynamic and unpredictable business environment?

3. *For application:* What financial controls would you advise Mullen to use in analyzing its yearly billing to clients for commercials? Use the Nextel spot starring Dennis Franz as a guide.

4. *For application:* What steps can managers take to maintain control over sensitive corporate information?

5. *For debate:* Mullen operates in the bucolic setting of New England in a 1920s mansion, far from the buzz of Madison Avenue and Wall Street. For 30 years, it has based its business on individual excellence, responsibility, integrity, and care. The firm's image has remained pristine during the recent financial scandals. As a result, there is no reason for management at Mullen to be concerned about the renewed zeal for more stringent corporate governance. Do you agree or disagree? Support your position.

Source: "Mullen PR" (video), *Pearson Prentice Hall Management Video Library*; D. Gianatasio, "Nextel Cuts to Four," *AdWeek*, March 5, 2003, http://www.adweek.com/aw/national/article_display.jsp?vnu_content_id=1830360 (accessed November 2, 2007); http://www.mullen.com (accessed November 8, 2007); and Z. Rodgers, "Execs and Accounts for June 11, 2003," *ClickZ*, June 11, 2003, http://www.clickz.com/2220811 (accessed November 8, 2007).

Modern Manners at the Ritz-Carlton

The Ritz-Carlton hotel chain is designed to provide the kind of luxury that most of us only dream about. The company was established in 1983 when it purchased the Ritz-Carlton in Boston, as well as the rights to the Ritz-Carlton name. It now has 66 hotels in 23 countries and 32 000 employees. The company operates as an independent division of Marriott International.

Recently, the company's management decided to make a slight change to their gold standard of service, which has twice been recognized with a Malcolm Baldridge Award. The motto of the gold standard is, "We are Ladies and Gentlemen serving Ladies and Gentlemen." Employees are now trained to purposely reduce the formality of their conversations with guests and to attempt to make each interaction less predictable and rehearsed. Employees strive to read the individual customer instead.

QUESTIONS

1. *For analysis:* What do you think are some of the external forces causing the changes at the Ritz-Carlton?

2. *For application:* If you were a manager at the Ritz-Carlton, what actions would you take to change employee behaviour from more to less formal?

3. *For analysis:* What are some of the characteristics revealed about the Ritz-Carlton in the video that you believe helped it in its ability to successfully make these changes?

Source: "Ritz Carlton" (video), Pearson Prentice Hall Management Video Library; http:// corporate.ritzcarlton.com/en/Default.htm (accessed November 8, 2007).

PRENTICE HALL

mymanagementlab

After you have completed your study of Part 5, do the following exercises at the MyManagementLab website (www.pearsoned.ca/mymanagementlab):

- *You're the Manager: Putting Ethics into Action* (Boston Scientific)
- *Passport, Scenario 1* (Nelson Naidoo, Diamonds International), *Scenario 2* (Kristen Mesicek, Global One Cellular), and *Scenario 3* (Danny Lim, 88WebCom)

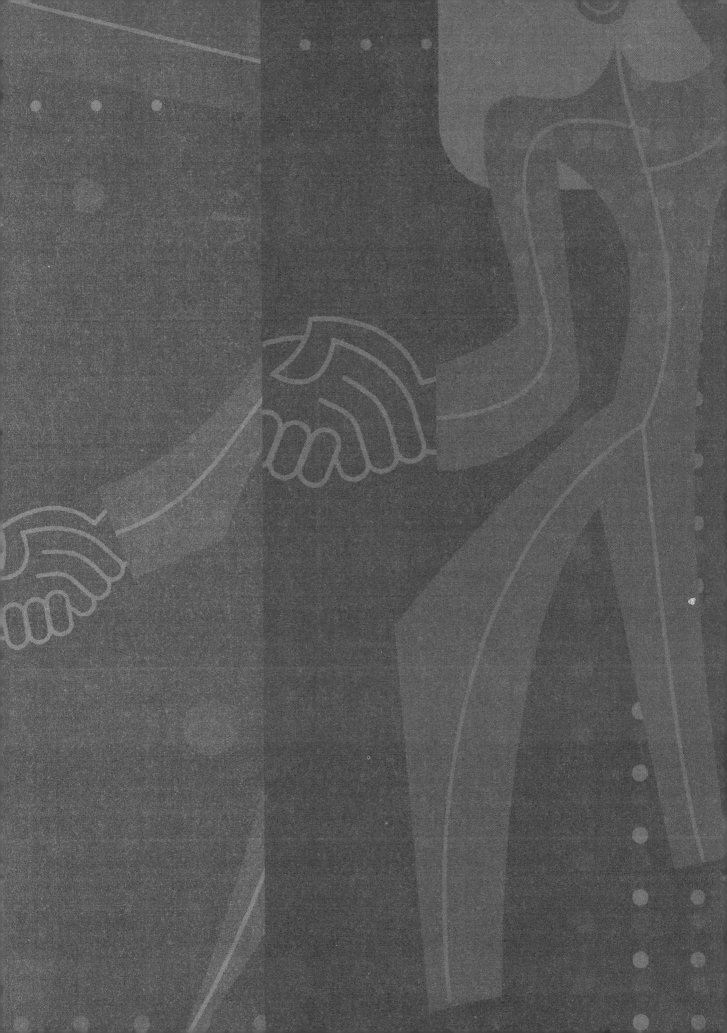

MANAGEMENT CASES

The case "The YMCA of London, Ontario" focuses on the need to engage in long-term strategic planning, while developing community relations. At the same time, the organization is facing a number of internal struggles because of the different business models of the core service areas. What can management do to effectively address the internal and external concerns raised in this case?

MC-1 The YMCA of London, Ontario

As Shaun Elliott, chief executive officer, prepared for the last senior management planning session in 2005, he reflected on what the YMCA of London (the London Y or the association) had achieved in the last four years. Since joining in 2001, Elliott had led the organization from a deficit of $230,000[1] to a projected surplus of almost $1 million by the end of this fiscal year. This turnaround had been accomplished through a careful balance of internal cost cutting and growth through partnering and program expansion. Innovative partnerships with other organizations had allowed the London Y to expand its programs and facilities with minimal capital investment. In addition to its now solid financial performance, the London Y was on track to exceed its targeted participation level of 46,500 individuals by the end of 2005. It was now time for Elliott to turn his attention to achieving the next level of growth: participation levels of 102,000 individuals by 2010. He knew that to achieve an increase of this magnitude, senior management would need to increase their focus and its capacity and that he would need to spend more time on longer term strategic initiatives and community relations. He wondered if this was possible given the current situation.

THE YMCA

The Young Men's Christian Association (YMCA) was an international federation of autonomous not-for-profit community service organizations dedicated to meeting the health and human service needs of men, women and children in their communities. The YMCA was founded in London, England in 1844, in response to the unhealthy social conditions resulting from the industrial revolution. Its founder, George Williams, hoped to substitute Bible study and prayer for life on the streets for the many rural young men who had moved to the cities for jobs. By 1851, there were 24 YMCAs in Great Britain and the first YMCA in North America had opened in Montreal. Three years later, in 1854, there were 397 separate YMCAs in seven nations, with a total of 30,400 members.[2]

From its start, the YMCA was unusual in that it crossed the rigid lines that separated the different churches and social classes in England at the time. This openness was a trait that would lead eventually to YMCAs including all men, women and children regardless of race, religion or nationality. In 2005, the YMCA was in more than 120 countries around the world and each association was independent and reflected its own unique social, political, economic and cultural situation. YMCAs worldwide shared a commitment to growth in spirit, mind and body, as well as a focus on community service, social change, leadership development and a passion for youth.[3]

A similar, although separate organization, the Young Women's Christian Association (YWCA) was founded in 1855 in England.[4] It remained a separate organization; however, some YMCA and YWCAs chose to affiliate in order to best serve the needs in their communities.

---

[1] All funds in Canadian dollars unless specified otherwise.

[2] http://www.ymca.net/about_the_ymca/history_of_the_ymca.html. Accessed February 23, 2006.

[3] http://www.ymca.ca/eng_worldys.htm. Accessed Feb. 23, 2006.

[4] http://www.ywca.org/site/pp.asp?c=djISI6PIKpG&b=281379. Accessed February 23, 2006.

IVEY

Richard Ivey School of Business
The University of Western Ontario

Pat MacDonald prepared this case under the supervision of W. Glenn Rowe solely to provide material for class discussion. The authors do not intend to illustrate either effective or ineffective handling of a managerial situation. The authors may have disguised certain names and other identifying information to protect confidentiality.

Ivey Management Services prohibits any form of reproduction, storage or transmittal without its written permission. This material is not covered under authorization from CanCopy or any reproduction rights organization.

Copyright © 2006, Ivey Management Services

Version: (A)2006-04-11.

One-time permission to reproduce granted by Ivey Management Services on January 14, 2008.

THE YMCA IN CANADA

The London Y was a member of YMCA Canada, the national body of the 61 Canadian member associations. YMCA Canada's role was to foster and stimulate the development of strong member associations and advocate on their behalf regionally, nationally and internationally. YMCA Canada was a federation governed by a national voluntary board of directors which oversaw national plans and priorities. Volunteer board members were nominated by the member associations. YMCA Canada's President and CEO was accountable to the board for national operations. The national office had only 20 employees in 2005, reflecting the relative autonomy of the member associations.

As in the rest of the world, YMCAs in Canada served people of all ages, backgrounds and abilities and through all stages of life. They were dedicated to helping people attain a healthy lifestyle and encouraging them to get involved in making their community a better place. As charities, the YMCA member associations relied on the support of their communities, the private sector, governments and other agencies. YMCA fundraising campaigns helped to provide better programs and facilities, as well as greater accessibility and financial assistance to include as many people as possible.[5]

Earlier in 2005, YMCA Canada, in conjunction with its member associations, had developed a strong association profile, which comprised a wide range of performance measures similar to a balanced scorecard. Implementation of this measurement tool was voluntary, although YMCA Canada encouraged individual associations to use it to assess their performance and to compare their performance with other associations. According to the YMCA Canada strong association profile, a strong YMCA position profile is as follows:

- demonstrates that it is having an impact on individuals' spirits, minds and bodies, while building strong kids, strong families and strong communities;
- assists people to participate in the YMCA who otherwise could not afford to be involved;
- is seen as a valued contributor to the community;
- has the capacity to influence the community relative to its strategic priorities;
- has quality programs that help members meet their personal goals;
- demonstrates growth in participation over time;
- offers a variety of programs that are accessible to the community;
- has a culture of involving their members continually by encouraging them to give their time, talent and treasure to the YMCA;

- has identified key audiences and has a communications plan that addresses each audience.

The London Y had piloted an earlier version of the strong association profile and had already set annual targets for 2005 through to 2010 (see Exhibit 1). The London Y planned to implement these targets and measures as part of its 2005 strategic planning cycle.

THE YMCA OF LONDON

Founded in 1856, the YMCA of London was a multi-service charity that described its mission as providing "opportunities for personal growth in spirit, mind and body for people of all backgrounds, beliefs and abilities."[6] Its articulated values and the principles by which it operates were:

- **Honesty:** to tell the truth, to act in such a way that you are worthy of trust, to have integrity, making sure your actions match your words.
- **Caring:** to accept others, to be sensitive to the well-being of others, to help others.
- **Respect:** to treat others as you would have them treat you, to value the worth of every person, including yourself.
- **Responsibility:** to do what is right, what you ought to do, to be accountable for your behaviour and obligations.

The association served almost 28,000 children annually through childcare and camping at 16 childcare locations, two residential camps, one outdoor education centre and numerous summer day camps and after school program locations. In 2004, the London Y had provided 13,025 health, fitness and recreation (HFR) memberships for children and adults at five branches: three in London, one in Strathroy and one in Woodstock. In addition, the St. Thomas YMCA was operated by London Y senior management under contract. To ensure that no one was turned away because of an inability to pay, in 2004, the association provided 2,994 assisted HFR memberships, 1,100 assisted "camperships" and assistance to 310 children in childcare. The association had a very positive brand position in the community and its internal research had shown that referrals were the number one source of new members and participants.

The last four years had been a time of renewal and change for the London Y (see Exhibit 2). Revenue had increased by 50 per cent and the association had transformed an operating deficit of $230,000 in 2001 to an expected $1 million operating surplus by the end of 2005 (see Exhibit 3). In 2004, childcare contributed 38 per cent of total revenue, HFR contributed 27 per cent and 16 per cent of revenue came from camping (see Exhibit 4 for The YMCA of London—Revenue). The remaining revenue sources included government programs

[5]http://www.ymca.ca/eng_abouty.htm. Accessed February 23, 2006.

[6]http://www.londony.ca/. Accessed February 24, 2006.

Exhibit 1

The YMCA of London Participation Targets

	2005	2006	2007	2008	2009	2010	5 yr inc	Avg inc
Childcare								
Infant	70	70	70	70	70	70	0%	0%
Toddler	140	140	140	140	140	140	0%	0%
Preschool	608	672	736	832	928	1,024	68%	14%
School Age	316	316	316	316	316	316	0%	0%
Childcare Total	**1,134**	**1,198**	**1,262**	**1,358**	**1,454**	**1,550**	**37%**	**7%**
Camping and Educational Services								
CQE	1,815	2,215	2,215	2,439	2,471	2,471	36%	7%
Day Camp	5,350	5,457	5,566	5,677	5,791	5,907	10%	2%
Outdoor Education	5,800	6,960	9,048	9.953	10,948	12,043	108%	22%
Children's Safety Village	12,000	13,500	14,000	14,000	14,000	14,000	17%	3%
Community School Programs	1,630	1,880	2,130	2,380	2,630	2,880	77%	15%
Camping Total	**26.595**	**30,012**	**32,959**	**34,449**	**35,840**	**37,301**	**40%**	**8%**
Health Fitness and Recreation								
CBY full fee	5,450	5,580	5,750	5,825	6,000	6,200	14%	3%
CBY assisted	2,210	2,330	2,450	2,500	2,525	2,650	20%	4%
CBY programs	4,200	4,580	4,975	5,750	6,875	8,050	92%	18%
BHY full fee	1,500	1,525	1,900	2,100	2,400	2,700	80%	16%
BHY assisted	300	305	380	420	480	540	80%	16%
BHY programs	1,600	7,565	9,100	10,195	11,480	13,125	720%	144%
ELY full fee		1,025	1,050	1,050	1,075	1,200		
ELY assisted		205	210	210	215	240		
ELY programs		4,085	5,010	5,280	5,755	6,225		
SCY full fee	481	865	1,155	1,155	1,155	1,155	140%	28%
SCY assisted	26	74	100	110	110	110	323%	65%
SCY programs	773	826	865	905	925	945	22%	4%
WDY full fee	1,822	1,844	1,879	1,913	2,400	3,040	67%	13%
WDY assisted	373	405	426	449	600	760	104%	21 %
WDY programs	4,900	5,680	6,480	6,935	8,140	9,375	91%	18%
New location full fee	n/a	n/a	n/a	5,000	7,000	7,000		
New location assisted	n/a	n/a	n/a	1,250	1,750	1,750		
HFR Total	**18,735**	**31,214**	**35,250**	**49,797**	**57,135**	**63,315**	**238%**	**48%**
Grand Total of Participants	**46,464**	**62,424**	**69,471**	**85,604**	**94,429**	**102,166**	**120%**	**24%**
Volunteers								
Childcare								
Camping								
CBY								
BHY		55	60	65	70	75		
ELY		15	20	25	30	35		
SCY	20	23	27	30	35	40	100%	20%
WDY	35	38	42	45	60	80		
Total	**55**	**131**	**149**	**165**	**195**	**230**		

Exhibit 1

continued

	2005	2006	2007	2008	2009	2010	5 yr inc	Avg inc
Member Retention Rate								
CBY		76%	76%	76%	76%	76%		
BHY		55%	64%	68%	69%	70%		
ELY		55%	64%	68%	69%	70%		
SCY		55%	65%	68%	72%	75%		
WDY		80%	80%	82%	82%	82%		
New Location								

Source: YMCA of London, 2005 Strategic Planning Documents.

and contracts, community programs, donations and the United Way. Almost 90 per cent of the London Y's revenue was self-generated through program and participation fees.

The responsibility for all development and fundraising activity was in the process of being moved into the YMCA of London Foundation, an affiliated but separate organization which had a strong record of investing and securing grants. In its newly expanded role, the foundation was expected to support capital campaigns, conduct annual campaigns and enhance planned giving.

The London Y's structure included the CEO who was accountable to a volunteer board of directors (the board). Seven general managers and one manager reported to the CEO along with three senior directors and one director. The general managers and manager were responsible for service areas or locations including camping and outdoor education, childcare, community services, London HFR, the Woodstock District YMCA, the St. Thomas Elgin Family YMCA, the Strathroy-Caradoc Family YMCA, overall facilities, and employment initiatives. The senior directors and director were responsible for

Exhibit 2

The YMCA of London Growth 2001 to 2005

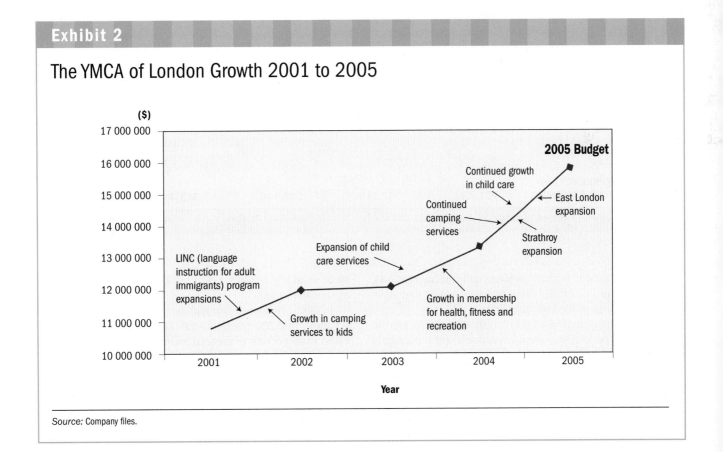

Source: Company files.

Exhibit 3

The YMCA of London Schedule of Operations

REVENUE	2005 Projected	Year ended Dec. 31, 2004	Year ended Dec. 31, 2003	Year ended Dec. 31, 2002	Year ended Dec. 31, 2001
Memberships	3,647,014	3,560,527	3,364,190	3,139,980	3,183,699
Childcare	6,811,401	4,958,138	4,037,612	4,516,214	4,576,632
Camp Fees	2,192,237	2,121,787	2,023,885	2,020,531	1,978,414
Community Programs	260,676	442,927	532,606	863,573	414,659
Program Service Fees	328,495	228,500	342,727	302,069	299,177
United Way	205,999	185,250	169,989	164,619	178,818
Ancillary Revenue	544,748	519,225	458,768	633,102	252,935
Donations & Fundraising	341,701	297,917	371,996	416,779	128,190
Employment Initiatives	989,141	891,815	792,983		
International Contributions & Grants				41,239	46,023
Total Revenue	15,321,412	13,206,086	12,094,756	12,098,106	11,058,547
EXPENSES					
Salaries & Benefits	9,550,594	8,525,862	7,663,975	7,718,093	7,288,194
Program Costs	973,935	1,357,277	1,237,143	946,329	1,013,640
Facilities	2,060,400	1,830,450	1,746,122	1,918,676	1,878,400
Promotion	165,180	178,053	140,143	183,441	164,600
Association Dues	163,543	157,570	137,985	136,795	132,777
Travel & Development	214,130	222,013	238,060		
Office Expenses	285,302	276,835	284,382		
Professional & Other Fees	247,592	247,430	302,695		
Miscellaneous	149,741	168,117	128,503		
Administration				840,048	763,095
International Development				41,239	46,023
Total expenses	14,399,676	12,963,607	11,879,008	11,784,621	11,286,729
EXCESS (DEFICIENCY) OF REVENUE OVER EXPENSES	921,736	242,279	215,748	313,485	-228,182

Source: The London YMCA Annual Reports 2004, 2003, 2002, 2001.

finance, development, human resources and communications, respectively (see Exhibit 5). The number of senior managers had not increased in the last four years.

With the introduction of the strong association profile framework for performance measurement, all senior managers would have performance agreements and work-plans that they had planned together. Measures of participation, program quality and financial performance would be tracked and accountability would be to the group. Once the measures and targets were well established, it was expected that compensation deci-sions would be based on each senior manager's performance against their plans.

In 2005, the association had over 500 permanent staff with an additional 200 seasonal staff. Full-time employees made up 35 to 40 per cent of the total and the remaining 60 to 65 per cent were part-time employees. Annual staff satisfaction surveys consistently showed high levels of both satisfaction and commitment to the association. However, wages were a persistent issue with staff in the childcare centres and finding suitable HFR staff had been particularly challenging.

Exhibit 4

The YMCA London Revenue 2004

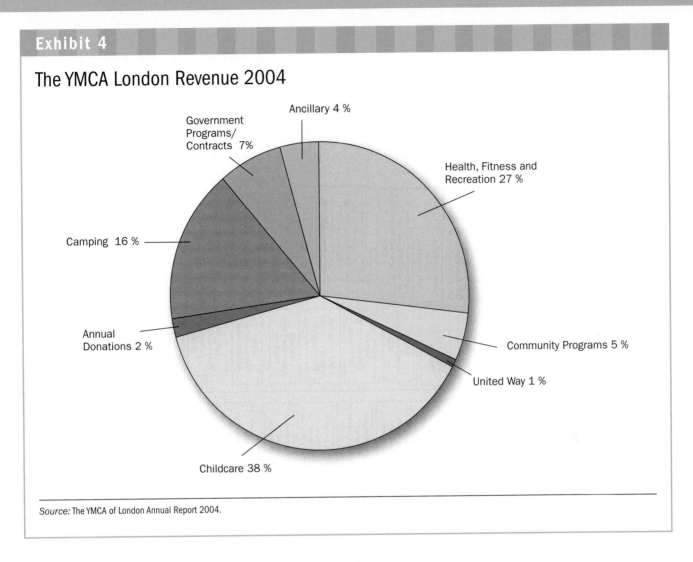

- Ancillary 4 %
- Government Programs/Contracts 7%
- Health, Fitness and Recreation 27 %
- Camping 16 %
- Annual Donations 2 %
- Community Programs 5 %
- United Way 1 %
- Childcare 38 %

Source: The YMCA of London Annual Report 2004.

During the last four years, the board and senior management of the London Y had identified partnering as a key strategy to achieve the association's long term strategic objectives in its three core service areas: HFR, childcare, and camping and outdoor education. Senior management moved quickly to seize opportunities for a number of new partnerships.[7] A new HFR facility in East London was developed in partnership with the London Public Library. Partnerships were established with Kellogg Canada Inc. and John Labatt Ltd. for the London Y to operate their on-site HFR facilities. Childcare services had grown more than 50 per cent, primarily as a result of a partnership with the University of Western Ontario.

Some partnerships were opportunistic or tactical but were nonetheless guided by their fit with the long term goals and values of the London Y. For example, a partnership with the Children's Safety Village made resources available to pursue a new full service HFR location in an underserved area of the city, thus expanding service and programs. In the absence of a significant capital infusion, senior management believed that new partnerships were critical to the London Y achieving its participation target of 102,000 individuals by 2010.

CORE SERVICE AREAS

Health, Fitness and Recreation

One of the longest standing services that the London Y provided was HFR. These services were offered through five branches each led by a general manager. These included: the London Centre YMCA (CBY), the Bob Hayward (BHY) and East London (ELY) all located in London; The Strathroy-Caradoc Family YMCA (SCY) located 40 kilometres west of London; and The YMCA of Woodstock and District (WDY) located 50 kilometres east of London. By 2005, the London Y had served more than 18,700 individuals through its HFR programs and

---

[7]All of the London Y's partnering relationships have approximately the same legal structure which involves a facilities lease and an operating or service provision agreement. There are no fees paid to the partners as all services are provided on a fee for service basis and the London Y covers the operating costs of the facility.

Exhibit 5

The YMCA of London Organization Chartt, September 2005

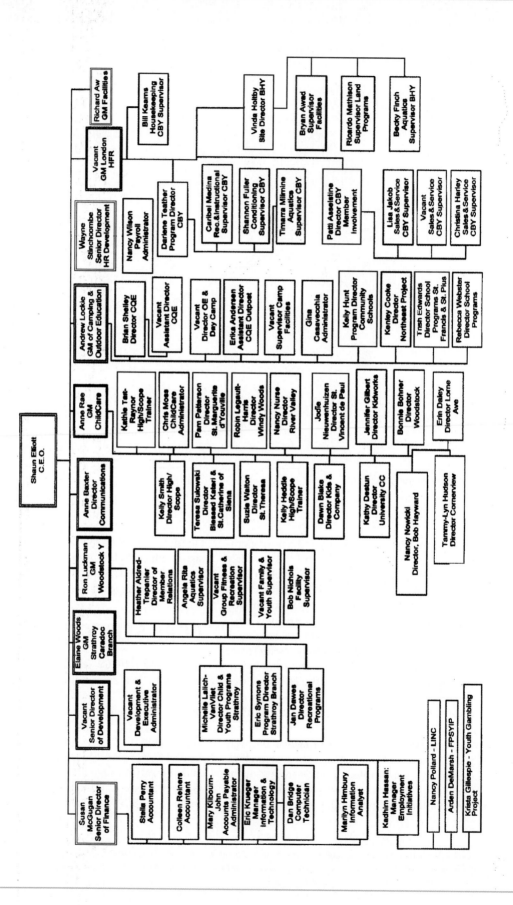

by 2010 the association had a target of serving more than 63,000 in six locations, an increase of 238 per cent. The St. Thomas Y was located 35 kilometres south of London.

The branches were membership-based and offered health and fitness programs for children, families and adults. Twenty-five per cent of the London Y's members received an assisted membership and paid one-third of the cost on average. Programs for children and youth were estimated to cost more than four times the association's programs for adults, yet generated lower fees. Children's programs and services often ran at a loss. The London Y depended on full fee paying adult HFR members to cross-subsidize assisted memberships and children's programs.

The largest challenge to the London Y attracting full fee adult members was the proliferation of fitness facilities for adults. Market-research commissioned by the London Y in 2002, indicated that approximately 30 per cent of the 193,845 adults in London would join a fitness facility and that 25.5 per cent of adults were already members of a fitness club. The potential for market growth was assessed as limited. The research also showed significant penetration of the market by private sector providers with the primary competition in London coming from the Good Life Clubs with 37 per cent market share and The Athletic Club with 22 per cent of the market. The London Y was third in the London market with a share of 12 per cent. The competition had increased recently with the entrance of the Premier/Mademoiselle chain of fitness clubs into the City of London.

The private clubs operated under a very different economic model than the London Y, typically leasing equipment and facilities. They targeted the adult market only and they did not offer pools or as wide a range of programming as the London Y. In contrast to the private operators, the London Y owned relatively large facilities with pools. Only the two newest branches in London and Strathroy (ELY and SCY) did not have pools, although interest in adding a pool to the SCY had already been raised in the community.

A number of the London Y facilities were aging and required significant capital reinvestment or replacement. The CBY was 25 years old and required ongoing maintenance and refurbishment. The BHY in East London and the WDY were each 50 years old and were not wheelchair accessible. Both buildings required significant capital investment to meet and maintain modern standards. Unfortunately, the BHY was not ideally located so the potential for new members would be limited. More positively, the City of Woodstock had expressed an interest in partnering with the association to develop a new community facility as part of the city's master recreational plan. Replacing the WDY building was considered to be an imperative and partnering with the city was the association's preferred strategy.

Senior management of the London Y believed that to remain relevant in the HFR market as well as meet its targets, the association must develop new facilities in London's north and west ends. The City of London's master recreational plan supported partnership in the delivery of recreational programs and the association had begun discussions with the city regarding development of a new HFR facility in the north end. The city's plan also identified the southwest of the city as a priority site for a HFR facility.

Retention was a key part of membership growth as research showed that two-thirds of new members leave within the first year. Currently, the London Y had relatively high retention rates for members that lasted beyond one year at CBY (76 per cent), WDY (80 per cent) and BHY (75 per cent). ELY and SCY had been in operation less than two years, and retention rates while high were expected to decrease. The association had targeted overall HFR retention rates of 55 per cent at BHY, ELY and SCY next year increasing to more than 70 per cent by 2010. While the association planned to continue its focus on families and to differentiate itself as a values-based organization, it also planned to offer specialized programs targeted at specific groups such as cardiac rehabilitation, weight loss, osteoporosis treatment etc. to enhance both member retention and new member attraction. This would require increased staff with increased qualifications, resulting in increased costs. To offset these expected cost increases HFR management would need to determine ways to increase revenues or fees.

Although the CEO managed most of the HFR facilities, each facility was run as a separate unit by its general manager. Each branch did its own hiring, staff training, uniform purchasing, program development, and sales and promotion materials. This had resulted in inconsistencies in program quality, program delivery, member service, staff management, facility maintenance and house-keeping between branches. There were significant economic and operational inefficiencies as well. Senior management believed that increased consistency would contribute to increased efficiency, allowing the association to serve more members and to retain more of the existing members. However, there were no coordinating mechanisms for HFR other than the CEO. With financial stability and revenue growth as his priorities, he had not had sufficient time to work with each of the HFR general managers. Also, the CEO was not himself an experienced HFR manager, having spent his career in financial services prior to joining the association.

HFR staff tended to be young and at the beginning of their careers. Finding and retaining appropriate HFR staff had been challenging for the London Y. Work had begun on developing relationships with the local Community College and University to establish a placement/apprentice program to identify strong candidates. Also a skill/aptitude profile of HFR staff was in development based on YMCA Canada's standards and training for HFR staff.

The senior management team had developed a number of strategic initiatives for HFR for the coming year. In summary they were:

- develop a new facility in London in partnership with the city of London
- develop a new facility in Woodstock
- manage and promote the Bob Hayward and East London facilities as one branch
- initiate discussions with the town of Strathroy for the development of a pool

- focus on program development and quality, and develop a new revenue structure to support increased quality of service

Childcare Services

Childcare services were the London Y's largest source of revenue. These services were offered through 16 childcare centres located in London (12 locations), Strathroy (two locations), St. Thomas and Woodstock (one location each). The centres were mostly located in leased premises with only the Woodstock centre operating in a facility owned by the association. In 2004, the London Y had served 1,139 children in three categories: infant, toddler and preschooler. By 2010, the association planned to serve an additional 415 preschoolers, for a total of 1,554 children. The London Y childcare centres were similar to other providers in offering full-time, part-time and flexible care options and its fees were set between the midpoint and the high end of fees charged in London. Infants are considerably more expensive to serve due to the higher staff to child ratios required.

Childcare is highly regulated through Ontario's Day Nursery Act (DNA). The DNA prescribes staff to children ratios by age, as well as physical space design, procedures, food preparation and all other aspects of operations. Wage enhancement subsidies were established by the provincial government 10 years ago, as private centres were made public and regulations were established. The subsidies were considered to be necessary for the financial feasibility of centres; however, they had remained at the same levels since their introduction in the early 1990s. Many levels of government were involved with the regulation and funding of childcare, including the Province of Ontario, the Ministry of Community and Social Services, the Ministry of Health, cities and counties, and in some instances, boards of education. It was expected that the landscape of childcare would undergo significant change in 2006 and beyond based on provincial initiatives and programs resulting from proposed increases in federal funding.

Subsidies for childcare fees are available to low income families through the cities and counties. These subsidies did not typically cover all of the fees and the London Y absorbed the shortfall as part of its support to the community.

There were two other large childcare providers in London: London Children's Connection with 13 centres and London Bridge with 11 centres. Unlike these service providers, the London Y offered unique programming through its use of the High Scope curriculum and its values-based programming. In fact, the London Y's curriculum and values focus were key reasons that The University of Western Ontario decided to partner with the association. In addition to the High Scope curriculum, the London Y also offered HFR memberships to each full-time child, discounts for HFR family memberships, summer day camp discounts for customers, swimming as part of their programs and family input through parent advisory committees.

The number of children aged zero to four was expected to decline until the year 2012 in the communities the association currently served. However, senior management believed that opportunities for expansion existed in some of the rural communities and counties that were near existing locations.

To continue to maintain full enrollment, the association would need to closely monitor local demographics, competitors' expansion and new subdivision development.

The London Y employed a large number of early childhood educators. Wage scales in the industry were lower than in many other industries. While the London Y had made every effort to provide reasonable compensation and reward good performance, staff satisfaction surveys consistently identified wages as an issue. It was now suspected that the London Y was paying slightly below the average childcare wages in the City of London. Management realized that they must carefully balance wage increases and additional managers against their goal of maintaining a surplus.

Communication and consistency among the centres seemed to require constant attention. Some operational processes had been centralized, such as subsidies and collections, while most processes remained with each centre, including the purchasing of supplies and food preparation. Procedures had been standardized with a common operation manual, although there were still many opportunities for greater consistency and standardization.

With more than 50 per cent growth in childcare since 2001, the general manager's scope of authority had become very large. By 2005, she had 18 people reporting directly to her, including all 16 centre directors. This created significant barriers to relationship-building, both internally with staff and externally with parents, potential partners, funding organizations and regulators. It was also a challenge during budget review when the general manager of Childcare had to review 16 centre budgets and the overall childcare budget in the same time frame as, for example, a general manager in HFR whose one budget might be smaller than one of the larger child care centres.

While the nature and the extent of the changes in programs and program funding were unclear, senior management believed that the complex regulatory environment gave a distinct advantage to an experienced and competent childcare provider. The London Y was confident that it had good working relationships with the cities of London, Woodstock, Strathroy and St. Thomas, the counties in which it operated, and with both the Public and the Roman Catholic School Boards.

Partially in response to the changes expected in the childcare environment, the London Y had begun to explore partnership or merger opportunities with other service providers. In addition to operating advantages, management believed a partnership might also enhance their ability to influence government funding.

The senior management team had developed a number of strategic initiatives for childcare services in the coming year. In summary they were:

- explore partnerships or mergers with other providers
- identify and initiate opportunities in rural areas
- enhance wage structure in balance with budget limitations
- monitor changes in government policy, acquire the best and earliest information and develop appropriate contingency plans.

Camping and Outdoor Education

The London Y expected to serve more than 26,500 participants through camping and education programs in 2005. Residential camping programs were delivered in July and August to almost 2,000 children aged six to 17 at two sites in Northern Ontario, Camp Queen Elizabeth and Camp Queen Elizabeth (CQE) Outpost. Summer day camps served more than 5,000 children aged three to 15 with a variety of programs running from traditional day camps to sports camps and other specialty camps. During the school year more than 1,500 children were served through community school programs delivered in cooperation with school boards. Another 12,000 children were served annually through programs given by police and firefighters at the Children's Safety Village located in the Upper Thames Conservation Authority area near the city of London. Finally, almost 6,000 children and adults participated in outdoor education programs including leadership and team building programs offered at various locations.

Camp Queen Elizabeth had been in operation for 50 years and had an excellent reputation. Each year the Camp was booked to capacity and each year those bookings occurred earlier. Similar to other residential camps, much of the activity was outdoors and programming included water sports, crafts and climbing. Fees were amongst the highest in YMCA camping and the return rate of campers was the highest of all YMCA camps in Ontario. Campers tended to be more homogeneous and from higher income families; however, assisted spots were made available for those unable to afford the fees.

Camp Queen Elizabeth was located on land leased from Parks Canada, a federal department. The current lease was due to expire in 2007 and the London Y had postponed capital investment in the facilities pending renewal of the lease. The association had now received assurance from Parks Canada that the lease would be renewed so a long-overdue refurbishment of the camp's infrastructure could be planned.

The CQE Outpost property had been purchased as a hedge against renewal of the Camp Queen Elizabeth lease as well as for additional capacity to serve older youth with adventure and canoe trips. Service to older youth had not increased as planned and there appeared to be little demand for this type of service. Management was now exploring the possibility of selling the property and using the proceeds towards the renovation of Camp Queen Elizabeth.

The London Y offered a wide variety of day camp and outdoor education programs during all weeks of the summer and, to a limited extent, in the shoulder seasons of spring and fall. During the summer, the association ran a bussing network throughout the City of London to collect and return participants to designated drop-off points. Programming was value-based and emphasized character development more than skill development. Other summer day camp providers included the local University, the City of London, a variety of private businesses and not-for-profit organizations, and churches. The London Y day camps offered the same size groups and staff ratios as other day camp providers and in some cases the offerings were quite undifferentiated. The service needs and selection processes for families and children were not clearly understood by the London Y, although it appeared to management that there were a number of different segments such as skills-based camps, traditional camps and camps that were more like a childcare service.

The association had recently invested some capital dollars in its outdoor education program and developed two new sites in partnership with Spencer Hall, run by the Richard Ivey School of Business and Spencer Lodge, run by the Boy Scouts of Canada. With these new partners and facilities the association hoped to increase the number of its outdoor education program participants by more than 100 per cent by 2010.

The community school program, funded by the United Way and the London Y, was an after school program aimed at improving the academic performance and the social skills of children in higher risk neighbourhoods. The focus was on literacy, social skills and recreation, and the programs were delivered in a number of designated schools. London Y staff worked closely with teachers to identify children who would benefit from participation in the program. This program continued to expand as much as funding and staffing would allow.

Each school year the Children's Safety Village targeted students in grades one to four with its programs on broad safety topics including pedestrian safety, bike safety, fire safety, electrical safety and other household hazards.[8] As a result of their partnership agreement, the London Y's Camping and Outdoor Education operations moved from their dilapidated offices at the association's outdoor education centre to the Children's Safety Village site and the London Y took over management of the site. While the London Y was responsible for the physical operation, the Children's Safety Village Board continued to govern the organization, resulting in some overlapping responsibilities.

Camping and outdoor education offered a wide variety of programs in a large number of locations under a number of different names. Each program produced its own sales and promotion materials and parent communications. A number of programs and facilities were not clearly identified as part of the YMCA, such as Camp Queen Elizabeth or the Children's Safety Village. Management believed that there were a number of opportunities to send a more consistent message to the community and to strengthen the London Y's brand.

The senior management team had developed a number of strategic initiatives for camping and outdoor education in the coming year. In summary they were:

- identify day camp market segments and deliver programs to meet identified needs

- sell the CQE Outpost site and use the proceeds to improve Camp Queen Elizabeth, ensuring that current and expected demand can be accommodated

---

[8]http://www.safetyvillage.ca/about.htm. Accessed February 28, 2006.

- negotiate a new governance model and transfer governance of the YMCA Children's Safety Village to the YMCA of London
- ensure that all facilities and programs are clearly identified as part of the London YMCA
- leverage opportunities to serve more individuals in outdoor education programs

ELLIOTT'S CONSIDERATION OF THE SITUATION

Elliott realized that each of the association's three main service areas had very different business models and dynamics and that this created challenges for organizational focus and expertise, resource allocation and communication. He also knew that while the challenges coming from this multi-service approach were abundant and the synergies limited, neither the board of the London Y nor the senior management wished to reduce the range of services that the association provided to the community. Elliott's challenge was how to best manage the association as a whole while appropriately nurturing each of the core service areas. He had a number of concerns.

The recent growth had put significant strain on both the capacity and capabilities of the senior managers. Elliott was concerned that there were simply not enough managers to deliver the targeted growth and, particularly, the new partnership relationships that would need to be established. Over the last few years Elliott felt that he was the "chief business development officer," searching out partnering opportunities with external organizations and developing both the opportunity and the relationship through to the final agreement. The service area leaders had been focusing on operations and did not have the time, or perhaps the inclination, to think about innovative ways for their areas to serve more people. He believed that it was now time for the service area leaders to take on the development role and to identify and create their own growth opportunities.

In addition to greater capacity, Elliott believed that the senior management team needed to increase its focus on higher level strategic issues affecting the whole association. With 12 people at the table, senior management team meetings were not as effective as they might have been and in fact some members only contributed when the discussion was about their specific location. Also, the meetings tended to over-emphasize day-to-day HFR operations simply because there were so many HFR general managers at the table. This meant that they were perhaps under-emphasizing the association's other key service areas of childcare and camping.

Along with decreasing senior management's focus on HFR, Elliott knew that he too needed to spend less time on day-to-day HFR operations and more time on strategic initiatives and community relations. However, with four HFR General Managers reporting to him and with HFR representing the biggest operational challenges and the largest growth target, he knew that HFR needed the undivided attention of a capable senior manager. Also, he did not know how the HFR General Managers would respond to any changes that might be perceived as a loss of status or position.

Elliott had real fears about creating a potentially unnecessary layer of management or, even worse, an elite group that became out of touch with the staff and the various locations. He worried about becoming out of touch with the operations himself. One of the first things that Elliott had done when he joined the association in 2001 was to eliminate most of the so called "head office" positions, including the chief operating officer, the head of HFR and the head of development. He did not think that the association could afford those roles at that time and he still believed in carefully balancing expenses and overhead with the need for resources to support expansion. Elliott also had concerns about how the community would perceive a charitable organization that significantly increased its senior management personnel. Finally, he worried about moving too quickly.

CONCLUSION

Elliott recognized that in trying to determine what was best for the London Y, he must consider the business model and strategy of each of the core service areas while taking into account the overall mission and values of the association. He needed to be confident that any changes would increase the management capacity and focus within each area as well as free him up to focus on longer term strategic initiatives. Elliott was concerned about introducing more overhead expense just when the association's financial performance was stable. He did not have much time left to ponder as he wanted the senior management team to consider any potential organizational changes in the last planning session which was scheduled for next week.

The case "Sarnia Food Fresh Grocery Store" focuses on the experiences of Krysta Lee Becker, a part-time cake decorator. She encounters a number of obstacles in learning to do her job, and then carrying it out. What organizational problems might lead to the experiences Becker has? What could the Assistant Bakery Department Manager and the Bakery Department Manager do to make sure that the next new employee does not have a similar negative experience at Food Fresh?

MC-2

Sarnia Food Fresh Grocery Store: The Icing on the Cake

In July 2002, Krysta Lee Becker, a part-time cake decorator, was working her usual Saturday shift at the local Food Fresh grocery store in Sarnia, Ontario, a shift she had worked regularly since the new store had opened four months before. Her duties for the day required her to complete custom cake orders for Sunday morning pick-up. At approximately 1:00 p.m., she had glanced at the order forms for cakes still to be completed and had realized that one of them, which had been prepared by another employee, had not been completely filled out. See Exhibit 1 for a sample order form. The order form did not specify the type of cake (chocolate or vanilla) or the flavour of icing (chocolate or vanilla). Becker knew this type of problem could often be resolved with a quick phone call to the customer, as the customer's phone number was required on the cake order form; however, on this particular form, no contact information for the customer had been recorded and the employee who took the order had not even written his or her name on the form. Unfortunately, this was not the first time that Becker had been caught in such a situation. The custom cake was due to be picked up at 10:00 a.m. the following day. Carrie Smith, the Bakery Department Manager, and Samantha Ochej, the Bakery Department Assistant Manager, were both also working this particular Saturday shift. This problem was simply the most recent that Becker had encountered in trying to do her job well since the store had opened—it was the "icing on the cake." Becker did not know how to complete the order as the customer required by the time the customer required it and, later in the shift at 2:30 p.m., she was still wondering what to do about it and all the other problems she had been experiencing on her job.

THE CITY AND THE COMPETITION

Sarnia is a relatively small city of 69,000 citizens located in Southwestern Ontario on the Canada–United States border. At the mouth of the St. Clair River where the river entered Lake Huron, Sarnia is a city surrounded by water. This superb geo-graphic location has attracted a large segment of seniors who have felt that Sarnia is an ideal community in which to retire. Historically, Sarnia has been known for its large oil refineries and manufacturing facilities. More recently, however, the tourism industry has been steadily increasing. When the Sarnia Food Fresh opened its doors for business in November 2001, it was in direct competition locally with eight other large grocery stores, namely, four discount retailers and four full-serve retailers.

SARNIA FOOD FRESH GROCERY STORE

Food Fresh's purpose was to create enduring value for customers, employees, suppliers and shareholders. In addition, Food Fresh was founded upon company values which consistently considered customers' interests as primary, as well as the need for employees to complete their tasks with passion and integrity. The Sarnia Food Fresh store was part of one of the two major national retail grocers in Canada, and when rumors that a Food Fresh store would be opening in Sarnia began to circulate, considerable hype and excitement was generated in the city. In November 2001, after much anticipation, Sarnia Food Fresh opened for business.

At the top of the Sarnia Food Fresh store hierarchy was the store manager to whom each of six department managers reported. The six departments included bakery as well as produce, seafood, deli, grocery, and customer service.

THE BAKERY DEPARTMENT

The bakery department manager, Carrie Smith, supervised the bakers, who completed all the daily baking of breads and pastries, the cake decorators, who maintained the display cases and filled custom cake orders, and the front end bakery clerks, who packaged all the goods and performed general cleaning in

Exhibit 1

Food Fresh Custom Cake Order Form

SPECIAL ORDER FORM

Customer Name _____   Customer Address _____
_____

Date Ordered _____   Date for Pickup _____   Time for Pickup _____

Customer's Telephone Number _____

Type of Cake (circle one)	Flavour of Icing (circle one)	Colour of Trim (circle one)	Colour of Flowers (circle one)
Chocolate Vanilla	Chocolate Vanilla	Pink, Yellow, Blue, Green, Other: _____	Pink, Yellow, Blue, Green, Other: _____

Size of Cake (circle one)

8" round (serves 8–10)

1/4 slab (approximately 8" × 12") (serves 12–15)

1/2 slab (approximately 16" × 12") (serves 20–30)

Full slab (approximately 16" × 24") (serves 50–60)

Image Cake ☐

Deco Pak ☐

Photo Image ☐

Message to be Written on Top of Cake

Price

Other Special Instructions

Order Taken by

Customer's Signature

FORM 1336 SG(R-7/01)

the department. Samantha Ochej, a full-time cake decorator, was also the assistant bakery manager and managed the department when Carrie Smith was not in the store. There was a mix of full-time and part-time staff. Five full-time employees worked the day shift, 7:00–16:00, Monday through Friday, and two or three part-time employees worked the night shift, 16:00–21:00, and the day shift on weekends. No bakery employees had been trained to perform the duties of more than one of the three jobs in the department.

KRYSTA LEE BECKER AND HER FIRST JOB IN THE FRONT END BAKERY CLERK POSITION

When Krysta Lee Becker was hired, in October 2001, as a part-time *Front End Bakery Clerk* for the new Food Fresh, she was seventeen years old and in high school with one more year to go before graduation. Her rate of pay when hired was the student minimum wage of $6.40. She actively participated in community and high school functions. Many of her teachers and supervisors at previous part-time jobs knew her to be an

ambitious, independent, and responsible young individual, who fully intended to go on to university in a couple of years upon completion of high school. The front end bakery clerk tasks included slicing and wrapping freshly baked breads, packaging and labeling baked goods, doing general clean-up of the bakery department, as well as providing consistent customer service. Becker was comfortable performing these tasks from the start because she had had previous bakery experience in a small independently owned bakery.

GRAND OPENING OF FOOD FRESH GROCERY STORE SARNIA

On opening day, in November of 2001, the new Sarnia Food Fresh was brimming with excited customers who had been waiting many months in anticipation for the grand opening. That day, the bakery department was staffed by the regional manager, experienced bakery employees from other Food Fresh stores who had been relocated temporarily to Sarnia to assist with the grand opening, and by employees newly hired to work in the Sarnia Food Fresh store.

Becker's first shift was 16:00 to 22:00 on opening day. She was one of several newly hired front end bakery clerks working that shift. Within seconds of stepping on to the department floor, each of the clerks was bombarded by questions from excited customers: "Can you slice my bread?" "What are the ingredients in these muffins?" "How much is this cake?" "How many will it feed?" "Do you recommend it?" The new clerks had received no previous training regarding product description, or how to slice and bag bread, or how to complete cake orders. As a result, the new clerks continually had to ask the experienced Food Fresh bakery personnel for advice and recommendations.

Later on her first shift, Becker was asked by the regional manager to complete a series of tasks. She quickly completed all the tasks and asked for additional work. The regional manager noticed that Becker was a hard-working individual and took her aside to ask her if she wanted to work as a cake decorator for the bakery department. He promised Becker that she would be formally trained for her position. Becker quickly agreed, believing that, with training, she could excel on that job, and started work immediately as a cake decorator.

THE TRAINING

One month following grand opening, Samantha Ochej, who was a full-time cake decorator and the Assistant Bakery Department Manager, decided that the time had come to train Becker formally to decorate cakes. On Becker's first day of formal training, Ochej took a large pile of chocolate 8-inch round cakes, one 45 pound container of chocolate fudge, a plastic container of chocolate cake garnish, a pile of cake containers, and a picture of a fully decorated chocolate fudge cake and placed all of these in front of Becker. Then she told Becker, "Have fun. If you have any questions, I will be counting inventory." Becker looked at the pile of cakes and simply did what she was told to the best of her ability.

Becker quickly noticed that the fudge was extremely difficult to spread on the cakes. Nevertheless, she continued the slow and tedious process of spreading fudge on cakes until her department manager, Carrie Smith, came by to check on her progress. Smith took one look at the pile of cakes and said, "You *do* know that you can warm the fudge before spreading it on the cakes, don't you?" Becker looked at her manager and shook her head, "no," in response. Smith said, "Oh, Ochej was probably just testing you." After this brief conversation with Smith, Becker began to warm the fudge before using it, and this made the task of decorating chocolate fudge cakes much easier and faster.

After three weeks of decorating only chocolate fudge cakes, and with no offer of further formal training, Becker was getting bored by the repetition and was looking for her next challenge. She noticed that Ochej was decorating classic birthday cakes, which included a flat base coat icing, icing roses, and trim. See Exhibit 2. Rather than decorating more of the chocolate fudge cakes that she had been assigned, Becker grabbed an icing bag and pin and stood watching Ochej create icing roses. Becker caught onto this

Exhibit 2

Classic Food Fresh Birthday Cake

method very quickly and, within a few minutes, she was able to create her own roses. The tough part for Becker now was to get the rose from the pin to the cake. Again, with a few failed attempts, Becker's roses were making it successfully onto the tops of birthday cakes. Becker's own method of learning by doing and watching enabled her to ice and trim cakes, to create icing roses, as well as to use all of the other required decorating techniques, without any further formal training.

THE INVENTORIES

By the end of June 2002, after nine months on the job, Becker was working the busiest shifts in the bakery department, that is, Thursday and Friday evenings, and during the day on Saturdays and Sundays. Because she was working these busy shifts, Becker was able to identify the products that sold well and those that did not, and she notified the bakery department manager of the inventories that required replenishment. For instance, on one occasion, Becker predicted that over the weekend there would be an increase in customer requests for specific *LaRocca Specialty Cakes*, such as *Brownie Chocolate Cheesecake* or *Chocolate Truffle Cake*. See Exhibit 3. Becker suggested to her manager prior to the start of the weekend that she reorder these specific popular cakes because inventories were low. To Becker's dismay, Smith replied that there were other kinds of cakes in the refrigerator or freezer for customers to select. Not

Chocolate Truffle Cake

Chocolate Brownie Cheesecake

surprisingly, over the course of the weekend, there were many customers who requested those specific popular cakes, who were annoyed to discover none were available, and who had to settle for a less desirable alternative.

In addition, on another occasion Becker informed Samantha Ochej, the full time cake decorator and Assistant Bakery Department Manager, that DecoPacs, including Disney Princess and Winnie-the-Pooh cakes, were low in inventory. Becker was aware of the animated figures children favoured at the time because she would listen when children visited the bakery with their parents to look at the DecoPac cake catalogue. Rather than ordering additional popular DecoPacs, Ochej told Becker that the current inventory was still too high and, therefore, that an order would not be placed. Consequently, Becker had to turn customers away because the desired DecoPac was not in stock.

TIME-OFF

Other part-time employees were allowed to swap shifts with one another to accommodate social and school related schedules without giving the department manager any notice. When other Bakery Department employees requested a scheduled shift off, their requests were usually granted even when their requests were made with just one week's notice.

If Becker ever wanted to have a scheduled day shift off, she was not permitted to simply swap shifts with other employees and she was required to give Smith three weeks notice. When Becker questioned these procedures, she was told by Smith that no other part-time bakery employee was cross-trained to decorate cakes. In addition, when Becker was granted the day off, the following week she would be scheduled for

only four and a half hours rather than her usual twenty-four hours. Becker thought that this pattern of scheduling was a form of punishment by her manager for requesting a day off.

On more than one occasion, the scheduled part-time front end bakery clerk did not report to work. Consequently, Becker was required to work late, as she was expected to perform the duties of the front end bakery clerk, as well as the duties of a cake decorator.

To provide a solution to these scheduling problems, Smith had attempted to cross-train interested part-time front end bakery clerks to decorate cakes. Although they wanted the prestige of becoming a cake decorator, the other part-time employees never wanted to put in the time and effort to learn how to perform the cake decorating job properly. As a result, Becker received more hours and more shifts than any other part-time worker in the department because no other part-time employee was qualified to perform her job. However, the scheduling problems continued.

DAY-TO-DAY WORK

When selecting icing colours to decorate cakes, Becker would typically use bright blues, oranges, yellows, pinks and greens. Her manager told her to use "dull" colours, rather than the bright colours that she had been using because customers preferred pastel coloured cakes to brightly coloured cakes. However, Becker refused to create cakes with pastel colours because she knew colourful cakes with bright colours were more popular among customers.

One Saturday in June, Smith asked Becker to make eight quarter-slab birthday cakes for the self-serve cake area. This was one of Becker's favourite tasks and she completed the cakes quickly, using her bright colour pallet. She then took her one-hour lunch break. When she returned, all but one of her cakes had been sold. Her manager approached her and said, "I thought I told you to make eight cakes and *then* take your lunch break." Becker responded, "I did. I am making more now to restock." Smith answered, "We sold seven of *your* cakes in an hour?" Becker replied, "Yes. Now do you believe me?" Smith said, "Fine," and walked away.

On another occasion, a distressed customer returned to the bakery department with a recently purchased cake. She told Becker, "I just purchased this cake and had asked another employee to have 'Congratulations Ashley' written on it." Becker quickly noticed that "Congratulations" had been spelled incorrectly, "Congradulations," with a "d", rather than a "t". This was not the first time in Becker's experience that a bakery employee had spelled "Congratulations" incorrectly. Becker retrieved the cake from the customer and told her that it would be fixed immediately.

On another occasion, Becker was required to use the bakery department's airbrush machine to spray coloured dye onto cakes. See Exhibit 4. Becker disliked using this particular airbrush machine for numerous reasons. The machine often dripped dye haphazardly onto the surface of the cake and many times the bottle which held the dye would drop from the machine onto the cake, ruining the cake. Becker would have to strip the icing completely off the cake and start again. Becker had repeatedly told Smith that she was not satisfied with the airbrush machine, but Smith always replied that the department could not afford a new one.

In spite of all these problems, Becker continued to work hard, doing her part to ensure that the bakery department was operating as efficiently and effectively as possible. She sometimes forgot to take her mandatory fifteen minute breaks during her shift because she was so busy. In addition, many times she did not take all of her one-hour lunch break because she was bored sitting around and wanted to get back to work. Returning to work early before the end of her break did not bother Becker because she truly enjoyed her job and the customers she served. Becker sometimes became annoyed with other employees in the department when they took extended breaks and lunch hours or additional smoke breaks during their shifts. These employees often did this during bakery rush hours, leaving Becker to serve more than one customer at a

Exhibit 4

Airbrush Machine Top

time. However, Becker did not let these employees know how she felt about their behaviour, and she did not tell her manager what was going on.

Becker also cleaned and organized the cake cupboards, washed the small cake refrigerators and swept floors. She went out of her way to help the other bakery employees if she noticed they were falling behind in their work. Becker was extremely proud of her position at the Sarnia Food Fresh, and would go "above and beyond" to ensure that each customer she served was satisfied with the product and with their entire shopping experience within the store.

THE DECISION

It was now 2:30 p.m. near the end of Becker's Saturday shift. She still had a number of custom cake orders to complete for Sunday morning pick up by customers, and she knew how to complete all of them except the cake on the order form that had been incorrectly filled out. Both Samantha Ochej, the full-time cake decorator and Assistant Bakery Department Manager, and Carrie Smith, the Bakery Department Manager, were working that particular Saturday shift. Becker knew that if she was going to do anything about the problem of the incomplete order form, she would have to do it within the hour. She also wondered what, if anything, she could do about the many other problems she had been experiencing at work.

ENDNOTES

Chapter 1

1 Based on S. Whittaker, "The Junk Man Cometh," *Gazette* (Montreal), June 5, 2006, p. B1; M. Haiken, "Employees: The Ultimate Partners," *Business 2.0 Magazine*, November 27, 2006; and http://www.1800gotjunk.com/us_en/Files/PRESS_KIT.pdf.

2 T. Schwartz, "The Greatest Sources of Satisfaction in the Workplace Are Internal and Emotional," *Fast Company*, November 2000, pp. 398–402; and K. Dobbs, "Plagued by Turnover? Train Your Managers," *Training*, August 2000, pp. 62–65.

3 "RBC Financial Group Again Selected by CEOs as Canada's Most Respected Corporation for 2003," *Canada NewsWire*, January 19, 2004.

4 Based on S. Whittaker, "The Junk Man Cometh," *Gazette* (Montreal), June 5, 2006, p. B1; and M. Villano, "Making a Cache of Cash Cleaning Up Others' Trash," *Globe and Mail*, May 5, 2006, p. G7.

5 D. J. Campbell, "The Proactive Employee: Managing Workplace Initiative," *Academy of Management Executive*, August 2000, pp. 52–66.

6 B. Scudamore, "The Out-of-Towners," *PROFIT*, May 2007, http://www.canadianbusiness.com/entrepreneur/columnists/brian_scudamore/article.jsp?content=20070405_145004_6148 (accessed July 1, 2007).

7 P. Drucker, *Management: Tasks, Responsibilities, Practices* (New York: Harper & Row, 1974).

8 H. Fayol, *Industrial and General Administration* (Paris: Dunod, 1916).

9 For a comprehensive review of this question, see C. P. Hales, "What Do Managers Do? A Critical Review of the Evidence," *Journal of Management*, January 1986, pp. 88–115.

10 H. Mintzberg, *The Nature of Managerial Work* (New York: Harper & Row, 1973); and J. T. Straub, "Put on Your Manager's Hat," *USA Today*, October 29, 2002, http://www.usatoday.com.

11 See, for example, L. D. Alexander, "The Effect Level in the Hierarchy and Functional Area Have on the Extent Mintzberg's Roles Are Required by Managerial Jobs," *Academy of Management Proceedings* (San Francisco, 1979), pp. 186–189; A. W. Lau and C. M. Pavett, "The Nature of Managerial Work: A Comparison of Public and Private Sector Managers," *Group and Organization Studies*, December 1980: pp. 453–466; M. W. McCall Jr. and C. A. Segrist, "In Pursuit of the Manager's Job: Building on Mintzberg," Technical Report No. 14 (Greensboro, NC: Center for Creative Leadership, 1980); C. M. Pavett and A. W. Lau, "Managerial Work: The Influence of Hierarchical Level and Functional Specialty," *Academy of Management Journal*, March 1983, pp. 170–177; C. P. Hales, "What Do Managers Do? A Critical Review of the Evidence," *Journal of Management*, January 1986, pp. 88–115; A. I. Kraut, P. R. Pedigo, D. D. McKenna, and M. D. Dunnette, "The Role of the Manager: What's Really Important in Different Management Jobs," *Academy of Management Executive*, November 1989, pp. 286–293; M. J. Martinko and W. L. Gardner, "Structured Observation of Managerial Work: A Replication and Synthesis," *Journal of Management Studies*, May 1990, pp. 330–357.

12 C. M. Pavett and A. W. Lau, "Managerial Work: The Influence of Hierarchical Level and Functional Specialty," *Academy of Management Journal*, March 1983, pp. 170–177.

13 S. J. Carroll and D. A. Gillen, "Are the Classical Management Functions Useful in Describing Managerial Work?" *Academy of Management Review*, January 1987, p. 48.

14 H. Koontz, "Commentary on the Management Theory Jungle—Nearly Two Decades Later," in *Management: A Book of Readings*, 6th ed., ed. H. Koontz, C. O'Donnell, and H. Weihrich (New York: McGraw-Hill, 1984); S. J. Carroll and D. A. Gillen, "Are the Classical Management Functions Useful in Describing Managerial Work?" *Academy of Management Review*, January 1987, p. 48; and P. Allan, "Managers at Work: A Large-Scale Study of the Managerial Job in New York City Government," *Academy of Management Journal*, September 1981, pp. 613–619.

15 R. L. Katz, "Skills of an Effective Administrator," *Harvard Business Review*, September–October 1974, pp. 90–102.

16 D. Nebenzahl, "People Skills Matter Most," *Gazette* (Montreal), September 20, 2004, p. B1.

17 Based on Industry Canada, "1-800-Got-Junk?: Branding Professionalism," November 2006, http://www.strategis.ic.gc.ca/epic/internet/inmfbs-gprea.nsf/en/lu00060e.html (accessed September 11, 2007).

18 H. G. Barkema, J. A. C. Baum, and E. A. Mannix, "Management Challenges in a New Time," *Academy of Management Journal*, October 2002, pp. 916–930; M. A. Hitt, "Transformation of Management for the New Millennium," *Organizational Dynamics*, Winter 2000, pp. 7–17; T. Aeppel, "Power Generation," *Wall Street Journal*, April 7, 2000, p. A11; "Rethinking Work," *Fast Company*, April 2000, p. 253; "Workplace Trends Shifting Over Time," *Springfield News Leader*, January 2, 2000, p. 7B1; "Expectations: The State of the New Economy," *Fast Company*, September 1999, pp. 251–264; T. J. Tetenbaum, "Shifting Paradigms: from Newton to Chaos," *Organizational Dynamics*, Spring 1998, pp. 21–33; T. A. Stewart, "Brain Power: Who Owns It... How They Profit from It," *Fortune*, March 17, 1997, pp. 105–110; G. P. Zachary, "The Right Mix," *Wall Street Journal*, March 13, 1997, p. A11; W. H. Miller, "Leadership at a Crossroads," *IndustryWeek*, August 19, 1996, pp. 42–56; M. Scott, "Interview with Dee Hock," *Business Ethics*, May–June 1996, pp. 37–41; and J. O. C. Hamilton, S. Baker, and B. Vlasic, "The New Workplace," *BusinessWeek*, April 29, 1996, pp. 106–117.

19 R. Spence, "Entrepreneurial Nation: How the Rise of Entrepreneurship Saved Canada's Economy," *PROFIT*, May 2007.

20 Statistics Canada, "Latest Release from the Labour Force Survey," June 8, 2007, http://www.statcan.ca/english/Subjects/Labour/LFS/lfs-en.htm.

21 Statistics Canada, "Latest Release from the Labour Force Survey," September 7, 2007, http://www.statcan.ca/english/Subjects/Labour/LFS/lfs-en.htm (accessed September 11, 2007).

22 See "Highlights of the 2006 Annual Report," *Canada Post*, http://www.canadapost.ca/business/corporate/about/annual_report/highlights2006-e.asp (accessed August 3, 2007); and "Top 1000 Publicly Traded Companies," *Report on Business*, http://www.reportonbusiness.com/v5/content/tp1000-2007/index.php?sort=employee&order=DESC&industry=all&company=Company+Name&x=18&y=5.

23 Based on E. McPhee, "Turning Junk into Gold: Scudamore Finds Midas Touch with 1-800-Got-Junk?" *North Shore News*, June 5, 2005, p. 24; and M. Johne, "Got Guts, and a Good Amount of Capital?" *Globe and Mail*, October 18, 2006, p. E8; J. Martin, "From Cash to

Trash," *Fortune*, November 8, 2003; B. Scudamore, "The Out-of-Towners," *PROFIT*, May 2007, http://www.canadianbusiness.com/entrepreneur/columnists/brian_scudamore/article.jsp?content=20070405_145004_6148 (accessed July 1, 2007); and E. Malykhina, "Maps on the Move," *Information Week*, September 12, 2005, http://64.233.167.104/search?q=cache:DNCOknpOqgkJ:www.informationweek.com/story/showArticle.jhtml%3FarticleID%3D170701926+1-800-got-junk+and+gps&hl=en&ct=clnk&cd=2.

24 "RCMP Needs Major Shakeup: Federal Investigator's Report," *CBCnews.ca*, June 15, 2007, http://www.cbc.ca/canada/story/2007/06/15/rcmp-pension-070615.html?ref=rss.

25 K. Davis and W. C. Frederick, *Business and Society: Management, Public Policy, Ethics*, 5th ed. (New York: McGraw-Hill, 1984), pp. 28–41, 76.

26 R. W. Judy and C. D'Amico, *Workforce 2020* (Indianapolis: Hudson Institute, August 1999).

27 Information for this paragraph is based on http//www.statcan.ca/Daily/English/071204/d071204a.htm (accessed December 31, 2007); and http://www12.statcan.ca/english/census06/data/profiles/community/search/List/Page.cfm?Lang=E&GeoCode=48 (accessed December 31, 2007).

28 J. E. Garten, "Globalism without Tears," *Strategy & Business*, Fourth Quarter 2002, pp. 36–45; and L. L. Bierema, J. W. Bing, and T. J. Carter, "The Global Pendulum," *Training & Development*, May 2002, pp. 70–78; C. Taylor, "Whatever Happened to Globalization?" *Fast Company*, September 1999, pp. 228–236; and S. Zahra, "The Changing Rules of Global Competitiveness in the 21st Century," *Academy of Management Executive*, February 1999, pp. 36–42.

29 "Is Corporate Canada Being 'Hollowed Out'?" *CBCnews.ca*, May 27, 2007.

30 "Fortune Globe 500 2006," *Fortune*, July 24, 2006, http://money.cnn.com/magazines/fortune/global500/2006/countries/C.html.

31 A. Shama, "Management Under Fire: The Transformation of Management in the Soviet Union and Eastern Europe," *Academy of Management Executive* 7, no. 1 (1993), pp. 22–35.

32 T. J. Mullaney, H. Green, M. Arndt, R. D. Hof, and L. Himelstein, "The E-Biz Surprise," *BusinessWeek*, May 12, 2003, pp. 60–68; R. D. Hof and S. Hamm, "How E-Biz Rose, Fell, and Will Rise Anew," *BusinessWeek*, May 13, 2002, pp. 64–72; "Companies Leading Online," *IQ Magazine*, November–December 2001, pp. 54–63.

33 D. A. Menasce and V. A. F. Almeida, *Scaling for E-Business* (Upper Saddle River, NJ: Prentice Hall PTR, 2000).

34 D. A. Menasce and V. A. F. Almeida, *Scaling for E-Business* (Upper Saddle River, NJ: Prentice Hall PTR, 2000); M. Lewis, "Boom or Bust," *Business 2.0*, April 2000, pp. 192–205; J. Davis, "How It Works," *Business 2.0*, February 2000, pp. 112–115; and S. Alsop, "e or Be Eaten," *Fortune*, November 8, 1999, pp. 86–98.

35 Cited in E. Naumann and D. W. Jackson Jr., "One More Time: How Do You Satisfy Customers?" *Business Horizons*, May–June 1999, p. 73.

36 K. A. Eddleston, D. L. Kidder, and B. E. Litzky, "Who's the Boss? Contending with Competing Expectations from Customers and Management," *Academy of Management Executive*, November 2002, pp. 85–95.

37 See, for instance, M. D. Hartline and O. C. Ferrell, "The Management of Customer-Contact Service Employees: An Empirical Investigation," *Journal of Marketing*, October 1996, pp. 52–70;

E. Naumann and D. W. Jackson Jr., "One More Time: How Do You Satisfy Customers?" *Business Horizons*, May–June 1999, p. 73; W. C. Tsai, "Determinants and Consequences of Employee Displayed Positive Emotions," *Journal of Management* 27, no. 4 (2001), pp. 497–512; S. D. Pugh, "Service with a Smile: Emotional Contagion in the Service Encounter," *Academy of Management Journal*, October 2001, pp. 1018–1027; S. D. Pugh, J. Dietz, J. W. Wiley, and S. M. Brooks, "Driving Service Effectiveness Through Employee-Customer Linkages," *Academy of Management Executive*, November 2002, pp. 73–84; K. A. Eddleston, D. L. Kidder, and B. E. Litzky, "Who's the Boss? Contending with Competing Expectations from Customers and Management," *Academy of Management Executive*, November 2002, pp. 85–95; and B. A. Gutek, M. Groth, and B. Cherry, "Achieving Service Success Through Relationships and Enhanced Encounters," *Academy of Management Executive*, November 2002, pp. 132–144.

38 R. A. Hattori and J. Wycoff, "Innovation DNA," *Training & Development*, January 2002, p. 24.

39 P. M. Senge, *The Fifth Discipline: The Art and Practice of Learning Organizations* (New York: Doubleday, 1990).

40 J. S. Brown and P. Duguid, "Balancing Act: How to Capture Knowledge without Killing It," *Harvard Business Review*, May–June 2000, pp. 73–80; J. Torsilieri and C. Lucier, "How to Change the World," *Strategy+Business*, Second Quarter, 2000, pp. 17–20; E. C. Wenger and W. M. Snyder, "Communities of Practice: The Organizational Frontier," *Harvard Business Review*, January–February 2000, pp. 139–145; S. R. Fisher and M. A. White, "Downsizing in a Learning Organization: Are There Hidden Costs?" *Academy of Management Review*, January 2000, pp. 244–251; R. Myers, "Who Knows?" *CFO*, December 1999, pp. 83–87; and M. T. Hansen, N. Nohria, and T. Tierney, "What's Your Strategy for Managing Knowledge?" *Harvard Business Review*, March–April 1999, pp. 106–116.

41 Based on J. B. Miner and N. R. Smith, "Decline and Stabilization of Managerial Motivation Over a 20-Year Period," *Journal of Applied Psychology*, June 1982, pp. 297–305; and J. B. Miner, B. Ebrahimi, and J. M. Wachtel, "How Deficiencies in Motivation to Manage Contribute to the United States' Competitiveness Problem (and What Can Be Done About It)," *Human Resource Management*, Fall 1995, pp. 363–386.

42 E. Church, "Market Recovery Delivers Executive Payout Bonanza," *Globe and Mail*, May 4, 2005, p. B1; and J. McFarland, "How Much Is Too Much?" *Globe and Mail*, May 9, 2006, p. B9.

43 See, for example, "Executive Hires and Compensations: Performance Rules," *HRfocus*, July 2003, p. 1; and H. B. Herring, "At the Top, Pay and Performance Are Often Far Apart," *New York Times*, August 17, 2003, p. B9.

44 L. Lavelle, "CEO Pay: Nothing Succeeds Like Failure," *BusinessWeek*, September 11, 2000, p. 48.

45 D. Dias, "Bang for the Buck: CEO Scorecard" *National Post Business*, November 2006, pp. 23–28.

46 Information from Lipschultz Levin & Gray website, http://www.thethinkers.com (accessed March 15, 2003); and N. K. Austin, "Tear Down the Walls," *Inc.*, April 1999, pp. 66–76.

47 Information from Symantec website, http://www.symantec.com, December 14, 2005; N. Rothbaum, "The Virtual Battlefield," *Smart Money*, January 2006, pp. 76–80; S. H. Wildstrom, "Viruses Get Smarter—and Greedy," *BusinessWeek*, November 22, 2005, http://www.businessweek.com/technology/content/nov2005/

tc20051122_735580.htm; and S. Kirsner, "Sweating in the Hot Zone," *Fast Company*, October 2005, pp. 60–65.

48 Based on H. Rothman, "The Boss as Mentor," *Nation's Business*, April 1993, pp. 66–67; J. B. Cunningham and T. Eberle, "Characteristics of the Mentoring Experience: A Qualitative Study," *Personnel Review*, June 1993, pp. 54–66; S. Crandell, "The Joys of Mentoring," *Executive Female*, March–April 1994, pp. 38–42; and W. Heery, "Corporate Mentoring Can Break the Glass Ceiling," *HRfocus*, May 1994, pp. 17–18.

49 Ford Motor Company, "Production Ends at Historic Windsor Casting Plant," news release, May 29, 2007, http://media.ford.com/newsroom/release_display.cfm?release=26091; "Chrysler to Eliminate 13,000 Jobs, Including 2,000 in Canada," *CBCnews.ca*, February 14, 2007, http://www.cbc.ca/money/story/2007/02/14/chrysler-cuts-070214.html; and "Canada's Struggling Forest Industry Needs Consumers' Help," *Huntsville Reporter*, July 11, 2007.

50 Statistics Canada, "The Retirement Wave," *The Daily*, February 21, 2003.

Supplement 1

1 Based on "Coffee Crisis Prompts Action from Aid Groups," *CTV News*, September 19, 2002; http://www.java-jazz.ca/ about_us.htm (accessed August 21, 2004); and G. Shaw, "No Turning Back Once the Money Rolls In: $30,000 Loan from a Friend Puts Jazzed-Up Coffee Van on the Road with Espresso Machine at the Ready," *Vancouver Sun*, August 21, 2004, p. J1.

2 C. S. George Jr., *The History of Management Thought*, 2nd ed. (Upper Saddle River, NJ: Prentice Hall, 1972), p. 4.

3 F. W. Taylor, *The Principles of Scientific Management* (New York: Harper, 1911), p. 44. For other information on F. W. Taylor, see M. Banta, *Taylored Lives: Narrative Productions in the Age of Taylor, Veblen, and Ford* (Chicago: University of Chicago Press, 1993); and R. Kanigel, *The One Best Way: Frederick Winslow Taylor and the Enigma of Efficiency* (New York: Viking, 1997).

4 See, for example, F. B. Gilbreth, *Motion Study* (New York: Van Nostrand, 1911); and F. B. Gilbreth and L. M. Gilbreth, *Fatigue Study* (New York: Sturgis and Walton, 1916).

5 G. Colvin, "Managing in the Info Era," *Fortune*, March 6, 2000, pp. F6–F9; and A. Harrington, "The Big Ideas," *Fortune*, November 22, 1999, pp. 152–153.

6 H. Fayol, *Industrial and General Administration* (Paris: Dunod, 1916).

7 M. Weber, *The Theory of Social and Economic Organizations*, ed. T. Parsons, trans. A. M. Henderson and T. Parsons (New York: Free Press, 1947).

8 E. Mayo, *The Human Problems of an Industrial Civilization* (New York: Macmillan, 1933); and F. J. Roethlisberger and W. J. Dickson, *Management and the Worker* (Cambridge, MA: Harvard University Press, 1939).

9 See, for example, A. Carey, "The Hawthorne Studies: A Radical Criticism," *American Sociological Review*, June 1967, pp. 403–416; R. H. Franke and J. Kaul, "The Hawthorne Experiments: First Statistical Interpretations," *American Sociological Review*, October 1978, pp. 623–643; B. Rice, "The Hawthorne Defect: Persistence of a Flawed Theory," *Psychology Today*, February 1982, pp. 70–74; J. A. Sonnenfeld, "Shedding Light on the Hawthorne Studies," *Journal of Occupational Behavior*, April 1985, pp. 111–130; S. R. G. Jones, "Worker Interdependence and Output: The Hawthorne Studies Reevaluated," *American Sociological Review*, April 1990, pp. 176–190; S. R. Jones,

"Was There a Hawthorne Effect?" *American Sociological Review*, November 1992, pp. 451–468; and G. W. Yunker, "An Explanation of Positive and Negative Hawthorne Effects: Evidence from the Relay Assembly Test Room and Bank Wiring Observation Room Studies" (paper presented at Academy of Management annual meeting, Atlanta, Georgia, August 1993).

10 With thanks to a reviewer who provided this example.

11 K. B. DeGreene, *Sociotechnical Systems: Factors in Analysis, Design, and Management* (Englewood Cliffs, NJ: Prentice Hall, 1973), p. 13.

Chapter 2

1 Based on C. Alphonso, "A Coast-to-Coast Cover-Up," *Globe and Mail*, April 3, 2004, p. F2; G. Richards, "School Dress Codes Cross Cultures," *Calgary Herald*, March 26, 2004, p. A12; and J. Colebourn and L. Sin, "Richmond Seeks to Curb 'Extreme' Dress in Schools," *Province*, March 26, 2004, p. A3.

2 S. Cruickshank, "Swim Canada Fires Coach after Poor Olympics," *National Post*, September 8, 2004, p. B9.

3 B. Cooper, "Blue Mantle Will Close on April 30: Other Closures Hurt Business," *Leader Post*, March 20, 2004, p. B2.

4 For insights into the symbolic view, see J. Pfeffer, "Management as Symbolic Action: The Creation and Maintenance of Organizational Paradigms," in *Research in Organizational Behavior*, vol. 3, ed. L. L. Cummings and B. M. Staw (Greenwich, CT: JAI Press, 1981), pp. 1–52; D. C. Hambrick and S. Finkelstein, "Managerial Discretion: A Bridge between Polar Views of Organizational Outcomes," in *Research in Organizational Behavior*, vol. 9, ed. L. L. Cummings and B. M. Staw (Greenwich, CT: JAI Press, 1987), pp. 369–406; J. A. Byrne, "The Limits of Power," *BusinessWeek*, October 23, 1987, pp. 33–35; J. R. Meindl and S. B. Ehrlich, "The Romance of Leadership and the Evaluation of Organizational Performance," *Academy of Management Journal*, March 1987, pp. 91–109; C. R. Schwenk, "Illusions of Management Control? Effects of Self-serving Attributions on Resource Commitments and Confidence in Management," *Human Relations*, April 1990, pp. 333–347; S. M. Puffer and J. B. Weintrop, "Corporate Performance and CEO Turnover: The Role of Performance Expectations," *Administrative Science Quarterly*, March 1991, pp. 1–19; and "Why CEO Churn Is Healthy," *BusinessWeek*, November 13, 2000, p. 230.

5 T. M. Hout, "Are Managers Obsolete?" *Harvard Business Review*, March–April 1999, pp. 161–168; and J. Pfeffer, "Management as Symbolic Action: The Creation and Maintenance of Organizational Paradigms," in *Research in Organizational Behavior*, vol. 3, ed. L. L. Cummings and B. M. Staw (Greenwich, CT: JAI Press, 1981), pp. 1–52.

6 Based on J. Colebourn and L. Sin, "Richmond Seeks to Curb 'Extreme' Dress in Schools," *Province*, March 26, 2004, p. A3.

7 Example based on D. Yedlin, "Home Field Advantage," *Report on Business Magazine*, March 26, 2004, p. 51. See also EnCana's corporate constitution, http://www.encana.com/aboutus/corporateconstitution/P1187982448043.html (accessed September 11, 2007).

8 L. Smircich, "Concepts of Culture and Organizational Analysis," *Administrative Science Quarterly*, September 1983, p. 339; D. R. Denison, "What Is the Difference between Organizational Culture and Organizational Climate? A Native's Point of View on a Decade of Paradigm Wars" (paper presented at Academy of Management Annual Meeting, Atlanta, Georgia, 1993); and

M. J. Hatch, "The Dynamics of Organizational Culture," *Academy of Management Review*, October 1993, pp. 657–693.

9 K. Shadur and M. A. Kienzle, "The Relationship between Organizational Climate and Employee Perceptions of Involvement," *Group & Organization Management*, December 1999, pp. 479–503; and A. M. Sapienza, "Believing Is Seeing: How Culture Influences the Decisions Top Managers Make," in *Gaining Control of the Corporate Culture*, ed. R. H. Kilmann, M. J. Saxton, and R. Serpa (San Francisco: Jossey-Bass, 1985), p. 68.

10 C. A. O'Reilly III, J. Chatman, and D. F. Caldwell, "People and Organizational Culture: A Profile Comparison Approach to Assessing Person-Organization Fit," *Academy of Management Journal*, September 1991, pp. 487–516; and J. A. Chatman and K. A. Jehn, "Assessing the Relationship between Industry Characteristics and Organizational Culture: How Different Can You Be?" *Academy of Management Journal*, June 1994, pp. 522–553.

11 See, for example, D. R. Denison, *Corporate Culture and Organizational Effectiveness* (New York: Wiley, 1990); G. G. Gordon and N. DiTomaso, "Predicting Corporate Performance from Organizational Culture," *Journal of Management Studies*, November 1992, pp. 793–798; J. P. Kotter and J. L. Heskett, *Corporate Culture and Performance* (New York: Free Press, 1992), pp. 15–27; J. C. Collins and J. I. Porras, *Built to Last* (New York: HarperBusiness, 1994); J. C. Collins and J. I. Porras, "Building Your Company's Vision," *Harvard Business Review*, September–October 1996, pp. 65–77; R. Goffee and G. Jones, "What Holds the Modern Company Together?" *Harvard Business Review*, November–December 1996, pp. 133–148; and J. B. Sorensen, "The Strength of Corporate Culture and the Reliability of Firm Performance," *Administrative Science Quarterly* 47, no. 1 (2002), pp. 70–91.

12 J. B. Sorensen, "The Strength of Corporate Culture and the Reliability of Firm Performance," *Administrative Science Quarterly* 47, no. 1 (2002), pp. 70–91.

13 See J. M. Jermier, J. Slocum, L. Fry, and J. Gaines, "Organizational Subcultures in a Soft Bureaucracy: Resistance Behind the Myth and Facade of an Official Culture," *Organization Science*, May 1991, pp. 170–194; S. A. Sackmann, "Culture and Subcultures: An Analysis of Organizational Knowledge," *Administrative Science Quarterly*, March 1992, pp. 140–161; R. F. Zammuto, "Mapping Organizational Cultures and Subcultures: Looking Inside and Across Hospitals" (paper presented at the 1995 National Academy of Management Conference, Vancouver, BC, August 1995); and G. Hofstede, "Identifying Organizational Subcultures: An Empirical Approach," *Journal of Management Studies*, January 1998, pp. 1–12.

14 T. A. Timmerman, "Do Organizations Have Personalities?" (paper presented at the 1996 National Academy of Management Conference, Cincinnati, OH, August 1996).

15 See http://thecanadianencyclopedia.com/index.cfm?PgNm=TCE&Params=M1ARTM0011001; http://www.magna.com/magna/en/about/ (accessed September 11, 2007); and B. Simon, "Work Ethic and the Magna Carta," *Financial Post Daily*, March 20, 1997, p. 14.

16 S. E. Ante, "The New Blue," *BusinessWeek*, March 17, 2003, p. 82.

17 See http://www.intuit.ca/en/intuit/careers_college.jsp.

18 Caption based on information in H. Dolezalek, "Outwit, Outlast, Outlearn," *Training*, January 2004, p. 18.

19 J. Forman, "When Stories Create an Organization's Future," *Strategy+Business*, Second Quarter 1999, pp. 6–9; D. M. Boje, "The Storytelling Organization: A Study of Story Performance in an Office-Supply Firm," *Administrative Science Quarterly*, March 1991: pp. 106–126; C. H. Deutsch, "The Parables of Corporate Culture," *New York Times*, October 13, 1991, p. F25; and T. Terez, "The Business of Storytelling," *Workforce*, May 2002, pp. 22–24.

20 J. Useem, "Jim McNerney Thinks He Can Turn 3M from a Good Company into a Great One—With a Little Help from His Former Employer, General Electric," *Fortune*, August 12, 2002, pp. 127–132.

21 A. M. Pettigrew, "On Studying Organizational Cultures," *Administrative Science Quarterly*, December 1979, p. 576.

22 A. M. Pettigrew, "On Studying Organizational Cultures," *Administrative Science Quarterly*, December 1979, p. 576.

23 Cited in J. M. Beyer and H. M. Trice, "How an Organization's Rites Reveal Its Culture," *Organizational Dynamics*, Spring 1987, p. 15; and "The 'Masculine' and 'Feminine' Sides of Leadership and Culture: Perception vs. Reality," *Knowledge@Wharton*, http://knowledge.wharton.upenn.edu/article.cfm?articleid=1287 (accessed July 3, 2007).

24 Thanks to one of my reviewers for reporting this story.

25 A. Bryant, "The New Power Breakfast," *Newsweek*, May 15, 2000, p. 52.

26 See B. Victor and J. B. Cullen, "The Organizational Bases of Ethical Work Climates," *Administrative Science Quarterly*, March 1988, pp. 101–125; L. K. Trevino, "A Cultural Perspective on Changing and Developing Organizational Ethics," in *Research in Organizational Change and Development*, vol. 4, ed. W. A. Pasmore and R. W. Woodman (Greenwich, CT: JAI Press, 1990); and M. W. Dickson, D. B. Smith, M. W. Grojean, and M. Ehrhart, "An Organizational Climate Regarding Ethics: The Outcome of Leader Values and the Practices That Reflect Them," *Leadership Quarterly*, Summer 2001, pp. 197–217.

27 P. P. Waldie and K. Howlett, "Reports Reveal Tight Grip of Ebbers on WorldCom," *Globe and Mail*, June 11, 2003, pp. B1, B7.

28 "Cirque du Soleil: Creating a Culture of Extraordinary Creativity," *Innovation Network*, http://www.thinksmart.com/iu/cirque.html (accessed March 14, 2003).

29 L. Simpson, "Fostering Creativity," *Training*, December 2001, p. 56.

30 J. Gray and R. Robin, "The Brothers in Law," *Canadian Business*, September 29, 2003, p. 75.

31 K. Aaserud, C. Cornell, J. McElgunn, K. Shiffman, and R. Wright, "The Golden Rules of Growth: Isadore Sharp," *PROFIT*, May 2007. http://www.canadianbusiness.com/entrepreneur/managing/article.jsp?content=20070419_095326_4460.

32 L. Gary, "Simplify and Execute: Words to Live By in Times of Turbulence," *Harvard Management Update*, January 2003, p. 12.

33 Based on M. J. Bitner, B. H. Booms, and L. A. Mohr, "Critical Service Encounters: The Employee's Viewpoint," *Journal of Marketing*, October 1994, pp. 95–106; M. D. Hartline and O. C. Ferrell, "The Management of Customer-Contact Service Employees: An Empirical Investigation," *Journal of Marketing*, October 1996, pp. 52–70; M. L. Lengnick-Hall and C. A. Lengnick-Hall, "Expanding Customer Orientation in the HR Function," *Human Resource Management*, Fall 1999, pp. 201–214; B. Schneider, D. E. Bowen, M. G. Ehrhart, and K. M. Holcombe, "The Climate for Service: Evolution of a Construct," in *Handbook of Organizational Culture and Climate*, ed. N. M. Ashkanasy, C. P. M. Wilderom, and M. F. Peterson (Thousand Oaks,

CA: Sage, 2000), pp. 21–36; M. D. Hartline, J. G. Maxham III, and D. O. McKee, "Corridors of Influence in the Dissemination of Customer-Oriented Strategy to Customer Contact Service Employees," *Journal of Marketing*, April 2000, pp. 35–50; L. A. Bettencourt, K. P. Gwinner, and M. L. Mueter, "A Comparison of Attitude, Personality, and Knowledge Predictors of Service-Oriented Organizational Citizenship Behaviors," *Journal of Applied Psychology*, February 2001, pp. 29–41; R. C. Ford and C. P. Heaton, "Lessons from Hospitality That Can Serve Anyone," *Organizational Dynamics*, Summer 2001, pp. 30–47; S. D. Pugh, J. Dietz, J. W. Wiley, and S. M. Brooks, "Driving Service Effectiveness Through Employee-Customer Linkages," *Academy of Management Executive*, November 2002, pp. 73–84; K. A. Eddleston, D. L. Kidder, and B. E. Litzky, "Who's the Boss? Contending with Competing Expectations from Customers and Management," *Academy of Management Executive*, November 2002, pp. 85–95; and B. A. Gutek, M. Groth, and B. Cherry, "Achieving Service Success Through Relationships and Enhanced Encounters," *Academy of Management Executive*, November 2002, pp. 132–144.

34 Thanks to a reviewer, Dr. Michelle Inness, University of Alberta, for providing this insight.

35 G. Richards, "School Dress Codes Cross Cultures," *Calgary Herald*, March 26, 2004, p. A12.

36 A. Kingston, "Green Report: It's So Not Cool," *Maclean's*, May 14, 2007, http://www.macleans.ca/article.jsp?content=20070514_105163_105163 (accessed July 1, 2007).

37 J. Greenwood, "Home Depot Runs into Vancouver Red Tape," *Financial Post (National Post)*, May 10, 2004, pp. FP1, FP11.

38 D. Calleja, "Equity or Else," *Canadian Business*, March 19, 2001, p. 31.

39 See http://strategis.ic.gc.ca/epic/internet/incb-bc.nsf/en/_ct02171e.html.

40 R. Annan, "Merger Remedies in Canada," *Competition Bureau*, June 20, 2006, http://www.competitionbureau.gc.ca/internet/index.cfm?itemID=2134&lg=e#25 (accessed September 24, 2006).

41 T. S. Mescon and G. S. Vozikis, "Federal Regulation—What Are the Costs?" *Business*, January–March 1982, pp. 33–39.

42 J. Thorpe, "Inter-Provincial Trade Barriers Still a Concern for Executives 'Handicapping Country Economically,'" *Financial Post (National Post)*, September 13, 2004, p. FP2.

43 C. Sands, "Canada's Problem: Domestic Trade Barriers," *American*, May 22, 2007, http://www.american.com/archive/2007/may-0507/canada2019s-problem-domestic-trade-barriers.

44 B. Constantineau, "Trans Fats Come Off the Menu at A&W," *Vancouver Sun*, January 4, 2007, p. C1.

45 See http://www.ctv.ca/servlet/ArticleNews/story/CTVNews/_1069789271153_26/?hub=Health.

46 G. Bonnell, "Food Industry Rushes to Drop Trans Fats," *Calgary Herald*, March 11, 2004, p. D1.

47 T. Donaldson and L. E. Preston, "The Stakeholder Theory of the Corporation: Concepts, Evidence, and Implications," *Academy of Management Review*, January 1995, pp. 65–91.

48 J. S. Harrison and C. H. St. John, "Managing and Partnering with External Stakeholders," *Academy of Management Executive*, May 1996, pp. 46–60.

49 A. J. Hillman and G. D. Keim, "Shareholder Value, Stakeholder Management, and Social Issues: What's the Bottom Line?" *Strategic Management Journal*, March 2001, pp. 125–139; and J. Kotter and J. Heskett, Corporate Culture and Performance (New York: Free Press, 1992).

50 J. S. Harrison and C. H. St. John, "Managing and Partnering with External Stakeholders," *Academy of Management Executive*, May 1996, pp. 46–60.

51 S. P. Robbins, *Organizational Behavior*, 8th ed. (Upper Saddle River, NJ: Prentice Hall, 1998), p. 617.

52 Situation adapted from information in "Two Admit to Securities Fraud," *Los Angeles Times*, April 25, 2006, p. C3; and "Software Chief Admits to Guilt in Fraud Case," *New York Times*, April 25, 2006, pp. A1+.

53 "2004 Report Warned of Low Morale in RCMP," *Edmonton Journal*, June 15, 2007, p. F7; "A Matter of Trust—Report of the Independent Investigator into Matters Relating to RCMP Pension and Insurance Plans," *Public Safety Canada*, June 25, 2007, http://www.ps-sp.gc.ca/rcmppension-retraitegrc/toc-en.asp; D. Butler and M. Fitzpatrick, "'Outsider' Facing Challenge at RCMP: Bureaucrat Selected to Fix 'Broken' Force," *National Post*, July 7, 2007, p. A1; C. Clark and D. Leblanc, "Fraser Puts Heat on PM," *Globe and Mail*, February 11, 2004; C. Clark and D. Leblanc, "RCMP 'Horribly Broken,'" *Globe and Mail*, June 16, 2007, p. A1; B. Cooper, "RCMP Chose Image over Effectiveness," *Ottawa Citizen*, June 20, 2007, p. A17; L. Greenberg, "RCMP Told of Air India Warning within Minutes: Bartleman," *CanWest News Service*, May 04, 2007; K. May, "A Tale of Two RCMPs," *Gazette* (Montreal), June 15, 2007, p. A3; K. May, "Mounties' Woes Pinned on Ex-Chief," *Gazette* (Montreal), June 16, 2007, p. A12; and L. Whittington, "'Daunting Task' Ahead, New RCMP Chief Says," *Toronto Star*, September 8, 2007, p. A23.

54 Based on http://www.southernco.com/mspower; Edison Electric Institute, "EEI Honors Mississippi Power with 'Emergency Response Award' for Hurricane Recovery Efforts," *PR Newswire*, January 11, 2006, http://www.prnewswire.com; S. Lewis, "Contractors to the Rescue," *Transmission & Distribution World*, December 1, 2005, http://tdworld.com/mag/power_contractors_rescue/index.html; D. Cauchon, "The Little Company That Could," *USA Today*, October 10, 2005, pp. 1B+; and S. Covey, The 7 Habits of Highly Effective People (New York: Free Press, 1989).

55 Based on N. Langton and S. P. Robbins, *Organizational Behavior*, 4th ed. (Toronto: Pearson Education Canada, 2007), p. 384.

56 Based on "Diversity at the Forefront," *BusinessWeek*, November 4, 2002, pp. 27–38; "Talking to Diversity Experts: Where Do We Go from Here?" *Fortune*, September 30, 2002, pp. 157–172; "Keeping Your Edge: Managing a Diverse Corporate Culture," *Fortune*, June 11, 2001, pp. S1–S18; "Diversity Today," *Fortune*, June 12, 2000, pp. S1–S24; O. C. Richard, "Racial Diversity, Business Strategy, and Firm Performance: A Resource-Based View," *Academy of Management Journal*, April 2000, pp. 164–177; A. Markels, "How One Hotel Manages Staff's Diversity," *Wall Street Journal*, November 20, 1996, pp. B1+; C. A. Deutsch, "Corporate Diversity in Practice," *New York Times*, November 20, 1996, pp. C1+; and D. A. Thomas and R. J. Ely, "Making Differences Matter: A New Paradigm for Managing Diversity," *Harvard Business Review*, September–October 1996, pp. 79–90.

57 Based on D. W. Brown, "Searching for Clues," *Black Enterprise*, November 2002, pp. 114–120; L. Bower, "Weigh Values to Decide if Working for 'Beasts' Worthwhile," *Springfield Business Journal*, November 4, 2002, p. 73; S. Shellenbarger, "How to Find Out if You're Going to Hate a New Job Before You Agree to Take It," *Wall Street Journal*, June 13, 2002, p. D1; and M. Boyle, "Just Right," *Fortune*, June 10, 2002, pp. 207–208.

Chapter 3

1 Based on D. Tetley, "Tension Rises as Recall List Grows," *Calgary Herald*, April 3, 2007, p. A3; and C. Gillis and A. Kingston, "The Great Pet Food Scandal," *Maclean's*, April 30, 2007, http://www.macleans. ca/business/companies/article.jsp?content=20070430_104326_ 104326 (accessed July 8, 2007).

2 N. Adler, *International Dimensions of Organizational Behavior*, 3rd ed. (Cincinnati, OH: South-Western, 1996).

3 M. R. F. Kets De Vries and E. Florent-Treacy, "Global Leadership from A to Z: Creating High Commitment Organizations," *Organizational Dynamics*, Spring 2002, pp. 295–309; P. R. Harris and R. T. Moran, *Managing Cultural Differences*, 4th ed. (Houston: Gulf Publishing, 1996); R. T. Moran, P. R. Harris, and W. G. Stripp, *Developing the Global Organization: Strategies for Human Resource Professionals* (Houston, TX: Gulf Publishing, 1993); Y. Wind, S. P. Douglas, and H. V. Perlmutter, "Guidelines for Developing International Marketing Strategies," *Journal of Marketing*, April 1973, pp. 14–23; and H. V. Perlmutter, "The Tortuous Evolution of the Multinational Corporation," *Columbia Journal of World Business*, January–February 1969, pp. 9–18.

4 A. K. Gupta and V. Govindarajan, "Cultivating a Global Mindset," *Academy of Management Executive*, February 2002, pp. 117–118.

5 "U.S. Legislators Could Side-Swipe Canada With Measures to Protect Food Supply," *Alaska Highway News*, May 11, 2007, p. C2; and R. Myers, "Food Fights: As Supply Chains Stretch to All Corners of the Globe, Producers Struggle to Guarantee Food Safety," *CFO Magazine*, June 01, 2007.

6 *WTO Policy Issues for Parliamentarians, World Trade Organization*, http://www.wto.org/english/res_e/booksp_e/parliamentarians_e.pdf (accessed September 3, 2004), p. 1.

7 B. Mitchener, "Ten New Members to Weigh in on Future of EU," *Wall Street Journal*, April 16, 2003, p. A16; C. Taylor, "Go East, Young Man," *Smart Money*, January 2003, p. 25; S. Miller and B. Grow, "A Bigger Europe? Not So Fast," *Wall Street Journal*, December 12, 2002, p. A15; http://europa.eu/abc/european_countries/index_ en.htm (accessed July 5, 2007); and http://europa.eu/abc/ european_countries/candidate_countries/index_en.htm (accessed July 5, 2007).

8 B. Mitchener, "A New EU, but No Operating Manual," *Wall Street Journal*, December 16, 2002, p. A10; and https://www.cia.gov/ library/publications/the-world-factbook/print/ee.html.

9 See http://europa.eu.int/euro (accessed March 18, 2007); H. Cooper, "The Euro: What You Need to Know," *Wall Street Journal*, January 4, 1999, p. A51.

10 P. Gumbel, "Euro-Division?" *Time Bonus Section*, July 2005, p. A18; N. Knox, "Leaders of Embattled EU Head to Washington," *USA Today*, June 20, 2005, p. A8; and N. Knox, "European Union Struggles with Constitution Rejection," *USA Today*, May 31, 2005, p. A10.

11 US Census Bureau, *Foreign Trade Statistics*, http://www.census. gov/foreign-trade/statistics/highlights/index.html.

12 Statistics Canada, "International Merchandise Trade: Annual Review," *The Daily*, May 8, 2007.

13 "Goods Going South? Think Mexico," http://www.edc.ca/ english/publications_9432.htm (accessed July 8, 2007).

14 Information from ASEAN website, http://www.aseansec.org/ stat/Table5.pdf.

15 "Ministerial Declaration," *Free Trade Area of the Americas*, http:// www.ftaa-alca.org (accessed April 4, 2003); and "NAFTA: Five-Year Anniversary," *Latin Trade*, January 1999, pp. 44–45.

16 "Ministerial Declaration," Free Trade Area of the Americas, http://www.ftaa-alca.org, January 23, 2006; and M. Moffett and J. D. McKinnon, "Failed Summit Casts Shadow on Global Trade Talks," *Wall Street Journal*, November 7, 2005, pp. A1+.

17 D. Kraft, "Leaders Question, Praise African Union," *Springfield News-Leader*, July 10, 2002, p. 8A.

18 SAARC website, http://www.saarc-sec.org; and N. George, "South Asia Trade Zone in Works," *Springfield News-Leader*, January 4, 2004, pp. 1E+.

19 This section is based on material from the World Trade Organization website, http://www.wto.org.

20 C. Gillis and A. Kingston, "The Great Pet Food Scandal," *Maclean's*, April 30, 2007, http://www.macleans.ca/business/ companies/article.jsp?content=20070430_104326_104326 (accessed July 8, 2007); see http://investing.businessweek.com/ research/stocks/snapshot/snapshot.asp?capId=3206215; D. George-Cosh, "Menu Foods Hammered as Customer Walks," *Globe and Mail*, June 13, 2007, p. B15; and http://www.menufoods.com/ about_us/distribution.html (accessed September 24, 2007).

21 C. A. Barlett and S. Ghoshal, *Managing Across Borders: The Transnational Solution*, 2nd ed. (Boston: Harvard Business School Press, 2002); and N. J. Adler, *International Dimensions of Organizational Behavior*, 4th ed. (Cincinnati, OH: South-Western, 2002), pp. 9–11.

22 D. A. Aaker, *Developing Business Strategies*, 5th ed. (New York: John Wiley & Sons, 1998); and J. A. Byrne et al., "Borderless Management," *BusinessWeek*, May 23, 1994, pp. 24–26.

23 G. A. Knight and S. T. Cavusgil, "A Taxonomy of Born-Global Firms," *Management International Review* 45, no. 3 (2005), pp. 15–35; S. A. Zahra, "A Theory of International New Ventures: A Decade of Research," *Journal of International Business Studies*, January 2005, pp. 20–28; and B. M. Oviatt and P. P. McDougall, "Toward a Theory of International New Ventures," *Journal of International Business Studies*, January 2005, pp. 29–41.

24 See http://www.blonnet.com/2006/10/17/stories/ 2006101701390400.htm.

25 Mega Brands, Annual Report, 2006; and http://communities. canada.com/nationalpost/blogs/tradingdesk/archive/2007/01/23/ good-news-for-mega-brands-put-in-context.aspx (figure is for 2006).

26 Statistics Canada, "Profile of Canadian Exporters," *The Daily*, March 22, 2004.

27 L. Frost, "Starbucks Lures French Café Society," *Associated Press*, January 16, 2004.

28 E. Malkin, "Founder Sees Lots of Room for Lots More Starbucks," *New York Times*, September 22, 2007.

29 B. Brown, "UAW Deal Hurts Canada's Auto Towns," *Washington Times*, October 2, 2007.

30 Based on C. Gillis and A. Kingston, "The Great Pet Food Scandal," *Maclean's*, April 30, 2007, http://www.macleans.ca/ business/companies/article.jsp?content=20070430_104326_ 104326 (accessed July 8, 2007); and D. Barboza and A. Barrionuevo, "Filler in Animal Feed Is Open Secret in China," *New York Times*, April 30, 2007.

31 Based on information from M. Javidan, P. W. Dorfman, M. S. deLuque, and R. J. House, "In the Eye of the Beholder: Cross-Cultural Lessons in Leadership from Project GLOBE," *Academy of Management Perspective*, February 2006, pp. 67–90; and M. Javidan, G. K. Stahl, F. Brodbeck, and C. P. M. Wilderon, "Cross-Border Transfer of Knowledge: Cultural Lessons from Project GLOBE," *Academy of Management Executive*, May 2005, pp. 59–76.

32 See G. Hofstede, *Culture's Consequences: International Differences in Work-Related Values*, 2nd ed. (Thousand Oaks, CA: Sage, 2001), pp. 9–15.

33 G. Hofstede, *Culture's Consequences: International Differences in Work-Related Values*, 2nd ed. (Thousand Oaks, CA: Sage, 2001), pp. 9–15; and G. Hofstede, "The Cultural Relativity of Organizational Practices and Theories," *Journal of International Business Studies*, Fall 1983, pp. 75–89.

34 Based on A. Daniels, "Wal-Mart Treading Softly in Japan: East Meets Western Retailer," *Arkansas Democrat-Gazette*, December 21, 2003, p. 67; K. Belson, "Wal-Mart Hopes It Won't Be Lost in Translation," *New York Times*, December 14, 2003, p. BU1; "Losses Increase at Wal-Mart Japan," August 22, 2006, *BBC News*, http://news.bbc.co.uk/2/hi/business/5273642.stm; and N. Maestri, "Wal-Mart Seeks Nimbler International Expansion," *Scotsman.com*, June 14, 2007, http://business.scotsman.com/latest.cfm?id=937142007.

35 Hofstede called this dimension *masculinity versus femininity* [italics added], but we have changed his terms because of their strong sexist connotation.

36 Hofstede, *Culture's Consequences: International Differences in Work-Related Values*, 2nd ed. (Thousand Oaks, CA: Sage, 2001), pp. 355–358.

37 R. J. House, P. J. Hanges, M. Javidan, P. W. Dorfman, and V. Gupta, *Culture Leadership, and Organizations: The GLOBE Study of 62 Societies* (Thousand Oaks, CA: Sage Publications), 2004; M. Javidan, P. W. Dorfman, M. S. deLuque, and R. J. House, "In the Eye of the Beholder: Cross-Cultural Lessons in Leadership from Project GLOBE," *Academy of Management Perspective*, February 2006, pp. 67–90; and M. Javidan, G. K. Stahl, F. Brodbeck, and C. P. M. Wilderon, "Cross-Border Transfer of Knowledge: Cultural Lessons from Project GLOBE," *Academy of Management Executive*, May 2005, pp. 59–76.

38 O. Ward, "Pop Goes Globalization," *Toronto Star*, March 13, 2004, http://www.thestar.com (accessed March 21, 2004).

39 A. Kreamer, "America's Yang Has a Yen for Asia's Yin," *Fast Company*, July 2003, p. 58; D. Yergin, "Globalization Opens Door to New Dangers," *USA Today*, May 28, 2003, p. 11A; K. Lowrey Miller, "Is It Globaloney?" *Newsweek*, December 16, 2002, pp. E4–E8; L. Gomes, "Globalization Is Now a Two-Way Street—Good News for the U.S.," *Wall Street Journal*, December 9, 2002, p. B1; J. Kurlantzick and J. T. Allen, "The Trouble with Globalism," *U.S. News & World Report*, February 11, 2002, pp. 38–41; and J. Guyon, "The American Way," *Fortune*, November 26, 2001, pp. 114–120.

40 J. Guyon, "The American Way," *Fortune*, November 26, 2001, pp. 114–120.

41 Adapted from G. M. Spreitzer, M. W. McCall Jr., and J. D. Mahoney, "Early Identification of International Executive Potential," *Journal of Applied Psychology*, February 1997, pp. 6–29.

42 Information from company website, http://www.inditex.com (accessed July 5, 2007); and M. Helft, "Fashion Fast-Forward," *Business 2.0*, May 2002, pp. 60–66.

43 Situation adapted from information in M. R. Cohn, "Indian Villagers Set to Battle Alcan," *Toronto Star*, July 3, 2004, pp. A1, A10–A12; A. Swift, "Alcan to Do Well in 2004, Says CEO," *Trail Times*, April 23, 2004, p. 14; L. Moore, "Alcan Sees Bright Year Ahead," *Gazette* (Montreal), April 23, 2004, p. B1; and http://www.alcan.com/web/publishing.nsf/Content/Alcan+Facts+2006 (accessed July 9, 2007).

44 See http://www.nba.com/canada/Canadians_in_the_NBA-Canada_Generic_Article-18022.html (accessed September 15, 2007); D. Eisenberg, "The NBA's Global Game Plan," *Time*, March 17, 2003, pp. 59–63; J. Tyrangiel, "The Center of Attention," *Time*, February 10, 2003, pp. 56–60; "Spin Master Stern," *Latin Trade*, July 2000, p. 32; Information from NBA website, http://www.nba.com (accessed July 1, 2004); J. Tagliabue, "Hoop Dreams, Fiscal Realities," *New York Times*, March 4, 2000, p. B11; D. Roth, "The NBA's Next Shot," *Fortune*, February 21, 2000, pp. 207–216; A. Bianco, "Now It's NBA All-the-Time TV," *BusinessWeek*, November 15, 1999, pp. 241–242; and D. McGraw and M. Tharp, "Going Out on Top," *U.S. News & World Report*, January 25, 1999, p. 55.

45 M. A. Prospero, "Attitude Adjustment," *Fast Company*, December 2005, p. 107; D. Roberts and M. Arndt, "It's Getting Hotter in the East," *BusinessWeek*, August 22/29, 2005, pp. 78–81; M. Champion, "Scotland Looks East for Labor," *Wall Street Journal*, July 7, 2005, p. A11; L. Bower, "Cultural Awareness Aids Business Relations," *Springfield Business Journal*, April 4–10, 2005, p. 59; R. Rosmarin, "Mountain View Masala," *Business 2.0*, March 2005, pp. 54–56; and P. W. Tam, "Culture Course," *Wall Street Journal*, May 25, 2004, pp. B1+.

46 C. Harvey and M. J. Allard, *Understanding and Managing Diversity: Readings, Cases, and Exercises*, 2nd ed. (Upper Saddle River, NJ: Prentice Hall, 2002); P. L. Hunsaker, *Training in Management Skills* (Upper Saddle River, NJ: Prentice Hall, 2001); and J. Greenberg, *Managing Behavior in Organizations: Science in Service to Practice*, 2nd ed. (Upper Saddle River, NJ: Prentice Hall, 1999).

Chapter 4

1 Based on G. Lamphier, "Syncrude Wins Aboriginal Business Award for Third Time," *Edmonton Journal*, February 15, 2007, p. G1; "Aboriginal Relations," *Syncrude Canada*, http://sustainability.syncrude.ca/sustainability2006/social/aboriginalRelations/aboriginalRelations.html; http://www.syncrude.com/community/aboriginal.html; *Syncrude Aboriginal Review, 2006*, http://www.syncrude.ca/aboreview/pdf/SyncrudeAboriginalRev2006.pdf; C. Petten, "Syncrude, Cameco Strike Gold With PAR," *Windspeaker*, March 2002, pp. B7–B8; and *Syncrude 2006 Aboriginal Review*, http://www.syncrude.ca/aboreview/relations-team.

2 M. Friedman, *Capitalism and Freedom* (Chicago: University of Chicago Press, 1962); and M. Friedman, "The Social Responsibility of Business Is to Increase Profits," *New York Times Magazine*, September 13, 1970, p. 33.

3 J. Bakan, *The Corporation* (Toronto: Big Picture Media Corporation, 2003).

4 Information from Avon's website, http://www.avoncompany.com/women/avoncrusade/index.html (accessed July 10, 2007).

5 E. P. Lima, "Seeding a World of Transformation," *IndustryWeek*, September 6, 1999, pp. 30–31.

6 "The McKinsey Global Survey of Business Executives: Business and Society," *McKinsey Quarterly*, January 2006, http://www.mckinseyquarterly.com.

7 The Triple Bottom Line was first introduced in J. Elkington, *Cannibals with Forks: The Triple Bottom Line of 21st-Century Business* (Stony Creek, CT: New Society Publishers, 1998).

8 See, for example, A. B. Carroll, "The Pyramid of Corporate Social Responsibility: Toward the Moral Management of Organizational Stakeholders," *Business Horizons*, July–August 1991, pp. 39–48.

9 This section has been influenced by K. B. Boal and N. Peery, "The Cognitive Structure of Social Responsibility," *Journal of Management*, Fall–Winter 1985, pp. 71–82.

10 This section is based on R. J. Monsen Jr., "The Social Attitudes of Management," in *Contemporary Management: Issues and Views*, ed. J. M. McGuire (Upper Saddle River, NJ: Prentice Hall, 1974), p. 616; and K. Davis and W. C. Frederick, *Business and Society: Management, Public Policy, Ethics*, 5th ed. (New York: McGraw-Hill, 1984), pp. 28–41.

11 A. B. Carroll, "A Three-Dimensional Conceptual Model of Corporate Performance," *Academy of Management Review*, October 1979, p. 499.

12 See S. P. Sethi, "A Conceptual Framework for Environmental Analysis of Social Issues and Evaluation of Business Response Patterns," *Academy of Management Review*, January 1979, pp. 68–74.

13 See, for example, D. J. Wood, "Corporate Social Performance Revisited," *Academy of Management Review*, October 1991, pp. 703–708.

14 Information from "How to Apply for Funding," *CIBC*, http://www.cibc.com/ca/inside-cibc/cibc-your-community/how-to-apply-for-funding.html (accessed July 12, 2007).

15 See http://www.mec.ca; and H. Hoag, "Blocks of Buildings of the Future," *Gazette* (Montreal), October 24, 2006, p. B3.

16 Information from http://www.purolator.com/media/news/may_01_07.html; and http://cassies.ca/caselibrary/winners/2006pdfs/_559Purolator_Web_DR.pdf.

17 S. L. Wartick and P. L. Cochran, "The Evolution of the Corporate Social Performance Model," *Academy of Management Review*, October 1985, p. 763.

18 See http://www.canada.com/national/features/raiseareader/index.html.

19 A. Kellogg, "Punch the Query 'Canada's Best Major Corporate Citizen' into Google on Your Computer and It's Likely the Image of Eric Newell Will Pop Up," *Calgary Herald*, November 30, 2003, p. C2; R. Yerema, *Canada's Top 100 Employers* (Toronto: Mediacorp Canada, 2000, 2001, 2002); and http://www.syncrude.ca/users/news_view.asp?FolderID=5690&NewsID=102 (accessed July 11, 2007).

20 See, for instance, D. O. Neubaum and S. A. Zahra, "Institutional Ownership and Corporate Social Performance: The Moderating Effects of Investment Horizon, Activism, and Coordination," *Journal of Management*, February 2006, pp. 108–131; P. C. Godfrey, "The Relationship between Corporate Philanthropy and Shareholder Wealth: A Risk Management Perspective," *Academy of Management Review*, October 2005, pp. 777–798; D. K. Peterson, "The Relationship between Perceptions of Corporate Citizenship and Organizational Commitment," *Business & Society*, September 2004, pp. 296–319; B. Seifert, S. A. Morris, and B. R. Bartkus, "Having, Giving, and Getting: Slack Resources, Corporate Philanthropy, and Firm Financial Performance," *Business & Society*, June 2004, pp. 135–161; S. L. Berman, A. Wicks, S. Kotha, and T. Jones, "Does Stakeholder Orientation Matter? The Relationship between Stakeholder Management Models and Firm Financial Performance,"

Academy of Management Journal, October 1999, pp. 488–506; S. A. Waddock and S. B. Graves, "The Corporate Social Performance–Financial Performance Link," *Strategic Management Journal*, April 1997, pp. 303–319; D. B. Turban and D. W. Greening, "Corporate Social Performance and Organizational Attractiveness to Prospective Employees," *Academy of Management Journal*, June 1996, pp. 658–672; J. B. McGuire, A. Sundgren, and T. Schneeweis, "Corporate Social Responsibility and Firm Financial Performance," *Academy of Management Journal*, December 1988, pp. 854–872; K. Aupperle, A. B. Carroll, and J. D. Hatfield, "An Empirical Examination of the Relationship between Corporate Social Responsibility and Profitability," *Academy of Management Journal*, June 1985, pp. 446–463; and P. Cochran and R. A. Wood, "Corporate Social Responsibility and Financial Performance," *Academy of Management Journal*, March 1984, pp. 42–56.

21 D. J. Wood and R. E. Jones, "Stakeholder Mismatching: A Theoretical Problem in Empirical Research on Corporate Social Performance," *International Journal of Organizational Analysis* 3 (1995), pp. 229–267.

22 See A. A. Ullmann, "Data in Search of a Theory: A Critical Examination of the Relationships Among Social Performance, Social Disclosure, and Economic Performance of U.S. Firms," *Academy of Management Review*, July 1985, pp. 540–557; R. E. Wokutch and B. A. Spencer, "Corporate Saints and Sinners: The Effects of Philanthropic and Illegal Activity on Organizational Performance," *California Management Review*, Winter 1987, pp. 62–77; R. Wolfe and K. Aupperle, "Introduction to Corporate Social Performance: Methods for Evaluating an Elusive Construct." Edited by J. E. Post. *Research in Corporate Social Performance and Policy* 12 (1991), pp. 265–268; and D. J. Wood and R. E. Jones, "Stakeholder Mismatching: A Theoretical Problem in Empirical Research on Corporate Social Performance," *International Journal of Organizational Analysis* 3 (1995), pp. 229–267.

23 M. Orlitzky, F. L. Schmidt, and S. L. Rynes, "Corporate Social and Financial Performance," *Organization Studies* 24, no. 3 (2003), pp. 403–441.

24 A. M. Odell, "Canadian SRI Assets Leap to More Than $500 Billion Canadian," http://www.socialfunds.com/news/article.cgi/2264.html (accessed April 03, 2007).

25 A. M. Odell, "Carrying the Shield for Responsible Investing in Canada," http://www.socialfunds.com/news/article.cgi/2248.html (accessed March 14, 2007).

26 D. Macfarlane, "Why Now?" *Report on Business*, March 2004, pp. 45–46.

27 J. Jedras, "Social Workers," *Silicon Valley North*, July 30, 2001, p. 1.

28 Based on http://sustainability.syncrude.ca/sustainability2006/environmental/air.html; "Syncrude Canada Ltd. and Aboriginal People Forge a Win-Win Partnership," *Grassroots*, Winter 2006, p. 6.

29 This section is based on K. Buysse and A. Verbeke, "Proactive Environmental Strategies: A Stakeholder Management Perspective," *Strategic Management Journal*, May 2003, pp. 453–470; D. A. Rondinelli and T. London, "How Corporations and Environmental Groups Cooperate: Assessing Cross-Sector Alliances and Collaborations," *Academy of Management Executive*, February 2003, pp. 61–76; J. Alberto Aragon-Correa and S. Sharma, "A Contingent Resource-Based View of Proactive Corporate Environmental Strategy," *Academy of Management Review*, January 2003, pp. 71–88; P. Christmann and G. Taylor, "Globalization and the Environment: Strategies for International Voluntary Environmental Initiatives," *Academy of Management Executive*, August 2002, pp. 121–135;

P. Bansal, "The Corporate Challenges of Sustainable Development," *Academy of Management Executive*, May 2002, pp. 122–131; M. Stark and A. A. Marcus, "Introduction to the Special Research Forum on the Management of Organizations in the Natural Environment: A Field Emerging from Multiple Paths, With Many Challenges Ahead," *Academy of Management Journal*, August 2000, pp. 539–546; P. Bansal and K. Roth, "Why Companies Go Green: A Model of Ecological Responsiveness," *Academy of Management Journal*, August 2000, pp. 717–736; S. L. Hart, "Beyond Greening: Strategies for a Sustainable World," *Harvard Business Review*, January–February 1997, pp. 66–76; S. L. Hart, "A Natural-Resource-Based View of the Firm," *Academy of Management Review*, December 1995, pp. 986–1014; and P. Shrivastava, "Environmental Technologies and Competitive Advantage," *Strategic Management Journal*, Summer 1995, pp. 183–200.

30 J. L. Seglin, "It's Not That Easy Going Green," *Inc.*, May 1999, pp. 28–32; W. H. Miller, "What's Ahead in Environmental Policy?" *IW*, April 19, 1999, pp. 19–24; and P. Shrivastava, "Environmental Technologies and Competitive Advantage," *Strategic Management Journal*, Summer 1995, p. 183.

31 S. L. Hart, "Beyond Greening: Strategies for a Sustainable World," *Harvard Business Review*, January–February 1997, p. 68.

32 The Worldwatch Institute, *State of the World 2006: China and India Hold World in Balance*, http://www.worldwatch.org/node/3894 (accessed July 12, 2007); "Is There a Green Movement in the Air?" *Fortune*, December 12, 2005, pp. 69–78; A. Aston and B. Helm, "The Race Against Climate Change," *BusinessWeek*, December 12, 2005, pp. 58–66; J. Kluger and A. Dorfman, "The Challenges We Face," *Time*, August 26, 2002, pp. A6–A12; Worldwatch Institute, "Earth Day 2000: What Humanity Can Do Now to Turn the Tide," http://www.worldwatch.org/node/483 (accessed July 12, 2007); and L. Brown and Staff of the Worldwatch Institute, *State of the World* (New York: Norton, 1987–1996).

33 A. White, "The Greening of the Balance Sheet," *Harvard Business Review*, March 2006, pp. 27–28; N. Guenster, Jeroen Derwall, R. Bauer, and K. Koedijk, "The Economic Value of Eco-Efficiency," *Academy of Management Conference*, August 2005; F. Bowen and S. Sharma, "Resourcing Corporate Environmental Strategy: Behavioral and Resource-Based Perspectives," *Academy of Management Conference*, August 2005; M. P. Sharfman, Teresa M. Shaft, and L. Tihanyi, "A Model of the Global and Institutional Antecedents of High-Level Corporate Environmental Performance," *Business & Society*, March 2004, pp. 6–36; S. L. Hart and M. B. Milstein, "Creating Sustainable Value," *Academy of Management Executive*, May 2003, pp. 56–67; K. Buysse and A. Verbeke, "Proactive Environmental Strategies: A Stakeholder Management Perspective" *Strategic Management Journal*, May 2003, pp. 453–470; C. Marsden, "The New Corporate Citizenship of Big Business: Part of the Solution to Sustainability?" *Business & Society Review*, Spring 2000, pp. 9–25; R. D. Klassen and D. C. Whybark, "The Impact of Environmental Technologies on Manufacturing Performance," *Academy of Management Journal*, December 1999, pp. 599–615; H. Bradbury and J. A. Clair, "Promoting Sustainable Organizations with Sweden's Natural Step," *Academy of Management Executive*, October 1999, pp. 63–73; F. L. Reinhardt, "Bringing the Environment Down to Earth," *Harvard Business Review*, July–August 1999, pp. 149–157; I. Henriques and P. Sadorsky, "The Relationship between Environmental Commitment and Managerial Perceptions of Stakeholder Importance," *Academy of Management Journal*, February 1999, pp. 87–99; and M. A. Berry and D. A. Rondinelli, "Proactive Corporate Environmental Management: A New Industrial Revolution," *Academy of Management Executive*, May 1998, pp. 38–50.

34 The concept of shades of green can be found in R. E. Freeman, J. Pierce, and R. Dodd, *Shades of Green: Business Ethics and the Environment* (New York: Oxford University Press, 1995).

35 See http://www.globalreporting.org/ReportingFramework/.

36 Information from ISO website, http://www.iso.org (accessed February 13, 2006).

37 Information from Global 100 website, www.global100.org (accessed July 11, 2007).

38 See http://www.syncrude.com/business/business_04.html#4b; http://sustainability.syncrude.ca/sustainability2006/social/aboriginalRelations/aboriginalRelations.html; and "Syncrude 2006 Aboriginal Review," http://www.syncrude.ca/aboreview/ (accessed July 12, 2007).

39 W. G. Bliss, "Why Is Corporate Culture Important?" *Workforce*, February 1999, pp. W8–W9; E. J. Giblin and L. E. Amuso, "Putting Meaning into Corporate Values," *Business Forum*, Winter 1997, pp. 14–18; R. Barrett, "Liberating the Corporate Soul," *HRfocus*, April 1997, pp. 15–16; K. Blanchard and M. O'Connor, *Managing by Values* (San Francisco: Berrett-Koehler Publishers, 1997); and G. P. Alexander, "Establishing Shared Values Through Management Training Programs," *Training & Development*, February 1987, pp. 45–47.

40 Based on Mary Lamey, "A Monument to the Environment: Focus on Recycling: Mountain Equipment Is Building First 'Green' Retail Outlet in Quebec," *Gazette* (Montreal), November 22, 2002, http://www.Canada.com/montreal.

41 W. G. Bliss, "Why Is Corporate Culture Important?" *Workforce*, February 1999, pp. W8–W9; E. J. Giblin and L. E. Amuso, "Putting Meaning into Corporate Values," *Business Forum*, Winter 1997, pp. 14–18; R. Barrett, "Liberating the Corporate Soul," *HRfocus*, April 1997, pp. 15–16; K. Blanchard and M. O'Connor, *Managing by Values* (San Francisco: Berrett-Koehler Publishers, 1997); G. P. Alexander, "Establishing Shared Values Through Management Training Programs," *Training & Development*, February 1987, pp. 45–47; J. L. Badaracco Jr. and R. R. Ellsworth, *Leadership and the Quest for Integrity* (Boston: Harvard Business School Press, 1989); and T. Chappell, *Managing Upside Down: The Seven Intentions of Values-Centered Leadership* (New York: William Morrow, 1999).

42 Information from Tom's of Maine website, http://www.tomsofmaine.com/about/statement.asp (accessed July 11, 2007).

43 R. Kamen, "Values: For Show or for Real?" *Working Woman*, August 1993, p. 10.

44 D. West, "Number 11 with a Bullet: Pacific Insight Cruises Down the Road of Success Powered by Employees," *Nelson Daily News*, December 14, 2006, p. 1.

45 See http://www.nrcan.gc.ca/mms/sociprac/syncrude_e.htm.

46 K. Davis and W. C. Frederick, *Business and Society: Management, Public Policy, Ethics*, 5th ed. (New York: McGraw-Hill, 1984), pp. 28–41, 76.

47 F. D. Sturdivant, *Business and Society: A Managerial Approach*, 3rd ed. (Homewood, IL: Richard D. Irwin, 1985), p. 128.

48 G. F. Cavanagh, D. J. Moberg, and M. Valasquez, "The Ethics of Organizational Politics," *Academy of Management Journal*, June 1981, pp. 363–374. See also F. N. Brady, "Rules for Making Exceptions to Rules," *Academy of Management Review*, July 1987, pp. 436–444, for an argument that the theory of justice is redundant with the prior two theories. See also T. Donaldson and T. W. Dunfee, "Toward a Unified Conception of Business Ethics: Integrative Social Contracts Theory," *Academy of Management Review*, April 1994, pp. 252–284;

M. Douglas, "Integrative Social Contracts Theory: Hype Over Hypernorms," *Journal of Business Ethics*, July 2000, pp. 101–110; and E. Soule, "Managerial Moral Strategies—In Search of a Few Good Principles," *Academy of Management Review*, January 2002, pp. 114–124, for discussions of integrative social contracts theory.

49 E. Soule, "Managerial Moral Strategies—In Search of a Few Good Principles," *Academy of Management Review*, January 2002, p. 117.

50 D. J. Fritzsche and H. Becker, "Linking Management Behavior to Ethical Philosophy—An Empirical Investigation," *Academy of Management Journal*, March 1984, pp. 166–175.

51 L. Kohlberg, *Essays in Moral Development: The Philosophy of Moral Development*, vol. 1 (New York: Harper & Row, 1981); L. Kohlberg, *Essays in Moral Development: The Psychology of Moral Development*, vol. 2 (New York: Harper & Row, 1984); J. W. Graham, "Leadership, Moral Development, and Citizenship Behavior," *Business Ethics Quarterly*, January 1995, pp. 43–54; and T. Kelley, "To Do Right or Just to Be Legal," *New York Times*, February 8, 1998, p. BU12.

52 See, for example, J. Weber, "Managers' Moral Reasoning: Assessing Their Responses to Three Moral Dilemmas," *Human Relations*, July 1990, pp. 687–702.

53 J. H. Barnett and M. J. Karson, "Personal Values and Business Decisions: An Exploratory Investigation," *Journal of Business Ethics*, July 1987, pp. 371–382; and W. C. Frederick and J. Weber, "The Value of Corporate Managers and Their Critics: An Empirical Description and Normative Implications," in *Business Ethics: Research Issues and Empirical Studies*, ed. W. C. Frederick and L. E. Preston (Greenwich, CT: JAI Press, 1990), pp. 123–144.

54 L. K. Trevino and S. A. Youngblood, "Bad Apples in Bad Barrels: A Causal Analysis of Ethical Decision-Making Behavior," *Journal of Applied Psychology*, August 1990, pp. 378–385; and M. E. Baehr, J. W. Jones, and A. J. Nerad, "Psychological Correlates of Business Ethics Orientation in Executives," *Journal of Business and Psychology*, Spring 1993, pp. 291–308.

55 R. L. Cardy and T. T. Selvarajan, "Assessing Ethical Behavior Revisited: The Impact of Outcomes on Judgment Bias" (paper presented at the Annual Meeting of the Academy of Management, Toronto, Ontario, 2000).

56 B. Z. Posner and W. H. Schmidt, "Values and the American Manager: An Update," *California Management Review*, Spring 1984, pp. 202–216; R. B. Morgan, "Self- and Co-Worker Perceptions of Ethics and Their Relationships to Leadership and Salary," *Academy of Management Journal*, February 1993, pp. 200–214; G. R. Weaver, L. K. Trevino, and P. L. Cochran, "Corporate Ethics Programs as Control Systems: Influences of Executive Commitment and Environmental Factors," *Academy of Management Journal*, February 1999, pp. 41–57; and G. R. Weaver, L. K. Trevino, and P. L. Cochran, "Integrated and Decoupled Corporate Social Performance: Management Commitments, External Pressures, and Corporate Ethics Practices," *Academy of Management Journal*, October 1999, pp. 539–552.

57 B. Victor and J. B. Cullen, "The Organizational Bases of Ethical Work Climates," *Administrative Science Quarterly*, March 1988, pp. 101–125; J. B. Cullen, B. Victor, and C. Stephens, "An Ethical Weather Report: Assessing the Organization's Ethical Climate," *Organizational Dynamics*, Autumn 1989, pp. 50–62; B. Victor and J. B. Cullen, "A Theory and Measure of Ethical Climate in Organizations," in *Business Ethics*, ed. W. Frederick and L. Preston, pp. 77–97 (Greenwich, CT: JAI Press, 1990); R. R. Sims, "The Challenge of Ethical Behavior in Organizations," *Journal of Business Ethics*, July 1992, pp. 505–513; and V. Arnold and J. C. Lampe, "Understanding the Factors Underlying Ethical Organizations: Enabling Continuous Ethical Improvement," *Journal of Applied Business Research*, Summer 1999, pp. 1–19.

58 T. M. Jones, "Ethical Decision Making by Individuals in Organizations: An Issue-Contingent Model," *Academy of Management Review*, April 1991, pp. 366–395; and T. Barnett, "Dimensions of Moral Intensity and Ethical Decision Making: An Empirical Study," *Journal of Applied Social Psychology*, May 2001, pp. 1038–1057.

59 T. M. Jones, "Ethical Decision Making by Individuals in Organizations: An Issue-Contingent Model," *Academy of Management Review*, April 1991, pp. 374–378.

60 M. McClearn, "African Adventure," *Canadian Business*, September 1, 2003.

61 "Corruption Still Tainting Asian Financial Picture, Study Says," *Vancouver Sun*, March 20, 2001, p. D18.

62 See http://www.transparency.ca/Readings/TI-C02.htm.

63 "Canadian Firms Ink New Ethics Code [for International Operations]," *Plant*, October 6, 1997, p. 4.

64 C. J. Robertson and W. F. Crittenden, "Mapping Moral Philosophies: Strategic Implications for Multinational Firms," *Strategic Management Journal*, April 2003, pp. 385–392.

65 Information from the Global Compact website, http://www.unglobalcompact.org (accessed July 11, 2007); J. Cohen, "Socially Responsible Business Goes Global," *In Business*, March–April 2000, p. 22; and C. M. Solomon, "Put Your Ethics to a Global Test," *Personnel Journal*, January 1996, pp. 66–74.

66 L. K. Trevino and S. A. Youngblood, "Bad Apples in Bad Barrels: A Causal Analysis of Ethical Decision-Making Behavior," *Journal of Applied Psychology*, August 1990, p. 384.

67 L. Bogomolny, "Good Housekeeping," *Canadian Business*, March 1, 2004, pp. 87–88.

68 See http://www.csa-acvm.ca/home.html.

69 W. Dabrowski, "Tighter Guidelines Issued on Disclosure: Canada's 'Sarbanes,'" *Financial Post (National Post)*, March 30, 2004, p. FP1.

70 "Global Ethics Codes Gain Importance as a Tool to Avoid Litigation and Fines," *Wall Street Journal*, August 19, 1999, p. A1; and J. Alexander, "On the Right Side," *World Business*, January–February 1997, pp. 38–41.

71 P. Richter, "Big Business Puts Ethics in Spotlight," *Los Angeles Times*, June 19, 1986, p. 29.

72 F. R. David, "An Empirical Study of Codes of Business Ethics: A Strategic Perspective" (paper presented at the 48th Annual Academy of Management Conference, Anaheim, California, August 1988).

73 "Ethics Programs Aren't Stemming Employee Misconduct," *Wall Street Journal*, May 11, 2000, p. A1.

74 L. Bogomolny, "Good Housekeeping," *Canadian Business*, March 1, 2004, pp. 87–88.

75 A. K. Reichert and M. S. Webb, "Corporate Support for Ethical and Environmental Policies: A Financial Management Perspective," *Journal of Business Ethics*, May 2000; G. R. Weaver, L. K. Trevino, and P. L. Cochran, "Corporate Ethics Programs as Control Systems: Influences of Executive Commitment and Environmental Factors," *Academy of Management Journal*, February 1999, pp. 41–57; G. R. Weaver, L. K. Trevino, and P. L. Cochran, "Integrated and

Decoupled Corporate Social Performance: Management Commitments, External Pressures, and Corporate Ethics Practices," *Academy of Management Journal*, October 1999, pp. 539–552; and B. Z. Posner and W. H. Schmidt, "Values and the American Manager: An Update," *California Management Review*, Spring 1984, pp. 202–216.

76 L. Nash, "Ethics Without the Sermon," *Harvard Business Review*, November–December 1981, p. 81.

77 J. B. Singh, "Ethics Programs in Canada's Largest Corporations," *Business and Society Review* 111, no. 2 (2006), pp. 119–136.

78 V. Wessler, "Integrity and Clogged Plumbing," *Straight to the Point*, newsletter of VisionPoint Corporation, Fall 2002, pp. 1–2.

79 J. B. Singh, "Ethics Programs in Canada's Largest Corporations," *Business and Society Review* 111, no. 2 (2006), pp. 119–136; and K. Doucet, "Canadian Organizations Not Meeting Ethics Expectations," *CMA Management* 74, no. 5 (2000), p. 10.

80 T. A. Gavin, "Ethics Education," *Internal Auditor*, April 1989, pp. 54–57.

81 L. Myyry and K. Helkama, "The Role of Value Priorities and Professional Ethics Training in Moral Sensitivity," *Journal of Moral Education* 31, no. 1 (2002), pp. 35–50; and W. Penn and B. D. Collier, "Current Research in Moral Development as a Decision Support System," *Journal of Business Ethics*, January 1985, pp. 131–136.

82 J. A. Byrne, "After Enron: The Ideal Corporation," *BusinessWeek*, August 19, 2002, pp. 68–71; D. Rice and C. Dreilinger, "Rights and Wrongs of Ethics Training," *Training & Development*, May 1990, pp. 103–109; and J. Weber, "Measuring the Impact of Teaching Ethics to Future Managers: A Review, Assessment, and Recommendations," *Journal of Business Ethics*, April 1990, pp. 182–190.

83 See, for instance, A. Wheat, "Keeping an Eye on Corporate America," *Fortune*, November 25, 2002, pp. 44–46; R. B. Schmitt, "Companies Add Ethics Training: Will It Work?" *Wall Street Journal*, November 4, 2002, p. B11; and P. F. Miller and W. T. Coady, "Teaching Work Ethics," *Education Digest*, February 1990, pp. 54–55.

84 The concept of shades of green can be found in R. E. Freeman, J. Pierce, and R. Dodd, *Shades of Green: Business Ethics and the Environment* (New York: Oxford University Press, 1995).

85 Adapted from A. Reichel and Y. Neumann, *Journal of Instructional Psychology*, March 1988, pp. 25–53. With permission of the authors.

86 Situation adapted from information in C. H. Deutsch, "Green Marketing: Label with a Cause," *New York Times*, June 15, 2003, sec. 3, p. 6; and B. Lloy, "Sierra Club Hits the Apparel Trail," *Daily News Record*, February 17, 2003, p. 104.

87 Based on J. Rupert, "Ottawa Probes City Hall Gift Complaint," *Ottawa Citizen*, June 10, 2007, http://www.canada.com/ottawacitizen/news/story.html?id=a8964f19-b94e-49d0-bf3c-32d78424358a (accessed September 25, 2007); "City's Auditor Investigates After Firm Gives Staff Gifts," *CBCnews.ca*, June 11, 2007, http://www.cbc.ca/canada/ottawa/story/2007/06/11/ticket-070611.html#skip300x250 (accessed September 25, 2007); and City of Ottawa, "The City's Employee Code of Conduct," March 2006, http://ottawa.ca/city_hall/policies/empl_codeconduct_en.html#P217_23046 (accessed September 25, 2007).

88 Situation adapted from information in J. O'Donnell, "CEO Left RadioShack with His Whole Life in Turmoil," *USA Today*, February 27, 2006, p. 3B; M. Morrison, "RadioShack's Lesson: Trust, But Verify," *BusinessWeek*, February 22, 2006, http://www.businessweek.com; B. Schlachter, "Few Surprised by Departure," *Fort Worth Star-Telegram*, February 21, 2006, p. C1; M. Schnurman, "How Did the Board, Roberts Miss Signs?" *Fort Worth Star-Telegram*, February 21,

2006, p. C1; F. Norris, "Radio Shack Chief Resigns After Lying," *New York Times*, February 21, 2006, http://www.nytimes.com; "RadioShack CEO Resigns in Resume Flap," *CNN Money*, February 21, 2006, http://www.cnnmoney.com; RadioShack, "RadioShack Corporation Board of Directors Accepts President and CEO Edmondson's Resignation," news release, February 20, 2006; F. Norris, "Under Fire, RadioShack Offers a Plan to Revamp," *New York Times*, February 18, 2006, http://www.nytimes.com; F. Norris, "At RadioShack, Some Questions (and Now, Answers)," *New York Times*, February 16, 2006, http://www.nytimes.com; and "Lies, Damn Lies, and Statistics," *Wired*, March 2004, p. 60.

89 Based on F. Bartolome, "Nobody Trusts the Boss Completely—Now What?" *Harvard Business Review*, March–April 1989, pp. 135–142; and J. K. Butler Jr., "Toward Understanding and Measuring Conditions of Trust: Evolution of a Condition of Trust Inventory," *Journal of Management*, September 1991, pp. 643–663.

Part 1 Continuing Case: Starbucks

1 Based on information from Starbucks website, http://www.starbucks.com; Hoover's Online, http://www.hoovers.com (accessed June 14, 2006); J. Simmons, *My Sister's a Barista: How They Made Starbucks a Home Away from Home* (London: Cyan Books, 2005); A. Serwer and K. Bonamici, "Hot Starbucks to Go," *Fortune*, January 26, 2004, pp. 60–74; S. Holmes, I. M. Kunii, J. Ewing, and K. Capell, "For Starbucks, There's No Place Like Home," *BusinessWeek*, June 9, 2003, p. 48; H. Schultz and D. Jones Yang, *Pour Your Heart into It; How Starbucks Built a Company One Cup at a Time* (New York: Hyperion, 1997); R. Gulati, S. Huffman, and G. Neilson, "The Barista Principle," *Strategy+Business*, Third Quarter 2002, pp. 58–69; J. Cummings, "Legislative Grind," *Wall Street Journal*, April 12, 2005, pp. A1+; B. Horovitz, "Starbucks Nation," *USA Today*, May 29, 2006, pp. A1+; J. Lawless, "Historian Studies Impact of Starbucks Globally," *Marketing News*, May 15, 2006, p. 44; K. M. Butler, "Examining the Benefits of Corporate Social Responsibility," *Employee Benefit News*, May 2006, p. 16; R. Tiplady, "Can Starbucks Blend into France?" *BusinessWeek*, April 21, 2006; A. Serwer, "Interview with Howard Schultz," *Fortune* (Europe), March 20, 2006, pp. 35–36; E. Barraclough, "Starbucks and Ferrero Celebrate China Victories," *Managing Intellectual Property*, February 2006, p. 12; K. Bonamici, S. Herman, and P. Jarvis, "Decoding the Dress Code," *Fortune*, January 23, 2006, pp. 130–131; A. Lustgarten, "A Hot, Steaming Cup of Customer Awareness," *Fortune*, November 15, 2004, p. 192; W. Meyers, "Conscience in a Cup of Coffee," *U.S. News & World Report*, October 31, 2005, pp. 48–50; M. Berglind and C. Nakata, "Cause-Related Marketing: More Buck Than Bang?" *Business Horizons*, September–October 2005, pp. 443–453; I. Mochari, "Coffee with Cream, Sugar, and Interest," *CFO*, September 2005, p. 23; C. Williamson, "Starbucks Calvert Support Fair Trade," *Pensions & Investments*, July 11, 2005, p. 8; T. Howard, "Starbucks Takes Up Cause for Safe Drinking Water," *USA Today*, August 3, 2005, p. 5B; P. Orsi, "Selling Charity in a Bottle," *Business 2.0*, October 2005, p. 38; P. L. Green, "US Firms Widen the Net," *Global Finance*, January 2006, pp. 28–29; http://www.starbucks.ca/en-ca/_About+Starbucks/Starbucks+in+Canada.htm (accessed September 28, 2007); http://www.starbucks.com/aboutus/Company_Factsheet.pdf; *Starbucks 2006 Annual Report*, http://investor.starbucks.com/phoenix.zhtml?c=99518&p=irol-IRHome (accessed September 28, 2007); and "Hero's Goodbye for McNaughton," *Province* (Vancouver), February 8, 2000, p. A4.

Chapter 5

1 Based on W. Stueck, "Builder of Toddler Shoe Empire Nudges Her Baby Out of the Nest," *Globe and Mail*, September 7, 2006, p. B1;

D. Drew, "She Turned a Crisis into a Success," *Cowichan Valley Citizen*, November 29, 2006, p. 12; and G. Shaw, "Robeez Shoes Sold for $30.5 Million," *Vancouver Sun*, September 7, 2006, p. C1.

2 I. Wylie, "Who Runs This Team Anyway?" *Fast Company*, April 2002, pp. 32–33.

3 D. A. Garvin and M. A. Roberto, "What You Don't Know about Making Decisions," *Harvard Business Review*, September 2001, pp. 108–116.

4 W. Pounds, "The Process of Problem Finding," *Industrial Management Review*, Fall 1969, pp. 1–19.

5 P. C. Nutt, *Why Decisions Fail: Avoiding the Blunders and Traps That Lead to Debacles* (San Francisco, CA: Berrett-Koehler Publishers, 2002).

6 W. Stueck, "Builder of Toddler Shoe Empire Nudges Her Baby Out of the Nest," *Globe and Mail*, September 7, 2006, p. B1; and Strategis, "Robeez Footwear, Better by Design," http://strategis.ic.gc.ca/epic/site/mfbs-gprea.nsf/en/lu00062e.html (accessed July 17, 2007).

7 T. A. Stewart, "Did You Ever Have to Make Up Your Mind?" *Harvard Business Review*, January 2006, p. 12; J. Pfeffer and R. I. Sutton, "Why Managing by Facts Works," *Strategy+Business*, Spring 2006, pp. 9–12; and E. Pooley, "Editor's Desk," *Fortune*, June 27, 2005, p. 16.

8 See H. A. Simon, "Rationality in Psychology and Economics," *Journal of Business*, October 1986, pp. 209–224; and A. Langley, "In Search of Rationality: The Purposes Behind the Use of Formal Analysis in Organizations," *Administrative Science Quarterly*, December 1989, pp. 598–631.

9 See, for example, J. G. March, *A Primer on Decision Making* (New York: Free Press, 1994), pp. 8–25; and A. Langley, H. Mintzberg, P. Pitcher, E. Posada, and J. Saint-Macary, "Opening Up Decision Making: The View from the Black Stool," *Organization Science*, May–June 1995, pp. 260–279.

10 See N. McK. Agnew and J. L. Brown, "Bounded Rationality: Fallible Decisions in Unbounded Decision Space," *Behavioral Science*, July 1986, pp. 148–161; B. E. Kaufman, "A New Theory of Satisficing," *Journal of Behavioral Economics*, Spring 1990, pp. 35–51; and D. R. A. Skidd, "Revisiting Bounded Rationality," *Journal of Management Inquiry*, December 1992, pp. 343–347.

11 W. Cole, "The Stapler Wars," *Time Inside Business*, April 2005, p. A5.

12 See K. R. Hammond, R. M. Hamm, J. Grassia, and T. Pearson, "Direct Comparison of the Efficacy of Intuitive and Analytical Cognition in Expert Judgment," in *IEEE Transactions on Systems, Man, and Cybernetics* SMC-17 no. 5 (1987): pp. 753–770; W. H. Agor, ed., *Intuition in Organizations* (Newbury Park, CA: Sage Publications, 1989); O. Behling and N. L. Eckel, "Making Sense Out of Intuition," *The Executive*, February 1991, pp. 46–47; L. A. Burke and M. K. Miller, "Taking the Mystery Out of Intuitive Decision Making," *Academy of Management Executive*, October 1999, pp. 91–99; A. L. Tesolin, "How to Develop the Habit of Intuition," *Training & Development*, March 2000, p. 76; and T. A. Stewart, "How to Think with Your Gut," *Business 2.0*, November 2002, pp. 98–104.

13 See M. H. Bazerman and D. Chugh, "Decisions without Blinders," *Harvard Business Review*, January 2006, pp. 88–97; C. C. Miller and R. D. Ireland, "Intuition in Strategic Decision Making: Friend or Foe in the Fast-Paced 21st Century," *Academy of Management Executive*, February 2005, pp. 19–30; E. Sadler-Smith and E. Shefy, "The Intuitive Executive: Understanding and Applying 'Gut Feel' in Decision-Making," *Academy of Management Executive*, November

2004, pp. 76–91; T. A. Stewart, "How to Think with Your Gut," *Business 2.0*, November 2002, pp. 98–104; A. L. Tesolin, "How to Develop the Habit of Intuition," *Training & Development*, March 2000, p. 76; L. A. Burke and M. K. Miller, "Taking the Mystery Out of Intuitive Decision Making," *Academy of Management Executive*, October 1999, pp. 91–99; O. Behling and N. L. Eckel, "Making Sense Out of Intuition," *The Executive*, February 1991, pp. 46–47; W. H. Agor, ed., *Intuition in Organizations* (Newbury Park, CA: Sage Publications, 1989); and K. R. Hammond, R. M. Hamm, J. Grassia, and T. Pearson, "Direct Comparison of the Efficacy of Intuitive and Analytical Cognition in Expert Judgment," *IEEE Transactions on Systems, Man, and Cybernetics* SMC-17, no. 5 (1987), pp. 753–770.

14 A. Dijksterhuis, M. W. Bos, L. F. Nordgren, R. B. van Baaren, "On Making the Right Choice: The Deliberation-without-Attention Effect," *Science* 311, no. 5763 (February 17, 2006), pp. 1005–1007.

15 S. Maich, "Promises, Promises but Tax Bill Grows," *Financial Post (National Post)*, June 1, 2004, p. FP1.

16 K. R. Brousseau, M. J. Driver, G. Hourihan, and R. Larsson, "The Seasoned Executive's Decision-Making Style," *Harvard Business Review*, February 2006, pp. 111–121.

17 M. Strauss, "Retailers Tap into War-Room Creativity of Employees," *Globe and Mail*, March 12, 2007, http://www.theglobeandmail.com.

18 A. J. Rowe and R. O. Mason, *Managing with Style* (San Francisco: Jossey-Bass, 1987); and A. J. Rowe, J. D. Boulgarides, and M. R. McGrath, *Managerial Decision Making, Modules in Management Series* (Chicago: SRA, 1984), pp. 18–22.

19 C. Shaffran, "Mind Your Meeting: How to Become the Catalyst for Culture Change," *Communication World*, February–March 2003, pp. 26–29.

20 I. L. Janis, *Victims of Groupthink* (Boston: Houghton Mifflin, 1972); R. J. Aldag and S. Riggs Fuller, "Beyond Fiasco: A Reappraisal of the Groupthink Phenomenon and a New Model of Group Decision Processes," *Psychological Bulletin,* May 1993, pp. 533–552; and T. Kameda and S. Sugimori, "Psychological Entrapment in Group Decision Making: An Assigned Decision Rule and a Groupthink Phenomenon," *Journal of Personality and Social Psychology*, August 1993, pp. 282–292.

21 I. L. Janis, *Victims of Groupthink* (Boston: Houghton Mifflin, 1972); R. J. Aldag and S. Riggs Fuller, "Beyond Fiasco: A Reappraisal of the Groupthink Phenomenon and a New Model of Group Decision Processes," *Psychological Bulletin,* May 1993, pp. 533–552; and T. Kameda and S. Sugimori, "Psychological Entrapment in Group Decision Making: An Assigned Decision Rule and a Groupthink Phenomenon," *Journal of Personality and Social Psychology*, August 1993, pp. 282–292.

22 D. D. Henningsen, M. L. M. Henningsen, J. Eden, and M. G.Cruz, "Examining the Symptoms of Groupthink and Retrospective Sensemaking," *Small Group Research* 37, no. 1 (2006), pp. 36–64; and R. S. Baron, "So Right It's Wrong: Groupthink and the Ubiquitous Nature of Polarized Group Decision Making," *Advances in Experimental Social Psychology* 37, 2005, pp. 219–253.

23 Based on J. Brockner, *Self Esteem at Work* (Lexington, MA: Lexington Books, 1988), chapters 1–4.

24 See, for example, L. K. Michaelson, W. E. Watson, and R. H. Black, "A Realistic Test of Individual vs. Group Consensus Decision Making," *Journal of Applied Psychology* 74, no. 5 (1989), pp. 834–839; R. A. Henry, "Group Judgment Accuracy: Reliability and Validity of Post-discussion Confidence Judgments," *Organizational Behavior and Human Decision Processes*, October 1993, pp. 11–27; P. W. Paese, M. Bieser, and M. E. Tubbs, "Framing Effects and Choice Shifts in

Group Decision Making," *Organizational Behavior and Human Decision Processes*, October 1993, pp. 149–165; N. J. Castellan Jr., ed., *Individual and Group Decision Making* (Hillsdale, NJ: Lawrence Erlbaum Associates, 1993); and S. G. Straus and J. E. McGrath, "Does the Medium Matter? The Interaction of Task Type and Technology on Group Performance and Member Reactions," *Journal of Applied Psychology*, February 1994, pp. 87–97.

25 E. J. Thomas and C. F. Fink, "Effects of Group Size," *Psychological Bulletin*, July 1963, pp. 371–384; F. A. Shull, A. L. Delbecq, and L. L. Cummings, *Organizational Decision Making* (New York: McGraw-Hill, 1970), p. 151; A. P. Hare, *Handbook of Small Group Research* (New York: Free Press, 1976); M. E. Shaw, *Group Dynamics: The Psychology of Small Group Behavior*, 3rd ed. (New York: McGraw-Hill, 1981); and P. Yetton and P. Bottger, "The Relationships among Group Size, Member Ability, Social Decision Schemes, and Performance," *Organizational Behavior and Human Performance*, October 1983, pp. 145–159.

26 D. Kahneman and A. Tversky, "Judgment under Uncertainty: Heuristics and Biases," *Science* 185 (1974), pp. 1124–1131.

27 Information for this section is taken from S. P. Robbins, *Decide & Conquer* (Upper Saddle River, NJ: Financial Times/Prentice Hall, 2004).

28 See, for example, B. M. Staw, "The Escalation of Commitment to a Course of Action," *Academy of Management Review*, October 1981, pp. 577–587; D. R. Bobocel and J. P. Meyer, "Escalating Commitment to a Failing Course of Action: Separating the Roles of Choice and Justification," *Journal of Applied Psychology*, June 1994, pp. 360–363; C. F. Camerer and R. A. Weber, "The Econometrics and Behavioral Economics of Escalation of Commitment: A Re-examination of Staw's Theory," *Journal of Economic Behavior and Organization*, May 1999, pp. 59–82; V. S. Rao and A. Monk, "The Effects of Individual Differences and Anonymity on Commitment to Decisions," *Journal of Social Psychology*, August 1999, pp. 496–515; and G. McNamara, H. Moon, and P. Bromiley, "Banking on Commitment: Intended and Unintended Consequences of an Organization's Attempt to Attenuate Escalation of Commitment," *Academy of Management Journal*, April 2002, pp. 443–452.

29 Based on W. McLellan, "Soled!: Born in a Basement, Robeez Matured into a Firm Worth $30.5M," *Province* (Vancouver), September 7, 2006, p. A29.

30 "Hurry Up and Decide!" *BusinessWeek*, May 14, 2001, p. 16.

31 J. Klayman, R. P. Larrick, and C. Heath, "Organizational Repairs," *Across the Board*, February 2000, pp. 26–31.

32 J. S. Hammond, R. L. Keeney, and H. Raiffa, *Smart Choices: A Practical Guide to Making Better Decisions* (Boston: Harvard Business School Press, 1999), p. 4.

33 This discussion is based on K. H. Hammonds, "5 Habits of Highly Reliable Organizations: An Interview with Karl Weick," *Fast Company*, May 2002, pp. 124–128.

34 Adapted from W. H. Agor, *AIM Survey* (El Paso, TX: ENP Enterprises, 1989), Part I. With permission.

35 Source unknown.

36 Situation adapted from information in N. Weinberg, "Holier Than Whom?" *Forbes*, June 23, 2003, p. 711; and E. Baum, "Schwab Campaign Bundles Controversy, Consistency," *Fund Marketing Alert*, March 10, 2003, p. 10.

37 Information from C. F. Martin's website, http://www.mguitar.com (accessed April 24, 2003 and July 18, 2007); D. Lieberman, "Guitar Sales Jam Despite Music Woes," *USA Today*, December 16, 2002, p. 2B; and S. Fitch, "Stringing Them Along," *Forbes*, July 26, 1999, pp. 90–91.

38 Based on A. Deslongchamps, "'Hard' to Raise Wages at Air Canada, ACE's Milton Warns," *National Post*, March 30, 2006, p. FP4; and "ACE Aviation to Pay Shareholders $266M in Aeroplan Units," *National Post*, February 17, 2006, p. FP6.

39 Based on J. Calano and J. Salzman, "Ten Ways to Fire Up Your Creativity," *Working Woman*, July 1989, p. 94; J. V. Anderson, "Mind Mapping: A Tool for Creative Thinking," *Business Horizons*, January–February 1993, pp. 42–46; M. Loeb, "Ten Commandments for Managing Creative People," *Fortune*, January 16, 1995, pp. 135–136; and M. Henricks, "Good Thinking," *Entrepreneur*, May 1996, pp. 70–73.

40 Information for this box comes from B. C. McDonald and D. Hutcheson, "Dealing with Diversity Is Key to Tapping Talent," *Atlanta Business Chronicle*, December 18, 1998, p. 45A1; P. M. Elsass and L. M. Graves, "Demographic Diversity in Decision-Making Groups: The Experience of Women and People of Color," *Academy of Management Review*, October 1997, pp. 946–973; and N. J. Adler, ed., *International Dimensions of Organizational Behavior*, 4th ed. (Cincinnati: South-Western College Publishing, 2001).

41 Information for this box comes from S. Caudron, "Some New Rules for the New World of Work," *Business Finance*, October 2001, p. 24; C. Kanchier, *Dare to Change Your Job and Your Life*, 2nd ed. (Indianapolis, IN: Jist Publishing, 2000); and S. Hagevik, "Responsible Risk Taking," *Journal of Environmental Health*, November 1999, p. 291.

Chapter 6

1 Based on R. Ouzounian, "Down the Tube," *Toronto Star*, January 7, 2007, p. C6; S. Sperounes, "A Sensation Rises from Out of the Blue," *Edmonton Journal*, September 30, 2003, p. C1; "Masters of Splatter May Turn Your Mood Indigo," *People Weekly*, June 8, 1992, pp. 108–110; and Blue Man Group website, http://www.blueman.com (accessed July 20, 2007).

2 V. Pilieci, "The Lost Generation of Business Talent," *Vancouver Sun*, May 2, 2001, pp. D1, D9.

3 See, for example, D. K. Sinha, "The Contribution of Formal Planning to Decisions," *Strategic Management Journal*, October 1990, pp. 479–492; N. Capon, J. U. Farley, and J. M. Hulbert, "Strategic Planning and Financial Performance: More Evidence," *Journal of Management Studies*, January 1994, pp. 22–38; C. C. Miller and L. B. Cardinal, "Strategic Planning and Firm Performance: A Synthesis of More Than Two Decades of Research," *Academy* of Management Journal, March 1994, pp. 1649–1685; P. J. Brews and M. R. Hunt, "Learning to Plan and Planning to Learn: Resolving the Planning School/Learning School Debate," *Strategic Management Journal*, December 1999, pp. 889–913; R. Wiltbank, N. Dew, S. Read, and S. D. Sarasvathy, "What to Do Next? The Case For Non-Predictive Strategy," *Strategic Management Journal* 27, no. 10 (October 2006), pp. 981–998; and EN.CITE.

4 S. Sperounes, "A Sensation Rises from Out of the Blue," *Edmonton Journal*, September 30, 2003, p. C1; K. Powers, "Blue Coup," *Forbes*, March 19, 2001, p. 136; and S. Hampson, "Blue Cogs in a Corporate Wheel," *Globe and Mail*, July 12, 2003, p. R3.

5 R. Molz, "How Leaders Use Goals," *Long Range Planning*, October 1987, p. 91.

6 P. N. Romani, "MBO by Any Other Name Is Still MBO," *Supervision*, December 1997, pp. 6–8; and A. W. Schrader and G. T. Seward, "MBO Makes Dollar Sense," *Personnel Journal*, July 1989, pp. 32–37.

7 P. N. Romani, "MBO by Any Other Name Is Still MBO," *Supervision*, December 1997, pp. 6–8; and R. Rodgers and J. E. Hunter, "Impact of Management by Objectives on Organizational Productivity," *Journal of Applied Psychology*, April 1991, pp. 322–336.

8 For additional information on goals, see, for instance, P. Drucker, *The Executive in Action* (New York: HarperCollins Books, 1996), pp. 207–214; and E. A. Locke and G. P. Latham, *A Theory of Goal Setting and Task Performance* (Upper Saddle River, NJ: Prentice Hall, 1990).

9 Based on J. McElgunn, "Staying on a Kicking Horse," PROFIT, November 2006.

10 J. D. Hunger and T. L. Wheelen, *Strategic Management and Business Policy*, 10th ed. (Upper Saddle River, NJ: Prentice Hall, 2006).

11 Several of these factors were suggested by J. S. Armstrong, "The Value of Formal Planning for Strategic Decisions: Review of Empirical Research," *Strategic Management Journal*, July–September 1982, pp. 197–211; and R. K. Bresser and R. C. Bishop, "Dysfunctional Effects of Formal Planning: Two Theoretical Explanations," *Academy of Management Review*, October 1983, pp. 588–599.

12 P. J. Brews and M. R. Hunt, "Learning to Plan and Planning to Learn: Resolving the Planning School/Learning School Debate," *Strategic Management Journal*, December 1999, pp. 889–913.

13 P. J. Brews and M. R. Hunt, "Learning to Plan and Planning to Learn: Resolving the Planning School/Learning School Debate," *Strategic Management Journal*, December 1999, pp. 889–913.

14 A. Campbell, "Tailored, Not Benchmarked: A Fresh Look at Corporate Planning," *Harvard Business Review*, March–April 1999, pp. 41–50.

15 J. H. Sheridan, "Focused on Flow," *IndustryWeek*, October 18, 1999, pp. 46–51.

16 J. K. Nestruck, "Blue Man Scoop: Founding Members Reveal How It All Began," *National Post*, June 8, 2005, p. AL1; S. Sperounes, " A Sensation Rises from Out of the Blue," *Edmonton Journal*, September 30, 2003, p. C1; K. Powers, "Blue Coup," *Forbes*, March 19, 2001, p. 136; and S. Hampson, "Blue Cogs in a Corporate Wheel," *Globe and Mail*, July 12, 2003, p. R3.

17 H. Mintzberg, *The Rise and Fall of Strategic Planning* (New York: Free Press, 1994).

18 H. Mintzberg, *The Rise and Fall of Strategic Planning* (New York: Free Press, 1994).

19 H. Mintzberg, *The Rise and Fall of Strategic Planning* (New York: Free Press, 1994).

20 G. Hamel and C. K. Prahalad, *Competing for the Future* (Boston: Harvard Business School Press, 1994).

21 D. Miller, "The Architecture of Simplicity," *Academy of Management Review*, January 1993, pp. 116–138.

22 M. C. Mankins and R. Steele, "Stop Making Plans—Start Making Decisions," *Harvard Business Review*, January 2006, pp. 76–84; L. Bossidy and R. Charan, *Execution: The Discipline of Getting Things Done* (New York: Crown/Random House, 2002); and P. Roberts, "The Art of Getting Things Done," *Fast Company*, June 2000, p. 162.

23 Associated Press, "Dow Jones to Shrink 'Wall Street Journal,' Cut Some Data," *USA Today*, October 12, 2005, http://www.usatoday.com.

24 P. J. Brews and M. R. Hunt, "Learning to Plan and Planning to Learn: Resolving the Planning School/Learning School Debate," *Strategic Management Journal*, December 1999, pp. 889–913.

25 Information on Wipro Limited from Hoover's Online, http://www.hoovers.com, (accessed March 21, 2006); R. J. Newman, "Coming and Going," *U.S. News & World Report*, January 23, 2006, pp. 50–52; T. Atlas, "Bangalore's Big Dreams," *U.S. News & World Report*, May 2, 2005, pp. 50–52; and K. H. Hammonds, "Smart, Determined, Ambitious, Cheap: The New Face of Global Competition," *Fast Company*, February 2003, pp. 90–97.

26 Adapted from N. T. Feather, "Attitudes toward the High Achiever: The Fall of the Tall Poppy," *Australian Journal of Psychology* 41 (1989), pp. 239–267.

27 Situation adapted from information in S. Leith, "Coke Faces Damage Control," *Atlanta Journal-Constitution*, June 19, 2003, p. C1; C. Terhume, "Coke Employees Acted Improperly in Marketing Test," *Wall Street Journal*, June 18, 2003, pp. A3, A6; and T. Howard, "Burger King, Coke May Face Off in Frozen Coke Suit," *USA Today*, June 6, 2003, http://www.usatoday.com/money/industries/food/ _2003-06-04.bk_x.htm.

28 Based on information on Lend Lease from Hoover's Online, http://www.hoovers.com (accessed November 8, 2004); Lend Lease website, http://www.lendlease.com (accessed November 8, 2004 and July 20, 2007); P. LaBarre, "A Company without Limits," *Fast Company*, September 1999, pp. 160–186; "Lend Lease Building on Its Success," *Business Asia*, March 15, 1999, p. 11; and http://www.lendlease.com/llweb/bll/main.nsf/images/pdf_2005_annualreport. pdf/$file/pdf_2005_annualreport.pdf.

29 Based on "Corporate Canada Preparing for Influenza Pandemic," *Canadian Press*, January 22, 2006; M. Siegel, "Is Yesterday's Swine Flu Today's Bird Flu?" *USA Today*, March 22, 2006, p. 13A; M. Warner, "Preparing for the Avian Flu Threat in the U.S.," *New York Times*, March 21, 2006, http://www.nytimes.com; E. Rosenthal and K. Bradsher, "Is Business Ready for a Flu Pandemic?" *New York Times*, March 16, 2006, http://www.nytimes.com; Deloitte Center for Health Solutions, "Business Preparations for Pandemic Flu," *Deloitte*, December 2005, http://www.deloitte.com/dtt/cda/doc/content/ PandemicFluSurvey%282%29.pdf (accessed July 20, 2007); and J. Carey, "Avian Flu: Business Thinks the Unthinkable," *BusinessWeek*, November 28, 2005, pp. 36–39.

30 Based on S. P. Robbins and D. A. DeCenzo, *Fundamentals of Management*, 4th ed. (Upper Saddle River, NJ: Prentice Hall, 2004), p. 85.

Chapter 7

1 Based on H. Shaw, "Indigo Pens Next Chapter," *Financial Post (National Post)*, June 22, 2007, http://www.canada.com/national post/financialpost/story.html?id=d1bc522d-712c-42f4-b2e4- fe71c0c5d0ba&k=68292 (accessed July 27, 2007); Indigo Books & Music website, http://www.chapters.indigo.ca (accessed July 27, 2007); and http://strategis.ic.gc.ca/epic/internet/incb-bc.nsf/en/ _ct02171e.html.

2 See http://www.hll.com/mediacentre/annualreport2006.pdf.

3 J. W. Dean Jr. and M. P. Sharfman, "Does Decision Process Matter? A Study of Strategic Decision-Making Effectiveness," *Academy of Management Journal*, April 1996, pp. 368–396.

4 Based on A. A. Thompson Jr., A. J. Strickland III, and J. E. Gamble, *Crafting and Executing Strategy*, 14th ed. (New York: McGraw-Hill Irwin, 2005).

5 J. Magretta, "Why Business Models Matter," *Harvard Business Review*, May 2002, pp. 86–92.

6 E. H. Bowman and C. E. Helfat, "Does Corporate Strategy Matter?" *Strategic Management Journal* 22 (2001), pp. 1–23; P. J. Brews and M. R. Hunt, "Learning to Plan and Planning to Learn: Resolving the Planning School–Learning School Debate," *Strategic Management Journal* 20 (1999), pp. 889–913; D. J. Ketchen Jr., J. B. Thomas, and R. R. McDaniel Jr., "Process, Content and Context; Synergistic Effects on Performance," *Journal* of Management 22, no. 2 (1996), pp. 231–257; C. C. Miller and L. B. Cardinal, "Strategic Planning and Firm Performance: A Synthesis of More Than Two Decades of Research," *Academy of Management Journal*, December 1994, pp. 1649–1665; and N. Capon, J. U. Farley, and J. M. Hulbert, "Strategic Planning and Financial Performance: More Evidence," *Journal of Management Studies*, January 1994, pp. 105–110.

7 "A Solid Strategy Helps Companies' Growth," *Nation's Business*, October 1990, p. 10.

8 See, for example, H. Mintzberg, *The Rise and Fall of Strategic Planning* (New York: Free Press, 1994); S. J. Wall and S. R. Wall, "The Evolution (Not the Death) of Strategy," *Organizational Dynamics*, Autumn 1995, pp. 7–19; J. A. Byrne, "Strategic Planning: It's Back!" *BusinessWeek*, August 26, 1996, pp. 46–52; and R. M. Grant, "Strategic Planning in a Turbulent Environment: Evidence from the Oil Majors," *Strategic Management Journal* 24, no. 6 (June 2003), pp. 491–517.

9 Based on information obtained from http://www.city.vancouver.bc.ca/commsvcs/socialplanning/_grants/PODGrants.htm; and http://www.centreforsustainability.ca/programs/ (accessed July 23, 2007).

10 Based on H. Shaw, "Indigo Pens Next Chapter," *Financial Post (National Post)*, June 22, 2007, http://www.canada.com/nationalpost/financialpost/story.html?id=d1bc522d-712c-42f4-b2e4-fe71c0c5d0ba&k=68292 (accessed July 27, 2007).

11 "About Our Company," *Indigo Books & Music*, http://www.chapters.indigo.ca/About-Indigo-Books-Music-Inc/chaptersinc-art.html (accessed July 23, 2007).

12 "About Us," *WorkSafeBC*, http://www.worksafebc.com/about_us/default.asp (accessed July 23, 2007).

13 "Company Overview," *eBay*, http://pages.ebay.ca/aboutebay/thecompany/companyoverview.html (accessed July 23, 2007).

14 See http://www.worksafebc.com/about_us/our_mandate/ (accessed September 26, 2007).

15 C. K. Prahalad and G. Hamel, "The Core Competence of the Corporation," *Harvard Business Review*, May–June 1990, pp. 79–91.

16 A. Taylor, "How Toyota Does It," *Fortune*, March 6, 2006, pp. 107–124; C. Woodyard, "Slow and Steady Drives Toyota's Growth," *USA Today*, December 21, 2005, pp. 1B+; I. M. Kunii, C. Dawson, and C. Palmeri, "Toyota Is Way Ahead of the Hybrid Pack," *BusinessWeek*, May 5, 2003, p. 48; and S. Spear and H. K. Bowen, "Decoding the DNA of the Toyota Production System," *Harvard Business Review*, September–October 1999, pp. 96–106.

17 See, for example, H. J. Cho and V. Pucik, "Relationship between Innovativeness, Quality, Growth, Profitability, and Market Value," *Strategic Management Journal* 26, no. 6 (2005), pp. 555–575; W. F. Joyce, "Building the 4+2 Organization," *Organizational Dynamics*, May 2005, pp. 118–129; R. S. Kaplan and D. P. Norton, "Measuring the Strategic Readiness of Intangible Assets," *Harvard Business Review*, February 2004, pp. 52–63; C. M. Fiol, "Managing Culture as a Competitive Resource: An Identity-Based View of Sustainable Competitive Advantage," *Journal of Management*, March

1991, pp. 191–211; T. Kono, "Corporate Culture and Long-Range Planning," *Long Range Planning*, August 1990, pp. 9–19; S. Green, "Understanding Corporate Culture and Its Relation to Strategy," *International Studies of Management and Organization*, Summer 1988, pp. 6–28; C. Scholz, "Corporate Culture and Strategy—The Problem of Strategic Fit," *Long Range Planning*, August 1987, pp. 78–87; and J. B. Barney, "Organizational Culture: Can It Be a Source of Sustained Competitive Advantage?" *Academy of Management Review*, July 1986, pp. 656–665.

18 J. P. Kotter and J. L. Heskett, *Corporate Culture and Performance* (New York: Free Press, 1992).

19 K. E. Klein, "Slogans That Are the Real Thing," *BusinessWeek*, August 4, 2005, http://www.businessweek.com/smallbiz/content/aug2005/sb20050804_867552.htm (accessed July 27, 2007); and T. Mucha, "The Payoff for Trying Harder," *Business 2.0*, July 2002, pp. 84–85.

20 A. Carmeli and A. Tischler, "The Relationships between Intangible Organizational Elements and Organizational Performance," *Strategic Management Journal* 25 (2004), pp. 1257–1278; P. W. Roberts and G. R. Dowling, "Corporate Reputation and Sustained Financial Performance," *Strategic Management Journal*, December 2002, pp. 1077–1093; and C. J. Fombrun, "Corporate Reputations as Economic Assets," in *Handbook of Strategic Management*, ed. M. A. Hitt, R. E. Freeman, and J. S. Harrison (Malden, MA: Blackwell Publishers, 2001), pp. 289–312.

21 Harris Interactive, "Johnson & Johnson Ranks No. 1 in National Corporate Reputation Survey for Seventh Consecutive Year," news release, December 7, 2005.

22 Based on G. Pitts, "Tide Turns for P&G Canada President," *Globe and Mail*, October 14, 2002, p. B3; and S. Heinrich, "P&G Still the Best Step Up," *National Post*, April 14, 2003, p. FP4; and http://www.pg.com/en_CA/index.jhtml (accessed July 23, 2007).

23 Based on Concentra Financial, "Concentra Financial—A 50 Best Managed Company, Again," news release, February 8, 2007; "Co-operative Trust Company of Canada," *Encyclopedia of Saskatchewan*, http://esask.uregina.ca/entry/co-operative_trust_company_of_canada.html (accessed July 24, 2007); A. Lopez-Pacheco, "Best Practices Grounded in Frontline Workers," *National Post*, January 12, 2004, p. SR03; and http://www.concentrafinancial.ca/forms/800-801.pdf (accessed September 26, 2007).

24 Based on H. Shaw, "Indigo Pens Next Chapter," *Financial Post (National Post)*, June 22, 2007, http://www.canada.com/nationalpost/financialpost/story.html?id=d1bc522d-712c-42f4-b2e4-fe71c0c5d0ba&k=68292 (accessed July 27, 2007); and Indigo Books & Music website, http://www.chapters.indigo.ca.

25 "Wal-Mart Announces Fiscal 2008 Growth Plans," *Wal-Mart Facts*, October 23, 2006, http://www.walmartfacts.com/articles/4549.aspx (accessed July 24, 2007).

26 See http://advisor.investopedia.com/news/06/Time_To_Double_Double_Down_On_Tim_Hortons.aspx (accessed September 26, 2007).

27 See http://www.prnewswire.co.uk/cgi/news/release?id=169402; and http://www.accor.com/gb/groupe/activites/autres/frantour_ag.asp.

28 G. Pitts, "Small Is Beautiful, Conglomerates Signal," *Globe and Mail*, April 1, 2002, pp. B1, B4; Brookfield Asset Management website, http://www.brookfield.com (accessed July 24, 2007); and *Brookfield Asset Management 2006 Annual Report*, http://www.brookfield.com/investorcenter/financialreports/annualreports/

resources/2006/2006%20Annual%20Report.pdf (accessed July 24, 2007).

29 V. Ramanujam and P. Varadarajan, "Research on Corporate Diversification: A Synthesis," *Strategic Management Journal* 10 (1989), pp. 523–551. Also see A. Shleifer and R. W. Vishny, "Takeovers in the 1960s and 1980s: Evidence and Implications," in *Fundamental Issues in Strategy*, ed. R. P. Rumelt, D. E. Schendel, and D. J. Teece (Boston: Harvard Business School Press, 1994).

30 G. Bellett, "Sears Getting Out of Automotive Business," *Vancouver Sun*, March 31, 2004, p. D5.

31 J. A. Pearce, II, "Retrenchment Remains the Foundation of Business Turnaround," *Strategic Management Journal* 15 (1994), pp. 407–417.

32 See http://www.nasrecruitment.com/TalentTips/NASinsights/CANLayoff02_07.pdf (accessed September 26, 2007).

33 *GM 2006 Annual Report*, http://www.gm.com/company/investor_information/docs/fin_data/gm05ar/download/gm05ar.pdf (accessed July 25, 2007).

34 *Kodak 2005 Annual Report*, http://library.corporate-ir.net/library/11/115/115911/items/189563/annualReport05.pdf (accessed July 25, 2007).

35 "GM to Offer Early Retirement to About 113,000 U.S. Workers," *CBCnews.ca*, March 22, 2006, http://www.cbc.ca/money/story/2006/03/22/gmretirement-060322.html (accessed July 25, 2007).

36 H. Quarls, T. Pernsteiner, and K. Rangan, "Love Your Dogs," *Strategy+Business*, Spring 2006, pp. 58–65; and P. Haspeslagh, "Portfolio Planning: Uses and Limits," *Harvard Business Review*, January–February 1982, pp. 58–73.

37 Boston Consulting Group, *Perspective on Experience* (Boston: Boston Consulting Group, 1970).

38 R. Rumelt, "Towards a Strategic Theory of the Firm," in *Competitive Strategic Management*, ed. R. Lamb (Upper Saddle River, NJ: Prentice Hall, 1984), pp. 556–570; M. E. Porter, *Competitive Advantage: Creating and Sustaining Superior Performance* (New York: Free Press, 1985); J. Barney, "Firm Resources and Sustained Competitive Advantage," *Journal of Management* 17, no. 1 (1991), pp. 99–120; M. A. Peteraf, "The Cornerstones of Competitive Advantage: A Resource-Based View," *Strategic Management Journal*, March 1993, pp. 179–191; and J. B. Barney, "Looking Inside for Competitive Advantage," *Academy of Management Executive*, November 1995, pp. 49–61.

39 T. C. Powell, "Total Quality Management as Competitive Advantage: A Review and Empirical Study," *Strategic Management Journal*, January 1995, pp. 15–37.

40 See R. J. Schonenberger, "Is Strategy Strategic? Impact of Total Quality Management on Strategy," *Academy of Management Executive*, August 1992, pp. 80–87; C. A. Barclay, "Quality Strategy and TQM Policies: Empirical Evidence," *Management International Review*, Special Issue (1993), pp. 87–98; T. E. Benson, "A Business Strategy Comes of Age," *IndustryWeek*, May 3, 1993, pp. 40–44; R. Jacob, "TQM: More Than a Dying Fad?" *Fortune*, October 18, 1993, pp. 66–72; R. Krishnan, A. B. Shani, R. M. Grant, and R. Baer, "In Search of Quality Improvement Problems of Design and Implementation," *Academy of Management Executive*, November 1993, pp. 7–20; B. Voss, "Quality's Second Coming," *Journal of Business Strategy*, March–April 1994, pp. 42–46; M. Barrier, "Raising TQM Consciousness," *Nation's Business*, April 1994, pp. 62–64; and special issue of *Academy of Management Review* devoted to TQM, July 1994, pp. 390–584.

41 See, for example, M. E. Porter, *Competitive Strategy: Techniques for Analyzing Industries and Competitors* (New York: Free Press, 1980); M. E. Porter, *Competitive Advantage: Creating and Sustaining Superior Performance* (New York: Free Press, 1985); G. G. Dess and P. S. Davis, "Porter's (1980) Generic Strategies as Determinants of Strategic Group Membership and Organizational Performance," *Academy of Management Journal*, September 1984, pp. 467–488; G. G. Dess and P. S. Davis, "Porter's (1980) Generic Strategies and Performance: An Empirical Examination with American Data—Part I: Testing Porter," *Organization Studies*, no. 1 (1986), pp. 37–55; G. G. Dess and P. S. Davis, "Porter's (1980) Generic Strategies and Performance: An Empirical Examination with American Data—Part II: Performance Implications," *Organization Studies*, no. 3 (1986), pp. 255–261; M. E. Porter, "From Competitive Advantage to Corporate Strategy," *Harvard Business Review*, May–June 1987, pp. 43–59; A. I. Murray, "A Contingency View of Porter's 'Generic Strategies,'" *Academy of Management Review*, July 1988, pp. 390–400; C. W. L. Hill, "Differentiation versus Low Cost or Differentiation and Low Cost: A Contingency Framework," *Academy of Management Review*, July 1988, pp. 401–412; I. Bamberger, "Developing Competitive Advantage in Small and Medium-Sized Firms," *Long Range Planning*, October 1989, pp. 80–88; D. F. Jennings and J. R. Lumpkin, "Insights between Environmental Scanning Activities and Porter's Generic Strategies: An Empirical Analysis," *Strategic Management Journal* 18, no. 4 (1992), pp. 791–803; N. Argyres and A. M. McGahan, "An Interview with Michael Porter," *Academy of Management Executive*, May 2002, pp. 43–52; and A. Brandenburger, "Porter's Added Value: High Indeed!" *Academy of Management Executive*, May 2002, pp. 58–60.

42 G. Pitts, "Ganong Boss Aims for Sweet Spot," *Globe and Mail*, March 3, 2003, p. B4.

43 Based on W. Hanley, "Mowat's Lefty Ways Pay Big Dividends," *National Post*, February 28, 2004, p. IN01.

44 See http://www.peicreditunions.com/news/article.php?ID=594 (accessed September 26, 2007).

45 D. Miller and J. Toulouse, "Strategy, Structure, CEO Personality, and Performance in Small Firms," *American Journal of Small Business*, Winter 1986, pp. 47–62.

46 *Bang & Olufsen 2005–2006 Annual Report*, http://www.bang-olufsen.com/graphics/bogo/reports/annualreport_2005-06_uk.pdf (accessed July 25, 2007).

47 C. W. L. Hill, "Differentiation versus Low Cost or Differentiation and Low Cost: A Contingency Framework," *Academy of Management Review*, July 1988, pp. 401–412; R. E. White, "Organizing to Make Business Unit Strategies Work," in *Handbook of Business Strategy*, 2nd ed., ed. H. E. Glass (Boston: Warren Gorham and Lamont, 1991), pp. 24.1–24.14; D. Miller, "The Generic Strategy Trap," *Journal of Business Strategy*, January–February 1991, pp. 37–41; S. Cappel, P. Wright, M. Kroll, and D. Wyld, "Competitive Strategies and Business Performance: An Empirical Study of Select Service Businesses," *International Journal of Management*, March 1992, pp. 1–11; and J. W. Bachmann, "Competitive Strategy: It's O.K. to Be Different," *Academy of Management Executive*, May 2002, pp. 61–65.

48 Based on H. Shaw, "Indigo Pens Next Chapter, *Financial Post (National Post)*, June 22, 2007, http://www.canada.com/nationalpost/financialpost/story.html?id=d1bc522d-712c-42f4-b2e4-fe71c0c5d0ba&k=68292 (accessed July 27, 2007).

49 See http://www.ifpi.org/site-content/statistics/worldsales.html; and G. Masson, "Music Sales Continue to Fall," *Variety*, July 4, 2007, http://www.variety.com/article/VR1117968039.html?categoryid=19&cs=1 (accessed July 25, 2007).

50 E. Gunderson, "Ringtone Sales Ring Up Music Profits," *USA Today*, January 25, 2006, http://www.usatoday.com/life/music/news/2006-01-25-ringtones_x.htm (accessed July 25, 2007).

51 D. Leonard, "Songs in the Key of Steve," *Fortune*, May 12, 2003, pp. 52–62; L. Grossman, "It's All Free!" *Time*, May 5, 2003, pp. 60–67; and "Everybody Hurts: Music Sales Fall 7.2%," *USA Today*, April 9, 2003, p. 1B.

52 K. Shimizu and M. A. Hitt, "Strategic Flexibility: Organizational Preparedness to Reverse Ineffective Decisions," *Academy of Management Executive*, November 2004, p. 44.

53 G. T. Lumpkin, S. B. Droege, and G. G. Dess, "E-commerce Strategies: Achieving Sustainable Competitive Advantage and Avoiding Pitfalls," *Organizational Dynamics*, Spring 2002, pp. 325–340.

54 E. Kim, D. Nam, and J. L. Stimpert, "The Applicability of Porter's Generic Strategies in the Digital Age: Assumptions, Conjectures, and Suggestions," *Journal of Management* 30, no. 5 (2004), pp. 569–589.

55 "Online Retailers Don't Click with Canadian Shoppers, Study Finds," *CBCNews.ca*, December 22, 2006, http://www.cbc.ca/news/yourview/2006/12/online_retailers_dont_click_wi.html (accessed July 26, 2007).

56 J. Gaffney, "Shoe Fetish," *Business 2.0*, March 2002, pp. 98–99.

57 J. Doebele, "The Engineer," *Forbes*, January 9, 2006, pp. 122–124.

58 S. Ellison, "P&G to Unleash Dental Adult-Pet Food," *Wall Street Journal*, December 12, 2002, p. B4.

59 P. C. Nutt, "The Tolerance for Ambiguity and Decision Making," Working Paper Series, WP88-291, Ohio State University College of Business, Columbus, Ohio; adapted from S. Budner, "Intolerance of Ambiguity as a Personality Variable," *Journal of Personality*, March 1962, pp. 29–50.

60 Situation adapted from information in J. Frederick, "War of Words," *Time International*, February 17, 2003, p. 33; and K. Regan, "Bugging Out Over Bezos' Bargain Book Bin," *E-commerce Times*, April 17, 2002, http://www.ecommercetimes.com.

61 Based on company information from Haier websites: http://www.haier.com, http://www.haieramerica.com, and http://www.haier.com.au (accessed March 30, 2006); S. Hamm and I. Rowley, "Speed Demons," *BusinessWeek*, March 27, 2006, pp. 68–76; E. Esfahani, "Thinking Locally, Succeeding Globally," *Business 2.0*, December 2005, pp. 96–98; Interbrand, "The Strategy for Chinese Brands," October 2005, http://www.brandchannel.com/images/papers/250_ChinaBrandStrategy.pdf (accessed July 27, 2007); Agence France-Presse, "Chinese Brands Coming to a Market Near You," *IndustryWeek*, April 14, 2005; and "Leadership in China: Haier's Zhang Ruimin," *Wharton Leadership Digest* 9, no. 6 (March 2005).

62 Based on B. Horovitz, "By Year's End, Regular Size Will Have to Do," *USA Today*, March 3, 2004, http://www.usatoday.com; and J. Woestendiek and A. Hirsch, "McDonald's to Trim Super Size," *Baltimore Sun*, March 4, 2004, http://www.baltimoresun.com.

63 Based on L. M. Fuld, *Monitoring the Competition* (New York: Wiley, 1988); E. H. Burack and N. J. Mathys, "Environmental Scanning Improves Strategic Planning," *Personnel Administrator*, 1989, pp. 82–87; and R. Subramanian, N. Fernandes, and E. Harper, "Environmental Scanning in U.S. Companies: Their Nature and Their Relationship to Performance," *Management International Review*, July 1993, pp. 271–286.

64 Based on R. J. Lewicki, D. D. Bowen, D. T. Hall, and F. Hall, *Experiences in Management and Organizational Behavior*, 3rd ed. (New York: John Wiley & Sons, 1988), pp. 261–267; A. Williams, "Career Planning: Build on Strengths, Strengthen Weaknesses," *Black Collegian*, September–October 1993, pp. 78–86; C. C. Campbell-Rock, "Career Planning Strategies That Really Work," *Black Collegian*, September–October 1993, pp. 88–93; B. Kaye, "Career Development—Anytime, Anyplace," *Training & Development*, December 1993, pp. 46–49; W. Wooten, "Using Knowledge, Skill, and Ability (KSA) Data to Identify Career Pathing Opportunities," *Public Personnel Management*, Winter 1993, pp. 551–563; C. Mossop, "Values Assessment: Key to Managing Careers," *CMA—The Management Accounting Magazine*, March 1994, p. 33; and A. D. Pinkney, "Winning in the Workplace," *Essence*, March 1994, pp. 79–80.

Chapter 8

1 Based on M. Hume, "On Time, On Budget: Games Cheaper Than Expected," *Globe and Mail*, May 8, 2007; D. Bramham, "Vancouver Games Hit First Hurdle," *Ottawa Citizen*, February 15, 2004, p. A12; D. Inwood, "Money Starts to Flow for Olympic Games," *Province* (Vancouver), February 18, 2004, p. A6; J. Lee, "John Furlong's Rockin' Life," *Vancouver Sun*, March 27, 2004, p. C1; J. Morris, "Long Road Ahead for 2010 Games," *Trail Times*, December 30, 2003, p. 4; "The Clock Is Ticking," *Maclean's*, July 14, 2003, p. 24; D. Saunders, "Olympics Put Greek Economy into a Tailspin," *Globe and Mail*, September 14, 2004, p. A1; and M. Bridge, "Athens Olympics May Have Been Best Ever," *Vancouver Sun*, October 15, 2004, p. B5.

2 S. C. Jain, "Environmental Scanning in U.S. Corporations," *Long Range Planning*, April 1984, pp. 117–128; see also L. M. Fuld, *Monitoring the Competition* (New York: John Wiley & Sons, 1988); E. H. Burack and N. J. Mathys, "Environmental Scanning Improves Strategic Planning," *Personnel Administrator*, April 1989, pp. 82–87; R. Subramanian, N. Fernandes, and E. Harper, "Environmental Scanning in U.S. Companies: Their Nature and Their Relationship to Performance," *Management International Review*, July 1993, pp. 271–286; B. K. Boyd and J. Fulk, "Executive Scanning and Perceived Uncertainty: A Multidimensional Model," *Journal of Management* 22, no. 1 (1996), pp. 1–21; D. S. Elkenov, "Strategic Uncertainty and Environmental Scanning: The Case for Institutional Influences on Scanning Behavior," *Strategic Management Journal* 18 (1997), pp. 287–302; K. Kumar, R. Subramanian, and K. Strandholm, "Competitive Strategy, Environmental Scanning and Performance: A Context Specific Analysis of Their Relationship," *International Journal of Commerce and Management*, Spring 2001, pp. 1–18; and C. G. Wagner, "Top 10 Reasons to Watch Trends," *Futurist*, March–April 2002, pp. 68–69.

3 T. L. Wheelen and J. D. Hunger, *Strategic Management*, 8th ed. (Upper Saddle River, NJ: Prentice Hall, 2001), pp. 52–53; and J. Barrett, "Can a '50s Icon Do It Again?" *Newsweek*, March 20, 2006, p. E20.

4 B. Gilad, "The Role of Organized Competitive Intelligence in Corporate Strategy," *Columbia Journal of World Business*, Winter 1989, pp. 29–35; L. Fuld, "A Recipe for Business Intelligence," *Journal of Business Strategy*, January–February 1991, pp. 12–17; J. P. Herring, "The Role of Intelligence in Formulating Strategy," *Journal of Business Strategy*, September–October 1992, pp. 54–60; K. Western, "Ethical Spying," *Business Ethics*, September–October 1995, pp. 22–23; D. Kinard, "Raising Your Competitive IQ: The Payoff of Paying Attention to Potential Competitors," *Association Management*, February 2003, pp. 40–44; and K. Girard, "Snooping on a Shoestring," *Business 2.0*, May 2003, pp. 64–66.

5 C. Davis, "Get Smart," *Executive Edge*, October–November 1999, pp. 46–50.

6 B. Ettore, "Managing Competitive Intelligence," *Management Review*, October 1995, pp. 15–19.

7 S. Myburgh, "Competitive Intelligence: Bridging Organizational Boundaries," *Information Management Journal* 38, no. 2 (2004), pp. 46–53.

8 C. Sorensen, "Cloak & Dagger Inc.," *Financial Post (National Post)*, July 8, 2004, p. FP1.

9 A. Serwer, "P&G's Covert Operation," *Fortune*, September 17, 2001, pp. 42–44.

10 K. Western, "Ethical Spying," *Business Ethics*, September–October 1995, pp. 22–23.

11 P. Vieira, "The Airline, the Analyst and the Secret Password," *Financial Post*, June 30, 2004, p. FP1; C. Wong, "WestJet Disputes Air Canada Allegations of Corporate Espionage," *Canadian Press*, July 1, 2004; K. Macklem, "Spies in the Skies," *Maclean's*, September 20, 2004, pp. 20–23; and B. Jang and P. Waldie, "Late Nights, 'Hush-Hush' E-mails and 007 Project," *GlobeAdvisor*, October 3, 2006, http://www.globeadvisor.com/servlet/ArticleNews/story/gam/20061003/RWESTJETPROJECT03 (accessed July 27, 2007).

12 W. H. Davidson, "The Role of Global Scanning in Business Planning," *Organizational Dynamics*, Winter 1991, pp. 5–16.

13 T. L. Wheelen and J. D. Hunger, *Strategic Management*, 8th ed. (Upper Saddle River, NJ: Prentice Hall, 2001), p. 67; and http://www.mitsubishi-motors.ca/Company/WhoWeAre.aspx?lng=2 (accessed September 27, 2007).

14 "Is Supply Chain Collaboration Really Happening?" *ERI Journal*, January–February 2006, http://www.eri.com; L. Denend and H. Lee, "West Marine: Driving Growth through Shipshape Supply Chain Management, A Case Study," *Stanford Graduate School of Business*, April 7, 2005, http://www.vics.org; N. Nix, A. G. Zacharia, R. F. Lusch, W. R. Bridges, and A. Thomas, "Keys to Effective Supply Chain Collaboration: A Special Report from the Collaborative Practices Research Program," *Neeley School of Business, Texas Christian University*, November 15, 2004, http://www.vics.org; Collaborative, Planning, Forecasting, and Replenishment Committee website, http://www.cpfr.org (accessed May 20, 2003); and J. W. Verity, "Clearing the Cobwebs from the Stockroom," *BusinessWeek*, October 21, 1996, p. 140.

15 L. Brannen, "Upfront: Global Planning Perspectives," *Business Finance*, March 2006, pp. 12+.

16 P. N. Pant and W. H. Starbuck, "Innocents in the Forest: Forecasting and Research Methods," *Journal of Management*, June 1990, pp. 433–460; F. Elikai and W. Hall Jr., "Managing and Improving the Forecasting Process," *Journal of Business Forecasting Methods & Systems*, Spring 1999, pp. 15–19; M. A. Giullian, M. D. Odom, and M. W. Totaro, "Developing Essential Skills for Success in the Business World: A Look at Forecasting," *Journal of Applied Business Research*, Summer 2000, pp. 51–65; and T. Leahy, "Turning Managers into Forecasters," *Business Finance*, August 2002, pp. 37–40.

17 K. Moore and S. Caney, "A Real Food Fight," *National Post*, May 10, 2003, p. FP11.

18 T. Leahy, "Turning Managers into Forecasters," *Business Finance*, August 2002, pp. 37–40.

19 J. Hope, "Use a Rolling Forecast to Spot Trends," *Harvard Business School Working Knowledge*, March 13, 2006, http://hbswk.hbs.edu/archive/5250.html (accessed August 1, 2007).

20 This section is based on Y. K. Shetty, "Benchmarking for Superior Performance," *Long Range Planning* 26, no. 1 (1993), pp. 39–44; G. H. Watson, "How Process Benchmarking Supports Corporate Strategy," *Planning Review*, January–February 1993, pp. 12–15; S. Greengard, "Discover Best Practices," *Personnel Journal*, November 1995, pp. 62–73; J. Martin, "Are You as Good as You Think You Are?" *Fortune*, September 30, 1996, pp. 142–152; R. L. Ackoff, "The Trouble with Benchmarking," *Across the Board*, January 2000, p. 13; V. Prabhu, D. Yarrow, and G. Gordon-Hart, "Best Practice and Performance within Northeast Manufacturing," *Total Quality Management*, January 2000, pp. 113–121; "E-benchmarking: The Latest E-Trend," *CFO*, March 2000, p. 7; and E. Krell, "Now Read This," *Business Finance*, May 2000, pp. 97–103.

21 "Newswatch," *CFO*, July 2002, p. 26.

22 I. Jack, "Ottawa Will Have to Pay if It Doesn't Deliver," *National Post (Financial Post)*, March 27, 2004, p. FP3.

23 Based on J. Lee, "Finances Are in Great Shape, Vanoc Says," *Vancouver Sun*, June 29, 2007, p. B1; "Frequently Asked Questions," *City of Vancouver*, http://www.city.vancouver.bc.ca/olympics/faq.htm (accessed June 28, 2007); D. Bramham, "Vancouver Games Hit First Hurdle," *Ottawa Citizen*, February 15, 2004, p. A12; D. Inwood, "Money Starts to Flow for Olympic Games," *Province*, February 18, 2004, p. A6; J. Lee, "John Furlong's Rockin' Life," *Vancouver Sun*, March 27, 2004, p. C1; J. Morris, "Long Road Ahead for 2010 Games," *Trail Times*, December 30, 2003, p. 4; and "The Clock Is Ticking," *Maclean's*, July 14, 2003, p. 24.

24 J. Hope and R. Fraser, "Who Needs Budgets?" *Harvard Business Review*, February 2003, pp. 108–115; T. Leahy, "The Top 10 Traps of Budgeting," *Business Finance*, November 2001, pp. 20–26; T. Leahy, "Necessary Evil," *Business Finance*, November 1999, pp. 41–45; J. Fanning, "Businesses Languishing in a Budget Comfort Zone?" *Management Accounting*, July–August 1999, p. 8; "Budgeting Processes: Inefficiency or Inadequate?" *Management Accounting*, February 1999, p. 5; A. Kennedy and D. Dugdale, "Getting the Most from Budgeting," *Management Accounting*, February 1999, pp. 22–24; G. J. Nolan, "The End of Traditional Budgeting," *Bank Accounting & Finance*, Summer 1998, pp. 29–36; and J. Mariotti, "Surviving the Dreaded Budget Process," *IndustryWeek*, August 17, 1998, p. 150.

25 See, for example, S. Stiansen, "Breaking Even," *Success*, November 1988, p. 16.

26 S. E. Barndt and D. W. Carvey, *Essentials of Operations Management* (Upper Saddle River, NJ: Prentice Hall, 1982), p. 134.

27 D. Bramham, "Vancouver Games Hit First Hurdle," *Ottawa Citizen*, February 15, 2004, p. A12; D. Inwood, "Money Starts to Flow for Olympic Games," *Province* (Vancouver), February 18, 2004, p. A6; J. Lee, "John Furlong's Rockin' Life," *Vancouver Sun*, March 27, 2004, p. C1; J. Morris, "Long Road Ahead for 2010 Games," *Trail Times*, December 30, 2003, p. 4; "The Clock Is Ticking," *Maclean's*, July 14, 2003, p. 24; and J. Lee, "Furlong Motivated by Olympic Challenge," *Vancouver Sun*, February 12, 2007, http://www.canada.com/vancouversun/features/2010/story.html?id=0b94e79e-433d-48ee-810b-0c5625684988 (accessed July 31, 2007).

28 E. E. Adam Jr. and R. J. Ebert, *Production and Operations Management*, 5th ed. (Upper Saddle River, NJ: Prentice Hall, 1992), p. 333.

29 See, for instance, C. Benko and F. W. McFarlan, *Connecting the Dots: Aligning Projects with Objectives in Unpredictable Times* (Boston: Harvard Business School Press, 2003); M. W. Lewis, M. A. Welsh, G. E. Dehler, and S. G. Green, "Product Development Tensions:

Exploring Contrasting Styles of Project Management," *Academy of Management Journal*, June 2002, pp. 546–564; C. E. Gray and E. W. Larsen, *Project Management: The Managerial Process* (Columbus, OH: McGraw-Hill Higher Education, 2000); and J. Davidson Frame, *Project Management Competence: Building Key Skills for Individuals, Teams, and Organizations* (San Francisco: Jossey-Bass, 1999).

30 For more information, see http://www.project-management -software.org; P. Gordon, "Track Projects on the Web," *Information Week*, May 22, 2000, pp. 88–89.

31 L. Fahey, "Scenario Learning," *Management Review*, March 2000, pp. 29–34; S. Caudron, "Frontview Mirror," *Business Finance*, December 1999, pp. 24–30; and J. R. Garber, "What if… ?," *Forbes*, November 2, 1998, pp. 76–79.

32 S. Caudron, "Frontview Mirror," *Business Finance*, December 1999, p. 30.

33 L. Ramsay, "Lessons Learned from SARS Crisis," *Globe and Mail*, May 22, 2003, p. B16.

34 L. Ramsay, "Lessons Learned from SARS Crisis," *Globe and Mail*, May 22, 2003, p. B16.

35 T. Murray, "Independence Key for Ontario's New MOH," *Medical Post*, February 10, 2004, p. 47.

36 R. E. Quinn, S. R. Faerman, M. P. Thompson, and M. McGrath, *Becoming a Master Manager: A Competency Framework* (New York: Wiley, 1990), pp. 33–34.

37 Situation adapted from information in J. Helyar, "The Bizarre Reign of King Richard," *Fortune*, July 7, 2002, pp. 76–86; and R. Abelson, "Scrushy Chided Staff about Profits, Tape Reveals," *New York Times*, May 22, 2003, p. C1.

38 Based on G. Pitts, "Peerless Stays Nimble, But Montreal Pays the Cost," *Globe and Mail*, June 30, 2007, p. B5; http://www. peerless-clothing.com (accessed August 1, 2007); G. Pitts, "Peerless on a Mission: Stop China Now," *Globe and Mail*, January 14, 2005, p. B8; P. Donnelly, A. Kaptainis, and S. Dougherty, "Some Faces They Can't Miss: Montrealers Have Made a Big Splash in Everything From Food and Clothing to Theatre and Finance," *Gazette* (Montreal), October 29, 2000, p. A12; A. D. Gray, "Hitting the U.S. with Suits; Peerless Taps Giant Men's-Wear Market," *Gazette* (Montreal), November 12, 1990, p. TWIB3; and B. McKenna, "Canadian Suit Firm Threatens to Unravel NAFTA Talks," *Globe and Mail*, August 05, 1992, p. B1.

39 Based on information from team website, http://tampabay. devilrays.mlb.com/index.jsp?c_id=tb (accessed April 7, 2006); S. Kirchhoff, "Batter Up! Sports Economics Hits Field," *USA Today*, July 27, 2006, pp. 1B+; L. Thomas Jr., "Case Study: Fix a Baseball Team," *New York Times*, April 2, 2006, http://www.nytimes.com; and A. Tillin, "Paul Podesta: The Stats Wonk Who Runs a Pro Sports Team," *Business 2.0*, November 2004, p. 103.

40 Based on R. N. Anthony, J. Dearden, and N. M. Bedford, *Management Control Systems*, 5th ed. (Homewood, IL: Irwin, 1984), Chapters 5–7.

Part 2 Continuing Case: Starbucks

1 Based on "Coffee Penetration," *Springfield Business Journal*, June 12–18, 2006, p. 70; B. Horovitz, "Starbucks Nation," *USA Today*, May 29, 2006, pp. A1+; S. E. Lockyer, "Operators Aim to Build More Than Restaurants When Adding Locations," *Nation's Restaurant News*, May 22, 2006, pp. 72–74; N. Ramachandran, "Java and a Shot of Hip-

Hop, *U.S. News & World Report*, May 22, 2006, pp. EE14–EE15; The Associated Press, "Starbucks Profit Climbs 27% in Quarter," *New York Times*, May 4, 2006, http://www.nytimes.com; S. Bradbury, "Rethinking Every Rule of Reinvention," *Advertising Age*, May 1, 2006, pp. 14–16; S. Waxman, "A Small Step at Starbucks from Mocha to Movies," *New York Times*, May 1, 2006, http://www.nytimes.com; Interview with Jim Donald, *Smart Money*, May 2006, pp. 31–32; P. R. LaMonica, "Coffee and Popcorn," *CNNMoney.com*, April 28, 2006; "Industry News," *National Petroleum News*, April 2006, p. 44; K. Macarthur, "Latte Reward: Cards Add Up at Starbucks," *Advertising Age*, March 20, 2006, p. S2; B. G. Francella, "Coffee Clash," *Convenience Store News*, March 6, 2006, pp. 43–46; D. Anderson, "Starbucks, Yahoo! Make a Match," *Brandweek*, February 20, 2006, p. 23; C. J. Farley, "A Tall Skinny Latte, a Nice, Comfy Chair and Now Kid Tunes," *Wall Street Journal*, February 14, 2006, pp. B1+; D. Anderson, "Starbucks Eyes Good Will from Times' Crosswords," *Brandweek*, February 13, 2006, p. 8; S. Thompson and K. MacArthur, "Starbucks, Kellogg Plot Cereal Killing," *Advertising Age*, February 6, 2006, pp. 1+; S. Gray and K. Kelly, "Starbucks Plans to Make Debut in Movie Business," *Wall Street Journal*, January 12, 2006, pp. A1+; "Hot Drink in the United States: Industry Profile," *DataMonitor*, December 2005; M. Moran, "Starbucks to Shutter Torrefazione Coffee Bars," *Gourmet Retailer*, August 2005, p. 10; interview with Jim Donald, *Fortune*, April 4, 2005, p. 30; A. Serwer and K. Bonamici, "Hot Starbucks to Go," *Fortune*, January 26, 2004, pp. 60–74; http:// www.starbucks.com/aboutus/Company_Factsheet.pdf (accessed October 1, 2007); http://www.starbucks.com/aboutus/Company_ Timeline.pdf (accessed October 1, 2007); http://www.starbucks.ca/ en-ca/_About+Starbucks/Starbucks+in+Canada.htm; and http:// www.secondcup.com/eng/about_us.php (accessed October 1, 2007).

Chapter 9

1 Based on "Corporate Info," *Air Canada Centre*, http://www. theaircanadacentre.com/peddie.html (accessed August 1, 2007); "Richard Peddie, President and CEO, Maple Leaf Sports & Entertainment," *Raptors*, http://www.nba.com/raptors/news/ richardpeddie_bio.html (accessed August 2, 2007); "Ownership," *MLSnet*, MLSnet.com, http://toronto.fc.mlsnet.com/t280/about/ ownership/ (accessed August 2, 2007); City of Toronto, "BMO Field Opens at Exhibition Place," news release, May 11, 2007, http://wx .toronto.ca/inter/it/newsrel.nsf/9da959222128b9e88525661800 6646d3/41b84cf6c5ef64fe852572db004bc010?OpenDocument (accessed August 2, 2007); "Maple Leaf Sports & Entertainment Unveils Toronto FC as 13th Major League Soccer Team," *CanadaSoccer.com*, May 11, 2006, http://www.canadasoccer.com/ eng/media/viewArtical.asp?Press_ID=2445 (accessed August 2, 2007); and "Contact Us," *Ricoh Coliseum*, http://www.ricohcoliseum .com/contact/ (accessed August 3, 2007).

2 See, for example, R. L. Daft, *Organization Theory and Design*, 6th ed. (St. Paul, MN: West Publishing, 1998).

3 S. Melamed, I. Ben-Avi, and M. S. Green, "Objective and Subjective Work Monotony: Effects on Job Satisfaction, Psychological Distress, and Absenteeism in Blue-Collar Workers," *Journal of Applied Psychology*, February 1995, pp. 29–42.

4 W. Hillier, "BC Forest Fires: A Time of Need," *Canadian Underwriter* 71, no. 1 (January 2004), pp. 22–23.

5 For a discussion of authority, see W. A. Kahn and K. E. Kram, "Authority at Work: Internal Models and Their Organizational Consequences," *Academy of Management Review*, January 1994, pp. 17–50.

6 B. Arthur, "Peddie Gives New GM 'Autonomy' for Change," *National Post*, June 8, 2004, p. S2.

7 See http://www.fan590.com/columnists/columnist1article. jsp?content=20060327_113940_4056 (accessed September 24, 2006).

8 "Senators Fire GM John Muckler: Report," *CBCnews.ca*, June 17, 2007, http://www.cbc.ca/sports/hockey/story/2007/06/17/ senators-fire-muckler.html (accessed August 2, 2007); and C. Iorfida, "Less Is More for Muckler, Burke," *CBCnews.ca*, May 25, 2007, http:// www.cbc.ca/sports/hockey/stanleycup2007/features/tradedeadline-fallout.html (accessed August 2, 2007).

9 D. Van Fleet, "Span of Management Research and Issues," *Academy of Management Journal*, September 1983, pp. 546–552.

10 See, for example, H. Mintzberg, *Power in and Around Organizations* (Upper Saddle River, NJ: Prentice Hall, 1983); and J. Child, *Organization: A Guide to Problems and Practices* (London: Kaiser & Row, 1984).

11 A. Ross, "BMO's Big Bang," *Canadian Business*, January 1994, pp. 58–63; and information on the company from Hoover's Online, http://www.hoovers.com (accessed May 25, 2003).

12 Based on L. Millan, "Who's Scoffing Now? The Lemaire Brothers Started Out Using Recycled Fibre in One Small Paper Mill in Rural Quebec," *Canadian Business*, March 27, 1998, pp. 74–77; "FAQ Corporate," *Cascades*, http://www.cascades.com/cas/en/0_0/ 0_2_1.jsp (accessed August 2, 2007); and *Cascades 2006 Annual Report*, http://www.cascades.com/document/en_129_2.pdf (accessed August 2, 2007).

13 E. W. Morrison, "Doing the Job Well: An Investigation of Pro-Social Rule Breaking," *Journal of Management*, February 2006, pp. 5–28.

14 E. W. Morrison, "Doing the Job Well: An Investigation of Pro-Social Rule Breaking," *Journal of Management*, February 2006, pp. 5–28.

15 T. Burns and G. M. Stalker, *The Management of Innovation* (London: Tavistock, 1961); and D. A. Morand, "The Role of Behavioral Formality and Informality in the Enactment of Bureaucratic versus Organic Organizations," *Academy of Management Review*, October 1995, pp. 831–872.

16 J. Dee, "All the News That's Fit to Print Out," *New York Times Magazine*, July 1, 2007, pp. 34–39; and wikipedia.com.

17 See, for instance, R. E. Miles and C. C. Snow, *Organizational Strategy, Structure, and Process* (New York: McGraw-Hill, 1978); D. Miller, "The Structural and Environmental Correlates of Business Strategy," *Strategic Management Journal*, January–February 1987, pp. 55–76; H. L. Boschken, "Strategy and Structure: Reconceiving the Relationship," *Journal of Management*, March 1990, pp. 135–150; H. A. Simon, "Strategy and Organizational Evolution," *Strategic Management Journal*, January 1993, pp. 131–142; R. Parthasarthy and S. P. Sethi, "Relating Strategy and Structure to Flexible Automation: A Test of Fit and Performance Implications," *Strategic Management Journal* 14, no. 6 (1993), pp. 529–549; D. C. Galunic and K. M. Eisenhardt, "Renewing the Strategy-Structure-Performance Paradigm," in *Research in Organizational Behavior*, vol. 16, ed. B. M. Staw and L. L. Cummings (Greenwich, CT: JAI Press, 1994), pp. 215–255; and D. Jennings and S. Seaman, "High and Low Levels of Organizational Adaptation: An Empirical Analysis of Strategy, Structure, and Performance," *Strategic Management Journal*, July 1994, pp. 459–475.

18 See, for instance, P. M. Blau and R. A. Schoenherr, *The Structure of Organizations* (New York: Basic Books, 1971); D. S. Pugh, "The Aston Program of Research: Retrospect and Prospect," in *Perspectives on Organization Design and Behavior*, ed. A. H. Van de Ven and W. F. Joyce, pp. 135–166 (New York: John Wiley, 1981); and R. Z. Gooding and J. A. Wagner III, "A Meta-Analytic Review of the Relationship between Size and Performance: The Productivity and Efficiency of Organizations and Their Subunits," *Administrative Science Quarterly*, December 1985, pp. 462–481.

19 J. Woodward, *Industrial Organization: Theory and Practice* (London: Oxford University Press, 1965).

20 See, for instance, C. Perrow, "A Framework for the Comparative Analysis of Organizations," *American Sociological Review*, April 1967, pp. 194–208; J. D. Thompson, *Organizations in Action* (New York: McGraw-Hill, 1967); J. Hage and M. Aiken, "Routine Technology, Social Structure, and Organizational Goals," *Administrative Science Quarterly*, September 1969, pp. 366–377; and C. C. Miller, W. H. Glick, Y. D. Wang, and G. P. Huber, "Understanding Technology-Structure Relationships: Theory Development and Meta-Analytic Theory Testing," *Academy of Management Journal*, June 1991, pp. 370–399.

21 D. Gerwin, "Relationships between Structure and Technology," in *Handbook of Organizational Design*, vol. 2, ed. P. C. Nystrom and W. H. Starbuck (New York: Oxford University Press, 1981), pp. 3–38; and D. M. Rousseau and R. A. Cooke, "Technology and Structure: The Concrete, Abstract, and Activity Systems of Organizations," *Journal of Management*, Fall–Winter 1984, pp. 345–361.

22 F. E. Emery and E. Trist, "The Causal Texture of Organizational Environments," *Human Relations*, February 1965, pp. 21–32; P. Lawrence and J. W. Lorsch, *Organization and Environment: Managing Differentiation and Integration* (Boston: Harvard Business School, Division of Research, 1967); and M. Yasai-Ardekani, "Structural Adaptations to Environments," *Academy of Management Review*, January 1986, pp. 9–21.

23 L. A. Perlow, G. A. Okhuysen, and N. P. Repenning, "The Speed Trap: Exploring the Relationship between Decision Making and Temporal Context," *Academy of Management Journal* 45 (2002), pp. 931–995.

24 Based on http://www.nba.com/raptors/news/mlsel_ management.html; http://www.mapleleafs.com/team/Management. asp; http://mapleleafs.nhl.com/team/app/?service=page& page=NHLPage&id=12839; http://www.torontomarlies.com/news/ News.asp?story_id=14; and http://www.torontomarlies.com/news/ news.asp?story_id=433.

25 H. Mintzberg, *Structure in Fives: Designing Effective Organizations* (Upper Saddle River, NJ: Prentice Hall, 1983), p. 157.

26 R. J. Williams, J. J. Hoffman, and B. T. Lamont, "The Influence of Top Management Team Characteristics on M-Form Implementation Time," *Journal of Managerial Issues*, Winter 1995, pp. 466–480.

27 See, for example, R. E. Hoskisson, C. W. L. Hill, and H. Kim, "The Multidivisional Structure: Organizational Fossil or Source of Value?" *Journal of Management* 19, no. 2 (1993), pp. 269–298; I. I. Mitroff, R. O. Mason, and C. M. Pearson, "Radical Surgery: What Will Tomorrow's Organizations Look Like?" *Academy of Management Executive*, February 1994, pp. 11–21; T. Clancy, "Radical Surgery: A View from the Operating Theater," *Academy of Management Executive*, February 1994, pp. 73–78; M. Hammer, "Processed Change: Michael Hammer Sees Process as 'the Clark Kent of Business Ideas'—A Concept That Has the Power to Change a Company's Organizational Design," *Journal of Business Strategy*,

November–December 2001, pp. 11–15; D. F. Twomey, "Leadership, Organizational Design, and Competitiveness for the 21st Century," *Global Competitiveness*, Annual 2002, pp. S31–S40; and G. J. Castrogiovanni, "Organization Task Environments: Have They Changed Fundamentally over Time?" *Journal of Management* 28, no. 2 (2002), pp. 129–150.

28 T. Starner, "Room for Improvement," *IQ Magazine*, March–April 2003, pp. 36–37.

29 Q. Hardy, "Google Thinks Small," *Forbes*, November 14, 2005, pp. 198–202.

30 See, for example, H. Rothman, "The Power of Empowerment," *Nation's Business*, June 1993, pp. 49–52; B. Dumaine, "Payoff from the New Management," *Fortune*, December 13, 1993, pp. 103–110; J. A. Byrne, "The Horizontal Corporation," *BusinessWeek*, December 20, 1993, pp. 76–81; J. R. Katzenbach and D. K. Smith, *The Wisdom of Teams* (Boston: Harvard Business School Press, 1993); L. Grant, "New Jewel in the Crown," *U.S. News & World Report*, February 28, 1994, pp. 55–57; D. Ray and H. Bronstein, *Teaming Up: Making the Transition to a Self-Directed Team-Based Organization* (New York: McGraw Hill, 1995); and D. R. Denison, S. L. Hart, and J. A. Kahn, "From Chimneys to Cross-Functional Teams: Developing and Validating a Diagnostic Model," *Academy of Management Journal*, December 1996, pp. 1005–1023.

31 C. Fishman, "Whole Foods Is All Teams," *Fast Company*, Greatest Hits, vol. 1, 1997, pp. 102–113.

32 W. Hillier, "BC Forest Fires: A Time of Need," *Canadian Underwriter*, January 2004, pp. 22–23.

33 P. LaBarre, "This Organization Is Dis-Organization," *Fast Company*, http://www.fastcompany.com (accessed April 16, 1997).

34 See, for example, G. G. Dess, A. Rasheed, K. J. McLaughlin, and R. L. Priem, "The New Corporate Architecture," *Academy of Management Executive*, August 1995, pp. 7–20.

35 For additional readings on boundaryless organizations, see M. Hammer and S. Stanton, "How Process Enterprises Really Work," *Harvard Business Review*, November–December 1999, pp. 108–118; T. Zenger and W. Hesterly, "The Disaggregation of Corporations: Selective Intervention, High-Powered Incentives, and Modular Units," *Organization Science* 8 (1997), pp. 209–222; R. Ashkenas, D. Ulrich, T. Jick, and S. Kerr, *The Boundaryless Organization: Breaking the Chains of Organizational Structure* (San Francisco: Jossey-Bass, 1997); R. M. Hodgetts, "A Conversation with Steve Kerr," *Organizational Dynamics*, Spring 1996, pp. 68–79; and J. Gebhardt, "The Boundaryless Organization," *Sloan Management Review*, Winter 1996, pp. 117–119. For another view of boundaryless organizations, see B. Victor, "The Dark Side of the New Organizational Forms: An Editorial Essay," *Organization Science*, November 1994, pp. 479–482.

36 S. C. Certo and S. T. Certo, *Modern Management*, 10th ed. (Upper Saddle River, NJ: Prentice Hall, 2006), p. 316; P. M. J. Christie and R. R. Levary, "Virtual Corporations: Recipe for Success," *Industrial Management*, July–August 1998, pp. 7–11; and C. C. Snow, R. E. Miles, and H. J. Coleman Jr., "Managing 21st Century Network Organizations," *Organizational Dynamics*, Winter 1992, pp. 5–20.

37 See, for instance, W. H. Davidow and M. S. Malone, *The Virtual Corporation* (New York: HarperCollins, 1992); H. Chesbrough and D. Teece, "When Is Virtual Virtuous? Organizing for Innovation," *Harvard Business Review*, January–February 1996, pp. 65–73; G. G. Dess, A. Rasheed, K. J. McLaughlin, and R. L. Priem, "The New Corporate Architecture," *Academy of Management Executive*, August 1995, pp. 7–20; M. Sawhney and D. Parikh, "Break Your Boundaries," *Business 2.0*, May 2000, pp. 198–207; D. Pescovitz, "The Company Where Everybody's a Temp," *New York Times Magazine*, June 11, 2000, pp. 94–96; W. F. Cascio, "Managing a Virtual Workplace," *Academy of Management Executive*, August 2000, pp. 81–90; D. Lyons, "Smart and Smarter," *Forbes*, March 18, 2002, pp. 40–41; and B. Hedberg, G. Dahlgren, J. Hansson, and N. Goran Olve, *Virtual Organizations and Beyond: Discovering Imaginary Systems* (New York: John Wiley, 2001).

38 Based on G. Shaw, "Vancouver Law Firm Opens Virtual Branch Office," *Vancouver Sun*, September 26, 2007, p. F4.

39 R. E. Miles and C. C. Snow, "Causes of Failures in Network Organizations," *California Management Review* 34, no. 4 (1992), pp. 53–72; R. E. Miles and C. C. Snow, "The New Network Firm: A Spherical Structure Built on Human Investment Philosophy," *Organizational Dynamics*, Spring 1995, pp. 5–18; C. Jones, W. Hesterly, and S. Borgatti, "A General Theory of Network Governance: Exchange Conditions and Social Mechanisms," *Academy of Management Review*, October 1997, pp. 911–945; and R. E. Miles, C. C. Snow, J. A. Mathews, G. Miles, and H. J. Coleman, "Organizing in the Knowledge Age: Anticipating the Cellular Form," *Academy of Management Executive*, November 1997, pp. 7–24.

40 S. Reed, A. Reinhardt, and A. Sains, "Saving Ericsson," *BusinessWeek*, November 11, 2002, pp. 64–68.

41 J. Barthelemy and D. Adsit, "The Seven Deadly Sins of Outsourcing," *Academy of Management Executive* 17, no. 2 (2003), pp. 87–100.

42 K. Restivo, "Most Canadian Tech Firms Prefer Not to Outsource, Study Shows," *Financial Post (National Post)*, June 11, 2004, p. FP5.

43 C. E. Connelly and D. G. Gallagher, "Emerging Trends in Contingent Work Research," *Journal of Management*, November 2004, pp. 959–983.

44 P. M. Senge, *The Fifth Discipline: The Art and Practice of Learning Organizations* (New York: Doubleday, 1990).

45 A. N. K. Chen and T. M. Edgington, "Assessing Value in Organizational Knowledge Creation: Considerations for Knowledge Workers," *MIS Quarterly*, June 2005, pp. 279–309; K. G. Smith, C. J. Collins, and K. D. Clark, "Existing Knowledge, Knowledge Creation Capability, and the Rate of New Product Introduction in High-Technology Firms," *Academy of Management Journal*, April 2005, pp. 346–357; B. Marr, "How to Knowledge Management," *Financial Management*, February 2003, pp. 26–27; R. Cross, A. Parker, L. Prusak, and S. P. Borgatti, "Supporting Knowledge Creation and Sharing in Social Networks," *Organizational Dynamics*, Fall 2001, pp. 100–120; M. Schulz, "The Uncertain Relevance of Newness: Organizational Learning and Knowledge Flows," *Academy of Management Journal*, August 2001, pp. 661–681; D. Zell, "Overcoming Barriers to Work Innovations: Lessons Learned at Hewlett-Packard," *Organizational Dynamics*, Summer 2001, pp. 77–86; G. Szulanski, "Exploring Internal Stickiness: Impediments to the Transfer of Best Practice within the Firm," *Strategic Management Journal*, Winter Special Issue, 1996, pp. 27–43; and J. M. Liedtka, "Collaborating Across Lines of Business for Competitive Advantage," *Academy of Management Executive*, April 1996, pp. 20–37.

46 N. M. Adler, *International Dimensions of Organizational Behavior*, 4th ed. (Cincinnati, OH: South-Western, 2002), p. 66.

47 P. B. Smith and M. F. Peterson, "Demographic Effects on the Use of Vertical Sources of Guidance by Managers in Widely Differing Cultural Contexts," *International Journal of Cross Cultural Management*, April 2005, pp. 5–26.

48 Based on J. F. Veiga and J. N. Yanouzas, *The Dynamics of Organization Theory: Gaining a Macro Perspective* (St. Paul, MN: West, 1979), pp. 158–160.

49 Situation adapted from information in "HR Pressured to Breach Ethics Policies, Says Survey," *HR Briefing*, June 1, 2003, p. 1; S. Pulliam, "A Staffer Ordered to Commit Fraud Balked, Then Caved," *Wall Street Journal*, June 23, 2003, pp. A1, A6; and J. Gilbert, "A Matter of Trust," *Sales & Marketing Management*, March 2003, pp. 30–31.

50 P. W. Tam, "System Reboot," *Wall Street Journal*, April 3, 2006, pp. A1+; A. Lashinsky, "Can HP Win Doing It the Hurd Way?" *Fortune*, April 3, 2006, p. 65; P. Burrows, "H-P Says Goodbye to Drama," *BusinessWeek*, September 12, 2005, pp. 83–86; A. Lashinsky, "Mark Hurd Takes His First Swing at H-P," *Fortune*, August 8, 2005, p. 24; P. Burrows and B. Elgin, "The Un-Carly Unveils His Game Plan," *BusinessWeek*, June 27, 2005, p. 36; and A. Lashinsky, "Take a Look at H-P," *Fortune*, June 13, 2005, pp. 117–120.

51 Based on N. George, "The Virtues of Being Local," *Financial Times*, October 8, 2003, pp. 4–5; "Svenska Handelsbanken Branches Out in the UK," *European Banker*, November 2003, p. 6; Svenska's website, http://www.handelsbanken.se (accessed 2004); and N. George, "Counting on the Spirit of Independent Branches," *Financial Times*, November 5, 2001, p. 10.

52 Based on P. L. Hunsaker, *Training in Management Skills* (Upper Saddle River, NJ: Prentice Hall, 2001), pp. 135–136 and 430–432; R. T. Noel, "What You Say to Your Employees When You Delegate," *Supervisory Management*, December 1993, p. 13; and S. Caudron, "Delegate for Results," *IndustryWeek*, February 6, 1995, pp. 27–30.

Chapter 10

1 Based on Hoover's online; "Canada Embraces Facebook as Web Site Reports 'Explosive' Growth," *National Post*, June 14, 2007, p. A6; B. McCrea, "A New Kind of Hookup," *Black Enterprise*, July 2007, p. 52; and J. N. Hoover, "Facebook, MySpace Become Work Tools for Some," *InformationWeek*, July 17, 2007, http://www.informationweek.com/internet/showArticle.jhtml?articleID=201001803 (accessed September 27, 2007).

2 P. G. Clampitt, *Communicating for Managerial Effectiveness*, 3rd ed. (Thousand Oaks, CA: Sage Publications, 2005); T. Dixon, *Communication, Organization, and Performance* (Norwood, NJ: Ablex Publishing Corporation, 1996), p. 281; P. G. Clampitt, *Communicating for Managerial Effectiveness* (Newbury Park, CA: Sage Publications, 1991); and L. E. Penley, E. R. Alexander, I. E. Jernigan, and C. I. Henwood, "Communication Abilities of Managers: The Relationship to Performance," *Journal of Management*, March 1991, pp. 57–76.

3 "Electronic Invective Backfires," *Workforce*, June 2001, p. 20; and E. Wong, "A Stinging Office Memo Boomerangs," *New York Times*, April 5, 2001, p. C11.

4 C. O. Kursh, "The Benefits of Poor Communication," *Psychoanalytic Review*, Summer–Fall 1971, pp. 189–208.

5 W. G. Scott and T. R. Mitchell, *Organization Theory: A Structural and Behavioral Analysis* (Homewood, IL: Richard D. Irwin, 1976).

6 Based on A. Shimo, "Why Is T.O. the Capital of Facebook?" *Toronto Star*, June 30, 2007, p. ID3; "City of Toronto Disconnects Workers from Facebook," *CBCnews.ca*, May 10, 2007, http://www.cbc.ca/technology/story/2007/05/10/facebook-toronto-city.html (accessed August 7, 2007); and "Face to Face Is Best," *GMTV*, August 20, 2007, http://www.gm.tv/index.cfm?articleid=26462.

7 D. K. Berlo, *The Process of Communication* (New York: Holt, Rinehart & Winston, 1960), pp. 30–32.

8 T. R. Kurtzberg, C. E. Naquin, and L. Y. Belkin, "Electronic Performance Appraisals: The Effects of E-Mail Communication on Peer Ratings in Actual and Simulated Environments," *Organizational Behavior and Human Decision Processes* 98, no. 2 (2005), pp. 216–226.

9 J. Kruger, N. Epley, J. Parker, and Z.-W. Ng, "Egocentrism over E-Mail: Can We Communicate as Well as We Think?" *Journal of Personality and Social Psychology* 89, no. 6 (2005), pp. 925–936.

10 Thanks to an anonymous reviewer for providing this elaboration.

11 P. G. Clampitt, *Communicating for Managerial Effectiveness* (Newbury Park, CA: Sage Publications, 1991).

12 A. Warfield, "Do You Speak Body Language?" *Training & Development*, April 2001, pp. 60–61; D. Zielinski, "Body Language Myths," *Presentations*, April 2001, pp. 36–42; and "Visual Cues Speak Loudly in Workplace," *Springfield News-Leader*, January 21, 2001, p. 8B.

13 C. Cavanagh, *Managing Your E-Mail: Thinking Outside the Inbox* (Hoboken, NJ: John Wiley & Sons, 2003).

14 K. Macklem, "You've Got Too Much Mail," *Maclean's*, January 30, 2006, pp. 20–21.

15 K. Macklem, "You've Got Too Much Mail," *Maclean's*, January 30, 2006, pp. 20–21.

16 D. K. Berlo, *The Process of Communication* (New York: Holt, Rinehart & Winston, 1960), p. 103.

17 Based on G. Robertson, "Goodbye, Buttonhole Makers. Hello, Tapas," May 22, 2007, *Globe and Mail*, p. B1.

18 A. Mehrabian, "Communication without Words," *Psychology Today*, September 1968, pp. 53–55.

19 L. Haggerman, "Strong, Efficient Leadership Minimizes Employee Problems," *Springfield Business Journal*, December 9–15, 2002, p. 23.

20 See, for instance, S. P. Robbins and P. L. Hunsaker, *Training in InterPersonal Skills*, 4th ed. (Upper Saddle River, NJ: Prentice Hall, 2006); M. Young and J. E. Post, "Managing to Communicate, Communicating to Manage: How Leading Companies Communicate with Employees," *Organizational Dynamics*, Summer 1993, pp. 31–43; J. A. DeVito, *The Interpersonal Communication Book*, 6th ed. (New York: HarperCollins, 1992); and A. G. Athos and J. J. Gabarro, *Interpersonal Behavior* (Upper Saddle River, NJ: Prentice Hall, 1978).

21 O. Thomas, "Best-Kept Secrets of the World's Best Companies: The Three Minute Huddle," *Business 2.0*, April 2006, p. 94.

22 V. Galt, "Top-Down Feedback," *Vancouver Sun*, February 15, 2003, pp. E1, E2.

23 Cited in "Heard It through the Grapevine," *Forbes*, February 10, 1997, p. 22.

24 See, for instance, A. Bruzzese, "What to Do about Toxic Gossip," *USA Today*, March 14, 2001, http://www.usatoday.com; N. B. Kurland and L. H. Pelled, "Passing the Word: Toward a Model of Gossip and Power in the Workplace," *Academy of Management Review*, April 2000, pp. 428–438; N. DiFonzo, P. Bordia, and R. L. Rosnow, "Reining in Rumors," *Organizational Dynamics*, Summer 1994, pp. 47–62; M. Noon and R. Delbridge, "News from Behind My Hand: Gossip in Organizations," *Organization Studies* 14, no. 1 (1993), pp. 23–26; and

J. G. March and G. Sevon, "Gossip, Information and Decision Making," in *Decisions and Organizations*, ed. G. March (Oxford: Blackwell, 1988), pp. 429–442.

25 "Effective Communication: A Leading Indicator of Financial Performance—2005/2006 Communication ROI Study," Watson Wyatt Worldwide, Washington, DC.

26 B. McCrea, "A New Kind of Hookup," *Black Enterprise*, July 2007, p. 52; and M. Stopforth, "Why You Should Let Your Employees Use Facebook," *Moneyweb*, August 5, 1007, http://www.moneyweb.co.za/mw/view/mw/en/page71?oid=151800&sn=Detail&ccs_clear_cache=1 (accessed October 9, 2007).

27 G. Buckler, "Instant Messaging Replacing Pagers in the Enterprise," *Computing Canada*, March 26, 2004, p. 18.

28 J. Rohwer, "Today, Tokyo: Tomorrow, the World," *Fortune*, September 18, 2000, pp. 140–152; J. McCullam and L. Torres, "Instant Enterprising," *Forbes*, September 11, 2000, p. 28; J. Guyon, "The World Is Your Office," *Fortune*, June 12, 2000, pp. 227–234; S. Baker, N. Gross, and I. M. Kunii, "The Wireless Internet," *BusinessWeek*, May 29, 2000, pp. 136–144; R. Lieber, "Information Is Everything..." *Fast Company*, November 1999, pp. 246–254; and "IM Is a Must in Lots of Offices," *MySA.com*, January 5, 2005, http://www.mysanantonio.com/business/stories/MYSA010205.1R.IM.55538bcc.html (accessed August 5, 2007).

29 M. Vallis, "Nasty E-mail from the Boss May Mean More Sick Days," *National Post*, January 9, 2004, pp. A1, A9. Study was done by George Fieldman, a psychologist at Buckinghamshire Chilterns University College, and presented at the 2004 Annual Occupational Psychology Conference of the British Psychological Society.

30 Derived from P. Kuitenbrouwer, "Office E-Mail Runs Amok," *Financial Post*, October 18, 2001, p. FP11.

31 F. Esker, "Employers Finding Business Applications for Instant Messaging" *New Orleans CityBusiness*, May 29, 2006, http://findarticles.com/p/articles/mi_qn4200/is_20060529/ai_n16432818 (accessed August 5, 2007).

32 Information on Second Life based on A. Athavaley, "A Job Interview You Don't Have to Show Up For," *Wall Street Journal*, June 20, 2007, p. D1.

33 "Be Careful about Your E-Trail," *Prince George Citizen*, June 22, 2007, p. 36.

34 M. Blanchard, "Johnson Inc. Relies on IP Telephony," *Globe and Mail*, May 13, 2004.

35 K. Hafner, "For the Well Connected, All the World's an Office," *New York Times*, March 30, 2000, p. D11.

36 R. D. Hof, "Your Undivided Attention Please," *BusinessWeek*, January 19, 2004, p. 14.

37 C. Tice, "You've Got E-mail—and a Lawsuit on Your Hands," *Home Channel News*, October 26, 1998, http://findarticles.com/p/articles/mi_m0VCW/is_1998_Oct_26/ai_53425670 (accessed August 6, 2007).

38 R. Gaffney-Rhys, "Do You Need an Email Policy?" *I.T. Wales*, August 24, 2005, http://www.itwales.com/998242.htm (accessed August 6, 2007).

39 J. Eckberg, "E-Mail: Messages Are Evidence," *Cincinnati Enquirer*, July 27, 2004, http://www.enquirer.com.

40 M. Conlin, "E-Mail Is So Five Minutes Ago," *BusinessWeek*, November 28, 2005, pp. 111–112.

41 J. Scanlon, "Woman of Substance," *Wired*, July 2002, p. 27.

42 E. Wenger, R. McDermott, and W. Snyder, *Cultivating Communities of Practice: A Guide to Managing Knowledge* (Boston: Harvard Business School Press, 2002), p. 4.

43 E. Wenger, R. McDermott, and W. Snyder, *Cultivating Communities of Practice: A Guide to Managing Knowledge* (Boston: Harvard Business School Press, 2002), p. 39.

44 B. A. Gutek, M. Groth, and B. Cherry, "Achieving Service Success through Relationship and Enhanced Encounters," *Academy of Management Executive*, November 2002, pp. 132–144.

45 R. C. Ford and C. P. Heaton, "Lessons from Hospitality That Can Serve Anyone," *Organizational Dynamics*, Summer 2001, pp. 30–47.

46 M. J. Bitner, B. H. Booms, and L. A. Mohr, "Critical Service Encounters: The Employee's Viewpoint," *Journal of Marketing*, October 1994, pp. 95–106.

47 S. D. Pugh, J. Dietz, J. W. Wiley, and S. M. Brooks, "Driving Service Effectiveness through Employee-Customer Linkages," *Academy of Management Executive*, November 2002, pp. 73–84.

48 Based on M. Strauss, "Mining Customer Feedback, Firms Go Undercover and On-Line," *Globe and Mail*, May 13, 2004.

49 Sears, Roebuck and Company, *Assisting Customers with Disabilities: A Summary of Policies and Guidelines Regarding the Assistance of Customers with Disabilities for the Sears Family of Companies*, pamphlet obtained at Springfield, Missouri, Sears store, May 28, 2003.

50 M. L. LaGanga, "Are There Words That Neither Offend nor Bore?" *Los Angeles Times*, May 18, 1994, pp. 11–27; J. Leo, "Language in the Dumps," *U.S. News & World Report*, July 27, 1998, p. 16.

51 Reprinted from *Supervisory Management*, January 1989. American Management Association, New York. http://www.amanet.org. All rights reserved.

52 Situation adapted from information in T. Weidlich, "The Corporate Blog Is Catching On," *New York Times*, June 22, 2003, sec. 3, p. 12; "CNN Shuts Down Correspondent's Blog," *EuropeMedia*, March 24, 2003, http://www.vandusseldorp.com; and see http://www.ozzie.net/blog/2002/08/24.html.

53 Based on E. Frauenheim, "Stop Reading This Headline and Get Back to Work," *C/Net*, July 13, 2005, http://news.com.com/Stop+reading+this+headline+and+get+back+to+work/2100-1022_3-5783552.html (accessed August 7, 2007); and R. Breeden, "More Employees Are Using the Web at Work," *Wall Street Journal*, May 10, 2005, p. B4.

54 Information on Voyant Technologies from Hoover's Online, http://www.hoovers.com (accessed April 14, 2006); and S. Clifford, "How to Get the Geeks and the Suits to Play Nice," *Business 2.0*, May 2002, pp. 92–93.

55 Case based on D. D. Hatch, J. E. Hall, and M. T. Miklave, "New EEOC Guidance on National-Origin Discrimination," *Workforce*, April 2003, p. 76; A. Piech, "Going Global: Speaking in Tongues," *Inc.*, June 2003, p. 50; E. Anderssen and M. Valpy, "Face the Nation: Canada Remade," *Globe and Mail*, June 7, 2003, pp. A10–A11; G. Schellenberg, *Immigrants in Canada's Census Metropolitan Areas*, Catalogue no. 89-613-MIE—No. 003 (Ottawa: Statistics Canada, August 2004); and http://www12.statcan.ca/english/census06/data/profiles/community (accessed January 1, 2008).

56 Based on C. R. Rogers and R. E. Farson, *Active Listening* (Chicago: Industrial Relations Center of the University of Chicago,

1976); and P. L. Hunsaker, *Training in Management Skills* (Upper Saddle River, NJ: Prentice Hall, 2001), pp. 61–62.

57 J. Langdon, "Differences between Males and Females at Work," *USA Today*, February 5, 2001, http://www.usatoday.com; J. Manion, "He Said, She Said," *Materials Management in Health Care*, November 1998, pp. 52–62; G. Franzwa and C. Lockhart, "The Social Origins and Maintenance of Gender Communication Styles, Personality Types, and Grid-Group Theory," *Sociological Perspectives* 41, no. 1 (1998), pp. 185–208; and D. Tannen, *Talking from 9 to 5: Women and Men in the Workplace* (New York: Avon Books, 1995).

Chapter 11

1 Based on Hoover's Online, http://www.hoovers.com; R. Waugh, "Getting More Leaders Is Hard Enough, but the Job Skills Needed Are Changing, Too," *Canadian HR Reporter*, January 26, 2004, p. 18; J. Kirby, "In the Vault," *Canadian Business*, March 1–14, 2004, pp. 68–72; S. Greengard, "Brett Ellison," *IQ Magazine*, November–December 2002, p. 52; http://www.scotiabank.com/cda/content/0,1608,CID821_LIDen,00.html; http://cgi.scotiabank.com/annrep2006/en/pdf/ScotiaAR06_ConsolidatedFinancialStatements.pdf; and http://www.scotiabank.com/cda/content/0,1608,CID11095_LIDen,00.html.

2 P. M. Wright and G. C. McMahan, "Theoretical Perspectives for Strategic Human Resource Management," *Journal of Management* 18, no. 1 (1992), pp. 295–320; A. A. Lado and M. C. Wilson, "Human Resource Systems and Sustained Competitive Advantage," *Academy of Management Review*, October 1994, pp. 699–727; J. Pfeffer, *Competitive Advantage through People* (Boston: Harvard Business School Press, 1994); and J. Pfeffer, *The Human Equation* (Boston: Harvard Business School Press, 1998).

3 "Maximizing the Return on Your Human Capital Investment: The 2005 Watson Wyatt Human Capital Index® Report," "WorkAsia 2004/2005: A Study of Employee Attitudes in Asia," and "European Human Capital Index 2002," *Watson Wyatt Worldwide*, http://www.watsonwyatt.com.

4 See, for example, Y. Y. Kor and H. Leblebici, "How Do Interdependencies among Human-Capital Deployment, Development, and Diversification Strategies Affect Firms' Financial Performance?" *Strategic Management Journal*, October 2005, pp. 967–985; D. E. Bowen and C. Ostroff, "Understanding HRM—Firm Performance Linkages: The Role of the 'Strength' of the HRM System," *Academy of Management Review*, April 2004, pp. 203–221; R. Batt, "Managing Customer Services: Human Resource Practices, Quit Rates, and Sales Growth," *Academy of Management Journal*, June 2002, pp. 587–597; A. S. Tsui, J. L. Pearce, L. W. Porter, and A. M. Tripoli, "Alternative Approaches to the Employee–Organization Relationship: Does Investment in Employees Pay Off?" *Academy of Management Journal*, October 1997, pp. 1089–1121; M. A. Huselid, S. E. Jackson, and R. S. Schuler, "Technical and Strategic Human Resource Management Effectiveness As Determinants of Firm Performance," *Academy of Management Journal*, January 1997, pp. 171–188; J. T. Delaney and M. A. Huselid, "The Impact of Human Resource Management Practices on Perceptions of Organizational Performance," *Academy of Management Journal*, August 1996, pp. 949–969; B. Becker and B. Gerhart, "The Impact of Human Resource Management on Organizational Performance: Progress and Prospects," *Academy of Management Journal*, August 1996, pp. 779–801; M. J. Koch and R. G. McGrath, "Improving Labor Productivity: Human Resource Management Policies Do Matter," *Strategic Management Journal*, May 1996, pp. 335–354; and M. A. Huselid, "The Impact of Human Resource Management Practices on Turnover, Productivity, and Corporate Financial Performance," *Academy of Management Journal*, June 1995, pp. 635–672.

5 "Human Capital a Key to Higher Market Value," *Business Finance*, December 1999, p. 15.

6 J. N. Baron and D. M. Kreps, "Consistent Human Resource Practices," *California Management Review* 41, no. 3 (Spring 1999), pp. 29–53.

7 Statistics Canada, "Fact-Sheet on Unionization in Canada," *The Daily*, August 28, 2003.

8 J. Visser, "Union Membership Statistics in 24 Countries," *Monthly Labor Review*, January 2006, pp. 38–49; and "Foreign Labor Trends—Mexico," *US Department of Labor*, 2002.

9 S. Premack and J. E. Hunter, "Individual Unionization Decisions," *Psychological Bulletin* 103, no. 2 (1988), pp. 223–234.

10 Based on M. King, "Union at Indigo," *Gazette* (Montreal), February 11, 2003, p. B3.

11 S. Armour, "Lawsuits Pin Target on Managers," *USA Today*, October 1, 2002, http://www.usatoday.com.

12 Canadian Human Rights Act, http://laws.justice.gc.ca/en/ShowFullDoc/cs/H-6///en.

13 See http://laws.justice.gc.ca/en/ShowDoc/cr/SOR-86-1082/bo-ga:s_1::bo-ga:s_2//en.

14 R. Waugh, "Getting More Leaders Is Hard Enough, But the Job Skills Needed Are Changing, Too," *Canadian HR Reporter*, January 26, 2004, p. 18.

15 J. Sullivan, "Workforce Planning: Why to Start Now," *Workforce*, September 2002, pp. 46–50.

16 Based on A. Tomlinson, "The Many Benefits of Online Job Boards," *Canadian HR Reporter*, July 15, 2002, pp. 17–18.

17 T. J. Bergmann and M. S. Taylor, "College Recruitment: What Attracts Students to Organizations?" *Personnel*, May–June 1984, pp. 34–46; and A. S. Bargerstock and G. Swanson, "Four Ways to Build Cooperative Recruitment Alliances," *HR Magazine*, March 1991, p. 49.

18 J. R. Gordon, *Human Resource Management: A Practical Approach* (Boston: Allyn and Bacon, 1986), p. 170.

19 F. Loyie, "Police in a Rush to Lure New Recruits," *Edmonton Journal*, April 24, 2004, p. B3.

20 S. Burton and D. Warner, "The Future of Hiring—Top 5 Sources for Recruitment Today," *Workforce Vendor Directory* 2002, p. 75.

21 C. Eustace, "VPD: Virtual Police Department," *Vancouver Sun*, May 29, 2007, pp. A1–A2.

22 G. Shaw, "An Offer That's Hard to Refuse," *Vancouver Sun*, November 12, 2003, p. D5.

23 See, for example, J. P. Kirnan, J. E. Farley, and K. F. Geisinger, "The Relationship between Recruiting Source, Applicant Quality, and Hire Performance: An Analysis by Sex, Ethnicity, and Age," *Personnel Psychology*, Summer 1989, pp. 293–308; and R. W. Griffeth, P. Hom, L. Fink, and D. Cohen, "Comparative Tests of Multivariate Models of Recruiting Sources Effects," *Journal of Management* 23, no. 1 (1997), pp. 19–36.

24 G. W. England, *Development and Use of Weighted Application Blanks*, rev. ed. (Minneapolis: Industrial Relations Center, University of Minnesota, 1971); J. J. Asher, "The Biographical Item: Can It Be

Improved?" *Personnel Psychology*, Summer 1972, p. 266; G. Grimsley and H. F. Jarrett, "The Relation of Managerial Achievement to Test Measures Obtained in the Employment Situation: Methodology and Results," *Personnel Psychology*, Spring 1973, pp. 31–48; E. E. Ghiselli, "The Validity of Aptitude Tests in Personnel Selection," *Personnel Psychology*, Winter 1973, p. 475; I. T. Robertson and R. S. Kandola, "Work Sample Tests: Validity, Adverse Impact, and Applicant Reaction," *Journal of Occupational Psychology* 55, no. 3 (1982), pp. 171–183; A. K. Korman, "The Prediction of Managerial Performance: A Review," *Personnel Psychology*, Summer 1986, pp. 295–322; G. C. Thornton, *Assessment Centers in Human Resource Management* (Reading, MA: Addison-Wesley, 1992); C. Fernandez-Araoz, "Hiring without Firing," *Harvard Business Review*, July–August, 1999, pp. 108–120; and A. M. Ryan and R. E. Ployhart, "Applicants' Perceptions of Selection Procedures and Decisions: A Critical Review and Agenda for the Future," *Journal of Management* 26, no. 3 (2000), pp. 565–606.

25 See, for instance, R. D. Arvey and J. E. Campion, "The Employment Interview: A Summary and Review of Recent Research," *Personnel Psychology* (Summer 1982), pp. 281–322; M. M. Harris, "Reconsidering the Employment Interview: A Review of Recent Literature and Suggestions for Future Research," *Personnel Psychology* (Winter 1989), pp. 691–726; J. H. Prager, "Nasty or Nice: 56-Question Quiz," *Wall Street Journal* (February 22, 2000), p. A4; and M. K. Zachary, "Labor Law for Supervisors," *Supervision* (March 2001), pp. 23–26.

26 See, for instance, G. Nicholsen, "Screen and Glean: Good Screening and Background Checks Help Make the Right Match for Every Open Position," *Workforce* (October 2000), p. 70.

27 E. White, "Walking a Mile in Another's Shoes," *Wall Street Journal*, January 16, 2006, p. B3; D. A. Waldman and T. Korbar, "Student Assessment Center Performance in the Prediction of Early Career Success," *Academy of Management Learning and Education*, June 2004, pp. 151–167; D. J. Woehr and W. Arthur Jr., "The Construct-Related Validity of Assessment Center Ratings: A Review and Meta-Analysis of the Role of Methodological Factors," *Journal of Management* 29, no. 2 (2003), pp. 231–258; and P. G. W. Jansen and B. A. M. Stoop, "The Dynamics of Assessment Center Validity: Results of a 7-Year Study," *Journal of Applied Psychology*, August 2001, pp. 741–753.

28 D. J. Woehr and W. Arthur Jr., "The Construct-Related Validity of Assessment Center Ratings: A Review and Meta-Analysis of the Role of Methodological Factors," *Journal of Management* 29, no. 2 (2003), pp. 231–258; P. G. W. Jansen, and B. A. M. Stoop, "The Dynamics of Assessment Center Validity: Results of a 7-Year Study," *Journal of Applied Psychology*, August 2001, pp. 741–753.

29 R. L. Dipboye, *Selection Interviews: Process Perspectives* (Cincinnati: South-Western Publishing, 1992), p. 6.

30 See, for instance, R. D. Arveny and J. E. Campion, "The Employment Interview: A Summary and Review of Recent Research," *Personnel Psychology*, Summer 1982, pp. 281–322; and M. M. Harris, "Reconsidering the Employment Interview: A Review of Recent Literature and Suggestions for Future Research," *Personnel Psychology*, Winter 1989, pp. 691–726.

31 J. Merritt, "Improv at the Interview," *BusinessWeek*, February 3, 2003, p. 63.

32 S. Caudron, "Who Are You Really Hiring?" *Workforce*, November 2002, pp. 28–32.

33 J. Middlemiss, "Bad Hires Can Be Costly," *Province* (Vancouver), February 4, 2007, p. A46.

34 See, for example, S. L. Premack and J. P. Wanous, "A Meta-Analysis of Realistic Job Preview Experiments," *Journal of Applied Psychology*, November 1985, pp. 706–720; J. A. Breaugh and M. Starke, "Research on Employee Recruitment: So Many Studies, So Many Remaining Questions," *Journal of Management* 26, no. 3 (2000), pp. 405–434; B. M. Meglino, E. C. Ravlin, and A. S. DeNisi, "A Meta-Analytic Examination of Realistic Job Preview Effectiveness: A Test of Three Counterintuitive Propositions," *Human Resource Management Review* 10, no. 4 (2000), pp. 407–434; and Y. Ganzach, A. Pazy, Y. Ohayun, and E. Brainin, "Social Exchange and Organizational Commitment: Decision-Making Training for Job Choice as an Alternative to the Realistic Job Preview," *Personnel Psychology*, Autumn 2002, pp. 613–637.

35 A. Wahl, "People Power," *Canadian Business*, March 29–April 11, 2004, p. 58.

36 D. G. Allen, "Do Organizational Socialization Tactics Influence Newcomer Embeddedness and Turnover?" *Journal of Management*, April 2006, pp. 237–256; C. L. Cooper, "The Changing Psychological Contract at Work: Revisiting the Job Demands–Control Model," *Occupational and Environmental Medicine*, June 2002, p. 355; D. M. Rousseau and S. A. Tijoriwala, "Assessing Psychological Contracts: Issues, Alternatives and Measures," *Journal of Organizational Behavior* 19 (1998), pp. 679–695; and S. L. Robinson, M. S. Kraatz, and D. M. Rousseau, "Changing Obligations and the Psychological Contract: A Longitudinal Study," *Academy of Management Journal*, February 1994, pp. 137–152.

37 "2006 Industry Report," *Training*, December 2006, http://www.trainingmag.com/managesmarter/images/pdfs/IndRep06.pdf (accessed September 6, 2007).

38 D. Sankey, "Canadian Companies Skimp on Training," *Canada.com*, June 27, 2007, http://www.canada.com/working/feeds/resources/atwork/story.html?id=30a5d031-8f8b-4f64-b607-2bcf11bead9d (accessed September 6, 2007); and "2006 Industry Report," *Training*, December 2006, http://www.trainingmag.com/managesmarter/images/pdfs/IndRep06.pdf (accessed September 6, 2007).

39 B. Hall, "The Top Training Priorities for 2003," *Training*, February 2003, p. 40; and T. Galvin, "2002 Industry Report," *Training*, October 2002, pp. 24–33.

40 H. Dolezalek, "2005 Industry Report," *Training*, December 2005, pp. 14–28.

41 B. Hall, "The Top Training Priorities for 2003," *Training*, February 2003, p. 40.

42 Based on K. Harding, "Once and Future Kings," *Globe and Mail*, April 9, 2003, pp. C1, C6.

43 V. Galt, "Training on Tap," *Globe and Mail*, November 20, 2002, pp. C1, C8.

44 U. Boser, "Gaming the System, One Click at a Time," *U.S. News & World Report*, October 28, 2002, p. 60.

45 L. Fowlie, "Online Training Takes the Slow Train: 'Next Big Thing' Fails to Live Up to Initial Hype," *Daily Townsman*, March 5, 2004, p. 11.

46 V. Peters, "Working and Training: First Results of the 2003 Adult Education and Training Survey," *Statistics Canada*: Culture, Tourism and the Centre for Education Statistics Division, 2004, Catalogue no. 81-595-MIE—No. 015.

47 S. Purba, "When Reviews Deserve a Failing Grade," *Globe and Mail*, June 11, 2004, p. C1.

48 K. Clark, "Judgment Day," *U.S. News & World Report*, January 13, 2003, pp. 31–32; E. E. Lawler III, "The Folly of Forced Ranking," *Strategy & Business*, Third Quarter 2002, pp. 28–32; K. Cross, "The Weakest Links," *Business2.Com*, June 26, 2001, pp. 36–37; J. Greenwald, "Rank and Fire," *Time*, June 18, 2001, pp. 38–39; D. Jones, "More Firms Cut Workers Ranked at Bottom to Make Way for Talent," *USA Today*, May 30, 2001, p. B11; and M. Boyle, "Performance Reviews: Perilous Curves Ahead," *Fortune*, May 28, 2001, pp. 187–188.

49 J. McGregor, "The Struggle to Measure Performance," *BusinessWeek*, January 9, 2006, pp. 26–28.

50 D. Jones, "Study: Thinning Herd from Bottom Helps," *USA Today*, March 14, 2005, p. 1B.

51 S. E. Cullen, P. K. Bergey, and L. Aiman-Smith, "Forced Distribution Rating Systems and the Improvement of Workforce Potential: A Baseline Simulation," *Personnel Psychology*, Spring 2005, pp. 1–32.

52 J. McGregor, "The Struggle to Measure Performance," *BusinessWeek*, January 9, 2006, pp. 26–28.

53 R. D. Bretz Jr., G. T. Milkovich, and W. Read, "The Current State of Performance Appraisal Research and Practice: Concerns, Directions, and Implications," *Journal of Management*, June 1992, p. 331.

54 M. Debrayen and S. Brutus, "Learning from Others' 360-Degree Experiences," *Canadian HR Reporter*, February 10, 2003, pp. 18–19.

55 M. Johne, "It's Good PR to Keep Employees Loyal," *Globe and Mail*, September 20, 2002, p. C1.

56 M. A. Peiperl, "Getting 360° Feedback Right," *Harvard Business Review*, January 2001, pp. 142–147.

57 This section is based on R. I. Henderson, *Compensation Management in a Knowledge-Based World*, 9th ed. (Upper Saddle River, NJ: Prentice Hall, 2003).

58 L. R. Gomez-Mejia, "Structure and Process of Diversification, Compensation Strategy, and Firm Performance," *Strategic Management Journal* 13 (1992), pp. 381–397; and E. Montemayor, "Congruence between Pay Policy and Competitive Strategy in High-Performing Firms," *Journal of Management* 22, no. 6 (1996), pp. 889–908.

59 J. D. Shaw, N. Gupta, A. Mitra, and G. E. Ledford Jr., "Success and Survival of Skill-Based Pay Plans," *Journal of Management*, February 2005, pp. 28–49; C. Lee, K. S. Law, and P. Bobko, "The Importance of Justice Perceptions on Pay Effectiveness: A Two-Year Study of a Skill-Based Pay Plan," *Journal of Management* 26, no. 6 (1999), pp. 851–873; G. E. Ledford, "Paying for the Skills, Knowledge and Competencies of Knowledge Workers," *Compensation and Benefits Review*, July–August 1995, pp. 55–62; and E. E. Lawler III, G. E. Ledford Jr., and L. Chang, "Who Uses Skill-Based Pay and Why," *Compensation and Benefits Review*, March–April 1993, p. 22.

60 J. D. Shaw, N. Gupta, A. Mitra, and G. E. Ledford Jr., "Success and Survival of Skill-Based Pay Plans," *Journal of Management*, February 2005, pp. 28–49.

61 M. Rowland, "It's What You Can Do That Counts," *New York Times*, June 6, 1993, p. F17.

62 Information from Hewitt Associates Studies, "Hewitt Study Shows Pay-for-Performance Plans Replacing Holiday Bonuses," December 6, 2005; "Salaries Continue to Rise in Asia Pacific," *Hewitt Annual Study Reports*, November 23, 2005; and "Hewitt Study Shows Base Pay Increases Flat for 2006 with Variable Pay Plans Picking Up the Slack," *Hewitt Associates*, August 31, 2005, http://www.hewitt.com.

63 L. Duxbury, L. Dyke, and N. Lam, "Career Development in the Federal Public Service: Building a World-Class Workforce," *Treasury Board of Canada*, January 1999.

64 An anonymous reviewer deserves credit for this insight.

65 D. E. Super and D. T. Hall, "Career Development: Exploration and Planning," in *Annual Review of Psychology*, vol. 29, ed. M. R. Rosenzweig and L. W. Porter (Palo Alto, CA: Annual Reviews, 1978), p. 334.

66 A. K. Smith, "Charting Your Own Course," *U.S. News & World Report*, November 6, 2000, pp. 56–65; S. E. Sullivan, "The Changing Nature of Careers: A Review and Research Agenda," *Journal of Management* 25, no. 3 (1999), pp. 457–484; D. T. Hall, "Protean Careers of the 21st Century," *Academy of Management Executive*, November 1996, pp. 8–16; M. B. Arthur and D. M. Rousseau, "A Career Lexicon for the 21st Century," *Academy of Management Executive*, November 1996, pp. 28–39; N. Nicholson, "Career Systems in Crisis: Change and Opportunity in the Information Age," *Academy of Management Executive*, November 1996, pp. 40–51; and K. R. Brousseau, M. J. Driver, K. Eneroth, and R. Larsson, "Career Pandemonium: Realigning Organizations and Individuals," *Academy of Management Executive*, November 1996, pp. 52–66.

67 A. K. Smith, "Charting Your Own Course," *U.S. News & World Report*, November 6, 2000, pp. 56–65; and D. T. Hall, "Protean Careers of the 21st Century," *Academy of Management Executive*, November 1996, pp. 8–16.

68 M. B. Arthur and D. M. Rousseau, *The Boundaryless Career: A New Employment Principle for a New Organizational Era* (New York: Oxford University Press, 1996).

69 M. Cianni and D. Wnuck, "Individual Growth and Team Enhancement: Moving toward a New Model of Career Development," *Academy of Management Executive*, February 1997, pp. 105–115.

70 D. E. Super, "A Life-Span Life Space Approach to Career Development," *Journal of Vocational Behavior*, Spring 1980, pp. 282–298. See also E. P. Cook and M. Arthur, *Career Theory Handbook* (Upper Saddle River, NJ: Prentice Hall, 1991), pp. 99–131; and L. S. Richman, "The New Worker Elite," *Fortune*, August 22, 1994, pp. 56–66.

71 R. Henkoff, "Winning the New Career Game," *Fortune*, July 12, 1993, pp. 46–49; "10 Tips for Managing Your Career," *Personnel*, October 1995, p. 106; A. Fisher, "Six Ways to Supercharge Your Career," *Fortune*, January 13, 1997, pp. 46–48; A. K. Smith, "Charting Your Own Course," *U.S. News & World Report*, November 6, 2000, pp. 56–65; and D. D. Dubois, "The 7 Stages of One's Career," *Training & Development*, December 2000, pp. 45–50.

72 Based on C. Petten, "Progressive Aboriginal Relations Important to Scotiabank," *Windspeaker*, March 2002, p. B7.

73 L. Crawford, "Motivation, Not a Degree Key at IKEA," *Financial Post (National Post)*, February 24, 2004, p. FP12; and interview with André de Wit, general manager of IKEA Ibérica, S.A., *Interes*, http://www.interes.org/icex/cda/controller/interes/0,5464,5322992_5325168_39745871_519802_0,00.html (accessed September 7, 2007).

74 A. Wahl, "Opening Doors," *Canadian Business*, March 29–April 11, 2004, p. 45.

75 J. Hickman, "50 Best Companies for Minorities," *Fortune*, June 28, 2004, http://money.cnn.com/magazines/fortune/fortune_archive/2004/06/28/374393/index.htm (accessed September 10, 2007); and J. Kahn, "Diversity Trumps the Downturn,"

Fortune, July 9, 2001, pp. 114–116; and http://www.dennys.com/en/cms/Diversity/36.html (accessed September 10, 2007).

76 "Employers Underestimate Extent of Sexual Harassment, Report Says," *Vancouver Sun*, March 8, 2001, p. D6.

77 J. Monchuk, "Female Mounties Allege Sex Harassment Not Investigated to Protect RCMP," *Canadian Press Newswire*, September 26, 2003.

78 D. Spears, "Is a Well Drafted Harassment Policy Enough?" *Ottawa Business Journal*, February 20, 2006, http://www.ottawabusinessjournal.com/293617634517614.php (accessed October 14, 2007).

79 "Employers Underestimate Extent of Sexual Harassment, Report Says," *Vancouver Sun*, March 8, 2001, p. D6.

80 Sexual Harassment Charges: FY 1992—FY 2005, *The U.S. Equal Employment Opportunity Commission*, http://www.eeoc.gov.

81 "U.S. Leads Way in Sex Harassment Laws, Study Says," *Evening Sun*, November 30, 1992, p. A11; and W. Hardman and J. Heidelberg, "When Sexual Harassment Is a Foreign Affair," *Personnel*, April 1996, pp. 91–97.

82 *Janzen v. Platy Enterprises Ltd.* (1989), 10 C.H.R.R. D/6205 (S.C.C.).

83 "Facts About Sexual Harassment," *U.S. Equal Employment Opportunity Commission*, http://www.eeoc.gov (accessed June 1, 2003).

84 A. Fisher, "After All This Time, Why Don't People Know What Sexual Harassment Means?" *Fortune*, January 12, 1998, p. 68; and A. R. Karr, "Companies Crack Down on the Increasing Sexual Harassment by E-Mail," *Wall Street Journal*, September 21, 1999, p. A1.

85 See T. S. Bland and S. S. Stalcup, "Managing Harassment," *Human Resource Management*, Spring 2001, pp. 51–61; K. A. Hess and D. R. M. Ehrens, "Sexual Harassment—Affirmative Defense to Employer Liability," *Benefits Quarterly*, Second Quarter 1999, p. 57; J. A. Segal, "The Catch-22s of Remedying Sexual Harassment Complaints," *HR Magazine*, October 1997, pp. 111–117; S. C. Bahls and J. E. Bahls, "Hands-Off Policy," *Entrepreneur*, July 1997, pp. 74–76; J. A. Segal, "Where Are We Now?" *HR Magazine*, October 1996, pp. 69–73; B. McAfee and D. L. Deadrick, "Teach Employees to Just Say No," *HR Magazine*, February 1996, pp. 86–89; G. D. Block, "Avoiding Liability for Sexual Harassment," *HR Magazine*, April 1995, pp. 91–97; and J. A. Segal, "Stop Making Plaintiffs' Lawyers Rich," *HR Magazine*, April 1995, pp. 31–35.

86 S. Jayson, "Workplace Romance No Longer Gets the Kiss-Off," *USA Today*, February 9, 2006, p. 9D.

87 R. Mano and Y. Gabriel, "Workplace Romances in Cold and Hot Organizational Climates: The Experience of Israel and Taiwan," *Human Relations*, January 2006, pp. 7–35; J. A. Segal, "Dangerous Liaisons," *HR Magazine*, December 2005, pp. 104–108; "Workplace Romance Can Create Unforeseen Issues for Employers," *HR Focus*, October 2005, p. 2; C. A. Pierce and H. Aguinis, "Legal Standards, Ethical Standards, and Responses to Social-Sexual Conduct at Work," *Journal of Organizational Behavior*, September 2005, pp. 727–732; and C. A. Pierce, B. J. Broberg, J. R. McClure, and H. Aguinis, "Responding to Sexual Harassment Complaints: Effects of a Dissolved Workplace Romance on Decision-Making Standards," *Organizational Behavior and Human Decision Processes*, September 2004, pp. 66–82.

88 J. A. Segal, "Dangerous Liaisons," *HR Magazine*, December 2005, pp. 104–108.

89 I. Towers, L. Duxbury, C. Higgins, and J. Thomas, "Time Thieves and Space Invaders: Technology, Work and the Organization," *Journal of Organizational Change Management* 19, no. 5 (2006), pp. 593–618; and L. Duxbury and C. Higgins, "Work–Life Conflict in Canada in the New Millennium: A Status Report." *Australian Canadian Studies* 21, no. 2 (2003), pp. 41–72.

90 C. Oglesby, "More Options for Moms Seeking Work-Family Balance," *CNN.com*, May 10, 2001, http://www.cnn.com.

91 J. Miller and M. Miller, "Get A Life!" *Fortune,* November 28, 2005, pp. 108–124.

92 M. Elias, "The Family-First Generation," *USA Today*, December 13, 2004, p. 5D.

93 F. Hansen, "Truths and Myths about Work/Life Balance," *Workforce*, December 2002, pp. 34–39.

94 J. H. Greenhaus and G. N. Powell, "When Work and Family Are Allies: A Theory of Work–Family Enrichment," *Academy of Management Review*, January 2006, pp. 72–92; L. Duxbury, C Higgins, and D. Coghill, "Voices of Canadians: Seeking Work–Life Balance," *HRSDC*, January 2003, http://www.hrsdc.gc.ca; and S. D. Friedman and J. H. Greenhaus, *Work and Family—Allies or Enemies?* (New York: Oxford University Press, 2000).

95 J. H. Greenhaus and G. N. Powell, "When Work and Family Are Allies: A Theory of Work–Family Enrichment," *Academy of Management Review*, January 2006, pp. 72–92.

96 L. B. Hammer, M. B. Neal, J. T. Newsom, K. J. Brockwood, and C. L. Colton, "A Longitudinal Study of the Effects of Dual-Earner Couples' Utilization of Family-Friendly Workplace Supports on Work and Family Outcomes," *Journal of Applied Psychology*, July 2005, pp. 799–810.

97 M. M. Arthur, "Share Price Reactions to Work–Family Initiatives: An Institutional Perspective," *Academy of Management Journal*, August 2003, pp. 497–505.

98 N. P. Rothbard, T. L. Dumas, and K. W. Phillips, "The Long Arm of the Organization: Work–Family Policies and Employee Preferences for Segmentation" (paper presented at the 61st Annual Academy of Management meeting, Washington, DC, August 2001).

99 L. T. Cullen, "Where Did Everyone Go?" *Time*, November 18, 2002, pp. 64–66.

100 S. Alleyne, "Stiff Upper Lips," *Black Enterprise*, April 2002, p. 59; C. Hymowitz, "Getting a Lean Staff to Do 'Ghost Work' of Departed Colleagues," *Wall Street Journal*, October 22, 2002, p. B1; and E. Krell, "Defusing Downsizing," *Business Finance*, December 2002, pp. 55–57.

101 P. P. Shah, "Network Destruction: The Structural Implications of Downsizing," *Academy of Management Journal*, February 2000, pp. 101–112.

102 See, for instance, K. A. Mollica and B. Gray, "When Layoff Survivors Become Layoff Victims: Propensity to Litigate," *Human Resource Planning*, January 2001, pp. 22–32.

103 S. Koudsi, "You're Stuck," *Fortune*, December 10, 2001, pp. 271–274.

104 L. A. Mainiero and C. L. Tromley, *Developing Managerial Skills in Organizational Behavior* (Upper Saddle River, NJ: Prentice Hall, 1994). Adapted by permission of Prentice Hall, Inc.

105 Situation adapted from information in J. Russell, "Older Goodyear Workers Who Say Age Played into Evaluations Get Day in Court," *Akron Beacon Journal*, July 3, 2003, http://www.ohio.com/bj; and K. Clark, "Judgment Day," *U.S. News & World Report*, January 13, 2003, pp. 31–32.

106 Information on company from Mitsubishi Motors North America website, http://www.mitsubishicars.com (accessed June 1, 2004); "Mitsubishi Plans Big Boost to U.S. Production," *IndustryWeek*, March 18, 2003, http://www.industryweek.com; D. Kiley, "Workplace Woes Almost Eclipse Mitsubishi Plant," *USA Today*, October 21, 2002, p. B11; "EEOC Responds to Final Report of Mitsubishi Consent Decree Monitors," *Equal Employment Opportunity Commission*, http://www.eeoc.gov (accessed May 23, 2001); and S. Greengard, "Zero Tolerance: Making It Work," *Workforce*, May 1999, pp. 28–34.

107 Based on S. P. Robbins and D. A. DeCenzo, *Fundamentals of Management*, 4th ed. (Upper Saddle River, NJ: Prentice Hall, 2004), p. 194.

Part 3 Continuing Case: Starbucks

1 A. Serwer and K. Bonamici, "Hot Starbucks to Go," *Fortune*, January 26, 2004, pp. 60–74; J. Cummings, "Legislative Grind," *Wall Street Journal*, April 12, 2005, pp. A1+; interview with Jim Donald, *Smart Money*, May 2006, pp. 31–32; A. Serwer "Interview with Howard Schultz," *Fortune (Europe)*, March 20, 2006, pp. 35–36; A. Lustgarten, "A Hot, Steaming Cup of Customer Awareness," *Fortune*, November 15, 2004, p. 192; W. Meyers, "Conscience in a Cup of Coffee," *U.S. News & World Report*, October 31, 2005, pp. 48–50; S. Gray, "Fill 'er Up—with Latte," *Wall Street Journal*, January 6, 2006, pp. A9+; S. Holmes, "A Bitter Aroma at Starbucks," *BusinessWeek*, June 6, 2005, p. 13; K. Maher and J. Adamy," Do Hot Coffee and 'Wobblies' Go Together?" *Wall Street Journal*, March 21, 2006, pp. B1+; P. Sellers, "Starbucks: The Next Generation," *Fortune*, April 4, 2005, p. 20; J. M. Cohn, R. Khurana, and L. Reeves, "Growing Talent as if Your Business Depended It," *Harvard Business Review*, October 2005, pp. 62–70; B. Nussbaum, R. Berner, and D. Brady, "Get Creative," *BusinessWeek*, August 1, 2005, pp. 60–68; "Training Top 100," *Training*, March 2006, pp. 40–59 and p. 72; P. Kafka, "Bean Counter," *Forbes*, February 28, 2005, pp. 78–80; and *Beyond the Cup: Corporate Social Responsibility, Fiscal 2005 Annual Report*, Starbucks Corporation.

Chapter 12

1 Based on "Magnotta: Breaking New Ground with Innovative Marketing Strategies," *Industry Canada*, http://strategis.ic.gc.ca/epic/site/mfbs-gprea.nsf/en/lu00057e.html (accessed July 2, 2007); S. Fife "Break the Competitive Roadblock: Three Canadian Success Stories," *Canadian Business*, May 18, 2007, http://www.canadianbusiness.com/innovation/article.jsp?content=20070518_094759_4716 (accessed July 2, 2007); and G. Stimmell, "Wine's Scrappy Duo," *Toronto Star*, January 24, 2007, p. D4.

2 R. N. Kanungo, "Leadership in Organizations: Looking Ahead to the 21st Century," *Canadian Psychology* 39, nos. 1–2 (1998), p. 77. For more evidence of this consensus, see N. Adler, *International Dimensions of Organizational Behavior*, 3rd ed. (Cincinnati, OH: South Western College Publishing, 1997); R. J. House, "Leadership in the Twenty-First Century," in *The Changing Nature of Work*, ed. A. Howard (San Francisco: Jossey-Bass, 1995), pp. 411–450; R. N. Kanungo and M. Mendonca, *Ethical Dimensions of Leadership* (Thousand Oaks, CA: Sage Publications, 1996); and A. Zaleznik, "The Leadership Gap," *Academy of Management Executive* 4, no. 1 (1990), pp. 7–22.

3 See, for instance, R. Lofthouse, "Herding the Cats," *EuroBusiness*, February 2001, pp. 64–65; and M. Delahoussaye, "Leadership in the 21st Century," *Training*, September 2001, pp. 60–72.

4 K. Y. Chan and F. Drasgow, "Toward a Theory of Individual Differences and Leadership: Understanding the Motivation to Lead," *Journal of Applied Psychology*, June 2001, pp. 481–498.

5 M. Sashkin, "The Visionary Leader," in *Charismatic Leadership*, ed. J. A. Conger and R. N. Kanungo (San Francisco: Jossey-Bass, 1988), p. 150.

6 Based on "Magnotta: Breaking New Ground with Innovative Marketing Strategies," *Industry Canada*, http://strategis.ic.gc.ca/epic/site/mfbs-gprea.nsf/en/lu00057e.html (accessed July 2, 2007); S. Fife "Break the Competitive Roadblock: Three Canadian Success Stories," *Canadian Business*, May 18, 2007, http://www.canadianbusiness.com/innovation/article.jsp?content=20070518_094759_4716 (accessed July 2, 2007); and G. Stimmell, "Wine's Scrappy Duo," *Toronto Star*, January 24, 2007, p. D4.

7 See S. A. Kirkpatrick and E. A. Locke, "Leadership: Do Traits Matter?" *Academy of Management Executive*, May 1991, pp. 48–60; and T. A. Judge, J. E. Bono, R. Ilies, and M. W. Gerhardt, "Personality and Leadership: A Qualitative and Quantitative Review," *Journal of Applied Psychology*, August 2002, pp. 765–780.

8 See T. A. Judge, J. E. Bono, R. Ilies, and M. Werner, "Personality and Leadership: A Review" (paper presented at the 15th Annual Conference of the Society for Industrial and Organizational Psychology, New Orleans, 2000); T. A. Judge, J. E. Bono, R. Ilies, and M. W. Gerhardt, "Personality and Leadership: A Qualitative and Quantitative Review," *Journal of Applied Psychology*, August 2002, pp. 765–780; and D. A. Hofmann and L. M. Jones, "Leadership, Collective Personality, and Performance," *Journal of Applied Psychology* 90, no. 3 (2005), pp. 509–522.

9 J. Kirby, "In the Vault," *Canadian Business*, March 1–March 14, 2004, pp. 68–72.

10 J. Kirby, "In the Vault," *Canadian Business*, March 1–March 14, 2004, pp. 68–72.

11 K. Lewin and R. Lippitt, "An Experimental Approach to the Study of Autocracy and Democracy: A Preliminary Note," *Sociometry* 1 (1938), pp. 292–300; K. Lewin, "Field Theory and Experiment in Social Psychology: Concepts and Methods," *American Journal of Sociology* 44, no. 6 (1939), pp. 868–896; K. Lewin, R. Lippitt, and R. K. White, "Patterns of Aggressive Behavior in Experimentally Created Social Climates," *Journal of Social Psychology* 10, 1939, pp. 271–301; R. Lippitt, "An Experimental Study of the Effect of Democratic and Authoritarian Group Atmospheres," *University of Iowa Studies in Child Welfare* 16, 1940, pp. 43–95.

12 B. M. Bass, *Stogdill's Handbook of Leadership* (New York: Free Press, 1981), pp. 289–299.

13 R. M. Stogdill and A. E. Coons, eds., *Leader Behavior: Its Description and Measurement*, Research Monograph No. 88 (Columbus: Ohio State University, Bureau of Business Research, 1951). For an updated literature review of Ohio State research, see S. Kerr, C. A. Schriesheirn, C. I. Murphy, and R. M. Stogdill, "Toward a Contingency Theory of Leadership Based upon the Consideration and Initiating Structure Literature," *Organizational Behavior and Human Performance*, August 1974, pp. 62–82; and B. M. Fisher, "Consideration and Initiating Structure and Their Relationships with Leader Effectiveness: A Meta-Analysis," in *Proceedings of the 48th Annual Academy of Management Conference*, ed. F. Hoy, pp. 201–205 (Anaheim, CA, 1988).

14 R. Kahn and D. Katz, "Leadership Practices in Relation to Productivity and Morale," in *Group Dynamics: Research and Theory*, 2nd ed., ed. D. Cartwright and A. Zander (Elmsford, NY: Row, Paterson, 1960).

15 R. R. Blake and J. S. Mouton, *The Managerial Grid III* (Houston, TX: Gulf Publishing, 1984).

16 L. L. Larson, J. G. Hunt, and R. N. Osborn, "The Great Hi-Hi Leader Behavior Myth: A Lesson from Occam's Razor," *Academy of Management Journal*, December 1976, pp. 628–641; and P. C. Nystrom, "Managers and the Hi-Hi Leader Myth," *Academy of Management Journal*, June 1978, pp. 325–331.

17 T. A. Judge, R. F. Piccolo, and R. Ilies, "The Forgotten Ones? The Validity of Consideration and Initiating Structure in Leadership Research," *Journal of Applied Psychology*, 89, no. 1 (February 2004), pp. 36–51; and R. T. Keller, "Transformational Leadership, Initiating Structure, and Substitutes for Leadership: A Longitudinal Study of Research and Development Project Team Performance," *Journal of Applied Psychology* 91, no. 1 (2006), pp. 202–210.

18 R. McQueen, "The Long Shadow of Tom Stephens: He Branded MacBlo's Crew as Losers, Then Made Them into Winners," *Financial Post (National Post)*, June 22, 1999, pp. C1, C5.

19 H. Wang, K. S. Law, R. D. Hackett, D. Wang, and Z. X. Chen, "Leader-Member Exchange As a Mediator of the Relationship between Transformational Leadership and Followers' Performance and Organizational Citizenship Behavior," *Academy of Management Journal* 48, no. 3 (June 2005), pp. 420–432.

20 F. E. Fiedler, *A Theory of Leadership Effectiveness* (New York: McGraw-Hill, 1967).

21 G. Johns and A. M. Saks, *Organizational Behaviour*, 5th ed. (Toronto: Pearson Education Canada, 2001), pp. 278–279.

22 L. H. Peters, D. D. Hartke, and J. T. Pholmann, "Fiedler's Contingency Theory of Leadership: An Application of the Meta-Analysis Procedures of Schmidt and Hunter," *Psychological Bulletin*, March 1985, pp. 274–285; C. A. Schriesheim, B. J. Tepper, and L. A. Tetrault, "Least-Preferred Co-Worker Score, Situational Control, and Leadership Effectiveness: A Meta-Analysis of Contingency Model Performance Predictions," *Journal of Applied Psychology*, August 1994, pp. 561–573; R. Ayman, M. M. Chemers, and F. Fiedler, "The Contingency Model of Leadership Effectiveness: Its Levels of Analysis," *Leadership Quarterly*, Summer 1995, pp. 147–167.

23 See E. H. Schein, *Organizational Psychology*, 3rd ed. (Upper Saddle River, NJ: Prentice Hall, 1980), pp. 116–117; and B. Kabanoff, "A Critique of Leader Match and Its Implications for Leadership Research," *Personnel Psychology*, Winter 1981, pp. 749–764.

24 P. Hersey and K. Blanchard, "So You Want to Know Your Leadership Style?" *Training & Development*, February 1974, pp. 1–15; and P. Hersey and K. Blanchard, *Management of Organizational Behavior: Leading Human Resources*, 8th ed. (Englewood Cliffs, NJ: Prentice Hall, 2001).

25 See, for instance, C. F. Fernandez and R. P. Vecchio, "Situational Leadership Theory Revisited: A Test of an Across-Jobs Perspective," *Leadership Quarterly* 8, no. 1 (1997), pp. 67–84; and C. L. Graeff, "Evolution of Situational Leadership Theory: A Critical Review," *Leadership Quarterly* 8, no. 2 (1997), pp. 153–170.

26 V. H. Vroom and P. W. Yetton, *Leadership and Decision-Making* (Pittsburgh, PA: University of Pittsburgh Press, 1973).

27 V. H. Vroom and A. G. Jago, *The New Leadership: Managing Participation in Organizations* (Upper Saddle River, NJ: Prentice Hall, 1988). See especially Chapter 8.

28 Based on V. H. Vroom, "Leadership and the Decision-Making Process," *Organizational Dynamics* 28, no. 4 (2000), p. 84.

29 V. H. Vroom, "Leadership and the Decision-Making Process," *Organizational Dynamics* 28, no. 4 (2000), pp. 82–94.

30 R. J. House, "A Path-Goal Theory of Leader Effectiveness," *Administrative Science Quarterly*, September 1971, pp. 321–338; R. J. House and T. R. Mitchell, "Path-Goal Theory of Leadership," *Journal of Contemporary Business*, Autumn 1974, p. 86; R. J. House, "Path-Goal Theory of Leadership: Lessons, Legacy, and a Reformulated Theory," *Leadership Quarterly*, Fall 1996, pp. 323–352.

31 J. C. Wofford and L. Z. Liska, "Path-Goal Theories of Leadership: A Meta-Analysis," *Journal of Management*, Winter 1993, pp. 857–376; A. Sagie and M. Koslowsky, "Organizational Attitudes and Behaviors as a Function of Participation in Strategic and Tactical Change Decisions: An Application of Path-Goal Theory," *Journal of Organizational Behavior*, January 1994, pp. 37–47.

32 Based on "Magnotta: Breaking New Ground with Innovative Marketing Strategies," *Industry Canada*, http://strategis.ic.gc.ca/epic/site/mfbs-gprea.nsf/en/lu00057e.html (accessed July 2, 2007); S. Fife 'Break the Competitive Roadblock: Three Canadian Success Stories," *Canadian Business*, May 18, 2007, http://www.canadianbusiness.com/innovation/article.jsp?content=20070518_094759_4716 (accessed July 2, 2007); and G. Stimmell, "Wine's Scrappy Duo," *Toronto Star*, Jan 24, 2007, p. D4.

33 B. M. Bass and R. E. Riggio, *Transformational Leadership*, 2nd ed. (Mahwah, NJ: Lawrence Erlbaum Associates, 2006), p. 3.

34 F. Vogelstein, "Mighty Amazon," *Fortune*, May 26, 2003, pp. 60–74.

35 J. A. Conger and R. N. Kanungo, "Behavioral Dimensions of Charismatic Leadership," in *Charismatic Leadership*, ed. J. A. Conger and R. N. Kanungo (San Francisco: Jossey-Bass, 1988), pp. 78–97; G. Yukl and J. M. Howell, "Organizational and Contextual Influences on the Emergence and Effectiveness of Charismatic Leadership," *Leadership Quarterly*, Summer 1999, pp. 257–283; and J. M. Crant and T. S. Bateman, "Charismatic Leadership Viewed from Above: The Impact of Proactive Personality," *Journal of Organizational Behavior*, February 2000, pp. 63–75.

36 J. A. Conger and R. N. Kanungo, *Charismatic Leadership in Organizations* (Thousand Oaks, CA: Sage, 1998).

37 K. S. Groves, "Linking Leader Skills, Follower Attitudes, and Contextual Variables via an Integrated Model of Charismatic Leadership," *Journal of Management*, April 2005, pp. 255–277; J. J. Sosik, "The Role of Personal Values in the Charismatic Leadership of Corporate Managers: A Model and Preliminary Field Study," *Leadership Quarterly*, April 2005, pp. 221–244; A. H. B. deHoogh, D. N. den Hartog, P. L. Koopman, H. Thierry, P. T. van den Berg, J. G. van der Weide, and C. P. M. Wilderom, "Leader Motives, Charismatic Leadership, and Subordinates' Work Attitudes in the Profit and Voluntary Sector," *Leadership Quarterly*, February 2005, pp. 17–38; J. M. Howell and B. Shamir, "The Role of Followers in the Charismatic Leadership Process: Relationships and Their Consequences," *Academy of Management Review*, January 2005, pp. 96–112; J. Paul, D. L. Costley, J. P. Howell, P. W. Dorfman, and D. Trafimow, "The Effects of Charismatic Leadership on Followers' Self-Concept Accessibility," *Journal of Applied Social Psychology*, September 2001, pp. 1821–1844; J. A. Conger, R. N. Kanungo, and S. T. Menon, "Charismatic Leadership and

Follower Effects," *Journal of Organizational Behavior* 21, 2000, pp. 747–767; R. W. Rowden, "The Relationship between Charismatic Leadership Behaviors and Organizational Commitment," *Leadership & Organization Development Journal*, January 2000, pp. 30–35; G. P. Shea and C. M. Howell, "Charismatic Leadership and Task Feedback: A Laboratory Study of Their Effects on Self-Efficacy," *Leadership Quarterly*, Fall 1999, pp. 375–396; S. A. Kirkpatrick and E. A. Locke, "Direct and Indirect Effects of Three Core Charismatic Leadership Components on Performance and Attitudes," *Journal of Applied Psychology*, February 1996, pp. 36–51; D. A. Waldman, B. M. Bass, and F. J. Yammarino, "Adding to Contingent-Reward Behavior: The Augmenting Effect of Charismatic Leadership," *Group & Organization Studies*, December 1990, pp. 381–394; and R. J. House, J. Woycke, and E. M. Fodor, "Charismatic and Noncharismatic Leaders: Differences in Behavior and Effectiveness," in *Charismatic Leadership*, ed. J. A. Conger and R. N. Kanungo (San Francisco: Jossey-Bass, 1988), pp. 103–104.

38 T. Dvir, D. Eden, B. J. Avolio, and B. Shamir, "Impact of Transformational Leadership on Follower Development and Performance: A Field Experiment," *Academy of Management Journal* 45, no. 4 (2002), pp. 735–744; R. J. House, J. Woycke, and E. M. Fodor, "Charismatic and Noncharismatic Leaders: Differences in Behavior and Effectiveness," in *Charismatic Leadership in Organizations*, ed. J. A. Conger and R. N. Kanungo (Thousand Oaks, CA: Sage, 1998), pp. 103–104; D. A. Waldman, B. M. Bass, and F. J. Yammarino, "Adding to Contingent-Reward Behavior: The Augmenting Effect of Charismatic Leadership," *Group & Organization Studies*, December 1990, pp. 381–394; S. A. Kirkpatrick and E. A. Locke, "Direct and Indirect Effects of Three Core Charismatic Leadership Components on Performance and Attitudes," *Journal of Applied Psychology*, February 1996, pp. 36–51; and J. A. Conger, R. N. Kanungo, and S. T. Menon, "Charismatic Leadership and Follower Outcome Effects" (paper presented at the 58th Annual Academy of Management Meetings, San Diego, CA, August 1998).

39 J. M. Howell and P. J. Frost, "A Laboratory Study of Charismatic Leadership," *Organizational Behavior & Human Decision Processes* 43, no. 2 (April 1989), pp. 243–269.

40 "Building a Better Boss," *Maclean's*, September 30, 1996, p. 41.

41 "Building a Better Boss," *Maclean's*, September 30, 1996, p. 41.

42 B. R. Agle, N. J. Nagarajan, J. A. Sonnenfeld, and D. Srinivasan, "Does CEO Charisma Matter? An Empirical Analysis of the Relationships Among Organizational Performance, Environmental Uncertainty, and Top Management Team Perceptions of CEO Charisma," *Academy of Management Journal*, February 2006, pp. 161–174.

43 A. Elsner, "The Era of CEO as Superhero Ends Amid Corporate Scandals," *Globe and Mail*, July 10, 2002, http://www.globeandmail.com.

44 J. A. Conger and R. N. Kanungo, "Training Charismatic Leadership: A Risky and Critical Task," in *Charismatic Leadership*, ed. J. A. Conger and R. N. Kanungo (San Francisco: Jossey-Bass, 1988), pp. 309–323; S. Caudron, "Growing Charisma," *IndustryWeek*, May 4, 1998, pp. 54–55; and R. Birchfield, "Creating Charismatic Leaders," *Management*, June 2000, pp. 30–31.

45 R. J. House, "A 1976 Theory of Charismatic Leadership" in *Leadership: The Cutting Edge*, ed. J. G. Hunt and L. L. Larson (Carbondale: Southern Illinois University Press); R. J. House and R. N. Aditya, "The Social Scientific Study of Leadership: Quo Vadis?" *Journal of Management* 23, no. 3 (1997), pp. 316–323; and J. G. Hunt, K. B. Boal, and G. E. Dodge, "The Effects of Visionary and Crisis-Responsive Charisma on Followers: An Experimental Examination," *Leadership Quarterly*, Fall 1999, pp. 423–448.

46 This definition is based on M. Sashkin, "The Visionary Leader," in *Charismatic Leadership*, ed. J. A. Conger and R. N. Kanungo, pp. 124–125 (San Francisco: Jossey-Bass, 1988); B. Nanus, *Visionary Leadership* (New York: Free Press, 1992), p. 8; N. H. Snyder and M. Graves, "Leadership and Vision," *Business Horizons*, January–February 1994, p. 1; and J. R. Lucas, "Anatomy of a Vision Statement," *Management Review*, February 1998, pp. 22–26.

47 B. Nanus, *Visionary Leadership* (New York: Free Press, 1992), p. 8.

48 Based on M. Sashkin, "The Visionary Leader," in *Charismatic Leadership*, ed. J. A. Conger and R. N. Kanungo (San Francisco: Jossey-Bass, 1988), pp. 128–130; and J. R. Baum, E. A. Locke, and S. A. Kirkpatrick, "A Longitudinal Study of the Relation of Vision and Vision Communication to Venture Growth in Entrepreneurial Firms," *Journal of Applied Psychology*, February 1998, pp. 43–54.

49 See http://www.newswire.ca/en/releases/archive/December2006/17/c8216.html.

50 J. M. Howell and B. Shamir, "The Role of Followers in the Charismatic Leadership Process: Relationships and Their Consequences," *Academy of Management Review* 30, no. 1 (2005), pp. 96–112.

51 B. M. Bass, "Theory of Transformational Leadership Redux," *Leadership Quarterly* 6, no. 4 (Winter 1995), pp. 463–478.

52 B. J. Avolio and B. M. Bass, "Transformational Leadership, Charisma, and Beyond" (working paper, School of Management, State University of New York, Binghamton, 1985), p. 14.

53 R. S. Rubin, D. C. Munz, and W. H. Bommer, "Leading from Within: The Effects of Emotion Recognition and Personality on Transformational Leadership Behavior," *Academy of Management Journal*, October 2005, pp. 845–858; T. A. Judge and J. E. Bono, "Five-Factor Model of Personality and Transformational Leadership," *Journal of Applied Psychology*, October 2000, pp. 751–765; B. M. Bass and B. J. Avolio, "Developing Transformational Leadership: 1992 and Beyond," *Journal of European Industrial Training*, January 1990, p. 23; and J. J. Hater and B. M. Bass, "Supervisors' Evaluation and Subordinates' Perceptions of Transformational and Transactional Leadership," *Journal of Applied Psychology*, November 1988, pp. 695–702.

54 R. F. Piccolo and J. A. Colquitt, "Transformational Leadership and Job Behaviors: The Mediating Role of Core Job Characteristics," *Academy of Management Journal*, April 2006, pp. 327–340; O. Epitropaki and R. Martin, "From Ideal to Real: A Longitudinal Study of the Role of Implicit Leadership Theories on Leader-Member Exchanges and Employee Outcomes," *Journal of Applied Psychology*, July 2005, pp. 659–676; J. E. Bono and T. A. Judge, "Self-Concordance at Work: Toward Understanding the Motivational Effects of Transformational Leaders," *Academy of Management Journal*, October 2003, pp. 554–571; T. Dvir, D. Eden, B. J. Avolio, and B. Shamir, "Impact of Transformational Leadership on Follower Development and Performance: A Field Experiment," *Academy of Management Journal*, August 2002, pp. 735–744; N. Sivasubramaniam, W. D. Murry, B. J. Avolio, and D. I. Jung, "A Longitudinal Model of the Effects of Team Leadership and Group Potency on Group Performance," *Group & Organization Management*, March 2002, pp. 66–96; J. M. Howell and B. J. Avolio, "Transformational Leadership, Transactional Leadership, Locus of Control, and Support for Innovation: Key Predictors of Consolidated-Business-Unit Performance," *Journal of Applied Psychology*, December

1993, pp. 891–911; R. T. Keller, "Transformational Leadership and the Performance of Research and Development Project Groups," *Journal of Management*, September 1992, pp. 489–501; and B. M. Bass and B. J. Avolio, "Developing Transformational Leadership: 1992 and Beyond," *Journal of European Industrial Training*, January 1990, p. 23.

55 R. Pillai, C. A. Schriesheim, and E. S. Williams, "Fairness Perceptions and Trust as Mediators of Transformational and Transactional Leadership: A Two-Sample Study," *Journal of Management* 25, 1999, pp. 897–933.

56 G. M. Spreitzer, K. H. Perttula, and K. Xin, "Traditionality Matters: An Examination of the Effectiveness of Transformational Leadership in the United States and Taiwan," *Journal of Organizational Behavior* 26, no. 3 (2005), pp. 205–227.

57 See J. R. P. French Jr. and B. Raven, "The Bases of Social Power," in *Group Dynamics: Research and Theory*, ed. D. Cartwright and A. F. Zander (New York: Harper & Row, 1960), pp. 607–623; P. M. Podsakoff and C. A. Schriesheim, "Field Studies of French and Raven's Bases of Power: Critique, Reanalysis, and Suggestions for Future Research," *Psychological Bulletin*, May 1985, pp. 387–411; R. K. Shukla, "Influence of Power Bases in Organizational Decision Making: A Contingency Model," *Decision Sciences*, July 1982, pp. 450–470; D. E. Frost and A. J. Stahelski, "The Systematic Measurement of French and Raven's Bases of Social Power in Workgroups," *Journal of Applied Social Psychology*, April 1988, pp. 375–389; and T. R. Hinkin and C. A. Schriesheim, "Development and Application of New Scales to Measure the French and Raven (1959) Bases of Social Power," *Journal of Applied Psychology*, August 1989, pp. 561–567.

58 See the Royal Australian Navy website, http://www.navy.gov.au.

59 J. Partridge and J. Saunders, "Milton's Right-Hand Man Quits Air Canada," *Globe and Mail*, April 7, 2004, p. A1.

60 J. M. Kouzes and B. Z. Posner, *Credibility: How Leaders Gain and Lose It, and Why People Demand It* (San Francisco: Jossey-Bass, 1993), p. 14.

61 Based on L. T. Hosmer, "Trust: The Connecting Link Between Organizational Theory and Philosophical Ethics," *Academy of Management Review*, April 1995, p. 393; R. C. Mayer, J. H. Davis, and F. D. Schoorman, "An Integrative Model of Organizational Trust," *Academy of Management Review*, July 1995, p. 712; and G. M. Spreitzer and A. K. Mishra, "Giving Up Control Without Losing Control," *Group & Organization Management*, June 1999, pp. 155–187.

62 P. L. Schindler and C. C. Thomas, "The Structure of Interpersonal Trust in the Workplace," *Psychological Reports*, October 1993, pp. 563–573.

63 H. H. Tan and C. S. F. Tan, "Toward the Differentiation of Trust in Supervisor and Trust in Organization," *Genetic, Social, and General Psychology Monographs*, May 2000, pp. 241–260.

64 R. C. Mayer and M. B. Gavin, "Trust in Management and Performance: Who Minds the Shop While the Employees Watch the Boss?" *Academy of Management Journal*, October 2005, pp. 874–888; and K. T. Dirks and D. L. Ferrin, "Trust in Leadership: Meta-Analytic Findings and Implications for Research and Practice," *Journal of Applied Psychology*, August 2002, pp. 611–628.

65 This section is based on F. Bartolome, "Nobody Trusts the Boss Completely—Now What?" *Harvard Business Review*, March–April 1989, pp. 135–142; J. K. Butler Jr., "Toward Understanding and Measuring Conditions of Trust: Evolution of a Conditions of Trust Inventory," *Journal of Management*, September 1991, pp. 643–663; and K. T. Dirks and D. L. Ferrin, "Trust in Leadership: Meta-Analytic Findings and Implications for Research and Practice," *Journal of Applied Psychology*, August 2002, pp. 611–628.

66 Based on "Magnotta: Breaking New Ground with Innovative Marketing Strategies," *Industry Canada*, http://strategis.ic.gc.ca/epic/site/mfbs-gprea.nsf/en/lu00057e.html (accessed July 2, 2007); S. Fife 'Break the Competitive Roadblock: Three Canadian Success Stories," *Canadian Business*, May 18, 2007, http://www.canadianbusiness.com/innovation/article.jsp?content=20070518_094759_4716 (accessed July 2, 2007); and G. Stimmell, "Wine's Scrappy Duo," *Toronto Star*, Jan 24, 2007, p. D4.

67 This section is based on R. B. Morgan, "Self- and Co-Worker Perceptions of Ethics and Their Relationships to Leadership and Salary," *Academy of Management Journal*, February 1993, pp. 200–214; E. P. Hollander, "Ethical Challenges in the Leader–Follower Relationship," *Business Ethics Quarterly*, January 1995, pp. 55–65; J. C. Rost, "Leadership: A Discussion about Ethics," *Business Ethics Quarterly*, January 1995, pp. 129–142; R. N. Kanungo and M. Mendonca, *Ethical Dimensions of Leadership* (Thousand Oaks, CA: Sage Publications, 1996); J. B. Ciulla, ed., *Ethics: The Heart of Leadership* (New York: Praeger Publications, 1998); J. D. Costa, *The Ethical Imperative: Why Moral Leadership Is Good Business* (Cambridge, MA: Perseus Press, 1999); and N. M. Tichy and A. McGill, eds., *The Ethical Challenge: How to Build Honest Business Leaders* (New York: John Wiley & Sons, 2003).

68 J. M. Burns, *Leadership* (New York: Harper & Row, 1978).

69 J. M. Avolio, S. Kahai, and G. E. Dodge, "The Ethics of Charismatic Leadership: Submission or Liberation?" *Academy of Management Executive*, May 1992, pp. 43–55.

70 L. K. Trevino, M. Brown, and L. P. Hartman, "A Qualitative Investigation of Perceived Executive Ethical Leadership: Perceptions from Inside and Outside the Executive Suite," *Human Relations*, January 2003, pp. 5–37.

71 C. Kleiman, "Virtual Teams Make Loyalty More Realistic," *Chicago Tribune*, January 23, 2001, p. B1.

72 B. J. Alge, C. Wiethoff, and H. J. Klein, "When Does the Medium Matter? Knowledge-Building Experiences and Opportunities in Decision-Making Teams," *Organizational Behavior and Human Decision Processes* 91, no. 1 (2003), pp. 26–37; C. O. Grosse, "Managing Communication within Virtual Intercultural Teams," *Business Communication Quarterly*, December 2002, pp. 22–38; M. M. Montoya-Weiss, A. P. Massey, and M. Song, "Getting It Together: Temporal Coordination and Conflict Management in Global Virtual Teams," *Academy of Management Journal*, December 2001, pp. 1251–1262; M. L. Maznevski and K. M. Chudoba, "Bridging Space Over Time: Global Virtual-Team Dynamics and Effectiveness," *Organization Science* 11, 2000, pp. 473–492; W. F. Cascio, "Managing a Virtual Workplace," *Academy of Management Executive*, August 2000, pp. 81–90; and A. M. Townsend, S. M. DeMarie, and A. R. Hendrickson, "'Virtual Teams' Technology and the Workplace of the Future," *Academy of Management Executive*, August 1998, pp. 17–29.

73 W. F. Cascio, "Managing a Virtual Workplace," *Academy of Management Executive*, August 2000, pp. 88–89.

74 N. Desmond, "The CEO Dashboard," *Business 2.0*, August 2002, p. 34.

75 W. A. Randolph, "Navigating the Journey to Empowerment," *Organizational Dynamics*, Spring 1995, pp. 19–32; R. C. Ford and M. D. Fottler, "Empowerment: A Matter of Degree," *Academy of*

Management Executive, August 1995, pp. 21–31; R. C. Herrenkohl, G. T. Judson, and J. A. Heffner, "Defining and Measuring Employee Empowerment," *Journal of Applied Behavioral Science*, September 1999, p. 373; C. Robert and T. M. Probst, "Empowerment and Continuous Improvement in the United States, Mexico, Poland, and India," *Journal of Applied Psychology*, October 2000, pp. 643–658; C. Gomez and B. Rosen, "The Leader-Member Link between Managerial Trust and Employee Empowerment," *Group & Organization Management*, March 2001, pp. 53–69; W. Alan Rudolph and M. Sashkin, "Can Organizational Empowerment Work in Multinational Settings?" *Academy of Management Executive*, February 2002, pp. 102–115; and P. K. Mills and G. R. Ungson, "Reassessing the Limits of Structural Empowerment: Organizational Constitution and Trust as Controls," *Academy of Management Review*, January 2003, pp. 143–153.

76 J. Schaubroeck, J. R. Jones, and J. L. Xie, "Individual Differences in Utilizing Control to Cope with Job Demands: Effects on Susceptibility to Infectious Disease," *Journal of Applied Psychology* 86, no. 2 (2001), pp. 265–278; and A. M. Owens, "Empowerment Can Make You Ill, Study Says," *National Post*, April 30, 2001, pp. A1, A8.

77 "Delta Promotes Empowerment," *Globe and Mail*, May 31, 1999, Advertising Supplement, p. C5.

78 S. Caminiti, "What Team Leaders Need to Know," *Fortune*, February 20, 1995, p. 93.

79 S. Caminiti, "What Team Leaders Need to Know," *Fortune*, February 20, 1995, p. 100.

80 N. Steckler and N. Fondas, "Building Team Leader Effectiveness: A Diagnostic Tool," *Organizational Dynamics*, Winter 1995, p. 20.

81 R. S. Wellins, W. C. Byham, and G. R. Dixon, *Inside Teams* (San Francisco: Jossey-Bass, 1994), p. 318.

82 N. Steckler and N. Fondas, "Building Team Leader Effectiveness: A Diagnostic Tool," *Organizational Dynamics*, Winter 1995, p. 21.

83 T. Kepner, "Jeter Shows Once Again Why He's the Captain," *New York Times*, July 3, 2004, http://www.nytimes.com (accessed July 3, 2004).

84 J. Schneider and R. F. Littrell, "Leadership Preferences of German and English Managers," *Journal of Management Development* 22, nos. 1–2 (2003), pp. 130–148.

85 R. J. House, "Leadership in the Twenty-First Century," in *The Changing Nature of Work*, ed. A. Howard (San Francisco: Jossey-Bass, 1995) p. 443; M. F. Peterson and J. G. Hunt, "International Perspectives on International Leadership," *Leadership Quarterly*, Fall 1997, pp. 203–231; and J. R. Schermerhorn and M. H. Bond, "Cross-Cultural Leadership in Collectivism and High Power Distance Settings," *Leadership & Organization Development Journal* 18, no. 4–5 (1997), pp. 187–193.

86 D. N. Hartog, R. J. House; P. J. Hanges; S. A. Ruiz-Quintanilla, and P. W. Dorfman, "Culture Specific and Cross-Culturally Generalizable Implicit Leadership Theories: Are the Attributes of Charismatic/Transformational Leadership Universally Endorsed?" *Leadership Quarterly*, Summer 1999, pp. 219–256; and D. E. Carl and M. Javidan, "Universality of Charismatic Leadership: A Multi-Nation Study" (paper presented at the National Academy of Management Conference, Washington, DC, August 2001).

87 D. E. Carl and M. Javidan, "Universality of Charismatic Leadership: A Multi-Nation Study" (paper presented at the National Academy of Management Conference, Washington, DC, August 2001), p. 29.

88 http://www.statcan.ca/english/freepub/89-503-XIE/0010589-503-XIE.pdf; and J. McFarland, "Women Still Find Slow Rise to Power Positions," *Globe and Mail*, March 13, 2003, pp. B1, B7.

89 L. Ramsay, "A League of Their Own," *Globe and Mail*, November 23, 2002, p. B11.

90 L. Ramsay, "A League of Their Own," *Globe and Mail*, November 23, 2002, p. B11.

91 All numbers are for 2005, except for Japan, which is 2004. United Nations, Statistics on Men and Women, http://mdgs.un.org/unsd/demographic/products/indwm/tab5d.htm (accessed October 8, 2007).

92 G. N. Powell, D. A. Butterfield, and J. D. Parent, "Gender and Managerial Stereotypes: Have the Times Changed?" *Journal of Management* 28, no. 2 (2002), pp. 177–193.

93 A. H. Eagly and B. T. Johnson, "Gender and Leadership Style: A Meta-Analysis," *Psychological Bulletin*, September 1990, pp. 233–256; A. H. Eagly and S. J. Karau, "Gender and the Emergence of Leaders: A Meta-Analysis," *Journal of Personality and Social Psychology*, May 1991, pp. 685–710; J. B. Rosener, "Ways Women Lead," *Harvard Business Review*, November–December 1990, pp. 119–125; A. H. Eagly, M. G. Makhijani, and B. G. Klonsky, "Gender and the Evaluation of Leaders: A Meta-Analysis," *Psychological Bulletin*, January 1992, pp. 3–22; A. H. Eagly, S. J. Karau, and B. T. Johnson, "Gender and Leadership Style among School Principals: A Meta-Analysis," *Educational Administration Quarterly*, February 1992, pp. 76–102; L. R. Offermann and C. Beil, "Achievement Styles of Women Leaders and Their Peers," *Psychology of Women Quarterly*, March 1992, pp. 37–56; R. L. Kent and S. E. Moss, "Effects of Size and Gender Role on Leader Emergence," *Academy of Management Journal*, October 1994, pp. 1335–1346; C. Lee, "The Feminization of Management," *Training*, November 1994, pp. 25–31; H. Collingwood, "Women as Managers: Not Just Different: Better," *Working Woman*, November 1995, p. 14; J. B. Rosener, *America's Competitive Secret: Women Managers* (New York: Oxford University Press, 1995); and J. Cliff, N. Langton, and H. Aldrich, "Walking the Talk? Gendered Rhetoric vs. Action in Small Firms," *Organizational Studies* 26, no. 1 (2005), pp. 63–91.

94 See F. J. Yammarino, A. J. Dubinsky, L. B. Comer, and M. A. Jolson, "Women and Transformational and Contingent Reward Leadership: A Multiple-Levels-of-Analysis Perspective," *Academy of Management Journal*, February 1997, pp. 205–222; M. Gardiner and M. Tiggemann, "Gender Differences in Leadership Style, Job Stress and Mental Health in Male- and Female-Dominated Industries," *Journal of Occupational and Organizational Psychology*, September 1999, pp. 301–315; C. L. Ridgeway, "Gender, Status, and Leadership," *Journal of Social Issues*, Winter 2001, pp. 637–655; W. H. Decker and D. M. Rotondo, "Relationships Among Gender, Type of Humor, and Perceived Leader Effectiveness," *Journal of Managerial Issues*, Winter 2001, pp. 450–465; J. M. Norvilitis and H. M. Reid, "Evidence for an Association Between Gender-Role Identity and a Measure of Executive Function," *Psychological Reports*, February 2002, pp. 35–45; N. Z. Selter, "Gender Differences in Leadership: Current Social Issues and Future Organizational Implications," *Journal of Leadership Studies*, Spring 2002, pp. 88–99; J. Becker, R. A. Ayman, and K. Korabik, "Discrepancies in Self/Subordinates' Perceptions of Leadership Behavior: Leader's Gender, Organizational Context, and Leader's Self-Monitoring," *Group & Organization Management*, June 2002, pp. 226–244; A. H. Eagly and S. J. Karau, "Role Congruity Theory of Prejudice Toward Female Leaders," *Psychological Review*, July 2002, pp. 573–598; and K. M. Bartol, D. C. Martin, and J. A. Kromkowski, "Leadership and the Glass

Ceiling: Gender and Ethnic Influences on Leader Behaviors at Middle and Executive Managerial Levels," *Journal of Leadership & Organizational Studies*, Winter 2003, pp. 8–19.

95 M. Gardiner and M. Tiggemann, "Gender Differences in Leadership Style, Job Stress and Mental Health in Male- and Female-Dominated Industries," *Journal of Occupational and Organizational Psychology*, September 1999, pp. 301–315.

96 "Women 'Take Care,' Men 'Take Charge:' Stereotyping of U.S. Business Leaders Exposed," *Catalyst* (New York, 2005).

97 C. Hymowitz, "Too Many Women Fall for Stereotypes of Selves, Study Says," *Wall Street Journal*, October 24, 2005, p. B1; B. Kantrowitz, "When Women Lead," *Newsweek*, October 24, 2005, pp. 46–61; and "Why Can't Women Be Leaders Too?" *Gallup Management Journal*, October 13, 2005, http://gmj.gallup.com/content/default.aspx?ci=19000.

98 J. Guyon, "The Art of the Decision," *Fortune*, November 14, 2005, p. 144; A. H. Eagly, S. J. Karau, and M. G. Makhijani, "Gender and the Effectiveness of Leaders: A Meta-Analysis," *Psychological Bulletin* 117, 1995, pp. 125–145; J. M. Norvilitis and H. M. Reid, "Evidence for an Association Between Gender-Role Identity and a Measure of Executive Function," *Psychological Reports*, February 2002, pp. 35–45; W. H. Decker and D. M. Rotondo, "Relationships among Gender, Type of Humor, and Perceived Leader Effectiveness," *Journal of Managerial Issues*, Winter 2001, pp. 450–465; H. Aguinis and S. K. R. Adams, "Social-Role versus Structural Models of Gender and Influence Use in Organizations: A Strong Inference Approach," *Group & Organization Management*, December 1998, pp. 414–446; and A. H. Eagly, S. J. Karau, and M. G. Makhijani, "Gender and the Effectiveness of Leaders: A Meta-Analysis," *Psychological Bulletin* 117, 1995, pp. 125–145.

99 A. H. Eagly, M. C. Johannesen-Schmidt, and M. L. van Engen, "Transformational, Transactional, and Laissez-Faire Leadership Styles: A Meta-Analysis Comparing Women and Men," *Psychological Bulletin* 129, no. 4 (July 2003), pp. 569–591; K. M. Bartol, D. C. Martin, and J. A. Kromkowski, "Leadership and the Glass Ceiling: Gender and Ethnic Influences on Leader Behaviors at Middle and Executive Managerial Levels," *Journal of Leadership & Organizational Studies*, Winter 2003, pp. 8–19; and R. Sharpe, "As Leaders, Women Rule," *BusinessWeek*, November 20, 2000, pp. 74–84.

100 K. M. Bartol, D. C. Martin, and J. A. Kromkowski, "Leadership and the Glass Ceiling: Gender and Ethnic Influences on Leader Behaviors at Middle and Executive Managerial Levels," *Journal of Leadership & Organizational Studies*, Winter 2003, pp. 8–19.

101 Adapted with permission from T. Sergiovanni, R. Metzcus, and L. Burden, "Toward a Particularistic Approach to Leadership Style: Some Findings," *American Educational Research Journal* 6, no. 1 (January 1969), American Educational Research Association, Washington, DC.

102 Situation adapted from information in J. Menn, "Ellison Talks Tough on Bid for PeopleSoft," *Los Angeles Times*, July 10, 2003, p. C11; M. Mangalindan, D. Clark, and R. Sidel, "Hostile Move Augurs High-Tech Consolidation," *Wall Street Journal*, June 9, 2003, p. A11; A. Pham, "Oracle's Merger Hurdles Get Higher," *Los Angeles Times*, June 30, 2003, p. C11; S. Pannill, "Smashmouth PR Meets High Tech," *Forbes*, May 28, 2001, p. 9; and F. Vogelstein, "Oracle's Ellison Turns Hostile," *Fortune*, June 23, 2003, p. 28.

103 Based on M. Henricks, "Kids These Days," *Entrepreneur*, May 2002, pp. 71–72.

104 L. M. Fisher, "Ricardo Semler Won't Take Control," *Strategy+Business*, Winter 2005, pp. 78–88; R. Semler, *The Seven-Day Weekend: Changing the Way Work Works* (New York: Penguin Group, 2004); A. J. Vogl, "The Anti-CEO," *Across the Board*, May–June 2004, pp. 30–36; G. Colvin, "The Anti-Control Freak," *Fortune*, November 26, 2001, p. 22; and R. Semler, "Managing without Managers," *Harvard Business Review*, September–October 1989, pp. 76–84.

105 Based on H. Mintzberg, *Power In and Around Organizations* (Upper Saddle River, NJ: Prentice Hall, 1983), p. 24; and P. L. Hunsaker, *Training in Management Skills* (Upper Saddle River, NJ: Prentice Hall, 2001), pp. 339–364.

106 Based on S. A. Culbert and J. J. McDonough, *The Invisible War: Pursuing Self-Interest at Work* (New York: John Wiley, 1980); J. Pfeffer, *Power in Organizations* (Marshfield, MA: Pitman, 1981); H. Mintzberg, *Power In and Around Organizations* (Upper Saddle River, NJ: Prentice Hall, 1983); and S. P. Robbins and P. L. Hunsaker, *Training in Interpersonal Skills: TIPS for Managing People at Work*, 3rd ed. (Upper Saddle River, NJ: Prentice Hall, 2003).

Chapter 13

1 Based on Hoover's Online, http://www.hoover.com; S. Butcher, "Relentless Rise in Pleasure Seekers," *Financial Times*, July 6, 2003, http://news.ft.com (accessed July 7, 2003); C. Blackhurst, "The Chris Blackhurst Interview: Sir Terry Leahy," *Management Today*, February 2004, pp. 32–34; and "Tesco at a Glance," *Tesco*, http://www.tescocorporate.com/page.aspx?pointerid=A8E0E60508F94A8DBA909E2ABB5F2CC7 (accessed September 20, 2007).

2 G. P. Latham and C. C. Pinder, "Work Motivation Theory and Research at the Dawn of the Twenty-First Century,"*Annual Review of Psychology* 56, no. 1 (2005), pp. 485–516; and C. C. Pinder, *Work Motivation in Organizational Behavior* (Upper Saddle River, NJ: Prentice Hall, 1998), p. 11. See also E. A. Locke and G. P. Latham, "What Should We Do About Motivation Theory? Six Recommendations for the Twenty-First Century," *Academy of Management Review* 29, no. 3 (July 1, 2004), pp. 388–403.

3 See, for instance, T. R. Mitchell, "Matching Motivational Strategies with Organizational Contexts," in *Research in Organizational Behavior*, vol. 19, ed. B. M. Staw and L. L. Cummings (Greenwich, CT: JAI Press, 1997), pp. 60–62; and R. Katerberg and G. J. Blau, "An Examination of Level and Direction of Effort and Job Performance," *Academy of Management Journal*, June 1983, pp. 249–257.

4 G. Shaw, "Canada Lags World on Job Quality," *Vancouver Sun*, September 18, 2004, p. F5.

5 Based on S. Butcher, "Relentless Rise in Pleasure Seekers," *Financial Times*, July 6, 2003, http://news.ft.com (accessed July 7, 2003).

6 A. Maslow, *Motivation and Personality* (New York: McGraw-Hill, 1954); A. Maslow, D. C. Stephens, and G. Heil, *Maslow on Management* (New York: John Wiley & Sons, 1998); M. L. Ambrose and C. T. Kulik, "Old Friends, New Faces: Motivation Research in the 1990s," *Journal of Management* 25, no. 3 (1999), pp. 231–292; and "Dialogue," *Academy of Management Review*, October 2000, pp. 696–701.

7 See, for example, D. T. Hall and K. E. Nongaim, "An Examination of Maslow's Need Hierarchy in an Organizational Setting," *Organizational Behavior and Human Performance*, February 1968, pp. 12–35; E. E. Lawler III and J. L. Suttle, "A Causal Correlational Test of the Need Hierarchy Concept," *Organizational Behavior and Human*

Performance, April 1972, pp. 265–287; R. M. Creech, "Employee Motivation," *Management Quarterly*, Summer 1995, pp. 33–39; J. Rowan, "Maslow Amended," *Journal of Humanistic Psychology*, Winter 1998, pp. 81–92; J. Rowan, "Ascent and Descent in Maslow's Theory," *Journal of Humanistic Psychology*, Summer 1999, pp. 125–133; and M. L. Ambrose and C. T. Kulik, "Old Friends, New Faces: Motivation Research in the 1990s," *Journal of Management* 25, no. 3 (1999), pp. 231–292.

8 D. McGregor, *The Human Side of Enterprise* (New York: McGraw-Hill, 1960). For an updated analysis of Theories X and Y, see R. J. Summers and S. F. Conshaw, "A Study of McGregor's Theory X, Theory Y and the Influence of Theory X, Theory Y Assumptions on Causal Attributions for Instances of Worker Poor Performance," in *Organizational Behavior*, ASAC 1988 Conference Proceedings, vol. 9, Part 5, ed. S. L. McShaneed (Halifax, NS: ASAC, 1988), pp. 115–123.

9 K. W. Thomas, *Intrinsic Motivation at Work* (San Francisco: Berrett-Koehler, 2000); and K. W. Thomas, "Intrinsic Motivation and How It Works," *Training*, October 2000, pp. 130–135.

10 F. Herzberg, B. Mausner, and B. Snyderman, *The Motivation to Work* (New York: John Wiley, 1959); F. Herzberg, *The Managerial Choice: To Be Effective or to Be Human*, rev. ed. (Salt Lake City: Olympus, 1982); R. M. Creech, "Employee Motivation," *Management Quarterly*, Summer 1995, pp. 33–39; and M. L. Ambrose and C. T. Kulik, "Old Friends, New Faces: Motivation Research in the 1990s," *Journal of Management* 25, no. 3 (1999), pp. 231–292.

11 Based on G. Bellett, "Firm's Secret to Success Lies in Treating Workers Right," *Vancouver Sun*, March 21, 2001, pp. D7, D11; V. Galt, "Getting Fit on the Job," *Globe and Mail*, November 6, 2002, p. C1; and C. Lochhead, "Healthy Workplace Programs at Pazmac Enterprises Ltd.," *Canadian Labour and Business Centre*, March 2002, http://www.clbc.ca/files/CaseStudies/pazmac.pdf (accessed September 20, 2007).

12 Based on S. Butcher, "Relentless Rise in Pleasure Seekers," *Financial Times*, July 6, 2003, http://news.ft.com (accessed July 7, 2003); A. Nottage, "Tesco," *Human Resources*, May 2003, p. 10; and C. Blackhurst, "The Chris Blackhurst Interview: Sir Terry Leahy," *Management Today*, February 2004, pp. 32–34.

13 M. L. Ambrose and C. T. Kulik, "Old Friends, New Faces: Motivation Research in the 1990s," *Journal of Management* 25, no. 3 (1999), pp. 231–292.

14 See, for example, R. W. Griffin, "Toward an Integrated Theory of Task Design," in *Research in Organizational Behavior*, vol. 9, ed. B. Staw and L. L. Cummings (Greenwich, CT: JAI Press, 1987), pp. 79–120; and M. Campion, "Interdisciplinary Approaches to Job Design: A Constructive Replication with Extensions," *Journal of Applied Psychology*, August 1988, pp. 467–481.

15 S. Caudron, "The De-Jobbing of America," *IndustryWeek*, September 5, 1994, pp. 31–36; W. Bridges, "The End of the Job," *Fortune*, September 19, 1994, pp. 62–74; and K. H. Hammonds, K. Kelly, and K. Thurston, "Rethinking Work," *BusinessWeek*, October 12, 1994, pp. 75–87.

16 M. A. Campion and C. L. McClelland, "Follow-Up and Extension of the Interdisciplinary Costs and Benefits of Enlarged Jobs," *Journal of Applied Psychology*, June 1993, pp. 339–351; M. L. Ambrose and C. T. Kulik, "Old Friends, New Faces: Motivation Research in the 1990s," *Journal of Management* 25, no. 3 (1999), pp. 231–292.

17 See, for example, J. R. Hackman and G. R. Oldham, *Work Redesign* (Reading, MA: Addison-Wesley, 1980); J. B. Miner, *Theories of Organizational Behavior*, pp. 231–266 (Hinsdale, IL: Dryden Press,

1980); R. W. Griffin, "Effects of Work Redesign on Employee Perceptions, Attitudes, and Behaviors: A Long-Term Investigation," *Academy of Management Journal*, June 1991, pp. 425–435; J. L. Cotton, *Employee Involvement* (Newbury Park, CA: Sage, 1993), pp. 141–172; and M. L. Ambrose and C. T. Kulik, "Old Friends, New Faces: Motivation Research in the 1990s," *Journal of Management* 25, no. 3 (1999), pp. 231–292.

18 J. R. Hackman and G. R. Oldham, "Development of the Job Diagnostic Survey," *Journal of Applied Psychology*, April 1975, pp. 159–170; and J. R. Hackman and G. R. Oldham, "Motivation through the Design of Work: Test of a Theory," *Organizational Behavior and Human Performance*, August 1976, pp. 250–279.

19 J. R. Hackman, "Work Design," in *Improving Life at Work*, ed. J. R. Hackman and J. L. Suttle (Glenview, IL: Scott, Foresman, 1977), p. 129; M. L. Ambrose and C. T. Kulik, "Old Friends, New Faces: Motivation Research in the 1990s," *Journal of Management* 25, no. 3 (1999), pp. 231–292.

20 "Entrepreneur Profile," *National Post*, http://www.canada.com/nationalpost/entrepreneur/ail.html (accessed September 20, 2007).

21 J. S. Adams, "Inequity in Social Exchanges," in *Advances in Experimental Social Psychology*, vol. 2, ed. L. Berkowitz (New York: Academic Press, 1965), pp. 267–300; and M. L. Ambrose and C. T. Kulik, "Old Friends, New Faces: Motivation Research in the 1990s," *Journal of Management* 25, no. 3 (1999), pp. 231–292.

22 See, for example, P. S. Goodman and A. Friedman, "An Examination of Adams' Theory of Inequity," *Administrative Science Quarterly*, September 1971, pp. 271–288; E. Walster, G. W. Walster, and W. G. Scott, *Equity: Theory and Research* (Boston: Allyn & Bacon, 1978); and J. Greenberg, "Cognitive Reevaluation of Outcomes in Response to Underpayment Inequity," *Academy of Management Journal*, March 1989, pp. 174–184.

23 See, for example, M. R. Carrell, "A Longitudinal Field Assessment of Employee Perceptions of Equitable Treatment," *Organizational Behavior and Human Performance*, February 1978, pp. 108–118; R. G. Lord and J. A. Hohenfeld, "Longitudinal Field Assessment of Equity Effects on the Performance of Major League Baseball Players," *Journal of Applied Psychology*, February 1979, pp. 19–26; and J. E. Dittrich and M. R. Carrell, "Organizational Equity Perceptions, Employee Job Satisfaction, and Departmental Absence and Turnover Rates," *Organizational Behavior and Human Performance*, August 1979, pp. 29–40.

24 Based on "Councillors Approve Own Pay Hike," *cbc.ca*, July 28, 2006; and Z. Ruryk, "Most T.O. Residents Against Council Raise," *TorontoSun.com*, September 9, 2007.

25 P. S. Goodman, "An Examination of Referents Used in the Evaluation of Pay," *Organizational Behavior and Human Performance*, October 1974, pp. 170–195; S. Ronen, "Equity Perception in Multiple Comparisons: A Field Study," *Human Relations*, April 1986, pp. 333–346; R. W. Scholl, E. A. Cooper, and J. F. McKenna, "Referent Selection in Determining Equity Perception: Differential Effects on Behavioral and Attitudinal Outcomes," *Personnel Psychology*, Spring 1987, pp. 113–127; and C. T. Kulik and M. L. Ambrose, "Personal and Situational Determinants of Referent Choice," *Academy of Management Review*, April 1992, pp. 212–237.

26 A. Wahl, "Canada's Best Workplaces: Overview," *Canadian Business*, April 26, 2007, http://www.canadianbusiness.com/managing/career/article.jsp?content=20070425_85420_85420 (accessed September 20, 2007).

27 See, for example, J. Brockner, "Why It's So Hard to Be Fair," *Harvard Business Review*, March 2006, pp. 122–129; J. A. Colquitt,

"Does the Justice of One Interact with the Justice of Many? Reactions to Procedural Justice in Teams," *Journal of Applied Psychology*, August 2004, pp. 633–646; M. A. Konovsky, "Understanding Procedural Justice and Its Impact on Business Organizations," *Journal of Management* 26, no. 3 (2000), pp. 489–511; R. C. Dailey and D. J. Kirk, "Distributive and Procedural Justice as Antecedents of Job Dissatisfaction and Intent to Turnover," *Human Relations*, March 1992, pp. 305–316; and D. B. McFarlin and P. D. Sweeney, "Distributive and Procedural Justice as Predictors of Satisfaction with Personal and Organizational Outcomes," *Academy of Management Journal*, August 1992, pp. 626–637.

28 G. P. Latham and C. C. Pinder, "Work Motivation Theory and Research at the Dawn of the Twenty-First Century," *Annual Review of Psychology* 56, 2005, pp. 485–516; P. S. Goodman, "Social Comparison Process in Organizations," in *New Directions in Organizational Behavior*, ed. B. M. Staw and G. R. Salancik (Chicago: St. Clair, 1977), pp. 97–132; and J. Greenberg, "A Taxonomy of Organizational Justice Theories," *Academy of Management Review*, January 1987, pp. 9–22.

29 V. H. Vroom, *Work and Motivation* (New York: John Wiley, 1964).

30 See, for example, H. G. Heneman III and D. P. Schwab, "Evaluation of Research on Expectancy Theory Prediction of Employee Performance," *Psychological Bulletin*, July 1972, pp. 1–9; and L. Reinharth and M. Wahba, "Expectancy Theory as a Predictor of Work Motivation, Effort Expenditure, and Job Performance," *Academy of Management Journal*, September 1975, pp. 502–537.

31 See, for example, V. H. Vroom, "Organizational Choice: A Study of Pre- and Postdecision Processes," *Organizational Behavior and Human Performance*, April 1966, pp. 212–225; L. W. Porter and E. E. Lawler III, *Managerial Attitudes and Performance* (Homewood, IL: Richard D. Irwin, 1968); W. Van Eerde and H. Thierry, "Vroom's Expectancy Models and Work-Related Criteria: A Meta-Analysis," *Journal of Applied Psychology*, October 1996, pp. 575–586; and M. L. Ambrose and C. T. Kulik, "Old Friends, New Faces: Motivation Research in the 1990s," *Journal of Management* 25, no. 3 (1999), pp. 231–292.

32 See, for instance, M. Siegall, "The Simplistic Five: An Integrative Framework for Teaching Motivation," *Organizational Behavior Teaching Review* 12, no. 4 (1987–1988), pp. 141–143.

33 S. Butcher, "Relentless Rise in Pleasure Seekers," *Financial Times*, July 6, 2003, http://news.ft.com (accessed July 7, 2003); "Tesco Pilots Student Benefits," *Employee Benefits*, November 7, 2003, p. P12; and http://www.tescocorporate.com/annualreview07/01_tescostory/tescostory3.html (accessed October 14, 2007).

34 J. R. Billings and D. L. Sharpe, "Factors Influencing Flextime Usage among Employed Married Women," *Consumer Interests Annual*, vol. 45 (Ames, IA: American Council on Consumer Interests, 1999), pp. 89–94; and I. Harpaz, "The Importance of Work Goals: An International Perspective," *Journal of International Business Studies*, First Quarter 1990, pp. 75–93.

35 N. Ramachandran, "New Paths at Work," *U.S. News & World Report*, March 20, 2006, p. 47; S. Armour, "Generation Y: They've Arrived at Work with a New Attitude," *USA Today*, November 6, 2005, pp. B1+; R. Kanfer and P. L. Ackerman, "Aging, Adult Development, and Work Motivation," *Academy of Management Review*, July 2004, pp. 440–458; and R. Bernard, D. Cosgrave, and J. Welsh, *Chips and Pop: Decoding the Nexus Generation* (Toronto: Malcolm Lester Books, 1998).

36 N. J. Adler, *International Dimensions of Organizational Behavior*, 4th ed. (Cincinnati, OH: South-Western, 2002), p. 174.

37 G. Hofstede, "Motivation, Leadership and Organization: Do American Theories Apply Abroad?" *Organizational Dynamics*, Summer 1980, p. 55.

38 J. K. Giacobbe-Miller, D. J. Miller, and V. I. Victorov, "A Comparison of Russian and U.S. Pay Allocation Decisions, Distributive Justice Judgments and Productivity Under Different Payment Conditions," *Personnel Psychology*, Spring 1998, pp. 137–163.

39 S. L. Mueller and L. D. Clarke, "Political-Economic Context and Sensitivity to Equity: Differences between the United States and the Transition Economies of Central and Eastern Europe," *Academy of Management Journal*, June 1998, pp. 319–329.

40 I. Harpaz, "The Importance of Work Goals: An International Perspective," *Journal of International Business Studies*, First Quarter 1990, pp. 75–93.

41 G. E. Popp, H. J. Davis, and T. T. Herbert, "An International Study of Intrinsic Motivation Composition," *Management International Review*, January 1986, pp. 28–35.

42 R. W. Brislin, B. MacNab, R. Worthley, F. Kabigting Jr., and B. Zukis, "Evolving Perceptions of Japanese Workplace Motivation: An Employee-Manager Comparison," *International Journal of Cross-Cultural Management*, April 2005, pp. 87–104.

43 P. Falcone, "Motivating Staff without Money," *HR Magazine*, August 2002, pp. 105–108.

44 P. Falcone, "Motivating Staff without Money," *HR Magazine*, August 2002, pp. 105–108.

45 See, for instance, S. R. Barley and G. Kunda, "Contracting: A New Form of Professional Practice," *Academy of Management Perspectives*, February 2006, pp. 45–66; T. J. Allen and R. Katz, "Managing Technical Professionals and Organizations: Improving and Sustaining the Performance of Organizations, Project Teams, and Individual Contributors," *Sloan Management Review*, Summer 2002, pp. S4–S5; G. Poole, "How to Manage Your Nerds," *Forbes ASAP*, December 1994, pp. 132–136; and M. Alpert, "The Care and Feeding of Engineers," *Fortune*, September 21, 1992, pp. 86–95.

46 "One CEO's Perspective on the Power of Recognition," *Workforce Management*, March 2, 2004, http://www.workforce.com; and R. Fournier, "Teamwork Is the Key to Remote Development—Inspiring Trust and Maintaining Motivation Are Critical for a Distributive Development Team," *InfoWorld*, March 5, 2001, p. 48.

47 R. J. Bohner Jr. and E. R. Salasko, "Beware the Legal Risks of Hiring Temps," *Workforce*, October 2002, pp. 50–57.

48 J. P. Broschak and A. Davis-Blake, "Mixing Standard Work and Nonstandard Deals: The Consequences of Heterogeneity in Employment Arrangements," *Academy of Management Journal*, April 2006, pp. 371–393; M. L. Kraimer, S. J. Wayne, R. C. Liden, and R. T. Sparrowe, "The Role of Job Security in Understanding the Relationship between Employees' Perceptions of Temporary Workers and Employees' Performance," *Journal of Applied Psychology*, March 2005, pp. 389–398; and C. E. Connelly and D. G. Gallagher, "Emerging Trends in Contingent Work Research," *Journal of Management*, November 2004, pp. 959–983.

49 D. W. Krueger, "Money, Success, and Success Phobia," in *The Last Taboo: Money as a Symbol and Reality in Psychotherapy and Psychoanalysis*, ed. D. W. Krueger (New York: Brunner/Mazel, 1986), pp. 3–16.

50 T. R. Mitchell and A. E. Mickel, "The Meaning of Money: An Individual-Difference Perspective," *Academy of Management Review*, July 1999, pp. 568–578.

51 This paragraph is based on Graham Lowe, "21st Century Job Quality: Achieving What Canadians Want," *Canadian Policy Research Networks*, Research Report W|37, September 2007.

52 D. Grigg and J. Newman, "Labour Researchers Define Job Satisfaction," *Vancouver Sun*, February 16, 2002, p. E2.

53 This paragraph is based on T. R. Mitchell and A. E. Mickel, "The Meaning of Money: An Individual-Difference Perspective," *Academy of Management Review*, July 1999, pp. 568–578. The reader may want to refer to the myriad references cited in the article.

54 F. Luthans and A. D. Stajkovic, "Provide Recognition for Performance Improvement," in *Principles of Organizational Behavior*, ed. E. A. Locke (Oxford, UK: Blackwell, 2000), pp. 166–180.

55 CNW Group, "Calgary Salary Increases Outpace Rest of Canada, According to Hewitt," news release, September 5, 2006, http://www.newswire.ca/en/releases/archive/September2006/05/c2519.html (accessed September 20, 2007).

56 "Secrets of Their Success (and Failure)," *Report on Business*, January 2006, pp. 54–55.

57 S. L. Rynes, B. Gerhart, and L. Parks, "Personnel Psychology: Performance Evaluation and Pay for Performance," *Annual Review of Psychology* 56, no. 1 (2005), p. 572; and A. M. Dickinson, "Are We Motivated by Money? Some Results from the Laboratory," *Performance Improvement* 44, no. 3 (March 2005), pp. 18–24.

58 R. K. Abbott, "Performance-Based Flex: A Tool for Managing Total Compensation Costs," *Compensation and Benefits Review*, March–April 1993, pp. 18–21; J. R. Schuster and P. K. Zingheim, "The New Variable Pay: Key Design Issues," *Compensation and Benefits Review*, March–April 1993, pp. 27–34; C. R. Williams and L. P. Livingstone, "Another Look at the Relationship between Performance and Voluntary Turnover," *Academy of Management Journal*, April 1994, pp. 269–298; and A. M. Dickinson and K. L. Gillette, "A Comparison of the Effects of Two Individual Monetary Incentive Systems on Productivity: Piece Rate Pay versus Base Pay Plus Incentives," *Journal of Organizational Behavior Management*, Spring 1994, pp. 3–82.

59 CNW Group, "Calgary Salary Increases Reach New Heights, According to Hewitt," news release, http://www.newswire.ca/en/releases/archive/September2007/06/c5734.html (accessed September 17, 2007); G. Teel, "City Leads Nation in Salary Increases," *Calgary Herald*, September 7, 2007, http://www.canada.com/calgaryherald/news/calgarybusiness/story.html?id=ba2ca066-5d60-4a67-b24b-969c32bcedfa&p=1 (accessed September 17, 2007); Hewitt Associates, "Hewitt Study Shows Pay-for-Performance Plans Replacing Holiday Bonuses," news release, December 6, 2005, http://was4.hewitt.com/hewitt/resource/newsroom/pressrel/2005/12-06-05eng.pdf (accessed April 29, 2006); and P. Brieger, "Variable Pay Packages Gain Favour: Signing Bonuses, Profit Sharing Taking Place of Salary Hikes," *Financial Post (National Post)*, September 13, 2002, p. FP5.

60 E. Beauchesne, "Pay Bonuses Improve Productivity, Study Shows," *Vancouver Sun*, September 13, 2002, p. D5; and the Conference Board of Canada, "Variable Pay Offers a Bonus for Unionized Workplaces," news release, September 12, 2002, http://www.conferenceboard.ca/press/2002/variable_pay.asp (accessed April 29, 2006).

61 "Hope for Higher Pay: The Squeeze on Incomes Is Gradually Easing Up," *Maclean's*, November 25, 1996, pp. 100–101.

62 Hewitt Associates, "Hewitt Study Shows Base Pay Increases Flat for 2006 with Variable Pay Plans Picking Up the Slack," August 31, 2005.

63 E. Beauchesne, "Pay Bonuses Improve Productivity, Study Shows," *Vancouver Sun*, September 13, 2002, p. D5; and "More Than 20 Percent of Japanese Firms Use Pay Systems Based on Performance," *Manpower Argus*, May 1998, p. 7.

64 M. Tanikawa, "Fujitsu Decides to Backtrack on Performance-Based Pay," *New York Times*, March 22, 2001, p. W1.

65 G. D. Jenkins Jr., N. Gupta, A. Mitra, and J. D. Shaw, "Are Financial Incentives Related to Performance? A Meta-Analytic Review of Empirical Research," *Journal of Applied Psychology*, October 1998, pp. 777–787.

66 T. Coupé, V. Smeets, and F. Warzynski, "Incentives, Sorting and Productivity Along the Career: Evidence from a Sample of Top Economists," *Journal of Law Economics & Organization* 22, no. 1 (April 2006), pp. 137–167.

67 A. Kauhanen and H. Piekkola, "What Makes Performance-Related Pay Schemes Work? Finnish Evidence," *Journal of Management and Governance* 10, no. 2 (2006), pp. 149–177.

68 E. Beauchesne, "Pay Bonuses Improve Productivity, Study Shows," *Vancouver Sun*, September 13, 2002, p. D5.

69 P. A. Siegel and D. C. Hambrick, "Pay Disparities within Top Management Groups: Evidence of Harmful Effects on Performance of High-Technology Firms," *Organization Science* 16, no. 3 (May–June 2005), pp. 259–276; S. Kerr, "Practical, Cost-Neutral Alternatives That You May Know, But Don't Practice," *Organizational Dynamics* 28, no. 1 (1999), pp. 61–70; E. E. Lawler, *Strategic Pay* (San Francisco: Jossey Bass, 1990); and J. Pfeffer, *The Human Equation: Building Profits by Putting People First* (Boston: Harvard Business School Press, 1998).

70 T. Reason, "Why Bonus Plans Fail," *CFO*, January 2003, p. 53; and "Has Pay for Performance Had Its Day?" *McKinsey Quarterly*, no. 4, 2002, via *Forbes* website, http://www.forbes.com/smallbusiness/2002/10/22/1022mckinsey.html (accessed September 20, 2007).

71 V. Sanderson, "Sweetening Their Slice: More Hardware and Lumberyard Dealers Are Investing in Profit-Sharing Programs as a Way to Promote Employee Loyalty," *Hardware Merchandising*, May–June 2003, p. 66.

72 R. J. Long, "Patterns of Workplace Innovations in Canada," *Relations Industrielles* 44, no. 4 (1989), pp. 805–826; R. J. Long, "Motives for Profit Sharing: A Study of Canadian Chief Executive Officers," *Relations Industrielles* 52, no. 4 (1997), pp. 712–723; and T. H. Wagar and R. J. Long, "Profit Sharing in Canada: Incidences and Predictors," *Proceedings of the Administrative Sciences Association of Canada (Human Resources Division)*, 1995, pp. 97–105.

73 J. Gray, "A Tale of Two CEOs," *Canadian Business*, April 26–May 9, 2004, pp. 35–36.

74 J. McFarland, "Missing Link: CEO Pay and Results," *Globe and Mail*, June 1, 2006, p. B1.

75 W. J. Duncan, "Stock Ownership and Work Motivation," *Organizational Dynamics*, Summer 2001, pp. 1–11.

76 P. Brandes, R. Dharwadkar, and G. V. Lemesis, "Effective Employee Stock Option Design: Reconciling Stakeholder, Strategic, and Motivational Factors," *Academy of Management Executive*, February 2003, pp. 77–95; and J. Blasi, D. Kruse, and A. Bernstein,

In the Company of Owners: The Truth About Stock Options (New York: Basic Books, 2003).

77 G. Shaw, "Top Gamers Kept on the Job With Array of Sweet Deals," *Vancouver Sun*, March 25, 2004, p. D1.

78 "Health Club Membership, Flextime Are Most Desired Perks," *Business West*, September 1999, p. 75.

79 "More than Base Pay Needed to Attract and Retain Employees," *Canada NewsWire*, http://www.newswire.ca/en/releases/archive/September2007/06/c5734.html (accessed October 21, 2007).

80 M. Arndt, "The Family That Flips Together ...," *BusinessWeek*, April 17, 2006, p. 14.

81 T. D. Golden and J. F. Veiga, "The Impact of Extent of Telecommuting on Job Satisfaction: Resolving Inconsistent Findings," *Journal of Management*, April 2005, pp. 301–318.

82 This paragraph is based on "Paying Workers Well Is Not Enough, Surveys Finds," *Financial Post (National Post)*, May 16, 2001, p. C10.

83 D. Penner, "Survey: Top Pay Trumps Work-Life Balance," *Gazette* (Montreal), March 10, 2007, p. G2.

84 "What Employees Want," *CMA Management* 75, no. 7 (October 2001), p. 8.

85 This paragraph is based on D. Grigg and J. Newman, "Labour Researchers Define Job Satisfaction," *Vancouver Sun*, February 16, 2002, p. E2.

86 J. Greenberg and R. Baron, *Behavior in Organizations*, 6th ed. (Upper Saddle River, NJ: Prentice Hall, 1995). Reprinted by permission of Prentice Hall, Inc., Upper Saddle River, NJ.

87 Situation adapted from information in W. Zellner, "They Took More Than They Needed from Us," *BusinessWeek*, June 2, 2003, p. 58; "Coffee, Tea, or Bile?" *BusinessWeek*, June 2, 2003, p. 56; "US Airways Pilots' Stand on Management," *New York Times*, May 24, 2003, p. C2; and "US Airways Flight Attendants Delay Concession Talks," *New York Times*, December 4, 2002, p. C4.

88 Based on J. Marquez, "Best Buy Offers Choice in Its Long-term Incentive Program to Keep the Best and Brightest," *Workforce Management*, April 24, 2006, pp. 42–43; M. Boyle, "Best Buy's Giant Gamble," *Fortune*, April 3, 2006, pp. 68–75; J. S. Lublin, "A Few Share the Wealth," *Wall Street Journal*, December 12, 2005, pp. B1+; J. Thotta, "Reworking Work," *Time*, July 25, 2005, pp. 50–55; and M. V. Copeland, "Best Buy's Selling Machine," *Business 2.0*, July 2004, pp. 92–102.

89 Based on A. C. Poe, "Keeping Hotel Workers," *HR Magazine*, February 2003, pp. 91–93.

90 Based on J. R. Hackman, "Work Design," in *Improving Life at Work*, ed. J. R. Hackman and J. L. Suttle (Santa Monica, CA: Goodyear, 1977), pp. 132–133.

91 Based on D. Jones, "Ford, Fannie Mae Tops in Diversity," *USA Today*, May 7, 2003, http://www.usatoday.com; S. N. Mehta, "What Minority Employees Really Want," *Fortune*, July 10, 2000, pp. 180–186; K. H. Hammonds, "Difference Is Power," *Fast Company*, July 2000, pp. 258–266; "Building a Competitive Workforce: Diversity, the Bottom Line," *Forbes*, April 3, 2000, pp. 181–194; and "Diversity: Developing Tomorrow's Leadership Talent Today," *BusinessWeek*, December 20, 1999, pp. 85–100.

92 Based on R. McNatt, "The Young and the Restless," *BusinessWeek*, May 22, 2000, p. 12; "On the Job," *Wall Street Journal*, April 11, 2000, p. B18; P. Kruger, "Does Your Job Work?"

Fast Company, November 1999, pp. 181–196; and M. A. Verespej, "What Each Generation Wants," *IndustryWeek*, October 18, 1999, pp. 14–15.

Chapter 14

1 Based on D. Cox, "Team Canada Has It All; Depth, Experience and, Oh Yes, Talent," *Toronto Star*, December 22, 2005, p. 1; M. MacDonald, "Teamwork Key to Gold—On and Off the Ice," *Nanaimo Daily News*, January 27, 2003, p. A9; S. Burnside and B. Beacon, "Lafleur Says Team Canada Well Chosen, Even if There's No Canadiens," *Canadian Press*, May 18, 2004; and "Primeau Looks Like Conn Man," *Star Phoenix*, May 17, 2004, p. C2.

2 See, for instance, E. Sunstrom, K. DeMeuse, and D. Futrell, "Work Teams: Applications and Effectiveness," *American Psychologist*, February 1990, pp. 120–133.

3 G. M. Spreitzer, S. G. Cohen, and G. E. Ledford Jr., "Developing Effective Self-Managing Work Teams in Service Organizations," *Group & Organization Management*, September 1999, pp. 340–366.

4 R. I. Beekun, "Assessing the Effectiveness of Sociotechnical Interventions: Antidote or Fad?" *Human Relations*, October 1989, pp. 877–897.

5 S. G. Cohen, G. E. Ledford, and G. M. Spreitzer, "A Predictive Model of Self-Managing Work Team Effectiveness," *Human Relations*, May 1996, pp. 643–676.

6 C. E. Nicholls, H. W. Lane, and M. Brehm Brechu, "Taking Self-Managed Teams to Mexico," *Academy of Management Executive*, August 1999, pp. 15–27.

7 R. Lepine and K. Rawson, "Strategic Savings on the Right Track: How Canadian Pacific Railway Has Saved Millions of Dollars in the Past Four Years through Strategic Sourcing," *CMA Management*, February 2003, pp. 20–23.

8 G. Shaw, "The New Home of Microsoft in Canada," *Vancouver Sun*, October 6, 2007, p. D1.

9 B. L. Kirkman and J. E. Mathieu, "The Dimensions and Antecedents of Team Virtuality," *Journal of Management,* October 2005, pp. 700–718; J. Gordon, "Do Your Virtual Teams Deliver Only Virtual Performance?" *Training*, June 2005, pp. 20–25; L. L. Martins, L. L. Gilson, and M. T. Maynard, "Virtual Teams: What Do We Know and Where Do We Go from Here?" *Journal of Management*, December 2004, pp. 805–835; S. A. Furst, M. Reeves, B. Rosen, and R. S. Blackburn, "Managing the Life Cycle of Virtual Teams," *Academy of Management Executive*, May 2004, pp. 6–20; B. L. Kirkman, B. Rosen, P. E. Tesluk, and C. B. Gibson, "The Impact of Team Empowerment on Virtual Team Performance: The Moderating Role of Face-to-Face Interaction," *Academy of Management Journal*, April 2004, pp. 175–192; F. Keenan and S. E. Ante, "The New Teamwork," *BusinessWeek e.biz*, February 18, 2002, pp. EB12–EB16; and G. Imperato, "Real Tools for Virtual Teams" *Fast Company*, July 2000, pp. 378–387.

10 S. Whittaker, "Being Part of the Team," *Gazette* (Montreal), April 30, 2005, p. B5.

11 See, for example, C. M. Fiol and E. J. O'Connor, "Identification in Face-to-Face, Hybrid, and Pure Virtual Teams: Untangling the Contradictions," *Organization Science* 16, no. 1 (January–February 2005), pp. 19–32; and L. L. Martins, L. L. Gilson, and M. T. Maynard, "Virtual Teams: What Do We Know and Where Do We Go From Here?" *Journal of Management* 30, no. 6 (December 2004), pp. 805–835.

12 J. M. Wilson, S. G. Straus, and B. McEvily. "All in Due Time: The Development of Trust in Computer-Mediated and Face-To-Face Teams," *Organizational Behavior and Human Decision Processes* 99, no. 1 (2006), pp. 16–33; and S. L. Jarvenpaa, K. Knoll, and D. E. Leidner, "Is Anybody Out There? Antecedents of Trust in Global Virtual Teams," *Journal of Management Information Systems*, Spring 1998, pp. 29–64.

13 P. J. Hinds and M. Mortensen, "Understanding Conflict in Geographically Distributed Teams: The Moderating Effects of Shared Identity, Shared Context, and Spontaneous Communication," *Organization Science* 16, no. 3 (2005), pp. 290–307.

14 B. W. Tuckman and M. C. Jensen, "Stages of Small-Group Development Revisited," *Group and Organizational Studies*, December 1977, pp. 419–427; and M. F. Maples, "Group Development: Extending Tuckman's Theory," *Journal for Specialists in Group Work*, Fall 1988, pp. 17–23.

15 L. N. Jewell and H. J. Reitz, *Group Effectiveness in Organizations* (Glenview, IL: Scott, Foresman, 1981); and M. Kaeter, "Repotting Mature Work Teams," *Training*, April 1994, pp. 54–56.

16 Based on B. Beacon, "Continuity Rules on Squad," *Leader Post*, December 22, 2005, p. C2.

17 See, for instance, J. E. Salk, and M. Y. Brannien, "National Culture, Networks, and Individual Influence in a Multinational Management Team," *Academy of Management Journal*, April 2000, p. 191; B. L. Kirkman, C. B. Gibson, and D. L. Shapiro, "Enhancing the Implementation and Effectiveness of Work Teams in Global Affiliates," *Organizational Dynamics*, Summer 2001, pp. 12–30; and B. L. Kirkman and D. L. Shapiro, "The Impact of Cultural Values on Employee Resistance to Teams: Towards a Model of Globalized Self-Managing Work Team Effectiveness," *Academy of Management Review*, July 1997, pp. 730–757.

18 S. Stern, "Teams That Work," *Management Today*, June 2001, p. 48.

19 McMurry, Inc., "The Roles Your People Play," *Managing People at Work*, October 2005, p. 4; G. Prince, "Recognizing Genuine Teamwork," *Supervisory Management*, April 1989, pp. 25–36; R. F. Bales, *SYMOLOG Case Study Kit* (New York: Free Press, 1980); and K. D. Benne and P. Sheats, "Functional Roles of Group Members," *Journal of Social Issues* 4, no. 2 (1948), pp. 41–49.

20 A. R. Jassawalla and H. C. Sashittal, "Strategies of Effective New Product Team Leaders," *California Management Review* 42, no. 2 (Winter 2000), pp. 34–51.

21 R. M. Yandrick, "A Team Effort," *HR Magazine*, June 2001, pp. 136–141.

22 R. M. Yandrick, "A Team Effort," *HR Magazine*, June 2001, pp. 136–141.

23 M. A. Marks, C. S. Burke, M. J. Sabella, and S. J. Zaccaro, "The Impact of Cross-Training on Team Effectiveness," *Journal of Applied Psychology*, February 2002, pp. 3–14; and M. A. Marks, S. J. Zaccaro, and J. E. Mathieu, "Performance Implications of Leader Briefings and Team Interaction for Team Adaptation to Novel Environments," *Journal of Applied Psychology*, December 2000, p. 971.

24 C. Garvey, "Steer Teams with the Right Pay: Team-Based Pay Is a Success When It Fits Corporate Goals and Culture, and Rewards the Right Behavior," *HR Magazine*, May 2002, pp. 71–77.

25 Based on "Canada Lacked Cohesion, Chemistry," *Edmonton Journal*, February 24, 2006, p. C3; and E. Duhatschek, "Under

Pressure, Gretzky Scores in Balancing Act," *Globe and Mail*, May 17, 2004, p. S1.

26 G. R. Jones and G. M. George, "The Experience and Evolution of Trust: Implications for Cooperation and Teamwork," *Academy of Management Review*, July 1998, pp. 531–546; A. R. Jassawalla and H. C. Sashittal, "Building Collaborative Cross-Functional New Product Teams," *Academy of Management Executive*, August 1999, pp. 50–63; R. Forrester and A. B. Drexler, "A Model for Team-Based Organization Performance," *Academy of Management Executive*, August 1999, pp. 36–49; V. U. Druskat and S. B. Wolff, "The Link between Emotions and Team Effectiveness: How Teams Engage Members and Build Effective Task Processes," *Academy of Management Proceedings*, CD-ROM, 1999; M. Mattson, T. Mumford, and G. S. Sintay, "Taking Teams to Task: A Normative Model for Designing or Recalibrating Work Teams," *Academy of Management Proceedings*, CD-ROM, 1999; J. D. Shaw, M. K. Duffy, and E. M. Stark, "Interdependence and Preference for Group Work: Main and Congruence Effects on the Satisfaction and Performance of Group Members," *Journal of Management* 26, no. 2 (2000), pp. 259–279; G. L. Stewart and M. R. Barrick, "Team Structure and Performance: Assessing the Mediating Role of Intrateam Process and the Moderating Role of Task Type," *Academy of Management Journal*, April 2000, pp. 135–148; J. E. Mathieu, T. S. Heffner, G. F. Goodwin, E. Salas, and J. A. Cannon-Bowers, "The Influence of Shared Mental Models on Team Process and Performance," *Journal of Applied Psychology*, April 2000, pp. 273–283; J. M. Phillips and E. A. Douthitt, "The Role of Justice in Team Member Satisfaction with the Leader and Attachment to the Team," *Journal of Applied Psychology*, April 2001, pp. 316–325; J. A. Colquitt, R. A. Noe, and C. L. Jackson, "Justice in Teams: Antecedents and Consequences of Procedural Justice Climate," *Personnel Psychology* 55, 2002, pp. 83–100; M. A. Marks, M. J. Sabella, C. S. Burke, and S. J. Zaccaro, "The Impact of Cross-Training on Team Effectiveness," *Journal of Applied Psychology*, February 2002, pp. 3–13; and S. W. Lester, B. W. Meglino, and M. A. Korsgaard, "The Antecedents and Consequences of Group Potency: A Longitudinal Investigation of Newly Formed Work Groups," *Academy of Management Journal*, April 2002, pp. 352–368.

27 D. R. Ilgen, J. R. Hollenbeck, M. Johnson, and D. Jundt, "Teams in Organizations: From Input-Process-Output Models to IMOI Models," *Annual Review of Psychology* 56, no. 1 (2005), pp. 517–543.

28 C. R. Evans and K. L. Dion, "Group Cohesion and Performance: A Meta-Analysis," *Small Group Research*, May 1991, pp. 175–186; B. Mullen and C. Copper, "The Relation between Group Cohesiveness and Performance: An Integration," *Psychological Bulletin*, March 1994, pp. 210–227; and P. M. Podsakoff, S. B. MacKenzie, and M. Ahearne, "Moderating Effects of Goal Acceptance on the Relationship between Group Cohesiveness and Productivity," *Journal of Applied Psychology*, December 1997, pp. 974–983.

29 See, for example, L. Berkowitz, "Group Standards, Cohesiveness, and Productivity," *Human Relations*, November 1954, pp. 509–519; and B. Mullen and C. Copper, "The Relation between Group Cohesiveness and Performance: An Integration," *Psychological Bulletin*, March 1994, pp. 210–227.

30 S. E. Seashore, *Group Cohesiveness in the Industrial Work Group* (Ann Arbor: University of Michigan, Survey Research Center, 1954).

31 Paragraph based on R. Kreitner and A. Kinicki, *Organizational Behavior*, 6th ed. (New York: Irwin, 2004), pp. 459–461.

32 This section is adapted from S. P. Robbins, *Managing Organizational Conflict: A Nontraditional Approach* (Upper Saddle River, NJ: Prentice Hall, 1974), pp. 11–14. See also D. Wagner-Johnson, "Managing Work Team Conflict: Assessment and

Preventative Strategies," *Center for the Study of Work Teams, University of North Texas*, http://www.workteams.unt.edu/reports/wagner.html (accessed November 3, 2000); and M. Kennedy, "Managing Conflict in Work Teams," *Center for the Study of Work Teams, University of North Texas*, http://www.workteams.unt.edu/reports/kennedy-m.html (accessed November 3, 2000).

33 See J. Weiss and J. Hughes, "Want Collaboration? Accept—and Actively Manage—Conflict," *Harvard Business Review*, March 2005, pp. 92–101; C. K. W. DeDreu and A. E. M. Van Vianen, "Managing Relationship Conflict and the Effectiveness of Organizational Teams," *Journal of Organizational Behavior*, May 2001, pp. 309–328; K. A. Jehn and E. A. Mannix, "The Dynamic Nature of Conflict: A Longitudinal Study of Intragroup Conflict and Group Performance," *Academy of Management Journal*, April 2001, pp. 238–251; K. A. Jehn, "A Multimethod Examination of the Benefits and Detriments of Intragroup Conflict," *Administrative Science Quarterly*, June 1995, pp. 256–282; K. A. Jehn, "A Qualitative Analysis of Conflict Type and Dimensions in Organizational Groups," *Administrative Science Quarterly*, September 1997, pp. 530–557; and K. A. Jehn, "Affective and Cognitive Conflict in Work Groups: Increasing Performance through Value-Based Intragroup Conflict," in *Using Conflict in Organizations,* ed. C. K. W. DeDreu and E. Van deVliert (London: Sage, 1997), pp. 87–100.

34 C. K. W. DeDreu, "When Too Little or Too Much Hurts: Evidence for a Curvilinear Relationship between Task Conflict and Innovation in Teams," *Journal of Management*, February 2006, pp. 83–107.

35 K. W. Thomas, "Conflict and Negotiation Processes in Organizations," in *Handbook of Industrial and Organizational Psychology,* vol. 3, 2nd ed., ed. M. D. Dunnette and L. M. Hough (Palo Alto, CA: Consulting Psychologists Press, 1992), pp. 651–717.

36 See D. R. Comer, "A Model of Social Loafing in Real Work Groups," *Human Relations*, June 1995, pp. 647–667.

37 S. G. Harkins and K. Szymanski, "Social Loafing and Group Evaluation," *Journal of Personality and Social Psychology*, December 1989, pp. 934–941.

38 See P. C. Earley, "Social Loafing and Collectivism: A Comparison of the United States and the People's Republic of China," *Administrative Science Quarterly*, December 1989, pp. 565–581; and P. C. Earley, "East Meets West Meets Mideast: Further Explorations of Collectivistic and Individualistic Work Groups," *Academy of Management Journal*, April 1993, pp. 319–348.

39 B. L. Kirkman, C. B. Gibson, and D. L. Shapiro, "Exporting Teams: Enhancing the Implementation and Effectiveness of Work Teams in Global Affiliates," *Organizational Dynamics*, Summer 2001, pp. 12–29; J. W. Bing and C. M. Bing, "Helping Global Teams Compete," *Training & Development*, March 2001, pp. 70–71; C. G. Andrews, "Factors That Impact Multi-Cultural Team Performance," *Center for the Study of Work Teams, University of North Texas*, November 3, 2000, http://www.workteams.unt.edu/reports; P. Christopher Earley and E. Mosakowski, "Creating Hybrid Team Cultures: An Empirical Test of Transnational Team Functioning," *Academy of Management Journal*, February 2000, pp. 26–49; J. Tata, "The Cultural Context of Teams: An Integrative Model of National Culture, Work Team Characteristics, and Team Effectiveness," *Academy of Management Proceedings*, CD-ROM, 1999; D. I. Jung, K. B. Baik, and J. J. Sosik, "A Longitudinal Investigation of Group Characteristics and Work Group Performance: A Cross-Cultural Comparison," *Academy of Management Proceedings*, CD-ROM, 1999; and C. B. Gibson, "They Do What They Believe They Can? Group-Efficacy Beliefs and Group Performance Across Tasks and Cultures," *Academy of Management Proceedings,* CD-ROM, 1996.

40 R. Bond and P. B. Smith, "Culture and Conformity: A Meta-Analysis of Studies Using Asch's [1952, 1956] Line Judgment Task," *Psychological Bulletin*, January 1996, pp. 111–137.

41 I. L. Janis, *Groupthink*, 2nd ed. (New York: Houghton Mifflin, 1982), p. 175.

42 See P. C. Earley, "East Meets West Meets Mideast: Further Explorations of Collectivistic and Individualistic Work Groups," *Academy of Management Journal*, April 1993, pp. 319–348; and P. C. Earley, "Social Loafing and Collectivism: A Comparison of the United States and the People's Republic of China," *Administrative Science Quarterly*, December 1989, pp. 565–581.

43 N. J. Adler, *International Dimensions of Organizational Behavior*, 4th ed. (Cincinnati, OH: Southwestern, 2002), p. 142.

44 N. J. Adler, *International Dimensions of Organizational Behavior*, 4th ed. (Cincinnati, OH: Southwestern, 2002), p. 142.

45 K. B. Dahlin, L. R. Weingart, and P. J. Hinds, "Team Diversity and Information Use," *Academy of Management Journal*, December 2005, pp. 1107–1123.

46 N. J. Adler, *International Dimensions of Organizational Behavior*, 4th ed. (Cincinnati, OH: Southwestern, 2002), p. 142.

47 S. Paul, I. M. Samarah, P. Seetharaman, and P. P. Mykytyn, "An Empirical Investigation of Collaborative Conflict Management Style in Group Support System-Based Global Virtual Teams," *Journal of Management Information Systems*, Winter 2005, pp. 185–222.

48 S. Chang and P. Tharenou, "Competencies Needed for Managing a Multicultural Workgroup," *Asia Pacific Journal of Human Resources* 42, no. 1 (2004), pp. 57–74; and N. J. Adler, *International Dimensions of Organizational Behavior*, 4th ed. (Cincinnati, OH: Southwestern, 2002), p. 153.

49 C. E. Nicholls, H. W. Lane, and M. Brehm Brechu, "Taking Self-Managed Teams to Mexico," *Academy of Management Executive*, August 1999, pp. 15–27.

50 D. Brown, "Innovative HR Ineffective in Manufacturing Firms," *Canadian HR Reporter*, April 7, 2003, pp. 1–2.

51 A. B. Drexler and R. Forrester, "Teamwork—Not Necessarily the Answer," *HR Magazine*, January 1998, pp. 55–58.

52 R. Forrester and A. B. Drexler, "A Model for Team-Based Organization Performance," *Academy of Management Executive*, August 1999, p. 47. See also S. A. Mohrman, with S. G. Cohen and A. M. Mohrman Jr., *Designing Team-Based Organizations* (San Francisco: Jossey-Bass, 1995); and J. H. Shonk, *Team-Based Organizations* (Homewood, IL: Business One Irwin, 1992).

53 Adapted from D. A. Whetten and K. S. Cameron, *Developing Management Skills*, 3rd ed. (New York: HarperCollins, 1995), pp. 534–535.

54 M. Fackler, "Raising the Bar at Samsung," *New York Times*, April 25, 2006, http://www.nytimes.com/2006/04/25/technology/25samsung.html (accessed September 21, 2007); B. Breen, "The Seoul of Design," *Fast Company*, December 2005, pp. 90–97; E. Ramstad, "Standing Firm," *Wall Street Journal*, March 16, 2005, pp. A1+; D. Rocks and M. Ihlwan, "Samsung Design," *BusinessWeek*, December 6, 2004, pp. 88–96; and Interbrand Consulting Group, "Best Global Brands 2006," http://www.ourfishbowl.com/images/surveys/BGB06Report_072706.pdf (accessed September 20, 2007).

55 Based on M. Moskowitz and R. Levering, "100 Best Companies to Work For: 10 Great Companies to Work for in Europe: Ferrari Good

Food, Good People, Lots of Fun—Sounds Like a European Holiday? No, It's a Great Job," *Fortune*, January 7, 2003, http://www.fortune.com; and http://www.ferrari.com (accessed 2004).

56 Based on P. L. Hunsaker, *Training in Management Skills* (Upper Saddle River, NJ: Prentice Hall, 2001), chapter 12.

57 Based on K. B. Dahlin, L. R. Weingart, and P. J. Hinds, "Team Diversity and Information Use," *Academy of Management Journal*, December 2005, pp. 1107–1123; B. L. Kirkman, P. E. Tesluk, and B. Rosen, "The Impact of Demographic Heterogeneity and Team Leader–Team Member Demographic Fit on Team Empowerment and Effectiveness," *Group & Organization Management*, June 2004, pp. 334–368; K. Lovelace, D. L. Shapiro, and L. R. Weingart, "Maximizing Cross-Functional New Product Teams' Innovativeness and Constraint Adherence: A Conflict Communications Perspective," *Academy of Management Journal*, August 2002, pp. 779–793; J. Jusko, "Diversity Enhances Decision Making," *IndustryWeek*, April 2, 2001, p. 9; F. Rice, "How to Make Diversity Pay," *Fortune*, August 8, 1994, pp. 78–86; M. L. Maznevski, "Understanding Our Differences: Performance in Decision-Making Groups with Diverse Members," *Human Relations*, May 1994, pp. 531–552; L. Strach and L. Wicander, "Fitting In: Issues of Tokenism and Conformity for Minority Women," *SAM Advanced Management Journal*, Summer 1993, pp. 22–25; C. R. Bantz, "Cultural Diversity and Group Cross-Cultural Team Research," *Journal of Applied Communication Research*, February 1993, pp. 1–19; and L. Copeland, "Making the Most of Cultural Differences at the Workplace," *Personnel*, June 1988, pp. 52–60.

Part 4 Continuing Case: Starbucks

1 A. Serwer and K. Bonamici, "Hot Starbucks to Go," *Fortune*, January 26, 2004, pp. 60–74; interview with Jim Donald, *Fortune*, April 4, 2005, p. 30; interview with Jim Donald, *Smart Money*, May 2006, pp. 31–32; A. Serwer, "Interview with Howard Schultz," *Fortune (Europe)*, March 20, 2006, pp. 35–36; W. Meyers, "Conscience in a Cup of Coffee," *U.S. News & World Report*, October 31, 2005, pp. 48–50; J. M. Cohn, R. Khurana, and L. Reeves, "Growing Talent As if Your Business Depended It," *Harvard Business Review*, October 2005, pp. 62–70; P. Kafka, "Bean Counter," *Forbes*, February 28, 2005, pp. 78–80; S. Gray, "Starbucks's CEO Announces Plan to Retire in March," *Wall Street Journal*, October 13, 2004, p. A6; *Beyond the Cup: Corporate Social Responsibility, Fiscal 2005 Annual Report*, Starbucks Corporation; and *Starbucks 2006 Annual Report*, http://investor.starbucks.com/phoenix.zhtml?c=99518&p=irol-IRHome (accessed September 28, 2007).

Chapter 15

1 Based on "Energy Roughneck," *Canadian Business*, August 1996, pp. 20+; Hoover's Online, http://www.hoovers.com; and C. Cattaneo, "Husky CEO Lau Reveals Intention to Retire," *National Post (Financial Post)*, April 23, 2004, p. FP4.

2 J. Kluger and B. Liston, "A Columbia Culprit?" *Time*, February 24, 2003, p. 13.

3 K. A. Merchant, "The Control Function of Management," *Sloan Management Review*, Summer 1982, pp. 43–55.

4 E. Flamholtz, "Organizational Control Systems as a Managerial Tool," *California Management Review*, Winter 1979, p. 55.

5 "The Top 1000: Canada's Power Book," *Globe and Mail*, http://www.globeinvestor.com/series/top1000.

6 S. Brearton and J. Daly, "50 Best Employers in Canada," *Globe and Mail*, December 29, 2003, p. 33; and "Study Guidelines," *Best Employers in Canada*, http://was7.hewitt.com/bestemployers/canada/study_guidelines.htm (accessed September 21, 2007).

7 See http://www.canadianbusiness.com/rankings/profit100/list.jsp?pageID=faq&type=about&listType=&year=2006&page=&content=faqen (accessed September 21, 2007).

8 P. Magnusson, "Your Jitters Are Their Lifeblood," *BusinessWeek*, April 14, 2003, p. 41; S. Williams, "Company Crisis: CEO Under Fire," *Hispanic Business*, March 2003, pp. 54–56; T. Purdum, "Preparing for the Worst," *IndustryWeek*, January 2003, pp. 53–55; and S. Leibs, "Lesson from 9/11: It's Not About Data," *CFO*, September 2002, pp. 31–32.

9 S. Kerr, "On the Folly of Rewarding A, While Hoping for B," *Academy of Management Journal*, December 1975, pp. 769–783.

10 Y. F. Jarrar and M. Zairi, "Future Trends in Benchmarking for Competitive Advantage: A Global Survey," *Total Quality Management*, December 2001, pp. 906–912.

11 M. Simpson and D. Kondouli, "A Practical Approach to Benchmarking in Three Service Industries," *Total Quality Management*, July 2000, pp. S623–S630.

12 K. N. Dervitsiotis, "Benchmarking and Paradigm Shifts," *Total Quality Management*, July 2000, pp. S641–S646.

13 See http://www.canada.com/nationalpost/entrepreneur/bouclair.html.

14 T. Leahy, "Extracting Diamonds in the Rough," *Business Finance*, August 2000, pp. 33–37.

15 "Recognizing Commitment to Diversity," *Canadian HR Reporter*, November 3, 2003, p. 12.

16 B. Bruzina, B. Jessop, R. Plourde, B. Whitlock, and L. Rubin, "Ameren Embraces Benchmarking as a Core Business Strategy," *Power Engineering*, November 2002, pp. 121–124; T. Leahy, "Extracting Diamonds in the Rough," *Business Finance*, August 2000, pp. 33–37.

17 Based on R. Luciw, "Firm's application of new management practices draws praise from analyst," *Globe and Mail*, March 2, 2005, p. B16, and T. Harbert, "Lean, Mean Six Sigma Machines," *Design News*, December 11, 2006.

18 H. Koontz and R. W. Bradspies, "Managing through Feedforward Control," *Business Horizons*, June 1972, pp. 25–36.

19 "An Open Letter to McDonald's Customers," *Wall Street Journal*, August 22, 2001, p. A5.

20 W. H. Newman, *Constructive Control: Design and Use of Control Systems* (Upper Saddle River, NJ: Prentice Hall, 1975), p. 33.

21 R. Ilies and T. A. Judge, "Goal Regulation across Time: The Effects of Feedback and Affect," *Journal of Applied Psychology* 90, no. 3 (May 2005), pp. 453–467.

22 Based on C. Cattaneo, "Li May Usher in Sea Change at Air Canada," *National Post (Financial Post)*, November 24, 2003, p. FP03.

23 W. G. Ouchi, "A Conceptual Framework for the Design of Organizational Control Mechanisms," *Management Science*, August 1979, pp. 833–838; and W. G. Ouchi, "Markets, Bureaucracies, and Clans," *Administrative Science Quarterly*, March 1980, pp. 129–141.

24 Based on P. Fitzpatrick, "Wacky WestJet's Winning Ways: Passengers Respond to Stunts That Include Races to Determine Who Leaves the Airplane First," *National Post*, October 16, 2000, p. C1.

25 C. Cattaneo, "Li May Usher in Sea Change at Air Canada," *National Post (Financial Post)*, November 24, 2003, p. FP03; C. Cattaneo, "Stranger in a Strange Land," *National Post (Financial Post)*, December 13, 2003, p. FP1F; Husky Energy, *Annual Report 2006*, p. 6, http://www.huskyenergy.ca/downloads/Investor Relations/2006/HSE_Annual2006.pdf (accessed September 22, 2007); and "Husky Energy [The Investor 500]," *Canadian Business*, http://www.canadianbusiness.com/rankings/investor500/index .jsp?pageID=profile&profile=16&year=2007&type=profile (accessed September 22, 2007).

26 F. Hansen, "The Value-Based Management Commitment," *Business Finance*, September 2001, pp. 2–5.

27 M. Acharya and T. Yew, "A New Kind of Top 10," *Toronto Star*, June 30, 2002, p. C01.

28 M. Acharya and T. Yew, "A New Kind of Top 10," *Toronto Star*, June 30, 2002, p. C01.

29 K. Lehn and A. K. Makhija, "EVA and MVA as Performance Measures and Signals for Strategic Change," *Strategy & Leadership*, May–June 1996, pp. 34–38.

30 S. Taub, "MVPs of MVA: Which Companies Created the Most Wealth for Shareholders Last Year? *CFO*, July 1, 2003, http://www .cfo.com (accessed June 22, 2004); and "America's Best Wealth Creators—2007 edition," EVA Dimensions, http://www .evadimensions.com/2007top20RankingSummary.pdf (accessed September 22, 2007).

31 Debra Black, "Rogers Data on Clients Found in Lot," *Toronto Star*, April 08, 2007, http://www.thestar.com/News/article/200727 (accessed May 20, 2007).

32 "When Wireless Works," *CIO*, February 12, 2002, http://www .cio.de (accessed July 2, 2004).

33 J. McPartlin, "Hackers Find Backers," *CFO*, January 2006, pp. 75–77; J. Swartz, "Data Losses Push Businesses to Encrypt Backup Tapes," *USA Today*, June 13, 2005, p. 1B; J. Goff, "New Holes for Hackers," *CFO*, May 2005, pp. 64–73; B. Grow, "Hacker Hunters," *BusinessWeek*, May 30, 2005, pp. 74–82; J. Swartz, "Crooks Slither into Net's Shady Nooks and Crannies," *USA Today*, October 21, 2004, pp. 1B+; J. Swartz, "Spam Can Hurt in More Ways Than One," *USA Today*, July 7, 2004, p. 3B; and T. Reason, "Stopping the Flow," *CFO*, September 2003, pp. 97–99.

34 D. Whelan, "Google Me Not," *Forbes*, August 16, 2004, pp. 102–104.

35 J. Levitz and J. Hechinger, "Laptops Prove Weakest Link in Data Security," *Wall Street Journal*, March 24, 2006, pp. B1+.

36 J. Markoff, "Study Says Chips in ID Tags Are Vulnerable to Viruses," *New York Times*, March 15, 2006, http://www.nytimes. com/2006/03/15/technology/15tag.html (accessed September 25, 2007).

37 Based on "Corporate Governance," *Husky Energy*, http://www. huskyenergy.ca/abouthusky/corporategovernance/ (accessed September 22, 2007).

38 J. Yaukey and C. L. Romero, "Arizona Firm Pays Big for Workers' Digital Downloads," *Springfield News-Leader*, May 6, 2002, p. 6B.

39 R. S. Kaplan and D. P. Norton, "How to Implement a New Strategy without Disrupting Your Organization," *Harvard Business Review*, March 2006, pp. 100–109; L. Bassi and D. McMurrer, "Developing Measurement Systems for Managing in the Knowledge Era," *Organizational Dynamics*, May 2005, pp. 185–196; G. M. J. de Koning, "Making the Balanced Scorecard Work (Part 2), *Gallup Brain*, August 12, 2004, http://brain.gallup.com; G. M. J. de Koning, "Making the Balanced Scorecard Work (Part 1), *Gallup* Brain, July 8, 2004, http://brain.gallup.com; Balanced Scorecard Collaborative, June 29, 2003, http://www.bscol.com; K. Graham, "Balanced Scorecard," *New Zealand Management*, March 2003, pp. 32–34; K. Ellis, "A Ticket to Ride: Balanced Scorecard," *Training*, April 2001, p. 50; T. Leahy, "Tailoring the Balanced Scorecard," *Business Finance*, August 2000, pp. 53–56; and R. S. Kaplan and D. P. Norton, "Using the Balanced Scorecard as a Strategic Management System," *Harvard Business Review*, 74, no. 1 (January–February 1996), pp. 75–85.

40 T. Leahy, "Tailoring the Balanced Scorecard," *Business Finance*, August 2000, pp. 53–56.

41 See http://www.oha.ca/client/oha/oha_lp4w_lnd_webstation .nsf/page/Hospital+Report (accessed October 14, 2007); and T. Leahy, "Tailoring the Balanced Scorecard," *Business Finance*, August 2000, pp. 53–56.

42 "A Revolution Where Everyone Wins: Worldwide Movement to Improve Corporate-Governance Standards," *BusinessWeek*, May 19, 2003, p. 72.

43 J. S. McClenahen, "Executives Expect More Board Input," *IndustryWeek*, October 2002, p. 12.

44 D. Salierno, "Boards Face Increased Responsibility," *Internal Auditor*, June 2003, pp. 14–15.

45 N. Shirouzu and J. Bigness, "7-Eleven Operators Resist System to Monitor Managers," *Wall Street Journal*, June 16, 1997, p. B1.

46 E. O'Connor, "Pulling the Plug on Cyberslackers," *StarPhoenix*, May 24, 2003, p. F22.

47 E. O'Connor, "Pulling the Plug on Cyberslackers," *StarPhoenix*, May 24, 2003, p. F22.

48 D. Hawkins, "Lawsuits Spur Rise in Employee Monitoring," *U.S. News & World Report*, August 13, 2001, p. 53; L. Guernsey, "You've Got Inappropriate Mail," *New York Times*, April 5, 2000, p. C11; and R. Karaim, "Setting E-Privacy Rules," *Cnnfn Online*, December 15, 1999, http://www.cnnfn.com.

49 E. Bott, "Are You Safe? Privacy Special Report," *PC Computing*, March 2000, pp. 87–88.

50 E. O'Connor, "Pulling the Plug on Cyberslackers," *StarPhoenix*, May 24, 2003, p. F22.

51 A. Tomlinson, "Heavy-Handed Net Policies Push Privacy Boundaries," *Canadian HR Reporter*, December 2, 2002, pp. 1–2.

52 C. Sorensen, "Canada Ranks High in Employee Theft: Global Survey Findings," *National Post*, May 28, 2004, p. FP9.

53 A. Perry, "Back-to-School Brings Pilfering: Some Employees Raid Office for Kids," *Toronto Star*, August 30, 2003, p. B01.

54 See http://www.tagcompany.com/filesttc/ Canadian%20Retail%20Security%20Report%202003.pdf (accessed October 15, 2007).

55 J. Greenberg, "The STEAL Motive: Managing the Social Determinants of Employee Theft," in *Antisocial Behavior in Organizations*, ed. R. Giacalone and J. Greenberg (Newbury Park, CA: Sage, 1997), pp. 85–108.

56 "Crime Spree," *BusinessWeek*, September 9, 2002, p. 8;
B. P. Niehoff and R. J. Paul, "Causes of Employee Theft and
Strategies That HR Managers Can Use for Prevention," *Human
Resource Management*, Spring 2000, pp. 51–64; and G. Winter,
"Taking at the Office Reaches New Heights: Employee Larceny Is
Bigger and Bolder," *New York Times*, July 12, 2000, p. C11.

57 This section is based on J. Greenberg, *Behavior in Organizations:
Understanding and Managing the Human Side of Work*, 8th ed. (Upper
Saddle River, NJ: Prentice Hall, 2003), pp. 329–330.

58 A. H. Bell and D. M. Smith, "Why Some Employees Bite the Hand
That Feeds Them," *Workforce*, May 16, 2000, http://www.workforce
.com (accessed December 3, 2000).

59 A. H. Bell and D. M. Smith, "Protecting the Company against
Theft and Fraud," *Workforce*, May 18, 2000, http://www.workforce
.com (accessed December 3, 2000); J. D. Hansen, "To Catch a
Thief," *Journal of Accountancy*, March 2000, pp. 43–46; and
J. Greenberg, "The Cognitive Geometry of Employee Theft," in
*Dysfunctional Behavior in Organizations: Nonviolent and Deviant
Behavior*, ed. S. B. Bacharach, A. O'Leary-Kelly, J. M. Collins, and
R. W. Griffin (Stamford, CT: JAI Press, 1998), pp. 147–193.

60 Information from company website, http://www.enterprise.com
(accessed June 29, 2003); A. Taylor, "Driving Customer Satisfaction,"
Harvard Business Review, July 2002, pp. 24–25.

61 S. D. Pugh, J. Dietz, J. W. Wiley, and S. M. Brooks, "Driving
Service Effectiveness through Employee-Customer Linkages,"
Academy of Management Executive, November 2002, pp. 73–84.

62 T. S. Bateman and J. M. Crant, "The Proactive Component of
Organizational Behavior: A Measure and Correlates," *Journal of
Organizational Behavior*, March 1993, p. 112; and J. M. Crant,
"Proactive Behavior in Organizations," *Journal of Management* 26,
no. 3 (2000), pp. 435–462.

63 Situation adapted from information in K. Cushing, "E-Mail Policy,"
Computer Weekly, June 24, 2003, p. 8; and "Spam Leads to Lawsuit
Fears, Lost Time," *InternetWeek*, June 23, 2003, http://www.
internetweek.com.

64 Based on P. Vieira, "The Airline, the Analyst and the Secret
Password," *Financial Post*, June 30, 2004, p. FP1; C. Wong, "WestJet
Disputes Air Canada Allegations of Corporate Espionage," *Canadian
Press*, July 1, 2004; and T. Gignac, "WestJet Settles Air Canada
Corporate-Espionage Suit," *Vancouver Sun*, May 30, 2006, p. D2.

65 Based on E. Baron and E. O'Connor, "Why So Far Off Course?"
Province (Vancouver), March 23, 2006, p. A3; W. Boei, M. Bridge, and
L. Pynn, "99 Escape after Ship Runs Aground, Slides into Depths,"
Vancouver Sun, March 23, 2006, p. A1; C. E. Harnett, "Ferry Brass,"
Times Colonist (Victoria), June 6, 2006, p. A3; C. E. Harnett, "Human
Error Sank B.C. Ferry," *Calgary Herald*, March 27, 2007, p. A5;
D. Meissner, "New Details in Queen of North Report," *Daily News*,
March 27, 2007, p. 1; C. Montgomery, "Loose Manifest Rules
Led to Miscount," *Province* (Vancouver), March 28, 2006, p. A4;
C. Montgomery and I. Austin, "Human Error Is Faulted for Ship
Sinking," *Province* (Vancouver), March 27, 2007, p. A6; and "Union
Will Defend Fired Ferry Workers," *Kamloops Daily News*, May 7, 2007,
p. A5.

66 With thanks to Denise Fortier, Bishop's University, who provided
this insight.

67 Based on P. L. Hunsaker, *Training in Management Skills* (Upper
Saddle River, NJ: Prentice Hall, 2001), pp. 60–61.

68 Based on J. Hickman, C. Tkaczyk, E. Florian, J. Stemple, and
D. Vazquez, "50 Best Companies for Minorities," *Fortune*, July 7,

2003, pp. 103–120; S. M. Mehta, "What Minority Employees Really
Want," *Fortune*, July 10, 2000, pp. 180–186; and "Why Diversity
Pays," *Canadian Business*, March 29–April 11, 2004, cover story.

Supplement 2

1 Information from Sepomex website, http://www.sepomex.gob.mx
(accessed February 24, 2006); and A. Guthrie, "Going Postal," *Latin
Trade*, July 2005, pp. 84–85.

2 D. McGinn, "Faster Food," *Newsweek*, April 19, 2004, pp. E20–E22;
and *World Fact Book 2006*, http://www.odci.gov/cia/publications.

3 D. Michaels and J. L. Lunsford, "Streamlined Plane Making," *Wall
Street Journal*, April 1, 2005, pp. B1+.

4 J. Ordonez, "McDonald's to Cut the Cooking Time of Its French
Fries," *Wall Street Journal*, May 19, 2000, p. B2.

5 C. Fredman, "The Devil in the Details," *Executive Edge*, April–May,
1999, pp. 36–39.

6 Information from Škoda website, http://www.skoda-auto.com
(accessed May 30, 2006); and T. Mudd, "The Last Laugh,"
IndustryWeek, September 18, 2000, pp. 38–44.

7 S. Levy, "The Connected Company," *Newsweek*, April 28, 2003,
pp. 40–48; and J. Teresko, "Plant Floor Strategy," *IndustryWeek*, July
2002, pp. 26–32.

8 S. Hemtasilpa, "Swiss Shoemaker Ready to Tap China's Domestic
Market," *Tribune Business News*, March 5, 2004, p. 1.

9 R. B. Chase and N. J. Aquilano, *Production and Operations
Management: A Life-Cycle Approach*, 3rd ed. (Homewood, IL: Irwin,
1981), pp. 34–41.

10 E. E. Adam Jr. and R. J. Ebert, *Production and Operations
Management: Concepts, Models, and Behavior*, 5th ed. (Upper Saddle
River, NJ: Prentice Hall, 1992), pp. 53–60.

11 E. E. Adam Jr. and R. J. Ebert, *Production and Operations
Management: Concepts, Models, and Behavior*, 5th ed. (Upper Saddle
River, NJ: Prentice Hall, 1992), pp. 231–233.

12 E. E. Adam Jr. and R. J. Ebert, *Production and Operations
Management: Concepts, Models, and Behavior*, 5th ed. (Upper Saddle
River, NJ: Prentice Hall, 1992), pp. 341–344.

13 E. E. Adam Jr. and R. J. Ebert, *Production and Operations
Management: Concepts, Models, and Behavior*, 5th ed. (Upper Saddle
River, NJ: Prentice Hall, 1992), p. 340; N. P. Lin, L. Krajewski,
K. Leong, and W. C. Benton, "The Effects of Environmental Factors on
the Design of Master Production Scheduling Systems," *Journal of
Operations Management*, March 1994, pp. 367–374.

14 D. Bartholomew, "MRP Upstaged," *IndustryWeek*, February 3,
1997, pp. 39–41.

15 Cited in *Fortune*, October 28, 1985, p. 47.

16 S. E. Barndt and D. W. Carvey, *Essentials of Operations
Management* (Upper Saddle River, NJ: Prentice Hall, 1982), p. 112.

17 R. B. Chase and N. J. Aquilano, *Production and Operations
Management: A Life-Cycle Approach*, 3rd ed. (Homewood, IL: Irwin,
1981), pp. 551–552.

18 ISO, *The ISO Survey—2005*, http://www.iso.org/iso/iso9000-
14000/pdf/survey2005.pdf (accessed September 27, 2007).

19 See http://www.iso.org/iso/iso_catalogue.htm (accessed
October 14, 2007).

20 G. Hasek, "Merger Marries Quality Efforts," *IndustryWeek*, October 16, 2000, pp. 79–80.

21 M. Arndt, "Quality Isn't Just for Widgets," *BusinessWeek*, July 22, 2002, pp. 72–73.

22 J. H. Sheridan, "Managing the Value Chain," *IndustryWeek*, September 6, 1999, http://www.industryweek.com/CurrentArticles/.

23 J. H. Sheridan, "Managing the Value Chain," *IndustryWeek*, September 6, 1999, http://www.industryweek.com/CurrentArticles/.

24 R. Normann and R. Ramirez, "From Value Chain to Value Constellation," in *Harvard Business Review on Managing the Value Chain*, ed. C. Baldwin, K. B. Clark, J. Magretta, J. H. Dyer, M. Fisher, and D. V. Fites (Boston: Harvard Business School Press, 2000), pp. 185–219.

25 J. Teresko, "The Dawn of E-Manufacturing," *IndustryWeek*, October 2, 2000, pp. 55–60.

26 "Made-to-Fit Clothes Are on the Way," *USA Today*, July 2002, pp. 8–9; L. Elliott, "Mass Customization Comes a Step Closer," *Design News*, February 18, 2002, p. 21.

27 E. Schonfeld, "The Customized, Digitized, Have-It-Your-Way Economy," *Fortune*, October 28, 1998, pp. 114–120.

Chapter 16

1 Based on K. J. Delaney, "Spreading Change: As Yahoo! Falters, Executive's Memo Calls for Overhaul," *Wall Street Journal*, November 18, 2006, p. A1; and R. D. Hof, "Back to the Future at Yahoo!" *BusinessWeek*, July 02, 2007, p. 34.

2 C. R. Leana and B. Barry, "Stability and Change as Simultaneous Experiences in Organizational Life," *Academy of Management Review*, October 2000, pp. 753–759.

3 Based on L. Tischler, "Sudden Impact," *Fast Company*, September 2002, pp. 106–113.

4 E. Nee, "The Hottest CEO in Tech," *Business 2.0*, June 2003, p. 86.

5 Based on R. D. Hof, "Back to the Future at Yahoo!" *BusinessWeek*, July 02, 2007, p. 34.

6 See http://www.techcrunch.com/2007/04/29/panama-not-enough-to-battle-google-yahoo-acquires-rightmedia (accessed October 14, 2007).

7 The idea for these metaphors came from J. E. Dutton, S. Ashford, K. O'Neill, and K. Lawrence, "Moves That Matter: Issue Selling and Organizational Change," *Academy of Management Journal*, August 2001, pp. 716–736; B. H. Kemelgor, S. D. Johnson, and S. Srinivasan, "Forces Driving Organizational Change: A Business School Perspective," *Journal of Education for Business*, January–February 2000, pp. 133–137; G. Colvin, "When It Comes to Turbulence, CEOs Could Learn a Lot from Sailors," *Fortune*, March 29, 1999, pp. 194–196; and P. B. Vaill, *Managing as a Performing Art: New Ideas for a World of Chaotic Change* (San Francisco: Jossey-Bass, 1989).

8 K. Lewin, *Field Theory in Social Science* (New York: Harper & Row, 1951).

9 For contrasting views on episodic and continuous change, see K. E. Weick and R. E. Quinn, "Organizational Change and Development," in *Annual Review of Psychology*, vol. 50, ed. J. T. Spence, J. M. Darley, and D. J. Foss (Palo Alto, CA: Annual Reviews, 1999) pp. 361–386.

10 G. Hamel, "Take It Higher," *Fortune*, February 5, 2001, pp. 169–170.

11 Information on Converse from website, http://www.converse.com, and Hoover's Online, http://www.hoovers.com (accessed June 6, 2003); and M. Davids, "Wanted: Strategic Planners," *Journal of Business Strategy*, May–June 1995, pp. 30–38.

12 Based on S. Rubin, "Blinded by the Dazzle of the Deal," *Financial Post (National Post)*, February 12, 2004, pp. FP8–FP9.

13 Based on R. D. Hof, "Back to the Future at Yahoo!" *BusinessWeek*, July 02, 2007, p. 34; and J. Thaw and A. Levy, "Yahoo! CEO Digs in for Slugfest With Google, *The Vancouver Sun*, June 20, 2007, p. D3.

14 Based on T. Belford, "Half Public, Half Private, It Beats Odds," *Financial Post (National Post)*, June 9, 2003, p. BE4; S. Tafler, "BC + X = P3: BC Struggles with the Partnering Numbers," *Summit: Canada's Magazine for Public Sector Purchasing*, September 2002, pp. 16–18; and P. Vieira, "RBC Pushes Public-Private Partnerships," *Financial Post (National Post)*, November 26, 2002, p. FP10.

15 S. Crock and J. Carey, "Storming the Streets of Baghdad," *BusinessWeek*, October 21, 2002, pp. 46–47.

16 J. Jesitus, "Change Management: Energy to the People," *IndustryWeek*, September 1, 1997, pp. 37, 40.

17 D. Lavin, "European Business Rushes to Automate," *Wall Street Journal*, July 23, 1997, p. A14.

18 See, for example, T. C. Head and P. F. Sorensen, "Cultural Values and Organizational Development: A Seven-Country Study," *Leadership & Organization Development Journal*, March 1993, pp. 3–7; A. H. Church, W. W. Burke, and D. F. Van Eynde, "Values, Motives, and Interventions of Organization Development Practitioners," *Group & Organization Management*, March 1994, pp. 5–50; W. L. French and C. H. Bell Jr., *Organization Development: Behavioral Science Interventions for Organization Improvement*, 6th ed. (Upper Saddle River, NJ: Prentice Hall, 1998); N. A. Worren, K. Ruddle, and K. Moore, "From Organizational Development to Change Management," *Journal of Applied Behavioral Science*, September 1999, pp. 273–286; G. Farias, "Organizational Development and Change Management," *Journal of Applied Behavioral Science*, September 2000, pp. 376–379; W. Nicolay, "Response to Farias and Johnson's Commentary," *Journal of Applied Behavioral Science*, September 2000, pp. 380–381; and S. Hicks, "What Is Organization Development?" *Training & Development*, August 2000, p. 65.

19 T. White, "Supporting Change: How Communicators at Scotiabank Turned Ideas into Action," *Communication World*, April 2002, pp. 22–24.

20 M. Javidan, P. W. Dorfman, M. S. deLuque, and R. J. House, "In the Eye of the Beholder: Cross-Cultural Lessons in Leadership from Project GLOBE," *Academy of Management Perspective*, February 2006, pp. 67–90; and E. Fagenson-Eland, E. A. Ensher, and W. W. Burke, "Organization Development and Change Interventions: A Seven-Nation Comparison," *Journal of Applied Behavioral Science*, December 2004, pp. 432–464.

21 E. Fagenson-Eland, E. A. Ensher, and W. W. Burke, "Organization Development and Change Interventions: A Seven-Nation Comparison," *Journal of Applied Behavioral Science*, December 2004, p. 461.

22 See, for example, A. Deutschman, "Making Change: Why Is It So Hard to Change Our Ways?" *Fast Company*, May 2005, pp. 52–62; S. B. Silverman, C. E. Pogson, and A. B. Cober, "When Employees at Work Don't Get It: A Model for Enhancing Individual Employee Change in Response to Performance Feedback," *Academy of Management Executive*, May 2005, pp. 135–147; C. E. Cunningham,

C. A. Woodward, H. S. Shannon, J. MacIntosh, B. Lendrum, D. Rosenbloom, and J. Brown, "Readiness for Organizational Change: A Longitudinal Study of Workplace, Psychological and Behavioral Correlates," *Journal of Occupational and Organizational Psychology*, December 2002, pp. 377–392; M. A. Korsgaard, H. J. Sapienza, and D. M. Schweiger, "Beaten Before Begun: The Role of Procedural Justice in Planning Change," *Journal of Management* 28, no. 4 (2002), pp. 497–516; R. Kegan and L. L. Lahey, "The Real Reason People Won't Change," *Harvard Business Review*, November 2001, pp. 85–92; S. K. Piderit, "Rethinking Resistance and Recognizing Ambivalence: A Multidimensional View of Attitudes toward an Organizational Change," *Academy of Management* Review, October 2000, pp. 783–794; C. R. Wanberg and J. T. Banas, "Predictors and Outcomes of Openness to Changes in a Reorganizing Workplace," *Journal of Applied Psychology*, February 2000, pp. 132–142; A. A. Armenakis and A. G. Bedeian, "Organizational Change: A Review of Theory and Research in the 1990s," *Journal of Management* 25, no. 3 (1999), pp. 293–315; and B. M. Staw, "Counterforces to Change," in *Change in Organizations*, ed. P. S. Goodman and Associates (San Francisco: Jossey-Bass, 1982), pp. 87–121.

23 J. P. Kotter and L. A. Schlesinger, "Choosing Strategies for Change," *Harvard Business Review*, March–April 1979, pp. 107–109; P. Strebel, "Why Do Employees Resist Change?" *Harvard Business Review*, May–June 1996, pp. 86–92; J. Mariotti, "Troubled by Resistance to Change," *IndustryWeek*, October 7, 1996, p. 30; and A. Reichers, J. P. Wanous, and J. T. Austin, "Understanding and Managing Cynicism About Organizational Change," *Academy of Management Executive*, February 1997, pp. 48–57.

24 J. P. Kotter and L. A. Schlesinger, "Choosing Strategies for Change," *Harvard Business Review*, March–April 1979, pp. 106–111; K. Matejka and R. Julian, "Resistance to Change Is Natural," *Supervisory Management*, October 1993, p. 10; C. O'Connor, "Resistance: The Repercussions of Change," *Leadership & Organization Development Journal*, October 1993, pp. 30–36; J. Landau, "Organizational Change and Barriers to Innovation: A Case Study in the Italian Public Sector," *Human Relations*, December 1993, pp. 1411–1429; A. Sagie and M. Koslowsky, "Organizational Attitudes and Behaviors as a Function of Participation in Strategic and Tactical Change Decisions: An Application of Path-Goal Theory," *Journal of Organizational Behavior*, January 1994, pp. 37–47; V. D. Miller, J. R. Johnson, and J. Grau, "Antecedents to Willingness to Participate in a Planned Organizational Change," *Journal of Applied Communication Research*, February 1994, pp. 59–80; P. Pritchett and R. Pound, *The Employee Handbook for Organizational Change* (Dallas, TX: Pritchett Publishing, 1994); R. Maurer, *Beyond the Wall of Resistance: Unconventional Strategies That Build Support for Change* (Austin, TX: Bard Books, 1996); D. Harrison, "Assess and Remove Barriers to Change," *HRfocus*, July 1999, pp. 9–10; L. K. Lewis, "Disseminating Information and Soliciting Input during Planned Organizational Change," *Management Communication Quarterly*, August 1999, pp. 43–75; J. P. Wanous, A. E. Reichers, and J. T. Austin, "Cynicism About Organizational Change," *Group & Organization Management*, June 2000, pp. 132–153; K. W. Mossholder, R. P. Settoon, A. A. Armenakis, and S. G. Harris, "Emotion during Organizational Transformations," *Group & Organization Management*, September 2000, pp. 220–243; and S. K. Piderit, "Rethinking Resistance and Recognizing Ambivalence: A Multidimensional View of Attitudes toward an Organizational Change," *Academy of Management Review*, October 2000, pp. 783–794.

25 M. Helft, "Yahoo!, Aiming for Agility, Shuffles Executives," *Business Day*, December 6, 2006.

26 R. M. Kanter, "From Spare Change to Real Change: The Social Sector as Beta Site for Business Innovation," *Harvard Business Review*, May–June 1999, pp. 122–132.

27 J. E. Perry-Smith and C. E. Shalley, "The Social Side of Creativity: A Static and Dynamic Social Network Perspective," *Academy of Management Review*, January 2003, pp. 89–106; and P. K. Jagersma, "Innovate or Die: It's Not Easy, but It Is Possible to Enhance Your Organization's Ability to Innovate," *Journal of Business Strategy*, January–February 2003, pp. 25–28.

28 Statistics Canada, "Corporate Failures, 1996," *The Daily*, August 8, 2003.

29 These definitions are based on T. M. Amabile, *Creativity in Context* (Boulder, CO: Westview Press, 1996).

30 R. W. Woodman, J. E. Sawyer, and R. W. Griffin, "Toward a Theory of Organizational Creativity," *Academy of Management Review*, April 1993, pp. 293–321.

31 T. M. Egan, "Factors Influencing Individual Creativity in the Workplace: An Examination of Quantitative Empirical Research," *Advances in Developing Human Resources*, May 2005, pp. 160–181; F. Damanpour, "Organizational Innovation: A Meta-Analysis of Effects of Determinants and Moderators," *Academy of Management Journal*, September 1991, pp. 555–590; S. D. Saleh and C. K. Wang, "The Management of Innovation: Strategy, Structure, and Organizational Climate," *IEEE Transactions on Engineering Management*, February 1993, pp. 14–22; G. R. Oldham and A. Cummings, "Employee Creativity: Personal and Contextual Factors at Work," *Academy of Management Journal*, June 1996, pp. 607–634; J. B. Sorensen and T. E. Stuart, "Aging, Obsolescence, and Organizational Innovation," *Administrative Science Quarterly*, March 2000, pp. 81–112; T. M. Amabile, C. N. Hadley, and S. J. Kramer, "Creativity Under the Gun," *Harvard Business Review*, August 2002, pp. 52–61; and N. Madjar, G. R. Oldham, and M. G. Pratt, "There's No Place Like Home? The Contributions of Work and Nonwork Creativity Support to Employees' Creative Performance," *Academy of Management Journal*, August 2002, pp. 757–767.

32 P. R. Monge, M. D. Cozzens, and N. S. Contractor, "Communication and Motivational Predictors of the Dynamics of Organizational Innovations," *Organization Science*, May 1992, pp. 250–274.

33 T. M. Amabile, C. N. Hadley, and S. J. Kramer, "Creativity Under the Gun," *Harvard Business Review*, August 2002, pp. 52–61.

34 N. Madjar, G. R. Oldham, and M. G. Pratt, "There's No Place Like Home? The Contributions of Work and Nonwork Creativity Support to Employees' Creative Performance," *Academy of Management Journal*, August 2002, pp. 757–767.

35 V. Galt, "Training on Tap," *Globe and Mail*, November 20, 2002, pp. C1, C8.

36 C. Salter, "Mattel Learns to 'Throw the Bunny,'" *Fast Company*, November 2002, p. 22.

37 See, for instance, J. E. Perry-Smith, "Social Yet Creative: The Role of Social Relationships in Facilitating Individual Creativity," *Academy of Management Journal*, February 2006, pp. 85–101; C. E. Shalley, J. Zhou, and G. R. Oldham, "The Effects of Personal and Contextual Characteristics on Creativity: Where Should We Go from Here?" *Journal of Management* 30, no. 6 (2004), pp. 933–958; M. Amabile, *Creativity in Context* (Boulder, CO: Westview Press, 1996); M. Tushman and D. Nadler, "Organizing for Innovation," *California Management Review*, Spring 1986, pp. 74–92; R. Moss Kanter, "When a Thousand Flowers Bloom: Structural, Collective, and Social Conditions for Innovation in Organization," in *Research in Organizational Behavior*, vol. 10, ed. B. M. Staw and L. L. Cummings (Greenwich, CT: JAI Press, 1988), pp. 169–211; G. Morgan, "Endangered Species: New Ideas," *Business Month*, April 1989, pp. 75–77; S. G. Scott and R. A. Bruce, "Determinants of Innovative People: A Path Model of Individual Innovation in the Workplace," *Academy of Management Journal*, June 1994, pp. 580–607; T. M. Amabile, R. Conti, H. Coon, J. Lazenby, and M. Herron, "Assessing the Work Environment for Creativity," *Academy of Management Journal*, October 1996, pp. 1154–1184; A. deGues, "The Living Company," *Harvard Business Review*, March–April 1997, pp. 51–59; J. Zhou, "Feedback Valence, Feedback Style, Task Autonomy, and Achievement Orientation: Interactive Effects on Creative Behavior," *Journal of Applied Psychology* 83, no. 2 (1998), pp. 261–276; G. Hamel, "Reinvent Your Company," *Fortune*, June 12, 2000, pp. 98–118; J. M. George and J. Zhou, "When Openness to Experience and Conscientiousness Are Related to Creative Behavior: An Interactional Approach," *Journal of Applied Psychology*, June 2001, pp. 513–524; and Perry-Smith and C. E. Shalley, "The Social Side of Creativity: A Static and Dynamic Social Network Perspective," *Academy of Management Review*, January 2003, pp. 89–106.

38 J. M. Howell and C. A. Higgins, "Champions of Change," *Business Quarterly*, Spring 1990, pp. 31–32; P. A. Carrow-Moffett, "Change Agent Skills: Creating Leadership for School Renewal," *NASSP Bulletin*, April 1993, pp. 57–62; T. Stjernberg and A. Philips, "Organizational Innovations in a Long-Term Perspective: Legitimacy and Souls-of-Fire as Critical Factors of Change and Viability," *Human Relations*, October 1993, pp. 1193–2023; and J. Ramos, "Producing Change That Lasts," *Across the Board*, March 1994, pp. 29–33.

39 Associated Press, "Mars Rover Is Launched on Voyage to Look for Water," *USA Today*, June 11, 2003, http://www.usatoday.com; NASA's website, http://www.nasa.gov (accessed June 11, 2003); and W. J. Broad, "A Tiny Rover, Built on the Cheap, Is Ready to Explore Distant Mars," *New York Times*, July 5, 1997, p. 9.

40 Based on K. J. Delaney and J. S. Lublin, "Can 'Chief Yahoo' Rise to Challenges As Yahoo Chief?" *Wall Street Journal*, June 20, 2007, p. B1; and http://yodel.yahoo.com/2007/06/18/my-new-job.

41 C. Hymowitz, "How Leader at 3M Got His Employees to Back Big Changes," *Wall Street Journal*, April 23, 2002, p. B1; and J. Useem, "Jim McNerney Thinks He Can Turn 3M from a Good Company into a Great One—With a Little Help from His Former Employer: General Electric," *Fortune*, August 12, 2002, pp. 127–132.

42 See T. H. Fitzgerald, "Can Change in Organizational Culture Really Be Managed?" *Organizational Dynamics*, Autumn 1988, pp. 5–15; B. Dumaine, "Creating a New Company Culture," *Fortune*, January 15, 1990, pp. 127–131; P. F. Drucker, "Don't Change Corporate Culture—Use It!" *Wall Street Journal*, March 28, 1991, p. A14; J. Martin, *Cultures in Organizations: Three Perspectives* (New York: Oxford University Press, 1992); D. C. Pheysey, *Organizational Cultures: Types and Transformations* (London: Routledge, 1993); C. G. Smith and R. P. Vecchio, "Organizational Culture and Strategic Management: Issues in the Strategic Management of Change," *Journal of Managerial Issues*, Spring 1993, pp. 53–70; P. Bate, *Strategies for Cultural Change* (Boston: Butterworth-Heinemann, 1994); and P. Anthony, *Managing Culture* (Philadelphia: Open University Press, 1994).

43 M. L. Wald and J. Schwartz, "Shuttle Inquiry Uncovers Flaws in Communication," *New York Times*, August 4, 2003, http://nytimes.com.

44 M. L. Wald and J. Schwartz, "Shuttle Inquiry Uncovers Flaws in Communication," *New York Times*, August 4, 2003, http://nytimes.com.

45 See, for example, R. H. Kilmann, M. J. Saxton, and R. Serpa, eds., *Gaining Control of the Corporate Culture* (San Francisco: Jossey-Bass, 1985); and D. C. Hambrick and S. Finkelstein, "Managerial

Discretion: A Bridge between Polar Views of Organizational Outcomes," in *Research in Organizational Behavior*, vol. 9, ed. B. M. Staw and L. L. Cummings (Greenwich, CT: JAI Press, 1987), p. 384.

46 M. A. Cavanaugh, W. Boswell, M. Roehling, and J. Boudreau, "An Empirical Examination of Self-Reported Work Stress among U.S. Managers," *Journal of Applied Psychology*, February 2000, pp. 65–74; M. A. Verespej, "Stressed Out," *IndustryWeek*, February 21, 2000, pp. 30–34; J. Laabs, "Time-Starved Workers Rebel," *Workforce*, October 2000, pp. 26–28; and C. Daniels, "The Last Taboo," *Fortune*, October 28, 2002, pp. 137–144.

47 I. Phaneuf, "Drug Company Study Finds Rise in Work-Related Stress," *Vancouver Sun*, May 5, 2001, p. D15.

48 Adapted from R. S. Schuler, "Definition and Conceptualization of Stress in Organizations," *Organizational Behavior and Human Performance*, April 1980, p. 189. For an updated review of definitions, see R. L. Kahn and P. Byosiere, "Stress in Organizations," in *Handbook of Industrial and Organizational Psychology*, vol. 3, 2nd ed., ed. M. D. Dunnette and L. J. Hough (Palo Alto, CA: Consulting Psychologists Press, 1992), pp. 573–580.

49 B. L. de Mente, "Karoshi: Death from Overwork," Asia Pacific Management Forum, May 2002, http://www.apmforum.com.

50 H. Benson, "Are You Working Too Hard?" *Harvard Business Review*, November 2005, pp. 53–58; B. Cryer, R. McCraty, and D. Childre, "Pull the Plug on Stress," *Harvard Business Review*, July 2003, pp. 102–107; C. Daniels, "The Last Taboo," *Fortune*, October 28, 2002, pp. 137–144; S. E. Jackson, "Participation in Decision Making as a Strategy for Reducing Job-Related Strain," *Journal of Applied Psychology*, February 1983, pp. 3–19; C. D. Fisher, "Boredom at Work: A Neglected Concept," *Human Relations*, March 1993, pp. 395–417; C. A. Heaney, B. A. Israel, S. J. Schurman, E. A. Baker, J. S. House, and M. Hugentobler, "Industrial Relations, Worksite Stress Reduction and Employee Well-Being: A Participatory Action Research Investigation," *Journal of Organizational Behavior*, September 1993, pp. 495–510; P. Froiland, "What Cures Job Stress?" *Training*, December 1993, pp. 32–36; C. L. Cooper and S. Cartwright, "Healthy Mind, Healthy Organization—A Proactive Approach to Occupational Stress," *Human Relations*, April 1994, pp. 455–471; and A. A. Brott, "New Approaches to Job Stress," *Nation's Business*, May 1994, pp. 81–82.

51 See R. S. Schuler, "Time Management: A Stress Management Technique," *Personnel Journal*, December 1979, pp. 851–855; and M. E. Haynes, *Practical Time Management: How to Make the Most of Your Most Perishable Resource* (Tulsa, OK: Penn Well Books, 1985).

52 "Employee Wellness," *Canadian HR Reporter*, February 23, 2004, pp. 9–12.

53 P. A. McLagan, "Change Leadership Today," *Training & Development*, November 2002, p. 29.

54 W. Pietersen, "The Mark Twain Dilemma: The Theory and Practice for Change Leadership," *Journal of Business Strategy*, September–October 2002, pp. 32–37; C. Hymowitz, "To Maintain Success, Managers Must Learn How to Direct Change," *Wall Street Journal*, August 13, 2002, p. B1; and J. E. Dutton, S. Ashford, K. O'Neill, and K. Lawrence, "Moves That Matter: Issue Selling and Organizational Change," *Academy of Management Journal*, August 2001, pp. 716–736.

55 P. A. McLagan, "The Change-Capable Organization," *Training & Development*, January 2003, pp. 50–58.

56 Adapted from P. B. Vaill, *Managing as a Performing Art: New Ideas for a World of Chaotic Change* (San Francisco: Jossey-Bass, 1989), pp. 8, 9.

57 Situation adapted from information in "HR Director Backs Team to Stay Focused During Boots Upheaval," *Personnel Today*, March 21, 2006, p. 2; "Boots' Revamp As Group to Shut 17 Depots," *Europe Intelligence Wire*, March 15, 2006.

58 Information from press kit on company's website, http://www.1800gotjunk.com; A. Wahl, "Canada's Best Workplaces: Overview," *Canadian Business*, April 26, 2007 (accessed May 20, 2007); "Fastest-Growing Franchises 2006 Rankings," *Entrepreneur*, April 29, 2006, http://www.entrepreneur.com; J. Hainsworth, The Associated Press, "Canadian Company Finds Treasures in People's Trash," *Springfield News-Leader*, April 24, 2006, p. 5B; J. Martin, "Cash from Trash," *Fortune*, November 2003, pp. 52–56; and M. Carbonaro, "1-800-GOT-JUNK? Quickly Opens Second Area Site," *CNY Business Journal*, August 10, 2007, http://findarticles.com/p/articles/mi_qa3718/is_20070810/ai_n19510769 (accessed October 2, 2007).

59 Based on M. Warner, "Under the Knife," *Business 2.0*, February 2004, http://www.business20.com.

60 Based on J. P. Kotter and L. A. Schlesinger, "Choosing Strategies for Change," *Harvard Business Review*, March–April 1979, pp. 106–114; and T. A. Stewart, "Rate Your Readiness to Change," *Fortune*, February 7, 1994, pp. 106–110.

61 Based on C. Lindsay, "Paradoxes of Organizational Diversity: Living within the Paradoxes," in *Proceedings of the 50th Academy of Management Conference*, ed. L. R. Jauch and J. L. Wall (San Francisco: Academy of Management, 1990), pp. 374–378.

62 Based on H. Ibarra, "How to Stay Stuck in the Wrong Career," *Harvard Business Review*, December 2002, pp. 40–47; "Before Uprooting Your Career," *BusinessWeek*, October 22, 2001, p. 131; N. G. Carr, "Being Virtual: Character and the New Economy," *Harvard Business Review*, May–June 1999, pp. 181–190; B. Kaye, "Career Development—Anytime, Anyplace," *Training & Development*, December 1993, pp. 46–49; A. D. Pinkney, "Winning in the Workplace," *Essence*, March 1994, pp. 79–80; C. B. Bardwell, "Career Planning & Job Search Guide 1994," *Black Collegian*, March–April 1994, pp. 59–64; and W. Kiechel III, "A Manager's Career in the New Economy," *Fortune*, April 4, 1994, pp. 68–72.

Part 5 Continuing Case: Starbucks

1 A. Serwer and K. Bonamici, "Hot Starbucks to Go," *Fortune*, January 26, 2004, pp. 60–74; interview with Jim Donald, *Smart Money*, May 2006, pp. 31–32; A. Serwer, "Interview with Howard Schultz," *Fortune (Europe)*, March 20, 2006, pp. 35–36; W. Meyers, "Conscience in a Cup of Coffee," *U.S. News & World Report*, October 31, 2005, pp. 48–50; S. Gray, "Fill 'er Up—With Latte," *Wall Street Journal*, January 6, 2006, pp. A9+; P. Kafka, "Bean Counter," *Forbes*, February 28, 2005, pp. 78–80; J. Schnack, L. Adamson, S. Brull, L. Conger, P. Paulden, and J. Sutherland, "Starbucks Shells Out to Safeguard Schultz," *Institutional Investor*, January 2006, p. 11; R. Ruggless, "Starbucks Exec: Security from Employee Theft Important When Implementing Gift Card Strategies," *Nation's Restaurant News*, December 12, 2005, p. 24; R. Ruggless, "Transaction Monitoring Boosts Safety, Perks Up Coffee Chain Profits," *Nation's Restaurant News*, November 28, 2005, p. 35; and Standards of Business Conduct, Starbucks, http://www.starbucks.com.

GLOSSARY/SUBJECT INDEX

Note: Page references in bold refer to pages on which key terms have been defined.

management by walking around, 477

market control, 479

meaning of, 467–470

measures of organizational performance, 468

methods of control, 478–480

operations, 508–510

performance standards, 468

planning-control link, 469f

quality control, 509–510, 509f

service profit train, 490, 491f

types of control, 477f

workplace concerns, 487–489

workplace privacy, 487–489, 488

Control methods, 478–480

Control process. A three-step process that includes measuring actual performance, comparing actual performance against a standard, and taking managerial action to correct deviations or inadequate standards. **470**

benchmarking, 473, 474f

corrective action, 474–475

described, 470f

managerial action, 473–475

performance measurement, 470–471, 471f

performance vs. standard, 471–473

revision of standard, 475

summary of managerial decisions, 476, 476f

Controlling. A management function that involves monitoring actual performance, comparing actual performance to a standard, and taking correct action when necessary. **10**, 289

see also Control

Coordination, 511

Core competencies. An organization's major value-creating skills, capabilities, and resources that determine its competitive advantage. **196**

Core values. The primary, or dominant, values that are accepted throughout the organization. **47**

Corporate blogs, 313

Corporate governance. The system used to govern a corporation so that the interests of corporate owners are protected. **486**–487, 486f

Corporate reputation, 196

Corporate rituals, 49

Corporate social responsibility. A firm's obligation, beyond that required by law and economics, to do the right things and act in ways that are good for society. **102**

arguments for and against, 102–104, 103f

classical view, 100

comparison of views of, 101–102

described, 100

and economic performance, 104–105

ethical imperative, 103

greening of management, 105–108

practice of, 104

vs. social responsiveness, 104f

socio-economic view, 100–101

two views of, 100–102

values-based management, 108–110

Corporate strategy. An organizational strategy that evaluates what businesses a company is in, should be in, or wants to be in, and what it wants to do with those businesses. **200**

BCG matrix, 204–205, 204f

corporate portfolio analysis, 204–205

described, 200–201

growth strategy, 201–203

renewal strategy, 203

retrenchment strategy, 203

stability strategy, 203

turnaround strategy, 203

The Corporation (Bakan), 100

Corrective action, 474–475

Corruption, 116

Cost centre. A unit in which managers are held responsible for all associated costs. **508**

Cost control, 508

Cost leadership strategy. A business strategy in which the organization sets out to be the lowest-cost producer in its industry. **207**–210, 208f

Cost minimization, 270

Costs

direct costs, 508

fixed costs, 236

indirect costs, 508

interpersonal communication, 292

used book sales, 218

variable costs, 236

Creative problem-solving, 164–165

Creativity. The ability to combine ideas in a unique way or to make unusual associations between ideas. 181, **527**

Credibility. The degree to which someone is perceived as honest, competent, and able to inspire. **385**

Critical incidents. A performance appraisal method in which the evaluator focuses on the critical behaviours that separate effective from ineffective job performance. **340**

Critical path. The longest or most time-consuming sequence of events and activities in a PERT network. **235**

Cross-cultural. See Cultural differences; Cultural environment

Cross-functional teams. Work teams made up of individuals who are experts in various functional specialties. **263**, **438**

Crown corporation. A commercial company owned by the government but independently managed. **15**

Cultural awareness, 95–96

Cultural differences

body language, 296

communication barriers, 296

and communications, 296

control, 487

dealing with, 94–95

and ethics, 115–116

motivation, 416–417

status, 449

Cultural environment

see also Workforce diversity

achievement, 86

assertiveness, 87

challenges of, 84

collectivism, 85, 87, 296

future orientation, 87

gender differentiation, 87

GLOBE framework for assessing cultures, 87, 88f

Hofstede's framework for assessing cultures, 85–86, 86f

humane orientation, 87

in-group collectivism, 87

individualism, 85, 87

leadership, 390–391

long-term orientation, 86

nurturing, 86

performance orientation, 87

power distance, 85, 87

short-term orientation, 86

uncertainty avoidance, 85, 87

Culture

national culture, 84

organizational culture. See Organizational culture

Customer departmentalization. Groups jobs on the basis of customers who have common needs or problems. **261**

Customer-responsive culture, 54

Customer service

feedback, 307

quality of, 307

strategies, 213–214

and VoIP, 304–305

Customers

bargaining power of buyers, 207

communication with, 306–307

and e-business, 19

and globalization, 19

interactions with, and control, 489–490

as management challenge, 19

service profit train, 490, 491f

specific environment, 55–56

D

Dark green approach, 107

Data. Raw, unanalyzed facts. **483**

Debates, 53

Decentralization. The degree to which lower-level employees provide input or actually make decisions. **266**–267, 266f

Decision. A choice from two or more alternatives. **138**

decision rules, 117–118, 118*f*

ego strength, 113

email, 305

employee selection, 117

ethical leadership, 118–119, 386

factors affecting employee ethics, 112–115, 112*f*

formal protective mechanisms, 120

four views of ethics, 111–112

Global Compact, 116

improvement of ethical behaviour, 116–120

independent social audits, 119

and individual characteristics, 113

information technology, 305

integrative social contracts theory, 111

international code of ethics, 116

international context, 115–116

issue intensity, 115, 115*f*

job goals, 119

locus of control, 113

as management challenge, 16–17

and moral development stages, 112–113*f*

and organizational culture, 114

and performance-appraisal systems, 114, 119

rights view of ethics, 111

self-assessment, 122–123

structural variables, 113–114

theory of justice view of ethics, 111

training, 119

utilitarian view of ethics, 111

values, 113

voice mail, 305

whistle-blowers, 120

Ethnocentric attitude. The belief that the best work approaches and practices are those of the home country. **74**

Euro. A single common European currency. **76**

European Union (EU). A union of 27 European countries that forms an economic and political entity. **76**–77, 76*f*

Evaluation of results, 200

Events. End points that represent the completion of major activities in a PERT network. **235**, 236*f*

Executive compensation, 25

Expectancy theory. The theory that an individual tends to act in a certain way based on the expectation that the act will be followed by a given outcome and on the attractiveness of that outcome to the individual. **414**–415, 414*f*, 415*f*

Expert power. The influence a leader has based on his or her expertise, special skills, or knowledge. **384**

Experts on the front-line, 157

Exporting. An approach to going global that involves making products at home and selling them abroad. **81**

External analysis, 197–198

External environment. Outside forces and institutions that potentially can affect the organization's performance. **55**, 56*f*

External forces for change, 516

External locus of control, 113

External support, 444

Extrinsic motivation. Motivation that comes from outside the person and includes such things as pay, bonuses, and other tangible rewards. **405**

F

Face-to-face communication style, 310–312

Facilities layout planning. Assessing and selecting among alternative layout options for equipment and workstations. **505**

Facilities location planning. The design and location of an operations facility. **504**

Family-friendly benefits. Benefits that accommodate employees' needs for work–life balance. **348**

Fayol, Henri, 33

Fayol's 14 principles of management, 33

Feasibility region, 238

Feedback. The degree to which carrying out work activities required by a job results in the individual's obtaining direct and clear information about the effectiveness of his or her performance. **410**

on customer service, 307

giving performance feedback, 352–353

interpersonal communication, 292

openning feedback channels, 411

to overcome communication barriers, 297

performance, 173

positive feedback, 529

providing feedback, 497–498

suggestions for giving feedback, 299

360-degree feedback, 341

Feedback control. A type of control that takes place after a work activity is done. **478**

Feedback loop, 292

Feedforward control. A type of control that focuses on preventing anticipated problems, since it takes place before the actual activity. **476**–477

Fiedler contingency model. A leadership theory that proposes effective group performance depends on the proper match between the leader's style of interacting with his or her followers and the degree to which the situation gives the leader control and influence, **374**–376, 374*f*, 376*f*

Filtering. The deliberate manipulation of information to make it appear more favourable to the receiver. **294**–295

Financial controls, 480–482

Financial ratios, 480–481, 481*f*

Financial reporting, 487

First-line manager. Managers at the lowest level of the organization who manage the work of nonmanagerial employees who

are directly or indirectly involved with the production or creation of the organization's products. **6**

First mover. An organization that is first to bring a product innovation to the market or to use a new process innovation. **214**

First-mover advantages and disadvantages, 215*f*

Five whys approach, 156

Fixed costs, 236

Fixed-position layout. A layout in which the product stays in place, and tools, equipment, and human skills are brought to it. **505**

Flexible manufacturing, 513

Flexible work hours. A scheduling option in which employees are required to work a specific number of hours per week but are free to vary those hours within certain limits, **423**

Flextime. A scheduling option in which employees are required to work a specific number of hours per week but are free to vary those hours within certain limits, **423**

Focus strategy. A business strategy in which a company pursues a cost or differentiation advantage in a narrow industry segment. **210**

Follower readiness, 377–378

Forecasting

accuracy, and shorter length of forecasts, 228

described, 227

effectiveness, 228

ethical dilemmas, 244–245

involvement of others in process, 228

multiple methods, reliance on, 228

no-change forecast, 228

qualitative forecasting, 227

quantitative forecasting, 227

revenue forecasts, 244–245

rolling forecasts, 228

simple forecasting methods, 228

techniques, 227–227*f*

turning points in trend, identification of, 228

Forecasts. Predictions of outcomes. **227**

Foreign subsidiary. An approach to going global that involves a direct investment in a foreign country by setting up a separate and independent production facility or office. **82**

Formal communication. Communication that follows the official chain of command or is part of the communication required to do one's job. **298**–299

Formal groups, 436, 436*f*

Formal planning, 170

see also Planning

Formal planning department. A group of planning specialists whose sole responsibility is to help write the various organizational plans. **179**

Formal protective mechanisms, 120

Formality, 292

Formalization. The degree to which jobs within the organization are standardized and the extent to which employee behaviour is guided by rules and procedures. **267**–268

Forming. The first stage of team development, in which people join the group and then define the team's purpose, structure, and leadership. **438**

Formulation of strategies, 198

Franchising. An approach to going global in which a service organization gives a person or group the right to sell a product, using specific business methods and practices that are standardized. **81**

Free Trade Area of the Americas (FTAA), 78

Freedom, 53

Functional conflicts. Conflicts that support the goals of the work group and improve its performance. **446**

Functional departmentalization. Groups jobs by functions performed. **261**

Functional strategy. A strategy used by a functional department to support the business strategy of the organization. **211**, 211*f*

Functional structure. An organizational structure that groups similar or related occupational specialties together. **272**

Functions. See Management functions

Future orientation, 87

G

Gantt chart. A scheduling chart developed by Henry Gantt that shows output, both planned and actual, over a period of time. **232**, 233*f*

Gender differences
  in communication styles, 316
  leadership, 391–392, 393*f*

Gender differentiation, 87

General administrative theorists. Writers who developed general theories of what managers do and what constitutes good management practice. **33**

General administrative theory
  described, 33
  Henri Fayol, 33
  important contributions, 33–34
  Max Weber, 34
  today's use of, 34

General Agreement on Tariffs and Trade (GATT), 78

General environment. Broad external conditions that may affect the organization. **57**
  demographic conditions, 60
  economic conditions, 58, 321
  legal-political conditions, 58–59, 322–323
  socio-cultural conditions, 59
  technological conditions, 60

Generation X, 60

Generation Y, 60

Geocentric attitude. A world-oriented view that focuses on using the best approaches and people from around the globe. **74**

Geographical departmentalization. Groups jobs on the basis of territory or geography. **261**

Gilbreth, Frank, 32

Gilbreth, Lillian, 32

Global 100 Most Sustainable Corporations in the World, 108

Global aptitudes, 92–93

Global attitudes, 74, 75*f*

Global business
  see also Global environment
  described, 78–79
  exporting, 81
  foreign subsidiary, 82
  franchising, 81
  Global Compact, 116
  global sourcing, 80
  importing, 81
  international organizations, types of, 79–80
  joint venture, 82
  licensing, 81
  methods of going international, 80–82, 80*f*
  strategic alliances, 81–82

Global Compact, 116

Global company. An international company that centralizes management and other decisions in the home country. **79**–80

Global environment
  see also Global business
  African Union, 78
  Association of Southeast Asian Nations (ASEAN), 77*f*, 77
  cultural environment, 84–87
  economic environment, 83
  ethics, 115–116
  European Union (EU), 76–77, 76*f*
  Free Trade Area of the Americas (FTAA), 78
  General Agreement on Tariffs and Trade (GATT), 78
  legal-political environment, 83
  management in, 82–88
  Mercosur, 78
  North American Free Trade Agreement (NAFTA), 77
  planning in, 182
  regional trading alliances, 76–78
  self-assessment quiz, 91–92
  South Asian Association for Regional Cooperation (SAARC), 78
  Southern Cone Common Market, 78
  understanding, 75–78
  World Trade Organization, 78

Global environment problems, 106

Global organizational development, 524

Global organizations, 79–80

Global outsourcing, 80

Global perspective, 74

Global scanning, 226

Global sourcing. Purchasing materials or labour from around the world wherever it is cheapest. **80**

Global structural issues, 278–279

Global teams
  advantages and disadvantages, 448*f*
  cohesivenss, 449
  conformity, 449
  described, 448
  group member resources, 448
  group processes, 449
  group structure, 448–449
  management of, 448–449, 448*f*
  manager, role of, 449
  social loafing, 449
  status, 449

Globalization
  anti-globalization groups, 89*f*
  and customers, 19
  as management challenge, 17
  pro-globalization groups, 89*f*
  pros and cons of, 87–88, 88*f*, 89*f*

GLOBE framework for assessing cultures, 87, 88*f*, 390

Goal specificity, 173

Goals. Desired outcomes for individuals, groups, or entire organizations. **172**
  ambiguous goals, 173
  in broad terms, 173
  effective teams, 443
  establishment of, 172–176
  focus on, 529
  goal setting, 189
  hierarchy of organizational goals, 173
  identification of, in strategic management process, 194–195
  management by objectives (MBO), 173–174, 174*f*
  open-ended goals, 174
  and planning, 170
  quality goals, 509–510
  steps in goal setting, 175–176
  traditional goal setting, 172–173, 173*f*
  well-designed goals, 174–175, 175*f*

Government legislation. See Legal conditions

Grapevine. The informal organizational communication network. **301**

Graphic rating scales. A performance appraisal method in which the evaluator rates an employee on a set of performance factors. **340**

Greening of management. The recognition by business of the close link between its decisions and activities and their impact on the natural environment. **106**
  activist approach, 107

job enlargement,   409

job enrichment,   409

job redesign guidelines,   411

job scope,   409

motivating jobs,   431

Job dissatisfaction,   407, 407f

Job enlargement. The horizontal expansion of a job through increasing job scope. **409**

Job enrichment. The vertical expansion of a job by adding planning and evaluating responsibilities. **409**

Job goals,   119

Job redesign guidelines,   411

Job satisfaction,   334, 407, 407f, 409

Job scope. The number of different tasks required in a job and the frequency with which these tasks are repeated. **409**

Job search,   344

Job search assistance,   349

Job sharing. The practice of having two or more people split a full-time job. **424**

Job specification. A statement of the minimum qualifications that a person must possess to perform a given job successfully. **325**

Joint venture. An approach to going global in which the partners agree to form a separate, independent organization for some business purpose; it is a type of strategic alliance. **82**

"Just following orders,"   282

K

Karoshi,   533

Knowledge enlargement actvities,   409

Knowledge management. Cultivating a learning culture in which an organization's members systematically gather knowledge and share it with others in the organization to achieve better performance. **20**

Knowledge resources, management of,   306

L

Labour market fluctuations,   517

Labour standards,   116

Labour union. An organization that represents employees and seeks to protect their interests through collective bargaining. **322**

Laissez-faire style. A leadership style where the leader tends to give the group complete freedom to make decisions and complete the work in whatever way it sees fit. **372**

Language,   295–296, 297

Language, and organizational culture,   50

Lateral communication. Communication that takes place among employees on the same organizational level. **299**

Laws,   58–59

Layoff-survivor sickness. A set of attitudes, perceptions, and behaviours of employees who remain after involuntary

employee reductions; it includes insecurity, guilt, depression, stress, fear, loss of loyalty, and reduced effort. **349**

Layout planning,   505

Leader. Someone who can influence others and provide vision and strategy to the organization. **368**

achievement-oriented leader,   380

becoming a leader,   368–369

charismatic leader,   381–382

directive leader,   380

employee-oriented leaders,   372

high-high leader,   372

leader-member relations,   375

vs. managers,   368, 368f

participative leader,   380

position power,   375

production-oriented leaders,   372

relationship-oriented leaders,   374

supportive leader,   380

task-oriented leaders,   374–375

task structure,   375

transactional leaders,   381

transformational leaders,   383

Leader-member relations. One of Fiedler's situational contingencies that describes the degree of confidence, trust, and respect employees have for their leader. **375**

Leader participation model. A leadership theory that relates leadership behaviour and participation to decision making. **378**, 379f

Leadership. The process of influencing individuals or groups toward the achievement of goals. **368**

autocratic style,   371–372

charismatic leadership,   381–382

consideration,   372

credibility,   385

cross-cultural leadership,   390–391

current issues,   385–392

democratic style,   371–372

effective teams,   444

employee empowerment,   388

ethical leadership,   118–119, 386

gender differences,   391–392, 393f

initiating structure,   372

laissez-faire style,   372

leading change,   381–383

necessity of,   369

online leadership,   386–388

power, management of,   384

radical leadership,   399

readiness,   377

team leadership,   388–390, 389f, 390, 452–453

transformational leadership,   383

trust,   384–385

and value chain management,   512

visionary leadership,   382–383

Leadership school,   336

Leadership style

see also Leadership; Leadership theories

autocratic style,   371–372

democratic style,   371–372

laissez-faire style,   372

managerial grid,   373–374, 373f

self-assessment of,   395–397

Leadership theories

behavioural theories,   371–374, 371f

contingency theories of leadership,   374–380

early leadership theories,   369–374

Fiedler contingency model,   374–376, 374f, 376f

leader participation model,   378–379f

Ohio State studies,   372

path-goal theory,   379–380, 380f

Situational Leadership (SL),   377–378, 377f

trait theories,   370, 370f

University of Iowa studies,   371–372

University of Michigan studies,   372

Leading. A management function that involves motivating subordinates, directing the work of individuals or teams, selecting the most effective communication channels, and resolving employee behaviour issues. **10**

Learning organization. An organization that has developed the capacity to continuously learn, adapt, and change. **19**

described,   19, 20f

and organizational design,   278

Svenska Handelsbanken,   283

Least-preferred co-worker (LPC) questionnaire. A questionnaire that measures whether a leader is task oriented or relationship oriented. **374**, 374f

Legal approach,   107

Legal conditions,   58–59, 322–323

Legal environment

and competitive intelligence,   225

described,   83

as impetus for change,   516

Legitimate power. The power a leader has as a result of his or her position in the organization. **384**

Levels of organizational strategy,   201f

Licensing. An approach to going global in which a manufacturer gives another organization the right to use its brand name, technology, or product specifications. **81**

Life or death situations,   161

Light green approach,   106–107

Limits,   157

Line authority,   264

Linear programming. A mathematical technique that solves resource allocation problems. **237**–238, 238f, 239f

Listening skills,   54

Load chart. A modified Gantt chart that schedules capacity by entire departments or specific resources. **233**–234, 234f

Locus of control. A personality attribute that reflects the degree to which people believe they control their own fate. **113**

Long-term orientation, 86

Long-term plans. Plans with a time frame beyond three years. **176**

Lower-order needs, 405

Loyalty, 385

M

Maastricht Treaty, 76

Maintenance control, 508

Maintenance roles. Roles performed by group members to maintain good relations within the group. **441**

Management. Coordinating work activities so that they are completed efficiently and effectively with and through other people. **8**

see also Managers

career opportunities, 28

challenges of. See Management challenges

control, amount of, 42–43

described, 8–12

effectiveness, 8, 9f

efficiency, 8, 9f

functions. See Management functions

in global environment. See Global environment

greening of management, 105–108

historical perspective. See Historical perspective

human resource management. See Human resource management

omnipotent view of management, 42

operating within constraints, 43

parameters of managerial discretion, 43f

and reality of work, 21

roles, 10–12

and self-employment, 21

skills, 12

of stakeholder relationships, 61–63

study of management, 20–21

symbolic view of management, 42, 43

universality of management, 20–21f

values-based management, 108–110

Management by objectives (MBO). An approach to setting goals in which specific performance goals are jointly determined by employees and their managers, progress toward accomplishing those goals is periodically reviewed, and rewards are allocated on the basis of this progress. **173–174, 174f, 341**

Management by walking around. A term used to describe a manager being out in the work area, interacting directly with employees. **477**

Management cases

see also Cases

Sarnia Food Fresh Grocery Store: The Icing on the Cake, 560–565

The YMCA of London, Ontario, 550–560

Management challenges

customers, 19

dealing with, 16

e-business, 17–19

ethics, 16–17

globalization, 17

innovation, 19

knowledge management, 20

learning organizations, 19, 20f

workforce diversity, 17

Management functions. Planning, organizing, leading, and controlling. **9**

controlling, 10

decision making, 143f

see also Decision making

described, 9f

leading, 10

vs. management roles, 12

organizing, 10

planning, 9–10

Management information system (MIS). A system used to provide management with needed information on a regular basis. **483**

Management roles. Specific categories of managerial behaviour. **10**

decisional roles, 11

informational roles, 11

interpersonal roles, 11

vs. management functions, 12

Mintzberg's management roles, 11f

validity of, 11

Management skills

conceptual skills, 12

human skills, 12

relationship of, to management level, 12, 12f

skill-building exercises, 13

technical skills, 12

Management theories

behavioural approach, 35–37

contingency approach, 38–39, 38f

development of, 32f

general administrative theory, 33–34

organizational behaviour (OB), 35–37

quantitative approach, 35

scientific management, 31–33

situational approach, 38–39, 38f

summarizing management theory, 39

systems approach, 37–38

Management trends, history of, 30–39

Manager. Someone who works with and through other people by coordinating their work activities in order to accomplish organizational goals. **6**

see also Management

Crown corporations, 15

as decision maker. See Decision making

described, 6–7

the environment, effect of, 60–63

first-line manager, 6

functions, 9–10

and global teams, 449

vs. leaders, 368, 368f

middle managers, 6

organizational culture, effect of, 50–51, 51f

in private sector, 15

project manager, 240–241

role of, 6

shift managers, 6

top managers, 6–7

types of, 6–7

Managerial action in control process, 473–475

Managerial discretion, 43f

Managerial grid. A two-dimensional grid of leadership behaviours - concern for people and concern for production - that results in five different leadership styles. **373–374, 373f**

Managerial levels, 7f

Manufacturing organizations. Organizations that produce physical goods. **501**

Market approach, 107

Market control. An approach to control that emphasizes the use of external market mechanisms, such as price competition and relative market share, to establish the standards used in the control system. **479**

Market economy. An economic system in which resources are primarily owned and controlled by the private sector. **83**

Market value added (MVA). A financial tool that measures the stock market's estimate of the value of a firm's past and expected capital investment projects. **482**

Maslow's hierarchy of needs theory, 405, 406f

Mass customization. Providing consumers with a product when, where, and how they want it. **513**

Mass production. The production of items in large batches. **270**

Master schedule. A schedule that specifies quality and type of each item to be produced; how, when, and where they should be produced; labour force levels; and inventory. **506–507, 507f**

Material requirements planning (MRP). A system that dissects products into the materials and parts necessary for purchasing, inventory, and priority planning purposes. **507**

Material symbols, 50

Matrix structure. An organizational structure that assigns specialists from different functional departments to work on one or more projects. **275, 275f**

Maximin choice, 148

McGregor's Theory X and Theory Y, 405–406

Means-ends chain. An integrated network of goals in which the accomplishment of goals at one level serves as the means for achieving the goals, or ends, at the next level. **173**

Mechanistic organization. An organizational design that is rigid and tightly controlled. **268**–269, 268*f*

Mentoring, 27–28

Mercosur, 78

Message. A purpose to be conveyed. **290**–291

Middle managers. Managers between the first-line level and the top level of the organization who manage the work of first-line managers. **6**

Military applications, 35

Minimax choice, 148

Minimum-wage employees, 417–418

Mission. The purpose of an organization. **175**

components of mission statement, 195*f*

identification of, in strategic management process, 194–195

Money, 419, 425

Monitoring in the workplace, 487–489, 488

Moral development stages, 112–113*f*

Motivation. An individual's willingness to exert high levels of effort to reach organizational goals, conditioned by the degree to which that effort satisfies some individual need. **404**

and communication, 289

contingent workers, 418–419

cultural differences, 416–417

current issues, 416–424

described, 403–404

equity in system, 425

extrinsic motivation, 405

individual differences, recognition of, 424

individualize rewards, 425

inspirational motivation, 383

intrinsic motivation, 405

link rewards to performance, 425

matching people to jobs, 424

minimum-wage employees, 417–418

money, 425

process, 404*f*

professional employees, 418

recognition, power of, 425

rewards programs, 419–422

suggestions for motivating employees, 424–425

technical employees, 418

work-life balance, 422–424

workforce diversity, 416–419

Motivation-hygiene theory. Herzberg's theory that intrinsic factors are related to job satisfaction and motivation, whereas extrinsic factors are related to job dissatisfaction. **406**–408, 407*f*

Motivation theories

contemporary theories, 408–415

early motivation theories, 404–408

equity theory, 412–414, 412*f*

expectancy theory, 414–415, 414*f*, 415*f*

hierarchy of needs theory, 405, 406*f*

job design, 409–411

motivation-hygiene theory, 406–408, 407*f*

Theory X, 405–406

Theory Y, 405–406

Motivators. Factors that increase job satisfaction and motivation. **407**

Multidomestic corporations. An international company that decentralizes management and other decisions to the local country. **79**

Multinational corporation (MNC). A broad term that refers to any and all types of international companies that maintain operations in multiple countries. **79**

Multiperson comparisons. A performance appraisal method by which one individual's performance is compared with that of others. **340**–341, 354

Mutual trust, 444

Mystery shoppers, 307

N

National culture. The values and attitudes shared by individuals from a specific country that shape their behaviour and beliefs about what is important. **84**

see also Cultural environment

Natural work units, 410

Need. An internal state that makes certain outcomes appear attractive. **404**

esteem needs, 405

higher-order needs, 405

lower-order needs, 405

physiological needs, 405

safety needs, 405

self-actualization needs, 405

social needs, 405

Negotiating skills, 444

Network organization. A small core organization that outsources major business functions. **277**–278

New entrants, threat of, 206

NGOs. An organization that is independent from government control and whose primary focus is on humanitarian, development, and environmental sustainability activities. **15**

No-change forecast, 228

Noise. Disturbances that interfere with the transmission, receipt, or feedback of a message. **290**

Nonprofit organizations, and strategic planning, 193–194

Nonprofit sector. The part of the economy that is run by organizations which operate for purposes other than making a profit (that is, providing charity or services). **15**

Nonprogrammed decisions. Decisions that are unique and nonrecurring and require custom-made solutions. **146**–147

Nonverbal communications. Communication transmitted without words. **292**

body language, 294, 296

vs. verbal communication, 294

verbal intonation, 294

Nonverbal cues, 298

Norming. The third stage of team development, which is characterized by close relationships and cohesiveness. **439**

North American Free Trade Agreement (NAFTA). An agreement among the Canadian, American, and Mexican governments in which barriers to free trade were reduced. **77**

Nurturing, 86

O

Occupational health and safety legislation, 323

Offensive email, 495

Office politics, 401

Ohio State studies, 372

Omnipotent view of management. The view that managers are directly responsible for an organization's success or failure. **42**

Online leadership

challenges, 386

communication, 387

defining performance, 387

encouragement of performance, 387

facilitation of performance, 387

performance management, 387

trust, 388

Open-system focus, 529

Open systems. Systems that dynamically interact with their environment. **37**, 37*f*

Openness, 53, 385

Operational plans. Plans that specify the details of how the overall goals are to be achieved. **176**

Operations management. The design, operation, and control of the transformation process that converts resources into goods and services. **501**

controlling operations, 508–510

cost control, 508

current issues, 510–513

importance of, 501–503

maintenance control, 508

manufacturing organizations, 501

mass customization, 513

operations system, 501*f*

planning operations. See Planning operations

productivity, management of, 501–502, 502*f*

quality control, 509–510, 509*f*

service organizations, 501

strategic role of, 502–503

technology, 512–513

value chain management, 510–512

Operations system, 501*f*

Opportunities. Positive trends in external environmental factors. **197**, 198*f*

Order, 33

organizational design decisions, 268–272

self-assessment, 280–281

and size, 270

span of control, 264–265, 265f

and strategy, 270

and technology, 270–271

work specialization, 260

Organizing. A management function that involves determining what tasks are to be done, who is to do them, how the tasks are to be grouped, who reports to whom, and where decisions are to be made. **10**, **260**, 260f

Orientation. Introduction of a new employee to his or her job and the organization. **335**–336, 346

Outplacement agencies, 350

Outsourcing, 277–278

Overconfidence bias, 153

Overlapping activities, 170

P

Paradox of diversity, 543

Paralinguistics, 294

Parameters of managerial discretion, 43f

Parochialism. A narrow view of the world; an inability to recognize the differences of other people. **74**

Participating, 377

Participative decision making, 173

Participative leader, 380

Path-goal theory. A leadership theory that says it's the leader's job to assist his or her followers in attaining their goals and to provide the necessary direction and/or support to ensure that their goals are compatible with the overall objectives of the group or organization. **379**–381, 380f

Pay-for-performance programs. Variable compensation plans that pay employees on the basis of some performance measure. **420**–421

Payoff matrix, 149f

Performance. The end result of an activity. **468**

appraisals. See Performance appraisal

benchmarking, 473, 474f

economic performance, and corporate social responsibility, 104–105

feedback, 173

management. See Performance management system

measurement of, 470–471, 471f

organizational performance, 468

and planning, 171

poor performance, 341

and rewards, 425

vs. standard, 471–473

Performance appraisal

behaviourally anchored rating scales (BARS), 340

challenges of, 339

critical incidents, 340

and ethics, 114, 119

graphic rating scales, 340

management by objectives, 341

methods, 340–341, 340f

multiperson comparisons, 340–341, 354

360-degree feedback, 341

written essay, 340

Performance management

discipline, 341

employee counselling, 341

online leadership, 387

Performance management system. A process of establishing performance standards and evaluating performance in order to arrive at objective human resource decisions, as well as to provide documentation to support those decisions. **339**

described, 339

performance appraisal methods, 340–341, 340f

Performance orientation, 87

Performance-simulation tests, 330–331

Performance standards, 468, 475

Performing. The fourth stage of team development, in which the team structure is fully functional and accepted by team members. **439**

Personal planning, 243–244

Personal SWOT analysis, 220–221

Personality tests, 330

Persons with disabilities, 308

PERT network. A flow chart diagram that depicts the sequence of activities needed to complete a project and the time or costs associated with each activity. **234**–235, 235f, 236f

Physical examinations, 334

Physiological needs. A person's need for food, drink, shelter, sexual satisfaction, and other physical requirements. **405**

Planning. A management function that involves defining goals, establishing a strategy for achieving those goals, and developing plans to integrate and coordinate activities. **9**, **169**

approaches to, 179

benefits of planning, 175

commitment concept, 179

and competition, 181

contingency factors, 178–179

criticisms of planning, 180–181

current issues in planning, 180

described, 9–10, 169–170

as direction, 170

disease outbreaks, planning for, 188

and dynamic environments, 180, 181–182

as formal planning, 170

formal planning department, 179

goals, establishment of, 172–176

in hierarchy of organizations, 178f

human resource planning, 325–326

international perspective, 182

vs. intuition and creativity, 181

involvement of organizational members, 179

methods of planning, 171–172

operations. See Planning operations

and performance, 171

personal planning, self-assessment of, 243–244

planning-control link, 469f

plans, development of, 176–178

and previously successful plans, 181

purposes of, 170

reasons for, 170

and rigidity, 180

tools and techniques. See Planning tools and techniques

top-down organizational planning processes, 179

Planning operations

aggregate planning, 505

capacity planning, 504

decisions, 503f

described, 503

facilities layout planning, 505

facilities location planning, 504

master schedule, 506–507, 507f

material requirements planning (MRP), 507

process planning, 504–505

Planning tools and techniques

assessment of environment, 224–229

benchmarking, 228–229, 229f

breakeven analysis, 236–237, 237f

budgeting, 231

contemporary planning techniques, 239–242

environmental scanning, 224–226

forecasting, 227–228

linear programming, 237–238, 238f, 239f

project management, 240–241

resource allocation, 230–239, 230f

scenario planning, 241–242

scheduling, 232–236

Plans. Documents that outline how goals are going to be met and describe resource allocations, schedules, and other necessary actions to accomplish the goals. **172**

development of, 176–178

directional plans, 177, 178f

long-term plans, 176

operational plans, 176

short-term plans, 176

single-use plan, 178

specific plans, 177, 178f

standing plans, 178

strategic plans, 176

types of, 176–178, 177f

Playfulness, 53

Policy. A guideline for making a decision. **146**

Political climate, 59

Political conditions, 58–59

Political environment, 83

Politically correct communication, 308

Polycentric attitude. The view that the managers in the host country know the best work approaches and practices for running their businesses. **74**

Pornography, 495

Position power. One of Fiedler's situational contingencies that describes the degree of influence a leader has over power-based activities such as hiring, firing, discipline, promotions, and salary increases. **375**

Positive feedback, 529

Post-War group, 60

Power
  acquisition of power, 400–401
  bargaining power, 207
  coercive power, 384
  expert power, 384
  legitimate power, 384
  management of, 384
  referent power, 384
  reward power, 384

Power distance, 85, 87

Preventive maintenance. Maintenance performed before a breakdown occurs. **508**

Principles of management. Fundamental rules of management that could be taught in schools and applied in all organizational situations. **34**

The Principles of Scientific Management (Taylor), 31

Privacy Act, 305

Privacy in the workplace, 487–489, 488

Private sector. The part of the economy that is run by organizations which are free from direct government control; organizations in this sector operate to make a profit. **15**

Private-sector pay, 342–343

Privately held organization. A company whose shares are not available on the stock exchange but are privately held. **15**

Pro-globalization groups, 89f

Proactive personality, 493–494

Problem. A discrepancy between an existing and a desired state of affairs. **138**
  creative problem-solving, 164–165
  described, 138
  nonprogrammed decisions, 146–147
  structured problems, 146
  types of problems, 145–147
  unstructured problems, 146–147

Problem-solving team. A work team of 5 to 12 employees from the same department or functional area who are involved in efforts to improve work activities or to solve specific problems. **436**

Procedural justice. Perceived fairness of the process used to determine the distribution of rewards. **413**

Procedure. A series of interrelated sequential steps that a decision maker can use to respond to a structured problem. **146**

Process conflict. Conflict over how the work gets done. **446**

Process departmentalization. Groups jobs on the basis of product or customer flow. **261**

Process layout. A layout that arranges components together according to similarity of function. **505**, 506f

Process planning. Determining how a product or service will be produced. **504**

Process production. The production of items in continuous processes. **270**

Product departmentalization. Groups jobs by product line. **261**

Product layout. A layout that arranges components according to the progressive steps by which a product is made. **505**, 506f

Production capacity numbers, 238

Production-oriented leaders, 372

Productivity. The overall output of goods or services produced divided by the inputs needed to generate that output. **468**, 501–**502**, 502f

Professional employees, 418

Profit-sharing plan. An organization-wide plan in which the employer shares profits with employees based on a predetermined formula. **421**

Programmed decisions. Repetitive decisions that can be handled by a routine approach. **146**

Prohibited grounds of discrimination, 324f

Project. A one-time-only set of activities that has a definite beginning and ending point in time. **240**

Project management. The task of getting a project's activities done on time, within budget, and according to specifications. **240**
  described, 240
  process, 240, 240f
  role of project manager, 241

Project manager, 240–241

Project structure. An organizational structure in which employees continuously work on projects. **275**–276

Public pressure groups, 57

Public-private partnerships, 523

Public sector. The part of the economy that is controlled by government. **15**

Public-sector pay, 342–343

Public Servants Disclosure Protection Act, 120

Publicly held organization. A company whose shares are available on the stock exchange for public trading by brokers/dealers. **15**

Punishment practices, 118

Q

Qualitative forecasting. Forecasting that uses the judgment and opinions of knowledge-able individuals to predict outcomes. **227**

Quality. The ability of a product or service to reliably do what it's supposed to do and to satisfy customer expectations. **509**

Quality control, 509–510, 509f

Quality goals, 509–510

Quantitative approach. The use of quantitative techniques to improve decision making. **35**

Quantitative forecasting. Forecasting that applies a set of mathematical rules to a series of past data to predict outcomes. **227**

Question marks, 204

R

Radical leadership, 399

Range of variation. The acceptable degree of variation between actual performance and the standard. **471**, 472f

Rational decision making. Making decisions that are consistent and value-maximizing within specified constraints. **143**

Readiness. The extent to which people have the ability and willingness to accomplish a specific task. **377**

Reading an organization's culture, 68–69

Realistic job preview (RJP). A preview of a job that includes both positive and negative information about the job and the company. **334**–335

Reality of work, 21

Recognition, 425

Recorded music industry, 212

Recruitment. The process of locating, identifying, and attracting capable applicants. **326**–328, 345–346, 353

Referent power. The power a leader has because of his or her desirable resources or personal traits. **384**

Referents. Those things individuals compare themselves against in order to assess equity. **413**

Regional trading alliances, 76–78

Regret matrix, 149f

Related diversification. When a company grows by combining with firms in different, but related, industries. **202**

Relationship conflict. Conflict based on interpersonal relationships. **446**

Relationship-oriented leaders, 374

Reliability. The ability of a selection device to measure the same thing consistently. **330**

Remedial maintenance. Maintenance that calls for the overhaul, replacement, or repair of equipment when it breaks down. **508**

Remuneration, 33

Renewal strategy. A corporate strategy designed to address organizational weaknesses that are leading to performance declines. **203**
  retrenchment strategy, 203
  turnaround strategy, 203

Resistance to change, 524–526, 526*f*, 541–543

Resource allocation

  breakeven analysis, 236–237, 237*f*

  budgeting, 231

  linear programming, 237–238, 238*f*, 239*f*

  scheduling, 232–236

  techniques for, 230–239, 230*f*

Resource availability, 176

Resources. An organization's assets - financial, physical, human, intangible - that are used to develop, manufacture, and deliver products or services to customers; the assets of the organization, including financial, physical, human, intangible, and structural/cultural factors. **196, 230**

Responsibility. The obligation or expectation to perform any assigned duties. **263**

Results, evaluation of, 200

Retrenchment strategy. A short-run renewal strategy. **203**

Revenue forecasts, 244–245

Reverse engineering, 225

Revision of standard, 475

Reward power. The power a leader has to give positive benefits or rewards. **384**

Reward practices, 118

Rewards, 414

Rewards programs

  employee recognition programs, 419–420

  money, role of, 419

  pay-for-performance programs, 420–421

  profit-sharing plan, 421

  self-assessment, 427–428

  stock option programs, 421–422, 422*f*

  work teams, 369–370

Rights view of ethics. A view of ethics that is concerned with respecting and protecting individual liberties and privileges. **111**

Rigidity, 180

Risk. A condition in which a decision maker is able to estimate the likelihood of certain outcomes. **147–148**

Risk-taking, 52–53, 166

Risk tolerance, 529

Rivalry, 207

Role. A set of expected behaviour patterns attributed to someone who occupies a given position in a social unit. **441**

Role clarity, 54

Roles. *See* Management roles

Rolling forecasts, 228

Romances in the workplace, 347

Rule. An explicit statement that tells a decision maker what he or she can or cannot do. **146**

Rules of thumb, 153–155

S

Safety needs. A person's need for security and protection from physical and emotional harm, as well as assurance that physical needs will continue to be met. **405**

Sarbanes-Oxley Act, 487

SARS outbreak, 241–242

Satisfice. To accept solutions that are "good enough." **144**

Scalar chain, 33

Scanability, 292

Scanning the environment, 220

Scenario. A consistent view of what the future is likely to be. **241**

Scenario planning, 241–242

Scheduling. Detailing what activities have to be done, the order in which they are to be completed, who is to do each, and when they are to be completed. **232**

  Gantt chart, 232–233*f*

  load charts, 233–234, 234*f*

  master schedule, 506–507, 507*f*

  PERT network analysis, 234–236, 235*f*, 236*f*

Scientific management. The use of the scientific method to determine the "one best way" for a job to be done. **31**

  contributions to theory, 31–33

  Frank and Lillian Gilbreth, 32

  Frederick W. Taylor, 31–32

  therbligs, 33

  today's use of, 33

Second Life, 277

Selection devices

  application forms, 330

  assessment centres, 331

  background investigations, 334

  choice of, 334–335

  interviews, 332, 332*f*

  performance-simulation tests, 330–331

  physical examinations, 334

  quality of, as predictors, 334*f*

  realistic job preview (RJP), 334–335

  types of, 330–335, 331*f*

  work sampling, 331

  written tests, 330

Selection process. The process of screening job applicants to ensure that the most appropriate candidates are hired. **328**

  reliability, 330

  selection, meaning of, 328–330

  selection decision outcomes, 329*f*

  selection devices, 330–335, 331*f*

  validity, 330

  work teams, 442

  workforce diversity, 346

Selective perception, 295

Selective perception bias, 153

Self-actualization needs. A person's need to grow and become what he or she is capable of becoming. **405**

Self-assessment

  achievement, attitude toward, 184–185

  ambiguity, 216–217

  building and leading a team, 452–453

  ethics, 122–123

  face-to-face communication style, 310–312

  giving performance feedback, 352–353

  global management, 91–92

  intuition, 159–160

  leadership style, 395–397

  motivation to manage, 23–24

  organizational culture, 64–65

  organizational structure, preferences for, 280–281

  personal planning, 243–244

  proactive personality, 493–494

  response to change, 537–538

  rewards, 427–428

Self-employment, 21

Self-managed team. A work team that operates without a manager and is responsible for a complete work process or segment. **437**

Self-serving bias, 154

Self-training, 338*f*

Selling, 377

Sender, 290

Service culture, 306–307

Service organizations. Organizations that produce nonphysical outputs in the form of services. **501**

Service profit chain. The service sequence from employees to customers to profit. **490**, 491*f*

Sexual harassment. Any unwelcome behaviour of a sexual nature in the workplace that negatively affects the work environment or leads to adverse job-related consequences for the employee. **346**–347, 354–355

Shaping team behaviour, 441–442

Shared values, 109, 109*f*

Shareholders, 15

Shift managers, 6

Short-term orientation, 86

Short-term plans. Plans with a time frame of one year or less. **176**

Simple structure. An organizational structure with low departmentalization, wide spans of control, authority centralized in a single person, and little formalization. **272**

Simplification of language, 297

Single-use plan. A one-time plan specifically designed to meet the needs of a unique situation. **178**

Situational approach, 38–39, 38*f*

Situational Leadership (SL). A leadership theory that focuses on the readiness of followers. **377**–378, 377*f*

Six Sigma. A quality standard that establishes a goal of no more than 3.4 defects per million units or procedures. **510**

Size of organization

  described, 14–15

  and organizational structure, 270

U

Uncertainty. A condition in which a decision maker is not certain about the outcomes and cannot even make reasonable probability estimates. **148–149, 170, 271**

see also Environmental uncertainty

Uncertainty avoidance, 85, 87

Unexpected circumstances, 157

Unexpected events, 242

Unified commitment, 444

Unit production. The production of items in units or small batches. **270**

Unity of command. The management principle that states every employee should receive orders from only one superior. 33, **263**

Unity of direction, 33

Universality of management. The reality that management is needed in all types and sizes of organizations, at all organizational levels, in all organizational work areas, and in organizations in all countries around the globe. **20, 21f**

University of Iowa studies, 371–372

University of Michigan studies, 372

Unrelated diversification. When a company grows by combining with firms in different and unrelated industries. **202**

Unstructured problems. Problems that are new or unusual and for which information is ambiguous or incomplete. **146–147**

Upward communication. Communication that flows upward from employees to managers. **299**

Utilitarian view of ethics. A view of ethics that says that ethical decisions are made solely on the basis of their outcomes or consequences. **111**

V

Validity. The proven relationship that exists between the selection device and some relevant job criterion. **330**

Value. The performance characteristics, features and attributes, and any other aspects of goods and services for which customers are willing to give up resources. **510**

Value chain. The entire series of organizational work activities that add value at each step, beginning with the processing of raw materials and ending with the finished product in the hands of end-users. **510**

Value chain management. The process of managing the entire sequence of integrated activities and information about product flows along the entire value chain. **511**

attitudes, 512

collaboration, 511

coordination, 511

employees, 512

leadership, 512

organizational culture, 512

organizational processes, 511

requirements for, 511–512, 511f

technology investment, 511

Values. Basic convictions about what is right and wrong. **113**

core values, 47

and ethics, 113

shared values, 109, 109f

Values-based management. An approach to managing in which managers establish and uphold an organization's shared values. **108**

described, 108

making a difference with, 110

purposes of shared values, 109, 109f

Variable costs, 236

Verbal intonation. An emphasis given to words or phrases that conveys meaning. **294**

Vertical expansion, 411

Vertical integration, 202

Virtual organization. An organization that has elements of a traditional organization, but also relies on recent developments in information technology to get work done. **276–277**

Virtual team. A type of work team that uses computer technology to link physically dispersed members in order to achieve a common goal. **438**

Visionary leadership. The ability to create and articulate a realistic, credible, and attractive vision of the future that improves upon the present situation. **382–383**

VoIP (Voice over Internet Protocol), 304–305

W

Wasteful activities, 170

Way of thinking, 150

Weak cultures, 45–46

Weaknesses. Activities the organization does not do well or resources it needs but does not possess. **196**

The Wealth of Nations (Smith), 31

Weber, Max, 34

Well-designed goals, 174–175, 175f

Wellness programs, 534

Wheel network, 300

Whistle-blowers. Individuals who raise ethical concerns or issues to others inside or outside the organization. **120**

White-water rapids metaphor, 519–520

Work-life balance

compressed workweek, 423

flexible work hours, 423

flexible work schedules, 423

human resource management challenge, 347–349

job sharing, 424

motivation and, 422–423

telecommuting, 424

Work sampling. A selection device in which job applicants are presented with a minia-ture model of a job and are asked to perform a task or set of tasks that are central to it. **331**

Work specialization. The degree to which activities in an organization are subdivided into separate job tasks; also known as *division of labour.* **260**

Work team. A group whose members work intensely on a specific common goal using their positive synergy, individual and mutual accountability, and complementary skills. **436**

adjourning, 439

building a team, 452–453

cross-functional teams, 263–438

effective teams. *See* Effective teams

forming, 438

global teams, 448–449, 448f

group-based performance incentives, 421

vs. groups, 437f

maintenance roles, 441

management challenges, 448–450

norming, 439

performing, 439

problem-solving teams, 436

rewards, 369–370

roles of team members, 441

selection, 442

self-managed teams, 437–438

shaping team behaviour, 441–442

stages of team development, 438–440, 439f

storming, 439

suitability of, 450

synergy, 436

task-oriented roles, 441

team leadership, 388–390, 389f, 390, 452–453

team players, 440–442, 454

team structure, 273–274

training, 369

types of teams, 436–438

virtual teams, 438

workforce diversity, 457

Work unit orientation, 335

Workflow layouts, 505

Workforce diversity. The mix of people in organizations in terms of gender, race, ethnicity, disability, sexual orientation, and age, and demographic characteristics such as education and socioeconomic status. **17**

see also Cultural environment

and decision making, 165

development of employee potential, 432

diverse work teams, 457

diversity success stories, 499

English-only rules, 314

and human resource management, 345–346

inclusive workplace culture, 69

as management challenge, 17

NAME AND ORGANIZATION INDEX

A

A& P Canada, 203
A& W Food Services of Canada, 59
ABC, 57
Aboriginal Human Resource Development
  Council of Canada, 345
ABS Manufacturing and Distributing, 229
Accentra, 145
Accenture, 182
Accenture Canada, 418
Accor, 202
Active Green & Ross, 202
Acxiom, 274
Adams, J. Stacey, 412
Adaptec, 94
Adidas, 57, 520
Advantica, 346
Aguilera, Christina, 55
AHL, 259
Air Canada, 14, 30, 37, 163–164, 197, 205,
  211, 225, 226, 349, 384, 429, 479,
  483, 489, 496, 508, 510, 531
Air Canada Centre, 259
Airbus, 501
AJ Bus Lines, 59
Alberta Energy Co. (AEC), 44
Alcatel-Lucent, 334, 432
Alcoa, 104
Alexander Keith's, 202, 336
Alliance of Manufacturers & Exporters Canada,
  116
Amazon.ca, 19, 211, 215, 513
Amazon.com, 215, 218, 381
America Online, 191, 313, 515
American Chamber of Commerce, 188
Anderson, Brad, 429
Andrus, Mark, 48
Anheuser-Busch, 81, 473
APM Group, 101
Apple Computer, 181, 382, 521
aQuantive, 518
Arar, Maher, 66
Araujo, Rafael, 94
Army and Navy, 43
ASB, 304
Asch, Solomon, 449
Ash, Mary Kay, 383
Ask Jeeves, 516
The Athletic Club, 555
Atkins, 423
Atkinson, Mike, 59
Atlantic Industries, 412

Au Premier Spa Urbain, 289
Audi, 410
The Authors Guild, 218
Avis, 196
Aviva Canada, 263, 274
Avon Products, 101
Axcelis Technologies, 94
Axworthy, Lloyd, 116

B

Babcock, Rob, 263
Back in Motion Rehab, 413
Baez, Danys, 246
Bagg, Geoff, 304
Bagg Group, 304
Bakan, Joel, 87, 100
Baldwin, Jerry, 128, 129, 358
Bang & Olufsen, 210
Bank of Montreal, 69, 266, 489, 499
Bank of Nova Scotia (Scotiabank), 77, 319,
  325, 326, 327, 335, 336, 345, 349,
  350, 351, 371, 499, 524
Banks, Tim, 101
Baptiste, Michele, 345, 349
Bard on the Beach Festival, 15
Barnard, Chester, 35
Barnes & Noble, 218
Barreñ, Graciela, 261
Barrett, Dave, 43
Barron, Millard, 374
Barrows, John, 291
BASF, 229
Basrur, Sheela, 242
Bata Shoes, 504
Bayer, 229
Bayer AG, 270
BC Ferries, 496, 497
BC Ferry and Marine Workers Union, 496
BC Hydro, 534
BCE, 77, 349
Beairsto, Bruce, 41, 44, 46, 54–55, 63
Becker, Krysta Lee, 560–565
Beddoe, Clive, 226, 479
Belanger, Dorys, 289
Bell, Don, 226, 496
Bell Canada, 80, 485
Bell Labs, 432
Benetton Group (BP), 524
Benimadhu, Prem, 420, 421
Bennett, Chris, 277
Bennett, Steve, 517

Bentley, Myrna, 199
Berker, Brandee, 287
Bertuzzi, Todd, 435
Best Buy, 19, 429, 430
Best Buy Canada, 307
Bethlehem Steel Company, 31
Bethune, Gordon M., 179
Better Business Bureau, 245
Bezos, Jeff, 381
BHY. *See* Bob Hayward (BHY)
Biovail, 421
Birk, Steve, 125
Birks, 58
BJ's Wholesale Club, 291
Black, Conrad, 16, 163
Blair, Bob, 467
Blake, R.R., 373
Blanchard, Ken, 377
Bloess, Rainer, 125
Bloomingdale's, 156
Blue Circle Industries, 187
Blue Man Group Productions, 169, 171, 180,
  182, 183
Blue Mantle, 43
Blue Water Café, 268, 269
BMO Field, 259
Bob Hayward (BHY), 555, 557
Bobbitt, Gordon, 482
The Body Shop, 47
Boeing Company, 114, 240, 501
Boman, Pär, 283
Bombardier, 80, 115, 240
Bookoff, 218
Boots, 539
Boralex, 267
Borden & Elliot, 53
Borden Ladner Gervais (BLG), 53
Borders Group, 224
BorderWare, 229
Born, Joe, 19
Boston Consulting Group, 204
Boston Market, 203
Boston Pizza International, 81, 336
Boston Red Sox, 390
BouClair, 473
Bowker, Gordon, 128, 129, 358
Boxboard Group, 267
Boy Scouts, 543
Boy Scouts of Canada, 559
Branson, Richard, 47
Brascan, 202
Brayer, Jean-Paul, 81

LIST OF CANADIAN COMPANIES BY PROVINCE

LIST OF INTERNATIONAL COMPANIES BY COUNTRY

Argentina

Indicom, 261

Australia

Alcoa, 104
Ford Australia, 261
Lend Lease Corporation, 187
Qantas Airways, 19
Toyo Ink Australia, 440

Belgium

Ecover, 107
Inbev, 202

Brazil

Natura Cosmeticos SA, 101
Semco Group, 399

Chile

Compania Chilena de Fosforos SA, 210

China

Fujian Sanming Dinghui Chemical Company, 83
Haier Group, 218
HSBC, 188
Turner International Asia Pacific, 188
Wahaha, 147
XuZhou Anying, 82

Czech Republic

Škoda, 502

Denmark

Bang & Olufsen, 210

Finland

Forum Nokia, 94, 77
Nokia, 77
Oticon Holding A/S, 275

France

Accor, 202
Airbus, 501

Club Med, 56
LVMH Möet Hennessy-Louis Vuitton SA, 205
Total SA, 106

Germany

Audi, 410
Bayer AG, 270
Daimler, 77, 212
Deutsche Bank, 188
Volkswagen AG, 502

India

Hindustan Lever, 192
Sitel India, 80
Wipro, 182, 229

Italy

Benetton Group, 524
Ferrari, 455
Filtea, 18

Japan

Bookoff, 218
DENSO, 104
Fujitsu, 420
Hitachi, 82
Kirin, 81
Matsushita, 479
Mitsubishi, 226
Nissin Foods, 49
Seiyu, 85
Seven & i Holdings, 487
Sharp Corp., 417
Sony Corporation, 45, 527
Toyota Motor Corporation, 59, 196, 229, 274, 473, 501
Trend Micro, 277

Korea

Hyundai Corportation, 47

Lithuania

IKI, 210

Luxembourg

Skype, 55

Mexico

Modelo, 81
Sepomex, 500

The Netherlands

StrawberryFrog, 276

New Zealand

ASB, 304

Singapore

Singapore Airlines, 214

South Korea

Samsung Electronics, 455, 477

Spain

Grupo VIPS, 81
Telefónica, 80
Zara, 93, 232

Sweden

Electrolux, 191
Ericsson, 277
IKEA, 345–346, 511
Svenska Handelsbanken, 283

Switzerland

Nestlé, 79

United Kingdom

BBC, 74
Blue Circle Industries, 187
BP, 524
British Telecom, 495
Kwintessential, 95
McTavish's Kitchens, 94
Norwich Union, 305
Tesco, 403, 404, 408, 416, 426
The Body Shop, 47
Unilever PC, 77
Virgin Group, 47
Virgin Atlantic Airways, 150
Western Provident Association, 305

United States

CREDITS

Author Photos

Page xxiv (top), Courtesy of Stephen P. Robbins; p. xxiv (middle), Courtesy of Mary Coulter; p. xxiv (bottom), Courtesy of Gary Schwartz.

Chapter 1

Page 5, Courtesy 1-800-GOT-JUNK; p. 7, Michael Quan/The New York Times; p. 16, Tom Mihalek/EPA/Landov; p. 18, Friedrich Stark/Das Fotoarchiv/Peter Arnold, Inc./"DEU, Deutschland, Wuppertal: Mitarbeiterin wickelt Baender auf [Bei Verwendung des Fotos ausserhalb journalistischer Zwecke bitte Ruecksprache mit der Agentur halten, NO M]"; p. 19, Saverio Truglia Photography.

Chapter 2

Page 41, Courtesy of Dr. J. A. B. Beairsto; p. 43, Don Healy/Leader Post; p. 48, K. Dooher Photography; p. 49, Chiaki Tsukumo/AP; p. 52, © Philippe Petit/Paris Match—Gamma/PONOPRESSE; p. 57, AP Wide World Photos; p. 58, Copyright © 2006 Yvonne Berg.

Chapter 3

Page 73, Norm Betts/Bloomberg News/Landov; p. 74, CPA/Topham/The Image Works; p. 82, Zhu Gang-Feature China/NewsCom; p. 84, Samantha Appleton/Aurora & Quanta Productions Inc.

Chapter 4

Page 99, Syncrude Canada Ltd.; p. 101, Photo: Heather Taweel; p. 107, Ric Ernst/The Province; p. 109, Mountain Equipment Co-op; p. 114, Courtesy of Boeing Aircraft Company; p. 119 (top), John Abbott Photography; p. 119 (bottom), Reprinted with permission of the CBC; p. 129, Scott Pitts © Dorling Kindersley; p. 130, AP Wide World Photos.

Chapter 5

Page 137, Wayne Leidenfrost/The Province; p. 140, Lee Jae-Won/Landov LLC; p. 145, Gerard Burkhart/The New York Times; p. 147, Quentin Shih aka Shi Xiaofan; p. 150, © 2002 Brian Smith.

Chapter 6

Page 169, AP/Wide World Photos; p. 170, Meredith Heuer/J Group Photo; p. 172, Don Hogan Charles/The New York Times; p. 176, Peter Battistoni; p. 181, Blake Little Photography.

Chapter 7

Page 191, Wayne Cuddington/The Ottawa Citizen; p. 197, Reprinted with permission from The Globe and Mail; p. 201, Jim Ross; p. 207, Colin O'Connor; p. 209, Glenn Lowson; p. 210, Piotr Malecki Photography.

Chapter 8

Page 223, Mark Van Manen/Vancouver Sun; p. 224, © Wyman IRA/CORBIS SYGMA; p. 229, Atul Loke; p. 231, Getty Images, Inc.; p. 232,

Xurxo Lobato/Cover/International Cover; p. 241, Chuck Stoody/CP Photo Archive; p. 251, David McNew/Getty Images, Inc-Liaison.

Chapter 9

Page 259, J.P. Moczulski/CP Photo Archive; p. 261, Photo by Michael Mendez Photography; p. 265, Xerox Canada Limited; p. 271, Jeff Sciortino Photography; p. 274, Acxiom Corporation; p. 277, Alan Levenson.

Chapter 10

Page 287, AP/Paul Sakuma; p. 289, Frederic Jorez/Getty Images; p. 291, Jenny Schulder; p. 295, Ann States; p. 301, Howard Cao; p. 304, Kim Christenson Photography.

Chapter 11

Page 319, CP/Marianne Helm; p. 327, The Vancouver Police Department; p. 329, Dick Loek/The Toronto Star; p. 337, Lucas Oleniuk/1The Toronto Star; p. 348, Bill Keay/Vancouver Sun; p. 349, Dauphin Friendship Centre; p. 359, AP Wide World Photos.

Chapter 12

Page 367, Magnotta Winery Corporation; p. 369, Mike Aporius/CP Photo Archive; p. 387, Randall Scott; p. 389, CP/Jim Young.

Chapter 13

Page 403, Andy Shaw/Bloomberg News/Landov; p. 410, Burkhard Schittny; p. 417, The Yomiuri Shimbun; p. 418, Mark Van Manen/Vancouver Sun; p. 425, Joei Page/The New York Times.

Chapter 14

Page 435, CP/Paul Chiasson; p. 437, Catherine Karnow/CORBIS-NY; p. 440, Courtesy of Toyo Inc.; p. 459, Courtesy of Nancy Langton.

Chapter 15

Page 467, Adrian Wyld/CP Photo Archive; p. 473, SYSCO Corporation; p. 475, REUTERS/Win McNamee/Landov LLC; p. 477, Ki Ho Park/Kistone Photography.

Chapter 16

Page 515, AP/Paul Sakuma; p. 516, Nelson Ching/New York Times Agency; p. 523, © 2002 Robert Houser (roberthouser.com); p. 530, Darryl James; p. 545, Michael Newman/Photo Edit Inc.

Management Cases

Page 563, Photodsic/MaXx Images; p. 564 (left), Stock Food/MaXx Images; p. 564 (right), FoodCollection/MaXx Images; p. 565, Courtesy J. David Whitehead and Jennifer Baker.